SOCIAL THEORY

Peter Xiao. *Intellectual Pursuits*

SOCIAL THEORY

ROOTS AND BRANCHES

FIFTH EDITION

Peter Kivisto
AUGUSTANA COLLEGE
University of Turku

NEW YORK   OXFORD
OXFORD UNIVERSITY PRESS

Oxford University Press is a department of the University of Oxford. It furthers the University's
objective of excellence in research, scholarship, and education by publishing worldwide.

Oxford   New York
Auckland   Cape Town   Dar es Salaam   Hong Kong   Karachi
Kuala Lumpur   Madrid   Melbourne   Mexico City   Nairobi
New Delhi   Shanghai   Taipei   Toronto

With offices in
Argentina   Austria   Brazil   Chile   Czech Republic   France   Greece
Guatemala   Hungary   Italy   Japan   Poland   Portugal   Singapore
South Korea   Switzerland   Thailand   Turkey   Ukraine   Vietnam

For titles covered by Section 112 of the US Higher Education Opportunity
Act, please visit www.oup.com/us/he for the latest information about
pricing and alternate formats.

Published by Oxford University Press.
198 Madison Avenue, New York, New York 10016
www.oup.com

ISBN: 978-0-19-993712-7

Printing number: 9   8   7   6   5   4   3   2   1

Printed in the United States of America
on acid-free paper

CONTENTS

*Indicates new to the fifth edition

PREFACE

NEW TO THE FIFTH EDITION

This edition of *Social Theory: Roots and Branches* contains 17 new selections, including 9 substitutions for entries by a particular author in the previous edition and 8 readings by theorists who are new to this collection. These include the following:

(1) Karl Marx and Friedrich Engels' passage from *The German Ideology*
(2) Émile Durkheim and Marcel Mauss' "Note on the Notion of Civilization"
(3) Georg Simmel's "The Adventurer"
(4) Georg Simmel's "The Metropolis and Mental Life"
(5) Harriet Martineau's "On Marriage"
(6) Alex de Tocqueville's "On Individualism"
(7) Thorstein Veblen's "Conspicuous Consumption"
(8) Charles Horton Cooley's "Social and Individual Aspects of Mind"
(9) Charles Tilly's "War Making and State Making as Organized Crime"
(10) Michael Hechter's "The Emergence of Cooperative Social Institutions"
(11) Catharine MacKinnon's "Difference and Dominance: On Sex Discrimination"
(12) Will Kymlicka's "The Rise and Fall of Multiculturalism?"
(13) Giorgio Agamben's "The Politicization of Life"
(14) Jean-François Lyotard's "The Postmodern Condition: A Report on Knowledge"
(15) Ulrich Beck's "The Cosmopolitan Condition: Why Methodological Nationalism Fails"
(16) Jeffrey Alexander's "Real Civil Societies: Dilemmas of Institutionalization"
(17) Steven Seidman's "Queering Sociology, Sociologizing Queer Theory."

ACKNOWLEDGMENTS

I have been teaching social theory for about a third of a century. First and foremost I would like to thank all of the students who have passed through my classes during that time. In particular, I would like to thank three exceptional students: Dan Pittman, Chad McPherson, and Sonia Hanson. In addition, I would like to thank a number of former professors who in rather different ways and with different results shaped my ability to think like a theorist. They include from my undergraduate days Max Heirich and Stephen Berkowitz and from my graduate school days David Apter, Norman Birnbaum, Niklas Luhmann, Stanford Lyman, Benjamin Nelson, Arthur Vidich, and R. Stephen Warner.

Sherith Pankratz has been involved in several of my book projects for more than a decade, and as I knew would be the case, it has been a real pleasure to have worked with her on this new edition. Sherith is a pro who knows what works. Thus, I always value her judgment and her generous advice. Caitlin Greene and I didn't know each other prior to commencing work on this project. She has proven to be masterful at keeping me on task while providing plenty of assistance along the way. To the reviewers who provided detailed comments, I extend my appreciation for their careful reading and insight provided:

Cynthia D. Anderson, Ohio University
Gretchen Arnold, St. Louis University
Barbara A. Arrigi, Northern Kentucky University
Emma Bailey, Western New Mexico University
David K. Brown, Illinois State Universtiy
Paula S. Brush, Radford University
Keith Doubt, Wittenberg University
Peter R. Grahame, Pennsylvania State University–Schuylkill
Gabe Ignatow, University of North Texas
Thomas J. Keil, Arizona State University
Hans-Herbert Koegler, University of North Florida
Matthew T. Loveland, Le Moyne College
Keumjae Park, William Paterson University
Chavella T. Pittman, Dominican University
Nancy Sonleitner, University of Tennessee–Martin
Adia Harvey Wingfield, Georgia State University

ABOUT THE EDITOR

Peter Kivisto is the Richard A. Swanson Professor of Social Thought and Chair of Sociology at Augustana College, and he is also Finland Distinguished Professor at the University of Turku. He is the author or editor of 28 books, including *Race and Ethnicity: The Basics; Beyond a Border; Citizenship: Discourse, Theory, and Transnational Prospects; Key Ideas in Sociology;* and *Illuminating Social Life.*

SOCIAL THEORY: CLASSICAL FOUNDATIONS AND CONTEMPORARY DEVELOPMENTS

PETER KIVISTO

Near the end of the past century, a century that had witnessed the institutionalization and dramatic growth of sociology in the academy, Alan Sica, the director of the Graduate Program in Social Thought at Pennsylvania State University and a well-known scholar of classical social theory, convened a panel of prominent scholars to probe the question, "What is social theory?" The result of the gathering was a book whose title posed that very question (Sica 1998). A little more than a decade later, two other prominent social theorists, Hans Joas and Wolfgang Knöbl, would begin *Social Theory: Twenty Introductory Lectures* (2009) with a chapter titled "What Is Theory?" Thus it is that a question inevitably raised by undergraduate sociology majors entering a required course in social theory is also a question that scholars who have made theory their vocation continue to ask.

Those who have asked this question repeatedly over the course of their careers are well aware of the fact that one of the reasons it remains germane is that sociologists are far from arriving at a consensus in articulating a reply. At a very general level, most would concur with various depictions of social theory. Thus, few would object to those who characterize theories, variously, as tools of analysis, or lenses into aspects of social reality. All would concur that theories offer something more than description or broad generalizations based on composites of cases.

But it is here that theorists of various persuasions begin to part company. Some advance theories that are interpretive, while others construct theories to explain. Some theorists prefer to focus on structure, while others concentrate on the agency of social actors. Indeed, some theorists begin with the individual while others think it quite all right to dispense altogether with individuals. Some theorists think the proper object of investigation ought to be social structures, while others are equally convinced that culture should be the main focus. In another theoretical divide, one side is intent on keeping social theory closely linked to social philosophy, while the other side urges the construction of formal mathematical models patterned after the natural sciences. Finally, for some theorists the purpose of theory extends no further than to understand some patch of reality, a view that was articulated by Erving Goffman (1982) in his presidential address to the American Sociological Association, where he contended that the reason one studies the social world is simply "because it is there." Others—indeed, if Goffman is right, a majority of the profession—think that theories ought to have some practical or applied import or, to use Marxist terminology, theory ought to be related to praxis (or, in other words, concrete social practices). It is thus not surprising that Donald Levine would speak in the plural of *Visions of the Sociological Tradition* (1995) rather than of a singular, shared vision.

Given such widely divergent assessments of the nature and functions of theory, it´s reasonable to ask what counts as theory and what doesn´t. It is also reasonable to ask whether the fragmented and contested discipline of sociology will ever move beyond being what George Ritzer (1975) has called a "multiple paradigm science." There are those who dream of the time that sociology will "mature" sufficiently to develop a commonly shared paradigm that serves to shape inquiry. To lay my cards on the table, I am not convinced that we are moving or someday will move toward consensus nor do I think it is necessary to do so. Indeed, part of the vitality of the discipline derives from the fact that it is engaged in attempting to make sense of what is invariably "contested knowledge" (Seidman 2013, Callinicos 2007). Sociology is a big-tent discipline. It relies on a wide range of research methodologies as well as a broad spectrum of theoretical approaches.

This fact, of course, poses challenges to anybody seeking to introduce students to social theory, for being as comprehensive as possible can make it difficult for students to be able to see the forest for the trees. Moreover, the need to be selective means that some theorists are being privileged over others. It is this issue that I want to address by explaining the structure and rationale for this particular collection of articles. Social theory encompasses a body of writing dating from the early nineteenth century that has informed and continues to inform the discipline of sociology. This anthology has a simple objective, which is to assist students in social theory classes to acquire an appreciation of its range and scope. A casual perusal of the 85 entries in this collection will reveal the remarkable variety of work that falls under the rubric "social theory." Looking a bit further, readers will find ample indications that social theory is indeed a contested terrain abounding in intellectual debates and controversies.

For the first three editions of this book, I used Peter Xiao´s painting titled "Intellectual Pursuits" for the cover (see page ii) because I think it manages to humorously convey the sense of urgency and importance that thinkers attach to ideas. While it is not often that intellectual disputes lead scholars to throw books at one another, it is true that social theorists are capable of being quite feisty! They take ideas seriously, and as such do not enter lightly into debates with those who have a different sense of the nature and purpose of theory.

Although the selection process necessarily excluded many significant theorists, I have tried to identify and include representatives of those theoretical approaches that have had the greatest impact on sociology. The history of sociology has been an ongoing process of defining disciplinary boundaries while remaining open to interdisciplinary dialogues. The readings I have selected reflect an attempt to show how sociology has developed as a distinctive enterprise while also revealing the ways in which voices from outside the discipline have continued to enrich it. While in the end I am responsible for the choices appearing within these two covers, this is far from a solo venture. On the contrary, anthologies that attempt to provide readers with a broad, ecumenical overview of a field are not possible without a sustained conversation with numerous other people, including prominent scholars,

professors who teach relevant courses, reviewers employed by the publisher, editors, and students. I have relied on dozens of such individuals and have benefited in many ways from the sage advice I have received for each previous edition as well as for this one. While many of these people are mentioned by name in the acknowledgments, the point here is simply that creating a theory reader is very much a cooperative enterprise.

CLASSICAL ROOTS AND THE EMERGENCE OF A CANON

This reader is divided into two sections, which I have termed "roots" and "branches." The former comprises the period from roughly 1840 to 1920, a time when sociology emerged as a distinctive enterprise, distinguishing itself from philosophy and the other social sciences. During this time, the first explicit advocates of this new field of inquiry appeared on the scene and created what might be seen as the infrastructure needed to sustain it, particularly the carving out of a legitimate place in the university system, with all that implies. This time frame represents sociology´s classical period. The individuals associated with this era were responsible, even when they were not trying to do so, for giving sociology its initial identity.

In this regard, it is important to note that left out of this collection are those philosophers who preceded the rise of sociology and social theory. These include classics in the history of philosophy, beginning with Plato and Aristotle, but in particular those that are associated with the rise of modern philosophical inquiry into the nature of social order, such as Niccolo Machiavelli; Charles Louis Montesquieu; the social contract theorists Thomas Hobbes, John Locke, and Jean-Jacques Rousseau; Claude Henri de Rouvroy Saint-Simon; the Scottish moralists such as Adam Smith and Adam Ferguson; Immanuel Kant; and Georg Wilhelm Friedrich Hegel. These and others constitute the central figures of the prehistory of sociology (Hawthorne 1976). According to Johan Heilbron in *The Rise of Social Theory* (1995), it was in the predisciplinary era from approximately 1600 to 1850 that such thinkers developed analytical tools that would become central to the sociological enterprise, including such basic concepts as society, economy and state. He sees the rise of social theory being made possible by the emergence of an intellectual space distinct from both church and state. In a related argument, Brian Singer (2004) contends that the birth of the social was made possible insofar as social theory began to be viewed as an enterprise distinct from political theory. These thinkers not only had a profound impact on the classic figures we take up in this collection, but continue to inform theorists (see, for example, contemporary theorists of civil society, who frequently begin by turning to the likes of Ferguson, or see in this collection the role of Hegel´s concept of recognition in the critical theory of Axel Honneth).

In a provocative article, R. W. Connell (1997) asked "Why Is Classical Theory Classical?" He claimed that, contrary to the standard view that sociology arose in order to make sense of the emergence of modern industrial societies, in fact the early figures associated with the formative years of the discipline were keenly interested in the worlds of the colonial Other and as such they engaged in the "imperial gaze" and granted legitimacy to the colonialism of the era. Sociology's linkage to issues concerning imperialism was reflected in its practitioners' preoccupation with the idea of progress, which was assessed by comparisons of "primitive" and "advanced" societies. In his pointed rejoinder to the article, Randall Collins (1997) insisted, quite accurately in my opinion, that early sociologists were far more preoccupied with changes occurring within their own societies than with what was happening elsewhere and thus the common narrative of the rise of sociology is an accurate depiction of that history. More to the point of this discussion, he observes that Connell "has no real explanation of canonicity, just a denunciation of it" (Collins 1997: 1558). He, in short, failed to answer the question posed in his article's title.

Before suggesting an answer to what makes something classical or canonical, we first turn to question of process: How does one become a classic, and, related to this question, how does a text become part of the canon? There is no simple answer to either of these questions. The reputations of early sociologists have often waxed and waned over time. Likewise, the canon, being a social construct, is subject to challenges and to change. There is no central sociological authority

that lays claim to being the final arbiter regarding who counts as a classic figure and who doesn´t and, similarly, which texts are canonical and which are not. Nevertheless, it is clear that influential and well-positioned sociological elites play a key role in making these determinations, acting as brokers.

This situation is no different than in other fields. Thus, in literature, the literary establishment— English professors at elite universities and critics writing for national newspapers and the most influential literary journals—once excoriated James Joyce, and his masterpiece, *Ulysses*, was prevented from entering the United States because it was considered pornographic. Today Joyce is comfortably located in the pantheon of the twentieth century´s greatest authors of fiction. Contemporary novelists such as Philip Roth and John Updike are highly regarded today, but exactly how they will be viewed in the long run is still to be determined—their precise place in the canon can only be surmised. On the other hand, today´s literary gatekeepers disparage Danielle Steel´s oeuvre, viewing it as nothing more than drivel for the masses. Given that this assessment is not likely to be overturned by subsequent critics, Steel will no doubt remain forever outside the canon, her only consolation being the fortune she has amassed as a result of her pandering.

While the financial stakes and prestige have never been quite so high in sociology, a similar process has been and continues to be at play. The gatekeepers are not all that different from those in the literary world. Professors at elite universities, journal editors, and the editorial decision makers at publishing houses have had a say in deciding which works enter the canon and which are excluded. This is at best an imperfect process, as honest considerations of the particular merits and weaknesses of any work inevitably mingle with the intellectual predilections and cultural prejudices of the critics in question. Nowhere are the latter more evident than in matters related to the gender and racial backgrounds of specific authors.

One way of determining whether someone ought to be considered a contender for the sociological pantheon is whether his or her work continues to be read today and in some fashion still informs the varied ways in which sociologists frame their patterns of inquiry. Early in the twenty-first century, there is fairly widespread consensus that four scholars have played especially significant roles in shaping what has come to be contemporary sociology: (1) Karl Marx (1818–1883), who never claimed to be a sociologist or suggested he wanted to advance sociology´s cause (he did, however, criticize the earliest proponent of sociology, Auguste Comte); (2) Émile Durkheim (1858–1917), who was single-minded in his determination to promote sociology as a science clearly distinct from competing social sciences; (3) Max Weber (1864–1920), who became a sociologist later in life but never gave up also considering himself to be a historian and economist; and (4) Georg Simmel (1858–1918), who until fairly recently was not considered in the league of the preceding trio but whose reputation in recent years has finally landed him in the pantheon of founding figures.

What exactly does it mean to say that this quartet is viewed as foundational to the discipline? Suffice it to say that all of them are widely read today, with all of their major works still in print in many languages. Moreover, in all cases there are virtual cottage industries devoted to exegeses, analyses, and assessments of their works. Parenthetically, the fact that we maintain such interest in individuals who were dead by 1920 and that we continue to read them indicates that sociologists disagree with Alfred North Whitehead´s (1938) claim that a science cannot progress unless it forgets its founders. We read them because whatever their shortcomings and however different our world is from theirs, they provide insights that continue to inform the discipline.

In examining how the work of certain social theorists came to be viewed as classical, one can get an implicit sense of what it means to be a classic. Whereas Connell skirted the question in his earlier noted article, Jeffrey C. Alexander (1987) has convincingly addressed it head on in perhaps as clear and concise an account as is possible:

> Classics are earlier works of human exploration which are given privileged status *vis-à-vis* contemporary explorations in the same field. The concept of privileged status means that contemporary practitioners of the discipline in question believe that they can learn as much

about their field through understanding this earlier work as they can from the work of their own contemporaries. To be accorded such a privileged status, moreover, implies that, in the day-to-day work of the average practitioner, this deference is accorded without prior demonstration; it is accepted as a matter of course that, as a classic, such a work establishes fundamental criteria in the particular field. It is because of this privileged position that exegesis and reinterpretation of the classics—within or without a historical context—become conspicuous currents in various disciplines, for what is perceived to be the "true meaning" of a classical work has broad repercussions. (pp. 11–12)

In other words, we examine these theorists because they get us thinking in intellectually productive ways. Their works are not construed as ends in themselves. If sociologists were to treat any or all of these scholars as providing something akin to revealed truth, they would be approaching works such as *Capital, The Division of Labor in Society, The Protestant Ethic and the Spirit of Capitalism,* and *The Philosophy of Money* in a manner analogous to the way Christian fundamentalists view the Bible—as inerrant and complete. Fortunately, few sociologists operate with such a perspective—and those who do tend to be adherents of an orthodox Marxism that is fast fading from the scene.

The appropriate reason for reading these canonical figures is that sociological theory does not arise out of nowhere, without context or history. Rather, it is always the product of responding to a tradition of thought, and in this regard theorists are no different from other writers who both look forward to what they want to produce and backward to whence they came. Much theoretical work is intended to be revisionist, by which I mean that it seeks to simultaneously build upon and correct those who came before. It sometimes wants to amend, while at other times to challenge, to embrace and refine, or to dismiss. Whatever the particular nature of the relationship with past theorists, all are motivated in part by what literary scholar Harold Bloom (1997) has called the "anxiety of influence."

When did Marx, Durkheim, Weber, and Simmel become classics? Certainly after their deaths, since death would appear to be a prerequisite. While this is not the place for intellectual history, I note simply that Durkheim and Weber were accorded classic status first. While the process of becoming part of the canon began rather quickly after their deaths, a most important point occurred with the publication of Talcott Parsons´ *The Structure of Social Action (SSA)* in 1937. Therein the young Harvard theorist, sensing an unappreciated convergence in their writing, placed them in the center of sociological theory. His book was to have a singularly important impact on their subsequent reputations. However, it was not altogether determinative in shaping the received wisdom of various theorists, for he also included two other theorists who are largely unread today: Alfred Marshall and Vilfredo Pareto. At the same time, it is worth mentioning that Parsons appeared to be ambivalent about Simmel. On the one hand, he treated him as a sufficiently compelling theorist to draft a chapter for the book. On the other hand, in the end he decided not to publish that particular chapter.

Marx was never considered for inclusion into Parsons´ first major work. Moreover, Marx´s move into the canon was stymied by the association of his work with the events surrounding the Russian Revolution and subsequent Marxist-inspired revolutions. During the Cold War, and especially during the McCarthy era, embracing Marx´s ideas could be a risky enterprise. Nonetheless, even before the events of the 1960s—the civil rights movement, the anti-Vietnam war movement, and the counterculture—Marx´s reputation was on the rise among sociologists. As Alvin Gouldner (1973) pointed out, two of the most significant theorists of the post–World War II era, Robert Merton and C. Wright Mills "kept open an avenue of access to Marxist theory" (pp. x–xi). This meant that two of the three major theory schools of the period—functionalism and conflict theory—made room for Marxist thought.

Finally, Simmel´s claim to canonical status occurred only in the late 1960s and early 1970s. In no small part, this was due to the promotional efforts of a small number of scholars, most notably the émigré scholar Kurt Wolfe and University of Chicago theorist Donald Levine. It is fair to say that, just like during his lifetime when he was highly regarded by many

influential sociologists ranging from Weber to the key figures associated with the early years of the Chicago School of sociology but still remained marginalized, so it is today. Indeed, if theorists continue to debate whether any of these four should be considered central founders of social theory, Simmel is clearly the one whose status is most insecure.

If these individuals have made the grade, who didn´t? I could provide a long list of also-rans, but among the more obvious are Auguste Comte, Herbert Spencer, William Graham Sumner, and Vilfredo Pareto. Comte was a prolific writer who bequeathed to us the name of our discipline, creating "sociology" out of two stems, the Latin *socius* and Greek *logos*. He had an impact, not the least on someone included in this collection: Harriett Martineau. Nonetheless, he is little read today, and when he is it is more out of historical curiosity than a desire to import his ideas into contemporary sociological discourse. A similar fate befell Spencer, who was widely read and respected during his lifetime. Nevertheless, by the time Parsons wrote *SSA*, he was increasingly ignored, in no small part because of his association with Social Darwinian ideology. Parsons (1937) famously began his book with the following sentence: "Who now reads Spencer?" A similar fate befell Sumner, who introduced sociology to Yale and was one of the first presidents of the American Sociological Society, and he was left out for similar reasons, as his politics were in main respects similar to those of Spencer. Pareto was an acerbic and lacerating critic of other theorists, including Marx and Durkheim, which made him controversial in his lifetime. Over time, his ideas (perhaps fairly, perhaps unfairly) became associated with Italian fascism, which did his reputation no good. In addition, many subsequent theorists concluded that in the end he really wasn´t a theorist. It should be noted that periodically calls have been made to reconsider the contribution of one or another of these largely ignored thinkers, as when Jonathan Turner (1985) proposed a reevaluation of Spencer´s legacy. It should also be noted that those calls have largely gone unheeded.

In recent decades the discipline at large has increasingly come to the realization that some scholars from the nineteenth and early twentieth centuries were not given their due during their lifetimes. These neglected figures are the products of the dual legacies of racism and sexism. In several instances, concerted efforts have been made to redress this situation, beginning with the civil rights and women´s movements in the 1960s. While many of the neglected voices made valuable contributions to one or another of sociology´s various subfields, they were not necessarily interested in advancing social theory.

In this collection, I have identified a few particularly significant individuals who because of their race or gender were marginalized from the mainstream of the emerging sociological profession and as a result failed to influence developments in theory the way they might have. The earliest such neglected voice that I have included is the British writer Harriet Martineau, whose thought, as noted earlier, was shaped by Comte. Viewed for decades as an entertaining travel writer and essayist, she has only recently—due in no small part to the efforts of historical sociologists such as Michael Hill and Susan Hoecker-Drysdale (2001)—been viewed as someone who made a contribution to social theory. The marginalization of W. E. B. DuBois is perhaps even more curious given that he was trained as a sociologist, becoming the first black to obtain a Ph.D. from Harvard (where he studied with such luminaries as William James), and the author of *The Philadelphia Negro* (1899), considered to be the first major empirical research study published by an American sociologist. Part of the reason that he was frequently forgotten as a sociologist is that he left academe (his job options were limited to historically black colleges) to become one of the founding members of the NAACP and spent his life, in the United States—and later, when he embraced Pan-Africanism, in Ghana—as a civil rights and political activist. Nonetheless, as has become clear due to renewed attention to his writings (see, for example, Zuckermann 2004), it is well worth the effort to explore how Du Bois can contribute to social theory—particularly, in an age of multiculturalism, to the ongoing salience of racial and ethnic identities.

For her part, Jane Addams, the founder of Hull House and recipient of the Nobel Peace Prize, had an ongoing relationship with the members of the Chicago School of sociology and as such was well positioned to be viewed as a sociologist in her own right, despite a lack of explicit training in the field. She is appropriately known as one of the most important founding figures of contemporary social work and as an activist supporting a variety of progressive causes, and these activities clearly overshadowed her contribution to sociology in general and theory in particular. Nevertheless, as Mary Jo Deegan (1988) and others have made clear, it is worth the effort to return to her work, particularly in coming to terms with changing gender roles brought about by the newly emerging industrial society and the birth of the welfare state. And thus it goes with another neglected figure. Charlotte Perkins Gilman, a student of early American sociologist Lester Ward, is better known today as an early feminist; whether she had anything to offer social theorists has only recently been explored.

In recent years, considerable intellectual energy has been expended attempting to include these and related figures as other important foundation voices. In this regard, they are no longer neglected the way they once were. Just as a consideration and intellectual appreciation of their work is underway, so there is a contemporary reconsideration of figures who were influential during their lifetime, but whose work bears scrutiny to determine to what extent they remain valuable precursors to contemporary social theorizing. Among such are two included herein: the iconoclastic economist and social critic Thorstein Veblen and the pragmatist sociologist usually considered to be an early spokesperson for what would become known as symbolic interactionism, Charles Horton Cooley.

In what is perhaps a place of his own, Alexis de Tocqueville has had a generally positive reputation over the long haul, due primarily to the continued interest in the book he produced after visiting the United States in the 1830s, *Democracy in America* (1969 [1853]). Among the most enduring topics of interest has been his discussion on individualism, which led, for example, to a major study by Robert Bellah and colleagues, *Habits of the Heart* (1985), that, in effect, sought to explore the themes Tocqueville raised about individualism 150 years later.

What is clear is that the canon developed slowly and fitfully. Borrowing an insight from social constructionism, we should treat the canon as an ongoing accomplishment and not as a fixed, stable, and unchanging "thing." While it would appear that from the vantage of the present the four European scholars accorded their own sections in this collection are firmly located in the pantheon of founding figures of modern social theory, there is also an appreciation of the fact that they are not the only intellectuals from the past who ought to inform present and future trends in social theory.

In this regard, I concur with John O'Neill and Bryan Turner, founders of the *Journal of Classical Sociology*, who in an editorial that launched that publication's first issue wrote, "A canon, however uncertain and contested, has been important as a common platform in the study of sociology, as a framework for teaching sociology to students and as one component in building a common research purpose." With this in mind, they suggested, "A constructive canon of sociology should have the normative goal of nurturing the sociological imagination rather than functioning as a narrow principle of professional exclusion" (O'Neill and Turner 2001: 6–7).

CONTEMPORARY BRANCHES OF A MULTIPLE-PARADIGM SCIENCE

No unified theoretical paradigm shapes sociology today. Nor is one looming on the horizon. In fact, many inside and outside the world of social theory would describe the situation as a cacophony of competing approaches. Some bemoan this reality, others embrace it as salutary, and still others simply see it as a fact of life. This is not to suggest that efforts have not been made to create a unified and singular theoretical paradigm. However, the experience of the past seven decades has led most sociologists to be rather circumspect about the prospects of becoming other than a multiple-paradigm science.

The boldest attempt to forge a one-paradigm science commenced with the publication of Parsons' *SSA*. The central claim of that work was that those classic theorists he was prepared to place in the canon, particularly Durkheim and Weber, had more in common than first met the eye. Indeed, in articulating what he was to call a "theory of action," Parsons explicitly intended to stress the commonalities of these figures (Camic 1989). He thought that none had managed to develop an entirely satisfactory basis for a

unified theoretical approach, but they had set the stage. Parsons then turned his attention to a sustained effort to establish that unified theory. Indeed, his goal in *Toward a General Theory of Action* (1951), which he edited with Edward Shils, was to create a theoretical paradigm that would serve to unite the various social sciences, particularly sociology, anthropology, and psychology. He found that paradigm in what was first defined as functionalism (he shifted to systems theory during the later phase of his life). Given his missionary zeal and his ecumenical outlook on those theory camps that differed from his approach (particularly symbolic interactionism and phenomenology), he managed for a time to establish a hegemonic theoretical stance, though not one without significant dissent. During the 1950s and 1960s, functionalism was the reigning orthodoxy. However, it never managed to eliminate all theoretical competitors. Rather, two competing schools during this time came to characterize what might be described as the loyal opposition: conflict theories and symbolic interactionism. Unlike the Parsonian effort to create a unified theoretical model, conflict theorists were a varied lot, some influenced primarily by Marx and Marxism and others aptly characterized by a neo-Weberian approach. What they shared in common was a conviction that structural functionalism presented a distorted portrait of social life that depicted individuals as overly socialized and society as overly integrated. This led to frontal assaults on Parsonian theory, evident in two influential works that appeared just as the Cold War consensus appeared to unravel: C. Wright Mills' *The Sociological Imagination* (1959), with its often sarcastic critique of "Grand Theory," and Alvin Gouldner's far more sustained challenge to "the world of Talcott Parsons" in *The Coming Crisis of Western Sociology* (1970). Symbolic interactionists did not tend to engage in similar frontal attacks on structural functionalism, but key exponents such as Herbert Blumer did express their misgivings about what they saw as the dominant tendencies in the discipline (see Vidich and Lyman 1985: 307). Thus it is that the first three sections of the "branches" part of this book represent each of these theoretical orientations.

Functionalism, structural functionalism, and systems theory are three analytically distinct but in historical practice interrelated theoretical positions, and since this package of theories achieved a certain level of hegemony in the two decades after World War II, we appropriately begin with them. The section titled Functionalism and Systems Theory begins with a classic statement from Robert K. Merton, one of the key exponents of functionalism during this era, on the unintended consequences of action. This is followed by an example of Talcott Parsons' articulation of systems theory, in this instance focusing on the subsystems of society. If functionalism was deemed useful in accounting for social consensus and solidarity, Lewis Coser's contribution on the functions of conflict indicates that functionalists thought, contrary to the critics, that they could account for conflict. The section is rounded out with an entry by the German systems theorist Niklas Luhmann, who carried this tradition on and moved it in new directions until his death in 1998. In contrast to Parsons' contention that the system was an analytical tool for understanding certain societal processes, Luhmann viewed systems ontologically.

Conflict theories comprise a variety of approaches that share one thing in common: the assumption that functionalism tended to gloss over the tensions, fissions, and problems—in short the conflictual tendencies and realities—in contemporary social life. Such was disputed, in differing ways, by the three theorists used to exemplify the conflict stance: C. Wright Mills, Ralf Dahrendorf, and Randall Collins. Collins, it should be noted, was responsible for the first significant effort to provide a systematic conflict theory. The section is rounded out by Charles Tilly's provocative, historically grounded argument that nation states should be seen as parallel institutions to criminal syndicates, both operating as protection rackets.

Symbolic interaction theory was deeply indebted to the work of philosopher George Herbert Mead, though it was sociologist Herbert Blumer who was responsible, in the selection included herein, for spelling out what a symbolic interactionist perspective might look like. Blumer rejected Parsons' claim that this theoretical stance could readily be incorporated into Parsons' own theoretical edifice. Symbolic interactionists became closely associated with ethnographic research methods and with the presentation of thick descriptions in attempts to uncover the interpretive work of actors creating their lives and their social worlds. For his part Erving Goffman would

probably have resisted being so labeled. Indeed, although in many respects he ought to be seen as offering a distinctive approach to theory, it is clear that subsequent symbolic interactionists like to claim Goffman as one of their own, and it is fair to conclude that if one has to categorize him, this is the most appropriate label to apply.

If symbolic interaction is a distinctly American theoretical branch, phenomenology's roots are European, located in particular in the philosopher Edmund Husserl's work. Among the most important scholars to bring phenomenology into sociology was the Austrian-born émigré scholar Alfred Schutz, who along with other European exile scholars taught at New York's New School for Social Research. Unlike Blumer, he actually sought to engage Parsons in an ongoing dialogue, but in the end he was frustrated by where it was leading. Certainly not to be confused with phenomenology, but bearing what might be called a family resemblance, ethnomethodology emerged, like symbolic interactionism, on American soil. Harold Garfinkel is the founding figure of ethnomethodology, and thus it is appropriate that an excerpt from his landmark book, *Studies in Ethnomethodology* (1967), be included in the section. Given the interest of many ethnomethodologists in conversational analysis, it is also appropriate that one of the early proponents of such a focus, Harvey Sacks, also be included.

The following section, Exchange Theory and Rational Choice Theory, like the preceding one, links two theoretical camps that are distinct but nonetheless are in some respects related or offer overlapping perspectives. Exchange theory is the oldest, generally associated with Parsons's Harvard colleague and theoretical rival, George Homans. He was an exponent of methodological individualism and a behavioralist approach to the social sciences and thus disagreed profoundly with Parsons's work. Indeed, in his autobiography, *Coming to My Senses* (1984) Homans wrote that Parsons asked him to read SSA. He went on to say, "I conscientiously read it, but did not criticize it, I hated it so much" (p. 323). Exchange theory was taken up by Richard Emerson, who utilized laboratory experiments to ground his theoretical work on "power-dependence relations." Peter Blau's contribution to exchange theory in this collection occurs in his effort to link the micro-level analysis characteristic of exchange theory to macro-level issues.

One of the selections in this section was penned by rational choice theorist James S. Coleman. Coleman's selection derives from his magnum opus, *Foundations of Social Theory* (1990), wherein he sought to do nothing less than point social theory in a new direction, specifically one that in many respects abandoned Parsons. Like exchange theorists, Coleman embraced methodological individualism. His excerpt sketches some of the fundamental grounding principles of the approach. To provide a concrete example of a rational choice theorist approaching a specific topic, Michael Hechter's essay seeks to illustrate how one might understand the way that cooperative social institutions are constructed and how they address the perennial problem of "free riders."

If the preceding two sections contain theoretical orientations that operate at fairly high levels of abstraction and at a remove from political engagements, such is not the case with the next two sections. Beginning with the first, feminist theories, a great outpouring of theoretical work developed during and in the wake of the 1960s women's movement. Feminist theories often have their origins in other theoretical perspectives, including but not limited to Marxism, neo-Freudianism, structuralism, symbolic interactionism, and postmodernism. This section provides readers with some indication of the range of feminist theories, beginning with Candace West and Don Zimmerman's symbolic interactionist-grounded article and including Catharine MacKinnon's brief on behalf of a dominance approach to sex discrimination, Patricia Hill Collins' attempt to link race and gender in outlining an Afrocentric feminist epistemology, and Dorothy Smith's explanation of what "standpoint" means for a theoretical approach that begins with the concrete experiences of women. Finally, the Australian feminist theorist Raewyn Connell (much of her work has been published under the names R. W. or Robert W.) develops a theory of the power dynamics inherent in gender relations, understood in terms of her concept of "hegemonic masculinity."

This is followed by a section first introduced in the preceding edition, one concerned with the interrelated concepts of race, ethnicity, and nationalism. Two of the selections focus explicitly on race, beginning with Michael Omi and Howard Winant's articulation of the outlines of a critical theory of race. This is followed by and counterposed to British theorist Paul Gilroy's interrogation of the idea of race from the perspective of a global humanism. Canadian philosopher Will Kymlicka is one of the primary exponents of liberal multiculturalism, a perspective on incorporating diverse cultural groups in liberal democracies in a way that expands the bounds of national solidarity without demanding the elimination of cultural differences. Of particular note in his first influential work on the subject, *Multicultural Citizenship* (1995), is his distinction between ethnonational minorities and indigenous peoples on the one hand and voluntary immigrants on the other. He contends that the former can appropriately make more far-reaching claims for cultural preservation than the latter. In the selection included herein, he takes stock of the multicultural condition today, after a period of sustained criticism of multicultural policies and practices in both Western Europe and North America. In a very different vein, Rogers Brubaker attempts to salvage ethnicity from reifying tendencies, arguing that "groupism" offers a theoretically suspect way of viewing social relations that are inherently dynamic and multifarious. The section is rounded out with an essay by Craig Calhoun on nationalism, which he contends offers an important source of solidarity needed to establish the idea of a "people" that is essential for the flourishing of democracy.

The next section contains selections from the key figures associated with the Frankfurt School who advanced a "critical theory" that was at once deeply indebted to Marx and also profoundly influenced (even when not explicitly acknowledged) by Weber. Actually, there is both a broad and a narrower definition of critical theory. The broad definition refers to theories in general that are concerned with overcoming domination, and have both a descriptive and a normative character. Thus, for example, the contemporary French theorist Luc Boltanski has recently written a book in this spirit, *On Critique: A Sociology of Emancipation* (2011). This selection is shaped by the narrow definition, which refers specifically to theorists who have been directly associated with the Frankfurt School. Although different from one another in many ways, what linked these individuals was an abiding critique of capitalism and a concern with the consequences of rationalization. This section includes an excerpt from Walter Benjamin's extremely influential article "Art in the Age of Mechanical Reproduction," Herbert Marcuse's critique of the new forms of control that he saw arising in the overly administered societies of the world's liberal democracies, and Max Horkheimer's comparison of traditional and critical theory. All three of these individuals were contemporaries and associated with the founding of the Frankfurt School. In contrast, Jürgen Habermas is the current heir of these founding figures. He has been concerned with the challenges confronting the public sphere since the earliest phase of his academic life and with their implications for democratic practice. He offers an alternative to what are generally posed as the two available democratic options—liberalism and republicanism—that he refers to as deliberative politics. Axel Honneth is the third-generation heir to Habermas' mantle. Arguing for the central significance of recognition and respect for identity, he charts a course that, among other things, has implications for conceptualizing multiculturalism.

The following section offers an array of articles by theorists seeking to account for aspects of the causes and consequences of modernity—viewing it, to borrow from Peter Wagner (2008), as experience and interpretation. It begins with an excerpt from Norbert Elias, a scholar who worked in relative obscurity for decades on the "civilizing process" but who by the 1970s was finally recognized as a major theorist of the rise of modernity. Guy Debord, a key figure of the French Situationist International, is an original thinker, though his work resembles in some respects both critical theory and postmodernism. His contribution to the collection provides a brief introduction to his concept of "the society of the spectacle." Anthony Giddens, one of the most influential theorists in the world during the past three decades, rejects the notion that we have entered a postmodern epoch, instead contending that we have moved to a higher stage of modernity. His focus in the selection contained here is on the reflexive character of modernity. Bruno Latour can be read as an iconoclast who sides neither with postmodernists nor the defenders of modernism, arguing instead that both camps have in fundamental ways gotten it all wrong. He declares as much in his provocative claim that "we have never been modern." Finally, this section is rounded out with an excerpt from Italian political theorist Giorgio Agamben's increasingly influential work on the political condition of the modern world, which he characterizes by what he refers to as "bare life."

Three distinct but often related theoretical strands define the next section: structuralism, poststructuralism, and postmodernism. In his discussion of structures and habitus, the late French theorist Pierre Bourdieu builds on both Marxism and structuralism in developing his own distinctive theoretical perspective which took shape in his relatively early work, *Outline of a Theory of Practice* (1977). The selection contained in this collection derives from perhaps his most widely read work, *Distinction* (1984), which makes use of his theoretical approach in a richly detailed account of the social production of taste, with a particular emphasis on its class-based character. Michel Foucault is the poststructuralist representative in the collection. His analysis of Jeremy Bentham's notion of the panopticon reveals something of his understanding of the relationship between knowledge, power, and control. Postmodernism has been a highly influential theoretical perspective in the social sciences and humanities, but because it is defined so variably by different advocates, it is often difficult to specify what one means in using the term. Two rather different representatives of postmodernism are included in order to illustrate this fact: the radical postmodernist Jean Baudrillard and the more moderate version of postmodernism associated with the writings of Zygmunt Bauman. In his most recent work, Bauman has begun to use "liquid" imagery, describing the present as novel insofar as everyday life and the culture that informs it are increasingly incapable of establishing anything resembling permanence or stability. Within this ambit, he has written brief essays that deal with liquid life, liquid modernity, liquid times, and liquid fear. This section is completed with a selection from what has become one of the classic statements on the epistemology of postmodernism, that of the late French theorist Jean-François Lyotard, a statement that, interestingly, was commissioned by a university advisory body in the Canadian province of Quebec.

Few would dispute the fact that we live in an increasingly interconnected world where what geographer David Harvey (1996) calls "time-space compression" has led to an emerging global economy, the increasing significance of transnational politics, and the ascendance of a global culture. It has become incumbent on theorists to increasingly frame their work with globalization in mind. The four authors in the section on world systems and globalization theory are among the most prominent exemplars of current developments. Immanuel Wallerstein's major project on world systems theory offers a Marxist-inspired approach to the emergence of a capitalist system that no longer operates primarily at the national level but has over several centuries managed to become a world-wide phenomenon. If his work is more explicitly associated with world systems theory, the other three authors in the section are globalization theorists, including German theorist Ulrich Beck, who has sought to link globalization theory to ideas associated with modernity, risk society, and more recently cosmopolitanism. While Arjun Appadurai is primarily interested in the cultural aspects of globalization, Douglas Kellner focuses his lens on the intersections of political and economic globalization, with a keen eye to the reconfigurations of power.

The final section contains selections from four particularly prominent contemporary theorists whose current work does not fit neatly into any of the existing section headings. In rather different ways, they point to new potential directions for theory development. French theorist Alain Touraine offers a theoretical account of the role of social movements in shaping the contours of change in post-industrial society. In his work, the subject is conceived in collective rather than individual terms. Jeffrey Alexander's *The Civil Sphere* (2006) constitutes the most significant effort to rethink a long legacy of civil society theorizing, locating his position in terms of major theorists from the eighteenth century through the twentieth and advancing the claim that the civil sphere is the institutional realm of solidarity and justice. Randall Collins, whose contribution to conflict sociology appears earlier in the collection, has recently built on the work of Durkheim and Goffman to advance what he calls "interaction ritual theory." Steven Seidman, one of the principal proponents of queer theory, builds on the work of Foucault and Dorothy Smith to lay out the implications of this perspective for sociology. Manuel

Castells offers a version of network theory quite different from that advanced by figures such as Harrison White. Castells offers a macro-sociological theoretical account of the contours of a network society in an information age. Finally, John Urry proposes that sociology ought to shift its focus from the study of society, which encourages a static approach to social life, to the study of mobility—or more specifically, mobilities.

CONCLUSION

As this overview reveals, social theory is a remarkably broad and diverse enterprise. I, quite frankly, would have liked to include far more theorists than I was able to within the confines of a single volume. Many of the reviewers for the fifth edition offered suggested theorists and readings, and in some instances I followed their advice. In the end, there were many excellent suggestions that I simply could not make room for. The choice of entries is further complicated by the fact that deciding what to include and what to exclude was partially dependent on any particular work's accessibility to student readers—an inherently difficult matter for all social theory anthologies. While I make no claim that the readings are easy, I do believe that careful attention has been paid to including seminal readings that can be made comprehensible to most students. Confidence in my judgment was reinforced by the fact that I received valuable advice from a number of people who currently teach theory courses in a variety of institutional settings.

It is my firm conviction that students cannot get a feel for what theory is or how theorists think without reading them in their own words. There are a number of fine textbooks on the market that can assist students in understanding the intellectual and social contexts that shaped various theoretical projects. These texts can also provide cogent and helpful overviews of the key issues motivating particular theorists and the characteristic elements of their respective theoretical approaches. However, these ought to be viewed as complementary—modes of assistance as one engages with the texts themselves. It is only after engaging the original works that one is in a position to begin to offer a compelling, if tentative, answer to the question, What is social theory?

REFERENCES

Alexander, Jeffrey C. 1987. "The Centrality of the Classics." Pp. 11–57 in Anthony Giddens and Jonathan H. Turner (eds.), *Social Theory Today*. Stanford, CA: Stanford University Press.

———— 2006. *The Civil Sphere*. New York: Oxford University Press.

Bellah, Robert, Richard Mardsen, William M. Sullivan, Ann Swidler, and Steven M. Tipton. 1985. *Habits of the Heart: Individualism and Commitment in American Life*. Berkeley: University of California Press.

Bloom, Harold. 1997. *The Anxiety of Influence: A Theory of Poetry*, 2nd edition. New York: Oxford University Press.

Boltanski, Luc. 2011. *On Critique: A Sociology of Emancipation*. Cambridge, UK: Polity.

Bourdieu, Pierre. 1977. *Outline of a Theory of Practice*. Cambridge, UK: Cambridge University Press.

———— 1984. *Distinction: A Social Critique of the Judgement of Taste*. Cambridge, MA: Harvard University Press.

Callinicos, Alex. 2007. *Social Theory: An Introduction*, 2nd edition. Cambridge, UK: Polity Press.

Camic, Charles. 1989. "Structure After 50 Years: The Anatomy of a Charter." *American Journal of Sociology*, 95(1): 38–107.

Coleman, James S. 1990. *Foundations of Social Theory*. Cambridge, MA: The Belknap Press of Harvard University Press.

Collins, Randall. 1997. "A Sociological Guilt Trip: Comment on Connell." *American Journal of Sociology*, 102(6): 1558–1564.

Connell, R. W. 1997. "Why Is Classical Theory Classical?" *American Journal of Sociology*, 102(6): 1511–1547.

Deegan, Mary Jo. 1988. *Jane Addams and the Men of the Chicago School, 1892–1918*. New Brunswick, NJ: Transaction Books.

DuBois, W. E. B. 1999 [1899]. *The Philadelphia Negro: A Social Study*. Philadelphia: University of Pennsylvania Press.

Goffman, Erving. 1982. "The Interaction Order." *American Sociological Review*, 48(1): 1–17.

Gouldner, Alvin W. 1970. *The Coming Crisis of Western Sociology*. New York: Avon Books.

Gouldner, Alvin. 1973. "Forward." Pp. ix–xiv in Ian Taylor, Paul Walton, and Jock Young (eds.), *The New Criminology: For a Social Theory of Deviance*. London: Routledge and Kegan Paul.

Harvey, David. 1996. *Justice, Nature, and the Geography of Difference*. Malden, MA: Blackwell Publishing.

Hawthorn, Geoffrey. 1976. *Enlightenment and Despair: A History of Sociology*. Cambridge, UK: Cambridge University Press.

Heilbron, Johan. 1995. *The Rise of Social Theory*. Cambridge, UK: Polity.

Hill, Michael R. and Susan Hoecker-Drysdale. 2001. *Harriet Martineau: Theoretical and Methodological Perspectives*. New York: Routledge.

Homans, George. 1984. *Coming to My Senses: The Autobiography of a Sociologist*. New Brunswick, NJ: Transaction Books.

Joas, Hans and Wolfgang Knöbl. 2009. *Social Theory: Twenty Introductory Lectures*. Cambridge, UK: Cambridge University Press.

Kymlicka, Will. 1995. *Multicultural Citizenship*. New York: Oxford University Press.

Levine, Donald. 1995. *Visions of the Sociological Tradition*. Chicago: University of Chicago Press.

Mills, C. Wright. 1959. *The Sociological Imagination*. New York: Oxford University Press.

O'Neill, John and Bryan S. Turner. 2001. "Introduction—The Fragmentation of Sociology." *Journal of Classical Sociology*, 1(1): 5–12.

Parsons, Talcott. 1937. *The Structure of Social Action*, vols. I and II. Glencoe, IL: The Free Press.

Parsons, Talcott and Edward A. Shils (eds.). 1951. *Toward a General Theory of Action*. Cambridge, MA: Harvard University Press.

Ritzer, George. 1975. *Sociology: A Multiple Paradigm Science*. Boston: Allyn and Bacon.

Seidman, Steven. 2013. *Contested Knowledge: Social Theory in a Postmodern Era*, 5th edition. Malden, MA: Blackwell Publishers.

Sica, Alan (ed.). 1998. *What Is Social Theory? The Philosophical Debates*. Malden, MA: Blackwell Publishers.

Singer, Brian C. J. 2004. "Montesquieu, Adam Smith, and the Discovery of the Social." *Journal of Classical Sociology*, 4(1): 31–57.

Tocqueville, Alexis de. 1969 [1853]. *Democracy in America*, edited by J. P. Mayer. Garden City, NY: Doubleday.

Turner, Jonathan. 1985. *Herbert Spencer: A Renewed Appreciation*. Newbury Park, CA: Sage.

Vidich, Arthur J. and Stanford M. Lyman, 1985. *American Sociology: Worldly Rejections of Religion and Their Directions*. New Haven, CT: Yale University Press.

Wagner, Peter. 2008. *Modernity as Experience and Interpretation: A New Sociology of Modernity*. Cambridge, UK: Polity Press.

Whitehead, Alfred North. 1938. *Science and the Modern World*. New York: Penguin.

Zuckerman, Phil (ed.). 2004. *The Social Theory of W. E. B. DuBois*. Thousand Oaks, CA: Pine Forge Press.

SOCIAL THEORY

PART ONE

THE ROOTS

Classical Social Theory

I. KARL MARX

1. ALIENATED LABOR

KARL MARX

Unpublished during Marx's lifetime (1818–1883), *The Economic and Philosophic Manuscripts* of 1844 provide key insights into the early period of his intellectual development. This excerpt concerns alienated labor; it allows the reader to see the Hegelian-inspired philosopher begin to link philosophy to the realm of economics. In this early critique of capitalism, alienation becomes the focus of Marx's analysis. He contends that as a result of a loss of control of the means of production, workers end up alienated not only from the goods that they produce and the process of work itself but from fellow humans, from themselves, and from nature. Wage labor means that workers are reduced to the level of a commodity—an object.

We started from the presuppositions of political economy. We accepted its vocabulary and its laws. We presupposed private property, the separation of labour, capital, and land, and likewise of wages, profit, and ground rent; also division of labour; competition; the concept of exchange value, etc. Using the very words of political economy we have demonstrated that the worker is degraded to the most miserable sort of commodity; that the misery of the worker is in inverse proportion to the power and size of his production; that the necessary result of competition is the accumulation of capital in a few hands, and thus a more terrible restoration of monopoly; and that finally the distinction between capitalist and landlord, and that between peasant and industrial worker disappears and the whole of society must fall apart into the two classes of the property owners and the propertyless workers.

Political economy starts with the fact of private property, it does not explain it to us. It conceives of the material process that private property goes through in reality in general abstract formulas which then have for it a value of laws. It does not understand these laws, i.e. it does not demonstrate how they arise from the nature of private property. Political economy does not afford us any explanation of the reason for the separation of labour and capital, of capital and land. When, for example, political economy defines the relationship of wages to profit from capital, the interest of the capitalist is the ultimate court of appeal, that is, it presupposes what should be its result. In the same way competition enters the argument everywhere. It is explained by exterior circumstances. But political economy tells us nothing about how far these exterior, apparently fortuitous circumstances are merely the expression of a necessary development. We have seen how it regards exchange itself as something fortuitous.

The only wheels that political economy sets in motion are greed and war among the greedy, competition.

It is just because political economy has not grasped the connections in the movement that new contradictions have arisen in its doctrines, for example, between that of monopoly and that of competition, freedom of craft and corporations, division of landed property and large estates. For competition, free trade, and the division of landed property were only seen as fortuitous circumstances created by will and force, not developed and comprehended as necessary, inevitable, and natural results of monopoly, corporations, and feudal property.

So what we have to understand now is the essential connection of private property, selfishness, the separation of labour, capital, and landed property, of exchange and competition, of the value and degradation of man, of monopoly and competition, etc.— the connection of all this alienation with the money system.

Let us not be like the political economist who, when he wishes to explain something, puts himself in an imaginary original state of affairs. Such an original stage of affairs explains nothing. He simply pushes the question back into a grey and nebulous distance. He presupposes as a fact and an event what he ought to be deducing, namely the necessary connection between the two things, for example, between the division of labour and exchange. Similarly, the theologian explains the origin of evil through the fall, i.e. he presupposes as an historical fact what he should be explaining.

We start with a contemporary fact of political economy:

The worker becomes poorer the richer is his production, the more it increases in power and scope. The worker becomes a commodity that is all the cheaper the more commodities he creates. The depreciation of the human world progresses in direct proportion to the increase in value of the world of things. Labour does not only produce commodities; it produces itself and the labourer as a commodity and that to the extent to which it produces commodities in general.

What this fact expresses is merely this: the object that labour produces, its product, confronts it as an alien being, as a power independent of the producer. The product of labour is labour that has solidified itself into an object, made itself into a thing, the objectification of labour. The realization of labour is its objectification. In political economy this realization of labour appears as a loss of reality for the worker, objectification as a loss of the object or slavery to it, and appropriation as alienation, as externalization.

The realization of labour appears as a loss of reality to an extent that the worker loses his reality by dying of starvation. Objectification appears as a loss of the object to such an extent that the worker is robbed not only of the objects necessary for his life but also of the objects of his work. Indeed, labour itself becomes an object he can only have in his power with the greatest of efforts and at irregular intervals. The appropriation of the object appears as alienation to such an extent that the more objects the worker produces, the less he can possess and the more he falls under the domination of his product, capital.

All these consequences follow from the fact that the worker relates to the product of his labour as to an alien object. For it is evident from this presupposition that the more the worker externalizes himself in his work, the more powerful becomes the alien, objective world that he creates opposite himself, the poorer he becomes himself in his inner life and the less he can call his own. It is just the same in religion. The more man puts into God, the less he retains in himself. The worker puts his life into the object and this means that it no longer belongs to him but to the object. So the greater this activity, the more the worker is without an object. What the product of his labour is, that he is not. So the greater this product the less he is himself. The externalization of the worker in his product implies not only that his labour becomes an object, an exterior existence but also that it exists outside him, independent and alien, and becomes a self-sufficient power opposite him, that the life that he has lent to the object affronts him, hostile and alien.

Let us now deal in more detail with objectification, the production of the worker, and the alienation, the loss of the object, his product, which is involved in it.

The worker can create nothing without nature, the sensuous exterior world. It is the matter in which his labour realizes itself, in which it is active, out of which and through which it produces.

But as nature affords the means of life for labour in the sense that labour cannot live without objects on which it exercises itself, so it affords a means of life in the narrower sense, namely the means for the physical subsistence of the worker himself.

Thus the more the worker appropriates the exterior world of sensuous nature by his labour, the more he doubly deprives himself of the means of subsistence, firstly since the exterior sensuous world increasingly ceases to be an object belonging to his work, a means of subsistence for his labour; secondly, since it increasingly ceases to be a means of subsistence in the direct sense, a means for the physical subsistence of the worker.

Thus in these two ways the worker becomes a slave to his object: firstly he receives an object of labour, that is he receives labour, and secondly, he receives the means of subsistence. Thus it is his object that permits him to exist first as a worker and secondly as a physical subject. The climax of this slavery is that only as a worker can he maintain himself as a physical subject and it is only as a physical subject that he is a worker.

(According to the laws of political economy the alienation of the worker in his object is expressed as follows: the more the worker produces the less he has to consume, the more values he creates the more valueless and worthless he becomes, the more formed the product the more deformed the worker, the more civilized the product, the more barbaric the worker, the more powerful the work the more powerless becomes the worker, the more cultured the work the more philistine the worker becomes and more of a slave to nature.)

Political economy hides the alienation in the essence of labour by not considering the immediate relationship between the worker (labour) and production. Labour produces works of wonder for the rich, but nakedness for the worker. It produces palaces, but only hovels for the worker; it produces beauty, but cripples the worker; it replaces labour by machines but throws a part of the workers back to a barbaric labour and turns the other part into machines. It produces culture, but also imbecility and cretinism for the worker.

The immediate relationship of labour to its products is the relationship of the worker to the objects of his production. The relationship of the man of means to the objects of production and to production itself is only a consequence of this first relationship. And it confirms it. We shall examine this other aspect later.

So when we ask the question: what relationship is essential to labour, we are asking about the relationship of the worker to production.

Up to now we have considered only one aspect of the alienation or externalization of the worker, his relationship to the products of his labour. But alienation shows itself not only in the result, but also in the act of production, inside productive activity itself. How would the worker be able to affront the product of his work as an alien being if he did not alienate himself in the act of production itself? For the product is merely the summary of the activity of production. So if the product of labour is externalization, production itself must be active externalization, the externalization of activity, the activity of externalization. The alienation of the object of labour is only the résumé of the alienation, the externalization in the activity of labour itself.

What does the externalization of labour consist of then?

Firstly, that labour is exterior to the worker, that is, it does not belong to his essence. Therefore he does not confirm himself in his work, he denies himself, feels miserable instead of happy, deploys no free physical and intellectual energy, but mortifies his body and ruins his mind. Thus the worker only feels a stranger. He is at home when he is not working and when he works he is not at home. His labour is therefore not voluntary but compulsory, forced labour. It is therefore not the satisfaction of a need but only a means to satisfy needs outside itself. How alien it really is is very evident from the fact that when there is no physical or other compulsion, labour is avoided like the plague. External labour, labour in which man externalizes himself, is a labour of self-sacrifice and mortification. Finally, the external character of labour for the worker shows itself in the fact that it is not his own but someone else´s, that it does not belong to him, that he does not belong to himself in his labour but to someone else. As in religion the human imagination´s own activity, the activity of man´s head and his heart, reacts independently on the individual as an alien activity of gods or devils, so the activity of the worker is not his own spontaneous activity. It belongs to another and is the loss of himself.

The result we arrive at then is that man (the worker) only feels himself freely active in his animal functions of eating, drinking, and procreating, at most also in his dwelling and dress, and feels himself an animal in his human functions.

Eating, drinking, procreating, etc. are indeed truly human functions. But in the abstraction that separates them from the other round of human activity and makes them into final and exclusive ends they become animal.

We have treated the act of alienation of practical human activity, labour, from two aspects. (1) The relationship of the worker to the product of his labour as an alien object that has power over him. This relationship is at the same time the relationship to the sensuous exterior world and to natural objects as to an alien and hostile world opposed to him. (2) The relationship of labour to the act of production inside labour. This relationship is the relationship of the worker to his own activity as something that is alien and does not belong to him; it is activity that is passivity, power that is weakness, procreation that is castration, the worker´s own physical and intellectual energy, his personal life (for what is life except activity?) as an activity directed against himself, independent of him and not belonging to him. It is self-alienation, as above it was the alienation of the object.

We now have to draw a third characteristic of alienated labour from the two previous ones.

Man is a species-being not only in that practically and theoretically he makes both his own and others species into his objects, but also, and this is only another way of putting the same thing, he relates to himself as to the present, living species, in that he relates to himself as to a universal and therefore free being.

Both with man and with animals the species-life consists physically in the fact that man (like animals) lives from inorganic nature, and the more universal man is than animals the more universal is the area of inorganic nature from which he lives. From the theoretical point of view, plants, animals, stones, air, light, etc. form part of human consciousness, partly as objects of natural science, partly as objects of art; they are his intellectual inorganic nature, his intellectual means of subsistence, which he must first prepare before he can enjoy and assimilate them. From the practical point of view, too, they form a part of human life and activity. Physically man lives solely from these products of

nature, whether they appear as food, heating, clothing, habitation, etc. The universality of man appears in practice precisely in the universality that makes the whole of nature into his inorganic body in that it is both (i) his immediate means of subsistence and also (ii) the material object and tool of his vital activity. Nature is the inorganic body of a man, that is, in so far as it is not itself a human body. That man lives from nature means that nature is his body with which he must maintain a constant interchange so as not to die. That man´s physical and intellectual life depends on nature merely means that nature depends on itself, for man is a part of nature.

While alienated labour alienates (1) nature from man, and (2) man from himself, his own active function, his vital activity, it also alienates the species from man; it turns his species-life into a means towards his individual life. Firstly it alienates species-life and individual life, and secondly in its abstraction it makes the latter into the aim of the former which is also conceived of in its abstract and alien form. For firstly, work, vital activity, and productive life itself appear to man only as a means to the satisfaction of a need, the need to preserve his physical existence. But productive life is species-life. It is life producing life. The whole character of a species, its generic character, is contained in its manner of vital activity, and free conscious activity is the species-characteristic of man. Life itself appears merely as a means to life.

The animal is immediately one with its vital activity. It is not distinct from it. They are identical. Man makes his vital activity itself into an object of his will and consciousness. He has a conscious vital activity. He is not immediately identical to any of his characterizations. Conscious vital activity differentiates man immediately from animal vital activity. It is this and this alone that makes man a species-being. He is only a conscious being, that is, his own life is an object to him, precisely because he is a species-being. This is the only reason for his activity being free activity. Alienated labour reverses the relationship so that, just because he is a conscious being, man makes his vital activity and essence a mere means to his existence.

The practical creation of an objective world, the working-over of inorganic nature, is the confirmation of man as a conscious species-being, that is, as a being that relates to the species as to himself and to himself as to the species. It is true that the animal, too, produces. It builds itself a nest, a dwelling, like the bee, the beaver, the ant, etc. But it only produces what it needs immediately for itself or its offspring; it produces one-sidedly whereas man produces universally; it produces only under the pressure of immediate physical need, whereas man produces freely from physical need and only truly produces when he is thus free; it produces only itself whereas man reproduces the whole of nature. Its product belongs immediately to its physical body whereas man can freely separate himself from his product. The animal only fashions things according to the standards and needs of the species it belongs to, whereas man knows how to produce according to the measure of every species and knows everywhere how to apply its inherent standard to the object; thus man also fashions things according to the laws of beauty.

Thus it is in the working over of the objective world that man first really affirms himself as a species-being. This production is his active species-life. Through it nature appears as his work and his reality. The object of work is therefore the objectification of the species-life of man; for he duplicates himself not only intellectually, in his mind, but also actively in reality and thus can look at his image in a world he has created. Therefore when alienated labour tears from man the object of his production, it also tears from him his species-life, the real objectivity of his species and turns the advantage he has over animals into a disadvantage in that his inorganic body, nature, is torn from him.

Similarly, in that alienated labour degrades man´s own free activity to a means, it turns the species-life of man into a means for his physical existence.

Thus consciousness, which man derives from his species, changes itself through alienation so that species-life becomes a means for him.

Therefore alienated labour:

(3) makes the species-being of man, both nature and the intellectual faculties of his species, into a being that is alien to him, into a means for his individual existence. It alienates from man his own body, nature exterior to him, and his intellectual being, his human essence.

(4) An immediate consequence of man´s alienation from the product of his work, his vital activity and his species-being, is the alienation of man from man. When man is opposed to himself, it is another man that is opposed to him. What is valid for the relationship of a man to his work, of the product of his work and himself, is also valid for the relationship of man to other men and of their labour and the objects of their labour.

In general, the statement that man is alienated from his species-being, means that one man is alienated from another as each of them is alienated from the human essence.

The alienation of man and in general of every relationship in which man stands to himself is first realized and expressed in the relationship with which man stands to other men.

Thus in the situation of alienated labour each man measures his relationship to other men by the relationship in which he finds himself placed as a worker.

We began with a fact of political economy, the alienation of the worker and his production. We have expressed this fact in conceptual terms: alienated, externalized labour. We have analysed this concept and thus analysed a purely economic fact.

Let us now see further how the concept of alienated, externalized labour must express and represent itself in reality.

If the product of work is alien to me, opposes me as an alien power, whom does it belong to then?

If my own activity does not belong to me and is an alien, forced activity to whom does it belong then?

To another being than myself.

Who is this being?

The gods? Of course in the beginning of history the chief production, as for example, the building of temples etc. in Egypt, India, and Mexico was both in the service of the gods and also belonged to them. But the gods alone were never the masters of the work. And nature just as little. And what a paradox it would be if, the more man mastered nature through his work and the more the miracles of the gods were rendered superfluous by the miracles of industry, the more man had to give up his pleasure in producing and the enjoyment in his product for the sake of these powers.

The alien being to whom the labour and the product of the labour belongs, whom the labour serves and who enjoys its product, can only be man himself. If the product of labour does not belong to the worker but stands over against him as an alien power, this is only possible in that it belongs to another man apart from the worker.

If his activity torments him it must be a joy and a pleasure to someone else. This alien power above man can be neither the gods nor nature, only man himself.

Consider further the above sentence that the relationship of man to himself first becomes objective and real to him through his relationship to other men. So if he relates to the product of his labour, his objectified labour, as to an object that is alien, hostile, powerful, and independent of him, this relationship implies that another man is the alien, hostile, powerful, and independent master of this object. If he relates to his own activity as to something unfree, it is a relationship to an activity that is under the domination, oppression, and yoke of another man.

Every self-alienation of man from himself and nature appears in the relationship in which he places himself and nature to other men distinct from himself. Therefore religious self-alienation necessarily appears in the relationship of layman to priest, or, because here we are dealing with a spiritual world, to a mediator, etc. In the practical, real world, the self-alienation can only appear through the practical, real relationship to other men. The means through which alienation makes progress are themselves practical. Through alienated labour, then, man creates not only his relationship to the object and act of production as to alien and hostile men; he creates too the relationship in which other men stand to his production and his product and the relationship in which he stands to these other men. Just as he turns his production into his own loss of reality and punishment and his own product into a loss, a product that does not belong to him, so he creates the domination of the man who does not produce over the production and the product. As he alienates his activity from himself, so he hands over to an alien person an activity that does not belong to him.

Up till now we have considered the relationship only from the side of the worker and we will later consider it from the side of the non-worker.

Thus through alienated, externalized labour the worker creates the relationship to this labour of a man who is alien to it and remains exterior to it. The relationship of the worker to his labour creates the relationship to it of the capitalist, or whatever else one wishes to call the master of the labour. Private property is thus the product, result, and necessary consequence of externalized labour, of the exterior relationship of the worker to nature and to himself.

Thus private property is the result of the analysis of the concept of externalized labour, i.e. externalized man, alienated work, alienated life, alienated man.

We have, of course, obtained the concept of externalized labour (externalized life) from political economy as the result of the movement of private property. But it is evident from the analysis of this concept that, although private property appears to be the ground and reason for externalized labour, it is rather a consequence of it, just as the gods are originally not the cause but the effect of the aberration of the human mind, although later this relationship reverses itself.

It is only in the final culmination of the development of private property that these hidden characteristics come once more to the fore, in that firstly it is the product of externalized labour and secondly it is the means through which labour externalizes itself, the realization of this externalization.

This development sheds light at the same time on several, previously unresolved contradictions.

1. Political economy starts from labour as the veritable soul of production, and yet it attributes nothing to labour and everything to private property. Proudhon has drawn a conclusion from this contradiction that is favourable to labour and against private property. But we can see that this apparent contradiction is the contradiction of alienated labour with itself and that political economy has only expressed the laws of alienated labour.

   We can therefore also see that wages and private property are identical: for wages, in which the product, the object of the labour, remunerates the labour itself, are just a necessary consequence of the alienation of labour. In the wage system the labour does not appear as the final aim but only as the servant of the wages. We will develop this later and for the moment only draw a few consequences.

An enforced raising of wages (quite apart from other difficulties, apart from the fact that, being an anomaly, it could only be maintained by force) would only mean a better payment of slaves and would not give this human meaning and worth either to the worker or to his labour.

Indeed, even the equality of wages that Proudhon demands only changes the relationship of the contemporary worker to his labour into that of all men to labour. Society is then conceived of as an abstract capitalist.

Wages are an immediate consequence of alienated labour and alienated labour is the immediate cause of private property. Thus the disappearance of one entails also the disappearance of the other.

2. It is a further consequence of the relationship of alienated labour to private property that the emancipation of society from private property, etc., from slavery, is expressed in its political form by the emancipation of the workers. This is not because only their emancipation is at stake but because general human emancipation is contained in their emancipation. It is contained within it because the whole of human slavery is involved in the relationship of the worker to his product and all slave relationships are only modifications and consequences of this relationship.

Just as we have discovered the concept of private property through an analysis of the concept of alienated, externalized labour, so all categories of political economy can be deduced with the help of these two factors. We shall recognize in each category of market, competition, capital, money, only a particular and developed expression of these first two fundamental elements.

However, before we consider this structure let us try to solve two problems:

1. To determine the general essence of private property as it appears as a result of alienated labour in its relationship to truly human and social property.
2. We have taken the alienation and externalization of labour as a fact and analysed this fact.

We now ask, how does man come to externalize, to alienate his labour? How is this alienation grounded in human development? We have already obtained much material for the solution of this problem, in that we have turned the question of the origin of private property into the question of the relationship of externalized labour to the development of human history. For when we speak of private property we think we are dealing with something that is exterior to man. When we speak of labour then we are dealing directly with man. This new formulation of the problem already implies its solution.

To take point 1, the general nature of private property and its relationship to truly human property.

Externalized labour has been broken down into two component parts that determine each other or are only different expressions of one and the same relationship. Appropriation appears as alienation, as externalization, and externalization as appropriation, and alienation as true enfranchisement. We have dealt with one aspect, alienated labour as regards the worker himself, that is, the relationship of externalized labour to itself. As a product and necessary result of this relationship we have discovered the property relationship of the non-worker to the worker and his labour.

As the material and summary expression of alienated labour, private property embraces both relationships, both that of the worker to his labour, the product of his labour and the non-worker, and that of the non-worker to the worker and the product of his labour.

We have already seen that for the worker who appropriates nature through his work, this appropriation appears as alienation, his own activity as activity for and of someone else, his vitality as sacrifice of his life, production of objects as their loss to an alien power, an alien man: let us now consider the relationship that this man, who is alien to labour and the worker, has to the worker, to labour and its object.

The first remark to make is that everything that appears in the case of the worker to be an activity of externalization, of alienation, appears in the case of the non-worker to be a state of externalization, of alienation.

Secondly, the real, practical behaviour of the worker in production and towards his product (as a state of mind) appears in the case of the non-worker opposed to him as theoretical behaviour. Thirdly, the non-worker does everything against the worker that the worker does against himself but he does not do against himself what he does against the worker.

Let us consider these three relationships in more detail. . . . [The manuscript breaks off unfinished here.]

2. THE GERMAN IDEOLOGY

KARL MARX AND FRIEDRICH ENGELS

The German Ideology is a sprawling work of over 700 pages, written largely between the fall of 1845 and the summer of 1846. It picks up where *The Economic and Philosophic Manuscripts* left off. In its pages one sees not only the continued settling of accounts with the German philosophic tradition, but the beginnings of what would become a distinctly Marxist vision of the social world created by industrial capitalism. In this particular selection Marx and Engels take aim at certain exponents of Hegelian idealism, and they do so with a certain acerbic flair, comparing the philosophical idealists known as the Young Hegelians with the person who thinks that people drown because they are "possessed with the idea of gravity." In their discussion of the production of consciousness, they begin to lay the foundations for an alternative, materialist theory of historical development. In so doing, they part company with Ludwig Feuerbach's version of materialism, which they find wanting because it is rooted in nature and not history.

PREFACE

Hitherto men have constantly made up for themselves false conceptions about themselves, about what they are and what they ought to be. They have arranged their relationships according to their ideas of God, of normal man, etc. The phantoms of their brains have got out of their hands. They, the creators, have bowed down before their creations. Let us liberate them from the chimeras, the ideas, dogmas, imaginary beings under the yoke of which they are pining away. Let us revolt against the rule of thoughts. Let us teach men, says one, to exchange these imaginations for thoughts which correspond to the essence of man; says the second, to take up a critical attitude to them; says the the third, to knock them out of their heads; and—existing reality will collapse.

These innocent and childlike fancies are the kernel of the modern Young Hegelian philosophy, which not only is received by the German public with horror and awe, but is announced by our philosophic heroes with the solemn consciousness of its cataclysmic dangerousness and criminal ruthlessness. The first volume of the present publication has the aim of uncloaking these sheep, who take themselves and are taken for wolves; of showing how their bleating merely imitates in a philosophic form the conceptions of the German middle class; how the boasting of these philosophic commentators only mirrors the wretchedness of the real conditions in Germany. It is its aim to debunk and discredit the philosophic struggle with the shadows of reality, which appeals to the dreamy and muddled German nation.

Once upon a time a valiant fellow had the idea that men were drowned in water only because they were possessed with the idea of gravity. If they were to knock this notion out of their heads, say by stating it to be a superstition, a religious concept, they would be sublimely proof against any danger from water. His whole life long he fought against the illusion of gravity, of whose harmful results all statistics brought him new and manifold evidence. This honest fellow was the type of the new revolutionary philosophers in Germany. . . .

THE PREMISSES OF THE MATERIALIST METHOD

The premisses from which we begin are not arbitrary ones, not dogmas, but real premisses from which abstraction can only be made in the imagination. They are the real individuals, their activity and the material conditions under which they live, both those which they find already existing and those produced by their activity. These premisses can thus be verified in a purely empirical way.

The first premiss of all human history is, of course, the existence of living human individuals. Thus the first fact to be established is the physical organization of these individuals and their consequent relation to the rest of nature. Of course, we cannot here go either into the actual physical nature of man, or into the natural conditions in which man finds himself—geological, oro-hydrographical, climatic, and so on. The writing of history must always set out from these natural bases and their modification in the course of history through the action of men.

Men can be distinguished from animals by consciousness, by religion, or anything else you like. They themselves begin to distinguish themselves from animals as soon as they begin to produce their means of subsistence, a step which is conditioned by their physical organization. By producing their means of subsistence men are indirectly producing their actual material life.

The way in which men produce their means of subsistence depends first of all on the nature of the actual means of subsistence they find in existence and have to reproduce. This mode of production must not be considered simply as being the production of the physical existence of the individuals. Rather it is a definite form of activity of these individuals, a definite form of expressing their life, a definite mode of life on their part. As individuals express their life, so they are. What they are, therefore, coincides with their production, both with *what* they produce and with *how* they produce. The nature of individuals thus depends on the material conditions determining their production.

This production only makes its appearance with the increase of population. In its turn this presupposes the intercourse of individuals with one another. The form of this intercourse is again determined by production.

The relations of different nations among themselves depend upon the extent to which each has developed its productive forces, the division of labour, and internal intercourse. This statement is generally recognized. But not only the relation of one nation to others, but also the whole internal structure of the nation itself depends on the stage of development reached by its production and its internal and external intercourse. How far the productive forces of a nation are developed is shown most manifestly by the degree to which the division of labour has been carried. Each new productive force, in so far as it is not merely a quantitative extension of productive forces already known (for instance the bringing into cultivation of fresh land), causes a further development of the division of labour.

The division of labour inside a nation leads at first to the separation of industrial and commercial from agricultural labour, and hence to the separation of town and country and to the conflict of their interests. Its further development leads to the separation of commercial from industrial labour. At the same time, through the division of labour inside these various branches there develop various divisions among the individuals co-operating in definite kinds of labour. The relative position of these individual groups is determined by the methods employed in agriculture, industry, and commerce (patriarchalism, slavery, estates, classes). These same conditions are to be seen (given a more developed intercourse) in the relations of different nations to one another.

The various stages of development in the division of labour are just so many different forms of ownership, i.e. the existing stage in the division of labour determines also the relations of individuals to one another with reference to the material, instrument, and product of labour.

The first form of ownership is tribal ownership. It corresponds to the undeveloped stage of production, at which a people lives by hunting and fishing, by the rearing of beasts, or, in the highest stage, agriculture. In the latter case it presupposes a great mass of uncultivated stretches of land. The division of labour is at this stage still very elementary and is confined to a further extension of the natural division of labour existing in the family. The social structure is, therefore, limited to an extension of the family; patriarchal family chieftains, below them the members of the tribe, finally slaves. The slavery latent in the family only develops gradually with the increase of population, the growth of wants, and with the extension of external relations, both of war and of barter.

The second form is the ancient communal and State ownership which proceeds especially from the union of several tribes into a city by agreement or by conquest, and which is still accompanied by slavery. Beside communal ownership we already find movable, and later also immovable, private property developing, but as an abnormal form subordinate to communal ownership. The citizens hold power over their labouring slaves only in their community, and on this account alone, therefore, they are bound to the form of communal ownership. It is the communal private property which compels the active citizens to remain in this spontaneously derived form of association over against their slaves. For this reason the whole structure of society based on this communal ownership, and with it the power of the people, decays in the same measure as, in particular, immovable private property evolves. The division of labour is already more developed. We already find the antagonism of town and country; later the antagonism between those states which represent town interests and those which represent country interests, and inside the towns themselves the antagonism between industry and maritime commerce. The class relation between citizens and slaves is now completely developed.

With the development of private property, we find here for the first time the same conditions which we shall find again, only on a more extensive scale, with modern private property. On the one hand, the concentration of private property, which began very early in Rome (as the Licinian agrarian law proves) and proceeded very rapidly from the time of the civil wars and especially under the Emperors; on the other hand, coupled with this, the transformation of the plebeian small peasantry into a proletariat, which, however, owing to its intermediate position between propertied

citizens and slaves, never achieved an independent development.

The third form of ownership is feudal or estate property. If antiquity started out from the town and its little territory, the Middle Ages started out from the country. This differing starting-point was determined by the sparseness of the population at that time, which was scattered over a large area and which received no large increase from the conquerors. In contrast to Greece and Rome, feudal development at the outset, therefore, extends over a much wider territory, prepared by the Roman conquests and the spread of agriculture at first associated with it. The last centuries of the declining Roman Empire and its conquest by the barbarians destroyed a number of productive forces; agriculture had declined, industry had decayed for want of a market, trade had died out or been violently suspended, the rural and urban population had decreased. From these conditions and the mode of organization of the conquest determined by them, feudal property developed under the influence of the Germanic military constitution. Like tribal and communal ownership, it is based again on a community; but the directly producing class standing over against it is not, as in the case of the ancient community, the slaves, but the enserfed small peasantry. As soon as feudalism is fully developed, there also arises antagonism towards the towns. The hierarchical structure of landownership, and the armed bodies of retainers associated with it, gave the nobility power over the serfs. This feudal organization was, just as much as the ancient communal ownership, an association against a subjected producing class; but the form of association and the relation to the direct producers were different because of the different conditions of production.

This feudal system of landownership had its counterpart in the towns in the shape of corporative property, the feudal organization of trades. Here property consisted chiefly in the labour of each individual person. The necessity for association against the organized robber barons, the need for communal covered markets in an age when the industrialist was at the same time a merchant, the growing competition of the escaped serfs swarming into the rising towns, the feudal structure of the whole country: these combined to bring about the guilds. The gradually accumulated small capital of individual craftsmen and their stable numbers, as against the growing population, evolved the relation of journeyman and apprentice, which brought into being in the towns a hierarchy similar to that in the country.

Thus the chief form of property during the feudal epoch consisted on the one hand of landed property with serf labour chained to it, and on the other of the labour of the individual with small capital commanding the labour of journeymen. The organization of both was determined by the restricted conditions of production—the small-scale and primitive cultivation of the land and the craft type of industry. There was little division of labour in the heyday of feudalism. Each country bore in itself the antithesis of town and country; the division into estates was certainly strongly marked; but apart from the differentiation of princes, nobility, clergy, and peasants in the country, and masters, journeymen, apprentices, and soon also the rabble of casual labourers in the towns, no division of importance took place. In agriculture it was rendered difficult by the strip-system, beside which the cottage industry of the peasants themselves emerged. In industry there was no division of labour at all in the individual trades themselves, and very little between them. The separation of industry and commerce was found already in existence in older towns; in the newer it only developed later, when the towns entered into mutual relations.

The grouping of larger territories into feudal kingdoms was a necessity for the landed nobility as for the towns. The organization of the ruling class, the nobility, had, therefore, everywhere a monarch at its head.

The fact is, therefore, that definite individuals who are productively active in a definite way enter into these definite social and political relations. Empirical observation must in each separate instance bring out empirically, and without any mystification and speculation, the connection of the social and political structure with production. The social structure and the State are continually evolving out of the life-process of definite individuals, but of individuals, not as they may appear in their own or other people's imagination, but as they really are, i.e. as they operate, produce materially, and hence as they work under definite material limits, presuppositions, and conditions independent of their will.

The production of ideas, of conceptions, of consciousness, is at first directly interwoven with the material activity and the material intercourse of men, the language of real life. Conceiving, thinking, the mental intercourse of men, appear at this stage as the direct efflux of their material behaviour. The same applies to mental production as expressed in the language of politics, laws, morality, religion, metaphysics, etc. of a people. Men are the producers of their conceptions, ideas, etc.—real, active men, as they are conditioned by a definite development of their productive forces and of the intercourse corresponding to these, up to its furthest forms. Consciousness can never be anything else than conscious existence, and the existence of men is their actual life-process. If in all ideology men and their circumstances appear upside-down as in a *camera obscura*, this phenomenon arises just as much from their historical life-process as the inversion of objects on the retina does from their physical life-process.

In direct contrast to German philosophy which descends from heaven to earth, here we ascend from earth to heaven. That is to say, we do not set out from what men say, imagine, conceive, nor from men as narrated, thought of, imagined, conceived, in order to arrive at men in the flesh. We set out from real, active men, and on the basis of their real life-process we demonstrate the development of the ideological reflexes and echoes of this life-process. The phantoms formed in the human brain are also, necessarily, sublimates of their material life-process, which is empirically verifiable and bound to material premisses. Morality, religion, metaphysics, all the rest of ideology and their corresponding forms of consciousness, thus no longer retain the semblance of independence. They have no history, no development; but men, developing their material production and their material intercourse, alter, along with this their real existence, their thinking and the products of their thinking. Life is not determined by consciousness, but consciousness by life. In the first method of approach the starting-point is consciousness taken as the living individual; in the second method, which conforms to real life, it is the real living individuals themselves, and consciousness is considered solely as their consciousness.

3. MANIFESTO OF THE COMMUNIST PARTY

KARL MARX AND FRIEDRICH ENGELS

The Communist Manifesto, coauthored by Marx and his close ally Friedrich Engels (1820–1895) in 1847 and published the following year, is one of the most important political tracts of all time. A stirring call to arms, the essay begins with the claim that all history is the history of class conflict, and it concludes with the injunction, "Workers of the world unite! You have nothing to lose but your chains." Thus, it is an appeal to workers to engage in the revolutionary overthrow of capitalism. However, the *Manifesto* is much more than this, for it offers a succinct and insightful analysis of the nature of the conflictual relationship between the two central classes in a capitalist class structure, the bourgeoisie and the proletariat. Moreover, as a part of this excerpt reveals, Marx and Engels maintained a keen appreciation of the historically progressive character of the bourgeoisie, who, they contend, have created a dynamic, innovative, and highly productive economic system that is capable of laying the groundwork for a post-scarcity society in which alienation and economic exploitation are overcome.

A spectre is haunting Europe—the spectre of Communism. All the Powers of old Europe have entered into a holy alliance to exorcise this spectre: Pope and Czar, Metternich and Guizot, French Radicals and German police-spies.

Where is the party in opposition that has not been decried as Communistic by its opponents in power? Where the Opposition that has not hurled back the branding reproach of Communism, against the more advanced opposition parties, as well as against its reactionary adversaries?

Two things result from this fact.

I. Communism is already acknowledged by all European Powers to be itself a Power.
II. It is high time that Communists should openly, in the face of the whole world, publish their views, their aims, their tendencies, and meet this nursery tale of the Spectre of Communism with a Manifesto of the party itself.

To this end, Communists of various nationalities have assembled in London, and sketched the following Manifesto, to be published in the English, French, German, Italian, Flemish and Danish languages.

BOURGEOIS AND PROLETARIANS[1]

The history of all hitherto existing society[2] is the history of class struggles.

Freeman and slave, patrician and plebian, lord and serf, guild-master[3] and journeyman, in a word, oppressor and oppressed, stood in constant opposition to one another, carried on an uninterrupted, now hidden, now open fight, a fight that each time ended, either in a revolutionary re-constitution of society at large, or in the common ruin of the contending classes.

In the earlier epochs of history, we find almost everywhere a complicated arrangement of society into various orders, a manifold gradation of social rank. In ancient Rome we have patricians, knights, plebeians, slaves; in the Middle Ages, feudal lords, vassals, guild-masters, journeymen, apprentices, serfs; in almost all of these classes, again, subordinate gradations.

The modern bourgeois society that has sprouted from the ruins of feudal society has not done away with class antagonisms. It has but established new classes, new conditions of oppression, new forms of struggle in place of the old ones.

Our epoch, the epoch of the bourgeoisie, possesses, however, this distinctive feature: it has simplified the class antagonisms: Society as a whole is more and more splitting up into two great hostile camps, into two great classes directly facing each other: Bourgeoisie and Proletariat.

From the serfs of the Middle Ages sprang the chartered burghers of the earliest towns. From these burgesses the first elements of the bourgeoisie were developed.

The discovery of America, the rounding of the Cape, opened up fresh ground for the rising bourgeoisie. The East-Indian and Chinese markets, the colonisation of America, trade with the colonies, the increase in the means of exchange and in commodities generally, gave to commerce, to navigation, to industry, an impulse never before known, and thereby, to the revolutionary element in the tottering feudal society, a rapid development.

The feudal system of industry, under which industrial production was monopolised by closed guilds, now no longer sufficed for the growing wants of the new markets. The manufacturing system took its place. The guild-masters were pushed on one side by the manufacturing middle class; division of labour between the different corporate guilds vanished in the face of division of labour in each single workshop.

Meantime the markets kept ever growing, the demand ever rising. Even manufacture no longer sufficed. Thereupon, steam and machinery revolutionised industrial production. The place of manufacture was taken by the giant, Modern Industry, the place of the industrial middle class, by industrial millionaires, the leaders of whole industrial armies, the modern bourgeois. Modern industry has established the world-market, for which the discovery of America paved the way. This market has given an immense development to commerce, to navigation, to communication by land. This development has, in its turn, reacted on the extension of industry: and in proportion as industry, commerce, navigation, railways extended, in the same proportion the bourgeoisie developed, increased its capital, and pushed into the background every class handed down from the Middle Ages.

We see, therefore, how the modern bourgeoisie is itself the product of a long course of development, of a series of revolutions in the modes of production and of exchange.

Each step in the development of the bourgeoisie was accompanied by a corresponding political advance of that class. An oppressed class under the sway of the feudal nobility, an armed and self-governing association in the mediaeval commune;[4] here independent urban republic (as in Italy and Germany), there taxable "third estate" of the monarchy (as in France), afterwards, in the period of manufacture proper, serving either the semi-feudal or the absolute monarchy as a counterpoise against the nobility, and, in fact, cornerstone of the great monarchies in general, the bourgeoisie has at last, since the establishment of Modern Industry and of the world-market, conquered for itself, in the modern representative State, exclusive political sway. The executive of the modern State is but a committee for managing the common affairs of the whole bourgeoisie.

The bourgeoisie, historically, has played a most revolutionary part.

The bourgeoisie, wherever it has got the upper hand, has put an end to all feudal, patriarchal, idyllic relations. It has pitilessly torn asunder the motley feudal ties that bound man to his "natural superiors," and has left remaining no other nexus between man and man than naked self-interest, than callous "cash payment." It has drowned the most heavenly ecstasies of religious fervour, of chivalrous enthusiasm, of philistine sentimentalism, in the icy water of egotistical calculation. It has resolved personal worth into exchange value, and in place of the numberless indefeasible chartered freedoms, has set up that single, unconscionable freedom—Free Trade. In one word, for exploitation, veiled by religious and political illusions, it has substituted naked, shameless, direct, brutal exploitation.

The bourgeoisie has stripped of its halo every occupation hitherto honoured and looked up to with reverent awe. It has converted the physician, the lawyer, the priest, the poet, the man of science, into its paid wage-labourers.

The bourgeoisie has torn away from the family its sentimental veil, and has reduced the family relation to a mere money relation.

The bourgeoisie has disclosed how it came to pass that the brutal display of vigour in the Middle Ages, which Reactionists so much admire, found its fitting complement in the most slothful indolence. It has been the first to show what man´s activity can bring about. It has accomplished wonders far surpassing Egyptian pyramids, Roman aqueducts, and Gothic cathedrals; it has conducted expeditions that put in the shade all former Exoduses of nations and crusades.

The bourgeoisie cannot exist without constantly revolutionising the instruments of production, and thereby the relations of production, and with them the whole relations of society. Conservation of the old modes of production in unaltered form, was, on the contrary, the first condition of existence for all earlier industrial classes. Constant revolutionising of production, uninterrupted disturbance of all social conditions, everlasting uncertainty and agitation distinguish the bourgeois epoch from all earlier ones. All fixed, fast-frozen relations, with their train of ancient and venerable prejudices and opinions, are swept away, all new-formed ones become antiquated before they can ossify. All that is solid melts into air, all that is holy is profaned, and man is at last compelled to face with sober senses, his real conditions of life, and his relations with his kind.

The need of a constantly expanding market for its products chases the bourgeoisie over the whole surface of the globe. It must nestle everywhere, settle everywhere, establish connexions everywhere.

The bourgeoisie has through its exploitation of the world-market given a cosmopolitan character to production and consumption in every country. To the great chagrin of Reactionists, it has drawn from under the feet of industry the national ground on which it stood. All old-established national industries have been destroyed or are daily being destroyed. They are dislodged by new industries, whose introduction becomes a life and death question for all civilised nations, by industries that no longer work up indigenous raw material, but raw material drawn from the remotest zones; industries whose products are consumed, not only at home, but in every quarter of the globe. In place of the old wants, satisfied by the productions of the country, we find new wants, requiring for their satisfaction the products of distant lands and climes. In place of the old local and national seclusion and self-sufficiency, we have intercourse in every direction, universal interdependence of nations. And as in material, so also in intellectual production. The intellectual creations of individual nations become common property. National one-sidedness and narrow-mindedness become more and more impossible, and from the numerous national and local literatures, there arises a world literature.

The bourgeoisie, by the rapid improvement of all instruments of production, by the immensely facilitated means of communication, draws all, even the most barbarian, nations into civilisation. The cheap prices of its commodities are the heavy artillery with which it batters down all Chinese walls, with which it forces the barbarians´ intensely obstinate hatred of foreigners to capitulate. It compels all nations, on pain of extinction, to adopt the bourgeois mode of production; it compels them to introduce what it calls civilisation into their midst, *i.e.*, to become bourgeois themselves. In one word, it creates a world after its own image.

The bourgeoisie has subjected the country to the rule of the towns. It has created enormous cities, has greatly increased the urban population as compared with the rural, and has thus rescued a considerable part of the population from the idiocy of rural life. Just as it has made the country dependent on the towns, so it has made barbarian and semi-barbarian countries dependent on the civilised ones, nations and peasants on nations of bourgeois, the East on the West.

The bourgeoisie keeps more and more doing away with the scattered state of the population, of the means of production, and of property. It has agglomerated population, centralised means of production, and has concentrated property in a few hands. The necessary consequence of this was political centralisation. Independent, or but loosely connected provinces, with separate interests, laws, governments and systems of taxation, became lumped together into one nation, with one government, one code of laws, one national class-interest, one frontier and one customs-tariff.

The bourgeoisie, during its rule of scarce one hundred years, has created more massive and more colossal productive forces than have all preceding generations together. Subjection of Nature's forces to man, machinery, application of chemistry to industry and agriculture, steam-navigation, railways, electric telegraphs, clearing of whole continents for cultivation, canalisation of rivers, whole populations conjured out of the ground—what earlier century had even a presentiment that such productive forces slumbered in the lap of social labour?

We see then: the means of production and of exchange, on whose foundation the bourgeoisie built itself up, were generated in feudal society. At a certain stage in the development of these means of production and of exchange, the conditions under which feudal society produced and exchanged, the feudal organisation of agriculture and manufacturing industry, in one word, the feudal relations of property became no longer compatible with the already developed productive forces; they became so many fetters. They had to be burst asunder; they were burst asunder.

Into their place stepped free competition, accompanied by a social and political constitution adapted to it, and by the economical and political sway of the bourgeois class.

A similar movement is going on before our own eyes. Modern bourgeois society with its relations of production, of exchange and of property, a society that has conjured up such gigantic means of production and of exchange, is like the sorcerer, who is no longer able to control the powers of the nether world whom he has called up by his spells. For many a decade past the history of industry and commerce is but the history of the revolt of modern productive forces against modern conditions of production, against the property relations that are the conditions for the existence of the bourgeoisie and of its rule. It is enough to mention the commercial crises that by their periodical return put on its trial, each time more threateningly, the existence of the entire bourgeois society. In these crises a great part not only of the existing products, but also of the previously created productive forces, are periodically destroyed. In these crises there breaks out an epidemic that, in all earlier epochs, would have seemed an absurdity—the epidemic of over-production. Society suddenly finds itself put back into a state of momentary barbarism; it appears as if a famine, a universal war of devastation had cut off the supply of every means of subsistence; industry and commerce seem to be destroyed; and why? Because there is too much civilisation, too much means of subsistence, too much industry, too much commerce. The productive forces at the disposal of society no longer tend to further the development of the conditions of bourgeois property; on the contrary, they have become too powerful for these conditions, by which they are fettered, and so soon as they overcome these fetters, they bring disorder into the whole of bourgeois society, endanger the existence of bourgeois property. The conditions of bourgeois society are too narrow to comprise the wealth created by them. And how does the bourgeoisie get over these crises? On the one hand by enforced destruction of a mass of productive forces; on the other, by the conquest of new markets, and by the more thorough exploitation of the old ones. That is to say, by paving the way for more extensive and more destructive crises, and by diminishing the means whereby crises are prevented.

The weapons with which the bourgeoisie felled feudalism to the ground are now turned against the bourgeoisie itself.

But not only has the bourgeoisie forged the weapons that bring death to itself; it has also called into existence the men who are to wield those weapons—the modern working class—the proletarians.

In proportion as the bourgeoisie, *i.e.,* capital, is developed, in the same proportion is the proletariat, the modern working class, developed—a class of labourers, who live only so long as they find work, and who find work only so long as their labour increases capital. These labourers, who must sell themselves piece-meal, are a commodity, like every other article of commerce, and are consequently exposed to all the vicissitudes of competition, to all the fluctuations of the market.

Owing to the extensive use of machinery and to division of labour, the work of the proletarians has lost all individual character, and consequently, all charm for the workman. He becomes an appendage of the machine, and it is only the most simple, most monotonous, and most easily acquired knack, that is required of him. Hence, the cost of production of a workman is restricted, almost entirely, to the means of subsistence that he requires for his maintenance, and for the propagation of his race. But the price of a commodity, and therefore also of labour,[5] is equal to its cost of production. In proportion, therefore, as the repulsiveness of the work increases, the wage decreases. Nay more, in proportion as the use of machinery and division of labour increases, in the same proportion the burden of toil also increases, whether by prolongation of the working hours, by increase of the work exacted in a given time or by increased speed of the machinery, etc.

Modern industry has converted the little workshop of the patriarchal master into the great factory of the industrial capitalist. Masses of labourers, crowded into the factory, are organised like soldiers. As privates of the industrial army they are placed under the command of a perfect hierarchy of officers and sergeants. Not only are they slaves of the bourgeois class, and of the bourgeois State; they are daily and hourly enslaved by the machine, by the over-looker, and, above all, by the individual bourgeois manufacturer himself. The more openly this despotism proclaims gain to be its end and aim, the more petty, the more hateful and the more embittering it is.

The less the skill and exertion of strength implied in manual labour, in other words, the more modern industry becomes developed, the more is the labour of men superseded by that of women. Differences of age and sex have no longer any distinctive social validity for the working class. All are instruments of labour, more or less expensive to use, according to their age and sex.

No sooner is the exploitation of the labourer by the manufacturer, so far, at an end, that he receives his wages in cash, than he is set upon by the other portions of the bourgeoisie, the landlord, the shopkeeper, the pawnbroker, etc.

The lower strata of the middle class—the small tradespeople, shopkeepers, and retired tradesmen generally, the handicraftsmen and peasants—all these sink gradually into the proletariat, partly because their diminutive capital does not suffice for the scale on which Modern Industry is carried on, and is swamped in the competition with the large capitalists, partly because their specialised skill is rendered worthless by new methods of production. Thus the proletariat is recruited from all classes of the population.

The proletariat goes through various stages of development. With its birth begins its struggle with the bourgeoisie. At first the contest is carried on by individual labourers, then by the workpeople of a factory, then by the operatives of one trade, in one locality, against the individual bourgeois who directly exploits them. They direct their attacks not against the bourgeois conditions of production, but against the instruments of production themselves; they destroy imported wares that compete with their labour, they smash to pieces machinery, they set factories ablaze, they seek to restore by force the vanished status of the workman of the Middle Ages.

At this stage the labourers still form an incoherent mass scattered over the whole country, and broken up by their mutual competition. If anywhere they unite to form more compact bodies, this is not yet the consequence of their own active union, but of the union of the bourgeoisie, which class, in order to attain its own political ends, is compelled to set the whole proletariat in motion, and is moreover yet, for a time, able to do so. At this stage, therefore, the proletarians do not fight their enemies, but the enemies of their enemies, the remnants of absolute monarchy, the landowners, the non-industrial bourgeois, the petty bourgeoisie. Thus the whole historical movement is concentrated in the hands of the bourgeoisie; every victory so obtained is a victory for the bourgeoisie. But with the development of industry the proletariat not only increases in number; it becomes concentrated in greater masses, its strength grows, and it feels that strength more. The various interests and conditions of life within the ranks of the proletariat are more and more equalised, in proportion as machinery obliterates all distinctions of labour, and nearly everywhere reduces wages to the same low level. The growing competition among the bourgeois, and the resulting commercial crises, make the wages of the workers ever more fluctuating. The unceasing improvement of machinery, ever more rapidly developing, makes their livelihood more and more precarious; the collisions between individual workmen and individual bourgeois take more and more the character of collisions between two classes. Thereupon the workers begin to form combinations (Trades Unions) against the bourgeois; they club together in order to keep up the rate of wages; they found permanent associations in order to make provision beforehand for these occasional revolts. Here and there the contest breaks out into riots.

Now and then the workers are victorious, but only for a time. The real fruit of their battles lies, not in the immediate result, but in the ever-expanding union of the workers. This union is helped on by the improved means of communication that are created by modern industry and that place the workers of different localities in contact with one another. It was just this contact that was needed to centralise the numerous local struggles, all of the same character, into one national struggle between classes. But every class struggle is a political struggle. And that union, to attain which the burghers of the Middle Ages, with their miserable highways, required centuries, the modern proletarians, thanks to railways, achieve in a few years.

This organisation of the proletarians into a class, and consequently into a political party, is continually being upset again by the competition between the workers themselves. But it ever rises up again, stronger, firmer, mightier. It compels legislative recognition of particular interests of the workers, by taking advantage of the divisions among the bourgeoisie itself. Thus the ten-hours' bill in England was carried.

Altogether collisions between the classes of the old society further, in many ways, the course of development of the proletariat. The bourgeoisie finds itself involved in a constant battle. At first with the aristocracy; later on, with those portions of the bourgeoisie itself, whose interests have become antagonistic to the progress of industry; at all times, with the bourgeoisie of foreign countries. In all these battles it sees itself compelled to appeal to the proletariat, to ask for its help, and thus, to drag it into the political arena. The bourgeoisie itself, therefore, supplies the proletariat with its own elements of political and general education, in other words, it furnishes the proletariat with weapons for fighting the bourgeoisie.

Further, as we have already seen, entire sections of the ruling classes are, by the advance of industry, precipitated into the proletariat, or are at least threatened in their conditions of existence. These also supply the proletariat with fresh elements of enlightenment and progress.

Finally, in times when the class struggle nears the decisive hour, the process of dissolution going on

within the ruling class, in fact within the whole range of society, assumes such a violent, glaring character, that a small section of the ruling class cuts itself adrift, and joins the revolutionary class, the class that holds the future in its hands. Just as, therefore, at an earlier period, a section of the nobility went over to the bourgeoisie, so now a portion of the bourgeoisie goes over to the proletariat, and in particular, a portion of the bourgeois ideologists, who have raised themselves to the level of comprehending theoretically the historical movement as a whole.

Of all the classes that stand face to face with the bourgeoisie today, the proletariat alone is a really revolutionary class. The other classes decay and finally disappear in the face of Modern Industry; the proletariat is its special and essential product. The lower middle class, the small manufacturer, the shopkeeper, the artisan, the peasant, all these fight against the bourgeoisie, to save from extinction their existence as fractions of the middle class. They are therefore not revolutionary, but conservative. Nay more, they are reactionary, for they try to roll back the wheel of history. If by chance they are revolutionary, they are so only in view of their impending transfer into the proletariat, they thus defend not their present, but their future interests, they desert their own standpoint to place themselves at that of the proletariat.

The "dangerous class," the social scum, that passively rotting mass thrown off by the lowest layers of old society, may, here and there, be swept into the movement by a proletarian revolution; its conditions of life, however, prepare it far more for the part of a bribed tool of reactionary intrigue.

In the conditions of the proletariat, those of old society at large are already virtually swamped. The proletarian is without property; his relation to his wife and children has no longer anything in common with the bourgeois family-relations; modern industrial labour, modern subjection to capital, the same in England as in France, in America as in Germany, has stripped him of every trace of national character. Law, morality, religion, are to him so many bourgeois prejudices, behind which lurk in ambush just as many bourgeois interests.

All the preceding classes that got the upper hand, sought to fortify their already acquired status by subjecting society at large to their conditions of appropriation. The proletarians cannot become masters of the productive forces of society, except by abolishing their own previous mode of appropriation, and thereby also every other previous mode of appropriation. They have nothing of their own to secure and to fortify; their mission is to destroy all previous securities for, and insurances of, individual property.

All previous historical movements were movements of minorities, or in the interests of minorities. The proletarian movement is the self-conscious, independent movement of the immense majority, in the interests of the immense majority. The proletariat, the lowest stratum of our present society, cannot stir, cannot raise itself up, without the whole superincumbent strata of official society being sprung into the air.

Though not in substance, yet in form, the struggle of the proletariat with the bourgeoisie is at first a national struggle. The proletariat of each country must, of course, first of all settle matters with its own bourgeoisie.

In depicting the most general phases of the development of the proletariat, we traced the more or less veiled civil war, raging within existing society, up to the point where that war breaks out into open revolution, and where the violent overthrow of the bourgeoisie lays the foundation for the sway of the proletariat.

Hitherto, every form of society has been based, as we have already seen, on the antagonism of oppressing and oppressed classes. But in order to oppress a class, certain conditions must be assured to it under which it can, at least, continue its slavish existence. The serf, in the period of serfdom, raised himself to membership in the commune, just as the petty bourgeois, under the yoke of feudal absolutism, managed to develop into a bourgeois. The modern labourer, on the contrary, instead of rising with the progress of industry, sinks deeper and deeper below the conditions of existence of his own class. He becomes a pauper, and pauperism develops more rapidly than population and wealth. And here it becomes evident, that the bourgeoisie is unfit any longer to be the ruling class in society, and to impose its conditions of existence upon society as an overriding law. It is unfit to rule because it is incompetent to assure an existence to its slave within his slavery, because it cannot help letting him sink into such a state, that it has to feed him, instead of being fed by him. Society can no longer live under this bourgeoisie, in other words, its existence is no longer compatible with society.

The essential condition for the existence, and for the sway of the bourgeois class, is the formation and augmentation of capital; the condition for capital is wage-labour. Wage-labour rests exclusively on competition between the labourers. The advance of industry, whose involuntary promoter is the bourgeoisie, replaces the isolation of the labourers, due to competition, by their revolutionary combination, due to association. The development of Modern Industry, therefore, cuts from under its feet the very foundation on which the bourgeoisie produces and appropriates products. What the bourgeoisie, therefore, produces, above all, is its own grave-diggers. Its fall and the victory of the proletariat are equally inevitable. . . .

NOTES

1. By bourgeoisie is meant the class of modern Capitalists, owners of the means of social production and employers of wage-labour. By proletariat, the class of modern wage-labourers who, having no means of production of their own, are reduced to selling their labour-power in order to live. [*Engels, English edition of 1888*]
2. That is, all *written* history. In 1847, the pre-history of society, the social organisation existing previous to recorded history, was all but unknown. Since then, Haxthausen discovered common ownership of land in Russia, Maurer proved it to be the social foundation from which all Teutonic races started in history, and by and by village communities were found to be, or to have been the primitive form of society everywhere from India to Ireland. The inner organisation of this primitive Communistic society was laid bare, in its typical form, by Morgan's crowning discovery of the true nature of the *gens* and its relation to the *tribe*. With the dissolution of these

primaeval communities society begins to be differentiated into separate and finally antagonistic classes. I have attempted to retrace this process of dissolution in: "Der Ursprung der Familie, des Privateigenthums und des Staats" [*The Origin of the Family, Private Property and the State*], 2nd edition, Stuttgart 1886. [*Engels, English edition of 1888*]

3. Guild-master, that is, a full member of a guild, a master within, not a head of a guild. [*Engels, English edition of 1888*]

4. "Commune" was the name taken, in France, by the nascent towns even before they had conquered from their feudal lords and masters local self-government and political rights as the "Third Estate." Generally speaking, for the economical development of the bourgeoisie, England is here taken as the typical country; for its political development, France. [*Engels, English edition of 1888*]

    This was the name given their urban communities by the townsmen of Italy and France, after they had purchased or wrested their initial rights of self-government from their feudal lords. [*Engels, German edition of 1890*]

5. Subsequently Marx pointed out that the worker sells not his labour but his labour power.

4. COMMODITIES

KARL MARX

During many years of intellectual labor in the British Museum, Marx produced a huge body of work designed to uncover and explicate the underlying dynamics of capitalism. These works include *The Grundrisse* (1857–58), the multivolume *Theories of Surplus Value* (1862–63), and the three-volume *Capital* (1867, 1885, 1894). The first volume of this last work is generally seen as his most important critique of capitalism. In this selection from that book, Marx presents his understanding of what is meant by the term *commodity*, discussing its dual-edged character as both a source of use-value and value. This discussion is an essential building block in the further elaboration of his economic theory of capitalism.

COMMODITIES: USE-VALUE AND EXCHANGE-VALUE

The wealth of those societies in which the capitalist mode of production prevails presents itself as 'an immense accumulation of commodities', its unit being a single commodity. Our investigation must therefore begin with the analysis of a commodity.

A commodity is, in the first place, an object outside us, a thing that by its properties satisfies human wants of some sort or another. The nature of such wants, whether, for instance, they spring from the stomach or from fancy, makes no difference. Neither are we here concerned to know how the object satisfies these wants, whether directly as means of subsistence, or indirectly as means of production.

Every useful thing, as iron, paper, etc., may be looked at from the two points of view: of quality and quantity. It is an assemblage of many properties, and may therefore be of use in various ways. To discover the various uses of things is the work of history. So also is the establishment of socially recognized standards of measure for the quantities of these useful objects. The diversity of these measures has its origin partly in the diverse nature of the objects to be measured, partly in convention.

The utility of a thing makes it a use-value. But this utility is not a thing of air. Being limited by the physical properties of the commodity, it has no existence apart from that commodity. A commodity, such as iron, corn, or a diamond, is therefore, so far as it is a material thing, a use-value, something useful. This property of a commodity is independent of the amount of labour required to appropriate its useful qualities. When treating of use-value, we always assume we are dealing with definite quantities, such as dozens of watches, yards of linen, or tons of iron. The use-values of commodities furnish the material for a special study, that of the commercial knowledge of commodities. Use-values become a reality only by use or consumption; they also constitute the substance of all wealth, whatever may be the social form of that wealth. In the form of society we are about to consider, they are, in addition, the material depositories of exchange-value.

Exchange-value, at first sight, presents itself as a quantitative relation, as the proportion in which values in use of one sort are exchanged for those of another sort, a relation constantly changing with time

Reprinted from Karl Marx, *Karl Marx: Selected Writings,* edited by David McLellan, pp. 421–435. Oxford: Oxford University Press. Copyright © 1977. Reprinted by permission of Oxford University Press. ✦

and place. Hence exchange-value appears to be something accidental and purely relative, and consequently an intrinsic value, i.e. an exchange-value that is inseparably connected with, inherent in, commodities, seems a contradiction in terms. Let us consider the matter a little more closely.

A given commodity, e.g., a quarter of wheat is exchanged for x blacking, y silk, or z gold, etc.—in short, for other commodities in the most different proportions. Instead of one exchange-value, the wheat has, therefore, a great many. But since x blacking, y silk, or z gold, etc., each represent the exchange-value of one quarter of wheat, x blacking, y silk, z gold, etc., must, as exchange-values, be replaceable by each other, or equal to each other. Therefore, first: the valid exchange-values of a given commodity express something equal; secondly, exchange-value, generally, is only the mode of expression, the phenomenal form, of something contained in it, yet distinguishable from it.

Let us take two commodities, e.g., corn and iron. The proportions in which they are exchangeable, whatever those proportions may be, can always be represented by an equation in which a given quantity of corn is equated to some quantity of iron: e.g., 1 quarter corn = x cwt. iron. What does this equation tell us? It tells us that in two different things—in 1 quarter of corn and x cwt. of iron, there exists in equal quantities something common to both. The two things must therefore be equal to a third, which in itself is neither the one nor the other. Each of them, so far as it is exchange-value, must therefore be reducible to this third.

A simple geometrical illustration will make this clear. In order to calculate and compare the areas of rectilinear figures, we decompose them into triangles. But the area of the triangle itself is expressed by something totally different from its visible figure, namely, by half the product of the base into the altitude. In the same way the exchange-values of commodities must be capable of being expressed in terms of something common to them all, of which thing they represent a greater or less quantity.

This common 'something' cannot be either a geometrical, a chemical, or any other natural property of commodities. Such properties claim our attention only in so far as they affect the utility of those commodities, make them use-values. But the exchange of commodities is evidently an act characterized by a total abstraction from use-value. Then one use-value is just as good as another, provided only it be present in sufficient quantity. Or, as old Barbon says, 'one sort of wares is as good as another, if the values be equal. There is no difference or distinction in things of equal value. . . . A hundred pounds' worth of lead or iron is of as great value as one hundred pounds' worth of silver or gold.' As use-values, commodities are, above all, of different qualities, but as exchange-values they are merely different quantities, and consequently do not contain an atom of use-value.

If then we leave out of consideration the use-value of commodities, they have only one common property left, that of being products of labour. But even the product of labour itself has undergone a change in our hands. If we make abstraction from its use-value, we make abstraction at the same time from the material elements and shapes that make the product a use-value; we see in it no longer a table, a house, yarn, or any other useful thing. Its existence as a material thing is put out of sight. Neither can it any longer be regarded as the product of the labour of the joiner, the mason, the spinner, or of any other definite kind of productive labour. Along with the useful qualities of the products themselves, we put out of sight both the useful character of the various kinds of labour embodied in them, and the concrete forms of that labour; there is nothing left but what is common to them all; all are reduced to one and the same sort of labour, human labour in the abstract.

Let us now consider the residue of each of these products; it consists of the same unsubstantial reality in each, a mere congelation of homogeneous human labour, of labour power expended without regard to the mode of its expenditure. All that these things now tell us is that human labour power has been expended in their production, that human labour is embodied in them. When looked at as crystals of this social substance, common to them all, they are—Values.

We have seen that when commodities are exchanged, their exchange-value manifests itself as something totally independent of their use-value. But if we abstract from their use-value, there remains their Value as defined above. Therefore, the common substance that manifests itself in the exchange-value of commodities, whenever they are exchanged, is their value. The progress of our investigation will show that exchange-value is the only form in which the value of commodities can manifest itself or be expressed. For the present, however, we have to consider the nature of value independently of this, its form.

A use-value, or useful article, therefore, has value only because human labour in the abstract has been embodied or materialized in it. How, then, is the magnitude of this value to be measured? Plainly, by the quantity of the value-creating substance, the labour, contained in the article. The quantity of labour, however, is measured by its duration, and labour time in its turn finds its standard in weeks, days, and hours.

Some people might think that if the value of a commodity is determined by the quantity of labour spent on it, the more idle and unskilful the labourer, the more valuable would his commodity be, because more time would be required in its production. The labour, however, that forms the substance of value, is homogeneous human labour, expenditure of one uniform labour power. The total labour power of society, which is embodied in the sum total of the values of all commodities produced by that society, counts here as one homogeneous mass of human labour power, composed though it be of innumerable individual units. Each of these units is the same as any other, so far as it has the character of the average labour power of society, and takes effect as such; that is, so far as it requires for producing a commodity no more time than is needed on average, no more than is socially necessary. The labour time socially necessary is that required to produce an article under the normal conditions of production, and with the average degree of skill and intensity prevalent at the time. The introduction of power-looms into England probably reduced by one-half the labour required to weave a given quantity of yarn into cloth. The hand-loom weavers, as a matter of fact, continued to require the same time as before; but for all that, the product of one hour of their labour represented after the change only half an hour's social labour, and consequently fell to one-half its former value.

We see then that that which determines the magnitude of the value of any article is the amount of labour socially necessary, or the labour time socially necessary for its production. Each individual commodity, in this connection, is to be considered as an average sample of its class. Commodities, therefore, in which equal quantities of labour are embodied, or which can be produced in the same time, have the same value. The value of one commodity is to the value of any other, as the labour time necessary for the production of the one is to that necessary for the production of the other. 'As values, all commodities are only definite masses of congealed labour time.'

The value of a commodity would therefore remain constant, if the labour time required for its production also remained constant. But the latter changes with every variation in the productiveness of labour. This productiveness is determined by various circumstances, among others, by the average amount of skill of the workmen, the state of science, and the degree of its practical application, the social organization of production, the extent and capabilities of the means of production, and by physical conditions. For example, the same amount of labour in favourable seasons is embodied in eight bushels of corn, and in unfavourable, only in four. The same labour extracts from rich mines more metal than from poor mines. Diamonds are of very rare occurrence on the earth's surface, and hence their discovery costs, on an average, a great deal of labour time. Consequently much labour is represented in a small compass. Jacob doubts whether gold has ever been paid for at its full value. This applies still more to diamonds. According to Eschwege, the total produce of the Brazilian diamond mines for the eighty years ending in 1823, had not realized the price of one-and-a-half years' average produce of the sugar and coffee plantations of the same country, although the diamonds cost much more labour, and therefore represented more value. With richer mines, the same quantity of labour would embody itself in more diamonds, and their value would fall. If we could succeed, at a small expenditure of labour, in converting carbon into diamonds, their value might fall below that of bricks. In general, the greater the productiveness of labour, the less is the labour time required for the production of an article, the less is the amount of labour crystallized in that article, and the less is its value; and vice versa, the less the productiveness of labour, the greater is the labour time required for the production of an article, and the greater is its value. The value of a commodity, therefore, varies directly as the quantity, and inversely as the productiveness, of the labour incorporated in it.

A thing can be a use-value, without having value. This is the case whenever its utility to man is not due to labour. Such are air, virgin soil, natural meadows, etc. A thing can be useful, and the product of human labour, without being a commodity. Whoever directly satisfies his wants with the produce of his own labour creates, indeed, use-values, but not commodities. In order to produce the latter, he must not only produce use-values, but use-values for others, social use-values. (And not only for others. The medieval peasant produced quit-rent-corn for his feudal lord and tithe-corn for his parson. But neither the quit-rent-corn nor the tithe-corn became commodities by reason of the fact that they had been produced for others. To become a commodity a product must be transferred to another, whom it will serve as a use-value, by means of an exchange.) Lastly, nothing can have value without being an object of utility. If the thing is useless, so is the labour contained in it; the labour does not count as labour, and therefore creates no value.

* * *

At first sight a commodity presented itself to us as a complex of two things—use-value and exchange-value. Later on, we saw also that labour, too, possesses the same twofold nature; for, so far as it finds expression in value, it does not possess the same characteristics that belong to it as a creator of use-values. I was the first to point out and to examine critically this twofold nature of the labour contained in commodities. As this point is the pivot on which a clear comprehension of Political Economy turns, we must go more into detail.

Let us take two commodities such as a coat and 10 yards of linen, and let the former be double the value of the latter, so that, if 10 yards of linen = W, the coat = 2W.

The coat is a use-value that satisfies a particular want. Its existence is the result of a special sort of productive activity, the nature of which is determined by its aim, mode of operation, subject, means, and result. The labour, whose utility is thus represented by the value in use of its product, or which manifests itself by making its product a use-value, we call useful labour. In this connection we consider only its useful effect.

As the coat and the linen are two qualitatively different use-values, so also are the two forms of labour that produce them, tailoring and weaving. Were these two objects not qualitatively different, not produced respectively by labour of different quality, they could not stand to each other in the relation of commodities. Coats are not exchanged for coats, one use-value is not exchanged for another of the same kind.

To all the different varieties of values in use there correspond as many different kinds of useful labour, classified according to the order, genus, species, and variety to which they belong in the social division of labour. This division of labour is a necessary condition for the production of commodities, but it does not follow, conversely, that the production of commodities is a necessary condition for the division of labour. In the primitive Indian community there is social division of labour, without production of commodities. Or, to take an example nearer home, in every factory the labour is divided according to a system, but this division is not brought about by the operatives mutually exchanging their individual products. Only such products can become commodities with regard to each other, as result from different kinds of labour, each kind being carried on independently and for the account of private individuals.

To resume, then: In the use-value of each commodity there is contained useful labour, i.e., productive activity of a definite kind and exercised with a definite aim. Use-values cannot confront each other as commodities, unless the useful labour embodied in them is qualitatively different in each of them. In a community, the produce of which in general takes the form of commodities, i.e., in a community of commodity producers, this qualitative difference between the useful forms of labour that are carried on independently by individual producers, each on their own account, develops into a complex system, a social division of labour.

Anyhow, whether the coat be worn by the tailor or by his customer, in either case it operates as a use-value. Nor is the relation between the coat and the labour that produced it altered by the circumstance that tailoring may have become a special trade, an independent branch of the social division of labour. Wherever the want of clothing forced them to it, the human race made clothes for thousands of years, without a single man becoming a tailor. But coats and linen, like every other element of material wealth that is not the spontaneous produce of Nature, must invariably owe their existence to a special productive activity, exercised with a definite aim, an activity that appropriates particular nature-given materials to particular human wants. So far therefore as labour is a creator of use-value, is useful labour, it is a necessary condition, independent of all forms of society for the existence of the human race; it is an eternal nature-imposed necessity, without which there can be no material exchanges between man and Nature, and therefore no life.

The use-values, coat, linen, etc., i.e., the bodies of commodities, are combinations of two elements—matter and labour. If we take away the useful labour expended upon them, a material substratum is always left, which is furnished by Nature without the help of man. The latter can work only as Nature does, that is by changing the form of matter. Nay more, in this work of changing the form he is constantly helped by natural forces. We see, then, that labour is not the only source of material wealth, of use-values produced by labour. As William Petty puts it, labour is its father and the earth its mother.

Let us now pass from the commodity considered as a use-value to the value of commodities.

By our assumption, the coat is worth twice as much as the linen. But this is a mere quantitative difference, which for the present does not concern us. We bear in mind, however, that if the value of the coat is double that of 10 yds of linen, 20 yds of linen must have the same value as one coat. So far as they are values, the coat and the linen are things of a like substance, objective expressions of essentially identical labour. But tailoring and weaving are, qualitatively, different kinds of labour. There are, however, states of society in which one and the same man does tailoring and weaving alternately, in which case these two forms of labour are mere modifications of the labour of the same individual, and not special and fixed functions of different persons; just as the coat which our tailor makes one day, and the trousers which he makes another day, imply only a variation in the labour of one and the same individual. Moreover, we see at a glance that, in our capitalist society, a given portion of human labour is, in accordance with the varying demand, at one time

supplied in the form of tailoring, at another in the form of weaving. This change may possibly not take place without friction, but take place it must.

Productive activity, if we leave out of sight its special form, viz., the useful character of the labour, is nothing but the expenditure of human labour power. Tailoring and weaving, though qualitatively different productive activities, are each a productive expenditure of human brains, nerves, and muscles, and in this sense are human labour. They are but two different modes of expending human labour power. Of course, this labour power, which remains the same under all its modifications, must have attained a certain pitch of development before it can be expended in a multiplicity of modes. But the value of a commodity represents human labour in the abstract, the expenditure of human labour in general. And just as in society, a general or a banker plays a great part, but mere man, on the other hand, a very shabby part, so here with mere human labour. It is the expenditure of simple labour power, i.e., of the labour power which, on an average, apart from any special development, exists in the organism of every ordinary individual. Simple average labour, it is true, varies in character in different countries and at different times, but in a particular society it is given. Skilled labour counts only as simple labour intensified, or rather, as multiplied simple labour, a given quantity of skilled being considered equal to a greater quantity of simple labour. Experience shows that this reduction is constantly being made. A commodity may be the product of the most skilled labour, but its value, by equating it to the product of simple unskilled labour, represents a definite quantity of the latter labour alone. The different proportions in which different sorts of labour are reduced to unskilled labour as their standard, are established by a social process that goes on behind the backs of the producers, and, consequently, appear to be fixed by custom. For simplicity's sake we shall henceforth account every kind of labour to be unskilled, simple labour; by this we do no more than save ourselves the trouble of making the reduction.

Just as, therefore, in viewing the coat and linen as values, we abstract from their different use-values, so it is with the labour represented by those values: we disregard the difference between its useful forms, weaving and tailoring. As the use-values, coat and linen, are combinations of special productive activities with cloth and yarn, while the values, coat and linen, are, on the other hand, mere homogeneous congelations of indifferentiated labour, so the labour embodied in these latter values does not count by virtue of its productive relation to cloth and yarn, but only as being expenditure of human labour power. Tailoring and weaving are necessary factors in the creation of the use-values, coat and linen, precisely because these two kinds of labour are of different qualities; but only in so far as abstraction is made from their special qualities, only in so far as both possess the same quality of being human labour, do tailoring and weaving form the substance of the values of the same articles.

Coats and linen, however, are not merely values, but values of definite magnitude, and according to our assumption, the coat is worth twice as much as the ten yards of linen. Whence this difference in their values? It is owing to the fact that the linen contains only half as much labour as the coat, and consequently, that in the production of the latter, labour power must have been expended during twice the time necessary for the production of the former.

While, therefore, with reference to use-value, the labour contained in a commodity counts only qualitatively, with reference to value it counts only quantitatively, and must first be reduced to human labour pure and simple. In the former case, it is a question of How and What, in the latter of How much? How long a time? Since the magnitude of the value of a commodity represents only the quantity of labour embodied in it, it follows that all commodities, when taken in certain proportions, must be equal in value.

If the productive power of all the different sorts of useful labour required for the production of a coat remains unchanged, the sum of the values of the coats produced increases with their number. If one coat represents x days' labour, two coats represent 2x days' labour, and so on. But assume that the duration of the labour necessary for the production of a coat becomes doubled or halved. In the first case, one coat is worth as much as two coats were before; in the second case, two coats are only worth as much as one was before, although in both cases one coat renders the same service as before, and the useful labour embodied in it

remains of the same quality. But the quantity of labour spent on its production has altered.

An increase in the quantity of use-values is an increase of material wealth. With two coats two men can be clothed, with one coat only one man. Nevertheless, an increased quantity of material wealth may correspond to a simultaneous fall in the magnitude of its value. This antagonistic movement has its origin in the twofold character of labour. Productive power has reference, of course, only to labour of some useful concrete form; the efficacy of any special productive activity during a given time being dependent on its productiveness. Useful labour becomes, therefore, a more or less abundant source of products, in proportion to the rise or fall of its productiveness. On the other hand, no change in this productiveness affects the labour represented by value. Since productive power is an attribute of the concrete useful forms of labour, of course it can no longer have any bearing on that labour, so soon as we make abstraction from those concrete useful forms. However then productive power may vary, the same labour, exercised during equal periods of time, always yields equal amounts of value. But it will yield, during equal periods of time, different quantities of values in use; more, if the productive power rise, fewer, if it fall. The same change in productive power, which increases the fruitfulness of labour, and, in consequence, the quantity of use-values produced by that labour, will diminish the total value of this increased quantity of use-values, provided such change shorten the total labour time necessary for their production; and vice versa.

On the one hand all labour is, speaking physiologically, an expenditure of human labour power, and in its character of identical abstract human labour, it creates and forms the value of commodities. On the other hand, all labour is the expenditure of human labour power in a special form and with a definite aim, and in this, its character of concrete useful labour, it produces use-values.

Commodities come into the world in the shape of use-values, articles, or goods, such as iron, linen, corn, etc. This is their plain, homely, bodily form. They are, however, commodities, only because they are something twofold, both objects of utility, and, at the same time, depositories of value. They manifest themselves therefore as commodities, or have the form of commodities, only in so far as they have two forms, a physical or natural form, and a value-form.

The reality of the value of commodities differs in this respect from Mistress Quickly, that we don't know 'where to have it'. The value of commodities is the very opposite of the coarse materiality of their substance, not an atom of matter enters into its composition. Turn and examine a single commodity, by itself, as we will, yet in so far as it remains an object of value, it seems impossible to grasp it. If, however, we bear in mind that the value of commodities has a purely social reality, and that they acquire this reality only in so far as they are expressions or embodiments of one identical social substance, viz., human labour, it follows as a matter of course, that value can only manifest itself in the social relation of commodity to commodity. In fact we started from exchange-value, or the exchange relation of commodities, in order to get at the value that lies hidden behind it. We must now return to this form under which value first appeared to us.

Everyone knows, if he knows nothing else, that commodities have a value-form common to them all, and presenting a marked contrast with the varied bodily forms of their use-values. I mean their money-form. Here, however, a task is set us, the performance of which has never yet even been attempted by bourgeois economy, the task of tracing the genesis of this money-form, of developing the expression of value implied in the value-relation of commodities, from its simplest, almost imperceptible outline, to the dazzling money-form. By doing this we shall, at the same time, solve the riddle presented by money.

The simplest value-relation is evidently that of one commodity to some one other commodity of a different kind. Hence the relation between the values of two commodities supplies us with the simplest expression of the value of a single commodity.

* * *

The whole mystery of the form of value lies hidden in this elementary form. Its analysis, therefore, is our real difficulty.

Here two different kinds of commodities (in our example the linen and the coat) evidently play two different parts. The linen expresses its value in the coat; the coat serves as the material in which that value is expressed. The former plays an active, the latter a passive, part. The value of the linen is represented as relative value, or appears in relative form. The coat officiates as equivalent, or appears in equivalent form.

The relative form and the equivalent form are two intimately connected, mutually dependent, and inseparable elements of the expression of value; but, at the same time, are mutually exclusive, antagonistic extremes—i.e., poles of the same expression. They are allotted respectively to the two different commodities brought into relation by that expression. It is not possible to express the value of linen in linen. 20 yards of linen = 20 yards of linen is no expression of value. On the contrary, such an equation merely says that 20 yards of linen are nothing else than 20 yards of linen, a definite quantity of the use-value linen. The value of the linen can therefore be expressed only relatively—i.e., in some other commodity. The relative form of the value of the linen presupposes, therefore, the presence of some other commodity—here the coat—under the form of an equivalent. On the other hand, the commodity that figures as the equivalent cannot at the same time assume the relative form. That second commodity is not the one whose value is expressed. Its function is merely to serve as the material in which the value of the first commodity is expressed.

No doubt, the expression 20 yards of linen = 1 coat, or 20 yards of linen are worth 1 coat, implies the opposite relation: 1 coat = 20 yards of linen, or 1 coat is worth 20 yards of linen. But, in that case, I must reverse the equation, in order to express the value of the coat relatively; and, so soon as I do that, the linen becomes the equivalent instead of the coat. A single commodity cannot, therefore, simultaneously assume, in the same expression of value, both forms. The very polarity of these forms makes them mutually exclusive.

Whether, then, a commodity assumes the relative form, or the opposite equivalent form, depends entirely upon its accidental position in the expression of value—that is, upon whether it is the commodity whose value is being expressed or the commodity in which value is being expressed.

* * *

In order to discover how the elementary expression of the value of a commodity lies hidden in the value-relation of two commodities, we must, in the first place, consider the latter entirely apart from its quantitative aspect. The usual mode of procedure is generally the reverse, and in the value-relation nothing is seen but the proportion between definite quantities of two different sorts of commodities that are considered equal to each other. It is apt to be forgotten that the magnitudes of different things can be compared quantitatively, only when those magnitudes are expressed in terms of the same unit. It is only as expressions of such a unit that they are of the same denomination, and therefore commensurable.

Whether 20 yards of linen = 1 coat or = 20 coats or = x coats—that is, whether a given quantity of linen is worth few or many coats, every such statement implies that the linen and coats, as magnitudes of value, are expressions of the same unit, things of the same kind. Linen = coat is the basis of the equation.

But the two commodities whose identity of quality is thus assumed, do not play the same part. It is only the value of the linen that is expressed. And how? By its reference to the coat as its equivalent, as something that can be exchanged for it. In this relation the coat is the mode of existence of value, is value embodied, for only as such is it the same as the linen. On the other hand, the linen's own value comes to the front, receives independent expression, for it is only as being value that it is comparable to the coat as a thing of equal value, or exchangeable with the coat. To borrow an illustration from chemistry, butyric acid is a different substance from propyl formate. Yet both are made up of the same chemical substances, carbon (C), hydrogen (H), and oxygen (O), and that, too, in like proportions—namely, $C_4H_8O_2$. If now we equate butyric acid to propyl formate, then, in the first place, propyl formate would be, in this relation, merely a form of existence of $C_4H_8O_2$; and in the second place, we should be stating that butyric acid also consists of $C_4H_8O_2$. Therefore, by thus equating the two substances, expression would be given to their chemical composition, while their different physical forms would be neglected.

If we say that, as values, commodities are mere congelations of human labour, we reduce them by our analysis, it is true, to the abstraction, value; but we ascribe to this value no form apart from their bodily form. It is otherwise in the value-relation of

one commodity to another. Here, the one stands forth in its character of value by reason of its relation to the other.

By making the coat the equivalent of the linen, we equate the labour embodied in the former to that in the latter. Now, it is true that the tailoring, which makes the coat, is concrete labour of a different sort from the weaving which makes the linen. But the act of equating it to the weaving reduces the tailoring to that which is really equal in the two kinds of labour, to their common character of human labour. In this roundabout way, then, the fact is expressed, that weaving also, in so far as it weaves value, has nothing to distinguish it from tailoring, and, consequently, is abstract human labour. It is the expression of equivalence between different sorts of commodities that alone brings into relief the specific character of value-creating labour, and this it does by actually reducing the different varieties of labour embodied in the different kinds of commodities to their common quality of human labour in the abstract.

There is, however, something else required beyond the expression of the specific character of the labour of which the value of the linen consists. Human labour power in motion, or human labour, creates value, but is not itself value. It becomes value only in its congealed state, when embodied in the form of some object. In order to express the value of the linen as a congelation of human labour, that value must be expressed as having objective existence, as being a something materially different from the linen itself, and yet a something common to the linen and all other commodities. The problem is already solved.

When occupying the position of equivalent in the equation of value, the coat ranks qualitatively as the equal of the linen, as something of the same kind, because it is value. In this position it is a thing in which we see nothing but value, or whose palpable bodily form represents value. Yet the coat itself, the body of the commodity, coat, is a mere use-value. A coat as such no more tells us it is value, than does the first piece of linen we take hold of. This shows that when placed in value-relation to the linen, the coat signifies more than when out of that relation, just as many a man strutting about in a gorgeous uniform counts for more than when in mufti.

In the production of the coat, human labour power, in the shape of tailoring, must have been actually expended. Human labour is therefore accumulated in it. In this aspect the coat is a depository of value, but though worn to a thread, it does not let this fact show through. And as equivalent of the linen in the value equation, it exists under this aspect alone, counts therefore as embodied value, as a body that is value. A, for instance, cannot be 'your majesty' to B, unless at the same time majesty in B's eyes assumes the bodily form of A, and, what is more, with every new father of the people, changes its features, hair, and many other things besides.

Hence, in the value equation, in which the coat is the equivalent of the linen, the coat officiates as the form of value. The value of the commodity linen is expressed by the bodily form of the commodity coat, the value of one by the use-value of the other. As a use-value, the linen is something palpably different from the coat; as value, it is the same as the coat, and now has the appearance of a coat. Thus the linen acquires a value-form different from its physical form. The fact that it is value is made manifest by its equality with the coat, just as the sheep's nature of a Christian is shown in his resemblance to the Lamb of God.

We see, then, that all that our analysis of the value of commodities has already told us is told us by the linen itself, as soon as it comes into communication with another commodity, the coat. Only it betrays its thoughts in that language with which alone it is familiar, the language of commodities. In order to tell us that its own value is created by labour in its abstract character of human labour, it says that the coat, in so far as it is worth as much as the linen, and therefore is value, consists of the same labour as the linen. In order to inform us that its sublime reality as value is not the same as its buckram body, it says that value has the appearance of a coat, and consequently that so far as the linen is value, it and the coat are as like as two peas. We may here remark, that the language of commodities has, besides Hebrew, many other more or less correct dialects. The German 'Wertsein', to be worth, for instance, expresses in a less striking manner than the Romance verbs 'valere', 'valer', 'valoir', that the equating of commodity B to commodity A is commodity A's own mode of expressing its value. *Paris vaut bien une messe.* [Paris is easily worth a Mass.]

By means, therefore, of the value-relation expressed in our equation, the bodily form of commodity B becomes the value-form of commodity A, or the body of commodity B acts as a mirror to the value of commodity A. By putting itself in relation with commodity B, as value *in propria persona* [in its own person] as the matter of which human labour is made up, the commodity A converts the value in use, B, into the substance in which to express its, A's, own value. The value of A, thus expressed in the use-value of B, has taken the form of relative value.

* * *

Every commodity, whole value it is intended to express, is a useful object of given quantity, as 15 bushels of corn, or 100 lb of coffee. And a given quantity of any commodity contains a definite quantity of human labour. The value-form must therefore not only express value generally, but also value in definite quantity. Therefore, in the value-relation of commodity A to commodity B, of the linen to the coat, not only is the latter, as value in general, made the equal in quality of the linen, but a definite quantity of coat (1 coat) is made the equivalent of a definite quantity (20 yards) of linen.

The equation, 20 yards of linen = 1 coat, or 20 yards of linen are worth one coat, implies that the same quantity of value-substance (congealed labour) is embodied in both; that the two commodities have each cost the same amount of labour or the same quantity of labour time. But the labour time necessary for the production of 20 yards of linen or 1 coat varies with every change in the productiveness of weaving or tailoring. We have now to consider the influence of such changes on the quantitative aspect of the relative expression of value.

I. Let the value of the linen vary, that of the coat remaining constant. If, say in consequence of the exhaustion of flax-growing soil, the labour time necessary for the production of the linen be doubled, the value of the linen will also be doubled. Instead of the equation, 20 yards of linen = 1 coat, we should have 20 yards of linen = 2 coats, since 1 coat would now contain only half the labour time embodied in

20 yards of linen. If, on the other hand, in consequence, say, of improved looms, this labour time were reduced by one-half, the value of the linen would fall by one-half. Consequently, we should have 20 yards of linen = ½ coat. The relative value of commodity A, i.e., its value expressed in commodity B, rises and falls directly as the value of A, the value of B being supposed constant.

II. Let the value of the linen remain constant, while the value of the coat varies. If, under these circumstances, in consequence, for instance, of a poor crop of wool, the labour time necessary for the production of a coat becomes doubled, we have instead of 20 yards of linen = 1 coat, 20 yards of linen = ½ coat. If, on the other hand, the value of the coat sinks by one-half, then 20 yards of linen = 2 coats. Hence, if the value of commodity A remains constant, its relative value expressed in commodity B rises and falls inversely as the value of B.

If we compare the different cases in I and II, we see that the same change of magnitude in relative value may arise from totally opposite causes. Thus, the equation, 20 yards of linen = 1 coat, becomes 20 yards of linen = 2 coats, either, because, the value of the linen has doubled, or because the value of the coat has fallen by one-half; and it becomes 20 yards of linen = ½ coat, either, because the value of the linen has fallen by one-half, or because the value of the coat has doubled.

III. Let the quantities of labour time respectively necessary for the production of the linen and the coat vary simultaneously in the same direction and in the same proportion. In this case 20 yards of linen continue equal to 1 coat, however much their values may have altered. Their change of value is seen as soon as they are compared with a third commodity, whose value has remained constant. If the values of all commodities rose or fell simultaneously, and in the same proportion, their relative values would remain unaltered. Their real change of value would appear from the diminished or increased quantity of commodities produced in a given time.

IV. The labour time respectively necessary for the production of the linen and the coat, and therefore the value of these commodities may simultaneously vary in the same direction, but at unequal rates, or in opposite directions, or in other ways. The effect of all these possible different variations, on the relative value of a commodity, may be deduced from the results of I, II, and III.

Thus real changes in the magnitude of value are neither unequivocally nor exhaustively reflected in their relative expression, that is, in the equation expressing the magnitude of relative value. The relative value of a commodity may vary, although its value remains constant. Its relative value may remain constant, although its value varies; and finally, simultaneous variations in the magnitude of value and in that of its relative expression by no means necessarily correspond in amount. . . .

5. THE GENERAL FORMULA FOR CAPITAL

KARL MARX

In this selection from *Capital*, volume I (1867), Marx sketches a general formula to account for the distinctive way that commodities circulate in capitalism. In a simple version of commodity circulation, C—M—C, one commodity is exchanged for another and money becomes a medium that allows one to compare corn and clothes. However, in capitalism, another form is evident: M—C—M', where M' is greater than M. In the first example, a transaction occurs that provides the seller with a good that he or she did not possess before, and that has personal use-value. With the second formula, the individual who has money puts it into circulation with the anticipation of having the money returned along with an additional increment, which Marx calls "surplus value." What, then, is the actual source of surplus value? Answering this question is a focal concern of Marx´s subsequent work.

The circulation of commodities is the starting-point of capital. The production of commodities, their circulation, and that more developed form of their circulation called commerce, these form the historical groundwork from which it rises. The modern history of capital dates from the creation in the 16th century of a world-embracing commerce and a world-embracing market.

If we abstract from the material substance of the circulation of commodities, that is, from the exchange of the various use-values, and consider only the economic forms produced by this process of circulation, we find its final result to be money: this final product of the circulation of commodities is the first form in which capital appears. As a matter of history, capital, as opposed to landed property, invariably takes the form at first of money: it appears as moneyed wealth, as the capital of the merchant and of the usurer. But we have no need to refer to the origin of capital in order to discover that the first form of appearance of capital is money. We can see it daily under our very eyes. All new capital, to commence with, comes on the stage, that is, on the market, whether of commodities, labour, or money, even in our days, in the shape of money that by a definite process has to be transformed into capital.

The first distinction we notice between money that is money only, and money that is capital, is nothing more than a difference in their form of circulation. The simplest form of the circulation of commodities is C—M—C, the transformation of commodities into money, and the change of the money back again into commodities; or selling in order to buy. But alongside of this form we find another specifically different form: M—C—M, the transformation of money into commodities, and the change of commodities back again into money; or buying in order to sell. Money that circulates in the latter manner is thereby transformed into, becomes capital, and is already potentially capital.

Now let us examine the circuit M—C—M a little closer. It consists, like the other, of two antithetical phases. In the first phase, M—C, or the purchase, the money is changed into a commodity.

In the second phase, C—M, or the sale, the commodity is changed back again into money. The combination of these two phases constitutes the single movement whereby money is exchanged for a commodity, and the same commodity is again exchanged for money; whereby a commodity is bought in order to

Reprinted from Karl Marx, *Karl Marx: Selected Writings*, edited by David McLellan, pp. 445–4451. Oxford: Oxford University Press. Copyright © 1977. Reprinted by permission of Oxford University Press. ✦

be sold, or, neglecting the distinction in form between buying and selling, whereby a commodity is bought with a commodity. The result, in which the phases of the process vanish, is the exchange of money for money, M—M. If I purchase 2,000 lbs. of cotton for £100, and resell the 2,000 lbs. of cotton for £110, I have, in fact, exchanged £100 for £110, money for money.

Now it is evident that the circuit M—C—M would be absurd and without meaning if the intention were to exchange by this means two equal sums of money, £100 for £100. The miser's plan would be far simpler and surer; he sticks to his £100 instead of exposing it to the dangers of circulation. And yet, whether the merchant who has paid £100 for his cotton sells it for £110, or lets it go for £100, or even £50, his money has, at all events, gone through a characteristic and original movement, quite different in kind from that which it goes through in the hands of the peasant who sells corn, and with the money thus set free buys clothes. We have therefore to examine first the distinguishing characteristics of the forms of the circuits M—C—M and C—M—C, and in doing this the real difference that underlies the mere difference of form will reveal itself.

Let us see, in the first place, what the two forms have in common.

Both circuits are resolvable into the same two antithetical phases, C—M, a sale, and M—C, a purchase. In each of these phases the same material elements—a commodity, and money, and the same economic dramatis personæ, a buyer and a seller—confront one another. Each circuit is the unity of the same two antithetical phases, and in each case this unity is brought about by the intervention of three contracting parties, of whom one only sells, another only buys, while the third both buys and sells.

What, however, first and foremost distinguishes the circuit C—M—C from the circuit M—C—M, is the inverted order of succession of the two phases. The simple circulation of commodities begins with a sale and ends with a purchase, while the circulation of money as capital begins with a purchase and ends with a sale. In the one case both the starting-point and the goal are commodities, in the other they are money. In the first form the movement is brought about by the intervention of money, in the second by that of a commodity.

In the circulation C—M—C, the money is in the end converted into a commodity, that serves as a use-value; it is spent once for all. In the inverted form, M—C—M, on the contrary, the buyer lays out money in order that, as a seller, he may recover money. By the purchase of his commodity he throws money into circulation, in order to withdraw it again by the sale of the same commodity. He lets the money go, but only with the sly intention of getting it back again. The money, therefore, is not spent, it is merely advanced.

In the circuit C—M—C, the same piece of money changes its place twice. The seller gets it from the buyer and pays it away to another seller. The complete circulation, which begins with the receipt, concludes with the payment, of money for commodities. It is the very contrary in the circuit M—C—M. Here it is not the piece of money that changes its place twice, but the commodity. The buyer takes it from the hands of the seller and passes it into the hands of another buyer. Just as in the simple circulation of commodities the double change of place of the same piece of money effects its passage from one hand into another, so here the double change of place of the same commodity brings about the reflux of the money to its point of departure.

Such reflux is not dependent on the commodity being sold for more than was paid for it. This circumstance influences only the amount of the money that comes back. The reflux itself takes place, so soon as the purchased commodity is resold, in other words, so soon as the circuit M—C—M is completed. We have here, therefore, a palpable difference between the circulation of money as capital, and its circulation as mere money.

The circuit C—M—C comes completely to an end, so soon as the money brought in by the sale of one commodity is abstracted again by the purchase of another.

If, nevertheless, there follows a reflux of money to its starting-point, this can only happen through a renewal or repetition of the operation. If I sell a quarter of corn of £3, and with this £3 buy clothes, the money, so far as I am concerned, is spent and done with. It belongs to the clothes merchant. If I now sell a second quarter of corn, money indeed flows back to me, not however as a sequel to the first transaction, but in consequence of its repetition. The money again leaves me, so soon as I complete this second transaction by a fresh purchase. Therefore, in the circuit C—M—C, the expenditure of money has nothing to do with its reflux. On the other hand, in M—C—M, the reflux of the money is conditioned by the very mode of its expenditure. Without this reflux, the operation fails, or the process is interrupted and incomplete, owing to the absence of its complementary and final phase, the sale.

The circuit C—M—C starts with one commodity, and finishes with another, which falls out of circulation and into consumption. Consumption, the satisfaction of wants, in one word, use-value, is its end and aim. The circuit M—C—M, on the contrary, commences with money and ends with money. Its leading motive, and the goal that attracts it, is therefore mere exchange-value.

In the simple circulation of commodities, the two extremes of the circuit have the same economic form. They are both commodities, and commodities of equal value. But they are also use-values differing in their qualities, as, for example corn and clothes. The exchange of products, of the different materials in which the labour of society is embodied, forms here the basis of the movement. It is otherwise in the circulation M—C—M, which at first sight appears purposeless, because tautological. Both extremes have the same economic form. They are both money, and therefore are not qualitatively different use-values; for money is but the converted form of commodities, in which their particular use-values vanish. To exchange £100 for cotton, and then this same cotton again for £110, is merely a roundabout way of exchanging money for money, the same for the same, and appears to be an operation just as purposeless as it is absurd. One sum of money is distinguishable from another only by its amount. The character and tendency of the process M—C—M, is therefore not due to any qualitative difference between its extremes, both being money, but solely to their quantitative difference. More money is withdrawn from circulation at the finish than was thrown into it at the start. The cotton that was bought for £100 is perhaps resold for £100+£10 or £110. The exact form of this process is therefore M—C—M′, where M′ = M+ ΔM = the original sum advanced, plus an increment. This increment or excess over the original value I call "surplus-value." The value originally advanced, therefore, not only remains intact while in circulation, but adds to itself a surplus-value or expands itself. It is this movement that converts it into capital.

Of course, it is also possible, that in C—M—C, the two extremes C—C, say corn and clothes, may represent different quantities of value. The farmer may sell his corn above its value, or may buy the clothes at less than their value. He may, on the other hand, "be done" by the clothes merchant. Yet, in the form of circulation now under consideration, such differences in value are purely accidental. The fact that the corn and the clothes are equivalents, does not deprive the process of all meaning, as it does in M—C—M. The equivalence of their values is rather a necessary condition to its normal course.

The repetition or renewal of the act of selling in order to buy, is kept within bounds by the very object it aims at, namely, consumption or the satisfaction of definite wants, an aim that lies altogether outside the sphere of circulation. But when we buy in order to sell, we, on the contrary, begin and end with the same thing, money, exchange-value; and thereby the movement becomes interminable. No doubt, M becomes M+ΔM, £100 become £110. But when viewed in their qualitative aspect alone, £110 are the same as £100, namely money; and considered quantitatively, £110 is, like £100, a sum of definite and limited value. If now, the £110 be spent as money, they cease to play their part. They are no longer capital. Withdrawn from circulation, they become petrified into a hoard, and though they remained in that state till doomsday, not a single farthing would accrue to them. If, then, the expansion of value is once aimed at, there is just the same inducement to augment the value of the £110 as that of the £100; for both are but limited expressions for exchange-value, and therefore both have the same vocation to approach, by quantitative increase, as near as possible to absolute wealth. Momentarily, indeed, the value originally advanced, the £100, is distinguishable from the surplus-value of £10, that is annexed to it during circulation; but the distinction vanishes immediately. At the end of the process, we do not receive with one hand the original £100, and with the other, the surplus-value of £10. We simply get a value of £110, which is in exactly the same condition and fitness for commencing the expanding process, as the original £100 was. Money ends the movement only to begin it again.[1] Therefore, the final result of every separate circuit, in which a purchase and consequent sale are completed, forms of itself the starting-point of a new circuit.

The simple circulation of commodities—selling in order to buy—is a means of carrying out a purpose unconnected with circulation, namely, the appropriation of use-values, the satisfaction of wants. The circulation of money as capital is, on the contrary, an end in itself, for the expansion of value takes place only within this constantly renewed movement. The circulation of capital has therefore no limits.[2]

As the conscious representative of this movement, the possessor of money becomes a capitalist. His person, or rather his pocket, is the point from which the money starts and to which it returns. The expansion of value, which is the objective basis or main-spring of the circulation M—C—M, becomes his subjective aim, and it is only in so far as the appropriation of ever more and more wealth in the abstract becomes the sole motive of his operations, that he functions as a capitalist, that is, as capital personified and endowed with consciousness and a will. Use-values must therefore never be looked upon as the real aim of the capitalist; neither must the profit on any single transaction. The restless never-ending process of profit-making alone is what he aims at. This boundless greed after riches, this passionate chase after exchange-value, is common to the capitalist and the miser; but while the miser is merely a capitalist gone mad, the capitalist is a rational miser. The never-ending augmentation of exchange-value, which the miser strives after, by seeking to save his money from circulation, is attained by the more acute capitalist, by constantly throwing it afresh into circulation.

The independent form, *i.e.*, the money-form, which the value of commodities assumes in the case of simple circulation, serves only one purpose, namely, their exchange, and vanishes in the final result of the movement. On the other hand, in the circulation M—C—M, both the money and the commodity represent only different modes of existence of value itself, the money its general mode, and the commodity its particular, or, so to say, disguised mode. It is constantly changing from one form to the other without thereby becoming lost, and thus assumes an automatically active character. If now we take in turn each of the two different forms which self-expanding value successively assumes in the course of its life, we then arrive at these two propositions: Capital is money: Capital is commodities. In truth, however, value is here the active factor in a process, in which, while constantly assuming the form in turn of money and commodities, it at the same time changes in magnitude, differentiates itself by throwing off surplus-value from itself; the original value, in other words, expands spontaneously. For the movement, in the course of which it adds surplus-value, is its own movement, its expansion, therefore, is automatic expansion. Because it is value, it has acquired the occult quality of being able to add value to itself. It brings forth living offspring, or, at the least, lays golden eggs.

Value, therefore, being the active factor in such a process, and assuming at one time the form of money, at another that of commodities, but through all these changes preserving itself and expanding, it requires some independent form, by means of which its identity may at any time be established. And this form it possesses only in the shape of money. It is under the form of money that value begins and ends, and begins again, every act of its own spontaneous generation. It began by being £100, it is now £110, and so on. But the money itself is only one of the two forms of value. Unless it takes the form of some commodity, it does not become capital. There is here no antagonism, as in the case of hoarding, between the money and commodities. The capitalist knows that all commodities, however scurvy they may look, or however badly they may smell, are in faith and in truth money, inwardly circumcised Jews, and what is more, a wonderful means whereby out of money to make more money.

In simple circulation, C—M—C, the value of commodities attained at the most a form independent of their use-values, *i.e.*, the form of money; but that same value now in the circulation M—C—M, or the circulation of capital, suddenly presents itself as an independent substance, endowed with a motion of its own, passing, through a life-process of its own, in which money and commodities are mere forms which it assumes and casts off in turn. Nay, more: instead of simply representing the relations of commodities, it enters now, so to say, into private relations with itself. It differentiates itself as original value from itself as surplus-value; as the father differentiates himself from himself quâ the son, yet both are one and of one age: for only by the surplus-value of £10 does the £100 originally advanced become capital, and so soon as this takes place, so soon as the son, and by the son, the father, is begotten, so soon does their difference vanish, and they again become one, £110.

Value therefore now becomes value in process, money in process, and, as such, capital. It comes out of circulation, enters into it again, preserves and multiplies itself within its circuit, comes back out of it with expanded bulk, and begins the same round ever afresh. M—M, money which begets money, such is the description of Capital from the mouths of its first interpreters, the Mercantilists.

Buying in order to sell, or, more accurately, buying in order to sell dearer, M—C—M, appears certainly to be a form peculiar to one kind of capital alone, namely merchants' capital. But industrial capital too is money, that is changed into commodities, and by the sale of these commodities, is re-converted into more money. The events that take place outside the sphere of circulation, in the interval between the buying and selling, do not affect the form of this movement. Lastly, in the case of interest-bearing capital, the circulation M—C—M appears abridged. We have its result without the intermediate stage, in the form M—M "en style lapidaire" so to say, money that is worth more money, value that is greater than itself.

M—C—M′ is therefore in reality the general formula of capital as it appears prima facie within the sphere of circulation.

NOTES

1. "Capital is divisible . . . into the original capital and the profit, the increment to the capital . . . although in practice this profit is immediately turned into capital, and set in motion with the original." (F. Engels, "Umrisse zu einer Kritik der Nationalökonomie," in the "Deutsch-Französische Jahrbücher," edited by Arnold Ruge and Karl Marx. Paris, 1844, p. 99.) [*Marx*]

2. Aristotle opposes Oeconomic to Chrematistic. He starts from the former. So far as it is the art of gaining a livelihood, it is limited to procuring those articles that are necessary to existence, and useful either to a household or the state. "True wealth consists of such values in use; for the quantity of possessions of this kind, capable of making life pleasant, is not unlimited. There is, however, a second mode of acquiring things, to which we may by preference and with correctness give the name of Chrematistic, and in this case there appear to be no limits to riches and possessions. Trade (literally retail trade, and Aristotle takes this kind because in it values in use predominate) does not in its nature belong to Chrematistic, for here the exchange has reference only to what is necessary to themselves (the buyer or seller)." Therefore, as he goes on to show, the original form of trade was barter, but with the extension of the latter, there arose the necessity for money. On the discovery of money, barter of necessity developed into trading in commodities, and this again, in opposition to its original tendency, grew into Chrematistic, into the art of making money. Now Chrematistic is distinguishable from Oeconomic in this way, that "in the case of Chrematistic circulation is the source of riches. And it appears to revolve about money, for money is the beginning and end of this kind of exchange. Therefore also riches, such as Chrematistic strives for, are unlimited. Just as every art that is not a means to an end, but an end in itself, has no limit to its aims, because it seeks constantly to approach nearer and nearer to that end, while those arts that pursue means to an end, are not boundless, since the goal itself imposes a limit upon them, so with Chrematistic, there are no bounds to its aims, these aims being absolute wealth. Oeconomic not Chrematistic has a limit . . . the object of the former is something different from money, of the latter the augmentation of money . . . . By confounding these two forms, which overlap each other, some people have been led to look upon the preservation and increase of money ad infinitum as the end and aim of Oeconomic." (Aristoteles, "De-rep." edit. Bekker. lib. I. c. 8, 9. passim.) [*Marx*]

SECTION I

1. Implicit in Marx´s analysis of alienated labor is a view of the significance of work for a meanngful life. How would you characterize his view?
2. How does capitalism alienate workers from the product of their work?
3. What distinguished Marx and Engels´ view of materialism from that of philosophers such as Feuerbach?
4. How would you summarize Marx and Engels´ understanding of the production of consciousness?
5. If the bourgeoisie is a revolutionary class, why do Marx and Engels want to see it overthrown?
6. What is a commodity in Marxist language?
7. What makes the circulation of commodities in capitalism unique?

II. ÉMILE DURKHEIM

6. ON MECHANICAL AND ORGANIC SOLIDARITY

ÉMILE DURKHEIM

Émile Durkheim (1858–1917) used two metaphors to describe the different bases of solidarity, or social order, in traditional preindustrial and modern industrial societies. He saw traditional society as characterized by mechanical solidarity and modern society as defined in terms of organic solidarity. In this excerpt from his first major book, *The Division of Labor in Society* (1893), Durkheim poses a fundamental question about modern society: How can it facilitate individual autonomy while people are increasingly more dependent on others? As the title of the book might suggest, the answer has to do with the ever more complex and differentiated division of labor in industrial societies.

• • • This work had its origins in the question of the relations of the individual to social solidarity. Why does the individual, while becoming more autonomous, depend more upon society? How can he be at once more individual and more solidary? Certainly, these two movements, contradictory as they appear, develop in parallel fashion. This is the problem we are raising. It appeared to us that what resolves this apparent antinomy is a transformation of social solidarity due to the steadily growing development of the division of labor. That is how we have been led to make this the object of our study. . . .

INTRODUCTION

THE PROBLEM

The division of labor is not of recent origin, but it was only at the end of the eighteenth century that social cognizance was taken of the principle, though, until then, unwitting submission had been rendered to it. To be sure, several thinkers from earliest times saw its importance;[1] but Adam Smith was the first to attempt a theory of it. Moreover, he adopted this phrase that social science later lent to biology.

Nowadays, the phenomenon has developed so generally it is obvious to all. We need have no further illusions about the tendencies of modern industry; it advances steadily towards powerful machines, towards great concentrations of forces and capital, and consequently to the extreme division of labor. Occupations are infinitely separated and specialized, not only inside the factories, but each product is itself a specialty dependent upon others. Adam Smith and John Stuart Mill still hoped that agriculture, at least, would be an exception to the rule, and they saw it as the last resort of small-scale industry. Although one must be careful not to generalize unduly in such matters, nevertheless it is hard to deny today that the principal branches of the agricultural industry are steadily being drawn into the general movement.[2] Finally, business itself is ingeniously following and reflecting in all its shadings the infinite diversity of industrial enterprises; and, while this evolution is realizing itself with unpremeditated spontaneity, the economists, examining its causes and appreciating its results, far from condemning or opposing it, uphold it as necessary. They see in it the supreme law of human societies and the condition of their progress. . .

* * *

. . .[T]he relations governed by co-operative law with restitutive sanctions and the solidarity which they express, result from the division of social labor. We have explained, moreover, that, in general, co-operative relations do not convey other sanctions. In fact, it is in the nature of special tasks to escape the action of the collective conscience, for, in order for a thing to be the object of common sentiments, the first condition is that it be common, that is to say, that it be present in all consciences and that all can represent it in one and the same manner. To be sure, in so far as functions have a certain generality, everybody can have some idea of them. But the more specialized they are, the more circumscribed the number of those cognizant of each of them. Consequently, the more marginal they are to the common conscience. The rules which determine them cannot have the superior force, the transcendent authority which, when offended, demands expiation. It is also from opinion that their authority comes, as is the case with penal rules, but from an opinion localized in restricted regions of society.

Moreover, even in the special circles where they apply and where, consequently, they are represented in people, they do not correspond to very active sentiments, nor even very often to any type of emotional state. For, as they fix the manner in which the different functions ought to concur in diverse combinations of circumstances which can arise, the objects to which they relate themselves are not always present to consciences. We do not always have to administer guardianship trusteeship,[3] or exercise the rights of creditor or buyer, etc., or even exercise them in such and such a condition. But the states of conscience are strong only in so far as they are permanent. The violation of these rules reaches neither the common soul of society in its living parts,

nor even, at least not generally, that of special groups, and, consequently, it can determine only a very moderate reaction. All that is necessary is that the functions concur in a regular manner. If this regularity is disrupted, it behooves us to re-establish it. Assuredly, that is not to say that the development of the division of labor cannot be affective of penal law. There are, as we already know, administrative and governmental functions in which certain relations are regulated by repressive law, because of the particular character which the organ of common conscience and everything that relates to it has. In still other cases, the links of solidarity which unite certain social functions can be such that from their break quite general repercussions result invoking a penal sanction. But, for the reason we have given, these counter-blows are exceptional.

This law definitely plays a role in society analogous to that played by the nervous system in the organism. The latter has as its task, in effect, the regulation of the different functions of the body in such a way as to make them harmonize. It thus very naturally expresses the state of concentration at which the organism has arrived, in accordance with the division of physiological labor. Thus, on different levels of the animal scale, we can measure the degree of this concentration according to the development of the nervous system. Which is to say that we can equally measure the degree of concentration at which a society has arrived in accordance with the division of social labor according to the development of co-operative law with restitutive sanctions. We can foresee the great services that this criterion will render us. . .

* * *

Since negative solidarity does not produce any integration by itself, and since, moreover, there is nothing specific about it, we shall recognize only two kinds of positive solidarity which are distinguishable by the following qualities:

1. The first binds the individual directly to society without any intermediary. In the second, he depends upon society, because he depends upon the parts of which it is composed.
2. Society is not seen in the same aspect in the two cases. In the first, what we call society is a more or less organized totality of beliefs and

sentiments common to all the members of the group: this is the collective type. On the other hand, the society in which we are solidary in the second instance is a system of different, special functions which definite relations unite. These two societies really make up only one. They are two aspects of one and the same reality, but none the less they must be distinguished.

3. From this second difference there arises another which helps us to characterize and name the two kinds of solidarity.

The first can be strong only if the ideas and tendencies common to all the members of the society are greater in number and intensity than those which pertain personally to each member. It is as much stronger as the excess is more considerable. But what makes our personality is how much of our own individual qualities we have, what distinguishes us from others. This solidarity can grow only in inverse ratio to personality. There are in each of us, as we have said, two consciences: one which is common to our group in its entirety, which, consequently, is not ourself, but society living and acting within us; the other, on the contrary, represents that in us which is personal and distinct, that which makes us an individual.[4] Solidarity which comes from likenesses is at its maximum when the collective conscience completely envelops our whole conscience and coincides in all points with it. But, at that moment, our individuality is nil. It can be born only if the community takes smaller toll of us. There are, here, two contrary forces, one centripetal, the other centrifugal, which cannot flourish at the same time. We cannot, at one and the same time, develop ourselves in two opposite senses. If we have a lively desire to think and act for ourselves, we cannot be strongly inclined to think and act as others do. If our ideal is to present a singular and personal appearance, we do not want to resemble everybody else. Moreover, at the moment when this solidarity exercises its force, our personality vanishes, as our definition permits us to say, for we are no longer ourselves, but the collective life.

The social molecules which can be coherent in this way can act together only in the measure that they have no actions of their own, as the molecules of inorganic bodies. That is why we propose to call this type of solidarity mechanical. The term does not signify that it is produced by mechanical and artificial means. We call it that only by analogy to the cohesion which unites the elements of an inanimate body, as opposed to that which makes a unity out of the elements of a living body. What justifies this term is that the link which thus unites the individual to society is wholly analogous to that which attaches a thing to a person. The individual conscience, considered in this light, is a simple dependent upon the collective type and follows those of its owner. In societies where this type of solidarity is highly developed, the individual does not appear, as we shall see later. Individuality is something which the society possesses. Thus, in these social types, personal rights are not yet distinguished from real rights.

It is quite otherwise with the solidarity which the division of labor produces. Whereas the previous type implies that individuals resemble each other, this type presumes their difference. The first is possible only in so far as the individual personality is absorbed into the collective personality; the second is possible only if each one has a sphere of action which is peculiar to him; that is, a personality. It is necessary, then, that the collective conscience leave open a part of the individual conscience in order that special functions may be established there, functions which it cannot regulate. The more this region is extended, the stronger is the cohesion which results from this solidarity. In effect, on the one hand, each one depends much more strictly on society as labor is more divided; and, on the other, the activity of each is much more personal as it is, more specialized. Doubtless, as circumscribed as it is, it is never completely original. Even in the exercise of our occupation, we conform to usages, to practices which are common to our whole professional brotherhood. But, even in this instance, the yoke that we submit to is much less heavy than when society completely controls us, and it leaves much more place open for the free play of our initiative. Here, then, the individuality of all grows at the same time as that of its parts. Society becomes more capable of collective movement, at the same time that each of its elements has more freedom of movement. This solidarity resembles that which we observe among the higher animals. Each organ, in effect, has its special physiognomy, its autonomy. And, moreover, the unity of the organism is as great as the individuation of the parts is more marked. Because of this analogy, we propose to call the solidarity which is due to the division of labor, organic. . .

* * *

Not only, in a general way, does mechanical solidarity link men less strongly than organic solidarity, but also, as we advance in the scale of social evolution, it grows ever slacker.

The force of social links which have this origin vary with respect to the three following conditions:

1. The relation between the volume of the common conscience and that of the individual conscience. The links are as strong as the first more completely envelops the second.
2. The average intensity of the states of the collective conscience. The relation between volumes being equal, it has as much power over the individual as it has vitality. If, on the other hand, it consists of only feeble forces, it can but feebly influence the collective sense. It will the more easily be able to pursue its own course, and solidarity will be less strong.
3. The greater or lesser determination of these same states. That is, the more defined beliefs and practices are, the less place they leave for individual divergencies. They are uniform moulds into which we all, in the same manner, couch our ideas and our actions. The *consensus* is then as perfect as possible; all consciences vibrate in unison. Inversely, the more general and indeterminate the rules of conduct and thought are, the more individual reflection must intervene to apply them to particular cases. But it cannot awaken without upheavals occurring, for, as it varies from one man to another in quality and quantity, everything that it produces has the same character. Centrifugal tendencies thus multiply at the expense of social cohesion and the harmony of its movements.

On the other hand, strong and defined states of the common conscience are the roots of penal law. But we are going to see that the number of these is less today than heretofore, and that it diminishes, progressively, as societies approach our social type. . . .

To prove this, it would avail us nothing to compare the number of rules with repressive sanctions in different social types, for the number of rules does not vary exactly with the sentiments the rules represent. The same sentiment can, in effect, be offended in several different ways, and thus give rise to several rules without diversifying itself in so doing. Because there are now more ways of acquiring property, there are also more ways of stealing, but the sentiment of respect for the property of another has not multiplied itself proportionally. . .

This is not to say, however, that the common conscience is threatened with total disappearance. Only, it more and more comes to consist of very general and very indeterminate ways of thinking and feeling, which leave an open place for a growing multitude of individual differences. There is even a place where it is strengthened and made precise: that is the way in which it regards the individual. As all the other beliefs and all the other practices take on a character less and less religious, the individual becomes the object of a sort of religion. We erect a cult in behalf of personal dignity which, as every strong cult, already has its superstitions. It is thus, if one wishes, a common cult, but it is possible only by the ruin of all others, and, consequently, cannot produce the same effects as this multitude of extinguished beliefs. There is no compensation for that. Moreover, if it is common in so far as the community partakes of it, it is individual in its object. If it turns all wills towards the same end, this end is not social. It thus occupies a completely exceptional place in the collective conscience. It is still from society that it takes all its force, but it is not to society that it attaches us; it is to ourselves. Hence, it does not constitute a true social link. That is why we have been justly able to reproach the theorists who have made this sentiment exclusively basic in their moral doctrine, with the ensuing dissolution of society. We can then conclude by saying that all social links which result from likeness progressively slacken.

This law, in itself, is already enough to show the tremendous grandeur of the role of the division of labor. In sum, since mechanical solidarity progressively becomes enfeebled, life properly social must decrease or another solidarity must slowly come in to take the place of that which has gone. The choice must be made. In vain shall we contend that the collective conscience extends and grows stronger at the same time as that of individuals. We have just proved that the two terms vary in a sense inverse to each other. Social progress, however, does not consist in a continual dissolution. On the contrary, the more we advance, the more profoundly do societies reveal the sentiment of self and of unity. There must, then, be some other social link which produces this result; this cannot be any other than that which comes from the division of labor.

If, moreover, one recalls that even where it is most resistant, mechanical solidarity does not link men with the same force as the division of labor, and that, moreover, it leaves outside its scope the major part of phenomena actually social, it will become still more evident that social solidarity tends to become exclusively organic. It is the division of labor which, more and more, fills the role that was formerly filled by the common conscience. It is the principal bond of social aggregates of higher types.

This is a function of the division of labor a good deal more important than that ordinarily assigned to it by economists.

NOTES

1. Aristotle, *Nichomachean Ethics*, E1133a, 16.
2. *Journal des Economistes*, November 1884, p. 211.
3. That is why the law which governs the relations of domestic functions is not penal, although these functions are very general.
4. However, these two consciences are not in regions geographically distinct from us, but penetrate from all sides.

7. WHAT IS A SOCIAL FACT?

ÉMILE DURKHEIM

Durkheim was intent on staking out a distinctive place for sociology among the human sciences. He took particular pains to indicate the ways in which sociology and psychology differ. In *The Rules of Sociological Method* (1895), his famous methodological treatise, he begins making his case by defining what he refers to as "social facts." These, he proceeds to argue, are the proper subject matter of sociology and are what serve to distinguish it from the other sciences. Central to his understanding of the proper domain of sociological inquiry is his claim that social facts are forces that have an impact on the behavior of individuals. This focus on the constraining character of social facts has led subsequent critics to charge that Durkheim's overemphasis on social structure resulted in a devaluation of agency. In other words, he failed to appreciate that although people are shaped by their social circumstances, they can affect those circumstances.

Before inquiring into the method suited to the study of social facts, it is important to know which facts are commonly called "social." This information is all the more necessary since the designation "social" is used with little precision. It is currently employed for practically all phenomena generally diffused, within society, however small their social interest. But on that basis, there are, as it were, no human events that may not be called social. Each individual drinks, sleeps, eats, reasons; and it is to society's interest that these functions be exercised in an orderly manner. If, then, all these facts are counted as "social" facts, sociology would have no subject matter exclusively its own, and its domain would be confused with that of biology and psychology.

But in reality there is in every society a certain group of phenomena which may be differentiated from those studied by the other natural sciences. When I fulfil my obligations as brother, husband, or citizen, when I execute my contracts, I perform duties which are defined, externally to myself and my acts, in law and in custom. Even if they conform to my own sentiments and I feel their reality subjectively, such reality is still objective, for I did not create them: I merely inherited them through my education. How many times it happens, moreover, that we are ignorant of the details of the obligations incumbent upon us, and that in order to acquaint ourselves with them we must consult the law and its authorized interpreters! Similarly, the church-member finds the beliefs and practices of his religious life ready-made at birth; their existence prior to his own implies their existence outside of himself. The system of signs I use to express my thought, the system of currency I employ to pay my debts, the instruments of credit I utilize in my commercial relations, the practices followed in my profession, etc., function independently of my own use of them. And these statements can be repeated for each member of society. Here, then, are ways of acting, thinking, and feeling that present the noteworthy property of existing outside the individual consciousness.

These types of conduct or thought are not only external to the individual but are, moreover, endowed with coercive power, by virtue of which they impose themselves upon him, independent of his individual will. Of course, when I fully consent and conform to them, this constraint is felt only slightly, if at all, and is therefore unnecessary. But it is, nonetheless, an intrinsic characteristic of these facts, the proof thereof being that it asserts itself as soon as I attempt to resist it. If I attempt to violate the law, it reacts against me so as to prevent my act before its accomplishment, or to nullify my violation by restoring the damage, if it is accomplished and reparable, or to make me expiate it if it cannot be compensated for otherwise.

In the case of purely moral maxims the public conscience exercises a check on every act which offends it by means of the surveillance it exercises over the conduct of citizens, and the appropriate penalties at its disposal. In many cases the constraint is less violent, but nevertheless it always exists. If I do not submit to the conventions of society, if in my dress I do not conform to the customs observed in my country and in my class, the ridicule I provoke, the social isolation in which I am kept, produce, although in an attenuated form, the same effects as a punishment in the strict sense of the word. The constraint is nonetheless efficacious for being indirect. I am not obliged to speak French with my fellow countrymen nor to use the legal currency, but I cannot possibly do otherwise. If I tried to escape this necessity, my attempt would fail miserably. As an industrialist, I am free to apply the technical methods of former centuries; but by doing so, I should invite certain ruin. Even when I free myself from these rules and violate them successfully, I am always compelled to struggle with them. When finally overcome, they make their constraining power sufficiently felt by the resistance they offer. The enterprises of all innovators, including successful ones, come up against resistance of this kind.

Here, then, is a category of facts with very distinctive characteristics: it consists of ways of acting, thinking, and feeling, external to the individual, and endowed with a power of coercion, by reason of which they control him. These ways of thinking could not be confused with biological phenomena, since they consist of representations and of actions; nor with psychological phenomena, which exist only in the individual consciousness and through it. They constitute, thus, a new variety of phenomena; and it is to them exclusively that the term "social" ought to be applied. And this term fits them quite well, for it is clear that, since their source is not in the individual, their substratum can be no other than society, either the political society as a whole or some one of the partial groups it includes, such as religious denominations, political, literary, and occupational associations, etc. On the other hand, this term "social" applies to them exclusively, for it has a distinct meaning only if it designates exclusively the phenomena which are not included in any of the categories of facts that have already been established and classified. These ways of thinking and acting therefore constitute the proper domain of sociology. It is true that, when we define them with this word "constraint," we risk shocking the zealous partisans of absolute individualism. For those who profess the complete autonomy of the individual, man's dignity is diminished whenever he is made to feel that he is not completely self-determinant. It is generally accepted today, however, that most of our ideas and our tendencies are not developed by ourselves but come to us from without. How can they become a part of us except by imposing themselves upon us? This is the whole meaning of our definition. And it is generally accepted, moreover, that social constraint is not necessarily incompatible with the individual personality.[1]

Since the examples that we have just cited (legal and moral regulations, religious faiths, financial systems, etc.) all consist of established beliefs and practices, one might be led to believe that social facts exist only where there is some social organization. But there are other facts without such crystallized form which have the same objectivity and the same ascendency over the individual. These are called "social currents." Thus the great movements of enthusiasm, indignation, and pity in a crowd do not originate in any one of the particular individual consciousnesses. They come to each one of us from without and can carry us away in spite of ourselves. Of course, it may happen that, in abandoning myself to them unreservedly, I do not feel the pressure they exert upon me. But it is revealed as soon as I try to resist them. Let an individual attempt to oppose one of these collective manifestations, and the emotions that he denies will turn against him. Now, if this power of external coercion asserts itself so clearly in cases of resistance, it must exist also in the first-mentioned cases, although we are unconscious of it. We are then victims of the illusion of having ourselves created that which actually forced itself from without. If the complacency with which we permit ourselves to be carried along conceals the pressure undergone, nevertheless it does not abolish it. Thus, air is no less heavy because we do not detect its weight. So, even if we ourselves have spontaneously contributed to the production of the common emotion, the impression we have received differs markedly from that which we would have experienced if we had been alone. Also, once the crowd has dispersed, that is, once these social influences have ceased to act upon us and we are alone again, the emotions which have passed through the mind appear strange to us, and we no longer recognize them as ours. We realize that these feelings have been impressed upon us to a much greater extent than they were created by us. It may even happen that they horrify us, so much were they contrary to our nature. Thus, a group of individuals, most of whom are perfectly inoffensive, may, when gathered in a crowd, be drawn into acts of atrocity. And what we say of these transitory outbursts applies similarly to those more permanent currents of opinion on religious, political, literary, or artistic matters which are constantly being formed around us, whether in society as a whole or in more limited circles.

To confirm this definition of the social fact by a characteristic illustration from common experience, one need only observe the manner in which children are brought up. Considering the facts as they are and as they have always been, it becomes immediately evident that all education is a continuous effort to impose on the child ways of seeing, feeling, and acting which he could not have arrived at spontaneously. From the very first hours of his life, we compel him to eat, drink, and sleep at regular hours; we constrain him to cleanliness, calmness, and obedience; later we exert pressure upon him in order that he may learn proper consideration for others, respect for customs and conventions, the need for work, etc. If, in time, this constraint ceases to be felt, it is because it gradually gives rise to habits and to

internal tendencies that render constraint unnecessary; but nevertheless it is not abolished, for it is still the source from which these habits were derived. It is true that, according to Spencer, a rational education ought to reject such methods, allowing the child to act in complete liberty; but as this pedagogic theory has never been applied by any known people, it must be accepted only as an expression of personal opinion, not as a fact which can contradict the aforementioned observations. What makes these facts particularly instructive is that the aim of education is, precisely, the socialization of the human being; the process of education, therefore, gives us in a nutshell the historical fashion in which the social being is constituted. This unremitting pressure to which the child is subjected is the very pressure of the social milieu which tends to fashion him in its own image, and of which parents and teachers are merely the representatives and intermediaries.

It follows that sociological phenomena cannot be defined by their universality. A thought which we find in every individual consciousness, a movement repeated by all individuals, is not thereby a social fact. If sociologists have been satisfied with defining them by this characteristic, it is because they confused them with what one might call the reincarnation in the individual. It is, however, the collective aspects of the beliefs, tendencies, and practices of a group that characterize truly social phenomena. As for the forms that the collective states assume when refracted in the individual, these are things of another sort. This duality is clearly demonstrated by the fact that these two orders of phenomena are frequently found dissociated from one another. Indeed, certain of these social manners of acting and thinking acquire, by reason of their repetition, a certain rigidity which on its own account crystallizes them, so to speak, and isolates them from the particular events which reflect them. They thus acquire a body, a tangible form, and constitute a reality in their own right, quite distinct from the individual facts which produce it. Collective habits are inherent not only in the successive acts which they determine but, by a privilege of which we find no example in the biological realm, they are given permanent expression in a formula which is repeated from mouth to mouth, transmitted by education, and fixed even in writing.

Such is the origin and nature of legal and moral rules, popular aphorisms and proverbs, articles of faith wherein religious or political groups condense their beliefs, standards of taste established by literary schools, etc. None of these can be found entirely reproduced in the applications made of them by individuals, since they can exist even without being actually applied.

No doubt, this dissociation does not always manifest itself with equal distinctness, but its obvious existence in the important and numerous cases just cited is sufficient to prove that the social fact is a thing distinct from its individual manifestations. Moreover, even when this dissociation is not immediately apparent, it may often be disclosed by certain devices of method. Such dissociation is indispensable if one wishes to separate social facts from their alloys in order to observe them in a state of purity. Currents of opinion, with an intensity varying according to the time and place, impel certain groups either to more marriages, for example, or to more suicides, or to a higher or lower birthrate, etc. These currents are plainly social facts. At first sight they seem inseparable from the forms they take in individual cases. But statistics furnish us with the means of isolating them. They are, in fact, represented with considerable exactness by the rates of births, marriages, and suicides, that is, by the number obtained by dividing the average annual total of marriages, births, suicides, by the number of persons whose ages lie within the range in which marriages, births, and suicides occur.[2] Since each of these figures contains all the individual cases indiscriminately, the individual circumstances which may have had a share in the production of the phenomenon are neutralized and, consequently, do not contribute to its determination. The average, then, expresses a certain state of the group mind (*l'âme collective*).

Such are social phenomena, when disentangled from all foreign matter. As for their individual manifestations, these are indeed, to a certain extent, social, since they partly reproduce a social model. Each of them also depends, and to a large extent, on the organopsychological constitution of the individual and on the particular circumstances in which he is placed. Thus they are not sociological phenomena in the strict sense of the word. They belong to two realms at once; one

could call them sociopsychological. They interest the sociologist without constituting the immediate subject matter of sociology. There exist in the interior of organisms similar phenomena, compound in their nature, which form in their turn the subject matter of the "hybrid sciences," such as physiological chemistry, for example.

The objection may be raised that a phenomenon is collective only if it is common to all members of society, or at least to most of them—in other words, if it is truly general. This may be true; but it is general because it is collective (that is, more or less obligatory), and certainly not collective because general. It is a group condition repeated in the individual because imposed on him. It is to be found in each part because it exists in the whole, rather than in the whole because it exists in the parts. This becomes conspicuously evident in those beliefs and practices which are transmitted to us ready-made by previous generations; we receive and adopt them because, being both collective and ancient, they are invested with a particular authority that education has taught us to recognize and respect. It is, of course, true that a vast portion of our social culture is transmitted to us in this way; but even when the social fact is due in part to our direct collaboration, its nature is not different. A collective emotion which bursts forth suddenly and violently in a crowd does not express merely what all the individual sentiments had in common; it is something entirely different, as we have shown. It results from their being together, a product of the actions and reactions which take place between individual consciousnesses; and if each individual consciousness echoes the collective sentiment, it is by virtue of the special energy resident in its collective origin. If all hearts beat in unison, this is not the result of a spontaneous and pre-established harmony but rather because an identical force propels them in the same direction. Each is carried along by all.

We thus arrive at the point where we can formulate and delimit in a precise way the domain of sociology. It comprises only a limited group of phenomena. A social fact is to be recognized by the power of external coercion which it exercises or is capable of exercising over individuals, and the presence of this power may be recognized in its turn either by the existence of some specific sanction or by the resistance offered against every individual effort that tends to violate it. One can, however, define it also by its diffusion within the group, provided that, in conformity with our previous remarks, one takes care to add as a second and essential characteristic that its own existence is independent of the individual forms it assumes in its diffusion. This last criterion is perhaps, in certain cases, easier to apply than the preceding one. In fact, the constraint is easy to ascertain when it expresses itself externally by some direct reaction of society, as is the case in law, morals, beliefs, customs, and even fashions. But when it is only indirect, like the constraint which an economic organization exercises, it cannot always be so easily detected. Generality combined with externality may, then, be easier to establish. Moreover, this second definition is but another form of the first; for if a mode of behavior whose existence is external to individual consciousnesses becomes general, this can only be brought about by its being imposed upon them.[3]

But these several phenomena present the same characteristic by which we defined the others. These "ways of existing" are imposed on the individual precisely in the same fashion as the "ways of existing" of which we have spoken. Indeed, when we wish to know how a society is divided politically, of what these divisions themselves are composed, and how complete is the fusion existing between them, we shall not achieve our purpose by physical inspection and by geographical observations; for these phenomena are social, even when they have some basis in physical nature. It is only by a study of public law that a comprehension of this organization is possible, for it is this law that determines the organization, as it equally determines our domestic and civil relations. This political organization is, then, no less obligatory than the social facts mentioned above. If the population crowds into our cities instead of scattering into the country, this is due to a trend of public opinion, a collective drive that imposes this concentration upon the individuals. We can no more choose the style of our houses than of our clothing—at least, both are equally obligatory. The channels of communication prescribe the direction of internal migrations and commerce, etc., and even their extent. Consequently, at the very most, it should be

necessary to add to the list of phenomena which we have enumerated as presenting the distinctive criterion of a social fact only one additional category, "ways of existing"; and, as this enumeration was not meant to be rigorously exhaustive, the addition would not be absolutely necessary.

Such an addition is perhaps not necessary, for these "ways of existing" are only crystallized "ways of acting." The political structure of a society is merely the way in which its component segments have become accustomed to live with one another. If their relations are traditionally intimate, the segments tend to fuse with one another, or, in the contrary case, to retain their identity. The type of habitation imposed upon us is merely the way in which our contemporaries and our ancestors have been accustomed to construct their houses. The methods of communication are merely the channels which the regular currents of commerce and migrations have dug, by flowing in the same direction. To be sure, if the phenomena of a structural character alone presented this permanence, one might believe that they constituted a distinct species. A legal regulation is an arrangement no less permanent than a type of architecture, and yet the regulation is a "physiological" fact. A simple moral maxim is assuredly somewhat more malleable, but it is much more rigid than a simple professional custom or a fashion. There is thus a whole series of degrees without a break in continuity between the facts of the most articulated structure and those free currents of social life which are not yet definitely molded. The differences between them are, therefore, only differences in the degree of consolidation they present. Both are simply life, more or less crystallized. No doubt, it may be of some advantage to reserve the term "morphological" for those social facts which concern the social substratum, but only on condition of not overlooking the fact that they are of the same nature as the others. Our definition will then include the whole relevant range of facts if we say: *A social fact is every way of acting, fixed or not, capable of exercising on the individual an external constraint;* or again, *every way of acting which is general throughout a given society, while at the same time existing in its own right independent of its individual manifestations.*[4]

NOTES

1. We do not intend to imply, however, that all constraint is normal. We shall return to this point later.
2. Suicides do not occur at every age, and they take place with varying intensity at the different ages in which they occur.
3. It will be seen how this definition of the social fact diverges from that which forms the basis of the ingenious system of M. Tarde. First of all, we wish to state that our researches have nowhere led us to observe that preponderant influence in the genesis of collective facts which M. Tarde attributes to imitation. Moreover, from the preceding definition, which is not a theory but simply a résumé of the immediate data of observation, it seems indeed to follow, not only that imitation does not always express the essential and characteristic features of the social fact, but even that it never expresses them. No doubt, every social fact is imitated; it has, as we have just shown, a tendency to become general, but that is because it is social, i.e., obligatory. Its power of expansion is not the cause but the consequence of its sociological character. If, further, only social facts produced this consequence, imitation could perhaps serve, if not to explain them, at least to define them. But an individual condition which produces a whole series of effects remains individual nevertheless. Moreover, one may ask whether the word "imitation" is indeed fitted to designate an effect due to a coercive influence. Thus, by this single expression, very different phenomena, which ought to be distinguished, are confused.
4. This close connection between life and structure, organ and function, may be easily proved in sociology because between these two extreme terms there exists a whole series of immediately observable intermediate stages which show the bond between them. Biology is not in the same favorable position. But we may well believe that the inductions on this subject made by sociology are applicable to biology and that, in organisms as well as in societies, only differences in degree exist between these two orders of facts.

8. ANOMIC SUICIDE

ÉMILE DURKHEIM

Durkheim has been depicted as a physician of society because of his interest in diagnosing the problems of contemporary society and offering prescriptions to remedy social ills. This approach is nowhere more evident than in his landmark empirical study of self-destruction, *Suicide* (1897). One reason for undertaking this particular study was Durkheim´s desire to meet psychology on what might seem to be its own turf, by examining a phenomenon that lends itself to psychological interpretations. As such, the book is a polemic in which he argues that sociology can offer unique insights beyond the access of psychological concepts. In this excerpt, Durkheim discusses what he means by anomic suicide, one of four types of suicide he identifies. He contends that anomie, which is often translated as "rulelessness" or "normlessness," is a characteristic social pathology of modern society.

If anomy never appeared except . . . in intermittent spurts and acute crisis, it might cause the social suicide rate to vary from time to time, but it would not be a regular, constant factor. In one sphere of social life, however—the sphere of trade and industry—it is actually in a chronic state.

For a whole century, economic progress has mainly consisted in freeing industrial relations from all regulation. Until very recently, it was the function of a whole system of moral forces to exert this discipline. First, the influence of religion was felt alike by workers and masters, the poor and the rich. It consoled the former and taught them contentment with their lot by informing them of the providential nature of the social order, that the share of each class was assigned by God himself, and by holding out the hope for just compensation in a world to come in return for the inequalities of this world. It governed the latter, recalling that worldly interests are not man´s entire lot, that they must be subordinate to other and higher interests, and that they should, therefore, not be pursued without rule or measure. Temporal power, in turn, restrained the scope of economic functions by its supremacy over them and by the relatively subordinate role it assigned them. Finally, within the business world proper, the occupational groups, by regulating salaries, the price of products and production itself, indirectly fixed the average level of income on which needs are partially based by the very force of circumstances. However, we do not mean to propose this organization as a model. Clearly it would be inadequate to existing societies without great changes. What we stress is its existence, the fact of its useful influence, and that nothing today has come to take its place.

Actually, religion has lost most of its power. And government, instead of regulating economic life, has become its tool and servant. The most opposite schools, orthodox economists and extreme socialists, unite to reduce government to the role of a more or less passive intermediary among the various social functions. The former wish to make it simply the guardian of individual contracts; the latter leave it the task of doing the collective bookkeeping, that is, of recording the demands of consumers, transmitting them to producers, inventorying the total revenue and distributing it according to a fixed formula. But both refuse it any power to subordinate other social organs to itself and to make them converge toward one dominant aim. On both sides nations are declared to have the single or chief purpose of achieving industrial prosperity; such is the implication of the dogma of economic materialism, the basis of both apparently opposed systems. And as these theories merely express the state of opinion, industry, instead of being still regarded as a means to an end transcending itself, has become the supreme end of individuals and societies alike. Thereupon the appetites thus excited have become freed of any limiting authority. By sanctifying them, so to speak, this apotheosis of well-being has placed them above all human law. Their restraint seems like a sort of sacrilege. For this reason, even, the purely utilitarian regulation of them exercised by the industrial world itself through the medium of occupational groups has been unable to persist. Ultimately, this liberation of desires has been made worse by the very development of industry and the almost infinite extension of the market. So long as the producer could gain his profits only in his immediate neighborhood, the restricted amount of possible gain could not much overexcite ambition. Now that he may assume to have almost the entire world as his customer, how could passions accept their former confinement in the face of such limitless prospects?

Such is the source of the excitement predominating in this part of society, and which has thence extended to the other parts. There, the state of crisis and anomy is constant and, so to speak, normal. From top to bottom of the ladder, greed is aroused without knowing where to find ultimate foothold. Nothing can calm it, since its goal is far beyond all it can attain. Reality seems valueless by comparison with the dreams of fevered imaginations; reality is therefore abandoned, but so too is possibility abandoned when it in turn becomes reality. A thirst arises for novelties, unfamiliar pleasures, nameless sensations, all of which lose their savor once known. Henceforth one has no strength to endure the least reverse. The whole fever subsides and the sterility of all this tumult is apparent, and it is seen that all these new sensations in their infinite quantity cannot form a solid foundation of happiness to support one during

days of trial. The wise man, knowing how to enjoy achieved results without having constantly to replace them with others, finds in them an attachment to life in the hour of difficulty. But the man who has always pinned all his hopes on the future and lived with his eyes fixed upon it, has nothing in the past as a comfort against the present's afflictions, for the past was nothing to him but a series of hastily experienced stages. What blinded him to himself was his expectation always to find further on the happiness he had so far missed. Now he is stopped in his tracks; from now on nothing remains behind or ahead of him to fix his gaze upon. Weariness alone, moreover, is enough to bring disillusionment, for he cannot in the end escape the futility of an endless pursuit.

We may even wonder if this moral state is not principally what makes economic catastrophes of our day so fertile in suicides. In societies where a man is subjected to a healthy discipline, he submits more readily to the blows of chance. The necessary effort for sustaining a little more discomfort costs him relatively little, since he is used to discomfort and constraint. But when every constraint is hateful in itself, how can closer constraint not seem intolerable? There is no tendency to resignation in the feverish impatience of men's lives. When there is no other aim but to outstrip constantly the point arrived at, how painful to be thrown back! Now this very lack of organization characterizing our economic condition throws doors wide to every sort of adventure. Since imagination is hungry for novelty, and ungoverned, it gropes at random. Setbacks necessarily increase with risks and thus crises multiply, just when they are becoming more destructive. Yet these dispositions are so inbred that society has grown to accept them and is accustomed to think them normal. It is everlastingly repeated that it is man's nature to be eternally dissatisfied, constantly to advance, without relief or rest, toward an indefinite goal. The longing for infinity is daily represented as a mark of moral distinction, whereas it can only appear within unregulated consciences which elevate to a rule the lack of rule from which they suffer. The doctrine of the most ruthless and swift progress has become an article of faith. But other theories appear parallel with those praising the advantages of instability, which,

TABLE 8.1 SUICIDES PER MILLION PERSONS OF DIFFERENT OCCUPATIONS

	Trade	Transportation	Industry	Agriculture	Liberal* Professions
France (1878–87)†	440	—	340	240	300
Switzerland (1876)	664	1,514	577	304	558
Italy (1866–76)	277	152.6	80.4	26.7	618‡
Prussia (1883–90)	754	—	456	315	832
Bavaria (1884–91)	465	—	369	153	454
Belgium (1886–90)	421	—	160	160	100
Wurttemberg (1873–78)	273	—	190	206	—
Saxony (1878)		341.59§		71.17	—

* When statistics distinguish several different sorts of liberal occupations, we show as a specimen the one in which the suicide-rate is highest.
† From 1826 to 1880 economic functions seem less affected (see *Compte-rendu* of 1880); but were occupational statistics very accurate?
‡ This figure is reached only by men of letters.
§ Figure represents Trade, Transportation and Industry combined for Saxony.—Ed.

generalizing the situation that gives them birth, declare life evil, claim that it is richer in grief than in pleasure and that it attracts men only by false claims. Since this disorder is greatest in the economic world, it has most victims there.

Industrial and commercial functions are really among the occupations which furnish the greatest number of suicides (see Table 8.1). Almost on a level with the liberal professions, they sometimes surpass them; they are especially more afflicted than agriculture, where the old regulative forces still make their appearance felt most and where the fever of business has least penetrated. Here is best recalled what was once the general constitution of the economic order. And the divergence would be yet greater if, among the suicides of industry, employers were distinguished from workmen, for the former are probably most stricken by the state of anomy. The enormous rate of those with independent means (720 per million) sufficiently shows that the possessors of most comfort suffer most. Everything that enforces subordination attenuates the effects of this state. At least the horizon of the lower classes is limited by those above them, and for this same reason their desires are more modest. Those who have only empty space above them are almost inevitably lost in it, if no force restrains them.

Anomy, therefore, is a regular and specific factor in suicide in our modern societies; one of the springs from which the annual contingent feeds. So we have here a new type to distinguish from the others. It differs from them in its dependence, not on the way in which individuals are attached to society, but on how it regulates them. Egoistic suicide results from man´s no longer finding a basis for existence in life; altruistic suicide, because this basis for existence appears to man situated beyond life itself. The third sort of suicide, the existence of which has just been shown, results from man´s activity´s lacking regulation and his consequent sufferings. By virtue of its origin we shall assign this last variety the name of *anomic suicide*.

Certainly, this and egoistic suicide have kindred ties. Both spring from society´s insufficient presence in individuals. But the sphere of its absence is not the same in both cases. In egoistic suicide it is deficient in truly collective activity, thus depriving the latter of object and meaning. In anomic suicide, society´s influence is lacking in the basically individual passions, thus leaving them without a check-rein. In spite of their relationship, therefore, the two types are independent of each other. We may offer society everything social in us, and still be unable to control our desires; one may live in an anomic state without being egoistic, and vice versa. These two sorts of suicide therefore do not draw their chief recruits from the same social environments; one has its principal field among intellectual careers, the world of thought—the other, the industrial or commercial world.

But economic anomy is not the only anomy which may give rise to suicide. The suicides occurring at the crisis of widowhood...are really due to domestic anomy resulting from the death of husband or wife. A family catastrophe occurs which affects the survivor. He is not adapted to the new situation in which he finds himself and accordingly offers less resistance to suicide.

But another variety of anomic suicide should draw greater attention, both because it is more chronic and because it will serve to illustrate the nature and functions of marriage.

In the *Annales de demographie internationale* (September 1882), Bertillon published a remarkable study of divorce, in which he proved the following proposition: throughout Europe the number of suicides varies with that of divorces and separations. If the different countries are compared from this twofold point of view, this parallelism is apparent (see Table 8.2). Not only is the relation between the averages evident, but the single irregular detail of any importance is that of Holland, where suicides are not as frequent as divorces.

The law may be yet more vigorously verified if we compare not different countries but different provinces of a single country. Notably, in Switzerland the agreement between phenomena is striking (see Table 8.3). The Protestant cantons have the most divorces and also the most suicides. The mixed cantons follow, from both points of view, and only then come the Catholic cantons. Within each group the same agreements appear. Among the Catholic cantons Solothurn and Inner Appenzell are marked by the high number of their divorces; they are likewise marked by the number of their suicides. Freiburg, although Catholic and French, has a considerable number of both divorces and suicides. Among the Protestant German cantons none has so many divorces as Schaffhausen; Schaffhausen also leads the list for suicides. Finally, the mixed cantons, with the one exception of Argau, are classed in exactly the same way in both respects.

The same comparison, if made between French departments, gives the same result. Having classified

TABLE 8.2 COMPARISON OF EUROPEAN STATES FROM THE POINT OF VIEW OF BOTH DIVORCE AND SUICIDE

	Annual Divorces per 1,000 Marriages	Suicides per Million Inhabitants
I. Countries Where Divorce and Separation Are Rare		
Norway	0.54 (1875–80)	73
Russia	1.6 (1871–77)	30
England and Wales	1.3 (1871–79)	68
Scotland	2.1 (1871–81)	—
Italy	3.05 (1871–73)	31
Finland	3.9 (1875–79)	30.8
Averages	2.07	46.5
II. Countries Where Divorce and Separation Are of Average Frequency		
Bavaria	5.0 (1881)	90.5
Belgium	5.1 (1871–80)	68.5
Holland	6.0 (1871–80)	35.5
Sweden	6.4 (1871–80)	81
Baden	6.5 (1874–79)	156.6
France	7.5 (1871–79)	150
Wurttemberg	8.4 (1871–78)	162.4
Prussia	—	133
Averages	6.4	109.6
III. Countries Where Divorce and Separation Are Frequent		
Kingdom of Saxony	26.9 (1876–80)	299
Denmark	38.0 (1871–80)	258
Switzerland	47.0 (1876–80)	216
Averages	37.3	257

TABLE 8.3 COMPARISON OF SWISS CANTONS FROM THE POINT OF VIEW OF DIVORCE AND SUICIDE

	Divorces and Separations per 1,000 Marriages	Suicides per Million		Divorces and Separations per 1,000 Marriages	Suicides per Million
			I. Catholic Cantons		
			French and Italian		
Tessina	7.6	57	Freiburg	15.9	119
Valais	4.0	47			
Averages	5.8	50	Averages	15.9	119
			German		
Uri	–	60	Solothurn	37.7	205
Upper Unterwalden	4.9	20	Inner Appenzell	18.9	158
Lower Unterwalden	5.2	1	Zug	14.8	87
Schwyz	5.6	70	Luzern	13.0	100
Averages	3.9	37.7	Averages	21.1	137.5
			II. Protestant Cantons		
			French		
Neufchâtel	42.4	560	Vaud	43.5	352
			German		
Bern	47.2	229	Schaffhausen	106.0	602
Basel (city)	34.5	323	Outer Appenzell	100.7	213
Basel (country)	33.0	288	Glaris	83.1	127
			Zurich	80.0	288
Averages	38.2	280	Averages	92.4	307
			III. Cantons Mixed as to Religion		
Argau	40.0	195	Geneva	70.5	360
Grisons	30.9	116	Saint Goll	57.6	179
Averages	36.9	155	Averages	64.0	269

them in eight categories according to the importance of their suicidal mortality, we discovered that the groups thus formed were arranged in the same order as with reference to divorces and separations (see Table 8.4): Having shown this relation, let us try to explain it.

We shall mention only as a note the explanation Bertillon summarily suggested. According to that author, the number of suicides and that of divorces vary in parallel manner because both depend on the same factor: the greater or less frequency of people with unstable equilibrium. There are actually, he says, more divorces in a country the more incompatible married couples it contains. The latter are recruited especially

TABLE 8.4

	Suicides per Million	Average of Divorces and Separations per 1,000 Marriages
1st group (5 departments)	Below 50	2.6
2nd group (18 departments)	From 51 to 75	2.9
3rd group (15 departments)	76 to 100	5.0
4th group (19 departments)	101 to 150	5.4
5th group (10 departments)	151 to 200	7.5
6th group (9 departments)	201 to 250	8.2
7th group (4 departments)	251 to 300	10.0
8th group (5 departments)	Above 300	12.4

from among people of irregular lives, persons of poor character and intelligence, whom this temperament predisposes to suicide. The parallelism would then be due, not to the influence of divorce itself upon suicide, but to the fact that these two phenomena derive from a similar cause which they express differently. But this association of divorce with certain psychopathic flaws is made arbitrarily and without proof. There is no reason to think that there are 15 times as many unbalanced people in Switzerland as in Italy and from 6 to 7 times as many as in France, and yet in the first of these countries divorces are 15 times as frequent as in the second and about 7 times as frequent as in the third. Moreover, so far as suicide is concerned, we know how far purely individual conditions are from accounting for it. Furthermore, all that follows will show the inadequacy of this theory.

One must seek the cause of this remarkable relation not in the organic predispositions of people but in the intrinsic nature of divorce. As our first proposition here we may assert: in all countries for which we have the necessary data, suicides of divorced people are immensely more numerous than those of other portions of the population.

Thus, divorced persons of both sexes kill themselves between three and four times as often as married persons, although younger (40 years in France as against 46 years), and considerably more often than widowed persons in spite of the aggravation resulting for the latter from their advanced age. What is the explanation?

There is no doubt that the change of moral and material regimen which is a consequence of divorce is of some account in this result. But it does not sufficiently explain the matter. Widowhood is indeed as complete a disturbance of existence as divorce; it usually even has much more unhappy results, since it was not desired by husband and wife, while divorce is usually a deliverance for both. Yet divorced persons who, considering their age, should commit suicide only one half as often as widowed persons, do so more often everywhere, even twice as often in certain countries. This aggravation, to be represented by a coefficient between 2.5 and 4, does not depend on their changed condition in any way.

Let us refer to one of the propositions established above to discover the causes of this fact. . . .[I]n a given society the tendency of widowed persons to suicide was a function of the corresponding tendency of married persons. While the latter are highly protected, the former enjoy an immunity less, to be sure, but still considerable, and the sex best protected by marriage is also that best protected in the state of widowhood. Briefly, when conjugal society is dissolved by the death of one of the couple, the effects which it had with reference to suicide continue to be felt in part by the survivor. . . . Then, however, is it not to be supposed that the same thing takes place when the marriage is interrupted, not by death, but by a judicial act, and that the aggravation which afflicts divorced persons is a result not of the divorce but of the marriage ended by

TABLE 8.5 SUICIDES IN A MILLION

	Unmarried Above 15 Years		Married		Widowed		Divorced	
	Men	Women	Men	Women	Men	Women	Men	Women
Prussia (1887–1889)*	360	120	430	90	1,471	215	1,875	290
Prussia (1883–1890)*	388	129	498	100	1,552	194	1,952	328
Baden (1885–1893)	45	93	460	85	1,172	171	1,328	—
Saxony (1847–1858)	—	—	481	120	1,242	240	3,102	312
Saxony (1876)	555.18[†]		821	146	—	—	3,252	389
Wurttemberg (1846–1860)	—	—	226	52	530	97	1,298	281
Wurttemberg (1873–1892)	251	—	218[†]		405[†]		796[†]	

* There appears to be some error in the figures for Prussia here.—Ed
[†] Men and women combined.—Ed

divorce? It must be connected with some quality of the matrimonial society, the influence of which the couple continue to experience even when separated. If they have so strong an inclination to suicide, it is because they were already strongly inclined to it while living together and by the very effect of their common life.

Admitting so much, the correspondence between divorces and suicides becomes explicable. Actually, among the people where divorce is common, this peculiar effect of marriage in which divorce shares must necessarily be very wide-spread; for it is not confined to households predestined to legal separation. If it

reaches its maximum intensity among them, it must also be found among the others, or the majority of the others, though to a lesser degree. For just as where there are many suicides, there are many attempted suicides, and just as mortality cannot grow without morbidity increasing simultaneously, so wherever there are many actual divorces there must be many households more or less close to divorce. The number of actual divorces cannot rise, accordingly, without the family condition predisposing to suicide also developing and becoming general in the same degree, and thus the two phenomena naturally vary in the same general direction.

9. NOTE ON THE NOTION OF CIVILIZATION

ÉMILE DURKHEIM AND MARCEL MAUSS

Durkheim published this essay in 1913 with his nephew Marcel Mauss, who would go on to a prominent career as an anthropologist. It was long forgotten and did not appear in an English-language version until Benjamin Nelson's translation appeared in *Social Research* nearly six decades later. The authors note that much of social analysis operates with the understanding that the proper unit of analysis is the nation-state, which is often seen as the same as what sociologists generally describe as society. While such a focus is deemed appropriate in some instances, Durkheim and Mauss make a case for the need to create a broader framework of analysis, one that operates at the civilizational level and takes into account intercivilizational encounters. Their thesis can be read as an early call to avoid what today is frequently described as methodological individualism.

One of the rules we follow here is that, in studying social phenomena in themselves and by themselves, we take care not to leave them in the air but always to relate them to a definite substratum, that is to say, to a human group occupying a determinate portion of geographically representable space. But, of all these groups, the largest—that which comprises all of the others in itself and which consequently comprises all forms of social activity—is, it would appear, that which forms the political society: tribe, clan, nation, city, state, and so on. It seems then, on first view, that collective life can develop only within political organisms having definite contours, within strictly marked limits, that is to say, that the national life is the highest form of social phenomenon and sociology cannot know one of a higher order.

There are, nonetheless, phenomena which do not have such well-defined limits; they pass beyond the political frontiers and extend over less easily determinable spaces. Although their complexity renders their study difficult, it nonetheless behooves us to acknowledge their existence and to indicate their place within the bounds of sociology.

Ethnography and prehistory, especially, have directed attention to this perspective.

The enormous work, which has been pursued for three decades in the ethnographic museums of America and Germany and in prehistoric museums of France and Sweden above all, has not remained without theoretical results. Especially on the ethnological side, scientific requirements of simplification and of cataloguing and even simple practical necessities of organization and exposition have produced classifications which are at the same time logical, geographical, and chronological: logical because, in the absence of a possible history, logic is the sole means of perceiving, at least hypothetically, historical sequences of tools, styles, and so on; chronological and geographical because these series develop in time as in space and extend to many different peoples. For a long time now American museums have displayed charts showing the extension of this or that type of art, and prehistoric museums have proposed geological schemas for the forms of certain tools.

Therefore, social phenomena that are not strictly attached to a determinate social organism do exist: they extend into areas that reach beyond the national

Reprinted from *Social Research*, 1971, vol. 38, no. 4, pp. 808–813, translated and with an introduction by Benjamin Nelson. Reprinted with permission of the New School for Social Research. ✦

territory or they develop over periods of time that exceed the history of a single society. They have a life which is in some ways supranational.

But these problems are not only posed by technology or esthetics. Several phenomena of the same genre have been known in linguistics for a long time. Languages spoken by different peoples have close links to one another—for example, certain verbal and grammatical forms that appear in different societies, which permit us to group these societies into families of people who are or have been in relationship with one another or who have the same origin; thus one now speaks of an Indo-European language. It is the same with institutions. The quite different Algonquin and Iroquois nations had similar sorts of totemism and a similar kind of magic or religion. Among all the Polynesian peoples one finds a similar type of political organization (power of the chief). The beginnings of the family have been identical among all peoples who speak an Indo-European language.

Moreover, it has been recognized that phenomena which present this degree of extension are not independent of one another; they are generally linked in an interdependent system. It often occurs that one of these phenomena involves the others and reveals their existence. Matrimonial classes are characteristic of an entire ensemble of beliefs and practices which appear throughout Australia. The absence of pottery is one of the distinctive traits of Polynesian industry. A certain form of the adze is an essentially Melanesian object. All peoples who speak an Indo-European language have a common fund of ideas and institutions. There exist not merely isolated instances, but also complex and interdependent systems, which without being limited to a determinate political organism are, however, localizable in time and space.

It becomes necessary to give a special name to those systems of facts that have their own unity and form of existence. Civilization seems to be the most appropriate name. Without doubt every civilization is susceptible to nationalization; it may assume particular characteristics with each people of each state; but its most essential elements are not the product of the state or of the people alone. Rather, they extend beyond these frontiers, whether they extend out from a determinate area by a power of expansion originating within

them, or whether they result from relationships established among different societies and so are the common product of these societies.

For example: we speak of a Christian civilization, which, while having different centers, has been developed by all Christian peoples. There is a Mediterranean civilization common to all the people who bordered the Mediterranean coast. There is a civilization of Northwest America common to the Tlinkit, to the Tsimshian and to the Haida, even though they speak various languages and have different customs. A civilization constitutes a kind of moral milieu encompassing a certain number of nations, each national culture being only a particular form of the whole.

It is noteworthy that these very general phenomena were the first to attract the attention of sociologists; and these served as material for emerging sociology. For Comte, it was not a question of particular societies, nations or states. What he studied was the general movement of civilization, abstracting national particularities. At least, the latter interested him only insofar as they could aid in establishing successive stages of human progress.

We have often had the occasion to show how this method is inadequate to the facts, for it leaves aside the concrete reality which the observer can better and more immediately grasp, that is, the social organism, the great collective personalities which are constituted in the course of history. It is to them that the sociologist has to relate above all. He must commit himself to describe them, to arrange them in genus and in species, to analyze and to explain the elements that compose them. One might say that the human milieu, the integral humanity of which Comte hoped to make a science, is only a construction of the spirit.

Nonetheless, it still remains that beyond these national groupings there are other wider and less clearly defined groupings, which do have individuality and which are the seat of a new sort of social life. If there does not exist one human civilization, there have been and there still are diverse civilizations which dominate and develop the collective life of each people. Here is an order of things which deserves to be studied by appropriate procedures.

All sorts of problems, neglected until now, could be connected with this subject. One could ask what are the diverse conditions which determine variations in the areas of civilizations, why have they stopped here or there, what forms have they taken and what factors determine these forms. As Ratzel has shown, these questions that are asked concerning political frontiers could be posed equally well with respect to symbolic frontiers *(frontières idéales)*.

Furthermore, not all social phenomena are equally apt to internationalize themselves. Political institutions, juridical institutions, the phenomena of social morphology constitute part of the specific character of each people. On the other hand, the myths, tales, money, commerce, fine arts, techniques, tools, language, words, scientific knowledge, literary forms and ideas—all of these travel and are borrowed. In short, they result from a process involving more than a determinate society.

It is justifiable, then, to ask on what this unequal coefficient of expansion and internationalization depends. These differences are not determined solely by the intrinsic nature of the social phenomena, but also by the diverse conditions influencing the societies. A certain form of collective life, then, may or may not be susceptible to internationalization depending on these circumstances. Christianity is essentially international, but there have also been some strictly national religions. There are some languages which are spread across vast territories; there are others which serve to distinguish nationalities, as is the case with those spoken by the great peoples of Europe.

All these problems are properly sociological. Undoubtedly, they cannot be approached unless other problems, which do not pertain to sociology, are resolved. It belongs to ethnography and to history to map these areas of civilization and to link diverse civilizations to their fundamental source. But once these preliminary tasks have sufficiently advanced, other more general questions, which do relate to sociology, become possible to consider. Some of these have been indicated above. It is a matter of arriving at causes and laws by means of methodical comparisons.

Also, one might question how writers—for example, Father Schmidt—have undertaken to separate the study of civilizations from sociology, reserving it for other disciplines, notably ethnography. First of all, ethnography does not suffice for the task. History has similar studies to make with respect to historic peoples. Moreover, civilization only expresses a collective life of a special genre, the substratum of which is a plurality of interrelated political bodies acting upon one another. International life is merely social life of a higher kind, and one which sociology needs to know. The exclusion of sociology from these studies would never have been considered if it were not still too often believed that to explain a civilization one need merely ask whence it comes, from what it has borrowed, and by what means it has passed from one point to another. In reality, the true manner of understanding all this is to determine the causes of which it is the result, that is to say, what collective interactions of diverse orders produced it.

10. THE HUMAN MEANING OF RELIGION

ÉMILE DURKHEIM

In his final—and what some take to be his most important—work, *The Elementary Forms of the Religious Life* (1912), Durkheim looks to "primitive" religions in order to ascertain the significance of religion for social life. The earliest manifestations of religious belief and practice are seen as the building blocks for later, more complex expressions of religious phenomena. Thus, if we want to get at the essence of religion, Durkheim thought it appropriate to go to the least complex articulation of the religious. In this passage, he offers a definition of religion that emphasizes not simply the socially constructed nature of the religious but makes the more controversial claim that religion is a mirror of society and that in fact what people take to be the realm of the sacred is society itself.

At the beginning of this work we announced that the religion whose study we were taking up contained within it the most characteristic elements of the religious life. The exactness of this proposition may now be verified. Howsoever simple the system which we have studied may be, we have found within it all the great ideas and the principal ritual attitudes which are at the basis of even the most advanced religions: the division of things into sacred and profane, the notions of the soul, of spirits, of mythical personalities, and of a national and even international divinity, a negative cult with ascetic practices which are its exaggerated form, rites of oblation and communion, imitative rites, commemorative rites and expiatory rites; nothing essential is lacking. We are thus in a position to hope that the results at which we have arrived are not peculiar to totemism alone, but can aid us in an understanding of what religion in general is.

It may be objected that one single religion, whatever its field of extension may be, is too narrow a base for such an induction. We have not dreamed for a moment of ignoring the fact that an extended verification may add to the authority of a theory, but it is equally true that when a law has been proven by one well-made experiment, this proof is valid universally. If in one single case a scientist succeeded in finding out the secret of the life of even the most protoplasmic creature that can be imagined, the truths thus obtained would be applicable to all living beings, even the most advanced. Then if, in our studies of these very humble societies, we have really succeeded in discovering some of the elements out of which the most fundamental religious notions are made up, there is no reason for not extending the most general results of our researches to other religions. In fact, it is inconceivable that the same effect may be due now to one cause, now to another, according to the circumstances, unless the two causes are at bottom only one. A single idea cannot express one reality here and another one there, unless the duality is only apparent. If among certain peoples the ideas of sacredness, the soul and God are to be explained sociologically, it should be presumed scientifically that, in principle, the same explanation is valid for all the peoples among whom these same ideas are found with the same essential characteristics. Therefore, supposing that we have not been deceived, certain at least of our conclusions can be legitimately generalized. The moment has come to disengage these. And an induction of this sort having at its foundation a clearly defined experiment, is less adventurous than many summary generalizations which, while attempting to reach the essence of religion at once, without resting upon the careful analysis of any religion in particular, greatly risk losing themselves in space.

* * *

The theorists who have undertaken to explain religion in rational terms have generally seen in it before all else a system of ideas, corresponding to some determined object. This object has been conceived in a multitude of ways: nature, the infinite, the unknowable, the ideal, etc.; but these differences matter but little. In any case, it was the conceptions and beliefs which were considered as the essential elements of religion. As for the rites, from this point of view they appear to be only an external translation, contingent and material, of these internal states which alone pass as having any intrinsic value. This conception is so commonly held that generally the disputes of which religion is the theme turn about the question whether it can conciliate itself with science or not, that is to say, whether or not, there is a place beside our scientific knowledge for another form of thought which would be specifically religious.

But the believers, the men who lead the religious life and have a direct sensation of what it really is, object to this way of regarding it, saying that it does not correspond to their daily experience. In fact, they feel that the real function of religion is not to make us think, to enrich our knowledge, nor to add to the conceptions which we owe to science others of another origin and another character, but rather, it is to make us act, to aid us to live. The believer who has communicated with his god is not merely a man who sees new truths of which the unbeliever is ignorant; he is a man who is *stronger*. He feels within him more force, either to endure the trials of existence, or to conquer them. It is as though he were raised above the miseries of the world, because he is raised above his condition as a mere man; he believes that he is saved from evil, under whatever form he may conceive this evil. The first article in every creed is the belief in salvation by faith. But it is hard to see how a mere idea could have this efficacy. An idea is in reality only a part of ourselves; then how could it confer upon us powers superior to those which we have of our own nature? Howsoever rich it

might be in affective virtues, it could add nothing to our natural vitality; for it could only release the motive powers which are within us, neither creating them nor increasing them. From the mere fact that we consider an object worthy of being loved and sought after, it does not follow that we feel ourselves stronger afterwards; it is also necessary that this object set free energies superior to these which we ordinarily have at our command and also that we have some means of making these enter into us and unite themselves to our interior lives. Now for that, it is not enough that we think of them; it is also indispensable that we place ourselves within their sphere of action, and that we set ourselves where we may best feel their influence; in a word, it is necessary that we act, and that we repeat the acts thus necessary every time we feel the need of renewing their effects. From this point of view, it is readily seen how that group of regularly repeated acts which form the cult get their importance. In fact, whoever has really practiced a religion knows very well that it is the cult which gives rise to these impressions of joy, of interior peace, of serenity, of enthusiasm which are, for the believer, an experimental proof of his beliefs. The cult is not simply a system of signs by which the faith is outwardly translated; it is a collection of the means by which this is created and recreated periodically. Whether it consists in material acts or mental operations, it is always this which is efficacious.

Our entire study rests upon this postulate that the unanimous sentiment of the believers of all times cannot be purely illusory. Together with a recent apologist of the faith[1] we admit that these religious beliefs rest upon a specific experience whose demonstrative value is, in one sense, not one bit inferior to that of scientific experiments, though different from them. We, too, think that "a tree is known by its fruits,"[2] and that fertility is the best proof of what the roots are worth. But from the fact that a "religious experience," if we choose to call it this, does exist and that it has a certain foundation—and, by the way, is there any experience which has none?—it does not follow that the reality which is its foundation conforms objectively to the idea which believers have of it. The very fact that the fashion in which it has been conceived has varied infinitely in different times is enough to prove that none of these conceptions express it adequately. If a scientist states it as an axiom that the sensations of heat and light which we feel correspond to some objective cause, he does not conclude that this is what it appears to the senses to be. Likewise, even if the impressions which the faithful feel are not imaginary, still they are in no way privileged intuitions; there is no reason for believing that they inform us better upon the nature of their object than do ordinary sensations upon the nature of bodies and their properties. In order to discover what this object consists of, we must submit them to an examination and elaboration analogous to that which has substituted for the sensuous idea of the world another which is scientific and conceptual. This is preceisely what we have tried to do, and we have seen that this reality, which mythologies have represented under so many different forms, but which is the universal and eternal objective cause of these sensations *sui generis* out of which religious experience is made, is society. We have shown what moral forces it develops and how it awakens this sentiment of a refuge, of a shield and of a guardian support which attaches the believer to his cult. It is that which raises him outside himself; it is even that which made him. For that which makes a man is the totality of the intellectual property which constitutes civilization, and civilization is the work of society. Thus is explained the preponderating rôle of the cult in all religions, whichever they may be. This is because society cannot make its influence felt unless it is in action, and it is not in action unless the individuals who compose it are assembled together and act in common. It is by common action that it takes consciousness of itself and realizes its position; it is before all else an active co-operation. The collective ideas and sentiments are even possible only owing to these exterior movements which symbolize them, as we have established.[3] Then it is action which dominates the religious life, because of the mere fact that it is society which is its source.

In addition to all the reasons which have been given to justify this conception, a final one may be added here, which is the result of our whole work. As we have progressed, we have established the fact that the fundamental categories of thought, and consequently of science, are of religious origin. We have seen that the same is true for magic and consequently for the different processes which have issued from it. On the other

hand, it has long been known that up until a relatively advanced moment of evolution, moral and legal rules have been indistinguishable from ritual prescriptions. In summing up, then, it may be said that nearly all the great social institutions have been born in religion.[4] Now in order that these principal aspects of the collective life may have commenced by being only varied aspects of the religious life, it is obviously necessary that the religious life be the eminent form and, as it were, the concentrated expression of the whole collective life. If religion has given birth to all that is essential in society, it is because the idea of society is the soul of religion.

Religious forces are therefore human forces, moral forces. It is true that since collective sentiments can become conscious of themselves only by fixing themselves upon external objects, they have not been able to take form without adopting some of their characteristics from other things: they have thus acquired a sort of physical nature; in this way they have come to mix themselves with the life of the material world, and then have considered themselves capable of explaining what passes there. But when they are considered only from this point of view and in this rôle, only their most superficial aspect is seen. In reality, the essential elements of which these collective sentiments are made have been borrowed by the understanding. It ordinarily seems that they should have a human character only when they are conceived under human forms;[5] but even the most impersonal and the most anonymous are nothing else than objectified sentiments.

It is only by regarding religion from this angle that it is possible to see its real significance. If we stick closely to appearances, rites often give the effect of purely manual operations: they are anointings, washings, meals. To consecrate something, it is put in contact with a source of religious energy, just as today a body is put in contact with a source of heat or electricity to warm or electrify it; the two processes employed are not essentially different. Thus understood, religious technique seems to be a sort of mystic mechanics. But these material manœuvres are only the external envelope under which the mental operations are hidden. Finally, there is no question of exercising a physical constraint upon blind and, incidentally, imaginary forces, but rather of reaching individual consciousnesses of giving them a direction and of disciplining them. It is sometimes said that inferior religions are materialistic. Such an expression is inexact. All religions, even the crudest, are in a sense spiritualistic: for the powers they put in play are before all spiritual, and also their principal object is to act upon the moral life. Thus it is seen that whatever has been done in the name of religion cannot have been done in vain: for it is necessarily the society that did it, and it is humanity that has reaped the fruits.

But, it is said, what society is it that has thus made the basis of religion? Is it the real society, such as it is and acts before our very eyes, with the legal and moral organization which it has laboriously fashioned during the course of history? This is full of defects and imperfections. In it, evil goes beside the good, injustice often reigns supreme, and the truth is often obscured by error. How could anything so crudely organized inspire the sentiments of love, the ardent enthusiasm and the spirit of abnegation which all religions claim of their followers? These perfect beings which are gods could not have taken their traits from so mediocre, and sometimes even so base a reality.

But, on the other hand, does someone think of a perfect society, where justice and truth would be sovereign, and from which evil in all its forms would be banished forever? No one would deny that this is in close relations with the religious sentiment; for, they would say, it is towards the realization of this that all religions strive. But that society is not an empirical fact, definite and observable; it is a fancy, a dream with which men have lightened their sufferings, but in which they have never really lived. It is merely an idea which comes to express our more or less obscure aspirations towards the good, the beautiful and the ideal. Now these aspirations have their roots in us; they come from the very depths of our being; then there is nothing outside of us which can account for them. Moreover, they are already religious in themselves; thus it would seem that the ideal society presupposes religion, far from being able to explain it.[6]

But, in the first place, things are arbitrarily simplified when religion is seen only on its idealistic side: in its way, it is realistic. There is no physical or moral ugliness, there are no vices or evils which do not have a special divinity. There are gods of theft and trickery, of lust and war, of sickness and of death. Christianity itself, howsoever high the idea which it has made of the divinity may be, has been obliged to give the spirit of evil a place in its

mythology. Satan is an essential piece of the Christian system; even if he is an impure being, he is not a profane one. The anti-god is a god, inferior and subordinated, it is true, but nevertheless endowed with extended powers; he is even the object of rites, at least of negative ones. Thus religion, far from ignoring the real society and making abstraction of it, is in its image; it reflects all its aspects, even the most vulgar and the most repulsive. All is to be found there, and if in the majority of cases we see the good victorious over evil, life over death, the powers of light over the powers of darkness, it is because reality is not otherwise. If the relation between these two contrary forces were reversed, life would be impossible; but, as a matter of fact, it maintains itself and even tends to develop.

But if, in the midst of these mythologies and theologies we see reality clearly appearing, it is nonetheless true that it is found there only in an enlarged, transformed and idealized form. In this respect, the most primitive religions do not differ from the most recent and the most refined. For example, we have seen how the Arunta place at the beginning of time was a mythical society whose organization exactly reproduces that which still exists today; it includes the same clans and phratries, it is under the same matrimonial rules and it practises the same rites. But the personages who compose it are ideal beings, gifted with powers and virtues to which common mortals cannot pretend. Their nature is not only higher, but it is different, since it is at once animal and human. The evil powers there undergo a similar metamorphosis: evil itself is, as it were, made sublime and idealized. The question now raises itself of whence this idealization comes.

Some reply that men have a natural faculty for idealizing, that is to say, of substituting for the real world another different one, to which they transport themselves by thought. But that is merely changing the terms of the problem; it is not resolving it or even advancing it. This systematic idealization is an essential characteristic of religions. Explaining them by an innate power of idealization is simply replacing one word by another which is the equivalent of the first; it is as if they said that men have made religions because they have a religious nature. Animals know only one world, the one which they perceive by experience, internal as well as external. Men alone have the faculty of conceiving the ideal, of adding something to the real. Now where does this singular privilege come from? Before making it an initial fact or a mysterious virtue which escapes science, we must be sure that it does not depend upon empirically determinable conditions.

The explanation of religion which we have proposed has precisely this advantage, that it gives an answer to this question. For our definition of the sacred is that it is something added to and above the real: now the ideal answers to this same definition; we cannot explain one without explaining the other. In fact, we have seen that if collective life awakens religious thought on reaching a certain degree of intensity, it is because it brings about a state of effervescence which changes the conditions of psychic activity. Vital energies are over-excited, passions more active, sensations stronger, there are even some which are produced only at this moment. A man does not recognize himself; he feels himself transformed and consequently he transforms the environment which surrounds him. In order to account for the very particular impressions which he receives, he attributes to the things with which he is in most direct contact properties which they have not: exceptional powers and virtues which the objects of everyday experience do not possess. In a word, above the real world where his profane life passes he has placed another which, in one sense, does not exist except in thought, but to which he attributes a higher sort of dignity than to the first. Thus, from a double point of view it is an ideal world.

The formation of the ideal world is therefore not an irreducible fact which escapes science; it depends upon conditions which observation can touch; it is a natural product of social life. For a society to become conscious of itself and maintain at the necessary degree of intensity the sentiments which it thus attains, it must assemble and concentrate itself. Now this concentration, brings about an exaltation of the mental life which takes form in a group of ideal conceptions where is portrayed the new life thus awakened; they correspond to this new set of psychical forces which is added to those which we have at our disposition for the daily tasks of existence. A society can neither create itself nor re-create itself without at the same time creating an ideal. This creation is not a sort of work of supererogation for it, by which it would complete itself, being already formed; it is the act by which it is periodically made and remade. Therefore when some oppose the ideal society to the real society, like two antagonists which would lead us in opposite directions, they materialize and oppose abstractions. The ideal society is not outside of the real society; it is a part of it. Far from being divided between them as between two poles which mutually repel each other, we cannot hold to one without holding to the other. For a society is not made up merely of the mass of individuals who compose it, the ground which they occupy, the things which they use and the movements which they perform, but above all is the idea which it forms of itself. It is undoubtedly true that it hesitates over the manner in which it ought to conceive itself; it feels itself drawn in divergent directions. But these conflicts which break forth are not between the ideal and reality, but between two different ideals, that of yesterday and that of today, that which has the authority of tradition and that which has the hope of the future. There is surely a place for investigating whence these ideals evolve; but whatever solution may be given to this problem, it still remains that all passes in the world of the ideal. Thus the collective ideal which religion expresses is far from being due to a vague innate power of the individual, but it is rather at the school of collective life that the individual has learned to idealize. It is in assimilating the ideals elaborated by society that he has become capable of conceiving the ideal. It is society which, by leading him within its sphere of action, has made him acquire the need of raising himself above the world of experience and has at the same time furnished him with the means of conceiving another. For society has constructed this new world in constructing itself, since it is society which this expresses. Thus both with the individual and in the group, the faculty of idealizing has nothing mysterious about it. It is not a sort of luxury which a man could get along without, but a condition of his very existence. He could not be a social being, that is to say, he could not be a man, if he had not acquired it. It is true that in incarnating themselves in individuals, collective ideals tend to individualize themselves. Each understands them after his own fashion and marks them with his own stamp; he suppresses certain elements and adds others. Thus the personal ideal disengages itself from the social ideal in proportion as the individual personality develops itself and becomes an autonomous source of action. But if we wish to understand this aptitude, so singular in appearance, of living outside of reality, it is enough to connect it with the social conditions upon which it depends.

Therefore it is necessary to avoid seeing in this theory of religion a simple restatement of historical materialism: that would be misunderstanding our thought to an extreme degree. In showing that religion is something essentially social we do not mean to say that it confines itself to translating into another language the material forms of society and its immediate vital necessities. It is true that we take it as evident that social life depends upon its material foundation and bears its mark, just as the mental life of an individual depends upon his nervous system and in fact his whole organism. But collective consciousness is something more than a mere epiphenomenon of its morphological basis, just as individual consciousness is something more than a simple efflorescence of the nervous system. In order that the former may appear, a synthesis *sui generis* of particular consciousnesses is required. Now this synthesis has the effect of disengaging a whole world of sentiments, ideas and images which, once born, obey laws all their own. They attract each other, repel each other, unite, divide themselves, and multiply, though these combinations are not commanded and necessitated by the condition of the underlying reality. The life thus brought into being even enjoys so great an independence that it sometimes indulges in manifestations with no purpose or utility of any sort, for the mere pleasure of affirming itself. We have shown that this is often precisely the case with ritual activity and mythological thought.[7]

But if religion is the product of social causes, how can we explain the individual cult and the universalistic character of certain religions? If it is born *in foro externo*, how has it been able to pass into the inner conscience of the individual and penetrate there ever more and more profoundly? If it is the work of definite and individualized societies, how has it been able to detach itself from them, even to the point of being conceived as something common to all humanity? In the course of our studies, we have met with the germs of individual religion and of religious cosmopolitanism, and we have seen how they were formed; thus we possess the more general

elements of the reply which is to be given to this double question. We have shown how the religious force which animates the clan particularizes itself, by incarnating itself in particular consciousnesses. Thus secondary sacred beings are formed; each individual has his own, made in his own image associated to his own intimate life, bound up with his own destiny; it is the soul, the individual totem, the protecting ancestor, etc. These beings are the object of rites which the individual can celebrate by himself, outside of any group; this is the first form of the individual cult. To be sure, it is only a very rudimentary cult; but since the personality of the individual is still only slightly marked, and but little value is attributed to it, the cult which expresses it could hardly be expected to be very highly developed as yet. But as individuals have differentiated themselves more and more and the value of an individual has increased, the corresponding cult has taken a relatively greater place in the totality of the religious life and at the same time it is more fully closed to outside influences.

Thus the existence of individual cults implies nothing which contradicts or embarrasses the sociological interpretation of religion; for the religious forces to which it addresses itself are only the individualized forms of collective forces. Therefore, even when religion seems to be entirely within the individual conscience, it is still in society that it finds the living source from which it is nourished. We are now able to appreciate the value of the radical individualism which would make religion something purely individual: it misunderstands the fundamental conditions of the religious life. If up to the present it has remained in the stage of theoretical aspirations which have never been realized, it is because it is unrealizable. A philosophy may well be elaborated in the silence of the interior imagination, but not so a faith. For, before all else, a faith is warmth, life, enthusiasm, the exaltation of the whole mental life, the raising of the individual above himself. Now how could he add to the energies which he possesses without going outside himself? How could he surpass himself merely by his own forces? The only source of life at which we can morally reanimate ourselves is that formed by the society of our fellow beings; the only moral forces with which we can sustain and increase our own are those which we get from others. Let us even admit that there really are beings more or less analogous to those which the mythologies represent. In order that they may exercise over souls the useful direction which is their reason for existence, it is necessary that men believe in them. Now these beliefs are active only when they are partaken by many. A man cannot retain them any length of time by a purely personal effort; it is not thus that they are born or that they are acquired; it is even doubtful if they can be kept under these conditions. In fact, a man who has a veritable faith feels an invincible need of spreading it: therefore he leaves his isolation, approaches others and seeks to convince them, and it is the ardour of the convictions which he arouses that strengthens his own. It would quickly weaken if it remained alone.

It is the same with religious universalism as with this individualism. Far from being an exclusive attribute of certain very great religions, we have found it, not at the base, it is true, but at the summit of the Australian system. Bunjil, Daramulum or Baiame are not simple tribal gods; each of them is recognized by a number of different tribes. In a sense, their cult is international. This conception is therefore very near to that found in the most recent theologies. So certain writers have felt it their duty to deny its authenticity, howsoever incontestable this may be.

And we have been able to show how this has been formed.

Neighboring tribes of a similar civilization cannot fail to be in constant relations with each other. All sorts of circumstances give an occasion for it: besides commerce, which is still rudimentary, there are marriages; these international marriages are very common in Australia. In the course of these meetings, men naturally become conscious of the moral relationship which united them. They have the same social organization, the same division into phratries, clans and matrimonial classes; they practise the same rites of initiation, or wholly similar

ones. Mutual loans and treaties result in reinforcing these spontaneous resemblances. The gods to which these mainfestly identical institutions were attached could hardly have remained distinct in their minds. Everything tended to bring them together and consequently, even supposing that each tribe elaborated the notion independently, they must necessarily have tended to confound themselves with each other. Also, it is probable that it was in inter-tribal assemblies that they were first conceived. For they are chiefly the gods of initiation, and in the initiation ceremonies, the different tribes are usually represented. So if sacred beings are formed which are connected with no geographically determined society, that is not because they have an extra-social origin. It is because there are other groups above these geographically determined ones, whose contours are less clearly marked: they have no fixed frontiers, but include all sorts of more or less neighbouring and related tribes. The particular social life thus created tends to spread itself over an area with no definite limits. Naturally the mythological personages who correspond to it have the same character; their sphere of influence is not limited; they go beyond the particular tribes and their territory. They are the great international gods.

Now there is nothing in this situation which it peculiar to Australian societies. There is no people and no state which is not a part of another society, more or less unlimited, which embraces all the peoples and all the states with which the first comes in contact, either directly or indirectly; there is no national life which is not dominated by a collective life of an international nature. In proportion as we advance in history, these international groups acquire a greater importance and extent. Thus we see how, in certain cases, this universalistic tendency has been able to develop itself to the point of affecting not only the higher ideas of the religious system, but even the principles upon which it rests....

NOTES

1. William James, *The Varieties of Religious Experience*.
2. Quoted by James, *op. cit.*, p. 20.
3. See above, pp. 262 ff.
4. Only one form of social activity has not yet been expressly attached to religion: that is economic activity. Sometimes processes that are derived from magic have, by that fact alone, an origin that is

indirectly religious. Also, economic value is a sort of power of efficacy, and we know the religious origins of the idea of power. Also, richness can confer *mana*; therefore it has it. Hence it is seen that the ideas of economic value and of religious value are not without connection. But the question of the nature of these connections has not yet been studied.

5. It is for this reason that Frazer and even Preuss set impersonal religious forces outside of, or at least on the threshold of religion, to attach them to magic.
6. Boutroux, *Science et Religion*, pp. 206–207.
7. See above, pp. 423ff. On this same question, see also our article, "Représentations individuelles et représentations collectives," in the *Revue de Métaphysique*, May, 1898.

SECTION II

1. What in Durkheim´s view is the significance of the division of labor in modern society for solidarity?
2. Describe the difference between mechanical and organic solidarity.
3. What is a social fact and why is it so central to Durkheim´s vision of sociology?
4. Define anomie in your own words and relate it to Marx´s understanding of alienation.
5. Based on Durkheim´s discussion of anomic suicide, explain why it is particularly common in modern societies.
6. What are civilizations and how should one understand their boundaries?
7. How does Durkheim define religion and explain its social function?

III. MAX WEBER

11. 'OBJECTIVITY' IN SOCIAL SCIENCE AND SOCIAL POLICY

MAX WEBER

Max Weber´s (1864–1920) quest for the construction of an empirical science of social life differed from Durkheim´s. Trained in both history and economics, Weber did not abandon these disciplines when he turned to sociology; instead, he sought to weave them into sociology. Thus, whereas Durkheim wanted to differentiate sociology from other disciplines, Weber was interested in interconnections among disciplines. Moreover, as this essay (first published in 1904) illustrates, his idea of an objective science was shaped by his convictions about the perspectival nature of knowledge and the relativity of values. He advocated a sociology concerned not merely with causal explanation, but with interpretation, or *Verstehen*. What the sociologist wants to learn, Weber suggests here, entails both explanation and interpretation. For Weber, causal analysis is a preliminary to inquiring into matters related to what he refers to in this passage as the cultural significance of social phenomena.

There is no absolutely "objective" scientific analysis of culture—or put perhaps more narrowly but certainly not essentially differently for our purposes—of "social phenomena" independent of special and "one-sided" viewpoints according to which—expressly or tacitly, consciously or unconsciously—they are selected, analyzed and organized for expository purposes. The reasons for this lie in the character of the cognitive goal of all research in social science which seeks to transcend the purely formal treatment of the legal or conventional norms regulating social life.

The type of social science in which we are interested is an *empirical science* of concrete *reality* (*Wirklichkeitswissenschaft*). Our aim is the understanding of the characteristic uniqueness of the reality in which we move. We wish to understand on the one hand the relationships and the cultural significance of individual events in their contemporary manifestations and on the other the causes of their being historically *so* and not *otherwise*. Now, as soon as we attempt to reflect about the way in which life confronts us in immediate concrete situations, it presents an infinite multiplicity of successively and coexistently emerging and disappearing events, both "within" and "outside" ourselves. The absolute infinitude of this multiplicity is seen to remain undiminished even when our attention is focused on a single "object," for instance, a concrete act of exchange, as soon as we seriously attempt an exhaustive description of *all* the individual components of this "individual phenomena," to say nothing of explaining it causally. All the analysis of infinite reality which the finite human mind can conduct rests on the tacit assumption that only a finite portion of this reality constitutes the object of scientific investigation, and that only it is "important" in the sense of being "worthy of being known." But what are the criteria by which this segment is selected? It has often been thought that the decisive criterion in the cultural sciences, too, was in the last analysis, the "regular" recurrence of certain causal relationship. The "laws" which we are able to perceive in the infinitely manifold stream of events must—according to this conception—contain the scientifically "essential" aspect of reality. As soon as we have shown some causal relationship to be a "law," i.e., if we have shown it to be universally valid by means of comprehensive historical induction or have made it immediately and tangibly plausible according to our subjective experience, a great number of similar cases order themselves under the formula thus attained. Those elements in each individual event which are left unaccounted for by the selection of their elements subsumable under the "law" are considered as scientifically unintegrated residues which will be taken care of in the further perfection of the system of "laws." Alternatively they will be viewed as "accidental" and therefore scientifically unimportant *because* they do not fit into the structure of the "law"; in other words, they are not typical of the event and hence can only be the objects of "idle curiosity." Accordingly, even among the followers of the Historical School we continually find the attitude which declares that the ideal which all the sciences, including the cultural sciences, serve and towards which they should strive even in the remote future is a system of propositions from which reality can be "deduced." As is well known, a leading natural scientist believed that he could designate the (factually unattainable) ideal goal of such a treatment of cultural reality as a sort of "*astronomical*" knowledge.

Let us not, for our part, spare ourselves the trouble of examining these matters more closely—however often they have already been discussed. The first thing that impresses one is that the "astronomical" knowledge which was referred to is not a system of laws at all. On the contrary, the laws which it presupposes have been taken from other disciplines like mechanics. But it too concerns itself with the question of the *individual* consequence which the working of these laws in an unique *configuration* produces, since it is these individual configurations which are *significant* for us. Every individual constellation which it "explains" or predicts is causally

explicable only as the consequence of another equally individual constellation which has preceded it. As far back as we may go into the grey mist of the far-off past, the reality to which the laws apply always remains equally *individual*, equally *undeducible* form laws. A cosmic "primeval state" which had no individual character or less individual character than the cosmic reality of the present would naturally be a meaningless notion. But is there not some trace of similar ideas in our field in those propositions sometimes derived from natural law and sometimes verified by the observation of "primitives," concerning an economic-social "primeval state" free from historical "accidents," and characterized by phenomena such as "primitive agrarian communism," sexual "promiscuity," etc., from which individual historical development emerges by a sort of fall from grace into concreteness?

The social-scientific interest has its point of departure, of course, in the *real*, i.e., concrete, individually-structured configuration of our cultural life in its universal relationships which are themselves no less individually structured, and in its development out of other social cultural conditions, which themselves are obviously likewise individually structured. It is clear here that the situation which we illustrated by reference to astronomy as a limiting case (which is regularly drawn on by logicians for the same purpose) appears in a more accentuated form. Whereas in astronomy, the heavenly bodies are of interest to us only in their *quantitative* and exact aspects, the *qualitative* aspect of phenomena concerns us in the social sciences. To this should be added that in the social sciences we are concerned with psychological and intellectual (*geistig*) phenomena the empathic understanding of which is naturally a problem of a specifically different type from those which the schemes of the exact natural sciences in general can or seek to solve. Despite that, this distinction in itself is not a distinction in principle, as it seems at first glance. Aside from pure mechanics, even the exact natural sciences do not proceed without qualitative categories. Furthermore, in our own field we encounter the idea (which is obviously distorted) that at least the phenomena characteristic of a money-economy—which are basic to our culture—are quantifiable and on that account subject to formulation as "laws." Finally it depends on the breadth or narrowness of one´s definition of "law" as to whether one will also include regularities which because they are not quantifiable are not subject to numerical analysis. Especially insofar as the influence of psychological and intellectual (*geistig*) factors is concerned, it does not in any case exclude the establishment of *rules* governing rational conduct. Above all, the point of view still persists which claims that the task of psychology is to play a role comparable to mathematics for the *Geisteswissenschaften* in the sense that it analyzes the complicated phenomena of social life into their psychic conditions and effects, reduces them to their most elementary possible psychic factors and then analyzes their functional interdependences. Thereby, a sort of "chemistry" if not "mechanics" of the psychic foundations of social life would be created. Whether such investigations can produce valuable and—what is something else—useful results for the cultural sciences, we cannot decide here. But this would be irrelevant to the question as to whether the aim of social-economic knowledge in our sense, i.e., knowledge of *reality* with respect to its cultural *significance* and its causal relationships can be attained through the quest for recurrent sequences. Let us assume that we have succeeded by means of psychology or otherwise in analyzing all the observed and imaginable relationships of social phenomena into some ultimate elementary "factors," that we have made an exhaustive analysis and classification of them and then formulated rigorously exact laws covering their behavior. What would be the significance of these results for our knowledge of the *historically* given culture or any individual phase thereof, such as capitalism, in its development and cultural significance? As an analytical tool, it would be as useful as a textbook of organic chemical combinations would be for our knowledge of the biogenetic aspect of the animal and plant world. In each case, certainly an important and useful preliminary step would have been taken. In neither case can concrete reality be deduced from "laws" and "factors." This is not because some higher mysterious powers reside in living phenomena (such as "dominants," "entelechies," or whatever they might be called). This, however, is a problem in its own right. The real reason is that the analysis of reality is concerned with the *configuration* into which those (hypothetical!) "factors" are arranged to form a cultural phenomenon which is historically significant to us. Furthermore, if we wish to "explain" this individual configuration "causally" we must invoke other equally individual configurations on the basis of which we will explain it with the aid of those (hypothetical!) "laws."

The determination of those (hypothetical) "laws" and "factors" would in any case only be the first of the many options which would lead us to the desired type of knowledge. The analysis of the historically given individual configuration of those "factors" and their *significant* concrete interaction, conditioned by their historical context and especially the *rendering intelligible* of the basis and type of this significance would be the next task to be achieved. This task must be achieved, it is true, by the utilization of the preliminary analysis but it is nonetheless an entirely new and *distinct* task. The tracing as far into the past as possible of the individual features of these historically evolved configurations which are *contemporaneously* significant, and their historical explanation by antecedent and equally individual configurations would be the third task. Finally the prediction of possible future constellations would be a conceivable fourth task.

For all these purposes, clear concepts and the knowledge of these (hypothetical) "laws" are obviously of great value as heuristic means—but only as such. Indeed they are quite indispensable for this purpose. But even in this function their limitations become evident at a decisive point. In stating this, we arrive at the decisive feature of the method of the cultural sciences. We have designated as "cultural sciences" those disciplines which analyze the phenomena of life in terms of their cultural significance. The *significance* of a configuration of cultural phenomena and the basis of this significance cannot however be derived and rendered intelligible by a system of analytical laws (*Gesetzesbegriffen*), however perfect it may be, since the significance of cultural events presupposes a *value-orientation* towards these events. The concept of culture is a *value-concept*. Empirical reality becomes "culture" to us because and insofar as we relate it to *value-ideas*. It includes those segments and only those segments of reality which have become significant to us because of this value-relevance. Only a small portion of existing concrete reality is colored by our value-conditioned interest and it alone is significant to us. It is significant because it reveals relationships which are important to us due to their connection with our values. Only because and to the extent that this is the case is it worthwhile for us to know it in its individual features. We cannot discover, however, what is meaningful to us by means of a "presuppositionless" investigation of empirical data. Rather perception of its meaningfulness to us is the presupposition of its becoming an *object* of investigation. Meaningfulness naturally does not coincide with laws as such, and the more general the law the less the coincidence. For the specific meaning which a phenomenon has for us is naturally *not* to be found in those relationships which it shares with many other phenomena.

The focus of attention on reality under the guidance of values which lend it significance and the selection and ordering of the phenomena which are thus affected in the light of their cultural significance is entirely different from the analysis of reality in terms of laws and general concepts. Neither of these two types of the analysis of reality has any necessary logical relationship with the other. They can coincide in individual instances but it would be most disastrous if their occasional coincidence caused us to think that they were not distinct *in principle*. The *cultural significance* of a phenomenon, e.g., the significance of exchange in a money economy, can be the fact that it exists on a mass scale as a fundamental component of modern culture. But the historical fact that it plays this role must be causally explained in order to render its cultural significance understandable. The analysis of the *general* aspects of exchange and the technique of the market is a—highly important and indispensable—*preliminary task*. For not only does this type of analysis leave unanswered the question as to how exchange historically acquired its fundamental significance in the modern world; but above all else, the fact with which we are primarily concerned, namely, the *cultural significance* of the money-economy, for the sake of which we are interested in the description of exchange technique and for the sake of which alone a science exists which deals with that technique—is not derivable from any "law." The *generic features* of exchange, purchase, etc., interest the jurist—but we are concerned with the analysis of the *cultural significance* of the concrete *historical* fact that today exchange exists on a mass scale. When we require an explanation, when we wish to understand what distinguishes the social-economic aspects of our culture for instance from that of antiquity in which exchange showed precisely the same generic traits as it does today

and when we raise the question as to where the significance of "money economy" lies, logical principles of quite heterogeneous derivation enter into the investigation. We will apply those concepts with which we are provided by the investigation of the general features of economic mass phenomena—indeed, insofar as they are relevant to the meaningful aspects of our culture, we shall use them as *means* of exposition. The *goal* of our investigation is not reached through the exposition of those laws and concepts, precise as it may be. The question as to what should be the object of universal conceptualization cannot be decided "presuppositionlessly" but only with reference to the *significance* which certain segments of that infinite multiplicity which we call "commerce" have for culture. We seek knowledge of an historical phenomenon, meaning by historical: significant in its individuality (*Eigenart*). And the decisive element in this is that only through the presupposition that a finite part alone of the infinite variety of phenomena is significant, does the knowledge of an individual phenomenon become logically meaningful. Even with the widest imaginable knowledge of "laws," we are helpless in the face of the question: how is the *causal explanation* of an *individual* fact possible—since a *description* of even the smallest slice of reality can never be exhaustive? The number and type of causes which have influenced any given event are always infinite and there is nothing in the things themselves to set some of them apart as alone meriting attention. A chaos of "existential judgments" about countless individual events would be the only result of a serious attempt to analyze reality "without presuppositions." And even this result is only seemingly possible, since every single perception discloses on closer examination an infinite number of constituent perceptions which can never be exhaustively expressed in a judgement. Order is brought into this chaos only on the condition that in every case only a *part* of concrete reality is interesting and *significant* to us, because only it is related to the *cultural values* with which we approach reality. Only certain sides of the infinitely complex concrete phenomenon, namely those to which we attribute a general *cultural significance*— are therefore worthwhile knowing. They alone are objects of causal explanation. And even this causal explanation evinces the same character; an *exhaustive* causal investigation of any concrete phenomenon in its full reality is not only practically impossible—it is simply nonsense. We select only those causes to which are to be imputed in the individual case, the "essential" feature of an event. Where the *individuality* of a phenomenon is concerned, the question of causality is not a question of *laws* but of concrete causal *relationships;* it is not a question of the subsumption of the event under some general rubric as a representative case but of its imputation as a consequence of some constellation. It is in brief a *question of imputation.* Wherever the causal explanation of a "cultural phenomenon"—a "historical individual"[1]—is under consideration, the knowledge of causal *laws* is not the *end* of the investigation but only a *means.* It facilitates and renders possible the causal imputation to their concrete causes of those components of a phenomenon the individuality of which is culturally significant. So far and only so far as it achieves this, is it valuable for our knowledge of concrete relationships. And the more "general," i.e., the more abstract the laws, the less they can contribute to the causal imputation of *individual* phenomena and, more indirectly, to the understanding of the significance of cultural events.

What is the consequence of all this?

Naturally, it does not imply that the knowledge of *universal* propositions, the construction of abstract concepts, the knowledge of regularities and the attempt to formulate *"laws"* have no scientific justification in the cultural sciences. Quite the contrary, if the causal knowledge of the historians consists of the imputation of concrete effects to concrete causes, a *valid* imputation of any individual effect without the application of *"nomological" knowledge*—i.e., the knowledge of recurrent causal sequences—would in general be impossible. Whether a single individual component of a relationship is, in a concrete case, to be assigned causal responsibility for an effect, the causal explanation of which is at issue, can in doubtful cases be determined only by estimating the effects which we *generally* expect from it and from the other components of the same complex which are relevant to the explanation. In other words, the *"adequate"* effects of the causal elements involved must be considered in arriving at any such conclusion. The extent to which the historian (in the widest sense of the word) can perform this imputation in a reasonably certain manner with his

imagination sharpened by personal experience and trained in analytic methods and the extent to which he must have recourse to the aid of special disciplines which make it possible, varies with the individual case. Everywhere, however, and hence also in the sphere of complicated economic processes, the more certain and the more comprehensive our general knowledge the greater is the *certainty* of imputation. This proposition is not in the least affected by the fact that even in the case of all so-called "economic laws" without exception, we are concerned here not with "laws" in the narrower exact natural science sense, but with *adequate* causal relationships expressed in rules and with the application of the category of "objective possibility." The establishment of such regularities is not the *end* but rather the *means* of knowledge. It is entirely a question of expediency, to be settled separately for each individual case, whether a regularly recurrent causal relationship of everyday experience should be formulated into a "law." Laws are important and valuable in the exact natural sciences, in the measure that those sciences are *universally valid.* For the knowledge of historical phenomena in their concreteness, the most general laws, because they are most devoid of content are also the least valuable. The more comprehensive the validity—or scope—of a term, the more it leads us away from the richness of reality since in order to include the common elements of the largest possible number of phenomena, it must necessarily be as abstract as possible and hence *devoid* of content. In the cultural sciences, the knowledge of the universal or general is never valuable in itself.

The conclusion which follows from the above is that an "objective" analysis of cultural events, which proceeds according to the thesis that the ideal of science is the reduction of empirical reality to "laws," is meaningless. It is not meaningless, as is often maintained, because cultural or psychic events for instance are "objectively" less governed by laws. It is meaningless for a number of other reasons. Firstly, because the knowledge of social laws is not knowledge of social reality but is rather one of the various aids used by our minds for attaining this end; secondly, because knowledge of *cultural* events is inconceivable except on a basis of the *significance* which the concrete constellations of reality have for us in certain *individual* concrete situations. In *which* sense and in *which* situations this is the case is not revealed to us by any laws; it is decided according to the *value-ideas* in the light of which we view "culture" in each individual case. "Culture" is a finite segment of the meaningless infinity of the world process, a segment on which *human beings* confer meaning and significance. This is true even for the human being who views a *particular* culture as a mortal enemy and who seeks to "return to nature." He can attain this point of view only after viewing the culture in which he lives from the standpoint of his values, and finding it "too soft." This is the purely logical-formal fact which is involved when we speak of the logically necessary rootedness of all historical entities (*historische Individuen*) in "evaluative ideas." The transcendental presupposition of every *cultural science* lies not in our finding a certain culture or any "culture" in general to be *valuable* but rather in the fact that we are *cultural beings*, endowed with the capacity and the will to take a deliberate attitude towards the world and to lend it *significance*. Whatever this significance may be, it will lead us to judge certain phenomena of human existence in its light and to respond to them as being (positively or negatively) meaningful. Whatever may be the content of this attitude—these phenomena have cultural significance for us and on this significance alone rests its scientific interest. Thus when we speak here of the conditioning of cultural knowledge through *evaluative* ideas (*Wertideen*) (following the terminology of modern logic), it is done in the hope that we will not be subject to crude misunderstandings such as the opinion that cultural significance should be attributed only to *valuable* phenomena. Prostitution is a *cultural* phenomenon just as much as religion or money. All three are cultural phenomena *only* because and *only* insofar as their existence and the form which they historically assume touch directly or indirectly on our cultural *interests* and arouse our striving for knowledge concerning problems brought into focus by the evaluative ideas which give *significance* to the fragment of reality analysed by those concepts....

NOTE

1. We will use the term which is already occasionally used in the methodology of our discipline and which is now becoming widespread in a more precise formulation in logic.

12. THE SPIRIT OF CAPITALISM

MAX WEBER

Weber's most famous and widely read work is *The Protestant Ethic and the Spirit of Capitalism* (1904–05). In this essay, he seeks to account for what he describes as an elective affinity between capitalism and Protestantism. The spirit of capitalism, according to Weber, encouraged a distinctive mentality that proved to be vital during the early stages of capitalist development. The capitalist was an ascetic—a rational miser—who was devoted to the task of making money, not in order to enjoy its fruits but to reinvest it to make more money. The question Weber poses is: Why would someone act in such a manner? The answer he develops hinges on the idea that a distinctly Protestant ethic served to provide a rationale for such conduct. While the thrust of the essay is to focus on the formative period of capitalism, Weber concludes with a pessimistic account of the future wrought by capitalism, depicted most graphically and poignantly by his metaphor of the "iron cage."

The title of this study uses a concept that sounds rather intimidating: the *"spirit* of **capitalism**."[1] What should be understood by it? An attempt to provide even an approximate "definition" immediately unveils certain difficulties that are embedded in the essence of this investigation's purpose. [1920]

If one can discover at all an object for which the utilization of this concept is meaningful, then it can only be a specific *historical case*. Such a singular entity is nothing more than a complex of relationships in historical reality. We join them together, from the vantage point of their *cultural significance*, into a conceptual unity.

Such a historical concept, however, cannot be defined according to how it is "demarcated" vis-à-vis other concepts (*genus proximum, differentia specifica*). This holds if only because the concept denotes a phenomenon that is of qualitative importance as a consequence of its individual *uniqueness*. Moreover, this concept must be gradually *put together* from its single component parts, each of which is taken out of historical reality. Therefore, the final formation of the concept cannot appear at the beginning of the investigation; rather, it must stand at its *conclusion*. In other words, how our understanding of a "spirit" of capitalism is to be best defined will have to unfold only in the course of our discussion and only as its main outcome. Only a definition formulated in this manner will be adequate to the particular vantage points of interest to us here.

In turn, it must be recognized that these vantage points (which are still to be discussed) by no means constitute the only ones possible in reference to which the historical cases under consideration can be analyzed. Other vantage points would identify other features of our historical cases as "essential," as is true with every historical case. From this premise it follows unequivocally that whatever one understands by a "spirit" of capitalism by no means necessarily can or must correspond to *that which we* will note as essential in our exegesis here.

This must be acknowledged, namely, the central role played by the researcher's particular vantage point in identifying what is essential to each case, as it

belongs to the very essence of the "formation of historical concepts." This endeavor does not aim, in terms of
its methodological goals, to trap reality in abstract,
general concepts (*Gattungsbegriffe*). Rather, when
forming historical concepts we strive to achieve something different: to order reality into tangible, causal
connections that are stable and, unavoidably, of a
unique character.[2]

That being said, and even if we succeed in demarcating the case we are attempting here to analyze and
explain historically, our concern now cannot be to offer
a conceptual definition. Instead, our focus at the beginning should be only to provide a provisional *illustration*
of the activity implied here by the term "spirit" of
capitalism. Indeed, such an illustration is indispensable
in order to attain our aim now of simply understanding
the object of our investigation. On behalf of this purpose we turn to a document that contains the spirit of
concern to us in near classical purity, and simultaneously offers the advantage of being detached from
all direct connection to religious belief—hence, for our
theme, of being "free of presuppositions."

Remember, that *time* is *money*. He that can earn ten
shillings a day by his labour, and goes abroad, or
sits idle one half of that day, though he spends but
sixpence during his diversion or idleness, ought
not to reckon that the only expense; he has really
spent or rather thrown away five shillings besides.

Remember, that *credit* is *money*. If a man lets his
money lie in my hands after it is due, he gives me
the interest, or so much as I can make of it during
that time. This amounts to a considerable sum
where a man has good and large credit, and
makes good use of it.

Remember, that money is of the *prolific,
generating nature*. Money can beget money, and
its offspring can beget more, and so on. Five
shillings turned is six, turned again it is seven
and threepence, and so on, till it becomes a
hundred pounds. The more there is of it, the
more it produces every turning, so that the
profits rise quicker and quicker. He that kills a
breeding-sow, destroys all her offspring to the
thousandth generation. He that murders a
crown, *destroys* all that it might have produced,
even scores of pounds....

Remember this saying: The good *paymaster* is
lord of another man's purse. He that is known to
pay punctually and exactly to the time he
promises, may at any time, and on any occasion,
raise all the money his friends can spare.

This is sometimes of great use. After industry
and frugality, nothing contributes more to the
raising of a young man in the world than punctuality and justice in all his dealings; therefore
never keep borrowed money an hour beyond the
time you promised, lest a disappointment shut
up your friend's purse for ever.

The most trifling actions that affect a man's
credit are to be regarded. The sound of your
hammer at five in the morning, or nine at night,
heard by a creditor, makes him easy six months
longer; but if he sees you at a billiard-table, or
hears your voice at a tavern, when you should
be at work, he sends for his money the next
day;...[he] demands it before you are able
to pay.

It shows, besides, that you are mindful of what
you owe; it makes you *appear* a careful as well as an
honest man, and that still increases your *credit*.

Beware of thinking that you own all that you
possess, and of living accordingly. It is a mistake
that many people who have credit fall into. To
prevent this, keep an exact account both of your
expenses and your income. If you make an effort
to attend to particular expenses, it will have this
good effect: you will discover how wonderfully
small, trifling expenses mount up to large sums,
and will discern what might have been, and may
for the future be saved, without occasioning any
great inconvenience.

For six pounds a year you may have the use of
one hundred pounds if you are a man of known
prudence and honesty.

He that spends a groat a day idly, spends idly
above six pounds a year, which is the price of
using one hundred pounds.

He that wastes idly a groat's worth of his time
per day, one day with another, wastes the privilege
of using one hundred pounds each year.

He that idly loses five shillings' worth of time,
loses five shillings and might as prudently throw
five shillings into the sea.

He that loses five shillings not only loses that sum, but all the advantage that might be made by turning it in dealing, which by the time that a young man becomes old, amounts to a comfortable bag of money.

It is *Benjamin Franklin*[3] [1706–90] who preaches to us in these sentences. As the supposed catechism of a Yankee, Ferdinand Kürnberger satirizes these axioms in his brilliantly clever and venomous *Picture of American Culture*.[4] That the "spirit of capitalism" is here manifest in Franklin's words, even in a characteristic manner, no one will doubt. It will not be argued here, however, that *all aspects* of what can be understood by this "spirit" are contained in them.

Let us dwell a moment upon a passage, the worldly wisdom of which is summarized thusly by Kürnberger: "They make tallow for candles out of cattle and money out of men." Remarkably, the real peculiarity in the "philosophy of avarice" contained in this maxim is the ideal of the *credit-worthy* man of honor and, above all, the idea of the *duty* of the individual to increase his wealth, which is assumed to be a self-defined interest in itself. Indeed, rather than simply a common-sense approach to life, a peculiar "ethic" is preached here: its violation is treated not simply as foolishness but as a sort of forgetfulness of *duty*. Above all, this distinction stands at the center of the matter. "Business savvy," which is found commonly enough, is here not *alone* taught; rather, an *ethos* is expressed in this maxim. Just *this* quality is of interest to us in this investigation.

A retired business partner of Jakob Fugger [1459–1525, an extremely wealthy German financier, export merchant, and philanthropist] once sought to convince him to retire. Yet his colleague's argument—that he had accumulated enough wealth and should allow others their chance—was rebuked by Fugger as "contemptible timidity." He "viewed matters differently," Fugger answered, and "wanted simply to make money as long as he could."[5]

Obviously, the "spirit" of this statement must be *distinguished* from Franklin's. Fugger's entrepreneurial daring and personal, morally indifferent proclivities[6] now take on the character, in Franklin, of an *ethically* oriented maxim for the **organization of life**. The expression "spirit of capitalism" will be used here in just this specific manner[7]—naturally the spirit of *modern* capitalism. That is, in light of the formulation of our theme, it must be evident that the Western European and American capitalism of the last few centuries constitutes our concern rather than the "capitalism" that has appeared in China, India, Babylon, the ancient world, and the Middle Ages. As we will see, *just that peculiar ethic was missing in all these cases.*

Nevertheless, all of Franklin's moral admonishments are applied in a utilitarian fashion: Honesty is *useful* because it leads to the availability of credit. Punctuality, industry, and frugality are also useful and are *therefore* virtues. It would follow from this that, for example, the *appearance* of honesty, wherever it accomplishes the same end, would suffice. Moreover, in Franklin's eyes an unnecessary surplus of this virtue must be seen as unproductive wastefulness. Indeed, whoever reads in his autobiography the story of his "conversion" to these virtues,[8] or the complete discussions on the usefulness of a strict preservation of the *appearance* of modesty and the intentional minimizing of one's own accomplishments in order to attain a general approval,[9] will necessarily come to the conclusion that all virtues, according to Franklin, become virtues *only to the extent* that they are useful to the individual. The surrogate of virtue—namely, its appearance only—is fully adequate wherever the same purpose is achieved. Indeed, this inseparability of motive and appearance is the inescapable consequence of all strict utilitarianism. The common German tendency to perceive the American virtues as "hypocrisy" appears here confirmed beyond a doubt.

In truth, however, matters are not so simple. Benjamin Franklin's own character demonstrates that the issue is more complex: his character appears clearly, however seldom, in his autobiography as one of candor and truthfulness. It is also evident in Franklin's tracing of his realization—virtues can be "useful"—back to a revelation from God that was designed, he believed, to guide him onto the path of righteousness. Something more is involved here than simply an embellishing of purely self-interested, egocentric maxims.

The complexity of this issue is above all apparent in the *summum bonum* ["supreme good"] of this "ethic": namely, the acquisition of money, and more and more money, takes place here simultaneously with the strictest avoidance of all spontaneous enjoyment of it. The pursuit of riches is fully stripped of all pleasurable (*eudämonistischen*), and surely all hedonistic, aspects.

Accordingly, this striving becomes understood completely as an end in itself—to such an extent that it appears as fully outside the normal course of affairs and simply irrational, at least when viewed from the perspective of the "happiness" or "utility" of the single individual.[10] Here, people are oriented to acquisition as the purpose of life; acquisition is no longer viewed as a means to the end of satisfying the substantive needs of life. Those people in possession of spontaneous, fun-loving dispositions experience this situation as an absolutely meaningless reversal of a "natural" condition (as we would say today). Yet this reversal constitutes just as surely a guiding principle of [modern] capitalism as incomprehension of this new situation characterizes all who remain untouched by [modern] capitalism's tentacles.

This reversal implies an internal line of development that comes into close contact with certain religious ideas. One can ask *why* then "money ought to be made out of persons." In his autobiography, and although he is himself a neutral Deist, Franklin answers with a maxim from the Bible that, as he says, his strict Calvinist father again and again drilled into him in his youth: "Seest thou a man vigorous in his **vocational calling** (*Beruf*)? He shall stand before kings" (Prov. 22:29). As long as it is carried out in a legal manner, the acquisition of money in the modern economic order is the result and manifestation of competence and proficiency in a *vocational calling. This competence and proficiency* is the actual alpha and omega of Franklin's morality, as now can be easily recognized. It presents itself to us both in the passages cited above and, without exception, in all his writings.[11]

In fact, this peculiar idea of a *duty to have a vocational calling*, so familiar to us today but actually not at all self-evident, is the idea that is characteristic of the "social ethic" of modern capitalist culture. In a certain sense, it is even of constitutive significance for it. It implies a notion of duty that individuals ought to experience, and do, vis-à-vis the content of their "vocational" activity. This notion appears regardless of the particular nature of the activity and regardless, especially, of whether this activity seems to involve (as it does for

people with a spontaneous, fun-loving disposition) nothing more than a simple utilization of their capacity for labor or their treatment of it as only a material possession (as "capital").

Nevertheless, it is surely not the case that the idea of a duty in one's vocational calling could grow *only* on the soil of [modern] capitalism. Rather, our attempt later to trace its roots will take us to a period prior to [modern] capitalism. Naturally it will be argued here even less that, under *today's* capitalism, the subjective acquisition of these ethical maxims by capitalism's particular social carriers (such as businesspersons or workers in modern capitalist companies) constitutes a condition for capitalism's further existence. Rather, the capitalist economic order of today is a vast cosmos into which a person is born. It simply exists, to each person, as a factually unalterable casing (*unabänderliches Gehäuse*) in which he or she must live. To the extent that people are interwoven into the context of capitalism's market forces, the norms of its economic action are forced onto them. Every factory owner who operates in the long term against these norms will inevitably be eliminated from the economy. With the same degree of inevitability, every worker who cannot or will not adapt to the norms of the marketplace will become unemployed.

Our analysis should have demonstrated that one of the constitutive components of the modern capitalist spirit and, moreover, generally of modern civilization was the rational organization of life on the basis of the *idea of the calling*. It was born out of the spirit of *Christian asceticism*. If we now read again the passages from Benjamin Franklin cited at the beginning of this essay, we will see that the essential elements of the frame of mind described as the "spirit of capitalism" are just those that we have conveyed above as the content of Puritan vocational asceticism.[12] In Franklin, however, this "spirit" exists without the religious foundation, which had already died out.

The idea that modern work in a vocational calling carries with it an *ascetic* imprint is, of course, also not new. The restriction of persons to specialized work, and the renunciation of the Faustian multidimensionality of the human species it requires, is in our world today the precondition for doing anything of value at all—that is, the "specialized task" and this "foresaking" unavoidably determine one another. *Goethe*, at the peak of his wisdom in his *Wilhelm Meister's Years of Travel* [1829] and in his depiction of Faust's final stage of life [1808], tried to teach us just this:[13] the middle-class way of ordering life, if it wishes to be directed at all rather than to be devoid of continuity, contains a basic component of asceticism. This realization for Goethe implied a resigned farewell to an era of full and beautiful humanity—and a foresaking of it. For such an era will repeat itself in the course of our civilizational development with as little likelihood as a reappearance of the epoch in which Athens bloomed.[14]

The Puritan *wanted* to be a person with a vocational calling; we *must* be. For to the extent that asceticism moved out of the monastic cell and was carried over into the life of work in a vocational calling, and then commenced to rule over this-worldly morality, it helped to do its part to build the mighty cosmos of the modern economic order. This economy is bound to the technical and economic conditions of mechanized, machine-based production.

This cosmos today determines the style of life *not* only of those directly engaged in economically productive activity, but of all born into this grinding mechanism. It does so with overwhelming force, and perhaps it will continue to do so until the last ton of fossil fuel has burnt to ashes. The concern for material goods, according to Baxter, should lie on the shoulders of his saints like "a lightweight coat that one can throw off at any time."[15] Yet fate allowed this coat to become a steel-hard casing (*stahlhartes Gehäuse*).[16] To the extent that asceticism undertook to transform and influence the world, the world's material goods acquired an increasing and, in the end, inescapable power over people—as never before in history.

Today asceticism's spirit has fled from this casing—whether with finality who knows? Victorious capitalism, in any case, ever since it came to rest on a mechanical foundation, no longer needs asceticism as a supporting pillar. Even the optimistic temperament of the Enlightenment, asceticism's joyful heir, appears finally to be fading. And the idea of an "obligation to search for and then accept a vocational calling" now wanders around in our lives as the ghost of past religious beliefs. Persons today usually reject entirely all attempts to make sense of a "fulfillment of one's calling" wherever this notion cannot be directly aligned with the highest spiritual and cultural values, or wherever, conversely, it is not experienced subjectively simply as economic coercion. The pursuit of gain, in the region where it has become most completely unchained and stripped of its religious-ethical meaning, the United States, tends to be associated with purely competitive passions. Not infrequently, these passions directly imprint this pursuit with the character of a sports event.[17]

No one any longer knows who will live in this casing and whether entirely new prophets or a mighty rebirth of ancient ideas and ideals will stand at the end of this monumental development. *Or*, however, if neither, whether a mechanized ossification, embellished with a sort of rigidly compelled sense of self-importance, will arise. Then, indeed, if ossification appears, the saying might be true for the "last humans"[18] in this long civilizational development:

> narrow specialists without minds, pleasure-seekers without heart: in its conceit this nothingness imagines it has climbed to a level of humanity never before attained.[19]

Here, however, we have fallen into the realm of value-judgments, with which this purely historical analysis should not be burdened. Nor should it be burdened by judgments rooted in faith. The further task is a different one: to chart the significance of ascetic rationalism.[20] The above sketch has only hinted at its importance.

Its significance for the content of a community-building, ethical *social policy* must now be outlined—that is, for the type of organization of social groups, ranging from the conventicle to the state, and their functions. Having done that we must analyze the relationship of ascetic rationalism to the ideals and cultural influences of humanistic rationalism.[21] Further, we must investigate the relationship of ascetic rationalism to the development of philosophical and scientific empiricism, to the unfolding of technology, and to the development of nonmaterial culture (*geistige Kulturgüter*) in general.[22] Finally, beginning with the first signs of this-worldly asceticism in the Middle Ages and moving all the way to its dissolution in pure utilitarianism, we need to pursue the historical course of ascetic rationalism. That is, in its *historical* manifestations and through the particular regions of the expansion of ascetic religious devotion. Only after the completion of such investigations can the *extent* of ascetic Protestantism's civilizational significance be demarcated in comparison to that of other elements of modern civilization that can be changed and shaped in response to the actions of persons.

This study has attempted, of course, merely to trace ascetic Protestantism's influence, and the particular *nature* of this influence, back to ascetic Protestantism's motives in regard to one—however important—point.[23] The way in which Protestant asceticism was in turn influenced in its development and characteristic

uniqueness by the entirety of societal-cultural conditions, and especially *economic* conditions, must also have its day.[24] For sure, even with the best will, the modern person seems generally unable to imagine *how* large a significance those components of our consciousness rooted in religious beliefs have actually had upon culture, national character, and the organization of life. Nevertheless, of course it cannot be the intention here to set a one-sided religion-oriented analysis of the causes of culture and history in place of an equally one-sided "materialistic" analysis. *Both* are *equally possible.*[25] Historical truth, however, is served equally little if either of these analyses claims to be the conclusion of an investigation rather than its preparatory stage.[26]

NOTES

1. Weber generally places the term *spirit* in quotation marks. By doing so he wishes (a) to express his awareness that controversy surrounded this term and (b) to emphasize that it is used in this study in a specific and unique manner (and thus to distance his usage, above all, from that of the major figure of German Idealism, G. W. F. Hegel [1770–1831]) [sk].

2. Weber here alludes to a few central aspects of his sociological methodology: (a) historical concepts must refer to "historical individuals" (unique cases); (b) classificatory schemes (*genus proximum, differentia specifica*) are too abstract to capture uniqueness and hence are useful *only* as preliminary conceptual tools; (c) concepts do not "replicate reality," for "reality" varies depending on the investigator's particular research question (or "vantage point" upon reality); and (d) following from the above, concepts can be formulated only after an assessment by researchers of the "cultural significance" of potential constituent elements and a selection accordingly. All the above points are central to Weber's sociological methodology based on "subjective meaning," "interpretive understanding," and "ideal types." See "'Objectivity' in Social Science and Social Policy," in *The Methodology of the Social Sciences*, translated and edited by Edward A. Shils and Henry A. Finch (New York: Free Press, 1949). See also the "Basic Concepts" chapter in *E&S* (pp. 3–22). See Fritz Ringer, *Max Weber's Methodology* (Cambridge, MA: Harvard University Press, 1997); John Drysdale, "How Are Social-Scientific Concepts Formed? A Reconstruction of Max Weber's Theory of Concept Formation," *Sociological Theory* 14 (March 1996): 71–88 [sk].

3. The final [five short] passages are from *Necessary Hints to Those That Would Be Rich*, in *Works* (1736) [Sparks ed. (Chicago, 1882), vol. 2, p. 80]. The earlier are passages from *Advice to a Young Tradesman* (1748) (Sparks ed., vol. 2, p. 87). [The italics in the text are Franklin's.]

4. This book, *Der Amerikamüde* (Frankfurt, 1855; Vienna and Leipzig, 1927), is well known to be a fictional paraphrase of Lenau's impressions of America. As a work of art, the book would today be somewhat difficult to enjoy. However, it is unsurpassed as a document of the differences (now long since blurred over) between German and American sensibilities; indeed, one could say, of the spiritual life of the Germans (which has remained *common* to all Germans since the German mysticism of the Middle Ages, despite all the differences between German Catholics

and German Protestants) in contrast to Puritan-capitalist "can-do" energy. [Italics in paragraphs one (*time*), two (*credit*), and four (the good *paymaster*) are Franklin's; the remainder are Weber's.]

5. Sombart has used this quotation as a motto for his section on "the genesis of capitalism" (*Der moderne Kapitalismus, op. cit.*, vol. 1 [see pp. 193–634], p. 193. See also p. 390.).

6. Which obviously does not mean either that Jakob Fugger was a morally indifferent or an irreligious man, or that Benjamin Franklin's ethic is *completely* covered by the above quotations. It scarcely required Brentano's quotations (*Die Anfänge des modernen Kapitalismus, op. cit.*, pp. 151 f.) to protect this well-known philanthropist from the misunderstanding that Brentano seems to attribute to me. The problem is actually just the reverse: how could such a philanthropist come to write precisely *these sentences* (the especially characteristic form of which Brentano neglected to reproduce) in the manner of a *moralist*? [1920]

7. This way of formulating the problem constitutes the basis for our differences with Sombart. The very considerable practical significance of this difference will become clear later. It should, however, be noted here that Sombart has by no means neglected this ethical aspect of the capitalist employer. However, in his train of thought, capitalism calls forth this ethical aspect. We must, on the contrary, for our purposes, take into consideration the opposite hypothesis. A final position on this difference can only be taken up at the end of this investigation. For Sombart's view see *op. cit.*, vol. 1, pp. 357, 380, etc. His reasoning here connects with the brilliant conceptualizations offered in [Georg] Simmel's *Philosophie des Geldes* [Leipzig: Duncker & Humblot, 1900] [*The Philosophy of Money* (London: Routledge, 1978)] (final chapter). I will speak later of the polemics which Sombart has brought forward against me in his *The Quintessence of Capitalism*. At this point any thorough discussion must be postponed.

8. "I grew convinced that *truth, sincerity*, and *integrity* in dealings between man and man were of the utmost importance *to the felicity of life*; and I formed written resolutions, which still remain *in my journal book* to practise them ever while I lived. Revelation had indeed no weight with me as such; but I entertained an opinion that, though certain actions might not be bad because they were forbidden by it, or good because it commanded them, yet probably these actions might be forbidden *because* they were bad for us, or commanded *because* they were beneficial to us in their own nature, all the circumstances of things considered" [*Autobiography*, ed. by F. W. Pine (New York: Henry Holt, 1916), p. 112].

9. "I therefore put myself as much as I could out of sight and started it"—that is, the project of a library which he had initiated—"as a scheme of a *number of friends*, who had requested me to go about and propose it to such as they thought lovers of reading. In this way my affair went on smoothly, and I ever after practised it on such occasions; and from my frequent successes, can heartily recommend it. The present little sacrifice of your vanity will afterwards be amply repaid. If it remains *awhile* uncertain to whom the merit belongs, someone more vain than yourself will be encouraged to claim it, and then even envy will be disposed to do you justice by plucking those assumed feathers and restoring them to their right owner" [*Autobiography, ibid.*, p. 140].

10. Brentano (*op. cit.*, pp. 125; 127, note I) takes this remark as an occasion to criticize the later discussion of "that rationalization and intensification of discipline" to which this-worldly asceticism has subjected men. That, he says, is a "rationalization" toward an "irrational" organization of life. This is in fact quite correct. Something is never "irrational" in itself but only from a particular "rational" vantage point. For the nonreligious person every religious way of organizing life is irrational; for the hedonist every ascetic organization of life is "irrational" even if it may be, measured against *its* ultimate values, a "rationalization." If this essay wishes to

make any contribution at all, may it be to unveil the many-sidedness of a concept—the "rational"—that only appears to be straightforward and linear. [1920] [see also Weber, 1946c, p. 326; 1946e, p. 293; Kalberg, 1980.]

11. In reply to Brentano's (*Die Anfänge des modernen Kapitalismus, op. cit*, pp. 150 f.) very detailed but somewhat imprecise defense of Franklin, which alleges that I have misunderstood his ethical qualities, I refer only to this statement. It should have been sufficient, in my opinion, to have rendered his defense unnecessary. [1920]

12. That even the components here (which have not yet been traced back to their religious roots)—namely, the maxim honesty is the best policy (Franklin's discussion of *credit*)—are also of Puritan origins is a theme that belongs in a somewhat different context (see the "Protestant Sects" essay below) [pp. 209–26]. Only the following observation of J. S. Rowntree (*Quakerism, Past and Present* [London: Smith, Elder and Co., 1859], pp. 95–96), to which Eduard Bernstein called my attention, needs to be repeated:

> Is it merely a *coincidence*, or is it a *consequence*, that the lofty profession of spirituality made by the Friends has gone hand in hand with shrewdness and tact in the transaction of mundane affairs? Real piety favours the success of a trader by insuring his integrity and fostering habits of prudence and forethought. [These are] important items in obtaining that standing and credit in the commercial world, which are requisite for the steady accumulation of wealth (see the "Protestant Sects" essay). [Original in English]

> "Honest as a Huguenot" was as proverbial in the seventeenth century as the respect for law of the Dutch (which Sir W. Temple admired) and, a century later, that of the English. The peoples of the European continent, in contrast, had not moved through this ethical schooling. [1920]

13. This theme is analyzed well in Albert Bielschowsky's *Goethe: sein Leben und seine Werke*, 3rd ed., vol. 2 (Munich: C. H. Beck, 1902–04), ch. 18. A related idea is articulated in regard to the development of the *scientific* "cosmos" by [Wilhelm] Windelband at the end of his *Blütezeit der deutschen Philosophie* [The Flowering Era of German Philosophy] (vol. 2 of his *Geschichte der neueren Philosophie* [Leipzig: Breitkopf und Hartel, 1899], pp. 428 ff.).

14. See Weber, "The Meaning of 'Ethical Neutrality," p. 18 (Weber 1949) [sk].

15. *Saints' Everlasting Rest, op. cit.* [ch. 4, note 62], p. 310. [The text varies slightly from Weber's quote. It reads: "Keep these things loose about thee like thy upper garments, that thou mayest lay them by whenever there is need."]

16. Translated by Parsons as "iron cage," this phrase has acquired near-mythical status in sociology. Weber elaborates upon its meaning in several passages in his "Parliament and Government in Germany" essay, which was unfortunately taken by the editors of *Economy and Society* from the corpus of his political writings and incorporated into this *analytic* treatise (see pp. 1400–03), and in "Prospects for Liberal Democracy in Tsarist Russia" (see *Weber: Selections in Translation*, ed. by W. G. Runciman [Cambridge, UK: Cambridge University Press, 1978], pp. 281–83). Parallel German expressions are translated in these passages as "housing," "shell of bondage," and "casing."

There are many reasons that speak in favor of "steel-hard casing." Not least, it is a literal rendering of the German. Had Weber wished to convey an "iron cage" to his German readership he could easily have done so by employing a commonly used phrase, *eiserner Käfig* (or even *eisenes Gefängnis* [iron prison]); see Stephen Kent, "Weber, Goethe, and the Nietzschean Allusion," *Sociological Analysis* 44 (1983): pp. 297–320 (esp. at pp. 299–300). Let us turn first to the adjective.

Weber's choice of *stahlhart* appropriately conveys (even more than *eisen*) the "hardness" of the constraining casing, as emphasized in the mechanistic images utilized in this paragraph to describe this new "powerful cosmos." This same image of hardness, however, is visible also in the "lightweight coat" metaphor above: once supple, it has now hardened into something (the power of material goods over the individual) that encases persons and cannot be thrown off. Appropriately, because ascetic Protestantism to Weber helped to call forth this cosmos, the same adjective is used to describe the Puritan merchant (see p. 125). This lineage is apparent, he argues, even though the dimension foremost for this "merchant saint"—the ethical—has today vanished and left, unforeseeably, in its wake instrumental (or "mechanical") modes of action devoid of genuine brotherhood and resistant to ethical regulation (see, again, the images above and below; see also Weber, 2009, pp. 426–30). Finally, although not directly apparent in this passage, "steel-hard" conveys a related theme crucial to Weber (as well as Marx and Simmel): the massively impersonal, coldly formal, harsh, and machine-like character of modern public sphere relationships whenever they remain uninfluenced by either traditions or values (see, e.g., the last page of "Science as a Vocation" [Weber, 2005, p. 339]).

Now let us turn to the noun. There are substantive reasons also to prefer "casing" over "cage." Almost without exception, the secondary literature has argued that *stahlhartes Gehäuse* is a phrase intended to call attention to a bleak future inevitably on the horizon. Once in place, this commentary asserts, according to Weber, a nightmare society is putatively permanent. He is then characterized as a dour prophet of doom who, heroically, performs the worthy service of analyzing in a realistic manner a civilization on its deathbed. However, through conditional terms such as "if," "perhaps," "might," "would," "potentially," and "possibly," the usages of this and similar expressions in Weber's other works (as noted above) stress that such a cosmos arises from a series of identifiable economic, religious, political, historical, etc., forces that have become juxtaposed in a unique manner rather than from an unstoppable unfolding of "bureaucratization and rationalization." In other words, if a *stahlhartes Gehäuse* does appear, it must be seen, Weber insists, as a contingent occurrence with, as other occurrences, a period of development and a period of decline (see 2009, pp. 313–430).

In my view, this interpretation conforms to the overall tenor of Weber's sociology—a body of work that attends on the one hand to configurations of forces and their unique contexts rather than to linear historical change and, on the other hand, sees change, conflict, dynamism, and upheaval nearly universally (see 1946e, 1968, and Kalberg, 1994b, pp. 71–78, 98–117, 168–77, 189–92). Of course, Weber notes that a few civilizations have been quite ossified, such as China for 1500 years and ancient Egypt. Yet their closed character did not result from an "inevitable development" or "evolutionary historical laws" (see above, pp. 97-98, 108-10). Rather, their rigidity must be understood as a consequence of an identifiable constellation of historical, political, etc., forces. (See also the paragraph below on "new prophets . . . ideas and ideals.") "Cage" implies great inflexibility and hence does not convey this contingency aspect as effectively as "casing" (which, under certain circumstances, can become less restrictive and even peeled off).

In general, in regard to *stahlhartes Gehäuse*, the commentary has vastly exaggerated the importance of this metaphorical image in Weber's works, in the process transforming him from a rigorous comparative-historical sociologist of near-universal breadth into a social philosopher of modernity (see Lawrence A. Scaff, *Fleeing the Iron Cage* [Berkeley: The University of California Press, 1989]). Notably, *stahlhartes Gehäuse*, and its equivalents, appear in Weber's works either at the end of an empirical study, where he cannot resist the temptation to offer more general speculations (this volume and this volume only), or in his political writings (see "Prospects" [1978b] and "Parliament and Government" [1968]), but only once in the body of his sociology; see above (p. 73). Not a single entry can be found in the detailed index to *E&S*, for example, nor in the comprehensive index to the German edition. On the "steel-hard cage" theme generally, see Kalberg, "The Modern World as a Monolithic Iron Cage? Utilizing Max Weber to Define the Internal Dynamics of the American Political Culture Today," in *Max Weber Studies* 1, 2 (2001): 178–97. See also Chalcraft (1994) [sk].

17. "Couldn't the old man be satisfied with his $75,000 a year and retire? No! The frontage of the store must be widened to 400 feet. Why? That beats everything, he says. Evenings, when his wife and daughter read together, he longs for bed. Sundays, in order to know when the day will be over, he checks his watch every five minutes. What a miserable existence!" In this manner the son-in-law (who had emigrated from Germany) of this prosperous dry-goods-man from a city on the Ohio River offered his judgment. Such a judgment would surely appear to the "old man" as completely incomprehensible. It could be easily dismissed as a symptom of the lack of energy of the Germans.

18. This phrase (*letzte Menschen*) is from Friedrich Nietzsche. It could as well be translated as "last people." It is normally rendered as "last men." See *Ecce Homo* (New York: Vintage Books; transl. by Walter Kaufmann, 1967), p. 330; see also *Thus Spoke Zarathustra* (New York: Penguin; transl. by R. J. Hollingdale, 1961), pp. 275–79, 296–311. The "last humans," to Nietzsche, are repulsive figures without emotion. Through their "little pleasures" they render everything small—yet they claim to have "invented happiness." Weber uses this phrase also in "Science as a Vocation." See *Weber*, 2005, p. 325 [sk].

19. Despite thorough investigations by many generations of Weber scholars, the source of this quotation has remained unidentified. Although it appears not to be directly from Nietzsche, as often believed, it is clearly formulated from the tenor of *Thus Spoke Zarathustra*. In full accord with the common usage in academic circles in his time, Weber is using the term *Geist* here to denote a thinker's "multidimensional" capacity to unify and integrate diverse ideas and concepts. This vital capacity was widely lamented in Germany as lacking among narrow specialists (*Fachmenschen*). This passage links back to the above paragraph on Goethe [sk].

20. This term is a synonym for "ascetic Protestantism" [sk].

21. This remark (which remains here unchanged) might have indicated to Brentano [*Die Anfänge des modernen Kapitalismus, op. cit.* (ch. 1, note 15)] that I never doubted the *independent* significance of humanistic rationalism. That even Humanism was not *pure* "rationalism" has been strongly emphasized recently again. See Karl Borinski, "Die Wiedergeburtsidee in den neueren Zeiten," in *Abhandlungen der Münchener Akademie der Wissenschaft* (1919). [1920] [Humanistic rationalism, which Weber is here contrasting to his subject, ascetic rationalism, refers to Humanism generally as it arose out of the Renaissance.]

22. This phrase (*geistige Kulturgüter*) refers to the entire spectrum of "products of the mind," ranging from mathematical ideas and philosophical theories to interpretations of art and history. In Weber's time, they were more frequently referred to as "cultural ideas" (*Kulturideen*) or, simply, "ideas" (*Ideen*) [sk].

23. Namely, the relationship between religious belief and economic activity [sk].

24. The university lecture by Georg von Below, *Die Ursachen der Reformation* [Munich: Oldenbourg, 1917], is not concerned with this problem, but with the Reformation in general, especially with

Luther. For the theme addressed *here*, and in particular the controversies that have tied into this study, the book from Heinrich Hermelink should be noted finally. See *Reformation und Gegenreformation* (Tübingen: Mohr, 1911). Nonetheless, this investigation primarily addresses other problems. [1920]

25. The sketch above has intentionally taken up only the relationships in which an effect on "material" life by components of a religious consciousness is actually beyond doubt. It would have been a simple matter to move beyond this theme to a formal "construction," according to which *all* that is "characteristic" of modern civilization is logically *deduced* out of Protestant rationalism. However, this sort of construction is better left to that type of dilettante who believes in the "unity" (*Einheitlichkeit*) of the "social psyche" and its reducibility to *one* formula. It should only further be noted that naturally the period of capitalist development *before* the development we have considered was *comprehensively co-*determined by Christian influences, both inhibiting and promoting. What type of influences these were belongs in a later chapter [see Weber, 2009, pp. 304–10, 370–76].

   Whether, by the way, of those further problems outlined above, one or another can be discussed in the pages of *this* journal remains, in light of its particular tasks, uncertain. [Weber was an editor of *Archiv für Sozialwissenschaft und Sozialpolitik* where *PE* was originally published.] I for one am not at all inclined to write large treatises that rest upon, as would occur if these "further problems" were to be pursued, unfamiliar (theological and historical) investigations. (I am allowing [1920] these sentences to stand unchanged [despite Weber's authorship over a decade-long period of a three-volume treatise, *Economy and Society*, and the three-volume EEWR series].)

   On the *tension* between life-ideals and reality in the "early capitalist" period before the Reformation, see now Jakob Strieder, *Studien zur Geschichte kapitalistischer Organisationformen*, vol. 2 (Munich: Duncker & Humblot, 1914). (This study stands against the earlier cited work of Franz Keller, which Sombart used [see ch. 1, note 25; ch. 2, note 32].) [1920]

26. I would have believed that this sentence and the directly preceding observations [in the text] and endnotes might well have sufficed to exclude every misunderstanding regarding what this investigation *wanted* to achieve—and I find *no occasion for any sort of supplement*. Instead of pursuing the originally intended, direct continuation of this study, in the sense of the *agenda* outlined above, I have decided to follow a different course. This conclusion was arrived at in part owing to accident (especially the publication of Ernst Troeltsch's *The Social Teachings of the Christian Churches*, which comes to conclusions on subjects I would have taken up; yet, as a nontheologian, I could not have addressed them adequately), and in part as a consequence of a decision to strip this study on the Protestant ethic of its isolation and to place it in relation to the entirety of civilizational development. In order to do so I decided at the time to write down first of all the results of several comparative studies on the *universal*-historical relationships between religion and society. [1920] [See the EEWR series and pp. 207–08.]

13. BUREAUCRACY

MAX WEBER

Weber was the first scholar to assess the impact of modern bureaucratic organizations, which he saw as an integral aspect of industrial capitalism, parallel in significance to the machine. He thought this to be the case because he understood that a successful capitalist had to make decisions based on such criteria as efficiency, calculability, predictability, and control. Bureaucracy, like the machine, was a reflection of a scientific and rational worldview. Bureaucracy was thus essential if capitalism was to expand productive capacity. In Weber's estimation, this novel form of modern bureaucracy was becoming so pervasive that it was appropriate to define the present era as the age of bureaucracy. In this selection from his magnum opus, *Economy and Society* (1921), Weber presents an ideal typical portrait of the most salient features of bureaucracy, paying particular attention to the nature and basis of authority in bureaucracy.

Modern officialdom functions in the following specific manner:

I.

There is the principle of fixed and official jurisdictional areas, which are generally ordered by rules, that is, by laws or administrative regulations.

1. The regular activities required for the purposes of the bureaucratically governed structure are distributed in a fixed way as official duties.
2. The authority to give the commands required for the discharge of these duties is distributed in a stable way and is strictly delimited by rules concerning the coercive means, physical, sacerdotal, or otherwise, which may be placed at the disposal of officials.
3. Methodical provision is made for the regular and continuous fulfilment of these duties and for the execution of the corresponding rights; only persons who have the generally regulated qualifications to serve are employed.

In public and lawful government these three elements constitute 'bureaucratic authority.' In private economic domination, they constitute bureaucratic 'management.' Bureaucracy, thus understood, is fully developed in political and ecclesiastical communities only in the modern state, and, in the private economy, only in the most advanced institutions of capitalism. Permanent and public office authority, with fixed jurisdiction, is not the historical rule but rather the exception. This is so even in large political structures such as those of the ancient Orient, the Germanic and Mongolian empires of conquest, or of many feudal structures of state. In all these cases, the ruler executes the most important measures through personal trustees, table-companions, or court-servants. Their commissions and authority are not precisely delimited and are temporarily called into being for each case.

II.

The principles of office hierarchy and of levels of graded authority mean a firmly ordered system of super- and

Reprinted from "Bureaucracy," from *From Max Weber: Essays in Sociology* by Max Weber, edited by H. H. Gerth & C. Wright Mills, translated by H. H. Gerth & C. Wright Mills. Translation copyright © 1946, 1958 by H. H. Gerth & C. Wright Mills. Used by permission of Oxford University Press, Inc. ✦

subordination in which there is a supervision of the lower offices by the higher ones. Such a system offers the governed the possibility of appealing the decision of a lower office to its higher authority, in a definitely regulated manner. With the full development of the bureaucratic type, the office hierarchy is monocratically organized. The principle of hierarchical office authority is found in all bureaucratic structures: in state and ecclesiastical structures as well as in large party organizations and private enterprises. It does not matter for the character of bureaucracy whether its authority is called `private´ or `public.´

When the principle of jurisdictional `competency´ is fully carried through, hierarchical subordination—at least in public office—does not mean that the `higher´ authority is simply authorized to take over the business of the `lower.´ Indeed, the opposite is the rule. Once established and having fulfilled its task, an office tends to continue in existence and be held by another incumbent.

III.

The management of the modern office is based upon written documents (`the files´), which are preserved in their original or draught form. There is, therefore, a staff of subaltern officials and scribes of all sorts. The body of officials actively engaged in a `public´ office, along with the respective apparatus of material implements and the files, make up a `bureau.´ In private enterprise, `the bureau´ is often called `the office.´

In principle, the modern organization of the civil service separates the bureau from the private domicile of the official and, in general, bureaucracy segregates official activity as something distinct from the sphere of private life. Public monies and equipment are divorced from the private property of the official. This condition is everywhere the product of a long development. Nowadays, it is found in public as well as in private enterprises; in the latter, the principle extends even to the leading entrepreneur. In principle, the executive office is separated from the household, business from private correspondence, and business assets from private fortunes. The more consistently the modern type of business management has been carried through the more are these separations the case. The beginnings of this process are to be found as early as the Middle Ages.

It is the peculiarity of the modern entrepreneur that he conducts himself as the `first official´ of his enterprise, in the very same way in which the ruler of a specifically modern bureaucratic state spoke of himself as `the first servant´ of the state.[1] The idea that the bureau activities of the state are intrinsically different in character from the management of private economic offices is a continental European notion and, by way of contrast, is totally foreign to the American way.

IV.

Office management, at least all specialized office management—and such management is distinctly modern—usually presupposes thorough and expert training. This increasingly holds for the modern executive and employee of private enterprises, in the same manner as it holds for the state official.

V.

When the office is fully developed, official activity demands the full working capacity of the official irrespective of the fact that his obligatory time in the bureau may be firmly delimited. In the normal case, this is only the product of a long development, in the public as well as in the private office. Formerly, in all cases, the normal state of affairs was reversed: official business was discharged as a secondary activity.

VI.

The management of the office follows general rules, which are more or less stable, more or less exhaustive, and which can be learned. Knowledge of these rules represents a special technical learning which the officials possess. It involves jurisprudence, or administrative or business management.

The reduction of modern office management to rules is deeply embedded in its very nature. The theory of modern public administration, for instance, assumes that the authority to order certain matters by decree—which has been legally granted to public authorities—does not entitle the bureau to regulate the matter by commands given for each case, but only to regulate the matter abstractly. This stands in extreme contrast to the regulation of all relationships through individual privileges and bestowals of favor, which is absolutely dominant in patrimonialism, at least in so far as such relationships are not fixed by sacred tradition.

THE POSITION OF THE OFFICIAL

All this results in the following for the internal and external position of the official:

I.

Office holding is a `vocation.´ This is shown, first, in the requirement of a firmly prescribed course of training, which demands the entire capacity for work for a long period of time, and in the generally prescribed and special examinations which are prerequisites of employment. Furthermore, the position of the official is in the nature of a duty. This determines the internal structure of his relations, in the following manner: Legally and actually, office holding is not considered a source to be exploited for rents or emoluments, as was normally the case during the Middle Ages and frequently up to the threshold of recent times. Nor is office holding considered a usual exchange of services for equivalents, as is the case with free labor contracts. Entrance into an office, including one in the private economy, is considered an acceptance of a specific obligation of faithful management in return for a secure existence. It is decisive for the specific nature of modern loyalty to an office that, in the pure type, it does not establish a relationship to a *person*, like the vassal´s or disciple´s faith in feudal or in patrimonial relations of authority. Modern loyalty is devoted to impersonal and functional purposes. Behind the functional purposes, of course, `ideas of culture-values´ usually stand. These are *ersatz* for the earthly or supramundane personal master: ideas such as `state,´ `church,´ `community,´ `party,´ or `enterprise´ are thought of as being realized in a community; they provide an ideological halo for the master.

The political official—at least in the fully developed modern state—is not considered the personal servant of a ruler. Today, the bishop, the priest, and the preacher are in fact no longer, as in early Christian times, holders of purely personal charisma. The supra-

mundane and sacred values which they offer are given to everybody who seems to be worthy of them and who asks for them. In former times, such leaders acted upon the personal command of their master; in principle, they were responsible only to him. Nowadays, in spite of the partial survival of the old theory, such religious leaders are officials in the service of a functional purpose, which in the present-day `church´ has become routinized and, in turn, ideologically hallowed.

II.

The personal position of the official is patterned in the following way:

1. Whether he is in a private office or a public bureau, the modern official always strives and usually enjoys a distinct *social esteem* as compared with the governed. His social position is guaranteed by the prescriptive rules of rank order and, for the political official, by special definitions of the criminal code against `insults of officials´ and `contempt´ of state and church authorities.

    The actual social position of the official is normally highest where, as in old civilized countries, the following conditions prevail: a strong demand for administration by trained experts; a strong and stable social differentiation, where the official predominantly derives from socially and economically privileged strata because of the social distribution of power; or where the costliness of the required training and status conventions are binding upon him. The possession of educational certificates—to be discussed elsewhere[2]—are usually linked with qualification for office. Naturally, such certificates or patents enhance the `status element´ in the social position of the official. For the rest this status factor in individual cases is explicitly and impassively acknowledged; for example, in the prescription that the acceptance or rejection of an aspirant to an official career depends upon the consent (`election´) of the members of the official body. This is the case in the German army with the officer corps. Similar phenomena, which promote this guild-like closure of officialdom, are typically found in patrimonial and, particularly, in prebendal officialdoms of the past. The desire to resurrect such phenomena in changed forms is by no menas infrequent among modern bureaucrats. For instance, they have played a role among the demands of the quite proletarian and expert officials (the *tretyj* element) during the Russian revolution.

Usually the social esteem of the officials as such is especially low where the demand for expert administration and the dominance of status conventions are weak. This is especially the case in the United States; it is often the case in new settlements by virtue of their wide fields for profit-making and the great instability of their social stratification.

2. The pure type of bureaucratic official is *appointed* by a superior authority. An official elected by the governed is not a purely bureaucratic figure. Of course, the formal existence of an election does not by itself mean that no appointment hides behind the election—in the state, especially, appointment by party chiefs. Whether or not this is the case does not depend upon legal statutes but upon the way in which the party mechanism functions. Once firmly organized, the parties can turn a formally free election into the mere acclamation of a candidate designated by the party chief. As a rule, however, a formally free election is turned into a fight, conducted according to definite rules, for votes in favor of one of two designated candidates.

In all circumstances, the designation of officials by means of an election among the governed modifies the strictness of hierarchical subordination. In principle, an official who is so elected has an autonomous position opposite the superordinate official. The elected official does not derive his position `from above´ but `from below,´ or at least not from a superior authority of the official hierarchy but from powerful party men (`bosses´), who also determine his further career. The career of the elected

official is not, or at least not primarily, dependent upon his chief in the administration. The official who is not elected but appointed by a chief normally functions more exactly, from a technical point of view, because, all other circumstances being equal, it is more likely that purely functional points of consideration and qualities will determine his selection and career. As laymen, the governed can become acquainted with the extent to which a candidate is expertly qualified for office only in terms of experience, and hence only after his service. Moreover, in every sort of selection of officials by election, parties quite naturally give decisive weight not to expert considerations but to the services a follower renders to the party boss. This holds for all kinds of procurement of officials by elections, for the designation of formally free, elected officials by party bosses when they determine the slate of candidates, or the free appointment by a chief who has himself been elected. The contrast, however, is relative: substantially similar conditions hold where legitimate monarchs and their subordinates appoint officials, except that the influence of the followings are then less controllable.

Where the demand for administration by trained experts is considerable, and the party followings have to recognize an intellectually developed, educated, and freely moving `public opinion,´ the use of unqualified officials falls back upon the party in power at the next election. Naturally, this is more likely to happen when the officials are appointed by the chief. The demand for a trained administration now exists in the United States, but in the large cities, where immigrant votes are `corraled,´ there is, of course, no educated public opinion. Therefore, popular elections of the administrative chief and also of his subordinate officials usually endanger the expert qualification of the official as well as the precise functioning of the bureaucratic mechanism. It also weakens the dependence of the officials upon the hierarchy. This holds at least for the large administrative bodies that are difficult to supervise. The superior qualification and integrity of federal judges, appointed by the President, as over against elected judges in the United States is well known, although both types of officials have been selected primarily in terms of party considerations. The great changes in American metropolitan administrations demanded by reformers have proceeded essentially from elected mayors working with an apparatus of officials who were appointed by them. These reforms have thus come about in a `Caesarist´ fashion. Viewed technically, as an organized form of authority, the efficiency of `Caesarism,´ which often grows out of democracy, rests in general upon the position of the `Caesar´ as a free trustee of the masses (of the army or of the citizenry), who is unfettered by tradition. The `Caesar´ is thus the unrestrained master of a body of highly qualified military officers and officials whom he selects freely and personally without regard to tradition or to any other considerations. This `rule of the personal genius,´ however, stands in contradiction to the formally `democratic´ principle of a universally elected officialdom.

3. Normally, the position of the official is held for life, at least in public bureaucracies; and this is increasingly the case for all similar structures. As a factual rule, *tenure for life* is presupposed, even where the giving of notice or periodic reappointment occurs. In contrast to the worker in a private enterprise, the official normally holds tenure. Legal or actual life-tenure, however, is not recognized as the official´s right to the possession of office, as was the case with many structures of authority in the past. Where legal guarantees against arbitrary dismissal or transfer are developed, they merely serve to guarantee a strictly objective discharge of specific office duties free from all personal considerations. In Germany, this is the case for all juridical and, increasingly, for all administrative officials.

Within the bureaucracy, therefore, the measure of `independence,´ legally guaranteed by tenure, is not always a source of increased status for the official whose position is thus secured. Indeed, often the reverse holds, especially in old cultures and communities that are highly differentiated. In such communities, the stricter the subordination under the arbitrary rule of the master, the more it guarantees the maintenance of the conventional seigneurial style of living for the official. Because of the very absence of these legal guarantees of tenure, the conventional esteem for the official may rise in the same way as, during the Middle Ages, the esteem of the nobility of office[3] rose at the expense of esteem for the freemen, and as the king´s judge surpassed that of the people´s judge. In Germany, the military officer or the administrative official can be removed from office at any time, or at least far more readily than the `independent judge,´ who never pays with loss of his office for even the grossest offense against the `code of honor´ or against social conventions of the salon. For this very reason, if other things are equal, in the eyes of the master stratum the judge is considered less qualified for social intercourse than are officers and administrative officials, whose greater dependence on the master is a greater guarantee of their conformity with status conventions. Of course, the average official strives for a civil-service law, which would materially secure his old age and provide increased guarantees against his arbitrary removal from office. This striving, however, has its limits. A very strong development of the `right to the office´ naturally makes it more difficult to staff them with regard to technical efficiency, for such a development decreases the career-opportunities of ambitious candidates for office. This makes for the fact that officials, on the whole, do not feel their dependency upon those at the top. This lack of a feeling of dependency, however, rests primarily upon the inclination to depend upon one´s equals rather than upon the socially inferior and governed strata. The present conservative movement among the Badenia clergy, occasioned by the anxiety of a presumably threatening separation of church and state, has been expressly determined by the desire not to be turned `from a master into a servant of the parish.´[4]

4. The official receives the regular pecuniary compensation of a normally fixed salary and the old age security provided by a pension. The salary is not measured like a wage in terms of work done, but according to `status,´ that is, according to the kind of function (the `rank´) and, in addition, possibly, according to the length of service. The relatively great security of the official´s income, as well as the rewards of social esteem, make the office a sought-after position, especially in countries which no longer provide opportunities for colonial profits. In such countries, this situation permits relatively low salaries for officials.

5. The official is set for a `career´ within the hierarchical of the public service. He moves from the lower, less important, and lower paid to the higher positions. The average official naturally desires a mechanical fixing of the conditions of promotion: if not of the offices, at least of the salary levels. He wants these conditions fixed in terms of `seniority,´ or possibly according to grades achieved in a developed system of expert examinations. Here and there, such examinations actually form a character indelebilis of the official and have lifelong effects on his career. To this is joined the desire to qualify the right to office and the increasing tendency toward status group closure and economic security. All of this makes for a tendency to consider the offices as `prebends´ of those who are qualified by educational certificates. The necessity of taking general personal and intellectual qualifications into consideration, irrespective of the often subaltern character of the educational certificate, has led to a condition in which the highest political offices, especially the positions of `ministers,´ are principally filled without reference to such certificates. . . .

NOTES

1. Frederick II of Prussia.
2. Cf. *Wirtschaft und Gesellschaft*, pp. 73 ff. and part II. (German Editor.)
3. `*Ministerialan.´*
4. Written before 1914. (German editor´s note.)

14. THE SOCIOLOGY OF CHARISMATIC AUTHORITY

MAX WEBER

In his political sociology, Weber identified three bases for legitimate authority or domination: traditional, charismatic, and legal-rational. In this selection from *Economy and Society* (1921), he discusses the characteristic features of charismatic authority. Borrowing the term from Rudolph Sohm´s depiction of religious leadership in early Christianity, he locates this type of authority in the perceived extraordinary character of the individual, who is viewed by followers as being endowed with grace. Charismatic leadership involves a profoundly emotional bond between the leader and followers, and in its purest form it is construed as being potentially disruptive, revolutionary, and anti-institutional, and thus a source of far-reaching social upheaval.

Bureaucracy, like the patriarchal system which is opposed to it in so many ways, is a structure of `the everyday´, in the sense that stability is among its most important characteristics. Patriarchal power, above all, is rooted in the supply of the normal, constantly recurring needs of everyday life and thus has its basis in the economy—indeed, in just those sections of the economy concerned with the supply of normal everyday requirements. The patriarch is the `natural leader´ in everyday life. In this respect, bureaucracy is the counterpart of patriarchalism, only expressed in more rational terms. Bureaucracy, moreover, is a permanent structure and is well adapted, with its system of rational rules, for the satisfaction of calculable long-term needs by normal methods. On the other hand, the supply of all needs which go beyond the economic requirements of everyday life is seen, the further back we go in history, to be based on a totally different principle, that of *charisma*. In other words, the `natural´ leaders in times of spiritual, physical, economic, ethical, religious or political emergency were neither appointed officials nor trained and salaried specialist `professionals´ (in the present-day sense of the word `profession´), but those who possessed specific physical and spiritual gifts which were regarded as supernatural, in the sense of not being available to everyone.

In this context, the concept of `charisma´ is being used in a completely `value-free´ way. The ability of the Nordic `Berserker´ to work himself up into an heroic trance, in which he bites his shield and his person like a rabid dog, eventually dashing off in a raving bloodlust (like the Irish hero Cuculain or Homer´s Achilles) is a form of manic attack, artificially induced, according to a theory long held about the Berserkers, by acute poisoning: in Byzantium, indeed, a number of `blond beasts´ with a talent for inducing such attacks were kept, in much the same way as war elephants had previously been. Shamanic trances, likewise, are connected with constitutional epilepsy, the possession of which, once confirmed, constitutes the charismatic qualification. Thus, both kinds of trance have nothing `uplifting´ about them to our way of thinking, any more than does the kind of `revelation´ to be found in the sacred book of the Mormons which must, at least in terms of its value, be considered a crude swindle. Such questions, however, do not concern sociology: the

Mormon leader, like the heroes and magicians already referred to, is certified as charismatically gifted by the beliefs of his followers. It was in virtue of possessing this gift or `charisma´ and (if a clear concept of god had already been formed) in virtue of the divine mission embodied therein that they practised their art and exercised their domination. This was as true of healers and prophets as of judges or leaders in war or great hunting expeditions. We have to thank Rudolph Sohm for having worked out the sociological features of this type of power-structure in relation to one particular case of great historical importance (the historical development of the power of the Christian Church in its early stages) in a way which is intellectually coherent and so, from a purely historical point of view, necessarily one-sided. But the same situation in all its essentials is repeated everywhere, even though often expressed in its purest form in the religious domain.

In contrast with all forms of bureaucratic administrative system, the charismatic structure recognises no forms or orderly procedures for appointment or dismissal, no `career´, no `advancement´, no `salary´; there is no organised training either for the bearer of charisma or his aides, no arrangements for supervision or appeal, no allocation of local areas of control or exclusive spheres of competence, and finally no standing institutions comparable to bureaucratic `governing bodies´ independent of persons and of their purely personal charisma. Rather, charisma recognises only those stipulations and limitations which come from within itself. The bearer of charisma assumes the tasks appropriate to him and requires obedience and a following in virtue of his mission. His success depends on whether he finds them. If those to whom he feels himself sent do not recognise his mission, then his claims collapse. If they do recognise him, then he remains their master for as long as he is able to retain their recognition by giving `proofs´. His right to rule, however, is not dependent on their will, as is that of an elected leader; on the contrary, it is the duty of those to whom he is sent to recognise his charismatic qualification. When the Emperor´s right to rule is said, in the Chinese theory, to depend on recognition by the people, that is no more a case of the acceptance of popular sovereignty than is the requirement of the early Christian Church that prophets should be `recognised´

by the faithful. Rather, it is a sign of the charismatic character of the monarch´s office, based as it is on personal qualification and proof. Charisma may be, and obviously often is, qualitatively specialised, in which case qualitative limitations are imposed on the mission and power of its bearer by the internal character of his charisma, not by external regulation. The meaning and content of the mission may be (and normally are) directed to a human group which is defined geographically, ethnically, socially, politically, occupationally, or in some other way; its limits are then set by the boundaries of that group.

Charismatic domination is diametrically opposed to bureaucratic in all respects, and hence in its economic sub-structure. Bureaucracy depends on constancy of income, and so *a fortiori* on a money economy and money taxation, while charisma lives in the world, but is certainly not of it. The true meaning of this remark needs to be understood. Frequently there is a completely conscious sense of horror at the possession of money and at money incomes as such, as in the case of St. Francis and many like him. But of course this is not the general rule. The domination exercised even by a gifted pirate may be `charismatic´ in the value-free sense of that term used here, and charismatic political heroes seek booty, above all in the form of money. But the important point is that charisma rejects as dishonourable all rational planning in the acquisition of money, and in general all rational forms of economy. In this it is sharply contrasted also with all `patriarchal´ structures, which are based on the orderly foundation of the `household´. In its `pure´ form, charisma is not a private source of income for its bearer, either in the sense of being economically exploited in the fashion of an exchange of services or in the other sense of being salaried; equally, it is without any organised levying of tribute to provide for the material needs of the mission. Rather, if its mission is a peaceful one, its requirements are economically provided either by individual patrons or by the donations, contributions or other voluntary services given by those to whom it is directed. Alternatively, in the case of charismatic war heroes, booty furnishes both one of the goals of the mission and a means of supplying its material needs. `Pure´ charisma is opposed to all forms of regulated economy—in contrast with all kinds of `patriarchal´ domination in the sense of that term used here: it is a, indeed *the*, anti-economic force, even (indeed precisely) when it seeks to obtain possession of material goods, as in the case of the charismatic war hero. This is possible because charisma, by its very essence, is not a permanent `institutional´ structure, but rather, when it is functioning in its `pure´ form, the exact opposite. Those who possess charisma—not only the master himself but his disciples and followers—must, in order to fulfil their mission, keep themselves free of all worldly ties, free from everyday occupations as well as from everyday family responsibilities. The prohibition against accepting payment for ecclesiastical office laid down in the statutes of the Jesuit order, the prohibition against owning property imposed on members of an order, or even, as in the original rule of the Franciscans, on the order itself, the rule of celibacy for priests and members of knightly orders, the actual celibacy of many bearers of prophetic or artistic charisma—all express the necessary `alienation from the world´ of those who have a share (`κλῆρος´) in charisma. The economic conditions of having such a share may, however, seem, from the outside to be opposed to each other, depending on the kind of charisma and the way of life which expresses its meaning (religious or artistic, for example). When modern charismatic movements of artistic origin suggest `those of independent means´ (or, putting it in plainer language, *rentiers*) as the persons normally best qualified to be followers of someone with a charismatic mission, this is just as logical as was the vow of poverty taken by the medieval monastic orders, which had precisely the opposite economic implications.

The continued existence of charismatic authority is, by its very nature, characteristically *unstable:* the bearer may lose his charisma, feel himself, like Jesus on the cross, to be `abandoned by his God´, and show himself to his followers as `bereft of his power´, and then his mission is dead, and his followers must hopefully await and search out a new charismatic leader. He himself, however, is abandoned by his following, for pure charisma recognises no `legitimacy´ other than that conferred by personal power, which must be constantly re-confirmed. The charismatic hero does not derive his authority from ordinances and statutes, as if it were an official `competence´, nor from customary usage or feudal fealty, as with patrimonial power: rather, he acquires it and retains it only by proving his

powers in real life. He must perform miracles if he wants to be a prophet, acts of heroism if he wants to be a leader in war. Above all, however, his divine mission must `prove´ itself in that those who entrust themselves to him must prosper. If they do not, then he is obviously not the master sent by the gods. This very serious conception of genuine charisma obviously stands in stark contrast with the comfortable pretensions of the modern theory of the `divine right of kings´, with its references to the `inscrutable´ decrees of God, `to whom alone the monarch is answerable´: the genuinely charismatic leader, by contrast, is answerable rather to his subjects. That is, it is for that reason and that reason alone that precisely he personally is the genuine master willed by God.

Someone who holds power in a way which still has important residual charismatic elements, as the Chinese monarchs did (at least in theory), will blame himself if his administration does not succeed in exorcising some calamity which has befallen his subjects, whether a flood or a defeat in war: openly, before the whole people, he will condemn his own sins and shortcomings, as we have seen even in the last few decades. If even this penitence does not appease the gods, then he resigns himself to dismissal and death, which is often the method of atonement. This is the very specific meaning of the proposition found, for instance, in Mencius that the voice of the people is `the voice of God´ (according to Mencius, this is the *only* way in which God speaks!): once he is no longer recognised by the people, the master becomes (as is expressly said) a simple private citizen, and, if he aspires to anything more, he is a usurper and deserves to be punished. The situation expressed in these phrases, with their extremely revolutionary resonance, can also be found, in forms which carry no hint of pathos, in primitive societies, where authority has the charismatic character to be found in almost all primitive authority, with the exception of domestic power in the strictest sense, and the chief is often simply deserted if success deserts him.

The purely *de facto* `recognition´, whether active or passive, of his personal mission by the subjects, on which the power of the charismatic lord rests, has its source in submission by faith to the extraordinary and unheard-of, to that which does not conform to any rule or tradition and is therefore regarded as divine—a submission born from distress and enthusiasm. In genuine charismatic domination, therefore, there are no abstract legal propositions and regulations and no `formalised´ legal judgments. `Objective´ law, in such a case, flows from concrete and intensely personal experience of heavenly grace and a semi-divine heroic stature: it means the rejection of the bonds of external organisation in favour of nothing but the ecstasy of the true prophet and hero. It thus leads to a revolutionary revaluation of everything and a sovereign break with all traditional or rational norms: `it is written, but I say unto you´. The specifically charismatic method of settling disputes is a revelation through the prophet or oracle, or the `Solomonic´ judgments of a charismatically qualified sage based on evaluations which, while extremely concrete and individual, yet claim absolute validity. This is the true home of `Kadi-justice´, in the proverbial rather than the historical sense of that word. For, as an actual historical phenomenon, the judgments of the Islamic *Kadi* were bound up with sacred traditions and their often extremely formalistic interpretation: they amounted in some situations, to be sure, to specific, rule-free evaluations of the individual case, but only where these sources of knowledge had failed. Genuinely charismatic justice is always rule-free in this sense: in its pure form it is completely opposed to all the bonds of formalism and tradition and is as free in its attitude to the sanctity of tradition as to rationalistic deductions from abstract concepts. There will be no discussion here of the relation of the reference to `*aequum et bonum*´ in Roman Law and the original sense of the term `equity´ in English law to charismatic justice in general and the theocratic Kadi-justice of Islam in particular. However, both are products in part of a system of justice which is already highly rationalised and in part of the abstract concepts of Natural Law: the phrase `*ex fide bona*´ contains in any case an allusion to good commercial `morality´ and so has as little to do with genuinely irrational justice as does our own `free judicial opinion´. To be sure, all forms of trial by ordeal are derived from charismatic justice. But to the extent that they substitute for the personal authority of a bearer of charisma a rule-bound mechanism for the formal determination of the divine will, they already belong to the domain of that `bringing down to earth´ of charisma which is shortly to be discussed.

As we saw, bureaucratic rationalisation can also be, and often has been, a revolutionary force of the first order in its relation to tradition. But its revolution is carried out by *technical* means, basically `from the outside´ (as is especially true of all economic reorganisation); first it revolutionises things and organisations, and then, in consequence, it changes people, in the sense that it alters the conditions to which they must adapt and in some cases increases their chances of adapting to the external world by rational determination of means and ends. The power of charisma, by contrast, depends on beliefs in revelation and heroism, on emotional convictions about the importance and value of a religious, ethical, artistic, scientific, political or other manifestation, on heroism, whether ascetic or military, or judicial wisdom or magical or other favours. Such belief revolutionises men `from within´ and seeks to shape things and organisations in accordance with its revolutionary will. This contrast must, to be sure, be rightly understood. For all the vast differences in the areas in which they operate, the psychological origins of ideas are essentially the same, whether they are religious, artistic, ethical, scientific or of any other kind: this is especially true of the organising ideas of social and political life. Only a purely subjective, `time-serving´ evaluation could attribute one sort of idea to `understanding´ and another to `intuition´ (or whatever other pair of terms one might care to use): the mathematical `imagination´ of a Weierstrass is `intuition´ in exactly the same sense as that of any artist, prophet or, for that matter, of any demagogue: that is not where the difference lies.[1] If we are to understand the true meaning of `rationalism´, we must emphasise that the difference does not lie in general in the person or in the inner `experiences´ of the creator of the ideas or the `work´, but in the manner in which it is inwardly `appropriated´ or `experienced´ by those whom he rules or leads. We have already seen that, in the process of rationalisation, the great majority of those who are led merely appropriate the external technical consequences which are of practical importance to their interests, or else adapt themselves to them (in the same way that we `learn´ our multiplication tables or as all too many jurists learn the techniques of the law): the actual content of their creator´s ideas remains irrelevant to them. This is the meaning of the assertion that rationalisation and rational organisation revolutionise `from the outside´, whereas charisma, wherever its characteristic influence is felt, on the contrary exerts its revolutionary power from within, by producing a fundamental change of heart (`metanoia´) in the ruled. The bureaucratic form of organisation merely replaces the belief in the holiness of what has always been—the traditional standards—with submission to deliberately created rules: everyone knows that anyone with sufficient power can always replace these rules with others, equally deliberately created, and so that they are not in any sense `sacred´. By contrast, charisma, in its highest forms, bursts the bonds of rules and tradition in general and overturns all ideas of the sacred. Instead of the pious following of time-hallowed custom, it enforces inner subjection to something which has never before existed, is absolutely unique and is therefore considered divine. It is in this purely empirical and value-free sense the characteristically `creative´ revolutionary force in history.

Although both charismatic and patriarchal power rest on personal submission to `natural leaders´ and personal exercise of authority by them (in contrast with the `appointed´ leaders of bureaucratic systems), the submission and the authority take very different forms in the two cases. The patriarch, like the bureaucratic official, holds his authority in virtue of a certain established order: the difference between this order and the laws and regulations of the bureaucracy is that it is not deliberately created by men but has been accepted as inviolably valid from time immemorial. The bearer of charisma holds his authority in virtue of a mission held to be incarnate in his person: this mission need not always or necessarily be of a revolutionary nature, dedicated to the subversion of all hierarchies of value and the overthrow of existing morality, law and tradition, but it certainly has been in its highest forms. However unstable the existence of patriarchal power may be in the case of any particular individual, it is nevertheless the structure of social domination which is appropriate to the demands of everyday life and which, like everyday life itself, continues to function without regard to changes in the individual holder of power or in the environment. In these respects it may be contrasted with the charismatic structure which is born of extraordinary situations of emergency and enthusiasm. Both kinds of structure may, in themselves, be suited to any sphere of life: many of the old German armies, for instance, fought patriarchally, divided into families each under the leadership of its head. The ancient colonising armies of Eastern monarchs and the contingents of small farmers in the Frankish army, marching under the leadership of their `seniores´, were patrimonially organised. The religious function of the head of the household and religious worship within the household persist alongside the official community cult on the one hand and the great movements of charismatic prophecy, which in the nature of the case are almost always revolutionary, on the other. Along with the peacetime leader who deals with the everyday economic business of the community, and the popular levy in times of war involving the whole community, there is found nevertheless, among the Germans as well as the Indians, the charismatic war hero, who takes the field with his volunteer force of followers; even in official national wars the normal peacetime authorities are very often replaced by the warprince, proclaimed as `Herzog´ on an *ad hoc* basis because he has proved himself as a hero in such adventures.

In the political sphere, as in the religious, it is traditional, customary, everyday needs which are served by the patriarchal structure, resting as it does on habit, respect for tradition, piety towards elders and ancestors and bonds of personal loyalty, in contrast with the revolutionary role of charisma. This holds likewise in the economic sphere. The economy, as an organised permanent system of transactions for the purpose of planned provision for the satisfaction of material needs, is the specific home of the patriarchal structure of domination, and of the bureaucratic structure as it becomes increasingly rationalised to the level of the `enterprise´. Nevertheless, even here there may be room for charisma. In primitive societies, charismatic features are often found in the organisation of hunting, which was at that time an important branch of the provision of material needs, even if it became less important as material culture increased: hunting was organised in a similar way to war, and even at a later stage was long treated in much the same way as war (even up to the time of the Assyrian royal inscriptions). But even in specifically capitalist economies the antagonism between charisma and the everyday can be found, except that here it is not charisma and `household´, but charisma and `enterprise´ which are opposed. When

Henry Villard, with the aim of pulling off a coup on the stock exchange involving the shares of the Northern Pacific Railroad, arranged the famous `blind pool´, asked the public, without stating his purpose, for fifty million pounds for an undertaking which he refused to specify any further, and got the loan without security on the basis of his reputation, his action was an example of grandiose booty-capitalism and economic brigandage which, like other similar examples, was fundamentally different in its whole structure and spirit from the rational management of a normal large capitalist `enterprise´, while on the other hand resembling the large financial undertakings and projects for colonial exploitation, or the `occasional trade´ combined with piracy and slave-hunting expeditions, which have been known since earliest times. One can only understand the double nature of what one might call `the spirit of capitalism´, and equally the specific features of the modern, professionalised, bureaucratic form of everyday capitalism if one learns to make the conceptual distinction between these two structural elements, which are thoroughly entangled with one another, but are in the last analysis distinct.

Although a `purely´ charismatic authority in the sense of the word used here cannot, to the extent that it preserves its purity, be understood as an `organisation´ in the usual sense of an ordering of men and things according to the principle of ends and means, nevertheless its existence implies, not an amorphous, unstructured condition, but a well-defined form of social structure with personal organs and a suitable apparatus for providing services and material goods for the mission of the bearer of charisma. The leader´s personal aides and, among them, a certain kind of charismatic aristocracy represent a narrower group of followers within the group, formed on principles of discipleship and personal loyalty and chosen according to personal charismatic qualification. The provision of material goods, though in theory voluntary, non-statutory and fluctuating, is regarded as a bounden duty of the charismatic ruler´s subjects to an extent sufficient to cover what is required, and such services are offered according to need and capacity. The more the purity of the charismatic structure is maintained, the less the followers or disciples receive their material means of support or social position in the form of prebends, stipends, or any form of remuneration or salary, or in the form of titles or places in an ordered hierarchy. As far as material needs are concerned, to the extent that individuals have no other means of support, the master, in a community under authoritarian leadership, shares with his followers, without any form of deduction or contract, the wealth which flows in, according to circumstances, in the form of donations, booty or bequests; in some cases, therefore, they have rights of commensality and claims to equipment and donations which he bestows on them. As for non-material needs, they have a right to share in the social, political and religious esteem and honour which is paid to the master himself. Every deviation from this sullies the purity of the charismatic structure and marks a step towards other structural forms.

Together with the household community (though distinct from it), charisma is thus the second great historical example of communism, if that term is taken to mean a lack of `calculation´ in the *consumption* of goods, rather than the rational organisation of the *production* of goods for some kind of common benefit (which might be called `socialism´). Every form of `communism´ in this sense which is known to history finds its true home either in traditional or patriarchal societies (household communism)—the only form in which it has been or is now a phenomenon of the everyday—or amongst charismatic modes of thought far removed from the everyday: in the latter case, when complete, it is either the camp-communism of the robber band or the love-communism of the monastery in all its varied forms and its tendency to degenerate into mere `charity´ or alms-giving. Camp-communism (in varying degrees of purity) can be found in charismatic warrior societies in all periods, from the pirate-state of the Ligurian islands to the organisation of Islam under the Caliph Omar and the warrior orders of Christendom and of Japanese Buddhism. Love-communism in one form or another is found at the origins of all religions, and lives on amongst the professional followers of the god, or monks; it is also to be found in the many pietistic sects (Labadie, for instance) and other extremist religious communities. Both the genuine heroic disposition and genuine sanctity, as it seems to their true advocates, can only be preserved by maintenance of the communistic basis and absence of the urge towards individual private property. In this they are right: charisma is a force which is essentially outside the everyday and so necessarily outside economics. It is immediately threatened in its innermost being when the economic interests of everyday life prevail, as always tends to happen: the first stage in its decline is the `prebend´, the `allowance´ granted in place of the earlier communistic mode of provision from the common store. Every possible means is used by the proponents of true charisma to set limits to this decline. All specifically warrior states—Sparta is a typical example—retained remnants of charismatic communism and sought (no less than religious orders) to protect the heroes from the `temptations´ presented by a concern for possessions, rational industry, and family cares. The adjustments achieved between these remnants of the older charismatic principles and individual economic interests, which enter with the introduction of prebends and are constantly hammering at the doors, take the most varied forms. In all cases, however, the limitless freedom to found families and acquire wealth which is finally given marks the end of the domination of true charisma. It is only the shared dangers of the military camp or the loving disposition of disciples who are withdrawn from the world which can hold communism together, and it is only communism in its turn which can ensure the purity of charisma against the interests of the everyday.

All charisma, however, in every hour of its existence finds itself on this road, from a passionate life in which there is no place for the economic to slow suffocation under the weight of material interests, and with every hour of its existence it moves further along it.

NOTE

1. And incidentally they correspond completely with each other also in the `value-sphere´, which does not concern us here, in that they all—even artistic intuition—in order to make themselves objective and so in general to prove their reality, imply `grasping´, or, if it is preferred, being `grasped´ by the claims of the `work´, and not a subjective `feeling´ or `experience´ like any other.

15. CLASS, STATUS, PARTY

MAX WEBER

Albert Salomon once wrote that Weber's sociology constitutes "a long and intense dialogue with the ghost of Marx." While this is something of an overstatement, Weber was in significant ways responding to Marxist theory. In this passage from *Economy and Society* (1921), Weber articulates at the conceptual level the basis of a critique of the economic determinism that he thought infected Marx's work. He identifies three discrete but interrelated realms: the economic, where class is the key concept; the social order (or culture), where status is the central notion; and power (or the political), where the party is the key associational mode. Weber was actually in agreement with Marx insofar as he believed that the economy has a particularly determinative impact on the social order and power, but he sought to correct what he thought was Marx's tendency to deny a relative autonomy to culture and politics.

ECONOMICALLY DETERMINED POWER AND THE SOCIAL ORDER

Law exists when there is a probability that an order will be upheld by a specific staff of men who will use physical or psychical compulsion with the intention of obtaining conformity with the order, or of inflicting sanctions for infringement of it.[1] The structure of every legal order directly influences the distribution of power, economic or otherwise, within its respective community. This is true of all legal orders and not only that of the state. In general, we understand by `power´ the chance of a man or of a number of men to realize their own will in a communal action even against the resistance of others who are participating in the action.

`Economically conditioned´ power is not, of course, identical with `power´ as such. On the contrary, the emergence of economic power may be the consequence of power existing on other grounds. Man does not strive for power only in order to enrich himself economically. Power, including economic power, may be valued `for its own sake.´ Very frequently the striving for power is also conditioned by the social `honor´ it entails. Not all power, however, entails social honor: The typical American boss, as well as the typical big speculator, deliberately relinquishes social honor. Quite generally, `mere economic´ power, and especially `naked´ money power, is by no means a recognized basis of social honor. Nor is power the only basis of social honor. Indeed, social honor, or prestige, may even be the basis of political or economic power, and very frequently has been. Power, as well as honor, may be guaranteed by the legal order, but, at least normally, it is not their primary source. The legal order is rather an additional factor that enhances the chance to hold power or honor; but it cannot always secure them.

The way in which social honor is distributed in a community between typical groups participating in this distribution we may call the `social order.´ The social order and the economic order are, of course, similarly related to the `legal order.´ However, the social and the economic order are not identical. The economic order is for us merely the way in which economic goods and services are distributed and used. The social order is of course conditioned by the economic order to a high degree, and in its turn reacts upon it.

Now: `classes,´ `status groups,´ and `parties´ are phenomena of the distribution of power within a community.

DETERMINATION OF CLASS-SITUATION BY MARKET-SITUATION

In our terminology, `classes´ are not communities; they merely represent possible, and frequent, bases for communal action. We may speak of a `class´ when (1) a number of people have in common a specific causal component of their life chances, in so far as (2) this component is represented exclusively by economic interests in the possession of goods and opportunities for income, and (3) is represented under the conditions of the commodity or labor markets. [These points refer to `class situation,´ which we may express more briefly as the typical chance for a supply of goods, external living conditions, and personal life experiences, in so far as this chance is determined by the amount and kind of power, or lack of such, to dispose of goods or skills for the sake of income in a given economic order. The term `class´ refers to any group of people that is found in the same class situation.]

It is the most elemental economic fact that the way in which the disposition over material property is distributed among a plurality of people, meeting competitively in the market for the purpose of exchange, in itself creates specific life chances. According to the law of marginal utility this mode of distribution excludes the non-owners from competing for highly valued goods; it favors the owners and, in fact, gives to them a monopoly to acquire such goods. Other things being equal, this mode of distribution monopolizes the opportunities for profitable deals for all those who, provided with goods, do not necessarily have to exchange them. It increases, at least generally, their power in price wars with those who, being propertyless, have nothing to offer but their services in native form or goods in a form constituted through their own labor, and who above all are compelled to get rid of these products in order barely to subsist. This mode of distribution gives to the propertied a monopoly on the possibility of transferring property from the sphere of use as a `fortune,´ to the sphere of `capital goods;´ that is, it gives them the

entrepreneurial function and all chances to share directly or indirectly in returns on capital. All this holds true within the area in which pure market conditions prevail. `Property´ and `lack of property´ are, therefore, the basic categories of all class situations. It does not matter whether these two categories become effective in price wars or in competitive struggles.

Within these categories, however, class situations are further differentiated: on the one hand, according to the kind of property that is usable for returns; and, on the other hand, according to the kind of services that can be offered in the market. Ownership of domestic buildings; productive establishments; warehouses; stores; agriculturally usable land, large and small holdings—quantitative differences with possibly qualitative consequences—; ownership of mines; cattle; men (slaves); disposition over mobile instruments of production, or capital goods of all sorts, especially money or objects that can be exchanged for money easily and at any time; disposition over products of one´s own labor or of others´ labor differing according to their various distances from consumability; disposition over transferable monopolies of any kind—all these distinctions differentiate the class situations of the propertied just as does the `meaning´ which they can and do give to the utilization of property, especially to property which has money equivalence. Accordingly, the propertied, for instance, may belong to the class of rentiers or to the class of entrepreneurs.

Those who have no property but who offer services are differentiated just as much according to their kinds of services as according to the way in which they make use of these services, in a continuous or discontinuous relation to a recipient. But always this is the generic connotation of the concept of class: that the kind of chance in the *market* is the decisive moment which presents a common condition for the individual´s fate. `Class situation´ is, in this sense, ultimately `market situation.´ The effect of naked possession *per se*, which among cattle breeders gives the non-owning slave or serf into the power of the cattle owner, is only a forerunner of real `class´ formation. However, in the cattle loan and in the naked severity of the law of debts in such communities, for the first time mere `possession´ as such emerges as decisive for the fate of the individual. This is very much in contrast to the agricultural communities based on labor. The creditor-debtor relation becomes the basis of `class situations´ only in those cities where a `credit market,´ however primitive, with rates of interest increasing according to the extent of dearth and a factual monopolization of credits, is developed by a plutocracy. Therewith `class struggles´ begin.

Those men whose fate is not determined by the chance of using goods or services for themselves on the market, e.g., slaves, are not, however, a `class´ in the technical sense of the term. They are, rather, a `status group.´

COMMUNAL ACTION FLOWING FROM CLASS INTEREST

According to our terminology, the factor that creates `class´ is unambiguously economic interest, and indeed, only those interests involved in the existence of the `market.´ Nevertheless, the concept of `class-interest´ is an ambiguous one: even as an empirical concept it is ambiguous as soon as one understands by it something other than the factual direction of interests following with a certain probability from the class situation for a certain `average´ of those people subjected to the class situation. The class situation and other circumstances remaining the same, the direction in which the individual worker, for instance, is likely to pursue his interests may vary widely, according to whether he is constitutionally qualified for the task at hand to a high, to an average, or to a low degree. In the same way, the direction of interests may vary according to whether or not a *communal* action of a larger or smaller portion of those commonly affected by the `class situation,´ or even an association among them, e.g., a `trade union,´ has grown out of the class situation from which the individual may or may not expect promising results. [Communal action refers to that action which is oriented to the feeling of the actors that they belong together. Societal action, on the other hand, is oriented to a rationally motivated adjustment of interests.] The rise of societal or even of communal action from a common class situation is by no means a universal phenomenon.

The class situation may be restricted in its effects to the generation of essentially *similar* reactions, that is to say, within our terminology, of `mass actions.´ However, it may not have even this result. Furthermore, often merely an amorphous communal action emerges.

For example, the `murmuring´ of the workers known in ancient oriental ethics: the moral disapproval of the work-master´s conduct, which in its practical significance was probably equivalent to an increasingly typical phenomenon of precisely the latest industrial development, namely, the `slow down´ (the deliberate limiting of work effort) of laborers by virtue of tacit agreement. The degree in which `communal action´ and possibly `societal action,´ emerges from the `mass actions´ of the members of a class is linked to general cultural conditions, especially to those of an intellectual sort. It is also linked to the extent of the contrasts that have already evolved, and is especially linked to the *transparency* of the connections between the causes and the consequences of the `class situation.´ For however different life chances may be, this fact in itself, according to all experience, by no means gives birth to `class action´ (communal action by the members of a class). The fact of being conditioned and the results of the class situation must be distinctly recognizable. For only then the contrast of life chances can be felt not as an absolutely given fact to be accepted, but as a resultant from either (1) the given distribution of property, or (2) the structure of the concrete economic order. It is only then that people may react against the class structure not only through acts of an intermittent and irrational protest, but in the form of rational association. There have been `class situations´ of the first category (1), of a specifically naked and transparent sort, in the urban centers of Antiquity and during the Middle Ages; especially then, when great fortunes were accumulated by factually monopolized trading in industrial products of these localities or in foodstuffs. Furthermore, under certain circumstances, in the rural economy of the most diverse periods, when agriculture was increasingly exploited in a profit-making manner. The most important historical example of the second category (2) is the class situation of the modern `proletariat.´

TYPES OF CLASS STRUGGLE

Thus every class may be the carrier of any one of the possibly innumerable forms of `class action,´ but this is not necessarily so. In any case, a class does not in itself constitute a community. To treat `class´ conceptually as having the same value as `community´ leads to distortion. That men in the same class situation regularly react in mass actions to such tangible situations as economic ones in the direction of those interests that are most adequate to their average number is an important and after all simple fact for the understanding of historical events. Above all, this fact must not lead to that kind of pseudo-scientific operation with the concepts of `class` and `class interests` so frequently found these days, and which has found its most classic expression in the statement of a talented author, that the individual may be in error concerning his interests but that the `class` is `infallible` about its interests. Yet, if classes as such are not communities, nevertheless class situations emerge only on the basis of communalization. The communal action that brings forth class situations, however, is not basically action between members of the identical class; it is an action between members of different classes. Communal actions that directly determine the class situation of the worker and the entrepreneur are: the labor market, the commodities market, and the capitalistic enterprise. But, in its turn, the existence of a capitalistic enterprise presupposes that a very specific communal action exists and that it is specifically structured to protect the possession of goods *per se*, and especially the power of individuals to dispose, in principle freely, over the means of production. The existence of a capitalistic enterprise is preconditioned by a specific kind of `legal order.` Each kind of class situation, and above all when it rests upon the power of property *per se*, will become most clearly efficacious when all other determinants of reciprocal relations are, as far as possible, eliminated in their significance. It is in this way that the utilization of the power of property in the market obtains its most sovereign importance.

Now `status groups` hinder the strict carrying through of the sheer market principle. In the present context they are of interest to us only from this one point of view. Before we briefly consider them, note that not much of a general nature can be said about the more specific kinds of antagonism between `classes` (in our meaning of the term). The great shift, which has been going on continuously in the past, and up to our times, may be summarized, although at the cost of some precision: the struggle in which class situations are effective has progressively shifted from consumption credit toward, first, competitive struggles in the commodity

market and, then, toward price wars on the labor market. The `class struggles` of antiquity—to the extent that they were genuine class struggles and not struggles between status groups—were initially carried on by indebted peasants, and perhaps also by artisans threatened by debt bondage and struggling against urban creditors. For debt bondage is the normal result of the differentiation of wealth in commercial cities, especially in seaport cities. A similar situation has existed among cattle breeders. Debt relationships as such produced class action up to the time of Cataline. Along with this, and with an increase in provision of grain for the city by transporting it from the outside, the struggle over the means of sustenance emerged. It centered in the first place around the provision of bread and the determination of the price of bread. It lasted throughout antiquity and the entire Middle Ages. The propertyless as such flocked together against those who actually and supposedly were interested in the dearth of bread. This fight spread until it involved all those commodities essential to the way of life and to handicraft production. There were only incipient discussions of wage disputes in antiquity and in the Middle Ages. But they have been slowly increasing up into modern times. In the earlier periods they were completely secondary to slave rebellions as well as to fights in the commodity market.

The propertyless of antiquity and of the Middle Ages protested against monopolies, pre-emption, forestalling, and the withholding of goods from the market in order to raise prices. Today the central issue is the determination of the price of labor.

This transition is represented by the fight for access to the market and for the determination of the price of products. Such fights went on between merchants and workers in the putting-out system of domestic handicraft during the transition to modern times. Since it is quite a general phenomenon we must mention here that the class antagonisms that are conditioned through the market situation are usually most bitter between those who actually and directly participate as opponents in price wars. It is not the rentier, the shareholder, and the banker who suffer the ill will of the worker, but almost exclusively the manufacturer and the business executives who are the direct opponents of workers in price wars. This is so in spite of the fact that it is precisely the cash boxes of the rentier, the share-holder, and the banker into which the more or less `unearned´ gains flow, rather than into the pockets of the manufacturers or of the business executives. This simple state of affairs has very frequently been decisive for the role the class situation has played in the formation of political parties. For example, it has made possible the varieties of patriarchal socialism and the frequent attempts—formerly, at least—of threatened status groups to form alliances with the proletariat against the `bourgeoisie.´

STATUS HONOR

In contrast to classes, *status groups* are normally communities. They are, however, often of an amorphous kind. In contrast to the purely economically determined `class situation´ we wish to designate as `status situation´ every typical component of the life fate of men that is determined by a specific, positive or negative, social estimation of *honor*. This honor may be connected with any quality shared by a plurality, and, of course, it can be knit to a class situation: class distinctions are linked in the most varied ways with status distinctions. Property as such is not always recognized as a status qualification, but in the long run it is, and with extraordinary regularity. In the subsistence economy of the organized neighborhood, very often the richest man is simply the chieftain. However, this often means only an honorific preference. For example, in the so-called pure modern `democracy,´ that is, one devoid of any expressly ordered status privileges for individuals, it may be that only the families coming under approximately the same tax class dance with one another. This example is reported of certain smaller Swiss cities. But status honor need not necessarily be linked with a `class situation.´ On the contrary, it normally stands in sharp opposition to the pretensions of sheer property.

Both propertied and propertyless people can belong to the same status group, and frequently they do with very tangible consequences. This `equality´ of social esteem may, however, in the long run become quite precarious. The `equality´ of status among the American `gentlemen,´ for instance, is expressed by the fact that outside the subordination determined by the different functions of `business,´ it would be considered strictly repugnant—wherever the old tradition still prevails—if even the richest `chief,´ while playing billiards or cards in his club in the evening, would not treat his `clerk´ as in every sense fully his equal in birthright. It would be repugnant if the American `chief´ would bestow upon his `clerk´ the condescending `benevolence´ marking a distinction of `position,´ which the German chief can never dissever from his attitude. This is one of the most important reasons why in America the German `clubby-ness´ has never been able to attain the attraction that the American clubs have. . . .

PARTIES

Whereas the genuine place of `classes´ is within the economic order, the place of `status groups´ is within the social order, that is, within the sphere of the distribution of `honor.´ From within these spheres, classes and status groups influence one another and they influence the legal order and are in turn influenced by it. But `parties´ live in a house of `power.´

Their action is oriented toward the acquisition of social `power,´ that is to say, toward influencing a communal action no matter what its content may be. In principle, parties may exist in a social `club´ as well as in a `state.´ As over against the actions of classes and status groups, for which this is not necessarily the case, the communal actions of `parties´ always mean a societalization. For party actions are always directed toward a goal which is striven for in planned manner. This goal may be a `cause´ (the party may aim at realizing a program for ideal or material purposes), or the goal may be `personal´ (sinecures, power, and from these, honor for the leader and the followers of the party). Usually the party action aims at all these simultaneously. Parties are, therefore, only possible within communities that are societalized, that is, which have some rational order and a staff of persons available who are ready to enforce it. For parties aim precisely at influencing this staff, and if possible, to recruit it from party followers.

In any individual case, parties may represent interests determined through `class situation´ or `status situation,´ and they may recruit their following respectively from one or the other. But they need be neither purely `class´ nor purely `status´ parties. In most cases they are partly class parties and partly status parties, but sometimes they are neither. They may represent ephemeral or enduring structures. Their means of attaining power may be quite varied, ranging from naked violence of any sort to canvassing for votes with coarse or subtle means: money, social influence, the force of speech, suggestion, clumsy hoax, and so on to the rougher or more artful tactics of obstruction in parliamentary bodies.

The sociological structure of parties differs in a basic way according to the kind of communal action which they struggle to influence. Parties also differ according to whether or not the community is stratified by status or by classes. Above all else, they vary according to the structure of domination within the community. For their leaders normally deal with the conquest of a community. They are, in the general concept which is maintained here, not only products of specially modern forms of domination. We shall also designate as parties the ancient and medieval `parties,´ despite the fact that their structure differs basically from the structure of modern parties. By virtue of these structural differences of domination it is impossible to say anything about the structure of parties without discussing the structural forms of social domination *per se.* Parties, which are always structures struggling for domination, are very frequently organized in a very strict `authoritarian´ fashion....

Concerning `classes,´ `status groups,´ and `parties,´ it must be said in general that they necessarily presuppose a comprehensive societalization, and especially a political framework of communal action, within which they operate. This does not mean that parties would be confined by the frontiers of any individual political community. On the contrary, at all times it has been the order of the day that the societalization (even when it aims at the use of military force in common) reaches beyond the frontiers of politics. This has been the case in the solidarity of interests among the Oligarchs and among the democrats in Hellas, among the Guelfs and among Ghibellines in the Middle Ages, and within the Calvinist party during the period of religious struggles. It has been the case up to the solidarity of the landlords (International Congress of Agrarian Landlords), and has continued among princes (Holy Alliance, Karlsbad Decrees), socialist workers, conservatives (the longing of Prussian conservatives for Russian intervention in 1850). But their aim is not necessarily the establishment of new international political, i.e. *territorial*, dominion. In the main they aim to influence the existing dominion.[2]

NOTES

1. *Wirtschaft und Gesellschaft*, part III, chap. 4, pp. 631–40. The first sentence in paragraph one and the several definitions in this chapter which are in brackets do not appear in the original text. They have been taken from other contexts of *Wirtschaft und Gesellschaft*.
2. The posthumously published text breaks off here. We omit an incomplete sketch of types of `warrior estates.´

SECTION III

1. According to Weber, what is the difference between explanation and interpretation in sociological inquiry?
2. What does Weber see as the relationship between causal analysis and Verstehen?
3. What do you see as the central characteristic features of the spirit of capitalism?
4. What does Weber mean when he says that it is the fate of people in modern societies to live in an "iron cage"?
5. Why, according to Weber, is bureaucracy so integral to capitalist development?
6. What is charismatic leadership, and why is it so inherently unstable?
7. In what ways does Weber's discussion of status and party call into question Marx's emphasis on class?

IV. GEORG SIMMEL

16. FASHION

GEORG SIMMEL

Georg Simmel (1858–1918) was the first classical figure in sociology to turn his attention to the realms of leisure and consumption. This interest is nowhere more evident than in this 1904 essay on fashion, in which he discusses the reason that fashions come into vogue and go out of style with such rapidity in modern social life. On the one hand, he explains this phenomenon in terms of the collective psyche of the times: We live, he says, in a "more nervous age" than the past. On the other hand, Simmel attributes changes in fashion to the wide expansion of consumer choices industrial society makes possible and to the fact that people increasingly seek to use fashions as ways to differentiate themselves from others. He also points out, however, that fashions are not merely reflections of individual choices but are structured by class and other social divisions.

The vital conditions of fashion as a universal phenomenon in the history of our race are circumscribed by these conceptions. Fashion is the imitation of a given example and satisfies the demand for social adaptation; it leads the individual upon the road which all travel, it furnishes a general condition, which resolves the conduct of every individual into a mere example. At the same time it satisfies in no less degree the need of differentiation, the tendency towards dissimilarity, the desire for change and contrast, on the one hand by a constant change of contents, which gives to the fashion of today an individual stamp as opposed to that of yesterday and of to-morrow, on the other hand because fashions differ for different classes—the fashions of the upper stratum of society are never identical with those of the lower; in fact, they are abandoned by the former as soon as the latter prepares to appropriate them. Thus fashion represents nothing more than one of the many forms of life by the aid of which we seek to combine in uniform spheres of activity the tendency towards social equalization with the desire for individual differentiation and change. Every phase of the conflicting pair strives visibly beyond the degree of satisfaction that any fashion offers to an absolute control of the sphere of life in question. If we should study the history of fashions (which hitherto have been examined only from the view-point of the development of their contents) in connection with their importance for the form of the social process, we should find that it reflects the history of the attempts to adjust the

Reprinted from *On Individuality & Social Forms*, by Georg Simmel, edited by Donald Levine. From the series *The Heritage of Sociology*, edited by Morris Janowitz. Copyright © 1971 by The University of Chicago. Reprinted from "Fashion," *American Journal of Sociology* 62 (May 1957); originally published in *International Quarterly* (New York), 10 (1904). Translator unknown. Published in German as *Philosophie der Mode* (Berlin: Pan-Verlag, 1905), and in slightly revised and enlarged form in *Philosophische Kultur* (Leipzig: W. Klinkhardt, 1911). Reprinted with permission of The University of Chicago Press. ✦

satisfaction of the two counter-tendencies more and more perfectly to the condition of the existing individual and social culture. The various psychological elements in fashion all conform to this fundamental principle.

Fashion, as noted above, is a product of class distinction and operates like a number of other forms, honor especially, the double function of which consists in revolving within a given circle and at the same time emphasizing it as separate from others. Just as the frame of a picture characterizes the work of art inwardly as a coherent, homogeneous, independent entity and at the same time outwardly severs all direct relations with the surrounding space, just as the uniform energy of such forms cannot be expressed unless we determine the double effect, both inward and outward, so honor owes its character, and above all its moral rights, to the fact that the individual in his personal honor at the same time represents and maintains that of his social circle and his class. These moral rights, however, are frequently considered unjust by those without the pale. Thus fashion on the one hand signifies union with those in the same class, the uniformity of a circle characterized by it, and, *uno actu*, the exclusion of all other groups.

Union and segregation are the two fundamental functions which are here inseparably united, and one of which, although or because it forms a logical contrast to the other, becomes the condition of its realization. Fashion is merely a product of social demands, even though the individual object which it creates or re-creates may represent a more or less individual need. This is clearly proved by the fact that very frequently not the slightest reason can be found for the creations of fashion from the standpoint of an objective, aesthetic, or other expediency. While in general our wearing apparel is really adapted to our needs, there is not a trace of expediency in the method by which fashion dictates, for example, whether wide or narrow trousers, colored or black scarfs shall be worn. As a rule the material justification for an action coincides with its general adoption, but in the case of fashion there is a complete separation of the two elements, and there remains for the individual only this general acceptance as the deciding motive to appropriate it. Judging from the ugly and repugnant things that are sometimes in vogue, it would seem as though fashion were desirous of exhibiting its power by getting us to adopt the most atrocious things for its sake alone. The absolute indifference of fashion to the material standards of life is well illustrated by the way in which it recommends something appropriate in one instance, something abstruse in another, and something materially and aesthetically quite indifferent in a third. The only motivations with which fashion is concerned are formal social ones. The reason why even aesthetically impossible styles seem *distingué*, elegant, and artistically tolerable when affected by persons who carry them to the extreme, is that the persons who do this are generally the most elegant and pay the greatest attention to their personal appearance, so that under any circumstances we would get the impression of something *distingué* and aesthetically cultivated. This impression we credit to the questionable element of fashion, the latter appealing to our consciousness as the new and consequently most conspicuous feature of the *tout ensemble*.

Fashion occasionally will affect objectively determined subjects such as religious faith, scientific interests, even socialism and individualism; but it does not become operative as fashion until these subjects can be considered independent of the deeper human motives from which they have risen. For this reason the rule of fashion becomes in such fields unendurable. We therefore see that there is good reason why externals—clothing, social conduct, amusements—constitute the specific field of fashion, for here no dependence is placed on really vital motives of human action. It is the field which we can most easily relinquish to the bent towards imitation, which it would be a sin to follow in important questions. We encounter here a close connection between the consciousness of personality and that of the material forms of life, a connection that runs all through history. The more objective our view of life has become in the last centuries, the more it has stripped the picture of nature of all subjective and anthropomorphic elements, and the more sharply has the conception of individual personality become defined. The social regulation of our inner and outer life is a sort of embryo condition, in which the contrasts of the purely personal and the purely objective are differentiated, the action being synchronous and reciprocal. Therefore wherever man appears essentially as a social being we observe neither strict objectivity in the view of life nor absorption and independence in the consciousness of personality.

Social forms, apparel, aesthetic judgment, the whole style of human expression, are constantly transformed by fashion, in such a way, however, that fashion—*i.e.*, the latest fashion—in all these things affects only the upper classes. Just as soon as the lower classes begin to copy their style, thereby crossing the line of demarcation the upper classes have drawn and destroying the uniformity of their coherence, the upper classes turn away from this style and adopt a new one, which in its turn differentiates them from the masses; and thus the game goes merrily on. Naturally the lower classes look and strive towards the upper, and they encounter the least resistance in those fields which are subject to the whims of fashion; for it is here that mere external imitation is most readily applied. The same process is at work as between the different sets within the upper classes, although it is not always as visible here as it is, for example, between mistress and maid. Indeed, we may often observe that the more nearly one set has approached another, the more frantic becomes the desire for imitation from below and the seeking for the new from above. The increase of wealth is bound to hasten the process considerably and render it visible, because the objects of fashion, embracing as they do the externals of life, are most accessible to the mere call of money, and conformity to the higher set is more easily acquired here than in fields which demand an individual test that gold and silver cannot affect.

We see, therefore, that in addition to the element of imitation the element of demarcation constitutes an important factor of fashion. This is especially noticeable wherever the social structure does not include any superimposed groups, in which case fashion asserts itself in neighboring groups. Among primitive peoples we often find that closely connected groups living under exactly similar conditions develop sharply differentiated fashions, by means of which each group establishes uniformity within, as well as difference without, the prescribed set. On the other hand, there exists a widespread predilection for importing fashions from without, and such foreign fashions assume a greater value within the circle, simply because they did not originate there. The prophet Zephaniah expressed his indignation at the aristocrats who affected imported apparel. As a matter of fact the exotic origin of fashions seems strongly to favor the exclusiveness of the groups which adopt them. Because of their external origin, these imported fashions create a special and significant form of socialization, which arises through mutual relation to a point without the circle. It sometimes appears as though social elements, just like the axes of vision, converge best at a point that is not too near. The currency, or more precisely the medium of exchange among primitive races, often consists of objects that are brought in from without. On the Solomon Islands, and at Ibo on the Niger, for example, there exists a regular industry for the manufacture of money from shells, etc., which are not employed as a medium of exchange in the place itself, but in neighboring districts, to which they are exported. Paris modes are frequently created with the sole intention of setting a fashion elsewhere.

This motive of foreignness, which fashion employs in its socializing endeavors, is restricted to higher civilization, because novelty, which foreign origin guarantees in extreme form, is often regarded by primitive races as an evil. This is certainly one of the reasons why primitive conditions of life favor a correspondingly infrequent change of fashions. The savage is afraid of strange appearances; the difficulties and dangers that beset his career cause him to scent danger in anything new which he does not understand and which he cannot assign to a familiar category. Civilization, however, transforms this affectation into its very opposite. Whatever is exceptional, bizarre, or conspicuous, or whatever departs from the customary norm, exercises a peculiar charm upon the man of culture, entirely independent of its material justification. The removal of the feeling of insecurity with reference to all things new was accomplished by the progress of civilization. At the same time it may be the old inherited prejudice, although it has become purely formal and unconscious, which, in connection with the present feeling of security, produces this piquant interest in exceptional and odd things. For this reason the fashions of the upper classes develop their power of exclusion against the lower in proportion as general culture advances, at least until the mingling of the classes and the leveling effect of democracy exert a counter-influence.

Fashion plays a more conspicuous *rôle* in modern times, because the differences in our standards of life have become so much more strongly accentuated, for the more numerous and the more sharply drawn these differences are, the greater the opportunities for emphasizing them at every turn. In innumerable instances this cannot be accomplished by passive inactivity, but only by the development of forms established by fashion; and this has become all the more pronounced since legal restrictions prescribing various forms of apparel and modes of life for different classes have been removed.

* * *

Two social tendencies are essential to the establishment of fashion, namely, the need of union on the one hand and the need of isolation on the other. Should one of these be absent, fashion will not be formed—its sway will abruptly end. Consequently the lower classes possess very few modes and those they have are seldom specific; for this reason the modes of primitive races are much more stable than ours. Among primitive races the socializing impulse is much more powerfully developed than the differentiating impulse. For, no matter how decisively the groups may be separated from one another, separation is for the most part hostile in such a way that the very relation the rejection of which within the classes of civilized races makes fashion reasonable, is absolutely lacking. Segregation by means of differences in clothing, manners, taste, etc., is expedient only where the danger of absorption and obliteration exists, as is the case among highly civilized nations. Where these differences do not exist, where we have an absolute antagonism, as for example between not directly friendly groups of primitive races, the development of fashion has no sense at all.

It is interesting to observe how the prevalence of the socializing impulse in primitive peoples affects various institutions, such as the dance. It has been noted quite generally that the dances of primitive races exhibit a remarkable uniformity in arrangement and rhythm. The dancing group feels and acts like a uniform organism; the dance forces and accustoms a number of individuals, who are usually driven to and fro without rime or reason by vacillating conditions and needs of life, to be guided by a common impulse and a single common motive. Even making allowances for the tremendous difference in the outward appearance of the dance, we are dealing here with the same element that

appears in socializing force of fashion. Movement, time, rhythm of the gestures, are all undoubtedly influenced largely by what is worn: similarly dressed persons exhibit relative similarity in their actions. This is of especial value in modern life with its individualistic diffusion, while in the case of primitive races the effect produced is directed within and is therefore not dependent upon changes of fashion. Among primitive races fashions will be less numerous and more stable because the need of new impressions and forms of life, quite apart from their social effect, is far less pressing. Changes in fashion reflect the dulness of nervous impulses: the more nervous the age, the more rapidly its fashions change, simply because the desire for differentiation, one of the most important elements of all fashion, goes hand in hand with the weakening of nervous energy. This fact in itself is one of the reasons why the real seat of fashion is found among the upper classes . . . .

The very character of fashion demands that it should be exercised at one time only by a portion of the given group, the great majority being merely on the road to adopting it. As soon as an example has been universally adopted, that is, as soon as anything done only by a few has really come to be practiced by all—as is the case in certain portions of our social conduct—we no longer speak of fashion. As fashion spreads, it gradually goes to its doom. The distinctiveness which in the early stages of a set fashion assures for it a certain distribution is destroyed as the fashion spreads, and as this element wanes, the fashion also is bound to die. By reason of this peculiar play between the tendency towards universal acceptance and the destruction of its very purpose to which this general adoption leads, fashion includes a peculiar attraction of limitation, the attraction of a simultaneous beginning and end, the charm of novelty coupled to that of transitoriness. The attractions of both poles of the phenomena meet in fashion, and show also here that they belong together unconditionally, although, or rather because, they are contradictory in their very nature. Fashion always occupies the dividing-line between the past and the future, and consequently conveys a stronger feeling of the present, at least while it is at its height, than most other phenomena. What we call the present is usually nothing more than a combination of a fragment of the past with a fragment of the future.

Attention is called to the present less often than collo- quial usage, which is rather liberal in its employment of the word, would lead us to believe.

Few phenomena of social life possess such a pointed curve of consciousness as does fashion. As soon as the social consciousness attains to the highest point designated by fashion, it marks the beginning of the end for the latter. This transitory character of fashion, however, does not on the whole degrade it, but adds a new element of attraction. At all events an object does not suffer degradation by being called fash- ionable, unless we reject it with disgust or wish to debase it for other, material reasons, in which case, of course, fashion becomes an idea of value. In the prac- tice of life anything else similarly new and suddenly disseminated is not called fashion, when we are con- vinced of its continuance and its material justification. If, on the other hand, we feel certain that the fact will vanish as rapidly as it came, then we call it fashion. We can discover one of the reasons why in these latter days fashion exercises such a powerful influence on our consciousness in the circumstance that the great, per- manent, unquestionable convictions are continually losing strength, as a consequence of which the transi- tory and vacillating elements of life acquire more room for the display of their activity. The break with the past, which, for more than a century, civilized mankind has been laboring unceasingly to bring about, makes the consciousness turn more and more to the present. This accentuation of the present evidently at the same time emphasizes the element of change, and a class will turn to fashion in all fields, by no means only in that of apparel, in proportion to the degree in which it sup- ports the given civilizing tendency. It may almost be considered a sign of the increased power of fashion, that it has overstepped the bounds of its original domain, which comprised only personal externals, and has acquired an increasing influence over taste, over theoretical convictions, and even over the moral foundations of life.

* * *

From the fact that fashion as such can never be generally in vogue, the individual derives the satisfac- tion of knowing that as adopted by him it still repre- sents something special and striking, while at the same time he feels inwardly supported by a set of persons who are striving for the same thing, not as in the case of other social satisfactions, by a set actually doing the same thing. The fashionable person is regarded with mingled feelings of approval and envy; we envy him as an individual, but approve of him as a member of a set or group. Yet even this envy has a peculiar coloring. There is a shade of envy which includes a species of ideal participation in the envied object itself. An instructive example of this is furnished by the conduct of the poor man who gets a glimpse of the feast of his rich neighbor. The moment we envy an object or a person, we are no longer absolutely excluded from it; some relation or other has been established—between both the same psychic content now exists—although in entirely different categories and forms of sensations. This quiet personal usurpation of the envied property contains a kind of antidote, which occasionally counter-acts the evil effects of this feeling of envy. The contents of fashion afford an especially good chance of the development of this conciliatory shade of envy, which also gives to the envied person a better con- science because of his satisfaction over his good for- tune. This is due to the fact that these contents are not, as many other psychic contents are, denied absolutely to any one, for a change of fortune, which is never entirely out of the question, may play them into the hands of an individual who had previously been con- fined to the state of envy.

From all this we see that fashion furnishes an ideal field for individuals with dependent natures, whose self-consciousness, however, requires a certain amount of prominence, attention, and singularity. Fashion raises even the unimportant individual by making him the representative of a class, the embodi- ment of a joint spirit. And here again we observe the curious intermixture of antagonistic values. Speaking broadly, it is characteristic of a standard set by a general body, that its acceptance by any one individual does not call attention to him; in other words, a positive adoption of a given norm signifies nothing. Whoever keeps the laws the breaking of which is punished by the penal code, whoever lives up to the social forms pre- scribed by his class, gains no conspicuousness or notoriety. The slightest infraction or opposition, how- ever, is immediately noticed and places the individual in an exceptional position by calling the attention of the public to his action. All such norms do not assume positive importance for the individual until he begins to depart from them. It is peculiarly characteristic of fashion that it renders possible a social obedience, which at the same time is a form of individual differentiation. Fashion does this because in its very nature it represents a standard that can never be accepted by all. While fashion postulates a certain amount of general acceptance, it nevertheless is not without significance in the characterization of the individual, for it emphasizes his personality not only through omission but also through observance. In the dude the social demands of fashion appear exaggerated to such a degree that they completely assume an individualistic and peculiar character. It is characteristic of the dude that he carries the elements of a particular fashion to an extreme; when pointed shoes are in style, he wears shoes that resemble the prow of a ship; when high collars are all the rage, he wears collars that come up to his ears; when scientific lectures are fashionable, you cannot find him anywhere else, etc., etc. Thus he represents something distinctly individual, which consists in the quantitative intensification of such elements as are qualitatively common property of the given set of class. He leads the way, but all travel the same road. Representing as he does the most recently conquered heights of public taste, he seems to be marching at the head of the general procession. In reality, however, what is so frequently true of the relation between individuals and groups applies also to him: as a matter of fact, the leader allows himself to be led . . . .

17. THE ADVENTURER

GEORG SIMMEL

In the world of routinization that characterized Weber's work, his contemporary Simmel indicates that there are possibilities for departing from that world, for most people in temporary ways, but for some as a way of life. This is the presupposition of his analysis of a particular social type: the adventurer. The essay begins by discussing the adventure and then moves on to the person for whom this becomes a dominant aspect of life. An adventure entails stepping out of the domain of mundane everyday life and entering a domain of activity with its own rules and rhythms, a domain of the present where linear time ceases. As such the adventure is an ahistorical moment that promises release from a disenchanted world, offering the prospect of excitement, novelty, and self-actualization. Simmel moves to a consideration of the social type of the adventurer, using Casanova as an example and comparing the adventurer as an ideal type to the gambler.

Each segment of our conduct and experience bears a twofold meaning: it revolves about its own center, contains as much breadth and depth, joy and suffering, as the immediate experiencing gives it, and at the same time is a segment of a course of life—not only a circumscribed entity, but also a component of an organism. Both aspects, in various configurations, characterize everything that occurs in a life. Events which may be widely divergent in their bearing on life as a whole may nonetheless be quite similar to one another; or they may be incommensurate in their intrinsic meanings but so similar in respect to the roles they play in our total existence as to be interchangeable.

One of two experiences which are not particularly different in substance, as far as we can indicate it, may nevertheless be perceived as an "adventure" and the other not. The one receives the designation denied the other because of this difference in the relation to the whole of our life. More precisely, the most general form of adventure is its dropping out of the continuity of life. "Wholeness of life," after all, refers to the fact that a consistent process runs through the individual components of life, however crassly and irreconcilably distinct they may be. What we call an adventure stands in contrast to that interlocking of life-links, to that feeling that those countercurrents, turnings, and knots still, after all, spin forth a continuous thread. An adventure is certainly a part of our existence, directly contiguous with other parts which precede and follow it; at the same time, however, in its deeper meaning, it occurs outside the usual continuity of this life. Nevertheless, it is distinct from all that is accidental and alien, merely touching life's outer shell. While it falls outside the context of life, it falls, with this same movement, as it were, back into that context again, as will become clear later; it is a foreign body in our existence which is yet somehow connected with the center; the outside, if only by a long and unfamiliar detour, is formally an aspect of the inside.

Because of its place in our psychic life, a remembered adventure tends to take on the quality of a dream. Everyone knows how quickly we forget dreams because they, too, are placed outside the meaningful context of life-as-a-whole. What we designate as "dreamlike" is nothing but a memory which is bound to the unified, consistent life-process by fewer threads than are ordinary experiences. We might say that we localize our inability to assimilate to this process something experienced by imagining a dream in which it took place. The more "adventurous" an adventure, that is, the more fully it realizes its idea, the more "dreamlike" it becomes in our memory. It often moves so far away from the center of the ego and the course of life which the ego guides and organizes that we may think of it as something experienced by another person. How far outside that course it lies, how alien it has become to that course, is expressed precisely by the fact that we might well feel that we could appropriately assign to the adventure a subject other than the ego.

We ascribe to an adventure a beginning and an end much sharper than those to be discovered in the other forms of our experiences. The adventure is freed of the entanglements and concatenations which are characteristic of those forms and is given a meaning in and of itself. Of our ordinary experiences, we declare that one of them is over when, or because, another starts; they reciprocally determine each other's limits, and so become a means whereby the contextual unity of life is structured or expressed. The adventure, however, according to its intrinsic meaning, is independent of the "before" and "after"; its boundaries are defined regardless of them. We speak of adventure precisely when continuity with life is thus disregarded on principle—or rather when there is not even any need to disregard it, because we know from the beginning that we have to do with something alien, untouchable, out of the ordinary. The adventure lacks that reciprocal interpenetration with adjacent parts of life which constitutes life-as-a-whole. It is like an island in life which determines its beginning and end according to its own formative powers and not—like the part of a continent —also according to those of adjacent territories. This factor of decisive boundedness, which lifts an adventure out of the regular course of a human destiny, is not mechanical but organic: just as the organism determines its spatial shape not simply by adjusting to obstacles confining it from right and left but by the propelling force of a life forming from inside out, so

does an adventure not end because something else begins; instead, its temporal form, its radical being-ended, is the precise expression of its inner sense.

Here, above all, is the basis of the profound affinity between the adventurer and the artist, and also, perhaps, of the artist's attraction by adventure. For the essence of a work of art is, after all, that it cuts out a piece of the endlessly continuous sequences of perceived experience, detaching it from all connections with one side or the other, giving it a self-sufficient form as though defined and held together by an inner core. A part of existence, interwoven with the uninterruptedness of that existence, yet nevertheless felt as a whole, as an integrated unit—this is the form common to both the work of art and the adventure. Indeed, it is an attribute of this form to make us feel that in both the work of art and the adventure the whole of life is somehow comprehended and consummated—and this irrespective of the particular theme either of them may have. Moreover, we feel this, not although, but because, the work of art exists entirely beyond life as a reality; the adventure, entirely beyond life as an uninterrupted course which intelligibly connects every element with its neighbors. It is because the work of art and the adventure stand over against life (even though in very different senses of the phrase) that both are analogous to the totality of life itself, even as this totality presents itself in the brief summary and crowdedness of a dream experience.

For this reason, the adventurer is also the extreme example of the ahistorical individual, of the man who lives in the present. On the one hand, he is not determined by any past (and this marks the contrast between him and the aged, of which more later); nor, on the other hand, does the future exist for him. An extraordinarily characteristic proof of this is that Casanova (as may be seen from his memoirs), in the course of his erotic-adventurous life, ever so often seriously intended to marry a woman with whom he was in love at the time. In the light of his temperament and conduct of life, we can imagine nothing more obviously impossible, internally and externally. Casanova not only had excellent knowledge of men but also rare knowledge of himself. Although he must have said to himself that he could not stand marriage even two weeks and that the most miserable consequences of such a step would be quite unavoidable, his perspective on the future was wholly obliterated in the rapture of the moment. (Saying this, I mean to put the emphasis on the moment rather than on the rapture.) Because he was entirely dominated by the feeling of the present, he wanted to enter into a future relationship which was impossible precisely because his temperament was oriented to the present.

In contrast to those aspects of life which are related only peripherally—by mere fate—the adventure is defined by its capacity, in spite of its being isolated and accidental, to have necessity and meaning. Something becomes an adventure only by virtue of two conditions: that it itself is a specific organization of some significant meaning with a beginning and an end; and that, despite its accidental nature, its extraterritoriality with respect to the continuity of life, it nevertheless connects with the character and identity of the bearer of that life—that it does so in the widest sense, transcending, by a mysterious necessity, life's more narrowly rational aspects.

At this point there emerges the relation between the adventurer and the gambler. The gambler, clearly, has abandoned himself to the meaninglessness of chance. In so far, however, as he counts on its favor and believes possible and realizes a life dependent on it, chance for him has become part of a context of meaning. The typical superstition of the gambler is nothing other than the tangible and isolated, and thus, of course, childish, form of this profound and all-encompassing scheme of his life, according to which chance makes sense and contains some necessary meaning (even though not by the criterion of rational logic). In his superstition, he wants to draw chance into his teleological system by omens and magical aids, thus removing it from its inaccessible isolation and searching in it for a lawful order, no matter how fantastic the laws of such an order may be.

The adventurer similarly lets the accident somehow be encompassed by the meaning which controls the consistent continuity of life, even though the accident lies outside that continuity. He achieves a central feeling of life which runs through the eccentricity of the adventure and produces a new, significant necessity of his life in the very width of the distance between its accidental, externally given content and the unifying

core of existence from which meaning flows. There is in us an eternal process playing back and forth between chance and necessity, between the fragmentary materials given us from the outside and the consistent meaning of the life developed from within.

The great forms in which we shape the substance of life are the syntheses, antagonisms, or compromises between chance and necessity. Adventure is such a form. When the professional adventurer makes a system of life out of his life's lack of system, when out of his inner necessity he seeks the naked, external accidents and builds them into that necessity, he only, so to speak, makes macroscopically visible that which is the essential form of every "adventure," even that of the non-adventurous person. For by adventure we always mean a third something, neither the sheer, abrupt event whose meaning—a mere given—simply remains outside us nor the consistent sequence of life in which every element supplements every other toward an inclusively integrated meaning. The adventure is no mere hodgepodge of these two, but rather that incomparable experience which can be interpreted only as a particular encompassing of the accidentally external by the internally necessary.

Occasionally, however, this whole relationship is comprehended in a still more profound inner configuration. No matter how much the adventure seems to rest on a differentiation within life, life as a whole may be perceived as an adventure. For this, one need neither be an adventurer nor undergo many adventures. To have such a remarkable attitude toward life, one must sense above its totality a higher unity, a super-life, as it were, whose relation to life parallels the relation of the immediate life totality itself to those particular experiences which we call adventures.

Perhaps we belong to a metaphysical order, perhaps our soul lives a transcendent existence, such that our earthly, conscious life is only an isolated fragment as compared to the unnamable context of an existence running its course in it. The myth of the transmigration of souls may be a halting attempt to express such a segmental character of every individual life. Whoever senses through all actual life a secret, timeless existence of the soul, which is connected with the realities of life only as from a distance, will perceive life in its given and limited wholeness as an adventure when compared to that transcendent and self-consistent fate. Certain religious moods seem to bring about such a perception. When our earthly career strikes us as a mere preliminary phase in the fulfillment of eternal destinies, when we have no home but merely a temporary asylum on earth, this obviously is only a particular variant of the general feeling that life as a whole is an adventure. It merely expresses the running together, in life, of the symptoms of adventure. It stands outside that proper meaning and steady course of existence to which it is yet tied by a fate and a secret symbolism. A fragmentary incident, it is yet, like a work of art, enclosed by a beginning and an end. Like a dream, it gathers all passions into itself and yet, like a dream, is destined to be forgotten; like gaming, it contrasts with seriousness, yet, like the *va banque* of the gambler, it involves the alternative between the highest gain and destruction.

Thus the adventure is a particular form in which fundamental categories of life are synthesized. Another such synthesis it achieves is that between the categories of activity and passivity, between what we conquer and what is given to us. To be sure, their synthesis in the form of adventure makes their contrast perceptible to an extreme degree. In the adventure, on the one hand, we forcibly pull the world into ourselves. This becomes clear when we compare the adventure with the manner in which we wrest the gifts of the world through work. Work, so to speak, has an organic relation to the world. In a conscious fashion, it develops the world's forces and materials toward their culmination in the human purpose, whereas in adventure we have a nonorganic relation to the world. Adventure has the gesture of the conqueror, the quick seizure of opportunity, regardless of whether the portion we carve out is harmonious or disharmonious with us, with the world, or with the relation between us and the world. On the other hand, however, in the adventure we abandon ourselves to the world with fewer defenses and reserves than in any other relation, for other relations are connected with the general run of our worldly life by more bridges, and thus defend us better against shocks and dangers through previously prepared avoidances and adjustments. In the adventure, the interweaving of activity and passivity which characterizes our life tightens these elements into a coexistence of conquest, which owes everything only to its own strength and

presence of mind, and complete self-abandonment to the powers and accidents of the world, which can delight us, but in the same breath can also destroy us. Surely, it is among adventure's most wonderful and enticing charms that the unity toward which at every moment, by the very process of living, we bring together our activity and our passivity—the unity which even in a certain sense *is* life itself—accentuates its disparate elements most sharply, and precisely in *this* way makes itself the more deeply felt, as if they were only the two aspects of one and the same, mysteriously seamless life.

If the adventure, furthermore, strikes us as combining the elements of certainty and uncertainty in life, this is more than the view of the same fundamental relationship from a different angle. The certainty with which—justifiably or in error—we know the outcome, gives our activity one of its distinct qualities. If, on the contrary, we are uncertain whether we shall arrive at the point for which we have set out, if we know our ignorance of the outcome, then this means not only a quantitatively reduced certainty but an inwardly and outwardly unique practical conduct. The adventurer, in a word, treats the incalculable element in life in the way we ordinarily treat only what we think is by definition calculable. (For this reason, the philosopher is the adventurer of the spirit. He makes the hopeless, but not therefore meaningless, attempt to form into conceptual knowledge an attitude of the soul, its mood toward itself, the world, God. He treats this insoluble problem as if it were soluble.) When the outcome of our activity is made doubtful by the intermingling of unrecognizable elements of fate, we usually limit our commitment of force, hold open lines of retreat, and take each step only as if testing the ground.

In the adventure, we proceed in the directly opposite fashion: it is just on the hovering chance, on fate, on the more-or-less that we risk all, burn our bridges, and step into the mist, as if the road will lead us on, no matter what. This is the typical fatalism of the adventurer. The obscurities of fate are certainly no more transparent to him than to others; but he proceeds as if they were. The characteristic daring with which he continually leaves the solidities of life underpins itself, as it were, for its own justification with a feeling of security and "it-must-succeed," which normally only belongs to the transparency of calculable events. This is only a subjective aspect of the fatalist conviction that we certainly cannot escape a fate which we do not know: the adventurer nevertheless believes that, as far as he himself is concerned, he is certain of this unknown and unknowable element in his life. For this reason, to the sober person adventurous conduct often seems insanity; for, in order to make sense, it appears to presuppose that the unknowable is known. The prince of Ligne said of Casanova, "He believes in nothing except in what is least believable." Evidently, such belief is based on that perverse or at least "adventurous" relation between the certain and the uncertain, whose correlate, obviously, is the skepticism of the adventurer—that he "believes in nothing": for him to whom the unlikely is likely, the likely easily becomes unlikely. The adventurer relies to some extent on his own strength, but above all on his own luck; more properly, on a peculiarly undifferentiated unity of the two. Strength, of which he is certain, and luck, of which he is uncertain, subjectively combine into a sense of certainty.

If it is the nature of genius to possess an immediate relation to these secret unities which in experience and rational analysis fall apart into completely separate phenomena, the adventurer of genius lives, as if by mystic instinct, at the point where the course of the world and the individual fate have, so to speak, not yet been differentiated from one another. For this reason, he is said to have a "touch of genius." The "sleepwalking certainty" with which the adventurer leads his life becomes comprehensible in terms of that peculiar constellation whereby he considers that which is uncertain and incalculable to be the premises of his conduct, while others consider only the calculable. Unshakable even when it is shown to be denied by the facts of the case, this certainty proves how deeply that constellation is rooted in the life conditions of adventurous natures.

The adventure is a form of life which can be taken on by an undetermined number of experiences. Nevertheless, our definitions make it understandable that one of them, more than all others, tends to appear in this form: the erotic—so that our linguistic custom hardly lets us understand by "adventure" anything but an erotic one. The love affair, even if short-lived, is by

no means always an adventure. The peculiar psychic qualities at whose meeting point the adventure is found must be added to this quantitative matter. The tendency of these qualities to enter such a conjuncture will become apparent step by step.

A love affair contains in clear association the two elements which the form of the adventure characteristically conjoins: conquering force and unextortable concession, winning by one's own abilities and dependence on the luck which something incalculable outside ourselves bestows on us. A degree of balance between these forces, gained by virtue of his sense of their sharp differentiation, can, perhaps, be found only in the man. Perhaps for this reason, it is of compelling significance that, as a rule, a love affair is an "adventure" only for men; for women it usually falls into other categories. In novels of love, the activity of woman is typically permeated by the passivity which either nature or history has imparted to her character; on the other hand, her acceptance of happiness is at the same time a concession and a gift.

The two poles of conquest and grace (which manifest themselves in many variations) stand closer together in woman than in man. In man, they are, as a matter of fact, much more decisively separated. For this reason, in man their coincidence in the erotic experience stamps this experience quite ambiguously as an adventure. Man plays the courting, attacking, often violently grasping role: this fact makes one easily overlook the element of fate, the dependence on something which cannot be predetermined or compelled, that is contained in every erotic experience. This refers not only to dependence on the concession on the part of the other, but to something deeper. To be sure, every "love returned," too, is a gift which cannot be "earned," not even by any measure of love—because to love, demand and compensation are irrelevant; it belongs, in principle, in a category altogether different from a squaring of accounts—a point which suggests one of its analogies to the more profound religious relation. But over and above that which we receive from another as a free gift, there still lies in every happiness of love—like a profound, impersonal bearer of those personal elements—a favor of fate. We receive happiness not only from the other: the fact that we do receive it from him is a blessing of destiny, which is incalculable. In the proudest, most self-assured event in this sphere lies something which we must accept with humility. When the force which owes its success to itself and gives all conquest of love some note of victory and triumph is then combined with the other note of favor by fate, the constellation of the adventure is, as it were, preformed.

The relation which connects the erotic content with the more general form of life as adventure is rooted in deeper ground. The adventure is the exclave of life, the "torn-off" whose beginning and end have no connection with the somehow unified stream of existence. And yet, as if hurdling this stream, it connects with the most recondite instincts and some ultimate intention of life as a whole—and this distinguishes it from the merely accidental episode, from that which only externally "happens" to us. Now, when a love affair is of short duration, it lives in precisely such a mixture of a merely tangential and yet central character. It may give our life only a momentary splendor, like the ray shed in an inside room by a light flitting by outside. Still, it satisfies a need, or is, in fact, only possible by virtue of a need which—whether it be considered as physical, psychic, or metaphysical—exists, as it were, timelessly in the foundation or center of our being. This need is related to the fleeting experience as our general longing for light is to that accidental and immediately disappearing brightness.

The fact that love harbors the possibility of this double relation is reflected by the twofold temporal aspect of the erotic. It displays two standards of time: the momentarily climactic, abruptly subsiding passion; and the idea of something which cannot pass, an idea in which the mystical destination of two souls for one another and for a higher unity finds a temporal expression. This duality might be compared with the double existence of intellectual contents: while they emerge only in the fleetingness of the psychic process, in the forever moving focus of consciousness, their logical meaning possesses timeless validity, an ideal significance which is completely independent of the instant of consciousness in which it becomes real for us. The phenomenon of adventure is such that its abrupt climax places its end into the perspective of its beginning. However, its connection with the center of life is

such that it is to be distinguished from all merely accidental happenings. Thus "mortal danger," so to speak, lies in its very style. This phenomenon, therefore, is a form which by its time symbolism seems to be predetermined to receive the erotic content.

These analogies between love and adventure alone suggest that the adventure does not belong to the lifestyle of old age. The decisive point about this fact is that the adventure, in its specific nature and charm, is a *form of experiencing.* The *content* of the experience does not make the adventure. That one has faced mortal danger or conquered a woman for a short span of happiness; that unknown factors with which one has waged a gamble have brought surprising gain or loss; that physically or psychologically disguised, one has ventured into spheres of life from which one returns home as if from a strange world—none of these are necessarily adventure. They become adventure only by virtue of a certain experiential tension whereby their substance is realized. Only when a stream flowing between the minutest externalities of life and the central source of strength drags them into itself; when the peculiar color, ardor, and rhythm of the life-process become decisive and, as it were, transform its substance—only then does an event change from mere experience to adventure. Such a principle of accentuation, however, is alien to old age. In general, only youth knows this predominance of the process of life over its substance; whereas in old age, when the process begins to slow up and coagulate, substance becomes crucial; it then proceeds or perseveres in a certain timeless manner, indifferent to the tempo and passion of its being experienced. The old person usually lives either in a wholly *centralized* fashion, peripheral interests having fallen off and being unconnected with his essential life and its inner necessity; or his center atrophies, and existence runs its course only in isolated petty details, accenting mere externals and accidentals. Neither case makes possible the relation between the outer fate and the inner springs of life in which the adventure consists; clearly, neither permits the perception of contrast characteristic of adventure, viz., that an action is completely torn out of the inclusive context of life and that simultaneously the whole strength and intensity of life stream into it. . . .

18. THE METROPOLIS AND MENTAL LIFE

GEORG SIMMEL

In this classic essay that first appeared in 1903, Simmel explores the social psychology of city dwellers. Given that urbanization, like industrialization, is a characteristic feature of modernity, he contends that one can find the distillation of modern consciousness most clearly in the metropolis. His essay echoes themes developed by both Durkheim and Weber, but articulated from his own distinctive perspective and in his unique voice. The former's focus on the interdependency of society is on display here, where Simmel speculates about what would happen to Berlin's commercial life if, even for an hour, all the watches in the city were out of sync with all the other watches. This theme also resonates with Weber's sense of the growing impact of rationalization. Simmel expresses his concern about the struggle individuals confront in maintaining individuality and offers a compelling account of the blasé attitude, not as an indication of coldness, apathy, or dullness, but rather as a safeguard for the individual's psychic well-being.

The deepest problems of modern life flow from the attempt of the individual to maintain the independence and individuality of his existence against the sovereign powers of society, against the weight of the historical heritage and the external culture and technique of life. This antagonism represents the most modern form of the conflict which primitive man must carry on with nature for his own bodily existence. The eighteenth century may have called for liberation from all the ties which grew up historically in politics, in religion, in morality and in economics in order to permit the original natural virtue of man, which is equal in everyone, to develop without inhibition; the nineteenth century may have sought to promote, in addition to man's freedom, his individuality (which is connected with the division of labor) and his achievements which make him unique and indispensable but which at the same time make him so much the more dependent on the complementary activity of others; Nietzsche may have seen the relentless struggle of the individual as the prerequisite for his full development, while Socialism found the same thing in the suppression of all competition—but in each of these the same fundamental motive was at work, namely the resistance of the individual to being levelled, swallowed up in the social-technological mechanism. When one inquires about the products of the specifically modern aspects of contemporary life with reference to their inner meaning—when, so to speak, one examines the body of culture with reference to the soul, as I am to do concerning the metropolis today—the answer will require the investigation of the relationship which such a social structure promotes between the individual aspects of life and those which transcend the existence of single individuals. It will require the investigation of the adaptations made by the personality in its adjustment to the forces that lie outside of it.

The psychological foundation, upon which the metropolitan individuality is erected, is the intensification of emotional life due to the swift and continuous

Reprinted from *On Individuality & Social Forms*, by Georg Simmel, edited by Donald Levine. From the series *Heritage of Sociology*, edited by Morris Janowitz. Copyright © 1971 by The University of Chicago. Reprinted with permission of The University of Chicago Press. ✦

shift of external and internal stimuli. Man is a creature whose existence is dependent on differences, i.e., his mind is stimulated by the difference between present impressions and those which have preceded. Lasting impressions, the slightness in their differences, the habituated regularity of their course and contrasts between them, consume, so to speak, less mental energy than the rapid telescoping of changing images, pronounced differences within what is grasped at a single glance, and the unexpectedness of violent stimuli. To the extent that the metropolis creates these psychological conditions—with every crossing of the street, with the tempo and multiplicity of economic, occupational and social life—it creates in the sensory foundations of mental life, and in the degree of awareness necessitated by our organization as creatures dependent on differences, a deep contrast with the slower, more habitual, more smoothly flowing rhythm of the sensory-mental phase of small town and rural existence. Thereby the essentially intellectualistic character of the mental life of the metropolis becomes intelligible as over against that of the small town which rests more on feelings and emotional relationships. These latter are rooted in the unconscious levels of the mind and develop most readily in the steady equilibrium of unbroken customs. The locus of reason, on the other hand, is in the lucid, conscious upper strata of the mind and it is the most adaptable of our inner forces. In order to adjust itself to the shifts and contradictions in events, it does not require the disturbances and inner upheavals which are the only means whereby more conservative personalities are able to adapt themselves to the same rhythm of events. Thus the metropolitan type—which naturally takes on a thousand individual modifications—creates a protective organ for itself against the profound disruption with which the fluctuations and discontinuities of the external milieu threaten it. Instead of reacting emotionally, the metropolitan type reacts primarily in a rational manner, thus creating a mental predominance through the intensification of consciousness, which in turn is caused by it. Thus the reaction of the metropolitan person to those events is moved to a sphere of mental activity which is least sensitive and which is furthest removed from the depths of the personality.

This intellectualistic quality which is thus recognized as a protection of the inner life against the domination of the metropolis, becomes ramified into numerous specific phenomena. The metropolis has always been the seat of money economy because the many-sidedness and concentration of commercial activity have given the medium of exchange an importance which it could not have acquired in the commercial aspects of rural life. But money economy and the domination of the intellect stand in the closest relationship to one another. They have in common a purely matter-of-fact attitude in the treatment of persons and things in which a formal justice is often combined with an unrelenting hardness. The purely intellectualistic person is indifferent to all things personal because, out of them, relationships and reactions develop which are not to be completely understood by purely rational methods—just as the unique element in events never enters into the principle of money. Money is concerned only with what is common to all, i.e., with the exchange value which reduces all quality and individuality to a purely quantitative level. All emotional relationships between persons rest on their individuality, whereas intellectual relationships deal with persons as with numbers, that is, as with elements which, in themselves, are indifferent, but which are of interest only insofar as they offer something objectively perceivable. It is in this very manner that the inhabitant of the metropolis reckons with his merchant, his customer, and with his servant, and frequently with the persons with whom he is thrown into obligatory association. These relationships stand in distinct contrast with the nature of the smaller circle in which the inevitable knowledge of individual characteristics produces, with an equal inevitability, an emotional tone in conduct, a sphere which is beyond the mere objective weighting of tasks performed and payments made. What is essential here as regards the economic-psychological aspect of the problem is that in less advanced cultures production was for the customer who ordered the product so that the producer and the purchaser knew one another. The modern city, however, is supplied almost exclusively by production for the market, that is, for entirely unknown purchasers who never appear in the actual field of vision of the producers themselves. Thereby, the interests of each party acquire a relentless matter-of-factness, and its rationally calculated economic egoism need not fear any divergence from its set path because of the imponderability of personal relationships. This is all the more the case in the money economy which dominates the metropolis in which the last remnants of domestic production and direct barter of goods have been eradicated and in which the amount of production on direct personal order is reduced daily. Furthermore, this psychological intellectualistic attitude and the money economy are in such close integration that no one is able to say whether it was the former that effected the latter or *vice versa*. What is certain is only that the form of life in the metropolis is the soil which nourishes this interaction most fruitfully, a point which I shall attempt to demonstrate only with the statement of the most outstanding English constitutional historian to the effect that through the entire course of English history London has never acted as the heart of England but often as its intellect and always as its money bag.

In certain apparently insignificant characters or traits of the most external aspects of life are to be found a number of characteristic mental tendencies. The modern mind has become more and more a calculating one. The calculating exactness of practical life which has resulted from a money economy corresponds to the ideal of natural science, namely that of transforming the world into an arithmetical problem and of fixing every one of its parts in a mathematical formula. It has been money economy which has thus filled the daily life of so many people with weighing, calculating, enumerating and the reduction of qualitative values to quantitative terms. Because of the character of calculability which money has there has come into the relationships of the elements of life a precision and a degree of certainty in the definition of the equalities and inequalities and an unambiguousness in agreements and arrangements, just as externally this precision has been brought about through the general diffusion of pocket watches. It is, however, the conditions of the metropolis which are cause as well as effect for this essential characteristic. The relationships and concerns of the typical metropolitan resident are so manifold and complex that, especially as a result of the agglomeration of so many persons with such differentiated interests, their relationships and activities intertwine with one another into a many-membered organism. In view of this fact, the lack of the most exact punctuality in promises and performances would cause the whole to break down into an inextricable chaos. If all the watches in Berlin suddenly went wrong in different ways even only as much as an hour, its entire economic and commercial life would be derailed for some time. Even though this may seem more superficial in its significance, it transpires that the magnitude of distances results in making all waiting and the breaking of appointments an ill-afforded waste of time. For this reason the technique of metropolitan life in general is not conceivable without all of its activities and reciprocal relationships being organized and coordinated in the most punctual way into a firmly fixed framework of time which transcends all subjective elements. But here too there emerge those conclusions which are in general the whole task of this discussion, namely, that every event, however restricted to this superficial level it may appear, comes immediately into contact with the depths of the soul, and that the most banal externalities are, in the last analysis, bound up with the final decisions concerning the meaning and the style of life. Punctuality, calculability, and exactness, which are required by the complications and extensiveness of metropolitan life are not only most intimately connected with its capitalistic and intellectualistic character but also color the content of life and are conducive to the exclusion of those irrational, instinctive, sovereign human traits and impulses which originally seek to determine the form of life from within instead of receiving it from the outside in a general, schematically precise form. Even though those lives which are autonomous and characterised by these vital impulses are not entirely impossible in the city, they are, none the less, opposed to it *in abstracto*. It is in the light of this that we can explain the passionate hatred of personalities like Ruskin and Nietzsche for the metropolis—personalities who found the value of life only in unschematized individual expressions which cannot be reduced to exact equivalents and in whom, on that account, there flowed from the same source as did that hatred, the hatred of the money economy and of the intellectualism of existence.

The same factors which, in the exactness and the minute precision of the form of life, have coalesced into a structure of the highest impersonality, have, on the other hand, an influence in a highly personal direction. There is perhaps no psychic phenomenon which is so unconditionally reserved to the city as the blasé outlook. It is at first the consequence of those rapidly shifting stimulations of the nerves which are thrown together in all their contrasts and from which it seems to us the intensification of metropolitan intellectuality seems to be derived. On that account it is not likely that stupid persons who have been hitherto intellectually dead will be blasé. Just as an immoderately sensuous life makes one blasé because it stimulates the nerves to their utmost reactivity until they finally can no longer produce any reaction at all, so, less harmful stimuli, through the rapidity and the contradictoriness of their shifts, force the nerves to make such violent responses, tear them about so brutally that they exhaust their last reserves of strength and, remaining in the same milieu, do not have time for new reserves to form. This incapacity to react to new stimulations with the required amount of energy constitutes in fact that blasé attitude which every child of a large city evinces when compared with the products of the more peaceful and more stable milieu.

Combined with this physiological source of the blasé metropolitan attitude there is another which derives from a money economy. The essence of the blasé attitude is an indifference toward the distinctions between things. Not in the sense that they are not perceived, as is the case of mental dullness, but rather that the meaning and the value of the distinctions between things, and therewith of the things themselves, are experienced as meaningless. They appear to the blasé person in a homogeneous, flat and gray color with no one of them worthy of being preferred to another. This psychic mood is the correct subjective reflection of a complete money economy to the extent that money takes the place of all the manifoldness of things and expresses all qualitative distinctions between them in the distinction of "how much." To the extent that money, with its colorlessness and its indifferent quality, can become a common denominator of all values it becomes the frightful leveler—it hollows out the core of things, their peculiarities, their specific values and their uniqueness and incomparability in a way which is

beyond repair. They all float with the same specific gravity in the constantly moving stream of money. They all rest on the same level and are distinguished only by their amounts. In individual cases this coloring, or rather this de-coloring of things, through their equation with money, may be imperceptibly small. In the relationship, however, which the wealthy person has to objects which can be bought for money, perhaps indeed in the total character which, for this reason, public opinion now recognizes in these objects, it takes on very considerable proportions. This is why the metropolis is the seat of commerce and it is in it that the purchasability of things appears in quite a different aspect than in simpler economies. It is also the peculiar seat of the blasé attitude. In it is brought to a peak, in a certain way, that achievement in the concentration of purchasable things which stimulates the individual to the highest degree of nervous energy. Through the mere quantitative intensification of the same conditions this achievement is transformed into its opposite, into this peculiar adaptive phenomenon—the blasé attitude—in which the nerves reveal their final possibility of adjusting themselves to the content and the form of metropolitan life by renouncing the response to them. We see that the self-preservation of certain types of personalities is obtained at the cost of devaluing the entire objective world, ending inevitably in dragging the personality downward into a feeling of its own valuelessness.

Whereas the subject of this form of existence must come to terms with it for himself, his self-preservation in the face of the great city requires of him a no less negative type of social conduct. The mental attitude of the people of the metropolis to one another may be designated formally as one of reserve. If the unceasing external contact of numbers of persons in the city should be met by the same number of inner reactions as in the small town, in which one knows almost every person he meets and to each of whom he has a positive relationship, one would be completely atomized internally and would fall into an unthinkable mental condition. Partly this psychological circumstance and partly the privilege of suspicion which we have in the face of the elements of metropolitan life (which are constantly touching one another in fleeting contact) necessitates in us that reserve, in consequence of which we do not know by sight neighbors of years standing and which permits us to appear to small-town folk so often as cold and uncongenial. Indeed, if I am not mistaken, the inner side of this external reserve is not only indifference but more frequently than we believe, it is a slight aversion, a mutual strangeness and repulsion which, in a close contact which has arisen any way whatever, can break out into hatred and conflict. The entire inner organization of such a type of extended commercial life rests on an extremely varied structure of sympathies, indifferences and aversions of the briefest as well as of the most enduring sort. This sphere of indifference is, for this reason, not as great as it seems superficially. Our minds respond, with some definite feeling, to almost every impression emanating from another person. The unconsciousness, the transitoriness and the shift of these feelings seem to raise them only into indifference. Actually this latter would be as unnatural to us as immersion into a chaos of unwished-for suggestions would be unbearable. From these two typical dangers of metropolitan life we are saved by antipathy which is the latent adumbration of actual antagonism since it brings about the sort of distanciation and deflection without which this type of life could not be carried on at all. Its extent and its mixture, the rhythm of its emergence and disappearance, the forms in which it is adequate—these constitute, with the simplified motives (in the narrower sense) an inseparable totality of the form of metropolitan life. What appears here directly as dissociation is in reality only one of the elementary forms of socialization.

This reserve with its overtone of concealed aversion appears once more, however, as the form or the wrappings of a much more general psychic trait of the metropolis. It assures the individual of a type and degree of personal freedom to which there is no analogy in other circumstances. It has its roots in one of the great developmental tendencies of social life as a whole; in one of the few for which an approximately exhaustive formula can be discovered. The most elementary stage of social organization which is to be found historically, as well as in the present, is this: a relatively small circle almost entirely closed against neighboring foreign or otherwise antagonistic groups but which has however within itself such a narrow

cohesion that the individual member has only a very slight area for the development of his own qualities and for free activity for which he himself is responsible. Political and familial groups began in this way as do political and religious communities; the self-preservation of very young associations requires a rigorous setting of boundaries and a centripetal unity and for that reason it cannot give room to freedom and the peculiarities of inner and external development of the individual. From this stage social evolution proceeds simultaneously in two divergent but none the less corresponding directions. In the measure that the group grows numerically, spatially, and in the meaningful content of life, its immediate inner unity and the definiteness of its original demarcation against others are weakened and rendered mild by reciprocal interactions and interconnections. And at the same time the individual gains a freedom of movement far beyond the first jealous delimitation, and gains also a peculiarity and individuality to which the division of labor in groups, which have become larger, gives both occasion and necessity. However much the particular conditions and forces of the individual situation might modify the general scheme, the state and Christianity, guilds and political parties and innumerable other groups have developed in accord with this formula. This tendency seems, to me, however to be quite clearly recognizable also in the development of individuality within the framework of city life. Small town life in antiquity as well as in the Middle Ages imposed such limits upon the movements of the individual in his relationships with the outside world and on his inner independence and differentiation that the modern person could not even breathe under such conditions. Even today the city dweller who is placed in a small town feels a type of narrowness which is very similar. The smaller the circle which forms our environment and the more limited the relationships which have the possibility of transcending the boundaries, the more anxiously the narrow community watches over the deeds, the conduct of life and the attitudes of the individual and the more will a quantitative and qualitative individuality tend to pass beyond the boundaries of such a community.

The ancient *polis* seems in this regard to have had a character of a small town. The incessant threat against its existence by enemies from near and far brought about that stern cohesion in political and military matters, that supervision of the citizen by other citizens, and that jealousy of the whole toward the individual whose own private life was repressed to such an extent that he could compensate himself only by acting as a despot in his own household. The tremendous agitation and excitement, and the unique colorfulness of Athenian life is perhaps explained by the fact that a people of incomparably individualized personalities were in constant struggle against the incessant inner and external oppression of a de-individualizing small town. This created an atmosphere of tension in which the weaker were held down and the stronger were impelled to the most passionate type of self-protection. And with this there blossomed in Athens, what, without being able to define it exactly, must be designated as "the general human character" in the intellectual development of our species. For the correlation, the factual as well as the historical validity of which we are here maintaining, is that the broadest and the most general contents and forms of life are intimately bound up with the most individual ones. Both have a common prehistory and also common enemies in the narrow formations and groupings, whose striving for self preservation set them in conflict with the broad and general on the outside, as well as the freely mobile and individual on the inside. Just as in feudal times the "free" man was he who stood under the law of the land, that is, under the law of the largest social unit, but he was unfree who derived his legal rights only from the narrow circle of a feudal community—so today in an intellectualized and refined sense the citizen of the metropolis is "free" in contrast with the trivialities and prejudices which bind the small town person. The mutual reserve and indifference, and the intellectual conditions of life in large social units are never more sharply appreciated in their significance for the independence of the individual than in the dense crowds of the metropolis because the bodily closeness and lack of space make intellectual distance really perceivable for the first time. It is obviously only the obverse of this freedom that, under certain circumstances, one never feels as lonely and as deserted as in this metropolitan crush of persons. For here, as elsewhere, it is by no means necessary that the freedom of

man reflect itself in his emotional life only as a pleasant experience.

It is not only the immediate size of the area and population which, on the basis of world-historical correlation between the increase in the size of the social unit and the degree of personal inner and outer freedom, makes the metropolis the locus of this condition. It is rather in transcending this purely tangible extensiveness that the metropolis also becomes the seat of cosmopolitanism. Comparable with the form of the development of wealth—(beyond a certain point property increases in ever more rapid progression as out of its own inner being)—the individual's horizon is enlarged. In the same way, economic, personal and intellectual relations in the city (which are its ideal reflection), grow in a geometrical progression as soon as, for the first time, a certain limit has been passed. Every dynamic extension becomes a preparation not only for a similar extension but rather for a larger one and from every thread which is spun out of it there continue, growing as out of themselves, an endless number of others. This may be illustrated by the fact that within the city the "unearned increment" of ground rent, through a mere increase in traffic, brings to the owner profits which are self-generating. At this point the quantitative aspects of life are transformed qualitatively. The sphere of life of the small town is, in the main, enclosed within itself. For the metropolis it is decisive that its inner life is extended in a wave-like motion over a broader national or international area. Weimar was no exception because its significance was dependent upon individual personalities and died with them, whereas the metropolis is characterised by its essential independence even of the most significant individual personalities; this is rather its antithesis and it is the price of independence which the individual living in it enjoys. The most significant aspect of the metropolis lies in this functional magnitude beyond its actual physical boundaries and this effectiveness reacts upon the latter and gives to it life, weight, importance and responsibility. A person does not end with limits of his physical body or with the area to which his physical activity is immediately confined but embraces, rather, the totality of meaningful effects which emanates from him temporally and spatially. In the same way the city exists only in the totality of the effects which transcend their immediate sphere. These really are the actual extent in which their existence is expressed. This is already expressed in the fact that individual freedom, which is the logical historical complement of such extension, is not only to be understood in the negative sense as mere freedom of movement and emancipation from prejudices and philistinism. Its essential characteristic is rather to be found in the fact that the particularity and incomparability which ultimately every person possesses in some way is actually expressed, giving form to life. That we follow the laws of our inner nature—and this is what freedom is—becomes perceptible and convincing to us and to others only when the expressions of this nature distinguish themselves from others; it is our irreplaceability by others which shows that our mode of existence is not imposed upon us from the outside.

Cities are above all the seat of the most advanced economic division of labor. They produce such extreme phenomena as the lucrative vocation of the *quatorzieme* in Paris. These are persons who may be recognized by shields on their houses and who hold themselves ready at the dinner hour in appropriate costumes so they can be called upon on short notice in case thirteen persons find themselves at the table. Exactly in the measure of its extension the city offers to an increasing degree the determining conditions for the division of labor. It is a unit which, because of its large size, is receptive to a highly diversified plurality of achievements while at the same time the agglomeration of individuals and their struggle for the customer forces the individual to a type of specialized accomplishment in which he cannot be so easily exterminated by the other. The decisive fact here is that in the life of a city, struggle with nature for the means of life is transformed into a conflict with human beings and the gain which is fought for is granted, not by nature, but by man. For here we find not only the previously mentioned source of specialization but rather the deeper one in which the seller must seek to produce in the person to whom he wishes to sell ever new and unique needs. The necessity to specialize one's product in order to find a source of income which is not yet exhausted and also to specialize a function which cannot be easily supplanted is conducive to differentiation, refinement and enrichment of the needs of the public which

obviously must lead to increasing personal variation within this public.

All this leads to the narrower type of intellectual individuation of mental qualities to which the city gives rise in proportion to its size. There is a whole series of causes for this. First of all there is the difficulty of giving one's own personality a certain status within the framework of metropolitan life. Where quantitative increase of value and energy has reached its limits, one seizes on qualitative distinctions, so that, through taking advantage of the existing sensitivity to differences, the attention of the social world can, in some way, be won for oneself. This leads ultimately to the strangest eccentricities, to specifically metropolitan extravagances of self-distanciation, of caprice, of fastidiousness, the meaning of which is no longer to be found in the content of such activity itself but rather in its being a form of "being different"—of making oneself noticeable. For many types of persons these are still the only means of saving for oneself, through the attention gained from others, some sort of self-esteem and the sense of filling a position. In the same sense there operates an apparently insignificant factor which in its effects however is perceptibly cumulative, namely, the brevity and rarity of meetings which are allotted to each individual as compared with social intercourse in a small city. For here we find the attempt to appear to-the-point, clear-cut and individual with extraordinarily greater frequency than where frequent and long association assures to each person an unambiguous conception of the other's personality.

This appears to me to be the most profound cause of the fact that the metropolis places emphasis on striving for the most individual forms of personal existence—regardless of whether it is always correct or always successful. The development of modern culture is characterised by the predominance of what one can call the objective spirit over the subjective; that is, in language as well as in law, in the technique of production as well as in art, in science as well as in the objects of domestic environment, there is embodied a sort of spirit [*Geist*], the daily growth of which is followed only imperfectly and with an even greater lag by the intellectual development of the individual. If we survey for instance the vast culture which during the last century has been embodied in things and in knowledge, in institutions and comforts, and if we compare them with the cultural progress of the individual during the same period—at least in the upper classes—we would see a frightful difference in rate of growth between the two which represents, in many points, rather a regression of the culture of the individual with reference to spirituality, delicacy and idealism. This discrepancy is in essence the result of the success of the growing division of labor. For it is this which requires from the individual an ever more one-sided type of achievement which, at its highest point, often permits his personality as a whole to fall into neglect. In any case this overgrowth of objective culture has been less and less satisfactory for the individual. Perhaps less conscious than in practical activity and in the obscure complex of feelings which flow from him, he is reduced to a negligible quantity. He becomes a single cog as over against the vast overwhelming organization of things and forces which gradually take out of his hands everything connected with progress, spirituality and value. The operation of these forces results in the transformation of the latter from a subjective form into one of purely objective existence. It need only be pointed out that the metropolis is the proper arena for this type of culture which has outgrown every personal element. Here in buildings and in educational institutions, in the wonders and comforts of space-conquering technique, in the formations of social life and in the concrete institutions of the State is to be found such a tremendous richness of crystallizing, depersonalized cultural accomplishments that the personality can, so to speak, scarcely maintain itself in the face of it. From one angle life is made infinitely more easy in the sense that stimulations, interests, and the taking up of time and attention, present themselves from all sides and carry it in a stream which scarcely requires any individual efforts for its ongoing. But from another angle, life is composed more and more of these impersonal cultural elements and existing goods and values which seek to suppress peculiar personal interests and incomparabilities. As a result, in order that this most personal element be saved, extremities and peculiarities and individualizations must be produced and they must be over-exaggerated merely to be brought into the awareness even of the individual himself. The atrophy of individual culture through the hypertrophy of

objective culture lies at the root of the bitter hatred which the preachers of the most extreme individualism, in the footsteps of Nietzsche, directed against the metropolis. But it is also the explanation of why indeed they are so passionately loved in the metropolis and indeed appear to its residents as the saviors of their unsatisfied yearnings.

When both of these forms of individualism which are nourished by the quantitative relationships of the metropolis, i.e., individual independence and the elaboration of personal peculiarities, are examined with reference to their historical position, the metropolis attains an entirely new value and meaning in the world history of the spirit. The eighteenth century found the individual in the grip of powerful bonds which had become meaningless—bonds of a political, agrarian, guild and religious nature—delimitations which imposed upon the human being at the same time an unnatural form and for a long time an unjust inequality. In this situation arose the cry for freedom and equality—the belief in the full freedom of movement of the individual in all his social and intellectual relationships which would then permit the same noble essence to emerge equally from all individuals as Nature had placed it in them and as it had been distorted by social life and historical development. Alongside of this liberalistic ideal there grew up in the nineteenth century from Goethe and the Romantics, on the one hand, and from the economic division of labor on the other, the further tendency, namely, that individuals who had been liberated from their historical bonds sought now to distinguish themselves from one another. No longer was it the "general human quality" in every individual but rather his qualitative uniqueness and irreplaceability that now became the criteria of his value. In the conflict and shifting interpretations of these two ways of defining the position of the individual within the totality is to be found the external as well as the internal history of our time. It is the function of the metropolis to make a place for the conflict and for the attempts at unification of both of these in the sense that its own peculiar conditions have been revealed to us as the occasion and the stimulus for the development of both. Thereby they attain a quite unique place, fruitful with an inexhaustible richness of meaning in the development of the mental life. They reveal themselves as one of those great historical struc- tures in which conflicting life-embracing currents find themselves with equal legitimacy. Because of this, how- ever, regardless of whether we are sympathetic or anti- pathetic with their individual expressions, they transcend the sphere in which a judge-like attitude on our part is appropriate. To the extent that such forces have been integrated, with the fleeting existence of a single cell, into the root as well as the crown of the totality of historical life to which we belong—it is our task not to complain or to condone but only to understand.

19. THE STRANGER

GEORG SIMMEL

"The Stranger" (1908) is one of Simmel's classic essays on social types. In it he describes the type of person who lives among and yet apart from—in but not of—a society. The stranger, as he writes in one crucial passage, is a person who "comes today and stays tomorrow." The stranger is both integrally part of the society and in some fashion appended onto it. As Simmel points out, the classic example of the stranger is the Jew in European society: Although part of the economy as trader, the Jew is also marginalized from that society, living in close physical proximity to non-Jews, but in a situation where the social distance between Jews and Christians is pronounced. This social type, recast as the "marginal man," became at the hands of Simmel's former student, the American sociologist Robert E. Park, an important concept in the study of immigration and ethnic relations.

If wandering, considered as a state of detachment from every given point in space, is the conceptual opposite of attachment to any point, then the sociological form of "the stranger" presents the synthesis, as it were, of both of these properties. (This is another indication that spatial relations not only are determining conditions of relationships among men, but are also symbolic of those relationships.) The stranger will thus not be considered here in the usual sense of the term, as the wanderer who comes today and goes tomorrow, but rather as the man who comes today and stays tomorrow—the potential wanderer, so to speak, who, although he has gone no further, has not quite got over the freedom of coming and going. He is fixed within a certain spatial circle—or within a group whose boundaries are analogous to spatial boundaries—but his position within it is fundamentally affected by the fact that he does not belong in it initially and that he brings qualities into it that are not, and cannot be, indigenous to it.

In the case of the stranger, the union of closeness and remoteness involved in every human relationship is patterned in a way that may be succinctly formulated as follows: the distance within this relation indicates that one who is close by is remote, but his strangeness indicates that one who is remote is near. The state of being a stranger is of course a completely positive relation; it is a specific form of interaction. The inhabitants of Sirius are not exactly strangers to us, at least not in the sociological sense of the word as we are considering it. In that sense they do not exist for us at all; they are beyond being far and near. The stranger is an element of the group itself, not unlike the poor and sundry "inner enemies"—an element whose membership within the group involves both being outside it and confronting it.

The following statements about the stranger are intended to suggest how factors of repulsion and distance work to create a form of being together, a form of union based on interaction.

In the whole history of economic activity the stranger makes his appearance everywhere as a trader, and the trader makes his as a stranger. As long as production for one's own needs is the general rule, or products are exchanged within a relatively small circle, there is no need for a middleman within the group. A trader is required only for goods produced outside the group. Unless there are people who wander out into foreign lands to buy these necessities, in which case they are themselves "strange" merchants in this other region, the trader *must* be a stranger; there is no opportunity for anyone else to make a living at it.

This position of the stranger stands out more sharply if, instead of leaving the place of his activity, he settles down there. In innumerable cases even this is possible only if he can live by trade as a middleman. Any closed economic group where land and handicrafts have been apportioned in a way that satisfies local demands will still support a livelihood for the trader. For trade alone makes possible unlimited combinations, and through it intelligence is constantly extended and applied in new areas, something that is much harder for the primary producer with his more limited mobility and his dependence on a circle of customers that can be expanded only very slowly. Trade can always absorb more men than can primary production. It is therefore the most suitable activity for the stranger, who intrudes as a supernumerary, so to speak, into a group in which all the economic positions are already occupied. The classic example of this is the history of European Jews. The stranger is by his very nature no owner of land—land not only in the physical sense but also metaphorically as a vital substance which is fixed, if not in space, then at least in an ideal position within the social environment.

Although in the sphere of intimate personal relations the stranger may be attractive and meaningful in many ways, so long as he is regarded as a stranger he is no "landowner" in the eyes of the other. Restriction to intermediary trade and often (as though sublimated from it) to pure finance gives the stranger the specific character of *mobility*. The appearance of this mobility within a bounded group occasions that synthesis of nearness and remoteness which constitutes the formal position of the stranger. The purely mobile person comes incidentally into contact with *every* single element but is not bound up organically, through established ties of kinship, locality, or occupation, with any single one.

Another expression of this constellation is to be found in the objectivity of the stranger. Because he is not bound by roots to the particular constituents and partisan dispositions of the group, he confronts all of these with a distinctly "objective" attitude, an attitude that does not signify mere detachment and nonparticipation, but is a distinct structure composed of remoteness and nearness, indifference and involvement. I refer to my analysis of the dominating positions gained by aliens, in the discussion of superordination and subordination,[1] typified by the practice in certain Italian cities of recruiting their judges from outside, because no native was free from entanglement in family interests and factionalism.

Connected with the characteristic of objectivity is a phenomenon that is found chiefly, though not exclusively, in the stranger who moves on. This is that he often receives the most surprising revelations and confidences, at times reminiscent of a confessional, about matters which are kept carefully hidden from everybody with whom one is close. Objectivity is by no means nonparticipation, a condition that is altogether outside the distinction between subjective and objective orientations. It is rather a positive and definite kind of participation, in the same way that the objectivity of a theoretical observation clearly does not mean that the mind is a passive tabula rasa on which things inscribe their qualities, but rather signifies the full activity of a mind working according to its own laws, under conditions that exclude accidental distortions and emphases whose individual and subjective differences would produce quite different pictures of the same object.

Objectivity can also be defined as freedom. The objective man is not bound by ties which could prejudice his perception, his understanding, and his assessment of data. This freedom, which permits the stranger to experience and treat even his close relationships as though from a bird's-eye view, contains many dangerous possibilities. From earliest times, in uprisings of all sorts the attacked party has claimed that there has been incitement from the outside, by foreign emissaries and agitators. Insofar as this has happened, it represents an exaggeration of the specific role of the stranger: he is the freer man, practically and theoretically; he examines conditions with less prejudice; he assesses them against standards that are more general and more objective; and his actions are not confined by custom, piety, or precedent.[2]

Finally, the proportion of nearness and remoteness which gives the stranger the character of objectivity also finds practical expression in the more *abstract* nature of the relation to him. That is, with the stranger one has only certain *more general* qualities in common, whereas the relation with organically connected persons is based on the similarity of just those specific traits which differentiate them from the merely universal. In fact, all personal relations whatsoever can be analyzed in terms of this scheme. They are not determined only by the existence of certain common characteristics which the individuals share in addition to their individual differences, which either influence the relationship or remain outside of it. Rather, the kind of effect which that commonality has on the relation essentially depends on whether it exists only among the participants themselves, and thus, although general within the relation, is specific and incomparable with respect to all those on the outside, or whether the participants feel that what they have in common is so only because it is common to a group, a type, or mankind in general. In the latter case, the effect of the common features becomes attenuated in proportion to the size of the group bearing the same characteristics. The commonality provides a basis for unifying the members, to be sure; but it does not specifically direct *these* particular persons to one another. A similarity so widely shared could just as easily unite each person with every possible other. This, too, is evidently a way in which a relationship includes both nearness and remoteness simultaneously. To the extent to which the similarities assume a universal nature, the warmth of the connection based on them will acquire an element of coolness, a sense of the contingent nature of precisely *this* relation—the connecting forces have lost their specific, centripetal character.

In relation to the stranger, it seems to me, this constellation assumes an extraordinary preponderance in principle over the individual elements peculiar to the relation in question. The stranger is close to us insofar as we feel between him and ourselves similarities of nationality or social position, of occupation or of general human nature. He is far from us insofar as these similarities extend beyond him and us, and connect us only because they connect a great many people.

A trace of strangeness in this sense easily enters even the most intimate relationships. In the stage of first passion, erotic relations strongly reject any thought of generalization. A love such as this has never existed before; there is nothing to compare either with the person one loves or with our feelings for that person. An estrangement is wont to set in (whether as cause or effect is hard to decide) at the moment when this feeling of uniqueness disappears from the relationship. A skepticism regarding the intrinsic value of the relationship and its value for us adheres to the very thought that in this relation, after all, one is only fulfilling a general human destiny, that one has had an experience that has occurred a thousand times before, and that, if one had not accidentally met this precise person, someone else would have acquired the same meaning for us.

Something of this feeling is probably not absent in any relation, be it ever so close, because that which is common to two is perhaps never common *only* to them but belongs to a general conception which includes much else besides, many *possibilities* of similarities. No matter how few of these possibilities are realized and how often we may forget about them, here and there, nevertheless, they crowd in like shadows between men, like a mist eluding every designation, which must congeal into solid corporeality for it to be called jealousy. Perhaps this is in many cases a more general, at least more insurmountable, strangeness than that due to differences and obscurities. It is strangeness caused by the fact that similarity, harmony, and closeness are accompanied by the feeling that they are actually not the exclusive property of this particular relation, but stem from a more general one—a relation that potentially includes us and an indeterminate number of others, and therefore prevents that relation which alone was experienced from having an inner and exclusive necessity.

On the other hand, there is a sort of "strangeness" in which this very connection on the basis of a general quality embracing the parties is precluded. The relation of the Greeks to the barbarians is a typical example; so are all the cases in which the general characteristics one takes as peculiarly and merely human are disallowed to the other. But here the expression "the stranger" no longer has any positive meaning. The relation with him is a non-relation; he is not what we have been discussing here: the stranger as a member of the group itself.

As such, the stranger is near and far *at the same time*, as in any relationship based on merely universal human similarities. Between these two factors of nearness and distance, however, a peculiar tension arises, since the consciousness of having only the absolutely general in common has exactly the effect of putting a special emphasis on that which is not common. For a stranger to the country, the city, the race, and so on, what is stressed is again nothing individual, but alien origin, a quality which he has, or could have, in common with many other strangers. For this reason strangers are not really perceived as individuals, but as strangers of a certain type. Their remoteness is no less general than their nearness.

This form appears, for example, in so special a case as the tax levied on Jews in Frankfurt and elsewhere during the Middle Ages. Whereas the tax paid by Christian citizens varied according to their wealth at any given time, for every single Jew the tax was fixed once and for all. This amount was fixed because the Jew had his social position as a *Jew*, not as the bearer of certain objective contents. With respect to taxes every other citizen was regarded as possessor of a certain amount of wealth, and his tax could follow the fluctuations of his fortune. But the Jew as taxpayer was first of all a Jew, and thus his fiscal position contained an invariable element. This appears most forcefully, of course, once the differing circumstances of individual Jews are no longer considered, limited though this consideration is by fixed assessments, and all strangers pay exactly the same head tax.

Despite his being inorganically appended to it, the stranger is still an organic member of the group. Its unified life includes the specific conditioning of this element. Only we do not know how to designate the characteristic unity of this position otherwise than by saying that it is put together of certain amounts of nearness and of remoteness. Although both these qualities are found to some extent in all relationships, a special proportion and reciprocal tension between them produce the specific form of the relation to the "stranger."

NOTES

1. Simmel refers here to a passage which may be found in *The Sociology of Georg Simmel*, pp. 216–21.
2. Where the attacked parties make such an assertion falsely, they do so because those in higher positions tend to exculpate inferiors who previously have been in a close, solidary relationship with them. By introducing the fiction that the rebels were not really guilty, but only instigated, so they did not actually start the rebellion, they exonerate themselves by denying that there were any real grounds for the uprising.

20. THE PHILOSOPHY OF MONEY

GEORG SIMMEL

Simmel is often remembered as a superb essayist, as someone whose métier was the short but incisive analysis of the fragments that constitute the modern world. He did, however, produce a magnum opus that offers his most sustained argument about the character of the modern world writ large: *The Philosophy of Money*, which was published in 1900 but wasn't translated into English until 1978. In this work one sees similarities in his theoretical framework to the theoretical positions advanced by both Marx and Weber. What was distinctive about his work was that he opted to focus on the varied ways that a money economy transforms culture and in turn the individual's relations with others. In this particular passage from the text, Simmel is intent on illustrating the possibilities that are generated by a money economy. Money is viewed as a tool that has no other purpose than to facilitate the exchange of goods and services. Indeed, as he puts it, money is "the purest example of the tool." One of the consequences of a money economy is that it expands the possibilities of social exchange with larger circles of people, which in turn transforms cultural expectations and ideals. Simmel concludes this passage by examining what he terms "the surplus value of wealth."

MONEY AS THE PUREST EXAMPLE OF THE TOOL

Here, finally, we reach the point at which money finds its place in the interweaving of purposes. I will begin with some generally accepted facts. All economic transactions rest upon the fact that I want something that someone else owns, and that he will transfer it to me if I give him something I own that he wants. It is obvious that the final link in this two-sided process will not always be present when the first link appears; on many occasions I want the object A which A possesses, but the object or service B which I am willing to give in return does not interest A; or else the goods offered are acceptable to both parties but no agreement can be reached about the respective quantities. Thus, it is of great value in the attainment of our purposes that an intermediate link should be introduced into the chain of purposes; something into which I can change B at any time and which can itself be changed into A in much the same way as any form of power, from water, wind, etc., can be transformed into another form of power by means of a dynamo. Just as my thoughts must take the form of a universally understood language so that I can attain my practical ends in this roundabout way, so must my activities and possessions take the form of money value in order to serve my more remote purposes. Money is the purest form of the tool, in the category mentioned above; it is an institution through which the individual concentrates his activity and possessions in order to attain goals that he could not attain directly. The fact that everyone works with it makes its character as a tool more evident than was the case in the examples given earlier. The nature and effectiveness of money is not to be found simply in the coin that I hold in my hand; its qualities are invested in the social

Reprinted with permission from *The Philosophy of Money*, by Georg Simmel, pp. 210–218. Copyright © 1990 by Routledge Publishing, London and New York. Translated by Tom Bottomore and David Frisby from a first draft by Kaethe Mengelberg. ✦

organizations and the supra-subjective norms that make this coin a tool of endlessly diverse and extensive uses despite its material limitations, its insignificance and rigidity. It is characteristic of the State and of religious rites that, since they are constituted entirely by mental powers and do not have to compromise with any independent material objects, they can express their purpose fully in themselves. Yet they are so close to their specific purposes, indeed almost identical with them, that we often hesitate to recognize that they are tools (which would make them instruments without value in themselves, brought to life only by the will behind them) and regard them as ultimate moral values. In the case of money, its character as an instrument is very rarely obscured. By contrast with the other institutions mentioned earlier, money has no inherent relation to the specific purpose the attainment of which it aids. Money is totally indifferent to the objects because it is separated from them by the fact of exchange. What money mediates is not the possession of an object but the exchange of objects. Money in its perfected forms is an absolute means because, on the one hand, it is completely teleologically determined and is not influenced by any determination from a different series, while on the other hand it is restricted to being a pure means and tool in relation to a given end, has no purpose of its own and functions impartially as an intermediary in the series of purposes. Money is perhaps the clearest expression and demonstration of the fact that man is a `tool-making´ animal, which, however, is itself connected with the fact that man is a `purposive´ animal. The concept of means characterizes the position of man in the world; he is not dependent as is an animal upon the mechanism of instinctual life and immediate volition and enjoyment, nor does he have unmediated power, such as we attribute to a god, such that his will is identical with its realization. He stands between the two in so far as he can extend his will far beyond the present moment, but can realize it only in a roundabout way through a teleological series which has several links. Love, which according to Plato is an intermediate stage between possessing and not-possessing, is in the inner subjective life what means are in the objective external world. For man, who is always striving, never satisfied, always becoming, love is the true human condition. Means, on the other hand, and their enhanced form, the tool, symbolize the human

genus. The tool illustrates or incorporates the grandeur of the human will, and at the same time its limitations. The practical necessity to introduce a series of intermediate steps between ourselves and our ends has perhaps given rise to the concept of the past, and so has endowed man with his specific sense of life, of its extent and its limits, as a watershed between past and future. Money is the purest reification of means, a concrete instrument which is absolutely identical with its abstract concept; it is a pure instrument. The tremendous importance of money for understanding the basic motives of life lies in the fact that money embodies and sublimates the practical relation of man to the objects of his will, his power and his impotence; one might say, paradoxically, that man is an indirect being. I am here concerned with the relation of money to the totality of human life only in so far as it illuminates our immediate problem, which is to comprehend the nature of money through the internal and external relationships that find their expression, their means or their effects in money. I shall add here to the functions previously discussed one that shows with particular clarity how the abstract character of money is transposed into practical reality.

THE UNLIMITED POSSIBILITIES FOR THE UTILIZATION OF MONEY

I noted earlier that the representation and provision of means does not always depend upon an already formed purpose; the availability of materials and forces often provokes us to form certain purposes which these means will enable us to attain. Once a purpose has engendered the idea of means, the means may produce the conception of a purpose. This relationship, frequently modified but enduring, may be seen in the case of tools, which I characterized as the purest kind of means. While ordinary, simple means are entirely used up in achieving the purpose, a tool continues to exist apart from its particular application and is capable of a variety of other uses that cannot be foreseen. This is true not only for thousands of cases in daily life that need not be exemplified, but also in much more complicated situations. How often are military organizations, which were intended for external deployment, used by a dynasty for internal political ends? How often does a relationship among individuals which was originally established for a particular purpose grow beyond this and become the bearer of altogether different contents, with the result that one may say of all enduring human associations— familial, economic, religious, political or social—that they have a tendency to acquire purposes for which they were not originally conceived? It is obvious that a tool will be more significant and valuable—*ceteris paribus*—if it has various and extensive uses. At the same time, it must then become more neutral and colourless, more objective in relation to particular interests and more remote from any specific purpose. Money as the means *par excellence* fulfils this condition perfectly; from this point of view its importance is enhanced. The matter can be put as follows. The value of a given quantity of money exceeds the value of the particular object for which it is exchanged, because it makes possible the choice of any other object in an unlimited area. Of course, the money can be used ultimately only for one of the objects, but the choice that it offers is a bonus which increases its value. Since money is not related at all to a specific purpose, it acquires a relation to the totality of purposes. Money is the tool that has the greatest possible number of unpredictable uses and so possesses the maximum value attainable in this respect. The mere possibility of unlimited uses that money has, or represents, on account of its lack of any content of its own, is manifested in a positive way by the restlessness of money, by its urge to be used, so to speak. As in the case of languages such as French, which have a limited vocabulary, the need to employ the same expression for different things makes possible a wealth of allusions, references and psychological overtones, and one might almost say that their wealth results from their poverty; so the absence of any inner significance of money engenders the abundance of its practical uses, and indeed provides the impulse to fill its infinite conceptual categories with new formations, to give new content to its form, because it is never a conclusion but only a transitional point for each content. In the last analysis, the whole vast range of commodities can only be exchanged for one value, namely money; but money can be exchanged for any one of the range of commodities. By contrast with labour, which can rarely change

its application, and the less easily the more specialized it is, capital in the form of money can almost always be transferred from one use to another, at worst with a loss, but often with a gain. The worker can hardly ever extricate his art and skill from his trade and invest it somewhere else. By comparison with the owner of money he is at a disadvantage so far as free choice is concerned, just as the merchant is. Thus, the value of a given amount of money is equal to the value of any object for which it might be exchanged plus the value of free choice between innumerable other objects, and this is an asset that has no analogy in the area of commodities or labour.

This surplus value of money appears all the more important if one considers the nature of the decision to which this power of choice leads in reality. It has been asserted that a commodity that is limited in quantity and has alternative uses will be valued by its owners with respect to its most important use; all other uses will appear uneconomic and unreasonable. On the other hand, a supply of goods that is sufficient or more than sufficient for all possible uses, so that the goods compete to be used, will be valued according to its least important use. The most important use becomes the measure of the object if there are competing uses. This is most fully and effectively demonstrated by money. Since money can be used for any economic purpose, a given amount of it can be used to satisfy the most important subjective need for the moment. The choice is not limited, as is the case with all other commodities, and, because human desires know no limit, a great variety of possible uses is always competing for any given quantity of money. Since the decision will always be in favour of the good that is desired most intensely, money must be valued at any moment as equivalent to the most important interest experienced at that moment. A supply of wood or a building plot that is adequate only for one of several desired uses, and which is therefore valued according to the most valuable of those uses cannot have a significance beyond the region of things of its own kind. Money, however, has no such limitation, and so its value corresponds with the most important universal interest of the individual that can be satisfied with the available supply.

The opportunity of choice which money as an abstract instrument provides applies not only to the goods offered at any one time, but also to the date when it can be used. The value of a commodity is not determined simply by its practical significance at the moment of its use. The relative freedom of choice in timing the use is a factor that can increase or diminish considerably the value placed upon the commodity. The first of these possibilities of choice results from the coexistence of different uses, the second from the existence of alternative uses over time. Other things being equal, that commodity is more valuable which I *can* but do not *have to* use immediately. The range of commodities falls into a graduated series of values between two extremes: at one end is the commodity that can be enjoyed later but not now. If, for example, fish caught during the summer is exchanged for furs that are going to be worn in the winter, then the value of the fish is increased by the fact that I can consume it immediately, whereas the value of the furs is affected by the fact that the delay in using them involves the risk of damage, loss or devaluation. On the other hand, the value of the fish is diminished because it will no longer be fresh tomorrow, and the value of the furs is increased because they will still be serviceable at a later date. An object used as a means of exchange is most suitable for money, if it possesses both of these value-enhancing qualities. Money as a pure instrument represents their highest possible synthesis because it has no specific quality for a specific use, but is only a tool for acquiring concrete values, and because the opportunities for using it are just as great at any point of time and for any object.

The superiority of the owner of money over the owner of commodities results from this unique quality of money as being unrelated to all particular characteristics of things or moments of time, dissociated from any purpose, and a purely abstract means. There are some exceptions to this, such as the refusal to sell on ideological grounds, boycotts and cartels, but these arise only when the objects of exchange in that particular situation cannot be replaced by other objects. The freedom of choice and also the particular advantage that money confers upon its owner are then eliminated precisely because there is a single object of desire instead of a choice. In general, the owner of money

enjoys this twofold liberty and he will demand a recompense if he relinquishes it in favour of the owner of goods. This is shown, for example, by the economically and psychologically interesting principle of the `supplement´. When goods that can be measured or weighed are purchased the merchant is expected to `measure liberally´, that is to add at least one additional unit, and he usually does so. It must be taken into account that a mistake is more likely in measuring goods than in counting money, but the important feature is that the buyer has the power to enforce an interpretation of this possibility in his own favour even though the chances of advantage or disadvantage are equal for both parties. It is significant that the advantage is given to the buyer even when the other party is also dealing in money. The customer expects the banker, the insured expects the insurance company in case of a claim, to deal `fairly´, that is to give a little more, even if only in a formal way, than what is enforceable by law. The bank and the insurance company also trade only in money, but the customer for his part does not think of being `fair´ or `liberal´; he only offers what has been agreed upon beforehand. The sums of money offered on each side have in fact quite a different significance. For the banker and the insurance company the money with which they operate is simply a commodity that they can use only in this particular way; for the customer it is `money´ in the sense with which we are here concerned, namely a value that he can, but need not necessarily, use for stock exchange business or insurance. The freedom to use the money for diverse purposes gives the customer an advantage which is compensated by the `fairness´ of the other party. Where a supplement is given by the owner of money, as in tipping waiters and taxi-drivers, this merely expresses the social superiority of the giver, which is the presupposition of tipping. Like all other monetary phenomena these are not occurrences isolated from the rest of human life; they display in a particularly clear and obvious manner a fundamental characteristic of life, namely that in every relationship the individual who has less interest in the substance of the relationship is at an advantage. This may appear paradoxical, since the more intense the desire to possess something or to establish a relationship, the more intense and passionate is the enjoyment of it. It is indeed the anticipated enjoyment that determines the strength of our desire. Yet it is just this situation that gives an advantage to the less interested party, for it is in the nature of things that the one who benefits less should be compensated by some concessions from the other party. This is apparent even in the most refined and intimate relations. In every love relationship, the one who is less involved has an advantage, because the other renounces from the very beginning any exploitation of the relationship, is more ready to make sacrifices, and offers a greater measure of devotion in exchange for the greater satisfaction that he derives. Equity is thus established: since the degree of desire corresponds with the degree of enjoyment it is right that the relationship should provide the individual who is less involved with a special gain, which he is able to exact because he is more hesitant, more reserved and more ready to make conditions. Thus the profit of the one who gives money is not altogether unfair; since he is usually less interested in the commodity–money transaction, an agreement between the two parties is brought about by the one who is more interested in the transaction giving to the other a gain over and above the objective equivalence of the exchange values. It should also be borne in mind that the owner of money has this advantage not because he possesses money, but because he is prepared to part with it.

The profit that accrues to money because it is detached from any particular content or process of the economy is also shown in other ways, and particularly in the fact that owners of money usually profit from violent and ruinous economic upheavals, often to an extraordinary extent. However many bankruptcies and business failures result from price slumps or from commodity market booms, experience has shown that the big bankers usually make a steady profit out of these dangers that confront sellers and buyers, creditors and debtors. The services of money, as the neutral tool of economic processes, have to be paid for regardless of the direction or pace of these processes. Of course, money has to pay something for this freedom; the uncommitted nature of money means that contradictory demands are made upon the dispenser of money from different sides, and that he excites the suspicion of betrayal more easily

than does the individual who deals in specific commodities. In early modern times, when the great financial powers—the Fuggers, the Welsers, the Florentine and Genoan bankers—entered the political arena, particularly during the great struggle between the Habsburgs and the French monarchy for European hegemony, they were regarded with permanent mistrust by all parties, including those to whom they had lent vast sums of money. One never could be sure of the financiers, whose money transactions did not commit them beyond the present moment; and even the enemy against whom they had lent their financial support did not regard this as an obstacle to approaching them himself with requests and propositions. Money has the very positive quality that is designated by the negative concept of lack of character. The individual whom we regard as a weak character is not directed by the inner worth of persons, things or thoughts, but by the external pressure that is brought to bear upon him. The fact that money is detached from all specific contents and exists only as a quantity earns for money and for those people who are only interested in money the quality of characterlessness. This is the almost logically necessary reverse side of the advantages of finance and of the over-valuation of money in relation to qualitative values. The superiority of money is expressed first in the fact that the seller is more interested and eager than the buyer. A very significant feature of our whole attitude towards objects is involved here; namely, when two opposing classes of values are considered as a whole, the first class may be distinctly superior to the second, while the individual objects or representatives of the second group may be superior to those of the first. Faced with a choice between the totality of material goods and the totality of ideal goods, we should probably be obliged to choose the first, because to renounce it would be to negate life, including all its ideal contents; but on the other hand, we might not hesitate to give up any single material good in exchange for an ideal good. In our relations with other people we do not question that one relationship is much more valuable and indispensable than another, when viewed as a whole; but on particular occasions and in particular aspects the less valuable relationship may be more enjoyable and attractive. This is how matters stand in the relation between money and concrete objects of value; a choice between the objects as a whole and money as a whole would immediately reveal the intrinsic valueless-ness of the latter, which provides us only with means, not with an end. Yet when a given sum of money is set against a given quantity of commodities, the exchange of the latter for the former is usually demanded much more strongly than vice-versa. This relationship exists not only between commodities and money in general, but also between money and particular categories of commodities. A single pin is almost worthless, but pins in general are almost indispensable and `worth their weight in gold´. The case is similar with many kinds of commodities; the ease with which a single specimen can be supplied in return for money devalues it in relation to money, which now appears as a ruling power disposing over the object. But the significance of the class of object as a whole seems incommensurable with money; it has a value independent of money which is often concealed from our notice by the fact that the single specimen can so easily be replaced. However, since our practical economic interests are almost exclusively concerned with single units or with a limited number of units, our sense of the value of objects generally employs the measuring rod of money. This is evidently connected with the overriding interest in possessing money rather than commodities.

THE UNEARNED INCREMENT OF WEALTH

This leads to a more general phenomenon, which might be termed the surplus value of wealth and which resembles the unearned rent of land. The wealthy man enjoys advantages beyond the enjoyment of what he can buy with his money. The merchant supplies him more reliably and more cheaply than he does poorer people; everyone he meets, whether likely to profit from his wealth or not, is more deferential; he moves in an ideal atmosphere of unquestioned privilege. One can observe everywhere all manner of small privileges being granted to the purchaser of expensive goods and to the first-class traveller; privileges that have as little connection with the objective value as has the

friendly smile of the merchant with the more expensive goods that he is selling. These privileges are a gratuitous supplement, and their most painful feature is perhaps that the consumer of cheaper goods, who is denied them, cannot complain that he is being cheated. This can be best illustrated by a very minor instance. The streetcars in some cities have two separate classes which differ in price, although the more expensive class offers no material advantage in the way of greater comfort. What the traveller buys with his first-class ticket is the right to join the exclusive company of those who pay such a higher price in order to be separated from the second-class passengers. Thus the well-to-do individual can acquire an advantage simply by spending more money, without necessarily receiving a material equivalent for his expenditure.

Viewed from the outside, it may seem that this is the opposite of an unearned increment, because the well-to-do individual receives relatively less, not relatively more, for his money. But the unearned increment of wealth appears here in a negative, but pure, form; the rich man gains an advantage without recourse to an object and exclusively by virtue of the fact that other people cannot spend as much money as he can. Wealth, indeed, is often regarded as a kind of moral merit, as is indicated by the term `respectability´ and by popular references to the well-to-do as `upright citizens´ or `the better-class public´. The same phenomenon is shown from the other side by the fact that the poor are treated as if they were guilty, that beggars are angrily driven away, and that even good-natured people consider themselves naturally superior to the poor. When it was decreed in 1536 that the journeyman locksmiths in Strasbourg who earned more than eight *kreuzer* should have a holiday on Monday afternoons, a bonus was given to those who were better off, when moral logic suggests that it should have been given to the needy. It is not uncommon for the unearned increment of wealth to attain such a degree of perversity: practical idealism, when it is manifested in the unpaid scientific work of a wealthy man, is generally more highly esteemed than is the work of a poor schoolteacher. This usurious interest upon wealth, these advantages that its possessor gains without being obliged to give anything in return, are bound up with the money form of value. For those phenomena obviously express or reflect that unlimited freedom of use which distinguishes money from all other values. This it is that creates the state of affairs in which a rich man has an influence not only by what he does but also by what he could do; a great fortune is encircled by innumerable possibilities of use, as though by an astral body, which extend far beyond the employment of the income from it on the benefits which the income brings to other people. The German language indicates this by the use of the word *Vermögen*, which means ʻto be able to do somethingʼ, for a great fortune. These possibilities, only a small number of which can be realized, are nevertheless put to account psychologically. They convey the impression of an indeterminate power which is not confined to the achievement of a particular result, and this impression is all the stronger the more mobile and more easily available for any purpose the possessions are; that is to say, the more the fortune consists of money or is convertible to money, and the more distinctly money itself has become a tool and a point of transition without any purpose of its own. The pure potentiality of money as a means is distilled in a general conception of power and significance which becomes effective as real power and significance for the owner of money. It is like the attraction of a work of art, which is produced not only by its content and the associated psychological reactions, but by all the accidental, individual and indirect complexes of feeling that it makes possible. Only the indeterminate sum of these feelings circumscribes the whole value and significance of a work of art.

SECTION IV

1. Explain why, according to Simmel, the success of any particular fashion spells its inevitable demise.
2. Why is fashion more characteristic of the modern world than the premodern world?
3. Simmel contends that a love affair contains the elements of an adventure. Summarize his argument and provide additional examples.
4. What is the blasé attitude, according to Simmel. Do you agree with his assessment? Why or why not?
5. Describe Simmel's depiction of the stranger and explain why, in his view, Jews constitute a primary example.
6. Provide examples from today's global economy to illustrate Simmel's claim that a money economy expands the possibility of potential exchange partners and discuss what this means in cultural rather than purely economic terms.
7. Compare Simmel's discussion on the philosophy of money with Marx's ideas on the circulation of capital.

V. OTHER FOUNDATIONAL VOICES

21. ON MARRIAGE

HARRIET MARTINEAU

A growing body of scholarly opinion has concluded that Harriet Martineau (1802–1876) ought to be seen—along with figures such as Auguste Comte and Herbert Spencer—as one of the critical formative influences on the subsequent development of sociology. She was a prolific author; included among her most important achievements are *Society in America* (1837), which has been compared favorably with Tocqueville´s *Democracy in America*, and *How to Observe Morals and Manners* (1838). Martineau´s writings evince a keen appreciation of the importance of social theory, which, like many of her contemporaries, she sought to advance by employing both historical and comparative perspectives. Moreover, she sought to connect theory to both empirical research and social reform. Far more consistently than her male counterparts, she attempted to explore the significance of gender relations. This interest is apparent in this essay, which concerns itself with the institution of marriage across cultures. Martineau contends that the observer will discover that in all cultures the marriage compact treats women unequally, which is releated to the limitations imposed on them in terms of occupational opportunities.

The Marriage compact is the most important feature of the domestic state on which the observer can fix his attention. If he be a thinker, he will not be surprised at finding much imperfection in the marriage state wherever he goes. By no arrangements yet attempted have purity of morals, constancy of affection, and domestic peace been secured to any extensive degree in society. Almost every variety of method is still in use, in one part of the world or another. The primitive custom of brothers marrying sisters still subsists in some Eastern regions. Polygamy is very common there, as every one knows. In countries which are too far advanced for this, every restraint of law, all sanction of opinion, has been tried to render that natural method,—the restriction of one husband to one wife, —successful, and therefore universal and permanent. Law and opinion have, however, never availed to anything like complete success. Even in thriving young countries, where no considerations of want, and few of ambition, can interfere with domestic peace,—where the numbers are equal, where love has the promise of a free and even course, and where religious sentiment is directed full upon the sanctity of the marriage state,—it is found to be far from pure. In almost all countries, the corruption of society in this department is so deep and wide-spreading, as to vitiate both moral sentiment and practice in an almost hopeless degree. It neutralizes almost all attempts to ameliorate and elevate the

Harriet Martineau, *How to Observe Morals and Manners.* (London: Charles Knight, 1838), 167–182. ✦

condition of the race.—There must be something fearfully wrong where the general result is so unfortunate as this. As in most other cases of social suffering, the wrong will be found to lie less in the methods ordained and put in practice, than in the prevalent sentiment of society, out of which all methods arise.

It is necessary to make mention (however briefly) of the kinds of false sentiment from which the evil of conjugal unhappiness appears to spring.—The sentiment by which courage is made the chief ground of honour in men, and chastity in women, coupled with the inferiority in which women have ever been sunk, was sure to induce profligacy. As long as men were brave nothing more was required to make them honourable in the eyes of society: while the inferior condition of women has ever exposed those of them who were not protected by birth and wealth to the profligacy of men. . . .

Marriage exists everywhere, to be studied by the moral observer. He must watch the character of courtships wherever he goes;—whether the young lady is negociated for and promised by her guardians, without having seen her intended; like the poor girl who, when she asked her mother to point out her future husband from among a number of gentlemen, was silenced with the rebuke, "What is that to you?"— or whether they are left free to exchange their faith "by flowing stream, through wood, or craggy wild," as in the United States;—or whether there is a medium between these two extremes, as in England. He must observe how fate is defied by lovers in various countries . . . Scotch lovers agree to come together after so many years spent in providing the "plenishing." Irish lovers conclude the business, in case of difficulty, by appearing before the priest the next morning. There is recourse to a balcony and rope-ladder in one country; a steam-boat and back-settlement in another; trust and patience in a third; and intermediate flirtations, to pass the time, in a fourth. He must note the degree of worldly ambition which attends marriages, and which may therefore be supposed to stimulate them, —how much space the house with two rooms in humble life, and the country-seat and carriages in higher life, occupy in the mind of bride or bridegroom.—He must observe whether conjugal infidelity excites horror and rage, or whether it is so much a

matter of course as that no jealousy interferes to mar the arrangements of mutual convenience.—He must mark whether women are made absolutely the property of their husbands, in mind and in estate; or whether the wife is treated more or less professedly as an equal party in the agreement.—He must observe whether there is an excluded class, victims to their own superstition or to a false social obligation, wandering about to disturb by their jealousy or licentiousness those whose lot is happier.—He must observe whether there are domestic arrangements for home enjoyments, or whether all is planned on the supposition of pleasure lying abroad; whether the reliance is on books, gardens, and play with children, or on the opera, parties, the ale-house, or dances on the green. —He must mark whether the ladies are occupied with their household cares in the morning, and the society of their husbands in the evening, or with embroidery and looking out of balconies; with receiving company all day, or gadding abroad; with the library or the nursery; with lovers or with children.—In each country, called civilized, he will meet with almost all these varieties: but in each there is such a prevailing character in the aspect of domestic life, that intelligent observation will enable him to decide, without much danger of mistake, as to whether marriage is merely an arrangement of convenience, in accordance with low morals, or a sacred institution, commanding the reverence and affection of a virtuous people. No high degree of this sanctity can be looked for till that moderation is attained which, during the prevalence of asceticism and its opposite, is reached only by a few. That it yet exists nowhere as the characteristic of any society,— that all the blessings of domestic life are not yet open to all, so as to preclude the danger of any one encroaching on his neighbour,—is but too evident to the travelled observer. He can only mark the degree of approximation to this state of high morals wherever he goes.

The traveller everywhere finds woman treated as the inferior party in a compact in which both parties have an equal interest. Any agreement thus formed is imperfect, and is liable to disturbance; and the danger is great in proportion to the degradation of the supposed weaker party. The degree of the degradation of woman is as good a test as the moralist can adopt for ascertaining the state of domestic morals in any country.

The Indian squaw carries the household burdens, trudging in the dust, while her husband on horseback paces before her, unencumbered but by his own gay trappings. She carries the wallet with food, the matting for the lodge, the merchandize (if they possess any), and her infant. There is no exemption from labour for the squaw of the most vaunted chief. In other countries the wife may be found drawing the plough, hewing wood and carrying water; the men of the family standing idle to witness her toils. Here the observer may feel pretty sure of his case. From a condition of slavery like this, women are found rising to the highest condition in which they are at present seen, in France, England, and the United States,—where they are less than half-educated, precluded from earning a subsistence, except in a very few ill-paid employments, and prohibited from giving or withholding their assent to laws which they are yet bound by penalties to obey. In France, owing to the great destruction of men in the wars of Napoleon, women are engaged, and successfully engaged, in a variety of occupations which have been elsewhere supposed unsuitable to the sex. Yet there remains so large a number who cannot, by the most strenuous labour in feminine employments, command the necessaries of life, while its luxuries may be earned by infamy, that the morals of the society are naturally bad. Great attention has of late been given to this subject in France: the social condition of women is matter of thought and discussion to a degree which promises some considerable amelioration. Already, women can do more in France than anywhere else; they can attempt more without ridicule or arbitrary hinderance: and the women of France are probably destined to lead the way in the advance which the sex must hereafter make. At present, society is undergoing a transition from a feudal state to one of mutual government; and women, gaining in some ways, suffer in others during the process. They have, happily for themselves, lost much of the peculiar kind of observance which was the most remarkable feature of the chivalrous age; and it has been impossible to prevent their sharing in the benefits of the improvement and diffusion of knowledge. All cultivation of their powers has secured to them the use of new power; so that their

condition is far superior to what it was in any former age. But new difficulties about securing a maintenance have arisen. Marriage is less general; and the husbands of the greater number of women are not secure of a maintenance from the lords of the soil, any more than women are from being married. The charge of their own maintenance is thrown upon large numbers of women, without the requisite variety of employments having been opened to them, or the needful education imparted. A natural consequence of this is, that women are educated to consider marriage the one object in life, and therefore to be extremely impatient to secure it. The unfavourable influence of these results upon the happiness of domestic life may be seen at a glance.

This may be considered the sum and substance of female education in England; and the case is scarcely better in France, though the independence and practical efficiency of women there are greater than in any other country. The women in the United States are in a lower condition than either, though there is less striving after marriage, from its greater frequency, and little restriction is imposed upon the book-learning which women may obtain. But the old feudal notions about the sex flourish there, while they are going out in the more advanced countries of Europe; and these notions, in reality, regulate the condition of women. American women generally are treated in no degree as equals, but with a kind of superstitious outward observance, which, as they have done nothing to earn it, is false and hurtful. Coexisting with this, there is an extreme difficulty in a woman's obtaining a maintenance, except by the exercise of some rare powers. In a country where women are brought up to be indulged wives, there is no hope, help, or prospect for such as have not money and are not married.

In America, women can earn a maintenance only by teaching, sewing, employment in factories, keeping boarding-houses, and domestic service. Some governesses are tolerably well paid,—comparing their earnings with those of men. Employment in factories, and domestic service, are well paid. Sewing is so wretched an occupation everywhere, that it is to be hoped that machinery will soon supersede the use of human fingers in a labour so unprofitable. In Boston, Massachusetts, a woman is paid ninepence (sixpence English) for making a shirt.—In England, besides these occupations, others are opening; and, what is of yet greater consequence, the public mind is awakening to the necessity of enlarging the sphere of female industry. Some of the inferior branches of the fine arts have lately offered profitable employment to many women. The commercial adversity to which the country has been exposed from time to time, has been of service to the sex, by throwing hundreds and thousands of them upon their own resources, and thus impelling them to urge claims and show powers which are more respected every day.—In France this is yet more conspicuously the case. There, women are shopkeepers, merchants, professional accountants, editors of newspapers, and employed in many other ways, unexampled elsewhere, but natural and respectable enough on the spot.

Domestic morals are affected in two principal respects by these differences. Where feminine occupations of a profitable nature are few, and therefore overstocked, and therefore yielding a scanty maintenance with difficulty, there is the strongest temptation to prefer luxury with infamy to hardship with unrecognized honour. Hence arises much of the corruption of cities,—less in the United States than in Europe, from the prevalence of marriage,—but awful in extent everywhere. Where vice is made to appear the interest of large classes of women, the observer may be quite sure that domestic morals will be found impure. If he can meet with any society where the objects of life are as various and as freely open to women as to men, there he may be sure of finding the greatest amount of domestic purity and peace; for, if women were not helpless, men would find it far less easy to be vicious.

The other way in which domestic morals are affected by the scope which is allowed to the powers of women, is through the views of marriage which are induced. Marriage is debased by being considered the one worldly object in life,—that on which maintenance, consequence, and power depend. Where the husband marries for connexion, fortune, or an heir to his estate, and the wife for an establishment, for consequence, or influence, there is no foundation for high domestic morals and lasting peace; and in a country where marriage is made the single aim of all women, there is no security against the influence of some of these motives even in the simplest and purest cases of attachment. The sordidness is infused from the earliest

years; the taint is in the mind before the attachment begins, before the objects meet; and the evil effects upon the marriage state are incalculable.

All this—the sentiment of society with regard to Woman and to Marriage, the social condition of Woman, and the consequent tendency and aim of her education,—the traveller must carefully observe. Each civilized society claims for itself the superiority in its treatment of woman. In one, she is indulged with religious shows, and with masquerades, or Punch, as an occasional variety. In another, she is left in honourable and undisputed possession of the housekeeping department. In a third, she is allowed to meddle, behind the scenes, with the business which is confided to her husband's management. In a fourth, she is satisfied in being the cherished domestic companion, unaware of the injury of being doomed to the narrowness of mind which is the portion of those who are always confined to the domestic circle. In a fifth, she is flattered at being guarded and indulged as a being requiring incessant fostering, and too feeble to take care of herself. In a sixth society, there may be found expanding means of independent occupation, of responsible employment for women; and here, other circumstances being equal, is the best promise of domestic fidelity and enjoyment.

It is a matter of course that women who are furnished with but one object,—marriage,—must be as unfit for anything when their aim is accomplished as if they had never had any object at all. They are no more equal to the task of education than to that of governing the state; and, if any unexpected turn of adversity befals them, they have no resource but a convent, or some other charitable provision. Where, on the other hand, women are brought up capable of maintaining an independent existence, other objects remain where the grand one is accomplished. Their independence of mind places them beyond the reach of the spoiler; and their cultivated faculty of reason renders them worthy guardians of the rational beings whose weal or woe is lodged in their hands. There is yet, as may be seen by a mere glance over society, only a very imperfect provision made anywhere for doing justice to the next generation by qualifying their mothers; but the observer of morals may profit by marking the degrees in which this imperfection approaches to barbarism.

Where he finds that girls are committed to convents for education, and have no alternative in life but marriage, in which their will has no share, and a return to their convent, he may safely conclude that there a plurality of lovers is a matter of course, and domestic enjoyments of the highest kind undesired and unknown. He may conclude that as are the parents, so will be the children; and that, for one more generation at least, there will be little or no improvement. But where he finds a variety of occupations open to women; where he perceives them not only pursuing the lighter mechanic arts, dispensing charity and organizing schools for the poor, but occupied in education, and in the study of science and the practice of the fine arts, he may conclude that here resides the highest domestic enjoyment which has yet been attained, and the strongest hope of a further advance....

From observation on these classes of facts,—the Occupation of the people, the respective Characters of the occupied classes, the Health of the population, the state of Marriage and of Women, and the character of Childhood,—the moralist may learn more of the private life of a community than from the conversation of any number of the individuals who compose it.

22. ON INDIVIDUALISM

ALEXIS DE TOCQUEVILLE

Alexis de Tocqueville, a 26-year-old Frenchman, made a nine-month sojourn to the United States in the early 1830s, traveling from the eastern seaboard to the Midwest and into the Deep South, thus seeing both the most settled parts of the nation and regions that were in most respects frontiers. The result of this excursion was *Democracy in America*, a two-volume work, the first volume published in 1835 and the second in 1840. Jon Elster describes Tocqueville as the "first social scientist," and most commentators speak of his work in the most positive of terms. At the same time, it is generally conceded that his book is sometimes ambiguous and contradictory. This selection, from volume II, addresses the issue of individualism, which was a word that had only recently been coined. Tocqueville's account is generally seen as the starting point for subsequent explorations of American individualism, including Robert Putnam's influential *Bowling Alone*. Seeking to distinguish individualism from selfishness, he proceeds to argue that individualism is a characteristic of democratic societies, and as such if democracy takes root in a nation, so too will individualism. The final section of this entry addresses the way that American individualism is channeled into public activities, thus protecting the society from a population solely concerned with private interests.

ON INDIVIDUALISM IN DEMOCRATIC COUNTRIES

I have brought out how, in centuries of equality, each man seeks his beliefs in himself; I want to show how, in the same centuries, he turns all his sentiments toward himself alone.

Individualism is a recent expression arising from a new idea. Our fathers knew only selfishness.

Selfishness is a passionate and exaggerated love of self that brings man to relate everything to himself alone and to prefer himself to everything.

Individualism is a reflective and peaceable sentiment that disposes each citizen to isolate himself from the mass of those like him and to withdraw to one side with his family and his friends, so that after having thus created a little society for his own use, he willingly abandons society at large to itself.

Selfishness is born of a blind instinct; individualism proceeds from an erroneous judgment rather than a depraved sentiment. It has its source in the defects of the mind as much as in the vices of the heart.

Selfishness withers the seed of all the virtues; individualism at first dries up only the source of public virtues; but in the long term it attacks and destroys all the others and will finally be absorbed in selfishness.

Selfishness is a vice as old as the world. It scarcely belongs more to one form of society than to another.

Individualism is of democratic origin, and it threatens to develop as conditions become equal.

In aristocratic peoples, families remain in the same state for centuries, and often in the same place. That renders all generations so to speak contemporaries. A man almost always knows his ancestors and respects them; he believes he already perceives his great-grandsons and he loves them. He willingly does his duty by both, and he frequently comes to sacrifice his personal enjoyments for beings who no longer exist or who do not yet exist.

In addition, aristocratic institutions have the effect of binding each man tightly to several of his fellow citizens.

Classes being very distinct and immobile within an aristocratic people, each of them becomes for whoever makes up a part of it a sort of little native country, more visible and dearer than the big one.

As in aristocratic societies all citizens are placed at a fixed post, some above the others, it results also that each of them always perceives higher than himself a man whose protection is necessary to him, and below he finds another whom he can call upon for cooperation.

Men who live in aristocratic centuries are therefore almost always bound in a tight manner to something that is placed outside of them, and they are often disposed to forget themselves. It is true that in these same centuries the general notion of *those like oneself* is obscure and that one scarcely thinks of devoting oneself to the cause of humanity; but one often sacrifices oneself for certain men.

In democratic centuries, on the contrary, when the duties of each individual toward the species are much clearer, devotion toward one man becomes rarer: the bond of human affections is extended and loosened.

In democratic peoples, new families constantly issue from nothing, others constantly fall into it, and all those who stay on change face; the fabric of time is torn at every moment and the trace of generations is effaced. You easily forget those who have preceded you, and you have no idea of those who will follow you. Only those nearest have interest.

As each class comes closer to the others and mixes with them, its members become indifferent and almost like strangers among themselves. Aristocracy had made of all citizens a long chain that went from the peasant up to the king; democracy breaks the chain and sets each link apart.

As conditions are equalized, one finds a great number of individuals who, not being wealthy enough or powerful enough to exert a great influence over the fates of those like them, have nevertheless acquired or preserved enough enlightenment and

goods to be able to be self-sufficient. These owe nothing to anyone, they expect so to speak nothing from anyone; they are in the habit of always considering themselves in isolation, and they willingly fancy that their whole destiny is in their hands.

Thus not only does democracy make each man forget his ancestors, but it hides his descendants from him and separates him from his contemporaries; it constantly leads him back toward himself alone and threatens finally to confine him wholly in the solitude of his own heart.

HOW INDIVIDUALISM IS GREATER AT THE END OF A DEMOCRATIC REVOLUTION THAN IN ANY OTHER PERIOD

It is above all at the moment when a democratic society succeeds in forming itself on the debris of an aristocracy that this isolation of men from one another and the selfishness resulting from it strike one's regard most readily.

These societies not only contain many independent citizens, they are filled daily with men who, having arrived at independence yesterday, are drunk with their new power: these conceive a presumptuous confidence in their strength, and not imagining that from now on they could need to call upon the assistance of those like them, they have no difficulty in showing that they think only of themselves.

An aristocracy ordinarily succumbs only after a prolonged struggle, during which implacable hatreds among the different classes are ignited. These passions survive victory, and one can follow their track in the midst of the democratic confusion that succeeds it.

Those among the citizens who were the first in the hierarchy that has been destroyed cannot immediately forget their former greatness; for a long time they consider themselves strangers within the new society. They see all the equals that this society gives them as oppressors whose destiny cannot excite their sympathy; they have lost sight of their former equals and no longer feel bound by a common interest to their fates; each, in withdrawing separately, therefore believes himself reduced to being occupied only with himself. Those, on the contrary, who were formerly placed at the bottom of the social scale, and whom a sudden revolution has brought to the common level, enjoy their newly acquired independence only with a sort of secret restiveness; if they find some of their former superiors at their side, they cast looks of triumph and fear at them, and draw apart from them.

It is, therefore, ordinarily at the origin of democratic societies that citizens show themselves the most disposed to isolate themselves.

Democracy inclines men not to get close to those like themselves; but democratic revolutions dispose them to flee each other and to perpetuate in the heart of equality the hatreds to which inequality gave birth.

The great advantage of the Americans is to have arrived at democracy without having to suffer democratic revolutions, and to be born equal instead of becoming so.

HOW THE AMERICANS COMBAT INDIVIDUALISM WITH FREE INSTITUTIONS

Despotism, which in its nature is fearful, sees the most certain guarantee of its own duration in the isolation of men, and it ordinarily puts all its care into isolating them. There is no vice of the human heart that agrees with it as much as selfishness: a despot readily pardons the governed for not loving him, provided that they do not love each other. He does not ask them to aid him in leading the state; it is enough that they do not aspire to direct it themselves. He calls those who aspire to unite their efforts to create common prosperity turbulent and restive spirits, and changing the natural sense of words, he names those who confine themselves narrowly to themselves good citizens.

Thus the vices to which despotism gives birth are precisely those that equality favors. These two things complement and aid each other in a fatal manner.

Equality places men beside one another without a common bond to hold them. Despotism raises barriers between them and separates them. It disposes them not to think of those like themselves, and for them it makes a sort of public virtue of indifference.

Despotism, which is dangerous in all times, is therefore particularly to be feared in democratic centuries.

It is easy to see that in these same centuries men have a particular need of freedom.

When citizens are forced to be occupied with public affairs, they are necessarily drawn from the midst of their individual interests, and from time to time, torn away from the sight of themselves.

From the moment when common affairs are treated in common, each man perceives that he is not as independent of those like him as he at first fancied, and that to obtain their support he must often lend them his cooperation.

When the public governs, there is no man who does not feel the value of public benevolence and who does not seek to capture it by attracting the esteem and affection of those in the midst of whom he must live.

Several of the passions that chill and divide hearts are then obliged to withdraw to the bottom of the soul and hide there. Haughtiness dissimulates; contempt does not dare come to light. Selfishness is afraid of itself.

Under a free government, since most public functions are elective, men who by the loftiness of their souls or the restiveness of their desires are cramped in private life, feel every day that they cannot do without the populace surrounding them.

It then happens that through ambition one thinks of those like oneself, and that often one's interest is in a way found in forgetting oneself. I know that one can object to me here with all the intrigues that arise in an election, the shameful means the candidates often make use of, and the calumnies their enemies spread. These are occasions for hatred, and they present themselves all the more often as elections become more frequent.

These evils are undoubtedly great, but they are passing, whereas the goods that arise with them stay.

The longing to be elected can momentarily bring certain men to make war on each other, but in the long term this same desire brings all men to lend each other a mutual support; and if it happens that an election accidentally divides two friends, the electoral system brings together in a permanent manner a multitude of citizens who would have always remained strangers to one another. Freedom creates particular hatreds, but despotism gives birth to general indifference.

The Americans have combated the individualism to which equality gives birth with freedom, and they have defeated it.

The legislators of America did not believe that, to cure a malady so natural to the social body in democratic times and so fatal, it was enough to accord to the nation as a whole a representation of itself; they thought that, in addition, it was fitting to give political life to each portion of the territory in order to multiply infinitely the occasions for citizens to act together and to make them feel every day that they depend on one another.

This was wisely done.

The general affairs of a country occupy only the principal citizens. They assemble in the same places only from time to time; and as it often happens that afterwards they lose sight of each other, lasting bonds among them are not established. But when it is a question of having the particular affairs of a district regulated by the men who inhabit it, the same individuals are always in contact and they are in a way forced to know each other and to take pleasure in each other.

Only with difficulty does one draw a man out of himself to interest him in the destiny of the whole state, because he understands poorly the influence that the destiny of the state can exert on his lot. But should it be necessary to pass a road through his property, he will see at first glance that he has come across a relation between this small public affair and his greatest private affairs, and he will discover, without anyone's showing it to him, the tight bond that here unites a particular interest to the general interest.

Thus by charging citizens with the administration of small affairs, much more than by leaving the government of great ones to them, one interests them in the public good and makes them see the need they constantly have for one another in order to produce it.

One can capture the favor of a people all at once by a striking action; but to win the love and respect of the populace that surrounds you, you must have a long succession of little services rendered, obscure good offices, a constant habit of benevolence, and a well-established reputation of disinterestedness.

Local freedoms, which make many citizens put value on the affection of their neighbors and those close to them, therefore constantly bring men closer to one another, despite the instincts that separate them, and force them to aid each other.

In the United States, the most opulent citizens take much care not to isolate themselves from the people; on the contrary, they constantly come close to them, they gladly listen to them and speak to them every day. They know that the rich in democracies always need the poor, and that in democratic times one ties the poor to oneself more by manners than by benefits. The very greatness of the benefits, which brings to light the difference in conditions, causes a secret irritation to those who profit from them; but simplicity of manners has almost irresistible charms: their familiarity carries one away and even their coarseness does not always displease.

At first this truth does not penetrate the minds of the rich. They ordinarily resist it as long as the democratic revolution lasts, and they do not accept it immediately even after this revolution is accomplished. They willingly consent to do good for the people, but they want to continue to hold them carefully at a distance. They believe that is enough; they are mistaken. They would thus ruin themselves without warming the hearts of the population that surrounds them. It does not ask of them the sacrifice of their money, but of their haughtiness.

One would say that in the United States there is no imagination that does not exhaust itself in inventing the means of increasing wealth and satisfying the needs of the public. The most enlightened inhabitants of each district constantly make use of their enlightenment to discover new secrets appropriate to increasing the common prosperity; and when they have found any, they hasten to pass them along to the crowd.

When examining up close the vices and weakness often displayed in America by those who govern, one is astonished at the growing prosperity of the people—and one is wrong. It is not the elected magistrate who makes American democracy prosper; but it prospers because the magistrate is elective.

It would be unjust to believe that the patriotism of the Americans and the zeal that each of them shows for the well-being of his fellow citizens have nothing real about them. Although private interest directs most human actions, in the United States as elsewhere, it does not rule all.

I must say that I often saw Americans make great and genuine sacrifices for the public, and I remarked a hundred times that, when needed, they almost never fail to lend faithful support to one another.

The free institutions that the inhabitants of the United States possess and the political rights of which they make so much use recall to each citizen constantly and in a thousand ways that he lives in society. At every moment they bring his mind back toward the idea that the duty as well as the interest of men is to render themselves useful to those like them; and as he does not see any particular reason to hate them, since he is never either their slave or their master, his heart readily leans to the side of benevolence. One is occupied with the general interest at first by necessity and then by choice; what was calculation becomes instinct; and by dint of working for the good of one's fellow citizens, one finally picks up the habit and taste of serving them.

Many people in France consider equality of conditions as the first evil and political freedom as the second. When they are obliged to submit to the one, they strive at least to escape the other. And I say that to combat the evils that equality can produce there is only one efficacious remedy: it is political freedom.

23. THE CONSERVATION OF RACES

W. E. B. DU BOIS

William Edward Burghardt Du Bois (1868–1963) was one of the monumental figures in the struggle for racial justice in America. He founded the Niagara Movement, was one of the creators of the National Association for the Advancement of Colored People (NAACP), and later became an advocate of Pan-Africanism. Du Bois was trained as a sociologist, the first African American to receive a Ph.D. from Harvard University. In "The Conservation of Races," first published in 1897, he argues that contrary to those who would contend that racial differences are inconsequential when seen in the light of the similarities that bind all humans, there are important differences that transcend the obvious physical differences. These he characterizes as spiritual and psychical differences, and out of these differences the races have contributed to civilization. With this in mind, and without resorting to such language, Du Bois argues against assimilation and in favor of cultural pluralism.

The American Negro has always felt an intense personal interest in discussions as to the origins and destinies of races: primarily because back of most discussions of race with which he is familiar, have lurked certain assumptions as to his natural abilities, as to his political, intellectual and moral status, which he felt were wrong. He has, consequently, been led to deprecate and minimize race distinctions, to believe intensely that out of one blood God created all nations, and to speak of human brotherhood as though it were the possibility of an already dawning to-morrow.

Nevertheless, in our calmer moments we must acknowledge that human beings are divided into races; that in this country the two most extreme types of the world's races have met, and the resulting problem as to the future relations of these types is not only of intense and living interest to us, but forms an epoch in the history of mankind.

It is necessary, therefore, in planning our movements, in guiding our future development, that at times we rise above the pressing, but smaller questions of separate schools and cars, wage-discrimination and lynch law, to survey the whole question of race in human philosophy and to lay, on a basis of broad knowledge and careful insight, those large lines of policy and higher ideals which may form our guiding lines and boundaries in the practical difficulties of every day. For it is certain that all human striving must recognize the hard limits of natural law, and that any striving, no matter how intense and earnest, which is against the constitution of the world, is vain. The question, then, which we must seriously consider is this: What is the real meaning of Race; what has, in the past, been the law of race development, and what lessons has the past history of race development to teach the rising Negro people?

When we thus come to inquire into the essential difference of races we find it hard to come at once to any definite conclusion. Many criteria of race differences have in the past been proposed, as color, hair, cranial measurements and language. And manifestly, in each of these respects, human beings differ widely. They vary in color, for instance, from the marble-like pallor of the Scandinavian to the rich, dark brown of the Zulu, passing by the creamy Slav, the yellow Chinese, the light brown Sicilian and the brown Egyptian. Men vary, too, in the texture of hair from the obstinately straight hair of the Chinese to the obstinately tufted and frizzled hair of the Bushman. In measurement of heads, again, men vary; from the broad-headed Tartar to the medium-headed European and the narrow-headed Hottentot; or, again in language, from the highly-inflected Roman tongue to the monosyllabic Chinese. All these physical characteristics are patent enough, and if they agreed with each other it would be very easy to classify mankind. Unfortunately for scientists, however, these criteria of race are most exasperatingly intermingled. Color does not agree with texture of hair, for many of the dark races have straight hair; nor does color agree with the breadth of the head, for the yellow Tartar has a broader head than the German; nor, again, has the science of language as yet succeeded in clearing up the relative authority of these various and contradictory criteria. The final word of science, so far, is that we have at least two, perhaps three, great families of human beings—the whites and Negroes, possibly the yellow race. That other races have arisen from the intermingling of the blood of these two. This broad division of the world's races which men like Huxley and Raetzel have introduced as more nearly true than the old five-race scheme of Blumenbach, is nothing more than an acknowledgment that, so far as purely physical characteristics are concerned, the differences between men do not explain all the differences of their history. It declares, as Darwin himself said, that great as is the physical unlikeness of the various races of men their likenesses are greater, and upon this rests the whole scientific doctrine of Human Brotherhood.

Although the wonderful developments of human history teach that the grosser physical differences of color, hair and bone go but a short way toward explaining the different roles which groups of men have played in Human Progress, yet there are differences—subtle, delicate and elusive, though they may be—which have silently but definitely separated men into groups. While these subtle forces have generally followed the natural cleavage of common blood, descent and physical peculiarities, they have at other times

swept across and ignored these. At all times, however, they have divided human beings into races, which, while they perhaps transcend scientific definition, nevertheless, are clearly defined to the eye of the Historian and Sociologist.

If this be true, then the history of the world is the history, not of individuals, but of groups, not of nations, but of races, and he who ignores or seeks to override the race idea in human history ignores and overrides the central thought of all history. What, then, is a race? It is a vast family of human beings, generally of common blood and language, always of common history, traditions and impulses, who are both voluntarily and involuntarily striving together for the accomplishment of certain more or less vividly conceived ideals of life.

Turning to real history, there can be no doubt, first, as to the widespread, nay, universal, prevalence of the race idea, the race spirit, the race ideal, and as to its efficiency as the vastest and most ingenious invention for human progress. We, who have been reared and trained under the individualistic philosophy of the Declaration of Independence and the laisser-faire philosophy of Adam Smith, are loath to see and loath to acknowledge this patent fact of human history. We see the Pharaohs, Caesars, Toussaints and Napoleons of history and forget the vast races of which they were but epitomized expressions. We are apt to think in our American impatience, that while it may have been true in the past that closed race groups made history, that here in conglomerate America *nous avons changer tout cela*—we have changed all that, and have no need of this ancient instrument of progress. This assumption of which the Negro people are especially fond, can not be established by a careful consideration of history.

We find upon the world's stage today eight distinctly differentiated races, in the sense in which History tells us the word must be used. They are, the Slavs of eastern Europe, the Teutons of middle Europe, the English of Great Britain and America, the Romance nations of Southern and Western Europe, the Negroes of Africa and America, the Semitic people of Western Asia and Northern Africa, the Hindoos of Central Asia and the Mongolians of Eastern Asia. There are, of course, other minor race groups, as the American Indians, the Esquimaux and the South Sea Islanders; these larger races, too, are far from homogeneous; the Slav includes the Czech, the Magyar, the Pole and the Russian; the Teuton includes the German, the Scandinavian and the Dutch; the English include the Scotch, the Irish and the conglomerate American. Under Romance nations the widely-differing Frenchman, Italian, Sicilian and Spaniard are comprehended. The term Negro is, perhaps, the most indefinite of all, combining the Mulattoes and Zamboes of America and the Egyptians, Bantus and Bushmen of Africa. Among the Hindoos are traces of widely differing nations, while the great Chinese, Tartar, Corean and Japanese families fall under the one designation—Mongolian.

The question now is: What is the real distinction between these nations? Is it the physical differences of blood, color and cranial measurements? Certainly we must all acknowledge that physical differences play a great part, and that, with wide exceptions and qualifications, these eight great races of to-day follow the cleavage of physical race distinctions; the English and Teuton represent the white variety of mankind; the Mongolian, the yellow; the Negroes, the black. Between these are many crosses and mixtures, where Mongolian and Teuton have blended into the Slav, and other mixtures have produced the Romance nations and the Semites. But while race differences have followed mainly physical race lines, yet no mere physical distinctions would really define or explain the deeper differences—the cohesiveness and continuity of these groups. The deeper differences are spiritual, psychical, differences—undoubtedly based on the physical, but infinitely transcending them. The forces that bind together the Teuton nations are, then, first, their race identity and common blood; secondly, and more important, a common history, common laws and religion, similar habits of thought and a conscious striving together for certain ideals of life. The whole process which has brought about these race differentiations has been a growth, and the great characteristic of this growth has been the differentiation of spiritual and mental differences between great races of mankind and the integration of physical differences.

The age of nomadic tribes of closely related individuals represents the maximum of physical differences. They were practically vast families, and there were as many groups as families. As the families came together to form cities the physical differences lessened, purity of blood was replaced by the requirement of domicile, and all who lived within the city bounds became gradually to be regarded as members of the group; *i.e.*, there was a slight and slow breaking down of physical barriers. This, however, was accompanied by an increase of the spiritual and social differences between cities. This city became husbandmen, this, merchants, another warriors, and so on. The *ideals of life* for which the different cities struggled were different. When at last cities began to coalesce into nations there was another breaking down of barriers which separated groups of men. The larger and broader differences of color, hair and physical proportions were not by any means ignored, but myriads of minor differences disappeared, and the sociological and historical races of men began to approximate the present division of races as indicated by physical researches. At the same time the spiritual and physical differences of race groups which constituted the nations became deep and decisive. The English nation stood for constitutional liberty and commercial freedom; the German nation for science and philosophy; the Romance nations stood for literature and art, and the other race groups are striving, each in its own way, to develop for civilization its particular message, its particular ideal, which shall help to guide the world nearer and nearer that perfection of human life for which we all long, that "one far off Divine event."

This has been the function of race differences up to the present time. What shall be its function in the future? Manifestly some of the great races of today—particularly the Negro race—have not as yet given to civilization the full spiritual message which they are capable of giving. I will not say that the Negro race has as yet given no message to the world, for it is still a mooted question among scientists as to just how far Egyptian civilization was Negro in its origin; if it was not wholly Negro, it was certainly very closely allied. Be that as it may, however the fact still remains that the full, complete Negro message of the whole Negro race has not as yet been given to the world: that the messages and ideal of the yellow race have not been completed, and that the striving of the mighty Slavs has but begun. The question is, then: How shall this message be delivered; how shall these various ideals be realized? The answer is plain: By the development of these race groups, not as individuals, but as races. For the development of Japanese genius, Japanese literature and art, Japanese spirit, only Japanese, bound and welded together, Japanese inspired by one vast ideal, can work out in its fullness the wonderful message which Japan has for the nations of the earth. For the development of Negro genius, of Negro literature and art, of Negro spirit, only Negroes bound and welded together, Negroes inspired by one vast ideal, can work out in its fullness the great message we have for humanity. We cannot reverse history; we are subject to the same natural laws as other races, and if the Negro is ever to be a factor in the world's history—if among the gaily-colored banners that deck the broad ramparts of civilization is to hang one uncompromising black, then it must be placed there by black hands, fashioned by black heads and hallowed by the travail of 200,000,000 black hearts beating in one glad song of jubilee.

For this reason, the advance guard of the Negro people—the 8,000,000 people of Negro blood in the United States of America—must soon come to realize that if they are to take their just place in the van of Pan-Negroism, then their destiny is *not* absorption by the white Americans. That if in America it is to be proven for the first time in the modern world that not only Negroes are capable of evolving individual men like Toussaint, the Saviour, but are a nation stored with wonderful possibilities of culture, then their destiny is not a servile imitation of Anglo-Saxon culture, but a stalwart originality which shall unswervingly follow Negro ideals.

It may, however, be objected here that the situation of our race in America renders this attitude impossible; that our sole hope of salvation lies in our being able to lose our race identity in the commingled blood of the nation; and that any other course would merely increase the friction of races which we call race prejudice, and against which we have so long and so earnestly fought.

Here, then, is the dilemma, and it is a puzzling one, I admit. No Negro who has given earnest thought to the situation of his people in America has failed, at some time in life, to find himself at these cross-roads; has failed to ask himself at some time: What, after all, am I? Am I an American or am I a Negro? Can I be both? Or is it my duty to cease to be a Negro as soon as possible and be an American? If I strive as a Negro, am I not perpetuating the very cleft that threatens and separates Black and White America? Is not my only possible practical aim the subduction of all that is Negro in me to the American? Does my black blood place upon me any more obligation to assert my nationality than German, or Irish or Italian blood would?

It is such incessant self-questioning and the hesitation that arises from it, that is making the present period a time of vacillation and contradiction for the American Negro; combined race action is stifled, race responsibility is shirked, race enterprises languish, and the best blood, the best talent, the best energy of the Negro people cannot be marshalled to do the bidding of the race. They stand back to make room for every rascal and demagogue who chooses to cloak his selfish deviltry under the veil of race pride.

Is this right? Is is rational? Is it good policy? Have we in America a distinct mission as a race—a distinct sphere of action and an opportunity for race development, or is self-obliteration the highest end to which Negro blood dare aspire?

If we carefully consider what race prejudice really is, we find it, historically, to be nothing but the friction between different groups of people; it is the difference in aim, in feeling, in ideals of two different races; if, now, this difference exists touching territory, laws, language, or even religion, it is manifest that these people cannot live in the same territory without fatal collision; but if, on the other hand, there is substantial agreement in laws, language and religion; if there is a satisfactory adjustment of economic life, then there is no reason why, in the same country and on the same street, two or three great national ideals might not thrive and develop, that men of different races might not strive together for their race ideals as well, perhaps even better, than in isolation. Here, it seems to me, is the reading of the riddle that puzzles so many of us. We are Americans, not only by birth and by citizenship, but by our political ideals, our language, our religion. Farther than that, our Americanism does not go. At that point, we are Negroes, members of a vast historic race that from the very dawn of creation has slept, but half awakening in the dark forests of its African fatherland. We are the first fruits of this new nation, the harbinger of that black to-morrow which is yet destined to soften the whiteness of the Teutonic to-day. We are that people whose subtle sense of song has given American its only American music, its only American fairy tales, its only touch of pathos and humor amid its mad money-getting plutocracy. As such, it is our duty to conserve our physical powers, our intellectual endowments, our spiritual ideals; as a race we must strive by race organization, by race solidarity, by race unity to the realization of that broader humanity which freely recognizes differences in men, but sternly deprecates inequality in their opportunities of development.

For the accomplishment of these ends we need race organizations: Negro colleges, Negro newspapers, Negro business organizations, a Negro school of literature and art, and an intellectual clearing house, for all these products of the Negro mind, which we may call a Negro Academy. Not only is all this necessary for positive advance, it is absolutely imperative for negative defense. Let us not deceive ourselves at our situation in this country. Weighted with a heritage of moral iniquity from our past history, hard pressed in the economic world by foreign immigrants and native prejudice, hated here, despised there and pitied everywhere; our one haven of refuge is ourselves, and but one means of advance, our own belief in our great destiny, our own implicit trust in our ability and worth. There is no power under God's high heaven that can stop the advance of eight thousand thousand honest, earnest, inspired and united people. But—and here is the rub—they *must* be honest, fearlessly criticising their own faults, zealously correcting them; they must be *earnest*. No people that laughs at itself, and ridicules itself, and wishes to God it was anything but itself ever wrote its name in history; it *must* be inspired with the Divine faith of our black mothers, that out of the blood and dust of battle will march a victorious host, a mighty nation, a peculiar people, to speak to the nations of earth a Divine truth that shall make them free. And such a people must be united; not merely united for the organized theft of political spoils, not united to disgrace religion with whoremongers and ward-heelers; not united merely to protest and pass resolutions, but united to stop the ravages of consumption among the Negro people, united to keep black boys from loafing, gambling and crime; united to guard the purity of black women and to reduce that vast army of black prostitutes that is today marching to hell; and united in serious organizations, to determine by careful conference and thoughtful interchange of opinion the broad lines of policy and action for the American Negro. . . .

24. THE DEPENDENCE OF WOMEN

CHARLOTTE PERKINS GILMAN

Charlotte Perkins Gilman (1860–1935) is best known today as a feminist theorist and novelist. Her personal account of her own descent into madness, *The Yellow Wallpaper*, along with her futuristic novel *Herland*, continue to be read today. Less well known is the fact that Gilman was interested in sociology, having been influenced in particular by the work of one of the founders of American sociology, Frank Lester Ward. In this descriptive passage from *Women and Economics* (1898), she discusses the implications of consigning women to household labor and child rearing—which, because these forms of work are uncompensated, means that they have no impact on the economic status of women. As a consequence of this situation, wives are dependent on their husbands for their status in the larger community. As contemporary feminists have frequently pointed out, this assessment by a turn-of-the-century feminist remains relevant today.

. . . Grateful return for happiness conferred is not the method of exchange in a partnership. The comfort a man takes with his wife is not in the nature of a business partnership, nor are her frugality and industry. A housekeeper, in her place, might be as frugal, as industrious, but would not therefore be a partner. Man and wife are partners truly in their mutual obligation to their children, their common love, duty, and service. But a manufacturer who marries, or a doctor, or a lawyer, does not take a partner in parenthood, unless his wife is also a manufacturer, a doctor, or a lawyer. In his business, she cannot even advise wisely without training and experience. To love her husband the composer, does not enable her to compose; and the loss of a man´s wife, though it may break his heart, does not cripple his business, unless his mind is affected by grief. She is in no sense a business partner, unless she contributes capital or experience or labor, as a man would in like relation. Most men would hesitate very seriously before entering a business partnership with any woman, wife or not.

If the wife is not, then, truly a business partner, in what way does she earn from her husband the food, clothing, and shelter she receives at his hands? By house service, it will be instantly replied. This is the general misty idea upon the subject,—that women earn all they get, and more, by house service. Here we come to a very practical and definite economic ground. Although not producers of wealth, women serve in the final processes of preparation and distribution. Their labor in the household has a genuine economic value.

For a certain percentage of persons to serve other persons, in order that the ones so served may produce more, is a contribution not to be overlooked. The labor of women in the house, certainly, enables men to produce more wealth than they otherwise could; and in this way women are economic factors in society. But so are horses. The labor of horses enables men to produce more wealth than they otherwise could. The horse is an economic factor in society. But the horse is not economically independent, nor is the woman. If a man plus a valet can perform more useful service than he could minus a valet, then the valet is performing useful service. But, if the valet is the property of the man, is obliged to perform this service, and is not paid for it, he is not economically independent.

The labor which the wife performs in the household is given as part of her functional duty, not as employment. The wife of the poor man, who works hard in a small house, doing all the work for the family, or the wife of the rich man, who wisely and gracefully manages a large house and administers its functions, each is entitled to fair pay for services rendered.

To take this ground and hold it honestly, wives, as earners through domestic service, are entitled to the wages of cooks, housemaids, nursemaids, seamstresses, or housekeepers, and to no more. This would of course reduce the spending money of the wives of the rich, and put it out of the power of the poor man to "support" a wife at all, unless, indeed, the poor man faced the situation fully, paid his wife her wages as house servant, and then she and he combined their funds in the support of their children. He would be keeping a servant: she would be helping keep the family. But nowhere on earth would there be "a rich woman" by these means. Even the highest class of private housekeeper, useful as her services are, does not accumulate a fortune. She does not buy diamonds and sables and keep a carriage. Things like these are not earned by house service.

But the salient fact in this discussion is that, whatever the economic value of the domestic industry of women is, they do not get it: The women who do the most work get the least money, and the women who have the most money do the least work. Their labor is neither given nor taken as a factor in economic exchange. It is held to be their duty as women to do this work; and their economic status bears no relation to their domestic labors, unless an inverse one. Moreover, if they were thus fairly paid,—given what they earned, and no more,—all women working in this way would be reduced to the economic status of the house servant. Few women—or men either—care to face this condition. The ground that women earn their living by domestic labor is instantly forsaken, and we are told that they obtain their livelihood as mothers. This is a peculiar position. We speak of it commonly enough, and often with deep feeling, but without due analysis.

In treating of an economic exchange, asking what return in goods or labor women make for the goods and labor given them,—either to the rate collectively or to their husbands individually,—what payment women make for their clothes and shoes and furniture and food and shelter, we are told that the duties and services of the mother entitle her to support.

If this is so, if motherhood is an exchangeable commodity given by women in payment for clothes and food, then we must of course find some relation between the quantity or quality of the motherhood and the quantity and quality of the pay. This being true, then the women who are not mothers have no economic status at all; and the economic status of those who are must be shown to be relative to their motherhood. This is obviously absurd. The childless wife has as much money as the mother of many—more; for the children of the latter consume what would otherwise be hers; and the inefficient mother is no less provided for than the efficient one. Visibly, and upon the face of it, women are not maintained in economic prosperity proportioned to their motherhood. Motherhood bears no relation to their economic status. Among primitive races, it is true,—in the patriarchal period, for instance,—there was some truth in this position. Women being of no value whatever save as bearers of children, their favor and indulgence did bear direct relation to maternity; and they had reason to exult on more grounds than one when they could boast a son. To-day, however, the maintenance of the woman is not conditioned upon this. A man is not allowed to discard his wife because she is barren. The claim of motherhood as a factor in economic exchange is false to-day. But suppose it were true. Are we willing to hold this ground, even in theory? Are we willing to consider motherhood as a business, a form of commercial exchange? Are the cares and duties of the mother, her travail and her love, commodities to be exchanged for bread?

It is revolting so to consider them; and, if we dare face our own thoughts, and force them to their logical conclusion, we shall see that nothing could be more repugnant to human feeling, or more socially and individually injurious, than to make motherhood a trade. Driven off these alleged grounds of women's economic independence; shown that women, as a class, neither produce nor distribute wealth; that women, as individuals, labor mainly as house servants, are not paid as such, and would not be satisfied with such an economic status if they were so paid; that wives are not business partners or co-producers of wealth with their husbands, unless they actually practise the same profession; that they are not salaried as mothers, and that it would be unspeakably degrading if they were,—what remains to those who deny that women are supported by men? This (and a most amusing position it is),—that the function of maternity unfits a woman for economic production, and, therefore, it is right that she should be supported by her husband.

The ground is taken that the human female is not economically independent, that she is fed by the male of her species. In denial of this, it is first alleged that she is economically independent,—that she does support herself by her own industry in the house. It being shown that there is no relation between the economic status of woman and the labor she performs in the home, it is then alleged that not as house servant, but as mother, does woman earn her living. It being shown that the economic status of woman bears no relation to her motherhood, either in quantity or quality, it is then alleged that motherhood renders a woman unfit for economic production, and that, therefore, it is right that she be supported by her husband. Before going farther, let us seize upon this admission,—that she *is* supported by her husband.

Without going into either the ethics or the necessities of the case, we have reached so much common ground: the female of genus homo is supported by the male. Whereas, in other species of animals, male and female alike graze and browse, hunt and kill, climb, swim, dig, run, and fly for their livings, in our species the female does not seek her own living in the specific activities of our race, but is fed by the male.

Now as to the alleged necessity. Because of her maternal duties, the human female is said to be unable to get her own living. As the maternal duties of other females do not unfit them for getting their own living and also the livings of their young, it would seem that the human maternal duties require the segregation of the entire energies of the mother to the service of the child during her entire adult life, or so large a proportion of them that not enough remains to devote to the individual interests of the mother.

Such a condition, did it exist, would of course excuse and justify the pitiful dependence of the human female, and her support by the male. As the queen bee, modified entirely to maternity, is supported, not by the male, to be sure, but by her co-workers, the "old maids," the barren working bees, who labor so patiently and lovingly in their branch of the maternal duties of the hive, so would the human female, modified entirely to maternity, become unfit for any other exertion, and a helpless dependant.

Is this the condition of human motherhood? Does the human mother, by her motherhood, thereby lose control of brain and body, lose power and skill and desire for any other work? Do we see before us the human race, with all its females segregated entirely to the uses of motherhood, consecrated, set apart, specially developed, spending every power of their nature on the service of their children?

We do not. We see the human mother worked far harder than a mare, laboring her life long in the service, not of her children only, but of men; husbands, brothers, fathers, whatever male relatives she has; for mother and sister also; for the church a little, if she is allowed; for society, if she is able; for charity and education and reform,—working in many ways that are not the ways of motherhood.

It is not motherhood that keeps the housewife on her feet from dawn till dark; it is house service, not child service. Women work longer and harder than most men, and not solely in maternal duties. The savage mother carries the burdens, and does all menial service for the tribe. The peasant mother toils in the fields, and the workingman's wife in the home. Many mothers, even now, are wage-earners for the family, as well as bearers and rearers of it. And the women who are not so occupied, the women who belong to rich men,—here perhaps is the exhaustive devotion to maternity which is supposed to justify an admitted economic dependence. But we do not find it even among these. Women of ease and wealth provide for their children better care than the poor woman can; but they do not spend more time upon it themselves, not more care and effort. They have other occupation.

In spite of her supposed segregation to maternal duties, the human female, the world over, works at extra-maternal duties for hours enough to provide her with an independent living, and then is denied independence on the ground that motherhood prevents her working!

If this ground were tenable, we should find a world full of women who never lifted a finger save in the service of their children, and of men who did *all* the work besides, and waited on the women whom motherhood prevented from waiting on themselves. The ground is not tenable. A human female, healthy, sound, has twenty-five years of life before she is a mother, and should have twenty-five years more after the period of such maternal service as is expected of her has been given. The duties of grandmotherhood are surely not alleged as preventing economic independence.

The working power of the mother has always been a prominent factor in human life. She is the worker *par excellence*, but her work is not such as to affect her economic status. Her living, all that she gets,—food, clothing, ornaments, amusements, luxuries,—these bear no relation to her power to produce wealth, to her services in the house, or to her motherhood. These things bear relation only to the man she marries, the man she depends on,—to how much he has and how much he is willing to give her. The women whose splendid extravagance dazzles the world, whose economic goods are the greatest, are often neither house-workers nor mothers, but simply the women who hold most power over the men who have the most money. The female of genus home is economically dependent on the male. He is her food supply.

25. CONSPICUOUS CONSUMPTION

THORSTEIN VEBLEN

The American-born son of Norwegian immigrants, Thorstein Veblen (1857–1929) proved to be one of the most original social thinkers of the late nineteenth and early twentieth centuries. Although appreciated for his creativity, his thought has often been misunderstood. This is in no small part due to its mode of presentation. Veblen was perhaps the most acerbic social critic of his era, but his criticism was couched in irony and sarcasm. Growing up in Minnesota, Veblen´s political thought was shaped by Midwestern populism rather than Marxism; he shared populism´s critique of the economic power of giant corporations and banks, which were seen as undermining democracy and economic justice. Among Veblen´s major works are *The Theory of the Leisure Class* (1899), *The Theory of Business Enterprise* (1904), *The Engineers and the Price System* (1921), and *The Higher Learning in America* (1924). His "theory of the leisure class" argued that the capitalist class was not innovative or dynamic, but rather lived off of rather than contributed to industrial society. Much of his book on the topic focuses on the culture of this class, in which he introduced such terms as "pecuniary canons of taste," "conspicuous leisure," and in the excerpt included here "conspicuous consumption." In focusing on the class character of consumption, his work can be read as a precursor to the more recent work of the French social theorist Pierre Bourdieu (see his entry in this collection).

Conspicuous consumption of valuable goods is a means of reputability to the gentleman of leisure. As wealth accumulates on his hands, his own unaided effort will not avail to sufficiently put his opulence in evidence by this method. The aid of friends and competitors is therefore brought in by resorting to the giving of valuable presents and expensive feasts and entertainments. Presents and feasts had probably another origin than that of naïve ostentation, but they acquired their utility for this purpose very early, and they have retained that character to the present; so that their utility in this respect has now long been the substantial ground on which these usages rest. Costly entertainments, such as the potlatch or the ball, are peculiarly adapted to serve this end. The competitor with whom the entertainer wishes to institute a comparison is, by this method, made to serve as a means to the end. He consumes vicariously for his host at the same time that he is a witness to the consumption of that excess of good things which his host is unable to dispose of single-handed, and he is also made to witness his host's facility in etiquette.

In the giving of costly entertainments other motives, of a more genial kind, are of course also present. The custom of festive gatherings probably originated in motives of conviviality and religion; these motives are also present in the later development, but they do not continue to be the sole motives. The latter-day leisure-class festivities and entertainments may continue in some slight degree to serve the religious need and in a higher degree the needs of recreation and conviviality, but they also serve an invidious purpose; and they serve it none the less effectually for having a colourable non-invidious ground in these more avowable motives. But the economic effect of these social amenities is not therefore lessened, either in the

Thorstein Veblen, *The Theory of the Leisure Class: An Economic Study of Institutions*. New York: B. W. Huebsch, 1924. ✦

vicarious consumption of goods or in the exhibition of difficult and costly achievements in etiquette.

As wealth accumulates, the leisure class develops further in function and structure, and there arises a differentiation within the class. There is a more or less elaborate system of rank and grades. This differentiation is furthered by the inheritance of wealth and the consequent inheritance of gentility. With the inheritance of gentility goes the inheritance of obligatory leisure; and gentility of a sufficient potency to entail a life of leisure may be inherited without the complement of wealth required to maintain a dignified leisure. Gentle blood may be transmitted without goods enough to afford a reputably free consumption at one's ease. Hence results a class of impecunious gentlemen of leisure, incidentally referred to already. These half-caste gentlemen of leisure fall into a system of hierarchical gradations. Those who stand near the higher and the highest grades of the wealthy leisure class, in point of birth, or in point of wealth, or both, outrank the remoter-born and the pecuniarily weaker. These lower grades, especially the impecunious, or marginal, gentlemen of leisure, affiliate themselves by a system of dependence or fealty to the great ones; by so doing they gain an increment of repute, or of the means with which to lead a life of leisure, from their patron. They become his courtiers or retainers, servants; and being fed and countenanced by their patron they are indices of his rank and vicarious consumers of his superfluous wealth. Many of these affiliated gentlemen of leisure are at the same time lesser men of substance in their own right; so that some of them are scarcely at all, others only partially, to be rated as vicarious consumers. So many of them, however, as make up the retainers and hangers-on of the patron may be classed as vicarious consumers without qualification. Many of these again, and also many of the other aristocracy of less degree, have in turn attached to their persons a more or less comprehensive group of vicarious consumers in the persons of their wives and children, their servants, retainers, etc.

Throughout this graduated scheme of vicarious leisure and vicarious consumption the rule holds that these offices must be performed in some such manner, or under some such circumstance or insignia, as shall point plainly to the master to whom this leisure or consumption pertains, and to whom therefore the resulting increment of good repute of right inures. The consumption and leisure executed by these persons for their master or patron represents an investment on his part with a view to an increase of good fame. As regards feasts and largesses this is obvious enough, and the imputation of repute to the host or patron here takes place immediately, on the ground of common notoriety. Where leisure and consumption is performed vicariously by henchmen and retainers, imputation of the resulting repute to the patron is effected by their residing near his person so that it may be plain to all men from what source they draw. As the group whose good esteem is to be secured in this way grows larger, more patent means are required to indicate the imputation of merit for the leisure performed, and to this end uniforms, badges, and liveries come into vogue. The wearing of uniforms or liveries implies a considerable degree of dependence, and may even be said to be a mark of servitude, real or ostensible. The wearers of uniforms and liveries may be roughly divided into two classes—the free and the servile, or the noble and the ignoble. The services performed by them are likewise divisible into noble and ignoble. Of course the distinction is not observed with strict consistency in practice; the less debasing of the base services and the less honorific of the noble functions are not infrequently merged in the same person. But the general distinction is not on that account to be overlooked. What may add some perplexity is the fact that this fundamental distinction between noble and ignoble, which rests on the nature of the ostensible service performed, is traversed by a secondary distinction into honorific and humiliating, resting on the rank of the person for whom the service is performed or whose livery is worn. So, those offices which are by right the proper employment of the leisure class are noble; such are government, fighting, hunting, the care of arms and accoutrements, and the like,—in short, those which may be classed as ostensibly predatory employments. On the other hand, those employments which properly fall to the industrious class are ignoble; such as handicraft or other productive labour, menial services, and the like. But a base service performed for a person of very high degree may become a very honorific office; as for instance the office of a

Maid of Honour or of a Lady in Waiting to the Queen, or the King's Master of the Horse or his Keeper of the Hounds. The two offices last named suggest a principle of some general bearing. Whenever, as in these cases, the menial service in question has to do directly with the primary leisure employments of fighting and hunting, it easily acquires a reflected honorific character. In this way great honour may come to attach to an employment which in its own nature belongs to the baser sort.

In the later development of peaceable industry, the usage of employing an idle corps of uniformed men-at-arms gradually lapses. Vicarious consumption by dependents bearing the insignia of their patron or master narrows down to a corps of liveried menials. In a heightened degree, therefore, the livery comes to be a badge of servitude, or rather of servility. Something of a honorific character always attached to the livery of the armed retainer, but this honorific character disappears when the livery becomes the exclusive badge of the menial. The livery becomes obnoxious to nearly all who are required to wear it. We are yet so little removed from a state of effective slavery as still to be fully sensitive to the sting of any imputation of servility. This antipathy asserts itself even in the case of the liveries or uniforms which some corporations prescribe as the distinctive dress of their employees. In this country the aversion even goes the length of discrediting—in a mild and uncertain way—those government employments, military and civil, which require the wearing of a livery or uniform.

With the disappearance of servitude, the number of vicarious consumers attached to any one gentleman tends, on the whole, to decrease. The like is of course true, and perhaps in a still higher degree, of the number of dependents who perform vicarious leisure for him. In a general way, though not wholly nor consistently, these two groups coincide. The dependent who was first delegated for these duties was the wife, or the chief wife; and, as would be expected, in the later development of the institution, when the number of persons by whom these duties are customarily performed gradually narrows, the wife remains the last. In the higher grades of society a large volume of both these kinds of service is required; and here the wife is of course still assisted in the work by a more or less numerous corps of menials.

But as we descend the social scale, the point is presently reached where the duties of vicarious leisure and consumption devolve upon the wife alone. In the communities of the Western culture, this point is at present found among the lower middle class.

And here occurs a curious inversion. It is a fact of common observation that in this lower middle class there is no pretence of leisure on the part of the head of the household. Through force of circumstances it has fallen into disuse. But the middle-class wife still carries on the business of vicarious leisure, for the good name of the household and its master. In descending the social scale in any modern industrial community, the primary fact—the conspicuous leisure of the master of the household—disappears at a relatively high point. The head of the middle-class household has been reduced by economic circumstances to turn his hand to gaining a livelihood by occupations which often partake largely of the character of industry, as in the case of the ordinary business man of to-day. But the derivative fact—the vicarious leisure and consumption rendered by the wife, and the auxiliary vicarious performance of leisure by menials—remains in vogue as a conventionality which the demands of reputability will not suffer to be slighted. It is by no means an uncommon spectacle to find a man applying himself to work with the utmost assiduity, in order that his wife may in due form render for him that degree of vicarious leisure which the common sense of the time demands.

The leisure rendered by the wife in such cases is, of course, not a simple manifestation of idleness or indolence. It almost invariably occurs disguised under some form of work or household duties or social amenities, which prove on analysis to serve little or no ulterior end beyond showing that she does not and need not occupy herself with anything that is gainful or that is of substantial use. As has already been noticed under the head of manners, the greater part of the customary round of domestic cares to which the middle-class housewife gives her time and effort is of this character. Not that the results of her attention to household matters, of a decorative and mundificatory character, are not pleasing to the sense of men trained in middle-class proprieties; but the taste to which these effects of household adornment and tidiness appeal is a taste which has been formed under the selective guidance of a canon of propriety that demands just these evidences of wasted effort. The effects are pleasing to us chiefly because we have been taught to find them pleasing. There goes into these domestic duties much solicitude for a proper combination of form and colour, and for other ends that are to be classed as æsthetic in the proper sense of the term; and it is not denied that effects having some substantial æsthetic value are sometimes attained. Pretty much all that is here insisted on is that, as regards these amenities of life, the housewife's efforts are under the guidance of traditions that have been shaped by the law of conspicuously wasteful expenditure of time and substance. If beauty or comfort is achieved,—and it is a more or less fortuitous circumstance if they are,—they must be achieved by means and methods that commend themselves to the great economic law of wasted effort. The more reputable, "presentable" portion of middle-class household paraphernalia are, on the one hand, items of conspicuous consumption, and on the other hand, apparatus for putting in evidence the vicarious leisure rendered by the housewife.

The requirement of vicarious consumption at the hands of the wife continues in force even at a lower point in the pecuniary scale than the requirement of vicarious leisure. At a point below which little if any pretence of wasted effort, in ceremonial cleanness and the like, is observable, and where there is assuredly no conscious attempt at ostensible leisure, decency still requires the wife to consume some goods conspicuously for the reputability of the household and its head. So that, as the latter-day outcome of this evolution of an archaic institution, the wife, who was at the outset the drudge and chattel of the man, both in fact and in theory,—the producer of goods for him to consume,—has become the ceremonial consumer of goods which he produces. But she still quite unmistakably remains his chattel in theory; for the habitual rendering of vicarious leisure and consumption is the abiding mark of the unfree servant.

This vicarious consumption practised by the household of the middle and lower classes can not be counted as a direct expression of the leisure-class scheme of life, since the household of this pecuniary grade does not belong within the leisure class. It is rather that the leisure-class scheme of life here comes to an expression at the second remove. The leisure class stands at the head of the social structure in point of reputability; and its manner of life and its standards of worth therefore afford the norm of reputability for the community. The observance of these standards, in some degree of approximation, becomes incumbent upon all classes lower in the scale. In modern civilized communities the lines of demarcation between social classes have grown vague and transient, and wherever this happens the norm of reputability imposed by the upper class extends its coercive influence with but slight hindrance down through the social structure to the lowest strata. The result is that the members of each stratum accept as their ideal of decency the scheme of life in vogue in the next higher stratum, and bend their energies to live up to that ideal. On pain of forfeiting their good name and their self-respect in case of failure, they must conform to the accepted code, at least in appearance.

The basis on which good repute in any highly organised industrial community ultimately rests is pecuniary strength; and the means of showing pecuniary strength, and so of gaining or retaining a good name, are leisure and a conspicuous consumption of goods. Accordingly, both of these methods are in vogue as far down the scale as it remains possible; and in the lower strata in which the two methods are employed, both offices are in great part delegated to the wife and children of the household. Lower still, where any degree of leisure, even ostensible, has become impracticable for the wife, the conspicuous consumption of goods remains and is carried on by the wife and children. The man of the household also can do something in this direction, and, indeed, he commonly does; but with a still lower descent into the levels of indigence—along the margin of the slums—the man, and presently also the children, virtually cease to consume valuable goods for appearances, and the woman remains virtually the sole exponent of the household's pecuniary decency. No class of society, not even the most abjectly poor, foregoes all customary conspicuous consumption. The last items of this category of consumption are not given up except under stress of the direst necessity. Very much of squalor and discomfort will be endured before the last trinket or the last pretence of pecuniary decency is put away. There is no class and no country that has yielded so abjectly before the pressure of physical want as to deny themselves all gratification of this higher or spiritual need.

26. UTILIZATION OF WOMEN IN CITY GOVERNMENT

JANE ADDAMS

Jane Addams (1860–1935) was perhaps the most prominent social reformer of her generation. As the founder of Hull House in Chicago, she was a leader in the settlement house movement. She was recognized for her work as a peace activist by being awarded the Nobel Peace Prize. Addams was also a social thinker who had close connections with the members of the Chicago School of Sociology. In "Utilization of Women in City Government" (1907), this influence is evident in her discussion of the modern industrial city. But Addams takes this analysis in an original direction by first arguing for the need to create a welfare state in order to address the myriad social problems that have emerged in urban settings. Moreover, she proceeds to contend that since many of the tasks the welfare state will need to perform involve the nurturing and caring jobs heretofore consigned to women in the domestic realm, it makes sense to utilize women, with their unique expertise, in the public arena as well.

As the city itself originated for the common protection of the people and was built about a suitable centre of defense which formed a citadel such as the Acropolis at Athens or the Kremlin at Moscow, so we can trace the beginning of the municipal franchise to the time when the problems of municipal government were still largely those of protecting the city against rebellion from within and against invasion from without. A voice in city government, as it was extended from the nobles, who alone bore arms, was naturally given solely to those who were valuable to the military system. . . . It was fair that only those who were liable to a sudden call to arms should be selected to decide as to the relations which the city should bear to rival cities, and that the vote for war should be cast by the same men who would bear the brunt of battle and the burden of protection. . . .

But rival cities have long since ceased to settle their claims by force of arms, and we shall have to admit, I think, that this early test of the elector is no longer fitted to the modern city. . . .

It has been well said that the modern city is a stronghold of industrialism, quite as the feudal city was a stronghold of militarism, but the modern city fears no enemies, and rivals from without, and its problems of government are solely internal. Affairs for the most part are going badly in these great new centres in which the quickly congregated population has not yet learned to arrange its affairs satisfactorily. Insanitary housing, poisonous sewage, contaminated water, infant mortality, the spread of contagion, adulterated food, impure milk, smoke-laden air, ill-ventilated factories, dangerous occupations, juvenile crime, unwholesome crowding, prostitution, and drunkenness are the enemies which the modern city must face and overcome would it survive. Logically, its electorate should be made up of those who can bear a valiant part in this arduous contest, of those who in the past have at least attempted to care for children, to clean houses, to prepare foods, to isolate the family from moral dangers, of those who have traditionally taken care of that side of life which, as soon as the population is congested, inevitably becomes the subject of municipal consideration and control.

To test the elector's fitness to deal with this situation by his ability to bear arms, is absurd. A city is in many respects a great business corporation, but in other respects it is enlarged housekeeping. If American cities have failed in the first, partly because office holders have carried with them the predatory instinct learned in competitive business, and cannot help "working a good thing" when they have an opportunity, may we not say that city housekeeping has failed partly because women, the traditional housekeepers, have not been consulted as to its multiform activities? The men of the city have been carelessly indifferent to much of this civic housekeeping, as they have always been indifferent to the details of the household. They have totally disregarded a candidate's capacity to keep the streets clean, preferring to consider him in relation to the national tariff or to the necessity for increasing the national navy, in a pure spirit of reversion to the traditional type of government which had to do only with enemies and outsiders.

It is difficult to see what military prowess has to do with the multiform duties, which, in a modern city, include the care of parks and libraries, superintendence of markets, sewers and bridges, the inspection of provisions and boilers, and the proper disposal of garbage. Military prowess has nothing to do with the building department which the city maintains to see to it that the basements be dry, that the bedrooms be large enough to afford the required cubic feet of air, that the plumbing be sanitary, that the gas-pipes do not leak, that the tenement-house court be large enough to afford light and ventilation, and that the stairways be fireproof. The ability to carry arms has nothing to do with the health department maintained by the city, which provides that children be vaccinated, that contagious diseases be isolated and placarded, that the spread of tuberculosis be curbed, and that the water be free from typhoid infection. Certainly the military conception of society is remote from the functions of the school boards, whose concern it is that children be educated, that they be supplied with kindergartens and be given a decent place in which to play. The very multifariousness and complexity of a city government demands the help of minds accustomed to detail and

variety of work, to a sense of obligation for the health and welfare of young children, and to a responsibility for the cleanliness and comfort of others.

Because all these things have traditionally been in the hands of women, if they take no part in them now, they are not only missing the education which the natural participation in civic life would bring to them, but they are losing what they have always had. From the beginning of tribal life women have been held responsible for the health of the community, a function which is now represented by the health department; from the days of the cave dwellers, so far as the home was clean and wholesome, it was due to their efforts, which are now represented by the bureau of tenement-house inspection; from the period of the primitive village, the only public sweeping performed was what they undertook in their own dooryards, that which is now represented by the bureau of street cleaning. Most of the departments in a modern city can be traced to woman's traditional activity, but in spite of this, so soon as these old affairs were turned over to the care of the city, they slipped from woman's hands, apparently because they then became matters for collective action and implied the use of the franchise. Because the franchise had in the first instance been given to the man who could fight, because in the beginning he alone could vote who could carry a weapon, the franchise was considered an improper thing for a woman to possess. . . .

It is so easy to believe that things that used to exist still go on long after they are passed; it is so easy to commit irreparable blunders because we fail to correct our theories by our changing experience. So many of the stumbling-blocks against which we fail are the opportunities to which we have not adjusted ourselves. Because it shocks an obsolete ideal, we keep hold of a convention which no longer squares with our genuine insight, and we are slow to follow a clue which might enable us to solace and improve the life about us.

Why is it that women do not vote upon the matters which concern them so intimately? Why do they not follow these vital affairs and feel responsible for their proper administration, even though they have become municipalized? What would the result have been could women have regarded the suffrage, not as a right or a privilege, but as a mere piece of governmental machinery without which they could not perform their traditional functions under the changed conditions of city life? Could we view the whole situation as a matter of obligation and of normal development, it would be much simplified. We are at the beginning of a prolonged effort to incorporate a progressive developing life founded upon a response to the needs of all the people, into the requisite legal enactments and civic institutions. To be in any measure successful, this effort will require all the intelligent powers of observation, all the sympathy, all the common sense which may be gained from the whole adult population. . . .

It is questionable whether women to-day, in spite of the fact that there are myriads of them in factories and shops, are doing their full share of the world´s work in the lines of production which have always been theirs. Even two centuries ago they did practically all the spinning, dyeing, weaving, and sewing. They carried on much of the brewing and baking and thousands of operations which have been pushed out of the domestic system into the factory system. But simply to keep on doing the work which their grandmothers did, was to find themselves surrounded by conditions over which they have no control.

Sometimes when I see dozens of young girls going into the factories of a certain biscuit company on the West Side of Chicago, they appear for the moment as a mere cross-section in the long procession of women who have furnished the breadstuffs from time immemorial, from the savage woman who ground the meal and baked a flat cake, through innumerable cottage hearths, kitchens, and bake ovens, to this huge concern in which they are still carrying on their traditional business. But always before, during the ages of this unending procession, women themselves were able to dictate concerning the hours and the immediate conditions of their work; even grinding the meal and baking the cake in the ashes was diversified by many other activities. But suddenly, since the application of steam to the processes of kneading bread and of turning the spindle, which really means only a different motor power and not in the least an essential change in her work, she has been denied the privilege of regulating the conditions which immediately surround her. . . .

Practically one-half of the working women in the United States are girls—young women under the age of twenty-five years. This increase in the number of young girls in industry is the more striking when taken in connection with the fact that industries of today differ most markedly from those of the past in the relentless speed which they require. This increase in speed is as marked in the depths of sweat-shop labor as in the most advanced New England mills, where the eight looms operated by each worker have increased to twelve, fourteen, and even sixteen looms. This speed, of course, brings a new strain into industry and tends inevitably to nervous exhaustion. Machines may be revolved more and more swiftly, but the girl workers have no increase in vitality responding to the heightened pressure. An ampler and more far-reaching protection than now exists, is needed in order to care for the health and safety of woman in industry. Their youth, their helplessness, their increasing numbers, the conditions under which they are employed, all call for uniform and enforceable statutes. The elaborate regulations of dangerous trades, enacted in England and on the Continent for both adults and children, find no parallel in the United States. The injurious effects of employments involving the use of poisons, acids, gases, atmospheric extremes, or other dangerous processes, still await adequate investigation and legislation in this country. How shall this take place, save by the concerted efforts of the women themselves, those who are employed, and those other women who are intelligent as to the worker´s needs and who possess a conscience in regard to industrial affairs? . . .

So far as women have been able, in Chicago at least, to help, the poorest workers in the sweatshops, it has been accomplished by women organized into trades unions. The organization of Special Order Tailors found that it was comparatively simple for an employer to give the skilled operatives in a clothing factory more money by taking it away from the wages of the seam-sewer and button-holer. The fact that it resulted in one set of workers being helped at the expense of another set did not appeal to him, so long as he was satisfying the demand of the union without increasing the total cost of production. But the Special Order Tailors, at the sacrifice of their own wages and growth, made a determined effort to include even the sweat-shop workers in the benefits they had slowly secured for themselves. By means of the use of the label they were finally able to insist that no goods should be given out for home-finishing save to women presenting union cards, and they raised the wages from nine and eleven cents a dozen for finishing garments, to the minimum wage of fifteen cents. They also made a protest against the excessive subdivision of the labor upon garments, a practice which enables the manufacturer to use children and the least skilled adults. Thirty-two persons are commonly employed upon a single coat, and it is the purpose of the Special Order Tailors to have all the machine work performed by one worker, thus reducing the number working on one coat to twelve or fourteen. As this change will at the same time demand more skill on the part of the operator, and will increase the variety and interest in his work, these garment-makers are sacrificing both time and money for the defence of Ruskinian principles—one of the few actual attempts to recover the "joy of work." . . . The poorest women are often but uncomprehending victims of this labor movement of which they understand so little, and which has become so much a matter of battle that helpless individuals are lost in the conflict.

A complicated situation occurs to me in illustration. A woman from the Hull-House Day Nursery came to me two years ago asking to borrow twenty-five dollars, a sum her union had imposed as a fine. She gave such an incoherent account of her plight that it was evident that she did not in the least understand what it was all about. A little investigation disclosed the following facts: The "Nursery Mother," as I here call her for purposes of identification, had worked for a long time in an unorganized overall factory, where the proprietor, dealing as he did in goods purchased exclusively by working-men, found it increasingly difficult to sell his overalls because they did not bear the union label. He finally made a request to the union that the employees in his factory be organized. This was done, he was given the use of the label, and upon this basis he prospered for several months.

Whether the organizer was "fixed" or not, the investigation did not make clear; for, although the "Nursery Mother," with her fellow-workers, had paid their union dues regularly, the employer was not compelled to pay the union scale of wages, but continued to pay the same wages as before. At the end of three months his employees discovered that they were not being paid the union scale, and demanded that their wages be raised to that amount. The employer, in the meantime having extensively advertised his use of the label, concluded that his purpose had been served, and that he no longer needed the union. He refused, therefore, to pay the union scale, and a strike ensued. The "Nursery Mother" went out with the rest, and within a few days found work in another shop, a union shop doing a lower grade of manufacturing. At that time there was no uniform scale in the garment trades, and although a trade unionist working for union wages, she received lower wages than she had under the non-union conditions in the overall factory. She was naturally much confused and, following her instinct to get the best wages possible, she went back to her old place. Affairs ran smoothly for a few weeks, until the employer discovered that he was again losing trade because his goods lacked the label, whereupon he once more applied to have his shop unionized. The organizer, coming back, promptly discovered the recreant "Nursery Mother," and, much to her bewilderment, she was fined twenty-five dollars. She understood nothing clearly, nor could she, indeed, be made to understand so long as she was in the midst of this petty warfare. Her labor was a mere method of earning money quite detached from her European experience, and failed to make for her the remotest connection with the community whose genuine needs she was supplying. No effort had been made to show her the cultural aspect of her work, to give her even the feeblest understanding of the fact that she was supplying a genuine need of the community, and that she was entitled to respect and a legitimate industrial position. It would have been necessary to make such an effort from the historic standpoint, and this could be undertaken only by the community as a whole and not by any one class in it. Protective legislation would be but the first step toward making her a more valuable producer and a more intelligent citizen. The whole effort would imply a closer connection between industry and government, and could be accomplished intelligently only if women were permitted to exercise the franchise.

A certain healing and correction would doubtless ensue could we but secure for the protection and education of industrial workers that nurture of health and morals which women have so long reserved for their own families and which has never been utilized as a directing force in industrial affairs.

When the family constituted the industrial organism of the day, the daughters of the household were carefully taught in reference to the place they would take in that organism, but as the household arts have gone outside the home, almost nothing has been done to connect the young women with the present great industrial system. This neglect has been equally true in regard to the technical and cultural sides of that system.

The failure to fit the education of women to the actual industrial life which is carried on about them has had disastrous results in two directions. First, industry itself has lacked the modification which women might have brought to it had they committed the entire movement to that growing concern for a larger and more satisfying life for each member of the community, a concern which we have come to regard as legitimate. Second, the more prosperous women would have been able to understand and adjust their own difficulties of household management in relation to the producer of factory products, as they are now utterly unable to do.

As the census of 1900 showed that more than half of the women employed in "gainful occupations" in the United States are engaged in households, certainly their conditions of labor lie largely in the hands of women employers. At a conference held at Lake Placid by employers of household labor, it was contended that future historical review may show that the girls who are today in domestic service are the really progressive women of the age; that they are those who are fighting conditions which limit their freedom, and although they are doing it blindly, at least they are demanding avenues of self-expression outside their work; and that this struggle from conditions detrimental to their highest life is the ever recurring story of the emancipation of first one class and then another. It was further contended that in this effort to become sufficiently educated to be able to understand the needs of an educated employer from an independent standpoint, they are really doing the community a great service, and did they but receive co-operation instead of opposition, domestic service would lose its social ostracism and attract a more intelligent class of women. And yet this effort, perfectly reasonable from the standpoint of historic development

and democratic tradition, receives little help from the employing housekeepers, because they know nothing of industrial development. . . .

If American women could but obtain a liberating knowledge of that history of industry and commerce which is so similar in every country of the globe, the fact that so much factory labor is performed by immigrants would help to bring them nearer to the immigrant woman. Equipped with "the informing mind" on the one hand and with experience on the other, we could then walk together through the marvelous streets of the human city, no longer conscious whether we are natives or aliens, because we have become absorbed in a fraternal relation arising from a common experience.

And this attitude of understanding and respect for the worker is necessary, not only to appreciate what he produces, but to preserve his power of production, again showing the necessity for making that substitute for war—human labor—more aggressive and democratic. We are told that the conquered races everywhere, in their helplessness, are giving up the genuine practise of their own arts. In India, for instance, where their arts have been the blossom of many years of labor, the conquered races are casting them aside as of no value in order that they may conform to the inferior art, or rather, lack of art, of their conquerors. Morris constantly lamented that in some parts of India the native arts were quite destroyed, and in many others nearly so; that in all parts they had more or less begun to sicken. This lack of respect and understanding of the primitive arts found among colonies of immigrants in a modern cosmopolitan city, produces a like result in that the arts languish and disappear. We have made an effort at Hull-House to recover something of the early industries from an immigrant neighborhood, and in a little exhibit called a labor museum, we have placed in historic sequence and order methods of spinning and weaving from a dozen nationalities in Asia Minor and Europe. The result has been a striking exhibition of the unity and similarity of the earlier industrial processes. Within the narrow confines of one room, the Syrian, the Greek, the Italian, the Russian, the Norwegian, the Dutch, and the Irish find that the differences in their spinning have been merely putting the distaff upon a frame or placing the old handspindle in a horizontal position. A group of women representing vast differences in religion, in language, in tradition, and in nationality, exhibit practically no difference in the daily arts by which, for a thousand generations, they have clothed their families. When American women come to visit them, the quickest method, in fact almost the only one of establishing a genuine companionship with them, is through this same industry, unless we except that still older occupation, the care of little children. Perhaps this experiment may claim to have made a genuine effort to find the basic experiences upon which a cosmopolitan community may unite at least on the industrial side. . . .

Can we learn our first lesson in modern industry from these humble peasant women who have never shirked the primitive labors upon which all civilized life is founded, even as we must obtain our first lessons in social morality from those who are bearing the brunt of the overcrowded and cosmopolitan city which is the direct result of modern industrial conditions? If we contend that the franchise should be extended to women on the ground that less emphasis is continually placed upon the military order and more upon the industrial order of society, we should have to insist that, if she would secure her old place in industry, the modern woman must needs fit her labors to the present industrial organization as the simpler woman fitted hers to the more simple industrial order. It has been pointed out that woman lost her earlier place when man usurped the industrial pursuits and created wealth on a scale unknown before. Since that time women have been reduced more and more to a state of dependency, until we see only among the European peasant women as they work in the fields, "the heavy, strong, enduring, patient, economically functional representative of what the women of our day used to be."

Cultural education as it is at present carried on in the most advanced schools, is to some extent correcting the present detached relation of women to industry but a sense of responsibility in relation to the development of industry would accomplish much more. As men earned their citizenship through their readiness and ability to defend their city, so perhaps woman, if she takes a citizen's place in the modern industrial city, will have to earn it by devotion and self-abnegation in the service of its complex needs.

The old social problems were too often made a cause of war in the belief that all difficulties could be settled by an appeal to arms. But certainly these subtler problems which confront the modern cosmopolitan city, the problems of race antagonisms and economic adjustments, must be settled by a more searching and genuine method than mere prowess can possibly afford. The first step toward their real solution must be made upon a past experience common to the citizens as a whole and connected with their daily living. As moral problems become more and more associated with our civic and industrial organizations, the demand for enlarged activity is more exigent. If one could connect the old maternal anxieties, which are really the basis of family and tribal life, with the candidates who are seeking offices, it would never be necessary to look about for other motive powers, and if to this we could add maternal concern for the safety and defence of the industrial worker, we should have an increasing code of protective legislation.

We certainly may hope for two results if women enter formally into municipal life. First, the opportunity to fulfill their old duties and obligations with the safeguard and the consideration which the ballot alone can secure for them under the changed conditions, and, second, the education which participation in actual affairs always brings. As we believe that woman has no right to allow what really belongs to her to drop away from her, so we contend that ability to perform an obligation comes very largely in proportion as that obligation is conscientiously assumed.

27. SOCIAL AND INDIVIDUAL ASPECTS OF MIND

CHARLES HORTON COOLEY

Charles Horton Cooley (1864–1929) is one of a group of American academics associated with the formative period of American pragmatism, a group that included William James, John Dewey, George Herbert Mead (see the essays of all three in this collection), and George Santayana. Born and raised in the university town of Ann Arbor, Cooley remained there throughout his entire career once he accepted a professorship at the University of Michigan. Cooley is sometimes seen as one of the precursors to the symbolic interactionist tradition, and he is often described as a microsociologist or a social psychologist. This is understandable given his interest in analyzing the linkages between consciousness and social context. His notion of the "looking-glass self" is a reflection of this concern. Much of his work focused on the relationship between the individual and others within the confines of the family and the intimacy of small groups—or what he referred to as "primary groups." These settings constituted the crucible for the forging of self-identity. In this selection from *Social Organization* (1909), Cooley takes issue with the position originating with Descartes' famous declaration "I think, hence I am." Cooley counters this by advancing the idea that self and society are intricately intertwined and the idea of a self that is independent from society is mistaken.

Mind is an organic whole made up of coöperating individualities, in somewhat the same way that the music of an orchestra is made up of divergent but related sounds. No one would think it necessary or reasonable to divide the music into two kinds, that made by the whole and that of particular instruments, and no more are there two kinds of mind, the social mind and the individual mind. When we study the social mind we merely fix our attention on larger aspects and relations rather than on the narrower ones of ordinary psychology.

The view that all mind acts together in a vital whole from which the individual is never really separate flows naturally from our growing knowledge of heredity and suggestion, which makes it increasingly clear that every thought we have is linked with the thought of our ancestors and associates, and through them with that of society at large. It is also the only view consistent with the general standpoint of modern science, which admits nothing isolate in nature.

The unity of the social mind consists not in agreement but in organization, in the fact of reciprocal influence or causation among its parts, by virtue of which everything that takes place in it is connected with everything else, and so is an outcome of the whole. Whether, like the orchestra, it gives forth harmony may be a matter of dispute, but that its sound, pleasing or otherwise, is the expression of a vital coöperation, cannot well be denied. Certainly everything that I say or think is influenced by what others have said or thought, and, in one way or another, sends out an influence of its own in turn.

This differentiated unity of mental or social life, present in the simplest intercourse but capable of infinite growth and adaptation, is what I mean in this work by social organization. It would be useless, I think, to

Charles Horton Cooley, *Social Organization: A Study of the Larger Mind*, New York: Schocken Books, 1962 [1909]. ✦

attempt a more elaborate definition. We have only to open our eyes to *see* organization; and if we cannot do that no definition will help us.

* * *

In the social mind we may distinguish—very roughly of course—conscious and unconscious relations, the unconscious being those of which we are not aware, which for some reason escape our notice. A great part of the influences at work upon us are of this character: our language, our mechanical arts, our government and other institutions, we derive chiefly from people to whom we are but indirectly and unconsciously related. The larger movements of society—the progress and decadence of nations, institutions and races—have seldom been a matter of consciousness until they were past. And although the growth of social consciousness is perhaps the greatest fact of history, it has still but a narrow and fallible grasp of human life.

Social consciousness, or awareness of society, is inseparable from self-consciousness, because we can hardly think of ourselves excepting with reference to a social group of some sort, or of the group except with reference to ourselves. The two things go together, and what we are really aware of is a more or less complex personal or social whole, of which now the particular, now the general, aspect is emphasized.

In general, then, most of our reflective consciousness, of our wide-awake state of mind, is social consciousness, because a sense of our relation to other persons, or of other persons to one another, can hardly fail to be a part of it. Self and society are twin-born, we know one as immediately as we know the other, and the notion of a separate and independent ego is an illusion.

This view, which seems to me quite simple and in accord with common-sense, is not the one most commonly held, for psychologists and even sociologists are still much infected with the idea that self-consciousness is in some way primary, and antecedent to social consciousness, which must be derived by some recondite process of combination or elimination. I venture, therefore, to give some further exposition of it, based in part on firsthand observation of the growth of social ideas in children.

Descartes is, I suppose, the best-known exponent of the traditional view regarding the primacy of self-consciousness. Seeking an unquestionable basis for philosophy, he thought that he found it in the proposition "I think, therefore I am" (*cogito, ergo sum*). This seemed to him inevitable, though all else might be illusion. "I observed," he says, "that, whilst I thus wished to think that all was false, it was absolutely necessary that I, who thus thought, should be somewhat; and as I observed that this truth, *I think, hence I am*, was so certain and of such evidence that no ground of doubt, however extravagant, could be alleged by the sceptics capable of shaking it, I concluded that I might, without scruple, accept it as the first principle of the philosophy of which I was in search."[1]

From our point of view this reasoning is unsatisfactory in two essential respects. In the first place it seems to imply that "I"-consciousness is a part of all consciousness, when, in fact, it belongs only to a rather advanced stage of development. In the second it is one-sided or "individualistic" in asserting the personal or "I" aspect to the exclusion of the social or "we" aspect, which is equally original with it.

* * *

Introspection is essential to psychological or social insight, but the introspection of Descartes was, in this instance, a limited, almost abnormal, sort of introspection—that of a self-absorbed philosopher doing his best to isolate himself from other people and from all simple and natural conditions of life. The mind into which he looked was in a highly technical state, not likely to give him a just view of human consciousness in general.

Introspection is of a larger sort in our day. There is a world of things in the mind worth looking at, and the modern psychologist, instead of fixing his attention wholly on an extreme form of speculative self-consciousness, puts his mind through an infinite variety of experiences, intellectual and emotional, simple and complex, normal and abnormal, sociable and private, recording in each ease what he sees in it. He does this by subjecting it to suggestions or incitements of various kinds, which awaken the activities he desires to study.

In particular he does it largely by what may be called *sympathetic introspection*, putting himself into intimate contact with various sorts of persons and allowing them to awake in himself a life similar to their own, which he afterwards, to the best of his ability, recalls and describes. In this way he is more or less able to understand—always by introspection—children, idiots, criminals, rich and poor, conservative and radical—any phase of human nature not wholly alien to his own.

This I conceive to be the principal method of the social psychologist.

* * *

One thing which this broader introspection reveals is that the "I"-consciousness does not explicitly appear until the child is, say, about two years old, and that when it does appear it comes in inseparable conjunction with the consciousness of other persons and of those relations which make up a social group. It is in fact simply one phase of a body of personal thought which is self-consciousness in one aspect and social consciousness in another.

The mental experience of a new-born child is probably a mere stream of impressions, which may be regarded as being individual, in being differentiated from any other stream, or as social, in being an undoubted product of inheritance and suggestion from human life at large; but is not aware either of itself or of society.

Very soon, however, the mind begins to discriminate personal impressions and to become both naïvely self-conscious and naïvely conscious of society; that is, the child is aware, in an unreflective way, of a group and of his own special relation to it. He does not say "I" nor does he name his mother, his sister or his nurse, but he has images and feelings out of which these ideas will grow. Later comes the more reflective consciousness which names both himself and other people, and brings a fuller perception of the relations which constitute the unity of this small world.[2]

And so on to the most elaborate phases of self-consciousness and social consciousness, to the metaphysician pondering the Ego, or the sociologist meditating on the Social Organism. Self and society go together, as phases of a common whole. I am aware of the social groups in which I live as immediately and authentically as I am aware of myself; and Descartes

might have said "We think," *cogitamus*, on as good grounds as he said *cogito*.

But, it may be said, this very consciousness that you are considering is after all located in a particular person, and so are all similar consciousnesses, so that what we see, if we take an objective view of the matter, is merely an aggregate of individuals, however social those individuals may be. Common-sense, most people think, assures us that the separate person is the primary fact of life.

If so, is it not because common-sense has been trained by custom to look at one aspect of things and not another? Common-sense, moderately informed, assures us that the individual has his being only as part of a whole. What does not come by heredity comes by communication and intercourse; and the more closely we look the more apparent it is that separateness is an illusion of the eye and community the inner truth. "Social organism," using the term in no abstruse sense but merely to mean a vital unity in human life, is a fact as obvious to enlightened common-sense as individuality.

I do not question that the individual is a differentiated centre of psychical life, having a world of his own into which no other individual can fully enter; living in a stream of thought in which there is nothing quite like that in any other stream, neither his "I," nor his "you," nor his "we," nor even any material object; all, probably, as they exist for him, have something unique about them. But this uniqueness is no more apparent and verifiable than the fact—not at all inconsistent with it—that he is in the fullest sense member of a whole, appearing such not only to scientific observation but also to his own untrained consciousness.

There is then no mystery about social consciousness. The view that there is something recondite about it and that it must be dug for with metaphysics and drawn forth from the depths of speculation, springs from a failure to grasp adequately the social nature of all higher consciousness. What we need in this connection is only a better seeing and understanding of rather ordinary and familiar facts.

* * *

We may view social consciousness either in a particular mind or as a coöperative activity of many minds.

The social ideas that I have are closely connected with those that other people have, and act and react upon them to form a whole. This gives us public consciousness, or to use a more familiar term, public opinion, in the broad sense of a group state of mind which is more or less distinctly aware of itself. By this last phrase I mean such a mutual understanding of one another's points of view on the part of the individuals or groups concerned as naturally results from discussion. There are all degrees of this awareness in the various individuals. Generally speaking, it never embraces the whole in all its complexity, but almost always some of the relations that enter into the whole. The more intimate the communication of a group the more complete, the more thoroughly knit together into a living whole, is its public consciousness.

In a congenial family life, for example, there may be a public consciousness which brings all the important thoughts and feelings of the members into such a living and coöperative whole. In the mind of each member, also, this same thing exists as a social consciousness embracing a vivid sense of the personal traits and modes of thought and feeling of the other members. And, finally, quite inseparable from all this, is each one's consciousness of himself, which is largely a direct reflection of the ideas about himself he attributes to the others, and is directly or indirectly altogether a product of social life. Thus all consciousness hangs together, and the distinctions are chiefly based on point of view.

The unity of public opinion, like all vital unity, is one not of agreement but of organization, of interaction and mutual influence. It is true that a certain underlying likeness of nature is necessary in order that minds may influence one another and so coöperate in forming a vital whole, but identity, even in the simplest process, is unnecessary and probably impossible. The consciousness of the American House of Representatives, for example, is by no means limited to the common views, if there are any, shared by its members, but embraces the whole consciousness of every member so far as this deals with the activity of the House. It would be a poor conception of the whole which left out the opposition, or even one dissentient individual. That all minds are different is a condition, not an obstacle, to the unity that consists in a differentiated and coöperative life.

Here is another illustration of what is meant by individual and collective aspects of social consciousness. Some of us possess a good many books relating to social questions of the day. Each of these books, considered by itself, is the expression of a particular social consciousness; the author has cleared up his ideas as well as he can and printed them. But a library of such books expresses social consciousness in a larger sense; it speaks for the epoch. And certainly no one who reads the books will doubt that they form a whole, whatever their differences. The radical and the reactionist are clearly part of the same general situation.

There are, then, at least three aspects of consciousness which we may usefully distinguish: self-consciousness, or what I think of myself; social consciousness (in its individual aspect), or what I think of other people; and public consciousness, or a collective view of the foregoing as organized in a communicating group. And all three are phases of a single whole.

NOTES

1. Discourse on Method, part iv.
2. There is much interest and significance in the matter of children's first learning the use of "I" and other self-words—just how they learn them and what they mean by them. Some discussion of the matter, based on observation of two children, will be found in Human Nature and the Social Order; and more recently I have published a paper in the Psychological Review (November, 1908) called A Study of the Early Use of Self-Words by a Child. "I" seems to mean primarily the assertion of will in a social medium of which the child is conscious and of which his "I" is an inseparable part. It is thus a social idea and, as stated in the text, arises by differentiation of a vague body of personal thought which is self-consciousness in one phase and social consciousness in another. It has no necessary reference to the body.

SECTION V

1. According to Martineau, only "incapables" can be excluded from democratic participation. How does she argue against figures such as Thomas Jefferson that women don´t fall into that category?
2. How is individualism different from selfishness and how is individualism related to democracy?
3. What are the racial differences that Du Bois considers to be truly consequential? What does this suggest about attempts to preserve racial group distinctiveness?
4. Do you agree or disagree with Du Bois´ argument against assimilation? Why?
5. In your view, to what extent is Gilman´s discussion of the negative impact of uncompensated labor on women´s independence still an issue today? What are the differences between her era and the present in this regards?
6. In your own words, describe what Veblen means by "conspicuous consumption."
7. Why does Addams think that women are particularly well suited for the new occupations that were emerging during her lifetime within city governments? Does her view reinforce existing stereotypes of what can be seen as women´s proper sphere?
8. What, according to Cooley, is the social mind? How does he see the relationship between self and society?

VI. VOICES OUTSIDE THE DISCIPLINE

28. THE MADMAN

FRIEDRICH NIETZSCHE

Friedrich Nietzsche (1844–1900) was a tormented but extremely influential German philosopher. His thought was held to be of particular consequence by Weber and Simmel in the classical period of social theory, and more recently it has been referred to by postmodernists. In these aphorisms from *The Gay Science* (first published in 1887), he proclaims his conviction that not only had the death of God occurred but that we were responsible for it. Moreover, he contends that most people have not yet begun to appreciate the full implications of the end of theistic religion—namely, that the religious grounding for a meaningful, purposeful, and moral life has disappeared. Indeed, as the final section suggests, those secularists who have turned to science as a substitute for religion fail to realize that they, too, have grounded their convictions in faith. They have not yet begun to struggle with the relativizing implications of the demise of God and the end of metaphysics.

Have you not heard of that madman who lit a lantern in the bright morning hours, ran to the market place, and cried incessantly, "I seek God! I seek God!"? As many of those who do not believe in God were standing around just them, he provoked much laughter. Why, did he get lost? said one. Did he lose his way like a child? said another. Or is he hiding? Is he afraid of us? Has he gone on a voyage? or emigrated? Thus they yelled and laughed. The madman jumped into their midst and pierced them with his glances.

"Whither is God" he cried. "I shall tell you. *We have killed him*—you and I. All of us are his murderers. But how have we done this? How were we able to drink up the sea? Who gave us the sponge to wipe away the entire horizon? What did we do when we unchained this earth from its sun? Whither is it moving now? Whither are we moving now? Away from all suns? Are we not plunging continually? Backward, sideward, forward, in all directions? Is there any up or down left? Are we not straying as through an infinite nothing? Do we not feel the breath of empty space? Has it not become colder? Is not night and more night coming on all the while? Must not lanterns be lit in the morning? Do we not hear anything yet of the noise of the gravediggers who are burying God? Do we not smell anything yet of God´s decomposition? Gods too decompose. God is dead. God remains dead. And we have killed him. How shall we, the murderers of all murders, comfort ourselves? What was holiest and most powerful of all that the world has yet owned has bled to death under our knives. Who will wipe this blood off us? What water is there for us to clean ourselves? What festivals of atonement, what sacred games shall we have to invent? Is not the greatness of this deed too great for us? Must not we ourselves become gods simply to seem worthy of it? There has never been a greater deed; and whoever will be born after us—for the sake of this deed he will be part of a higher history than all history hitherto."

Here the madman fell silent and looked again at his listeners; and they too were silent and stared at him in astonishment. At last he threw his lantern on the ground, and it broke and went out. "I come too early," he said then; "my time has not come yet. This tremendous event is still on its way, still wandering—it has not yet reached the ears of man. Lightning and thunder require time, the light of the stars requires time, deeds require time even after they are done, before they can be seen and heard. This deed is still more distant from them than the most distant stars—*and yet they have done it themselves.*"

It has been related further that on that same day the madman entered divers churches and there sang his *requiem aeternam deo.* Led out and called to account, he is said to have replied each time. "What are these churches now if they are not the tombs and sepulchers of God?" . . .

* * *

The background of our cheerfulness. The greatest recent event—that "God is dead," that the belief in the Christian God has ceased to be believable—is even now beginning to cast its first shadows over Europe. For the few, at least, whose eyes, whose *suspicion* in their eyes, is strong and sensitive enough for this spectacle, some sun seems to have set just now. . . . In the main, however, this may be said: the event itself is much too great, too distant, too far from the comprehension of the many even for the tidings of it to be thought of as having *arrived* yet, not to speak of the notion that many people might know what has really happened here, and what must collapse now that this belief has been undermined—all that was built upon it, leaned on it, grew into it; for example, our whole European morality. . . .

Even we born guessers of riddles who are, as it were, waiting on the mountains, put there between today and tomorrow and stretched in the contradiction between today and tomorrow, we firstlings and premature births of the coming century, to whom the shadows that must soon envelop Europe really *should* have appeared by now—why is it that even we look forward to it without

any real compassion for this darkening, and above all without any worry and fear for *ourselves?* Is it perhaps that we are still too deeply impressed by the first consequences of this event—and these first consequences, the consequences for *us,* are perhaps the reverse of what one might expect: not at all sad and dark, but rather like a new, scarcely describable kind of light, happiness, relief, exhilaration, encouragement, dawn? Indeed, we philosophers and "free spirits" feel as if a new dawn were shining on us when we receive the tidings that "the old god is dead"; our heart overflows with gratitude, amazement, anticipation, expectation. At last the horizon appears free again to us, even granted that it is not bright; at last our ships may venture out again, venture out to face any danger; all the daring of the lover of knowledge is permitted again; the sea, *our* sea, lies open again; perhaps there has never yet been such an "open sea." . . .

* * *

How far we too are still pious. In science, convictions have no rights of citizenship, as is said with good reason. Only when they decide to descend to the modesty of a hypothesis, of a provisional experimental point of view, of a regulative fiction, may they be granted admission and even a certain value within the realm of knowledge—though always with the restriction that they remain under police supervision, under the police of mistrust. But does this not mean, more precisely considered, that a conviction may obtain admission to science only when it *ceases* to be a conviction? Would not the discipline of the scientific spirit begin with this, no longer to permit oneself any convictions? Probably that is how it is. But one must still ask whether it is not the case that, *in order that this discipline could begin,* a conviction must have been there already, and even such a commanding and unconditional one that it sacrificed all other convictions for its own sake. It is clear that science too rests on a faith; there is no science "without presuppositions." The question whether truth is needed must not only have been affirmed in advance, but affirmed to the extent that the principle, the faith, the conviction is expressed: "*nothing* is needed *more* than truth, and in relation to it everything else has only second-rate value."

This unconditional will to truth: what is it? . . . What do you know in advance of the character of existence, to be able to decide whether the greater advantage is on the side of the unconditionally mistrustful or of the unconditionally trusting? Yet if both are required, much trust *and* much mistrust: whence might science then take its unconditional faith, its conviction, on which it rests, that truth is more important than anything else, even than any other conviction? Just this conviction could not have come into being if both truth *and* untruth showed themselves to be continually useful, as is the case. Thus, though there undeniably exists a faith in science, it cannot owe its origin to such a utilitarian calculus but it must rather have originated *in spite* of the fact that the inutility and dangerousness of the "will to truth," of "truth at any price," are proved to it continually....

Consequently, "will to truth" does *not* mean "I will not let myself be deceived" but—there is no choice—"I will not deceive, not even myself": *and with this we are on the ground of morality*. For one should ask one-self carefully: "Why don´t you want to deceive?" especially if it should appear—and it certainly does appear—that life depends on appearance; I mean, on error, simulation, deception, self-deception; and when life has, as a matter of fact, always shown itself to be on the side of the most unscrupulous *polytropoi*. Such an intent, charitably interpreted, could perhaps be a quixotism, a little enthusiastic impudence; but it could also be something worse, namely, a destructive principle, hostile to life. "Will to truth"—that might be a concealed will to death.

Thus the question "Why science?" leads back to the moral problem, "For what end any morality at all" if life, nature, and history are "not moral"?... But one will have gathered what I am driving at, namely, that it always remains a *metaphysical faith* upon which our faith in science rests—that even we devotees of knowledge today, we godless ones and anti-metaphysicians, still take *out* fire too from the flame which a faith thousands of years old has kindled: that Christian faith, which was also Plato´s faith, that God is truth, that truth is divine....

29. WHAT PRAGMATISM MEANS

WILLIAM JAMES

William James (1842–1910), the brother of novelist Henry James, was an American philosopher who, along with Charles S. Peirce and John Dewey, is considered one of the founders of a distinctly American school of philosophy called "pragmatism." In this selection from Chapter 2 of *Pragmatism* (1907), James offers in characteristically straightforward and unambiguous language what he means by the term. His argument entails a major shift from traditional philosophy's understanding of its purpose. James contends that pragmatism offers not answers, but a method of inquiry. Moreover, rather than being preoccupied with first principles that serve as the requisite basis for traditional philosophy, pragmatism is concerned from the outset with the implications or consequences of any theoretical position. Such an orientation implies that philosophy ought to be less grandiose in its aims, content to assist in obtaining insights that are both more limited and more provisional than the goal of most philosophers, yet still having the potential for actually affecting people in their everyday lives.

Some years ago, being with a camping party in the mountains, I returned from a solitary ramble to find every one engaged in a ferocious metaphysical dispute. The *corpus* of the dispute was a squirrel—a live squirrel supposed to be clinging to one side of a tree-trunk; while over against the tree's opposite side a human being was imagined to stand. This human witness tries to get sight of the squirrel by moving rapidly round the tree, but no matter how fast he goes, the squirrel moves as fast in the opposite direction, and always keeps the tree between himself and the man, so that never a glimpse of him is caught. The resultant metaphysical problem now is this: *Does the man go round the squirrel or not?* He goes round the tree, sure enough, and the squirrel is on the tree; but does he go round the squirrel? In the unlimited leisure of the wilderness, discussion had been worn threadbare. Every one had taken sides, and was obstinate; and the numbers on both sides were even. Each side, when I appeared therefore appealed to me to make it a majority. Mindful of the scholastic adage that whenever you meet a contradiction you must make a distinction, I immediately sought and found one, as follows: "Which party is right," I said, "depends on what you *practically mean* by `going round´ the squirrel. If you mean passing from the north of him to the east, then to the south, then to the west, and then to the north of him again, obviously the man does go round him, for he occupies these successive positions. But if on the contrary you mean being first in front of him, then on the right of him, then behind him, then on his left, and finally in front again, it is quite as obvious that the man fails to go round him, for by the compensating movements the squirrel makes, he keeps his belly turned towards the man all the time, and his back turned away. Make the distinction, and there is no occasion for any farther dispute. You are both right and both wrong according as you conceive the verb `to go round´ in one practical fashion or the other."

Although one or two of the hotter disputants called my speech a shuffling evasion, saying they wanted no quibbling or scholastic hairsplitting, but meant just plain honest English `round,´ the majority seemed to think that the distinction had assuaged the dispute.

I tell this trivial anecdote because it is a peculiarly simple example of what I wish now to speak of as *the pragmatic method*. The pragmatic method is primarily a method of settling metaphysical disputes that otherwise might be interminable. Is the world one or many?—fated or free?—material or spiritual?—here are notions either of which may or may not hold good of the world; and disputes over such notions are unending. The pragmatic method in such cases is to try to interpret each notion by tracing its respective practical consequences. What difference would it practically make to any one if this notion rather than that notion were true? If no practical difference whatever can be traced, then the alternatives mean practically the same thing, and all dispute is idle. Whenever a dispute is serious, we ought to be able to show some practical difference that must follow from one side or the other's being right. A glance at the history of the idea will show you still better what pragmatism means. The term is derived from the same Greek word *pragma*, meaning action, from which our words `practice´ and `practical´ come. It was first introduced into philosophy by Mr. Charles Peirce in 1878. In an article entitled `How to Make Our Ideas Clear,´ in the *Popular Science Monthly* for January of that year, Mr. Peirce, after pointing out that our beliefs are really rules for action, said that, to develop a thought's meaning, we need only determine what conduct it is fitted to produce: that conduct is for us its sole significance. And the tangible fact at the root of all our thought-distinctions, however subtle, is that there is no one of them so fine as to consist in anything but a possible difference of practice. To attain perfect clearness in our thoughts of an object, then, we need only consider what conceivable effects of a practical kind the object may involve—what sensations we are to expect from it, and what reactions we must prepare. Our conception of these effects, whether immediate or remote, is then for us the whole of our conception of the object, so far as that conception has positive significance at all.

This is the principle of Peirce, the principle of pragmatism. It lay entirely unnoticed by any one for twenty years, until I, in an address before Professor Howison's philosophical union at the University of California, brought it forward again and made a special application of it to religion. By that date (1898) the times seemed ripe for its reception. The word `pragmatism´ spread, and at present it fairly spots the pages of the philosophic journals. On all hands we find the `pragmatic movement´ spoken of, sometimes with respect, sometimes with contumely, seldom with clear understanding. It is evident that the term applies itself conveniently to a number of tendencies that hitherto have lacked a collective name, and that it has `come to stay.´

To take in the importance of Peirce's principle, one must get accustomed to applying it to concrete cases. I found a few years ago that Ostwald, the illustrious Leipzig chemist, had been making perfectly distinct use of the principle of pragmatism in his lectures on the philosophy of science, though he had not called it by that name.

"All realities influence our practice," he wrote me, "and that influence is their meaning for us. I am accustomed to put questions to my classes in this way: In what respects would the world be different if this alternative or that were true? If I can find nothing that would become different, then the alternative has no sense."

That is, the rival views mean practically the same thing, and meaning, other than practical, there is for us none. Ostwald in a published lecture gives this example of what he means. Chemists have long wrangled over the inner constitution of certain bodies called `tautomerous.´ Their properties seemed equally consistent with the notion that an instable hydrogen atom oscillates inside of them, or that they are instable mixtures of two bodies. Controversy raged, but never was decided. "It would never have begun," says Ostwald, "if the combatants had asked themselves what particular experimental fact could have been made different by one or the other view being correct. For it would then have appeared that no difference of fact could possibly ensue; and the quarrel was as unreal as if, theorizing in primitive times about the raising of dough by yeast, one party should have invoked a `brownie,´ while another insisted on an `elf´ as the true cause of the phenomenon."[1]

It is astonishing to see how many philosophical disputes collapse into insignificance the moment you subject them to this simple test of tracing a concrete consequence. There can *be* no difference anywhere that doesn't *make* a difference elsewhere—no difference in abstract truth that doesn't express itself in a difference in concrete fact and in conduct consequent upon that fact, imposed on somebody, somehow, somewhere, and somewhen. The whole function of philosophy ought to be to find out what definite difference it will make to you and me, at definite instants of our life, if this world-formula or that world-formula be the true one.

There is absolutely nothing new in the pragmatic method. Socrates was an adept at it. Aristotle used it methodically. Locke, Berkeley, and Hume made momentous contributions to truth by its means. Shadworth Hodgson keeps insisting that realities are only what they are `known as.´ But these forerunners of pragmatism used it in fragments: they were preluders only. Not until in our time has it generalized itself, become conscious of a universal mission, pretended to a conquering destiny. I believe in that destiny, and I hope I may end by inspiring you with my belief.

Pragmatism represents a perfectly familiar attitude in philosophy, the empiricist attitude, but it represents it, as it seems to me, both in a more radical and in a less objectionable form than it has ever yet assumed. A pragmatist turns his back resolutely and once for all upon a lot of inveterate habits dear to professional philosophers. He turns away from abstraction and insufficiency, from verbal solutions, from bad *a priori* reasons, from fixed principles, closed systems, and pretended absolutes and origins. He turns towards concreteness and adequacy, towards facts, towards action and towards power. That means the empiricist temper regnant and the rationalist temper sincerely given up. It means the open air and possibilities of nature, as against dogma, artificiality, and the pretense of finality in truth.

At the same time it does not stand for any special results. It is a method only. But the general triumph of that method would mean an enormous change in what I called in my last lecture the `temperament´ of philosophy. Teachers of the ultra-rationalistic type would be frozen out, much as the courtier type is frozen out in republics, as the ultramontane type of priest is frozen out in protestant lands. Science and metaphysics would come much nearer together, would in fact work absolutely hand in hand.

Metaphysics has usually followed a very primitive kind of quest. You know how men have always hankered after unlawful magic, and you know what a great part in magic *words* have always played. If you have his name, or the formula of incantation that binds him, you can control the spirit, genie, afrite, or whatever the power may be. Solomon knew the names of all the spirits, and having their names, he held them subject to his will. So the universe has always appeared to the natural mind as a kind of enigma, of which the key must be sought in the shape of some illuminating or power-bringing word or name. That word names the universe's *principle*, and to possess it is after a fashion to possess the universe itself. `God,´ `Matter,´ `Reason,´ `the Absolute,´ `Energy,´ are so many solving names. You can rest when you have them. You are at the end of your metaphysical quest.

But if you follow the pragmatic method, you cannot look on any such word as closing your quest. You must bring out of each word its practical cash-value, set it at work within the stream of your experience. It appears less as a solution, then, than as a program for more work, and more particularly as an indication of the ways in which existing realities may be *changed*.

Theories thus become instruments, not answers to enigmas, in which we can rest. We don't lie back upon them, we move forward, and, on occasion, make nature over again by their aid. Pragmatism unstiffens all our theories, limbers them up and sets each one at work. Being nothing essentially new, it harmonizes with many ancient philosophic tendencies. It agrees with nominalism for instance, in always appealing to particulars; with utilitarianism in emphasizing practical aspects; with positivism in its disdain for verbal solutions, useless questions and metaphysical abstractions.

All these, you see, are *anti-intellectualist* tendencies. Against rationalism as a pretension and a method pragmatism is fully armed and militant. But, at the outset, at least, it stands for no particular results. It has no dogmas, and no doctrines save its method. As the young Italian pragmatist Papini has well said, it lies in the midst of our theories, like a corridor in a hotel.

Innumerable chambers open out of it. In one you may find a man writing an atheistic volume; in the next some one on his knees praying for faith and strength; in a third a chemist investigating a body's properties. In a fourth a system of idealistic metaphysics is being excogitated; in a fifth the impossibility of metaphysics is being shown. But they all own the corridor, and all must pass through it if they want a practicable way of getting into or out of their respective rooms.

No particular results then, so far, but only an attitude of orientation, is what the pragmatic method means. *The attitude of looking, away from first things, principles, `categories,´ supposed necessities; and of looking towards last things, fruits, consequences, facts.*

So much for the pragmatic method! You may say that I have been praising it rather than explaining it to you, but I shall presently explain it abundantly enough by showing how it works on some familiar problems. Meanwhile the word pragmatism has come to be used in a still wider sense, as meaning also a certain *theory of truth.* I mean to give a whole lecture to the statement of that theory, after first paving the way, so I can be very brief now. But brevity is hard to follow, so I ask for your redoubled attention for a quarter of an hour. If much remains obscure, I hope to make it clearer in the later lectures.

One of the most successfully cultivated branches of philosophy in our time is what is called inductive logic, the study of the conditions under which our sciences have evolved. Writers on this subject have begun to show a singular unanimity as to what the laws of nature and elements of fact mean, when formulated by mathematicians, physicists and chemists. When the first mathematical, logical, and natural uniformities, the first *laws,* were discovered, men were so carried away by the clearness, beauty and simplification that resulted, that they believed themselves to have deciphered authentically the eternal thoughts of the Almighty. His mind also thundered and reverberated in syllogisms. He also thought in conic sections, squares and roots and ratios, and geometrized like Euclid. He made Kepler's laws for the planets to follow; he made velocity increase proportionally to the time in falling bodies; he made the law of the sines for light to obey when refracted; he established the classes, orders, families and genera of plants and animals, and fixed the distances between them. He thought the archetypes of all things, and devised their variations; and when we rediscover any one of these his wondrous institutions, we seize his mind in its very literal intention.

But as the sciences have developed farther, the notion has gained ground that most, perhaps all, of our laws are only approximations. The laws themselves, moreover, have grown so numerous that there is no counting them; and so many rival formulations are proposed in all the branches of science that investigators have become accustomed to the notion that no theory is absolutely a transcript of reality, but that any one of them may from some point of view be useful. Their great use is to summarize old facts and to lead to new ones. They are only a man-made language, a conceptual shorthand, as some one calls them, in which we write our reports of nature; and languages, as is well known, tolerate much choice of expression and many dialects.

Thus human arbitrariness has driven divine necessity from scientific logic. If I mention the names of Sigwart, Mach, Ostwald, Pearson, Milhaud, Poincaré, Duhem, Ruyssen, those of you who are students will easily identify the tendency I speak of, and will think of additional names.

Riding now on the front of this wave of scientific logic Messrs. Schiller and Dewey appear with their pragmatistic account of what truth everywhere signifies. Everywhere, these teachers say, `truth´ in our ideas and beliefs means the same thing that it means in science. It means, they say, nothing but this, *that ideas (which themselves are but parts of our experience) become true just in so far as they help us to get into satisfactory relation with other parts of our experience,* to summarize them and get about among them by conceptual shortcuts instead of following the interminable succession of particular phenomena. Any idea upon which we can ride, so to speak; any idea that will carry us prosperously from any one part of our experience to any other part, linking things satisfactorily, working securely, simplifying, saving labor; is true for just so much, true in so far forth, true *instrumentally.* This is the `instrumental´ view of truth taught so successfully at Chicago, the view that truth in our ideas means their power to `work,´ promulgated so brilliantly at Oxford.

Messrs. Dewey, Schiller and their allies, in reaching this general conception of all truth, have only followed the example of geologists, biologists and philologists. In the establishment of these other sciences, the successful stroke was always to take some simple process actually observable in operation—as denudation by weather, say, or variation from parental type, or change of dialect by incorporation of new words and pronunciations—and then to generalize it, making it apply to all times, and produce great results by summating its effects through the ages.

The observable process which Schiller and Dewey particularly singled out for generalization is the familiar one by which any individual settles into *new opinions*. The process here is always the same. The individual has a stock of old opinions already, but he meets a new experience that puts them to a strain. Somebody contradicts them; or in a reflective moment he discovers that they contradict each other; or he hears of facts with which they are incompatible; or desires arise in him which they cease to satisfy. The result is an inward trouble to which his mind till then had been a stranger, and from which he seeks to escape by modifying his previous mass of opinions. He saves as much of it as he can, for in this matter of belief we are all extreme conservatives. So he tries to change first this opinion, and then that (for they resist change very variously), until at last some new idea comes up which he can graft upon the ancient stock with a minimum of disturbance of the latter, some idea that mediates between the stock and the new experience and runs them into one another most felicitously and expediently.

This new idea is then adopted as the true one. It preserves the older stock of truths with a minimum of modification, stretching them just enough to make them admit the novelty, but conceiving that in ways as familiar as the case leaves possible. An *outrée* explanation, violating all our preconceptions, would never pass for a true account of a novelty. We should scratch round industriously till we found something less eccentric. The most violent revolutions in an individual's beliefs leave most of his old order standing. Time and space, cause and effect, nature and history, and one's own biography remain untouched. New truth is always a go-between, a smoother-over of transitions. It marries old opinion to new fact so as ever to show a minimum of jolt, a maximum of continuity. We hold a theory true just in proportion to its success in solving this `problem of maxima and minima.´ But success in solving this problem is eminently a matter of approximation. We say this theory solves it on the whole more satisfactorily than that theory; but that means more satisfactorily to ourselves, and individuals will emphasize their points of satisfaction differently. To a certain degree, therefore, everything here is plastic.

The point I now urge you to observe particularly is the part played by the older truths. Failure to take account of it is the source of much of the unjust criticism levelled against pragmatism. Their influence is absolutely controlling. Loyalty to them is the first principle—in most cases it is the only principle; for by far the most usual way of handling phenomena so novel that they would make for a serious re-arrangement of our preconception is to ignore them altogether, or to abuse those who bear witness for them.

You doubtless wish examples of this process of truth's growth, and the only trouble is their superabundance. The simplest case of new truth is of course the mere numerical addition of new kinds of facts, or of new single facts of old kinds, to our experience—an addition that involves no alteration in the old beliefs. Day follows day, and its contents are simply added. The new contents themselves are not true, they simply, *come* and *are*. Truth is *what we say about them*, and when we say that they have come, truth is satisfied by the plain additive formula.

But often the day's contents oblige a re-arrangement. If I should now utter piercing shrieks and act like a maniac on this platform, it would make many of you revise your ideas as to the probable worth of my philosophy. `Radium´ came the other day as part of the day's content, and seemed for a moment to contradict our ideas of the whole order of nature, that order having come to be identified with what is called the conservation of energy. The mere sight of radium paying heat away indefinitely out of its own pocket seemed to violate that conservation. What to think? If the radiations from it were nothing but an escape of unsuspected `potential´ energy, pre-existent inside of the atoms, the principle of conservation would be saved. The discovery of `helium´ as the radiation's outcome, opened a way to this belief. So Ramsay's view is generally held to be true, because, although it extends our old ideas of energy, it causes a minimum of alteration in their nature.

I need not multiply instances. A new opinion counts as `true´ just in proportion as it gratifies the individual's desire to assimilate the novel in his experience to his beliefs in stock. It must both lean on old truths and grasp new fact; and its success (as I said a moment ago) in doing this, is a matter for the individual's appreciation. When old truth grows, then, by new truth's addition, it is for subjective reasons. We are in the process and obey the reasons. That new idea is truest which performs most felicitously its function of satisfying our double urgency. It makes itself true, gets itself classed as true, by the way it works; grafting itself then upon the ancient body of truth, which thus grows much as a tree grows by the activity of a new layer of cambium.

Now Dewey and Schiller proceed to generalize this observation and to apply it to the most ancient parts of truth. They also once were plastic. They also were called true for human reasons. They also mediated between still earlier truths and what in those days were novel observations. Purely objective truth, truth in whose establishment the function of giving human satisfaction in marrying previous parts of experience with newer parts played no rôle whatever, is nowhere to be found. The reason why we call things true is the reason why they *are* true, for `to be true´ *means* only to perform this marriage-function.

The trail of the human serpent is thus over everything. Truth independent; truth that we *find* merely; truth no longer malleable to human need; truth incorrigible, in a word; such truth exists indeed superabundantly—or is supposed to exist by rationalistically minded thinkers; but then it means only the dead heart of the living tree, and its being there means only that truth also has its paleontology, and its `prescription,´ and may grow stiff with years of veteran service and petrified in men's regard by sheer antiquity. But how plastic even the oldest truths nevertheless really are has been vividly shown in our day by the transformation of logical and mathematical ideas, a transformation which seems even to be invading physics. The ancient formulas are reinterpreted as special expressions of much wider principles, principles that our ancestors never got a glimpse of in their present shape and formulation . . . .

NOTE

1. `Theorie und Praxis,´ *Zeitsch. des Oesterreichischen Ingenieur u. Architecten-Vereines*, 1905, Nr. 4 u. 6. I find a still more radical pragmatism than Ostwald's in an address by Professor W. S. Franklin: "I think that the sickliest notion of physics, even if a student gets it, is that it is `the science of masses, molecules, and the ether.´ And I think that the healthiest notion, even if a student does not wholly get it, is that physics is the science of the ways of taking hold of bodies and pushing them!" (*Science*, January 2, 1903.)

30. THE ECLIPSE OF THE PUBLIC

JOHN DEWEY

The most influential public intellectual in the United States during the first half of the twentieth century, philosopher John Dewey (1859–1952) was one of the key proponents of pragmatism. Commentators often view Dewey and William James (see his essay herein) as the two most consequential philosophical pragmatists. Moreover, in recent years interest in his work has witnessed a revival, with a rather disparate group of intellectuals embracing aspects of his thought, including the late philosopher Richard Rorty, sociologist Robert Bellah, and critical theorist Jürgen Habermas (see his essay in the section on critical theory). Dewey´s interests and impact were broad. He was involved in educational philosophy as a spokesperson for progressive education, and he supported women´s suffrage and other social movements promoting social justice and international peace. He was associated with Jane Addams (see her essay in the preceding section) and her work at Hull House. Given these intellectual and political commitments, it is not surprising that Dewey would become a major theorist of democracy. A key component of democratic practice, in his view, was the opportunity to facilitate public discourse. In the essay below, derived from *The Public and Its Problems* (1927), Dewey expresses his concern that the autonomy of public opinion was eroding.

Optimism about democracy is to-day under a cloud. We are familiar with denunciation and criticism which however, often reveal their emotional source in their peevish and undiscriminating tone. Many of them suffer from the same error into which earlier laudations fell. They assume that democracy is the product of an idea, of a single and consistent intent. Carlyle was no admirer of democracy, but in a lucid moment he said: "Invent the printing press and democracy is inevitable." Add to this: Invent the railway, the telegraph, mass manufacture and concentration of population in urban centers, and some form of democratic government is, humanly speaking, inevitable. Political democracy as it exists to-day calls for adverse criticism in abundance. But the criticism is only an exhibition of querulousness and spleen or of a superiority complex, unless it takes cognizance of the conditions out of which popular government has issued. All intelligent political criticism is comparative. It deals not with all-or-none situations, but with practical alternatives; an absolutistic indiscriminate attitude, whether in praise or blame, testifies to the heat of feeling rather than the light of thought.

American democratic polity was developed out of genuine community life, that is, association in local and small centers where industry was mainly agricultural and where production was carried on mainly with hand tools. It took form when English political habits and legal institutions worked under pioneer conditions. The forms of association were stable, even though their units were mobile and migratory. Pioneer conditions put a high premium upon personal work, skill, ingenuity, initiative and adaptability, and upon neighborly sociability. The township or some not much larger area was the political unit, the town meeting the political medium, and roads, schools, the peace of the community, were the political objectives. The state was a sum of such units,

John Dewey, *The Public and Its Problems*. Athens, OH: Swallow Press & Ohio University Press, 1954 [1927]. ✦

and the national state a federation—unless perchance a confederation—of states. The imagination of the founders did not travel far beyond what could be accomplished and understood in a congeries of self-governing communities. The machinery provided for the selection of the chief executive of the federal union is illustrative evidence. The electoral college assumed that citizens would choose men locally known for their high standing; and that these men when chosen would gather together for consultation to name some one known to them for his probity and public spirit and knowledge. The rapidity with which the scheme fell into disuse is evidence of the transitoriness of the state of affairs that was predicated. But at the outset there was no dream of the time when the very names of the presidential electors would be unknown to the mass of the voters, when they would plump for a "ticket" arranged in a more or less private caucus, and when the electoral college would be an impersonal registering machine, such that it would be treachery to employ the personal judgment which was originally contemplated as the essence of the affair.

The local conditions under which our institutions took shape is well indicated by our system, apparently so systemless, of public education. Any one who has tried to explain it to a European will understand what is meant. One is asked, say, what method of administration is followed, what is the course of study and what the authorized methods of teaching. The American member to the dialogue replies that in this state, or more likely county, or town, or even some section of a town called a district, matters stand thus and thus; somewhere else, so and so. The participant from this side is perhaps thought by the foreigner to be engaged in concealing his ignorance; and it would certainly take a veritable cyclopedic knowledge to state the matter in its entirety. The impossibility of making any moderately generalized reply renders it almost indispensable to resort to a historical account in order to be intelligible. A little colony, the members of which are probably mostly known to one another in advance, settle in what is almost, or quite, a wilderness. From belief in its benefits and by tradition, chiefly religious, they wish their children to know at least how to read, write and figure. Families can only rarely provide a tutor; the neighbors over a certain area, in New England an area smaller even than the township,

combine in a "school district." They get a school house built, perhaps by their own labor, and hire a teacher by means of a committee, and the teacher is paid from the taxes. Custom determines the limited course of study, and tradition the methods of the teacher, modified by whatever personal insight and skill he may bring to bear. The wilderness is gradually subdued; a network of highways, then of railways, unite the previously scattered communities. Large cities grow up; studies grow more numerous and methods more carefully scrutinized. The larger unit, the state, but not the federal state, provides schools for training teachers and their qualifications are more carefully looked into and tested. But subject to certain quite general conditions imposed by the state-legislature, but not the national state, local maintenance and control remain the rule. The community pattern is more complicated, but is not destroyed. The instance seems richly instructive as to the state of affairs under which our borrowed, English, political institutions were reshaped and forwarded.

We have inherited, in short, local town-meeting practices and ideas. But we live and act and have our being in a continental national state. We are held together by non-political bonds, and the political forms are stretched and legal institutions patched in an ad hoc and improvised manner to do the work they have to do. Political structures fix the channels in which non-political, industrialized currents flow. Railways, travel and transportation, commerce, the mails, telegraph and telephone, newspapers, create enough similarity of ideas and sentiments to keep the thing going as a whole, for they create interaction and interdependence. The unprecedented thing is that states, as distinguished from military empires, can exist over such a wide area. The notion of maintaining a unified state, even nominally self-governing, over a country as extended as the United States and consisting of a large and racially diversified population would once have seemed the wildest of fancies. It was assumed that such a state could be found only in territories hardly larger than a city-state and with a homogeneous population. It seemed almost self-evident to Plato—as to Rousseau later—that a genuine state could hardly be larger than the number of persons capable of personal acquaintance with one another. Our modern state-unity is due to the consequences of technology employed so as to facilitate the rapid and easy circulation of opinions and information, and so as to generate constant and intricate interaction far beyond the limits of face-to-face communities. Political and legal forms have only piece-meal and haltingly, with great lag, accommodated themselves to the industrial transformation. The elimination of distance, at the base of which are physical agencies, has called into being the new form of political association.

The wonder of the performance is the greater because of the odds against which it has been achieved. The stream of immigrants which has poured in is so large and heterogeneous that under conditions which formerly obtained it would have disrupted any semblance of unity as surely as the migratory invasion of alien hordes once upset the social equilibrium of the European continent. No deliberately adopted measures could have accomplished what has actually happened. Mechanical forces have operated, and it is no cause for surprise if the effect is more mechanical than vital. The reception of new elements of population in large number from heterogeneous peoples, often hostile to one another at home, and the welding them into even an outward show of unity is an extraordinary feat. In many respects, the consolidation has occurred so rapidly and ruthlessly that much of value has been lost which different peoples might have contributed. The creation of political unity has also promoted social and intellectual uniformity, a standardization favorable to mediocrity. Opinion has been regimented as well as outward behavior. The temper and flavor of the pioneer have evaporated with extraordinary rapidity; their precipitate, as is often noted, is apparent only in the wild-west romance and the movie. What Bagehot called the cake of custom formed with increasing acceleration, and the cake is too often flat and soggy. Mass production is not confined to the factory.

The resulting political integration has confounded the expectations of earlier critics of popular government as much as it must surprise its early backers if they are gazing from on high upon the present scene. The critics predicted disintegration, instability. They foresaw the new society falling apart, dissolving into mutually repellent animated grains of sand. They, too, took seriously the theory of "Individualism" as the basis of democratic government. A stratification of society into immemorial classes within which each person performed his stated duties according to his fixed position seemed to them the only warrant of stability. They had no faith that human beings released from the pressure of this system could hold together in any unity. Hence they prophesied a flux of governmental régimes, as individuals formed factions, seized power, and then lost it as some newly improvised faction proved stronger. Had the facts conformed to the theory of Individualism, they would doubtless have been right. But, like the authors of the theory, they ignored the technological forces making for consolidation.

In spite of attained integration, or rather perhaps because of its nature, the Public seems to be lost; it is certainly bewildered.[1] The government, officials and their activities, are plainly with us. Legislatures make laws with luxurious abandon; subordinate officials engage in a losing struggle to enforce some of them; judges on the bench deal as best they can with the steadily mounting pile of disputes that come before them. But where is the public which these officials are supposed to represent? How much more is it than geographical names and official titles? The United States, the state of Ohio or New York, the county of this and the city of that? Is the public much more than what a cynical diplomat once called Italy: a geographical expression? Just as philosophers once imputed a substance to qualities and traits in order that the latter might have something in which to inhere and thereby gain a conceptual solidity and consistency which they lacked on their face, so perhaps our political "common-sense" philosophy imputes a public only to support and substantiate the behavior of officials. How can the latter be public officers, we despairingly ask, unless there is a public? If a public exists, it is surely as uncertain about its own whereabouts as philosophers since Hume have been about the residence and make-up of the self. The number of voters who take advantage of their majestic right is steadily decreasing in proportion to those who might use it. The ratio of actual to eligible voters is now about one-half. In spite of somewhat frantic appeal and organized effort, the endeavor to bring voters to a sense of their privileges and duties has so far been noted for failure. A few preach the impotence of all politics; the many nonchalantly practice abstinence and indulge in indirect action. Skepticism regarding the efficacy of voting is openly expressed, not only in the theories of intellectuals, but in the words of lowbrow masses: "What difference does it make whether I vote or not? Things go on just the same anyway. My vote never changed anything." Those somewhat more reflective add: "It is nothing but a fight between the ins and the outs. The only difference made by an election is as to who get the jobs, draw the salaries and shake down the plum tree."

Those still more inclined to generalization assert that the whole apparatus of political activities is a kind of protective coloration to conceal the fact that big business rules the governmental roost in any case. Business is the order of the day, and the attempt to stop or deflect its course is as futile as Mrs. Partington essaying to sweep back the tides with a broom. Most of those who hold these opinions would profess to be shocked if the doctrine of economic determinism were argumentatively expounded to them, but they act upon a virtual belief in it. Nor is acceptance of the doctrine limited to radical socialists. It is implicit in the attitude of men of big business and financial interests, who revile the former as destructive "Bolshevists." For it is their firm belief that "prosperity"—a word which has taken on religious color—is the great need of the country, that they are its authors and guardians, and hence by right the determiners of polity. Their denunciations of the "materialism" of socialists is based simply upon the fact that the latter want a different distribution of material force and well-being than that which satisfies those now in control.

The unfitness of whatever public exists, with respect to the government which is nominally its organ, is made manifest in the extra-legal agencies which have grown up. Intermediary groups are closest to the political conduct of affairs. It is interesting to compare the English literature of the eighteenth century regarding factions with the status actually occupied by parties. Factionalism was decried by all thinkers as the chief enemy to political stability. Their voice of condemnation is rechoed in the writing of early nineteenth-century American writers on politics. Extensive and consolidated factions under the name of parties are now not only a matter of course, but popular imagination can conceive of no other way by which officials may be selected and governmental affairs carried on. The centralizing movement has reached a point where even a third party can lead only a spasmodic and precarious existence. Instead of individuals who in the privacy of their consciousness make choices which are carried into effect by personal volition, there are citizens who have the blessed opportunity to vote for a ticket of men mostly unknown to them, and which is made up for them by an undercover machine in a caucus whose operations constitute a kind of political predestination. There are those who speak as if ability to choose between two tickets were a high exercise of individual freedom. But it is hardly the kind of liberty contemplated by the authors of the individualistic doctrine. "Nature abhors a vacuum." When the public is as uncertain and obscure as it is to-day, and hence as remote from government, bosses with their political machines fill the void between government and the public. Who pulls the strings which move the bosses and generates power to run the machines is a matter of surmise rather than of record, save for an occasional overt scandal.

NOTE

1. See Walter Lippmann´s "The Phantom Public." To this as well as to his "Public Opinion," I wish to acknowledge my indebtedness, not only as to this particular point, but for ideas involved in my entire discussion even when it reaches conclusions diverging from his.

31. CIVILIZATION AND ITS DISCONTENTS

SIGMUND FREUD

Sigmund Freud (1856–1939), the founder of psychoanalysis, was an intellectual giant whose influence transcended psychology and the other social sciences to shape literature, art, and the general culture. He was known to Weber, who was rather critical of Freud´s work, and to Simmel, who was more appreciative. Freud´s work has had a profound impact on subsequent theorists, ranging from critical theorists to Parsons, from feminists to postmodernists. In this selection from his classic work *Civilization and Its Discontents* (1930), Freud argues that, although it is worth it, we pay a steep psychological price for civilization because it demands that we repress instinctual drives circumscribing the limits of human happiness. Freud´s tragic view of life is nowhere better articulated than in this passage.

Our enquiry concerning happiness has not so far taught us much that is not already common knowledge. And even if we proceed from it to the problem of why it is so hard for men to be happy, there seems no greater prospect of learning anything new. We have given the answer already . . . by pointing to the three sources from which our suffering comes: the superior power of nature, the feebleness of our own bodies and the inadequacy of the regulations which adjust the mutual relationships of human beings in the family, the state and society. In regard to the first two sources, our judgement cannot hesitate long. It forces us to acknowledge those sources of suffering and to submit to the inevitable. We shall never completely master nature; and our bodily organism, itself a part of that nature, will always remain a transient structure with a limited capacity for adaptation and achievement. This recognition does not have a paralysing effect. On the contrary, it points the direction for our activity. If we cannot remove all suffering, we can remove some, and we can mitigate some: the experience of many thousands of years has convinced us of that. As regards the third source, the social source of suffering, our attitude is a different one. We do not admit it at all; we cannot see why the regulations made by ourselves should not, on the contrary, be a protection and a benefit for every one of us. And yet, when we consider how unsuccessful we have been in precisely this field of prevention of suffering, a suspicion dawns on us that here, too, a piece of unconquerable nature may lie behind—this time a piece of our own psychical constitution.

When we start considering this possibility, we come upon a contention which is so astonishing that we must dwell upon it. This contention holds that what we call our civilization is largely responsible for our misery, and that we should be much happier if we gave it up and returned to primitive conditions. I call this contention astonishing because, in whatever way we may define the concept of civilization, it is a certain fact that all the things with which we seek to protect ourselves against the threats that emanate from the sources of suffering are part of that very civilization.

How has it happened that so many people have come to take up this strange attitude of hostility to civilization?[1] I believe that the basis of it was a deep and long-standing dissatisfaction with the then existing state of civilization and that on that basis a condemnation of it was built up, occasioned by certain specific historical events. I think I know what the last and the last but one of those occasions were. I am not learned enough to trace the chain of them far back enough in the history of the human species; but a factor of this kind hostile to civilization must already have been at work in the victory of Christendom over the heathen religions. For it was very closely related to the low estimation put upon earthly life by the Christian doctrine. The last but one of these occasions was when the progress of voyages of discovery led to contact with primitive peoples and races. In consequence of insufficient observation and a mistaken view of their manners and customs, they appeared to Europeans to be leading a simple, happy life with few wants, a life such as was unattainable by their visitors with their superior civilization. Later experience has corrected some of those judgements. In many cases the observers had wrongly attributed to the absence of complicated cultural demands what was in fact due to the bounty of nature and the ease with which the major human needs were satisfied. The last occasion is especially familiar to us. It arose when people came to know about the mechanism of the neuroses, which threaten to undermine the modicum of happiness enjoyed by civilized men. It was discovered that a person becomes neurotic because he cannot tolerate the amount of frustration which society imposes on him in the service of its cultural ideals, and it was inferred from this that the abolition or reduction of those demands would result in a return to possibilities of happiness.

There is also an added factor of disappointment. During the last few generations mankind has made an extraordinary advance in the natural sciences and in their technical application and has established his control over nature in a way never before imagined. The single steps of this advance are common knowledge and it is unnecessary to enumerate them. Men are proud of those achievements, and have a right to be. But they seem to have observed that this newly-won power over space and time, this subjugation of the forces of nature, which is the fulfilment of a longing that goes back thousands of years, has not increased the amount of pleasurable satisfaction which they may expect from life and has not made them feel happier. From the recognition of this fact we ought to be content

to conclude that power over nature is not the *only* precondition of human happiness, just as it is not the *only* goal of cultural endeavour; we ought not to infer from it that technical progress is without value for the economics of our happiness. One would like to ask: is there, then, no positive gain in pleasure, no unequivocal increase in my feeling of happiness, if I can, as often as I please, hear the voice of a child of mine who is living hundreds of miles away or if I can learn in the shortest possible time after a friend has reached his destination that he has come through the long and difficult voyage unharmed? Does it mean nothing that medicine has succeeded in enormously reducing infant mortality and the danger of infection for women in childbirth, and, indeed, in considerably lengthening the average life of a civilized man? And there is a long list that might be added to benefits of this kind which we owe to the much-despised era of scientific and technical advances. But here the voice of pessimistic criticism makes itself heard and warns us that most of these satisfactions follow the model of the `cheap enjoyment´ extolled in the anecdote—the enjoyment obtained by putting a bare leg from under the bedclothes on a cold winter night and drawing it in again. If there had been no railway to conquer distances, my child would never have left his native town and I should need no telephone to hear his voice; if travelling across the ocean by ship had not been introduced, my friend would not have embarked on his sea-voyage and I should not need a cable to relieve my anxiety about him. What is the use of reducing infantile mortality when it is precisely that reduction which imposes the greatest restraint on us in the begetting of children, so that, taken all round, we nevertheless rear no more children than in the days before the reign of hygiene, while at the same time we have created difficult conditions for our sexual life in marriage, and have probably worked against the beneficial effects of natural selection? And, finally, what good to us is a long life if it is difficult and barren of joys, and if it is so full of misery that we can only welcome death as a deliverer?

It seems certain that we do not feel comfortable in our present-day civilization, but it is very difficult to form an opinion whether and in what degree men of an earlier age felt happier and what part their cultural conditions played in the matter. We shall always tend to consider people´s distress objectively—that is, to place ourselves, with our own wants and sensibilities, in *their* conditions, and then to examine what occasions we should find in them for experiencing happiness or unhappiness. This method of looking at things, which seems objective because it ignores the variations in subjective sensibility, is, of course, the most subjective possible, since it puts one´s own mental states in the place of any others, unknown though they may be. Happiness, however, is something essentially subjective. No matter how much we may shrink with horror from certain situations—of a galley-slave in antiquity, of a peasant during the Thirty Years´ War, of a victim of the Holy Inquisition, of a Jew awaiting a pogrom—it is nevertheless impossible for us to feel our way into such people—to divine the changes which original obtuseness of mind, a gradual stupefying process, the cessation of expectations, and cruder or more refined methods of narcotization have produced upon their receptivity to sensations of pleasure and unpleasure. Moreover, in the case of the most extreme possibility of suffering, special mental protective devices are brought into operation. It seems to me unprofitable to pursue this aspect of the problem any further.

It is time for us to turn our attention to the nature of this civilization on whose value as a means to happiness doubts have been thrown. We shall not look for a formula in which to express that nature in a few words, until we have learned something by examining it. We shall therefore content ourselves with saying once more that the word `civilization´[2] describes the whole sum of the achievements and the regulations which distinguish our lives from those of our animal ancestors and which serve two purposes—namely to protect men against nature and to adjust their mutual relations.[3] In order to learn more, we will bring together the various features of civilization individually, as they are exhibited in human communities. In doing so, we shall have no hesitation in letting ourselves be guided by linguistic usage or, as it is also called, linguistic feeling, in the conviction that we shall thus be doing justice to inner discernments which still defy expression in abstract terms.

The first stage is easy. We recognize as cultural all activities and resources which are useful to men for making the earth serviceable to them, for protecting them against the violence of the forces of nature, and so on. As regards this side of civilization, there can be scarcely any doubt. If we go back far enough, we find that the first acts of civilization were the use of tools, the gaining of control over fire and the construction of dwellings. Among these, the control over fire stands out as a quite extraordinary and unexampled achievement,[4] while the others opened up paths which man has followed ever since, and the stimulus to which is easily guessed. With every tool man is perfecting his own organs, whether motor or sensory, or is removing the limits to their functioning. Motor power places gigantic forces at his disposal, which, like his muscles, he can employ in any direction; thanks to ships and aircraft neither water nor air can hinder his movements; by means of spectacles he corrects defects in the lens of his own eye; by means of the telescope he sees into the far distance; and by means of the microscope he overcomes the limits of visibility set by the structure of his retina. In the photographic camera he has created an instrument which retains the fleeting visual impressions, just as a gramophone disc retains the equally fleeting auditory ones; both are at bottom materializations of the power he possesses of recollection, his memory. With the help of the telephone he can hear at distances which would be respected as unattainable even in a fairy tale. Writing was in its origin the voice of an absent person; and the dwelling-house was a substitute for the mother´s womb, the first lodging, for which in all likelihood man still longs, and in which he was safe and felt at ease.

These things that, by his science and technology, man has brought about on this earth, on which he first appeared as a feeble animal organism and on which each individual of his species must once more make its entry (`oh inch of nature!´[5]) as a helpless suckling—these things do not only sound like a fairy tale, they are an actual fulfillment of every—or of almost every—fairy-tale wish. All these assets he may lay claim to as his cultural acquisition. Long ago he formed an ideal conception of omnipotence and omniscience which he embodied in his gods. To these gods he attributed everything that seemed unattainable to his wishes, or that was forbidden to him. One may say, therefore, that these gods were cultural ideals. Today he has come very close to the attainment of this ideal, he has almost become a god himself. Only, it is true, in the fashion in which ideals are usually attained according to the general judgement of humanity. Not completely; in some respects not at all, in others only half way. Man has, as it were, become a kind of prosthetic[6] God. When he puts on all his auxiliary organs he is truly magnificent; but those organs have not grown on to him and they still give him much trouble at times. Nevertheless, he is entitled to console himself with the thought that this development will not come to an end precisely with the year 1930 A.D. Future ages will bring with them new and probably unimaginably great advances in this field of civilization and will increase man´s likeness to God still more. But in the interests of our investigations, we will not forget that present-day man does not feel happy in his Godlike character.

We recognize, then, that countries have attained a high level of civilization if we find that in them everything which can assist in the exploitation of the earth by man and in his protection against the forces of nature—everything, in short, which is of use to him—is attended to and effectively carried out. In such countries rivers which threaten to flood the land are regulated in their flow, and their water is directed through canals to places where there is a shortage of it. The soil is carefully cultivated and planted with the vegetation which it is suited to support; and the mineral wealth below ground is assiduously brought to the surface and fashioned into the required implements and utensils. The means of communication are ample, rapid and reliable. Wild and dangerous animals have been exterminated, and the breeding of domesticated animals flourishes. But we demand other things from civilization besides these, and it is a noticeable fact that we hope to find them realized in these same countries. As though we were seeking to repudiate the first demand we made, we welcome it as a sign of civilization as well if we see people directing their care too to what has no practical value whatever, to what is useless—if for instance, the green spaces necessary in a town as playgrounds and as reservoirs of fresh air are also laid out with flower-beds, or if the windows of the houses are decorated with pots of flowers. We soon observe that this useless thing which we expect civilization to value is beauty. We require civilized man to reverence beauty wherever he sees it in nature and to create it in the objects of his handiwork so far as he is able. But this is far from exhausting our demands on civilization. We expect besides to see the signs of cleanliness and order. We do not think highly of the cultural level of an English country town in Shakespeare´s time when we read that there was a big dungheap in front of his father´s house in Stratford; we are indignant and call it `barbarous´ (which is the opposite of civilized) when we find the paths in the Wiener Wald[7] littered with paper. Dirtiness of any kind seems to us incompatible with civilization. We extend our demand for cleanliness to the human body too. We are astonished to learn of the objectionable smell which emanated from the *Roi Soleil;*[8] and we shake our heads on the Isola Bella[9] when we are shown the tiny washbasin in which Napoleon made his morning toilet. Indeed, we are not surprised by the idea of setting up the use of soap as an actual yardstick of civilization. The same is true of order. It, like cleanliness, applies solely to the works of man. But whereas cleanliness is not to be expected in nature, order, on the contrary, has been imitated from her. Man´s observation of the great astronomical regularities not only furnished him with a model for introducing order into his life, but gave him the first points of departure for doing so. Order is a kind of compulsion to repeat which, when a regulation has been laid down once and for all, decides when, where and how a thing shall be done, so that in every similar circumstance one is spared hesitation and indecision. The benefits of order are incontestable. It enables men to use space and time to the best advantage, while conserving their psychical forces. We should have a right to expect that order would have taken its place in human activities from the start and without difficulty; and we may well wonder that this has not happened—that, on the contrary, human beings exhibit an inborn tendency to carelessness, irregularity and unreliability in their work, and that a laborious training is needed before they learn to follow the example of their celestial models.

Beauty, cleanliness and order obviously occupy a special position among the requirements of civilization. No one will maintain that they are as important for life as control over the forces of nature or as some other factors with which we shall become acquainted. And yet no one would care to put them in the background as trivialities. That civilization is not exclusively taken up with what is useful is already shown by the example of beauty, which we decline to omit from among the interests of civilization. The usefulness of order is quite evident. With regard to cleanliness, we must bear in mind that it is demanded of us by hygiene as well, and we may suspect that even before the days of scientific prophylaxis the connection between the two was not altogether strange to man. Yet utility does not entirely explain these efforts; something else must be at work besides.

No feature, however, seems better to characterize civilization than its esteem and encouragement of man's higher mental activities—his intellectual, scientific and artistic achievements—and the leading role that it assigns to ideas in human life. Foremost among those ideas are the religious systems, on whose complicated structure I have endeavoured to throw light elsewhere.[10] Next come the speculations of philosophy; and finally what might be called man's `ideals'—his ideas of a possible perfection of individuals, or of peoples or of the whole of humanity, and the demands he sets up on the basis of such ideas. The fact that these creations of his are not independent of one another, but are on the contrary closely interwoven, increases the difficulty not only of describing them but of tracing their psychological derivation. If we assume quite generally that the motive force of all human activities is a striving towards the two confluent goals of utility and a yield of pleasure, we must suppose that this is also true of the manifestations of civilization which we have been discussing here, although this is easily visible only in scientific and aesthetic activities. But it cannot be doubted that the other activities, too, correspond to strong needs in men—perhaps to needs which are only developed in a minority. Nor must we allow ourselves to be misled by judgements of value concerning any particular religion, or philosophic system, or ideal. Whether we think to find in them the highest achievements of the human spirit, or whether we deplore them as aberrations, we cannot but recognize that where they are present, and, in especial, where they are dominant, a high level of civilization is implied.

The last, but certainly not the least important, of the characteristic features of civilization remains to be assessed: the manner in which the relationships of men to one another, their social relationships, are regulated—relationships which affect a person as a neighbour, as a source of help, as another person's sexual object, as a member of a family and of a State. Here it is especially difficult to keep clear of particular ideal demands and to see what is civilized in general. Perhaps we may begin by explaining that the element of civilization enters on the scene with the first attempt to regulate these social relationships. If the attempt were not made, the relationships would be subject to the arbitrary will of the individual: that is to say, the physically stronger man would decide them in the sense of his own interests and instinctual impulses. Nothing would be changed in this if this stronger man should in his turn meet someone even stronger than he. Human life in common is only made possible when a majority comes together which is stronger than any separate individual, and which remains united against all separate individuals. The power of this community is then set up as `right' in opposition to the power of the individual, which is condemned as `brute force'. This replacement of the power of the individual by the power of a community constitutes the decisive step of civilization. The essence of it lies in the fact that the members of the community restrict themselves in their possibilities of satisfaction, whereas the individual knew no such restrictions. The first requisite of civilization, therefore, is that of justice—that is, the assurance that a law once made will not be broken in favour of an individual. This implies nothing as to the ethical value of such a law. The further course of cultural development seems to tend towards making the law no longer an expression of the will of a small community—a caste or a stratum of the population or a racial group—which, in its turn, behaves like a violent individual towards other, and perhaps more numerous, collections of people. The final outcome should be a rule of law to which all—except those who are not capable of entering a community—have contributed by a sacrifice of their instincts, and which leaves no one—again with the same exception—at the mercy of brute force.

The liberty of the individual is no gift of civilization. It was greatest before there was any civilization, though then, it is true, it had for the most part no value, since the individual was scarcely in a position to defend it. The development of civilization imposes restrictions on it, and justice demands that no one shall escape those restrictions. What makes itself felt in a human community as a desire for freedom may be their revolt against some existing injustice, and so may prove favourable to a further development of civilization; it may remain compatible with civilization. But it may also spring from the remains of their original personality, which is still untamed by civilization and may thus become the basis in them of hostility to civilization. The urge for freedom, therefore, is directed against particular forms and demands of civilization or against civilization altogether. It does not seem as though any influence could induce a man to change his nature into a termite´s. No doubt he will always defend his claim to individual liberty against the will of the group. A good part of the struggles of mankind centre round the single task of finding an expedient accommodation—one, that is, that will bring happiness—between this claim of the individual and the cultural claims of the group; and one of the problems that touches the fate of humanity is whether such an accommodation can be reached by means of some particular form of civilization or whether this conflict is irreconcilable.

By allowing common feeling to be our guide in deciding what features of human life are to be regarded as civilized, we have obtained a clear impression of the general picture of civilization; but it is true that so far we have discovered nothing that is not universally known. At the same time we have been careful not to fall in with the prejudice that civilization is synonymous with perfecting, that it is the road to perfection pre-ordained for men. But now a point of view presents itself which may lead in a different direction. The development of civilization appears to us as a peculiar process which mankind undergoes, and in which several things strike us as familiar. We may characterize this process with reference to the changes which it brings about in the familiar instinctual dispositions of human beings, to satisfy which is, after all, the economic task of our lives. A few of these instincts are used up in such a manner that something appears in their place which, in an individual, we describe as a character-trait. The most remarkable example of such a process is found in the anal erotism of young human beings. Their original interest in the excretory function, its organs and products, is changed in the course of their growth into a group of traits which are familiar to us as parsimony, a sense of order and cleanliness—qualities which, though valuable and welcome in themselves, may be intensified till they become markedly dominant and produce what is called the anal character. How this happens we do not know, but there is no doubt about the correctness of the finding.[11] Now we have seen that order and cleanliness are important requirements of civilization, although their vital necessity is not very apparent, any more than their suitability as sources of enjoyment. At this point we cannot fail to be struck by the similarity between the process of civilization and the libidinal development of the individual. Other instincts [besides anal erotism] are induced to displace the conditions for their satisfaction, to lead them into other paths. In most cases this process coincides with that of the *sublimation* (of instinctual aims) with which we are familiar, but in some it can be differentiated from it. Sublimation of instinct is an especially conspicuous feature of cultural development; it is what makes it possible for higher psychical activities, scientific, artistic or ideological, to play such an important part in civilized life. If one were to yield to a first impression, one would say that sublimation is a vicissitude which has been forced upon the instincts entirely by civilization. But it would be wiser to reflect upon this a little longer. In the third place,[12] finally, and this seems the most important of all, it is impossible to overlook the extent to which civilization is built up upon a renunciation of instinct, how much it presupposes precisely the non-satisfaction (by suppression, repression or some other means?) of powerful instincts. This `cultural frustration´ dominates the large field of social relationships between human beings. As we already know, it is the cause of the hostility against which all civilizations have to struggle. It will also make severe demands on our scientific work, and we shall have much to explain here. It is not easy to understand how it can become possible to deprive an instinct of satisfaction. Nor is doing so without danger. If the loss is not compensated for economically, one can be certain that serious disorders will ensue.

But if we want to know what value can be attributed to our view that the development of civilization is a special process, comparable to the normal maturation of the individual, we must clearly attack another problem. We must ask ourselves to what influences the development of civilization owes its origin, how it arose, and by what its course has been determined. . . .

NOTES

1. [Freud had discussed this question at considerable length two years earlier, in the opening chapters of *The Future of an Illusion* (1927c).]
2. `Kultur.` For the translation of this word see the Editor's Note to *The Future of an Illusion.*
3. See *The Future of an Illusion.*
4. Psycho-analytic material, incomplete as it is and not susceptible to clear interpretation, nevertheless admits of a conjecture—a fantastic-sounding one—about the origin of this human feat. It is as though primal man had the habit, when he came in contact with fire, of satisfying an infantile desire connected with it, by putting it out with a stream of his urine. The legends that we possess leave no doubt about the originally phallic view taken of tongues of flame as they shoot upwards. Putting out fire by micturating—a theme to which modern giants, Gulliver in Lilliput and Rabelais' Gargantua, still hark back—was therefore a kind of sexual act with a male, an enjoyment of sexual potency in a homosexual competition. The first person to renounce this desire and spare the fire was able to carry it off with him and subdue it to his own use. By damping down the fire of his own sexual excitation, he had tamed the natural force of fire. This great cultural conquest was thus the reward for his renunciation of instinct. Further, it is as though woman had been appointed guardian of the fire which was held captive on the domestic hearth, because her anatomy made it impossible for her to yield to the temptation of this desire. It is remarkable, too, how regularly analytic experience testifies to the connection between ambition, fire and urethral erotism.—[Freud had pointed to the connection between urination and fire as early as in the `Dora` case history (1905e [1901]). The connection with ambition came rather later. A full list of references will be found in the Editor's Note to the later paper on the subject, `The Acquisition and Control of Fire` (1932a).]
5. [In English in the original. This very Shakespearean phrase is not in fact to be found in the canon of Shakespeare. The words `Poore inch of Nature` occur, however, in a novel by George Wilkins, *The Painfull Adventures of Pericles Prince of Tyre*, where they are addressed by Pericles to his infant daughter. This work was first printed in 1608, just after the publication of Shakespeare's play, in which Wilkins has been thought to have had a hand. Freud's unexpected acquaintance with the phrase is explained by its appearance in a discussion of the origins of *Pericles* in Georg Brandes's well-known book on Shakespeare, a copy of the German translation of which had a place in Freud's library (Brandes, 1896). He is known to have greatly admired the Danish critic (cf. Jones, 1957, 120), and the same book is quoted in his paper on the three caskets (1913f)].
6. [A prosthesis is the medical term for an artificial adjunct to the body, to make up for some missing or inadequate part: e.g. false teeth or a false leg.]
7. [The wooded hills on the outskirts of Vienna.]
8. [Louis XIV of France.]
9. [The well-known island in Lake Maggiore, visited by Napoleon a few days before the battle of Marengo.]
10. [Cf. *The Future of an Illusion* (1927c).]
11. Cf. my `Character and Anal Erotism` (1908b), and numerous further contributions, by Ernest Jones [1918] and others.
12. [Freud had already mentioned two other factors playing a part in the `process` of civilization: character-formation and sublimation.]

32. THE FUSION OF THE 'I' AND THE 'ME' IN SOCIAL ACTIVITIES

GEORGE HERBERT MEAD

George Herbert Mead (1863–1931), a philosopher at The University of Chicago, was a brilliant conversationalist, preferring to present his ideas orally rather than in writing. Thus, many of his books that have had an enduring impact were actually posthumous publications compiled from former students´ lecture notes. This is the case with the book from which the following selection derives: *Mind, Self, and Society* (1934). Mead distinguished two aspects of the self, which he rather prosaically referred to as the "I" and the "me." The former includes the spontaneous, dynamic, and autonomous aspects of selfhood, while the latter is the socialized self that is shaped by external social conditions and is responsive to them. The "I" is the aspect of self responsible for initiative, creativity, and novelty, while the "me" provides selfhood with stability and continuity. In this passage, Mead discusses the ways these two aspects of the self working together make possible action in social life.

In a situation where persons are all trying to save someone from drowning, there is a sense of common effort in which one is stimulated by the others to do the same thing they are doing. In those situations one has a sense of being identified with all because the reaction is essentially an identical reaction. In the case of team work, there is an identification of the individual with the group; but in that case one is doing something different from the others, even though what the others do determines what he is to do. If things move smoothly enough, there may be something of the same exaltation as in the other situation. There is still the sense of directed control. It is where the "I" and the "me" can in some sense fuse that there arises the peculiar sense of exaltation which belongs to the religious and patriotic attitudes in which the reaction which one calls out in others is the response which one is making himself. I now wish to discuss in more detail than previously the fusion of the "I" and the "me" in the attitudes of religion, patriotism, and team work.

In the conception of universal neighborliness, there is a certain group of attitudes of kindliness and helpfulness in which the response of one calls out in the other and in himself the same attitude. Hence the fusion of the "I" and the "me" which leads to intense emotional experiences. The wider the social process in which this is involved, the greater is the exaltation, the emotional response, which results. We sit down and play a game of bridge with friends or indulge in some other relaxation in the midst of our daily work. It is something that will last an hour or so, and then we shall take up the grind again. We are, however, involved in the whole life of society; its obligations are upon us; we have to assert ourselves in various situations; those factors are all lying back in the self. But under the situations to which I am now referring that which lies in the background is fused with what we are all doing. This, we feel, is the meaning of life—and one experiences an exalted religious attitude. We get into an attitude in which everyone is at one with each other in so far as all belong to the same community. As long as we can retain that attitude we have for the time being freed ourselves of that sense of control which hangs over us all because of the responsibilities we have to meet in difficult and trying social conditions. Such is the normal situation in our social activity, and we have its problems back in our minds; but in such a situation as this, the religious situation, all seem to be lifted into the attitude of accepting everyone as belonging to the same group. One´s interest is the interest of all. There is complete identification of individuals. Within the individual there is a fusion of the "me" with the "I."

The impulse of the "I" in this case is neighborliness, kindliness. One gives bread to the hungry. It is that social tendency which we all have in us that calls out a certain type of response: one wants to give. When one has a limited bank account, one cannot give all he has to the poor. Yet under certain religious situations, in groups with a certain background, he can get the attitude of doing just that. Giving is stimulated by more giving. He may not have much to give, but he is ready to give himself completely. There is a fusion of the "I" and the "me." The time is not there to control the "I," but the situation has been so constructed that the very attitude aroused in the other stimulates one to do the same thing. The exaltation in the case of patriotism presents an analogous instance of this fusion.

From the emotional standpoint such situations are peculiarly precious. They involve, of course, the successful completion of the social process. I think that the religious attitude involves this relation of the social stimulus to the world at large, the carrying-over of the social attitude to the larger world. I think that that is the definite field within which the religious experience appears. Of course, where one has a clearly marked theology in which there are definite dealings with the deity, with whom one acts as concretely as with another person in the room, then the conduct which takes place is simply of a type which is comparable to the conduct with reference to another social group, and it may be one which is lacking in that peculiar mystical character which we generally ascribe to the religious attitude. It may be a calculating attitude in which a person makes a vow, and carries it out providing the deity gives him a particular favor. Now, that attitude would normally come under the general statement of religion, but in addition it is generally recognized that the attitude has to be one that carries that particular extension of the social attitude to the universe at large. I think it is that which we generally refer to as the religious experience, and that this is the situation out of which the mystical experience of religion arises. The social situation is spread over the entire world.

It may be only on certain days of the week and at certain hours of that day that we can get into that attitude of feeling at one with everybody and everything about us. The day goes around; we have to go into the market to compete with other people and to hold our heads above the water in a difficult economic situation. We cannot keep up the sense of exaltation, but even then we may still say that these demands of life are only a task which is put on us, a duty which we must perform in order to get at particular moments the religious attitude. When the experience is attained, however, it comes with this feeling of complete identification of the self with the other.

It is a different, and perhaps higher, attitude of identification which comes in the form of what I have referred to as "team work." Here one has the sort of satisfaction which comes from working with others in a certain situation. There is, of course, still a sense of control; after all, what one does is determined by what other persons are doing; one has to be keenly aware of the positions of all the others; he knows what the others are going to do. But he has to be constantly awake to the way in which other people are responding in order to do his part in the team work. That situation has its delight, but it is not a situation in which one simply throws himself, so to speak, into the stream where he can get a sense of abandonment. That experience belongs to the religious or patriotic situation. Team work carries, however, a content which the other does not carry. The religious situation is abstract as far as the content is concerned. How one is to help others is a very complicated undertaking. One who undertakes to be a universal help to others is apt to find himself a universal nuisance. There is no more distressing person to have about than one who is constantly seeking to assist everybody else. Fruitful assistance has to be intelligent assistance. But if one can get the situation of a well-organized group doing something as a unit, a sense of the self is attained which is the experience of team work, and this is certainly from an intellectual stand-point higher than mere abstract neighborliness. The sense of team work is found where all are working towards a common end and everyone has a sense of the common end interpenetrating the particular func-tion which he is carrying on.

The frequent attitude of the person in social ser-vice who is trying to express a fundamental attitude of neighborliness[1] may be compared with the attitude of the engineer, the organizer, which illustrates in extreme form the attitude of team work. The engineer has the attitudes of all the other individuals in the group, and it is because he has that participation that he is able to direct. When the engineer comes out of the machine shop with the bare blue print, the machine does not yet exist; but he must know what the people are to do, how long it should take them, how to measure the processes involved, and how to eliminate waste. That sort of taking the attitudes of everyone else as fully and completely as possible, entering upon one's own action from the standpoint of such a complete taking of the rôle of the others, we may perhaps refer to as the "attitude of the engineer." It is a highly intelligent attitude; and if it can be formed with a profound interest in social team work, it belongs to the high social processes and to the significant experiences. Here the full concreteness of the "me" depends upon a man's capacity to take the attitude of everybody else in the process which he directs. Here is gained the concrete content not found in the bare emotional identification of one's self with everyone else in the group.

These are the different types of expressions of the "I" in their relationship to the "me" that I wanted to bring out in order to complete the statement of the relation of the "I" and the "me." The self under these circumstances is the action of the "I" in harmony with the taking of the rôle of others in the "me." The self is both the "I" and the "me"; the "me" setting the situa-tion to which the "I" responds. Both the "I" and "me"

are involved in the self, and here each supports the other.

I wish now to discuss the fusion of the "I" and the "me" in terms of another approach, namely, through a comparison of the physical object with the self as a social object.

The "me," I have said, presents the situation within which conduct takes place, and the "I" is the actual response to that situation. This twofold separation into situation and response is characteristic of any intelligent act even if it does not involve this social mechanism. There is a definite situation which presents a problem, and then the organism responds to that situation by an organization of the different reactions that are involved. There has to be such an organization of activities in our ordinary movements among dif-ferent articles in a room, or through a forest, or among automobiles. The stimuli present tend to call out a great variety of responses; but the actual response of the organism is an organization of these tendencies, not a single response which mediates all the others. One does not sit down in a chair, one does not take a book, open a window, or do a great variety of things to which in a certain sense the individual is invited when he enters a room. He does some specific thing; he perhaps goes and takes a sought paper out of a desk and does not do anything else. Yet the objects exist there in the room for him. The chair, the windows, tables, exist as such because of the uses to which he normally puts these objects. The value that the chair has in his perception is the value which belongs to his response; so he moves by a chair and past a table and away from a window. He builds up a landscape there, a scene of objects which make possible his actual move-ment to the drawer which contains the paper that he is after. This landscape is the means of reaching the goal he is pursuing; and the chair, the table, the window, all enter into it as objects. The physical object is, in a certain sense, what you do not respond to in a consum-matory fashion. If the moment you step into a room, you drop into a chair you hardly do more than direct your attention to the chair; you do not view it as a chair in the same sense as when you just recognize it as a chair and direct your movement toward a distant object. The chair that exists in the latter case is not one you are sitting down in; but it is a something that will receive you after you do drop into it, and that gives it the character of an object as such.

Such physical objects are utilized in building up the field in which the distant object is reached. The same result occurs from a temporal standpoint when one carries out a more distant act by means of some precedent act which must be first carried through. Such organization is going on all the time in intelligent conduct. We organize the field with reference to what we are going to do. There is now, if you like, a fusion of the getting of the paper out of the drawer and the room through which we move to accomplish that end, and it is this sort of fusion that I referred to previously, only in such instances as religious experiences it takes place in the field of social mediation, and the objects in the mechanism are social in their character and so represent a different level of experience. But the process is analogous: we are what we are in our relationship to other individuals through taking the attitude of the other individuals toward ourselves so that we stimulate ourselves by our own gesture, just as a chair is what it is in terms of its invitation to sit down; the chair is something in which we might sit down, a physical "me," if you like. In a social "me" the various attitudes of all the others are expressed in terms of our own gesture, which represents the part we are carrying out in the social cooperative activity. Now the thing we actually do, the words we speak, our expressions, our emotions, those are the "I"; but they are fused with the "me" in the same sense that all the activities involved in the articles of furniture of the room are fused with the path followed toward the drawer and the taking out of the actual paper. The two situations are identical in that sense.

The act itself which I have spoken of as the "I" in the social situation is a source of unity of the whole, while the "me" is the social situation in which this act can express itself. I think that we can look at such conduct from the general standpoint of intelligent conduct; only, as I say, conduct is taking place here in this social field in which a self arises in the social situation in the group, just as the room arises in the activity of an individual in getting to this particular object he is after. I think the same view can be applied to the appearance of the self that applies to the appearance of an object in a field that constitutes in some sense a problem; only the peculiar character of it lies in the fact that it is a

social situation and that this social situation involves the appearance of the "me" and the "I" which are essentially social elements. I think it is consistent to recognize this parallelism between what we call the "physical object" over against the organism, and the social object over against the self. The "me" does definitely answer to all the different reactions which the objects about us, tend to call out in us. All such objects call out responses in ourselves, and these responses are the meanings or the natures of the objects: the chair is something we sit down in, the window is something that we can open, that gives us light or air. Likewise the "me" is the response which the individual makes to the other individuals in so far as the individual takes the attitude of the other. It is fair to say that the individual takes the attitude of the chair. We are definitely in that sense taking the attitude of the objects about us; while normally this does not get into the attitude of communication in our dealing with inanimate objects, it does take that form when we say that the chair invites us to sit down, or the bed tempts us to lie down. Our attitude under those circumstances is, of course, a social attitude. We have already discussed the social attitude as it appears in the poetry of nature, in myths, rites, and rituals. There we take over the social attitude toward nature itself. In music there is perhaps always some sort of a social situation, in terms of the emotional response involved; and the exaltation of music would have, I suppose, reference to the completeness of the organization of the response that answers to those emotional attitudes. The idea of the fusion of the "I" and the "me" gives a very adequate basis for the explanation of this exaltation. I think behavioristic psychology provides just the opportunity for such development of aesthetic theory. The significance of the response in the aesthetic experience has already been stressed by critics of painting and architecture.

The relationship of the "me" to the "I" is the relationship of a situation to the organism. The situation that presents the problem is intelligible to the organism that responds to it, and fusion takes place in the act. One can approach it from the "I" if one knows definitely what he is going to do. Then one looks at the whole process simply as a set of means for reaching the known end. Or it can be approached from the point of view of the means and the problem appears then as a decision among a set of different ends. The attitude of one individual calls out this response, and the attitude of another individual calls out another response. There are varied tendencies, and the response of the "I" will be one which relates all of these together. Whether looked at from the viewpoint of a problem which has to be solved or from the position of an "I" which in a certain sense determines its field by its conduct, the fusion takes place in the act itself in which the means expresses the end.

NOTE

1. "Philanthropy from the Point of View of Ethics," *Intelligent Philanthropy*, edited by Faris, Lane, and Dodd.

SECTION VI

1. Why does Nietzsche´s madman think we have killed God?
2. Explain what James means when his advocacy of pragmatism leads him to claim that theories should be seen as "instruments" rather than as "answers to enigmas."
3. Summarize in your own words what James means by the "pragmatic method."
4. Sharing an interest about public opinion with his contemporary, Cooley, Dewey expressed his concern that it was eroding. Why did he believe this to be the case?
5. Why does Freud think that various forms of discontent and unhappiness are the inevitable result of the creation of civilization?
6. How does Freud reply to those social critics who have taken up a "strange attitude of hostility to civilization"?
7. Summarize Mead´s discussion of the "I" and the "me," first defining the terms and then indicating how in conjunction they come to constitute the self.

PART TWO

THE BRANCHES

Contemporary Social Theory

VII. FUNCTIONALISM AND SYSTEMS THEORY

33. THE UNANTICIPATED CONSEQUENCES OF SOCIAL ACTION

ROBERT K. MERTON

Appearing in the first issue of the *American Sociological Review*, Robert K. Merton's (1910–2003) "The Unanticipated Consequences of Social Action" (1936) has become one of the most frequently cited essays in the discipline. What makes this all the more remarkable is that it was composed by a 26-year-old Harvard graduate student. Merton, a student of Talcott Parsons, became one of the central figures associated with structural functionalism. The article revealed a writer whose penetrating analyses were matched by a stylistic virtuosity quite uncharacteristic of most sociologists. Merton elevated what at one level is an obvious fact to a matter of central concern to the sociological enterprise: that our actions often turn out other than what we thought they would, or that they have, for better or worse, implications of which we were not originally aware. The sociologist is called upon to examine not only the intended outcomes of actions but those outcomes that were unanticipated, and Merton suggested a variety of factors that contribute to unintended consequences.

In some one of its numerous forms, the problem of the unanticipated consequences of purposive action has been touched upon by virtually every substantial contributor to the long history of social thought.[1] The diversity of context[2] and variety of terms[3] by which this problem has been known, however, have tended to obscure any continuity in its consideration. In fact, this diversity of context—ranging from theology to technology—has been so pronounced that not only has the substantial identity of the problem been overlooked, but no systematic, scientific analysis of it has as yet been made. The failure to subject the problem to thoroughgoing investigation has perhaps resulted in part from its having been linked historically with transcendental and ethical considerations. Obviously, the ready solution provided by ascribing uncontemplated consequences of action to the inscrutable will of God or Providence or Fate precludes, in the mind of the believer, any need for scientific analysis. Whatever the actual reasons, the fact remains that although the process has been widely recognized and its importance appreciated, it still awaits systematic treatment.

FORMULATION OF THE PROBLEM

Although the phrase, unanticipated consequences of purposive social action, is in a measure self-explanatory, the setting of the problem demands further specification. In the first place, the greater part of this paper deals with isolated purposive acts rather than with their integration into a coherent system of action (though some reference will be made to the latter). This limitation is prescribed by expediency; a treatment of systems of action would introduce further unmanageable complications. Furthermore, *unforeseen* consequences should not be identified with consequences which are necessarily *undesirable* (from the standpoint of the actor). For though these results are unintended, they are not upon their occurrence always deemed axiologically negative. In short, undesired effects are not always undesirable effects. The intended and anticipated outcomes of purposive action, however, are always, in the very nature of the case, relatively desirable to the actor, though they may seem axiologically negative to an outside observer. This is true even in the polar instance where the intended result is "the lesser of two evils" or in such cases as suicide, ascetic mortification and self-torture which, in given situations, are deemed desirable relative to other possible alternatives.

Rigorously speaking, the *consequences* of purposive action are limited to those elements in the resulting situation that are exclusively the outcome of the action, that is, that would not have occurred had the action not taken place. Concretely, however, the consequences result from the interplay of the action and the objective situation, the conditions of action.[4] We shall be primarily concerned with a pattern of results of action under certain conditions. This still involves the problems of causal imputation (of which more later) though to a less pressing degree than consequences in the rigorous sense. These relatively concrete consequences may be differentiated into (a) consequences to the actor(s), (b) consequences to other persons mediated through the social structure, the culture, and the civilization.[5]

In considering *purposive* action, we are concerned with "conduct" as distinct from "behavior," that is, with action that involves motives and consequently a choice between alternatives.[6] For the time being, we take purposes as given, so that any theories that "reduce" purpose to conditioned reflexes or tropisms, which assert that motives are simply compounded of instinctual drives, may be considered as irrelevant. Psychological considerations of the source or origin of motives, although undoubtedly important for a more complete understanding of the mechanisms involved in the development of unexpected consequences of conduct, will be ignored.

Moreover, it is not assumed that social action always involves clear-cut, explicit purpose. Such awareness of purpose may be unusual, the aim of action more often than not being nebulous and hazy. This is certainly the case with habitual action which, though it may originally have been induced by conscious purpose, is characteristically performed without such awareness. The significance of habitual action will be discussed later.

Above all, it must not be inferred that purposive action implies "rationality" of human action (that persons always use the objectively most adequate means for the attainment of their end).[7] In fact, part of my analysis is devoted to identifying those elements which account for concrete deviations from rationality of action. Moreover, rationality and irrationality are not to be identified with the success and failure of action, respectively. For in a situation where the number of *possible* actions for attaining a given end is severely limited, one acts rationally by selecting the means which, on the basis of the available evidence, has the greatest probability of attaining this goal[8] even though the goal may actually *not* be attained . . . . Contrariwise, an end may be attained by action that, on the basis of the knowledge available to the actor, is irrational (as in the case of "hunches").

Turning now to *action*, we differentiate this into two kinds: unorganized and formally organized. The first refers to actions of individuals considered distributively out of which may grow the second when like-minded individuals form an association in order to achieve a common purpose. Unanticipated consequences follow both types of action, although the second type seems to afford a better opportunity for sociological analysis since the processes of formal organization more often make for explicit statements of purpose and procedure.

Before turning to the actual analysis of the problem it is advisable to indicate two methodological pitfalls that are, moreover, common to all sociological investigations of purposive action. The first involves the problem of causal imputation, the problem of ascertaining the extent to which "consequences" can justifiably be attributed to certain actions. For example, to what extent has the recent increase in economic production in this country resulted from governmental measures? To what extent can the spread of organized crime be attributed to Prohibition? This ever-present difficulty of causal imputation must be solved for every empirical case.

The second problem is that of ascertaining the actual purposes of a given action. There is the difficulty, for instance, of discriminating between rationalization and truth in those cases where apparently unintended consequences are *ex post facto* declared to have been intended.[9] Rationalizations may occur in connection with nationwide social planning just as in the classical instance of the horseman who, on being thrown from his steed, declared that he was "simply dismounting." This difficulty, though not completely obviated, is significantly reduced in cases of organized group action since the circumstance of organized action customarily demands explicit (though not always "true") statements of goal and procedure. Furthermore, it is easily possible to exaggerate this difficulty since in many, if indeed not in most, cases, the observer's own experience and knowledge of the situation enables him to arrive at a solution. Ultimately, the final test is this: does the juxtaposition of the overt action, our general knowledge of the actor(s) and the specific situation and the inferred or avowed purpose "make sense," is there between these, as Weber puts it, a "verständliche Sinnzusammenhang?" If the analyst self-consciously subjects these elements to such probing, conclusions about purpose can have evidential value. The evidence available will vary, and the probable error of the imputation of purpose will likewise vary.

Although these methodological difficulties are not discussed further in this paper, an effort has been made to take them into account in the substantive analysis.

Last, a frequent source of misunderstanding will be eliminated at the outset if it is realized that the factors involved in unanticipated consequences are—precisely—factors, and that none of these serves by itself to explain any concrete case.

SOURCES OF UNANTICIPATED CONSEQUENCES

The most obvious limitation to a correct anticipation of consequences of action is provided by the existing state of knowledge. The extent of this limitation can be best appreciated by assuming the simplest case where the lack of adequate knowledge is the sole barrier to a correct anticipation.[10] Obviously, a very large number of concrete reasons for inadequate knowledge may be found, but it is also possible to summarize several classes of factors that are most important.

IGNORANCE

The first class derives from the type of knowledge—usually, perhaps exclusively—attained in the sciences of human behavior. The social scientist usually finds stochastic, not functional relationships.[11] This is to say, in the study of human behavior, there is found a set of different values of one variable associated with each value of the other variable(s), or in less formal language, the set of consequences of any repeated act is not constant but there is a range of possible consequences, *any one of which may follow the act in a given case*. In some instances, we have sufficient knowledge of the limits of the range of possible consequences, and even adequate knowledge for ascertaining the statistical (empirical) probabilities of the various possible consequences, but it is impossible to predict with certainty the results in any particular case. Our classifications of acts and situations never involve completely homogeneous categories nor even categories whose approximate degree of homogeneity is sufficient for the prediction of particular events.[12] We have here the paradox that whereas past experiences are the guide to our expectations on the assumption that certain past, present and future acts are sufficiently alike to be grouped in the same category, these experiences are in fact different. To the extent that these differences are pertinent to the outcome of the action and appropriate corrections for these differences are not adopted, the actual results will differ from the expected. As Poincaré has put it, "...small differences in the initial conditions produce very great ones in the final phenomena.... Prediction becomes impossible, and we have the fortuitous phenomenon."[13]

However, deviations from the usual consequences of an act can be anticipated by the actor who recognizes in the given situation some differences from previous similar situations. But insofar as these differences can themselves not be subsumed under general rules, the direction and extent of these deviations cannot be anticipated.[14] It is clear, then, that the partial knowledge in the light of which action is commonly carried on permits a varying range of unexpected outcomes of conduct.

Although we do not know the *amount* of knowledge necessary for foreknowledge, one may say in general that consequences are fortuitous when an exact knowledge of many details and facts (as distinct from general principles) is needed for even a highly approximate prediction. In other words, "chance consequences" are those occasioned by the interplay of forces and circumstances that are so numerous and complex that prediction of them is quite beyond our reach. This area of consequences should perhaps be distinguished from that of "ignorance," since it is related not to the knowledge actually in hand but to knowledge that can conceivably be obtained.[15]

The importance of ignorance as a factor is enhanced by the fact that the exigencies of practical life frequently compel us to act with some confidence even though it is manifest that the information on which we base our action is not complete. We usually act, as Knight has properly observed, not on the basis of scientific knowledge, but on that of opinion and estimate: Thus, situations that demand (or what is for our purposes tantamount to the same thing, that appear to the actor to demand) immediate action of some sort, will usually involve ignorance of certain aspects of the situation and will the more likely bring about unexpected results.

Even when immediate action is not required there is the *economic* problem of distributing our fundamental resources, time and energy. Time and energy are scarce means and economic behavior is concerned with the rational allocation of these means among alternative wants, only one of which is the anticipation of consequences of action.[16] An economy of social engineers is no more practicable than an economy of laundrymen. It is the fault of the extreme antinoetic activists who promote the idea of action above all else

to exaggerate this limit and to claim (in effect) that practically no resources be devoted to the acquisition of knowledge. On the other hand, the grain of truth in the anti-intellectualist position is that there are decided economic limits to the advisability of not acting until uncertainty is eliminated, and also psychological limits since, after the manner of Hamlet, excessive "forethought" of this kind precludes any action at all.

ERROR

A second major factor in unexpected consequences of conduct, perhaps as pervasive as ignorance, is error. Error may intrude itself, of course, in any phase of purposive action: we may err in our appraisal of the present situation, in our inference from this to the future, objective situation, in our selection of a course of action, or finally in the execution of the action chosen. A common fallacy is frequently involved in the too-ready assumption that actions which have in the past led to the desired outcome will continue to do so. This assumption is often fixed in the mechanism of habit and there often finds pragmatic justification. But precisely because habit is a mode of activity that has previously led to the attainment of certain ends, it tends to become automatic and undeliberative through continued repetition so that the actor fails to recognize that procedures which have been successful *in certain circumstances* need not be so *under any and all conditions.* [17] Just as rigidities in social organization often balk and block the satisfaction of new wants, so rigidities in individual behavior block the satisfaction of old wants in a changing social environment.

Error may also be involved in instances where the actor attends to only one or some of the pertinent aspects of the situation that influence the outcome of the action. This may range from the case of simple neglect (lack of thoroughness in examining the situation) to pathological obsession where there is a determined refusal or inability to consider certain elements of the problem. This last type has been extensively dealt with in the psychiatric literature. In cases of wishfulfilment, emotional involvements lead to a distortion of the objective situation and of the probable future course of events; action predicated upon imaginary conditions must have unexpected consequences.

IMPERIOUS IMMEDIACY OF INTEREST

A third general type of factor, the "imperious immediacy of interest," refers to instances where the actor's paramount concern with the foreseen immediate consequences excludes consideration of further or other consequences of the same act. The most prominent elements in such immediacy of interest range from physiological needs to basic cultural values. Thus, Vico's imaginative example of the "origin of the family," which derived from the practice of men carrying their mates into caves to satisfy their sex drive out of the sight of God, might serve as a somewhat fantastic illustration of the first. Another kind of example is provided by that doctrine of classical economics in which the individual endeavoring to employ his capital where most profitable to him and thus tending to render the annual revenue of society as great as possible is, in the words of Adam Smith, led "by an invisible hand to promote an end which was no part of his intention."

However, after the acute analysis by Max Weber, it goes without saying that action motivated by interest is not antithetical to an intensive investigation of the conditions and means of successful action. On the contrary, it would seem that interest, if it is to be satisfied, requires objective analysis of situation and instrumentality, as is assumed to be characteristic of "economic man." The irony is that intense interest often tends to preclude such analysis precisely because strong concern with the satisfaction of the immediate interest is a psychological generator of emotional bias, with consequent lopsidedness or failure to engage in the required calculations. It is as much a fallacious assumption to hold that interested action necessarily entails a rational calculation of the elements in the situation[18] as to deny rationality any and all influence over such conduct. Moreover, action in which the element of immediacy of interest is involved may be rational in terms of the values basic to that interest but irrational in terms of the life organization of the individual. Rational, in the sense that it is an action which may be expected to lead to the attainment of the specific goal; irrational, in the sense that it may defeat the pursuit or attainment of other values not, at the moment, paramount but which nonetheless form an integral part of the individual's scale of values. Thus, *precisely because a particular action is not carried out in a psychological or social vacuum, its effects will ramify into other spheres of value and interest.* For example, the practice of birth control for "economic reasons" influences the age-composition and size of sibships with profound consequences of a psychological and social character and, in larger aggregations, of course, affects the rate of population growth.

BASIC VALUES

Superficially similar to the factor of immediacy of interest, but differing from it in a significant theoretical sense, is that of basic values. This refers to instances where further consequences of action are not considered because of the felt necessity of the action enjoined by fundamental values. The classical analysis is Weber's study of the Protestant Ethic and the spirit of capitalism. He has properly generalized this case, saying that active asceticism paradoxically leads to its own decline through the accumulation of wealth and possessions entailed by the conjunction of intense productive activity and decreased consumption.

The process contributes much to the dynamic of social and cultural change, as has been recognized with varying degrees of cogency by Hegel, Marx, Wundt, and many others. The empirical observation is incontestable: activities oriented toward certain values release processes that so react as to change the very scale of values which precipitated them. This process can come about when a system of basic values enjoins certain *specific* actions, and adherents are concerned not with the objective consequences of these actions but with the subjective satisfaction of duty well performed. Or, action in accordance with a dominant set of values tends to be focused upon that particular value-area. But with the complex interaction that constitutes society, action ramifies. Its consequences are not restricted to the specific area in which they are intended to center and occur in interrelated fields explicitly ignored at the time of action. Yet it is because these fields are in fact interrelated that the further consequences in adjacent areas tend to *react* upon the fundamental value-system. It is this usually unlooked-for reaction that constitutes a most important element in the process of secularization, of the transformation or breakdown of basic value-systems. Here is the essential paradox of social action—the "realization" of values may lead to their renunciation. We may paraphrase Goethe and speak of "Die Kraft, die stets das Gute will, und stets das Böse schafft."

SELF-DEFEATING PREDICTIONS

There is one other circumstance, peculiar to human conduct, that stands in the way of successful social prediction and planning. Public predictions of future social developments are frequently not sustained precisely because the prediction has become a new element in the concrete situation, thus tending to change the initial course of developments. This is not true of prediction in fields that do not pertain to human conduct. Thus the prediction of the return of Halley's comet does not in any way influence the orbit of that comet; but, to take a concrete social example, Marx' prediction of the progressive concentration of wealth and increasing misery of the masses did influence the very process predicted. For at least one of the consequences of socialist preaching in the nineteenth century was the spread of organization of labor, which, made conscious of its unfavorable bargaining position in cases of individual contract, organized to enjoy the advantages of collective bargaining, thus slowing up, if not eliminating, the developments that Marx had predicted.[19]

Thus, to the extent that the predictions of social scientists are made public and action proceeds with full cognizance of these predictions, the "other-things-being-equal" condition tacitly assumed in all forecasting is not fulfilled. Other things will not be equal just because the scientist has introduced a new "other thing"—his prediction.[20] This contingency may often account for social movements developing in utterly unanticipated directions, and it hence assumes considerable importance for social planning.

The foregoing discussion represents no more than the briefest exposition of the major elements involved in one fundamental social process. It would take us too far afield, and certainly beyond the compass of this paper, to examine exhaustively the implications of this analysis for social prediction, control, and planning. We may maintain, however, even at this preliminary juncture, that no blanket statement categorically affirming or denying the practical feasibility of *all* social planning is warranted. Before we may indulge in such generalizations, we must examine and classify the *types* of social action and organization with reference to the elements here discussed and then refer our generalizations to these essentially different types. If the present analysis has served to set the problem, even in only its paramount aspects, and to direct attention toward the need for a systematic and objective study of the elements involved in the development of unanticipated consequences of purposive social action, the treatment of which has for much too long been consigned to the realm of theology and speculative philosophy, then it has achieved its avowed purpose.

NOTES

1. Some of the theorists, though their contributions are by no means of equal importance, are: Machiavelli, Vico, Adam Smith (and some later classical economists), Marx, Engels, Wundt, Pareto, Max Weber, Graham Wallas, Cooley, Sorokin, Gini, Chapin, von Schelting.
2. This problem has been related to such heterogeneous subjects as: the problem of evil (theodicy), moral responsibility, free will, predestination, deism, teleology, fatalism, logical, illogical and nonlogical behavior, social prediction, planning and control, social cycles, the pleasure- and reality principles, and historical "accidents."
3. Some of the terms by which the whole or certain aspects of the process have been known are: Providence (immanent or transcendental), Moira, *Paradoxie der Folgen, Schicksal*, social forces, heterogony of ends, immanent causation, dialectical movement, principle of emergence and creative synthesis.

4. Cf. Frank H. Knight, *Risk, Uncertainty and Profit* (Boston and New York: Houghton Mifflin Co., 1921), pp. 201–2. Professor Knight´s doctoral dissertation represents by far the most searching treatment of certain phases of this problem that I have yet seen.

5. For the distinction between society, culture and civilization, see Alfred Weber, "Prinzipielles zur Kultursoziologie: Gesellschaftsprozess, Civilisationsprozess und Kulturbewegung," *Archiv für Sozialwissenschaft und Sozialpolitik*, 47, 1920, pp. 1–49; R. K. Merton, "Civilization and Culture," *Sociology and Social Research* 21 (1936), pp. 103–13.

6. Knight, *op. cit.*, p. 52.

7. Max Weber, *Wirtschaft und Gesellschaft* (Tübingen: J. C. B. Mohr, 1925), pp. 3 ff.

8. See J. Bertrand, *Calcul des probabilités* (Paris, 1889), pp. 90 ff.; J. M. Keynes, *A Treatise on Probability* (London: The Macmillan Co., 1921), Chap. XXVI.

9. This introduces the problem of "chance," which will be treated in another connection. It should be realized that the aim of an action and the circumstances that actually ensue may coincide without the latter being a consequence of the action. Moreover, the longer the interval of time between the action and the circumstances in view, the greater the probability (in the absence of contrary evidence) that these circumstances have happened "by chance." Lastly, if this interval is greatly extended, the probability that the desired circumstances will occur fortuitously may increase until virtually the point of certainty. This reasoning is perhaps applicable to the case of governmental action "restoring prosperity." Compare V. Pareto, *Traité de sociologie générale* (Paris: Payot, 1917), II, par. 1977.

10. Most discussions of unanticipated consequences limit the explanation of unanticipated consequences to this one factor of ignorance. Such a view either reduces itself to a sheer tautology or exaggerates the role of only one of many factors. In the first instance, the argument runs in this fashion: "if we had only known enough, we could have anticipated the consequences which, as it happens, were unforeseen." The evident fallacy in this *post mortem* argument rests in the word "enough" which is implicitly taken to mean "enough knowledge to foresee" the consequences of our action. It is then no difficult matter to uphold the contention. This viewpoint is basic to several schools of educational theory, just as it was to Comte´s dictum, *savoir pour prevoir, prevoir pour pouvoir*. This intellectualist stand has gained credence partly because of its implicit optimism and because of the indubitable fact that sheer ignorance does actually account for the occurrence of some unforeseen consequences *in some cases*.

11. Cf. A. A. Tschuprow, *Grundbegriffe und Grund-probleme der Korrelationstheorie* (Leipzig: B. G. Teubner, 1925), pp. 20 ff., where he introduces the term "stochastic." It is apparent that stochastic associations are obtained because we have not ascertained, or having ascertained, have not controlled the other variables in the situation that influence the final result.

12. A classification into completely homogeneous categories would, of course, lead to functional associations and would permit successful prediction, but the aspects of social action which are of practical importance are too varied and numerous to permit such homogeneous classification.

13. Henri Poincaré, *Calcul des probabilités* (Paris, 1912), p. 2.

14. The actor´s awareness of his ignorance and its implications is perhaps most acute in the type of conduct which Thomas and Znaniecki attribute to the wish for "new experience." This is the case where unforeseen consequences actually constitute the purpose of action, but there is always the tacit assumption that the consequences will be desirable.

15. Cf. Keynes, *op. cit.*, p. 295. This distinction corresponds to that made by Keynes between "subjective chance" (broadly, ignorance) and "objective chance" (where even additional wide

knowledge of general principles would not suffice to foresee the consequences of a particular act). Much the same distinction appears in the works of Poincaré and Venn, among others.

16. Cf. Knight, *op. cit.*, p. 348. The reasoning is also applicable to cases where the occupation of certain individuals (e.g., social engineers and scientists) is devoted solely to such efforts, since then it is a correlative question of the distribution of the resources of society. Furthermore, there is the practical problem of the communicability of knowledge so obtained, since it may be very complex; the effort to assimilate such knowledge leads back to the same problem of distribution of resources [and costs of information].

17. Similar fallacies in the field of thought have been variously designated as "the philosophical fallacy" (Dewey), the "principle of limits" (Sorokin, Bridgman) and, with a somewhat different emphasis, "the fallacy of misplaced concreteness" (Whitehead). [For an application of the general idea to the case of organizations, see ... "Bureaucratic Structure and Personality," in Merton, *Social Theory and Social Structure* (New York: The Free Press, 1968, enlarged ed.), pp. 249–60.]

18. The assumption is tenable only in a normative sense. Obviously such calculation, within the limits specified in our previous discussion, *should* be made if the probability of satisfying the interest is to be at a maximum. The error lies in confusing norm with actuality.

19. Corrado Gini, *Prime linée di patologia economica* (Milan: A. Giuffè, 1935), pp. 72–75. John Venn uses the picturesque term "suicidal prophecies" to refer to this process and properly observes that it represents a class of considerations which have been much neglected by the various sciences of human conduct. See his *Logic of Chance* (London, 1888), pp. 225–26.

20. For the correlative process, see the paper, "The Self-Fulfilling Prophecy" first published a dozen years after this one, and reprinted in Merton, *op. cit.*, 1968, pp. 475–90.

34. THE SUBSYSTEMS OF SOCIETY

TALCOTT PARSONS

Talcott Parsons (1902–1979) was the preeminent social theorist of his generation, and during the two decades after World War II his home institution, Harvard, became in effect the center of the sociological universe. His theoretical work has carried several labels, including functionalism, structuralism, and systems theory. His first major book, *The Structure of Social Action* (1937), was an exegesis of the works of key figures in the formative years of the discipline. Despite their manifold differences, Parsons examined them in order to articulate what he saw as a theoretical convergence that set the foundation for his subsequent work. His first effort to offer a comprehensive theoretical synthesis of these various strands of thought appeared in *The Social System* (1951). It was an example of what C. Wright Mills would rather disparagingly refer to as "grand theory." Part of the problem Parsons had in making his theoretical case was that his prose style, as he well knew, left something to be desired. Despite this tendency, in the section below, deriving from his 1971 book, *The System of Modern Societies*, Parsons reveals a capacity to write lucidly. Here he is concerned with societal subsystems, focusing on what he sees as the "core," which he defines as the "societal community." Its primary function is to promote social integration, which occurs through a process of inclusion. After defining it, he links the societal community to the three other subsystems—pattern maintenance, polity, and economy.

In the context of cultural legitimation, a society is self-sufficient to the extent that its institutions are legitimized by values that its members hold with relative consensus *and* that are in turn legitimized by their congruence with other components of the cultural system, especially its constitutive symbolism.

It is essential to remember that cultural systems do not correspond exactly with social systems, including societies. The more important cultural systems generally become institutionalized, in varying patterns, in a number of societies, though there are also subcultures within societies. For example, the cultural system centering on Western Christianity has, with certain qualifications and many variations, been common to the whole European system of modernized societies. Two modes of the relation of one society to other societies are discussed. First, all societies we speak of as "politically organized" are involved with various other societies in "international relations" of various types, friendly or hostile. We shall extend this conception and regard these relations as themselves constituting a social system which can be analyzed with the same general concepts as other types of social system. Second, a social system may be involved with the social structure and/or the members and/or the culture of two or more societies. Such social systems are numerous and of many different kinds. American immigrant families often retain effective kinship relations with people in the "old country," so that their kinship systems have both American and foreign "branches." Something similar can be said of many business firms, professional associations, and religious collectivities. Although the Roman Catholic Church, for example, is a social system, it clearly is not a society since its self-sufficiency is very low by our criteria. Its control of economic

Talcott Parsons *The System of Modern Societies*. Englewood Cliffs, NJ: Prentice-Hall, 1971. ✦

resources through the organization of production is minimal; it lacks autonomous political control of territorial areas; in many societies, its members constitute a minority. Thus we must take account of both social systems which are "supersocietal" in being comprised of a plurality of societies and social systems that are "cross-societal" in that their members belong to a plurality of different societies.

THE SUBSYSTEMS OF SOCIETY

In accord with our four-function scheme for analyzing systems of action, we treat a society as analytically divisible into four *primary* subsystems (as shown in Table 34.1). Thus, the pattern-maintenance subsystem is particularly concerned with the relations of the society to the cultural system and, through it, ultimate reality; the goal-attainment subsystem or the polity, to the personalities of individual members; the adaptive subsystem, or the economy, to the behavioral organism and, through it, the physical world. These divisions are clearest and most important for societies advanced on the scale of modernity. However, the complexity of the relationships, both among subsystems of action and among subsystems of society, prevent these divisions from ever being very neat. For example, kinship structures must be located in all three of the above-mentioned subsystems. Through their relation to food, sex, biological descent, and residence, they are involved with the organism and the physical environment. As the individual´s primary

source of early learning of values, norms, and modes of communication, they are very much involved with the pattern-maintenance system. As the primary source of socialized services, they are involved with the polity.

Within this framework, the core of a society as a social system is the fourth component, its integrative subsystem. Because we treat the social system as integrative for action systems generally, we must pay special attention to the ways in which it achieves—or fails to achieve—various kinds and levels of internal integration. We will call the integrative subsystem of a society the *societal community*.

Perhaps the most general function of a societal community is to articulate a *system* of norms with a collective organization that has unity and cohesiveness. Following Weber, we call the normative aspect the system of legitimate order; the collective aspect is the societal community as a single, bounded collectivity.[1] Societal order requires clear and definite integration in the sense, on the one hand, of normative coherence and, on the other hand, of societal "harmony" and "coordination." Moreover, normatively defined obligations must on the whole be accepted while conversely, collectivities must have normative sanction in performing their functions and promoting their legitimate interests. Thus, normative order at the societal level contains a "solution" to the problem posed by Hobbes—of preventing human relations from degenerating into a "war of all against all."

It is important not to treat a structure of societal norms as a monolithic entity. Hence we distinguish

TABLE 34.1   SOCIETY (MORE GENERALLY, SOCIAL SYSTEM)

Subsystems	Structural Components	Aspects of Developmental Process	Primary Function
Societal Community	Norms	Inclusion	Integration
Pattern Maintenance or Fiduciary	Values	Value Generalization	Pattern Maintenance
Polity	Collectivities	Differentiation	Goal Attainment
Economy	Roles	Adaptive Upgrading	Adaptation

This table attempts to spell out, a little more elaborately, a four-function paradigm for the *society*, or other type of social system, conceived as an integrative subsystem of a general system of action. The societal community, which is the primary subsystem of reference for the present analysis, is placed in the left hand column; the other three follow it. Corresponding to this set is a classification in the second column, by the same functional criteria, of four main structural components of social systems. In the third column follows a corresponding classification of aspects of process of developmental change in social systems which will be used extensively in the analysis that follows. Finally, the fourth column repeats the designation of four primary functional categories.

Except for the developmental paradigm, this schema was first fully presented in the author´s "General Introduction, Part II: An Outline of the Social System" in *Theories of Society*.

four components analytically, even though they overlap greatly in specific content. Our distinctions concern the grounds of obligations and rights as well as the nature of sanctioning noncompliance and rewarding compliance or unusual levels of performance.

THE CORE: THE SOCIETAL COMMUNITY

Our core category, the societal community, is relatively unfamiliar—probably because it is generally discussed in religious and political rather than social terms. In our view the primary function of this integrative subsystem is to define the obligations of *loyalty* to the societal collectivity, both for the membership as a whole and for various categories of differentiated status and role within the society. Thus in most modern societies willingness to perform military service is a test of loyalty for men, but not for women. Loyalty is a readiness to respond to properly "justified" appeals in the name of the collective or "public" interest or need. The normative problem is the definition of occasions when such a response constitutes an obligation. In principle loyalty is required in any collectivity, but it has a special importance for the societal community. Organs of government are generally the agents of appeals to societal loyalty as well as agents of implementation of the associated norms. However, there are many instances in which government and justified community agency do not directly coincide.

Particularly important are the relations between subgroups´ and individual´s loyalties to the societal collectivity and to other collectivities of which they are members. *Role-pluralism*, the involvment of the same persons in several collectivities, is a fundamental feature of all human societies. On the whole, an increase in role-pluralism is a major feature of the differentiation processes leading toward modern types of society. Therefore, the regulation of the loyalties, to the community itself and to various other collectivities, is a major problem of integration for a societal community.

Individualistic social theory has persistently exaggerated the significance of individual "self-interest" in a psychological sense as an obstacle to the integration of social systems. The self-interested motives of individuals are, on the whole, effectively channeled into the social system through a variety of memberships and loyalties to collectivities. The most immediate problem for most individuals is the adjustment of obligations among the competing loyalties in cases of conflict. For example, the normal adult male in modern societies is both an employee and a member of a family household. Although the demands of these two roles often conflict, most men have a heavy stake in fulfilling loyalties to *both*.

A societal community is a complex network of interpenetrating collectivities and collective loyalties, a system characterized by both functional differentiation and segmentation. Thus kinship-household units, business firms, churches, governmental units, educational collectivities, and the like are differentiated from each other. Moreover, there are a number of each type of collective unit—for example, a very large number of households, each comprised of only a few persons, and many local communities.

Loyalty to the societal community must occupy a high position in any stable hierarchy of loyalties and as such, is a primary focus of societal concern. However it does not occupy the highest place in the hierarchy. We have stressed the importance of cultural legitimation of a society's normative order because it occupies a superordinate position. It operates in the first instance through the institutionalization of a value-system, which is part of both the societal and the cultural systems. Then its subvalues, which are specifications of general value patterns, become parts of every concrete norm that is integrated into the legitimate order. The system of norms governing loyalties, then, must integrate the rights and obligations of various collectivities and their members not only with each other, but also with the bases of legitimation of the order as a whole.[2]

In its hierarchial aspect, the normative ordering of the societal community in terms of memberships comprises its *stratification* scale, the scale of the accepted—and, so far as values and norms are integrated, legitimized—*prestige* of subcollectivities, statuses, and roles and of persons as social members. It must be coordinated both with universal norms governing the status of membership and with the elements of differentiation among the functions of subcollectivities, statuses, and roles, which do not as such imply a hierarchy. The concrete stratification system, then, is a complex function of all these components.

Role-pluralism renders the problem of the status of individuals in a stratification system especially complex. Stratification mechanisms have generally treated individuals as diffusely integrated in large collective systems, membership in which defines their status. Lineages, ethnic groups, "estates," and social classes have operated in this way. However modern society requires a differentiation of individual statuses from diffuse background solidarities, giving modern systems of stratification a distinctive character.[3]

The position of a subcollectivity or individual in the stratification system is measured by the level of its or his *prestige* or capacity to exercise *influence*. Influence we conceive to be a generalized symbolic medium of societal interchange, in the same general class as money and power. It consists in capacity to bring about desired decisions on the part of other social units without directly offering them a valued quid pro quo as an inducement or threatening them with deleterious consequences. Influence must operate through persuasion, however, in that its object must be convinced that to decide as the influencer suggests is to act in the interest of a collective system with which both are solidary. Its primary appeal is to the collective interest, but generally on the assumption that the parties involved have particular interests in promoting the collective interest and their mutual solidarity. Typical uses of influence are persuasion to enter into a contractual relation "in good faith" or to vote for a specific political candidate. Influence may be exchanged for ad hoc benefits or for other forms of influence, in a sense parallel to that in which monetary resources may either be used to obtain goods or pooled or exchanged. Influence may also be exchanged for other generalized media such as money or power.[4]

SOCIETAL COMMUNITY AND PATTERN-MAINTENANCE

The bases of cultural legitimation transcend direct contingencies of influence, interests, and solidarity, being grounded at the societal level in *value commitments*. By contrast with loyalty to collectivities, the hallmark of a value-commitment is greater independence from considerations of cost, relative advantage or disadvantage, and social or environmental exigency in the meeting of obligations. The violation of a commitment is defined as illegitimate: its fulfillment is a matter of honor or conscience which may not be comprised without dishonor and/or guilt.

Although this may sound very restrictive, as indeed such commitments often are, the degree and kind of restrictiveness involved depends on a variety of factors. Commitment to values in general implies the assumption of an obligation to help implement them in concrete action. Especially where the value system is "activistic," as it generally is in modern societies, this implies realistic acceptance of certain conditions of collective action.

Thus, value *systems* contain a category of commitments to "valued association," solidarity in legitimate collective relationships and enterprises. What associations are valued is a matter that varies widely among societies. It is almost impossible to ensure the legitimacy of association by restricting legitimation to quite specifically defined acts, however, because actors need scope for considerable discretion if they are to implement their values under varying circumstances. One major factor in setting the breadth of this scope is the level of generality of the legitimating values. For example, an injunction not to exploit others in economic transactions is very different from a specific prohibition of lending money at interest. The *generalization* of value systems, so that they can effectively regulate social action without relying upon particularistic prohibitions, has been a central factor in the modernization process.

At the cultural level, the relevant aspect of values is what we ordinarily call moral. It concerns the evaluation of the objects of experience in the context of social relationships. A moral act implements a cultural value in a social situation involving interaction with other actors. As a matter of interaction, it must involve standards which bind the interactors reciprocally.

Moral values comprise only one component of the value-content of a cultural system, others being, for example, aesthetic, cognitive, or specifically religious values. Cultures also become differentiated on bases other than the moral, so that religion, art as expressive symbolization, empirical knowledge (eventually science), also become independent, differentiated cultural systems. A highly differentiated cultural system along with complex modes of articulation, is a hallmark of modern societies.[5]

SOCIETAL COMMUNITY AND THE POLITY

In addition to the aspects of a societal normative order centering about membership and loyalty and about cultural legitimation, we must consider a third. Influence and value-commitments operate voluntarily, through persuasion and appeal to honor or conscience. However, no large and complex social system can endure unless compliance with large parts of its normative order is *binding*, that is negative situational sanctions attach to noncompliance. Such sanctions both deter noncompliance—in part by "reminding" the good citizen of his obligations—and punish infraction if, as, and when it occurs. The socially organized and regulated exercise of negative sanctions, including threats of using them when intentions of noncompliance are suspected, we call the function of *enforcement*. The more highly differentiated a society, the more likely enforcement is to be performed by specialized agencies such as police forces and military establishments.[6]

Regulated enforcement requires some mode of determining the actual fact, agency, and circumstances of the infraction of norms. Among the specialized agencies that operate in this connection are courts of law and the legal profession. A complex normative order requires not only enforcement, however, but also authoritative interpretation. Court systems have very generally come to combine the determination of obligations, penalties, and the like for specific cases with interpretation of the meaning of norms, often a very general problem.[7] Less developed societies tend to reserve the latter function to religious agencies, but modern societies entrust it increasingly to secular courts.

These problems raise questions about the relation between a societal community and the polity. In our analytical terms, the concept *political* includes not only the primary functions of government, in its relation to a societal community, but also corresponding aspects of any collectivity.[8] We treat a phenomenon as political in so far as it involves the organization and mobilization of resources for the attainment of the goals of a particular collectivity. Thus business firms, universities, and churches have political aspects. In the development of modern societies, however, government has increasingly become differentiated from the societal community as a specialized organ of the society that is at the core of the polity.

As it has become differentiated, government has tended to center on two primary sets of functions. The first concerns responsibility for maintaining the integrity of the societal community against generalized threats, with special but not exclusive reference to its legitimate normative order. This includes the function of enforcement and a share in the function of interpretation, at least. Moreover, the general process of governmental differentiation creates spheres within which it becomes admissible explicitly to formulate and promulgate new norms, making legislation part of this function also. The second primary function, the executive, concerns collective action in whatever situations indicate that relatively specific measures should be undertaken in the "public" interest. This responsibility ranges from certain inherently essential matters, such as defense of territorial control and maintenance of public order, to almost any issue deemed to be "affected with a public interest."[9]

The basic relations between government and the societal community may be ascribed. Even early modern societies defined the common people as simply "subjects" of a monarch, ascriptively obligated to obey his authority. Fully modern levels of differentiation, however, have tended to make the power of political leadership contingent on the support of very extensive proportions of the population. In so far as this is true, we shall distinguish roles of political leadership from positions of authority more generally.

Differentiation between leadership and authority necessitates special generalization of the medium we call power.[10] We define power as capacity to make—and "make stick"—decisions which are *binding* on the collectivity of reference and on its members in so far as their statuses carry obligations under the decisions. Power must be distinguished from influence for the promulgation of binding decisions differs importantly from attempts to persuade. By our definition, a citizen exercises power when he casts his vote because the aggregate of votes bindingly determines the electoral outcome. Only a little power still is power, just as one dollar, through only a little money, very definitely is money.

SOCIETAL COMMUNITY AND THE ECONOMY

A fourth component of the normative order concerns matters of practicality. Its most obvious fields of application are the economic and technological; its governing principle is the desirability of efficient management of resources. Even where issues of collective loyalty, binding obligations, and morality are not involved, the action of an individual or collectivity will be disapproved if it is unnecessarily wasteful or careless. In modern societies, the normative aspect of these considerations is especially clear in the regulation of the use of labor as a factor of production in the economic sense. Commitment to the labor force involves an obligation to work effectively within the legitimate conditions of employment.[11] As Weber noted, there is a crucial moral element in this obligation. But short of the moral emphasis, rational economic and technological action is very generally

approved, while deviation from the relevant standards of rationality is disapproved.

The differentiation of autonomous structures necessitates the development of a generalized monetary medium in association with a market system. Money and markets operate where there is a sufficiently complex division of labor and where spheres of action are sufficiently differentiated from political, communal, or moral imperatives.[12] Of the generalized mechanisms of societal interchange, money and markets is the least directly involved with the normative order as it centers in the societal community. Hence, practical rationality is regulated mainly by institutional norms, above all the institutions of property and contract which have other bases of sanction.[13]

NOTES

1. Max Weber, *The Theory of Social and Economic Organization* (New York: Oxford University Press, 1947).
2. On these matters, see Robert N. Bellah, "Epilogue," in *Religion and Progress in Modern Asia* (New York: Free Press, 1965).
3. Talcott Parsons, "Equality and Inequality in Modern Society, or Social Stratification Revisited," *Sociological Inquiry*, 40/2 (Spring 1970).
4. Talcott Parsons, "On the Concept of Influence," *Politics and Social Structure* (New York: Free Press, 1969).
5. Talcott Parsons, "Introduction" to "Culture and the Social System" in *Theories of Society*.
6. Talcott Parsons, "Some Reflections on the Place of Force in Social Process" in *Sociological Theory and Modern Society* (New York: Free Press, 1967).
7. Extremely suggestive in this regard is Lon Fuller, *The Morality of Law* (New Haven: Yale University Press, 1964).
8. Talcott Parsons, "The Political Aspect of Social Structure and Process" in David Easton (ed.), *Varieties of Political Theory* (Englewood Cliffs, N.J.: Prentice-Hall, 1966). (Reprinted in *Politics and Social Structure*.)
9. *Ibid*; see also Gabriel A. Almond and G. Bingham Powell, *Comparative Politics; A Developmental Approach* (Boston: Little, Brown, 1966).
10. Talcott Parsons, "On the Concept of Political Power," in *Politics and Social Structure*.
11. Neil J. Smelser, *The Sociology of Economic Life* (Englewood Cliffs, N.J.: Prentice-Hall, 1963).
12. *Ibid*; see also Talcott Parsons and Neil J. Smelser, *Economy and Society* (New York: Free Press, 1956).
13. The classic analysis of the significance of property and contract for social systems was developed by Émile Durkheim in *The Division of Labor in Society* (New York: Macmillan, 1933).

35. THE FUNCTIONS OF SOCIAL CONFLICT

LEWIS COSER

Although Lewis Coser (1913–2003) wrote this essay from a functionalist perspective, he took up a topic that critics contended was generally ignored by its Parsonian variant: conflict. In fact, Coser was indebted not only to Parsonian theory but to such classic figures as Simmel, who was concerned with the varied ways that conflict can draw antagonistic parties into webs of group affiliation. While Coser realizes that conflict can be destructive to groups and to intergroup relations, and thus agrees that attempts at conflict resolution are generally appropriate, he focuses in this essay on the functions of conflict not only in reinforcing group solidarity but in serving as a safety-valve, channeling tensions in constructive ways rather than letting them build up to such a point that when conflict is unleashed, it is unleashed with destructive force.

Conflict within a group...may help to establish unity or to reestablish unity and cohesion where it has been threatened by hostile and antagonistic feelings among the members. Yet, not *every* type of conflict is likely to benefit group structure, nor that conflict can subserve such functions for *all* groups. Whether social conflict is beneficial to internal adaptation or not depends on the type of issues over which it is fought as well as on the type of social structure within which it occurs. However, types of conflict and types of social structure are not independent variables.

Internal social conflicts which concern goals, values or interests that do not contradict the basic assumptions upon which the relationship is founded tend to be positively functional for the social structure. Such conflicts tend to make possible the readjustment of norms and power relations within groups in accordance with the felt needs of its individual members or subgroups.

Internal conflicts in which the contending parties no longer share the basic values upon which the legitimacy of the social system rests threaten to disrupt the structure.

One safeguard against conflict disrupting the consensual basis of the relationship, however, is contained in the social structure itself: it is provided by the institutionalization and tolerance of conflict. Whether internal conflict promises to be a means of equilibration of social relations or readjustment of rival claims, or whether it threatens to "tear apart," depends to a large extent on the social structure within which it occurs.

In every type of social structure there are occasions for conflict, since individuals and subgroups are likely to make from time to time rival claims to scarce resources, prestige or power positions. But social structures differ in the way in which they allow expression to antagonistic claims. Some show more tolerance of conflict than others.

Closely knit groups in which there exists a high frequency of interaction and high personality involvement of the members have a tendency to suppress conflict. While they provide frequent occasions for hostility (since both sentiments of love and hatred are intensified through frequency of interaction), the acting out of such feelings is sensed as a danger to such intimate relationships, and hence there is a tendency to suppress rather than to allow expression of hostile feelings. In close-knit groups, feelings of hostility tend, therefore, to accumulate and hence to intensify. If conflict breaks out in a group that has consistently tried to prevent expression of hostile feelings, it will be particularly intense for two reasons: First, because the conflict does not merely aim at resolving the immediate issue which led to its outbreak; all accumulated grievances which were denied expression previously are apt to emerge at this occasion. Second, because the total personality involvement of the group members makes for mobilization of all sentiments in the conduct of the struggle.

Hence, the closer the group, the more intense the conflict. Where members participate with their total personality and conflicts are suppressed, the conflict, if it breaks out nevertheless, is likely to threaten the very root of the relationship.

In groups comprising individuals who participate only segmentally, conflict is less likely to be disruptive. Such groups are likely to experience a multiplicity of conflicts. This in itself tends to constitute a check against the breakdown of consensus: the energies of group members are mobilized in many directions and hence will not concentrate on *one* conflict cutting through the group. Moreover, where occasions for hostility are not permitted to accumulate and conflict is allowed to occur wherever a resolution of tension seems to be indicated, such a conflict is likely to remain focused primarily on the condition which led to its outbreak and not to revive blocked hostility; in this way, the conflict is limited to "the facts of the case." One may venture to say that multiplicity of conflicts stands in inverse relation to their intensity.

So far we have been dealing with internal social conflict only. At this point we must turn to a consideration of external conflict, for the structure of the group is itself affected by conflicts with other groups in which it engages or which it prepares for. Groups which are engaged in continued struggle tend to lay claim on the total personality involvement of their members so that internal conflict would tend to mobilize all energies and affects of the members. Hence such groups are unlikely to tolerate more than limited departures from the group unity. In such groups there is a tendency to suppress conflict, where it occurs, it leads the group to break up through splits or through forced withdrawal of dissenters.

Groups which are not involved in continued struggle with the outside are less prone to make claims on total personality involvement of the membership and are more likely to exhibit flexibility of structure. The multiple internal conflicts which they tolerate may in turn have an equilibrating and stabilizing impact on the structure.

In flexible social structures, multiple conflicts crisscross each other and thereby prevent basic cleavages along one axis. The multiple group affiliations of individuals makes them participate in various group conflicts so that their total personalities are not involved in any single one of them. Thus segmental participation in a multiplicity of conflicts constitutes a balancing mechanism within the structure.

In loosely structured groups and open societies, conflict, which aims at a resolution of tension between antagonists, is likely to have stabilizing and integrative functions for the relationship. By permitting immediate and direct expression of rival claims, such social systems are able to readjust their structures by eliminating the sources of dissatisfaction. The multiple conflicts which they experience may serve to eliminate the causes for dissociation and to re-establish unity. These systems avail themselves, through the toleration and institutionalization of conflict, of an important stabilizing mechanism.

In addition, conflict within a group frequently helps to revitalize existent norms; or it contributes to the emergence of new norms. In this sense, social conflict is a mechanism for adjustment of norms adequate to new conditions. A flexible society benefits from conflict because such behavior, by helping to create and modify norms, assures its continuance under changed conditions. Such mechanism for readjustment of norms is hardly available to rigid systems: by suppressing conflict, the latter smother a useful warning signal, thereby maximizing the danger of catastrophic breakdown.

Internal conflict can also serve as a means for ascertaining the relative strength of antagonistic interests within the structure, and in this way constitutes a mechanism for the maintenance or continual readjustment of the balance of power. Since the outbreak of the conflict indicates a rejection of a previous accommodation between parties, once the respective power of the contenders has been ascertained through conflict, a new equilibrium can be established and the relationship can proceed on this new basis. Consequently, a social structure in which there is room for conflict disposes of an important means for avoiding or redressing conditions of disequilibrium by modifying the terms of power relations.

Conflicts with some produce associations or coalitions with others. Conflicts through such associations or coalitions, by providing a bond between the members, help to reduce social isolation or to unite individuals and groups otherwise unrelated or antagonistic to each other. A social structure in which there can exist a multiplicity of conflicts contains a mechanism for bringing together otherwise isolated, apathetic or mutually hostile parties and for taking them into the field of public social activities. Moreover, such a structure fosters a multiplicity of associations and coalitions whose diverse purposes crisscross each other, we recall, thereby preventing alliances along one major line of cleavage.

Once groups and associations have been formed through conflict with other groups, such conflict may further serve to maintain boundary lines between them and the surrounding social environment. In this way, social conflict helps to structure the larger social environment by assigning position to the various subgroups within the system and by helping to define the power relations between them.

Not all social systems in which individuals participate segmentally allow the free expression of antagonistic claims. Social systems tolerate or institutionalize conflict to different degrees. There is no society in which any and every antagonistic claim is allowed immediate expression. Societies dispose of mechanisms to channel discontent and hostility while keeping intact the relationship within which antagonism arises. Such mechanisms frequently operate through "safety-valve" institutions which provide substitute objects upon which to displace hostile sentiments as well as means of abreaction of aggressive tendencies.

Safety-valve institutions may serve to maintain both the social structure and the individual's security system, but they are incompletely functional for both of them. They prevent modification of relationships to meet changing conditions and hence the satisfaction they afford the individual can be only partially or momentarily adjustive. The hypothesis has been suggested that the need for safety-valve institutions increases with the rigidity of the social structure, i.e., with the degree to which it disallows direct expression of antagonistic claims.

Safety-valve institutions lead to a displacement of goal in the actor: he need no longer aim at reaching a solution of the unsatisfactory situation, but merely at releasing the tension which arose from it. Where safety-valve institutions provide substitute objects for the displacement of hostility, the conflict itself is channeled away from the original unsatisfactory relationship into one in which the actor's goal is no longer the attainment of specific results, but the release of tension.

This affords us a criterion for distinguishing between realistic and nonrealistic conflict.

Social conflicts that arise from frustrations of specific demands within a relationship and from estimates of gains of the participants, and that are directed at the presumed frustrating object, can be called realistic conflicts. Insofar as they are means toward specific results, they can be replaced by alternative modes of interaction with the contending party if such alternatives seem to be more adequate for realizing the end in view.

Nonrealistic conflicts, on the other hand, are not occasioned by the rival ends of the antagonists, but by the need for tension release of one or both of them. In this case the conflict is not oriented toward the attainment of specific results. Insofar as unrealistic conflict is an end in itself, insofar as it affords only tension release, the chosen antagonist can be substituted for by any other "suitable" target.

In realistic conflict, there exist functional alternatives with regard to the means of carrying out the conflict, as well as with regard to accomplishing desired results short of conflict; in nonrealistic conflict, on the other hand, there exist only functional alternatives in the choice of antagonists.

Our hypothesis, that the need for safety-valve institutions increases with the rigidity of the social system, may be extended to suggest that unrealistic conflict may be expected to occur as a consequence of rigidity present in the social structure.

Our discussion of the distinction between types of conflict, and between types of social structures, leads us to conclude that conflict tends to be dysfunctional for a social structure in which there is no or insufficient toleration and institutionalization of conflict. The intensity of a conflict which threatens to "tear apart," which attacks the consensual basis of a social system, is related to the rigidity of the structure. What threatens the equilibrium of such a structure is not conflict as such, but the rigidity itself which permits hostilities to accumulate and to be channeled along one major line of cleavage once they break out in conflict.

36. FUNCTIONAL DIFFERENTIATION

NIKLAS LUHMANN

Niklas Luhmann (1927–1998) was perhaps the most important German thinker associated with systems theory. His work is indebted to, while seeking to go beyond, that of Talcott Parsons. In addition, Luhmann was influenced by cybernetic theories. He had an ongoing dialogue with his German contemporary Jürgen Habermas, but unlike the writings of that sociologist, which offer a neo-Marxist critique of modern capitalism, the political implications of Luhmann's work are not immediately evident. In this essay from 1986, he explores the ways complex advanced industrial societies, characterized by considerable structural and functional differentiation, address societal problems. In focusing on issues related to environmental concerns, he contends that the tendency to think that problems such as air and water pollution can be resolved by recourse to value commitments to a clean environment are overly simplistic. Instead, he suggests, we must realize that the ways we look at such issues are a consequence of the structure of a society in which we can no longer presume to speak about the unity of the system.

The preceding... discussed the existence of ecological problems and the ways in which they trigger resonance in the function systems of modern society. But in the analysis of particular systems the sociologist should not lose sight of the unity of society. Indeed, the comparability of function systems and certain agreements in the structures of their differentiation—we examined the differentiation of codes and programs but this is only one of many viewpoints—point to this. The unity of the entire system resides in the way it operates and the form of its differentiation. The more clearly social evolution approaches a specific kind of operation, namely, meaningful communication, and the primacy of functional differentiation *vis-à-vis* other forms of internal system-formation the more obvious its corresponding structures become. If one eliminates all anachronisms, the conceptual and theoretical means by which society describes itself in its scientific system—in this case in sociology—have to be adapted to this.

Above all, one must realize that theories of hierarchy, delegation or decentralization that begin from an apex or center are incapable of grasping contemporary society adequately. They presuppose a channelling of the communication flow that does not exist nor can even be produced. Furthermore, the attempts to describe the relation of state and economy according to the model of centralization and decentralization and then, when it is politically expedient, to praise the advantages of decentralized decision-making and to warn against its disadvantages is unrealistic. In reality, the economy is a system that is highly centralized by the money-mechanism but with a concomitant, extensive decentralization of decision-making, whereas the political system organizes the political organisation more or less centrally and handles political influences according to entirely different models, like those of social movements. These systems distinguish themselves through the way in which they try to combine and reinforce centralization and decentralization according to their respective media of communication. But their independencies cannot be understood according to the model of centralization and decentralization.

Thus it is pointless to try to conceive the unity of modern society as the organization of a network of channels of communication, steering-centers and impulse receivers. One immediately gets the impression that good intentions cannot be realized because somewhere something is directed against them[1] which frequently ends up in mythical explanations in terms of capitalism, bureaucracy or complexity. With the help of a theory of system differentiation it is evident, however, that every formation of a subsystem is nothing more than a *new expression for the unity of the whole system.*[2] Every formation of a subsystem breaks the unity of the whole system down into a specific difference of system and environment, i.e., of the subsystem and its environment within the encompassing system. Every subsystem therefore, can use such a boundary line to reflect the entire system, in its own specific way; one that leaves other possibilities of subsystem formation open. For example, a political system can interpret society as the relation of consensus and the exercise of force and then attempt to optimize its own relation to these conditions. On one hand, consensus and force are specific operations, but on the other, they are also all-encompassing formulas and horizons for social conditions and consequences that can never be made completely transparent in the political subsystem.

Every function system, together with *its* environment, reconstructs *society.* Therefore, every function system can plausibly presume to be society *for itself*, if and in so far as it is open to its *own* environment. With the closure of its own autopoiesis it serves *one* function of *the* societal system (society). With openness to environmental conditions and changes it realizes that this has to occur *in the* societal system because society cannot specialize *itself* to one function alone. This is a matter of the operationalization of a paradox. Presented as the difference of system and environment the function system is and is not society at the same time. It operates closed and open at the same time and confers exclusivity on its own claim to reality, even if only in the sense of a necessary, operative illusion. It confers bivalence upon its own code and excludes third values that lurk in the environment´s opacity and the

susceptibility to surprise. In this way society reproduces itself as unity and difference at the same time. Of course, this does not eliminate the paradox of *unitas multiplex.* It reappears within the system as opacities, illusions, disturbances and the need for screening-off— as transcendence in immanence, to put it in terms of the religious system´s selective coding.

This systems-theoretical analysis highlights the significance and the preference of modern society for institutions like the market or democracy. Such descriptions symbolize the unity of closure and openness, of functional logic and sensibility. Of course, the market is not a real one (as it could be seen to be from the cousin´s corner window)[3] and democracy no longer means that the people rule. This is a matter of a semantic coding of an ultimately paradoxical state of affairs. It explains the meaning and the illusionary components of these concepts, explains the weakness of the corresponding theories and explains why, since the beginning of the eighteenth century, a kind of self-critique has accompanied this.

Yet the unity of this order is already necessarily given by evolution, i.e., through the continual adjustment of possibilities. Evolution does not guarantee either the selection of the best of all possible worlds nor `progress´ in any sense. At first evolutionary selection produces a very improbable, highly complex order. It transforms an improbable order into a probable (functional) one. This is exactly what concepts like negentropy or complexity intend. But it does not mean that the improbability disappears or is inactualized as prehistory. It is co-transformed and `aufgehoben´ in Hegel´s famous sense. It remains a structurally precipitated risk that cannot be negated.

Stratified societies already had to deal with problematical consequences of their own structural decisions. These were expressed, for example, as the constant conflict between inherited honors and distinctions and new ones, as the unfulfillable obligation to prescribe a class-specific endogamy and not least of all as the conflicts that result from centralizing the control of access to scarce resources, above all of the ownership of land. Compared to modern society these are relatively harmless problems for which historically stable solutions were found in many cases. The transition to primarily functional differentiation leads to a completely different constellation with higher risks and more intensified problems resulting from structural achievements. Society´s self-exposure to ecological dangers is therefore not a completely new problem. But it is a problem that, today, is coming dramatically to the fore.

With functional differentiation the principle of elastic adaptation through processes of substitution becomes the principle of the specification of subsystems. Its consequence is that, more than ever before, functional equivalents can be projected and actualized *but only in the context of the subsystems and their coding.* Extreme elasticity is purchased at the cost of the peculiar rigidity of its contextual conditions. Everything appears as contingent. But the realization of other possibilities is bound to specific system references. Every binary code claims universal validity, but only for its own perspective. Everything, for example, can be either true or false, but only true or false according to the specific theoretical programs of the scientific system. Above all, this means that no function system can step in for any other. None can replace or even relieve any other. Politics cannot be substituted for the economy, nor the economy for science, nor science for law or religion nor religion for politics, etc., in any conceivable intersystem relations.

Of course, this structural barrier does not exclude corresponding attempts. But they must be purchased at the price of dedifferentiation (*Entdifferenzierung*), i.e., with the surrender of the advantages of functional differentiation. This can be seen clearly in socialism´s experiments with the politization of the productive sector of the economy or even in tendencies towards the `Islamization´ of politics, the economy and law. Moreover, these are carried out only partially. For example, they do not touch on money (but, at best, the purely economic calculation of capital investment and prices) and are arrested by an immune reaction of the system of the world society.

The structurally imposed non-substitutability of function systems does not exclude interdependencies of every kind. A flowering economy is also a political blessing—and vice versa. This does not mean that the economy could fulfill a political function, namely, to produce collectively binding decisions (to whose profit?). Instead, the non-substitutability of functions (i.e., the regulation of substitution by functions) is compensated by increasing interdependencies. Precisely

because function systems cannot replace one another they support and burden one another reciprocally. It is their irreplaceability that imposes the continual displacement of problems from one system into another. The result is a simultaneous intensification of independencies and interdependencies (dependencies) whose operative and structural balance inflates the individual systems with an immense uncontrollable complexity.

This same state of affairs can be characterized as a progressive resolution and reorganization of the structural redundancies of society. The certainties that lay in multifunctional mechanisms and that specified systems for different functions and programmed them to `not only/but also´ were abandoned. This is shown very clearly by the reduction of the social relevance of the family and morality. Instead, new redundancies were created that rested on the differentiation of functional perspectives and `ceteris paribus´ clauses. But this does not safeguard the interdependencies between the function systems and the social effects of the change of one for the other. Time, then, becomes relevant: the consequences result only after a certain amount of time and then they have to be handled with new means that are, once again, specific to the system. This is accomplished without being able to go back to the initiating causes. Complexity is temporalized[4] and so are the ideas of certainty. The future becomes laden with hopes and fears, in any event, with the expectation that it will be different. The transformation of results into problems is accelerated, and structural precautions (for example, for sufficient liquidity or for invariably functional legislation) are established so that such a reproblematization of the solution is always possible.

The rejection of substitutability has to be understood essentially as the rejection of redundancy, i.e., as the rejection of multiple safeguarding. As we know, the rejection of redundancy restricts the system´s possibilities of learning from disturbances and environmental `noises´.[5] This implies that a functionally differentiated system cannot adapt itself to environmental changes as well as systems that are constructed more simply although it increasingly initiates concomitant environmental changes. But this is only part of the truth. For, through abstract coding and the functional specification of subsystems, functional differentiation makes a large measure of sensibility and learning possible on this level. This state of affairs becomes quite compli-cated when many system levels have to be kept in view at the same time. Society´s rejection of redundancy is compensated on the level of subsystems, and the pro-blem is that this is the only place that this can occur. Family households, moralities and religious cosmolo-gies are replaced by an arrangement in which highly organized capacities for substitution and recuperation remain bound to specific functions that operate at the cost of ignoring other functions. Because of this the consequences of adaptive changes are situated within a complex net of dependencies and independencies. In part, they lead to unforeseen extensions, in part they are absorbed. In such cases simple estimations and simple comparisons of the efficiency of different social formations are insufficient and inadvisable.

A further consequence of functional differentiation resides in the intensification of apparent contingencies on the structural level of all function systems. Examples of this are the replacement of natural by positive law, the democratic change of governments, the still merely hypothetical character of the validity of theories, the possibility of the free choice of a spouse and not least of all everything that is experienced as a `a market deci-sion´ (with whoever or whatever may decide) and is subjected to criticism. The result is that much of what was previously experienced as nature is presented as a decision and needs justification. Thus a need arises for new `inviolate levels´.... for a more rational and justifi-able a priori or, finally, for `values´.[6] Evidently, the stran-gely non-binding compulsion of values correlates to a widespread discontent with contingencies as much as to the fact that decisions become more exposed to criticism through structural critique and statistical analyses than facts. Indeed, even if we cannot determine that someone has decided (for example, about the number of deaths from accidents or about the increase of the rate of unem-ployment) decisions are still necessary to redress these unsatisfactory conditions. To require decisions means to appeal to values, explicitly or implicitly. Consequently, structural contingency generates an order of values without considering the possibilities of concretely causing effects, i.e., without considering the attainability of the corresponding conditions.

It is probable that ecological communication will intensify this inflation of values even more. For if society has to ascribe environmental changes to itself then it is quite natural to reduce them to decisions that would have to be corrected: decisions about emissions quotas, total consumption amounts, new technologies whose consequences are still unknown, etc.... [S]uch ascriptions are based on simplifying, illuminating and obscuring causal attributions. This does not prevent them from being carried out and communicated, but, if nothing else, it permits values to surface.[7]

At first, one might think that the value of clean air and water, trees and animals could be placed alongside the values of freedom and equality, and since this is only a matter of lists we could include pandas, Tamils, women, etc. But viewed essentially and in the long run this would be much too simple an answer. The proble-matic of the inflation of values as a symbolically gen-eralized medium of communication—an idea of Parsons[8]—results from its influence on society´s obser-vation and description of itself.

Actually the descriptions of society are steered by the problems that result from structural decisions and, therefore, they have a tendency to evoke values and see `crises´. Contrary to the mature phase of bourgeois-socialist theories in the first two-thirds of the nine-teenth century disadvantages are deferred for a time, are read off in values and are understood as the indefi-nite obligation to act. In any event, they are no longer understood as digressions of the spirit or matter on the way to perfection. Instead, they are the inescapable result of evolution. According to the theory proposed here, they are consequences of the principle of system differentiation and of its making probable what is improbable.

Moreover, the critical self-observation and descrip-tion that constantly accompanies society has to renounce moral judgements or end up getting lost in a factional morass.[9] Instead, a new kind of schematism, namely, manifest or latent (conscious or unconscious, intentional or unintentional) takes its place. Only manifest functions can be used to differentiate and specify because only these can be transformed into points of comparison or goal-formulas. This means that the critique is formed as a scheme of difference that also illuminates the other side, the counterpart. Straightforward striving toward a goal is viewed as naive. This even undermines the straightfor-ward intention of enlightenment.[10] A mirror is, as it were, held up to society, assuming that it cannot look through it because that which is latent can fulfill its function only latently. This is the way sociology, too, pursues `enlightenment´ [*Aufklärung*] and explains its ineffectuality in the same process.[11] In this sense ideology, the unconscious, latent structures and functions and unintended side-effects all become themes without a clarification of the status of this shadow world—note especially the reversal of Platonic metaphysics. One can therefore use this distinction only to discover that society enlightens itself about itself.

The problem of reintroducing the unity of society within society or even of expressing it in it is extended to the forms of the system´s critical self-description. Equally symptomatic are all attempts at judging and condemning society from the exalted standpoint of the subject, i.e., *ab extra*. This signifies nothing more than placing the unity of society in a principle outside itself.[12] A systems-theoretical analysis of such attempts, however, enjoys the advantage of being able to retrace this problematic back to the structure of modern society (which changes nothing about the fact that this must occur in society).

Essentially, every attempt within the system to make the unity of the system the object of a system operation encounters a paradox because this operation must exclude and include itself. As long as society was differentiated according to center/periphery or rank, positions could be established where it was possible, as it never has been since, to represent the system´s unity, i.e., in the center or at the apex of the hierarchy. The transition to functional differentiation destroys this possibility when it leaves it to the many function systems to represent the unity of society through their respective subsystem/environment differences and exposes them in this respect to competition among themselves while there is no superordinate standpoint of representation for them all. To be sure, one can observe and describe this too. But the unity of society is nothing more than this difference of function systems. It is nothing more than their reciprocal autonomy and non-substitutability; nothing more than the transformation of this structure into a togetherness of inflated independence and dependence. In other words, it is the resulting complexity, which is highly improbable evolutionarily.

NOTES

1. Cf., among others Jeffrey L. Pressman/Aaron Wildavsky, *Implementation: How Great Expectations in Washington are Dashed in Oakland*, Berkeley Ca. 1973.

2. Cf., Niklas Luhmann, *Soziale Systeme*, Frankfurt 1984, pp. 37ff.

3. According to E. T. A. Hoffmann, `Des Vetters Eckfenster´, *Werke*, Berlin-Leipzig, no date, vol. 12, pp. 142–64.

4. Cf., for a historico-semantic context Niklas Luhmann. `Temporalisierung von Komplexitaet: Zur Semantik neuzeitlicher Zeitbegriffe´, in Luhmann, *Gesellschaftsstruktur und Semantik*, vol. 1, Frankfurt 1980, pp. 235–300.

5. Cf., André Béjin, `Différenciation, complexification, évolution des sociétés´, in *Communications*, vol. 22 (1974), pp. 109–18 (114) in connection with Henri Atlan, *L´Organisation biologique et la théorie de l´information*, Paris 1972, pp. 270ff.

6. The still unclear semantic career of the concept of value (especially prior to the middle of the nineteenth century) might have one of its sources here. To be sure, it is incorrect to say that the concept of value was appropriated by morality, literature, aesthetics and philosophy from economics only in the middle of the nineteenth century. (The Abbé Morellet, *Prospectus d´un nouveau dictionnaire de commerce*, Paris 1769, reprint Munich 1980, pp. 98ff., observes a restriction to economic profit. But the entire eighteenth century used it in a much more general sense.) It is equally clear, however, that the concept of value has been used as an ultimate guarantee for meaning and therefore non-contradictably in the last hundred years.

7. This happens in any event. But it is also required in many respects and viewed as the precondition for the solutions of problems. Cf., Karl-Heinz Hillmann, *Umweltkrise und Wertwande: Die Umwertung der Werte als Strategie des Überlebens*, Frankfurt-Bern 1981.

8. Cf., Talcott Parsons, `On the Concept of Value-Commitments´, in *Sociological Inquiry*, vol. 38 (1968), pp. 135–60 (153ff.)

9. For a comparison: the self-description of stratified societies had always used a moral schematism—whether in the direct moral criticism of typical behavior in the individual strata or in the formulation of types of perfection from which everyone could measure their distance.

10. Cf., for example, Simon-Nicolas-Henri Linquet, *Le Fanatisme des philosophes*, London-Abbeville 1764; Peter Villaume, *Über das Verhältnis der Religion zur Moral und zum Staate*, Libau 1791, and of course, the widespread critique of the French Revolution as the outbreak of a naive faith in principles.

11. This led many to the conclusion of `revolution´—with very little support for possibilities and consequences. One finds typically that the manifest/latent schema is introduced without further reflection as a description of facts and forms the basis for analyses. This has been the case especially since Robert K. Merton, `The Unanticipated Consequences of Purposive Social Action´, in *American Sociological Review*, vol. 1 (1936), pp. 894–904.

12. Jürgen Habermas judges much more sharply and leaves more room for hope. He views this as the theory-immanent *problem* of the Enlightenment´s erroneous semantic guidance by the theory of the subject and its object and therefore sees the solution of the problem in the transition to a new paradigm of intersubjective agreement. Cf., *Der philosophische Diskurs der Moderne: Zwölf Vorlesungen*, Frankfurt 1985. To make this useful sociologically, one must still clarify how this erroneous guidance and the possibility of correcting it are connected with the structure of modern society.

SECTION VII

1. What are the sources that contribute to unintended consequences of action and in what ways do such consequences reveal the relevance of sociological, as opposed to psychological, analysis?

2. Select one of the sources of unintended consequences identified by Merton and provide your own examples to illustrate it.

3. According to Parsons, what is the primary purpose of the societal community, and how does it achieve this objective?

4. What is the relationship between the societal community and the polity?

5. Offer your own assessment of Coser´s claim that conflict can be functionally beneficial in some circumstances. Provide an example to illustrate his argument.

6. Using his understanding of differentiation, explain why Luhmann doesn´t think that value commitments to a clean environment alone can resolve our environmental problems.

VIII. CONFLICT THEORIES

37. CULTURE AND POLITICS

C. WRIGHT MILLS

C. Wright Mills (1916–1962), who has been referred to as "the angry Texan," is in many respects the heir of Marx and Weber. Writing during the Cold War of the 1950s, Mills was a vocal and persistent critic of those figures in the social scientific community who thought we had entered a new age in which the old conflicts of the preceding era had been overcome. One of the first sociological theorists to use the term "post-modern," Mills contends that we have entered a new and dangerous age characterized by large unresolved questions in the economic and political realms and by the threat of future large-scale violence at a time of continual war preparedness.

We are at the ending of what is called The Modern Age. Just as Antiquity was followed by several centuries of Oriental ascendancy which Westerners provincially call The Dark Ages, so now The Modern Age is being succeeded by a post-modern period. Perhaps we may call it: The Fourth Epoch.

The ending of one epoch and the beginning of another is, to be sure, a matter of definition. But definitions, like everything social, are historically specific. And now our basic definitions of society and of self are being overtaken by new realities. I do not mean merely that we *feel* we are in an epochal kind of transition. I mean that too many of our explanations are derived from the great historical transition from the Medieval to the Modern Age; and that when they are generalized for use today, they become unwieldy, irrelevant, not convincing. And I mean also that our major orientations—liberalism and socialism—have virtually collapsed as adequate explanations of the world and of ourselves.

I

These two ideologies came out of The Enlightenment, and they have had in common many assumptions and two major values: in both, freedom and reason are supposed to coincide: increased rationality is held to be the prime condition of increased freedom. Those thinkers who have done the most to shape our ways of thinking have proceeded under this assumption; these values lie under every movement and nuance of the work of Freud: to be free, the individual must become more rationally aware; therapy is an aid to giving reason its chance to work freely in the course of an individual´s life. These values underpin the main line of Marxist work: men, caught in the irrational anarchy of production, must become rationally aware of their position in society; they must become "class conscious"—the Marxian meaning of which is as rationalistic as any term set forth by Bentham.

Liberalism has been concerned with freedom and reason as supreme facts about the individual; Marxism as supreme facts about man´s role in the political making of history. But what has been happening in the world makes evident, I believe, why the ideas of freedom and of reason now so often seem so ambiguous in both the capitalist and the communist societies of our time: why Marxism has so often become a dreary rhetoric of bureaucratic defense and political abuse; and liberalism, a trivial and irrelevant way of masking social reality. The major developments of our time can be adequately understood in terms of neither the liberal nor the Marxian interpretation of politics and culture. These ways of thought, after all, arose as guidelines to reflection about types of society which do not now exist. John Stuart Mill never examined the kinds of political economy now arising in the capitalist world. Karl Marx never analyzed the kinds of society now arising in the Communist bloc. And neither of them ever thought through the problems of the so-called underdeveloped countries in which seven out of ten men are trying to exist today.

The ideological mark of The Fourth Epoch—that which sets it off from The Modern Age—is that the ideas of freedom and of reason have become moot; that increased rationality may not be assumed to make for increased freedom.

II

The underlying trends are well known. Great and rational organizations—in brief, bureaucracies—have indeed increased, but the substantive reason of the individual at large has not. Caught in the limited milieux of their everyday lives, ordinary men often cannot reason about the great structures—rational and irrational—of which their *milieux* are subordinate parts. Accordingly, they often carry out series of apparently rational actions without any ideas of the ends they serve, and there is the increasing suspicion that those at the top as well—like Tolstoy´s generals—only pretend they know. That the techniques and the rationality of science are given a central place in a society does not mean that men live reasonably and without myth, fraud and superstition. Science, it turns out, is not a technological Second Coming. Universal education

may lead to technological idiocy and nationalist provinciality, rather than to the informed and independent intelligence. Rationally organized social arrangements are not necessarily a means of increased freedom—for the individual or for the society. In fact, often they are a means of tyranny and manipulation, a means of expropriating the very chance to reason, the very capacity to act as a free man.

The atrocities of The Fourth Epoch are committed by men as "functions" of a rational social machinery—men possessed by an abstracted view that hides from them the humanity of their victims and as well their own humanity. The moral insensibility of our times was made dramatic by the Nazis, but is not the same lack of human morality revealed by the atomic bombing of the peoples of Hiroshima and Nagasaki? And did it not prevail, too, among fighter pilots in Korea, with their petroleum-jelly broiling of children and women and men? Auschwitz and Hiroshima—are they not equally features of the highly rational moral-insensibility of The Fourth Epoch? And is not this lack of moral sensibility raised to a higher and technically more adequate level among the brisk generals and gentle scientists who are now rationally—and absurdly—planning the weapons and the strategy of the third world war? These actions are not necessarily sadistic; they are merely businesslike; they are not emotional at all; they are efficient, rational, technically clean-cut. They are inhuman acts because they are impersonal.

III

In the meantime, ideology and sensibility quite apart, the compromises and exploitations by which the nineteenth-century world was balanced have collapsed. In this sixth decade of the twentieth century the structure of a new world is indeed coming into view.

The ascendancy of the USA, along with that of the USSR, has relegated the scatter of European nations to subsidiary status. The world of The Fourth Epoch is divided. On either side, a superpower now spends its most massive and co-ordinated effort in the highly scientific preparation of a third world war.

Yet, for the first time in history, the very idea of victory in war has become idiotic. As war becomes total, it becomes absurd. Yet in both the superstates, virtually all policies and actions fall within the perspective of war; in both, elites and spokesmen—in particular, I must say, those of the United States—are possessed by the military metaphysic, according to which all world reality is defined in military terms. By both, the most decisive features of reality are held to be the state of violence and the balance of fright.

Back of this struggle there is the world-encounter of two types of political economy, and in this encounter capitalism is losing. Some higher capitalists of the USA are becoming aware of this, and they are very much frightened. They fear, with good justification, that they are going to become an isolated and a second-rate power. They represent utopian capitalism in a world largely composed of people whose experiences with real capitalism, if any, have been mostly brutal. They profess "democracy" in a nation where it is more a formal outline than an actuality, and in a world in which the great majority of people have never experienced the bourgeois revolutions, in a world in which the values deposited by the Renaissance and the Reformation do not restrain the often brutal thrust to industrialize.

United States foreign policy and lack of foreign policy is firmly a part of the absurdity of this world scene, and it is foremost among the many defaults of the Western societies. During the last few years, confronting the brinks, I have often suspected that the world is not at the third world war largely because of the calculation and the forbearance of the Soviet elite.

IV

What kind of a society is the USA turning out to be in the middle of the twentieth century? Perhaps it is possible to characterize it as a prototype of at least "The West." To locate it within its world context in The Fourth Epoch, perhaps we may call it The Overdeveloped Society.

The *Underdeveloped Country* as you know, is one in which the focus of life is necessarily upon economic subsistence; its industrial equipment is not sufficient to meet Western standards of minimum comfort. Its style of life and its system of power are dominated by the struggle to accumulate the primary means of industrial production.

In a *Properly Developing Society*, one might suppose that deliberately cultivated styles of life would be central; decisions about standards of living would be made in terms of debated choices among such styles; the industrial equipment of such a society would be maintained as an instrument to increase the range of choice among styles of life.

But in *The Overdeveloped Nation*, the standard of living dominates the style of life; its inhabitants are possessed, as it were, by its industrial and commercial apparatus: collectively, by the maintenance of conspicuous production; individually, by the frenzied pursuit and maintenance of commodities. Around these fetishes, life, labor and leisure are increasingly organized. Focused upon these, the struggle for status supplements the struggle for survival; a panic for status replaces the proddings of poverty.

In underdeveloped countries, industrialization, however harsh, may be seen as man conquering nature and so freeing himself from want. But in the overdeveloped nation, as industrialization proceeds, the economic emphasis moves from production to merchandizing, and the economic system which makes a fetish of efficiency becomes highly inefficient and systematically wasteful. The pivotal decade for this shift in the United States was the twenties, but it is since the ending of the second world war that the overdeveloped economy has truly come to flourish.

Surely there is no need to elaborate this theme in detail; since Thorstein Veblen formulated it, it has been several times "affluently" rediscovered. Society in brief has become a great sales-room—and a network of rackets: the gimmick of success becomes the yearly change of model, as in the mass-society fashion becomes universal. The marketing apparatus transforms the human being into the ultimately-saturated man—the cheerful robot—and makes "anxious obsolescence" the American way of life.

V

But all this—although enormously important to the quality of life—is, I suppose, merely the obvious surface. Beneath it there are institutions which in the United States today are as far removed from the images of Tocqueville as is Russia today from the classic expectations of Marx.

The power structure of this society is based upon a privately incorporated economy that is also a permanent war economy. Its most important relations with the state now rest upon the coincidence of military and corporate interests—as defined by generals and businessmen, and accepted by politicians and publics. It is an economy dominated by a few hundred corporations, economically and politically interrelated, which together hold the keys to economic decision. These dominating corporation-hierarchies probably represent the highest concentration of the greatest economic power in human history, including that of the Soviet Union. They are firmly knit to political and military institutions, but they are dogmatic—even maniacal—in their fetish of the "freedom" of their private and irresponsible power.

I should like to put this matter in terms of certain parallel developments in the USA and the USSR. The very terms of their world antagonism are furthering their similarities. Geographically and ethnically both are super-societies; unlike the nations of Europe, each has amalgamated on a continental domain great varieties of peoples and cultures. The power of both is based upon technological development. In both, this development is made into a cultural and a social fetish, rather than an instrument under continual public appraisal and control. In neither is there significant craftsmanship in work or significant leisure in the non-working life. In both, men at leisure and at work are subjected to impersonal bureaucracies. In neither do workers control the process of production or consumers truly shape the process of consumption. Workers´ control is as far removed from both as is consumers´ sovereignty.

In both the United States and the Soviet Union, as the political order is enlarged and centralized, it becomes less political and more bureaucratic; less the locale of a struggle than an object to be managed. In neither are there nationally responsible parties which debate openly and clearly the issues which these nations, and indeed the world, now so rigidly confront. Under some conditions, must we not recognize that the two-party state can be as irresponsible as is a one-party state?

In neither the USA nor the USSR is there a senior civil service firmly linked to the world of knowledge and sensibility and composed of skilled men who, in their careers and in their aspirations, are truly independent—in the USA of corporation interests, in the USSR of party dictation.

In neither of these superpowers are there, as central facts of power, voluntary associations linking individuals, smaller communities and publics, on the one hand, with the state, the military establishment, the economic apparatus on the other. Accordingly, in neither are there readily available vehicles for reasoned opinions and instruments for the national exertion of public will. Such voluntary associations are no longer a dominant feature of the political structure of the overdeveloped society.

The classic conditions of democracy, in summary, do not exactly flourish in the overdeveloped society; democratic formations are not now ascendant in the power structure of the United States or of the Soviet Union. Within both, history-making decisions and lack of decisions are virtually monopolized by elites who have access to the material and cultural means by which history is now powerfully being made.

VI

I stress these parallels, and perhaps exaggerate them, because of the great nationalist emphasis upon the differences between the two world antagonists. The parallels are, of course, due in each case to entirely different sources; and so are the great differences. In the capitalist societies the development of the means of power has occurred gradually, and many cultural traditions have restrained and shaped them. In most of the Communist societies they have happened rapidly and brutally and from the beginning under tightly centralized authority; and without the cultural revolutions which in the West so greatly strengthened and gave political focus to the idea of human freedom.

You may say that all this is an immoderate and biased view of America, that America also contains many good features. Indeed that is so. But you must not expect me to provide A Balanced View. I am not a sociological bookkeeper. Moreover, "balanced views" are now usually surface views which rest upon the homogeneous absence of imagination and the passive avoidance of reflection. A balanced view is usually, in the phrase of Royden Harrison, merely a vague point of equilibrium between platitudes.

I feel no need for, and perhaps am incapable of arranging for you, a lyric upsurge, a cheerful little pat on the moral back. Yet perhaps, by returning to my point of beginning, I can remind you of the kinds of problems you might want to confront. I must make two points only: one about fate and the making of history; the other about the roles many intellectuals are now enacting.

Fate has to do with events in history that are the summary and unintended results of innumerable decisions of innumerable men. Each of their decisions is minute in consequence and subject to cancellation or reinforcement by other such decisions. There is no link between any one man´s intention and the summary result of the innumerable decisions. Events are beyond human decisions: history is made, behind men´s backs.

So conceived, fate is not a universal fact; it is not inherent in the nature of history or in the nature of man. In a society in which the ultimate weapon is the rifle; in which the typical economic unit is the family farm and shop; in which the national-state does not yet exist or is merely a distant framework; and in which communication is by word of mouth, handbill, pulpit—in *such* a society, history is indeed fate.

But consider now the major clue to our condition, to the shape of the overdeveloped society in The Fourth Epoch. In modern industrial society the means of economic production are developed and centralized, as peasants and artisans are replaced by private corporations and government industries. In the modern nation-state the means of violence and of administration undergo similar developments, as kings control nobles and self-equipped knights are replaced by standing armies and now by fearful military machines. The *post-modern* climax of all three developments—in economics, in politics, and in violence—is now occurring most dramatically in the USA and the USSR. In the polarized world of our time, international as well as national, means of history-making are being centralized. Is it not thus clear that the scope and the chance for conscious human agency in history-making are just now uniquely available? Elites of power in charge of

these means do now make history—to be sure, "under circumstances not of their own choosing"—but compared to other men and other epochs, these circumstances themselves certainly do not appear to be overwhelming.

And surely here is the paradox of our immediate situation: the facts about the newer means of history-making are a signal that men are not necessarily in the grip of fate, that men *can* now make history. But this fact stands ironically alongside the further fact that just now those ideologies which offer men the hope of making history have declined and are collapsing in the overdeveloped nation of the United States. That collapse is also the collapse of the expectations of the Enlightenment, that reason and freedom would come to prevail as paramount forces in human history. It also involves the abdication of many Western intellectuals.

VII

In the overdeveloped society, where is the intelligentsia that is carrying on the big discourse of the Western world *and* whose work as intellectuals is influential among parties and publics and relevant to the great decisions of our time? Where are the mass media open to such men? Who among those in charge of the two-party state and its ferocious military machines are alert to what goes on in the world of knowledge and reason and sensibility? Why is the free intellect so divorced from decisions of power? Why does there now prevail among men of power such a higher and irresponsible ignorance?

In The Fourth Epoch, must we not face the possibility that the human mind, as a social fact might be deteriorating in quality and cultural level, and yet not many would notice it because of the overwhelming accumulation of technological gadgets? Is not that the meaning of rationality without reason? Of human alienation? Of the absence of any role for reason in human affairs? The accumulation of gadgets hides these meanings: those who use them do not understand them; those who invent and maintain them do not understand much else. That is why we may not, without great ambiguity, use technological abundance as the index of human quality and cultural progress.

VIII

To formulate any problem requires that we state the values involved and the threat to these values. For it is the felt threat to cherished values—such as those of freedom and reason—that is the necessary moral substance of all significant problems of social inquiry, and as well of all public issues and private troubles.

The values involved in the cultural problem of freedom and individuality are conveniently embodied in all that is suggested by the ideal of The Renaissance Man. The threat to that ideal is the ascendancy among us of The Cheerful Robot, of the man with rationality but without reason. The values involved in the political problem of history-making are embodied in the Promethean ideal of its human making. The threat to that ideal is twofold: On the one hand, history-making may well go by default,

men may continue to abdicate its willful making, and so merely drift. On the other hand, history may indeed be made—but by narrow elite circles without effective responsibility to those who must try to survive the consequences of their decisions and of their defaults.

I do not know the answer to the question of political irresponsibility in our time or to the cultural and political question of The Cheerful Robot; but is it not clear that no answers will be found unless these problems are at least confronted? Is it not obvious that the ones to confront them, above all others, are the intellectuals, the scholars, the ministers, the scientists of the rich societies? That many of them do not now do so, with moral passion, with intellectual energy, is surely the greatest human default being committed by privileged men in our times.

38. CONFLICT GROUPS AND GROUP CONFLICTS

RALF DAHRENDORF

Ralf Dahrendorf (1929–2009) is a German-born social theorist who spent much of his academic career in England, where he rose to the directorship of the London School of Economics. Dahrendorf, like Lewis Coser, addresses the topic of the functions of social conflict, but he does so in an effort to examine the future of one particular type of conflict in advanced industrial societies: class conflict. He is also more attentive to the potential negative, or dysfunctional, consequences of conflict than Coser is. The potential for conflict, according to Dahrendorf, is contingent on the particular configurations of authority in a given society. In this essay, he sketches out some of the variables that must be considered in assessing both the potential for violence and the intensity of conflict in various situations.

THE 'FUNCTIONS' OF SOCIAL CONFLICT

Classes, understood as conflict groups arising out of the authority structure of imperatively coordinated associations, are in conflict. What are—so we must ask if we want to understand the lawfulness of this phenomenon—the social consequences, intended or unintended, of such conflicts? The discussion of this question involves, almost inevitably, certain value judgments. I think that R. Dubin is right in summarizing at least one prominent attitude toward the functions of social conflict as follows:

> From the standpoint of the social order, conflict is viewed from two positions: (*a*) it may be destructive of social stability and therefore `bad´ because stability is good; (*b*) it may be evidence of the breakdown of social control and therefore symptomatic of an underlying instability in the social order. Both positions express a value preference for social stability. (2, p. 183)

I would also agree with Dubin´s own position:

> Conflict may be labeled dysfunctional or symptomatic of an improperly integrated society.

> The empirical existence of conflict, however, is not challenged by the stability argument. . . . The fact of the matter is that group conflict cannot be wished out of existence. It is a reality with which social theorists must deal in constructing their general models of social behaviour. (p. 184)

But I think that in two respects Dubin might have been rather less cautious. First, I should not hesitate, on the level of value judgments, to express a strong preference for the concept of societies that recognizes conflict as an essential feature of their structure and process. Secondly, and quite apart from value judgments, a strong case can be made for group conflict having consequences which, if not "functional," are utterly necessary for the social process. This case rests on the distinction between the two faces of society—a distinction which underlies our discussions throughout this study. It is perhaps the ultimate proof of the necessity of distinguishing these two faces that conflict itself, the crucial category in terms of the coercion model, has two faces, i.e., that of contributing to the integration of social "systems" and that of making for change.

Both these consequences have been admirably expressed by L. Coser. (Although, to my mind, Coser is rather too preoccupied with what he himself tends to call the "positive" or "integrative functions" of conflict.) On the one hand, Coser states in the unmistakable terminology of the integration theory of society (for which see my italics):

> Conflict may serve to remove dissociating elements in a relationship and to *reestablish* unity. Insofar as conflict is the resolution of tension between antagonists it has *stabilizing functions* and becomes an *integrating component* of the relationship. However, not all conflicts are *positively functional* for the relationship.... Loosely structured groups, and open societies, by allowing conflicts, institute safeguards against the type of conflict which would *endanger basic consensus* and thereby *minimize the danger of divergences* touching core values. The interdependence of antagonistic groups and the crisscrossing within such societies of conflicts, which *serve to `sew the social system together´* by cancelling each other out, thus *prevent disintegration* along one primary line of cleavage. (4, p. 80)

On the other hand, Coser follows Sorel in postulating "the idea that conflict ... prevents the ossification of the social system by exerting pressure for innovation and creativity" and states:

> This conception seems to be more generally applicable than to class struggle alone. Conflict within and between groups in a society can prevent accommodations and habitual relations from progressively impoverishing creativity. The dash of values and interests, the tension between what is and what some groups feel ought to be, the conflict between vested interests and new strata and groups demanding their share of power, wealth and status, have been productive of vitality. (3, pp. 197 f.)

Conflict may, indeed, from a Utopian point of view, be conceived as one of the patterns contributing to the maintenance of the *status quo*. To be sure, this holds only for regulated conflicts, some of the conditions of which we shall try to explore presently. Coser´s analysis of Simmel (4) has convincingly demonstrated that there is no need to abandon the integration theory of society simply because the phenomenon of conflict "cannot be wished away" but is a fact of observation. In this sense, conflict joins role allocation, socialization, and mobility as one of the "tolerable" processes which foster rather than endanger the stability of social systems. There seems little doubt, however, that from this point of view we can barely begin to understand the phenomenon of group conflicts. Were it only for its "positive functions," for which Coser found so many telling synonyms, class conflict would continue to be rather a nuisance which the sociologist would prefer to dispense with since it may, after all, "endanger basic consensus." So far as the present study is concerned, "continuing group conflict" will be regarded as "an important way of giving direction to social change" (Dubin, 2, p. 194). Societies are essentially historical creatures, and, because they are, they require the motive force of conflict—or, conversely, because there is conflict, there is historical change and development. The dialectics of conflict and history provide the ultimate reason of our interest in this phenomenon and at the same time signify the consequences of social conflict with which we are concerned.

Dubin´s observation that conflict is a stubborn fact of social life is undoubtedly justified. Earlier, we have made the assertion explicit that social conflict is ubiquitous; in fact, this is one of the premises of our analysis. Possibly, this premise permits even further generalization. There has been in recent years some amount of interdisciplinary research on problems of conflict. In specific features the results of these interdisciplinary efforts remain as yet tentative; but one conclusion has been brought out by them with impressive clarity: it appears that not only in social life, but wherever there is life, there is conflict.[1] May we perhaps go so far as to say that conflict is a condition necessary for life to be possible at all? I would suggest, in any case, that all that is creativity, innovation, and development in the life of the individual, his group, and his society is due, to no small extent, to the operation of conflicts between group and group, individual and individual, emotion and emotion within one individual. This fundamental fact alone seems to me to justify the value judgment that conflict is essentially "good" and "desirable."

If I here assume social conflict, and the particular type of group conflict with which we are concerned in the present study, to be ubiquitous, I want this statement to be understood more rigidly than is usual. At an earlier point I have intimated what I mean by rigidity in this sense. One or two remarks in addition to these earlier hints seem in order. In summarizing earlier research, Mack and Snyder state with some justice that by most authors "competition is not regarded as conflict or a form of conflict" (2, p. 217). The alleged difference between the two is identified differently by different authors. T. H. Marshall emphasizes common interests, rather than divergent interests, as characteristic of states of competition or conflict (1, p. 99). For Mack and Snyder,

> competition involves striving for scarce objects . . . according to established rules which strictly limit what the competitors can do to each other in the course of striving; the chief objective is the scarce object, not the injury or destruction of an opponent per se. (2, p. 217)

It seems to me, however, that it is not accidental if Mack and Snyder state a little later that "conflict arises from `position scarcity` and `resource scarcity,`" and that therefore "conflict relations always involve attempts to gain control of scarce resources and positions" (pp. 218 f.). Despite terminological traditions, I can see no reason why a conceptual distinction between competition and conflict should be necessary or, indeed, desirable.[2] Like competition, conflict involves a striving for scarce resources. From the point of view of linguistic usage, it is perfectly proper to say that conflicting interest groups compete for power. As far as the "established rules" of competition are concerned, they emphasize but one type of conflict, namely, regulated conflict. In the present study, the notion of conflict is intended to include relations such as have been described by many other authors as competitive.

Another distinction almost general in the literature is that between changes "within" and changes "of" or conflicts "within" and conflicts "about" the system. Many authors have been at pains to define these differences. Coser, e.g., proposes "to talk of a change *of* system when all major structural relations, its basic institutions and its prevailing value system have been drastically altered," but admits that "in concrete historical reality, no clear-cut distinctions exist" (3, p. 202). Marshall distinguishes more specifically "conflict that arises out of the division of labor, conflict, that is to say, over the terms on which cooperation is to take place, as illustrated by a wage dispute between employer and employed," from "conflict over the system itself upon which the allocation of functions and the distribution of benefits are based" (1, p. 99). Thinking in terms of inclusive epochs like "feudalism" and "capitalism" as well as in terms of the existence of political parties that propose to change "the whole system" can probably explain the widespread feeling that a distinction between "changes within" and "changes of" is necessary. But apart from these, it is surely no coincidence that it was Parsons who emphasized that "it is necessary to distinguish clearly between the processes *within* the system and processes of change *of* the system." This very distinction betrays traces of the integration approach to social analysis. If conflict and change are assumed to be ubiquitous, there is no relevant difference between "changes within" and "changes of," because the "system" is no longer the frame of reference. It may be useful to distinguish more or less intense or violent conflicts and major and minor changes, but these are gradations to be accounted for in terms of intervening variables of an empirical nature. In the present study, no assumption is implied as to the type of change or conflict effected by the antagonism of conflict groups. Wage disputes as well as political conflicts "over the system itself" will be regarded as manifestations of class conflict, i.e., of clashes of interest arising out of and concerned with the distribution of authority in associations.

As with the theory of class formation, the real problems of the theory of class conflict consist in the identification of the empirical variables delimiting the range of variability of forms and types. Change and conflict are equally universal in society. But in historical reality we always encounter particular changes and specific conflicts, and these, even in the more limited sphere of class conflict, present a varied picture of manifold types and forms. Assuming the ubiquity of conflict and change, we have to try to discover some of the factors that influence its concrete shapes.

INTENSITY AND VIOLENCE: THE VARIABILITY OF CLASS CONFLICT

The substance of the theory of class action, or class conflict, can be summarized in one statement: conflict groups in the sense of this study, once they have organized themselves, engage in conflicts that effect structure changes. The theory of class action presupposes the complete formation of conflict groups and specifies their interrelations. However, this tautological statement is evidently not all that can be said about group conflicts, nor is it all that one would expect a theory of group conflict to provide. Beyond a basic assumption of this kind, a theory of class conflict has to identify and systematically interrelate those variables that can be shown to influence patterns of intergroup conflict. In the present chapter several such variables will be discussed in some detail, their selection being guided by the significance they suggest for the course and outcome of class conflict. Before we embark upon this discussion, however, there is one preliminary question that has to be settled. The statement that class conflicts are empirically variable is sufficiently vague to be almost meaningless. What is it—we must ask—about class conflicts that is variable and therefore subject to the influence of factors to be identified? In this question, the categories of intensity and violence are essential. In some connection or other, the terms "intensity" and "violence" can be found present in any discussion of conflict. Here is one example. Mack and Snyder, in their summary of earlier research, on the one hand derive the proposition "a high degree of intimacy between the parties, as contrasted with a high degree of functional interdependence, will *intensify* conflict" (2, p. 225), while, on the other hand, they suggest "the more integrated into the society are the parties to conflict, the less likely will conflict be *violent*" (p. 227). The distinction between the two concepts is not perhaps entirely clear from these statements, and, indeed, many authors use them almost synonymously. Yet there is an important difference between them, as Simmel knew when he said:

> It is almost inevitable that an element of commonness injects itself into . . . enmity once the stage of open *violence* yields to another

relationship, even though this new relation may contain a completely undiminished sum of *animosity* between the two parties. (see 4, p. 121)

That conflict is variable means that its intensity and violence are variable; but the two may vary independently and are, therefore, distinct aspects of any conflict situation.[3]

The category of intensity refers to the energy expenditure and degree of involvement of conflicting parties. A particular conflict may be said to be of high intensity if the cost of victory or defeat is high for the parties concerned. The more importance the individual participants of a conflict attach to its issues and substance, the more intense is this conflict. For class conflict a continuum might be constructed ranging, e.g., from a conflict within a chess club which involves but a small segment of the individual personalities concerned to the overriding class conflict, in Marx´s analyses, in which individuals are engaged with almost their entire personalities. In operational terms, the cost aspect is here crucial. Members of a group that strives to upset the authority structure of a chess club stand to lose less in case of defeat than members of a trade union who endeavor to change the authority structure of the enterprise (or their own social conditions by way of this authority structure).[4] The cost of defeat, and with it the intensity of conflict, differs in these cases.

By contrast to its intensity, the violence of conflict relates rather to its manifestations than to its causes; it is a matter of the weapons that are chosen by conflict groups to express their hostilities. Again, a continuum can be constructed ranging from peaceful discussions to militant struggles such as strikes and civil wars. Whether or not class conflict expresses itself in militant dashes of interest is in principle independent of the intensity of involvement of the parties. The scale of degree of violence, including discussion and debate, contest and competition, struggle and war, displays its own patterns and regularities.[5] Violent class struggles, or class wars, are but one point on this scale.

While violence and intensity of conflict vary independently, several of the factors shortly to be discussed affect both. This fact can be illustrated with reference to one factor which has been mentioned already and which need not therefore be discussed again at any length.... [T]he conditions of organization of interest groups continue to affect group conflict even after the complete formation of conflict groups. They are, in this sense, a factor which, among others, accounts for variations of intensity and violence. With respect to the intensity of class conflict, the political conditions of organization appear especially relevant. It may be suggested that, for the individuals concerned, involvement in conflicts decreases as the legitimacy of conflicts and, by implication, their issues become recognized. However, in the ensemble of factors affecting intensity of conflict, the specific weight of the conditions of organization is probably not very great. By contrast, it is considerable among the variables involved in determining the violence of conflict manifestations. As soon as conflict groups have been permitted and been able to organize themselves, the most uncontrollably violent form of conflict, that of guerrilla warfare, is excluded. Moreover, the very fact of organization presupposes some degree of recognition which in turn makes the most violent forms of conflict unnecessary and, therefore, unlikely. This is not to say, of course, that conflicts between organized groups cannot be highly intense and violent. The conditions of organization are but one, and not the most important, factor among many. Of these I have selected four which seem to me of particular importance and which will be dealt with separately in the following sections of this chapter.

PLURALISM VERSUS SUPERIMPOSITION: CONTEXTS AND TYPES OF CONFLICT

One of the crucial elements of the theory of group conflict consists in the strict relation of conflicts to particular associations. Any given conflict can be explained only in terms of the association in which it arose and, conversely, any given association can be analyzed in terms of the conflicts to which it gives rise. In theory, this approach would suggest that inclusive societies present the picture of a multitude of competing conflicts and conflict groups. The two-class model applies not to total societies but only to specific associations within societies (including, of course, the inclusive association of the state, i.e.,

the whole society in its political aspect). If, in a given society, there are fifty associations, we should expect to find a hundred classes, or conflict groups in the sense of the present study. Apart from these, there may be an undetermined number of conflict groups and conflicts arising from antagonisms other than those based on the authority structure of associations. In fact, of course, this extreme scattering of conflicts and conflict groups is rarely the case. Empirical evidence shows that different conflicts may be, and often are, superimposed in given historical societies, so that the multitude of possible conflict fronts is reduced to a few dominant conflicts. I suggest that this phenomenon has considerable bearing on the degree of intensity and violence of empirical conflicts.

The pluralism-superimposition scale which might thus be constructed has two distinct dimensions. One of these relates to the separation or combination of conflicts of the class type in different associations. Let us restrict ourselves, for purposes of illustration, to the three associations of the state, industry, and the church in countries in which one church dominates the sphere of religious institutions. It is conceivable that the ruling and the subjected groups of each of these associations are largely separate aggregations. The dignitaries of the church may be mere citizens of the state and may have no industrial property or authority. Similarly, the citizens of the state may be church dignitaries or industrial managers. This is the kind of situation here described as pluralistic. Within each of the three associations there are (class) conflicts, but, as between these, there is dissociation rather than congruence. Evidently, complete dissociation and pluralism are, in the case mentioned, empirically rather unlikely. It is more probable that the workers of industry are at the same time mere members of the church and mere citizens of the state. One might expect that the dignitaries of the church are in some ways connected with the rulers of the state and possibly even with the owners or managers of industry. If this is the case, (class) conflicts of different associations appear superimposed; i.e., the opponents of one association meet again—with different tides, perhaps, but in identical relations—in another association. In this case, the personel of the conflict groups of different associations is the same.

Such congruence may also occur with conflict groups of different types. Again, a realistic example may serve to illustrate the point. We might suppose that in a given country there are three dominant types of social conflict: conflict of the class type, conflict between town and country, and conflict between Protestants and Catholics. It is of course conceivable that these lines of conflict cut across each other in a random fashion, so that, e.g., there are as many Protestants among the ruling groups of the state as there are Catholics and as many townspeople in either denomination as there are countrypeople. However, here, too, we might suspect that dissociation and pluralism are empirically rather unlikely to occur. One would not be surprised to find that most Protestants live in towns and most Catholics in the country, or that only one of the denominations commands the instruments of political control. If this is so, we are again faced with a phenomenon of superimposition in the sense of the same people meeting in different contexts but in identical relations of conflict.

With respect to the violence of manifestations of conflict, the pluralism-superimposition scale is not likely to be a factor of great significance. While there is a possible (negative) correlation between the degree of pluralism and the violence of conflicts in a given society, there is little reason to believe that dissociation of types and contexts of conflict makes industrial strikes, for example, impossible. Only in the inclusive association of the state would there seem to be a probability of pluralism reducing and superimposition increasing the violence of interest clashes.

At the same time, this scale is of the utmost importance for variations in the intensity of class conflict. The proposition seems plausible that there is a close positive correlation between the degree of superimposition of conflicts and their intensity. When conflict groups encounter each other in several associations and in several clashes, the energies expended in all of them will be combined and one overriding conflict of interests will emerge. The situation with which Marx dealt is a case in point. If incumbents of subjected positions in industry are also subjected in all other associations; if they are, moreover, identical with conflict groups other than those determined by authority relations, a "division of society into two large hostile classes" may indeed result—a situation, that is, in which one inclusive conflict dominates the picture of the total society. If, on the other hand, the inevitable pluralism of associations is accompanied by a pluralism of fronts of conflict, none of these is likely to develop the intensity of class conflicts of the Marxian type. There is in this case, for every member of the subjected class of one association, the promise of gratification in another association. Every particular conflict remains confined to the individual in one of his many roles and absorbs only that part of the individual's personality that went into this role.[6] The empirical analysis of pluralism and superimposition of contexts and types of conflict is one of the important problems suggested by the theory of social classes and class conflicts.

PLURALISM VERSUS SUPERIMPOSITION: AUTHORITY AND THE DISTRIBUTION OF REWARDS AND FACILITIES

. . . It is evident that in the context of a theory of group conflict of the type under discussion, "class situation" is an unnecessary concept. It means no more than what we have described as the authority position of aggregates in associations. The condition of a quasi-group in terms of the distribution of authority signifies the "situation" that underlies class conflict. However, the traditional concept of class situation includes a number of elements which, while irrelevant for the formation of social classes, affect their patterns of conflict in ways to be defined. Property, economic status, and social status are no determinants of class, but they do belong to the factors influencing the empirical course of clashes of interest between conflict groups.

As with contexts and types of conflict, the problem of rewards and facilities can be seen in terms of a contrast between divergence and parallelism, or pluralism and superimposition. Thus, property can, but need not, be associated with the exercise of authority. It is conceivable that those who occupy positions of domination in industry do not own industrial property—and, indeed, that those in positions of subjection do own such property. The separation of ownership and control, and certain systems of the distribution of shares to industrial workers, are cases in point. While neither of these structural arrangements eliminates the causes of (industrial) conflict, they have an impact on its intensity and violence. Once again, a certain parallelism between authority and property ownership may seem more probable, but it is not necessary.

The same holds for the economic status of persons in different authority positions. By economic status I shall here understand status in terms of strictly occupational rewards such as income, job security, and general social security as it accrues from occupational position. It is both possible and reasonably probable that those in positions of domination enjoy a somewhat higher economic status, and that these two attributes of social position are in this sense superimposed. But numerous illustrations could also be given for divergences between the two. In the early labor unions, and for many shop stewards and local union secretaries today, authority involves a comparative loss of income and security. In the Roman Catholic church, authority is supposed, in theory if not in practice, to be accompanied by low economic status. In totalitarian countries, political authority usually conveys high incomes but also a high degree of insecurity which lowers the economic status of dominant groups. Such divergences of authority position and economic status make for a plurality of noncongruent scales of position in a society, which constitutes one of the critical facts of class analysis.

Divergences of position are even more evident if we contrast authority positions with people´s social status in the sense of the prestige attached to their position by themselves and by others in relevant universes of ranking. The prestige of power is a highly precarious quantity in all societies. Unless all existing studies are wrong in their findings, there would in fact seem to be, for persons in the upper ranges of the status scale, an inverse relation between the authority and the prestige. The judge (United States), the doctor (Britain), and the university professor (Germany) enjoy a markedly higher prestige than the cabinet minister or the large-scale entrepreneur.[7] Probably, the theory of class conflict with its assumption of opposing role interests would account for this phenomenon. On the other hand, there are and have been associations in which the division of authority and the scale of prestige followed identical lines. In the industrial enterprise, this would still seem to be the case in most countries (and with the possible exception of scientifically trained staff members). Thus, we also find here an empirically variable relation that is likely to affect the course of class conflict.

All examples chosen in the preceding paragraphs serve to illustrate the phenomenon of relative deprivation, i.e., the situation in which those subjected to authority are at the same time relatively worse placed in terms of socioeconomic status. However, in nineteenth-century Europe, and in some countries even today, we encounter what by contrast may be called an absolute deprivation of groups of people in socioeconomic terms. If the social condition of industrial workers, who are as such excluded from authority, falls below a physiological subsistence minimum or "poverty line," the effects of such deprivation are likely to be different in kind from those of relative deprivation. I would suggest that in this case, and in this case only, the superimposition of scales of status and the distribution of authority is likely to increase the violence of class conflict. This is a subtle and complex relation. So far as we know, oppression and deprivation may reach a point at which militant conflict motivation gives way to apathy and lethargy. Short of this point, however, there is reason to believe that absolute deprivation coupled with exclusion from authority makes for greater violence in conflict relations.

Relative deprivation, on the other hand, tends to affect the intensity of conflict rather than its violence. If incumbents of positions of subjection enjoy the countervailing gratification of a relatively high socioeconomic status, they are unlikely to invest as much energy in class conflicts arising out of the authority structure of associations as they would if they were deprived of both authority and socioeconomic status. Dominant groups are correspondingly not so likely to be as involved in the defense of their authority unless their high socioeconomic status is simultaneously involved. In terms of the intensity of conflict, pluralism would again seem to make for a decrease, and superimposition or congruence for an increase:[8] the lower the correlation is between authority position and other aspects of socioeconomic status, the less intense are class conflicts likely to be, and vice versa . . . .

NOTES

1. This and numerous other statements in the present chapter are based on discussions with and publications of psychologists, anthropologists, lawyers, and social psychologists at the Center for Advanced Study in the Behavioral Sciences, Stanford, California. John Bowlby, M.D., and Professor Frank Newman, LL.D., have been particularly helpful in making suggestions. In support of the statement in the text I might also refer, however, to the symposium published in *Conflict Resolution* (2), which includes contributions by economists, sociologists, social psychologists, anthropologists, and psychologists, and strongly supports my point.

2. At least, no such reason has been put forward. It might be argued, of course, that the concept of competition employed in economic theory is rather different from that defined by Marshall or Mack and Snyder, and does not carry any conflict connotation. I am not entirely sure that this argument is justified, but for purposes of the present analysis competition in a technical economic sense will be excluded.

3. All italics in the quotations of this paragraph are mine.

4. I have as yet not given a systematic exposition of the patterns of change effected by class conflict; the formulation in the text may therefore give rise to misunderstandings. . . .

5. In terms of the distinction thus introduced, we are now able to reformulate the contrast between the conception of conflict here assumed and that of several other authors. The latter tend to confine the term "conflict" to one point on the scale of degree of violence, namely, highly violent clashes. In the present study, however, conflict is conceived as including the whole scale, i.e., any clash of interest independent of the violence of its expressions.

6. This type of analysis seems to me to provide one of the answers to the question why there is no socialism in the United States. Throughout her history, the pluralism of associations and conflicts has made inclusive conflict groups held together by quasi-religious ideologies unnecessary. There has been no single group that enjoyed universal privilege or suffered universal alienation.

7. For relevant data, cf. the studies by the National Opinion Research Center (120), Glass (107), and Bolte (103).

8. This proposition must be opposed to the assumption of integration theorists that the congruence of different scales of social position is a requisite of stable, integrated societies (cf. Parsons, in 35). The exact opposite seems true, even from the point of view of integration theory. I cannot help feeling that this is one of the points at which integration theorists display—unwillingly, to be sure—almost totalitarian convictions.

REFERENCES

1. T. H. Marshall, *The Nature of Class Conflict*, in *Class Conflict and Social Stratification*, T. H. Marshall, ed., London, 1938.

2. "Approaches to the Study of Social Conflict: A Colloquium," *Conflict Resolution*, Vol. I, No. 2 (June 1957).

3. L. A. Coser, "Social Conflict and Social Change," *British Journal of Sociology*, Vol. VII, No. 3 (September 1957).

4. ———. *The Functions of Social Conflict*. London, 1956.

39. THE BASICS OF CONFLICT THEORY

RANDALL COLLINS

Randall Collins (b. 1941), in his book *Conflict Sociology* (1975), attempted to free conflict theory from its roots in structural functionalism while offering the first formal theoretical presentation of this paradigm. Open to the influences of a wide range of theorists, perhaps most importantly Marx, Weber, and Goffman, Collins sought to articulate an integrative theoretical approach that avoided the political polemics of someone like C. Wright Mills while establishing theoretical links between the micro level and the macro level. In this selection from his book, Collins outlines a conflict theory of stratification, looking not only at class (as Dahrendorf did), but also at the more Durkheimian concern with occupations.

The level of interpersonal interaction is all-inclusive; by the same token, it is highly abstract. To reduce its myriad complexities to causal order requires theory on another level of analysis. The most fruitful tradition of explanatory theory is the conflict, running from Machiavelli and Hobbes to Marx and Weber. If we abstract out its main causal propositions from extraneous political and philosophical doctrines, it looks like the following.

Machiavelli and Hobbes initiated the basic stance of cynical realism about human society. Individuals' behaviour is explained in terms of their self-interests in a material world of threat and violence. Social order is seen as being founded on organized coercion. There is an ideological realm of belief (religion, law), and an underlying world of struggles over power: ideas and morals are not prior to interaction but are socially created, and serve the interests of parties to the conflict.

Marx added more specific determinants of the lines of division among conflicting interests, and indicated the material conditions that mobilize particular interests into action and that make it possible for them to articulate their ideas. He also added a theory of economic evolution which turns the wheels of this system toward a desired political outcome; but that is a part of Marx's work that lies largely outside his contributions to conflict sociology, and hence will receive no attention here. Put schematically, Marx's sociology states:

1. Historically, particular forms of property (slavery, feudal landholding, capital) are upheld by the coercive power of the state; hence classes formed by property divisions (slaves and slave-owners, serfs and lords, capitalists and workers) are the opposing agents in the struggle for political power—the underpinning of their means of livelihood.

2. Material contributions determine the extent to which social classes can organize effectively to fight for their interests; such conditions of mobilization are a set of intervening variables between class and political power.

3. Other material conditions—the means of mental production—determine which interests will be able to articulate their ideas and hence to dominate the ideological realm.

In all of these spheres, Marx was primarily interested in the determinants of political power, and only indirectly in what may be called a "theory of stratification." The same principles imply, however:

1. The material circumstances of making a living are the main determinant of one´s style of life; since property relations are crucial for distinguishing ways of supporting oneself, class cultures and behaviors divide up along opposing lines of control over, or lack of, property.

2. The material conditions for mobilization as a coherent, intercommunicating group also vary among social classes; by implication, another major difference among class lifestyles stems from the differing organization of their communities and their differing experience with the means of social communication.

3. Classes differ in their control of the means of mental production; this produces yet another difference in class cultures—some are more articulated symbolically than others, and some have the symbolic structures of an other class imposed upon them from outside.

These Marxian principles, with certain modifications, provide the basis for a conflict theory of stratification. Weber may be seen as developing this line of analysis: adding complexity to Marx´s view of conflict, showing that the conditions involved in mobilization and "mental production" are analytically distinct from property, revising the fundamentals of conflict, and adding another major set of resources. Again making principles more explicit than they are in the original presentation, we may summarize Weber as showing several different forms of property conflict coexisting in the same society, and hence, by implication, the existence of multiple class divisions; elaborating the principles of organizational intercommunication and control in their own right, thereby adding a theory of organization and yet another sphere of interest conflict, this time intraorganizational factions; emphasizing that the violent coercion of the state is analytically prior to the economy, and thus transferring the center of attention to the control of the material means of violence.

Weber also opens up yet another area of resources in these struggles for control, what might be called the "means of emotional production." It is these that underlie the power of religion and make it an important ally of the state; that transform classes into status groups, and do the same to territorial communities under particular circumstances (ethnicity); and that make "legitimacy" a crucial focus for efforts at domination. Here, Weber comes to an insight parallel to those of Durkheim, Freud, and Nietzsche: not only that man is an animal with strong emotional desires and susceptibilities, but that particular forms of social interaction designed to arouse emotions operate to create strongly held beliefs and a sense of solidarity within the community constituted by participation in these rituals. I have put this formulation in a much more Durkheimian fashion than Weber himself, for Durkheim´s analysis of rituals can be incorporated at this point to show the mechanisms by which emotional bonds are created. There involves especially the emotional contagion that results from physical copresense, the focusing of attention on a common object, and the coordination of common actions or gestures. To invoke Durkheim also enables me to bring in the work of Goffman (1959, 1967), which carries on his microlevel analysis of social rituals, with an emphasis on the materials and techniques of stage-setting that determine the effectiveness of appeals for emotional solidarity.

Durkheim and Goffman are to be seen as amplifying our knowledge of the mechanisms of emotional production, but within the framework of Weber´s conflict theory. For Weber retains a crucial emphasis: The creation of emotional solidarity does not supplant conflict, but is one of the main weapons used in conflict. Emotional rituals can be used for domination within a group or organization; they are a vehicle by which alliances are formed in the struggle against other groups; and they can be used to impose a hierarchy of status prestige in which some groups dominate others by providing an ideal to emulate under inferior conditions. Weber´s theory of religion incorporates all of these aspects of domination through the manipulation of emotional solidarity, and thereby provides an archetype for the various forms of community stratification. Caste, ethnic group, feudal estate (Stand), educational-cultural group, or class "respectability" lines are all forms of stratified solidarities, depending on varying distributions of the resources for emotional production. The basic dynamics are captured in the hierarchy implicit in any religion between ritual leaders, ritual followers, and nonmembers of the community.

From this analytical version of Weber, incorporating the relevant principles of Marx, Durkheim, and Goffman, we can move into an explicit theory of stratification. It should be apparent that there are innumerable possible types of stratified societies; our aim is not to classify them, but to state the set of causal principles that go into various empirical combinations. Our emphasis is on the cutting tools of a theory, whatever the complexity of their application in the historical world.

For conflict theory, the basic insight is that human beings are sociable but conflict-prone animals. Why is there conflict? Above all else, there is conflict because violent coercion is always a potential resource, and it is a zero-sum sort. This does not imply anything about the inherence of drives to dominate; what we do know firmly is that being coerced is an intrinsically unpleasant experience, and hence that any use of coercion, even by a small minority, calls forth conflict in the form of antagonism to being dominated. Add to this the fact that coercive power, especially as represented in the state, can be used to bring one economic goods and emotional gratification—and to deny them to others—and we can see that the availability of coercion as a resource ramifies conflicts throughout the entire society. The simultaneous existence of emotional bases for solidarity—which may well be the basis of cooperation, as Durkheim emphasized—only adds group divisions and tactical resources to be used in these conflicts.

The same argument may be transposed into the realm of social phenomenology. Every individual maximizes his subjective status according to the resources available to him and to his rivals. This is a general principle that will make sense out of the variety of evidence. By this I mean that one's subjective experience of reality is the nexus of social motivation; that everyone constructs his own world with himself in it; but this reality construction is done primarily by communication, real or imaginary, with other people; and hence people hold the keys to each other's identities. These propositions will come as no surprise to readers of George Herbert Mead or Erving Goffman. Add to this an emphasis from conflict theories: that each individual is basically pursuing his own interests and that

there are many situations, notably ones where power is involved, in which those interests are inherently antagonistic. The basic argument, then, has three strands: that men live in self-constructed subjective worlds; that others pull many of the strings that control one's subjective experience; and that there are frequent conflicts over control. Life is basically a struggle for status in which no one can afford to be oblivious to the power of others around him. If we assume that everyone uses what resources are available to have others aid him in putting on the best possible face under the circumstances, we have a guiding priniciple to make sense out of the myriad variations of stratification.[1]

The general principles of conflict analysis may be applied to any empirical area. (*1*) Think through abstract formulations to a sample of the typical real-life interactions involved. Think of people as animals maneuvering for advantage, susceptible to emotional appeals, but steering a self-interested course toward satisfactions and away from dissatisfactions. (*2*) Look for the material arrangements that affect interaction: the physical places, the modes of communication, the supply of weapons, devices for staging one's public impression, tools, and goods. Assess the relative resources available to each individual: their potential for physical coercion, their access to other persons with whom to negotiate, their sexual attractiveness, their store of cultural devices for invoking emotional solidarity, as well as the physical arrangements just mentioned. (*3*) Apply the general hypothesis that inequalities in resources result in efforts by the dominant party to take advantage of the situation; this need not involve conscious calculation but a basic propensity of feeling one's way toward the areas of greatest immediate reward, like flowers turning to the light. Social structures are to be explained in terms of the behavior following from various lineups of resources, social change from shifts in resources resulting from previous conflicts. (*4*) Ideals and beliefs likewise are to be explained in terms of the interests which have the resources to make their viewpoint prevail. (*5*) Compare empirical cases; test hypotheses by looking for the conditions under which certain things occur versus the conditions under which other things occur. Think causally; look for generalizations. Be awake to multiple causes—the resources for conflict are complex.

Nowhere can these principles be better exemplified than on the materials of stratification. Especially in modern socities, we must separate out multiple spheres of social interaction and multiple causes in each one. These influences may be reduced to order through the principles of conflict theory. We can make a fair prediction of what sort of status shell each individual constructs around himself if we know how he deals with people in earning a living; how he gets along in the household in which he lives; how he relates to the population of the larger community, especially as determined by its political structures; and the ways in which he associates with friends and recreational companions. The conventional variables of survey research are all reflected in this list: occupation, parental occupation, education, ethnicity, age, and sex are cryptic references to how one's associations are structured at work, in the household, and in community and recreational groups. In each sphere, we look for the actual pattern of personal interaction, the resources available to persons in different positions, and how these affect the line of attack they take for furthering their personal status. The ideals and beliefs of persons in different positions thus emerge as personal ideologies, furthering their dominance or serving for their psychological protection.

I begin with occupational situations, as the most pervasively influential of all stratification variables. They are analyzed into several causal dimensions, elaborating a modified version of Marx, Weber, and Durkheim. Other stratified milieux are treated in terms of other resources for organizing social communities; here we find parallel applications of conflict principles as well as interaction with the occupational realm. The sum of these stratified milieux makes up the concrete social position of any individual.

OCCUPATIONAL INFLUENCES ON CLASS CULTURES

Occupations are the way people keep themselves alive. This is the reason for their fundamental importance. Occupations shape the differences among people, however, not merely by the fact that work is essential for survival, but because people relate to each other in different ways in this inescapable area of their lives. Occupations are the major basis of class cultures; these cultures, in turn, along with material resources for inter-communication, are the mechanisms that organize classes as communities, i.e., as kind of status group. The first process is dealt with here and the second takes up a later part of this chapter. The complexity of a system of class cultures depends on how many dimensions of difference we can locate among occupations. In order of importance, these are dominance relationships, position in a network of communication, and some additional variables, including the physical nature of the work and the amount of wealth it produces.

DOMINANCE RELATIONSHIPS

Undoubtedly, the most crucial difference among work situations is the power relations involved (the ways that men give or take orders). Occupational classes are essentially power classes within the realm of work. In stating this, I am accepting Ralf Dahrendorf's (1959) modification of Marx. Marx took property as the power relation par excellence. The dividing line between possessors and nonpossessors of property marked the crucial breaks in the class structure; changes among different sorts of property—slaves, land, industrial capital—made the difference among historical eras. But, although property classes might be the sharpest social distinctions in certain periods, the twentieth century has shown that other types of power can be equally important. In capitalist societies, the salaried managerial employee has remained socially distinct from the manual worker, although a strictly Marxist interpretation would put both of them in the working class. In socialist countries where conventional property classes do not exist, the same sorts of social distinctions and conflicts of interest appear among various levels of the occupational hierarchy. As Dahrendorf points out, Marx mistook an historically limited form of power for power relations in general; his theory of class divisions and class conflict can be made useful for a wider range of situations if we seek its more abstract form.[2]

Max Weber (1968:53) defined power as the ability to secure compliance against someone's will to do otherwise. This is not the only possible use of the word "power," but it is the most useful one if we are looking for ways to explain people's outlooks. There is power like the engineer's over inanimate objects; there is power like the scholar's over ideas and words; there is the power of the planner to affect future events. But, since men encountering men is the whole observable referent of "social causation," a social power that will directly affect someone's behavior is that of a man giving orders to another. It affects the behavior of the man who gives orders, for he must take a certain bearing, think certain thoughts, and speak certain formulas. It affects the man who must listen to orders, even though he may not accept too many of them or carry them out, for he accepts at least one thing—to put up with standing before someone who is giving him orders and with deferring to him at least for the moment. One animal cows another to its heels: That is the archetypal situation of organizational life and the shaper of classes and cultures.

The situations in which authority is acted out are the key experiences of occupational life. Since one cannot avoid having an occupation or being cared for by someone who does, it influences everyone. On this basis, three main classes can be distinguished: those who take orders from few or none, but give orders to many; those who must defer to some people, but can command others; and those who are order-takers only. The readily understood continuum from upper class through middle class to working class corresponds to this dimension. This is especially clear if we note how the middle-class-working-class break is commonly assigned: not so much on the basis of the cleanliness of the work, or of the income derived from it; certainly not, today, on the basis of property distinctions; but on the basis of where one stands when orders are given.

Upper middle class and lower middle class correspond to relative positions within the middle group, based on the ratio of order-giving to order-taking. Lower class can be distinguished from working class as a marginal group who work only occasionally and at the most menial positions. Farmers and farm laborers can be fitted into this categorization at a variety of middle-class and working-class levels. Prosperous farmers are similar to other businessmen; tenant farmers and laborers are not unlike the urban working class, with differences attributable to the different community structure rather than to occupational conditions per se. The power situation is similar, too, if one understands that the people who give orders are not

necessarily all in the same organization and that one need not be an actual employee to be a subordinate; the small farmer or businessman meets the banker with much the same face as the foreman meets his supervisor. There are some differences too, of course. First, I want to show that the most powerful effects on a man's behavior are the sheer volume of occupational deference he gives and gets. Then I will show how some different types of situations at about the same class level can add variations on the pattern.

Dahrendorf's (1959) revision of Marx converges here with Weber's emphasis on power relations. It should be noted that this formulation brings us into the universe of Durkheimian sociology as well, at least in its Goffmanian variant. If the successful application of power is a matter of personal bearing (in which sanctions are implied but not called upon), Goffman's analysis of the ritual dramatization of status provides us with detailed evidence on the mechanism. In a sense, the apocryphal Weberian principle of the "means of emotional production" applies not only in the realm of community formation but in the heart of the occupational relationship. Hence, it happens that Weber's historical summary of the religious propensities of various classes epitomizes later evidence on class cultures.

NETWORKS OF OCCUPATIONAL COMMUNICATION

Another dimension of occupational cultures comes from the sheer volume and diversity of personal contacts. The politician must see diverse audiences and the king receive the awe of crowds, whereas the tenant farmer and the servant rarely see outsiders, and the workman regularly deals with few besides his boss and a little-changing circle of friends and family. The greater cosmopolitanism of the higher occupational levels is one key to their outlooks. Cosmopolitanism is generally correlated with power because power is essentially the capacity to keep up relations with a fairly large number of persons in such a way as to draw others to back one up against whoever he happens to be with at the moment. But communications are also a separate variable, as we can see in the case of occupations that have greater contacts than power, such as salesmen, entertainers, intellectuals, and professionals generally. This variable accounts for horizontal variants within classes, and for their complex internal hierarchies (e.g., within professions or in the intellectual world) that stratify whole sectors over and above their actual order-giving power.

This dimension has its classic theoretical antecedents. Marx´s (1963: 123–124) principle of class mobilization by differential control of the means of transportation and communication applies not only to politics but to the differentiation of class cultures themselves. Weber´s extensions of this principle to the internal structure of organizations reinforces the implication, for organizational evidence not only documents the crucial distinctions in outlook and power derived from control over information and communications . . . but provides a look from a different angle at the *empirically* same phenomenon of occupational stratification. Durkheim´s model of ritual interactions and their effects on the "collective conscience" provides a finer specification of the mechanisms involved. In the *Division of Labor in Society*, Durkheim shows that the content of social beliefs, and especially the pressure for group conformity and respect for symbols, varies with the intensity and diversity of social contacts. In *The Elementary Forms of the Religious Life*, Durkheim examines the mechanisms at the high-intensity end of the continuum and shows that the highly reified conception of collective symbols, and the intense loyalties to the immediate group, are produced by ceremonial interactions within a group of unchanging characters, in a situation of close physical proximity and highly concentrated attention. By abstraction, we can see that not only entire historical eras but particular occupational milieus vary along these dimensions and hence produce different sorts of cultural objects and personal loyalties. Weber´s distinction between bureaucratic and patrimonial cultures captures this dimension, with its different centers of loyalty and standards of ethics; the bureaucratic and entrepreneurial sectors of the modern

occupational world represent these variations across the dimension of class power.[3]

WEALTH AND PHYSICAL DEMANDS

Besides the main variables of power and communications networks, occupations vary in additional ways that add to the explanation of class cultures and hence to their potential variety. One is the wealth produced and another is the kind of physical demands made. To insist on the importance of money as the main difference among social classes, of course, is vulgar Marxism. It is the organizational forms of power that produce the income that are crucial in determining basic distinctions in outlook. But money is important as one intervening link between occupational position and many aspects of lifestyle that set classes apart; as such it can have some independent effects. Income is not always commensurate with power. Some men make less or more than others of their power level. Power of position and power of money can be separate ways of controlling others, and hence have alternative or additive effects on one´s outlook. Moreover, income can be saved, collected, or inherited so that an aspect of power can be passed on—and so preserve its accompanying culture—when its organizational basis is no longer present.

On the physical side, some work calls for more exertion than others; some is more dirty or more dangerous. These aspects tend to be correlated with power, since it can be used to force others to do the harder and more unpleasant labor. But physical demands do influence lifestyle, making the lower classes more immured to hardship and dirt, and allowing the upper to be more effete and fastidious. Physical demands also vary independently of class power, and help account for variations between more military and more pacific eras and occupations, and between rural and urban milieux. . .

NOTES

1. The proposition that individuals *maximize* their subjective status appears to contradict March and Simon´s (1958) organizational principle that men operate by *satisficing*—setting minimal levels of payoff in each area of concern, and then troubleshooting where crises arise. The contradiction is only apparent. Satisficing refers to a strategy for dealing with the *cognitive* problem produced by

inherent limits on the human capacity for processing information. The principle of maximizing subjective status is a *motivational* principle, telling us what are the goals of behavior. Any analysis of cognitive strategies is incomplete without some motivational principle such as the latter to tell us what are the purposes of action, and what areas of concern are most emphasized. In other words, it is one thing to predict what goals someone will pursue, another to predict what strategies he will use in pursuing them, given the inability to see very far into the future or deal with very many things at once.

2. This is not to say that Dahrendorf´s (1959) position is completely satisfactory. Power organized as property, and power organized within a government or corporate structure, are not entirely equivalent. Men whose power depends on one of these forms are likely to be politically committed to maintaining it. The political differences among capitalists and socialists remain, even though the elites of both systems may have similar outlooks, in much the same way as holders of landed and industrial property have fought bitter political battles over whose organizational form should dominate. Dahrendorf´s formulation is a product of the period of Cold War liberalism; he argued for decreasing international hostilities by focusing on those things that might be taken as structural convergence among all modern societies.

   Ideological considerations aside, it is useful to retain both levels of analysis. Differences in power position, in whatever kind of organization, are the most fundamental determinant of men´s outlooks, and hence of where solidarity groups will form. Within the same general level of power, differences in the organizational basis of power—different forms of economic property or government organization—result in different political and ideological commitments. Men of power all resemble each other in general, but the specific source of power makes for some specific differences in political culture and creates definite political factions.

3. Patrimonial organization, most characteristic of traditional societies, centers around families, patrons and their clients, and other personalistic networks. The emphasis is on traditional rituals that demonstrate the emotional bonds among men; the world is divided into those whom one can trust because of strongly legitimated personal connections, and the rest of the world from whom nothing is to be expected that cannot be exacted by cold-blooded bargaining or force. In modern bureaucratic organization, by contrast, personal ties are weaker, less ritualized, and emotionally demonstrative; in their place is the allegiance to a set of abstract rules and positions. The different class cultures in patrimonial and bureaucratic organizations are accordingly affected. Patrimonial elites are more ceremonious and personalistic. Bureaucratic elites emphasize a colder set of ideals.

   The contrast is not merely an historical one. There are many elements of bureaucracy in premodern societies, notably in China; in Europe, bureaucracy gradually set in within the heart of the aristocracy, especially in France and Germany, around the seventeenth century. Patrimonial forms of organization exist in modern society as well, alongside and within bureaucracies. They are prominent in the entrepreneurial sector of modern business, especially in volatile areas like entertainment, construction, real estate, speculative finance, and organized crime, as well as in the politics of a complex, federated governmental system like the United States. Weber (1958: 57–58) caught the contrast between the two ways of doing business when he pointed out two kinds of business ethos throughout history. One has existed in all major societies: it emphasizes trickery, cleverness, and speculation aimed at making the greatest possible immediate profit. A second form is rationalistic, ascetic capitalism, which approaches business in a methodical and routinized fashion. Work and production are more ends in themselves, a way of life, rather than a means to get rich quick. In Weber's famous theory, capitalism developed in Europe precisely because business was dominated not merely by the entrepreneurial ethic, as in ancient and oriental societies, but by a sizable group holding the ascetic business ethic. The entrepreneurial type does not disappear once the modern economy is established, of course. He survives to skim the cream off of a system he could not have created.

REFERENCES

Dahrendorf, R. 1959. *Class and class conflict in industrial society*. Stanford, California: Stanford University Press.

Goffman, Erving. 1959. *The presentation of self in everyday life*. Garden City, NY: Doubleday.

——— 1967. *Interaction ritual*. Garden City, NY: Doubleday.

March, J. G., and H. A. Simon. 1958. *Organizations*. New York: Wiley.

Marx, K. 1963. *The eighteenth brumaire of Louis Napoleon*. New York: International Publishers (Originally published 1852).

Weber, M. 1958. *The Protestant ethic and the spirit of capitalism*. New York: Scribner's (Originally published 1904–1905).

——— 1968. *Economy and Society*. New York: Bedminster Press (Originally published 1922).

40. WAR MAKING AND STATE MAKING AS ORGANIZED CRIME

CHARLES TILLY

Charles Tilly (1929–2008) was a prolific scholar who published over 50 books and over 600 scholarly articles. He was trained as a sociologist, but his long and productive scholarly career constituted an ongoing interdisciplinary dialogue among three disciplines: sociology, history, and political science. Moreover, his rich body of empirical work was complemented by his contributions to theoretical inquiry. While his interests ranged far and wide, his most well known and sustained body of work concentrated on the formation of European nation-states and the contentious politics that were part of that long historical process. In this provocative article, he contends that nation-states function in a parallel way to criminal syndicates, and just as the latter often construct for their own benefit protection rackets, so too do the former. As part of his thesis, he discusses the significance of violence—be it construed as legitimate or illegitimate.

WARNING

If protection rackets represent organized crime at its smoothest, then war making and state making—quintessential protection rackets with the advantage of legitimacy—qualify as our largest examples of organized crime. Without branding all generals and statespeople as murderers or thieves, I want to urge the value of that analogy. At least for the European experience of the past few centuries, a portrait of war makers and state makers as coercive and self-seeking entrepreneurs bears a far greater resemblance to the facts than do its chief alternatives: the idea of a social contract, the idea of an open market in which operators of armies and states offer services to willing consumers, the idea of a society the shared norms and expectations of which call forth a certain kind of government.

The reflections that follow merely illustrate the analogy of war making and state making with organized crime from a few hundred years of European experience and offer tentative arguments concerning principles of change and variation underlying the experience. My reflections grow from contemporary concerns: worries about the increasing destructiveness of war, the expanding role of great powers as suppliers of arms and military organization to poor countries, and the growing importance of military rule in those same countries. They spring from the hope that the European experience, properly understood, will help us to grasp what is happening today, perhaps even to do something about it.

The Third World of the twentieth century does not greatly resemble Europe of the sixteenth or the seventeenth century. In no simple sense can we read the future of Third World countries from the pasts of European countries. Yet a thoughtful exploration of European experience will serve us well. It will show us that coercive exploitation played a large part in the creation of the European states. It will show us that popular resistance to coercive exploitation forced would-be power holders to concede protection and

The full version of this text was originally published as "War Making and State Making as Organized Crime" in Peter Evans, Dietrich Rueschemeyer, and Theda Skocpol, eds., *Bringing the State Back In*. Copyright © Cambridge University Press. Reprinted with permission.◆

constraints on their own action. It will therefore help us to eliminate faulty implicit comparisons between today's Third World and yesterday's Europe. That clarification will make it easier to understand exactly how today's world is different and what we therefore have to explain. It may even help us to explain the current looming presence of military organization and action throughout the world. Although that result would delight me, I do not promise anything so grand.

This essay, then, concerns the place of organized means of violence in the growth and change of those peculiar forms of government we call national states: relatively centralized, differentiated organizations the officials of which more or less successfully claim control over the chief concentrated means of violence within a population inhabiting a large, contiguous territory. The argument grows from historical work on the formation of national states in Western Europe, especially on the growth of the French state from 1600 onward. But it takes several deliberate steps away from that work, wheels, and stares hard at it from theoretical ground. The argument brings with it few illustrations and no evidence worthy of the name.

Just as one repacks a hastily filled rucksack after a few days on the trail—throwing out the waste, putting things in order of importance, and balancing the load—I have repacked my theoretical baggage for the climb to come; the real test of the new packing arrives only with the next stretch of the trail. The trimmed-down argument stresses the interdependence of war making and state making and the analogy between both of those processes and what, when less successful and smaller in scale, we call organized crime. War makes states, I shall claim. Banditry, piracy, gangland rivalry, policing, and war making all belong on the same continuum—that I shall claim as well. For the historically limited period in which national states were becoming the dominant organizations in Western countries, I shall also claim that mercantile capitalism and state making reinforced each other.

DOUBLE-EDGED PROTECTION

In contemporary American parlance, the word *protection* surrounds two contrasting tones. One is com-

forting, the other ominous. With one tone, protection calls up images of the shelter against danger provided by a powerful friend, a large insurance policy, or a sturdy roof. With the other, it evokes the racket in which a local strongman forces merchants to pay tribute in order to avoid damage—damage the strongman himself threatens to deliver. The difference, to be sure, is a matter of degree: A hell-and-damnation priest is likely to collect contributions from his parishioners only to the extent that they believe his predictions of brimstone for infidels; our neighborhood mobster may actually be, as he claims to be, a brothel's best guarantee of operation free of police interference.

Which image the word *protection* brings to mind depends mainly on our assessment of the reality and externality of the threat. Someone who produces both the danger and, at a price, the shield against it is a racketeer. Someone who provides a needed shield but has little control over the danger's appearance qualifies as a legitimate protector, especially if his price is no higher than his competitors'. Someone who supplies reliable, low-priced shielding both from local racketeers and from outside marauders makes the best offer of all.

Apologists for particular governments and for government in general commonly argue, precisely, that they offer protection from local and external violence. They claim that the prices they charge barely cover the costs of protection. They call people who complain about the price of protection "anarchists," "subversives," or both at once. But consider the definition of a racketeer as someone who creates a threat and then charges for its reduction. Governments' provision of protection, by this standard, often qualifies as racketeering. To the extent that the threats against which a given government protects its citizens are imaginary or are consequences of its own activities, the government has organized a protection racket. Since governments themselves commonly simulate, stimulate, or even fabricate threats of external war, and since the repressive and extractive activities of governments often constitute the largest current threats to the livelihoods of their own citizens, many governments operate in essentially the same way as racketeers. There is, of course, a difference: racketeers, by the conventional definition, operate without the sanctity of governments.

How do racketeer governments themselves acquire authority? As a question of fact and of ethics, that is one of the oldest conundrums of political analysis. Back to Machiavelli and Hobbes, nevertheless, political observers have recognized that, whatever else they do, governments organize and, wherever possible, monopolize violence. It matters little whether we take violence in a narrow sense, such as damage to persons and objects, or in a broad sense, such as violation of people's desires and interests; by either criterion, governments stand out from other organizations by their tendency to monopolize the concentrated means of violence. The distinction between "legitimate" and "illegitimate" force, furthermore, makes no difference to the fact. If we take legitimacy to depend on conformity to an abstract principle or on the assent of the governed (or both at once), these conditions may serve to justify, perhaps even to explain, the tendency to monopolize force, they do not contradict the fact.

In any case, Arthur Stinchcombe's agreeably cynical treatment of legitimacy serves the purposes of political analysis much more efficiently. Legitimacy, according to Stinchcombe, depends rather little on abstract principle or assent of the governed: "The person *over whom power is exercised* is not usually as important as *other power-holders*."[1] Legitimacy is the probability that other authorities will act to confirm the decisions of a given authority. Other authorities, I would add, are much more likely to confirm the decisions of a challenged authority that controls substantial force; not only fear of retaliation, but also desire to maintain a stable environment recommend that general rule. The rule underscores the importance of the authority's monopoly of force. A tendency to monopolize the means of violence makes a government's claim to provide protection, in either the comforting or the ominous sense of the word, more credible and more difficult to resist.

Frank recognition of the central place of force in governmental activity does not require us to believe that governmental authority rests "only" or "ultimately" on the threat of violence. Nor does it entail the assumption that a government's only service is protection. Even when a government's use of force imposes a large cost, some people may well decide that the government's other services outbalance the costs of acceding to its monopoly of violence.

Recognition of the centrality of force opens the way to an understanding of the growth and change of governmental forms.

Here is a preview of the most general argument: power holders' pursuit of war involved them willy-nilly in the extraction of resources for war making from the populations over which they had control and in the promotion of capital accumulation by those who could help them borrow and buy. War making, extraction, and capital accumulation interacted to shape European state making. Power holders did not undertake those three momentous activities with the intention of creating national states—centralized, differentiated, autonomous, extensive political organizations. Nor did they ordinarily foresee that national states would emerge from war making, extraction, and capital accumulation.

Instead, the people who controlled European states and states in the making warred in order to check or overcome their competitors and thus to enjoy the advantages of power within a secure or expanding territory. To make more effective war, they attempted to locate more capital. In the short run, they might acquire that capital by conquest, by selling off their assets, or by coercing or dispossessing accumulators of capital. In the long run, the quest inevitably involved them in establishing regular access to capitalists who could supply and arrange credit and in imposing one form of regular taxation or another on the people and activities within their spheres of control.

As the process continued, state makers developed a durable interest in promoting the accumulation of capital, sometimes in the guise of direct return to their own enterprises. Variations in the difficulty of collecting taxes, in the expense of the particular kind of armed force adopted, in the amount of war making required to hold off competitors, and so on, resulted in the principal variations in the forms of European states. It all began with the effort to monopolize the means of violence within a delimited territory adjacent to a power holder's base.

VIOLENCE AND GOVERNMENT

What distinguished the violence produced by states from the violence delivered by anyone else? In the long run, enough distinguished them to make the division between "legitimate" and "illegitimate" force credible. Eventually, the personnel of states purveyed violence on a larger scale, more effectively, more efficiently, with wider assent from their subject populations, and with readier collaboration from neighboring authorities than did the personnel of other organizations. But it took a long time for that series of distinctions to become established. Early in the state-making process, many parties shared the right to use violence, the practice of using it routinely to accomplish their ends, or both at once. The continuum ran from bandits and pirates to kings via tax collectors, regional power holders, and professional soldiers.

The uncertain, elastic line between "legitimate" and "illegitimate" violence appeared in the upper reaches of power. Early in the state-making process, many parties shared the right to use violence, its actual employment, or both at once. The long love/hate affair between aspiring state makers and pirates or bandits illustrates the division. "Behind piracy on the seas acted cities and city-states," writes Fernand Braudel of the sixteenth century. "Behind banditry, that terrestrial piracy, appeared the continual aid of lords."[2] In times of war, indeed, the managers of full-fledged states often commissioned privateers, hired sometime bandits to raid their enemies, and encouraged their regular troops to take booty. In royal service, soldiers and sailors were often expected to provide for themselves by preying on the civilian population: commandeering, raping, looting, taking prizes. When demobilized, they commonly continued the same practices, but without the same royal protection; demobilized ships became pirate vessels, demobilized troops, bandits.

It also worked the other way: a king's best source of armed supporters was sometimes the world of outlaws. Robin Hood's conversion to royal archer may be a myth, but the myth records a practice. The distinctions between "legitimate" and "illegitimate" users of violence came clear only very slowly, in the process during which the state's armed forces became relatively unified and permanent.

Up to that point, as Braudel says, maritime cities and terrestrial lords commonly offered protection, or even sponsorship, to freebooters. Many lords who did not pretend to be kings, furthermore, successfully

claimed the right to levy troops and maintain their own armed retainers. Without calling on some of those lords to bring their armies with them, no king could fight a war; yet the same armed lords constituted the king's rivals and opponents, his enemies' potential allies. For that reason, before the seventeenth century, regencies for child sovereigns reliably produced civil wars. For the same reason, disarming the great stood high on the agenda of every would-be state maker.

The Tudors, for example, accomplished that agenda through most of England. "The greatest triumph of the Tudors," writes Lawrence Stone,

> was the ultimately successful assertion of a royal monopoly of violence both public and private, an achievement which profoundly altered not only the nature of politics but also the quality of daily life. There occurred a change in English habits that can only be compared with the further step taken in the nineteenth century, when the growth of a police force finally consolidated the monopoly and made it effective in the greatest cities and the smallest villages.[3]

Tudor demilitarization of the great lords entailed four complementary campaigns: eliminating their great personal bands of armed retainers, razing their fortresses, taming their habitual resort to violence for the settlement of disputes, and discouraging the cooperation of their dependents and tenants. In the Marches of England and Scotland, the task was more delicate, for the Percys and Dacres, who kept armies and castles along the border, threatened the Crown but also provided a buffer against Scottish invaders. Yet they, too, eventually fell into line.

In France, Richelieu began the great disarmament in the 1620s. With Richelieu's advice, Louis XIII systematically destroyed the castles of the great rebel lords, Protestant and Catholic, against whom his forces battled incessantly. He began to condemn dueling, the carrying of lethal weapons, and the maintenance of private armies. By the later 1620s, Richelieu was declaring the royal monopoly of force as doctrine. The doctrine took another half century to become effective.

> Once more the conflicts of the Fronde had witnessed armies assembled by the "grands." Only the last of the regencies, the one after the

death of Louis XIV, did not lead to armed uprisings. By that time Richelieu's principle had become a reality. Likewise in the Empire after the Thirty Years' War only the territorial princes had the right of levying troops and of maintaining fortresses. . . . Everywhere the razing of castles, the high cost of artillery, the attraction of court life, and the ensuing domestication of the nobility had its share in this development.[4]

By the later eighteenth century, through most of Europe, monarchs controlled permanent, professional military forces that rivaled those of their neighbors and far exceeded any other organized armed force within their own territories. The state's monopoly of large-scale violence was turning from theory to reality.

The elimination of local rivals, however, posed a serious problem. Beyond the scale of a small city-state, no monarch could govern a population with his armed force alone, nor could any monarch afford to create a professional staff large and strong enough to reach from him to the ordinary citizen. Before quite recently, no European government approached the completeness of articulation from top to bottom achieved by imperial China. Even the Roman Empire did not come close. In one way or another, every European government before the French Revolution relied on indirect rule via local magnates. The magnates collaborated with the government without becoming officials in any strong sense of the term, had some access to government-backed force, and exercised wide discretion within their own territories: junkers, justices of the peace, lords. Yet the same magnates were potential rivals, possible allies of a rebellious people.

Eventually, European governments reduced their reliance on indirect rule by means of two expensive but effective strategies: (a) extending their officialdom to the local community and (b) encouraging the creation of police forces that were subordinate to the government rather than to individual patrons, distinct from war-making forces, and therefore less useful as the tools of dissident magnates. In between, however, the builders of national power all played a mixed strategy: eliminating, subjugating, dividing, conquering, cajoling, buying as the occasions presented themselves. The buying manifested itself in exemptions from taxation, creations of honorific offices, the

establishment of claims on the national treasury, and a variety of other devices that made a magnate's welfare dependent on the maintenance of the existing structure of power. In the long run, it all came down to massive pacification and monopolization of the means of coercion.

PROTECTION AS BUSINESS

In retrospect, the pacification, cooptation, or elimination of fractious rivals to the sovereign seems an awesome, noble, prescient enterprise, destined to bring peace to a people; yet it followed almost ineluctably from the logic of expanding power. If a power holder was to gain from the provision of protection, his competitors had to yield. As economic historian Frederic Lane put it decades ago, governments are in the business of selling protection . . . whether people want it or not. Lane argued that the very activity of producing and controlling violence favored monopoly, because competition within that realm generally raises costs, instead of lowering them. The production of violence, he suggested, enjoyed large economies of scale.

Working from there, Lane[5] distinguished between (a) the monopoly profit, or *tribute*, coming to owners of the means of producing violence as a result of the difference between production costs and the price exacted from "customers," and (b) the *protection rent* accruing to those customers—for example, merchants—who drew effective protection against outside competitors. Lane, a superbly attentive historian of Venice, allowed specifically for the case of a government that generates protection rents for its merchants by deliberately attacking their competitors. In their adaptation of Lane's scheme, furthermore, Edward Ames and Richard Rapp[6] substitute the apt word *extortion* for Lane's *tribute*. In this model, predation, coercion, piracy, banditry, and racketeering share a home with their upright cousins in responsible government.

This is how Lane's model worked: if a prince could create a sufficient armed force to hold off his and his subjects' external enemies and to keep the subjects in line for 50 megapounds but was able to extract 75 megapounds in taxes from those subjects for that purpose, he gained a tribute of (75 − 50 =) 25 megapounds. If the 10-pound share of those taxes paid by one of the prince's merchant-subjects gave him assured access to world markets at less than the 15-pound shares paid by the merchant's foreign competitors to *their* princes, the merchant also gained a protection rent of (15 − 10 =) 5 pounds by virtue of his prince's greater efficiency. That reasoning differs only in degree and in scale from the reasoning of violence-wielding criminals and their clients. Labor racketeering (in which, for example, a shipowner holds off trouble from long-shoremen by means of a timely payment to the local union boss) works on exactly the same principle: the union boss receives tribute for his no-strike pressure on the longshoremen, while the shipowner avoids the strikes and showdowns longshoremen impose on his competitors.

Lane pointed out the different behavior we might expect of the managers of a protection-providing government owned by

1. citizens in general
2. a single self-interested monarch
3. the managers themselves

If citizens in general exercised effective ownership of the government—O distant ideal!—we might expect the managers to minimize protection costs and tribute, thus maximizing protection rent. A single self-interested monarch, in contrast, would maximize tribute, set costs so as to accomplish that maximization of tribute, and be indifferent to the level of protection rent. If the managers owned the government, they would tend to keep costs high by maximizing their own wages, to maximize tribute over and above those costs by exacting a high price from their subjects, and likewise to be indifferent to the level of protection rent. The first model approximates a Jeffersonian democracy, the second a petty despotism, and the third a military junta.

Lane did not discuss the obvious fourth category of owner: a dominant class. If he had, his scheme would have yielded interesting empirical criteria for evaluating claims that a given government was "relatively autonomous" or strictly subordinate to the interests of a dominant class. Presumably, a subordinate government would tend to maximize monopoly profits—returns to the dominant class resulting from the difference between the costs of protection and the price received for it—as well as tuning protection rents nicely to the economic interests of the dominant class. An autonomous government, in contrast, would tend to maximize managers' wages and its own size as well and would be indifferent to protection rents. Lane's analysis immediately suggests fresh propositions and ways of testing them.

Lane also speculated that the logic of the situation produced four successive stages in the general history of capitalism:

1. a period of anarchy and plunder;
2. a stage in which tribute takers attracted customers and established their monopolies by struggling to create exclusive, substantial states;
3. a stage in which merchants and landlords began to gain more from protection rents than governors did from tribute; and
4. a period (fairly recent) in which technological changes surpassed protection rents as sources of profit for entrepreneurs.

In their new economic history of the Western world, Douglass North and Robert Paul Thomas[7] make the second and third stages—those in which state makers created their monopolies of force and established property rights that permitted individuals to capture much of the return from their own growth-generating innovations—the pivotal moment for sustained economic growth. Protection, at this point, overwhelms tribute. If we recognize that the protected property rights were mainly those of capital and that the development of capitalism also facilitated the accumulation of the wherewithal to operate massive states, that extension of Lane's analysis provides a good deal of insight into the coincidence of war making, state making, and capital accumulation.

Unfortunely, Lane did not take full advantage of his own insight. Wanting to contain his analysis neatly within the neoclassical theory of industrial organization, Lane cramped his treatment of protection: treating all taxpayers as "customers" for the "service" provided by protection-manufacturing governments, brushing aside the objections to the idea of a forced sale by insisting that the "customer" always had the choice of not paying and taking the consequences of nonpayment, minimizing the problems of divisibility created by the public-goods character of protection, and deliberately neglecting the distinction between the costs of producing the means of violence in general and the costs of giving "customers" protection by means of that violence. Lane's ideas suffocate inside the neoclassical box and breathe easily outside it. Nevertheless, inside or outside, they properly draw the economic analysis of government back to the chief activities that real governments have carried on historically: war, repression, protection, adjudication.

NOTES

1. Arthur L. Stinchcombe, *Constructing Social Theories* (New York: Harcourt, Brace & World, 1968), p. 150; italics in the original.
2. Fernand Braudel, *La Méditerranée et le monde méditerranéen à l'époque de Philippe II* (Paris: Armand Colin, 1966), vol. 2, pp. 88–89.
3. Lawrence Stone, *The Crisis of the Aristocracy* (Oxford: Clarendon Press, 1965), p. 200.
4. Dietrich Gerhard, *Old Europe: A Study of Continuity, 1000–1800* (New York: Academic Press, 1981), pp. 124–125.
5. Frederic C. Lane, *Venice and History: The Collected Papers of Frederic C. Lane* (Baltimore, MD: Johns Hopkins University Press, 1966, originally 1942).
6. Edward Ames and Richard T. Rapp, "The Birth and Death of Taxes: A Hypothesis," *Journal of Economic History* 37 (1977): 161–178.
7. Douglass C. North and Robert Paul Thomas, *The Rise of the Western World: A New Economic History* (Cambridge: Cambridge University Press, 1973).

SECTION VIII

1. Mills' argument was written during the height of the cold war. What aspects of his analysis may no longer be applicable, and which aspects remain relevant today?
2. What does Mills mean by an "overdeveloped nation"? Is this a fair assessment of your nation? Why or why not?
3. According to Dahrendorf, what are the main factors that contribute to the intensification of class conflict? What are the factors that work at reducing levels of conflict?
4. Dahrendorf's class structure was that of industrial society. Apply his perspective to the contemporary postindustrial landscape.
5. Offer an overview and critical assessment of Collins' discussion of the relevance of conflict theory to a Durkheimian perspective on occupations.
6. Summarize in your own words what Tilly means when he characterizes protection as double-edged. Give an example to illustrate his point.

IX. SYMBOLIC INTERACTION, PHENOMENOLOGY, AND ETHNOMETHODOLOGY

41. SOCIETY AS SYMBOLIC INTERACTION

HERBERT BLUMER

Herbert Blumer (1900–1987) coined the term *symbolic interactionism* to describe a theoretical approach to sociology different from the reigning orthodoxies of the day, which in his view included behaviorism, functionalism, and other deterministic theoretical approaches. Noting his intellectual debt not only to the key figures associated with the Chicago School of Sociology but to social philosophers William James, John Dewey, and George Herbert Mead, in this 1962 essay Blumer urges a sociology that treats human beings as authors of their own lives insofar as they imbue their actions with meaning and purpose. He believes that competing theoretical paradigms tend to treat people as the products or effects of social forces. To the extent that they do so, they fail to take seriously the idea of the self and the interpretive work that selves do in constructing their social lives— not in isolation, but through complex processes of interaction.

A view of human society as symbolic interaction has been followed more than it has been formulated. Partial, usually fragmentary, statements of it are to be found in the writings of a number of eminent scholars, some inside the field of sociology and some outside. Among the former we may note such scholars as Charles Horton Cooley, W. I. Thomas, Robert E. Parks, E. W. Burgess, Florian Znaniecki, Ellsworth Faris, and James Mickel Williams. Among those outside the discipline we may note William James, John Dewey, and George Herbert Mead. None of these scholars, in my judgment, has presented a systematic statement of the nature of human group life from the standpoint of symbolic interaction. Mead stands out among all of them in laying bare the fundamental premises of the approach, yet he did little to develop its methodological implications for sociological study. Students who seek to depict the position of symbolic interaction may easily give different pictures of it. What I have to present should be regarded as my personal version. My aim is to present the basic premises of the point of view and to develop their methodological consequences for the study of human group life.

The term "symbolic interaction" refers, of course, to the peculiar and distinctive character of interaction as it takes place between human beings. The peculiarity consists in the fact that human beings interpret or "define" each other's actions instead of merely reacting to each other's actions. Their "response" is not made directly to the actions of one another but instead is based on the meaning which they attach to such actions. Thus, human interaction is mediated by the use of symbols, by interpretation, or by ascertaining the meaning of one another's actions. This mediation is equivalent to inserting a process of interpretation between stimulus and response in the case of human behavior.

The simple recognition that human beings interpret each other's actions as the means of acting toward one another has permeated the thought and writings of many scholars of human conduct and of human group life. Yet few of them have endeavored to analyze what such interpretation implies about the nature of the human being or about the nature of human association. They are usually content with a mere recognition that "interpretation" should be caught by the student, or with a simple realization that symbols, such as cultural norms or values, must be introduced into their analyses. Only G. H. Mead, in my judgment, has sought to think through what the act of interpretation implies for an understanding of the human being, human action and human association. The essentials of his analysis are so penetrating and profound and so important for an understanding of human group life that I wish to spell them out, even though briefly.

The key feature in Mead's analysis is that the human being has a self. This idea should not be cast aside as esoteric or glossed over as something that is obvious and hence not worthy of attention. In declaring that the human being has a self, Mead had in mind chiefly that the human being can be the object of his own actions. He can act toward himself as he might act toward others. Each of us is familiar with actions of this sort in which the human being gets angry with himself, rebuffs himself, takes pride in himself, argues with himself, tries to bolster his own courage, tells himself that he should "do this" or not "do that," sets goals for himself, makes compromises with himself, and plans what he is going to do. That the human being acts toward himself in these and countless other ways is a matter of easy empirical observation. To recognize that the human being can act toward himself is no mystical conjuration.

Mead regards this ability of the human being to act toward himself as the central mechanism with which the human being faces and deals with his world. This mechanism enables the human being to make indications to himself of things in his surroundings and thus to guide his actions by what he notes. Anything of which a human being is conscious is something which he is indicating to himself—the ticking of a clock, a knock at the door, the appearance of a friend, the remark made by a companion, a recognition that he has a task to perform, or the realization that he has a cold. Conversely, anything of which he is not conscious is, ipso facto, something which he is not indicating to himself. The conscious life of the human being, from the time that he awakens until he falls asleep, is a continual flow of self-indications—notations of the things with which he deals and takes into account. We are given, then, a picture of the human being as an organism which confronts its world with a mechanism for making indications to itself. This is the mechanism that is involved in interpreting the actions of others. To interpret the actions of another is to point out to oneself that the action has this or that meaning or character.

Now, according to Mead, the significance of making indications to oneself is of paramount importance. The importance lies along two lines. First, to indicate something is to extricate it from its setting, to hold it apart, to give it a meaning or, in Mead's language, to make it into an object. An object—that is to say, anything that an individual indicates to himself—is different from a stimulus; instead of having an intrinsic character which acts on the individual and which can be identified apart from the individual, its character or meaning is conferred on it by the individual. The object is a product of the individual's disposition to act instead of being an antecedent stimulus which evokes the act. Instead of the individual being surrounded by an environment of pre-existing objects which play upon him and call forth his behavior, the proper picture is that he constructs his objects on the basis of his ongoing activity. In any of his countless acts—whether minor, like dressing himself, or major, like organizing himself for a professional career—the individual is designating different objects to himself, giving them meaning, judging their suitability to his action, and making decisions on the basis of the judgment. This is what is meant by interpretation or acting on the basis of symbols.

The second important implication of the fact that the human being makes indications to himself is that his action is constructed or built up instead of being a mere release. Whatever the action in which he is engaged, the human individual proceeds by pointing out to himself the divergent things which have to be taken into account in the course of his action. He has to note what he wants to do and how he is to do it; he has to point out to himself the various conditions which may be instrumental to his action and those which may obstruct his action; he has to take account of the demands, the expectations, the prohibitions, and the threats as they may arise in the situation in which he is acting. His action is built up step by step through a process of such self-indication. The human individual pieces together and guides his action by taking account of different things and interpreting their significance for his prospective action. There is no instance of conscious action of which this is not true.

The process of constructing action through making indications to oneself cannot be swallowed up in any of the conventional psychological categories. This process is distinct from and different from what is spoken of as the "ego"—just as it is different from any other conception which conceives of the self in terms of composition or organization. Self-indication is a moving communicative process in which the individual notes things, assesses them, gives them a meaning, and decides to act on the basis of the meaning. The human being stands over against the world, or against "alters," with such a process and not with a mere ego. Further, the process of self-indication cannot be subsumed under the forces, whether from the outside or inside, which are presumed to play upon the individual to produce his behavior. Environmental pressures, external stimuli, organic drives, wishes, attitudes, feelings, ideas, and their like do not cover or explain the process of self-indication. The process of self-indication stands over against them in that the individual points out to himself and interprets the appearance or expression of such things, noting a given social demand that is made on him, recognizing a command, observing that he is hungry, realizing that he wishes to buy something, aware that he has a given feeling, conscious that he

dislikes eating with someone he despises, or aware that he is thinking of doing some given thing. By virtue of indicating such things to himself, he places himself over against them and is able to act back against them, accepting them, rejecting them, or transforming them in accordance with how he defines or interprets them. His behavior, accordingly, is not a result of such things as environmental pressures, stimuli, motives, attitudes, and ideas but arises instead from how he interprets and handles these things in the action which he is constructing. The process of self-indication by means of which human action is formed cannot be accounted for by factors which precede the act. The process of self-indication exists in its own right and must be accepted and studied as such. It is through this process that the human being constructs his conscious action.

Now Mead recognizes that the formation of action by the individual through a process of self-indication always takes place in a social context. Since this matter is so vital to an understanding of symbolic interaction it needs to be explained carefully. Fundamentally, group action takes the form of a fitting together of individual lines of action. Each individual aligns his action to the action of others by ascertaining what they are doing or what they intend to do—that is, by getting the meaning of their acts. For Mead, this is done by the individual "taking the role" of others—either the role of a specific person or the role of a group (Mead's "generalized other"). In taking such roles the individual seeks to ascertain the intention or direction of the acts of others. He forms and aligns his own action on the basis of such interpretation of the acts of others. This is the fundamental way in which group action takes place in human society.

The foregoing are the essential features, as I see them, in Mead's analysis of the bases of symbolic interaction. They presuppose the following: that human society is made up of individuals who have selves (that is, make indications to themselves); that individual action is a construction and not a release, being built up by the individual through noting and interpreting features of the situations in which he acts; that group or collective action consists of the aligning of individuals' interpreting or taking into account each other's actions. Since my purpose is to present and not to defend the position of symbolic interaction I shall not endeavor in this essay to advance support for the three premises which I have just indicated. I wish merely to say that the three premises can be easily verified empirically. I know of no instance of human group action to which the three premises do not apply. The reader is challenged to find or think of a single instance which they do not fit. I wish now to point out that sociological views of human society are, in general, markedly at variance with the premises which I have indicated as underlying symbolic interaction. Indeed, the predominant number of such views, especially those in vogue at the present time, do not see or treat human society as symbolic interaction. Wedded, as they tend to be, to some form of sociological determinism, they adopt images of human society, of individuals in it, and of group action which do not square with the premises of symbolic interaction. I wish to say a few words about the major lines of variance.

Sociological thought rarely recognizes or treats human societies as composed of individuals who have selves. Instead, they assume human beings to be merely organisms with some kind of organization, responding to forces which play upon them. Generally, although not exclusively, these forces are lodged in the make-up of the society, as in the case of "social system," "social structure," "culture," "status position," "social role," "custom," "institution," "collective representation," "social situation," "social norm," and "values." The assumption is that the behavior of people as members *of a society* is an expression of the play on them of these kinds of factors or forces. This, of course, is the logical position which is necessarily taken when the scholar explains their behavior or phases of their behavior in terms of one or another of such social factors. The individuals who compose a human society are treated as the media through which such factors operate, and the social action of such individuals is regarded as an expression of such factors. This approach or point of view denies, or at least ignores, that human beings have selves—that they act by making indications to themselves. Incidentally, the "self" is not brought into the picture by introducing such items as organic drives, motives, attitudes, feelings, internalized social factors, or psychological components. Such psychological factors have the same status as the social factors mentioned: they are regarded as factors which play on the individual to produce his action. They do not constitute the process of self-indication. The process of self-indication stands over against them, just as it stands over against the social factors which play on the human being. Practically all sociological conceptions of human society fail to recognize that the individuals who compose it have selves in the sense spoken of.

Correspondingly, such sociological conceptions do not regard the social actions of individuals in human society as being constructed by them through a process of interpretation. Instead, action is treated as a product of factors which play on and through individuals. The social behavior of people is not seen as built up by them through an interpretation of objects, situations, or the actions of others. If a place is given to "interpretation," the interpretation is regarded as merely an expression of other factors (such as motives) which precede the act, and accordingly disappears as a factor in its own right. Hence, the social action of people is treated as an outward flow or expression of forces playing on them rather than as acts which are built up by people through their interpretation of the situations in which they are placed.

These remarks suggest another significant line of difference between general sociological views and the position of symbolic interaction. These two sets of views differ in where they lodge social action. Under the perspective of symbolic interaction, social action is lodged in acting individuals who fit their respective lines of action to one another through a process of interpretation; group action is the collective action of such individuals. As opposed to this view, sociological conceptions generally lodge social action in the action of society or in some unit of society. Examples of this are legion. Let me cite a few. Some conceptions, in treating societies or human groups as "social systems," regard group action as an expression of a system, either in a state of balance or seeking to achieve balance. Or group action is conceived as an expression of the "functions" of a society or of a group. Or group action is regarded as the outward expression of elements lodged in society or the group, such as cultural demands, societal purposes, social values, or institutional stresses.

These typical conceptions ignore or blot out a view of group life or of group action as consisting of the collective or concerted actions of individuals seeking to meet their life situations. If recognized at all, the efforts of people to develop collective acts to meet their situations are subsumed under the play of underlying or transcending forces which are lodged in society or its parts. The individuals composing the society or the group become "carriers," or media for the expression of such forces; and the interpretative behavior by means of which people form their actions is merely a coerced link in the play of such forces.

The indication of the foregoing lines of variance should help to put the position of symbolic interaction in better perspective. In the remaining discussion I wish to sketch somewhat more fully how human society appears in terms of symbolic interaction and to point out some methodological implications.

Human society is to be seen as consisting of acting people, and the life of the society is to be seen as consisting of their actions. The acting units may be separate individuals, collectivities whose members are acting together on a common quest, or organizations acting on behalf of a constituency. Respective examples are individual purchasers in a market, a play group or missionary band, and a business corporation or a national professional association. There is no empirically observable activity in a human society that does not spring from some acting unit. This banal statement needs to be stressed in light of the common practice of sociologists of reducing human society to social units that do not act—for example, social classes in modern society. Obviously, there are ways of viewing human society other than in terms of the acting units that compose it. I merely wish to point out that in respect to concrete or empirical activity human society must necessarily be seen in terms of the acting units that form it. I would add that any scheme of human society claiming to be a realistic analysis has to respect and be congruent with the empirical recognition that a human society consists of acting units.

Corresponding respect must be shown to the conditions under which such units act. One primary condition is that action takes place in and with regard to a situation. Whatever be the acting unit—an individual, a family, a school, a church, a business firm, a labor union, a legislature, and so on–any particular action is formed in the light of the situation in which it takes place. This leads to the recognition of a second major condition, namely, that the action is formed or constructed by interpreting the situation. The acting unit necessarily has to identify the things which it has to take into account—tasks, opportunities, obstacles, means, demands, discomforts, dangers, and the like; it has to assess them in some fashion and it has to make decisions on the basis of the assessment. Such interpretative behavior may take place in the individual guiding his own action, in a collectivity of individuals acting in concert, or in "agents" acting on behalf of a group or organization. Group life consists of acting units developing acts to meet the situations in which they are placed.

Usually, most of the situations encountered by people in a given society are defined or "structured" by them in the same way. Through previous interaction they develop and acquire common understandings or definitions of how to act in this or that situation. These common definitions enable people to act alike. The common repetitive behavior of people in such situations should not mislead the student into believing that no process of interpretation is in play; on the contrary, even though fixed, the actions of the participating people are constructed by them through a process of interpretation. Since ready-made and commonly accepted definitions are at hand, little strain is placed on people in guiding and organizing their acts. However, many other situations may not be defined in a single way by the participating people. In this event, their lines of action do not fit together readily and collective action is blocked. Interpretations have to be developed and effective accommodation of the participants to one another has to be worked out. In the case of such "undefined" situations, it is necessary to trace and study the emerging process of definition which is brought into play.

Insofar as sociologists or students of human society are concerned with the behavior of acting units, the position of symbolic interaction requires the student to catch the process of interpretation through which they construct their actions. This process is not to be caught merely by turning to conditions which are antecedent to the process. Such antecedent conditions are helpful in understanding the process insofar as they enter into it, but as mentioned previously they do not constitute the process. Nor can one catch the process merely by inferring its nature from the overt action which is its product. To catch the process, the student must take the role of the acting unit whose behavior he is studying. Since the interpretation is being made by the acting unit in terms of objects designated and appraised, meanings acquired, and decisions made, the process has to be seen from the standpoint of the acting unit. It is the recognition of this fact that makes the research work of such scholars as R. E. Park and W. I. Thomas so notable. To try to catch the interpretative process by remaining aloof as a so-called "objective" observer and refusing to take the role of the acting unit is to risk the worst kind of subjectivism—the objective observer is likely to fill in the process of interpretation with his own surmises in place of catching the process as it occurs in the experience of the acting unit which uses it.

By and large, of course, sociologists do not study human society in terms of its acting units. Instead, they are disposed to view human society in terms of structure or organization and to treat social action as an expression of such structure or organization. Thus, reliance is placed on such structural categories as social system, culture, norms, values, social stratification, status positions, social roles and institutional organization. These are used both to analyze human society and to account for social action within it. Other major interests of sociological scholars center around this focal theme of organization. One line of interest is to view organization in terms of the functions it is supposed to perform. Another line of interest is to study societal organization as a system seeking equilibrium; here the scholar endeavors to detect mechanisms which are indigenous to the system. Another line of interest is to identify forces which play upon organization to bring about changes in it; here the scholar endeavors, especially through comparative study, to isolate a relation between causative factors and structural results. These various lines of sociological perspective and interest, which are so strongly entrenched today, leap over the acting units of a society and bypass the interpretative process by which such acting units build up their actions.

These respective concerns with organization on one hand and with acting units on the other hand set the essential difference between conventional views of human society and the view of it implied in symbolic interaction. The latter view recognizes the presence of organization to human society and respects its importance. However, it sees and treats organization differently. The difference is along two major lines. First, from the standpoint of symbolic interaction the organization of a human society is the framework inside of which social action takes place and is not the determinant of that action. Second, such organization and changes in it are the product of the activity of acting units and not of "forces" which leave such acting units out of account. Each of these two major lines of difference should be explained briefly in order to obtain a better understanding of how human society appears in terms of symbolic interaction.

From the standpoint of symbolic interaction, social organization is a framework inside of which acting units develop their actions. Structural features, such as "culture," "social systems," "social stratification," or "social roles," set conditions for their action but do not determine their action. People—that is, acting units—do not act toward culture, social structure or the like; they act toward situations. Social organization enters into action only to the extent to which it shapes situations in which people act, and to the extent to which it supplies fixed sets of symbols which people use in interpreting their situations. These two forms of influence of social organization are important. In the case of settled and stabilized societies, such as isolated primitive tribes and peasant communities, the influence is certain to be profound. In the case of human societies, particularly modern societies, in which streams of new situations arise and old situations become unstable, the influence of organization decreases. One should bear in mind that the most important element confronting an acting unit in situations is the actions of other acting units. In modern society, with its increasing criss-crossing of lines of action, it is common for situations to arise in which the actions of participants are not previously regularized and standardized. To this extent, existing social organization does not shape the situations. Correspondingly, the symbols or tools of interpretation used by acting units in such situations may vary and shift considerably. For these reasons, social action may go beyond, or depart from, existing organization in any of its structural dimensions. The organization of a human society is not to be identified with the process of interpretation used by its acting units; even though it affects that process, it does not embrace or cover the process.

Perhaps the most outstanding consequence of viewing human society as organization is to overlook the part played by acting units in social change. The conventional procedure of sociologists is (a) to identify human society (or some part of it) in terms of an established or organized form, (b) to identify some factor or condition of change playing upon the human society or the given part of it, and (c) to identify the new form assumed by the society following upon the play of the factor of change. Such observations permit the student to couch propositions to the effect that a given factor of change playing upon a given organized form results in a given new organized form. Examples ranging from crude to refined statements are legion, such as that an economic depression increases solidarity in the families of working-men or that industrialization replaces extended families by nuclear families. My concern here is not with the validity of such propositions but with the methodological position which they presuppose. Essentially, such propositions either ignore the role of the interpretive behavior of acting units in the given instance of change, or else regard the interpretative behavior as coerced by the factor of change. I wish to point out that any line of social change, since it involves change in human action, is necessarily mediated by interpretation on the part of the people caught up in the change—the change appears in the form of new situations in which people have to construct new forms of action. Also, in line with

what has been said previously, interpretations of new situations are not predetermined by conditions antecedent to the situations but depend on what is taken into account and assessed in the actual situations in which behavior is formed. Variations in interpretation may readily occur as different acting units cut out different objects in the situation, or give different weight to the objects which they note, or piece objects together in different patterns. In formulating propositions of social change, it would be wise to recognize that any given line of such change is mediated by acting units interpreting the situations with which they are confronted.

Students of human society will have to face the question of whether their preoccupation with categories of structure and organization can be squared with the interpretative process by means of which human beings, individually and collectively, act in human society. It is the discrepancy between the two which plagues such students in their efforts to attain scientific propositions of the sort achieved in the physical and biological sciences. It is this discrepancy, further, which is chiefly responsible for their difficulty in fitting hypothetical propositions to new arrays of empirical data. Efforts are made, of course, to overcome these shortcomings by devising new structural categories, by formulating new structural hypotheses, by developing more refined techniques of research, and even by formulating new methodological schemes of a structural character. These efforts continue to ignore or to explain away the interpretative process by which people act, individually and collectively, in society. The question remains whether human society or social action can be successfully analyzed by schemes which refuse to recognize human beings as they are, namely, as persons constructing individual and collective action through an interpretation of the situations which confront them.

42. PERFORMANCES

ERVING GOFFMAN

Erving Goffman (1922–1982) has been described as the most important American sociological theorist in the second half of the twentieth century. Moreover, because of the literary character of his writing, his influence has extended well beyond the discipline. As a dramaturgical sociologist, he is sometimes seen as a perceptive, if somewhat cynical, chronicler of the contemporary "human comedy." In this selection from *The Presentation of Self in Everyday Life*, Goffman uses the metaphor of social life as theater in outlining his dramaturgical perspective. In a play, actors attempt to convey to an audience a particular impression of both the actor and the social scene. Through the use of scripted dialogue, gestures, props, costumes, and so on, actors create a new reality for the audience to consider. Goffman is concerned here with the ways in which actors convey a sense of personal identity. He begins with an intriguing discussion about whether the individual is taken in by her role performance, embracing it with sincerity or viewing it cynically, and then moves on to an analysis of the nature and function of the "front"— which he describes as the "expressive equipment" used to convince the other about the authenticity of the individual's performance. Goffman concludes by observing that fronts—along with other theatrical props—tend to be embedded in our social worlds. Rather than social life being improvisational, much of it is predicated on routines that actors select when deemed appropriate.

BELIEF IN THE PART ONE IS PLAYING

When an individual plays a part he implicitly requests his observers to take seriously the impression that is fostered before them. They are asked to believe that the character they see actually possesses the attributes he appears to possess, that the task he performs will have the consequences that are implicitly claimed for it, and that, in general, matters are what they appear to be. In line with this, there is the popular view that the individual offers his performance and puts on his show "for the benefit of other people." It will be convenient to begin a consideration of performances by turning the question around and looking at the individual's own belief in the impression of reality that he attempts to engender in those among whom he finds himself.

At one extreme, one finds that the performer can be fully taken in by his own act; he can be sincerely convinced that the impression of reality which he stages is the real reality. When his audience is also convinced in this way about the show he puts on—and this seems to be the typical case—then for the moment at least, only the sociologist or the socially disgruntled will have any doubts about the "realness" of what is presented.

At the other extreme, we find that the performer may not be taken in at all by his own routine. This possibility is understandable, since no one is in quite as good an observational position to see through the act as the person who puts it on. Coupled with this, the performer may be moved to guide the conviction of his audience only as a means to other ends, having no ultimate concern in the conception that they have of him or of the situation. When the individual has no belief in his own act and no ultimate concern with the beliefs of his audience, we may call him cynical, reserving the term "sincere" for individuals who believe in the impression fostered by their own performance. It should be understood that the cynic, with all his professional disinvolvement, may obtain unprofessional pleasures from his masquerade, experiencing a kind of gleeful spiritual aggression from the fact that he can toy at will with something his audience must take seriously.[1]

It is not assumed, of course, that all cynical performers are interested in deluding their audiences for purposes of what is called "self-interest" or private gain. A cynical individual may delude his audience for what he considers to be their own good, or for the good of the community, etc. For illustrations of this we need not appeal to sadly enlightened showmen such as Marcus Aurelius or Hsun Tzu. We know that in service occupations practitioners who may otherwise be sincere are sometimes forced to delude their customers because their customers show such a heartfelt demand for it. Doctors who are led into giving placebos, filling station attendants who resignedly check and recheck tire pressures for anxious women motorists, shoe clerks who sell a shoe that fits but tell the customer it is the size she wants to hear—these are cynical performers whose audiences will not allow them to be sincere. Similarly, it seems that sympathetic patients in mental wards will sometimes feign bizarre symptoms so that student nurses will not be subjected to a disappointingly sane performance.[2] So also, when inferiors extend their most lavish reception for visiting superiors, the selfish desire to win favor may not be the chief motive; the inferior may be tactfully attempting to put the superior at ease by simulating the kind of world the superior is thought to take for granted.

I have suggested two extremes: an individual may be taken in by his own act or be cynical about it. These extremes are something a little more than just the ends of a continuum. Each provides the individual with a position which has its own particular securities and defenses, so there will be a tendency for those who have traveled close to one of these poles to complete the voyage. Starting with lack of inward belief in one's role, the individual may follow the natural movement described by Park:

> It is probably no mere historical accident that the word person, in its first meaning, is a mask. It is rather a recognition of the fact that everyone is always and everywhere, more or less consciously, playing a role . . . It is in these roles that we know each other; it is in these roles that we know ourselves.[3]

In a sense, and in so far as this mask represents the conception we have formed of ourselves—the role we are striving to live up to—this mask is our truer self, the self we would like to be. In the end, our conception of our role becomes second nature and an integral part of our personality. We come into the world as individuals, achieve character, and become persons.[4]

This may be illustrated from the community life of Shetland.[5] For the last four or five years the island's tourist hotel has been owned and operated by a married couple of crofter origins. From the beginning, the owners were forced to set aside their own conceptions as to how life ought to be led, displaying in the hotel a full round of middle-class services and amenities. Lately, however, it appears that the managers have become less cynical about the performance that they stage; they themselves are becoming middle class and more and more enamored of the selves their clients impute to them.

Another illustration may be found in the raw recruit who initially follows army etiquette in order to avoid physical punishment and eventually comes to follow the rules so that his organization will not be shamed and his officers and fellow soldiers will respect him.

As suggested, the cycle of disbelief-to-belief can be followed in the other direction, starting with conviction or insecure aspiration and ending in cynicism. Professions which the public holds in religious awe often allow their recruits to follow the cycle in this direction, and often recruits follow it in this direction not because of a slow realization that they are deluding their audience—for by ordinary social standards the claims they make may be quite valid—but because they can use this cynicism as a means of insulating their inner selves from contact with the audience. And we may even expect to find typical careers of faith, with the individual starting out with one kind of involvement in the performance he is required to give, then moving back and forth several times between sincerity and cynicism before completing all the phases and turning-points of self-belief for a person of his station. Thus, students of medical schools suggest that idealistically oriented beginners in medical school typically lay aside their holy aspirations for a period of time. During the first two years the students find that their interest in medicine must be dropped that they may give all their time to the task of learning how to get through examinations. During the next two years they are too busy learning about diseases to show much concern for the persons who are diseased. It is only after their medical schooling has ended that their original ideals about medical service may be reasserted.[6]

While we can expect to find natural movement back and forth between cynicism and sincerity, still we must not rule out the kind of transitional point that can be sustained on the strength of a little self-illusion. We find that the individual may attempt to induce the audience to judge him and the situation in a particular way, and he may seek this judgment as an ultimate end in itself, and yet he may not completely believe that he deserves the valuation of self which he asks for or that the impression of reality which he fosters is valid. Another mixture of cynicism and belief is suggested in Kroeber's discussion of shamanism:

> Next there is the old question of deception. Probably most shamans or medicine men, the world over, help along with sleight-of-hand in curing and especially in exhibitions of power. This sleight-of-hand is sometimes deliberate; in many cases awareness is perhaps not deeper than foreconscious. The attitude, whether there has been repression or not, seems to be as toward a pious fraud. Field ethnographers seem quite generally convinced that even shamans who know that they add fraud nevertheless also believe in their powers, and especially in those of other shamans: they consult them when they themselves or their children are ill.[7]

FRONT

I have been using the term "performance" to refer to all the activity of an individual which occurs during a period marked by his continuous presence before a particular set of observers and which has some influence on the observers. It will be convenient to label as "front" that part of the individual's performance which regularly functions in a general and fixed fashion to define the situation for those who observe the performance. Front, then, is the expressive equipment of a standard kind intentionally or unwittingly employed by the individual during his performance. For preliminary purposes, it will be convenient to distinguish and label what seem to be the standard parts of front.

First, there is the "setting," involving furniture, decor, physical layout, and other background items which supply the scenery and stage props for the spate of human action played out before, within, or upon it. A setting tends to stay put, geographically speaking, so that those who would use a particular setting as part of their performance cannot begin their act until they have brought themselves to the appropriate place and must terminate their performance when they leave it. It is only in exceptional circumstances that the setting follows along with the performers; we see this in the funeral cortège, the civic parade, and the dream-like processions that kings and queens are made of. In the main, these exceptions seem to offer some kind of extra protection for performers who are, or who have momentarily become, highly sacred. These worthies are to be distinguished, of course, from quite profane performers of the peddler class who move their place of work between performances, often being forced to do so. In the matter of having one fixed place for one's setting, a ruler may be too sacred, a peddler too profane.

In thinking about the scenic aspects of front, we tend to think of the living room in a particular house and the small number of performers who can thoroughly identify themselves with it. We have given insufficient attention to assemblages of sign-equipment which large numbers of performers can call their own for short periods of time. It is characteristic of Western European countries, and no doubt a source of stability for them, that a large number of luxurious settings are available for hire to anyone of the right kind who can afford them. One illustration of this may be cited from a study of the higher civil servant in Britain:

> The question how far the men who rise to the top in the Civil Service take on the 'tone' or 'color' of a class other than that to which they belong by birth is delicate and difficult. The only definite

information bearing on the question is the figures relating to the membership of the great London clubs. More than three-quarters of our high administrative officials belong to one or more clubs of high status and considerable luxury, where the entrance fee might be twenty guineas or more, and the annual subscription from twelve to twenty guineas. These institutions are of the upper class (not even of the upper-middle) in their premises, their equipment, the style of living practiced there, their whole atmosphere. Though many of the members would not be described as wealthy, only a wealthy man would unaided provide for himself and his family space, food and drink, service, and other amenities of life to the same standard as he will find at the Union, the Travellers´, or the Reform.[8]

Another example can be found in the recent development of the medical profession where we find that it is increasingly important for a doctor to have access to the elaborate scientific stage provided by large hospitals, so that fewer and fewer doctors are able to feel that their setting is a place that they can lock up at night.[9]

If we take the term "setting" to refer to the scenic parts of expressive equipment, one may take the term "personal front" to refer to the other items of expressive equipment, the items that we most intimately identify with the performer himself and that we naturally expect will follow the performer wherever he goes. As part of personal front we may include: insignia of office or rank; clothing; sex, age, and racial characteristics; size and looks; posture; speech patterns; facial expressions; bodily gestures; and the like. Some of these vehicles for conveying signs, such as racial characteristics, are relatively fixed and over a span of time do not vary for the individual from one situation to another. On the other hand, some of these sign vehicles are relatively mobile or transitory, such as facial expression, and can vary during a performance from one moment to the next.

It is sometimes convenient to divide the stimuli which make up personal front into "appearance" and "manner," according to the function performed by the information that these stimuli convey. "Appearance" may be taken to refer to those stimuli which function at the time to tell us of the performer´s social statuses. These stimuli also tell us of the individual´s temporary ritual state, that is, whether he is engaging in formal social activity, work, or informal recreation, whether or not he is celebrating a new phase in the season cycle or in his life-cycle. "Manner" may be taken to refer to those stimuli which function at the time to warn us of the interaction role the performer will expect to play in the oncoming situation. Thus a haughty, aggressive manner may give the impression that the performer expects to be the one who will initiate the verbal interaction and direct its course. A meek, apologetic manner may give the impression that the performer expects to follow the lead of others, or at least that he can be led to do so.

We often expect, of course, a confirming consistency between appearance and manner; we expect that the differences in social statuses among the interactants will be expressed in some way by congruent differences in the indications that are made of an expected interaction role. This type of coherence of front may be illustrated by the following description of the procession of a mandarin through a Chinese city:

> Coming closely behind . . . the luxurious chair of the mandarin, carried by eight bearers, fills the vacant space in the street. He is mayor of the town, and for all practical purposes the supreme power in it. He is an ideal-looking official, for he is large and massive in appearance, whilst he has that stern and uncompromising look that is supposed to be necessary in any magistrate who would hope to keep his subjects in order. He has a stern and forbidding aspect, as though he were on his way to the execution ground to have some criminal decapitated. This is the kind of air that the mandarins put on when they appear in public. In the course of many years´ experience, I have never once seen any of them, from the highest to the lowest, with a smile on his face or a look of sympathy for the people whilst he was being carried officially through the streets.[10]

But, of course, appearance and manner may tend to contradict each other, as when a performer who appears to be of higher estate than his audience acts in a manner that is unexpectedly equalitarian, or intimate, or apologetic, or when a performer dressed in the garments of a high position presents himself to an individual of even higher status.

In addition to the expected consistency between appearance and manner, we expect, of course, some coherence among setting, appearance, and manner.[11] Such coherence represents an ideal type that provides us with a means of stimulating our attention to and interest in exceptions. In this the student is assisted by the Journalist, for exceptions to expected consistency among setting, appearance, and manner provide the piquancy and glamor of many careers and the salable appeal of many magazine articles. For example, a *New Yorker* profile on Roger Stevens (the real estate agent who engineered the sale of the Empire State Building) comments on the startling fact that Stevens has a small house, a meager office, and no letter-head stationery.[12]

In order to explore more fully the relations among several parts of social front, it will be convenient to consider here a significant characteristic of the information conveyed by front, namely, its abstractness and generality.

However specialized and unique a routine is, its social front, with certain exceptions, will tend to claim facts that can be equally churned and asserted of other, somewhat different routines. For example, many service occupations offer their clients a performance that is illuminated with dramatic expressions of cleanliness, modernity, competence, and integrity. While in fact these abstract standards have a different significance in different occupational performances, the observer is encouraged to stress the abstract similarities. For the observer this is a wonderful, though sometimes disastrous, convenience. Instead of having to maintain a different pattern of expectation and responsive treatment for each slightly different performer and performance, he can place the situation in a broad category around which it is easy for him to mobilize his past experience and stereotypical thinking. Observers then need only be familiar with a small and hence manageable vocabulary of fronts, and know how to respond to them, in order to orient themselves in a wide variety of situations. Thus in London the current tendency for chimney sweeps[13] and perfume clerics to wear white lab coats tends to provide the client with an understanding that the delicate tasks performed by these persons will be performed in what has become a standardized, clinical, confidential manner.

There are grounds for believing that the tendency for a large number of different acts to be presented from behind a small number of fronts is a natural development in social organization. Radcliffe-Brown has suggested this in his claim that a "descriptive" kinship system which gives each person a unique place may work for very small communities, but, as the number of persons becomes large, clan segmentation becomes necessary as a means of providing a less complicated system of identifications and treatments.[14] We see this tendency illustrated in factories, barracks, and other large social establishments. Those who organize these establishments find it impossible to provide a special cafeteria, special modes of payment, special vacation rights, and special sanitary facilities for every line and staff status category in the organization, and at the same time they feel that persons of dissimilar status ought not to be indiscriminately thrown together or classified together. As a compromise, the full range of diversity is cut at a few crucial points, and all those within a given bracket are allowed or obliged to maintain the same social front in certain situations.

In addition to the fact that different routines may employ the same front, it is to be noted that a given social front tends to become institutionalized in terms of the abstract stereotyped expectations to which it gives rise, and tends to take on a meaning and stability apart from the specific tasks which happen at the time to be performed in its name. The front becomes a "collective representation" and a fact in its own right.

When an actor takes on an established social role, usually he finds that a particular front has already been established for it. Whether his acquisition of the role was primarily motivated by a desire to perform the given task or by a desire to maintain the corresponding front, the actor will find that he must do both.

Further, if the individual takes on a task that is not only new to him but also unestablished in the society, or if he attempts to change the light in which his task is viewed, he is likely to find that there are already several well-established fronts among which he must choose. Thus, when a task is given a new front we seldom find that the front it is given is itself new.

Since fronts tend to be selected, not created, we may expect trouble to arise when those who perform a given task are forced to select a suitable front for themselves from among several quite dissimilar ones. Thus in military organizations, tasks are always developing which (it is felt) require too much authority and skill to be carried out behind the front maintained by one grade of personnel and too little authority and skill to be carried out behind the front maintained by the next grade in the hierarchy. Since there are relatively large jumps between grades, the task will come to "carry too much rank" or to carry too little.

NOTES

1. Perhaps the real crime of the confidence man is not that he takes money from his victims but that he robs all of us of the belief that middle-class manners and appearance can be sustained only by middle-class people. A disabused professional can be cynically hostile to the service relation his clients expect him to extend to them; the confidence man is in a position to hold the whole "legit" world in this contempt.

2. See Taxel, op. cit., p. 4. Harry Stack Sullivan has suggested that the tact of institutionalized performers can operate in the other direction, resulting in a kind of noblesse-oblige sanity. See his "Socio-Psychiatric Research," *American Journal of Psychiatry*, X, pp. 987–88.
   "A study of 'social recoveries' in one of our large mental hospitals some years ago taught me that patients were often released from care because they had learned not to manifest symptoms to the environing persons; in other words, had integrated enough of the personal environment to realize the prejudice opposed to their delusions. It seemed almost as if they grew wise enough to be tolerant of the imbecility surrounding them, having finally discovered that it was stupidity and not malice. They could then secure satisfaction from contact with others, while discharging a part of their cravings by psychotic means."

3. Robert Ezra Park, *Race and Culture* (Glencoe, IL: The Free Press, 1950), p. 249.

4. Ibid., p. 250.

5. Shetland Isle study.

6. H. S. Becker and Blanche Greer, "The Fate of Idealism in Medical School," *American Sociological Review*, 23, pp. 50–56.

7. A. L. Kroeber, *The Nature of Culture* (Chicago: University of Chicago Press, 1952), p. 311.

8. H. E. Dale, *The Higher Civil Service of Great Britain* (Oxford: Oxford University Press, 1941), p. 50.

9. David Solomon, "Career Contingencies of Chicago Physicians" (unpublished Ph.D. dissertation, Department of Sociology, University of Chicago, 1952), p. 74.

10. J. Macgowan, *Sidelights on Chinese Life* (Philadelphia: Lippincott, 1908), p. 187.

11. Cf. Kenneth Burke's comments on the "scene-act-agent ratio," *A Grammar of Motives* (New York: Prentice-Hall, 1945), pp. 6–9.

12. E. J. Kahn, Jr., "Closings and Openings," *The New Yorker*, February 13 and 20, 1954.

13. See Mervyn Jones, "White as a Sweep," *The New Statesman and Nation*, December 6, 1952.

14. A. R. Radcliffe-Brown, "The Social Organization of Australian Tribes," *Oceania*, I, 440.

43. INDIRECT SOCIAL RELATIONSHIPS

ALFRED SCHUTZ

Alfred Schutz (1899–1959) was an Austrian émigré scholar who, after fleeing his native land when the Nazis invaded, found a position at the New School for Social Research in New York City. From this institution, he became an important sociological exponent of a phenomenological theory derived primarily from the work of the philosopher Edmund Husserl. In this essay, Schutz describes the characteristic features of social relationships other than those that are direct or face to face. After discussing a spectrum of possible mediate relationships, such as moving from face-to-face encounters to telephone conversations and letters, he turns to a range of types of relatedness that include people one once encountered, people one expects to encounter in the future, and people one encounters not as individuals but in the roles they play (e.g., the clerk in a store). In understanding such types of relationships, Schutz argues for the centrality of the concept of anonymity.

DERIVED RELATIONSHIPS

In none of them does the self of the other become accessible to the partner as a unity. The other appears merely as a partial self, as originator of these and those acts, which I do not share in a vivid present. The shared vivid present of the We-relation presupposes co-presence of the partners. To each type of derived social relationship belongs a particular type of time perspective which is derived from the vivid present. There is a particular quasi-present in which I interpret the mere outcome of the other's communicating—the written letter, the printed book—without having participated in the ongoing process of communicating acts. There are other time dimensions in which I am connected with contemporaries I never met, or with predecessors or with successors; another, the historical time, in which I experience the actual present as the outcome of past events; and many more. All of these time perspectives can be referred to a vivid present: my own actual or former one, or the actual or former vivid present of my fellow-man with whom, in turn, I am connected in an originary or

derived vivid present and all this in the different modes of potentiality or quasi-actuality, each type having its own forms of temporal diminution and augmentation and its appurtenant style of skipping them in a direct move or "knight's move." There are furthermore the different forms of overlapping and interpenetrating of these different perspectives, their being put into and out of operation by a shift from one to the other and a transformation of one into the other, and the different types of synthesizing and combining or isolating and disentangling them. Manifold as these different time perspectives and their mutual relations are, they all originate in an intersection of *durée* and cosmic time.

In and by our social life with the natural attitude they are apprehended as integrated into one single supposedly homogeneous dimension of time which embraces not only the individual time perspectives of each of us during his wide-awake life but which is common to all of us. We shall call it the civic or *standard time*.

FROM DIRECT TO INDIRECT SOCIAL EXPERIENCE

In the face-to-face situation, directness of experience is essential, regardless of whether our apprehension of the Other is central or peripheral and regardless of how adequate our grasp of him is. I am still "Thou-oriented" even to the man standing next to me in the subway. When we speak of "pure" Thou-orientation or "pure" We-relationship, we are ordinarily using these as limiting concepts referring to the simple givenness of the Other in abstraction from any specification of the degree of concreteness involved. But we can also use these terms for the lower limits of experience obtainable in the face-to-face relationship, in other words, for the most peripheral and fleeting kind of awareness of the other person.

We make the transition from direct to indirect social experience simply by following this spectrum of decreasing vividness. The first steps beyond the realm of immediacy are marked by a decrease in the number of perceptions I have of the other person and a narrowing of the perspectives within which I view him. At one moment I am exchanging smiles with my friend, shaking hands with him, and bidding him farewell. At the next moment he is walking away. Then from the far distance I hear a faint good-by, a moment later I see a vanishing figure give a last wave, and then he is gone. It is quite impossible to fix the exact instant at which my friend left the world of my direct experience and entered the shadowy realm of those who are merely my contemporaries. As another example, imagine a face-to-face conversation, followed by a telephone call, followed by an exchange of letters, and finally messages exchanged through a third party. Here too we have a gradual progression from the world of immediately experienced social reality to the world of contemporaries. In both examples the total number of the other person's reactions open to my observation is progressively diminished until it reaches a minimum point. It is clear, then, that the world of contemporaries is itself a variant function of the face-to-face situation. They may even be spoken of as two poles between which stretches a continuous series of experiences. . . .

In everyday life there seems to be no practical problem of where the one situation breaks off and the other begins. This is because we interpret both our own behavior and that of others within contexts of meaning that far transcend the immediate here and now. For this reason, the question whether a social relationship we participate in or observe is direct or indirect seems to be an academic one. But there is a yet deeper reason for our customary indifference to this question. Even after the face-to-face situation has receded into the past and is present only in memory, it still retains its essential characteristics, modified only by an aura of pastness. Normally we do not notice that our just-departed friend, with whom we have a moment ago been interacting, perhaps affectionately or perhaps in an annoyed way, now appears to us in a quite different perspective. Far from seeming obvious, it actually seems absurd that someone we are close to has somehow become "different" now that he is out of sight, except in the trite sense that our experiences of him bear the mark of pastness. However, we must still sharply distinguish between such memories of face-to-face situations, on the one hand, and an intentional Act directed toward a mere contemporary, on the other. The recollections we have of another bear all the marks of direct experience. When I have a recollection of you, for instance, I remember you as you were in the concrete We-relationship with me. I remember you as a unique person in a concrete situation, as one who interacted with me in the mode of "mutual mirroring" described above. I remember you as a person vividly present to me with a maximum of symptoms of inner life, as one whose experiences I witnessed in the actual process of formation. I remember you as one whom I was for a time coming to know better and better. I remember you as one whose conscious life flowed in one stream with my own. I remember you as one whose consciousness was continuously changing in content. However, now that you are out of my direct experience, you are no more than my contemporary, someone who merely inhabits the same planet that I do. I am no longer in contact with the living you, but with the you of yesterday. You, indeed, have not ceased to be a living self, but you have a "new self" now; and, although I am contemporaneous with it, I am cut off from vital contact with it. Since the time we were last together, you have met with new experiences and have looked at them from new points of view. With each change of experience and outlook you have become a slightly different person. But somehow I fail to keep this in mind as I go about my daily round. I carry your image with me, and it remains the same. But then, perhaps, I hear that you have changed. I then begin to look upon you as a contemporary—not any contemporary, to be sure, but one whom I once knew intimately.

REGIONS OF ANONYMITY

We have been describing the intermediate zone between the face-to-face situation and the situation involving mere contemporaries. Let us continue our journey. As we approach the outlying world of contemporaries, our experience of others becomes more and more remote and anonymous. Entering the world of contemporaries itself, we pass through one region after another: (1) the region of those whom I once encountered face to face and could encounter again (for instance, my absent friend); then (2) comes the region of those once encountered by the person I am now talking to (for instance, your friend, whom you are promising to introduce to me); next (3) the region of those who are as yet pure contemporaries but whom I will soon meet (such as the colleague whose books I have read and whom I am now on my way to visit); then (4) those contemporaries of whose existence I know, not as concrete individuals, but as points in social space as defined by a certain function (for instance, the postal employee who will process my letter); then (5) those collective entities whose function and organization I know while not being able to name any of their members, such as the Canadian Parliament; then (6) collective entities which are by their very nature anonymous and of which I could never in principle have direct experience, such as "state" and "nation"; then (7) objective configurations of meaning which have been instituted in the world of my contemporaries and which live a kind of anonymous life of their own, such as the interstate commerce clause and the rules of French grammar; and finally (8) artifacts of any kind which bear witness to the subjective meaning-context of some unknown person. The farther out we get into the world of contemporaries, the more anonymous its inhabitants become, starting with the innermost region, where

they can almost be seen, and ending with the region where they are by definition forever inaccessible to experience.

MEDIATE EXPERIENCE OF CONTEMPORARIES

My mere contemporary (or "contemporary") . . . is one who I know coexists with me in time but whom I do not experience immediately. This kind of knowledge is, accordingly, always indirect and impersonal. I cannot call my contemporary "Thou" in the rich sense that this term has within the We-relationship. Of course, my contemporary may once have been my consociate or may yet become one, but this in no way alters his present status.

Let us now examine the ways in which the world of contemporaries is constituted and the modifications which the concepts "Other-orientation" and "social relationship" undergo in that world. These modifications are necessitated by the fact that the contemporary is only indirectly accessible and that his subjective experiences can only be known in the form of *general types* of subjective experience.

That this should be the case is easy to understand if we consider the difference between the two modes of social experience. When I encounter you face to face I know you as a person in one unique moment of experience. While this We-relationship remains unbroken, we are open and accessible to each other's intentional Acts. For a little while we grow older together, experiencing each other's flow of consciousness in a kind of intimate mutual possession.

It is quite otherwise when I experience you as my contemporary. Here you are not prepredicatively given to me at all. I do not even directly apprehend your existence (*Dasein*). My whole knowledge of you is mediate and descriptive. In this kind of knowledge your "characteristics" are established for me by inference. From such knowledge results the indirect We-relationship.

To become clear about this concept of "mediacy," let us examine two different ways in which I come to know a contemporary. The first way we have already mentioned: my knowledge is derived from a previous face-to-face encounter with the person in question. But this knowledge has since become mediate or indirect because he has moved outside the range of my direct observation. For I make inferences as to what is going on in his mind under the assumption that he remains much the same since I saw him last, although, in another sense, I know very well that he must have changed through absorbing new experiences or merely by virtue of having grown older. But, as to how he has changed, my knowledge is either indirect or nonexistent.

A second way in which I come to know a contemporary is to construct a picture of him from the past direct experience of someone with whom I am now speaking (for example, when my friend describes his brother, whom I do not know). This is a variant of the first case. Here too I apprehend the contemporary by means of a fixed concept, or type, derived ultimately from direct experience but now held invariant. But there are differences. First, I have no concrete vivid picture of my own with which to start: I must depend on what my friend tells me. Second, I have to depend on my friend´s assumption, not my own, that the contemporary he is describing has not changed.

These are the modes of constitution of all the knowledge we have of our contemporaries derived from our own past experience, direct or indirect, and of all the knowledge we have acquired from others, whether through conversation or through reading. It is clear, then, that indirect social experiences derive their original validity from the direct mode of apprehension. But the instances cited above do not exhaust all the ways by which I can come to know my contemporaries. There is the whole world of cultural objects, for instance, including everything from artifacts to institutions and conventional ways of doing things. These, too, contain within themselves implicit references to my contemporaries. I can "read" in these cultural objects the subjective experiences of others whom I do not know. Even here, however, I am making inferences on the basis of my previous direct experience of others. Let us say that the object before me is a finished product. Once, perhaps, I stood by the side of a man who was manufacturing something just like this. As I watched him work, I knew exactly what was going on in his mind. If it were not for this experience I would not know what to make of the finished product of the same kind that I now see. I might even fail to recognize

it as an artifact at all and would treat it as just another natural object, like a stone or a tree. For what we have called the general thesis of the alter ego, namely, that the Thou coexists with me and grows older with me, can only be discovered in the We-relationship. Even in this instance, therefore, I have only an indirect experience of the other self, based on past direct experiences either of a Thou as such or of a particular Thou. My face-to-face encounters with others have given me a deep prepredicative knowledge of the Thou as a self. But the Thou who is *merely* my contemporary is never experienced personally as a self and never prepredicatively. On the contrary, all experience (*Erfahrung*) of contemporaries is predicative in nature. It is formed by means of interpretive judgments involving all my knowledge of the social world, although with varying degrees of explicitness.

Now this is real Other-orientation, however indirect it may be.

THEY-ORIENTATION

Under this indirect Other-orientation we will find the usual forms of simple Other-orientation, social behavior and social interaction. Let us call all such intentional Acts directed toward contemporaries cases of "They-orientation," in contrast to the "Thou-orientation" of the intentional Acts of direct social experience.

The term "They-orientation" serves to call attention to the peculiar way in which I apprehend the conscious experiences of my contemporaries. For I apprehend them as anonymous processes. Consider the contrast to the Thou-orientation. When I am Thou-oriented, I apprehend the other person´s experiences within their setting in his stream of consciousness. I apprehend them as existing within a subjective context of meaning, as being the unique experiences of a particular person. All this is absent in the indirect social experience of the They-orientation. Here I am not aware of the ongoing flow of the Other´s consciousness. My orientation is not toward the existence (*Dasein*) of a concrete individual Thou. It is not toward any subjective experiences now being constituted in all their uniqueness in another´s mind nor toward the subjective configuration of meaning in which they are taking place. Rather, the object of my

They-orientation is my own experience (*Erfahrung*) of social reality in general, of human beings and their conscious processes as such, in abstraction from any individual setting in which they may occur. My knowledge of my contemporaries is, therefore, inferential and discursive. It stands, by its essential nature, in an objective context of meaning and only in such. It has within it no intrinsic reference to persons nor to the subjective matrix within which the experiences in question were constituted. However, it is due to this very abstraction from subjective context of meaning that they exhibit the property which we have called their "again and again" character. They are treated as typical conscious experiences of "someone" and, as such, as basically homogeneous and repeatable. The unity of the contemporary is not constituted originally in his own stream of consciousness. . . . Rather, the contemporary's unity is constituted in my own stream of consciousness, being built up out of a synthesis of my own interpretations of his experiences. This synthesis is a synthesis of recognition in which I monothetically bring within one view my own conscious experiences of someone else. Indeed, these experiences of mine may have been of more than one person. And they may have been of definite individuals or of anonymous "people." It is in this synthesis of recognition that the *personal ideal type* is constituted.

PERSONAL IDEAL TYPES

We must be quite clear as to what is happening here. The subjective meaning-context has been abandoned as a tool of interpretation. It has been replaced by a series of highly complex and systematically interrelated objective meaning-contexts. The result is that the contemporary is anonymized in direct proportion to the number and complexity of these meaning-contexts. Furthermore, the synthesis of recognition does not apprehend the unique person as he exists within his living present. Instead it pictures him as always the same and homogeneous, leaving out of account all the changes and rough edges that go along with individuality. Therefore, no matter how many people are subsumed under the ideal type, it corresponds to no one in particular. It is just this fact that justified Weber in calling it "ideal."

Let us give a few examples to clarify this point. When I mail a letter, I assume that certain contemporaries of mine, namely, postal employees, will read the address and speed the letter on its way. I am not thinking of these postal employees as individuals. I do not know them personally and never expect to. Again, as Max Weber pointed out, whenever I accept money I do so without any doubt that others, who remain quite anonymous, will accept it in turn from me. To use yet another Weberian example, if I behave in such a way as to avoid the sudden arrival of certain gentlemen with uniforms and badges, in other words, to the extent that I orient myself to the laws and to the apparatus which enforces them, here, too, I am relating myself socially to my contemporaries conceived under ideal types.

On occasions like these I am always expecting others to behave in a definite way, whether it be postal employees, someone I am paying, or the police. My social relationship to them consists in the fact that I interact with them, or perhaps merely that, in planning my actions, I keep them in mind. But they, on their part, never turn up as real people, merely as anonymous entities defined exhaustively by their functions. Only as bearers of these functions do they have any relevance for my social behavior. How they happen to feel as they cancel my letter, process my check, or examine my income tax return—these are considerations that never even enter into my mind. I just assume that there are "some people" who "do these things." Their behavior in the conduct of their duty is from my point of view defined purely through an objective context of meaning. In other words, when I am They-oriented, I have "types" for partners.

ANONYMITY OF THE CONTEMPORARY

The They-orientation is the pure form of understanding the contemporary in a predicative fashion, that is, in terms of his typical characteristics. Acts of They-orientation are, therefore, intentionally directed toward another person imagined as existing at the same time as oneself but conceived in terms of an ideal type. And just as in the cases of the Thou-orientation and the We-relationship, so also with the They-orientation can we speak of different *stages of concretization* and *actualization*.

In order to distinguish from one another the various stages of concretization of the We-relationship, we established as our criterion the degree of closeness to direct experience. We cannot use this criterion within the They-orientation. The reason is that the latter possesses by definition a high degree of remoteness from direct experience, and the other self which is its object possesses a corresponding higher degree of anonymity.

It is precisely this degree of anonymity which we now offer as the criterion for distinguishing between the different levels of concretization and actualization that occur in the They-orientation. The more anonymous the personal ideal type applied in the They-orientation, the greater is the use made of objective meaning-contexts instead of subjective ones, and likewise, we shall find, the more are lower-level personal ideal types and objective meaning-contexts pregiven. (The latter have in turn been derived from other stages of concretization of the They-orientation.)

Let us get clear as to just what we mean by the anonymity of the ideal type in the world of contemporaries. The pure Thou-orientation consists of mere awareness of the existence of the other person, leaving aside all questions concerning the characteristics of that person. On the other hand, the pure They-orientation is based on the presupposition of such characteristics in the form of a type. Since these characteristics are genuinely typical, they can in principle be presupposed again and again. Of course, whenever I posit such typical characteristics, I assume that they now exist or did once exist. However, this does not mean that I am thinking of them as existing in a particular person in a particular time and place. The contemporary alter ego is therefore anonymous in the sense that its existence is only the individuation of a type, an individuation which is merely supposable or possible. Now since the very existence of my contemporary is always less than certain, any attempt on my part to reach out to him or influence him may fall short of its mark, and, of course, I am aware of this fact.

The concept which we have been analyzing is the concept of the anonymity of the partner in the world of contemporaries. It is crucial to the understanding of the nature of the indirect social relationship.

44. RULES OF CONVERSATIONAL SEQUENCE[1]

HARVEY SACKS

Harvey Sacks (1935–1975) studied sociology with Erving Goffman at Berkeley but is generally known as one of the earliest ethnomethodologists, and thus he is typically associated more with the work of Harold Garfinkel than with that of Goffman. This essay, put together posthumously by former students from Sacks´ lecture notes, is a good example of the attention ethnomethodologists pay to conversational analysis. In this particular case, Sacks is dissecting telephone conversations he recorded at a psychiatric hospital between staff and persons calling from outside the facility. What he is attempting to get at—in a fairly provisional way—are the rules or "ethnomethods" people use to achieve orderly and stable interactional exchanges.

I´ll start off by giving some quotations.

(1) *A:* Hello
     B: Hello

(2) *A:* This is Mr Smith may I help you
     B: Yes, this is Mr Brown

(3) *A:* This is Mr Smith may I help you
     B: I can´t hear you.
     A: This is Mr *Smith*.
     B: Smith.

These are some first exchanges in telephone conversations I collected at an emergency psychiatric hospital. They are occurring between persons who haven´t talked to each other before. One of them, A, is a staff member of this psychiatric hospital. B can be either somebody calling about themselves, that is to say in trouble in one way or another, or somebody calling about somebody else.

I have a large collection of these conversations, and I got started looking at these first exchanges as follows. A series of persons who called this place would not give their names. The hospital´s concern was, can anything be done about it? One question I wanted to address

was, where in the course of the conversation could you tell that somebody would not give their name? So I began to look at the materials. It was in fact on the basis of that question that I began to try to deal in detail with conversations.

I found something that struck me as fairly interesting quite early. And that was that if the staff member used "This is Mr Smith may I help you" as their opening line, then overwhelmingly, any answer other than "Yes, this is Mr Brown" (for example, "I can´t hear you," "I don´t know," "How do you spell your name?") meant that you would have serious trouble getting the caller´s name, if you got the name at all.

I´m going to show some of the ways that I´ve been developing of analyzing stuff like this. There will be series of ways fitted to each other, as though one were constructing a multi-dimensional jigsaw puzzle. One or another piece can be isolated and studied, and also the various pieces can be studied as to how they fit together. I´ll be focussing on a variety of things, starting off with what I´ll call `rules of conversational sequence.´

Looking at the first exchange compared to the second, we can be struck by two things. First of all,

From *Lectures on Conversation*, vol. 1, pp. 3–11, by Harvey Sacks. Copyright © 1992, 1995, The Estate of Harvey Sacks. Reprinted by permission of Blackwell Publishers. ✦

there seems to be a fit between what the first person who speaks uses as their greeting, and what the person who is given that greeting returns. So that if A says "Hello," then B tends to say "Hello." If A says "This is Mr Smith may I help you," B tends to say "Yes, this is Mr Brown." We can say there´s a procedural rule there, that a person who speaks first in a telephone conversation can choose their form of address, and in choosing their form of address they can thereby choose the form of address the other uses.

By ´form´ I mean in part that the exchanges occur as ´units.´ That is, "Hello" "Hello" is a unit, and "This is Mr Smith may I help you" "Yes, this is Mr Brown," is a unit. They come in pairs. Saying "This is Mr Smith may I help you" thereby provides a ´slot´ to the other wherein they properly would answer "Yes, this is Mr Brown." The procedural rule would describe the occurrences in the first two exchanges. It won´t describe the third exchange, but we´ll come to see what is involved in such materials.

Secondly, if it is so that there is a rule that the person who goes first can choose their form of address and thereby choose the other´s, then for the unit, "This is Mr Smith, may I help you" "Yes, this is Mr Brown," if a person uses "This is Mr Smith . . ." they have a way of asking for the other´s name—without, however, asking the question, "What is your name?" And there is a difference between saying "This is Mr Smith may I help you"—thereby providing a slot to the other wherein they properly would answer "Yes, this is Mr Brown"—and asking the question "What is your name?" at some point in the conversation. They are very different phenomena.

For one, in almost all of the cases where the person doesn´t give their name originally, then at some point in the conversation they´re asked for their name. One way of asking is just the question "Would you give me your name?" To that, there are alternative returns, including "No" and "Why?" If a caller says "Why?" the staff member may say something like, "I want to have something to call you" or "It´s just for our records." If a caller says "No," then the staff member says "Why?" and may get something like "I´m not ready to do that" or "I´m ashamed."

Now, I´ll consider many times the use of "Why?" What I want to say about it just to begin with, is that

what one does with "Why?" is to propose about some action that it is an ´accountable action.´ That is to say, "Why?" is a way of asking for an account. Accounts are most extraordinary. And the use of accounts and the use of requests for accounts are very highly regulated phenomena. We can begin to cut into these regularities by looking at what happens when "May I have your name?" is followed by "Why?" Then you get an account; for example, "I need something to call you." The other might then say, "I don´t mind." Or you might get an account, "It´s just for our records." To which the other might say, "Well I´m not sure I want to do anything with you, I just want to find out what you do"— so that the records are not relevant.

What we can see is that there are ways that accounts seem to be dealable with. If a person offers an account, which they take it provides for the action in question being done—for example, the caller´s name being given—then if the other can show that the interest of that account can be satisfied without the name being given, the name doesn´t have to be given. That is, if the account is to control the action, then if you can find a way that the account controls the alternative action than it proposed to control, you can use it that way.

It seems to be quite important, then, who it is that offers the account. Because the task of the person who is offered the account can then be to, in some way, counter it. Where, alternatively, persons who offer an account seem to feel that they´re somehow committed to it, and if it turns out to be, for example, inadequate, then they have to stand by it.

The fact that you could use questions—like "Why?"—to generate accounts, and then use accounts to control activities, can be marked down as, I think, one of the greatest discoveries in Western civilization. It may well be that that is what Socrates discovered. With his dialectic he found a set of procedures by which this thing, which was not used systematically, could become a systematic device. Socrates will constantly ask "Why?," there will be an answer, and he´ll go on to show that that can´t be the answer. And that persons were terribly pained to go through this whole business is clear enough from the Dialogues. And it´s also clear in our own experiences. And in the materials I´ll present.

We see, then, one clear difference between providing a slot for a name, and asking for a name. Asking for a name tends to generate accounts and counters. By providing a slot for a name, those activities do not arise.

We can also notice that, as a way of asking for the other's name, "This is Mr Smith . . ." is, in the first place, not an accountable action. By that I mean to say, it's not required that staff members use it and they don't always use it, but when they do, the caller doesn't ask why. "This is Mr Smith . . ." gets its character as a non-accountable action simply by virtue of the fact that this is a place where, routinely, two persons speak who haven't met. In such places the person who speaks first can use that object. And we could say about that kind of item that the matters discriminated by its proper use are very restricted. That is to say, a call is made; the only issue is that two persons are speaking who presumably haven't met, and this object can be used.

Furthermore, the matters are discriminated in different terms than those which the agency is constructed for. That is, they are discriminated in terms of `two people who haven't met' rather than, for example, that an agency staff member is speaking to someone calling the agency for help. And where one has some organization of activities which sets out to do some task—and in this case it's important for the agency to get names—then if you find a device which discriminates in such a restricted fashion, you can use that device to do tasks for you.

Now, given the fact that such a greeting as "This is Mr Smith . . ." provides for the other giving his own name as an answer, one can see what the advantage of "Hello" is for someone who doesn't want to give their name. And I found in the first instance that while sometimes the staff members use "Hello" as their opening line, if it ever occurred that the persons calling the agency spoke first, they always said "Hello."

Persons calling could come to speak first because at this agency, caller and staff member are connected by an operator. The operator says "Go ahead please" and now the two parties are on an open line, and one can start talking or the other can start talking. This stands in contrast to, for example, calling someone's home. There, the rights are clearly assigned; the person who answers the phone speaks first. If they speak first, they have the right to choose their form. If they have the right to choose their form, they have the right thereby to choose the other's. Here, where the rights are not clearly assigned, the caller could move to speak first and thereby choose the form. And when callers to this agency speak first, the form they choose is the unit "Hello" "Hello." Since such a unit involves no exchange of names, they can speak without giving their name and be going about things in a perfectly appropriate way.

Now, there are variant returns to "This is Mr Smith may I help you?" one of which is in our set of three exchanges: "I can't hear you." I want to talk of that as an `occasionally usable' device. That is to say, there doesn't have to be a particular sort of thing preceding it; it can come at any place in a conversation. Here is one from the middle of a conversation, from a different bunch of materials.

> A: Hey you got a cigarette Axum. I ain't got, I ain't got a good cigarette, and I can't roll one right now. Think you can afford it maybe?
> B: I am not here to support your habits.
> A: Huh? My helplessness?
> B: I am not responsible for supporting your habits ( )
> A: My habits ((laughing))

Our third exchange from the psychiatric hospital has the device used at the beginning of the conversation,

> A: This is Mr Smith may I help you
> B: I can't hear you.
> A: This is Mr *Smith*.
> B: Smith.

What kind of a device is it? What you can see is this. When you say "I can't hear you," you provide that the other person can repeat what they said. Now what does that repetition do for you? Imagine you're in a game. One of the questions relevant to the game would be, is there a way in that game of skipping a move? It seems that something like "I can't hear you" can do such a job. If you introduce it you provide for the other to do some version of a repeat following which you yourself can repeat. And then it's the other's turn to talk again. What we find is that the slot where the return would go— your name in return to "This is Mr Smith . . ."—never occurs.

It is not simply that the caller ignores what they properly ought to do, but something rather more exquisite. That is, they have ways of providing that the place where the return name fits is never opened. So that their name is not absent. Their name would be absent if they just went ahead and talked. But that very rarely occurs. The rules of etiquette—if you want to call them that, though we take etiquette to be something very light and uninteresting and to be breached as you please—seem to be quite strong. Persons will use ways to not ignore what they properly ought to do by providing that the place for them to do it is never opened.

I hope it can also be seen that a device like "I can't hear you"—the repeat device, providing for a repetition of the thing that was first said, which is then repeated by the person who said "I can't hear you"—is not necessarily designed for skipping a move. It is not specific to providing a way of keeping in the conversation and behaving properly while not giving one's name. It can be used for other purposes and do other tasks, and it can be used with other items. That's why I talk about it as an `occasional device.´ But where that is what one is trying to do, it's a rather neat device.

Let me turn now to a consideration which deals with a variant return to "May I help you?" That is, not "Yes . . ." but "I don't know." I'll show a rather elaborate exchange in which the staff member opens with a version of "This is Mr Smith may I help you" but the combination gets split. The name is dealt with, and when the "can I help you" is offered, it occurs in such a way that it can be answered independent of the name.[2]

Op: Go ahead please
A: This is Mr Smith (*B*: Hello) of the Emergency Psychiatric Center can I help you.
B: Hello?
A: Hello
B: I can't hear you.
A: I see. Can you hear me, now?
B: Barely. Where are you, in the womb?
A: Where are you calling from?
B: Hollywood.
A: Hollywood.
B: I can hear you a little better.

A: Okay. Uh I was saying my name is Smith and I'm with the Emergency Psychiatric Center.
B: Your name is what?
A: Smith.
B: Smith?
A: Yes.
A: Can I help you?
B: I don't know hhhch. . .I hope you can.
A: Uh hah . . . Tell me about your problems.
B: I uh . . . Now that you're here I'm embarrassed to talk about it. I don't want you telling me I'm emotionally immature cause I know I am.

I was very puzzled by "I don't know" in return to "May I help you." I couldn't figure out what they were doing with it. And the reason I was puzzled was that having listened to so many of these things and having been through the scene so many times, I heard "May I help you" as something like an idiom. I'm going to call these idiom-like things `composites.´ That means you hear the whole thing as a form, a single unit. And as a single unit, it has a proper return. As a composite, "May I help you" is a piece of etiquette; a way of introducing oneself as someone who is in the business of helping somebody, the answer to which is "Yes" and then some statement of what it is one wants. We can consider this item in terms of what I'll call the `base environment´ of its use.

By `base environment´ I mean, if you go into a department store, somebody is liable to come up to you and say "May I help you." And in business-type phone calls this item is routinely used. And if you come into a place and you don't know what it's like, and somebody comes up to you and uses such an item, that's one way of informing you what kind of a place it is. So, if a new institution is being set up, then there are available in the society whole sets of ways that persons go about beginning conversations, and one could, for example, adopt one or another of a series of them as the ones that are going to be used in this place.

Now the thing about at least some composites is that they can be heard not only as composites, but as ordinary sentences, which we could call `constructives,´ which are understood by taking the pieces and adding them up in some way. As a composite, "May I help you" is a piece of etiquette, a signal for stating your request—what you want to be helped with. Alternatively, as a constructive, "May I help you" is a question. If one hears it as a question, the piece of etiquette and its work hasn't come up, and "I don't know" is a perfectly proper answer.

Further, "I don't know" may be locating a problem which "May I help you" is designed, in the first place, to avoid. In its base environment, for example a department store, it's pretty much the case that for a customer, the question of whether some person "can help" is a matter of the department store having made them the person who does that. That is to say, lots of things, like telling you whether you can find lingerie in a certain size, is something anybody can do, and as long as the department store says this person is going to do it, that's enough. But we're dealing with a psychiatric hospital. In a department store, being selected to do a job and having credentials to do it are essentially the same thing. In a psychiatric hospital and lots of other places, however, they are very different things. That is, whether somebody can help you if you have a mental disorder, is not solved or is not even presumptively solved by the fact that they've been selected by somebody to do that job. The way it's solved in this society is by reference to such things as having been trained in a particular fashion, having gotten degrees, having passed Board examinations, etc.

Now, in the base environment of the use of "May I help you?" there is, as I say, no difference essentially between having credentials and being selected. If one can formulate the matter in a psychiatric hospital such that those things come on as being the same, then one needn't start off by producing one's credentials at the beginning of the conversation. And in my materials, again and again, when "May I help you" is used the person calling says "Yes" and begins to state their troubles.

As a general matter, then, one can begin to look for kinds of objects that have a base environment, that, when they get used in that environment perform a rather simple task, but that can be used in quite different environments to do quite other tasks. So, a matter like `credentials´ can be handled by this "May I help you" device. There will be lots of other devices which have a base environment, which do some other task in some other environment.

Before moving off of "May I help you" I want to mention one other thing about it. If the base environment is something like a department store, then, when it's used in other places—for example, a psychiatric hospital—one of the pieces of information it seems to convey is that whatever it is you propose to do, you do routinely. To whomsoever that calls. That is, it's heard as standardized utterance. How is that relevant? It can be relevant in alternative ways. First of all, it can be a very reassuring thing to hear. Some persons feel that they have troubles, and they don't know if anybody else has those troubles; or, if others do have those troubles, whether anybody knows about them. If someone knows about them, then there may be a known solution to them. Also and relatedly, a lot of troubles—like mental diseases—are things that persons feel very ambivalent about. That is, they're not sure whether it's some defect of their character, or something else. That, in part, is why they're hesitant to talk about it. And it seems that one of the ways one begins to tell people that they can talk, that you know what they have and that you routinely deal with such matters, is to use manifestly organizational talk.

"May I help you," then, can be a reassuring way to begin. It can alternatively be something else. Consider the exchange I just showed, in which such standardized utterances as "May I help you" and "Tell me about your problems" are used.

A: Can I help you?

B: I don't know hhheh. . . I hope you can

A: Uh hah . . . Tell me about your problems

B: I uh . . . Now that you're here I'm embarrassed to talk about it. I don't want you telling me I'm emotionally immature `cause I know I am

That is, the use of standardized, manifestly organizational talk can provide for the person calling that they're going to get routine treatment. But `routine,´ for them, may not be such a happy thing. Because, for example, they've been through it before. But they may have gone through it, as psychiatrists would say, part way. For example, they were in analysis for three years and ran out of money, or the psychiatrist wouldn't keep them on, or they didn't want to stay.

Part way, they may have come to some point in the analysis where they `knew what was wrong with them.´ That is, they knew the diagnostic term. But that diagnostic term may have had a lay affiliate. By that I mean, if a psychiatrist says you´re regressed, it´s a technical term. But `regressed´ is also a lay term, and as a lay term it doesn´t have a great deal of attractiveness. If one finds oneself living with a lay understanding of such a term, where the term is not a very nice thing to have in its lay sense, then when you hear someone using such an item as "May I help you," you can hear that some procedure will be gone through, the upshot of which will be the discovery of what you `already know´—the knowing of which doesn´t do you any good.

Related to that are such things as, some people seem to feel very much disturbed about the fact that their relationship to a psychiatrist or to other doctors is monetary. What they want, they say, is a personal solution. Ask them what they want, "Well, that you don´t have to pay for it." When they hear "May I help you," they hear `a professional.´ But they feel that the way you get cured is by getting an affiliation to somebody which is like the affiliations that they failed to get in their lives. That is, they may already have come to learn from some other psychiatrist that the failure of love by their parents is the cause of their troubles. Then, what they come to see is that they need the love of somebody else. And they can´t get that from a therapist. Because as soon as they don´t pay, that´s the end of the relationship.

Now let me just make a few general points. Clearly enough, things like "This is Mr Smith," "May I help you?" and "I can´t hear you" are social objects. And if you begin to look at what they do, you can see that they, and things like them, provide the makings of activities. You assemble activities by using these things. And now when you, or I, or sociologists, watching people do things, engage in trying to find out what they do and how they do it, one fix which can be used is: Of the enormous range of activities that people do, all of them are done with something. Someone says "This is Mr Smith" and the other supplies his own name. Someone says "May I help you" and the other states his business. Someone says "Huh?" or "What did you say?" or "I can´t hear you," and then the thing said before gets repeated.

What we want then to find out is, can we first of all construct the objects that get used to make up ranges of activities, and then see how it is those objects do get used.

Some of these objects can be used for whole ranges of activities, where for different ones a variety of the properties of those objects will get employed. And we begin to see alternative properties of those objects. That´s one way we can go about beginning to collect the alternative methods that persons use in going about doing whatever they have to do. And we can see that these methods will be reproducible descriptions in the sense that any scientific description might be, such that the natural occurrences that we´re describing can yield abstract or general phenomena which need not rely on statistical observability for their abstractness or generality.

There was a very classical argument that it would not be that way; that singular events were singular events, given a historian´s sort of argument, that they just happen and they get more or less accidentally thrown together. But if we could find that there are analytically hard ways of describing these things—where, that is, we´re talking about objects that can be found elsewhere, that get placed, that have ways of being used; that are abstract objects which get used on singular occasions and describe singular courses of activity—then that´s something which is exceedingly non-trivial to know.

One final note. When people start to analyze social phenomena, if it looks like things occur with the sort of immediacy we find in some of these exchanges, then, if you have to make an elaborate analysis of it—that is to say, show that they did something as involved as some of the things I have proposed—then you figure that they couldn´t have thought that fast. I want to suggest that you have to forget that completely. Don´t worry about how fast they´re thinking. First of all, don´t worry about whether they´re `thinking.´ Just try to come to terms with how it is that the thing comes off. Because you´ll find that they can do these things. Just take any other area of natural science and see, for example, how fast molecules do things. And they don´t have very good brains. So just let the materials fall as they may. Look to see how it is that persons go about producing what they do produce.

NOTES

1. A combination of Fall 1964, tape 1, side 2 and tape 2, side 1, with brief extract from Winter 1965, lecture (1)—the parentheses indicate that the original transcripts were unnumbered, the current numbering likely but not certain—pp. 1 and 11–12 (transcriber unknown) and Spring 1965 (´64–´65), lecture 3, pp. 6–7 (transcriber unknown). . . .

2. The fragment of data is reproduced pretty much as Sacks transcribed it, preserving his attempts to deal with simultaneous talk (i.e., *A*: This is Mr Smith (*B*: Hello) of the Emergency Psychiatric Center) and silence (e.g., *B*: I uh . . . Now that you´re here. . . .). . . .

45. STUDIES OF THE ROUTINE GROUNDS
OF EVERYDAY ACTIVITIES

HAROLD GARFINKEL

Harold Garfinkel (1929–2011) coined the term "ethnomethodology" and offered its initial portrayal as a distinctive theory school in his influential 1967 book, *Studies in Ethnomethodology*. The term refers to the methods people use to make sense of and find ways to act in the routine situations of their everyday lives. As Garfinkel notes, he was significantly influenced by Alfred Schutz, so it is not surprising that phenomenology and ethnomethodology bear a family resemblance. In his own unique way, and with his own distinctive terminology, Garfinkel urges sociologists to refrain from imposing their interpretive frames to explain the subjects of their empirical research. Instead, as an alternative he calls for attentiveness to the structured ways in which the subjects themselves use what is typically referred to as "common sense." In this particular excerpt, he stresses the importance of attempting to make visible those routine aspects of everyday life that are generally taken for granted, and thus are not really noticed.

THE PROBLEM

For Kant the moral order "within" was an awesome mystery; for sociologists the moral order "without" is a technical mystery. From the point of view of sociological theory the moral order consists of the rule governed activities of everyday life. A society´s members encounter and know the moral order as perceivedly normal courses of action—familiar scenes of everyday affairs, the world of daily life known in common with others and with others taken for granted.

They refer to this world as the "natural facts of life" which for members, are through and through moral facts of life. For members not only are matters so about familiar scenes, but they are so because it is morally right or wrong that they are so. Familiar scenes of everyday activities, treated by members as the "natural facts of life," are massive facts of the members´ daily existence both as a real world and as the product of activities in a real world. They furnish the "fix," the "this is it" to which the waking state returns one, and are the points of departure and return for every modification of the world of daily life that is achieved in play, dreaming, trance, theater, scientific theorizing, or high ceremony.

In every discipline, humanistic or scientific, the familiar common sense world of everyday life is a matter of abiding interest. In the social sciences, and in sociology particularly, it is a matter of essential preoccupation. It makes up sociology´s problematic subject matter, enters the very constitution of the sociological attitude, and exercises an odd and obstinate sovereignty over sociologists´ claims to adequate explanation.

Despite the topic´s centrality, an immense literature contains little data and few methods with which the essential features of socially recognized "familiar scenes" may be detected and related to dimensions of social organization. Although sociologists take socially structured scenes of everyday life as a point of departure they rarely see,[1] as a task of sociological inquiry in its

---

own right, the general question of how any such common sense world is possible. Instead, the possibility of the everyday world is either settled by theoretical representation or merely assumed. As a topic and methodological ground for sociological inquiries, the definition of the common sense world of everyday life, though it is appropriately a project of sociological inquiry, has been neglected. My purposes in this paper are to demonstrate the essential relevance, to sociological inquiries, of a concern for common sense activities as a topic of inquiry in its own right and, by reporting a series of studies, to urge its "rediscovery."

MAKING COMMONPLACE SCENES VISIBLE

In accounting for the stable features of everyday activities sociologists commonly select familiar settings such as familial households or work places and ask for the variables that contribute to their stable features. Just as commonly, one set of considerations are unexamined: the socially standardized and standardizing, "seen but unnoticed," expected, background features of everyday scenes. The member of the society uses background expectancies as a scheme of interpretation. With their use actual appearances are for him recognizable and intelligible as the appearances-of-familiar-events. Demonstrably he is responsive to this background, while at the same time he is at a loss to tell us specifically of what the expectancies consist. When we ask him about them he has little or nothing to say.

For these background expectancies to come into view one must either be a stranger to the "life as usual" character of everyday scenes, or become estranged from them. As Alfred Schutz pointed out, a "special motive" is required to make them problematic. In the sociologists´ case this "special motive" consists in the programmatic task of treating a societal member´s practical circumstances, which include from the member´s point of view the morally necessary character of many of its background features, as matters of theoretic interest. The seen but unnoticed backgrounds of everyday activities are made visible and are described from a perspective in which persons live out the lives they do, have the children they do, feel the feelings, think the thoughts, enter

the relationships they do, all in order to permit the sociologist to solve his theoretical problems.

Almost alone among sociological theorists, the late Alfred Schutz, in a series of classical studies[2] of the constitutive phenomenology of the world of everyday life, described many of these seen but unnoticed background expectancies. He called them the "attitude of daily life." He referred to their scenic attributions as the "world known in common and taken for granted." Schutz´ fundamental work makes it possible to pursue further the tasks of clarifying their nature and operation, of relating them to the processes of concerted actions, and assigning them their place in an empirically imaginable society.

The studies reported in this paper attempt to detect some expectancies that lend commonplace scenes their familiar, life-as-usual character, and to relate these to the stable social structures of everyday activities. Procedurally it is my preference to start with familiar scenes and ask what can be done to make trouble. The operations that one would have to perform in order to multiply the senseless features of perceived environments; to produce and sustain bewilderment, consternation, and confusion; to produce the socially structured affects of anxiety, shame, guilt, and indignation; and to produce disorganized interaction should tell us something about how the structures of everyday activities are ordinarily and routinely produced and maintained.[3]

A word of reservation. Despite their procedural emphasis, my studies are not properly speaking experimental. They are demonstrations, designed, in Herbert Spiegelberg´s phrase, as "aids to a sluggish imagination." I have found that they produce reflections through which the strangeness of an obstinately familiar world can be detected.

SOME ESSENTIAL FEATURES OF COMMON UNDERSTANDINGS

Various considerations dictate that common understandings cannot possibly consist of a measured amount of shared agreement among persons on certain topics. Even if the topics are limited in number and scope and every practical difficulty of assessment is forgiven, the notion that we are dealing with an amount of shared agreement remains essentially incorrect. This may be demonstrated as follows.

Students were asked to report common conversations by writing on the left side of a sheet what the parties actually said and on the right side what they and their partners understood that they were talking about. A student reported the following colloquy between himself and his wife. (See Text Box.)

An examination of the colloquy reveals the following. (a) There were many matters that the partners understood they were talking about that they did not mention. (b) Many matters that the partners understood were understood on the basis not only of what was actually said but what was left unspoken. (c) Many matters were understood through a process of attending to the temporal series of utterances as documentary evidences of a developing conversation rather than as a string of terms. (d) Matters that the two understood in common were understood only in and through a course of understanding work that consisted of treating an actual linguistic event as "the document of," as "pointing to," as standing on behalf of an underlying pattern of matters that each already supposed to be the matters that the person, by his speaking, could be telling the other about. The underlying pattern was not only derived from a course of individual documentary evidences but the documentary evidences in their turn were interpreted on the basis of "what was known" and anticipatorily knowable about the underlying patterns.[4] Each was used to elaborate the other. (e) In attending to the utterances as events-in-the-conversation each party made references to the biography and prospects of the present interaction which each used and attributed to the other as a common scheme of interpretation and expression. (f) Each waited for something more to be said in order to hear what had previously been talked about, and each seemed willing to wait.

Common understandings would consist of a measured amount of shared agreement if the common understandings consisted of events coordinated with the successive positions of the hands of the clock, i.e., of events in standard time. The foregoing results, because they deal with the exchanges of the colloquy as events-in-a-conversation, urge that one more time parameter, at least, is required: the role of time as it is constitutive of "the matter talked about" as a developing and developed event over the course of action that produced it, as both the process and product were known *from within* this development by both parties, each for himself as well as on behalf of the other.

The colloquy reveals additional features. (1) Many of its expressions are such that their sense cannot be decided by an auditor unless he knows or assumes something about the biography and the purposes of the speaker, the circumstances of the utterance, the previous course of the conversation, or the particular

HUSBAND:	Dana succeeded in putting a penny in a parking meter today without being picked up.	This afternoon as I was bringing Dana, our four-year-old son, home from the nursery school, he succeeded in reaching high enough to put a penny in a parking meter when we parked in a meter parking zone, whereas before he has always had to be picked up to reach that high.
WIFE:	Did you take him to the record store?	Since he put a penny in a meter that means that you stopped while he was with you. I know that you stopped at the record store either on the way to get him or on the way back. Was it on the way back, so that he was with you or did you stop there on the way to get him and somewhere else on the way back?
HUSBAND:	No, to the shoe repair shop.	No, I stopped at the record store on the way to get him and stopped at the shoe repair shop on the way home when he was with me.
WIFE:	What for?	I know of one reason why you might have stopped at the shoe repair shop. Why did you in fact?
HUSBAND:	I got some new shoe laces for my shoes.	As you will remember I broke a shoe lace on one of my brown oxfords the other day so I stopped to get some new laces,
WIFE:	Your loafers need new heels badly.	Something else you could have gotten that I was thinking of. You could have taken in your black loafers which need heels badly. You'd better get them taken care of pretty soon.

relationship of actual or potential interaction that exists between user and auditor. The expressions do not have a sense that remains identical through the changing occasions of their use. (2) The events that were talked about were specifically vague. Not only do they not frame a clearly restricted set of possible determinations but the depicted events include as their essentially intended and sanctioned features an accompanying "fringe" of determinations that are open with respect to internal relationships, relationships to other events, and relationships to retrospective and prospective possibilities. (3) For the sensible character of an expression, upon its occurrence each of the conversationalists as auditor of his own as well as the other's productions had to assume as of any present accomplished point in the exchange that by waiting for what he or the other person might have said at a later time the present significance of what had already been said would have been clarified. Thus many expressions had the property of being progressively realized and realizable through the further course of the conversation. (4) It hardly needs to be pointed out that the sense of the expressions depended upon where the expression occurred in serial order, the expressive character of the terms that comprised it, and the importance to the conversationalists of the events depicted.

These properties of common understandings stand in contrast to the features they would have if we disregarded their temporally constituted character and treated them instead as precoded entries on a memory drum, to be consulted as a definite set of alternative meanings from among which one was to select, under predecided conditions that specified in which of some set of alternative ways one was to understand the situation upon the occasion that the necessity for a decision arose. The latter properties are those of strict rational discourse as these are idealized in the rules that define an adequate logical proof.

For the purposes of *conducting their everyday affairs* persons refuse to permit each other to understand "what they are really talking about" in this way. The anticipation that persons *will* understand, the occasionality of expressions, the specific vagueness of references, the retrospective-prospective sense of a present occurrence, waiting for something later in order to see what was meant before, are sanctioned properties of common discourse. They furnish a background of seen but unnoticed features of common discourse whereby actual utterances are recognized as events of common, reasonable, understandable, plain talk. Persons require these properties of discourse as conditions under which they are themselves entitled and entitle others to claim that they know what they are talking about, and that what they are saying is understandable and ought to be understood. In short, their seen but unnoticed presence is used to entitle persons to conduct their common conversational affairs without interference. Departures from such usages call forth immediate attempts to restore a right state of affairs.

NOTES

1. The work of Alfred Schutz, cited in endnote 2, is a magnificent exception. Readers who are acquainted with his writings will recognize how heavily this paper is indebted to him.
2. Alfred Schutz, *Der Sinnhafte Aufbau Der Sozialen Welt* (Wien: Verlag von Julius Springer, 1932); *Collected Papers I: The Problem of Social Reality*, ed. Maurice Natanson (The Hague: Martinus Nijhoff, 1962), *Collected Papers II: Studies in Social Theory*, ed. Arvid Broderson (The Hague: Martinus Nijhoff, 1964); *Collected Papers III: Studies in Phenomenological Philosophy*, ed. I. Schutz (The Hague: Martinus Nijhoff, 1966).
3. Obversely, a knowledge of how the structures of everyday activities are routinely produced should permit us to tell how we might proceed for the effective production of desired disturbances.
4. Karl Mannheim, in his essay "On the Interpretation of `Weltanschauung´ " (in *Essays on the Sociology of Knowledge*, trans. and ed. Paul Kecskemeti [New York: Oxford University Press, 1952], pp. 33–83), referred to this work as the "documentary method of interpretation.". . .

SECTION IX

1. What exactly does Blumer have in mind when he contends that we ought to view "society as symbolic interaction?"
2. From Blumer´s symbolic interactionist perspective, what is the place of human agency and how should we understand social structure?
3. Describe in your own words what Goffman means by "front," and provide an example from your own life.
4. What does sincerity indicate about a person´s presentation of self?
5. Describe the key factors, according to Schutz, that distinguish indirect social relations from direct ones.
6. Telephone conversations are a mundane part of all of our lives. Why is Sacks interested in turn taking in such conversations? What does he think this phenomenon reveals about the way people confront their everyday lives?
7. How does Garfinkel suggest we ought to view what most would describe as the use of common sense in dealing with life´s daily routines?

X. EXCHANGE THEORY AND RATIONAL CHOICE THEORY

46. SOCIAL BEHAVIOR AS EXCHANGE

GEORGE C. HOMANS

George C. Homans (1910–1989), a Boston Brahmin, was one of the key figures associated with the development of modern exchange theory, which he intended as an alternative to the grand sociological theorizing of his Harvard colleague, Talcott Parsons. Homans argues that sociological theory ought to be grounded in neoclassical economic theory and in behaviorist psychology, associated with figures such as B. F. Skinner. As such he advocates a form of psychological reductionism. In this essay, published in 1958, Homans sketches an outline of an exchange paradigm, which in its most elementary form seeks to explain social behavior in terms of costs and rewards. He sees social exchange as offering sociology a set of general propositions that, in explaining human behavior, constitute an essential starting point for examining issues related to social structure.

THE PROBLEMS OF SMALL-GROUP RESEARCH

This essay will hope to honor the memory of George Simmel in two different ways. So far as it pretends to be suggestive rather than conclusive, its tone will be Simmel´s; and its subject, too, will be one of his. Because Simmel, in essays such as those on sociability, games, coquetry, and conversation, was an analyst of elementary social behavior, we call him an ancestor of what is known today as small-group research. For what we are really studying in small groups is elementary social behavior: what happens when two or three persons are in a position to influence one another, the sort of thing of which those massive structures called "classes," "firms," "communities," and "societies" must ultimately be composed.

As I survey small-group research today, I feel that, apart from just keeping on with it, three sorts of things need to be done. The first is to show the relation between the results of experimental work done under laboratory conditions and the results of *quasi*-anthropological field research on what those of us who do it are pleased to call "real-life" groups in industry and elsewhere. If the experimental work has anything to do with real life—and I am persuaded that it has everything to do—its propositions cannot be inconsistent with those discovered through the field work. But the consistency has not yet been demonstrated in any systematic way.

George Homans, "Social Behavior as Exchange." *The American Journal of Sociology*, 63:6 (1958), pp. 597–606. Copyright © 1958 by The University of Chicago. Reprinted with permission of The University of Chicago Press. ✦

The second job is to pull together in some set of general propositions the actual results from the laboratory and from the field, of work on small groups—propositions that at least sum up, to an approximation, what happens in elementary social behavior, even though we may not be able to explain why the propositions should take the form they do. A great amount of work has been done, and more appears every day, but what it all amounts to in the shape of a set of propositions from which, under specified conditions, many of the observational results might be derived, is not at all clear—and yet to state such a set is the first aim of science.

The third job is to begin to show how the propositions that empirically hold good in small groups may be derived from some set of still more general propositions. "Still more general" means only that empirical propositions other than ours may also be derived from the set. This derivation would constitute the explanatory stage in the science of elementary social behavior, for explanation *is* derivation.[1] (I myself suspect that the more general set will turn out to contain the propositions of behavioral psychology. I hold myself to be an "ultimate psychological reductionist," but I cannot know that I am right so long as the reduction has not been carried out.)

I have come to think that all three of these jobs would be furthered by our adopting the view that interaction between persons is an exchange of goods, material and non-material. This is one of the oldest theories of social behavior, and one that we still use every day to interpret our own behavior, as when we say, "I found so-and-so rewarding"; or "I got a great deal out of him"; or, even, "Talking with him took a great deal out of me." But, perhaps just because it is so obvious, this view has been much neglected by social scientists. So far as I know, the only theoretical work that makes explicit use of it is Marcel Mauss's *Essai sur le don*, published in 1925, which is ancient as social science goes.[2] It may be that the tradition of neglect is now changing and that, for instance, the psychologists who interpret behavior in terms of transactions may be coming back to something of the sort I have in mind.[3]

An incidental advantage of an exchange theory is that it might bring sociology closer to economics—that science of man most advanced, most capable of application, and, intellectually, most isolated. Economics

studies exchange carried out under special circumstances and with a most useful built-in numerical measure of value. What are the laws of the general phenomenon of which economic behavior is one class?

In what follows I shall suggest some reasons for the usefulness of a theory of social behavior as exchange and suggest the nature of the propositions such a theory might contain.

AN EXCHANGE PARADIGM

I start with the link to behavioral psychology and the kind of statement it makes about the behavior of an experimental animal such as the pigeon.[4] As a pigeon explores its cage in the laboratory, it happens to peck a target, whereupon the psychologist feeds it corn. The evidence is that it will peck the target again; it has learned the behavior, or, as my friend Skinner says, the behavior has been reinforced, and the pigeon has undergone *operant conditioning*. This kind of psychologist is not interested in how the behavior was learned: "learning theory" is a poor name for his field. Instead, he is interested in what determines changes in the rate of emission of learned behavior, whether pecks at a target or something else.

The more hungry the pigeon, the less corn or other food it has gotten in the recent past, the more often it will peck. By the same token, if the behavior is often reinforced, if the pigeon is given much corn every time it pecks, the rate of emission will fall off as the pigeon gets *satiated*. If, on the other hand, the behavior is not reinforced at all, then, too, its rate of emission will tend to fall off, though a long time may pass before it stops altogether, before it is *extinguished*. In the emission of many kinds of behavior the pigeon incurs *aversive stimulation*, or what I shall call "cost" for short, and this, too, will lead in time to a decrease in the emission rate. Fatigue is an example of a "cost." Extinction, satiation, and cost, by decreasing the rate of emission of a particular kind of behavior, render more probable the emission of some other kind of behavior, including doing nothing. I shall only add that even a hard-boiled psychologist puts "emotional" behavior, as well as such things as pecking, among the unconditioned responses that may be reinforced in operant conditioning. As a statement of the propositions of behavioral psychology, the foregoing is, of course, inadequate for any purpose except my present one.

We may look on the pigeon as engaged in an exchange—pecks for corn—with the psychologist, but let us not dwell upon that, for the behavior of the pigeon hardly determines the behavior of the psychologist at all. Let us turn to a situation where the exchange is real, that is, where the determination is mutual. Suppose we are dealing with two men. Each is emitting behavior reinforced to some degree by the behavior of the other. How it was in the past that each learned the behavior he emits and how he learned to find the other's behavior reinforcing we are not concerned with. It is enough that each does find the other's behavior reinforcing, and I shall call the reinforcers—the equivalent of the pigeon's corn—*values*, for this, I think, is what we mean by this term. As he emits behavior, each man may incur costs, and each man has more than one course of behavior open to him.

This seems to me the paradigm of elementary social behavior, and the problem of the elementary sociologist is to state propositions relating the variations in the values and costs of each man to his frequency distribution of behavior among alternatives, where the values (in the mathematical sense) taken by these variables for one man determine in part their values for the other.[5]

I see no reason to believe that the propositions of behavioral psychology do not apply to this situation, though the complexity of their implications in the concrete case may be great indeed. In particular, we must suppose that, with men as with pigeons, an increase in extinction, satiation, or aversive stimulation of any one kind of behavior will increase the probability of emission of some other kind. The problem is not, as it is often stated, merely, what a man's values are, what he has learned in the past to find reinforcement but how much of any one value his behavior is getting him now. The more he gets, the less valuable any further unit of that value is to him, and the less often he will emit behavior reinforced by it.

THE INFLUENCE PROCESS

We do not, I think, possess the kind of studies of two-person interaction that would either bear out these propositions or fail to do so. But we do have studies of larger numbers of persons that suggest that they may apply, notably the studies by Festinger, Schachter, Back, and their associates on the dynamics of influence. One of the variables they work with they call *cohesiveness*, defined as anything that attracts people to take part in a group. Cohesiveness is a value variable; it refers to the degree of reinforcement people find in the activities of the group. Festinger and his colleagues consider two kinds of reinforcing activity: the symbolic behavior we call "social approval" (sentiment) and activity valuable in other ways, such as doing something interesting.

The other variable they work with they call *communication* and others call *interaction*. This is a frequency variable: it is a measure of the frequency of emission of valuable and costly verbal behavior. We must bear in mind that, in general, the one kind of variable is a function of the other.

Festinger and his co-workers show that the more cohesive a group is, that is, the more valuable the sentiment or activity the members exchange with one another, the greater the average frequency of interaction of the members.[6] With men, as with pigeons, the greater the reinforcement, the more often is the reinforced behavior emitted. The more cohesive a group, too, the greater the change that members can produce in the behavior of other members in the direction of rendering these activities more valuable.[7] That is, the more valuable the activities that members get, the more valuable those that they must give. For if a person is emitting behavior of a certain kind, and other people do not find it particularly rewarding, these others will suffer their own production of sentiment and activity, in time, to fall off. But perhaps the first person has found their sentiment and activity rewarding, and, if he is to keep on getting them, he must make his own behavior more valuable to the others. In short, the propositions of behavioral psychology imply a tendency toward a certain proportionality between the value to others of the behavior a man gives them and the value to him of the behavior they give him.[8]

Schachter also studied the behavior of members of a group toward two kinds of other members, "conformers" and "deviates."[9] I assume that conformers are people whose activity the other members find valuable. For conformity is behavior that coincides to a degree with some group standard or norm, and the only meaning I can assign to *norm* is "a verbal description of behavior that many members find it valuable for the actual behavior of themselves and others to conform to." By the same token, a deviate is a member whose behavior is not particularly valuable. Now Schachter shows that, as the members of a group come to see another member as a deviate, their interaction with him—communication addressed to getting him to change his behavior—goes up, the faster the more cohesive the group. The members need not talk to the other conformers so much; they are relatively satiated by the conformers' behavior: they have gotten what they want out of them. But if the deviate, by failing to change his behavior, fails to reinforce the members, they start to withhold social approval from him: the deviate gets low sociometric choice at the end of the experiment. And in the most cohesive groups—those Schachter calls "high cohesive-relevant"—interaction with the deviate also falls off in the end and is lowest among those members that rejected him most strongly, as if they had given him up as a bad job. But how plonking can we get? These findings are utterly in line with everyday experience.

PRACTICAL EQUILIBRIUM

At the beginning of this paper I suggested that one of the tasks of small-group research was to show the relation between the results of experimental work done under laboratory conditions and the results of field research on real-life small groups. Now the latter often appear to be in practical equilibrium, and by this I mean nothing fancy. I do not mean that all real-life groups are in equilibrium. I certainly do not mean that all groups must tend to equilibrium. I do not mean that groups have built-in antidotes to change: there is no homeostasis here. I do not mean that we assume equilibrium. I mean only that we sometimes *observe* it, that for the time we are with a group—and it is often short—there is no great change in the values of the variables we choose to measure. If, for instance, person A is interacting with B more than with C both at the beginning and at the end of the study, then at least by this crude measure the group is in equilibrium.

Many of the Festinger-Schachter studies are experimental, and their propositions about the process of influence seem to me to imply the kind of proposition that empirically holds good of real-life groups in practical equilibrium. For instance, Festinger *et al.* find that, the more cohesive a group is, the greater the change that members can produce in the behavior of other members. If the influence is exerted in the direction of conformity to group norms, then, when the process of influence has accomplished all the change of which it is capable, the proposition should hold good that, the more cohesive a group is, the larger the number of members that conform to its norms. And it does hold good.[10]

Again, Schachter found, in the experiment I summarized above, that in the most cohesive groups and at the end, when the effort to influence the deviate had failed, members interacted little with the deviate and gave him little in the way of sociometric choice. Now two of the propositions that hold good most often of real-life groups in practical equilibrium are precisely that the more closely a member's activity conforms to the norms the more interaction he receives from other members and the more liking choices he gets from them too. From these main propositions a number of others may be derived that also hold good.[11]

Yet we must ever remember that the truth of the proposition linking conformity to liking may on occasion be masked by the truth of other propositions. If, for instance, the man that conforms to the norms most closely also exerts some authority over the group, this may render liking for him somewhat less than it might otherwise have been.[12]

Be that as it may, I suggest that the laboratory experiments on influence imply propositions about the behavior of members of small groups, when the process of influence has worked itself out, that are identical with propositions that hold good of real-life groups in equilibrium. This is hardly surprising if all we mean by equilibrium is that all the change of which the system is, under present conditions, capable has been effected, so that no further change occurs. Nor would this be the first time that statics has turned out to be a special case of dynamics.

PROFIT AND SOCIAL CONTROL

Though I have treated equilibrium as an observed fact, it is a fact that cries for explanation. I shall not, as structural-functional sociologists do, use an assumed equilibrium as a means of explaining or trying to explain, why the other features of a social system should be what they are. Rather, I shall take practical equilibrium as something that is itself to be explained by the other features of the system.

If every member of a group emits at the end of, and during, a period of time much the same kinds of behavior and in much the same frequencies as he did at the beginning, the group is for that period in equilibrium. Let us then ask why any one member's behavior should persist. Suppose he is emitting behavior of value A_1. Why does he not let his behavior get worse (less valuable or reinforcing to the others) until it stands at $A_1 - \Delta A$? True, the sentiments expressed by others toward him are apt to decline in value (become less reinforcing to him), so that what he gets from them may be $S_1 - \Delta S$. But it is conceivable that, since most activity carries cost, a decline in the value of what he emits will mean a reduction in cost to him that more than offsets his losses in sentiment. Where, then, does he stabilize his behavior? This is the problem of social control.[13]

Mankind has always assumed that a person stabilizes his behavior, at least in the short run, at the point where he is doing the best he can for himself under the circumstances, though his best may not be a "rational" best, and what he can do may not be at all easy to specify, except that he is not apt to think like one of the theoretical antagonists in the *Theory of Games*. Before a sociologist rejects this answer out of hand for its horrid profit-seeking implications, he will do well to ask himself if he can offer any other answer to the question posed. I think he will find that he cannot. Yet experiments designed to test the truth of the answer are extraordinarily rare.

I shall review one that seems to me to provide a little support for the theory, though it was not meant to do so. The experiment is reported by H. B. Gerard, a member of the Festinger-Schachter team, under the title "The Anchorage of Opinions in Face-to-Face Groups."[14] The experimenter formed artificial groups whose members met to discuss a case in industrial relations and to express their opinions about its probable outcome. The groups were of two kinds: high-attraction groups, whose members were told that they would like one another very much, and low-attraction

groups, whose members were told that they would not find one another particularly likable.

At a later time the experimenter called the members in separately, asked them again to express their opinions on the outcome of the case, and counted the number that had changed their opinions to bring them into accord with those of other members of their groups. At the same time, a paid participant entered into a further discussion of the case with each member, always taking, on the probable outcome of the case, a position opposed to that taken by the bulk of the other members of the group to which the person belonged. The experimenter counted the number of persons shifting toward the opinion of the paid participant.

The experiment had many interesting results, from which I choose only those summed up in Tables 46.1 and 46.2. The three different agreement classes are made up of people who, at the original sessions, expressed different degrees of agreement with the opinions of other members of their groups. And the figure 44, for instance, means that, of all members of high-attraction groups whose initial opinions were strongly in disagreement with those of other members, 44 per cent shifted their opinion later toward that of others.

TABLE 46.1   PERCENTAGE OF SUBJECTS CHANGING TOWARD SOMEONE IN THE GROUP

	Agreement	Mild Disagreement	Strong Disagreement
High Attraction....	0	12	44
Low Attraction....	0	15	9

TABLE 46.2   PERCENTAGE OF SUBJECTS CHANGING TOWARD THE PAID PARTICIPANT

	Agreement	Mild Disagreement	Strong Disagreement
High Attraction....	7	13	25
Low Attraction....	20	38	8

In these results the experimenter seems to have been interested only in the differences in the sums of the rows, which show that there is more shifting toward the group, and less shifting toward the paid participant, in the high-attraction than in the low-attraction condition. This is in line with a proposition suggested earlier. If you think that the members of a group can give you much—in this case, liking—you are apt to give them much—in this case, a change to an opinion in accordance with their views—or you will not get the liking. And, by the same token, if the group can give you little of value, you will not be ready to give it much of value. Indeed, you may change your opinion so as to depart from agreement even further, to move, that is, toward the view held by the paid participant.

So far so good, but, when I first scanned these tables, I was less struck by the difference between them than by their similarity. The same classes of people in both tables showed much the same relative propensities to change their opinions, no matter whether the change was toward the group or toward the paid participant. We see, for instance, that those who change least are the high-attraction, strong-disagreement people and the low-attraction, mild-disagreement ones.

How am I to interpret these particular results? Since the experimenter did not discuss them, I am free to offer my own explanation. The behavior emitted by the subjects is opinion and changes in opinion. For this behavior they have learned to expect two possible kinds of reinforcement. Agreement with the group gets the subject favorable sentiment (acceptance) from it, and the experiment was designed to give this reinforcement a higher value in the high-attraction condition than in the low-attraction one. The second kind of possible reinforcement is what I shall call the "maintenance of one's personal integrity," which a subject gets by sticking to his own opinion in the face of disagreement with the group. The experimenter does not mention this reward, but I cannot make sense of the results without something much like it. In different degrees for different subjects, depending on their initial positions, these rewards are in competition with one another: they are alternatives. They are not absolutely scarce goods, but some persons cannot get both at once.

Since the rewards are alternatives, let me introduce a familiar assumption from economics—that the cost of a particular course of action is the equivalent of the foregone value of an alternative[15]—and then add the definition: Profit = Reward − Cost.

Now consider the persons in the corresponding cells of the two tables. The behavior of the high-attraction, agreement people gets them much in the way of acceptance by the group, and for it they must give up little in the way of personal integrity, for their views are from the start in accord with those of the group. Their profit is high, and they are not prone to change their behavior. The low-attraction, strong-disagreement people are getting much in integrity and they are not giving up for it much in valuable acceptance, for they are members of low-attraction groups. Reward less cost is high for them, too, and they change little. The high-attraction, strong-disagreement people are getting much in the way of integrity, but their costs in doing so are high, too, for they are in high-attraction groups and thus foregoing much valuable acceptance by the group. Their profit is low, and they are very apt to change, either toward the group or toward the paid participant, from whom they think, perhaps, they will get some acceptance while maintaining some integrity. The low-attraction, mild-disagreement people do not get much in the way of integrity, for they are only in mild disagreement with the group, but neither are they giving up much in acceptance, for they are members of low-attraction groups. Their rewards are low; their costs are low too, and their profit—the difference between the two—is also low. In their low profit they resemble the high-attraction, strong-disagreement people, and, like them, they are prone to change their opinions, in this case, more toward the paid participant. The subjects in the other two cells, who have medium profits, display medium propensities to change.

If we define profit as reward less cost, and if cost is value foregone, I suggest that we have here some evidence for the proposition that change in behavior is greatest when perceived profit is least. This constitutes no direct demonstration that change in behavior is least when profit is greatest, but if, whenever a man's behavior brought him a balance of reward and cost, he changed his behavior away from what got him, under the circumstances, the less profit, there might well come a time when his behavior would not change further. That is, his behavior would be stabilized, at least for the time being. And, so far as this were true for every member of a group, the group would have a social organization in equilibrium.

I do not say that a member would stabilize his behavior at the point of greatest conceivable profit to himself, because his profit is partly at the mercy of the behavior of others. It is a commonplace that the short-run pursuit of profit by several persons often lands them in positions where all are worse off than they might conceivably be. I do not say that the paths of behavioral change in which a member pursues his profit under the condition that others are pursuing theirs too are easy to describe or predict; and we can readily conceive that in jockeying for position they might never arrive at any equilibrium at all.

DISTRIBUTIVE JUSTICE

Yet practical equilibrium is often observed, and thus some further condition may make its attainment, under some circumstance, more probable than would the individual pursuit of profit left to itself. I can offer evidence for this further condition only in the behavior of subgroups and not in that of individuals. Suppose that there are two subgroups, working close together in a factory, the job of one being somewhat different from that of the other. And suppose that the members of the first complain and say: "We are getting the same pay as they are. We ought to get just a couple of dollars a week more to show that our work is more responsible." When you ask them what they mean by "more responsible," they say that, if they do their work wrong, more damage can result, and so they are under more pressure to take care.[16] Something like this is a common feature of industrial behavior. It is at the heart of disputes not over absolute wages but over wage differentials—indeed, at the heart of disputes over rewards other than wages.

In what kind of proposition may we express observations like these? We may say that wages and responsibility give status in the group, in the sense that a man who takes high responsibility and gets high wages is admired, other things equal. Then, if the members of one group score higher on responsibility than do the members of another, there is a felt need on the part of the first to score higher on pay too. There is a pressure, which shows itself in complaints, to bring the *status factors*, as I have called them, into line with one another. If they are in line, a condition of *status congruence* is said to exist. In this condition the workers may find their jobs dull or irksome, but they will not complain about the relative position of groups.

But there may be a more illuminating way of looking at the matter. In my example I have considered only responsibility and pay, but these may be enough, for they represent the two kinds of thing that come into the problem. Pay is clearly a reward: responsibility may be looked on, less clearly, as a cost. It means constraint and worry—or peace of mind foregone. Then the proposition about status congruence becomes this: If the costs of the members of one group are higher than those of another, distributive justice requires that their rewards should be higher too. But the thing works both ways: If the rewards are higher, the costs should be higher too. This last is the theory of *noblesse oblige*, which we all subscribe to, though we all laugh at it, perhaps because the *noblesse* often fails to *oblige*. To put the matter in terms of profit: though the rewards and costs of two persons or the members of two groups may be different, yet the profits of the two—the excess of reward over cost—should tend to equality. And more than "should." The less-advantaged group will at least try to attain greater equality, as, in the example I have used, the first group tried to increase its profit by increasing its pay.

I have talked of distributive justice. Clearly, this is not the only condition determining the actual distribution of rewards and costs. At the same time, never tell me that notions of justice are not a strong influence on behavior, though we sociologists often neglect them. Distributive justice may be one of the conditions of group equilibrium.

EXCHANGE AND SOCIAL STRUCTURE

I shall end by reviewing almost the only study I am aware of that begins to show in detail how a stable and differentiated social structure in a real-life group might arise out of a process of exchange between members. This is Peter Blau´s description of the behavior of sixteen agents in a federal law-enforcement agency.[17]

The agents had the duty of investigating firms and preparing reports on the firms´ compliance with the law. Since the reports might lead to legal action against the firms, the agents had to prepare them carefully, in the proper form, and take strict account of the many regulations that might apply. The agents were often in doubt what they should do, and then they were supposed to take the question to their supervisor. This they were reluctant to do, for they naturally believed that thus confessing to him their inability to solve a problem would reflect on their competence, affect the official ratings he made of their work, and so hurt their chances for promotion. So agents often asked other agents for help and advice, and, though this was nominally forbidden, the supervisor usually let it pass.

Blau ascertained the ratings the supervisor made of the agents, and he also asked the agents to rate one another. The two opinions agreed closely. Fewer agents were regarded as highly competent than were regarded as of middle or low competence; competence, or the ability to solve technical problems, was a fairly scarce good. One or two of the more competent agents would not give help and advice when asked, and so received few interactions and little liking. A man that will not exchange, that will not give you what he has when you need it, will not get from you the only thing you are, in this case, able to give him in return, your regard.

But most of the more competent agents were willing to give help, and of them Blau says:

> A consultation can be considered an exchange of values: both participants gain something, and both have to pay a price. The questioning agent is enabled to perform better than he could otherwise have done, without exposing his difficulties to his supervisor. By asking for advice, he implicitly pays his respect to the superior proficiency of his colleague. This acknowledgement of inferiority is the cost of receiving assistance. The consultant gains prestige, in return for which he is willing to devote some time to the consultation and permit it to disrupt his own work. The following remark of an agent illustrates this: `I like giving advice. It´s flattering, I suppose, if you feel that others come to you for advice.´[18]

Blau goes on to say: "All agents liked being consulted, but the value of any one of very many consultations became deflated for experts, and the price they paid in frequent interruptions became inflated."[19] This implies that, the more prestige an agent received, the less was the increment of value of that prestige; the more advice an agent gave, the greater was the increment of cost of that advice, the cost lying precisely in the forgone value of time to do his own work. Blau suggests that something of the same sort was true of an agent who went to a more competent colleague for advice: the more often he went, the more costly to him, in feelings of inferiority, became any further request. "The repeated admission of his inability to solve his own problems ... undermined the self-confidence of the worker and his standing in the group."[20]

The result was that the less competent agents went to the more competent ones for help less often than they might have done if the costs of repeated admissions of inferiority had been less high and that, while many agents sought out the few highly competent ones, no single agent sought out the latter much. Had they done so (to look at the exchange from the other side), the costs to the highly competent in interruptions to their own work would have become exorbitant. Yet the need of the less competent for help was still not fully satisfied. Under these circumstances they tended to turn for help to agents more nearly like themselves in competence. Though the help they got was not the most valuable, it was of a kind they could themselves return on occasion. With such agents they could exchange help and liking, without the exchange becoming on either side too great a confession of inferiority.

The highly competent agents tended to enter into exchanges, that is, to interact with many others. But, in the more equal exchanges I have just spoken of, less competent agents tended to pair off as partners. That is, they interacted with a smaller number of people, but interacted often with these few. I think I could show why pair relations in these more equal exchanges would be more economical for an agent than a wider distribution of favors. But perhaps I have gone far enough. The final pattern of this social structure was one in which a small number of highly competent agents exchanged advice for prestige with a large number of others less competent and in which the less competent agents exchanged, in pairs and in trios, both help and liking on more nearly equal terms.

Blau shows, then, that a social structure in equilibrium might be the result of a process of exchanging behavior rewarding and costly in different degrees, in which the increment of reward and cost varied with the frequency of the behavior, that is, with the frequency of interaction. Note that the behavior of the agents seems also to have satisfied my second condition of equilibrium: the more competent agents took more responsibility for the work, either their own or others´, than did the less competent ones, but they also got more for it in the way of prestige. I suspect that the same kind of explanation could be given for the structure of many "informal" groups.

SUMMARY

The current job of theory in small-group research is to make the connection between experimental and real-life studies, to consolidate the propositions that empirically hold good in the two fields, and to show how these propositions might be derived from a still more general set. One way of doing this job would be to revive and make more rigorous the oldest of theories of social behavior—social behavior as exchange.

Some of the statements of such a theory might be the following. Social behavior is an exchange of goods, material goods but also non-material ones, such as the symbols of approval or prestige. Persons that give much to others try to get much from them, and persons that get much from others are under pressure to give much to them. This process of influence tends to work out at equilibrium to a balance in the exchanges. For a person engaged in exchange, what he gives may be a cost to him, just as what he gets may be a reward, and his behavior changes less as profit, that is, reward less cost, tends to a maximum. Not only does he seek a maximum for himself, but he tries to see to it that no one in his group makes more profit than he does. The cost and the value of what he gives and of what he gets vary with the quantity of what he gives and gets. It is surprising how familiar these propositions are; it is surprising, too, how propositions about the dynamics of exchange can begin to generate the static thing we call "group structure" and, in so doing, generate also some of the propositions about group structure that students of real-life groups have stated.

In our unguarded moments we sociologists find words like "reward" and "cost" slipping into what we say. Human nature will break in upon even our most elaborate theories. But we seldom let it have its way with us and follow up systematically what these words imply.[21] Of all our many "approaches" to social behavior, the one that sees it as an economy is the most neglected, and yet it is the one we use every moment of our lives—except when we write sociology.

NOTES

1. See R. B. Braithwaite, *Scientific Explanation* (Cambridge: Cambridge University Press, 1953).
2. Translated by I. Cunnison as *The Gift* (Glencoe, Ill.: Free Press, 1954).
3. In social anthropology D. L. Oliver is working along these lines, and I owe much to him. See also T. M. Newcomb, "The Prediction of Interpersonal Attraction," *American Psychologist*, XI (1956), 575–86.
4. B. F. Skinner, *Science and Human Behavior* (New York: Macmillan Co., 1953).
5. *Ibid.*, pp. 297–329. The discussion of "double contingency" by T. Parsons and E. A. Shils could easily lead to a similar paradigm (see *Toward a General Theory of Action* [Cambridge, Mass.: Harvard University Press, 1951], pp. 14–16).
6. K. W. Back, "The Exertion of Influence through Social Communication," in L. Festinger, K. Back, S. Schachter, H. H. Kelley, and J. Thibaut (eds.), *Theory and Experiment in Social Communication* (Ann Arbor: Research Center for Dynamics, University of Michigan, 1950), pp. 21–36.

7. S. Schachter, N. Ellertson, D. McBride, and D. Gregory, "An Experimental Study of Cohesiveness and Productivity," *Human Relations*, IV (1951), 229–38.

8. Skinner, *op. cit.*, p. 100.

9. S. Schachter, "Deviation, Rejection, and Communication," *Journal of Abnormal and Social Psychology*, XLVI (1951), 190–207.

10. L. Festinger, S. Schachter, and K. Back, *Social Pressures in Informal Groups* (New York: Harper & Bros., 1950), pp. 72–100.

11. For propositions holding good of groups in practical equilibrium see G. C. Homans, *The Human Group* (New York: Harcourt, Brace & Co., 1950), and H. W. Riecken and G. C. Homans, "Psychological Aspects of Social Structure," in G. Lindzey (ed.), *Handbook of Social Psychology* (Cambridge, Mass.: Addison-Wesley Publishing Co., 1954), II, 786–832.

12. See Homans, *op. cit.*, pp. 244–48, and R. F. Bales, "The Equilibrium Problem in Small Groups," in A. P. Hare, E. F. Borgatta, and R. F. Bales (eds.), *Small Groups* (New York: A. A. Knopf, 1953), pp. 450–56.

13. Homans, *op. cit.*, pp. 281–301.

14. *Human Relations*, VII (1954), 313–25.

15. G. J. Stigler, *The Theory of Price* (rev. ed.; New York: Macmillan Co., 1952), p. 99.

16. G. C. Homans, "Status among Clerical Workers," *Human Organization*, XII (1953), 5–10.

17. Peter M. Blau, *The Dynamics of Bureaucracy* (Chicago: University of Chicago Press, 1955), 99–116.

18. *Ibid.*, p. 108.

19. *Ibid.*, p. 108.

20. *Ibid.*, p. 109.

21. *The White-Collar Job* (Ann Arbor: Survey Research Center, University of Michigan, 1953), pp. 115–27.

47. POWER-DEPENDENCE RELATIONS

RICHARD M. EMERSON

Early in his career, Richard Emerson (1925–1982) sought to advance exchange theory by developing a parsimonious theory of power/dependence that was amenable to a quantitative research program. Unlike many sociologists, he considered laboratory experiments with humans to hold considerable potential in developing such a program. In so doing, he extended Homans' efforts to ground social exchange theory in behaviorist psychology. In this classic essay—one of the more widely cited articles in sociology—Emerson attempts to provide a link among the concepts of "power," "authority," "legitimacy," and "structure" by articulating a view of power that emphasizes its relational character. More specifically, he sees power as predicated on "ties of mutual dependence." At its most fundamental level, this means that B's power is proportionally related to A's dependency on B for particular rewards or resources. Power is a potential that is realized in social exchange. Much of Emerson's interest in this essay focuses on exchanges that he calls "balancing operations." These operations consist of various options that A can attempt in responding to situations in which power is unbalanced in favor of B. Moreover, these operations constitute the core focus of the research agenda he stakes out.

Judging from the frequent occurrence of such words as *power, influence, dominance* and *submission, status* and *authority*, the importance of power is widely recognized, yet considerable confusion exists concerning these concepts.[1] There is an extensive literature pertaining to power, on both theoretical and empirical levels, and in small group[2] as well as large community contexts.[3] Unfortunately, this already large and rapidly growing body of research has not achieved the cumulative character desired. Our *integrated* knowledge of power does not significantly surpass the conceptions left by Max Weber.[4]

This suggests that there is a place at this moment for a systematic treatment of social power. The underdeveloped state of this area is further suggested by what appears, to this author, to be a recurrent flaw in common conceptions of social power; a flaw which helps to block adequate theoretical development as well as meaningful research. That flaw is the implicit treatment of power as though it were an attribute of a person or group ("X is an influential person," "Y is a powerful group," etc.). Given this conception, the natural research question becomes "Who in community X are the power *holders*?" The project then proceeds to rank-order persons by some criterion of power, and this ordering is called the *power-structure*. This is a highly questionable representation of a "structure," based upon a questionable assumption of generalized power.[5]

It is commonly observed that some person X dominates Y, while being subservient in relations with Z. Furthermore, these power relations are frequently intra-sensitive! Hence, to say that "X has power" is vacant, unless we specify "over whom." In making these necessary qualifications we force ourselves to face up to the obvious: power is a property of the social relation; it is not an attribute of the actor.[6]

Reprinted from Richard M. Emerson, "Power-Dependence Relations," *American Sociological Review*, 27(1), pp. 31–41, February, 1962. Copyright © by the American Sociological Association. ✦

In this paper, an attempt is made to construct a sample theory of the power aspects of social relations. Attention is focused upon characteristics of the relationship as such, with little or no regard for particular features of the persons or groups engaged in such relations. Personal traits, skills or possessions (such as wealth) which might be relevant in one relation are infinitely variable across the set of possible relations, and hence have no place in a general theory.

THE POWER-DEPENDENCE RELATION

While the theory presented here is anchored most intimately in small groups research, it is meant to apply to more complex community relations as well. In an effort to make these conceptions potentially as broadly applicable as possible, we shall speak of relations among *actors*, where an actor can be a person or a group. Unless otherwise indicated, any relation discussed might be a person-person, group-person or group-group relation.

Social relations commonly entail *ties of mutual dependence* between the parties. A depends upon B if he aspires to goals or gratifications whose achievement is facilitated by appropriate actions on B's part. By virtue of mutual dependency, it is more or less imperative to each party that he be able to control or influence the other's conduct. At the same time, these ties of mutual dependence imply that each party is in position, to some degree, to grant or deny, facilitate or hinder, the other's gratification. Thus, it would appear that the power to control or influence the other resides in control over the things he values, which may range all the way from oil resources to ego-support, depending upon the relation in question. In short, *power resides implicitly in the other's dependency*. When this is recognized, the analysis will of necessity revolve largely around the concept of dependence.[7]

Two variables appear to function jointly in fixing the dependence of one actor upon another. Since the precise nature of this joint function is an empirical question our proposition can do no more than specify the directional relationships involved:

Dependence (Dab). The dependence of actor A upon actor B is (1) directly proportional to A's *motivational investment* in goals mediated by B,

and (2) inversely proportional to the *availability* of those goals outside of the A-B relation.

In this proposition "goal" is used in the broadest possible sense to refer to gratifications consciously sought as well as rewards unconsciously obtained through the relationship. The "availability" of such goals outside of the relation refers to alternative avenues of goal-achievement, most notably other social relations. The costs associated with such alternatives must be included in any assessment of dependency.[8]

If the dependence of one party provides the basis for the power of the other, that power must be defined as a potential influence:

Power (Pab). The power of actor A over actor B is the amount of resistance on the part of B which can be potentially overcome by A.

Two points must be made clear about this definition. First, the power defined here will not be, of necessity, observable in every interactive episode between A and B, yet we suggest that it exists nonetheless as a potential, to be explored, tested, and occasionally employed by the participants. Pab will be empirically manifest only *if* A makes some demand, and only if this demand runs counter to B's desires (resistance to be overcome). Any operational definition must make reference to *change* in the conduct of B attributable to demands made by A.

Second, we define power as the "resistance" which can be overcome, without restricting it to any one domain of action. Thus, if A is dependent upon B for love and respect, B might then draw A into criminal activity which he would normally resist. The reader might object to this formulation, arguing that special power is in fact restricted to certain channels. If so, the reader is apparently concerned with "legitimized power" embedded in a social structure. Rather than begin at this more evolved level, we hope to derive legitimized power in the theory itself.

The premise we began with can now be stated as Pab = Dba; the power of A over B is equal to, and based upon, the dependence of B upon A.[9] Recognizing the reciprocity of social relations, we can represent a power-dependence relation as a pair of equations:

$$Pab = Dba$$
$$Pba = Dab.$$

Before proceeding further we should emphasize that these formulations have been so worded in the hope that they will apply across a wide range of social life. At a glance our conception of dependence contains two variables remarkably like supply and demand ("availability" and "motivational investment," respectively).[10] We prefer the term *dependency* over these economic terms because it facilitates broader application, for all we need to do to shift these ideas from one area of application to another is change the motivational basis of dependency. We can speak of the economic dependence of a home builder upon a loan agency as varying directly with his desire for the home, and hence capital, and inversely with the "availability" of capital from other agencies. Similarly, a child may be dependent upon another child based upon motivation toward the pleasures of collective play, the availability of alternative playmates, etc. The same generic power-dependence relation is involved in each case. The dependency side of the equation may show itself in "friendship" among playmates, in "filial love" between parent and child, in "respect for treaties" among nations. On the other side of the equation, I am sure no one doubts that mothers, lovers, children, and nations enjoy the power to influence their respective partners, within the limit set by the partner´s dependence upon them.

Finally, because these concepts are meant to apply across a wide variety of social situations, operational definitions cannot be appropriately presented here. Operational definitions provide the necessary bridge between generalizing concepts on the one hand, and the concrete features of a specific research situation on the other hand. Hence, there is no one proper operational definition for a theoretical concept.[11]

BALANCE AND IMBALANCE

The notion of reciprocity in power-dependency relations raises the question of equality or inequality of power in the relation. If the power of A over B (Pab) is confronted by equal opposing power of B over A, is power then neutralized or canceled out? We suggest that in such a balanced condition, power is in no way removed from the relationship. A pattern of "dominance" might not emerge in the interaction among these actors, but that does not imply that power is inoperative in either or both directions. A *balanced* relation and an *unbalanced* relation are represented respectively as follows:

$$Pab = Dba \qquad Pab = Dba$$
$$\| \qquad \| \qquad V \qquad V$$
$$Pba = Dab \qquad Pba = Dab$$

Consider two social relations, both of which are balanced, but at *different levels* of dependency (say Loeb and Leopold, as compared with two casual friends). A moment´s thought will reveal the utility of the argument that balance does not neutralize power, for each party may continue to exert profound control over the other. It might even be meaningful to talk about the parties being controlled by the relation itself.

Rather than canceling out considerations of power, reciprocal power provides the basis for studying three more features of power-relations: first, a power advantage can be defined as Pab minus Pba, which can be either positive or negative (a power disadvantage);[12] second, the *cohesion* of a relationship can be defined as the average of Dab and Dba, though this definition can be refined;[13] and finally, it opens the door to the study *balancing operations* as structural changes in power-dependence relations which tend to reduce power advantage.

Discussion of balancing tendencies should begin with a concrete illustration. In the unbalanced relation represented symbolically above, A is the more powerful party because B is the more dependent of the two. Let actor B be a rather "unpopular" girl, with puritanical upbringing, who wants desperately to date; and let A be a young man who occasionally takes her out, while dating other girls as well. (The reader can satisfy himself about A´s power advantage in this illustration by referring to the formulations above.) Assume further that A "discovers" this power advantage, and, in exploring for the limits of his power, makes sexual advances. In this simplified illustration, these advances should encounter resistance in B´s puritanical values. Thus, when a power advantage is used, the weaker member will achieve one value at the expense of other values.

In this illustration the tensions involved in an unbalanced relation need not be long endured. They can be reduced in either of two ways: (1) the girl might reduce the psychic costs involved in continuing the relation by redefining her moral values, with appropriate rationalizations and shifts in reference group attachments; or (2) she might renounce the value of dating, develop career aspirations, etc., thus reducing A's power. Notice that the first solution does not of necessity alter the unbalanced relation. The weaker member has sidestepped one painful demand but she is still vulnerable to new demands. By contrast, the second solution alters the power relation itself, in general, it appears that an unbalanced relation is unstable for it encourages the use of power which in turn sets in motion processes which we will call (a) cost reduction and (b) balancing operations.[14]

COST REDUCTION

The "cost" referred to here amounts to the "resistance" to be overcome in our definition of power—the cost involved for one party in meeting the demands made by the other. The process of cost reduction in power dependence relations shows itself in many varied forms. In the courting relation above it took the form of alteration in moral attitudes on the part of a girl who wanted to be popular; in industry it is commonly seen as the impetus for improved plant efficiency and technology in reducing the cost of production. What we call the "mark of oppression" in the character structure of members of low social castes (the submissive and "painless" loss of freedom) might well involve the same power processes, as does the "internalization of parental codes" in the socialization process. In fact, the oedipal conflict might be interpreted as a special case of the tensions of imbalance in a power-dependence relation, and cost reduction takes the form of identification and internalization classically described. "Identification with the aggressor" in any context would appear to be explainable in terms of cost reduction.

In general, *cost reduction* is a process involving change in values (personal, social, economic) which reduces the pains incurred in meeting the demands of a powerful other. It must be emphasized, however, that these adjustments do not necessarily alter the balance or imbalance of the relation, and, as a result, they must be distinguished from more fundamental *balancing operations* described below. It must be recognized that cost reducing tendencies will take place under conditions of balance, and while this is obvious in economic transactions, it is equally true of other social relations, where the "costs" involved are anchored in modifiable attitudes and values. The intense cohesion of a lasting social relation like the Loeb-Leopold relation mentioned above can be attributed in part to the cost reduction processes involved in the progressive formation of their respective personalities, taking place in the interest of preserving the valued relation. We suggest that cost reducing tendencies generally will function to deepen and stabilize social relations over and above the condition of balance.

BALANCING OPERATIONS

The remainder of this paper will deal with balancing processes which operate through changes in the variables which define the structure of the power-dependence relation as such. The formal notation adopted here suggests exactly four generic types of balancing operation. In the unbalanced relation

$$\begin{array}{ccc} P_{ab} &=& D_{ba} \\ V & & V \\ P_{ba} &=& D_{ab} \end{array}$$

balance can be restored either by an increase in D_{ab} or by a decrease in D_{ba}. If we recall that dependence is a joint function of two variables, the following alterations will move the relation toward a state of balance:

1. If B reduces motivational investment in goals mediated by A;
2. If B cultivates alternative sources for gratification of those goals;
3. If A increases motivational investment in goals mediated by B;
4. If A is denied alternative sources for achieving those goals.

While these four types of balancing operation are dictated by the logic of the scheme, we suggest that each corresponds to well known social processes. The first operation yields balance through motivational withdrawal by B, the weaker member. The second involves the cultivation of alternative social relations by B. The third is based upon "giving status" to A, and the fourth involves coalition and group formation.

In some of these processes the role of power is well known, while in others it seems to have escaped notice. In discussing any one of these balancing operations it must be remembered that a prediction of which one (or what combination) of the four will take place must rest upon analysis of conditions involved in the concrete case at hand.

In the interest of simplicity and clarity, we will illustrate each of the four generic types of balancing operation in relations among children in the context of play. Consider two children equally motivated toward the pleasures of collective play and equally capable of contributing to such play. These children, A and B, form a balanced relation if we assume further that each has the other as his only playmate, and the give-and-take of their interactions might well be imagined, involving the emergence of such equalitarian rules as "taking turns," etc. Suppose now that a third child, C, moves into the neighborhood and makes the acquaintance of A, but *not* B. The A-B relation will be thrown out of balance by virtue of A's decreased dependence upon B. The reader should convince himself of this fact by referring back to the proposition on dependence. Without any of these parties necessarily "understanding" what is going on, we would predict that A would slowly come to dominate B in the pattern of their interactions. On more frequent occasions B will find himself deprived of the pleasures A can offer, thus slowly coming to sense his own dependency more acutely. By the same token A will more frequently find B saying "yes" instead of "no" to his proposals, and he will gain increased awareness of his power over B. The growing self-images of these children will surely reflect and perpetuate this pattern.

OPERATION NUMBER ONE: WITHDRAWAL

We now have the powerful A making demands on the dependent B. One of the processes through which the tensions in the unbalanced A-B relation can be reduced is *motivational withdrawal* on the part of B, for this will

reduce Dba and Pab. In this illustration, child B might lose some of his interest in collective play under the impact of frustrations and demands imposed by A. Such a withdrawal from the play relation would presumably come about if the other three balancing operations were blocked by the circumstances peculiar to the situation. The same operation was illustrated above in the case of the girl who might renounce the value of dating. It would seem to be involved in the dampened level of aspiration associated with the "mark of oppression" referred to above.

In general, the denial of dependency involved in this balancing operation will have the effect of moving actors away from relations which are unbalanced to their disadvantage. The actor's motivational orientations and commitments toward different areas of activity will intimately reflect this process.

OPERATION NUMBER TWO: EXTENSION OF POWER NETWORK

Withdrawal as a balancing operation entails subjective alterations in the weaker actor. The second operation takes place through alterations in a structure we shall call a *power network*, defined as two or more connected power-dependence relations. As we have seen in our illustration, when the C-A relation is connected through A with the A-B relation, forming a simple linear network C-A-B, the properties of A-B are altered. In this example, a previously balanced A-B relation is thrown out of balance, giving A a power advantage. This points up the general fact that while each relation in a network will involve interactions which appear to be independent of other relations in the network (e.g., A and B are seen to play together in the absence of C; C and A in the absence of B), the internal features of one relation are nonetheless a function of the entire network. Any adequate conception of a "power structure" must be based upon this fact.

In this illustration the form of the network throws both relations within it out of balance, thus stimulating one or several of the balancing operations under discussion. If balancing operation number two takes place, *the network* will be extended by the formation of new relationships. The tensions of imbalance in the A-B and A-C relations will make B and C "ready" to form new friendships (1) with additional children D and E, thus lengthening a linear network, or (2) with each other, thus "closing" the network. It is important to notice that the lengthened network balances some relations, but not the network as a whole, while the closed network is completely balanced under the limiting assumptions of this illustration. Thus, we might offer as a corollary to operation number two: Power networks tend to achieve closure.[15]

If the reader is dissatisfied with this illustration in children's play relations, let A be the loan agent mentioned earlier, and B, C, ... be home builders or others dependent upon A for capital. This is the familiar monopoly situation with the imbalance commonly attributed to it. As a network, it is a set of relations connected only at A. Just as the children were "ready" to accept new friends, so the community of actors B, C, ... is ready to receive new loan agencies. Balancing operation number 2 involves in all cases the *diffusion* of dependency into new relations in a network. A final illustration of this principle can be found in institutionalized form in some kinship systems involving the extended family. In the case of Hopi, for example, Dorothy Eggan has described at length the diffusion of child dependency among many "mothers," thus draining off much of the force of oedipal conflicts in that society.[16] We have already suggested that oedipal conflict may be taken as a special case of the tension of imbalance, which in this case appears to be institutionally handled in a manner resembling operation number two. This is not to be taken, however, as an assertion that the institution evolved as a balancing process, though this is clearly open for consideration.

It is convenient at this juncture to take my balancing operation number 4, leaving number 3 to the last.

OPERATION NUMBER FOUR: COALITION FORMATION

Let us continue with the same illustration. When the B-C relation forms, closing the C-A-B network in the process of balancing, we have what appears to be a coalition of the two weaker against the one stronger. This, however, is not technically the case, for A is not involved in the B-C interactions; he simply exists as an alternative playmate for both B and C.

The proper representation of coalitions in a triad would be (AB)-C, (AC)-B, or (BC)-A. That is, a triadic network reduces to a coalition only if two members unite as a single actor in the process of dealing directly with the third. The difference involved here may be very small in behavioral terms and the distinction may seem overly refined, but it goes to the heart of an important conceptual problem (the difference between a closed "network" and a "group"), and it rests upon the fact that two very different balancing operations are involved. The C-A-B network is balanced through the addition of a third relation (C-B) in operation number 2, but it is still just a power network. In operation number 4 it achieves balance through collapsing the two-relational network into one group-person relation with the emergence of a "collective actor." Operation number two reduces the power of the stronger actor, while number 4 increases the power of weaker actors through collectivization. If the rewards mediated by A are such that they can be jointly enjoyed by B and C, then the tensions of imbalance in the A-B and A-C relations can be resolved in the (BC)-A coalition.

In a general way, Marx was asking for balancing operation number 4 in his call to "Workers of the world," and the collectivization of labor can be taken as an illustration of this balancing tendency as an historic process. Among the balancing operations described here, coalition formation is the one most commonly recognized as a power process. However, the more general significance of this balancing operation seems to have escaped notice, for the typical coalition is only one of the many forms this same operation takes. For this reason the next section will explore coalition processes further.

THE ORGANIZED GROUP

We wish to suggest that the coalition process is basically involved in all organized group functioning, whether the group be called a coalition or not. We believe this illuminates the role which power processes play in the emergence and maintenance of group structure in general.

In the typical coalition pattern, (AB)-C, A and B constitute a collective actor in the sense that they act as one, presenting themselves to their common environment as a single unit. A coalition, as one *type* of group, is characterized by the fact that (a) the common environment is an actor to be controlled, and (b) its unity is historically based upon efforts to achieve that control. Now, all we need do to blend this type of group with groups in general is to *dehumanize* the environmental problem which the group collectively encounters. Thus, instead of having the control of actor C as its end, the group attempts to control C in the interest of achieving X, some "group goal." Now, if C also aspires toward X, and if C is dependent upon the group for achieving X, C might well be one of the group members—any member. Thus, in a three-member group we have three coalition structures as *intra-group* relations, each representable as ([AB]-C)-X, with A, B and C interchangeable.

The situation involved here is reminiscent of the rapidly forming and reforming coalitions in unconsolidated children's play groups. As the group consolidates, these coalitions do not drop out of the picture; they become stabilized features of group structure, and the stabilization process is identical with "norm formation." In fact, the demands made by (AB) of C in the power process within ([AB]-C) are exactly what we normally call *group norms* and *role-prescriptions*. Such norms are properly viewed as the "voice" of a collective actor, standing in coalition against the object of its demands. This reasoning suggests an idealized conception of group structure, based upon two types of collective demands:

(1) *Role-Prescriptions*. Specifications of behavior which all group members expect (demand) of one or more but not all members.
(2) *Group Norms*. Specifications of behavior which all group members expect of all group members.

Certain actions, when performed by some member or members, need not be performed by all other members to properly facilitate group functioning. These will tend to be incorporated in role-prescriptions, which, taken together, provide a division of labor in a role structure. Roles are defined and enforced through a consolidation of power in coalition formation. Likewise with group norms. Thus, the structure of a group (its norms and prescriptions) will specify the makeup of the coalition a member would face for any group-relevant act he might perform.

This conception of group structure is idealized in the sense that it describes complete consensus among members, even to the point of group identification and internalization of collective demands (members expect things of themselves in the above definitions). Balancing operations, along with cost reduction, should move group structure toward this ideal.

AUTHORITY

It should be clear that in introducing conceptions of group *structure* we have in no way digressed from our discussion of power processes, for the emergence of these structural forms is attributed directly to operation number four, closely resembling coalition formation. Even the most formalized role-prescription is properly viewed as the "voice" of all members standing as a coalition in making its demand of the occupant of the role. Whenever a specific member finds occasion to remind another member of his "proper" job in terms of such prescriptions, he speaks with the *authority* of the group behind him; he is "authorized" to speak for them. In this sense, every member has authority of a kind (as in civil arrest), but authority is usually used to refer to power vested in an office or role. The situation is basically the same, however, in either case. The occupant of such a role has simply been singled out and commissioned more explicitly to speak for the group in the group's dealings with its members. That authority is *limited*, power follows from logical necessity when role-prescriptions are treated as they are here. A dean, for example, can force faculty member A to turn in his grades on time because the demand is "legitimate," that is, supported by a coalition of all other faculty members joining with the dean in making the demand. If that dean, however, were to employ sanctions in an effort to induce that member to polish the dean's private car, the "coalition" would immediately re-form around the faculty member, as expressed in role-prescriptions defining the boundary of "legitimate power" or authority. The dean's authority is power contained and restricted through balancing operation number four, coalition formation.

The notion of legitimacy is important, for authority is more than balanced power; it is *directed* power which can be employed (legitimately) only in channels defined by the norms of the group. A person holding such authority is commissioned; he does not simply have the right to rule or govern—he is obliged to. Thus, authority emerges as a transformation of power in a process called "legitimation," and that process is one special case of balancing operation number four.[17]

Earlier in this section we referred to the common phenomenon of rapidly forming and re-forming coalitions in children's play groups. Our reasoning suggests that it is precisely through these coalition processes that unifying norms emerge. These fluctuating coalitions can be taken as the prototype of organized group life wherein the tempo of coalition realignment is accelerated to the point of being a blur before our eyes. Stated more accurately, the norms and prescriptions define implicitly the membership of the coalition which would either support or oppose any member if he were to perform any action relevant to those norms.

OPERATION NUMBER THREE: EMERGENCE OF STATUS

One important feature of group structure remains to be discussed: status and status hierarchies. It is interesting that the one remaining balancing operation provided in this theory takes us naturally to the emergence of status ordering. Operation number three increases the weaker member's power to control the formerly more powerful member through increasing the latter's motivational investment in the relation. This is normally accomplished through giving him status recognition in one or more of its many forms, from ego-gratifications to monetary differentials. The ego-rewards, such as prestige, loom large in this process because they are highly valued by many recipients while given at low cost to the giver.

The discussion of status hierarchies forces us to consider *intra*-group relations, and how this can be done in a theory which treats the group in the singular as an actor. The answer is contained in the idealized conception of group structure outlined above. That conception implies that every intra-group relation involves at once every member of the group. Thus, in a group with members A, B, C, and D, the relations A-B, A-C, etc. do not exist. Any interactions between A and B, for example, lie outside of the social system in

question unless one or both of these persons "represents" the group in his actions, as in the coalition pattern discussed at length above. The relations which do exist are (ABCD)-A, (ABCD)-B, (ABCD)-C and (ABCD)-D as a minimum, plus whatever relations of the (ABCD)-(AB) type may be involved in the peculiar structure of the group in question. Thus, in a group of N members we have theoretical reason for dealing with N *group-member* relations rather than considering all of the $\frac{N(N-1)}{2}$ possible member-member relations. Each of these group-member relations can now be expressed in the familiar equations for a power-dependence relation:

$$Pgm_i = Dm_ig$$
$$Pm_ig = Dgm_i.$$

To account for the emergence of a status hierarchy within a group of N members, we start with a set of N group-member relations of this type and consider balancing operations in these relations.

Let us imagine a five member group and proceed on three assumptions: (1) *status* involves differential valuation of members (or roles) by the group, and this valuation is equivalent to, or an expression of, Dgm_i; (2) a member who is highly valued by the group is highly valued in other *similar* groups he belongs to or might freely join; and (3) all five members have the same motivational investment in the group at the outset. Assumptions 2 and 3 are empirical, and when they are true they imply that Dgm and Dmg are inversely related across the N group-member relations. This in turn implies a state of imbalance of a very precarious nature so far as group stability is concerned. The least dependent member of a group will be the first to break from the group, and these members are precisely the most valued members. It is this situation which balancing operation number three alleviates through "giving status" to the highly valued members, thus gaining the power to keep and control those members.

These ideas are illustrated with hypothetical values in Table 47.1, with imbalance represented as power advantage (PA). Balancing operations will tend to move PA toward zero, as shown in column 6 after the highly valued members A and B have come to depend

TABLE 47.1 HYPOTHETICAL VALUES SHOWING THE RELATION BETWEEN DGM AND DMG IN A GROUP WITH FIVE MEMBERS

	Before Balancing			After Operation #3			After Operation #1		
	1	2	3	4	5	6	7	8	9
Member	Dgm	Dmg*	PAgm**	Dgm	Dmg	PAgm**	Dgm	Dmg	PAgm**
A	5	1	–4	5	5	0	5	5	0
B	4	2	–2	4	4	0	4	4	0
C	3	3	0	3	3	0	3	3	0
D	2	4	2	2	4	2	2	2	0
E	1	5	4	1	5	4	1	1	0

*Assuming that all members have the same motivational investment in the group at the outset, and that highly valued members (A and B) are valued in other groups as well.

** Power Advantage PAgm=Dmg–Dgm.

upon the group for the special rewards of status, and in column 9 after the least valued members D and E have withdrawn some of their original motivational investment in the group. The table presents three stages in status crystallization, and the process of crystallization is seen as a balancing process. The final stage (columns 7, 8, and 9) should be achieved only in groups with very low membership turnover. The middle stage might well be perpetual in groups with new members continually coming in at the lower levels. In such "open" groups, status striving should be a characteristic feature and can be taken as a direct manifestation of the tensions of imbalance. In the final stage, such strivers have either succeeded or withdrawn from the struggle.

Among the factors involved in status ordering, this theory focuses attention upon the extreme importance of the *availability factor* in dependency as a determinant of status position and the values employed in status ordering. In considering Dgm (the relative value or importance the group attaches to member roles), it is notably difficult to rely upon a functional explanation. Is the pitcher more highly valued than the center fielder because he is functionally more important or because good pitchers are harder to find? Is the physicist valued over the plumber because of a "more important" functional contribution to the social system, or because physicists are more difficult to replace, more costly to obtain, etc.? The latter considerations involve the availability factor. We suggest here that the *values* people use in ordering roles or persons express the dependence of

the system upon those roles, and that the availability factor in dependency plays the decisive part in historically shaping those values.[18]

CONCLUSION

The theory put forth in this paper is in large part contained implicitly in the ties of mutual dependence which bind actors together in social systems. Its principal value seems to be its ability to pull together a wide variety of social events, ranging from the internalization of parental codes to society-wide movements, like the collectivization of labor, in terms of a few very simple principles. Most important, the concepts involved are subject to operational formulation. Two experiments testing certain propositions discussed above led to the following results:

1. Conformity (Pgm) varies directly with motivational investment in the group;
2. Conformity varies inversely with acceptance in alternative groups;
3. Conformity is high at both status extremes in groups with membership turnover (see column 5, Table 47.1);
4. Highly valued members of a group are strong conformers only if they are valued by other groups as well. (This supports the notion that special status rewards are used to hold the highly valued member who does not depend heavily

upon the group, and that in granting him such rewards power is obtained over him.);

5. Coalitions form among the weak to control the strong (balancing operation number three);

6. The greatest rewards within a coalition are given to the less dependent member of the coalition (balancing operation number three, analogous to "status giving").

Once the basic ideas in this theory have been adequately validated and refined, both theoretical and empirical work must be extended in two main directions. First, the interaction process should be studied to locate carefully the factors leading to *perceived* power and dependency in self and others, and the conditions under which power, as a potential, will be employed in action. Secondly, and, in the long run, more important, will be study of *power networks* more complex than those referred to here, leading to more adequate understanding of complex power structures. The theory presented here does no more than provide the basic underpinning to the study of complex networks. There is every reason to believe that modern mathematics, graph theory in particular,[19] can be fruitfully employed in the analysis of complex networks and predicting the outcome of power plays within such networks.

NOTES

1. See the Communications by Jay Butler and Paul Harrison on "On Power and Authority: An Exchange on Concepts," *American Sociological Review*, 25 (October, 1960), pp. 731–732. That both men can be essentially correct in the points they make yet fail to reconcile these points, strongly suggests the need for conceptual development in the domain of power relations.

2. Among many studies, see Ronald Lippitt, Norman Polansky, Fritz Redl and Sidney Rosen, "The Dynamics of Power," *Human Relations*, 5 (February, 1952), pp. 37–64.

3. Floyd Hunter, *Community Power Structure*, Chapel Hill: University of North Carolina Press, 1953.

4. Max Weber, in *The Theory of Social and Economic Organization*, New York: Oxford University Press, 1947, presents what is still a classic formulation of power, authority and legitimacy. However, it is characteristic of Weber that he constructs a typology rather than an organized theory of power.

5. Hence see Raymond E. Wolfinger, "Reputation and Reality in the Study of `Community Power`," *American Sociological Review*, 25 (October, 1960), pp. 636–644, for a well-taken critical review of Floyd Hunter's work on these very points. The notion of "generalized power" which is not restricted to specific social relations, if taken literally, is probably meaningless. Power may indeed be generalized across a finite set of relations in a power network, but this notion too requires very careful analysis. Are you dealing with some kind of halo effect (reputations if you wish), or are the range and boundary of generalized power anchored in the power structure itself? These are questions which must be asked and answered.

6. Just as power is often treated as though it were a property of the person, so leadership, conformity, etc., are frequently referred to the personal traits of "leaders," "conformers" and so on, as if there were distinguishable types of people. In a sociological perspective such behavior should be explicitly treated as an attribute of a relation rather than a person.

7. The relation between power and dependence is given similar emphasis in the systematic treatment by J. Thibaut and H. H. Kelley, *The Social Psychology of Groups*, New York: John Wiley and Sons, 1959.

8. The notion of "opportunity costs" in economics is a similar idea. If an employee has alternative employment opportunities, and if these opportunities have low associated cost (travel, etc.), the employee's dependence upon his current employer is reduced.

9. In asserting that power is based upon the dependency of the other, it might appear that we are dealing with *one* of the bases of power ("reward power") listed by John R. P. French, Jr. and Bertram Raven, "The Bases of Social Power," *Studies in Social Power*, D. Cartwright, editor, Ann Arbor, Michigan: Institute for Social Research, 1959. However, careful attention to our highly generalized conception of dependence will show that it covers most if not all of the forms of power listed in that study.

10. Professor Alfred Kuhn, Department of Economics, University of Cincinnati, has been working on a theory for power analysis soon to be published. The scheme he develops, though very similar to the one presented here, is put together in a different way. It is anchored more tightly to economic concepts, and hence its implications lead off in different directions from those presented below.

11. Many different operational definitions can serve one theoretical concept, and there is no reason to require that they produce intercorrelated results when applied in the same research situation. While the controversies surrounding "operationalism" have now been largely resolved, there remains some confusion on this point. See, for example, Bernice Eisman, "Some Operational Measures of Cohesiveness and Their Interrelations," *Human Relations*, 12 (May, 1959), pp. 183–189.

12. J. Thibaut and H. H. Kelley, *op. cit.*, pp. 107–108.

13. This definition of cohesion, based upon dependency seems to have one advantage over the definition offered by Leon Festinger, et al., *Theory and Experiment in Social Communication*, Ann Arbor: Research Center for Group Dynamics, University of Michigan Press, 1950. The Festinger definition takes into account only one of the two variables involved in dependency.

14. The "tensions of imbalance" which are assumed to make an unbalanced relation unstable, are closely related to the idea of "distributive justice" discussed by George C. Homans, *Social Behavior: Its Elementary Forms*, New York: Harcourt, Brace and World, Inc., 1961. All of what Homans has to say around this idea could be fruitfully drawn into the present formulation.

15. The notion of closed versus open networks as discussed here can be directly related to research dealing with communication networks, such as that reported by Harold J. Leavitt, "Some Effects of Communication Patterns on Group Performance," *Journal of Abnormal and Social Psychology*, 46 (January, 1951), pp. 38–50, in which the limiting assumptions involved in this discussion are fully met by experimental controls. In discussing those experiments in terms of the concepts in this theory we would consider each actor's dependence upon other actors for information. A formal treatment of such networks is suggested by A. Bavelas, "A Mathematical Model For Group Structure," *Applied Anthropology*, 7 (Summer, 1948), pp. 16–30.

16. Dorothy Eggan, "The General Problem of Hopi Adjustment," *American Anthropologist*, 45 (July-September, 1943), pp. 357–373.

17. The process of legitimation has sometimes been described as a tactic employed by a person aspiring to power or trying to hold his power, rather than a process through which persons are granted restricted power. For example, C. Wright Mills states: "Those in authority attempt to justify their rule over institutions by linking it, as if it were a necessary consequence, with widely believed in moral symbols, sacred emblems, legal formulae. These central conceptions may refer to God or gods, the `vote of the majority,´ `the will of the people,´ `the aristocracy of talent or wealth,´ to the `divine right of kings,´ or to the allegedly extraordinary endowments of the ruler himself. Social scientists, following Weber, call such conceptions `legitimations,´ or sometimes `symbols of justification´ " (*The Sociological Imagination*, New York: Oxford University Press,

1959, p. 36). Whether we view the process of legitimation in the context of the formation of such collective conceptions, or in the context of calling upon them to justify action, the process is fundamentally that of mobilizing collective support to oppose those who challenge power. Power so supported is authority, and the process fits the general model of coalition formation.

18. "Motivational investment" and "availability," which jointly determine dependency at any point in time, are functionally related through time. This is implied in our balancing operations. While these two variables can be readily distinguished in the case of Dmg, they are too intimately fused in Dgm to be clearly separated. The values by which a group sees a given role as "important" at time 2, evolve from felt scarcity in that role and similar roles at time 1.

19. F. Harary and R. Norman, *Graph Theory as a Mathematical Model in the Social Sciences*, Ann Arbor: Institute for Social Research, 1953. An effort to apply such a model to power relations can be found in John R. P. French, Jr., "A Formal Theory of Social Power," *The Psychological Review*, 63 (May, 1956), pp. 181–194.

48. HUMAN CAPITAL AND SOCIAL CAPITAL

JAMES S. COLEMAN

In *Foundations of Social Theory* (1990), a lengthy theoretical treatise written near the end of a long and varied sociological career, James S. Coleman (1926–1995) emerged as the most important spokesperson in sociology for rational choice theory, an orientation that has had a major impact in economics and political science. As with Homans´ exchange theory, the starting point for Coleman´s paradigm is the individual; he endorses a conceptual orientation known as "methodological individualism." The two elementary concepts in Coleman´s theory are actors and resources. In this selection from the book, two key resources—human capital and social capital—are described. The former refers to the skills and knowledge an individual possesses, while the latter refers to social relations.

Probably the most important and most original development in the economics of education in the past thirty years has been the idea that the concept of physical capital, as embodied in tools, machines, and other productive equipment, can be extended to include human capital as well (see Schultz, 1961; Becker, 1964). Just as physical capital is created by making changes in materials so as to form tools that facilitate production, human capital is created by changing persons so as to give them skills and capabilities that make them able to act in new ways.

Social capital, in turn, is created when the relations among persons change in ways that facilitate action. Physical capital is wholly tangible, being embodied in observable material form; human capital is less tangible, being embodied in the skills and knowledge acquired by an individual; social capital is even less tangible, for it is embodied in the *relations* among persons. Physical capital and human capital facilitate productive activity, and social capital does so as well. For example, a group whose members manifest trustworthiness and place extensive trust in one another will be able to accomplish much more than a comparable group lacking that trustworthiness and trust.

The distinction between human capital and social capital can be exhibited by a diagram such as Figure 48.1, which represents the relations of three persons (A, B, and C); the human capital resides in the nodes, and the social capital resides in the lines connecting the nodes. Social capital and human capital are often complementary. For example, if B is a child and A is an adult who is a parent of B, then for A to further the cognitive development of B, there must be capital in both the node and the link. There must be human capital held by A and social capital in the relation between A and B.

Using the concept of social capital will uncover no processes that are different in fundamental ways from those discussed in other chapters. This concept groups some of those processes together and blurs distinctions between types of social relations, distinctions that are important for other purposes. The value of the concept lies primarily in the fact that it identifies certain aspects of social structure by their function, just as the concept "chair" identifies certain physical objects by their function, disregarding differences in form, appearance, and construction. The function identified by the concept "social capital" is the value of those aspects of social

---

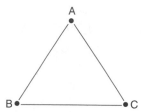

FIGURE 48.1 Three-Person Structure: Human Capital in Nodes and Social Capital in Relations

structure to actors, as resources that can be used by the actors to realize their interests.

By identifying this function of certain aspects of social structure, the concept of social capital aids in both accounting for different outcomes at the level of individual actors and making the micro-to-macro transition without elaborating the social-structural details through which this occurs. For example, characterizing the clandestine study circles of South Korean radical students as constituting social capital that these students can use in their revolutionary activities is an assertion that the groups constitute a resource which aids in moving the students from individual protest to organized revolt. If a resource that accomplishes this task is held to be necessary in a theory of revolt ... then the study circles can be grouped with other organizational structures, of different origins, which have fulfilled the same function for individuals with revolutionary goals in other contexts, such as the *comités d'action lycéen* of the French student revolt of 1968 or the workers' cells in czarist Russia described and advocated by Lenin (1973 [1902]).

It is true, of course, that for other purposes one wants to investigate the details of such organizational resources, to understand the elements that are critical to their usefulness as resources for a given purpose, and to examine how they came into being in a particular case. But the concept of social capital can allow showing how such resources can be combined with other resources to produce different system-level behavior or, in other cases, different outcomes for individuals. Whether

social capital will come to be as useful a quantitative concept in social science as are the concepts of financial capital, physical capital, and human capital remains to be seen; its current value lies primarily in its usefulness for qualitative analyses of social systems and for those quantitative analyses that employ qualitative indicators.

... ['I']he concept of social capital will be left unanalyzed (as it was in the brief descriptions given above as examples). In this chapter, however, I will examine just what it is about social relations that can constitute useful capital resources for individuals.

OBLIGATIONS AND EXPECTATIONS

... [I]f A does something for B and trusts B to reciprocate in the future, this establishes an expectation in A and an obligation on the part of B to keep the trust. This obligation can be conceived of as a "credit slip" held by A to be redeemed by some performance by B. If A holds a large number of these credit slips from a number of persons with whom he has relations, then the analogy to financial capital is direct: The credit slips constitute a large body of credit on which A can draw if necessary—unless, of course, the placement of trust has been unwise, and the slips represent bad debts that will not be repaid. In some social structures (such as, for example, the neighborhoods discussed by Willmott and Young, 1967) it is said that people are "always doing things for each other." There are a large number of these credit slips outstanding, often on both sides of a relation (for these credit slips often appear to be not fungible across different areas of activity, so credit slips from B held by A and those from A held by B are not fully used to cancel each other out). ... In other social structures where individuals are more self-sufficient, depending on each other less, there are fewer of these credit slips outstanding at any time.

Two elements are critical to this form of social capital: the level of trustworthiness of the social environment, which means that obligations will be repaid, and the actual extent of obligations held. Social structures differ in both of these dimensions, and actors within a particular structure differ in the second.

A case which illustrates the value of trustworthiness is the rotating credit association found in Southeast Asia and elsewhere. These associations are groups of friends and neighbors who typically meet monthly; each person contributes the same amount of money to a central fund, which is then given to one of the members (through bidding or by lot). After n months each of the n persons has made n contributions and received one payout. As Geertz (1962) points out, these associations serve as efficient institutions for amassing savings for small capital expenditures, an important aid to economic development. Without a high degree of trustworthiness among the members of the group, such a credit association could not exist—for a person who received a payout early in the sequence of meetings could abscond, leaving the others with a loss. One could not imagine such a rotating credit association operating successfully in urban areas marked by a high degree of social disorganization—or, in other words, by a lack of social capital.

Another situation in which extreme trustworthiness facilitates actions that would not otherwise be possible is that of heads of state. Various accounts of the experiences of heads of state suggest that for persons in this position it is extremely valuable to have an extension of one's self, an agent one can trust absolutely to act as one would in a given situation. Many heads of state have such a person, who may not occupy a formal position of power but may be a member of a personal staff. The fact that these persons are often old friends, or cronies, rather than persons who have distinguished themselves in some political activity, is derivative from this: The most important attribute of such a person is that trust can be placed in him, and this requirement often dictates choosing a long-term personal friend. Such persons often come to have enormous power due to their proximity to a head of state and the trust placed in them; and there are many recorded accounts of the use of that power. What is of interest here is the social capital this relation provides for the head of state, assuming that the trust is well placed. The trusted other is virtually an extension of self, allowing the head of state to expand his capacity for action.

Still another case that illustrates the importance of trustworthiness as a form of social capital is a system of

mutual trust. The extreme example of such a system is a couple, each of whom places extensive trust in the other, whether they are deeply in love or not. For both members of such a couple, the relation has extraordinary psychological value. Each can confide in the other, can expose inner doubts, can be completely forthright with the other, can raise sensitive issues—all without fear of the other's misuse of the trust.

Differences in social structures with respect to the extent of outstanding obligations arise for a variety of reasons. These include, besides the general level of trustworthiness that leads obligations to be repaid, the actual needs that persons have for help, the existence of other sources of aid (such as government welfare services), the degree of affluence (which reduces the amount of aid needed from others), cultural differences in the tendency to lend aid and ask for aid (see Banfield, 1967), the degree of closure of social networks, the logistics of social contacts (see Festinger, Schachter, and Back, 1963), and other factors. Individuals in social structures with high levels of obligations outstanding at any time, whatever the source of those obligations, have greater social capital on which they can draw. The density of outstanding obligations means, in effect, that the overall usefulness of the tangible resources possessed by actors in that social structure is amplified by their availability to other actors when needed.

In a farming community such as . . . where one farmer got his hay baled by another and where farm tools are extensively borrowed and lent, the social capital allows each farmer to get his work done with less physical capital in the form of tools and equipment. Such a social structure is analogous to an industrial community in which bills of exchange (that is, debts) are passed around, serving as money and effectively reducing the financial capital necessary to carry out a given level of manufacturing activity. (See Ashton, 1945, for a description of this in Lancashire in the 1790s, before a centralized monetary system was well established in England.)

Individual actors in a social system also differ with respect to the extent of credit slips on which they can draw at any time. For example, in hierarchically structured extended family settings, a patriarch often holds an extraordinarily large set of such credit slips, which he can call in at any time to get done what he wants done. Another clear example occurs in villages in traditional settings that are highly stratified, where certain wealthy families, because of their wealth, have built up extensive credits on which they can call at any time. (It is the existence of such asymmetries that can make some families immune to sanctions that can be used to regulate the actions of others in the community . . . .)

Similarly, in a political setting such as a legislature, a legislator in a position that brings extra resources (such as the Speaker of the House of Representatives or the Majority Leader of the Senate in the U.S. Congress) can, by effective use of those resources, build up a set of credits from other legislators so that it becomes possible for him to get legislation passed that would otherwise be defeated. This concentration of obligations constitutes social capital that is useful not only for the powerful legislator, but also in increasing the level of action of the legislature. Thus those members of legislatures who have extensive credit slips should be more powerful than those who do not because they can use the credits to produce bloc voting on many issues. It is well recognized, for example, that in the U.S. Senate, some senators are members of what is called the Senate Club, and others are not. This in effect means that some senators are embedded in a system of credits and debts, and others (outside the Club) are not. It is also well recognized that those in the Club are more powerful than those outside it.

Another example showing asymmetry in the sets of obligations and expectations is the one . . . about the crisis in medical care in the United States due to liability suits. Traditionally physicians have been in control of events having literally life-and-death importance to patients, who in turn often felt unable to adequately compensate them for the extreme benefits they brought about. Part of a physician´s payment was in the form of gratitude, deference, and high occupational prestige. These constituted a felt obligation to the physician, a form of social capital which inhibited patients dissatisfied with the outcome of their medical treatments from taking action against the physician.

But several factors have changed. One is that physicians´ monopoly on medical knowledge has been lessened by an expansion of education. A second is a reduction in the likelihood that there is a personal relation between physician and patient, since a patient is less likely to use a family doctor or even a general practitioner and more likely to see specialists for particular medical problems. A third is the high income of many physicians, which reduces the perceived asymmetry between service and compensation. A fourth is the increased use of liability insurance, which transfers the financial cost of a lawsuit from physician to insurer. The combination of these and other factors has reduced the social capital that protected the physician from becoming a target when patients experienced undesirable medical outcomes.

* * *

Why do rational actors create obligations? Although some of the variation in the extent of outstanding obligations arises from social changes of the sort described above, some appears to arise from the intentional creation of obligation by a person who does something for another. For example, Turnbull (1972), who studied the Ik, a poverty-ridden tribe in Africa, describes an occasion when a man arrived home to find his neighbors, unasked, on the roof of his house fixing it. Despite his not wanting this aid, he was unable to induce them to stop. In this case and others there appears to be, not the creation of obligations through necessity, but a purposive creation of obligations. The giving of gifts has been interpreted in this light (see Mauss, 1954), as have the potlatches of the Kwakiutl tribe in the Pacific Northwest. In rural areas persons who do favors for others often seem to prefer that these favors not be repaid immediately, and those for whom a favor is done sometimes seem anxious to relieve themselves of the obligation.

Although the motives for freeing oneself from obligations may be readily understood (especially if the existence of obligations consumes one´s attention), the motives for creating obligations toward oneself are less transparent. If there is a nonzero chance that the obligation will not be repaid, it would appear that rational persons would extend such credit only if they expect to receive something greater in return—just as a bank makes a loan only at sufficient interest to realize a profit after allowing for risk. The question then becomes whether there is anything about social obligations to make a rational person interested in establishing and maintaining such obligations on the part of others toward himself.

A possible answer is this: When I do a favor for you, this ordinarily occurs at a time when you have a need and involves no great cost to me. If I am rational and purely self-interested, I see that the importance to you of this favor is sufficiently great that you will be ready to repay me with a favor in my time of need that will benefit me more than this favor costs me—unless, of course, you are also in need at that time. This does not apply when the favor is merely the lending of money, since a unit of money holds about the same interest to a person over time.[1] When the favor involves services, expenditure of time, or some other nonfungible resource, however, or when it is of intrinsically more value to the recipient than to the donor (such as help with a task that can be done by two persons but not by one), this kind of mutually profitable exchange is quite possible. The profitability for the donor depends on the recipient's not repaying the favor until the donor is in need.

Thus creating obligations by doing favors can constitute a kind of insurance policy for which the premiums are paid in inexpensive currency and the benefit arrives as valuable currency. There may easily be a positive expected profit.

There is one more point: A rational, self-interested person may attempt to prevent others from doing favors for him or may attempt to relieve himself of an obligation at a time he chooses (that is, when repaying the favor costs him little), rather than when the donor is in need, because the call for his services may come at an inconvenient time (when repaying the obligation would be costly). Thus in principle there can be a struggle between a person wanting to do a favor for another and the other not wanting to have the favor done for him or a struggle between a person attempting to repay a favor and his creditor attempting to prevent repayment.

INFORMATION POTENTIAL

An important form of social capital is the potential for information that inheres in social relations. Information is important in providing a basis for action. But acquisition of information is costly. The minimum it requires is attention, which is always in short supply. One means by which information can be acquired is to use social relations that are maintained for other purposes. Katz and Lazarsfeld (1955) show how this operates for women in several areas of life; for example, a woman who has an interest in being in style but not at the leading edge of fashion can use certain friends, who do stay on the leading edge, as sources of information. As another example, a person who is not deeply interested in current events but who is interested in being informed about important developments can save the time required to read a newspaper if he can get the information he wants from a friend who pays attention to such matters. A social scientist who is interested in being up to date on research in related fields can make use of his everyday interactions with colleagues to do so, if he can depend on them to be up to date in their fields.

All these are examples of social relations that constitute a form of social capital in providing information that facilitates action. The relations in this case are valuable for the information they provide, not for the credit slips they provide in the form of obligations that one holds for others' performance.

NORMS AND EFFECTIVE SANCTIONS

... When an effective norm does exist, it constitutes a powerful, but sometimes fragile, form of social capital. Effective norms that inhibit crime in a city make it possible for women to walk freely outside at night and for old people to leave their homes without fear. Norms in a community that support and provide effective rewards for high achievement in school greatly facilitate the school's task. A prescriptive norm that constitutes an especially important form of social capital within a collectivity is the norm that one should forgo self-interests to act in the interests of the collectivity. A norm of this sort, reinforced by social support, status, honor, and other rewards, is the social capital which builds young nations (and which dissipates as they grow older), strengthens families by leading members to act selflessly in the family's interest, facilitates the development of nascent social movements from a small group of dedicated, inward-looking, and mutually rewarding persons, and in general leads persons to work for the public good.

In some of these cases the norms are internalized; in others they are largely supported through external rewards for selfless actions and disapproval for selfish actions. But whether supported by internal or external sanctions, norms of this sort are important in overcoming the public-good problem that exists in conjoint collectivities.

As all these examples suggest, effective norms can constitute a powerful form of social capital. This social capital, however, like the forms described earlier, not only facilitates certain actions but also constrains others. Strong and effective norms about young persons´ behavior in a community can keep them from having a good time. Norms which make it possible for women to walk alone at night also constrain the activities of criminals (and possibly of some noncriminals as well). Even prescriptive norms that reward certain actions, such as a norm which says that a boy who is a good athlete should go out for football, are in effect directing energy away from other activities. Effective norms in an area can reduce innovativeness in that area, can constrain not only deviant actions that harm others but also deviant actions that can benefit everyone. (See Merton, 1968, pp. 195–203, for a discussion of how this can come about.)

AUTHORITY RELATIONS

If actor A has transferred rights of control of certain actions to another actor, B, then B has available social capital in the form of those rights of control. If a number of actors have transferred similar rights of control to B, then B has available an extensive body of social capital, which can be concentrated on certain activities. Of course, this puts extensive power in B´s hands. What is not quite so straightforward is that the very concentration of these rights in a single actor increases the total social capital by overcoming (in principle, if not always entirely in fact) the free-rider problem experienced by individuals with similar interests but without a common authority. It appears, in fact, to be precisely the desire to bring into being the social capital needed to solve common problems that leads persons under certain circumstances to vest authority in a charismatic leader (as discussed . . . in Zablocki, 1980, and Scholem, 1973).

APPROPRIABLE SOCIAL ORGANIZATION

Voluntary organizations are brought into being to further some purpose of those who initiate them. In a housing project built during World War II in a city in the eastern United States, there were many physical problems caused by poor construction, such as faulty plumbing, crumbling sidewalks, and other defects (Merton, n.d.). Residents organized to confront the builders and to address these problems in other ways. Later, when the problems were solved, the residents´ organization remained active and constituted available social capital which improved the quality of life in the project. Residents had available to them resources that were seen as unavailable where they had lived before. (For example, despite the fact that there were *fewer* teenagers in the community, residents were *more* likely to express satisfaction concerning the availability of babysitters.)

Members of the New York Typographical Union who were monotype operators formed a social club called the Monotype Club (Lipset, Trow, and Coleman, 1956). Later, as employers looked for monotype operators and as monotype operators looked for jobs, both found this organization to be an effective employment referral service and utilized it for this purpose. Still later, when the Progressive Party came into power in the New York Typographical Union, the Monotype Club served as an organizational resource for the ousted Independent Party. The Monotype Club subsequently served as an important source of social capital for the Independents, sustaining their party as an organized opposition while they were out of office.

In an example used earlier in this chapter, the study circles of South Korean student radicals were described as being groups of students who came from the same high school or hometown or church. In this case also, organization that was initiated for one purpose is appropriable for other purposes, constituting important social capital for the individuals who have available to them the organizational resources.

These examples illustrate the general point that organization brought into existence for one set of purposes can also aid others, thus constituting social capital that is available for use.[2] It may be that this form of social capital can be dissolved, with nothing left over, into elements that are discussed under other headings in this section, that is, obligations and expectations, information potential, norms, and authority relations. If so, listing this form of social capital is redundant. But the phenomenon of social organization being appropriated as existing social capital for new purposes is such a pervasive one that separate mention appears warranted.

INTENTIONAL ORGANIZATION

A major use of the concept of social capital depends on its being a by-product of activities engaged in for other purposes. ... [T]here is often little or no direct investment in social capital. There are, however, forms of social capital which are the direct result of investment by actors who have the aim of receiving a return on their investment.

The most prominent example is a business organization created by the owners of financial capital for the purpose of earning income for them. These organizations ordinarily take the form of authority structures composed of positions connected by obligations and expectations and occupied by persons.... In creating such an organization, an entrepreneur or capitalist transforms financial capital into physical capital in the form of buildings and tools, social capital in the form of the organization of positions, and human capital in the form of persons occupying positions. Like the other forms of capital, social capital requires investment in the designing of the structure of obligations and expectations, responsibility and authority, and norms

(or rules) and sanctions which will bring about an effectively functioning organization.

Another form of intentional organization is a voluntary association which produces a public good. For example, a group of parents whose children attend a school forms a PTA chapter where one did not exist before. This organization constitutes social capital not only for the organizers but for the school, the students, and other parents. Even if the organization serves only the original purpose for which it is organized and is not appropriated for other purposes, as is the case for organizations described in an earlier section, it serves this purpose, by its very nature, for a wider range of actors than those who initiated it. Such an organization is, concretely, of the same sort as those described earlier. The PTA is the same kind of organization as the Monotype Club, the residents' association formed to deal with faulty plumbing, and the church groups of South Korean Youth. All are voluntary associations. As it functions, however, the organization creates two kinds of by-products as social capital. One is the by-product described in the preceding section, the appropriability of the organization for other purposes. A second is the by-product described here: Because the organization produces a public good, its creation by one subset of persons makes its benefits available to others as well, whether or not they participate. For example, the disciplinary standards promulgated by an active PTA change a school in ways that benefit nonparticipants as well as participants....

NOTES

1. It is interesting that, for persons whose interest in money fluctuates wildly over time, this sort of exchange is possible. In a rural county in West Virginia, the county clerk would lend money to the three town drunks when their need for money was great and then collect from them, with exorbitant interest, when they received their welfare checks, when money was of less interest to them.
2. A classic instance of this is described by Sills (1957). The March of Dimes was originally dedicated to the elimination of polio. When Salk's vaccine virtually eradicated polio, the March of Dimes organization did not go out of existence but directed its efforts toward other diseases.

REFERENCES

Ashton, T. S. 1945. The bill of exchange and private banks in Lancashire, 1790–1830. *Economic History Review* 15, nos. 1, 2:25–35.

Banfield, E. 1967. *The moral basis of a backward society*. New York: Free Press.

Becker, G. 1964. *Human capital*. New York: National Bureau of Economic Research, Columbia University Press.

Festinger, L., S. Schachter, and K. Back. 1963. *Social pressures in informal groups*. Stanford: Stanford University Press.

Geertz, C. 1962. The rotating credit association: a "middle rung" in development. *Economic Development and Cultural Change* 10:240–263.

Katz, E., and P. F. Lazarsfeld. 1955. *Personal influence*. New York: Free Press.

Lenin, V. I. 1973 (1902). *What is to be done?* Peking: Foreign Language Press.

Lipset, M., M. A. Trow, and J. S. Coleman. 1956. *Union democracy*. New York: Free Press.

Mauss, M. 1954. *The gift*. New York: Free Press.

Merton, R. K. 1968. *Social theory and social structure*. 3rd ed. New York: Free Press.

———. n.d. Study of World War II housing projects. Unpublished manuscript. Columbia University, Department of Sociology.

Scholem, G. 1973. *Sabbatai Sevi, the mystical messiah*. Princeton: Princeton University Press.

Schultz, T. 1961. Investment in human capital. *American Economic Review* 51 (March):1–17.

Sills, D. 1957. *The volunteers, means and ends in a national organization*. New York: Free Press.

Turnbull, C. 1972. *The mountain people*. New York: Simon and Schuster.

Willmott, P., and M. Young. 1967. *Family and class in a London suburb*. London: New English Library.

Zablocki, B. 1980. *Alienation and charisma*. New York: Free Press.

49. THE EMERGENCE OF COOPERATIVE SOCIAL INSTITUTIONS

MICHAEL HECHTER

From a rational choice perspective, Michael Hechter (b. 1943) attempts in this essay to offer an account of the manner in which social institutions arise. Rejecting what he terms the "invisible hand" approach, which treats institutions as the spontaneous outcome of the actions of self-interested individuals in interaction with others, he opts for a "solidaristic" approach. Of the two variants of solidaristic explanation—the imposition of institutions by powerful rulers versus the voluntary construction of institutions by relatively equal individuals—Hechter turns to the latter, since it raises the more interesting theoretical issues. Not the least of these issues is the matter of the "free-rider problem," a major focus of attention in this selection.

The origin of social institutions is a very old concern in social theory. Currently it has reemerged as one of the most intensely debated issues in social science. Among economists and rational choice theorists, there is growing awareness that most, if not all, of the social outcomes that are of interest to explain are at least partly a function of institutional constraints. Yet the role of institutions is negligible both in general equilibrium theory and in most neoclassical economic models. Among other social scientists, there is a burgeoning substantive interest in institutions ranging from social movements, to formal organizations, to states, and even international regimes.

This chapter discusses the two principal approaches to the problem of institutional genesis—*invisible-hand* and *solidaristic*. It further argues that the second of these is likely to afford us with a better means of attacking the problem than the first. Finally, one particular solidaristic explanation that holds promise for future research on institutional genesis is introduced.

THE CONCEPT OF SOCIAL INSTITUTIONS

Although the term *institution* is bandied about quite liberally in contemporary social science, no consensual definition of it has as yet emerged. The ambiguity of the term gives authors both the obligation and the license to adopt their favorite definition. At the most general level, I will take the existence of a social institution to be revealed by the appearance of *some regularity in collective behavior*. *Collective behavior* may be said to occur if different individuals behave similarly when placed in the same social situation;[1] *regularity*, for its part, indicates that this collective behavior endures over some long but indefinite period of time.

If institutions are revealed by the appearance of collective behavioral regularities, then one naturally wonders both about their origins and about the mechanisms responsible for their persistence. In institutionally rich environments, new institutions can arise from old ones through modification or diffusion processes (White, 1981; DiMaggio and Powell, 1983).

Such solutions to the problem of institutional genesis are limited, however, because they are exogenous and thus beg the question of the prime mover.

What is most challenging to account for theoretically is just how institutions emerge out of anarchy, that is, from a state of nature. How, in other words, do institutions ever arise from a *noninstitutional* environment? Two types of explanations have been advanced to address this hoary old Hobbesian problem.

The *invisible-hand* approach to institutional genesis, advocated to a greater or lesser degree by Menger [1883] (1963), Hayek (1973; 1976), and Nozick (1974), among others, views the emergence of institutions as a spontaneous by-product of the voluntary actions of self-interested individuals who share *no common ends or values* (see Hayek, 1976:111). In such accounts, existing social institutions are usually conceived as Pareto-efficient equilibria; therefore they are self-sustaining (because no one who is subject to them has an incentive to change them), rather than dependent on some third-party enforcement apparatus (like the state) whose existence, in turn, requires additional explanation.

Since invisible-hand arguments can offer an entirely endogenous explanation for the emergence of social institutions, they are to be admired for their parsimony and elegance (Nozick, 1974:18–22; Ullmann-Margalit, 1978). Their principal advantage is that they rely on fewer assumptions than do other kinds of explanations.

The alternative approach to the problem of institutional genesis rests on quite different premises. Rather than emerging spontaneously among self-interested actors each pursuing their own ends, institutions in this view are a product of *solidarity*. Solidarity can only arise among individuals who share some common end (Hechter, 1987). To attain this common end, actors must establish a set of obligations as well as a mechanism that enforces compliance to these obligations (Hobbes, [1651] 1968; Durkheim [1897] 1951; Blau, 1964:253; Hayek, 1976). From the solidaristic perspective, institutions persist not because they constitute self-enforcing equilibria, but because they are supported by consciously-designed controls.

There are two varieties of solidaristic explanations. On the one hand, institutions can be *imposed* upon a given population by some conqueror or overlord. Since it is easy to explain institutional emergence in the face of significant power differentials among individuals, this solution begs too many questions to be theoretically interesting (as Hobbes well understood). On the other hand, individuals with roughly equal power can create institutions *voluntarily*, in effect binding themselves to a joint project. This contractarian process is theoretically interesting precisely because it is such a problematic outcome.

Which approach is superior, the invisible-hand or solidaristic one? There is a great deal of debate in the literature on this question. Most of the advocates of invisible-hand explanations of institutional genesis rest their arguments on repeated game theory.

Yet, these arguments only suffice for the establishment and maintenance of *conventions* (Lewis, 1969)—such as the rule that we all drive on the right hand side of the road[2]—rather than for the establishment of *n*-person *cooperative institutions*. By cooperative institution, I refer to an institution, principally serving non-closely related kin,[3] that enables those who are subject to it to reap a surplus by agreeing on a jointly maximizing strategy that is otherwise unavailable due to the absence or inappropriateness of markets.

There is an essential difference between conventions and cooperative institutions. Cooperation is the dominant strategy in conventions because there is no free-rider problem. Compliance with a convention provides its own private reward: for example, drivers who ignore conventional rules of the road take their own lives in hand. Hence, conventions indeed can be conceived of as equilibria. In cooperative institutions (which resemble Prisoner's Dilemmas), however, defection is the dominant strategy. Hence, these institutions can persist only by precluding free riders, or by assuring would-be cooperators that they are not liable to be exploited by defectors.

Contrary to the rhetoric of Taylor (1976), Hardin (1982), and Axelrod (1984), repeated game theory offers no adequate solution to the emergence of cooperation among *n* players of a Prisoner's Dilemma supergame (Hechter, 1990). The inadequacy of repeated game theory in this respect is due to two separate problems. In the first place, there are multiple equilibria in the supergame, some of which are efficient and some inefficient (Aumann, 1985).[4] Yet under most conditions it is difficult to determine which of these multiple equilibria will be realized. In the second place, unique cooperative solutions to the supergame rest on a most unrealistic assumption—that players are endowed with perfect monitoring capacity (Bendor and Mookherjee, 1987). This assumption limits the application of game-theoretic solutions to the evolution of cooperative institutions to the smallest of groups.[5]

In the wake of these current difficulties with the invisible-hand approach, it is best to consider the merits of solidaristic explanations, even though they require much stronger initial conditions. From a solidaristic point of view, the emergence of cooperative institutions requires individual agreement on some common end, acceptance of corporate obligations, and the establishment of formal controls to preclude free riding.

Can these admittedly strong initial conditions be explained on the basis of the typical self-interested behavioral assumptions of rational choice theory?[6] I believe that the answer to this question is a qualified *yes*. Using the relatively weak assumptions that are traditional in rational choice, it is indeed possible to explain the emergence of cooperative institutions on the basis of solidaristic logic. The remainder of this chapter sketches out the basic argument, and then suggests that the argument can be applied to several types of empirical situations.

A SOLIDARISTIC APPROACH TO THE EMERGENCE OF COOPERATIVE INSTITUTIONS

Briefly, the genesis of cooperative institutions depends on the conjunction of (1) individuals' *demands* to provide themselves with jointly-produced private (that is, excludable) goods, as well as on (2) these individuals' potential *control capacity*—that is, their opportunities either to dissuade each other from free riding, or to assure each other of their intent to cooperate. Both demand and control capacity are necessary for the emergence of cooperative institutions; without either, this kind of institutional genesis is doomed.

The demand for cooperative institutions arises from individuals' desires to consume jointly-produced

private goods (hereafter termed *joint goods*) that cannot be obtained by following individual strategies. Cooperative institutions are generally formed to take advantage of positive externalities, such as increasing returns to scale, risk-sharing, and cost-sharing. The demand for joint goods is heightened by contextual events like wars, invasions, epidemics, and natural disasters, as well as by endogenous processes like rapid demographic growth. These events and processes are commonly experienced by a number of people, and on this account stimulate demand for goods that spread risk—such as the protection afforded by walls around a settlement, and the insurance provided the establishment of a mutual benefit society.

But the mere existence of demand for a joint good is insufficient to guarantee its production. One of the firmest conclusions of rational choice is that whereas the production of private goods is hardly problematic, in general public goods will not be produced at optimal levels, if they are produced at all. Whether a joint good is public or private is largely a function of its excludability from potential consumers. With respect to producers, both the protection afforded by town walls and the insurance offered by mutual benefit associations are *collective* goods, but with respect to consumers they are *private* goods in that these consumers (under certain conditions) can be readily excluded from them.

Whether or not a joint good is excludable is, at least in part, due to the control capacity of the potential producers of the good. This control capacity depends upon formal controls that must emerge endogenously. The establishment of these formal controls may be seen as a series of solutions to a three-tier free-rider problem. All three of these free-rider problems must be solved before a cooperative institution can emerge. Since the first two of these problems are already well-appreciated in the literature, this chapter focuses on the third of these.

THE FIRST TIER FREE-RIDER PROBLEM—DESIGN-MAKING

In the first place, at least one design or plan must be devised that promises to yield the joint good. Each plan must comprise a set of *production rules* that specify what must get done by whom in order to provide an adequate supply of the good.[7] Yet since these designs are themselves a collective good, who will devise them? Although X is eager to consume the joint good, X can spend her time more profitably by attempting to add to her resource endowment than by thinking up designs for newfangled institutions.

The solution to this first-order free-rider problem is the entrepreneurial one; it lies in the individuals' incentive to think up designs that—were their design implemented—would provide them with private benefits greatly exceeding the cost of design-making. For example, ambitious individuals would gamble by formulating plans whose adoption requires either expertise or resources that they alone can claim to have.

THE SECOND TIER FREE-RIDER PROBLEM: ESTABLISHMENT OF AN INITIAL CONSTITUTION

One particular design then must be selected by the relevant population. The desire to consume the joint good motivates individuals to make such a selection, for if they fail to do so, too little of the good will be produced. It is probable that each rational individual will prefer a realistic design that seems to offer the greatest amount of the good at the least (private) cost. These individual preferences must then be aggregated into a collective design. Under the conditions of the state of nature—that is, in the absence of any prior institutional framework, and in the absence of any significant resource imbalance among participants— agreement on a unanimity rule is likeliest among a relatively small group of rational egoists, because this kind of rule is most consistent with each member's private interest (Buchanan and Tullock, 1962).

THE THIRD TIER FREE-RIDER PROBLEM: IMPLEMENTATION OF THE DESIGN

Even though all institution-builders want to consume the joint good, each rational actor will prefer to free ride on the others' contributions. This preference may not however, characterize those contingent cooperators who would willingly contribute to the establishment of a cooperative institution if they were assured that others would do likewise (this is often known as the *assurance problem*). If there is no means of deterring free riders, then there will be suboptimal production of the joint good—either because everyone prefers to free ride, or because the assurance problem cannot be resolved to the satisfaction of contingent cooperators.[8]

Whatever its specific causes, suboptimal production of the joint good leads the group to unravel. In order to attain optimal production, formal controls that assure high levels of compliance with production (and distribution) rules by monitoring and sanctioning group members must be adopted.

Yet since these controls are themselves a collective good, their establishment has been difficult to explain from choice-theoretic premises. One solution (the solution I have been working on) flows from the *visibility* of the production and distribution of the joint good.

For a joint good to be maximally excludable, both individual production and distribution must be highly visible. In the absence of visibility, neither free riding (a production problem), nor overconsumption (a distribution problem) can be precluded. Production visibility is at a maximum when individual effort can be well-measured by output assessment. Distribution visibility, however, is at a maximum when individuals must draw measurable shares of the joint good publicly from some central store or repository.

Most (if not all) of the positive externalities of cooperative institutions rest on the advantages of pooling individual assets so that a common central store, or bank, is thereby established. The individual depositor expects to draw some net private benefit from this central store (either interest, or—most likely in the state of nature—access to a wholly different kind of good than that deposited, such as a share of the meat of a large game animal, or insurance against some loss).

Two examples should suffice to illustrate how control is attained in cooperative institutions. In hunting and gathering societies hunters pool individual inputs of time and labor in drives to kill large game that yield meat. Both the production and distribution of killed meat is highly visible to the other hunters. The effort that each hunter contributes to the drive is difficult to conceal: individual roles in the drive are agreed upon before it takes place, and whether a given person is performing his assigned role is relatively visible (although this is a less accurate way to judge his contribution than output assessment would provide). As for distribution, the meat that is produced by the drive is usually spatially concentrated—and thereby constitutes a central fund—for, given the technology of hunter-gatherers, the most efficient way to kill large animals is to stampede them into shallow arroyos or pits (Wheat, 1967; Lee, 1979).

In rotating credit associations (Hechter, 1987: Chap. 6), individuals pool a given amount of money (which is maximally visible because it is an archetypical output) for the right to draw upon the common store of money to increase their purchasing power. In this way the monetary contributions of individual participants generate what is in effect a credit line, access to which is highly visible to all other participants.

Once individual assets are pooled in a central place, however, another free-rider problem occurs: how is it possible to stop a depositor from taking more than her fair share, or from consuming the entire central fund? This is a question that faces all rational investors—would you be likely to deposit your paycheck in a bank that you believe will soon be robbed? Presumably, only if you had some assurance that your deposit is secure. *Hence it is rational for individuals to establish formal controls in cooperative institutions so as to preserve the integrity of their investment* (which, after all, is a private good). By establishing these controls, individuals inadvertently provide themselves with a collective good—namely, security of the common fund.

But who will monitor the depositors; who will sanction them; and how will the requisite sanctioning resources be produced?

All members will take on the burden of monitoring in the initial cooperative institution. Since anyone who consumes more than their fair share of the common fund appropriates some of my own assets, I am motivated to try to get my own (augmented) investment back. There is no free-rider problem here. Whereas I can assume that other members also have an interest in getting their own investment back, I have no assurance that they won't take my share, split it among themselves, and claim that my share was never found. There is no guarantee that anyone else will look after my interests.

Likewise, *all members* will sanction the noncompliant depositor; no depositor has anything to gain by associating with a rule-breaker whose assets have already been stripped—and presumably much to lose (if it is discovered that the deviant has been helped, the

helper herself is then subject to sanctioning).[9] Finally, the ultimate sanctioning resource is easily produced, for it lies entirely within the control of the members themselves—ostracism from the group.[10]

BY-PRODUCTS OF EXTANT COOPERATIVE INSTITUTIONS: A FOURTH TIER IN INSTITUTIONAL GENESIS

It is likely that the institutionalized group may come to produce different goods than those providing its initial rationale. This is because the group now has the immense comparative advantage that it is *already organized*[11] and therefore can produce new joint goods much more efficiently than can unorganized individuals.[12]

In certain situations, the group may even come to produce *public* (nonexcludable) goods. This can occur if members gain so much from the production of a public good that they are willing to provide it even to non-contributors.[13] In larger groups, this can also occur due to *agency* considerations. This will happen if the agent is not fully constrained by her principals, and if she can increase her own reputation by transforming some of the assets of the central fund into public goods.[14]

All told, this analysis suggests that cooperative institutions indeed can arise from the interaction of rational egoists in a state of nature. In such an environment, however, cooperative institutions will emerge only in a contractarian fashion. Without prior cooperative institutions, there can be no entrepreneurial route to new ones. This is why the earliest institutions tend to be of the "primitive communist" variety.[15] In institutionally rich environments where, for example, individual private property rights have been established, it is far simpler for these institutions to emerge via an entrepreneurial rather than a contractarian route on account of decision-making costs, and of the costs of specifying fully adequate contracts (Williamson, 1975; North, 1981).

This discussion of the emergence of cooperative institutions has two principal implications. If institutions emerge as a result of the demand for joint private goods, then *shifts in a variety of environmental and demographic conditions will heighten demand for certain kinds of joint goods and favor the emergence of institutions supplying these goods.*

Thus, the members of foraging societies tend to form local groups in the dry season—when the scarcity of water increases the benefits of cooperation among different nuclear families—but these groups disband when there is sufficient water to meet the subsistence needs of individual families (Johnson and Earle, 1987). Likewise, as markets penetrate into economically isolated territories this leads to the establishment of insurance institutions (Hechter, 1987). Finally, the rise of insecurity (due to the threat of invasion, piracy, and so forth) promotes the establishment of protective associations. Other kinds of shifts will diminish the demand for such institutions. Hence the growth of insurance markets in the late nineteenth century is associated with the decline of fraternal insurance institutions. If some public good-providing organization in a territory did not go through the first stage (that is, if it did not grow from the roots of some private good-producing institution), such evidence would contradict the thrust of this analysis.

Yet demand alone is insufficient to produce cooperative institutions: *both in their roles as producers and consumers, individuals must be highly visible to one another in order to reduce the severity of the free-rider and assurance problems.*

In the state of nature, bulky goods that must be cooperatively acquired are likely to promote both kinds of visibility. This is consistent with the finding that meat (at least some of which is often cooperatively acquired) is more widely shared among hunter-gatherers than other types of food (Kaplan and Hill, 1985). Irrigation systems provide a graphic example of a cooperative institution that develops to provide access to a bulky joint good. Wittfogel (1957:18), for example, notes that water is a distinctive resource in that it has a tendency to gather in bulk.[16] Further research into the visibility of the production of different kinds of joint goods, and of the potential centricity of these goods, doubtless will provide a richer body of empirical implications for the genesis of cooperative institutions.

It should be emphasized that the analysis in this chapter is quite different from Mancur Olson's (1965) well-known explanation of the development of collective goods-seeking organizations like trade unions and farm organizations. Insofar as these groups sought to raise the wages of whole classes of workers, they aimed to produce a collective good. Given this, the optimal strategy for any given worker is to free ride and cash in on the (presumably successful) efforts of union organizers and their credulous followers. How, then, did these groups emerge? Olson's explanation is that the early trade unions (in the days before the passage of closed-shop legislation) could lure members only if they provided them with desirable selective incentives, including insurance. In Olson's account, therefore, insurance is considered to be the by-product of trade unions.

The problem with Olson's explanation is that, like formal controls, selective incentives are themselves a collective good. This means that they, too, have to be produced by rational egoists. How is it that a group aiming to provide a public good can attract any rational members at all, let alone manage to produce selective incentives? As the previous analysis shows, the rise of groups providing immanent joint goods entails no such liability. Since they are formed for the provision of *private* goods, there is no initial free-rider problem. To obtain their goods, members are led to adopt formal controls that make possible production of the goods. Once the goods have been produced, they can be used in a variety of ways. For example, there is no inherent reason why the members of an insurance group cannot convert their common assets into a strike fund and reconstitute themselves as a trade union....

NOTES

1. Consider an elevator having male and female passengers. If male passengers are observed to allow the females to exit first, this is a collective behavioral regularity. Whether this behavioral regularity is due to the presence of a norm or to explicit rules is beside the point.
2. For the purposes of this chapter, language itself may be considered to be a convention.

3. This restriction is due to the fact that the rise of institutions among close relations can be explained easily by evolutionary arguments based on genetic relatedness. Such reasoning is, however, generally insufficient to account for institutions whose scope surpasses the members of a nuclear family.

4. The problem of multiple equilibria is double-barrelled. On the one hand, cooperation may not emerge because some of these equilibria are inefficient. On the other hand, cooperation may not emerge even if the various equilibria are all efficient, since they are unlikely to be equally preferred by all the players or the game. This situation then leads to a noncooperative bargaining problem.

5. In the absence of perfect monitoring capacity, a player can never be certain of the moves that other players have taken in past plays of the game. Thus, she cannot infer that cooperation is ever rational.

6. This question is critical, for if we suspend self-interested behavioral assumptions—and allow individuals to have internalized values or some small but positive amount of altruism—then there is an all too easy way to overcome the assurance problem, and thereby to account for the emergence of cooperative institutions. This strategy is akin to invoking a *deus ex machina*, but there can be no theoretical justification for so doing.

7. I ignore the obvious complication that the initial production functions for the joint good will be estimates, and that disagreements may well result about the accuracy of these estimates.

8. There is a growing experimental literature on the use of provision points and money-back guarantees as means of resolving the assurance problem. Whereas there is evidence that some of these arrangements do, in fact, result in the production of greater public goods, each of them is imposed *exogenously* in the experiments. Hence these solutions to the free-rider and assurance problems are inconsistent with the premises of this analysis.

9. In more complex situations where there are alternative benefit-providing institutions, deviant actors often gain a negative reputation that makes them unsuitable for admission to any such institution. After other participants get their investment back, what is their incentive to ruin the deviant's reputation? Why should rational egoists be concerned about the fortunes of the participants in *other* institutions? This kind of problem is endemic in academic hiring situations, where the members of sending departments often provide misleading information to receiving departments in hopes of getting rid of a troublesome colleague or a sub-par student. The only force that can counter this free-rider problem is the damage that such deceit might bring to the information provider in further repeat dealings. Hence, the less frequent the contact between the members of two academic departments, the less reliable the information supplied about potential colleagues and students, *ceteris paribus*. The multiplexity of ties between groups increases the probability of this intergroup sanctioning.

10. It should be noted that this solution to the emergence of cooperative institutions is practicable only in relatively small groups. In essence, the creation of a central store of resources commits participants to involvement in a repeated game. As such, many of the mechanisms that produce cooperation in the literature on repeated games (Taylor, 1976; Axelrod, 1984) are employed here to the same effect. The reader may wonder wherein this approach differs from the invisible-hand approach. Whereas repeated game theorists take the existence of the supergame (and sometimes the existence of a specific discount rate) as a given, this analysis explains how it is that rational egoists voluntarily commit themselves to social situations involving repeated exchange.

11. The connection between pre-existing organizations founded to produce joint private goods and public good-providing organizations often has been stressed in the literature on social

movements (Oberschall, 1973; McAdam *et al.*, 1988). Thus in her analysis of the emergence of the contemporary women's movement, Evans (1980) locates its roots in informal networks of women who had come to know one another in the context of prior civil rights and New Left political organizations. Black churches (which offered insurance benefits) played an important crystallizing role in the development of the civil rights movement (Oberschall, 1973:126–27; McAdam, 1982; Morris, 1984). Fraternal-service groups played a similar role in the emergence of local anti-pornography movements (Curtis and Zurcher, 1973:56); and mosques played this kind of role in the early days of the Iranian Revolution (Snow and Marshall, 1984).

12. Naturally, this kind of an argument has its limits, otherwise all production would be concentrated in just one institution. For an interesting discussion of the limits of integration in firms, see Hart (1987).

13. Thus, to satisfy his desire to watch movies in the middle of the night, Howard Hughes bought a local Las Vegas station (Hardin, 1982).

14. For example, the agents of some American ethnically-based fraternal societies had political aspirations in their communities, and by judiciously investing these funds they could further these political aspirations (Stolarik, 1980). Likewise, the managers of large Minneapolis corporations are motivated to provide charitable donations in the community by the access to high prestige social circles that these donations uniquely provide (Galaskiewicz, 1985). The provision of public goods also can be a by-product of relatively homogeneous groups. In such groups, access to the joint good may be limited only to those members who contribute to specific public goods that are unrelated to the group's initial rationale. Thus some Pittsburgh fraternal associations expelled members who had committed crimes or treason, or who hired out as strikebreakers (Galey, 1977). This then explains how the self-interest of rational egoists can lead them to produce collective (and sometimes even public) goods.

15. In contrast, the Marxian explanation for primitive communism rests on questionable arguments about the absence of a surplus beyond that necessary for subsistence.

16. Clearly, the demand for a predictable water supply is insufficient to account for actual irrigation works, for many peoples who would have gained from it did not adopt such practices. Whether the adopters of irrigation had a visibility advantage over nonadoptors remains to be explored in further research.

REFERENCES

Aumann, Robert J. (1985). "Repeated Games." Pp. 209–242 in George R. Feiwel, ed., *Issues in Contemporary Microeconomics and Welfare*. Albany, NY: State University of New York Press.

Axelrod, Robert. (1984). *The Evolution of Cooperation*. New York: Basic Books.

Bendor, Jonathan, and Dilip Mookherjee. (1987). "Institutional structure and the logic of ongoing collective action." *American Political Science Review*, 81(1):129–54.

Blau, Peter M. (1964). *Exchange and Power in Social Life*. New York: John Wiley.

Buchanan, James M. and Gordon Tullock. (1962). *The Calculus of Consent*. Ann Arbor: University of Michigan Press.

Curtis, Russell L. and Louis A. Zurcher, Jr. (1973). "Stable resources of protest movement: The multi-organizational field." *Social Forces*, 52(1):53–60.

DiMaggio, Paul J. and Walter W. Powell. (1983). "Institutional isomorphism." *American Sociological Review*, 48(2):147–160.

Durkheim, Émile. (1951). *Suicide*. New York: Free Press. [Originally published 1897.]

Evans, Sarah. (1980). *Personal Politics*. New York: Vintage Books.

Galaskiewicz, Joseph. (1985). *Social Organization of an Urban Grants Economy: A Study of Business Philanthropy and Nonprofit Organizations*. Orlando, FL: Academic Press.

Galey, Margaret E. (1977). "Ethnicity, fraternalism, social and mental health." *Ethnicity*, 4(1):19–53.

Hardin, Russell. (1982). *Collective Action*. Baltimore: Johns Hopkins University Press (for Resources for the Future).

Hart, Oliver. (1987). "Incomplete contracts and the theory of the firm." Paper presented at the Conference on Knowledge and Institutional Change, University of Minnesota.

Hayek, Friedrich A. (1973). *Law, Legislation and Liberty*, Vol. I. Chicago: University of Chicago Press.

———. (1976). *Law, Legislation and Liberty*, Vol. II. Chicago: University of Chicago Press.

Hechter, Michael. (1987). *Principles of Group Solidarity*. Berkeley and London: University of California Press.

———. (1990). "On the inadequacy of game theory for the resolution of real-world collective action problems." In M. Levi and K. S. Cook, eds., *The Limits of Rationality*. Chicago: University of Chicago Press. In press.

Hobbes, Thomas. (1968). *Leviathan*, edited by C. B. Macpherson. Harmondsworth, England: Penguin. [Originally published 1651.]

Johnson, Allen W. and Timothy Earle. (1987). *The Evolution of Human Societies*. Stanford: Stanford University Press.

Kaplan, Hillard and Kim Hill. (1985). "Food sharing among Ache foragers: Tests of explanatory hypotheses." *Current Anthropology*, 26(2):223–239.

Lee, Richard B. (1979). *The !Kung San*. Cambridge: Cambridge University Press.

Lewis, David. (1969). *Convention: A Philosophical Study*. Cambridge: Harvard University Press.

McAdam, Doug. (1982). *Political Process and the Development of Black Insurgency, 1930–1970*. Chicago: University of Chicago Press.

McAdam, Doug, John D. McCarthy, and Mayer N. Zald. (1988). "Social movements and collective behavior: Building micro-macro bridges." Pp. 695–738 in Neil J. Smelser, ed., *Handbook of Sociology*. Newbury Park, CA: Sage.

Menger, Carl. (1963). *Investigations into the Method of the Social Sciences with Special Reference to Economics*, edited by Louis Schneider. Translated by Francis J. Nock. Champaign-Urbana: University of Illinois Press. [Originally published 1883.]

Morris, Aldon. (1984). *The Origins of the Civil Rights Movement*. New York: Free Press.

North, Douglass C. (1981). *Structure and Change in Economic History*. New York: Norton.

Nozick, Robert. (1974). *Anarchy, State and Utopia*. New York: Basic Books.

Oberschall, Anthony. (1973). *Social Conflict and Social Movements*. Englewood Cliffs, N.J.: Prentice-Hall.

Olson, Mancur. (1965). *The Logic of Collective Action*. Cambridge: Harvard University Press.

Snow, David A. and Susan Marshall. (1984). "Cultural imperialism, social movements, and the Islamic revival." Pp. 131–152 in Louis Kriesberg, ed., *Social Movements, Conflicts and Change*, Vol. 7. Greenwich, CT: JAI Press.

Stolarik, M. Mark. (1980). "Slovak fraternal benefit societies." Pp. 130–145 in Scott Cummings, ed., *Urban Self-Help in America*. Port Washington, NY: Kennikat Press.

Taylor, Michael. (1976). *Anarchy and Cooperation*. London: John Wiley.

Ullman-Margalit, Edna. (1978). "Invisible hand explanations." *Synthese*, 39:263–91.

Wheat, J. B. (1967). "A Paleo-Indian bison kill." *Scientific American*, January.

White, Harrison C. (1981). "Where do markets come from?" *American Journal of Sociology*, 87 (3):517–547.

Williamson, Oliver. (1975). *Markets and Hierarchies*. New York: Free Press.

Wittfogel, Karl A. (1957). *Oriental Despotism: A Comparative Study of Total Power*. New Haven: Yale University Press.

50. FORMULATION OF EXCHANGE THEORY

PETER BLAU

Peter Blau (1918–2002), who was born in Vienna and emigrated to the United States during the Nazi era, was a key exponent of exchange theory for over three decades. During this time he attempted to go beyond the general propositional stage articulated by George Homans in order to focus on social structure. In this excerpt from *Structural Contexts of Opportunities* (1994), Blau builds on micro-level exchange theory while articulating an appreciation of both the difference between economic and social exchange and the factors that make the macro level different from the micro level. One of the issues he addresses is the paradoxical fact that social exchange both facilitates social bonding and gives rise to status differentiation.

A fundamental difference between social life in small isolated communities and that in large complex societies is the declining significance of the groups into which one is born and the growing significance of reciprocated choices for human relations. To be sure, the significance of ascribed positions has by no means disappeared in contemporary complex societies. Most people´s closest relations are with their parents and children. Other ascribed positions continue to exert a major influence on social relations, notably one´s kin and the ethnic group and social class into which one is born. Yet, even for quite close relatives, except one´s immediate family, the extent of social interaction and the intimacy of the relation are not ascribed but depend on reciprocal choices. Larger ascribed affiliations, like ethnic and class background, affect the likelihood of choice but do not predetermine who selects whom as close associate, which depends on reciprocated choices.

Thus, ascribed as well as achieved positions govern probabilities of association, which are generally higher for ascribed than achieved affiliations, but they do not determine specific associates (with the exception of parents and children), let alone the extent of social interaction and the closeness of the relation. Their probabilistic influences on ingroup associations are similar to those of a community´s population structure. The population distributions in a community also influence only the probabilities of ingroup and intergroup relations of various kinds, but the specific dyads within which these probabilities find expression depend on mutual choices.

Dependence on reciprocated choice implies that, if I want to associate with someone, I cannot realize my goal unless I make him interested in associating with me. For our social relation to persist once it has been established, both of us have to sustain an interest in its continuation. To determine what brings these conditions about is the objective of exchange theory, which analyzes the processes that establish reciprocity in social relations and sustain it, and which thereby dissects the dynamics of social interaction.

Structural conditions impose limits on the exchange relations that can develop. The population structure of an entire society or large community, however, is far removed from the daily social life of individuals and hence does not affect it directly but indirectly. Multilevel structural analysis traces these indirect limiting influences. It discloses how macro-structural conditions are transmitted to successive levels and which ones reach the lowest level on which direct social interaction and exchange occur. It may indicate, for example, that society's racial heterogeneity penetrates into small substructures or that it is reflected in segregation of different races in different suburbs and neighborhoods with much homogeneity within them. The former situation would make intergroup relations more likely than the latter, but neither would determine which specific social relations occur.

Many, if not most, human gratifications are obtained in relations with other human beings. Intellectual stimulation and relaxing conversation, sexual pleasures and the enchantment of love, academic recognition and a happy family life, satisfying the lust for power and the need for acceptance—all of these are contingent on eliciting responses from others. Exchange theory analyzes the mutual gratifications persons provide one another that sustain social relations.

* * *

The basic assumption of the theory of social exchange is that persons establish social associations because they expect them to be rewarding and that they continue social interaction and expand it because they experience it to be rewarding. This assumption that two parties associate with one another not owing to normative requirements but because they both expect rewards from doing so implies that the exchange of rewards is a starting mechanism of social relations that is not contingent on norms prescribing obligations. If a person is attracted to others because she expects associating with them to be rewarding, she will want to associate with them to obtain the expected rewards. For them to associate with her, they must be interested in doing so, which depends, according to the initial assumption, on their expecting such association to be rewarding to them. Consequently, for the first person to realize the rewards expected from the association with others, she must impress them as a desirable associate with whom interaction will be rewarding.

Individuals are often hesitant to take the first step for fear of rejection. A widely used early strategy is for people to impress others in whom they are interested with their outstanding qualities—their wit, charm, intelligence, knowledge of the arts—which implicitly promises that associating with them would be a rewarding experience. If the early steps are successful, they tend to become self-fulfilling prophecies. As each person puts his best foot forward, associating with him turns out to be an enjoyable experience. In due course, people start doing favors for one another. In a work situation, the more experienced may give their colleagues advice or help with a difficult job. Neighbors may lend one another tools. People who met socially may issue invitations to dinner or a party.

Most people enjoy doing favors for others, usually without any thought of return, at least initially. Nevertheless, a person who benefits from an association is under an obligation to reciprocate. If the benefits are recurrent—whether involving merely the enjoyment of the other's company or getting frequently needed advice about one's work from a colleague—the self-imposed obligation to reciprocate is sustained by the interest in continuing to obtain the benefits. It is further reinforced by the fear of not seeming ungrateful. Even when there is no initial thought of return, failure to reciprocate when the occasion arises invites such an accusation, which will be experienced though it remains unspoken.

Imagine a neighbor lends you her lawn mower in the summer, but when she asks you next winter to borrow your snow blower you refuse. The neighbor and others who learn of your refusal undoubtedly will consider you ungrateful, and whether they do or not, you yourself will feel ungrateful and surely will be hesitant to ask to borrow her lawn mower again. The feelings and possible accusations of ingratitude indicate that favors freely given are not entirely free but create obligations in one's own mind to reciprocate as well as possible social pressures to discharge the obligations.

A fundamental distinction between social and economic exchange is that social exchange engenders diffuse obligations, whereas those in economic exchange are specified in an implicit or explicit contract. For economic transactions that are not immediately completed, like purchases in stores, the terms of the exchange are agreed upon in advance by both parties, and major agreements are formalized in a contract that specifies the precise nature of the obligations of both parties and when any outstanding debts are due. The favors in social exchange, by contrast, create diffuse obligations, to be discharged at some unspecified future date. If a couple give a dinner party, for instance, they have no agreement on when and where or even whether the guests will invite them back, though their relations may be weakened if they do not, or if they do so too late or too soon. The diffuseness of the obligations implies that large-scale social exchange is not likely to occur unless firm social bonds rooted in trust have been established.

In the absence of legal obligations to make a return for benefits received, the initial problem of new acquaintances is to prove themselves trustworthy in social exchange. This typically occurs as exchange relations evolve in a slow process, starting with minor transactions entailing little risk and requiring little trust. The mutual discharge of obligations and reciprocation profit both parties and prove them increasingly trustworthy as favors are regularly reciprocated. The growing mutual advantages gained from the association fortify their social bond. This may appear to be merely a by-product of social exchange, but it is, in fact, its most important product.

Implicit in discussions of social exchange is an element of rationality, if not calculation, which may give the impression that social exchange theory is simply a version of rational choice theory. However, this impression is misleading. To be sure, social exchange does imply some rational pursuit of rewards, but the prime benefit sought, once the friendship bond of mutual support and trust is clearly established, is the rewarding experience derived from the association itself. Any material benefits exchanged are incidental and of significance largely as tokens of the friendship.

* * *

I conceptualize processes of social association as occurring in the relation between two persons. Accordingly, the exchange theory just presented analyzes exchange processes in dyads. . . . Ekeh (1974) has criticized my and Homans's (1961) exchange theory as individualistic, ignoring the difference between my concern with social structure and Homans's psychological reductionism. His criticism centers on the analysis of dyadic exchange. He contrasts the concept of restricted or two-party exchange unfavorably with Lévi-Strauss's (1949) generalized or multiparty exchange. Ekeh (1974: 62–65) considers the latter (multiparty) exchange more Durkheimian, owing to its concern with structural integration, whereas he dismisses dyadic exchange as individualistic and thus lacking a structural focus.

There is good reason that I, as a structural sociologist, prefer restricted dyadic to generalized multiparty exchange. Generalized exchange refers to the prevailing practice that all members of a tribe or group freely provide benefits to other members without looking for any return from the person to whom the contribution is made. Since doing favors for others is socially expected, it is in effect a group norm. Conformity with this norm is the reason that all group members receive favors in the long run and solidarity is strengthened. My criticism of generalized exchange is that it is simply another name for conformity to group norms and consequently commits the tautological fallacy of explaining social conduct in terms of social norms demanding this conduct.[1] Generalized exchange thereby dispenses with the crucial insight of exchange theory that interpersonal relations are not contingent on social norms, because gradually expanding reciprocity supplies a mechanism for establishing and maintaining them and engendering trust to boot.

That my analysis of social exchange is confined to exchange processes that occur in dyads does not mean that the social context in which these processes occur can be ignored, since it does influence them. Actually, exchange processes are affected by several contexts of widening social circles. The most immediate social context is the groups to which the dyads belong, which exert two distinct influences on dyadic exchange.

First, a group's network structure defines the alternative opportunities for exchange relations various persons have and thereby affects the outcomes of persons in different network positions. (Exchange processes, in turn, may alter the network structure.) Experiments performed by Cook and her colleagues indicate that networks that provide alternative exchange partners to one person but not to others increase the bargaining power of this person in dyadic exchanges (see, for example, Cook, Gillmore, and Tamagishi 1983).

A second influence of the immediate social context is that it discourages failure to reciprocate for benefits received by social disapproval of such ingratitude. I realize that my reference to social disapproval, which implies social pressure, sounds as if I attributed exchange to group norms, for which I criticized the principle of generalized exchange. There is a major difference, however. If the practice of making a contribution freely to any group member without expecting a return from that member is explained by the cultural norm to do so, the *explicans* cannot explain the *explicandum*, because the two are redundant. But exchange is explained not by social pressures but by the returns it brings, including pleasant company or friendship as well as possibly tangible benefits. Social exchange, however, cannot prevail if trust, once established, is violated, and social disapproval discourages its violation. Social pressures do not explain—account for—reciprocal exchange, but they help to sustain it.

The influence of the wider social circles—the population structure of a neighborhood, community, or entire society—depends on the extent to which the population distributions of the encompassing social structure penetrate into the substructures of face-to-face groups. Many of the differences in society's population structure are the result of differences among rather than within substructures on successive levels. As a result, face-to-face groups are less differentiated than their encompassing social structures. Multilevel structural analysis discloses how much differentiation in various dimensions penetrates into the substructures of interpersonal relations. Greater homophily in segregated substructures promotes ingroup relations, but despite much segregation, some differentiation penetrates to the lowest level of interpersonal relations. Consequently, although ingroup relations prevail in daily social intercourse, intergroup relations also regularly occur.

The common occurrence of intergroup relations is revealed in a study by Marsden (1990) that applies my theoretical scheme to the egocentric face-to-face networks of a sample of the American population. He initially distinguishes a demand-side view of networks in terms of preferences for various kinds of associates from a supply-side view, like my theory's, in terms of opportunities for associating with diverse others. On the basis of previous research on the composition of families and work places, we know that families are more diverse in age and sex but less diverse in ethnic and religious affiliation than associates at work. Accordingly, Marsden hypothesizes more intergroup relations in respect to age and sex and fewer intergroup relations in respect to ethnic and religious affiliation between relatives than between fellow workers. The results support these hypotheses, which stipulate intergroup as well as ingroup relations even between close associates. Marsden concludes that my macro-structural opportunity theory is applicable to the study of the relations in microstructures, contrary to what I myself had stated.

I am pleased that the theory can be used in the investigation of face-to-face networks, which I had questioned. One should note, however, that confining network analysis to the supply-side approach would fail to take full advantage of the possibilities for analysis the small scope of these networks provides. In the study of large populations, analysis and research cannot proceed without ignoring the complexities of social life by having to aggregate specific observations into gross concepts and measures, like heterogeneity, intersection, or intergroup relations. The subtle processes that govern face-to-face relations are admittedly (but inevitably) obscured by such aggregations. The study of interpersonal relations and small networks can directly analyze these processes and thereby contribute to our understanding of them.

IMBALANCE IN EXCHANGE

A paradox of social exchange is that it gives rise to both social bonds between peers and differentiation of status. This was the case for the ceremonial exchange of gifts in nonliterate societies, and it is the case for exchange processes in advanced industrial societies. To start by exemplifying the former, the Kula ceremonial gift exchange of the Trobriand Islanders, as discussed by Malinowski (1961: 92), "provides every man within its ring with a few friends near at hand, and with some friendly allies in far away, dangerous, foreign districts." A few pages later he states that "among the natives of the Kula . . . wealth is the indispensable appanage of social rank" (p. 97). Probably the extreme case of the significance of social exchange for differentiation of status is the famous potlatch of the Kwakiutl, a feast of reckless spending in which "status in associations and clans, and rank of every kind, are determined by the war of property" (Mauss 1954: 35).

A contemporary case of status differentiation resulting from social exchange was observed in the office of a federal government agency responsible for the enforcement of certain laws. The duties of the agents involved investigating private firms by auditing their books and conducting interviews, determining any legal violations and the action to be taken, and negotiating a settlement with the employer or a top manager. The work was quite complex, and agents often encountered problems. When they did, they were expected to consult their supervisor, but they tended to be reluctant to do so for fear of adversely affecting their annual rating by their supervisor. Instead, they usually consulted colleagues. Whereas officially prohibited, this practice was widespread and evidently tolerated. Although agents worked on different cases, one could observe all day long pairs or small clusters of persons in deep discussions, most of which dealt with problems of their cases. Lunch periods were filled with such discussions.

The observation of these consultations originally gave me the idea of social exchange. To cite the central passage (Blau 1955: 108):[2]

> A consultation can be considered an exchange of values; both participants gain something and both have to pay a price. The questioning agent is enabled to perform better than he could otherwise have done, without exposing his difficulties to the supervisor. By asking for advice, he implicitly pays his respect to the superior proficiency of his colleague. This acknowledgment of inferiority is the cost of receiving assistance. The consultant gains prestige, in return for which he is willing to devote some time to the consultation and permit it to disrupt his own work. The following remark illustrates this: `I like giving advice. It's flattering, I suppose, if you feel that the others come to you for advice.´

The principle of marginal utility applies to these exchanges. Although most agents liked being consulted, for those frequently asked for advice the gain in informal status of an additional consultation diminished and the cost in repeated interruptions of one's own work increased. As the most popular consultant said to me when asked about being consulted, "I never object, although sometimes it's annoying." The principle also applies to agents who frequently need advice, but in reverse, of course.

Repeated admissions of needing advice undermine one's self-confidence and standing in the group, particularly if an oft-interrupted consultant expresses some impatience or annoyance. To forestall such experiences, most agents establish partnerships of mutual consultation, reserving consulting the most expert colleagues for their most difficult problems. Since agents often have tentative solutions for their problems and need not so much an answer as assurance that theirs is correct, a colleague whose expertise is not superior to one's own can provide such support.

The most expert agents face a different dilemma: asking for advice or even for confirmation of their tentative solutions may well endanger their superior standing as experts. Making official decisions in a difficult case on one's own can easily raise doubts and questions in a person's mind, even an expert's. One way to cope with this situation is to stop going over it again and again in one's head and instead telling some colleagues about the interesting problems that have arisen in a given case and discussing how they might be solved, possibly over lunch if not in the office.

Such "thinking out loud" may well stimulate new associations and ideas one would not have come up with on one's own, particularly as the listeners are also experienced agents, who might raise objections if one is on the wrong track, and whose assent implicit in attentive listening and interested questions conveys approval. In contrast to asking for advice, telling colleagues about interesting problems in a case and how they might be solved enhances the respect of one's colleagues, though it is, in effect, a subtle form of asking colleagues to corroborate one's own provisional decisions.

* * *

To put the underlying principles of imbalanced and balanced exchange into general terms, rendering important services or providing valued benefactions is a claim to superior status. Reciprocation denies this claim, and excessive returns make a counterclaim, which can lead to a potlatch-like war of seeking to outdo one another to stay ahead. Failure to reciprocate by discharging one's obligations validates the claim and acknowledges the other's superiority in return for the benefits received and in the hope of continuing to receive them. Thus, the contingency that determines whether social exchanges lead to friendships between peers or superordination and subordination is whether benefits received are reciprocated or not. This, in turn, depends on whether one of the two parties has superior resources of the kind that are in contention (which was professional competence in the case of agents).[3]

In a seminal article, Emerson (1962) specified conditions in which balance in social exchange can be restored. I have slightly modified his scheme to conceptualize it as four alternatives to becoming dependent on a person's influence who has some services to offer that others need or want. First, they can give him something he needs or wants enough to reciprocate by satisfying their wishes, provided that they have resources that meet his needs. Second, they can obtain the needed benefits elsewhere, assuming that they have access to alternative sources of these benefits. These two possibilities, if recurring, result in reciprocal exchange relations between peers. Third, they can coerce him to give them what they want. This involves domination by force and is outside the purview of exchange. Fourth, they can resign themselves to do without what they thought they needed, which is Diogenes' solution for remaining independent.

If none of these four alternatives is available, the others become dependent on the supplier of the needed services and must defer to her to reciprocate for the benefits received lest she lose interest in continuing to provide them. Deference implies not only paying respect to another's superior ability, implicit in asking her help, but also deferring to her wishes in everyday intercourse. Thus, the social interaction among colleagues or in other groups that involves imbalances in social exchange gives rise to differentiation in the power to influence as well as in prestige, which is reflected in a stratified structure of informal status.

The illustration of instrumental assistance in a work group may have left the misleading impression that most social exchange involves instrumental benefits. Much of the social interaction, even among co-workers and still more outside a work situation, is social intercourse engaged in for its own sake. Hechter (1987: 33) states that people often join groups to pursue joint goods or common objectives, and he stresses that their joint achievement and, particularly, the intrinsic gratifications obtained from social associations among fellow members are the sources of group solidarity.[4]

Workers who organize in order to bargain collectively with their employer for higher wages exemplify joint efforts to achieve a common objective. It is in the interest of the group as a whole if workers who devote more energy to and prove more adept in this endeavor are allowed to take the leading role in their organizing effort. Thus, superior status based on past services prompts other workers to acknowledge and submit to the leadership of the one who seems to be most effective in making contributions to organizing the nascent union. Informal leadership is legitimated by the social approval of the rest of the group, and this approval is the return for past services and for the future contributions the leader is expected to make to the welfare of the group by helping to organize them.[5]

This fictitious description may well be idealized, but it is not completely inaccurate for the initial stage of workers getting together on their own to organize themselves for joint bargaining. To be sure, it is not applicable to formal positions of leadership, particularly not to the impersonal power their incumbents exercise. Thus, the description is not intended to depict the leadership of large national unions; indeed, it is designed as a contrast to them. Once a union has become a large, formal organization and its leaders have become persons of great power, a handful of workers with a grievance cannot on their own decide upon a course of action if the powerful leader is opposed. All they can do is organize a wildcat strike informally, as workers originally did, but now against both the union leadership and management. The point of this illustration is that the interpersonal power that develops in face-to-face relations is fundamentally different from the impersonal power to dominate large numbers, even in the rare cases when the latter emerged from the former.[6]

NOTES

1. Cultural theories that explain social patterns in terms of norms and values are prone to commit this tautology. It is the same fallacy as that of psychological explanations of behavior in terms of instincts to engage in such behavior.

2. As indicated by the publication date, this was written long before the women´s movement called attention to the implicit bias involved in referring to some unspecified person always by the masculine pronoun instead of using either he/she or even s/he (which I find deplorable) or alternating between feminine and masculine pronouns, as I have done....

3. This analysis applies to processes of differentiation in informal status among persons whose formal status is essentially the same.

4. The achievement of joint goods raises the well-known free-rider problem (that persons may benefit from public goods without contributing to their production), which Hechter considers to have solved by distinguishing partly excludable goods from public goods. The former are not available to the entire public but only to group members. His major illustration is that one cannot enjoy the sociability in a group without having become a member and thus a contributor to that sociability. But this solution does not work for instrumental objectives, as indicated by the case next discussed in the text.

5. Workers who fail to contribute to the organizing efforts of the new union would also benefit from its success, which illustrates the criticism I made in the last sentence of the preceding footnote that Hechter´s (1987) concept of partial excludability does not solve the freeloader problem for joint instrumental objectives.

6. I am particularly critical of the inference made by conservative social scientists that the elite´s domination of society´s economy and government is earned as a return for the great contributions they have made to society. It is the counterpart of the assumption that oligopolistic corporations achieved their position in free competition.

REFERENCES

Blau, Peter M. 1955. *The Dynamics of Bureaucracy*. Chicago: University of Chicago Press.

Cook, Karen S., Mary R. Gillmore, and Toshio Tamagishi. 1983. "The Distribution of Power in Exchange Networks." *American Journal of Sociology* 89:275–305.

Ekeh, Peter P. 1974. *Social Exchange Theory*. Cambridge, Mass.: Harvard University.

Emerson, Richard M. 1962. "Power-Dependence Relations." *American Sociological Review* 27:31–41.

Hechter, Michael. 1987. *Principles of Group Solidarity*. Berkeley: University of California Press.

Homans, George C. 1961. *Social Behavior*. New York: Harcourt, Brace, & World.

Lévi-Strauss, Claude. 1949. *Les structures élémentaires de la parenté*. Paris: Press Universitaires de France.

Malinowski, Bronislaw. 1961 (1922). *Argonauts of the Western Pacific*. New York: Dutton.

Marsden, Peter V. 1990. "Network Diversity, Substructures, and Opportunities for Contact." Pp. 396–410 in C. Calhoun, M. W. Meyer, and W. R. Scott (eds.), *Structures of Power and Constraint*. Cambridge: University Press.

Mauss, Marcel. 1954 (1925). *The Gift*. Glencoe, Ill.: Free Press.

SECTION X

1. Summarize Homans´ view of what he refers to as a "social exchange paradigm," and offer examples to illustrate it from your own life.
2. Why does Emerson think that power is predicated on relations of dependence, and how does he go about attempting to support this claim?
3. What are the circumstances in which Emerson thinks coalitions are formed and by whom? Provide an example of such a coalition.
4. What does Coleman mean by human capital? What does he mean by social capital?
5. What is the significance of the role of trust in social capital? After reviewing the examples Coleman cites, offer one of your own.
6. Hechter stresses the problematic nature of the "free rider." What does this term mean and how is it overcome in the creation of cooperative institutions?
7. How does Blau depict the difference between balanced and imbalanced exchanges and what is the signifiance of this distinction?

XI. FEMINIST THEORY

51. DOING GENDER

CANDACE WEST AND DON H. ZIMMERMAN

Distinguishing between sex and gender, Candace West (b. 1942) and Don H. Zimmerman (b. 1937) borrow insights from both Erving Goffman and Harold Garfinkel in making the claim that gender is the product of social interaction. They begin by stressing the fact that although in everyday life sex and gender are intertwined, it is necessary to analytically distinguish them. Gender is socially constructed, and in this regard it is appropriate to speak about "doing gender," for it ought to be construed as "a routine accomplishment embedded in everyday interaction." Central to their efforts at theoretical rethinking is an emphasis on the display of gender (borrowing from Goffman), sex categorization (using the insights of Garfinkel´s famous study on the sex reassignment of Agnes), and accountability.

PERSPECTIVES ON SEX AND GENDER

In Western societies, the accepted cultural perspective on gender views women and men as naturally and unequivocally defined categories of being (Garfinkel 1967, pp. 116–18) with distinctive psychological and behavioral propensities that can be predicted from their reproductive functions. Competent adult members of these societies see differences between the two as fundamental and enduring—differences seemingly supported by the division of labor into women´s and men´s work and an often elaborate differentiation of feminine and masculine attitudes and behaviors that are prominent features of social organization. Things are the way they are by virtue of the fact that men are men and women are women—a division perceived to be natural and rooted in biology, producing in turn profound psychological, behavioral, and social consequences. The structural arrangements of a society are presumed to be responsive to these differences.

Analyses of sex and gender in the social sciences, though less likely to accept uncritically the naive biological determinism of the view just presented, often retain a conception of sex-linked behaviors and traits as essential properties of individuals (for good reviews, see Hochschild 1973; Tresemer 1975; Thorne 1980; Henley 1985). The "sex differences approach" (Thorne 1980) is more commonly attributed to psychologists than to sociologists, but the survey researcher who determines the "gender" of respondents on the basis of the sound of their voices over the telephone is also making trait-oriented assumptions. Reducing gender to a fixed set of psychological traits or to a unitary "variable" precludes serious consideration of the ways it is used to structure distinct domains of social experience (Stacey and Thorne 1985, pp. 307–8).

Taking a different tack, role theory has attended to the social construction of gender categories, called "sex roles" or, more recently, "gender roles" and has

---

Reprinted from *Gender & Society*, June 1987, with permission of Sage Publications. ✦

analyzed how these are learned and enacted. Beginning with Linton (1936) and continuing through the works of Parsons (Parsons 1951; Parsons and Bales 1955) and Komarovsky (1946, 1950), role theory has emphasized the social and dynamic aspect of role construction and enactment (Thorne 1980; Connell 1983). But at the level of face-to-face interaction, the application of role theory to gender poses problems of its own (for good reviews and critiques, see Connell 1983, 1985; Kessler, Ashendon, Connell, and Dowsett 1985; Lopata and Thorne 1978; Thorne 1980; Stacey and Thorne 1985). Roles are *situated* identities—assumed and relinquished as the situation demands—rather than *master identities* (Hughes 1945), such as sex category, that cut across situations. Unlike most roles, such as "nurse," "doctor," and "patient" or "professor" and "student," gender has no specific site or organizational context.

Moreover, many roles are already gender marked, so that special qualifiers—such as "female doctor" or "male nurse"—must be added to exceptions to the rule. Thorne (1980) observes that conceptualizing gender as a role makes it difficult to assess its influence on other roles and reduces its explanatory usefulness in discussions of power and inequality. Drawing on Rubin (1975), Thorne calls for a reconceptualization of women and men as distinct social groups, constituted in "concrete, historically changing—and generally unequal—social relationships" (Thorne 1980, p. 11).

We argue that gender is not a set of traits, nor a variable, nor a role, but the product of social doings of some sort. What then is the social doing of gender? It is more than the continuous creation of the meaning of gender through human actions (Gerson and Peiss 1985). We claim that gender itself is constituted through interaction.[1] To develop the implications of our claim, we turn to Goffman's (1976) account of "gender display." Our object here is to explore how gender might be exhibited or portrayed through interaction, and thus be seen as "natural," while it is being produced as a socially organized achievement.

GENDER DISPLAY

Goffman contends that when human beings interact with others in their environment, they assume that each possesses an "essential nature"—a nature that can be discerned through the "natural signs given off or expressed by them" (1976, p. 75). Femininity and masculinity are regarded as "prototypes of essential expression—something that can be conveyed fleetingly in any social situation and yet something that strikes at the most basic characterization of the individual" (1976, p. 75). The means through which we provide such expressions are "perfunctory, conventionalized acts" (1976, p. 69), which convey to others our regard for them, indicate our alignment in an encounter, and tentatively establish the terms of contact for that social situation. But they are also regarded as expressive behavior, testimony to our "essential natures."

Goffman (1976, pp. 69–70) sees *displays* as highly conventionalized behaviors structured as two-part exchanges of the statement-reply type, in which the presence or absence of symmetry can establish deference or dominance. These rituals are viewed as distinct from but articulated with more consequential activities, such as performing tasks or engaging in discourse. Hence, we have what he terms the "scheduling" of displays at junctures in activities, such as the beginning or end, to avoid interfering with the activities themselves. Goffman (1976, p. 69) formulates *gender display* as follows:

> If gender be defined as the culturally established correlates of sex (whether in consequence of biology or learning), then gender display refers to conventionalized portrayals of these correlates.

These gendered expressions might reveal clues to the underlying, fundamental dimensions of the female and male, but they are, in Goffman's view, optional performances. Masculine courtesies may or may not be offered and, if offered, may or may not be declined (1976, p. 71). Moreover, human beings "themselves employ the term `expression´, and conduct themselves to fit their own notions of expressivity" (1976, p. 75). Gender depictions are less a consequence of our "essential sexual natures" than interactional portrayals of what we would like to convey about sexual natures, using conventionalized gestures. Our *human* nature gives us the ability to learn to produce and recognize masculine and feminine gender displays—"a capacity [we] have by virtue of being persons, not males and females" (1976, p. 76).

Upon first inspection, it would appear that Goffman's formulation offers an engaging sociological corrective to existing formulations of gender. In his view, gender is a socially scripted dramatization of the culture's *idealization* of feminine and masculine natures, played for an audience that is well schooled in the presentational idiom. To continue the metaphor, there are scheduled performances presented in special locations, and like plays, they constitute introductions to or time out from more serious activities.

There are fundamental equivocations in this perspective. By segregating gender display from the serious business of interaction, Goffman obscures the effects of gender on a wide range of human activities. Gender is not merely something that happens in the nooks and crannies of interaction, fitted in here and there and not interfering with the serious business of life. While it is plausible to contend that gender displays—construed as conventionalized expressions—are optional, it does not seem plausible to say that we have the option of being seen by others as female or male.

It is necessary to move beyond the notion of gender display to consider what is involved in doing gender as an ongoing activity embedded in everyday interaction. Toward this end, we return to the distinctions among sex, sex category, and gender introduced earlier.

SEX, SEX CATEGORY, AND GENDER

Garfinkel's (1967, pp. 118–40) case study of Agnes, a transsexual raised as a boy who adopted a female identity at age 17 and underwent a sex reassignment operation several years later, demonstrates how gender is created through interaction and at the same time structures interaction. Agnes, whom Garfinkel characterized as a "practical methodologist," developed a number of procedures for passing as a "normal, natural female" both prior to and after her surgery. She had the practical task of managing the fact that she possessed male genitalia and that she lacked the social resources a girl's biography would presumably provide in everyday interaction. In short, she needed to display herself as a woman, simultaneously learning what it was to be a woman. Of necessity, this full-time pursuit took place at a time when most people's gender would be well-accredited and routinized. Agnes had to consciously contrive what the vast majority of women do without thinking. She was not "faking" what "real" women do naturally. She was obliged to analyze

and figure out how to act within socially structured circumstances and conceptions of femininity that women born with appropriate biological credentials come to take for granted early on. As in the case of others who must "pass," such as transvestites, Kabuki actors, or Dustin Hoffman's "Tootsie," Agnes's case makes visible what culture has made invisible—the accomplishment of gender.

Garfinkel's (1967) discussion of Agnes does not explicitly separate three analytically distinct, although empirically overlapping, concepts—sex, sex category, and gender.

SEX

Agnes did not possess the socially agreed upon biological criteria for classification as a member of the female *sex*. Still, Agnes regarded herself as a female, albeit a female with a penis, which a woman ought not to possess. The penis, she insisted, was a "mistake" in need of remedy (Garfinkel 1967, pp. 126–27, 131–32). Like other competent members of our culture, Agnes honored the notion that there *are* "essential" biological criteria that unequivocally distinguish females from males. However, if we move away from the commonsense viewpoint, we discover that the reliability of these criteria is not beyond question (Money and Brennan 1968; Money and Erhardt 1972; Money and Ogunro 1974; Money and Tucker 1975). Moreover, other cultures have acknowledged the existence of "cross-genders" (Blackwood 1984; Williams 1986) and the possibility of more than two sexes (Hill 1935; Martin and Voorhies 1975, pp. 84–107; but see also Cucchiari 1981, pp. 32–35).

More central to our argument is Kessler and McKenna's (1978, pp. 1–6) point that genitalia are conventionally hidden from public inspection in everyday life; yet we continue through our social rounds to "observe" a world of two naturally, normally sexed persons. It is the *presumption* that essential criteria exist and would or should be there if looked for that provides the basis for sex categorization. Drawing on Garfinkel, Kessler and McKenna argue that "female" and "male" are cultural events—products of what they term the "gender attribution process"—rather than some collection of traits, behaviors, or even physical attributes. Illustratively they cite the child who, viewing a picture of someone clad in a suit and a tie, contends, "It's a man, because he has a pee-pee" (Kessler and McKenna 1978, p. 154). Translation: "He must have a pee-pee [an essential characteristic] because I see the *insignia* of a suit and tie." Neither initial sex assignment (pronouncement at birth as a female or male) nor the actual existence of essential criteria for that assignment (possession of a clitoris and vagina or penis and testicles) has much—if anything—to do with the identification of sex category in everyday life. There, Kessler and McKenna note, we operate with a moral certainty of a world of two sexes. We do not think, "Most persons with penises are men, but some may not be" or "Most persons who dress as men have penises." Rather, we take it for granted that sex and sex category are congruent—that knowing the latter, we can deduce the rest.

SEX CATEGORIZATION

Agnes's claim to the categorical status of female, which she sustained by appropriate identificatory displays and other characteristics, could be *discredited* before her transsexual operation if her possession of a penis became known and after by her surgically constructed genitalia (see Raymond 1979, pp. 37, 138). In this regard, Agnes had to be continually alert to actual or potential threats to the security of her sex category. Her problem was not so much living up to some prototype of essential femininity but preserving her categorization as female. This task was made easy for her by a very powerful resource, namely, the process of commonsense categorization in everyday life.

The categorization of members of society into indigenous categories such as "girl" or "boy," or "woman" or "man," operates in a distinctively social way. The act of categorization does not involve a positive test, in the sense of a well-defined set of criteria that must be explicitly satisfied prior to making an identification. Rather, the application of membership categories relies on an "if-can" test in everyday interaction (Sacks 1972, pp. 332–35). This test stipulates that if people *can be seen* as members of relevant categories, *then categorize them that way*. That is, use the category that seems appropriate, except in the presence of discrepant information or obvious features that would rule out its

use. This procedure is quite in keeping with the attitude of everyday life, which has us take appearances at face value unless we have special reason to doubt (Schutz 1943; Garfinkel 1967, pp. 272–77; Bernstein 1986).[2] It should be added that it is precisely when we have special reason to doubt that the issue of applying rigorous criteria arises, but it is rare, outside legal or bureaucratic contexts, to encounter insistence on positive tests (Garfinkel 1967, pp. 262–83; Wilson 1970).

Agnes's initial resource was the predisposition of those she encountered to take her appearance (her figure, clothing, hair style, and so on) as the undoubted appearance of a normal female. Her further resource was our cultural perspective on the properties of "natural, normally sexed persons." Garfinkel (1967, pp. 122–28) notes that in everyday life, we live in a world of two—and only two—sexes. This arrangement has a moral status, in that we include ourselves and others in it as "essentially, originally, in the first place, always have been, always will be, once and for all, in the final analysis, either `male´ or `female´" (Garfinkel 1967, p. 122).

Consider the following case:

This issue reminds me of a visit I made to a computer store a couple of years ago. The person who answered my questions was truly a *salesperson*. I could not categorize him/her as a woman or a man. What did I look for? (1) Facial hair: She/he was smooth skinned, but some men have little or no facial hair. (This varies by race, Native Americans and Blacks often have none.) (2) Breasts: She/he was wearing a loose shirt that hung from his/her shoulders. And, as many women who suffered through a 1950s' adolescence know to their shame, women are often flat-chested. (3) Shoulders: His/hers were small and round for a man, broad for a woman. (4) Hands: Long and slender fingers, knuckles a bit large for a woman, small for a man. (5) Voice: Middle range, unexpressive for a woman, not at all the exaggerated tones some gay males affect. (6) His/her treatment of me: Gave off no signs that would let me know if I were of the same or different sex as this person. There were not even any signs that he/she knew his/her sex would be difficult to categorize and I wondered about that even as I did my best to hide these questions so I would not embarrass him/her while we talked of computer paper. I left still not knowing the sex of my salesperson, and was disturbed by that unanswered question (child of my culture that I am). (Diane Margolis, personal communication)

What can this case tell us about situations such as Agnes's (cf. Morris 1974; Richards 1983) or the process of sex categorization in general? First, we infer from this description that the computer salesclerk's identificatory display was ambiguous, since she or he was not dressed or adorned in an unequivocally female or male fashion. It is when such a display *fails* to provide grounds for categorization that factors such as facial hair or tone of voice are assessed to determine membership in a sex category. Second, beyond the fact that this incident could be recalled after "a couple of years," the customer was not only "disturbed" by the ambiguity of the salesclerk's category but also assumed that to acknowledge this ambiguity would be embarrassing to the salesclerk. Not only do we want to know the sex category of those around us (to see it at a glance, perhaps), but we presume that others are displaying it for us, in as decisive a fashion as they can.

GENDER

Agnes attempted to be "120 percent female" (Garfinkel 1967, p. 129), that is, unquestionably in all ways and at all times feminine. She thought she could protect herself from disclosure before and after surgical intervention by comporting herself in a feminine manner, but she also could have given herself away by overdoing her performance. Sex categorization and the accomplishment of gender are not the same. Agnes's categorization could be secure or suspect, but did not depend on whether or not she lived up to some ideal conception of femininity. Women can be seen as unfeminine, but that does not make them "unfemale." Agnes faced an ongoing task of *being* a woman—something beyond style of dress (an identificatory display) or allowing men to light her cigarette (a gender display). Her problem was to produce configurations of behavior that would be seen by others as normative gender behavior.

Agnes's strategy of "secret apprenticeship," through which she learned expected feminine decorum by carefully attending to her fiancé's criticisms of other women, was one means of masking incompetencies and simultaneously acquiring the needed skills (Garfinkel 1967, pp. 146–147). It was through her fiancé that Agnes learned that sunbathing on the lawn in front of her apartment was "offensive" (because it put her on display to other men). She also learned from his critiques of other women that she should not insist on having things her way and that she should not offer her opinions or claim equality with men (Garfinkel 1967, pp. 147–148). (Like other women in our society, Agnes learned something about power in the course of her "education.")

Popular culture abounds with books and magazines that compile idealized depictions of relations between women and men. Those focused on the etiquette of dating or prevailing standards of feminine comportment are meant to be of practical help in these matters. However, the use of any such source *as a manual of procedure* requires the assumption that doing gender merely involves making use of discrete, well-defined bundles of behavior that can simply be plugged into interactional situations to produce recognizable enactments of masculinity and femininity. The man "does" being masculine by, for example, taking the woman's arm to guide her across a street, and she "does" being feminine by consenting to be guided and not initiating such behavior with a man.

Agnes could perhaps have used such sources as manuals, but, we contend, doing gender is not so easily regimented (Mithers 1982; Morris 1974). Such sources may list and describe the sorts of behaviors that mark or display gender, but they are necessarily incomplete (Garfinkel 1967, pp. 66–75; Wieder 1974, pp. 183–214; Zimmerman and Wieder 1970, pp. 285–98). And to be successful, marking or displaying gender must be finely fitted to situations and modified or transformed as the occasion demands. Doing gender consists of managing such occasions so that, whatever the particulars, the outcome is seen and seeable in context as gender-appropriate or, as the case may be, gender-*in*appropriate, that is, *accountable*.

GENDER AND ACCOUNTABILITY

As Heritage (1984, pp. 136–37) notes, members of society regularly engage in "descriptive accountings of states of affairs to one another," and such accounts are both serious and consequential. These descriptions name, characterize, formulate, explain, excuse, excoriate, or merely take notice of some circumstance or activity and thus place it within some social framework (locating it relative to other activities, like and unlike).

Such descriptions are themselves accountable, and societal members orient to the fact that their activities are subject to comment. Actions are often designed with an eye to their accountability, that is, how they might look and how they might be characterized. The notion of accountability also encompasses those actions undertaken so that they are specifically unremarkable and thus not worthy of more than a passing remark, because they are seen to be in accord with culturally approved standards.

Heritage (1984, p. 179) observes that the process of rendering something accountable is interactional in character:

> [This] permits actors to design their actions in relation to their circumstances so as to permit others, by methodically taking account of circumstances, to recognize the action for what it is.

The key word here is *circumstances*. One circumstance that attends virtually all actions is the sex category of the actor. As Garfinkel (1967, p. 118) comments:

> [T]he work and socially structured occasions of sexual passing were obstinately unyielding to [Agnes's] attempts to routinize the grounds of daily activities. This obstinacy points to the *omnirelevance* of sexual status to affairs of daily life as an invariant but unnoticed background in the texture of relevances that compose the changing actual scenes of everyday life, (italics added)

If sex category is omnirelevant (or even approaches being so), then a person engaged in virtually any activity may be held accountable for performance of that activity as a *woman* or a *man*, and their incumbency in one or the other sex category can be used to legitimate or discredit their other activities (Berger, Cohen, and Zelditch 1972; Berger, Conner, and Fisek 1974; Berger, Fisek, Norman, and Zelditch 1977; Humphreys and Berger 1981). Accordingly, virtually any activity can be assessed as to its womanly or manly nature. And note, to "do" gender is not always to live up to normative conceptions of femininity or masculinity; it is to engage in behavior *at the risk of gender assessment*. While it is individuals who do gender, the enterprise is fundamentally interactional and institutional in character, for accountability is a feature of social relationships and its idiom is drawn from the institutional arena in which those relationships are enacted. If this be the case, can we ever *not* do gender? Insofar as a society is partitioned by "essential" differences between women and men and placement in a sex category is both relevant and enforced, doing gender is unavoidable.

NOTES

1. This is not to say that gender is a singular "thing," omnipresent in the same form historically or in every situation. Because normative conceptions of appropriate attitudes and activities for sex categories can vary across cultures and historical moments, the management of situated conduct in light of those expectations can take many different forms.
2. Bernstein (1986) reports an unusual case of espionage in which a man passing as a woman convinced a lover that he/she had given birth to "their" child, who, the lover thought, "looked like" him.

REFERENCES

Berger, Joseph, Bernard P. Cohen, and Morris Zelditch, Jr. 1972. "Status Characteristics and Social Interaction." *American Sociological Review* 37:241–55.

Berger, Joseph, Thomas L. Conner, and M. Hamit Fisek, eds. 1974. *Expectation States Theory: A Theoretical Research Program*. Cambridge: Winthrop.

Berger, Joseph, M. Hamit Fisek, Robert Z. Norman, and Morris Zelditch, Jr. 1977. *Status Characteristics and Social Interaction: An Expectation States Approach.* New York: Elsevier.

Bernstein, Richard. 1986. "France Jails 2 in Odd Case of Espionage." *New York Times* (May 11).

Blackwood, Evelyn. 1984. "Sexuality and Gender in Certain Native American Tribes: The Case of Cross-Gender Females." *Signs: Journal of Women in Culture and Society* 10:27–42.

Connell, R. W. 1983. *Which Way Is Up?* Sydney: Allen & Unwin.

———. 1985. "Theorizing Gender." *Sociology* 19:260–72.

Cucchiari, Salvatore. 1981. "The Gender Revolution and the Transition From Bisexual Horde to Patrilocal Band: The Origins of Gender Hierarchy." Pp. 31–79 in *Sexual Meanings: The Cultural Construction of Gender and Sexuality*, edited by S. B. Ortner and H. Whitehead. New York: Cambridge.

Garfinkel, Harold. 1967. *Studies in Ethnomethodology.* Englewood Cliffs, NJ: Prentice-Hall.

Gerson, Judith M., and Kathy Peiss. 1985. "Boundaries, Negotiation, Consciousness: Reconceptualizing Gender Relations." *Social Problems* 32:317–31.

Goffman 1976. "Gender Display." *Studies in the Anthropology of Visual Communication* 3:69–77.

Henley, Nancy M. 1985. "Psychology and Gender." *Signs: Journal of Women in Culture and Society* 11:101–119.

Heritage, John. 1984. *Garfinkel and Ethnomethodology.* Cambridge, England: Polity Press.

Hill, W. W. 1935. "The Status of the Hermaphrodite and Transvestite in Navaho Culture." *American Anthropologist* 37:273–79.

Hochschild, Arlie R. 1973. "A Review of Sex Roles Research." *American Journal of Sociology* 78:1011–29.

Hughes, Everett C. 1945. "Dilemmas and Contradictions of Status." *American Journal of Sociology* 50:353–59.

Humphreys, Paul, and Joseph Berger. 1981. "Theoretical Consequences of the Status Characteristics Formulation." *American Journal of Sociology* 86:953–83.

Kessler, Suzanne J., and Wendy McKenna. 1978. *Gender: An Ethnomethodological Approach.* New York: Wiley.

Kessler, S., D. J. Ashendon, R. W. Connell, and G. W. Dowsett. 1985. "Gender Relations in Secondary Schooling." *Sociology of Education* 58:34–48.

Komarovsky, Mirra. 1946. "Cultural Contradictions and Sex Roles." *American Journal of Sociology* 52:184–89.

———. 1950. "Functional Analysis of Sex Roles." *American Sociological Review* 15:508–16.

Linton, Ralph. 1936. *The Study of Man.* New York: Appleton-Century.

Lopata, Helen Z., and Barrie Thorne. 1978. "On the Term `Sex Roles.´" *Signs: Journal of Women in Culture and Society* 3:718–21.

Martin, M. Kay, and Barbara Voorhies. 1975. *Female of the Species.* New York: Columbia University Press.

Mithers, Carol L. 1982. "My Life as a Man." *The Village Voice* 27 (October 5):1ff.

Money, John, and John G. Brennan. 1968. "Sexual Dimorphism in the Psychology of Female Transsexuals." *Journal of Nervous and Mental Disease* 147:487–99.

Money, John, and Charles Ogunro. 1974. "Behavioral Sexology: Ten Cases of Genetic Male Intersexuality with Impaired Prenatal and Pubertal Androgenization," *Archives of Sexual Behavior* 3:181–206.

Money, John, and Patricia Tucker. 1975. *Sexual Signatures.* Boston: Little, Brown.

Money, John, and Anke A. Erhardt. 1972. *Man and Woman/Boy and Girl.* Baltimore: Johns Hopkins.

Morris, Jan. 1974. *Conundrum.* New York: Harcourt Brace Jovanovich.

Parsons, Talcott. 1951. *The Social System.* New York: Free Press.

Parsons, Talcott, and Robert F. Bales. 1955. *Family, Socialization and Interaction Process.* New York: Free Press.

Raymond, Janice G. 1979. *The Transsexual Empire*. Boston: Beacon.

Richards, Renee (with John Ames). 1983. *Second Serve: The Renee Richards Story*. New York: Stein and Day.

Rubin, Gayle. 1975. "The Traffic in Women: Notes on the `Political Economy´ of Sex." Pp. 157–210 in *Toward an Anthropology of Women*, edited by R. Reiter. New York: Monthly Review Press.

Sacks, Harvey. 1972. "On the Analyzability of Stories by Children." Pp. 325–45 in *Directions in Sociolinguistics*, edited by J. J. Gumperz and D. Hymes. New York: Holt, Rinehart & Winston.

Schutz, Alfred. 1943. "The Problem of Rationality in the Social World." *Economics* 10:130–49.

Stacey, Judith, and Barrie Thorne. 1985. "The Missing Feminist Revolution in Sociology." *Social Problems* 32:301–16.

Thorne, Barrie. 1980. "Gender . . . How Is It Best Conceptualized?" Unpublished manuscript.

Tresemer, David. 1975. "Assumptions Made About Gender Roles." Pp. 308–39 in *Another Voice: Feminist Perspectives on Social Life and Social Science*, edited by M. Millman and R. M. Kantex. New York: Anchor/Doubleday.

Wieder, D. Lawrence. 1974. *Language and Social Reality: The Case of Telling the Convict Code*. The Hague: Mouton.

Williams, Walter L. 1986. *The Spirit and the Flesh: Sexual Diversity in American Indian Culture*. Boston: Beacon.

Wilson, Thomas P. 1970. "Conceptions of Interaction and Forms of Sociological Explanation." *American Sociological Review* 35:697–710.

Zimmerman, Don H., and D. Lawrence Wieder. 1970. "Ethnomethodology and the Problem of Order: Comment on Denzin." Pp. 287–95 in *Understanding Everyday Life*, edited by J. Denzin. Chicago: Aldine.

52. DIFFERENCE AND DOMINANCE: ON SEX DISCRIMINATION

CATHARINE MACKINNON

Catharine MacKinnon (b. 1946) is an influential feminist legal scholar currently teaching at the University of Michigan's Law School. Some of her work has proven to be controversial both outside of and within feminist circles, particularly her writing on pornography and her role in advocating for local anti-pornography ordinances. Her work on sexual harassment law has had substantial policy ramifications, used, for example, by the Equal Employment Opportunity Commission in shaping its guidelines on harassment. Central to all of her work is the question of gender inequality, the topic addressed in this excerpt from her 1987 book, *Feminism Unmodified: Discourses on Life and Law*. Here she first takes issue with what she refers to as the sameness/difference theory of sex equality—which she considers to be the theory most consequential in shaping sex discrimination discourse. This leads to her outline of an alternative theoretical account, the dominance approach that factors power differentials resulting from male dominance and female subordination into explanations of actual instances of sexual discrimination.

What is a gender question a question of? What is an inequality question a question of? These two questions underlie applications of the equality principle to issues of gender, but they are seldom explicitly asked. I think it speaks to the way gender has structured thought and perception that mainstream legal and moral theory tacitly gives the same answer to them both: these are questions of sameness and difference. The mainstream doctrine of the law of sex discrimination that results is, in my view, largely responsible for the fact that sex equality law has been so utterly ineffective at getting women what we need and are socially prevented from having on the basis of a condition of birth: a chance at productive lives of reasonable physical security, self-expression, individuation, and minimal respect and dignity. Here I expose the sameness/difference theory of sex equality, briefly show how it dominates sex discrimination law and policy and underlies its discontents, and propose an alternative that might do something.

According to the approach to sex equality that has dominated politics, law, and social perception, equality is an equivalence, not a distinction, and sex is a distinction. The legal mandate of equal treatment—which is both a systemic norm and a specific legal doctrine—becomes a matter of treating likes alike and unlikes unlike; and the sexes are defined as such by their mutual unlikeness. Put another way, gender is socially constructed as difference epistemologically; sex discrimination law bounds gender equality by difference doctrinally. A built-in tension exists between this concept of equality, which presupposes sameness, and this concept of sex, which presupposes difference. Sex equality thus becomes a contradiction in terms, something of an oxymoron, which may suggest why we are having such a difficult time getting it.

Upon further scrutiny, two alternate paths to equality for women emerge within this dominant approach, paths that roughly follow the lines of this tension. The leading one is: be the same as men. This path is termed gender neutrality doctrinally and the single standard philosophically. It is testimony to how substance gets itself up as form in law that this rule is considered formal equality. Because this approach mirrors the ideology of the social world, it is considered abstract, meaning transparent of substance; also for this reason it is considered not only to be *the* standard, but *a* standard at all. It is so far the leading rule that the words "equal to" are code for, equivalent to, the words "the same as"—referent for both unspecified.

To women who want equality yet find that you are different, the doctrine provides an alternate route: be different from men. This equal recognition of difference is termed the special benefit rule or special protection rule legally, the double standard philosophically. It is in rather bad odor. Like pregnancy, which always calls it up, it is something of a doctrinal embarrassment. Considered an exception to true equality and not really a rule of law at all, this is the one place where the law of sex discrimination admits it is recognizing something substantive. Together with the Bona Fide Occupational Qualification (BFOQ), the unique physical characteristic exception under ERA policy, compensatory legislation, and sex-conscious relief in particular litigation, affirmative action is thought to live here.[1]

The philosophy underlying the difference approach is that sex *is* a difference, a division, a distinction, beneath which lies a stratum of human commonality, sameness. The moral thrust of the sameness branch of the doctrine is to make normative rules conform to this empirical reality by granting women access to what men have access to: to the extent that women are no different from men, we deserve what they have. The differences branch, which is generally seen as patronizing but necessary to avoid absurdity, exists to value or compensate women for what we are or have become distinctively as women (by which is meant, unlike men) under existing conditions.

My concern is not with which of these paths to sex equality is preferable in the long run or more appropriate to any particular issue, although most discourse on sex discrimination revolves about these questions as if that were all there is. My point is logically prior: to treat issues of sex equality as issues of sameness and difference *is to take a particular approach*. I call this the difference approach because it is obsessed with the sex difference. The main theme in the fugue is "we're the same, we're the same, we're the same." The counterpoint theme (in a higher register) is "but we're different, but we're different, but we're different." Its underlying story is: on the first day, difference was; on the second day, a division was created upon it; on the third day, irrational instances of dominance arose. Division may be rational or irrational. Dominance either seems or is justified. Difference *is*.

There is a politics to this. Concealed is the substantive way in which man has become the measure of all things. Under the sameness standard, women are measured according to our correspondence with man, our equality judged by our proximity to his measure. Under the difference standard, we are measured according to our lack of correspondence with him, our womanhood judged by our distance from his measure. Gender neutrality is thus simply the male standard, and the special protection rule is simply the female standard, but do not be deceived: masculinity, or maleness, is the referent for both. Think about it like those anatomy models in medical school. A male body is the human body; all those extra things women have are studied in ob/gyn. It truly is a situation in which more is less. Approaching sex discrimination in this way—as if sex questions are difference questions and equality questions are sameness questions—provides two ways for the law to hold women to a male standard and call that sex equality.

* * *

Having been very hard on the difference answer to sex equality questions, I should say that it takes up a very important problem: how to get women access to everything we have been excluded from, while also valuing everything that women are or have been allowed to become or have developed as a consequence of our struggle either not to be excluded from most of life's pursuits or to be taken seriously under the terms that have been permitted to be our terms. It negotiates what we have managed in relation to men. Legally articulated as the need to conform normative standards to existing reality, the strongest doctrinal expression of its sameness idea would prohibit taking gender into account in any way.

Its guiding impulse is: we're as good as you. Anything you can do, we can do. Just get out of the way. I have to confess a sincere affection for this approach. It has gotten women some access to employment[2] and education,[3] the public pursuits, including academic,[4] professional,[5] and blue-collar work;[6] the military;[7] and more than nominal access to athletics.[8] It has moved to change the dead ends that were all we were seen as good for and has altered what passed for women's lack of physical training, which was really serious training in passivity and enforced weakness. It makes you want to cry sometimes to know that it has had to be a mission for many women just to be permitted to do the work of this society, to have the dignity of doing jobs a lot of other people don't even want to do.

The issue of including women in the military draft[9] has presented the sameness answer to the sex equality question in all its simple dignity and complex equivocality. As a citizen, I should have to risk being killed just like you. The consequences of my resistance to this risk should count like yours. The undercurrent is: what's the matter, don't you want me to learn to kill . . . just like you? Sometimes I see this as a dialogue between women in the afterlife. The feminist says to the soldier, "we fought for your equality." The soldier says to the feminist, "oh, no, *we* fought for *your* equality."

Feminists have this nasty habit of counting bodies and refusing not to notice their gender. As applied, the sameness standard has mostly gotten men the benefit of those few things women have historically had—for all the good they did us. Almost every sex discrimination case that has been won at the Supreme Court level has been brought by a man.[10] Under the rule of gender neutrality, the law of custody and divorce has been transformed, giving men an equal chance at custody of children and at alimony.[11] Men often look like better "parents" under gender-neutral rules like level of income and presence of nuclear family, because men

make more money and (as they say) initiate the building of family units.[12] In effect, they get preferred because society advantages them before they get into court, and law is prohibited from taking that preference into account because that would mean taking gender into account. The group realities that make women more in need of alimony are not permitted to matter, because only individual factors, gender-neutrally considered, may matter. So the fact that women will live their lives, as individuals, as members of the group women, with women's chances in a sex-discriminatory society, may not count, or else it is sex discrimination. The equality principle in this guise mobilizes the idea that the way to get things for women is to get them for men. Men have gotten them. Have women? We still have not got equal pay,[13] or equal work,[14] far less equal pay for equal work,[15] and we are close to losing separate enclaves like women's schools through this approach.[16]

Here is why. In reality, which this approach is not long on because it is liberal idealism talking to itself, virtually every quality that distinguishes men from women is already affirmatively compensated in this society. Men's physiology defines most sports,[17] their needs define auto and health insurance coverage, their socially designed biographies define workplace expectations and successful career patterns, their perspectives and concerns define quality in scholarship, their experiences and obsessions define merit, their objectification of life defines art, their military service defines citizenship, their presence defines family, their inability to get along with each other—their wars and rulerships—defines history, their image defines god, and their genitals define sex. For each of their differences from women, what amounts to an affirmative action plan is in effect, otherwise known as the structure and values of American society. But whenever women are, by this standard, "different" from men and insist on not having it held against us, whenever a difference is used to keep us second class and we refuse to smile about it, equality law has a paradigm trauma and it's crisis time for the doctrine.

What this doctrine has apparently meant by sex inequality is not what happens to us. The law of sex discrimination that has resulted seems to be looking only for those ways women are kept down that have *not* wrapped themselves up as a difference—whether original, imposed, or imagined. Start with original: what to do about the fact that women actually have an ability men still lack, gestating children in utero. Pregnancy therefore is a difference. Difference doctrine says it is sex discrimination to give women what we need, because only women need it. It is not sex discrimination not to give women what we need because then only women will not get what we need.[18] Move into imposed: what to do about the fact that most women are segregated into low-paying jobs where there are no men. Suspecting that the structure of the marketplace will be entirely subverted if comparable worth is put into effect, difference doctrine says that because there is no man to set a standard from which women's treatment is a deviation, there is no sex discrimination here, only sex difference. Never mind that there is no man to compare with because no man would do that job if he had a choice, and of course he has because he is a man, so he won't.[19]

Now move into the so-called subtle reaches of the imposed category, the de facto area. Most jobs in fact require that the person, gender neutral, who is qualified for them will be someone who is not the primary caretaker of a preschool child.[20] Pointing out that this raises a concern of sex in a society in which women are expected to care for the children is taken as day one of taking gender into account in the structuring of jobs. To do that would violate the rule against not noticing situated differences based on gender, so it never emerges that day one of taking gender into account was the day the job was structured with the expectation that its occupant would have no child care responsibilities. Imaginary sex differences—such as between male and female applicants to administer estates or between males aging and dying and females aging and dying[21]—I will concede, the doctrine can handle.

I will also concede that there are many differences between women and men. I mean, can you imagine elevating one half of a population and denigrating the other half and producing a population in which everyone is the same? What the sameness standard fails to notice is that men's differences from women are equal to women's differences from men. There is an *equality* there. Yet the sexes are not socially equal. The difference approach misses the fact that hierarchy of

power produces real as well as fantasied differences, differences that are also inequalities. What is missing in the difference approach is what Aristotle missed in his empiricist notion that equality means treating likes alike and unlikes unlike, and nobody has questioned it since. Why should you have to be the same as a man to get what a man gets simply because he is one? Why does maleness provide an original entitlement, not questioned on the basis of *its* gender, so that it is women—women who want to make a case of unequal treatment in a world men have made in their image (this is really the part Aristotle missed)—who have to show in effect that they are men in every relevant respect, unfortunately mistaken for women on the basis of an accident of birth?

The women that gender neutrality benefits, and there are some, show the suppositions of this approach in highest relief. They are mostly women who have been able to construct a biography that somewhat approximates the male norm, at least on paper. They are the qualified, the least of sex discrimination's victims. When they are denied a man's chance, it looks the most like sex bias. The more unequal society gets, the fewer such women are permitted to exist. Therefore, the more unequal society gets, the *less* likely the difference doctrine is to be able to do anything about it, because unequal power creates both the appearance and the reality of sex differences along the same lines as it creates its sex inequalities.

The special benefits side of the difference approach has not compensated for the differential of being second class. The special benefits rule is the only place in mainstream equality doctrine where you get to identify as a woman and not have that mean giving up all claim to equal treatment—but it comes close. Under its double standard, women who stand to inherit something when their husbands die have gotten the exclusion of a small percentage of the inheritance tax, to the tune of Justice Douglas waxing eloquent about the difficulties of all women's economic situation.[22] If we're going to be stigmatized as different, it would be nice if the compensation would fit the disparity. Women have also gotten three more years than men get before we have to be advanced or kicked out of the military hierarchy, as compensation for being precluded from combat, the usual way to advance.[23]

Women have also gotten excluded from contact jobs in male-only prisons because we might get raped, the Court taking the viewpoint of the reasonable rapist on women's employment opportunities.[24] We also get protected out of jobs because of our fertility. The reason is that the job has health hazards, and somebody who might be a real person some day and therefore could sue—that is, a fetus—might be hurt if women, who apparently are not real persons and therefore can't sue either for the hazard to our health or for the lost employment opportunity, are given jobs that subject our bodies to possible harm.[25] Excluding women is always an option if equality feels in tension with the pursuit itself. They never seem to think of excluding men. Take combat.[26] Somehow it takes the glory out of the foxhole, the buddiness out of the trenches, to imagine us out there. You get the feeling they might rather end the draft, they might even rather not fight wars at all than have to do it with us.

The double standard of these rules doesn't give women the dignity of the single standard; it also does not (as the differences standard does) suppress the gender of its referent, which is, of course, the female gender. I must also confess some affection for this standard. The work of Carol Gilligan on gender differences in moral reasoning[27] gives it a lot of dignity, more than it has ever had, more, frankly, than I thought it ever could have. But she achieves for moral reasoning what the special protection rule achieves in law: the affirmative rather than the negative valuation of that which has accurately distinguished women from men, by making it seem as though those attributes, with their consequences, really are somehow ours, rather than what male supremacy has attributed to us for its own use. For women to affirm difference, when difference means dominance, as it does with gender, means to affirm the qualities and characteristics of powerlessness.

Women have done good things, and it is a good thing to affirm them. I think quilts are art. I think women have a history. I think we create culture. I also know that we have not only been excluded from making what has been considered art; our artifacts have been excluded from setting the standards by which art is art. Women have a history all right, but it is a history both of what was and of what was not allowed to be. So I am critical of affirming what we have been, which necessarily is what we have been

permitted, as if it is women's, ours, possessive. As if equality, in spite of everything, already ineluctably exists.

I am getting hard on this and am about to get harder on it. I do not think that the way women reason morally is morality "in a different voice."[28] I think it is morality in a higher register, in the feminine voice. Women value care because men have valued us according to the care we give them, and we could probably use some. Women think in relational terms because our existence is defined in relation to men. Further, when you are powerless, you don't just speak differently. A lot, you don't speak. Your speech is not just differently articulated, it is silenced. Eliminated, gone. You aren't just deprived of a language with which to articulate your distinctiveness, although you are; you are deprived of a life out of which articulation might come. Not being heard is not just a function of lack of recognition, not just that no one knows how to listen to you, although it is that; it is also silence of the deep kind, the silence of being prevented from having anything to say. Sometimes it is permanent. All I am saying is that the damage of sexism is real, and reifying that into differences is an insult to our possibilities.

So long as these issues are framed this way, demands for equality will always appear to be asking to have it both ways: the same when we are the same, different when we are different. But this is the way men have it: equal and different too. They have it the same as women when they are the same and want it, and different from women when they are different and want to be, which usually they do. Equal and different too would only be parity.[29] But under male supremacy, while being told we get it both ways, both the specialness of the pedestal and an even chance at the race, the ability to be a woman and a person, too, few women get much benefit of either.

* * *

There is an alternative approach, one that threads its way through existing law and expresses, I think, the reason equality law exists in the first place. It provides a second answer, a dissident answer in law and philosophy, to both the equality question and the gender question. In this approach, an equality question is a question of the distribution of power. Gender is also a question of power, specifically of male supremacy and female subordination. The question of equality, from the standpoint of what it is going to take to get it, is at root a question of hierarchy, which—as power succeeds in constructing social perception and social reality—derivatively becomes a categorical distinction, a difference. Here, on the first day that matters, dominance was achieved, probably by force. By the second day, division along the same lines had to be relatively firmly in place. On the third day, if not sooner, differences were demarcated, together with social systems to exaggerate them in perception and in fact, *because* the systematically differential delivery of benefits and deprivations required making no mistake about who was who. Comparatively speaking, man has been resting ever since. Gender might not even code as difference, might not mean distinction epistemologically, were it not for its consequences for social power.

I call this the dominance approach, and it is the ground I have been standing on in criticizing mainstream law. The goal of this dissident approach is not to make legal categories trace and trap the way things are. It is not to make rules that fit reality. It is critical of reality. Its task is not to formulate abstract standards that will produce determinate outcomes in particular cases. Its project is more substantive, more jurisprudential than formulaic, which is why it is difficult for the mainstream discourse to dignify it as an approach to doctrine or to imagine it as a rule of law at all. It proposes to expose that which women have had little choice but to be confined to, in order to change it.

The dominance approach centers on the most sex-differential abuses of women as a gender, abuses that sex equality law in its difference garb could not confront. It is based on a reality about which little of a systematic nature was known before 1970, a reality that calls for a new conception of the problem of sex inequality. This new information includes not only the extent and intractability of sex segregation into poverty, which has been known before, but the range of issues termed violence against women, which has not been. It combines women's material desperation, through being relegated to categories of jobs that pay nil, with the massive amount of rape and attempted rape—44 percent of all women—about which virtually nothing is done;[30] the sexual assault of children—38 percent of girls and 10 percent of boys—which is

apparently endemic to the patriarchal family;[31] the battery of women that is systematic in one quarter to one third of our homes;[32] prostitution, women's fundamental economic condition, what we do when all else fails, and for many women in this country, all else fails often;[33] and pornography, an industry that traffics in female flesh, making sex inequality into sex to the tune of eight billion dollars a year in profits largely to organized crime.[34]

These experiences have been silenced out of the difference definition of sex equality largely because they happen almost exclusively to women. Understand: for this reason, they are considered *not* to raise sex equality issues. Because this treatment is done almost uniquely to women, it is implicitly treated as a difference, the sex difference, when in fact it is the socially situated subjection of women. The whole point of women's social relegation to inferiority as a gender is that for the most part these things aren't done to men. Men are not paid half of what women are paid for doing the same work on the basis of their equal difference. Everything they touch does not turn valueless because they touched it. When they are hit, a person has been assaulted. When they are sexually violated, it is not simply tolerated or found entertaining or defended as the necessary structure of the family, the price of civilization, or a constitutional right.

Does this differential describe the sex difference? Maybe so. It does describe the systematic relegation of an entire group of people to a condition of inferiority and attribute it to their nature. If this differential were biological, maybe biological intervention would have to be considered. If it were evolutionary, perhaps men would have to evolve differently. Because I think it is political, I think its politics construct the deep structure of society. Men who do not rape women have nothing wrong with their hormones. Men who are made sick by pornography and do not eroticize their revulsion are not under-evolved. This social status in which we can be used and abused and trivialized and humiliated and bought and sold and passed around and patted on the head and put in place and told to smile so that we look as though we're enjoying it all is not what some of us have in mind as sex equality.

This second approach—which is not abstract, which is at odds with socially imposed reality and therefore does not look like a standard according to the standard for standards—became the implicit model for racial justice applied by the courts during the sixties. It has since eroded with the erosion of judicial commitment to racial equality. It was based on the realization that the condition of Blacks in particular was not fundamentally a matter of rational or irrational differentiation on the basis of race but was fundamentally a matter of white supremacy, under which racial differences became invidious as a consequence.[35] To consider gender in this way, observe again that men are as different from women as women are from men, but socially the sexes are not equally powerful. To be on the top of a hierarchy is certainly different from being on the bottom, but that is an obfuscatingly neutralized way of putting it, as a hierarchy is a great deal more than that. If gender were merely a question of difference, sex inequality would be a problem of mere sexism, of mistaken differentiation, of inaccurate categorization of individuals. This is what the difference approach thinks it is and is therefore sensitive to. But if gender is an inequality first, constructed as a socially relevant differentiation in order to keep that inequality in place, then sex inequality questions are questions of systematic dominance, of male supremacy, which is not at all abstract and is anything but a mistake.

If differentiation into classifications, in itself, is discrimination, as it is in difference doctrine, the use of law to change group-based social inequalities becomes problematic, even contradictory. This is because the group whose situation is to be changed must necessarily be legally identified and delineated, yet to do so is considered in fundamental tension with the guarantee against legally sanctioned inequality. If differentiation is discrimination, affirmative action, and any legal change in social inequality, is discrimination—but the existing social differentiations which constitute the inequality are not? This is only to say that, in the view that equates differentiation with discrimination, changing an unequal status quo is discrimination, but allowing it to exist is not.

Looking at the difference approach and the dominance approach from each other's point of view clarifies some otherwise confusing tensions in sex equality debates. From the point of view of the dominance approach, it becomes clear that the difference approach adopts the point of view of male supremacy on the status of the sexes. Simply by treating the status quo

as "the standard," it invisibly and uncritically accepts the arrangements under male supremacy. In this sense, the difference approach is masculinist, although it can be expressed in a female voice. The dominance approach, in that it sees the inequalities of the social world from the standpoint of the subordination of women to men, is feminist.

If you look through the lens of the difference approach at the world as the dominance approach imagines it—that is, if you try to see real inequality through a lens that has difficulty seeing an inequality as an inequality if it also appears as a difference—you see demands for change in the distribution of power as demands for special protection. This is because the only tools that the difference paradigm offers to comprehend disparity equate the recognition of a gender line with an admission of lack of entitlement to equality under law. Since equality questions are primarily confronted in this approach as matters of empirical fit[36]— that is, as matters of accurately shaping legal rules (implicitly modeled on the standard men set) to the way the world is (also implicitly modeled on the standard men set)—any existing differences must be negated to merit equal treatment. For ethnicity as well as for gender, it is basic to mainstream discrimination doctrine to preclude any true diversity among equals or true equality within diversity.

To the difference approach, it further follows that any attempt to change the way the world actually is looks like a moral question requiring a separate judgment of how things ought to be. This approach imagines asking the following disinterested question that can be answered neutrally as to groups: against the weight of empirical difference, should we treat some as the equals of others, even when they may not be entitled to it because they are not up to standard? Because this construction of the problem is part of what the dominance approach unmasks, it does not arise with the dominance approach, which therefore does not see its own foundations as moral. If sex inequalities are approached as matters of imposed status, which are in need of change if a legal mandate of equality means anything at all, the question whether women should be treated unequally means simply whether women should be treated as less. When it is exposed as a naked power question, there is no separable question of what ought to be. The only real question is what is and is not a gender question. Once no amount of difference justifies treating women as subhuman, eliminating that is what equality law is for. In this shift of paradigms, equality propositions become no longer propositions of good and evil, but of power and powerlessness, no more disinterested in their origins or neutral in their arrival at conclusions than are the problems they address.

There came a time in Black people's movement for equality in this country when slavery stopped being a question of how it could be justified and became a question of how it could be ended. Racial disparities surely existed, or racism would have been harmless, but at that point—a point not yet reached for issues of sex —no amount of group difference mattered anymore. This is the same point at which a group's characteristics, including empirical attributes, become constitutive of the fully human, rather than being defined as exceptions to or as distinct from the fully human. To one-sidedly measure one group's differences against a standard set by the other incarnates partial standards. The moment when one's particular qualities become part of the standard by which humanity is measured is a millenial moment.

To summarize the argument: seeing sex equality questions as matters of reasonable or unreasonable classification is part of the way male dominance is expressed in law. If you follow my shift in perspective from gender as difference to gender as dominance, gender changes from a distinction that is presumptively valid to a detriment that is presumptively suspect. The difference approach tries to map reality; the dominance approach tries to challenge and change it. In the dominance approach, sex discrimination stops being a question of morality and starts being a question of politics.

You can tell if sameness is your standard for equality if my critique of hierarchy looks like a request

for special protection in disguise. It's not. It envisions a change that would make possible a simple equal chance for the first time. To define the reality of sex as difference and the warrant of equality as sameness is wrong on both counts. Sex, in nature, is not a bipolarity; it is a continuum. In society it is made into a bipolarity. Once this is done, to require that one be the same as those who set the standard—those which one is already socially defined as different from—simply means that sex equality is conceptually designed never to be achieved. Those who most need equal treatment will be the least similar, socially, to those whose situation set the standard as against which one's entitlement to be equally treated is measured. Doctrinally speaking, the deepest problems of sex inequality will not find women "similarly situated"[37] to men. Far less will practices of sex inequality require that acts be intentionally discriminatory.[38] All that is required is that the status quo be maintained. As a strategy for maintaining social power first structure reality unequally, then require that entitlement to alter it be grounded on a lack of distinction in situation; first structure perception so that different equals inferior, then require that discrimination be activated by evil minds who *know* they are treating equals as less.

I say, give women equal power in social life. Let what we say matter, then we will discourse on questions of morality. Take your foot off our necks, then we will hear in what tongue women speak. So long as sex equality is limited by sex difference, whether you like it or don't like it, whether you value it or seek to negate it, whether you stake it out as a grounds for feminism or occupy it as the terrain of misogyny, women will be born, degraded, and die. We would settle for that equal protection of the laws under which one would be born, live, and die, in a country where protection is not a dirty word and equality is not a special privilege.

NOTES

The most memorable occasions on which I delivered a version of this speech were: Harvard Law School, Cambridge, Massachusetts, Oct. 24, 1984; Conference on the Moral Foundations of Civil Rights Policy, Center for Philosophy and Public Policy, University of Maryland, College Park, Maryland, Oct. 19, 1984; and the James McCormick Mitchell Lecture, State University of Buffalo Law School, Buffalo, New York, Oct. 19, 1984. I thank the students of Harvard Law School for their response to so many of my initial thoughts.

1. The Bona Fide Occupational Qualification (BFOQ) exception to Title VII of the Civil Rights Act of 1964, 42 U.S.C. § 2000 e-(2)(e), permits sex to be a job qualification when it is a valid one. The leading interpretation of the proposed federal Equal Rights Amendment would, pursuing a similar analytic structure, permit a "unique physical characteristic" exception to its otherwise absolute embargo on taking sex into account. Barbara Brown, Thomas I. Emerson, Gail Falk, and Ann E. Freedman, "The Equal Rights Amendment: A Constitutional Basis for Equal Rights for Women," 80 *Yale Law Journal* 893 (1971).

2. Title VII of the Civil Rights Act of 1964, 42 U.S.C. § 2000 c; Phillips v. Martin-Marietta, 400 U.S. 542 (1971). Frontiero v. Richardson, 411 U.S. 484 (1974) is the high-water mark of this approach. See also City of Los Angeles v. Manhart, 435 U.S. 702 (1978): Newport News Shipbuilding and Dry Dock Co. v. EEOC, 462 U.S. 669 (1983).

3. Title IX of the Education Amendments of 1972, 20 U.S.C. § 1681; Cannon v. University of Chicago, 441 U.S. 677 (1981): Mississippi University for Women v. Hogan, 458 U.S. 718 (1982); see also De La Cruz v. Torney, 582 F.2d 45 (9th Cir. 1978).

4. My impression is that women appear to lose most academic sex discrimination cases that go to trial, although I know of no systematic or statistical study on the subject. One case that won eventually, elevating the standard of proof in the process, is Sweeney v. Board of Trustees of Keene State College, 439 U.S. 29 (1979). The ruling for the plaintiff was affirmed on remand, 604 F.2d 106 (1st Cir. 1979).

5. Hishon v. King & Spalding, 467 U.S. 69 (1984).

6. See, e.g., Vanguard Justice v. Hughes, 471 F. Supp. 670 (D. Md. 1979); Meyer v. Missouri State Highway Commission, 567 F.2d 804, 891 (8th Cir. 1977). Payne v. Travenol Laboratories Inc., 416 F. Supp. 248 (N.D. Mass. 1976). See also Dothard v. Rawlinson, 433 U.S. 321 (1977) (height and weight requirements invalidated for prison guard contact positions because of disparate impact on sex).

7. Frontiero v. Richardson, 411 U.S. 484 (1974); Schlesinger v. Ballard, 419 U.S. 498 (1975).

8. This situation is relatively complex. See Gomes v. R.I. Interscholastic League, 469 F. Supp. 659 (D. R.I. 1979); Brenden v. Independent School District, 477 F.2d 1292 (8th Cir. 1973); O'Connor v. Board of Education of School District No. 23, 645 F.2d 578 (7th Cir. 1981); Cape v. Tennessee Secondary School Athletic Association, 424 F. Supp. 732 (E.D. Tenn. 1976), rev'd, 563 F.2d 793 (6th Cir. 1977); Yellow Springs Exempted Village School District Board of Education v. Ohio High School Athletic Association, 443 F. Supp. 753 (S.D. Ohio 1978); Aiken v. Lieuallen, 593 P.2d 1243 (Or. App. 1979).

9. Rostker v. Goldberg, 453 U.S. 57 (1981). See also Lori S. Kornblum, "Women Warriors in a Men's World: The Combat Exclusion," 2 *Law and Inequality: A Journal of Theory and Practice* 353 (1984).

10. David Cole, "Strategies of Difference: Litigating for Women's Rights in a Man's World," 2 *Law & Inequality: A Journal of Theory and Practice* 34 n.4 (1984) (collecting cases).

11. Devine v. Devine, 398 So. 2d 686 (Ala. Sup. Ct. 1981); Danielson v. Board of Higher Education, 358 F. Supp. 22 (S.D.N.Y. 1972); Weinberger v. Wiesenfeld, 420 U.S. 636 (1975); Stanley v. Illinois, 405 U.S. 645 (1971); Caban v. Mohammed, 441 U.S. 380 (1979); Orr v. Orr, 440 U.S. 268 (1979).

12. Lenore Weitzman, "The Economics of Divorce: Social and Economic Consequences of Property, Alimony and Child Support Awards," 28 *U.C.L.A. Law Review* 1118, 1251 (1982), documents a

decline in women's standard of living of 73 percent and an increase in men's of 42 percent within a year after divorce.

13. Equal Pay Act, 29 U.S.C. § 206(d)(1) (1976) guarantees pay equality, as does case law, *but cf.* data on pay gaps, "Introduction," note 2. MacKinnon, *Feminism Unmodified.* Cambridge, Mass: Harvard University Press, 1987.

14. Examples include Christenson v. State of Iowa, 563 F.2d 353 (8th Cir. 1977); Gerlach v. Michigan Bell Tel. Co., 501 F. Supp. 1300 (E.D. Mich. 1980); Odomes v. Nucare, Inc., 653 F.2d 246 (6th Cir. 1981) (female nurse's aide denied Title VII remedy because her job duties were not substantially similar to those of better-paid male orderly): Power v. Barry County, Michigan, 539 F. Supp. 721 (W.D. Mich. 1982); Spaulding v. University of Washington, 740 F.2d 686 (9th Cir. 1984).

15. County of Washington v. Gunther, 452 U.S. 161 (1981) permits a comparable worth-type challenge where pay inequality can be proven to be a correlate of intentional job segregation. See also Lemons v. City and County of Denver, 17 FEP Cases 910 (D. Colo. 1978), aff'd, 620 F.2d 228 (10th Cir. 1977), cert. denied, 449 U.S. 888 (1980); AFSCME v. State of Washington, 770 F.2d 1401 (9th Cir. 1985). See generally Carol Jean Pint, "Value, Work and Women," 1 *Law & Inequality: A Journal of Theory and Practice* 159 (1983).

16. Combine the result in Bob Jones University v. United States, 461 U.S. 547 (1983) with Mississippi University for Women v. Hogan, 458 U.S. 718 (1982), and the tax-exempt status of women-only schools is clearly threatened.

17. A particularly pungent example comes from a case in which the plaintiff sought to compete in boxing matches with men, since there were no matches sponsored by the defendant among women. A major reason that preventing the woman from competing was found not to violate her equality rights was that the "safety rules and precautions [were] developed, designed, and tested in the context of all-male competition." Lafler v. Athletic Board of Control, 536 F. Supp. 104, 107 (W.D. Mich. 1982). As the court put it: "In this case, the real differences between the male and female anatomy are relevant in considering whether men and women may be treated differently with regard to their participating in boxing. The plaintiff *admits* that she wears a protective covering for her breasts while boxing. Such a protective covering ... would violate Rule Six, Article 9 of the Amateur Boxing Federation rules currently in effect. The same rule *requires* contestants to wear a protective cup, a rule obviously designed for the unique anatomical characteristics of men." Id. at 106 (emphasis added). The rule is based on the male anatomy, therefore not a justification for the discrimination but an example of it. This is not considered in the opinion, nor does the judge discuss whether women might benefit from genital protection, and men from chest guards, as in some other sports.

18. This is a reference to the issues raised by several recent cases which consider whether states' attempts to compensate pregnancy leaves and to secure jobs on return constitute sex discrimination. California Federal Savings and Loan Assn. v. Goerra, 758 F.2d 390 (9th Cir. 1985), cert. granted 54 U.S.L.W. 3460 (U.S. Jan. 13, 1986); see also Miller-Wohl v. Commissioner of Labor, 515 F. Supp. 1264 (D. Montana 1981), vacated and dismissed, 685 F.2d 1088 (9th Cir. 1982). The position argued in "Difference and Dominance" here suggests that if these benefits are prohibited under Title VII, Title VII is unconstitutional under the equal protection clause.

This argument was not made directly in either case. The American Civil Liberties Union argued that the provisions requiring pregnancy to be compensated in employment, without comparable coverage for men, violated Title VII's prohibition on pregnancy-based classifications and on sex. Montana had made it illegal for an employer to "terminate a woman's employment because of her pregnancy" or to "refuse to grant to the employee a reasonable leave of absence for such pregnancy." Montana Maternity Leave Act § 49-2-310(1) and (2). According to the ACLU this provision "grants pregnant workers certain employment rights not enjoyed by other workers . . . Legislation designed to benefit women has . . . perpetuated destructive stereotypes about their proper roles and operated to deny them rights and benefits enjoyed by men. The [Montana provision] deters employers from hiring women who are or may become pregnant, causes resentment and hostility in the workplace, and penalizes men." Brief of American Civil Liberties Union, et al. *amicus curiae*, Montana Supreme Court No. 84–172, at 7. The National Organization for Women argued that the California provision, which requires employers to give pregnant workers unpaid disability leave with job security for up to four months, would violate Title VII should Title VII be interpreted to permit it. Brief of National Organization for Women, et al., United States Court of Appeals for the Ninth Circuit, 685 F.2d 1088 (9th Cir. 1982).

When Congress passed the Pregnancy Discrimination Act, amending Title VII, 42 U.S.C. § 2000 e(k), it defined "because of sex" or "on the basis of sex" to include "because of or on the basis of pregnancy, childbirth, or related medical conditions; and women affected by pregnancy, childbirth, or related medical conditions shall be treated the same for all employment-related purposes." In so doing. Congress arguably decided that one did not have to be the same as a man to be treated without discrimination, since it guaranteed freedom from discriminatory treatment on the basis of a condition that is not the same for men as it is for women. It even used the word "women" in the statute.

Further, Congress made this decision expressly to overrule the Supreme Court decision in General Electric v. Gilbert, 429 U.S. 125 (1976), which had held that failure to cover pregnancy as a disability was not sex discrimination because the line between pregnant and nonpregnant was not the line between women and men. In rejecting this logic, as the Court found it did expressly in Newport News Shipbuilding and Dry Dock Co. v. EEOC, 462 U.S. 669, 678 (1983), Congress rejected the implicit measuring of women's entitlement to equality by a male standard. Nor need all women be the same, that is, pregnant or potentially so, to have pregnancy-based discrimination be sex-based discrimination.

Upholding the California pregnancy leave and job security law, the Ninth Circuit opinion did not require sameness for equality to be delivered: "The PDA does not require states to ignore pregnancy. It requires that women be treated equally . . . [E]quality under the PDA must be measured in employment opportunity, not necessarily in amounts of money expended—or in amounts of days of disability leave expended. Equality . . . compares coverage to actual need, not coverage to hypothetical identical needs." California Federal v. Guerra, 758 F.2d 390 (9th Cir. 1985) (Ferguson, J.). "We are not the first court to announce the goal of Title VII is equality of employment opportunity, not necessarily sameness of treatment." Id. at 396 n.7.

19.   Most women work at jobs mostly women do, and most of those jobs are paid less than jobs that mostly men do. See, e.g., Pint, note 15 above, at 162–63 nn.19, 20 (collecting studies). To the point that men may not meet the male standard themselves, one court found that a union did not fairly represent its women in the following terms: "As to the yard and driver jobs, defendants suggest not only enormous intellectual requirements, but that the physical demands of those jobs are so great as to be beyond the capacity of any female. Again, it is noted that plaintiffs' capacity to perform those jobs was never tested, despite innumerable requests therefor. It is also noted that defendants have never suggested *which* of the innumerable qualifications they list for

these jobs (for the first time) the plaintiffs might fail to meet. The court, however, will accept without listing here the extraordinary catalogue of feats which defendants argue must be performed in the yard, and as a driver. That well may be. However, one learns from this record that one cannot be too weak, too sick, too old and infirm, or too ignorant to perform these jobs, *so long as one is a man.* The plaintiffs appear to the layperson's eye to be far more physically fit than many of the drivers who moved into the yard, over the years, according to the testimony of defense witnesses . . . In short, they were all at least as fit as the men with serious physical deficits and disabilities who held yard jobs." Jones v. Cassens Transport, 617 F. Supp. 869, 892 (1985) (emphasis in original).

20. Phillips v. Martin-Marietta, 400 U.S. 542 (1971).
21. Reed v. Reed, 404 U.S. 71 (1971) held that a statute barring women from administering estates is sex discrimination. If few women were taught to read and write, as used to be the case, the gender difference would not be imaginary in this case, yet the social situation would be even more sex discriminatory than it is now. Compare City of Los Angeles v. Manhart, 434 U.S. 815 (1978), which held that requiring women to make larger contributions to their retirement plan was sex discrimination, in spite of the allegedly proven sex difference that women on the average outlive men.
22. Kahn v. Shevin, 416 U.S. 351, 353 (1974).
23. Schlesinger v. Ballard, 419 U.S. 498 (1975).
24. Dothard v. Rawlinson, 433 U.S. 321 (1977); see also Michael M. v. Sonoma County Superior Court, 450 U.S. 464 (1981).
25. Doerr v. B.F. Goodrich, 484 F. Supp. 320 (N.D. Ohio 1979). Wendy Webster Williams, "Firing the Woman to Protect the Fetus: The Reconciliation of Fetal Protection with Employment Opportunity Goals Under Title VII," 69 *Georgetown Law Journal* 641 (1981). See also Hayes v. Shelby Memorial Hospital, 546 F. Supp. 259 (N.D. Ala. 1982); Wright v. Olin Corp., 697 F.2d 1172 (4th Cir. 1982).
26. Congress requires the Air Force (10 U.S.C. § 8549 [1983]) and the Navy (10 U.S.C. § 6015 [1983]) to exclude women from combat, with some exceptions. Owens v. Brown, 455 F. Supp. 291 (D.D.C. 1978), had previously invalidated the prior Navy combat exclusion because it prohibited women from filling jobs they could perform and inhibited Navy's discretion to assign women on combat ships. The Army excludes women from combat based upon its own policies under congressional authorization to determine assignment (10 U.S.C. § 3012 [e] [1983]).
27. Carol Gilligan, *In a Different Voice* (1982).
28. Id.
29. I argued this in Appendix A of my *Sexual Harassment of Working Women: A Case of Sex Discrimination* (1979). That book ends with "Women want to be equal and different, too." I could have added "Men are." As a standard, this would have reduced women's aspirations for equality to some corresponding version of men's actualities. But as an observation, it would have been true.
30. Diana Russell and Nancy Howell, "The Prevalence of Rape in the United States Revisited," 8 *Signs: Journal of Women in Culture and Society* 689 (1983) (44 percent of women in 930 households were victims of rape or attempted rape at some time in their lives).
31. Diana Russell, "The Incidence and Prevalence of Intrafamilial and Extrafamilial Sexual Abuse of Female Children." 7 *Child Abuse & Neglect: The International Journal* 133 (1983).

32.   R. Emerson Dobash and Russell Dobash, *Violence against Wives: A Case against the Patriarchy* (1979); Bruno v. Codd, 90 Misc. 2d 1047, 396 N.Y.S. 2d 974 (Sup. Ct. 1977), rev'd. 64 A.D. 2d 582, 407 N.Y.S. 2d 165 (1st Dep't 1978), aff'd 47 N.Y. 2d 582, 393 N.E. 2d 976, 419 N.Y.S. 2d 901 (1979).

33.   Kathleen Barry, *Female Sexual Slavery* (1979); Moira K. Griffin, "Wives, Hookers and the Law: The Case for Decriminalizing Prostitution," 10 *Student Lawyer* 18 (1982); Report of Jean Fernand-Laurent, Special Rapporteur on the Suppression of the Traffic in Persons and the Exploitation of the Prostitution of Others (a United Nations report), in *International Feminism: Networking against Female Sexual Slavery* 130 (Kathleen Barry, Charlotte Bunch, and Shirley Castley eds.) (Report of the Global Feminist Workshop to Organize against Traffic in Women, Rotterdam, Netherlands, Apr. 6–15, 1983 [1984]).

34.   Galloway and Thornton. "Crackdown on Pornography—A No-Win Battle," *U.S. News and World Report*, June 4, 1984, at 84. See also "The Place of Pornography," *Harper's*, November 1984, at 31 (citing $7 billion per year).

35.   Loving v. Virginia, 388 U.S. 1 (1967), first used the term "white supremacy" in invalidating an antimiscegenation law as a violation of equal protection. The law equally forbade whites and Blacks to intermarry. Although going nowhere near as far, courts in the athletics area have sometimes seen that "same" does not necessarily mean "equal" nor does "equal" require "same." In a context of sex inequality like that which has prevailed in athletic opportunity, allowing boys to compete on girls' teams may diminish overall sex equality. "Each position occupied by a male reduces the female participation and increases the overall disparity of athletic opportunity which generally exists." Petrie v. Illinois High School Association, 394 N. E. 2d 855, 865 (Ill. 1979). "We conclude that to furnish exactly the same athletic opportunities to boys as to girls would be most difficult and would be detrimental to the compelling governmental interest of equalizing general athletic opportunities between the sexes." Id.

36.   The scholars Tussman and tenBroek first used the term "fit" to characterize the necessary relation between a valid equality rule and the world to which it refers. J. Tussman and J. tenBroek, "The Equal Protection of the Laws," 37 *California Law Review* 341 (1949).

37.   Royster Guano Co. v. Virginia, 253 U.S. 412, 415 (1920): "[A classification] must be reasonable, not arbitrary, and must rest upon some ground of difference having a fair and substantial relation to the object of the legislation, so that all persons similarly circumstanced shall be treated alike." Reed v. Reed, 404 U.S. 71, 76 (1971): "Regardless of their sex, persons within any one of the enumerated classes . . . are similarly situated . . . By providing dissimilar treatment for men and women who are thus similarly situated, the challenged section violates the Equal Protection Clause."

38.   Washington v. Davis, 426 U.S. 229 (1976) and Personnel Administrator of Massachusetts v. Feeney, 442 U.S. 256 (1979) require that intentional discrimination be shown for discrimination to be shown.

STUDY QUESTIONS

MacKinnon sketches two approaches to sex equality, viz., the *difference* approach and the *dominance* approach. Note that she also speaks of a "differences" (or "special benefits") path and a "sameness" path, both under the rubric of the *difference* approach. This can be confusing, so beware.

1. According to MacKinnon, how are sex and equality understood within the difference approach to sex equality? What does MacKinnon mean when she asserts that, given these definitions, "sex equality" is an oxymoron?
2. On the "sameness path" of the difference approach, how does one argue for equal treatment of women? And on the "differences path"?
3. State one criticism made by MacKinnon of the difference approach as a whole and one criticism of each of its paths.
4. According to MacKinnon, how are sex and equality understood within the dominance approach to sex equality? Why, according to MacKinnon, is this approach superior to the difference approach?
5. Do the "sameness path" and "difference path" map meaningfully onto the sameness and difference approaches outlined in this text? Do MacKinnon's criticisms of those paths apply to the works grouped under those headings in this text?

53. TOWARD AN AFROCENTRIC FEMINIST EPISTEMOLOGY

PATRICIA HILL COLLINS

Patricia Hill Collins (b. 1948) is the most important advocate within sociology proper of what she terms in this essay, from her book *Black Feminist Thought* (1990), "an Afrocentric feminist epistemology." The essay begins with a critique of Eurocentric and masculinist thought, which, particularly in its positivist articulation (she contends), seeks to divorce the researcher from the object of investigation, enforce a notion of objectivity by preventing emotions from entering in, and promote a value-free research process. The remainder of the essay is devoted to sketching a black feminist epistemology as an alternative. Key to this approach is recognizing and appreciating the concrete experiences of daily life as the basis for meaning construction and the notion of understanding, not as an individual accomplishment, but as the result of the collective efforts resulting from sisterhood.

A small girl and her mother passed a statue depicting a European man who had barehandedly subdued a ferocious lion. The little girl stopped, looked puzzled and asked, `Mama, something's wrong with that statue. Everybody knows that a man can't whip a lion.´ `But darling,´ her mother replied, `you must remember that the man made the statue.´

—As told by Katie G. Cannon

Black feminist thought, like all specialized thought, reflects the interests and standpoint of its creators. Tracing the origin and diffusion of any body of specialized thought reveals its affinity to the power of the group that created it (Mannheim 1936). Because elite white men and their representatives control structures of knowledge validation, white male interests pervade the thematic content of traditional scholarship. As a result, Black women's experiences with work, family, motherhood, political activism, and sexual politics have been routinely distorted in or excluded from traditional academic discourse.

Black feminist thought as specialized thought reflects the thematic content of African-American women's experiences. But because Black women have had to struggle against white male interpretations of the world in order to express a self-defined standpoint, Black feminist thought can best be viewed as subjugated knowledge. The suppression of Black women's efforts for self-definition in traditional sites of knowledge production has led African-American women to use alternative sites such as music, literature, daily conversations, and everyday behavior as important locations for articulating the core themes of a Black feminist consciousness.

Investigating the subjugated knowledge of subordinate groups—in this case a Black women's standpoint and Black feminist thought—requires more ingenuity than that needed to examine the standpoints and thought of dominant groups. I found my training as a social scientist inadequate to the task of studying the subjugated knowledge of a Black women's standpoint. This is because subordinate groups have long had to use alternative ways to create independent self-definitions and self-valuations and to rearticulate them through our own specialists. Like other subordinate groups, African-American women have not only developed a distinctive Black women´s standpoint, but have done so by using alternative ways of producing and validating knowledge.

Epistemology is the study of the philosophical problems in concepts of knowledge and truth. The techniques I use in this volume to rearticulate a Black women´s standpoint and to further Black feminist thought may appear to violate some of the basic epistemological assumptions of my training as a social scientist. In choosing the core themes in Black feminist thought that merited investigation, I consulted established bodies of academic research. But I also searched my own experiences and those of African-American women I know for themes we thought were important. My use of language signals a different relationship to my material than that which currently prevails in social science literature. For example, I often use the pronoun "our" instead of "their" when referring to African-American women, a choice that embeds me in the group I am studying instead of distancing me from it. In addition, I occasionally place my own concrete experiences in the text. To support my analysis, I cite few statistics and instead rely on the voices of Black women from all walks of life. These conscious epistemological choices signal my attempts not only to explore the thematic content of Black feminist thought but to do so in a way that does not violate its basic epistemological framework.

One key epistemological concern facing Black women intellectuals is the question of what constitutes adequate justifications that a given knowledge claim, such as a fact or theory, is true. In producing the specialized knowledge of Black feminist thought, Black women intellectuals often encounter two distinct epistemologies: one representing elite white male interests and the other expressing Afrocentric feminist concerns. Epistemological choices about who to trust, what to believe, and why something is true are not benign academic issues. Instead, these concerns tap the fundamental question of which versions of truth will prevail and shape thought and action.

THE EUROCENTRIC, MASCULINIST KNOWLEDGE VALIDATION PROCESS

Institutions, paradigms, and other elements of the knowledge validation procedure controlled by elite white men constitute the Eurocentric masculinist knowledge validation process. The purpose of this process is to represent a white male standpoint. Although it reflects powerful white male´s interest, various dimensions of the process are not necessarily managed by white men themselves. Scholars, publishers, and other experts represent specific interests and credentialing processes, and their knowledge claims must satisfy the political and epistemological criteria of the contexts in which they reside (Kuhn 1962; Mulkay 1979).

Two political criteria influence the knowledge validation process. First, knowledge claims are evaluated by a community of experts whose members represent the standpoints of the groups from which they originate. Within the Eurocentric masculinist process this means that a scholar making a knowledge claim must convince a scholarly community controlled by white men that a given claim is justified. Second, each community of experts must maintain its credibility as defined by the larger group in which it is situated and from which it draws its basic, taken-for-granted knowledge. This means that scholarly communities that challenge basic beliefs held in the culture at large will be deemed less credible than those which support popular perspectives.

When white men control the knowledge validation process, both political criteria can work to suppress Black feminist thought. Given that the general culture shaping the taken-for-granted knowledge of the community of experts is permeated by widespread notions of Black and female inferiority, new knowledge claims that seem to violate these fundamental assumptions are likely to be viewed as anomalies (Kuhn 1962). Moreover, specialized thought challenging notions of Black and female inferiority is unlikely to be generated from within a white-male-controlled academic community because both the kinds of questions that could be asked and the explanations that would be found satisfying would necessarily reflect a basic lack of familiarity with Black women´s reality. The experiences of African-American women scholars illustrate how individuals who wish to rearticulate a Black women´s standpoint through Black feminist thought can be suppressed by a white-male-controlled knowledge validation process. Exclusion from basic literacy, quality educational experiences, and faculty and administrative positions has limited Black women´s access to influential academic positions (Zinn et al. 1986). While Black women can produce knowledge claims that contest those advanced by the white male community, this community does not grant that Black women scholars have competing knowledge claims based in another knowledge validation process. As a consequence, any credentials controlled by white male academicians can be denied to Black women producing Black feminist thought on the grounds that it is not credible research.

Black women with academic credentials who seek to exert the authority that our status grants us to propose new knowledge claims about African-American women face pressures to use our authority to help legitimate a system that devalues and excludes the majority of Black women. When an outsider group—in this case, African-American women—recognizes that the insider group—namely, white men—requires special privileges from the larger society, a special problem arises of keeping the outsiders out and at the same time having them acknowledge the legitimacy of this procedure. Accepting a few "safe" outsiders addresses this legitimation problem (Berger and Luckmann 1966). One way of excluding the majority of Black women from the knowledge validation process is to permit a few Black women to acquire positions of authority in institutions that legitimate knowledge, and to encourage us to work within the taken-for-granted assumptions of Black female inferiority shared by the scholarly community and by the culture at large. Those Black women who accept these assumptions are likely to be rewarded by their institutions, often at significant personal cost. Those challenging the assumptions run the risk of being ostracized.

African-American women academicians who persist in trying to rearticulate a Black women´s standpoint also face potential rejection of our knowledge claims on epistemological grounds. Just as the material realities of the powerful and the dominated produce separate standpoints, each group may also have distinctive epistemologies or theories of knowledge. Black women scholars may know that something is true but be unwilling or unable to legitimate our claims using Eurocentric, masculinist criteria for consistency with substantiated knowledge and criteria for methodological adequacy. For any body of knowledge, new knowledge claims must be consistent with an existing body of knowledge that the group controlling the interpretive context accepts as true. The methods used to validate knowledge claims must also be acceptable to the group controlling the knowledge validation process.

The criteria for the methodological adequacy of positivism illustrate the epistemological standards that Black women scholars would have to satisfy in legitimating Black feminist thought using a Eurocentric masculinist epistemology. While I describe Eurocentric masculinist approaches as a single process, many schools of thought or paradigms are subsumed under this one process. Moreover, my focus on positivism should be interpreted neither to mean that all dimensions of positivism are inherently problematic for Black women nor that nonpositivist frameworks are better. For example, most traditional frameworks that women of color internationally regard as oppressive to women are not positivist, and Eurocentric feminist critiques of positivism may have less political importance for women of color, especially those in traditional societies than they have for white feminists (Narayan 1989).

Positivist approaches aim to create scientific descriptions of reality by producing objective generalizations. Because researchers have widely differing values, experiences, and emotions, genuine science is thought to be unattainable unless all human characteristics except rationality are eliminated from the research process. By following strict methodological rules, scientists aim to distance themselves from the values, vested interests, and emotions generated by their class, race, sex, or unique situation. By decontextualizing themselves, they allegedly become detached observers and manipulators of nature (Jaggar 1983; Harding 1986). Moreover, this researcher decontextualization is paralleled by comparable efforts to remove the objects of study from their contexts. The result of this entire process is often the separation of information from meaning (Fausto-Sterling 1989).

Several requirements typify positivist methodological approaches. First, research methods generally require a distancing of the researcher from her or his "object" of study by defining the researcher as a "subject" with full human subjectivity and by objectifying the "object" of study (Keller 1985; Asante 1987; Hooks 1989). A second requirement is the absence of emotions from the research process (Hochschild 1975; Jaggar 1983). Third, ethics and values are deemed inappropriate in the research process, either as the reason for scientific inquiry or as part of the research process itself (Richards 1980; Haan et al. 1983). Finally, adversarial debates, whether written or oral, become the preferred method of ascertaining truth: the arguments that can withstand the greatest assault and survive intact become the strongest truths (Moulton 1983).

Such criteria ask African-American women to objectify ourselves, devalue our emotional life, displace our motivations for furthering knowledge about Black women, and confront in an adversarial relationship those with more social, economic and professional power. It therefore seems unlikely that Black women would use a positivist epistemological stance in rearticulating a Black women's standpoint. Black women are more likely to choose an alternative epistemology for assessing knowledge claims, one using different standards that are consistent with Black women's criteria for substantiated knowledge and with our criteria for methodological adequacy. If such an epistemology exists, what are its contours? Moreover, what is its role in the production of Black feminist thought?

THE CONTOURS OF AN AFROCENTRIC FEMINIST EPISTEMOLOGY

Africanist analyses of the Black experience generally agree on the fundamental elements of an Afrocentric standpoint (Okanlawon 1972). Despite varying histories, Black societies reflect elements of a core African value system that existed prior to and independently of racial oppression (Jahn 1961; Mbiti 1969; Diop 1974; Zahan 1979; Sobel 1979; Richards 1980, 1990; Asante 1987; Myers 1988). Moreover, as a result of colonialism, imperialism, slavery, apartheid, and other systems of racial domination, Black people share a common experience of oppression. These two factors

foster shared Afrocentric values that permeate the family structure, religious institutions, culture, and community life of Blacks in varying parts of Africa, the Caribbean, South America, and North America (Walton 1971; Gayle 1971; Smitherman 1977; Shimkin et al. 1978; Walker 1980; Sudarkasa 1981; Thompson 1983; Mitchell and Lewter 1986; Asante 1987; Brown 1989). This Afrocentric consciousness permeates the shared history of people of African descent through the framework of a distinctive Afrocentric epistemology (Turner 1984).

Feminist scholars advance a similar argument by asserting that women share a history of gender oppression, primarily through sex/gender hierarchies (Eisenstein 1983; Hartsock 1983b; Andersen 1988). These experiences transcend divisions among women created by race, social class, religion, sexual orientation, and ethnicity and form the basis of a women's standpoint with a corresponding feminist consciousness and epistemology (Rosaldo 1974; D. Smith 1987; Hartsock 1983a; Jaggar 1983).

Because Black women have access to both the Afrocentric and the feminist standpoints, an alternative epistemology used to rearticulate a Black women's standpoint should reflect elements of both traditions. The search for the distinguishing features of an alternative epistemology used by African-American women reveals that values and ideas Africanist scholars identify as characteristically "Black" often bear remarkable resemblance to similar ideas claimed by feminist scholars as characteristically "female." This similarity suggests that the material conditions of race, class, and gender oppression can vary dramatically and yet generate some uniformity in the epistemologies of subordinate groups. Thus the significance of an Afrocentric feminist epistemology may lie in how such an epistemology enriches our understanding of how subordinate groups create knowledge that fosters resistance.

The parallels between the two conceptual schemes raise a question: Is the worldview of women of African descent more intensely infused with the overlapping feminine/Afrocentric standpoints than is the case for either African-American men or white women? While an Afrocentric feminist epistemology reflects elements of epistemologies used by African-Americans and women as groups, it also paradoxically demonstrates features that may be unique to Black women. On certain dimensions Black women may more closely resemble Black men; on others, white women; and on still others Black women may stand apart from both groups. Black women´s both/and conceptual orientation, the act of being simultaneously a member of a group and yet standing apart from it, forms an integral part of Black women´s consciousness. Black women negotiate these contradictions, a situation Bonnie Thornton Dill (1979) labels the "dialectics of Black womanhood," by using this both/and conceptual orientation.

Rather than emphasizing how a Black women´s standpoint and its accompanying epistemology are different from those in Afrocentric and feminist analyses, I use Black women´s experiences to examine points of contact between the two. Viewing an Afrocentric feminist epistemology in this way challenges additive analyses of oppression claiming that Black women have a more accurate view of oppression than do other groups. Such approaches suggest that oppression can be quantified and compared and that adding layers of oppression produces a potentially clearer standpoint (Spelman 1982). One implication of standpoint approaches is that the more subordinated the group, the purer the vision of the oppressed group. This is an outcome of the origins of standpoint approaches in Marxist social theory, itself an analysis of social structure rooted in Western either/or dichotomous thinking. Ironically, by quantifying and ranking human oppressions, standpoint theorists invoke criteria for methodological adequacy characteristic of positivism. Although it is tempting to claim that Black women are more oppressed than everyone else and therefore have the best standpoint from which to understand the mechanisms, processes, and effects of oppression, this simply may not be the case.

Like a Black women´s standpoint, an Afrocentric feminist epistemology is rooted in the everyday experiences of African-American women. In spite of diversity that exists among women, what are the dimensions of an Afrocentric feminist epistemology?

CONCRETE EXPERIENCE AS A CRITERION OF MEANING

"My aunt used to say, `A heap see, but a few know,´" remembers Carolyn Chase, a 31-year-old inner-city Black woman (Gwaltney 1980, 83). This saying depicts two types of knowing—knowledge and wisdom—and taps the first dimension of an Afrocentric feminist epistemology. Living life as Black women requires wisdom because knowledge about the dynamics of race, gender, and class oppression has been essential to Black women´s survival. African-American women give such wisdom high credence in assessing knowledge.

Allusions to these two types of knowing pervade the words of a range of African-American women. Zilpha Elaw, a preacher of the mid-1800s, explains the tenacity of racism:

> The pride of a white skin is a bauble of great value with many in some parts of the United States, who readily sacrifice their intelligence to their prejudices, and possess more knowledge than wisdom. (Andrews 1986, 85)

In describing differences separating African-American and white women, Nancy White invokes a similar rule: "When you come right down to it, white women just think they are free. Black women *know* they ain´t free" (Gwaltney 1980, 147). Geneva Smitherman, a college professor specializing in African-American linguistics, suggests that

> from a black perspective, written documents are limited in what they can teach about life and survival in the world. Blacks are quick to ridicule `educated fools,´... they have `book learning´ but no `mother wit,´ knowledge, but not wisdom. (Smitherman 1977, 76)

Mabel Lincoln eloquently summarizes the distinction between knowledge and wisdom:

> To black people like me, a fool is funny—you know, people who love to break bad, people you can´t tell anything to, folks that would take a shotgun to a roach. (Gwaltney 1980, 68)

African-American women need wisdom to know how to deal with the "educated fools" who would "take a shotgun to a roach." As members of a subordinate group, Black women cannot afford to be fools of any type, for our objectification as the Other denies us the protections that white skin, maleness, and wealth confer. This distinction between knowledge and wisdom, and the use of experience as the cutting edge dividing them, has been key to Black women´s survival. In the context of race, gender, and class oppression, the distinction is essential. Knowledge without wisdom is adequate for the powerful, but wisdom is essential to the survival of the subordinate.

For most African-American women those individuals who have lived through the experiences about which they claim to be experts are more believable and credible than those who have merely read or thought about such experiences. Thus concrete experience as a criterion for credibility frequently is invoked by Black women when making knowledge claims. For instance, Hannah Nelson describes the importance personal experience has for her:

> Our speech is most directly personal, and every black person assumes that every other black person has a right to a personal opinion. In speaking of grave matters, your personal experience is considered very good evidence. With us, distant statistics are certainly not as important as the actual experience of a sober person. (Gwaltney 1980, 7).

Similarly, Ruth Shays uses her concrete experiences to challenge the idea that formal education is the only route to knowledge:

> I am the kind of person who doesn´t have a lot of education, but both my mother and my father had good common sense. Now, I think that´s all you need. I might not know how to use thirty-four words where three would do, but that does not mean that I don´t know what I´m talking about.... I know what I´m talking about because I´m talking about myself. I´m talking about what I have lived. (Gwaltney 1980, 27, 33)

Implicit in Ms. Shays´s self-assessment is a critique of the type of knowledge that obscures the truth, the "thirty-four words" that cover up a truth that can be expressed in three.

Even after substantial mastery of white masculinist epistemologies, many Black women scholars invoke our own concrete experiences and those of other African-American women in selecting topics for investigation and methodologies used. For example, Elsa

Barkley Brown (1986) subtitles her essay on Black women´s history, "how my mother taught me to be an historian in spite of my academic training." Similarly, Joyce Ladner (1972) maintains that growing up as a Black woman in the South gave her special insights in conducting her study of Black adolescent women. Lorraine Hansberry alludes to the potential epistemological significance of valuing the concrete:

> In certain peculiar ways, we have been conditioned to think not small—but tiny. And the thing, I think, which has strangled us most is the tendency to turn away from the world in search of the universe. That is chaos in science—can it be anything else in art? (1969, 134).

Experience as a criterion of meaning with practical images as its symbolic vehicles is a fundamental epistemological tenet in African-American thought systems (Mitchell and Lewter 1986). "Look at my arm!" Sojourner Truth proclaimed: "I have ploughed, and planted, and gathered into barns, and no man could head me! And ain´t I a woman?" (Loewenberg and Bogin 1976, 235). By invoking concrete practical images from her own life to symbolize new meanings, Truth deconstructed the prevailing notions of woman. Stories, narratives, and Bible principles are selected for their applicability to the lived experiences of African-Americans and become symbolic representations of a whole wealth of experience. Bible tales are often told for the wisdom they express about everyday life, so their interpretation involves no need for scientific historical verification. The narrative method requires that the story be told, not torn apart in analysis, and trusted as core belief, not "admired as science" (Mitchell and Lewter 1986, 8).

June Jordan´s essay about her mother´s suicide illustrates the multiple levels of meaning that can occur when concrete experiences are used as a criterion of meaning. Jordan describes her mother, a woman who literally died trying to stand up, and the effect her mother´s death had on her own work:

> I think all of this is really about women and work. Certainly this is all about me as a woman and my life work. I mean I am not sure my mother´s suicide was something extraordinary. Perhaps

most women must deal with a similar inheritance, the legacy of a woman whose death you cannot possibly pinpoint because she died so many, many times and because, even before she became your mother, the life of that woman was taken. . . . I came too late to help my mother to her feet. By way of everlasting thanks to all of the women who have helped me to stay alive I am working never to be late again. (Jordan 1985, 26)

While Jordan has knowledge about the concrete act of her mother's death, she also strives for wisdom concerning the meaning of that death.

Some feminist scholars offer a similar claim that women as a group are more likely than men to use concrete knowledge in assessing knowledge claims. For example, a substantial number of the 135 women in a study of women's cognitive development were "connected knowers" and were drawn to the sort of knowledge that emerges from first-hand observation (Belenky et al. 1986). Such women felt that because knowledge comes from experience, the best way of understanding another person's ideas was to develop empathy and share the experiences that led the person to form those ideas.

In valuing the concrete, African-American women invoke not only an Afrocentric tradition but a women's tradition as well. Some feminist theorists suggest that women are socialized in complex relational nexuses where contextual rules versus abstract principles govern behavior (Chodorow 1978; Gilligan 1982). This socialization process is thought to stimulate characteristic ways of knowing (Hartsock 1983a; Belenky et al. 1986). These theorists suggest that women are more likely to experience two modes of knowing: one located in the body and the space it occupies and the other passing beyond it. Through their child-rearing and nurturing activities, women mediate these two modes and use the concrete experiences of their daily lives to assess more abstract knowledge claims (D. Smith 1987).

Although valuing the concrete may be more representative of women than men, social class differences among women may generate differential expression of this women's value. One study of working-class women's ways of knowing found that both white and African-American women rely on common sense and

intuition (Luttrell 1989). These forms of knowledge allow for subjectivity between the knower and the known, rest in the women themselves (not in higher authorities), and are experienced directly in the world (not through abstractions).

Amanda King, a young African-American mother, describes how she used the concrete to assess the abstract and points out how difficult mediating these two modes of knowing can be:

> The leaders of the ROC [a labor union] lost their jobs too, but it just seemed like they were used to losing their jobs. . . . This was like a lifelong thing for them, to get out there and protest. They were like, what do you call them—intellectuals. . . . You got the ones that go to the university that are supposed to make all the speeches, they're the ones that are supposed to lead, you know, put this little revolution together, and then you got the little ones . . . that go to the factory everyday, they be the ones that have to fight. I had a child and I thought I don't have the time to be running around with these people. . . . I mean I understand some of that stuff they were talking about, like the bourgeoisie, the rich and the poor and all that, but I had surviving on my mind for me and my kid. (Byerly 1986, 198)

For Ms. King abstract ideals of class solidarity were mediated by the concrete experience of motherhood and the connectedness it involved.

In traditional African-American communities Black women find considerable institutional support for valuing concrete experience. Black women's centrality in families, churches, and other community organizations allows us to share our concrete knowledge of what it takes to be self-defined Black women with younger, less experienced sisters. "Sisterhood is not new to Black women," asserts Bonnie Thornton Dill, but "while Black women have fostered and encouraged sisterhood, we have not used it as the anvil to forge our political identities" (1983, 134). Though not expressed in explicitly political terms, this relationship of sisterhood among Black women can be seen as a model for a whole series of relationships African-American women have with one another (Gilkes 1985; Giddings 1988).

Given that Black churches and families are both woman-centered, Afrocentric institutions, African-American women traditionally have found considerable institutional support for this dimension of an Afrocentric feminist epistemology. While white women may value the concrete, it is questionable whether white families—particularly middle-class nuclear ones—and white community institutions provide comparable types of support. Similarly, while Black men are supported by Afrocentric institutions, they cannot participate in Black women's sisterhood. In terms of Black women's relationships with one another, African-American women may find it easier than others to recognize connectedness as a primary way of knowing, simply because we are encouraged to do so by a Black women's tradition of sisterhood.

REFERENCES

Andersen, Margaret. 1988. *Thinking about Women: Sociological Perspectives on Sex and Gender.* 2d ed. New York: Macmillan.

Andrews, William L. 1986. *Sisters of the Spirit: Three Black Women's Autobiographies of the Nineteenth Century.* Bloomington: Indiana University Press.

Asante, Molefi Kete. 1987. *The Afrocentric Idea.* Philadelphia: Temple University Press.

Belenky, Mary Field, Blythe McVicker Clinchy, Nancy Rule Goldberger, and Jill Mattuck Tarule. 1986. *Women's Ways of Knowing.* New York: Basic Books.

Berger, Peter L. and Thomas Luckmann. 1966. *The Social Construction of Reality.* New York: Doubleday.

Brown, Elsa Barkley. 1986. *Hearing Our Mothers' Lives.* Atlanta: Fifteenth Anniversary of African-American and African Studies, Emory University. (unpublished)

———. 1989. "African-American Women's Quilting: A Framework for Conceptualizing and Teaching African-American Women's History." *Signs* 14(4): 921–29.

Byerly, Victoria. 1986. *Hard Times Cotton Mills Girls.* Ithaca, NY: Cornell University Press.

Chodorow, Nancy. 1978. *The Reproduction of Mothering.* Berkeley: University of California Press.

Dill, Bonnie Thornton. 1979. "The Dialectics of Black Womanhood." *Signs* 4(3): 543–55.

———. 1983. "Race, Class, and Gender: Prospects for an All-Inclusive Sisterhood." *Feminist Studies* 9(1): 131–50.

Diop, Cheikh. 1974. *The African Origin of Civilization: Myth or Reality.* New York: L. Hill.

Eisenstein, Hester: 1983. *Contemporary Feminist Thought.* Boston: G. K. Hall.

Fausto-Sterling, Anne. 1989. "Life in the XY Corral." *Women's Studies International Forum* 12(3): 319–31.

Gayle, Addison, ed. 1971. *The Black Aesthetic.* Garden City, NY: Doubleday.

Giddings, Paula. 1988. *In Search of Sisterhood: Delta Sigma Theta and the Challenge of the Black Sorority Movement.* New York: William Morrow.

Gilkes, Cheryl Townsend. 1985. "'Together and in Harness': Women's Traditions in the Sanctified Church." *Signs* 10(4): 678–99.

Gilligan, Carol. 1982. *In a Different Voice.* Cambridge, MA: Harvard University Press.

Gwaltney, John Langston. 1980. *Drylongso, A Self-Portrait of Black America.* New York: Vintage.

Haan, Norma, Robert Bellah, Paul Rabinow, and William Sullivan, eds. 1983. *Social Science as Moral Inquiry.* New York: Columbia University Press.

Hansberry, Lorraine. 1969. *To be Young, Gifted and Black.* New York: Signet.

Harding, Sandra. 1986. *The Science Question in Feminism.* Ithaca, NY: Cornell University Press.

Hartsock, Nancy M. 1983a. "The Feminist Standpoint: Developing the Ground for a Specifically Feminist Historical Materialism." In *Discovering Reality,* edited by Sandra Harding and Merrill B. Hintikka, 283–310. Boston: D. Reidel.

———. 1983b. *Money, Sex and Power.* Boston: Northeastern University Press.

Hochschild, Arlie Russell. 1975. "The Sociology of Feeling and Emotion: Selected Possibilities." In *Another Voice: Feminist Perspectives on Social Life and Social Science,* edited by Marcia Millman and Rosabeth Kanter, 280–307. Garden City, NY: Anchor.

Hooks, Bell. 1989. *Talking Back: Thinking Feminist, Thinking Black.* Boston: South End Press.

Jaggar, Alison M. 1983. *Feminist Politics and Human Nature.* Totowa, NJ: Rowman & Allanheld.

Jahn, Janheinz. 1961. *Muntu: An Outline of Neo-African Culture.* London: Faber and Faber.

Jordan, June. 1985. *On Call.* Boston: South End Press.

Keller, Evelyn Fox. 1985. *Reflections on Gender and Science.* New Haven, CT: Yale University Press.

Kuhn, Thomas. 1962. *The Structure of Scientific Revolutions.* 2d ed. Chicago: University of Chicago Press.

Ladner, Joyce. 1972. *Tomorrow's Tomorrow.* Garden City, NY: Doubleday.

Loewenberg, Bert J., and Ruth Bogin, eds. 1976. *Black Women in Nineteenth-Century American Life.* University Park: Pennsylvania State University Press.

Luttrell, Wendy. 1989. "Working-Class Women's Ways of Knowing: Effects of Gender, Race, and Class." *Sociology of Education* 62(1): 33–46.

Mannheim, Karl. 1936. *Ideology and Utopia.* New York: Harcourt, Brace & World.

Mbiti, John S. 1969. *African Religions and Philosophy.* London: Heinemann.

Mitchell, Henry H., and Nicholas Cooper Lewter. 1986. *Soul Theology: The Heart of American Black Culture.* San Francisco: Harper & Row.

Moulton, Janice. 1983. "A Paradigm of Philosophy: The Adversary Method." In *Discovering Reality,* edited by Sandra Harding and Merrill B. Hintikka, 149–64. Boston: D. Reidel.

Mulkay, Michael. 1979. *Science and the Sociology of Knowledge.* Boston: Unwin Hyman.

Myers, Linda James. 1988. *Understanding an Afrocentric World View: Introduction to an Optimal Psychology.* Dubuque, IA: Kendall/Hunt.

Narayan, Uma. 1989. "The Project of Feminist Epistemology: Perspectives from a Non-western Feminist." In *Gender/Body/Knowledge: Feminist Reconstructions of Being and Knowing,* edited by Alison M. Jaggar and Susan R. Bordo, 256–69. New Brunswick, NJ: Rutgers University Press.

Okanlawon, Alexander. 1972. "Africanism—A Synthesis of the African World-View." *Black World* 21 (9): 40–44, 92–97.

Richards, Dona. 1980. "European Mythology: The Ideology of `Progress.'" In *Contemporary Black Thought,* edited by Molefi Kete Asante and Abdulai Sa. Vandi, 59–79. Beverly Hills, CA: Sage.

———. 1990. "The Implications of African-American Spirituality." In *African Culture: The Rhythm of Unity,* edited by Molefi Kete Asante and Kariamu Welsh Asante, 207–31. Trenton, NJ: Africa World Press.

Rosaldo, Michelle Z. 1974. "Women, Culture and Society: A Theoretical Overview." In *Woman, Culture and Society,* edited by Michelle Rosaldo and Louise Lamphere, 17–42. Stanford: Stanford University Press.

Shimkin, Demitri B., Edith M. Shimkin, and Dennis A. Frate, eds. 1978. *The Extended Family in Black Societies.* Chicago: Aldine.

Smith, Dorothy. 1987. *The Everyday World as Problematic.* Boston: Northeastern University Press.

Smitherman, Geneva. 1977. *Talkin and Testifyin: The Language of Black America.* Boston: Houghton Mifflin.

Sobel, Mechal. 1979. *Trabelin' On: The Slave Journey to an Afro-Baptist Faith.* Princeton: Princeton University Press.

Spelman, Elizabeth V. 1982. "Theories of Race and Gender: The Erasure of Black Women." *Quest* 5(4): 36–62.

Sudarkasa, Niara. 1981. "Interpreting the African Heritage in Afro-American Family Organization." In *Black Families*, edited by Harriette Pipes McAdoo, 37–53. Beverly Hills, CA: Sage.

Thompson, Robert Farris. 1983. *Flash of the Spirit: African and Afro-American Art and Philosophy*. New York: Vintage.

Turner, James E. 1984. "Foreword: Africana Studies and Epistemology: A Discourse in the Sociology of Knowledge." In *The Next Decade: Theoretical and Research Issues in Africana Studies*, edited by James E. Turner, v–xxv. Ithaca, NY: Cornell University Africana Studies and Research Center.

Walker, Sheila S. 1980. "African Gods in the Americas: The Black Religious Continuum." *Black Scholar* 11(8): 25–36.

Walton, Ortiz M. 1971. "Comparative Analysis of the African and Western Aesthetics." In *The Black Aesthetic*, edited by Addison Gayle, 154–64. Garden City, NY: Doubleday.

Zahan, Dominique. 1979. *The Religion, Spirituality, and Thought of Traditional Africa*. Chicago: University of Chicago Press.

Zinn, Maxine Baca, Lynn Weber Cannon, Elizabeth Higginbotham, and Bonnie Thornton Dill. 1986. "The Costs of Exclusionary Practices in Women's Studies." *Signs* 11(2): 290–303.

54. SOCIOLOGY FROM WOMEN´S EXPERIENCE: A REAFFIRMATION

DOROTHY E. SMITH

Dorothy E. Smith (b. 1926), trained at the University of California, Berkeley, was for years unknown to the larger sociological community because of the demands of raising a family coupled with the sexism of the discipline during the earlier years of her career. In recent years, however, she has been "discovered," and her argument on behalf of a sociological theory that begins with women´s concrete experiences has had a significant impact on feminist thinking (its influence on the work of Patricia Hill Collins, for example, is obvious). This particular essay, published in the journal *Sociological Theory* in 1992, is the result of a symposium on her work. In it she is asked to reflect on the comments and criticisms of others and in the process to rearticulate her position. Central to her theory is the notion of "standpoint," which means that although her sociology begins with women´s concrete experiences, it does not end there. Smith concludes with a discussion of her suspicions about political opposition beginning within the realm of social theory.

The discussion of my work by Pat Hill Collins, Bob Connell, and Charles Lemert is generous and very much appreciated. My difficulty in responding is that each develops a critique from a very different theoretical stance.[1] Lemert brings to bear his interest in what he describes as the sociological dilemma of the subject-object relation, and the postmodernist critique of modernity and its unitary subject. Pat Hill Collins draws on the tradition of critical theory, strikingly informed by her experience of and commitment to recovering the suppressed feminist thought of black women. Connell works within a Marxist tradition and with specific concerns about the relation of sociology to political practice. Also, each constructs her or his own straw Smith. Lemert reads the project of an inquiry *beginning from* women´s experience as a sociology of women´s *subjective* experience. Collins reads into my project her objective of creating a transformative knowledge. Connell confounds beginning from experience with individualism, and interprets my rather careful (and critical)

explications of the conceptual practices of power as an abhorrence of abstractions in general.

In response I will clarify how I´ve understood and worked for a sociology beginning from women´s experience. It is not, I insist, a totalizing theory. Rather it is a *method of inquiry*, always ongoing, opening things up, discovering. In addition, to reemphasize its character as inquiry relevant to the politics and practice of progressive struggle, whether of women or of other oppressed groups, this essay refers to some of the work being done from this approach.

STANDPOINT

The very intellectual successes of the women´s movement have created their own contradictions. Though they follow from the powerful discovery of a world split apart—we learned to see, act, and speak from a ground in our experience as women—the intellectual achievements of feminism have woven texts over that original moment. Indeed Connell´s question "If the `standpoint of women' is not an extralocal abstraction, what would be?" reflects (as criticism) the distance between the theorizing of "standpoint" and what I thought I was talking about, working from, trying to build into a sociology.

My project is a sociology that begins in the actualities of women's experience. It builds on that earlier extraordinary moment, unlike anything I've experienced before or since, a giving birth to ourselves—slow, remorseless, painful, and powerful. It attempts to create a method of inquiry beginning from the site of being that we discovered as we learned to center ourselves as speaking, knowing subjects in our experience as women. When I first began this sociological project, I and others used notions such as "women's perspective," "women's experience," "women's standpoint" to express this singular move—the foundation of this phase of the women's movement. Particularly since Sandra Harding's (1986) study of *The Science Question in Feminism*, the concept of "standpoint" has been used to formalize such notions and subject them to a critique. Formalization is inevitable, but it also breaks connection with the original experience that sought expression in a variety of terms. My own attempts to express the project probably contribute to this process, though I wish they would not. Only when I encounter critiques, for example those of Lemert and of Harding herself, or Connell's version, which seems both to be correct and to miss the point altogether, do I become aware that in my own thinking I still rely on the original and extraordinary discovery. Can I explicate it better than I have, in this new context, where feminist theorizing has developed to such a sophisticated level and where even the notion of subject that we used to rely on (see Schutz 1962, for example) is called into question?

The experience, of course, was complex, individualized, various. It's hard to recall now that at that time we did not even have a language for our experiences of oppression as women. But we shared a method. We learned in consciousness-raising groups, through the writings of other women (I relied a great deal on the rich and marvelous poetry that feminists were writing at that time), in talk, and through an inner work that transformed our external and internal relationships. We explored *our experience as women* with other

women—not that we necessarily agreed or shared our experiences.

In those early days, taking the standpoint of women transformed how we thought and worked, how we taught, the social relationships of the classroom, almost every aspect of our lives. Remaking sociology was a matter that arose out of practical demands. Established sociology distorted, turned things upside down, turned us into objects, wasn't much use. I thought we could have a sociology responding to people's lack of knowledge of how our everyday worlds are hooked into and shaped by social relations, organization, and powers beyond the scope of direct experience. The theorizing of "standpoint" within feminist discourse displaces the practical politics that the notion of "standpoint" originally captured. The concept is moved upstairs, so to speak, and is reduced to a purely discursive function.

In exploring our experiences we talked with, wrote to and for, women, beginning with what we shared as women, our sexed bodies. Here was and is the site of women's oppression, whether of violence, of rape, of lack of control over our choices to have children, through our connectedness to our children, or through childbirth and suckling. To declare this is not to formulate essentialism or biological determinism. Women's experience of oppression, whatever its form and focus, was grounded in male control, use, domination of our bodies. No transcendence for us. We were irremediably (as it seemed) defined by our bodies' relevance for and uses to men.

I emphasize this embodied ground of our experiencing as women. Much feminist theorizing since this original moment has taken up the standpoint in text-mediated discourse for which Descartes wrote the constitution. The Cartesian subject escapes the body, hence escaping the limitations of the local historical particularities of time, place, and relationship. When we began with our experiences as women, however, we were always returning to ourselves and to each other as subjects *in our bodies*.

I'm not talking about *reflecting* on our bodily existence or describing our bodily experience. The consciousness raising of this phase of the women's movement did not *reflect* on the body from a discursive standpoint. But the sexed body was always the common ground in relation to which we could find ourselves with each other *as women*, even if only to discover the depth of our differences. Of course our experiences in this mode were multiple and various, and as we sought in them a common ground, we also disagreed, sometimes bitterly—fierce fights and divisions were endemic. It was a lot of work to arrive at shared political projects. But what we could have in common was explored through experiences grounded in our sexed bodies, our women's bodies. Exploring the varieties of our experience returned us to the site of our bodily being to rediscover, remake ourselves, stripping away the inner and outer restraints and constraints. We sought our grounding in what was there for us when we took up the particularized, localized, *felt* experiencing of a subject who is not divorced from her bodily site of being.

I certainly think that other sociological transformations may be created from other sites of oppression, although I don't think (as Connell seems to do) that it is the oppositional which defines the standpoint. I am so bold as to believe that there's something distinctive about the standpoint of women as I've expressed and experienced it, and have tried to build it into a method of sociological inquiry. Its distinction is this: that the standpoint of women situates inquiry in the actualities of people's living, beginning with their experience of living, and understands that inquiry and its product are in and of the same actuality.

For me, then, the standpoint of women locates a place to begin inquiry before things have shifted upwards into the transcendent subject. Once you've gone up there, settled into text-mediated discourse, irremediably stuck on the reading side of the textual surface, you can't peek round it to find the other side where you're actually *doing* your reading. You can reflect back, but you're already committed to a standpoint other than that of actual people's experience.

I'm not arguing against abstractions, as Connell seems to think (this would indeed be a contradiction). And I'm not concerned merely with "discrediting" (Connell) or "deconstructing" (Collins) the relations of ruling. I'm concerned with examining and explicating how "abstractions" are put together, with concepts, knowledge, facticity, as socially organized practices. Making these processes visible also makes

visible how we participate in and incorporate them into our own practices (see "The Politics and the Product" below). In explicating the social relations of knowledge, I am concerned also with redesigning them. My notion of an everyday world as problematic is just such an attempt—to redesign the social organization of our systematically developed knowledge of society.

Theorizing the standpoint of women contradicts the project I am addressing. Interpreting that project in those terms misinterprets it. All three critics argue that my project necessarily privileges a particular experience. Lemert, for example, asks whether I do not do "sociology with exceptional, if not exclusive, attention to one specific and gendered subjective experience of the actual world[.]" It's true that I begin with what I learned from my own experience of two worlds of consciousness and their relations (so, incidentally, did Descartes), but the formulation of a method of inquiry that I developed in fact works to make a space into which anyone's experience, however various, could become a beginning-place inquiry. "Anyone" could be an Afro- or Chinese or Caucasian Canadian, an individual from one of the First Nations, an old woman or man, a lesbian or a gay man, a member of the ruling class, or any other man.

I draw a contrast between beginning with the standpoint of women and standpoints constituted in text-mediated discourse. The categories that identify diversity (race, gender, class, age, and so forth) for Collins, oppositional sites for Connell, and fragmented identities for Lemert are categories of such discourse and of discursively embedded political organization and activism. To begin with the categories is to begin in discourse. Experiencing as a woman of color, as Himani Bannerji (1987) has pointed out, does not break down into experience as a woman and experience as a person of color. Roxana Ng (1990) has explored how the category "immigrant women" is constituted in the social relations of the Canadian state and labor market. The latter study in particular calls into question Haraway's (1985) derivation of identities from the discursive fragmentation of social categories (cited by Lemert). Are we really to be stuck with Althusser's (1971) condemnation of the subject to lasting dependency on being interpellated by "ideological state apparatuses"? Of course no one's citing Althusser these days, but Haraway follows the same path from discourse to subjectivity, from discursive category to identity. I want to go another way.

If I could think of a term other than "standpoint," I'd gladly shift, especially now that I've been caged in Harding's (1986) creation of the category of "standpoint theorists" and subjected to the violence of misinterpretation, replicated many times in journals and reviews, by those who speak of Hartsock and Smith but have read only Harding's version of us (or have read us through her version). My notion of standpoint doesn't privilege a knower. It does something rather different. It shifts the ground of knowing, the place where inquiry begins. Since knowledge is essentially socially organized, it can never be an act or an attribute of individual consciousness.

As I see it, the notion of standpoint works like this: Social scientific inquiry ordinarily begins from a standpoint in a text-mediated discourse or organization; it operates to claim a piece of the actual for the relations of ruling of which that discourse or organization is part; it proceeds from a concept or theory expressing those relations and it operates selectively in assembling observations of the world that are ordered discursively. The standpoint of women proposes a different *point d'appui*: It begins one step back before the Cartesian shift that forgets the body. The body isn't forgotten; hence the actual site of the body isn't forgotten. Inquiry starts with the knower who is actually located; she is active; she is at work; she is connected with particular other people in various ways; she thinks, laughs, desires, sorrows, sings, curses, loves just here; she reads here; she watches television. Activities, feelings, experiences, hook her into extended social relations linking her activities to those of other people and in ways beyond her knowing. Whereas a standpoint beginning in text-mediated discourse begins with the concepts or schema of that discourse and turns towards the actual to find its object, the standpoint of women never leaves the actual. The knowing subject is always located in a particular spatial and temporal site, a particular configuration of the everyday/everynight world. Inquiry is directed towards exploring and explicating what she does not know—the social relations and organization pervading her world but invisible in it.

A METHOD OF INQUIRY

Central to this particular sociology for women (I take for granted there's more than one) is a method of inquiry. The notion of a standpoint of women doesn't stand by itself as a theoretical construct; it is a place to begin inquiry. I argue that proceeding (and I emphasize the activity here) according to established methods of inquiry in sociology, beginning in discourse with *its* concepts, and relying on standard good social scientific methodologies produces people as objects. This is an effect of its methods of thinking and inquiry; it is not an effect of the sociologist's intentions. Sociologists' intentions may be as oppositional and as progressive as any of us could wish, but if they work with standard methods of thinking and inquiry, they import the relations of ruling into the texts they produce. (Note, as an aside, that this is not an issue of quantitative versus qualitative method.)

Hence the importance of the method of inquiry, as a method both of thinking about society and social relations, and of doing research—or, as I sometimes prefer to put it, of writing the social into discursive texts. Unlike sociologies that seek to generate a totalizing system, this sociology is always in the making. From different sites of women's experience, different social relations or different aspects of the same complex are brought into view and their organization is explicated. Far from being a dead end, as Connell suggests, it is a lively, unfolding, fascinating, and very productive method. I am not talking now about my own work, but am referring to the growing body of work, mostly in Canada, that is exploring contemporary social relations by using this approach, an enterprise that is ongoing and not exclusively mine. Those who have taken up such methods of inquiry have taken them in their own direction; there's no orthodoxy. From innovations made in different courses of inquiry, we learn how to do things that we didn't know how to do before, or we see flaws and problems in how we were working. I am struck by the extraordinary expansion of our grasp of how the relations of ruling are put together, and by the effectiveness with which this knowledge can be put to practical use in a variety of contexts.

So let me try to characterize this method of inquiry briefly:

1. The subject/knower of inquiry is not a transcendent subject but is situated in the actualities of her own living, in relations with others. Lemert is quite right when he says that "key to the position is the somewhat open term `actual.'" Yes, it is a key, and it is not defined. I don´t give it content because I use it like the arrow you see on maps of malls, which tells you, "You are here!" I want the term *actual* to be always directing us back to the "outside the text" in which living goes on and in which the text is being read. Of course the text is always in the actual, though we seem to feel that we can escape through the text, riding it like the magic carpet of legend. The "open" term *actual* reminds us of the actuality of the flying carpet, of us who are riding it, and of the ground below.

2. In this method, we´re talking about the actual ongoing practices of actual individuals. This ontology is based on Marx and Engels´s formulation in *The German Ideology*. Yet we´re not concerned just with what individuals do. The sociology I´m proposing is interested in the social as people´s ongoing concerting and coordinating of activities. Here I mark a shift away from the social as order or as rules or as meaning, to the social as actually happening and hence as investigatable. This notion owes much to ethnomethodology, except that I want to extend it to macro relations.

3. What I´ve called the standpoint of women locates us in bodily sites—local, actual, particular. The idea is not to reenact the theory/practice split and opt for practice, but to locate the knower in a lived world in which both theory and practice go on, in which theory is itself a practice, and in which the divide between the two can itself be brought under examination. The entry into text-mediated discourse and the relations of text-mediated discourse are themselves actual. They are the activity of people together, happening, always now. Concepts, beliefs, ideas, knowledge, and so on (what Marxists know as

consciousness) are included in this ontology. They are practices, they happen, they are ongoing, and they are integral to the concerting and coordinating of people´s activities.

4. Inquiry and its product are forms of social organization. They enter into and may become constituents of social relations. Knowledge itself is not distinct from yet dependent on social practices and contexts, as Flax (quoted by Lemert) holds; rather, it is understood as socially organized. Hence the importance, for this sociology, of investigating social relations as a critique of its own practices as well as those of others. Designing a new organization for sociological knowledge is the project of a sociology for women, and of making the everyday/everynight world a problematic of inquiry.

5. Texts, text mediation, textuality, are central. The text is the bridge between the actual and the discursive. It is a material object that brings into actual contexts of reading a fixed form of meaning that can be and may be read in many other settings by many other people at the same time or at other times. It creates something like an escape hatch out of the actual and is foundational to any possibility of abstraction of whatever kind including this one written here. The preceding clauses can be read as a set of procedures for writing the social into texts, and hence for exploiting the power of the textual to analyze and isolate dimensions of organization that are fully embedded in the actualities of living. Of course that writing, that text, its reading, are always ongoing and in the actual. The act of reading is very deceitful in this respect; it conceals its particularity, its being in time and place.

6. Text-mediated relations are the forms in which power is generated and held in contemporary societies. Marx argued that economic relations are a specialization of interdependencies which were previously embedded in direct personal relationships, as in feudalism. With the emergence of money, markets, and capital, these

relations become distinct, specialized, and autonomic. Similarly, in contemporary societies, the functions of organization and control are increasingly vested in distinct, specialized, and (to some extent) autonomic forms of organization and relations mediated by texts. I've called these "the relations of ruling." The materiality of the text and its indefinite replicability create a peculiar ground in which it can seem that language, thought, culture, formal organization have their own being outside lived time and the actualities of people's living—other than as the latter become objects of action or investigation from within the textual. But from the viewpoint of this method of inquiry, the textual mediation of these relations and forms of organization has the miraculous effect of creating a join between the local and particular (on one hand) and the generalizing and generalized organization of the relations of ruling (on the other), hence making the latter investigatable in a new way.

From this very summary formulation of the method of inquiry, we return to issues raised by the critics. Lemert thematizes subjective and objective, representing what I'm doing as a sociology of women's, perhaps of anyone's, *subjective* experience. But the standpoint of women locates the knowing subject in the actual, before the differentiation between subjective and objective—a conceptualization of objectifying institutions. To respond to another issue Lemert raises, I do hold that texts or textual technologies are essential to the objectification both of organization and of knowledge, but not, as he seems to suggest, that texts necessarily result in objectification.

Lemert suggests that the postmodernist sealing off of an escape hatch out of text-mediated discourse is merely an issue of postmodernism's "willingness to tolerate the irony and uncertain possibilities of life in a world without comforting certitudes." I disagree. The issue, as far as I'm concerned, isn't comfort or tolerance for ambiguity or appreciation of irony. Rather it is an issue of the reliability and accuracy of the products of inquiry, beginning from the standpoint of women. The product I imagine is an explication, an unfolding, of how things actually are being put together, of actual ongoing social organization. I am also increasingly formulating the enterprise of inquiry as a kind of ongoing dialogue with society, with people, in which the inquirer is always exposed to the discipline of the other—sometimes the other's direct response, but more often how people's activities are actually coordinated. The language of dominant discourse, to use Collins's term, is continually displaced and reworked in the process of trying to "get it right." It is necessarily destabilized because it is always open to being rewritten as it is disciplined by its engagement with the actual.

All three critics treat what I'm doing as derived from or as a synthesis of previous sociological theories. Collins is critical of my "grounding . . . work in sociological theories, yet refusing to embrace fully any one theoretical perspective," and describes it as eclecticism. Connell views it as "synthesis." But if we're talking about actual people and the actual ongoing concerting of activities, there's a common ground—a real world, if you like—to which we can refer. If you're seeking to learn how things actually are put together, that dialogue with the world constrains you. You or I draw on what is available in sociology that we can use in developing inquiry and methods of inquiry. This is neither synthesis nor eclecticism. Obviously I think of what I'm doing as sociology, and use what I've learned from sociology. But to situate the standpoint governing inquiry in the theoretical organization of sociological discourse contradicts the project of beginning from the standpoint of women "in real life" (to use Marx and Engels's phrase in *The German Ideology*).

If we are going to do a sociology that serves women, perhaps people in general, it is crucial to get it right. This objective makes no claim to a unitary, absolute, or final truth (hence Lemert's application of the Flax paradox doesn't apply). I've used the analogy of a map. We have maps, we use maps, we rely on maps in a perfectly ordinary and mundane way. I'm not aiming for the one truth. I'm aiming rather to produce sociological accounts and analyses that can have this kind of credence: Here is how you get from the Bloor-Bathurst intersection to Ossington on the subway line. The map extends my capacity to move about effectively in the city. It does not tell me everything about the subway system in Toronto (its technology, operations, organization), but it does tell me the sequence of stations and gives me some idea of the distance between them. I´d like to develop a sociology that would tie people´s sites of experience and action into accounts of social organization and relations which have that ordinarily reliable kind of faithfulness to "how it works."[2]

The project of inquiry from the standpoint of women is always reflexive. Also, it is always about ourselves as inquirers—not just our personal selves, but our selves as participants. The metaphor of insider and outsider contains an ambiguity that I should be more watchful of, for I disagree with Collins´s view and Connell´s implication that there is an outside in society. They are directing our attention to issues of marginality, exclusion, suppressed and oppositional cultures and positions—being outside in that general sense. But as I´ve used the metaphor, I´ve wanted to stress that those outside positions are inside. In the sense I´m trying to capture, we are inside necessarily, and so there are no modes of investigation other than those beginning from within. This is as true of established sociology as of a sociology developing inquiry from women´s standpoint. Established sociology has powerful ways of writing the social into the text, which produce society as seen from an Archimedean point. A sociology for women says: "You can´t have that wish." There is no other way than beginning from the actual social relations in which we are participants. This fact can be concealed, but not avoided.

Therefore I´m in general agreement with Collins, who suggests that "assuming the language of dominant discourses, even using the language of objectified knowledge to critique its terms, weds the thinker to the relations of ruling supported by objectified knowledge." Yet my proposed critique is not just in language—one set of terms against another—but in an inquiry disciplined by its commitment to explore how things actually work, including language not as terms but as actual practice. Such inquiry explores "dominant discourses" and discovers, among other matters, how we may be implicated in those discourses. A sociology from the standpoint of women insists that there is no place outside; hence it must be an insider´s sociology. It may be Connell´s failure to grasp my insistence on critique through inquiry which allows him to draw

the odd conclusion that I make feminism as such "the principle of anarchy" outside and opposed to the patriarchal power structure. In the sense I mean "insider," there are no outsiders. We are all participants. We discover ourselves in exploring the relations in which we participate and that shape how we participate. The project locates itself in a dialectic between actual people located just as we are and social relations, in which we participate and to which we contribute, that have come to take on an existence and a power over against us.

THE POLITICS AND THE PRODUCT

Connell makes a major and, in my view, unjustified shift from the feminist sociology I´m putting forward to a vaguely defined "oppositional mode of doing sociology." It is indeed true that my feminism is generally oppositional, but I´d have got nowhere if I´d stuck with the radical tradition of European sociology, as Connell suggests, which for the most part is embedded as deeply in the male-dominated standpoints of ruling as is American sociology.

Much of my earlier work as a feminist sociologist was in critical dialogue with the deeply masculine values of the Marxism that pervaded the activism of the 1960s, 1970s, and early 1980s. My critique of the ideological practice of sociology (Smith 1990a) is equally applicable to the thinking of the Marxist theorizing of that period and earlier. In fact, an original and much earlier version was directed primarily towards the Marxist thinking of that time. I came to see that the oppositional stance of Marxism did not preclude adopting a standpoint in the relations of ruling. Relevant here is the poststructuralist insight that the language and concepts of a discourse always speak more and other than our intentions. Though I address this effect quite differently, preserving an ontology of the actual and proposing to explore discourse as actual ongoing textually mediated relations among actual people, the point is the same. Marxists might have an oppositional intention, but in taking up modes of thinking, reasoning, inquiry, and explanation within the established discourses of social science, humanities, and philosophy, they have imported into their oppositional work a standpoint or standpoints within the relations of ruling. The thoroughly masculinist stance consolidated this approach. Whatever their intentions, the organization of the discourse drew the Marxists into relations that contradicted what they sought, perhaps even to the point of locating them in class relations on the side opposite that to which they claimed allegiance.

I do not suggest for one moment that Marxists were dishonest—only that they did not have methods of analysis, or perhaps a standpoint, from which such contradictions might become visible. Characteristically, the working class was other and object (analyses of women were always of their place in the working class). Characteristically, drawing on Lenin and Lukacs, Marxists viewed the working class as the political constituency of revolution, to be led by an "oppositional" intelligentsia. Characteristically, Althusser's theorizing empowered a "scientific" intelligentsia and, in a new day, recreated an ideology enabling a revolutionary intelligentsia to represent itself as the proper leaders of its constituency, the working class. Characteristically, the Marxist-Leninist organizations—at least those I was familiar with in Canada and the United States—were led by university-educated and mostly middle-class male members of the intelligentsia, while middle-class women and working-class women and men played various subordinate roles. When the feminist critique finally was launched internally, it precipitated the collapse of the movement in Canada.

Oppositional modes of doing sociology do not of themselves entail a shift of standpoint from the ruling relations. These relations are built into methods of thinking, reasoning, and inquiry that have been powerfully influential in Europe as well as in North America, and have invaded oppositional thinking, rather like a computer virus, on these two continents.

Opposition as such is not what I'm doing. Nor am I convinced, as Collins is, that knowledge as such can be transformative. She sees my work as failing when measured against her own objective, and indeed against her achievement (in *Black Feminist Thought* [1990]), of a transformed knowledge. Perhaps relations of dominance, such as those of white over nonwhite or of men over women, can be transformed through knowing them. The unyoking of black women's subjugated knowledge that has been Pat Hill Collins's own enterprise is surely empowering, but when we turn to

the practice of change, how shall we proceed? Collins is concerned to transform the consciousness of the oppressed. My concern is with what we confront in transforming oppressive relations.

I've never seen resistance or opposition as beginning in theory, much less in sociology. Rather I've thought of "revolution" and organization for change as needing a division of labor in which the production of knowledge plays an essential, though not a leading, part. But the social organization of such knowledge must not reclaim the enterprise for the established relations of ruling. I want a sociology capable of exploring and mapping actual organization and relations that are invisible but active in the everyday/everynight sites where people take up resistance and struggle, capable of producing a knowledge that extends and expands their and our grasp of how things are put together and hence their and our ability to organize and act effectively.

Universities and colleges already are political; teaching in the social sciences and the humanities is a practical politics. Teaching the canon is patriarchal activism. I take this fact seriously. Of course I want a sociology for women to provide useful research services to organizations working for women's issues, but I want more as well.

I take the view that when we employ standard sociological methods of work, we inadvertently realign the issues that concern us with those of the relations of ruling. I want to build a sociology that opens up the social relations and forms of organization shaping our lives from the standpoint of women. You cannot get there directly from the kinds of applied participatory research that Connell recommends for me, though such a sociology would serve participatory research well. The long exclusion of women's knowledge and thought from universities and schools makes me very wary of proposals that would confine the focus of a sociology for women to immediate practical issues. Yes, I presuppose an "agentic professional," but I want her to be able to work very differently than she is able to with established sociological strategies of thinking and inquiry. I want her to know methods of inquiry beginning from a standpoint outside the relations of ruling and to be able to call on a sociological knowledge put together the same way.

Far from representing the limitations of the method of inquiry I propose, as Connell seems to suggest, my micro analyses of ideology open up the ways in which we social scientists participate as subjects in the orders of ruling. The latter aren´t just literary matters or demonstrations of how the schemata of psychiatry generate accounts. An example is Adele Mueller´s (1987) investigation showing how research on peasant women in the Third World, done by feminist researchers and theorized in the "women and development" discourse of the United States, is tied into the latter´s development policies. The ideological organization I examined at the micro level in *The Conceptual Practices of Power* is shown to operate in the organization of relations of state, researchers, and the local realities of Third World woman. Gillian Walker (1990) also investigates ideological organization at the institutional level. She explores the process through which the concept of "family violence" was established as the conceptual organizer of state administrative and welfare practice, of the work of professionals, of the research and theoretical discourses concerned, and of the work of "transition houses."

This doesn´t mean merely exploring relations in which intellectuals are active. The text-mediated relations of ruling are indeed pervasive. Alison Griffith and I (Griffith and Smith 1987), in the course of an inquiry into the work that mothers do in relation to their children´s schooling, came to recognize in our own lives as single parents and in our talk with other mothers the pervasive organizing effect of a mothering discourse that was founded in North America in the 1920s and 1930s. I´ve written too about "femininity" as a text-mediated discourse in which women participate actively (Smith 1990b).

My research concern is to build an ordinary good knowledge of the text-mediated organization of power from the standpoint of women in contemporary capitalism. Not for one moment do I suggest that this is all there is to be done or indeed all that this method of inquiry makes possible, but it is powerfully relevant to making change in our kind of society. Work produced from this approach has been relevant and has been used in a variety of contexts of struggle for change, including collective bargaining, issues of racial inequality in Canada, pay and employment equity,

environmental activism, social policy, and gay activism—very much the kind of knowledge that Australian "femocrats" would find useful in their bridging of the gap between women´s experience outside the bureaucracy and their efforts to make change from within. Studies exploring specific contexts build a more general knowledge of how the ruling relations are put together and how to investigate them. Of special importance is an increasing knowledge of how textuality operates in the organization of power and of how concepts and ideology enter directly into the organization of ruling, replicating organizational controls across multiple sites.

People working from this approach have investigated the text-based organization of nursing and how it articulates the work of nurses on the ward with the new systems of financial accounting in health care (Campbell 1984); how public service systems of job descriptions organize gender-differentiated career lines (Cassin forthcoming; Reimer 1988); how the process of planning legislation and the operations of planning departments at municipal levels work to defeat local activists´ opposition to development even when the activists win (Turner 1991); how government policies involving changing funding practices transform the accounting practices of community colleges and hence their internal systems of control over and use of teaching staff (McCoy 1991); how to reorganize the availability of treatment for people with AIDS and who are HIV-positive so as to make "possible" clinical knowledge widely available (G. Smith 1990); the ideology of the "single parent" as organizer of multiple sites (parent-teacher contact, classroom, administration, newspaper features) in education (Griffith 1986); and the formation and practice of social work consciousness as an agent of ruling (De Montigny 1989). I have mentioned other issues earlier.

It is also possible to deploy this method of inquiry on topics other than the text-based relations of ruling, as demonstrated by Himani Bannerji´s (1988) brilliant study of late nineteenth-century Bengali theater in the formation of ruling-class consciousness in colonial Bengal; by Ann Manicom´s (1988) marvelous investigation of how teachers´ work is shaped by the economic status of the homes of the children they teach; and by George Smith´s (1991) investigation of the experience of gay students in high school, which explores through that experience the distinctive social organization of their oppression.

Fragmentary as these studies may seem, they teach us more and more about the complex and interwoven organization of the relations of ruling, and more and more about how institutional processes are coordinated and "run." Directly or indirectly, most of this work provides a knowledge of the processes and relations of ruling that at least some collectivities have found invaluable. And after all, there is a politics of inquiry that goes beyond direct service to organized struggles. We teach, and teaching sociology, as Sally Hacker (1990: 158) once told me, is essentially a political act, both in substance and in classroom practice.

NOTES

1. My responses are based on drafts of the critical essays, not on the final versions.
2. Of course sociological maps could not be as representationally simple as subway system maps, though indeed the latter are highly artful and indeed are interesting and sophisticated as translators of properties of local spatial and social organizational relations to a visual text. It is also important epistemologically to recognize that quite different maps or diagrams could be produced to represent the same actuality. A diagram of the subway's electrical system would be quite different.

REFERENCES

Althusser, Louis. 1971. "Ideology and Ideological State Apparatuses." Pp. 127–86 in *Lenin and Philosophy: Other Essays*. New York: Monthly Review Press.

Bannerji, Himani. 1987. "Introducing Racism: Notes towards an Anti-Racist Feminism." *Resources for Feminist Research* 16: 10–12.

———. 1988. "The Politics of Representation: A Study of Class and Class Struggle in the Political Theatre of West Bengal." PhD dissertation, University of Toronto.

Campbell, Marie. 1984. "Information Systems and Management of Hospital Nursing: A Study in the Social Organization of Knowledge." PhD dissertation. University of Toronto.

Cassin, A. Marguerite. Forthcoming. "Pay Equity and the Routine Production of Inequality." *Canadian Journal of Women and the Law*.

Collins, Patricia Hill. 1990. *Black Feminist Thought*. London: Unwin Hyman.

De Montigny, Gerald. 1989. "Accomplishing Professional Reality: An Ethnography of Social Workers' Practice." PhD dissertation, University of Toronto.

Griffith, Alison. 1986. "Reporting the Facts: Media Accounts of Single Parent Families." *Resources for Feminist Research* 15: 32–43.

Griffith, Alison and Dorothy E. Smith. 1987. "Constructing Cultural Knowledge: Mothering as Discourse." Pp. 87–103 in *Women and Education*, edited by J. Gaskell and A. McLaren. Calgary: Detselig.

Hacker, Sally. 1990. *Doing It the Hard Way: Investigations of Gender and Technology*, edited by Dorothy E. Smith and Susan Turn. Boston: Unwin Hyman.

Haraway, Donna. 1985. "A Manifesto for Cyborgs: Science, Technology, and Socialist Feminism in the 1980s." *Socialist Review* 15: 65–108.

Harding, Sandra. 1986. *The Science Question in Feminism*. Ithaca: Cornell University Press.

Manicom, Ann. 1988. "Constituting Class Relations: The Social Organization of Teachers' Work." PhD dissertation. University of Toronto.

McCoy, Liza. 1991. "Accounting as Interorganizational Organization." Paper presented at the annual meetings of the Society for the Study of Social Problems, Cincinnati.

Mueller, Adele. 1987. "Peasants and Professionals: The Social Organization of Women and Development Knowledge." PhD dissertation. University of Toronto.

Ng, Roxana. 1990. "Immigrant Women: The Construction of a Labour Market Category." *Canadian Journal of Women and the Law* 4: 96–112.

Reimer, Marilee. 1988. "The Social Organization of the Labour Process: A Case Study of the Documentary Management of Clerical Labour in the Public Service." PhD dissertation, University of Toronto.

Schutz, Alfred. 1962. "On Multiple Realities." Pp. 207–59 in *Collected Papers,* Vol. 1. The Hague: Martinus Nijhoff.

Smith, Dorothy E. 1990a. *The Conceptual Practices of Power: A Feminist Sociology of Knowledge.* London: Routledge.

———. 1990b. *Texts, Facts, and Femininity: Exploring the Relations of Ruling.* London: Routledge.

Smith, George W. 1990. "Political Activist as Ethnographer." *Social Problems* 37: 401–21.

———. 1991. "The Ideology of `Fag´: Barriers to Education for Gay Students." Paper presented at the annual meetings of the Society for the Study of Social Problems, Cincinnati.

Turner, Susan M. 1991. "Rendering the Site Developable: Textual Organization in the Planning Process." Paper presented at the annual meetings of the Canadian Sociology and Anthropology Association, Kingston, Ontario.

Walker, Gillian. 1990. *Family Violence: The Politics of Conceptualization in the Women´s Movement.* Toronto: University of Toronto Press.

55. FEMININITY AND MASCULINITY

RAEWYN CONNELL

Raewyn Connell (b. 1944; formerly Robert William Connell) is an Australian theorist who currently holds a position as university professor at the University of Sydney. She has taught at various universities in Australia, Canada, Germany, and the United States. Connell has published two of the most widely cited works in gender studies: *Gender and Power* (1987) and *Masculinities* (1995). The selection below derives from the former book, in which she developed the concept of "hegemonic masculinity." The idea of hegemony derives from the work of the Italian Marxist Antonio Gramsci, who applied it to class relations. Connell offers an original application of the concept to gender rather than class (a parallel application to race can be found in the work of Howard Winant and Michael Omi; they have an entry in the following section). Hegemony refers to domination brought about not simply by the application of force or coercion, but by its linkage to ideology. The result is a mode of domination that involves both coercion and the consent of dominated groups. In her discussion of masculinity and femininity, Connell stresses the structured character of gendered power relations, noting that the situation is always further complicated by the fact that there are multiple types of both masculinity and femininity. Thus, hegemonic masculinity is situated both in terms of varied patterns of relations to women and in its relationships with subordinated masculinities.

MULTIPLE MODELS: FROM TYPOLOGY TO RELATIONSHIP

Scalar models of personality have often stemmed from theories of personality "types." Extraversion-introversion scales and the famous "F scale" of authoritarianism both derive from such typologies, devised by Jung and the Frankfurt school respectively. M/F scales similarly derive from unitary models of sexual character, in effect `dimensionalizing´ them by adding a range of possibilities in between. But this is not the only way diversity can be recognized in a theory of types. One may hold to the conception of a whole personality rather than a dimension, and subdivide or multiply the types.

In the case of sexual character the classic of this approach is Simone de Beauvoir´s account of femininity in Book Two of *The Second Sex*. Starting with a general difference in the social situation and ontological status of women and men, she goes on to develop a subtle account of half-a-dozen types of femininity in literature and French social life: the lesbian, the married woman, the prostitute, the independent woman, etc. Her types are partly based on social circumstances, partly on the patterns of inner dynamics.

In principle the same kind of thing can be done for types of masculinity, though no Simone de Beauvoir has appeared to do it. Andrew Tolson´s *The Limits of Masculinity* makes a beginning. Going through the (mostly British) research in community studies and industrial sociology, Tolson draws out connections between economic circumstance, life cycle and sexual identity in a broad distinction between a working-class type and a middle-class type of masculinity.

R. W. Connell *Gender and Power: Society, The Person and Sexual Politics*. Stanford, CA: Stanford University Press, 1995. ✦

Both de Beauvoir and Tolson assume a one-to-one correspondence between character type and milieu. This is a step forward from unitary models of sexual character, but not a long one. Character is still treated as unitary within a given setting. The logic is the same as in "national character" or culture-and-personality research that described the "modal personalities" supposed to characterize Germany, Japan, Samoa. The same treatment of sexual character is found in the cross-cultural contrasts made by Margaret Mead in *Male and Female*.

The next step is to recognize that qualitatively different types are produced within the same social setting. Evidence for this is not difficult to find. Here is an example taken from the collection of working-class autobiographies. The author, Bim Andrews, is talking about growing up and going to work at Cambridge in the 1920s:

> In the mid-twenties, I learned how to become a clerk at the Co-op, and after evening classes in shorthand and typing, a higher grade office worker. A dutiful, heads-down-all-day, worker, with no ideas at all about my rights. Not even my basic rights as a human being, never mind my rights as part of a deal involving my work and their money. True, there was some talk of a Trades Union, but no girl or woman ever thought it applied to her. Some of my work kept me standing up all day, and when I had bad menstrual cramps, as I often did, I would slink off to the lavatory to sit down for as long as I dared. No rest room, not even a chair in our crowded cloakroom.
>
> Some new ideas did take root—the Co-op was quite an evangelical movement then, and it was their evening classes which I joined. But my emotions and understanding were still at sixes and sevens. Which was the right way to live? Like Nellie, with her placid face and her engagement ring, and her pieces of linen and underclothes in tissue paper, brought for display to the girls before settling in her bottom drawer? Or like Jessie, coy and nudging—what we would now call sexy—surrounded by men, single and married? Or like Miss Marshall, the General Manager's secretary and our immediate boss. Composed, and sharp with us, the owner of a little car, involved in a sly relationship with the Manager of the Grocery Dept?

Nellie, Jessie, Miss Marshall and indeed the earnest Bim herself, are present in her mind as types—real types, not ideal or abstracted types—standing for different "ways to live." Yet they do not float free from each other. Bim experiences a relationship between them. It is a kind of rivalry between alternatives, confronting her with an existential and to some extent moral choice. She can become a certain kind of woman, enter a certain kind of femininity, by throwing herself forward along one path in life.

The important point is that the types exist in a relationship with each other. In the research which first raised this question for me, in an Australian ruling-class boys' school, the connections take the definite form of a hierarchy. A teacher whom we call Angus Barr described to us an episode, some details of which we could confirm from other sources, of what he thought of as "bullying" between two groups of boys:

> There are a group ['the Bloods'] which I suppose you can say is a traditional one, the sporting group, they are more active physically ... And sometimes they ride a bit rough over another group who have been called, and now call themselves, 'the Cyrils', the conshies. [From 'conscientious'.] Who are the ones who don't play any games. Who have this year [had] a particularly bad time from the Blood group ... And about the middle of the year I had to—it hasn't arisen in past years, I've taken the form for a number of years so I think I know—had to intervene. And say, Well now, what is being done by some of you to some others has reached limits where it has got to stop, it is going too far ... [The Cyrils] were these quite clever little boys who are socially totally inadequate, and yet who have got very good brains. They've all got glasses, short, very fat and that sort of thing ... I think I was reasonably successful in stopping it. I tried to ask discreetly some of the Cyrils how things had been getting on, and they said, Well it had been better. And I spoke to one or two of the Bloods, said that it's got to stop.

In contrast to Bim Andrews's perceptions, the difference between these masculinities is not a matter of free choice by the boys: an unathletic way of life may for instance be imposed by a boy's understanding of his physique. Larger cultural dynamics can be detected here. But the crucial point is that entering one group does not make the other irrelevant. Far from it: an active relationship is constructed. The Bloods persecute the Cyrils, because being a Blood *involves* an active rejection of what they see as effeminacy.

This particular pattern of conflict does not arise by chance. The school in question is noted for its attachment to a fiercely competitive body-contact sport, football. Both official school policy, and the ethos among staff, parents and Old Boys, encourage activities in which the kind of aggressive, physically dominant masculinity represented by the Bloods is at a premium. The boys are obliged to define their attitude to this demand, either for or against. Hence they polarize along the axis described by Mr Barr. Yet those boys who react against the model embraced by the Bloods are not simply pushed into limbo. For the school not only wants football glory, it also must have academic success. A high rate of performance in matriculation examinations is necessary if the school is to hold its position in the now strongly competitive secondary-education market. In short, the school needs the Cyrils too. Within their own sphere it gives them honour: acknowledging examination success by means of prizes, giving awards to the chess club as well as the football team. And it protects their interests, as Mr Barr's intervention to stop the "bullying" neatly shows.

The production of multiple masculinities and femininities can be seen in studies of other schools. In one of the earlier school ethnographies, *Social Relations in a Secondary School*, David Hargreaves portrayed the production of a semi-delinquent "subculture" in the lower streams of a British secondary modern school. One of its components was a rough, aggressive masculinity, strongly and no doubt deliberately contrasted with the more compliant behaviour of boys in the upper streams. A similar pattern in a similar school a decade later is traced by Paul Willis in *Learning to Labour*, a contrast between "the lads" and "the ear'oles." Willis is more explicit about the construction of masculinity and its connection with class fate, as the two groups of boys head for factory jobs on the one hand and white-collar jobs on the other.

In the Australian girls' private school we call Auburn College, there is not only a differentiation between several kinds of femininity, but also a recent change in the pattern of hegemony among them. An academic renovation of the school, undertaken by a new headmistress and new staff, has altered the context of the girls' peer-group life. The prestige formerly enjoyed by a "social" set of girls has been broken and their place in the sun taken by academically successful girls headed for university and professional careers.

The pattern of differentiation and relation appears in other institutions besides schools. The fashion industry is an important case, given the significance of clothes and cosmetics as markers of gender. Here there is a constant interplay between the economic need of a turnover of styles—the basis of "fashion" itself—and the need to sustain the structures of motive that constitute their markets.

In the aftermath of the new feminism, the promotion of a "liberated" femininity became the basis of many marketing strategies. "Charlie" perfumes and cosmetics (introduced by Revlon in 1973) and "Virginia Slims" cigarettes were among the most heavily promoted examples. Yet a femininity that gets "liberated" too completely loses the need to present itself through cosmetics and fashionable clothes. Thus an oscillation: on one poster "Charlie" strides out boldly in trousers; on another, "Pretty Polly" advertises its fragile pantihose with the caption "For girls who don't want to wear the trousers." Some marketers take the contradiction inside the one promotion: thus "natural look" *cosmetics*; or a magazine that uses a feminist name, *Ms London*, as a vehicle for wholly stereotyped advertising.

The fashion industry works through competition of images, but also on the assumption that the competition is always being resolved. A leading designer emerges; a "look" is settled on; a particular presentation of femininity made normative. In cases such as Dior and the "New Look" of 1947, a trend lasting over a number of seasons may be set. Moreover, the brilliantly lit centre stage of high fashion is only a small part of the clothing industry's sales. The bulk of the business concerns cheap, drab, and poorly made clothing for the mass market in styles that change slowly. Two centuries ago this was called bluntly "slop cloathing"; it is now called in the rag trade "dumb fashion." So the currently exalted style does not eliminate all other styles. Rather it subordinates them.

There need not be any psychological traits which all femininities have in common and which distinguish them from all masculinities, or vice versa. The character structure of the academic high-flyers at Auburn College is probably closer to that of Milton's "Cyrils" than to socialite femininities. What unites the femininities of a given social milieu is the double *context* in which they are formed: on the one hand in relation to the image and experience of a female body, on the other to the social definitions of a woman's place and the cultural oppositions of masculinity and femininity. Femininity and masculinity are not essences: they are ways of living certain relationships. It follows that static typologies of sexual character have to be replaced by histories, analyses of the joint production of sets of psychological forms.

THE EFFECT OF STRUCTURES

To this point I have discussed the production of sexual character as if each milieu were independent of all others. It is time to bring into the analysis the structures that interrelate milieux and their historical composition into a gender order for the society as a whole.

To start with the structure of power, workplace studies show that face-to-face relations are strongly conditioned by the general power situation between employers and employees and its materialization in particular labour processes. A notable case is the job of personal "secretary" in business. An apparently very individualized relationship of mutual dependence and trust between the executive (generally a man) and the personal secretary (almost always a woman) in fact rests on sharp differences of income, the industrial vulnerability of the employee, and the overall social power and authority of men. A specific version of femininity is called for, in which technical competence and the social presentation of attractiveness, social skill and interpersonal compliance are fused. This kind of femininity has to be produced, and is by the informal training documented in Chris Griffin's study of British girls moving from school into office work.

The power hierarchy among men in the industrial enterprise is clear enough, from managers and professionals at the top to unqualified manual workers at the bottom. In sharp contrast to the situation of personal secretaries, the men in manual industrial work are often

in situations that allow a countervailing solidarity (one of the bases of unionism) and with it a rejection of the masculinity of the dominant group. John Lippert provides a striking description of the aggressive, sometimes violent, heterosexual masculinity produced among motor manufacturing workers in Detroit. The description can be matched in other countries: Meredith Burgmann's account of "machismo" among radical builders' labourers in Sydney and Paul Willis's account of masculine "shop-floor culture" among metal workers in Birmingham. The common elements are a cult of masculinity centring on physical prowess, and sexual contempt directed at managers, and men in office work generally, as being effete.

These examples also point to the gender structuring of production. Elements of sexual character are embedded in the distinctive sets of practices sometimes called "occupational cultures." Professionalism is a case in point. The combination of theoretical knowledge with technical expertise is central to a profession's claim to competence and to a monopoly of practice. This has been constructed historically as a form of masculinity: emotionally flat, centred on a specialized skill, insistent on professional esteem and technically based dominance over other workers, and requiring for its highest (specialist) development the complete freedom from childcare and domestic work provided by having wives and maids to do it. The masculine character of professionalism has been supported by the simplest possible mechanism, the exclusion of women. Women have had a long struggle even to get the basic training, and are still effectively excluded from professions like accountancy and engineering.

In manual trades, and manual work more broadly, the claim to competence is rather different. Here the most competent are not the most specialized but the most versatile—those with a range of skills, able to tackle any job that offers. This too is often constructed as a form of masculinity dependent on a domestic division of labour. Tradesmen have often been prepared to move around from place to place, even from country to country, to increase their range of experience, the wife's willingness to stay or go being assumed. Fathers have taken care to provide their sons with a range of skills as insurance against economic fluctuations. To quote another British working-class autobiography, from a miner's son called Fred Broughton who grew up in the years before World War I, "Father used to say, `I shall not leave you much money, but I will teach you every job, then you can always get work.´ He showed us every job in the garden and on the farm, including how to get stone in the quarry and trim it and build stone walls."

The construction of nursing has an element of the sexual division of labour, and is an occupation blending a particular version of femininity with the technical requirements of the job.

Finally the structure of cathexis is involved. This is the most obvious of structural determinations of sexual character because of the prominence of heterosexual couple relationships in everyday life. It is folklore that "opposites attract." One of the most familiar features of sexual display is behaviour and clothing that emphasizes stereotyped sex differences. Studs display their biceps and pectorals, suave charmers grow their pencil moustaches; "girls" emphasize their vulnerability in tight skirts and high-heeled shoes, sheer stockings and make-up that is constantly in need of repair. So much emotion is adrift around these marks of difference that they can get cathected in their own right. These stereotypes are so familiar that it is necessary to stress that they are not the whole story. Alongside the Errol Flynns and John Waynes are figures like Cary Grant, whose appeal is specially as a model of sympathetic (though not effeminate) masculinity. In a study of images of masculinity in Australian television, Glen Lewis has pointed to the prominence of "soft" men as presenters, especially in daytime programs directed at women.

Desire may be organized around identification and similarity rather than around difference. Homosexual love is the obvious case. The attempt to reduce this to attraction-of-opposites by assuming it is based on a butch/femme pattern is now generally discredited. Gay liberation theory lays emphasis instead on the *solidarity* created by love between women or between men. The point is that there are many more possibilities than the standard dichotomy or complete structurelessness. Works like Pat Califia's *Sapphistry* explore a variety of erotic constructions of femininity (homosexuality still presupposes gender division) based on identification and shared experience; the same can be done for masculinity.

There is a related possibility among heterosexual people, for powerful desire can exist between those whose character structure is similar. An *interplay* between identification and reciprocity, and a literal playing with similarity and difference, becomes possible as a basis of eroticism. On such a basis heterosexual masculinity and femininity might be recomposed as various kinds of psychological hermaphroditism.

To sum up: it is possible to see how each of the major structures impinges on the way femininity and masculinity are formed in particular milieux. Conversely, these structures must be seen as the vehicles for the constitution of femininity and masculinity as collective patterns on a scale far beyond that of an individual setting. We have moved from particular gender regimes to the society-wide gender order. The question now to be faced is how, at the level of a whole society, the elements are composed, interrelated and ordered.

HEGEMONIC MASCULINITY AND EMPHASIZED FEMININITY

The central argument can be put in a few paragraphs. There is an ordering of versions of femininity and masculinity at the level of the whole society, in some ways analogous to the patterns of face-to-face relationship within institutions. The possibilities of variation, of course, are vastly greater. The sheer complexity of relationships involving millions of people guarantees that ethnic differences and generational differences as well as class patterns come into play. But in key respects the organization of gender on the very large scale must be more skeletal and simplified than the human relationships in face-to-face milieux. The forms of femininity and masculinity constituted at this level are stylized and impoverished. Their interrelation is centred on a single structural fact, the global dominance of men over women.

This structural fact provides the main basis for relationships among men that define a hegemonic form of masculinity in the society as a whole. "Hegemonic masculinity" is always constructed in relation to various subordinated masculinities as well as in relation to women. The interplay between different forms of masculinity is an important part of how a patriarchal social order works.

There is no femininity that is hegemonic in the sense that the dominant form of masculinity is hegemonic among men. This is not a new observation. Viola Klein´s historical study of conceptions of "the feminine character" noted wryly how little the leading theorists could agree on what it was: "we find not only contradiction on particular points but a bewildering variety of traits considered characteristic of women by the various authorities." More recently the French analyst Luce Irigaray, in a celebrated essay "This Sex Which Is Not One," has emphasized the absence of any clear-cut definition for women´s eroticism and imagination in a patriarchal society.

At the level of mass social relations, however, forms of femininity are defined clearly enough. It is the global subordination of women to men that provides an essential basis for differentiation. One form is defined around compliance with this subordination and is oriented to accommodating the interests and desires of men. I will call this "emphasized femininity." Others are defined centrally by strategies of resistance or forms of non-compliance. Others again are defined by complex strategic combinations of compliance, resistance and co-operation. The interplay among them is a major part of the dynamics of change in the gender order as a whole.

The rest of this section will examine more closely the cases of hegemonic masculinity and emphasized femininity, making brief comments on subordinated and marginalized forms.

In the concept of hegemonic masculinity, "hegemony" means (as in Gramsci´s analyses of class relations in Italy from which the term is borrowed) a social ascendancy achieved in a play of social forces that extends beyond contests of brute power into the organization of private life and cultural processes. Ascendancy of one group of men over another achieved at the point of a gun, or by the threat of unemployment, is not hegemony. Ascendancy which is embedded in religious doctrine and practice, mass media content, wage structures, the design of housing, welfare/taxation policies and so forth, is.

Two common misunderstandings of the concept should be cleared up immediately. First, though "hegemony" does not refer to ascendancy based on force, it is not incompatible with ascendancy based on force. Indeed it is common for the two to go together. Physical or economic violence backs up a dominant cultural pattern (for example beating up "perverts"), or ideologies justify the holders of physical power ("law and order"). The connection between hegemonic masculinity and patriarchal violence is close, though not simple.

Second, "hegemony" does not mean total cultural dominance, the obliteration of alternatives. It means ascendancy achieved within a balance of forces, that is, a state of play. Other patterns and groups are subordinated rather than eliminated. If we do not recognize this it would be impossible to account for the everyday contestation that actually occurs in social life, let alone for historical changes in definitions of gender patterns on the grand scale.

Hegemonic masculinity, then, is very different from the notion of a general "male sex role" though the concept allows us to formulate more precisely some of the sound points made in the sex-role literature. First, the cultural ideal (or ideals) of masculinity need not correspond at all closely to the actual personalities of the majority of men. Indeed the winning of hegemony often involves the creation of models of masculinity which are quite specifically fantasy figures, such as the film characters played by Humphrey Bogart, John Wayne and Sylvester Stallone. Or real models may be publicized who are so remote from everyday achievement that they have the effect of an unattainable ideal, like the Australian Rules footballer Ron Barassi or the boxer Muhammed Ali.

As we move from face-to-face settings to structures involving millions of people, the easily symbolized aspects of interaction become more prominent. Hegemonic masculinity is very public. In a society of mass communications it is tempting to think that it exists only as publicity. Hence the focus on media images and media discussions of masculinity in the "Books About Men" of the 1970s and 1980s, from Warren Farrell´s *The Liberated Man* to Barbara Ehrenreich´s *The Hearts of Men*.

To focus on the media images alone would be a mistake. They need not correspond to the actual characters of the men who hold most social power—in contemporary societies the corporate and state elites. Indeed a ruling class may allow a good deal of sexual dissent. A minor but dramatic instance is the tolerance for homosexuality that the British diplomat Guy Burgess could assume from other men of his class during his career as a Soviet spy. The public face of hegemonic masculinity is not necessarily what powerful men are, but what sustains their power and what large numbers of men are motivated to support. The notion of "hegemony" generally implies a large measure of consent. Few men are Bogarts or Stallones, many collaborate in sustaining those images.

There are various reasons for complicity, and a thorough study of them would go far to illuminate the whole system of sexual politics. Fantasy gratification is one—nicely satirized in Woody Allen's Bogart take-off, *Play it Again, Sam*. Displaced aggression might be another—and the popularity of very violent movies from *Dirty Harry* to *Rambo* suggest that a great deal of this is floating around. But it seems likely that the major reason is that most men benefit from the subordination of women, and hegemonic masculinity is the cultural expression of this ascendancy.

This needs careful formulation. It does not imply that hegemonic masculinity means being particularly nasty to women. Women may feel as oppressed by non-hegemonic masculinities, may even find the hegemonic pattern more familiar and manageable. There is likely to be a kind of "fit" between hegemonic masculinity and emphasized femininity. What it does imply is the maintenance of practices that institutionalize men's dominance over women. In this sense hegemonic masculinity must embody a successful collective strategy in relation to women. Given the complexity of gender relations no simple or uniform strategy is possible: a "mix" is necessary. So hegemonic masculinity can contain at the same time, quite consistently, openings towards domesticity and openings towards violence, towards misogyny and towards heterosexual attraction.

Hegemonic masculinity is constructed in relation to women and to subordinated masculinities. These other masculinities need not be as clearly defined—indeed, achieving hegemony may consist precisely in preventing alternatives gaining cultural definition and recognition as alternatives, confining them to ghettos, to privacy, to unconsciousness.

The most important feature of contemporary hegemonic masculinity is that it is heterosexual, being closely connected to the institution of marriage; and a key form of subordinated masculinity is homosexual. This subordination involves both direct interactions and a kind of ideological warfare. Some of the interactions include police and legal harassment, street violence, economic discrimination. These transactions are tied together by the contempt for homosexuality and homosexual men that is part of the ideological package of hegemonic masculinity. The AIDS scare has been marked less by sympathy for gays as its main victims than by hostility to them as the bearers of a new threat. The key point of media concern is whether the "gay plague" will spread to "innocent," i.e., straight, victims.

In other cases of subordinated masculinity the condition is temporary. Cynthia Cockburn's splendid study of printing workers in London portrays a version of hegemonic masculinity that involved ascendancy over young men as well as over women. The workers recalled their apprenticeships in terms of drudgery and humiliation, a ritual of induction into trade and masculinity at the same time. But once they were in, they were "brothers."

Several general points about masculinity also apply to the analysis of femininity at the mass level. These patterns too are historical: relationships change, new forms of femininity emerge and others disappear. The ideological representations of femininity draw on, but do not necessarily correspond to, actual femininities as they are lived. What most women support is not necessarily what they are.

There is however a fundamental difference. All forms of femininity in this society are constructed in the context of the overall subordination of women to men. For this reason there is no femininity that holds among women the position held by hegemonic masculinity among men.

This fundamental asymmetry has two main aspects. First, the concentration of social power in the hands of men leaves limited scope for women to construct institutionalized power relationships over other women. It does happen on a face-to-face basis, notably in mother–daughter relationships. Institutionalized power hierarchies have also existed in contexts like the girls´ schools pictured in *Mädchen in Uniform* and *Frost in May*. But the note of domination that is so important in relations between kinds of masculinity is muted. The much lower level of violence between women than violence between men is a fair indication of this. Second, the organization of a hegemonic form around dominance over the other sex is absent from the social construction of femininity. Power, authority, aggression, technology are not thematized in femininity at large as they are in masculinity. Equally important, no pressure is set up to negate or subordinate other forms of femininity in the way hegemonic masculinity must negate other masculinities. It is likely therefore that actual femininities in our society are more diverse than actual masculinities.

The dominance structure which the construction of femininity cannot avoid is the global dominance of heterosexual men. The process is likely to polarize around compliance or resistance to this dominance.

The option of compliance is central to the pattern of femininity which is given most cultural and ideological support at present, called here "emphasized femininity." This is the translation to the large scale of patterns already discussed in particular institutions and milieux, such as the display of sociability rather than technical competence, fragility in mating scenes, compliance with men´s desire for titillation and ego-stroking in office relationships, acceptance of marriage and childcare as a response to labour-market discrimination against women. At the mass level these are organized around themes of sexual receptivity in relation to younger women and motherhood in relation to older women.

Like hegemonic masculinity, emphasized femininity as a cultural construction is very public, though its content is specifically linked with the private realm of the home and the bedroom. Indeed it is promoted in mass media and marketing with an insistence and on a scale far beyond that found for any form of masculinity. The articles and advertisements in mass-circulation women´s magazines, the "women´s pages" of mass-circulation newspapers and the soap operas and "games" of daytime television, are familiar cases.

Most of this promotion, it might be noted, is organized, financed and supervised by men.

To call this pattern "emphasized femininity" is also to make a point about how the cultural package is used in interpersonal relationships. This kind of femininity is performed, and performed especially to men. There is a great deal of folklore about how to sustain the performance. It is a major concern of women´s magazines from *Women´s Weekly* to *Vogue*. It is even taken up and turned into highly ambivalent comedy by Hollywood (*How to Marry a Millionaire*; *Tootsie*). Marilyn Monroe was both archetype and satirist of emphasized femininity. Marabel Morgan´s "total woman," an image that somehow mixes sexpot and Jesus Christ, uses the same tactics and has the same ambivalences.

Femininity organized as an adaptation to men´s power, and emphasizing compliance, nurturance and empathy as womanly virtues, is not in much of a state to establish hegemony over other kinds of femininity. There is a familiar paradox about anti-feminist women´s groups like "Women Who Want to be Women" who exalt the *Kinder, Kirche und Küche* version of femininity: they can only become politically active by subverting their own prescriptions. They must rely heavily on religious ideology and on political backing from conservative men. The relations they establish with other kinds of femininity are not so much domination as attempted marginalization.

Central to the maintenance of emphasized femininity is practice that prevents other models of femininity gaining cultural articulation. When feminist historiography describes women´s experience as "hidden from history," in Sheila Rowbotham´s phrase, it is responding partly to this fact. Conventional historiography recognizes, indeed presupposes, conventional femininity. What is hidden from it is the experience of spinsters, lesbians, unionists, prostitutes, madwomen, rebels and maiden aunts, manual workers, midwives and witches. And what is involved in radical sexual politics, in one of its dimensions, is precisely a reassertion and recovery of marginalized forms of femininity in the experience of groups like these.

SECTION XI

1. How do West and Zimmerman distinguish sex and gender, and what do they see as the nature of the relationship between the two? What exactly do they mean when they write about "doing gender?"
2. Why is the example of Agnes so important to West and Zimmerman´s thesis?
3. Summarize MacKinnon's differentiation between sameness/difference theory and dominance theory. Do you agree with her critique of the former and advocacy for the latter? Why?
4. Summarize Collins´ advocacy of an Afrocentric feminist epistemology. Do you agree or disagree with critics who would contend that such a position undermines the ability of people to see the world from the perspective of a shared humanity? Why?
5. What does Smith mean by standpoint, and what is the argument she advances on its behalf?
6. What does Connell mean by "hegemonic masculinity," and what is its role in shaping gender power relations?
7. Discuss and offer an example of what Connell means by the structured character of gender power relations.

XII. THEORIES OF RACE, ETHNICITY, AND NATIONALISM

56. THE THEORETICAL STATUS OF THE CONCEPT OF RACE

MICHAEL OMI AND HOWARD WINANT

Michael Omi (b. 1951), who teaches in the Ethnic Studies Department at the University of California, Berkeley, and Howard Winant (b. 1946), a professor at the University of California, Santa Barbara, introduced the idea of "racial formation" in their highly influential book on *Racial Formation in the United States*. The book was an attempt to provide a theoretical framework for understanding the social significance of race in the post–civil rights era, after the demise of Jim Crow. It extrapolates from Italian Marxist Antonio Gramsci´s concept of hegemony and applies it to race (see the preceding entry by Raewyn Connell for a parallel effort with gender), contending that race needs to be construed as a social construct that constitutes a fundamental organizing principle in social life—and that as such it cannot be reduced to other categories such as class or ethnicity. In this essay, which appeared in various versions during the early 1990s, Omi and Winant disagree with the argument that race should be viewed as ideology, if that means a form of false consciousness, and with the competing claim that it should be viewed as objective condition if that essentializes race. As an alternative to both approaches, the authors lay out the contours of a critical theory of race that views it as an unstable, historically contingent, and highly variable construct that arises and is sustained or changed by what they refer to as "racial projects." The essay ends with a discussion of the spatial and temporal parameters of race today.

INTRODUCTION

Race used to be a relatively intelligible concept; only recently have we seriously challenged its theoretical coherence. Today there are deep questions about what we actually mean by the term. But before (roughly) World War II, before the rise of Nazism, before the end of the great European empires and particularly before the decolonization of Africa, before the urbanization of the U.S. black population and the rise of the modern civil rights movement, race was still largely seen in Europe and North America (and elsewhere as well) as an essence, a natural phenomenon, whose meaning was fixed, as constant as a southern star.

Michael Omi and Howard Winant "The Theoretical Status of the Concept of Race." Unpublished version of an article used by permission of the authors 2002. ✦

In the earlier years of this century, only a handful of pioneers, people like W. E. B. Du Bois and Franz Boas, and Robert E. Park of the "Chicago School," conceived of race in a more social and historical way. Other doubters included avant-garde racial theorists emerging from the intellectual and cultural ferment of the Negritude movement and the Harlem renaissance, pan-Africanists and nationalists, and Marxists electrified by the Russian revolution. Many of these had returned from the battlefields of France to a Jim Crow United States, swept in 1919 by antiblack race riots. Others went back to a colony—Senegal, India, Trinidad, the Philippines or elsewhere—where they found the old racist imperialism proceeding undisturbed. So now they sought to apply to the mother continent of Africa or other colonial outposts, or to the United States or Europe itself, the rhetorics of national self-determination expressed at Versailles, in the Comintern, in the various pan-Africanist conferences that had been occurring, or in the music, art, and literature that was now being produced by colored hearts and minds all around the world.

These were but the early upsurges of twentieth-century challenges to the naturalistic and essentialized concept of race that had dominated Western thought for centuries; that had indeed been invented in Europe and had evolved in tandem with the Enlightenment and European imperial rule. To be sure, doubts about the eternality of racial categories, however important, were still very much on the margins of accepted knowledge. Early racial critics were not only peripheral to the global system of racial hierarchy; they too were marked, still marked, by its power and ubiquity. Even the pioneers just mentioned still paid homage to race-theories we would now view as archaic at best.[1] All made incomplete breaks with essentialist notions of race, whether biologistic or otherwise deterministic.

As do we still today. But that was then; this is now. Although racial essentialism remains very much with us, at the dawn of the twenty-first century the theory of race has been significantly transformed. The social construction of race, which we have labeled the *racial formation* process (Omi and Winant 1994), is widely recognized today, so much so that it is now often *conservatives* who argue that race is an illusion. The main task facing racial theory today, in fact, is no longer to critique the

seemingly "natural" or "common sense" concept of race—although that effort has not been entirely completed by any means. Rather the central task is to focus attention on the continuing significance and changing meaning of race. It is to argue against the recent discovery of the illusory nature of race; against the supposed contemporary transcendence of race; against the widely reported death of the concept of race; and against the replacement of the category of race by other, supposedly more objective categories like ethnicity, nationality, or class. All these initiatives are mistaken at best, and intellectually dishonest at worst.

In order to substantiate these assertions, we must first ask, what is race? Is it merely an illusion: an ideological construct utilized to manipulate, divide, and deceive? This position has been taken by many theorists, and activists as well, including many who have served the cause of racial and social justice in the United States. Or is race something real, material, objective? This view too has its adherents, including both racial reactionaries and racial radicals.

In our view both of these approaches miss the boat. The concept of race is neither an ideological construct, nor does it reflect an objective condition. Here we first reflect critically on these two opposed viewpoints on the contemporary theory of race. Then we offer an alternative perspective based on racial formation theory.

RACE AS AN IDEOLOGICAL CONSTRUCT

The assertion that race is an ideological construct—understood in the sense of an "illusion" that explains other "material" relationships in distorted fashion—seems highly problematic. Though today it is usually seen as a core tenet of conservative racial theory—think of "colorblindness" (Connerly 2000) and the main neoconservative positions (Murray 1984; Thernstrom 1997; Glazer 1997; see also Winant 1997), as noted this view is held across the political spectrum from right to left. For example the prominent radical historian Barbara Fields takes this view in her 1990 article "Slavery, Race and Ideology in the United States of America." Although Fields inveighs against various uses of the race concept, she directs her critical barbs most forcefully against historians who "invoke race as a historical explanation" (Fields 101).

According to Fields, the concept of race arose to meet an ideological need: its original effectiveness lay in its ability to reconcile freedom and slavery. The idea of race provided "the means of explaining slavery to people whose terrain was a republic founded on radical doctrines of liberty and natural rights. . . ." (Fields 114).

But, Fields says, to argue that race—once framed as a category in thought, an ideological explanation for certain distinct types of social inequality—"takes on a life of its own" in social relationships, is to transform (or "reify") an illusion into a reality. Such a position could be sustained

> ". . . [o]nly if *race* is defined as innate and natural prejudice of color. . . ." [S]ince race is not genetically programmed, racial prejudice cannot be genetically programmed either, but must arise historically. . . . The preferred solution is to suppose that, having arisen historically, race then ceases to be a historical phenomenon and becomes instead an external motor of history; according to the fatuous but widely repeated formula, it "takes on a life of its own." In other words, once historically acquired, race becomes hereditary. The shopworn metaphor thus offers camouflage for a latter-day version of Lamarckism (Fields 101, emphasis in original).

Thus race is either an illusion which does ideological work, or an objective biological fact. Since it is certainly not the latter, it must be the former. No intermediate possibility—consider for example the Durkheimian notion of a "social fact" – is considered.[2]

Some of this account—for example the extended discussion of the origins of North American race-thinking—can be accepted without major objection.[3] Furthermore, Fields effectively demonstrates the absurdity of many commonly held ideas about race. But her position at best can only account for the *origins* of race-thinking, and then only in one social context. To examine how race-thinking evolved from these origins, how it responded to changing sociocultural circumstances, is ruled out. Why and how did race-thinking survive after emancipation? Fields cannot answer, because the very perpetuation of the concept of race is ruled out by her theoretical approach. As a relatively orthodox Marxist, Fields could argue that changing "material conditions" continued to give rise to changes in racial "ideology," except that even the limited autonomy this would attach to the concept of race would exceed her standards. Race cannot take on "a life of its own"; it is a pure ideology, an illusion.

Fields simply skips from emancipation to the present, where she disparages opponents of "racism" for unwittingly perpetuating it. In denunciatory terms Fields concludes by arguing for the concept's abolition:

> Nothing handed down from the past could keep race alive if we did not constantly reinvent and re-ritualize it to fit our own terrain. If race lives on today, it can do so only because we continue to create and re-create it in our social life, continue to verify it, and thus continue to need a social vocabulary that will allow us to make sense, not of what our ancestors did then, but of what we choose to do now (Fields 118).

Fields is unclear about how "we" should jettison the ideological construct of race, and one can well understand why. By her own logic, racial ideologies cannot be abolished by acts of will. One can only marvel at the ease with which she distinguishes the bad old slavery days of the past from the present, when "we" anachronistically cling, as if for no reason, to the illusion that race retains any meaning. We foolishly "throw up our hands" and acquiesce in race-thinking, rather than . . . doing what? Denying the racially demarcated divisions in society? Training ourselves to be "color-blind?"[4]

In any case the view that race is an illusion or piece of false consciousness is held not only by intellectuals, based on both well-intentioned and ulterior motivations; it also has a common-sense character. One hears in casual discussion, for example, or in introductory social science classes, variations on the following statement: "I don't care if a person is black, white, or purple, I treat them exactly the same; a person's just a person to me. . . ." etc. Furthermore, some of the integrationist aspirations of racial minority movements, especially the civil rights movement, invoke this sort of idea. Consider the famous line from the "I Have a Dream" speech, the line that made Shelby Steele's career: ". . . that someday my four little children will be judged, not by the color of their skin, but by the content of their character. . . ."

Our core criticisms of this "race as ideology" approach are two: first, it fails to recognize the salience a social construct can develop over half a millennium or more of diffusion, or should we say enforcement, as a fundamental principle of social organization and identity formation. The longevity of the race concept, and the enormous number of effects race-thinking (and race-acting) have produced, guarantee that race will remain a feature of social reality across the globe, and *a fortiori* in the United States, despite its lack of intrinsic or scientific merit (in the biological sense).[5] Second, and related, this approach fails to recognize that at the level of experience, of everyday life, race is a relatively impermeable part of our identities. For example, U.S. society is so thoroughly racialized that to be without racial identity is to be in danger of having no identity. To be raceless is akin to being genderless. It is to be invisible or ghostly.[6] Indeed, when one cannot identify another's race, a micro sociological "crisis of interpretation" results, something perhaps best interpreted in ethnomethodological or Goffmanian terms. To complain about such a situation may be understandable, but it does not advance understanding.

RACE AS AN OBJECTIVE CONDITION

On the other side of the coin, it is clearly problematic to assign objectivity to the race concept. Such theoretical practice puts us in quite heterogeneous, and sometimes unsavory, company. Of course the biologistic racial theories of the past do this: here we are thinking of the prototypes of fascism such as Gobineau and Chamberlain (Mosse 1978), of the eugenicists such as Lothrop Stoddard and Madison Grant, and of the "founding fathers" of scientific racism such as Agassiz, Broca, Terman, and Yerkes (Kevles, 1985; Chase, 1977; Gould, 1981). Indeed an extensive legacy of this sort of thinking extends right up to the present.

But much liberal and even radical social science, though firmly committed to a social as opposed to biological interpretation of race, nevertheless also slips into a kind of objectivism about racial identity and racial meaning. This is true because race is all too frequently treated as discrete variable. It is considered, investigated, or "controlled for" as if it were an objective phenomenon, rather than a sociohistorical construct that is deeply unstable and internally contradictory

(Zuberi 2001). Thus, to select only prominent examples, Daniel Moynihan, William Julius Wilson, Milton Gordon, and many other mainstream thinkers theorize race in terms which downplay its variability and historically contingent character. So even these major writers, whose explicit rejection of biologistic forms of racial theory would be unquestioned, fall prey to a kind of creeping objectivism of race. For in their analyses a modal explanatory approach emerges as follows: sociopolitical circumstances change over historical time, racially defined groups adapt or fail to adapt to these changes, achieving mobility or remaining mired in poverty, etc. In this logic there is no reconceptualization of group identities, of the constantly shifting parameters through which race is thought about, group interests are assigned, statuses are ascribed, agency is attained, and roles performed.

Contemporary racial theory, then, is often "objectivistic" about its fundamental category. Although abstractly acknowledged to be a sociohistorical construct, race in practice is often treated as an objective fact: one simply *is* one's race; in the contemporary United States for example, if we discard euphemisms, we have five color-based racial categories: black, white, brown, yellow, or red.

This is problematic, indeed ridiculous, in numerous ways. Nobody really belongs in these boxes; they are patently absurd reductions of human variation. But even accepting the nebulous "rules" of racial classification—what Harris (1964) calls "hypodescent," for example—many people don't fit anywhere: into what categories should we place Arab Americans? Brazilians? Argentinians? South Asians? Such a list could be extended indefinitely; every racial identity is unstable. Objectivist treatments, lacking a critique of the constructed character of racial meanings, also clash with experiential dimensions of the issue. If one doesn't *act* black, white, etc., that's just deviance from the norm, etc. There is in these approaches an insufficient appreciation of the performative aspect of race, as postmodernists or pragmatists might call it.[7]

To summarize the critique of this "race as objective condition" approach, then, it fails on three counts: first, it cannot grasp the processual and relational character of racial identity and racial meaning. Second, it denies the historicity and social comprehensiveness of the race concept. And third, it cannot account for the way actors, both individual and collective, have to manage incoherent and conflictual racial meanings and identities in everyday life. It has no concept, in short, of what we have labeled *racial formation*.

TOWARD A CRITICAL THEORY OF THE CONCEPT OF RACE

The foregoing clearly sets forth the agenda which any adequate theorization of the race concept must fulfill. Such an approach must be theoretically constructed so as to steer between the Scylla of "race as illusion" and the Charybdis of "racial objectivism." Such a critical theory can be consistently developed, we suggest, drawing upon racial formation theory. Such a theoretical formulation must be explicitly historicist: it must recognize the importance of historical context and contingency in the framing of racial categories and the social construction of racially defined experiences.

What would be the minimum conditions for the development of such a critical, processual theory of race? Beyond addressing the standard issues to which we have already referred—such as equality, domination/resistance, and micro-macro linkages—we suggest three such conditions for such a theory:

> It must apply to contemporary *politics*;
> It must apply in an increasingly *global* context;
> It must apply across *historical* time.[8]

Contemporary Political Relationships: The meaning and salience of race is forever being reconstituted in the present. In the last half century new racial politics emerged in a process, usually decades-long, that constituted a hegemonic shift or postcolonial transition. Along the lines of what we have called the "trajectory of racial politics" (Omi and Winant 1994, 84-88) the meanings of race, and the political articulations of race, have proliferated.

Examples include the appearance of competing racial projects, by which we mean efforts to institutionalize racial meanings and identities in particular social structures: notably those of individual, family, community, and state. As equality-and difference-oriented movements contend with racial "backlash" over

sustained periods of time, as binary logics of racial antagonism (white/black, ladino/indio, settler/native, etc.) become more complex and decentered, political deployment of the concept of race comes to signal qualitatively new types of political domination, as well as new types of opposition.

Consider the U.S. example. In the United States today it is now possible to perpetuate racial domination without making any explicit reference to race at all. Subtextual or "coded" racial signifiers, or the mere denial of the continuing significance of race, usually suffice. Similarly, in terms of opposition, it is now possible to resist racial domination in entirely new ways, particularly by limiting the reach and penetration of the political system into everyday life, by generating new identities, new collectivities, new (imagined) communities that are relatively less permeable to the hegemonic system.[9] Much of the rationale for Islamic currents among blacks in the United States and to some extent for the Afrocentric phenomenon, can be found here. Thus the old political choices, integration vs. separatism, assimilation vs. nationalism, are no longer the only options.[10]

In the "underdeveloped" world, proliferation of so-called postcolonial phenomena also have significant racial dimensions, as the entire Fanonian tradition (merely to select one important theoretical current) makes clear. Crucial debates have now been occurring for decades on the question of postcolonial subjectivity and identity, the insufficiency of the simple dualism of "Europe and its others," the subversive and parodic dimensions of political culture at and beyond the edges of the old imperial boundaries, etc. (Said 1978; Bhabha 1990).

The Global Context of Race: Once seen in terms of imperial reach, in terms of colonization, conquest, and migration, racial space has always been globalized. In the postcolonial period, however, a new kind of racial globalization has become visible.[11]

Today the distinction "developed/underdeveloped" has been definitively overcome. Obviously by this we don´t mean that now there are no disparities between North and South, rich and poor. Rather we mean that the movement of capital and labor has internationalized all nations, all regions. Today we have reached the point where "the empire strikes back," as former (neo)colonial subjects, now redefined as "migrants" and "undocumented" persons (sometimes called "denizens") challenge the majoritarian status or cultural domination of the formerly metropolitan group (the whites, the Europeans, the "Americans," the "French," etc.).[12] Meanwhile such phenomena as the rise of "diasporic" models of blackness, the creation of "panethnic" communities of Latinos and Asians (in such countries as the United Kingdom or the United States), and the breakdown of borders in both Europe and North America, all seem to be internationalizing and racializing previously national polities, cultures, and identities.[13] To take just one example, popular culture now divulgates racial awareness almost instantaneously, as reggae, rap, samba, or various African pop styles leap from continent to continent.

Comparing hegemonic racial formations in the contemporary global context suggests that diasporic solidarity and race-consciousness is taking new forms as it emerges (or re-emerges) in the twenty-first century. There are also new theoretical and practical efforts to understand national and regional racial dynamics in light of the globalization framework. For example, the attention given to "the black Atlantic" as an evolving sociohistorical complex of domination and resistance (Gilroy 1993; Linebaugh and Rediker 2001) is being supplemented by work on regional diasporas like the Luso-Brazilian Atlantic (Miller 1988; Stam 1997), and the Caribbean (James 1998). Recent scholarship on Africa situates the Motherland much more centrally in global political economic development than was previously the case (Cooper 1993).[14] In similar fashion, African ideas and "the idea of Africa" (Mudimbe 1994; see also Appiah 1992) now challenge formerly hegemonic Northern and Western worldviews much more comprehensively than could ever have been imagined in the past. A burgeoning new literature on processes of continuity and change in the African diaspora points to the unrecognized (and ongoing) political dynamism of that global complex (Patterson and Kelley 2000). The world is learning once again—as it has over and over throughout the modern age—about the centrality of race on the global stage: racial identity continues to shape "life-chances" worldwide; transnational organizing along racial lines is evident among indigenous, black, and many dispersed/diasporic peoples; and racial stigma is

continually being reallocated (and resisted) everywhere. Although space is not available to develop these points fully here, we can offer two brief examples of the latter: resurgent Islamophobia and the increasing racialization of white identities.

By *Islamophobia* (Halliday 1999) we mean anti-Islamic (and by extension, anti-Muslim) prejudice. Although religious bigotry and hostility are certainly at work here, the racial components of Islamophobia should now be obvious, particularly in the United States but elsewhere in the world as well. Very old patterns are resurfacing here: for example, the United States affords itself a civilizing mission in the Arab world, the Muslim world, much as the British and French (not to mention the Crusades) did in the past. Arabs in the United States and Europe are subject to widespread racial profiling; this is particularly true after the September 11, 2001 attacks. The United States has been deluged with a flood of periodical ink and broadcast soundbites devoted to the problematic and mysterious essence of Islam—political Islam, fundamentalist Islam, sex and gender under Islam, the putative "backwardness" of Islam in comparison to the enlightened and democratic West, the tutelary role of Christianity and obligation of proselytization in the Islamic world, etc. All this signals a regression in the West, and particularly in the United States, to orientalism at its worst (Said 1978). It hardly needs repeating that, like the nineteenth-century phenomenon Said analyzed so influentially, twenty-first-century orientalism is also a discursive set of variations on the theme of racial rule; it is redolent of the old colonial and imperial arrogance. The uplifting mission of the West is proclaimed—in the values of "freedom," "democracy," "pluralism," "secularism," etc.—while underneath the surface the old agendas advance: most notably political-military power and the capture of natural resources.

The dissolution of the transparent racial identity of the formerly dominant group, that is to say, the *increasing racialization of whites* in Europe, the United States, and elsewhere, must also be recognized as proceeding from the increasingly globalized dimensions of race. As previous assumptions erode, white identity loses its transparency, the easy elision with "racelessness" that accompanies racial domination. "Whiteness" enters into crisis; it becomes a matter of anxiety and concern.[15] Harking back to the eugenic panics that swept the United States and the colonial "mother countries" a century ago (Grant 1970 [1916]), mainstream political thinkers now lament the demise of colonial order, hanker for a new imperial system (Ignatieff 2003) that would bring order to the chaotic postcolonial "ends of the Earth" (Kaplan 1997), and worry about racial "swamping," the loss of cultural integrity, and declining white fertility in the world's West and North (Brimelow 1995).

The Emergence of Racial Time: Some final notes are in order regarding the question of the epochal nature of racial time. Classical social theory had an enlightenment-based view of time, a perspective which understood the emergence of modernity in terms of the rise of capitalism and the bourgeoisie. This view was by no means limited to Marxism. Weberian disenchantment and the rise of the Durkheimian division of labor also partake of this temporal substrate. Only rarely does the racial dimension of historical temporality appear in this body of thought, as for example in Marx's excoriation of the brutalities of "primitive accumulation":

> The discovery of gold and silver in America, the extirpation, enslavement, and entombment in mines of the aboriginal population, the beginning of the conquest and looting of the East Indies, the turning of Africa into a warren for the commercial hunting of blackskins, signalized the rosy dawn of the era of capitalist production. These idyllic proceedings are the chief momenta of primitive accumulation. On their heels treads the commercial war of the European nations with the globe for a theater. It begins with the revolt of the Netherlands from Spain, assumes giant dimensions in England's AntiJacobin War, and is still going on in the opium wars with China, etc. (Marx 1967; 351).

Yet even Marx frequently legitimated such processes as the inevitable and ultimately beneficial birth-pangs of classlessness—by way of the ceaselessly revolutionary bourgeoisie.

Today such teleological accounts seem hopelessly outmoded. Historical time could well be interpreted in terms of something like a racial *longue duree*: for has there not been an immense historical rupture represented by the rise of Europe, the onset of African enslavement, the *conquista*, and the subjugation of much of Asia? We take the point of much poststructural scholarship on these matters to be quite precisely an effort to explain "Western" or colonial time as a huge project demarcating human "difference," or more globally as Todorov, say, would argue, of framing partial collective identities in terms of externalized "others" (Todorov 1985). Just as, for example, the writers of the *Annales* school sought to locate the deep logic of historical time in the means by which material life was produced—diet, shoes, etc.—so we might usefully think of a racial *longue duree* in which the slow inscription of phenotypical signification took place upon the human body, in and through conquest and enslavement to be sure, but also as an enormous act of expression, of narration.[16]

In short, just as the noise of the "big bang" still resonates through the universe, so the overdetermined construction of world "civilization" as a product of the rise of Europe and the subjugation of the rest of us still defines the race concept. Such speculative notes as these, to be sure, can be no more than provocations. Nor can we conclude this effort to reframe the agenda of racial theory with a neat summation. There was a long period—centuries—in which race was seen as a natural condition, an essence. This was gradually supplanted, although not entirely superseded, during the twentieth century by a new way of thinking about race: it was now seen as subordinate to the supposedly more concrete, "material" relationships of culture, economic interest, and national identity. Centuries of essentialist and "naturalizing" views of race were replaced (though not entirely) with more critical perspectives that envisioned dispensing with the "illusion" of race. Perhaps now we are approaching the end of that racial epoch too.

To our dismay, we may have to give up our familiar ways of thinking about race once more. If so, there may also be some occasion for delight. For it may be possible to glimpse yet another view of race, in which the concept operates neither as a signifier of comprehensive identity, nor of fundamental difference, both of which are patently absurd, but rather as a marker of the infinity of variations we humans hold as a common heritage and hope for the future.

NOTES

1. Du Bois´s invocations in *The Souls of Black Folk* of Germanic concepts of race derived from Herder and Fichte are but one example of this. Boas´s critique of the physical anthropology of his time also preserved some of its racial stereotypes. Marxism´s eurocentric elements contained significant racist residues, and pan-Africanism and Negritude often appealed to quasi-religious or non-rational black or African essences (e.g., *nomo*), in their accounts of racial difference.

2. For a similar "left" argument against the usefulness of the concept, see Appiah 1985 (1992).

3. Minor objections would have to do with Fields´s functionalist view of ideology, and her claim that the race concept only "came into existence" (Fields 101) when needed by whites in North American colonies beginning in the late 17th century. The concept of race, of course, has a longer history than that.

4. David Roediger – generally in agreement with Fields – also criticizes her on this point. "At times she nicely balances the ideological creation of racial attitudes with their manifest and ongoing importance and their (albeit ideological) *reality*. . . . But elsewhere, race disappears into the `reality´ of class" (Roediger 1991, 7–8; emphasis original).

5. A famous sociological dictum holds that "If men (sic) define situations as real, they are real in their consequences" (Thomas and Thomas 1928, 572), a claim that would clearly apply to racial "situations" of all sorts.

6. Avery Gordon has suggested that race "haunts" US society and culture as a consequence of the fierce contradictions it embodies: its simultaneous omnipresence and disavowal throughout American life (Gordon 1997).

7. "The question of identification is never the affirmation of a pregiven identity, never a self-fulfilling prophecy—it is always the production of an image of identity and the transformation of the subject in assuming that image" (Bhabha 1990, 188).

8. Although only in passing. There can be no extended racial theorizing here. In other work we have developed a more systematic theoretical approach to race. See Omi and Winant 1994.

9. The work of Paul Gilroy (1991) on the significance of black music in Afro-Diasporic communities is particularly revealing on this point.

10. Our point here is that previously marginalized identities and positions are now politically more salient, have more "voice," and influence current political conflicts more than they did in the past. Of course there is nothing new about the particular examples we have cited. Islam has always been present among African Americans (as well as in every other racially-identified group). For all its controversies and problems (Moses 1994), Afrocentrism justifiably claims its heritage in pan-Africanism, Ethiopianism, etc.

11. For a more extensive treatment of these large issues, see Winant 2001.

12. We borrow this phrase, not from George Lucas but from the book of that title edited at the Centre for Contemporary Cultural Studies, 1982.

13. David Lopez and Yen Le Espiritu define panethnicity as ". . . the development of bridging organizations and solidarities among subgroups of ethnic collectivities that are often seen as homogeneous by outsiders." Such a development, they claim, is a crucial feature of ethnic change: "supplanting both assimilation and ethnic particularism as the direction of change for racial/ethnic minorities." They conclude that while panethnic formation is facilitated by an ensemble of cultural factors (e.g., common language and religion) and structural factors (e.g., class, generation, and geographical concentration), a specific concept of race is fundamental to the construction of panethnicity (Lopez and Le Espiritu 1990, 198).

14. Thus confirming Du Bois's claims to this effect ("Semper novi quid ex Africa") nearly a century after he made them (Du Bois 1995 [1915]).
15. Once again this is an old story. Among a vast literature, see Roediger 1991, Harris 1993, Jacobson 1999.
16. For example the magisterial work of Fernand Braudel 1975.

REFERENCES

Appiah, Kwame Anthony. "The Uncompleted Argument: DuBois and the Illusion of Race," *Critical Inquiry* 12 (Autumn 1985); also in idem, *In My Father's House: Africa in the Philosophy of Culture*. New York: Oxford University Press, 1992.

Bhabha, Homi K. "Interrogating Identity." In David Theo Goldberg, ed., *Anatomy of Racism*. Minneapolis: University of Minnesota Press, 1990.

Braudel, Fernand. *Capitalism and Material Life, 1400–1800*. Translated by Miriam Kochan. New York: Harper Colophon, 1975.

Centre for Contemporary Cultural Studies. *The Empire Strikes Back: Race in 70s Britain*. London: Hutchinson, 1982.

Brimelow, Peter. *Alien Nation: Common Sense About America's Immigration Disaster*. New York: Random House, 1995.

Chase, Allan. *The Legacy of Malthus: The Social Costs of the New Scientific Racism*. New York: Knopf, 1977.

Connerly, Ward. *Creating Equal: My Fight Against Race Preferences*. San Francisco: Encounter Books, 2000.

Cooper, Frederick. "Africa and the World Economy." In Frederick Cooper et al., eds. *Confronting Historical Paradigms: Peasants, Labor, and the Capitalist World System in Africa and Latin America*. Madison: University of Wisconsin Press, 1993.

Du Bois, W. E. B. "The African Roots of the War" 1915. In David Levering Lewis, ed. *W. E. B. Du Bois: A Reader*. New York: Henry Holt, 1995.

Fields, Barbara. "Slavery, Race and Ideology in the United States of America." *New Left Review*, May/June 1990.

Gilroy, Paul. *There Ain't No Black in the Union Jack: The Cultural Politics of Race and Nation*. Chicago: University of Chicago Press, 1991.

Gilroy, Paul. *The Black Atlantic: Modernity and Double Consciousness*. Cambridge, Massachusetts: Harvard University Press, 1993.

Glazer, Nathan. *We Are All Multiculturalists Now*. Cambridge, MA: Harvard University Press, 1997.

Gordon, Avery F. *Ghostly Matters: Haunting and the Sociological Imagination*. Minneapolis: University of Minnesota Press, 1997.

Gould, Stephen Jay. *The Mismeasure of Man*. New York: Norton, 1981.

Grant, Madison. *The Passing of the Great Race*. New York: Arno, 1970 [1916].

Halliday, Fred. "`Islamophobia' Reconsidered." *Ethnic and Racial Studies*. Vol 22, no. 5 (September 1999).

Harris, Cheryl. "Whiteness as Property." 106 *Harvard Law Review* 1707 (1993).

Harris, Marvin. *Patterns of Race in the Americas*. New York: Walker, 1964.

Ignatieff, Michael. "American Empire (Get Used to It)." *The New York Times Magazine*, January 5, 2003.

Jacobson, Matthew Frye. *Whiteness of a Different Color: European Immigrants and the Alchemy of Race*. Cambridge, MA: Harvard University Press, 1999.

James, Winston. *Holding Aloft the Banner of Ethiopia: Caribbean Radicalism in Early Twentieth-Century America*. New York: Verso, 1998.

Kaplan, Robert B. *The Ends of the Earth: From Togo to Turkmenistan, from Iran to Cambodia, a Journey to the Frontiers of Anarchy*. New York: Vintage, 1997.

Kevles, Daniel J. *In the Name of Eugenics: Genetics and the Uses of Human Heredity*. New York: Knopf, 1985.

Linebaugh Peter, and Marcus Rediker. *The Many-Headed Hydra: The Hidden History of the Revolutionary Atlantic*. Boston: Beacon, 2001.

Lopez, David, and Yen Le Espiritu. "Panethnicity in the United States: A Theoretical Framework." *Ethnic and Racial Studies* 13 (1990).

Marx, Karl, *Capital* Vol. I. New York: International, 1967.

Miller, Joseph C. *Way of Death: Merchant Capitalism and the Angolan Slave Trade, 1730–1830*. Madison: University of Wisconsin Press, 1988.

Moses, Wilson Jeremiah. *Afrotopia: The Roots of African American Popular History*. New York: Cambridge University Press, 1998.

Mosse, George L. *Toward the Final Solution: A History of European Racism*. New York: Howard Fertig, 1978.

Mudimbe, V.Y. *The Idea of Africa*. Bloomington: Indiana University Press, 1994.

Murray, Charles A. *Losing Ground: American Social Policy, 1950–1980*. New York: Basic Books, 1984.

Omi, Michael and Howard Winant. *Racial Formation in the United States: From the 1960s to the 1990s*. rev. ed. New York: Routledge, 1994.

Patterson, Tiffany Ruby, and Robin D. G. Kelley. "Unfinished Migrations: Reflections on the African Diaspora and the Making of the Modern World." *African Studies Review*, Vol. 43, no. 1 (April 2000).

Roediger, David R. *The Wages of Whiteness: Race and the Making of the American Working Class*. New York: Verso, 1991.

Said, Edward W. *Orientalism*. New York: Viking, 1978.

Stam, Robert. *Tropical Multiculturalism: A Comparative History of Race in Brazilian Cinema and Culture*. Durham: Duke University Press, 1997.

Thernstrom, Stephan, and Abigail Thernstrom. *America in Black and White: One Nation, Indivisible*. New York: Simon & Schuster, 1997.

Thomas, W. I., and Dorothy Swaine Thomas. *The Child in America*. New York: Knopf, 1928.

Todorov, Tsvetan. *The Conquest of America: The Question of the Other*. Translated by Richard Howard. New York: Harper and Row, 1984.

Winant, Howard. *The World Is a Ghetto: Race and Democracy Since World War II*. New York: Basic, 2001.

———"Behind Blue Eyes: Contemporary White Racial Politics." *New Left Review* 225, September–October 1997.

Zuberi, Tukufu. *Thicker Than Blood: How Racial Statistics Lie*. Minneapolis: University of Minnesota Press, 2001.

57. BETWEEN CAMPS: RACE AND CULTURE IN POSTMODERNITY

PAUL GILROY

Currently the holder of the Anthony Giddens Professorship in Social Theory at the London School of Economics, Paul Gilroy (b. 1956) was early in his career affiliated with the Centre for Contemporary Cultural Studies at the University of Birmingham, where he was part of a collective that produced the acclaimed work on postcolonialism, *The Empire Strikes Back: Race and Racism in 1970s Britain* (1982). In *Their Ain't No Black in the Union Jack* (1987) and *The Black Atlantic* (1993) he further pursued his interest in exploring the political culture of the Black Atlantic Diaspora. Gilroy´s essay below derives from his 1997 inaugural address at Goldsmith´s College, University of London. In it he lays out the contours of an argument that would be more fully developed in his book published in the United Kingdom in 2000 as *Between Camps* and in the United States the same year with the title *Against Race: Imagining Political Culture Beyond the Color Line*. The thesis he offers is provocative and has led some critics to contend that he has fallen into the trap of accepting the "color-blind" argument prevalent among conservatives. This criticism represents a serious misreading of his work. Gilroy contends that nationalism and racial formations operate in terms of "camps," a word he chooses not only to "emphasize their hierarchical and regimented qualities," but to stress the pernicious consequences of the camp mentality in its most grotesque expression during the Nazi era, with its death camps. As an antidote, he promotes a cosmopolitan humanism based on interculturalism.

This is an uncomfortable experience for me. The genre requires that I use the word "I" more than I would normally want to do. Fortunately, it is one rare and special occasion on which I do not have to keep my discomfort to myself. This discomfort turns out to be a complex thing. It has been formed, in part at least, by seeing Britain´s institutions of higher learning being destroyed and devalued since 1978 when my own post-graduate work—it was not called training in those days—began. Believing that education is a good in itself, something which just cannot be translated into the terms of economic rationality, is now a perversely conservative position for a dissident to hold. The desire to celebrate on nights like these should not lead us to overlook the problems we share as scholars and as academics but more profoundly as political

intellectuals with utopian aspirations that are patently out of season. Of course, we care about our "customers" the students—tired, ill-prepared and under-resourced though they are—but we also care about the world of which they are but one part. There are other, in a sense less immediate but no less important, issues to contend with, things that resist the awful jargon of targets, budgets, missions and monitoring that claims so much of our precious time and saps our dwindling energy.

I´d like to think that this might also be a variety of discomfort shaped by a good sense of how little what we do matters in the wider scheme of things, by a realistic understanding of how insignificant and immaterial most of our efforts are doomed to be.

The gulf between work and the world yawns at the best of times but it can be especially wide for those of us

Paul Gilroy, "Between Camps: Race and Culture in Modernity." *Economy and Society, vol. 28*, number 2, May 1999: 183–197. ✦

who have maintained a commitment to writing about the unspeakable evils perpetrated under the banners of "race" and nation. Apprehending the fissures between our *is* and our *ought* contributes a powerful, lingering corrective, an antidote to the temptation of hubris. That gap is not the sort of problem I can pretend to solve, but I know that writing and teaching are an important part of what makes it bearable. I want to lay that pseudo-insight before you, in good faith, as something like the centre of my own understanding of my work. It consti-tutes the context in which I would like you to consider what I do: not, I should add, for any alibis it might afford me but, if you like, in mitigation for the failures, the incompleteness, the silences, evasions and provisional formulations, the speculations, the incon-sistencies and the errors that characterize what I have published and which have brought me to this happy but uncomfortable point. If this is a discomfort that can too easily become despair, it is also a discomfort that must be transformed into a resource of hope if only because it requires that we look outside the beleaguered walls of the university in order to find the tools, the concepts, that we need in order to maintain our serious work inside it.

An academic friend and colleague in the United States is fond of saying that most members of the professoriate have one or, if we are lucky, perhaps two worthwhile ideas in a lifetime of tenured scholarship. At best then, the bulk of what we do involves the re-cycling and recoding of those rare insights, often in language that is progressively more forbidding. I am not ready to succumb to that diagnosis of our profes-sion's ills, but I cannot deny that it passed through my mind while searching around for what I would say tonight and trying to find something to tie the threads of my presentation together. I took my difficulties as a sign that I must still be waiting for my big idea to arrive. Then it dawned on me that it might be possible to synthesize all my work and articulate it clearly as a single, quite simple project. It is unified by my antip-athy towards nationalism in all its forms and a related concern with the responsibility of intellectuals to act ethically, justly, when faced with the challenges that nationalisms represent. That critical disposition, some-thing I appreciate as the fortunate product of my London cosmopolitan upbringing by two intellectuals,

a migrant and a pacifist, connects almost everything I have written. As I have become more conscious of its power and value, it has given form to the later stages of my writing, as it reaches its urgent conclusion in an exploration of the location of black politics not in relation to England, Britain, the Americas or even the intercultural black Atlantic, but in relation to Europe past and future. Reading Frantz Fanon's work in my second term at Sussex University under the thoughtful guidance of the historian Donald Wood, I remember being struck by his repeated calls for the inauguration of a new humanism that was not blind to Europe's crimes. I do not share Fanon's masculinism, his Hegelianism or his faith in psychoanalysis but it is towards that end that I would like to direct my remarks tonight.

Before I begin, I would also like to express my gratitude to all my teachers, especially Stuart Hall and the late Gillian Rose; to my students here and at the other places where I have taught, to Miriam Glucksmann, Barbara Harrison and Stina Lyon for being prepared to give me my first chance at an academic job when I was on the brink of giving up and to my colleagues in different sociology depart-ments who have wanted me around and given me space and support to get on with my work, even though it is often remote from the doxa that defines the discipline and wins it institutional validity.

Long before I acquired an academic career, it had become commonplace for sociologically minded thinkers analysing the development of political and economic institutions to employ the concept of modernity. At some cost, it is now an indispensable part of professional shorthand. For those outside our masonic circle, I should say that modernity is used loosely to refer to the confluence of capitalism, indus-trialization and democracy, the emergence of modern government, the appearance of the nation state and numerous other social and cultural changes: in the registration of time, the experience of the metropolis, the configuration of gendered public and private spheres and the quality of ethical life. The development of territorial sovereignty and the cultural and commu-nicative apparatuses that correspond to it was also bound up with the struggle to consolidate the trans-parent, rational working of states and governmental powers to which the term modernity refers. That combination promoted a new sense of the relationship between place, community and what we are now able to call identity. It merits recognition as what I have come to call a distinctive ecology of belonging.

Though "race" thinking certainly existed in earlier times, modernity transformed the ways in which "race" was understood and acted upon. I am broadly sympathetic to the account which emerges from the rich work of scholars like Eric Voegelin, Martin Bernal and, most recently, the late Ivan Hannaford. From quite different political positions, all argue in complementary ways, that "race" as we routinely comprehend it, simply did not exist until the nineteenth century. Though it is presented as a permanent, inevitable and extra-historical principle of differentiation, there is nothing natural or spontaneous about "race" and the differences it makes. It is a short step from de-naturing "race" and appreciating the ways that "races" have been invented and imagined to seeing how modernity catalysed a distinctive regime of truths, of discourses that I want to call raciology. This was a novel way of understanding the anatomy, hierarchy and temporality. It made previously mute bodies communicate the truths of an irrevocable otherness that were being confirmed by new science and new semiotics just as the struggle against racial slavery was being won. Though it is not acknowledged as often as it should be, this close connection between "race" and modernity can be apprehended with special clarity if we allow our understanding of modernity to travel, to move with the workings of the great imperial systems it battled to control. Though they were centred on Europe, these systems, both exploitative and communicative, extended far beyond Europe's changing geo-body. That point need not be over-emphasized in this location: a stone's throw from the Thames, "the jugular vein of empire," and those distinctively modern technologies once represented by the operations of the Royal Dockyard in Deptford that have been so beautifully recaptured for us in the luminous work of the activist historian Peter Linebaugh.

Anthropology and geography are usually understood as the terminal points of the cognitive aspects of this social and cultural revolution but its effects were not confined to these new disciplinary perspectives. This large-scale historical change was given additional philosophical currency by the notion that character and talent could be distinguished unevenly and had been distributed along national and racial lines. These ideas are powerfully articulated in important texts like Kant's *Anthropology from a Pragmatic Point of View* and "On the different races of man" that are too little read these days because they are deemed to embarrass or even compromise the worthy democratic aspirations to which the critical Kant also gave expression. It is noteworthy that, when it comes to specifying what he calls "the distinctiveness of races in general" Kant's critical insight ebbs away: "The reason for assuming the Negroes and Whites to be fundamental races is self-evident" (1950: 19). Before we judge Kant too harshly we should recall that the view of national characteristics of this country which he derived from the seafarers of Koenigsberg has an interesting contemporary resonance:

> For his own countrymen the Englishman establishes great benevolent institutions unheard of among all other peoples. But the foreigner who has been driven to England's shores by fate, and has fallen into dire need, will be left to die on the dunghill because he is not an Englishman, that is not a human being.
>
> (Kant 1978: 230)

Kant is the first theorist rather than taxonomist of "race." His prolific writings show how raciology requires that enlightenment and myth are intertwined. Indeed, "race" and nationality supply the logic and mechanism of their interconnection. This complex tale deserves to be reconstructed in a more detailed manner than this occasion permits. It matters to me not only because it suggests the integral significance of "race" in the constitution of modernity, but also because it points towards the ways that raciology became linked to statecraft and modern political theory annexed by the exigencies of imperial power in its emergent phase.

Richard Wright, the first black writer I found who used the word modernity as part of his critical commentary, the philosopher Berel Lang and, from contrasting political standpoints, Aimé Césaire and Hannah Arendt have contributed much to my own grasp of these problems. All of them have something important to say about the complex and delicate historical processes that culminated in the order of the nation that is also a state. This was a new pattern of power that re-wrote the rules of political and ethical conduct according to novel principles opposed to ancient notions of political rationality, self-possession and citizenship.

Though these resources should not be disposed of lightly, my real point of departure tonight is the heretical notion that modernity´s new political codes must also be acknowledged as having been deeply compromised by the raciological drives that partly formed them and which endowed their exciting universal promises with a deadly exclusionary force. Perhaps, without sounding overly defensive, I can identify Adorno´s insightful remarks on the value of heresy as a guiding thread for my own wanderings in the labyrinth of "race" politics. "Through violations of the orthodoxy of thought, something in the object becomes visible which it is orthodoxy´s secret and objective aim to keep invisible" (Adorno 1993: 23).

I hope it is not too obvious to point out that the ideal of humanity, too narrowly defined, emerged from this revolution in thinking in filleted form. It was not only something to be monopolized by Europeans, it could exist only in neatly bounded, integral units. The national principle that rationalized this peculiar notion was founded, as Claude Lefort has pointed out, on the idea of "the people as one" which would later put hinges on the doorway into totalitarian possibilities. It denied "that division is constitutive of society." It accentuated the interchangeability and disposability of the nation´s members—its population. In time, they would also be discovered to exist in the strict organic patterns of a natural hierarchy that continued and extended the pre-modern typologies of race thinking in the direction of a totalizing bio-social science.

By this point, as numerous scholars have observed, "race" would be secure as a central philosophical, economic and historical concept. In some national traditions, it summoned up a political ontology so fundamental that it could supply unsentimental form and ruthless logic to the unfolding of history itself (Connerton 1983: 110). History with a capital letter was reconceptualized in geographical and geo-political designs. Inferior, no longer merely different, races were

excluded from its compass. Their exclusion by means of racialized rationality had the clearest implications for the folly of imagining human beings to be an essentially undifferentiated collectivity. Hegel understood the implications of this point when, in his geographical theory of history, he wrote these words: "The peculiarly African character is difficult to comprehend, for the very reason that in reference to it we must give up the principle which naturally accompanies all *our* ideas— the category of universality" (Hegel 1900: 93). There it is, his own symptomatic apprehension that raciology cut the modern political imaginary to the core. This primal ontology of "race" would become so powerful that the necessarily unnatural world of formal politics could only seem trivial and insubstantial by comparison. In *The Black Atlantic* (1993), I have tried to show that it can be answered by a primal, counter-history of modernity that takes the lives of slaves and their descendants as a privileged point of departure.

The racialization of the nation state and the consequent transformation of the national community involved a comprehensive negation and repudiation of politics as it had been practised in the past. Of course, the effects of this were not confined to the victims of raciology, who had, in any case, been deterred from cultivating or exercising themselves in any polity. I want to emphasize that it had important consequences for the beneficiaries of this new hierarchy as well. As we saw with Kant earlier, their consciousness was, as Fanon might have put it, amputated at this point. In many cases, they were offered an ideology of superiority, the glamour of whiteness, or Aryan-ness for example, as a form of compensation for the loss of that universal humanity. It bears repetition that the elaboration of raciology was toxic to the workings of politics, of political *culture*. Today, surveying its development affords a good means to observe the transformation of the nation into a new type of collective body, integrated spiritually as well as politically.

The spiritual, mystical and irrational aspects that gain in power under the constellation of raciology should not be underplayed in relation to the rational components in its anthropological and geographical schemes. Especially when closely bound to the workings of imperial nations, the concept of "race" can be appreciated as a successor to what Voegelin calls previous "body ideas"—the Greek polis and the idea of the mystical body of the Christian church. Right at the summit of imperial power, the nation was invested with characteristics associated with an equivalent type of bio-cultural kinship. The integrity of properly historic nations was imagined to derive from the activities of ancient sylvan tribes (MacDougall 1982). The damage done by these ideas is visible from Croatia to Canning Town.

I want to call the national and racial formations that resulted "camps," a name that emphasizes their hierarchical and regimented qualities rather than any organic features. The organic dimension has been widely commented upon as an antidote it supplied to mechanized modernity and its dehumanizing effects. In some cases, the final stages in the transformation of the nation into an embattled camp coincides with the rise of fascism as a distinctive political and cultural technology. However, I want to suggest that these developments have a wider currency. They are not adequately grasped if they are reduced too swiftly to an argument about the components of fascism as a generic phenomenon. I propose that we see them instead as associated with the perils and possibilities of modernity at a certain point in its unfolding. They communicate not only the entrance of "race" into the operations of modern political culture but also the confluence of "race" and nation in the service of authoritarian ends. It should be immediately apparent that nation states have often comprised camps in this straightforward descriptive sense. They are involutionary complexes in which the utterly fantastic idea of transmuting heterogeneity into homogeneity can be organized and amplified outwards and inwards.

Especially where "race" and nation become closely articulated, with each register of discourse conferring important legitimation on the other, the national principle can be recognized as forming an important bond between different and even opposing nationalisms that can become trapped in an embrace of mutual parasitism. The dominant varieties are bound to the subordinate by their shared notions of what nationality entails. Think, for example, of the recent history of Chief Buthelezi´s Inkatha Party, the strange ultra-nationalist alliances constructed in the cause of Holocaust denial or, even closer to home, of the connections made during the late 1980s between "third positionists" in the British National Front and the Nation of Islam in the USA.

What we can call camp thinking has distinctive rules and codes. However bitterly its practitioners may conflict with each other, their common approach to the problems of belonging and collective solidarity is betrayed by shared patterns for organizing thought about self and other, about the institution of collectivities to which one can be compelled to belong. That unexpected connection between sworn foes defines one axis of "race" politics in the twentieth century. What might be more properly termed the (anti) politics of "race" is deeply implicated in the institution of the camp and the emergence of national statecraft as an alternative to more traditional conceptions of politics, Politics is thus reconceptualized and reconstituted in a dualistic conflict between friends and enemies. At worst, citizenship becomes soldiery alone and the political imaginary is comprehensively militarized. The exaltation of war and spontaneity, the cults of youth and violence, the explicitly anti-modern sacralization of the political sphere, its colonization by the civil religion of nationalism: uniforms, flags and mass spectacles, all underline that what I call camps are fundamentally militaristic phenomena. These camps are armed and protected spaces that offer, at best, only a temporary break in unforgiving motion towards the next demanding phase of active conflict.

Marx and Engels appropriated this conception of solidarity in opposition to nation states when, at the start of *The Communist Manifesto*, they described the world they saw progressively divided "into two great hostile camps ... facing each other" and aspired to break the allegiance of their universal class to its national bourgeoisies (1973: 68). They believed that antagonistic social forces more profound than those of the nation were constituted in this distinctive arrangement. It would be foolish to deny that the internal organization of class consciousness and class struggle can also foster what Alexander Kluge and Oscar Negt, in their discussion of the history of the proletarian public sphere, call a "camp mentality" (1993). Kluge´s and Negt´s concerns differ from mine in that they are directed towards histories of class and party as sources of camp thinking. They contrast the oppositional but nonetheless antidemocratic moods fostered in the sealed-off space of the class-based camp with the open vitality that a public culture can accumulate even in the most beleaguered circumstances.

It should be obvious that camp solidarity can be constituted and fortified around dimensions of division, apart from class, especially when the resources of communicative technology—print, radio, film and now digital media—mediate solidarity-building. However, the camp mentalities constituted by appeals to "race" nation and ethnic difference, by the lore of blood, bodies and fantasies of absolute cultural identity, have some distinctive qualities. They revive a simple, pre-bourgeois homology between the state and the body and gain great authority through appeals to the ideal of purity which is accorded an inflated value. Their bio-political potency immediately raises questions of prophylaxis and hygiene: "as if the [social] body had to assure itself of its own identity by expelling waste matter" (Lefort 1986: 298). They demand the regulation of fertility as readily as they command the labour power of affiliates. Where the nation is a kin group supposedly composed of symmetrical and interchangeable family groups, the bodies of women are the favoured testing grounds for the principles of obligation, deference and duty that the camp demands. The debates about immigration and nationality that dominated British racial politics until quite recently have regularly presented the illegitimate presence of blacks as an invasion. They could also be used to illustrate each of these unsavoury features.

The camp mentality is also betrayed by its crude theories of culture and defined by the aspirations towards homogeneity, purity and unanimity that it nurtures. These words from James Callaghan's Home Office bi-centenary lecture from 1982 have stayed in my mind since I first encountered them while writing *There Ain't No Black*: "whatever their politics, Home Secretaries sprang from the same culture, a culture it was their duty to preserve if the country was to remain a good place to live in" (Gilroy 1987). Inside the fortifications of the national camp, culture is required to assume an artificial texture and an impossibly even consistency. Encampment puts an end to any sense of its development. Culture as process is arrested. Petrified and sterile, it is impoverished by a national obligation

not to change but to recycle the past in essentially unmodified form.

In his unwholesome nineteenth-century raciological enquiries into the meaning of nationality, Ernst Renan argued that there was an active contradiction between the demands of nation building and those of historical study. The nation and its new temporal order involved, for him, socialized forms of forgetting and historical error. These can be identified as further symptoms of the camp mentality. An orchestrated and enforced amnesia supplies the climate in which the national camp's principles of belonging and solidarity become attractive and powerful.

The idea of diaspora becomes significant here. I have used it to conjure up an altogether different cultural ecology. It introduces the possibility of an historical and experiential rift between the location of residence and the location of belonging. Diaspora demands the recognition of interculture. The complex and ambivalent identifications it promotes exist outside and sometimes in opposition to the political forms and codes of modern citizenship in its debased, camp form. The national encampment has regularly been presented as the institutional means to terminate diaspora dispersal. At one end of the communicative circuit this is to be accomplished by the assimilation of those who are out of place. At the other, a similar outcome is realized through the prospect of building a bigger and better camp in the place of origin. The fundamental equilibrium of natural nationality and civil society can thus be restored. In both options, it is the operation of an encamped nation-state that brings diaspora time to an end. Diaspora yearning and ambivalence are transformed into a simple unambiguous exile once the possibility of easy reconciliation with either the place of sojourn or the place of origin exists.

The national camp also represents the negation of diaspora because the latter places a premium on commemorative work. In diaspora culture has to be remembered and remade. Its determining powers cannot just be assumed to govern the reproduction of monolithic identity. The diaspora opposes the camp where it becomes comfortable in the in-between locations that camp thinking deprives of any significance.

For the members of the ethnic, national or racial camp, chronic conflict, a war in the background, latent as well as manifest hostility sanction some stern patterns of discipline, authority and deference. The camp operates under martial rules. Even if its ideologues speak the language of organic wholeness, it is stubbornly a place of mechanical solidarity. As it moves towards the totalitarian condition of permanent emergency, the camp is overdetermined by the terrifying sense that anything is possible.

Deliberately adopting a position between camps of this sort is not a sign of indecision or equivocation. It is a timely choice and it can, as I hope the diaspora example makes clear, be a positive if limited gesture against the patterns of authority, government and conflict that characterize raciological modernity's geometry of power. It can also yield richer theoretical understanding of culture as a travelling phenomenon.

Of course, occupying a space between camps means also that you are in danger of getting hostility from both sides, of being caught in the pincers of camp thinking. Responding to this perilous predicament involves re-thinking the practice of politics. We are immediately required to move outside the frustratingly simple binary categories we have inherited: left and right, racist and anti-racist. We need a political analysis that is alive to the fluidity and contingency of a situation that seems to lack precedents. The ultra-nationalists huddle together in cyberspace. The *Daily Mail* and the prime minister loudly join the family of Stephen Lawrence in the pursuit of justice. Diane Abbott MP acts the part of Alf Garnett in a local struggle against foreign nurses. Black and white boys in East London band together in the name of locality against alien Bengalis. We could say, in the interests of simplicity, that this is a political climate in which the prefix in words like postmodernity and post-traditional has begun to assert its presence. Whether we fasten on to the idea of postmodernity as something more than a provisional element in the enumeration of these novelties cannot be settled here, but the debate which that question raises is still useful.

If we are going to be able to operate in these new circumstances, it helps to approach the problem of camps from another angle. We must understand them not only as a means to comprehend the interrelation of space, identity and power with modern raciology but as sociological and historical features of a period in which that same raciology has constituted the most profound challenge to the deepest values of Occidental modernity.

I have already identified camps as locations in which particular versions of solidarity, belonging, kinship and identity have been devised, practised and policed. Now I want to turn away from the camp as a *metaphor* for the modern pathologies of "race" and nation and move towards a brief reflection upon actually existing camps. These were and are concrete institutions of radical evil, useless suffering and modern misery rather than odious if somehow routine expressions of the bad habits of power. To identify a connection between these different kinds of camp—in effect, to specify links between normal racism and nationalism and the exceptional state represented by genocidal fascisms—may be regarded as oversimple, even far-fetched. In recent British history, nationalism has sometimes been part of the best populist responses to menacing neofascisms that have been exposed as alien and unpatriotic. I endeavoured to answer arguments of that sort in *There Ain't No Black in the Union Jack*.

Tonight, I want to invoke a somewhat different case for that fateful linkage. This case is supported by the profane and bewildering tangles of recent post-colonial and post-imperial history. It was a case that, as the Martiniquean surrealist poet, philosopher and statesman Aimé Césaire has made clear, went to the bottom of the relationship between modern civilization and modern barbarism. The general message is certainly confirmed in the history of Rwanda where, in conjunction with modern cultural technologies and the civilizing mission of colonial power, raciology hardened pre-colonial conflicts into fully fledged neo-colonial ethnic absolutism. There too the emergence of camp thinking, camp nationality and encamped ethnicity— the key features of the first kind of camp—have been implicated in the institution of camps of the second variety: first, genocidal death camps and then, bewilderingly, refugee camps in which yesterday's killers become today's victims and reach out to us to seek aid and compassion.

Understanding these connections entails more than seeing these camps as epiphanies of catastrophic modernity and focusing on the colonial precedents for the genocidal killing that has happened within Europe. It necessitates recognizing our own predicament, caught not only between metaphorical camps but amid the uncertainties and anxieties that real camps both feed on and create. We are not inmates but their testimony calls out to us and we must answer it. Their moral claims might provide important reorientation in a world to which traditional moralities now say next to nothing. This prospect also means being alive to the camps out there now and the camps around the corner, the camps that are being prepared. With his own version of misanthropic humanism in mind, Zygmunt Bauman has suggested that our unstable time could, one day, be remembered as the Age of Camps. Camps are confirmation of the fact that cruelty has itself been modernized, sundered even from outmoded modern morality. Bauman, for whom a reconfigured humanism is neither explicitly post-anthropological nor post-colonial, makes no secret of his Europe-centredness. He has Auschwitz and the Gulag in mind rather than Kigali and Kisangani. I think that weakens his case but there is something valuable and eminently translatable in his polemical observation, especially if it does not prompt simplistic speculation about some easily accessible essence of modernity. In moving towards a different goal, I want to acknowledge the grave dangers that are involved in instrumentalizing extremity. However, I am going to set those important inhibitions cautiously aside in pursuit of a different role for the critical intellectual that is premised upon the way that the camps rupture modernity and constitute significant points of entry into an ethical and cultural climate associated with the repudiation of its more extravagant though nonetheless colour-coded promises. Adorno´s acute sense of the unhappy obligations that these novel circumstances placed upon the committed artist have a wider applicability and should be studied carefully by the committed academic lest "political reality is sold short for the sake of political commitment; that decreases the political impact as well" (Adorno 1992: 88–9).

I want to take the risk of identifying those camps: refugee camps, labour camps, punishment camps, concentration camps, even death camps, as providing opportunities for moral and political reflection in the careful sense described by the philosopher Stuart Hampshire who employs an explicit consideration of

Nazism as a means to refine his understanding of justice (Hampshire 1989: 66–72). Other writers, particularly the German sociologist of the concentration camps Wolfgang Sofsky and the Ugandan political philosopher Mahmood Mamdani who adapted the concept of fascism in his analysis of the Amin regime, have guided and inspired me.

To link together the very different historical examples to which this diverse body of work is addressed is already to have transgressed against the prescriptive uniqueness invoked to protect the special status of the Nazi genocide. Without being drawn deeply into the question of what; if anything, constitutes a common denominator at an experiential level, we can observe that the camp and its extreme wrongs have been strongly associated with the demand for justice and with important attempts to clarify the normal moral and historical order of modernity where the state of emergency has become an everyday reality. A condition of social death is common to inmates in regimes of unfreedom, coercion and systematic brutality. If genocide is not already under way, modern raciologies bring it closer and promote it as a rational solution. It is "race," to borrow some terms from Primo Levi, which explains how the outrage motive triumphs over modernity´s signature: the profit motive. The death factory is not itself a camp—its inmates are not alive long enough. But camps gain something from their proximity to the death factory. Tadeusz Borowski´s work springs to mind as our most vivid exploration of the articulation of the camp and the death factory. We can proceed heuristically by arguing that the camp is not always a death factory though it can easily become one and that the death factory is one possible variation on the patterns of rational administration that the camp initializes. The procedures of the death factory might also be thought of as partially derivative of the camps that preceded them in Europe and outside it. The definitive statement of this argument is found, of course, in Césaire´s angry and moving indictment of the West´s inability to live a humanism "made to the measure of the world" in his *Discourse on Colonialism*.

I have already hinted that the second type of camp is especially important to me because it has provided some stern tests for the critical intellectual. Jean Améry, Primo Levi's most profound, though not his most unsettling, interlocutor—that title is reserved for Borowski—describes the shock of discovering the redundancy of his own egg-head learning in the camp where, without technical or practical skills and religious certainties, intellectuals were less well equipped and more vulnerable than many of their fellows.

> Not only was rational-analytic thinking in the camp and, particularly in Auschwitz of no help, but it led straight into a tragic dialectic of self-destruction.... First of all the intellectual did not so easily acknowledge the unimaginable conditions as a given fact as did the nonintellectual. Long practice in questioning the phenomena of everyday reality prevented him from simply adjusting to the realities of the camp, because these stood in all-too-sharp a contrast to everything that he had regarded until then as possible and humanly acceptable.
>
> (Améry 1980: 10)

It is interesting too that Améry was driven to discover the power of even limited counter-violence in the restoration of the human dignity of which he had been deprived. He points to another of those resonant connections which produces hesitation, shuffling and embarrassed silences. In these circumstances, it should be noted, his body did not spontaneously manifest the absolute truths of its "racial" otherness. His words are all the more notable because they make no concessions to the veracity of racial difference coded into the body by nature rather than human endeavour:

> Painfully beaten, I was satisfied with myself. But not, as one might think, for reasons of courage and honor, but only because I had grasped well that there are situations in life in which our body is our entire self and our entire fate. I was my body and nothing else: in hunger, in the blow that I suffered, in the blow that I dealt. My body, debilitated and crusted with filth, was my calamity. My body, when it tensed to strike, was my physical and metaphysical dignity. In situations like mine, physical violence is the sole means for restoring a disjointed personality. In the punch I was myself—for myself and for my opponent.

What I later read in Frantz Fanon's *Les damnés de la terre*, in a theoretical analysis of the behaviour of colonised peoples, I anticipated back then when I gave concrete form to my dignity by punching a human face. To be a Jew meant the acceptance of the death sentence imposed by the world as a world verdict. To flee before it by withdrawing into oneself would have been nothing but a disgrace, whereas acceptance was simultaneously the physical revolt against it. I became a person not by subjectively appealing to my abstract humanity but by discovering myself within the given social reality as a rebelling Jew and by realising myself as one.

> (Améry 1980: 90–1)

His extraordinary account of his experiences in Auschwitz Monowitz and a number of other camps might be provocatively placed alongside the reflections of Léopold Sédar Senghor. The Senegalese poet, philosopher statesman and influential theorist of Négritude was confined in the prison camp Frontstalag 230 with other colonial troops drawn from very different social backgrounds from his own élite formation. Saved from a racist massacre that took the lives of his fellow colonials by the intervention of a French officer, Senghor sought comfort in the songs, poems and stories of his fellow Africans but also in the classic works of European philosophy and literature. This did not redeem the camp, but it does help him to reconstitute his sense of humanity out of absolutism's reach but still under its nose. He describes how his reading—particularly of Goethe—triggered a "veritable conversion" that enabled him to live with the complex transcultural patterns of his own hybrid mentality and to see that inter-mixture as something more than the loss and betrayal we are always told it must be. His comprehension of the relationship between the particular and the universal was thus transformed along with his understanding of the project Négritude itself. In one essay, "Goethe's message to the new Negroes" he describes how, standing at the camp's barbed wire, he arrived at these important insights under the uncomprehending gaze of a Nazi sentinel:

> I had been in the camp for "colonial" prisoners of war for one year.... My progress in German had at last enabled me to read Goethe's poetry in the original.... The defeat of France and of the West

in 1940 had, at first, stupefied black intellectuals. We soon awoke under the sting of the catastrophe naked and sober.... It is thus, I thought close to the barbed wire of the camp, that our most incarnate voice, our most Negro works would be at the same time our most human...and the Nazi sentry looked me up and down with an imbecilic air. And I smiled at him, and he didn't understand.

Strange meeting, significant lesson.

(Senghor 1964: 84–6, my translation)

These are only tiny examples. Many more could be drawn from the brave and strange lives of other, perhaps lesser known, black witnesses to European barbarity. Their complex consciousness of the dangers of camp thinking and good understanding of the anti-toxins that can be discovered and celebrated in crossing cultures provide important resources which today's post-colonial peoples will require if we are to weather the storms that lie ahead as we leave the century of the colour line. The need to find responses to globalization has stimulated some new and even more desperate varieties of camp thinking.

One of the many important things that examples drawn from the generation that faced European fascism can communicate today is an invitation to contemplate the precarious nature of our own political environments. Reflecting on the brutal context in which these testimonies were first uttered and thinking about the institutional patterns that fitted around them makes it easier to grasp that we inhabit a precious but nonetheless beleaguered niche in what used to be, but is no longer, a state of emergency. Modernity's limited

triumphs are besieged. As democracy, as creativity and as cosmopolitan hope, they are pitted against a moribund system of formal politics and its numbing representational codes; against the corrosive values of economic rationality and the abjection of post-industrial urban life. The persistence of fascism and the widespread mimicry of its styles is only the most alarming sign that the best of modernity is assailed from all sides by political movements and technological forces that work towards the erasure of ethical considerations and the deadening of aesthetic sensibilities. The resurgent power of racist and racializing language, of raciology in its new genomic form, is a strong link between the perils of our own time and the enduring effects of the past horrors that continue to haunt us in Europe.

Modernity is on trial and fascism is on hold. We must debate the value of the term postmodernity as an interpretative device turned towards these novel conditions. However that problem is resolved, the camp experiences I have recovered and briefly commemorated are addressed to it, if only because they promote a reflexive, untrusting perspective towards the truth claims made by modernity's complacent advocates as well as its sworn foes and their latter-day inheritors. We must claim that legacy now. It helps to appreciate that the achievements of modernity are in continual jeopardy but it might be even more important to be able to welcome their incomplete and suspended state as a further source of insight and moral inspiration. Perhaps it is possible to recognize in that vulnerable condition a new sense of moral agency and the stirrings of an appropriate response to the wrongs that raciology has sanctioned in the "age of camps"?

REFERENCES

Adorno, T. W. (1992) `Commitment´, in *Notes on Literature 2*, trans. Shierry Weber Nicholson, New York: Columbia University Press.

——(1993) `The essay as form´, in *Notes On Literature I*, trans. Shierry Weber Nicholson, New York: Columbia University Press.

Améry, J. (1980) *At The Mind's Limits*, trans. S. and S. P. Rosenfeld, Bloomington, IN: Indiana University Press.

Césaire, A. (1972) *Discourse on Colonialism*, trans. Joan Pinkham, New York: Monthly Review Press.

Connerton, P. (1983) *The Tragedy of Enlightenment*, Cambridge: Cambridge University Press.

Gilroy, P. (1987) *Ain't No Black in the Union Jack: The Cultural Politics of Race and Nation*, London: Hutchinson.

——(1993) *Black Atlantic: Modernity and Double Consciousness*, Cambridge, MA: Harvard University Press.

Hampshire, S. (1989) *Innocence and Experience*, Cambridge, MA: Harvard University Press.

Hegel, G. W. F. (1900) *The Philosophy of History*, trans. J. Sibree, New York: Dover.

Kant, I. (1950) `On the different races of man´, in Count, E. W. (ed.) *This is Race*, Henry Schuman.

——(1978) *Anthropology from a Pragmatic Point of View*, trans. Victor Lyle Dowdell, Southern Illinois Press.

Kluge, A. and Negt, O. (1993) *Public Sphere and Experience*, trans. P. Labanyi *et al.*, Minneapolis: University of Minnesota Press.

Lefort, C. (1986) *The Political Forms of Modern Society*, Cambridge: Polity.

MacDougall, H. A. (1982) *Racial Myth in English History: Trojans, Teutons and Anglo-Saxons.* University Press of New England.

Marx, K. and Engels, F. (1973) `The Manifesto of the Communist Party´, in *Political Writings*, Vol. 1, edited and introduced by David Fernback, Harmondsworth: Pelican Books.

Senghor, L. S. (1964) `Le Message de Goethe aux Nègres nouveaux´, in *Liberté 1 Négritude et Humanisme*, Paris: Seuil.

58. THE RISE AND FALL OF MULTICULTURALISM?

WILL KYMLICKA

Will Kymlicka (b. 1962) is currently the Canadian Research Professor in Political Philosophy at Queen's University. Along with fellow Canadian philosopher Charles Taylor, Kymlicka is one of the world's preeminent theorists of multiculturalism, beginning with his influential book *Multicultural Citizenship* (1995), in which he articulated a normative rationale for what he called liberal multiculturalism. Since then he has attempted in a variety of ways to connect normative claims to careful empirical analyses of multicultural policies and practices. Recently, along with Keith Banting, he has created the Multicultural Policy Index to assess multicultural policies in Western democracies. In this article, Kymlicka reacts to the increasingly common narrative that the dramatic rise of multiculturalism near the end of the past century has been followed by an equally spectacular fall. Disputing this narrative, he summarizes his understanding of what multiculturalism actually is and then proceeds to argue that claims about its presumed demise are off the mark.

Ideas about the legal and political accommodation of ethnic diversity have been in a state of flux for the past 40 years around the world. A familiar way of describing these changes is in terms of the rise and fall of multiculturalism. Indeed, this has become a kind of master narrative, widely invoked by scholars, journalists and policy-makers alike to explain the evolution of contemporary debates about diversity. Although people disagree about what comes after multiculturalism, there is a surprising consensus that we are indeed in a post-multicultural era.

My goal in this article will be to explore and critique this master narrative and to suggest an alternative framework for thinking about the choices we face. In order to make progress, I suggest, we need to dig below the surface of the master narrative. Both the rise and fall of multiculturalism have been very uneven processes, depending on the nature of the issue and the country involved, and we need to understand these variations if we are to identify a more sustainable model for accommodating diversity.

In its simplest form, the master narrative goes like this (for influential academic statements of this rise and fall narrative, claiming that it applies across the western democracies, see Brubaker 2001; Joppke 2004; cf. Baubock 2002. There are also many accounts of the decline, retreat, or crisis of multiculturalism in particular countries, such as The Netherlands (Entzinger 2003; Koopmans 2006; Prins and Slijper 2002), the UK (Back *et al.* 2002; Hansen 2007; Vertovec 2005), Australia (Ang and Stratton 2001) and Canada (Wong *et al.* 2005):

- From the 1970s to mid-1990s there was a clear trend across western democracies towards the increased recognition and accommodation of diversity through a range of multiculturalism policies and minority rights. These policies were endorsed both at the domestic level in various states and by international organisations, and involved a rejection of earlier ideas of unitary and homogenous nationhood.
- Since the mid-1990s, however, we have seen a backlash and retreat from multiculturalism, and a re-assertion of ideas of nation building, common values and identity, and unitary citizenship – even a return of assimilation.

- This retreat is partly driven by fears amongst the majority group that the accommodation of diversity has gone too far and is threatening their way of life. This fear often expresses itself in the rise of nativist and populist right-wing political movements, such as the Danish People's Party, defending old ideas of "Denmark for the Danish".
- But the retreat also reflects a belief amongst the centre-left that multiculturalism has failed to help the intended beneficiaries – namely, minorities themselves – because it has failed to address the underlying sources of their social, economic and political exclusion, and may indeed have unintentionally contributed to their social isolation. As a result, even the centre-left political movements that had initially championed multiculturalism, such as the social democratic parties in Europe, have backed away from it and shifted to a discourse that emphasizes ideas of integration, social cohesion, common values, and shared citizenship (For an overview of the attitudes of European social democratic parties to these issues, see Cuperus *et al.* 2003. There are also political perspectives on multiculturalism beyond the populist right and the social-democratic left. For example, the radical left has traditionally viewed multiculturalism as a state-led reformist project that seeks to contain the transformative potential of subaltern political movements and thereby forecloses the possibility of a more radical critique of the capitalist nation-state (Day 2000; Žižek 1997). The French republican tradition, in both its right and left strands, has also generally opposed multiculturalism as an obstacle to its vision of equality and emancipation (Laborde 2009). However, since the radical left and the republicans were never in favour of multiculturalism their opposition does not explain the rise and fall narrative. This narrative presupposes that former supporters of multiculturalism have now lost faith in it, and I believe that it is predominantly amongst the social democrats that one can see this sort of rise and fall).
- The social-democratic discourse of national integration differs from the radical right discourse in emphasising the need to develop a more inclusive national identity and to fight racism and discrimination, but nonetheless distances itself from the rhetoric and policies of multiculturalism. The term "post-multiculturalism" has often been invoked to signal this new approach, which seeks to overcome the perceived limits of a naive or misguided multiculturalism while avoiding the oppressive reassertion of homogenising nationalist ideologies. For references to post-multiculturalism by progressive intellectuals and academics, who distinguish it from the radical right's anti-multiculturalism, see Alibhai-Brown (2000, 2003, 2004) re the UK, Ley (2005), Jupp (2007) re Australia, and King (2004) and Hollinger (2006) re the USA.

This, in brief, is the master narrative of the rise and fall of multiculturalism. It helpfully captures important features of our current debates. Yet in some respects it is misleading and may obscure the real challenges and opportunities we face.

In the rest of this article, I will argue that the master narrative (a) mischaracterises the nature of the experiments in multiculturalism that have been undertaken over the past 40 years, (b) exaggerates the extent to which they have been abandoned and (c) misidentifies the genuine difficulties and limitations they have encountered.

WHAT IS MULTICULTURALISM?

In much of the post-multiculturalism literature, multiculturalism is characterised as a feel-good celebration of ethno-cultural diversity, encouraging citizens to acknowledge and embrace the panoply of customs, traditions, music and cuisine that exist in a multi-ethnic society. Alibhai-Brown calls this the 3S model of multiculturalism in Britain – samosas, steel drums and saris (Alibhai-Brown 2000). Multiculturalism takes these familiar cultural markers of ethnic groups – cuisine, music and clothing – and treats them as authentic cultural practices to be preserved by their members and safely consumed as cultural spectacles by others. So they are taught in multicultural school curricula, performed in multicultural festivals, displayed in multicultural media and museums, and so on.

This 3S picture of multiculturalism has been subject to many powerful critiques:

- It entirely ignores issues of economic and political inequality. Even if all Britons come to enjoy Jamaican steel drum music or Indian samosas, this by itself would do nothing to address the real problems facing Caribbean and South-Asian communities in Britain – problems of unemployment, poor educational outcomes, residential segregation, poor English language skills and political marginalisation. These economic and political issues cannot be solved simply by celebrating cultural difference.
- Even with respect to the (legitimate) goal of promoting greater understanding of cultural difference, the focus on celebrating discrete authentic cultural practices that are unique to each group is potentially dangerous and misleading. Firstly, not all customs that may be traditionally practiced in a particular group are worthy of being celebrated or even of being legally tolerated, such as forced marriage. To avoid this risk, there is a tendency to choose safely inoffensive practices as the focus of multicultural celebrations – such as cuisine or music – practices that can be enjoyably consumed by members of the larger society. But this runs the opposite risk of the trivialisation or Disneyfying of cultural difference (Bissoondath 1994), ignoring the real challenges that differences in cultural values and religious doctrine can raise.
- Secondly, the 3S model of multiculturalism can encourage a conception of groups as hermetically sealed and static, each reproducing its own distinct authentic practices. Multiculturalism may be intended to encourage people to share their distinctive customs, but the very assumption that each group has its own distinctive customs ignores processes of cultural adaptation, mixing and mélange, and renders invisible emerging cultural commonalities, thereby potentially reinforcing perceptions of minorities as eternally "Other".
- Thirdly, this model can end up reinforcing power inequalities and cultural restrictions within minority groups. In deciding which traditions are authentic and how to interpret and display them, the state generally consults the traditional elites within the group – typically older men – while ignoring the way these traditional practices (and traditional elites) are often challenged by internal reformers, who have different views about how, say, a good Muslim should act. It can therefore imprison people in cultural scripts that they are not allowed to question or dispute.

According to post-multiculturalists, it is the gradual recognition of these flaws that explains the retreat from multiculturalism and the search for new post-multicultural models of citizenship that emphasise the priority of political participation and economic opportunities over the symbolic politics of cultural recognition, the priority of human rights and individual freedom over respect for cultural traditions, the priority of building inclusive common national identities over the recognition of ancestral cultural identities, and the priority of cultural change and cultural mixing over the reification of static cultural differences.

Is this post-multiculturalist critique accurate and justified? If multiculturalism was fundamentally about celebrating cultural difference in the form of discrete folk practices, then the critique would indeed be justified. However, I will argue that the 3S account is a caricature of the reality of multiculturalism as it has developed over the past 40 years in western democracies, at least as multiculturalism is affirmed and embodied in public policy. To be sure, the 3S picture does accurately describe a certain sort of ethos or sensibility that exists in certain circles in modern societies. Within these circles, being able to enjoy a wide range of cuisines and cultural products from around the world is seen as a sign of sophistication and open-mindedness. But multiculturalism as a set of public policies has never been exclusively, or even primarily, about inculcating such an ethos of cultural consumption. If we focus on multiculturalism as a set of public policies rather than as a particular cultural sensibility, I believe that we will find a very different story from that presented in the post-multiculturalist critique.

In the rest of this article, therefore, I will be focusing on the rise and fall of multiculturalism policies – that is, on multiculturalism as a political project that attempts to redefine the relationship between ethno-cultural minorities and the state through the adoption of new laws, policies or institutions. (Thus, unless otherwise indicated, references to multiculturalism should be understood as references to multiculturalism policies). My focus is on why multiculturalism in this sense arose, what forms it has taken, what effects it has had and what obstacles it faces.

I cannot rehearse the full history of multiculturalism here, but I think it is important to situate it in its historical context. In one sense, multiculturalism is as old as humanity – different cultures have always found ways of co-existing and respect for diversity was a familiar feature of many empires throughout history, such as the Ottoman Empire. But the sort of multiculturalism that is said to have had a rise and fall is a much more specific historical phenomenon, emerging first in the western democracies in the late 1960s. This timing is important, for it helps us situate multiculturalism in relation to the larger social transformations of the post-war era.

More specifically, multiculturalism can be seen as part of a larger human rights revolution in relation to ethnic and racial diversity (for a more detailed discussion of the linkage between multiculturalism and the human rights revolution, from which these three paragraphs are taken, see Kymlicka 2007). Prior to the Second World War, ethno-cultural and religious diversity in the west was characterised by a range of illiberal and undemocratic relations – including the relations of conqueror and conquered, coloniser and colonised, master and slave, settler and indigenous, racialised and unmarked, normalised and deviant, orthodox and heretic, civilised and primitive, ally and enemy. These hierarchical relationships were justified by racialist ideologies that explicitly propounded the superiority of some peoples and cultures, and their right to rule over others. These ideologies were widely accepted throughout the western world, and underpinned both domestic laws (for example, racially biased immigration and citizenship policies) and foreign policies (for example, in relation to overseas colonies).

After the Second World War, however, the world recoiled against Hitler's fanatical and murderous use of such ideologies and the UN decisively repudiated them

in favour of a new ideology of racial and ethnic equality. And this new assumption of human equality has generated a series of political movements designed to contest the lingering presence or enduring effects of older hierarchies. We can distinguish three waves of such movements: (a) the struggle for decolonisation, concentrated in the period 1948 to 1965; (b) the struggle against racial segregation and discrimination, initiated and exemplified by the African–American civil rights movement from 1955 to 1965 and (c) the struggle for multiculturalism and minority rights that emerged from the late 1960s.

Each of these movements draws upon the human rights revolution and its foundational ideology of the equality of races and peoples, to challenge the legacies of earlier ethnic and racial hierarchies. Indeed, the human rights revolution plays a double role here: not just as the inspiration for struggle but also as a constraint on the permissible goals and means of that struggle. In so far as historically excluded or stigmatised groups struggle against earlier hierarchies in the name of equality, they too have to renounce their own traditions of exclusion or oppression in the treatment of, say, women, gays, people of mixed race, religious dissenters, and so on. The framework of human rights, and of liberal-democratic constitutionalism more generally, provides the overarching framework within which these struggles are debated and addressed.

Each of these movements, therefore, can be seen as contributing to a process of democratic "citizenisation" – that is, turning the earlier catalogue of hierarchical relations into relationships of liberal-democratic citizenship, both in terms of the vertical relationship between the members of minorities and the state and the horizontal relationships amongst the members of different groups. In the past it was often assumed that the only way to engage in this process of citizenisation was to impose a single undifferentiated model of citizenship on all individuals. But the ideas and policies of multiculturalism that emerged from the 1960s start from the assumption that this complex history inevitably and appropriately generates group-differentiated ethno-political claims. The key to citizenisation is not to suppress these differential claims but to filter and frame them through the language of human rights, civil liberties and democratic accountability. This is what multiculturalist movements have aimed to do.

The precise character of the resulting multicultural reforms varies from group to group, as befits the distinctive history that each has faced. They all start from the anti-discrimination principle that underpinned the second wave but go beyond it to challenge other forms of exclusion or stigmatisation. In most western countries explicit state-sponsored discrimination against ethnic, racial or religious minorities had largely ceased by the 1960s and 1970s, under the influence of the second wave of human rights struggles. Yet evidence of ethnic and racial hierarchies remained and continues to be clearly visible in many societies, whether measured in terms of economic inequalities, political underrepresentation, social stigmatisation or cultural invisibility. Various forms of multiculturalism have been developed to help overcome these lingering inequalities.

We can broadly distinguish three patterns of multiculturalism that have emerged in the western democracies. Firstly, we see new forms of empowerment of indigenous peoples such as the Maori in New Zealand; Aboriginals in Canada and Australia; American Indians; Sami in Scandinavia or Inuit of Greenland. These new models of multicultural citizenship for indigenous peoples often include some combination of the following nine policies. (This and the following lists of multicultural policies are taken from the index of multicultural policies developed in Banting and Kymlicka 2006):

- recognition of land rights and title
- recognition of self-government rights
- upholding historic treaties and/or signing new treaties
- recognition of cultural rights (language; hunting and fishing, sacred sites)
- recognition of customary law
- guarantees of representation and consultation in the central government
- constitutional or legislative affirmation of the distinct status of indigenous peoples
- support and ratification for international instruments on indigenous rights
- affirmative action

Secondly, we see new forms of autonomy and power-sharing for sub-state national groups, such as the Basques and Catalans in Spain, the Flemish and Walloons in Belgium, the Scots and Welsh in Britain, Quebecois in Canada, Germans in South Tyrol, Swedish in Finland and so on. These new forms of multicultural citizenship for national minorities typically include some combination of the following six elements:

- federal or quasi-federal territorial autonomy
- official language status, either in the region or nationally
- guarantees of representation in the central government or on constitutional courts
- public funding of minority language universities, schools and the media
- constitutional or parliamentary affirmation of multinationalism
- accorded an international personality (for example, allowing the sub-state region to sit on international bodies, or sign treaties, or have their own Olympic team)

Finally, we see new forms of multicultural citizenship for immigrant groups, which may include a combination of the following eight policies:

- constitutional, legislative or parliamentary affirmation of multiculturalism at central, regional and municipal levels;
- the adoption of multiculturalism in school curriculum;
- the inclusion of ethnic representation and sensitivity in the mandate of public media or media licensing;
- exemptions from dress codes, Sunday-closing legislation and so on (either by statute or by court cases)
- allowed dual citizenship
- the funding of ethnic group organisations to support cultural activities
- the funding of bilingual education or mother-tongue instruction
- affirmative action for disadvantaged immigrant groups

While there are important differences between these three modes of multiculturalism, each of them has been defended as a means to overcome the legacies of earlier hierarchies and to help build fairer and more inclusive democratic societies.

In my view, therefore, multiculturalism is first and foremost about developing new models of democratic citizenship, grounded in human rights ideals, to replace earlier uncivil and undemocratic relations of hierarchy and exclusion. Needless to say, this account of multiculturalism as citizenisation differs dramatically from the 3S account of multiculturalism as the celebration of static cultural differences. The citizenisation account says that multiculturalism is precisely about constructing new civic and political relations to overcome the deeply entrenched inequalities that have persisted after the abolition of formal discrimination.

It is obviously important to determine which of these accounts provides a more accurate description of the western experience with multiculturalism. Before we can decide whether to celebrate or lament the fall of multiculturalism or to replace it with post-multiculturalism, we need first to make sure we know what multiculturalism has in fact been. I have elsewhere tried to give a fuller defence of my account (Kymlicka 2007, pp. 63–167), so let me here just note three ways in which the 3S account is misleading.

Firstly, the claim that multiculturalism is solely or primarily about symbolic cultural politics depends on a complete misreading of the actual policies. If we look at the three lists of policies above, it is immediately apparent that they combine economic, political, social and cultural dimensions. Take the case of land claims for indigenous peoples. While regaining control of their traditional territories certainly has cultural and religious significance for many indigenous peoples, it also has profound economic and political significance. Land is the material basis for both economic opportunities and political self-government. Or consider language rights for national minorities. According official language status to a minority's language is partly valued as a form of symbolic recognition of a historically stigmatised language. But it is also a form of economic and political empowerment: the more a minority's language is used in public institutions, the more its speakers have access to employment opportunities and decision-making procedures. Indeed, the political and economic dimensions of the multiculturalist struggles of indigenous peoples and national minorities are obvious: they are precisely about restructuring state institutions, including redistributing political control over important public and natural resources.

The view that multiculturalism is about the apolitical celebration of ethnic folk customs, therefore, has plausibility only in relation to immigrant groups. And indeed, representations of cuisine, dress and music are often the most visible manifestations of multiculturalism in the schools and the media. It is not surprising, therefore, that when post-multiculturalists discuss multiculturalism they almost invariably ignore the issue of indigenous peoples and national minorities and focus only on the case of immigrant groups, where the 3S account has more initial plausibility.

But even in this context, if we look back at the list of eight multiculturalism policies adopted in relation to immigrant groups, we quickly see that they too involve a complex mixture of economic, political and cultural elements. While immigrants are (rightly) concerned to contest the historical stigmatisation of their cultures, immigrant multiculturalism also includes policies that are centrally concerned with access to political power and to economic opportunities – for example, policies of affirmative action, mechanisms of political consultation, funding for ethnic self-organisation or facilitated access to citizenship.

All three familiar patterns of multiculturalism, therefore – for indigenous peoples, national minorities and immigrant groups – combine cultural recognition, economic redistribution and political participation. In this respect, the post-multiculturalist critique that multiculturalism ignores economic and political inequality is simply off the mark. Nevertheless, the fact that multiculturalism policies were designed with an awareness of these inequalities and sought to address them does not show that they have been effective in redressing inequalities. Multiculturalism policies, like all public policies, can have perverse and unintended effects and it is possible that multiculturalism has unintentionally obscured or exacerbated inequalities or weakened the welfare state. However, a major cross-national study of the impact of multiculturalism on the welfare state shows no evidence of such unintended effects (Banting and Kymlicka 2006).

Secondly, the post-multiculturalists' claim that multiculturalism ignores the importance of universal human rights is equally misplaced. On the contrary, as we've seen, multiculturalism is itself a human rights-based movement, inspired and constrained by principles of universal human rights and liberal-democratic constitutionalism. Its goal is to challenge the sorts of traditional ethnic and racial hierarchies that have been discredited by the post-war human rights revolution. Understood in this way, multiculturalism as citizenisation offers no support for protecting or accommodating the sorts of illiberal cultural practices in minority groups that have also been discredited by this human rights revolution. The same human rights-based reasons we have for endorsing multiculturalism as citizenisation are the same reasons we have for rejecting cultural practices that violate human rights. And indeed, this is what we see throughout the western democracies. Wherever multiculturalist public policies have been adopted they have been tied conceptually and institutionally to larger human rights norms and have been subject to the overarching principles of the liberal-democratic constitutional order. No western democracy has exempted immigrant groups from constitutional norms of human rights in order to maintain practices of, say, forced marriage, the criminalisation of apostasy or cliterodectomy. Here again, the post-multiculturalist claim that human rights should take precedence over the recognition of cultural traditions simply reasserts what has been integral to the theory and practice of multiculturalism.

This in turn points out the flaws in the post-multiculturalists' claim that multiculturalism ignores or denies the reality of cultural change. On the contrary, multiculturalism as citizenisation is a deeply (and intentionally) transformative project, both for minorities and majorities. It demands that both dominant and historically subordinated groups engage in new practices, enter new relationships and embrace new concepts and discourses, all of which profoundly transform people's identities and practices.

This is perhaps most obvious in the case of the historically dominant majority nation in each country which is required to renounce fantasies of racial superiority, to relinquish claims to exclusive ownership of the state and to abandon attempts to fashion public institutions solely in its own national image. In fact, much of multiculturalism's long march through the institutions consists precisely in identifying and attacking those deeply rooted traditions, customs and symbols that have historically excluded or stigmatised minorities. Much has been written about the transformations in majority identities and practices this has required and the backlash it can create.

But multiculturalism is equally transformative of the identities and practices of minority groups. Many of these groups have their own histories of ethnic and racial prejudice, of anti-Semitism, of caste and gender exclusion, of religious triumphalism and of political authoritarianism, all of which are delegitimised by the norms of liberal-democratic multiculturalism and minority rights. Moreover, even where the traditional practices of a minority group are free of illiberal or undemocratic elements they may involve a level of cultural closure that becomes unattractive and unsustainable under multiculturalism. These practices may have initially emerged as a response to earlier experiences of discrimination, stigmatisation, or exclusion at the hands of the majority and may lose their attractiveness as that motivating experience fades in people's memories. For example, some minority groups have developed distinctive norms of self-help, endogamy and internal conflict resolution because they have been excluded from or discriminated against in the institutions of the larger society. Those norms may lose their rationale as ethnic and racial hierarchies break down and as group members feel more comfortable interacting with members of other groups and participating in state institutions. Far from guaranteeing the protection of the traditional ways of life of either the majority or minorities, multiculturalism poses multiple challenges to them. Here again, the post-multiculturalists' claim about recognising the necessity of cultural change simply reasserts a long-standing part of the multicultural agenda.

In short, I believe that the post-multiculturalist critique is largely off target, primarily because it misidentifies the nature and goals of the multiculturalism policies and programmes that have emerged over the past 40 years during the rise of multiculturalism.

THE RETREAT FROM MULTICULTURALISM?

But this then raises a puzzle. If post-multiculturalist claims about the flaws of multiculturalism are largely misguided, then what explains the fall of multiculturalism? If, as I claim, multiculturalism is inspired by human rights norms and seeks to deepen relations of democratic citizenship, why has there been such a retreat from it?

Part of the answer is that reports of multiculturalism's death are very much exaggerated. Here again, we need to keep in mind the different forms that multiculturalism takes, only some of which have faced a serious backlash. For example, there has been no retreat from the commitment to new models of multicultural citizenship for indigenous peoples. On the contrary, the trend towards enhanced land rights, self-government powers and customary law for indigenous peoples remains fully in place across the western democracy and was recently reaffirmed by the UN's General Assembly through the adoption of the Declaration of the Rights of Indigenous Peoples in 2007. Similarly, there has been no retreat from the commitment to new models of multicultural citizenship for national minorities. On the contrary, the trend towards enhanced language rights and regional autonomy for sub-state national groups remains fully in place in the western democracies (although there has been a retreat from attempts to formulate the rights of national minorities at the level of international law: see Kymlicka 2007, pp. 173–246). Indeed, these two trends are increasingly firmly entrenched in law and public opinion, backed by growing evidence that the adoption of multicultural reforms for indigenous peoples and national minorities has in fact contributed to building relations of democratic freedom and equality (I survey the evidence in Kymlicka 2007, pp. 135–167). Few people today, for example, would deny that regional autonomy for Catalonia has contributed to the democratic consolidation of Spain or that indigenous rights are helping to deepen democratic citizenship in Latin America.

So it is only with respect to immigrant groups that we see any serious retreat. Here, without question, there has been a backlash against multiculturalism policies relating to post-war migrants in several western democracies. And there is also greater scholarly dispute about the impact of these policies. For example, while studies have shown that immigrant multiculturalism policies in Canada have had strongly beneficial effects in relation to citizenisation (Bloemraad 2006), other studies suggest that immigrant multiculturalism in the Netherlands has had deleterious effects (Koopmans et al. 2005; Sniderman and Hagendoorn 2007) (I discuss these Dutch studies in Kymlicka 2008).

It is an important question why immigrant multiculturalism in particular has been so controversial, and I will return to this below. But we can begin by dismissing one popular explanation. Various commentators have suggested that the retreat from immigrant multiculturalism reflects a return to the traditional liberal and republican belief that ethnicity belongs in the private sphere, and that citizenship should be unitary and undifferentiated. On this view, the retreat from immigrant multiculturalism reflects a rejection of the whole idea of multiculturalism as citizenisation (for example, Brubaker 2001; Joppke 2004).

But this cannot be the explanation. If western democracies were rejecting the very idea of multicultural citizenship, they would have rejected the claims of sub-state national groups and indigenous peoples as well as immigrants. After all, the claims of national groups and indigenous peoples typically involve a much more dramatic insertion of ethno-cultural diversity into the public sphere, and a more dramatic degree of differentiated citizenship than is demanded by immigrant groups. Whereas immigrants typically seek modest variations or exemptions in the operation of mainstream institutions, historically national minorities and indigenous peoples typically seek a much wider level of recognition and accommodation, including such things as land claims, self-government powers, language rights, separate educational systems and even separate legal systems. These claims involve a much more serious challenge to ideas of undifferentiated citizenship and the privatisation of ethnicity than is involved in accommodating immigrant groups. Yet western democracies have not retreated at all from their commitment to accommodating these historic minorities.

Most western democracies are, in fact, increasingly comfortable with claims to differentiated citizenship and the public recognition of difference, when these claims are advanced by historic minorities. So it is not the very idea of multicultural citizenship per se that has come under attack. Commentators who argue that western democracies are rejecting multicultural citizenship per se typically simply ignore the obvious counter-examples of national minorities and indigenous peoples — see, for example Joppke (2004) and Barry (2001). The problem, rather, is specific to immigration. What we need to sort out, therefore, is why multiculturalism has proved to be so much more controversial in relation to this particular form of ethno-cultural diversity.

But even that way of phrasing the question is too general. The retreat from immigrant multiculturalism is not universal — it has affected some countries more than others. Public support for immigrant multiculturalism in Canada, for example, remains at an all-time high. And even in countries that are considered the paradigm cases of a retreat from immigrant multiculturalism, such as The Netherlands or Australia the story is more complicated. The Dutch military, for example, which in the 1990s had resisted ideas of accommodating diversity, has recently embraced the idea of multiculturalism, even as other public institutions are now shying away from it. And in Australia, while the former conservative federal government backed away from multiculturalism, the state governments (governed by the Labor party) have moved in to adopt their own new multiculturalism policies. What we see, in short, is a lot of uneven advances and retreats in relation to immigrant multiculturalism, both within and across countries.

So the post-multiculturalists' narrative of a retreat from multiculturalism is overstated and misdiagnosed. Many new forms of multicultural citizenship have taken root and not faced any significant backlash or retreat. This is true of the main reforms relating to both national minorities and indigenous peoples, backed by evidence of their beneficial effects. Even with respect to immigrant multiculturalism, claims of policy failure and retreat are overstated, obscuring a much more variable record in terms of policy outcomes and public support.

I now turn to some possible explanations for the distinctive fate of immigrant multiculturalism. But notice that we cannot start to identify these factors until we set aside the post-multiculturalists' assumption that what is being rejected is multiculturalism as such. What is happening here is not a general or principled rejection of the public recognition of ethnocultural diversity. On the contrary, many of the countries that are retreating from immigrant multiculturalism are actually strengthening the institutional recognition of their old minorities. For example, while The Netherlands is retreating from immigrant multiculturalism it is strengthening the rights of its Frisian minority; while France retreated from its brief flirtation with immigrant multiculturalism in education (see Bleich 1998), it is strengthening recognition of its long-standing regional minority languages; while Germany is retreating from immigrant multiculturalism, it is celebrating the 50th anniversary of the special status of its historic Danish minority; while Britain is retreating from immigrant multiculturalism, it has accorded new self-government powers to its historic nations in Scotland and Wales; and so on. None of this makes any sense if we explain the retreat from immigrant multiculturalism as somehow a return of orthodox liberal or republican ideas of undifferentiated citizenship and the privatisation of ethnicity.

In short, contrary to the post-multiculturalists' narrative, the ideal of multiculturalism as citizenisation is alive and well, and remains a salient option in the toolkit of democracies, in part because we now have 40 years of experience to show that it can indeed contribute to citizenisation. However, particular uses of this approach, in relation to particular forms of diversity in particular countries, have run into serious obstacles. Not all attempts to adopt new models of multicultural citizenship have taken root or succeeded in achieving their intended effects of promoting citizenisation.

The crucial question, therefore, is why multicultural citizenship works in some times and places and not others. This is aimed not only at explanations for the variable fate of multicultural citizenship in the west but also at exploring its potential role as a model for thinking about diversity in post-colonial and post-communist societies. Unfortunately, the post-multiculturalist debate is largely unhelpful in answering this question. Since post-multiculturalists ignore the extent to which multiculturalism ever aspired to citizenisation and also over-generalise the retreat from multiculturalism, they do not shed light on the central question of why multicultural citizenisation has flourished in some times and places and failed elsewhere.

REFERENCES

Alibhai-Brown, Y., 2000. *After multiculturalism*. London: Foreign Policy Centre.

—— 2003. Post-multiculturalism and citizenship values. Paper presented to Immigrant Council of Ireland Conference on Immigration, Ireland's Future, 11 December.

—— 2004. Beyond multiculturalism. *Canadian Diversity/Diversité Canadienne*, 3 (2), 51–54.

Ang, I. and Stratton, J., 2001. Multiculturalism in crisis: the new politics of race and national identity in Australia. *In:* I. Ang ed. *On not speaking Chinese: living between Asia and the west*. London: Routledge, 95–111.

Back, L., Keith, M., Khan, A., Shukra, K. and Solomos, J., 2002. New Labour's white heart: politics, multiculturalism and the return of assimilation. *Political Quarterly*, 73 (4), 445–454.

Banting, K. and Kymlicka, W., eds 2006. *Multiculturalism and the welfare state: recognition and redistribution in contemporary democracies*. (Oxford University Press, Oxford).

Baubock, R., 2002. Farewell to multiculturalism? Sharing values and identities in societies of immigration. *Journal of International Migration and Immigration*, 3 (1), 1–16.

Bissondath, N., 1994. *Selling illusions: the cult of multiculturalism in Canada*. Toronto: Penguin.

Bleich, E., 1998. From international ideas to domestic policies: educational multiculturalism in England and France. *Comparative Politics*, 31 (1), 81–100.

Bloemraad, I., 2006. *Becoming a citizen: incorporating immigrants and refugees in the United States and Canada*. Berkeley, CA: University of California Press.

Brubaker, R., 2001. The return of assimilation? *Ethnic and Racial Studies*, 24 (4), 531–548.

Cuperus, R., Duffek, K. and Kandel, J., eds 2003. *The challenge of diversity: European social democracy facing migration, integration and multiculturalism*. Innsbruck: Studien Verlag.

Day, R., 2000. *Multiculturalism and the history of Canadian diversity*. Toronto: University of Toronto Press.

Entzinger, H., 2003. The rise and fall of multiculturalism in the Netherlands. *In:* C. Joppke and E. Morawska eds *Toward assimilation and citizenship: immigrants in liberal nation-states*. London: Palgrave, 59–86.

Hansen, R., 2007. Diversity, integration and the turn from multiculturalism in the United Kingdom. *In:* K. Banting, T. Courchene and L. Seidle eds *Belonging? Diversity, recognition and shared citizenship in Canada*. Montreal: Institute for Research on Public Policy, 35–86.

Hollinger, D., 2006. *Post-ethnic America: beyond multiculturalism*. New York: Basic Books – revised edition.

Joppke, C., 2004. The retreat of multiculturalism in the liberal state: theory and policy. *British Journal of Sociology*, 55 (2), 237–257.

Jupp, J., 2007. *From white Australia to Woomera: the story of Australian immigration*. 2nd edn. Cambridge: Cambridge University Press.

King, D., 2004. *The liberty of strangers: making the American nation*. Oxford: Oxford University Press.

Koopmans, R., 2006. Trade-offs between equality and difference: the crisis of Dutch multiculturalism in cross-national perspective. Brief, December. Berlin: Danish Institute for International Affairs.

Koopmans, R., Statham, P., Guigni, M. and Passy, F., 2005. *Contested citizenship: immigration and cultural diversity in Europe*. Minneapolis, MI: University of Minnesota Press.

Kymlicka, W., 2007. Multicultural odysseys: navigating the new international politics of diversity. Oxford: Oxford University Press.

—— 2008. Review of Paul Sniderman and Louk Hagendoorn: when ways of life collide: multiculturalism and its discontents. *Perspectives on Politics*, 6 (4), 804–807.

Laborde, C., 2009. *Critical republicanism*. Oxford: Oxford University Press.

Ley, D., 2005. Post-multiculturalism? Working Paper 05–18. Vancouver: Metropolis British Columbia.

Prins, B. and Sluper, B., 2002. Multicultural society under attack. *Journal of International Migration and Immigration*, 3 (3–4), 313–328.

Sniderman, P. and Hagendoorn, L., 2007. *When ways of life collide*. Princeton. NJ: Princeton University Press.

Vertovec, S., 2005. *Pre-, high-, anti- and post-multiculturalism*. ESRC Centre on Migration, Policy and Society. Oxford: University of Oxford.

Wong, L., Garcea, J. and Kirova, A., 2005. An analysis of the anti- and post-multiculturalism discourses: the fragmentation position. Alberta: Prairie Centre for Excellence in Research on Immigration and Integration.

Žižek, S., 1997. Multiculturalism, or the cultural logic of multinational capitalism. *New Left Review*, 225, 28–51.

59. ETHNICITY WITHOUT GROUPS

ROGERS BRUBAKER

Rogers Brubaker (b. 1956) is currently a professor of sociology at UCLA, and was recently elected to the American Academy of Arts and Sciences. Previously, he was awarded a MacArthur Fellowship (popularly known as the "Genius Award"). While his early publications focused on the theme of rationality in the thought of Max Weber and on the work of Pierre Bourdieu, his more recent focus has been on ethnicity, nationalism, and citizenship. His book on *Citizenship and Nationhood in France and Germany* (1992) provided a model for exploring different citizenship regimes by contrasting France's civic nationalism to Germany's ethnic nationalism and exploring the implications of these differences for immigrants seeking to become naturalized citizens. Most recently, he coauthored *Nationalist Politics and Everyday Ethnicity in a Transylvanian Town* (2006), which offers a richly detailed account of the significance of ethnicity in the city of Cluj, Romania. He has also written a number of articles that attempt to clarify theoretical issues associated with ethnic and immigration studies, including assimilation, diaspora, identity, and ethnicity. "Ethnicity Without Groups," first published in 2002, has quickly become a widely cited article, one that takes aim at the essentializing and homogenizing tendency that treats ethnicity as a "thing" in much that is published in ethnic studies and seeks to offer as a corrective a perspective that stresses ethnicity's "relational, processual, and dynamic" character.

I. COMMON SENSE GROUPISM

Few social science concepts would seem as basic, even indispensable, as that of group. In disciplinary terms, "group" would appear to be a core concept for sociology, political science, anthropology, demography and social psychology. In substantive terms, it would seem to be fundamental to the study of political mobilization, cultural identity, economic interests, social class, status groups, collective action, kinship, gender, religion, ethnicity, race, multiculturalism, and minorities of every kind.

Yet despite this seeming centrality, the concept "group" has remained curiously unscrutinized in recent years. There is, to be sure, a substantial social psychological literature addressing the concept (Hamilton *et al.* 1998, McGrath 1984), but this has had little resonance outside that sub-discipline. Elsewhere in the social sciences, the recent literature addressing the concept "group" is sparse, especially by comparison with the immense literature on such concepts as class, identity, gender, ethnicity, or multiculturalism—topics in which the concept "group" is implicated, yet seldom analyzed in its own terms.[1] "Group" functions as a seemingly unproblematic, taken-for-granted concept, apparently in no need of particular scrutiny or explication. As a result, we tend to take for granted not only the concept "group" but also "groups"—the putative things-in-the-world to which the concept refers.

My aim in this paper is not to enter into conceptual or definitional casuistry about the concept of group. It is rather to address one problematic consequence of this tendency to take groups for granted in the study of ethnicity, race and nationhood, and in the study of ethnic, racial and national conflict in particular. This is what I will call groupism: the tendency to take discrete, sharply

Rogers Brubaker, "Ethnicity Without Groups" *Arch. Europ. Sociol.* vol. XLIII, no. 2, 2002, pp. 163–189. ✦

differentiated, internally homogeneous and externally bounded groups as basic constituents of social life, chief protagonists of social conflicts, and fundamental units of social analysis.[2] In the domain of ethnicity, nationalism and race, I mean by "groupism" the tendency to treat ethnic groups, nations and races as substantial entities to which interests and agency can be attributed. I mean the tendency to reify such groups, speaking of Serbs, Croats, Muslims and Albanians in the former Yugoslavia, of Catholics and Protestants in Northern Ireland, of Jews and Palestinians in Israel and the occupied territories, of Turks and Kurds in Turkey, or of Blacks, Whites, Asians, Hispanics and Native Americans in the United States as if they were internally homogeneous, externally bounded groups, even unitary collective actors with common purposes. I mean the tendency to represent the social and cultural world as a multichrome mosaic of monochrome ethnic, racial or cultural blocs.

From the perspective of broader developments in social theory, the persisting strength of groupism in this sense is surprising. After all, several distinct traditions of social analysis have challenged the treatment of groups as real, substantial things-in-the-world. These include such sharply differing enterprises as ethnomethodology and conversation analysis, social network theory, cognitive theory, feminist theory, and individualist approaches such as rational choice and game theory. More generally, broadly structuralist approaches have yielded to a variety of more "constructivist" theoretical stances, which tend—at the level of rhetoric, at least—to see groups as constructed, contingent, and fluctuating. And a diffuse postmodernist sensibility emphasizes the fragmentary, the ephemeral, and the erosion of fixed forms and clear boundaries. These developments are disparate, even contradictory in analytical style, methodological orientation and epistemological commitments. Network theory, with its methodological (and sometimes ontological) relationalism (Emirbayer and Goodwin 1994; Wellman 1988) is opposed to rational choice theory, with its methodological (and sometimes ontological) individualism; both are sharply and similarly opposed, in analytical style and epistemological commitments, to postmodernist approaches. Yet these and other developments have converged in problematizing groupness and undermining axioms of stable group being.

Challenges to "groupism" however, have been uneven. They have been striking—to take just one example—in the study of class, especially in the study of the working class, a term that is hard to use today without quotation marks or some other distancing device. Yet ethnic groups continue to be understood as entities and cast as actors. To be sure, constructivist approaches of one kind or another are now dominant in academic discussions of ethnicity. Yet everyday talk, policy analysis, media reports, and even much ostensibly constructivist academic writing routinely frame accounts of ethnic, racial and national conflict in groupist terms as the struggles "of" ethnic groups, races, and nations.[3] Somehow, when we talk about ethnicity, and even more so when we talk about ethnic conflict, we almost automatically find ourselves talking about ethnic groups.

Now it might be asked: "What's wrong with this?" After all, it seems to be mere common sense to treat ethnic struggles as the struggles of ethnic groups, and ethnic conflict as conflict between such groups. I agree that this is the—or at least a—common-sense view of the matter. But we cannot rely on common sense here. Ethnic common sense—the tendency to partition the social world into putatively deeply constituted, quasi-natural intrinsic kinds (Hirschfeld 1996)—is a key part of what we want to explain, not what we want to explain things *with*; it belongs to our empirical data, not to our analytical toolkit.[4] Cognitive anthropologists and social psychologists have accumulated a good deal of evidence about common-sense ways of carving up the social world—about what Lawrence Hirschfeld (1996) has called "folk sociologies." The evidence suggests that some common sense social categories—and notably common sense ethnic and racial categories—tend to be essentializing and naturalizing (Rothbart and Taylor 1992; Hirschfeld 1996; Gil White 1999). They are the vehicles of what has been called a "participants' primordialism" (Smith 1998: 158) or a "psychological essentialism" (Medin 1989). We obviously cannot ignore such common sense primordialism. But that does not mean we should simply replicate it in our scholarly analyses or policy assessments. As "analysts *of* naturalizers," we need not be `analytic naturalizers´ (Gil-White 1999: 803).

Instead, we need to break with vernacular categories and common sense understandings. We need to break, for example, with the seemingly obvious and uncontroversial point that ethnic conflict involves conflict between ethnic groups. I want to suggest that ethnic conflict—or what might better be called ethnicized or ethnically framed conflict—need not, and should not, be understood as conflict *between ethnic groups,* just as racial or racially framed conflict need not be understood as conflict between *races,* or nationally framed conflict as conflict between *nations.*

Participants, of course, regularly do represent ethnic, racial and national conflict in such groupist, even primordialist terms. They often cast ethnic groups, races or nations as the protagonists—the heroes and martyrs—of such struggles. But this is no warrant for analysts to do so. We must, of course, take vernacular categories and participants´ understandings seriously, for they are partly constitutive of our objects of study. But we should not uncritically adopt *categories of ethnopolitical practice* as our *categories of social analysis.* Apart from the general unreliability of ethnic common sense as a guide for social analysis, we should remember that participants´ accounts—especially those of specialists in ethnicity such as ethnopolitical entrepreneurs, who, unlike nonspecialists, may live "off" as well as "for" ethnicity—often have what Pierre Bourdieu has called a *performative* character. By *invoking* groups, they seek to *evoke* them, summon them, call them into being. Their categories are *for doing*—designed to stir, summon, justify, mobilize, kindle and energize. By reifying groups, by treating them as substantial things-in-the-world, ethnopolitical entrepreneurs may, as Bourdieu notes, "contribute to producing what they apparently describe or designate" (1991a: 220).[5]

Reification is a social process, not simply an intellectual bad habit. As a social process, it is central to the *practice* of politicized ethnicity. And appropriately so. To criticize ethnopolitical entrepreneurs for reifying ethnic groups would be a kind of category mistake. Reifying groups is precisely what ethnopolitical entrepreneurs are in the business of doing. When they are successful, the political fiction of the unified group can be momentarily yet powerfully realized in practice. As analysts, we should certainly try to *account* for the ways in which—and conditions under which—

this practice of reification, this powerful crystallization of group feeling, can work. This may be one of the most important tasks of the theory of ethnic conflict. But we should avoid unintentionally *doubling* or *reinforcing* the reification of ethnic groups in ethnopolitical practice with a reification of such groups in social analysis.

II. BEYOND GROUPISM

How, then, are we to understand ethnic conflict, if not in common sense terms as conflict between ethnic groups? And how can we go beyond groupism? Here I sketch eight basic points and then, in the next section, draw out some implications of them. In the final section, I illustrate the argument by considering one empirical case.

RETHINKING ETHNICITY

We need to rethink not only ethnic conflict, but also what we mean by ethnicity itself. This is not a matter of seeking agreement on a definition. The intricate and ever-recommencing definitional casuistry in studies of ethnicity, race and nationalism has done little to advance the discussion, and indeed can be viewed as a symptom of the non-cumulative nature of research in the field. It is rather a matter of critically scrutinizing our conceptual tools. Ethnicity, race and nation should be conceptualized not as substances or things or entities or organisms or collective individuals—as the imagery of discrete, concrete, tangible, bounded and enduring "groups" encourages us to do—but rather in relational, processual, dynamic, eventful and disaggregated terms. This means thinking of ethnicity, race and nation not in terms of substantial groups or entities but in terms of *practical categories, cultural idioms, cognitive schemas, discursive frames, organizational routines, institutional forms, political projects* and *contingent events.* It means thinking of *ethnicization, racialization* and *nationalization* as political, social, cultural and psychological *processes.* And it means taking as a basic analytical category not the "group" as an entity but *groupness* as a contextually fluctuating conceptual variable. Stated baldly in this fashion, these are of course mere slogans; I will try to fill them out a bit in what follows.

THE REALITY OF ETHNICITY

To rethink ethnicity, race and nationhood along these lines is in no way to dispute their reality, minimize their power or discount their significance; it is to construe their reality, power and significance in a different way. Understanding the reality of race, for example, does not require us to posit the existence of races. Racial idioms, ideologies, narratives, categories and systems of classification and racialized ways of seeing, thinking, talking and framing claims are real and consequential, especially when they are embedded in powerful organizations. But the reality of race—and even its overwhelming coercive power in some settings—does not depend on the existence of "races." Similarly, the reality of ethnicity and nationhood—and the overriding power of ethnic and national identifications in some settings—does not depend on the existence of ethnic groups or nations as substantial groups or entities.

GROUPNESS AS EVENT

Shifting attention from groups to groupness and treating groupness as variable and contingent rather than fixed and given,[6] allows us to take account of—and, potentially, to account for—phases of extraordinary cohesion and moments of intensely felt collective solidarity, without implicitly treating high levels of groupness as constant, enduring or definitionally present. It allows us to treat groupness as an *event*, as something that "happens," as E. P. Thompson famously said about class. At the same time, it keeps us analytically attuned to the possibility that groupness may *not* happen, that high levels of groupness may *fail* to crystallize, despite the group-making efforts of ethnopolitical entrepreneurs and even in situations of intense elite-level ethnopolitical conflict. Being analytically attuned to "negative" instances in this way enlarges the domain of relevant cases and helps correct for the bias in the literature toward the study of striking instances of high groupness, successful mobilization or conspicuous violence—a bias that can engender an "overethnicized" view of the social world, a distorted representation of whole world regions as "seething cauldrons" of ethnic tension (Brubaker 1998) and an overestimation of the incidence of ethnic violence (Fearon and Laitin 1996).

Sensitivity to such negative instances can also direct potentially fruitful analytical attention toward the problem of explaining failed efforts at ethnopolitical mobilization.

GROUPS AND CATEGORIES

Much talk about ethnic, racial or national groups is obscured by the failure to distinguish between groups and categories. If by "group" we mean a mutually interacting, mutually recognizing, mutually oriented, effectively communicating, bounded collectivity with a sense of solidarity, corporate identity and capacity for concerted action, or even if we adopt a less exigent understanding of "group," it should be clear that a category is not a group (Sacks 1995, I: 41, 401; Handelman 1977; McKay and Lewins 1978; Jenkins 1997: 53*ff*).[7] It is at best a potential basis for group-formation or "groupness."[8]

By distinguishing consistently between categories and groups, we can problematize—rather than presume—the relation between them. We can ask about the degree of groupness associated with a particular category in a particular setting and about the political, social, cultural and psychological processes through which categories get invested with groupness (Petersen 1987). We can ask how people—and organizations—*do things* with categories. This includes limiting access to scarce resources or particular domains of activity by excluding categorically distinguished outsiders (Weber 1968 [1922]: 43*ff*, 341*ff*; Barth 1969; Brubaker 1992; Tilly 1998), but it also includes more mundane actions such as identifying or classifying oneself or others (Levine 1999) or simply "doing being ethnic" in an ethnomethodological sense (Moerman 1968). We can analyze the organizational and discursive careers of categories—the processes through which they become institutionalized and entrenched in administrative routines (Tilly 1998) and embedded in culturally powerful and symbolically resonant myths, memories and narratives (Armstrong 1982; Smith 1986). We can study the politics of categories, both from above and from below. From above, we can focus on the ways in which categories are proposed, propagated, imposed, institutionalized, discursively articulated, organizationally entrenched and generally embedded in multifarious forms of "governmentality" (Noiriel 1991; Slezkine 1994; Brubaker 1994; Torpey 2000; Martin 2001). From below, we can study the "micropolitics" of categories, the ways in which the categorized appropriate, internalize, subvert, evade or transform the categories that are imposed on them (Dominguez 1986). And drawing on advances in cognitive research, ethnomethodology and conversation analysis, we can study the sociocognitive and interactional processes through which categories are used by individuals to make sense of the social world;[9] linked to stereotypical beliefs and expectations about category members.[10] invested with emotional associations and evaluative judgments; deployed as resources in specific interactional contexts; and activated by situational triggers or cues. A focus on categories, in short, can illuminate the multifarious ways in which ethnicity, race and nationhood can exist and "work" without the existence of ethnic groups as substantial entities. It can help us envision ethnicity without groups.

GROUP-MAKING AS PROJECT

If we treat groupness as a variable and distinguish between groups and categories, we can attend to the dynamics of *group-making* as a social, cultural and political project, aimed at transforming categories into groups or increasing levels of groupness (Bourdieu 1991a, 1991b). Sometimes this is done in quite a cynical fashion. Ethnic and other insurgencies, for example, often adopt what is called in French a *politique du pire*, a politics of seeking the worst outcome in the short run so as to bolster their legitimacy or improve their prospects in the longer run. When the small, ill-equipped, ragtag Kosovo Liberation Army stepped up its attacks on Serb policemen and other targets in early 1998, for example, this was done as a deliberate—and successful—strategy of provoking massive regime reprisals. As in many such situations, the brunt of the reprisals was borne by civilians. The cycle of attacks and counterattacks sharply increased groupness among both Kosovo Albanians and Kosovo Serbs, generated greater support for the KLA among both Kosovo and diaspora Albanians and bolstered KLA recruitment and funding. This

enabled the KLA to mount a more serious challenge to the regime, which in turn generated more brutal regime reprisals and so on. In this sense, group crystallization and polarization were the result of violence, not the cause (Brubaker 1999).

Of course, this group-making strategy employed in the late 1990s did not start from scratch. It had already begun with relatively high levels of groupness, a legacy of earlier phases of conflict. The propitious "raw materials" the KLA had to work with no doubt help explain the success of its strategy. Not all group-making projects succeed and those that do succeed (more or less) do so in part as a result of the cultural and psychological materials they have to work with. These materials include not only, or especially, "deep," *longue-durée* cultural structures such as the *mythomoteurs* highlighted by Armstrong (1982) and Smith (1986), but also the moderately durable ways of thinking and feeling that represent "middle-range" legacies of historical experience and political action. Yet while such raw materials—themselves the product and precipitate of past struggles and predicaments—constrain and condition the possibilities for group-making in the present, there remains considerable scope for deliberate group-making strategies. Certain dramatic events, in particular, can serve to galvanize and crystallize a potential group, or to ratchet up pre-existing levels of groupness. This is why deliberate violence, undertaken as a strategy of provocation, often by a very small number of persons, can sometimes be an exceptionally effective strategy of group-making.

GROUPS AND ORGANIZATIONS

Although participants' rhetoric and common sense accounts treat ethnic groups as the protagonists of ethnic conflict, in fact the chief protagonists of most ethnic conflict—and a fortiori of most ethnic violence—are not ethnic groups as such but various kinds of organizations, broadly understood and their empowered and authorized incumbents. These include states (or more broadly autonomous polities) and their organizational components such as particular ministries, offices, law enforcement agencies and armed forces units; they include terrorist groups, paramilitary organizations, armed bands and loosely structured gangs; and they include political parties, ethnic associations, social movement organizations, churches, newspapers, radio and television stations and so on. Some of these organizations may represent themselves, or may be seen by others, as organizations of and for particular ethnic groups.[11] But even when this is the case, organizations cannot be equated with ethnic groups. It is because and insofar as they are organizations and possess certain material and organizational resources, that they (or more precisely their incumbents) are capable of organized action and thereby of acting as more or less coherent protagonists in ethnic conflict.[12] Although common sense and participants´ rhetoric attribute discrete existence, boundedness, coherence, identity, interest and agency to ethnic groups, these attributes are in fact characteristic of organizations. The IRA, KLA and PKK claim to speak and act in the name of the (Catholic) Irish, the Kosovo Albanians and the Kurds; but surely analysts must differentiate between such organizations and the putatively homogeneous and bounded groups in whose name they claim to act. The point applies not only to military, paramilitary and terrorist organizations, of course, but to all organizations that claim to speak and act in the name of ethnic, racial or national groups (Heisler 1991).

A fuller and more rounded treatment of this theme, to be sure, would require several qualifications that I can only gesture at here. Conflict and violence vary in the degree to which, as well as the manner in which, organizations are involved. What Donald Horowitz (2001) has called the deadly ethnic riot, for example, differs sharply from organized ethnic insurgencies or terrorist campaigns. Although organizations (sometimes ephemeral ones) may play an important role in preparing, provoking and permitting such riots, much of the actual violence is committed by broader sets of participants acting in relatively spontaneous fashion and in starkly polarized situations characterized by high levels of groupness. Moreover, even where organizations are the core protagonists, they may depend on a penumbra of ancillary or supportive action on the part of sympathetic non-members. The "representativeness" of organizations—the degree to which an organization can justifiably claim to represent the will, express the interests and enjoy the active or passive support of its constituents—is enormously variable, not only

between organizations, but also over time and across domains. In addition, while organizations are ordinarily the *protagonists* of conflict and violence, they are not always the *objects* or *targets* of conflict and violence. Entire population categories—or putative groups—can be the objects of organized action, much more easily than they can be the subjects or undertakers of such action. Finally, even apart from situations of violence, ethnic conflict may be at least partly amorphous, carried out not by organizations as such but spontaneously by individuals through such everyday actions as shunning, insults, demands for deference or conformity, or withholdings of routine interactional tokens of acknowledgment or respect (Bailey 1997). Still, despite these qualifications, it is clear that organizations, not ethnic groups as such, are the chief protagonists of ethnic conflict and ethnic violence and that the relationship between organizations and the groups they claim to represent is often deeply ambiguous.

FRAMING AND CODING

If the protagonists of ethnic conflict cannot, in general, be considered ethnic groups, then what makes such conflict count as *ethnic* conflict?[13] And what makes violence count as ethnic violence? Similar questions can be asked about racial and national conflict and violence. The answer cannot be found in the intrinsic properties of behavior. The "ethnic" quality of "ethnic violence" for example, is not intrinsic to violent conduct itself; it is attributed to instances of violent behavior by perpetrators, victims, politicians, officials, journalists, researchers, relief workers or others. Such acts of framing and narrative encoding do not simply *interpret* the violence; they *constitute* it *as ethnic*.

Framing may be a key mechanism through which groupness is constructed. The metaphor of framing was popularized by Goffman (1974), drawing on Bateson 1985 [1955]. The notion has been elaborated chiefly in the social movement literature (Snow *et al.* 1986; Snow and Benford 1988; Gamson and Modigliani 1989; Gamson 1992; uniting rational choice and framing approaches, Esser 1999). When ethnic framing is successful, we may "see" conflict and violence not only in ethnic, but in groupist terms. Although such imputed groupness is the product of prevailing interpretive frames, not necessarily a measure of the groupness felt and experienced by the participants in an event, a compelling *ex post* interpretive framing or encoding may exercise a powerful feedback effect, shaping subsequent experience and increasing levels of groupness. A great deal is at stake, then, in struggles over the interpretive framing and narrative encoding of conflict and violence.

Interpretive framing, of course, is often contested. Violence—and more generally, conflict—is regularly accompanied by social struggles to label, interpret and explain it. Such "metaconflicts" or "conflict[s] over the nature of the conflict," as Donald Horowitz has called them (1991: 2), do not simply shadow conflicts from the outside, but are integral and consequential parts of the conflicts. To impose a label or prevailing interpretive frame—to cause an event to be seen as a "pogrom" or a "riot" or a "rebellion"—is no mere matter of external interpretation, but a constitutive act of social definition that can have important consequences (Brass 1996b). Social struggles over the proper coding and interpretation of conflict and violence are therefore important subjects of study in their own right (Brass 1996a, 1997, Abelmann and Lie 1995).

Coding and framing practices are heavily influenced by prevailing interpretive frames. Today, ethnic and national frames are accessible and legitimate, suggesting themselves to actors and analysts alike. This generates a "coding bias" in the ethnic direction. And this, in turn, may lead us to overestimate the incidence of ethnic conflict and violence by unjustifiably seeing ethnicity everywhere at work (Bowen 1996). Actors may take advantage of this coding bias and of the generalized legitimacy of ethnic and national frames, by strategically using ethnic framing to mask the pursuit of clan, clique or class interests. The point here is not to suggest that clans, cliques or classes are somehow more real than ethnic groups, but simply to note the existence of structural and cultural incentives for strategic framing.

ETHNICITY AS COGNITION

These observations about the constitutive significance of coding and framing suggest a final point about the cognitive dimension of ethnicity.[14] Ethnicity, race and nationhood exist only in and through our perceptions, interpretations, representations, categorizations and identifications. They are not things *in* the world, but perspectives *on* the world.[15] These include ethnicized ways of seeing (and ignoring), of construing (and misconstruing), of inferring (and misinferring), of remembering (and forgetting). They include ethnically oriented frames, schemas and narratives and the situational cues that activate them, such as the ubiquitous televised images that have played such an important role in the latest intifada. They include systems of classification, categorization and identification, formal and informal. And they include the tacit, taken-for-granted background knowledge, embodied in persons and embedded in institutionalized routines and practices, through which people recognize and experience objects, places, persons, actions or situations as ethnically, racially or nationally marked or meaningful.

Cognitive perspectives, broadly understood, can help advance constructivist research on ethnicity, race and nationhood, which has stalled in recent years as it has grown complacent with success.[16] Instead of simply asserting *that* ethnicity, race and nationhood are constructed, they can help specify *how* they are constructed. They can help specify how—and when—people identify themselves, perceive others, experience the world and interpret their predicaments in racial, ethnic or national rather than other terms. They can help specify how "groupness" can "crystallize" in some situations while remaining latent and merely potential in others. And they can help link macro-level outcomes with micro-level processes.

NOTES

1. Foundational discussions include Cooley 1962 [1909], chapter 3 and Homans 1950 in sociology; Nadel 1957, chapter 7 in anthropology; Bentley 1908, chapter 7 and Truman 1951 in political science. More recent discussions include Olson 1965, Tilly 1978 and Hechter 1987.

2. In this very general sense, groupism extends well beyond the domain of ethnicity, race and nationalism to include accounts of putative groups based on gender, sexuality, age, class, abledness, religion, minority status, and any kind of "culture", as well as putative groups based on

combinations of these categorical attributes. Yet while recognizing that it is a wider tendency in social analysis, I limit my discussion here to groupism in the study of ethnicity, race and nationalism.

3. For useful critical analyses of media representations of ethnic violence, see the collection of essays in Allen and Seaton 1999, as well as Seaton 1999.

4. This is perhaps too sharply put. To the extent that such intrinsic-kind categories are indeed constitutive of common-sense understandings of the social world, to the extent that such categories are used as a resource for participants, and are demonstrably deployed or oriented to by participants in interaction, they can also serve as a resource for analysts. But as Emanuel Schegloff notes in another context, with respect to the category "interruption", the fact that this is a vernacular, common-sense category for participants, `does not make it a first-order category usable for professional analysis. Rather than being employed *in* professional analysis, it is better treated as a target category *for* professional analysis´ (2000: 27). The same might well be said of common sense ethnic categories.

5. Such performative, group-making practices, of course, are not specific to ethnic entrepreneurs, but generic to political mobilization and representation (Bourdieu 1991b: 248–251).

6. For accounts (not focused specifically on ethnicity) that treat groupness as variable, see Tilly 1978: 62*ff*; Hechter 1987: 8; Hamilton *et al.* 1998. These accounts, very different from one another, focus on variability in groupness across cases; my concern is primarily with variability in groupness over time.

7. Fredrik Barth´s introductory essay to the collection *Ethnic Groups and Boundaries* (1969) was extraordinarily influential in directing attention to the workings of categories of self- and other-ascription. But Barth does not distinguish sharply or consistently between categories and groups and his central metaphor of "boundary" carries with it connotations of boundedness, entitativity and groupness.

8. This point was already made by Max Weber, albeit in somewhat different terms. As Weber argued—in a passage obscured in the English translation—ethnic commonality, based on belief in common descent, is "in itself mere (putative) commonality [(geglaubte) Gemeinsamkeit], not community [Gemeinschaft] [...] but only a factor facilitating communal action [Vergemeinschaftung]" (1964: 307; *cf.* 1968: 389). Ethnic commonality means more than mere category membership for Weber. It is—or rather involves—a category that is employed by members themselves. But this shows that even self-categorization does not create a "group".

9. Ethnomethodology and conversation analysis have not focused on the use of ethnic categories as such, but Sacks, Schegloff and others have addressed the problem of situated categorization in general, notably the question of the procedures through which participants in interaction, in deploying categories, choose among alternative sets of categories (since there is always more than one set of categories in terms of which any person can be correctly described). The import of this problem has been formulated as follows by Schegloff (2000: 30–31): "And given the centrality of [...] categories in organizing vernacular cultural `knowledge´, this equivocality can be profoundly consequential, for *which* category is employed will carry with it the invocation of common-sense knowledge about *that* category of person and bring it to bear on the person referred to on some occasion, rather than bringing to bear the knowledge implicated with *another* category, of which the person being referred to is equally a member". For Sacks on categories, see 1995; I, 40–48, 333–340, 396–403, 578–596; II, 184–187.

10. The language of "stereotypes" is, of course, that of cognitive social psychology (for a review of work in this tradition, see Hamilton and Sherman 1994). But the general ethnomethodological emphasis on the crucial importance of the rich though tacit background knowledge that

    participants bring to interaction and—more specifically—Harvey Sacks´ discussion of the "inference-rich" categories in terms of which much everyday social knowledge is stored (1995: I, 40*ff et passim; cf.* Schegloff 2000: 29*ff*) and of the way in which the knowledge thus organized is "protected against induction" (*ibid.*, 336*ff*), suggest a domain of potentially converging concern between cognitive work on the one hand and ethnomethodological and conversation-analytic work on the other—however different their analytic stances and methodologies.

11. One should remember, though, that organizations often compete with one another for the monopolization of the right to represent the same (putative) group.

12. In this respect the resource mobilizaition perspective on social movements, eclipsed in recent years by identity-oriented new social movement theory, has much to offer students of ethnicity. For an integrated statement, see McCarthy and Zald 1977.

13. These paragraphs draw on Brubaker and Laitin 1998.

14. These paragraphs draw on Brubaker *et al.* 2001.

15. As Emanuel Schegloff reminded me in a different context, this formulation is potentially misleading, since perspectives *on* the world—as every Sociology I student is taught—are themselves *in* the world and every bit as "real" and consequential as other sorts of things.

16. Cognitive perspectives, in this broad sense, include not only those developed in cognitive psychology and cognitive anthropology but also those developed in the post- (and anti-) Parsonian "cognitive turn" (DiMaggio and Powell 1991) in sociological and (more broadly) social theory, especially in response to the influence of phenomenological and ethnomethodological work (Schutz 1962; Garfinkel 1967; Heritage 1984). Cognitive perspectives are central to the influential syntheses of Bourdieu and Giddens and—in a very different form—to the enterprise of conversation analysis.

REFERENCES

Abelmann, Nancy and John Lie, 1995, *Blue Dreams: Korean Americans and the Los Angeles Riots* (Cambridge: Harvard University Press).

Adevărul de Cluj, 1999, Confruntarea dintre România și Uñgaria a continuat și după meci [The confrontation between Romania and Hungary continued also after the match], June 7, 1999.

Allen, Tim and Jean Seaton (eds), 1999, *The Media of Conflict: War Reporting and Representations of Ethnic Violence* (London: Zed Books).

Armstrong, John A., 1982, *Nations Before Nationalism* (Chapel Hill: University of North Carolina Press).

Bailey, Benjamin, 1997, Communication of Respect in Interethnic Service Encounters, *Language in Society* 26, 327–356.

Barth, Fredrik, 1969, Introduction, *in* Fredrik Barth (ed.), *Ethnic Groups and Boundaries: The Social Organization of Culture Difference* (London: George Allen & Unwin), 9–38.

Bateson, Gregory, 1985 [1955], A Theory of Play and Fantasy, *in* Robert E. Innis (ed.), *Semiotics: An Introductory Anthology*, 131–144.

Bauman, Zygmunt, 2000 [1989], *Modernity and the Holocaust* (Ithaca: Cornell University Press).

Bentley, Arthur F., 1908, *The Process of Government: A Study of Social Pressures (Chicago: University of Chicago Press).*

Bourdieu, Pierre, 1991a, Identity and Representation: Elements for a Critical Reflection on the Idea of Region, *in* Pierre Bourdieu, *Language and Symbolic Power* (Cambridge: Harvard University Press), 220–228.

———, 1991b, Social Space and the Genesis of "Classes", *in* Pierre Bourdieu, *Language and Symbolic Power* (Cambridge: Harvard University Press), 229–251.

Bowen, John R., 1996, The Myth of Global Ethnic Conflict, *Journal of Democracy* 7(4), 3–14.

Brass, Paul R. (ed.), 1996a, *Riots and Pogroms* (Washington Square: New York University Press).

——, 1996b, Introduction: Discourse of Ethnicity, Communalism and Violence, *in* Paul R. Brass (ed.), *Riots and Pogroms* (Washington Square: New York University Press), 1–55.

——, 1997, *Theft of an Idol: Text and Context in the Representation of Collective Violence* (Princeton: Princeton University Press).

Brubaker, Rogers, 1992, *Citizenship and Nationhood in France and Germany* (Cambridge, MA: Harvard University Press).

——, 1994, Nationhood and the National Question in the Soviet Union and Post-Soviet Eurasia, *Theory and Society* 23(1), 47–78.

——, 1998, Myths and Misconceptions in the Study of Nationalism, *in* John Hall (ed.), *The State of the Nation: Ernest Gellner and the Theory of Nationalism* (New York: Cambridge University Press), 272–306.

——, 1999, A Shameful Debacle, *UCLA Magazine*, Summer 1999, 15–16.

Brubaker, Rogers and Margit Feischmidt, 2002, 1848 in 1998: The Politics of Commemoration in Hungary, Romania, and Slovakia, in *Comparative Studies in Society and History* 44(4), 700–744.

Brubaker, Rogers and David D. Laitin, 1998, Ethnic and Nationalist Violence, *Annual Review of Sociology* 24, 423–452.

Brubaker, Rogers, Mara Loveman and Peter Stamatov, 2001, "Beyond Social Construction: The Case for a Cognitive Approach to Race, Ethnicity and Nationalism". Unpublished manuscript.

Collier, Paul, 1999, Doing Well Out of War. http://www.worldbank.org./research/conflict/papers/econagenda.htm.

Cooley, Charles H., 1962 [1909], *Social Organization* (New York: Schocken Books).

DiMaggio, Paul J. and Walter W. Powell, 1991, Introduction, *in* Walter W. Powell and Paul J. DiMaggio (eds), *The New Institutionalism in Organizational Analysis* (Chicago: University of Chicago Press), 1–38.

Dominguez, Virginia R., 1986, *White by Definition: Social Classification in Creole Louisiana* (New Brunswick: Rutgers University Press).

Emirbayer, Mustafa and Jeff Goodwin, 1994, Network Analysis, Culture and the Problem of Agency, *American Journal of Sociology* 99(6), 1411–1454.

Esser, Hartmut, 1999, Die Situationslogik ethnischer Konflikte: Auch eine Anmerkung zum Beitrag "Ethnische Mobilisierung und die Logik von Identitätskämpfen" von Klaus Eder und Oliver Schmidtke, *Zeitschrift für Soziologie* 28(4), 245–262.

Fearon, James and David D. Laitin, 1996, Explaining Interethnic Cooperation, *American Political Science Review* 90(4), 715–735.

Feischmidt, Margit, 2001, Zwischen Abgrenzung und Vermischung: Ethnizität in der siebenbürgischen Stadt Cluj (Kolozsvár, Klausenburg). Ph.D. dissertation (Humboldt University, Berlin).

Fox, Jon E., 2001, Nationness and Everyday Life: Romanian and Hungarian University Students in Transylvania. Paper presented to the Center for Comparative Social Analysis Workshop, Department of Sociology, UCLA.

Gamson, William A., 1992, *Talking Politics* (New York: Cambridge University Press).

Gamson, William A. and Andre Modigliani, 1989, Media Discourse and Public Opinion on Nuclear Power: A Constructionist Approach, *American Journal of Sociology* 95, 1–37.

Gans, Herbert J., 1979, Symbolic Ethnicity: The Future of Ethnic Groups and Cultures in America, *Ethnic and Racial Studies* 2, 1–20.

Garfinkel, Harold, 1967, *Studies in Ethnomethodology* (Englewood Cliffs, NJ.: Prentice-Hall, Inc.).

Gil-White, Francisco, 1999, How Thick Is Blood? The Plot Thickens. . .: If Ethnic Actors Are Primordialists, What Remains of the Circumstantialist/Primordialist Controversy? *Ethnic and Racial Studies* 22(5), 789–820.

Goffman, Erving, 1974, *Frame Analysis* (San Francisco: Harper Colophon Books).

Hamilton, David L. and Jeffrey W. Sherman, 1994, Stereotypes, *in* Robert S. Wyer and Thomas K. Srull (eds), *Handbook of Social Cognition*, 2nd ed. (Hillsdale, NJ: L. Erlbaum Associates), 1–68.

Hamilton, David L., Steven J. Sherman and Brian Lickel, 1998, Perceiving Social Groups: The Importance of the Entitativity Continuum, *in* Constantine Sedikides, John Schopler and Chester A. Insko (eds), *Intergroup Cognition and Intergroup Behavior* (Mahwah, NJ: Lawrence Erlbaum Associates), 47–74.

Handelman, Don, 1977, The Organization of Ethnicity, *Ethnic Groups* 1, 187–200.

Hechter, Michael, 1987, *Principles of Group Solidarity* (Berkeley: University of California Press).

Heisler, Martin, 1991, Ethnicity and Ethnic Relations in the Modern West, *in* Joseph Montville (ed.), *Conflict and Peacemaking in Multiethnic Societies* (Lexington: Lexington Books), 21–52.

Heritage, John, 1984, *Garfinkel and Ethnomethodology* (Cambridge: Polity Press).

Hirschfeld, Lawrence A., 1996, *Race in the Making: Cognition, Culture and the Child´s Construction of Human Kinds* (Cambridge, MA: MIT Press).

Hollinger, David A., 1995, *Postethnic America: Beyond Multiculturalism* (New York: Basic Books).

Holquist, Peter, 1997, Conduct Merciless "Mass Terror": Decossackization on the Don, 1919, *Cahiers du Monde russe* 38(1-2), 127–162.

Homans, George C., 1950, *The Human Group* (New York: Harcourt, Brace & World, Inc.)

Horowitz, Donald L., 1985, *Ethnic Groups in Conflict* (Berkeley, CA: University of California Press).

———, 1991, *A Democratic South Africa?: Constitutional Engineering in a Divided Society* (Berkeley: University of California Press).

———, 2001, *The Deadly Ethnic Riot* (Berkeley, CA: University of California Press).

Jenkins, Richard, 1997, *Rethinking Ethnicity* (London: Sage).

Kuran, Timur, 1998, Ethnic Norms and their Transformation through Reputational Cascades, *Journal of Legal Studies* 27, 623–659.

Laitin, David D., 1995, National Revivals and Violence, *Archives européennes de sociologie* xxxvi, 3–43.

Levine, Hal B., 1999, Reconstructing Ethnicity, *Journal of the Royal Anthropological Institute* (New Series) 5, 165–180.

Magyari-Nandor, László and László Péter, 1997, Az egyetemröl magyar diákszemmel [Hungarian students´ views on the university], *Korunk* 1997/4, 112–119.

Martin, Terry, 2001, *The Affirmative Action Empire* (Ithaca: Cornell University Press).

McCarthy, John D. and Mayer N. Zald, 1977, Resource Mobilization and Social Movements: A Partial Theory, *American Journal of Sociology* 82(6), 1212–1241.

McGrath, Joseph E., 1984, *Groups: Interaction and Performance* (New Jersey: Prentice-Hall).

McKay, James and Frank Lewins, 1978, Ethnicity and the Ethnic Group: A Conceptual Analysis and Reformulation, *Ethnic and Racial Studies* 1(4), 412–427.

Medin, Douglas L., 1989, Concepts and Conceptual Structure, *The American Psychologist* 44, 1469–1481.

Moerman, Michael, 1968, Being Lue: Uses and Abuses of Ethnic Identification, in June Helm (ed.), *Essays on the Problem of Tribe* (Washington: University of Washington Press).

Mueller, John, 2000, The Banality of "Ethnic War", *International Security* 25, 42–70.

Nadel, S. F., 1957, *A Theory of Social Structure* (London: Cohen & West).

Noiriel, Gérard, 1991, *La Tyrannie du national: le droit d´asile en Europe 1793–1993* (Paris: Calmann-Lévy).

Office of Management and Budget, 1994, Standards for the classification of federal data on race and ethnicity, http://www.whitehouse.gov/omb/fedreg/notice-15.html.

Olson, Mancur, 1965, The Logic of Collective Action: Public Goods and the Theory of Groups (Cambridge: Harvard University Press).

Petersen, William, 1987, Politics and the Measurement of Ethnicity, *in* William Alonso and Paul Starr (eds), *The Politics of Numbers* (New York: Russell Sage Foundation), 187–233.

Rothbart, Myron and Marjorie Taylor, 1992, Category Labels and Social Reality: Do We View Social Categories As Natural Kinds? *in* Gün R. Semin and Klaus Fiedler (eds), *Language, Interaction and Social Cognition* (London: Sage Publications).

Rothschild, Joseph, 1981, *Ethnopolitics: A Conceptual Framework* (New York: Columbia University Press).

Sacks, Harvey, 1995, *Lectures on Conversation* (Oxford, Blackwell Publishers).

Schegloff, Emanuel A., 2000, Accounts of Conduct in Interaction: Interruption, Overlap and Turn-Taking, *in* J. H. Turner (ed.), *Handbook of Sociological Theory* (New York: Plenum). Forthcoming.

Schutz, Alfred, 1962, *Collected Papers I: The Problem of Social Reality*, Maurice Natanson (ed.) (The Hague: Martinus Nijhoff).

Seation, Jean, 1999, Why Do We Think the Serbs Do It? The New "Ethnic" Wars and the Media, *Political Quarterly* 70(3), 254–270.

Slezkine, Yuri, 1994, The USSR As a Communal Apartment, or How a Socialist State Promoted Ethnic Particularlism, *Slavic Review* 53(4), 414–452.

Smith, Anthony D., 1986, *The Ethnic Origins of Nations* (Oxford: Basil Blackwell).

———, 1998, *Nationalism and Modernism: A Critical Survey of Recent Theories of Nations and Nationalism* (London: Routledge).

Snow, David A. and Robert D. Benford, 1988, Ideology, Frame Resonance and Participant Mobilization, *International Social Movement Research* 1, 197–217.

Snow, David A., E. B. Rochford Jr., Steven K. Worden and Robert D. Benford, 1986, Frame Alignment Processes, Micromobilization and Movement Participation, *American Sociological Review* 51, 464–481.

Sperber, Dan, 1985, Anthropology and Psychology: Towards an Epidemiology of Representations, *Man* 20, 73–89.

Tilly, Charles, 1978, From Mobilization to Revolution (Reading, Mass.: Addison-Wesley Publishing Company).

———, 1998, *Durable Inequality* (Berkeley: University of California Press).

Torpey, John, 2000, *The Invention of the Passport: Surveillance, Citizenship and the State* (Cambridge: Cambridge University Press).

Truman, David B., 1951, *The Governmental Process: Political Interests and Public Opinion*. 2nd ed. (New York: Alfred A. Knopf).

Weber, Max, 1946, *From Max Weber: Essays in Sociology*, H. H. Gerth and Wright Mills (eds) (New York: Oxford University Press).

———, 1964, *Wirtschaft und Gesellschaft*. 4th ed. (Köln: Kiepenheurer & Witsch).

Weber, Max, 1968 [1922], *Economy and Society*, Guenther Roth and Claus Wittich (eds) (Berkeley: University of California Press).

Weiner, Amir, 2001, *Making Sense of War: The Second World War and the Fate of the Bolshevik Revolution* (Princeton: Princeton University Press).

Wellman, Barry, 1988, Structural Analysis: From Method and Metaphor to Theory and Substance, *in* Barry Wellman and S. D. Berkowitz (eds), *Social Structures: A Network Approach* (Cambridge: Cambridge University Press), 19–61.

60. NATIONALISM AND THE CULTURES OF DEMOCRACY

CRAIG CALHOUN

Craig Calhoun (b. 1952) is currently Director of the London School of Economics and Political Science. His research interests and major publications have been wide ranging, including a book on class struggle during the Industrial Revolution, an analysis of the struggle for democracy in China culminating in the occupation of Tiananmen Square, and studies of the theoretical contributions of three major theorists included in this collection: Robert Merton, Pierre Bourdieu, and Jürgen Habermas. Expanding this range, there are several themes that have proven to be major preoccupations for him: democracy and citizenship, social movements, cosmopolitanism, and the continuing significance of nationalism. The selection included herein, deriving from his recent book, *Nations Matter* (2007), is a reflection of these concerns. Calhoun is critical of postnationalist and other theorists who argue that nationalism is being or should be overcome. As he provocatively begins the essay, "If nationalism is over, we shall miss it." Not only does he disagree with those who underestimate the continued power of nationalism, but he also criticizes them for failing to appreciate the role nationalism plays in facilitating social integration and solidarity, prerequisites for democratic practice. In making this claim, he is well aware of the fact that nationalism can also be deployed in the service of antidemocratic projects.

If nationalism is over, we shall miss it. Revolution may be the project of a vanguard party acting on behalf of its masses. Resistance to capitalist globalization may be pursued by a multifarious and inchoate multitude. But imagining democracy requires thinking of "the people" as active and coherent and oneself as both a member and an agent. Liberalism informs the notion of individual agency, but provides weak purchase at best on membership and on the collective cohesion and capacity of the *demos*. In the modern era, the discursive formation that has most influentially underwritten these dimensions of democracy is nationalism.[1]

Nationalists have exaggerated and naturalized the historical and never more than partial unity of the nation. The hyphen in nation-state tied the modern polity—with enormously more intense and effective internal administration than any large-scale

precursors—to the notion of a historically or naturally unified people who intrinsically belong together. The idea that nations give states clearly identifiable and meaningfully integrated populations, which in turn are the bases of their legitimacy, is as problematic as it is influential.[2] It is of course an empirically tendentious claim. But it is part of a discursive formation that structures the world, not simply an external description of it.

To be sure, nationalism has also been mobilized in sharply antidemocratic projects; it has often organized disturbingly intolerant attitudes; it has led to distorted views of the world and excesses of both pride and imagined insults. It has also been a recipe for conflicts both internal and external. Populations straddle borders or move long distances to new states while retaining allegiances to old nations. Dominant groups

Craig Calhoun, *Nations Matter: Culture, History, and the Cosmopolitan Dream.* New York: Routledge, 2007 pp. 147–157. ✦

demand that governments enforce cultural conformity, challenging both the individual freedom and the vitality that comes from cultural creativity. These faults have made it easier for liberals to dismiss nationalism from their theories of democracy. But this has not made it less important in the real world.

There are of course also many problems that affect everyone on earth—environmental degradation, for example, or small arms trade. Nationalist rhetoric is commonly employed in excuses for governmental failures to address these problems. Transnational movements press for action. But for the most part the action comes, if it does, from national states.

Likewise, there is no non-national and cosmopolitan solution available to "complex humanitarian emergencies" like that in Darfur. International humanitarian action is vitally important, but more a compensation for state failures and evils than as a substitute for better states. More generally, lacking a capable state may be as much a source of disaster as state violence. National integration and identity are also basic to many efforts at economic development and to contesting the imposition of a neoliberal model of global economic growth that ignores or undermines local quality of life and inhibits projects of self-government. Nations also remain basic units of international cooperation.

Though a secular decline in the capacity and importance of nation-states has often been asserted—or at least predicted—as a result of globalization, this is not evident. Certainly nation-states face new challenges: multinational corporations and global markets organize production, exchange, and even real estate markets across borders. It is harder for any state to control its fiscal policy autonomously, for example, and harder for most to control their borders (as not only migrants but money, media, and a variety of goods cross them). The popularity of neoliberal privatization programs has challenged state enterprises and provision of services that sometimes played an integrating role. The extent to which the integration of nations matches that of states, has never been complete, and now faces challenges from calls for greater regional, ethnic, and religious autonomy. Proponents of cultural diversity have often challenged assimilationist approaches to the cultural integration of immigrants. Migration has been organized into diasporic circuits linking communities in several

countries and making returning migrants and remittances significant issues in sender states.

Yet nationalism and nation-states retain considerable power and potential. Rather than their general decline, what we see today is loss of faith in progress through secular and civic nationalism and state building projects. This makes it harder to appreciate the positive work that nationalism has done and still does (alongside its evil uses). Nations provide for structures of belonging that build bridges between local communities and mediate between these and globalization. Nations organize the primary arenas for democratic political participation. Nationalism helps mobilize collective commitment to public institutions, projects, and debates. Nationalism encourages mutual responsibility across divisions of class and region. We may doubt both the capacities of nation-states and the morality of many versions of nationalism, but we lack realistic and attractive alternatives.

Crucially, we are poorly prepared to theorize democracy if we cannot theorize the social solidarity of democratic peoples. Substituting ethical attention to the obligations all human beings share does not fill the void. This effort lacks an understanding of politics as the active creation of ways of living together, not only distributing power but developing institutions. And, accordingly, it lacks a sense of democracy as a human creation necessarily situated in culture and history, always imperfect and open to improvement, and therefore always also variable.

A deep mutual relationship has tied nationalism to democracy throughout the modern era. Nationalism was crucial to collective democratic subjectivity, providing a basis for the capacity to speak as "we the people," the conceptualization of constitution-making as collective self-empowerment, and commitment to accept the judgment of citizens in general on contentious questions. As important, democracy encouraged the formation of national solidarity. When states were legitimated on the basis of serving the commonwealth, when collective struggles won improved institutions, when a democratic public sphere spanned class, regional, religious, and other divisions this strengthened national solidarity. It is a pernicious illusion to think of national identity as the prepolitical basis for a modern state—an illusion certainly encouraged by some nationalists. It is equally true that national identity is (like all collective identity) inherently political; created in speech, action, and recognition. A democratic public is not merely contingent on political solidarity, it can be productive of it.

Of course political community can be and is constructed on bases other than nations. Most people live in multiple, overlapping zones of solidarity. There are varying degrees of local autonomy within nation-states, and varying degrees of integration among neighboring states. And of course nations can be transformed; they need not be treated as prepolitically given but can be recognized as always made—culturally as well as politically—and therefore remarkable. But the idea of democracy requires some structures of integration, some cultural capacity for internal communication, some social solidarity of "the people."

LIBERALISM WITHIN OR BEYOND NATIONS

Political liberalism developed largely in the effort to theorize the transition from pre-national empires, monarchies, and aristocracies to nations. Nations were the primary political structures in which liberal individuals would be equals and have more or less universal rights.

The same liberalism was well attuned, of course, to recognizing the failures of actually existing nations, including especially failures to extend equal rights to all citizens. Liberals generally respond to these failings of nations and nationalism by abandoning reliance on historically achieved solidarities and subjectivities. This tendency has been reinforced by recognition of the ways in which globalization limits states. Seeking greater justice and liberty than actual nations have offered, they apply liberal ideas about the equality of and relations among individuals at the scale of humanity as a whole. But it is not clear that ratcheting up universalism makes it any more readily achievable.

In addition, this attempt to pursue liberal equality and justice at a more global level reveals a tension previously beneath the surface of liberalism. So long as liberalism could rely (explicitly or implicitly) on the idea of nation to supply a prepolitical constitution of "the people" it could be a theory both of democracy

and universal rights. But the pursuit of greater universalism commonly comes at the expense of solidarity, for solidarity is typically achieved in more particularistic formations. Since there is no democracy without social solidarity, as liberalism is transposed to the global level it becomes more a theory of universal rights or justice and less a theory of democratic politics.

Liberalism has been pervasive in democratic theory—enough so that its blind spots have left the democratic imaginary impoverished. This shows up in thinking about (or thinking too little about) solidarity, social cohesion, collective identity, and boundaries. With its concerns focused overwhelmingly on freedom, equality, and justice for individual persons, liberalism has had at best a complicated relationship with nationalism. For much of the modern era, liberalism worked within the tacit assumption that nation-states defined the boundaries of citizenship. John Rawls made the assumption explicit:

> we have assumed that a democratic society, like any political society, is to be viewed as a complete and closed social system. It is complete in that it is self-sufficient and has a place for all the main purposes of human life. It is also closed, in that entry into it is only by birth and exit from it is only by death.[3]

This "Westphalian" understanding incorporated a distinction of properly "domestic" from properly international matters that was closely related to the distinction of public from private emerging more generally in modern social thought.[4] It underwrote, among other things, the exclusion of religion from allegedly "realist" international relations, a treatment of religion as essentially a domestic matter (and often by implication a private choice) that has informed not only liberal political theory but the entire discipline of international relations. This has been closely related to liberalism´s difficulties with "strong" or "thick" accounts of culture as constitutive for human subjectivity. Liberalism typically presumes a theory of culture that it does not recognize as such, but instead treats somewhat ironically as an escape from culture into a more direct access to the universal—whether conceived as human nature, or human rights, or political process in the abstract.

More recently, pressed by the porousness of state borders in an era of intensified globalization, many liberals have recognized the difficulties with relying uncritically on nation-states to provide the framework within which liberal values are to be pursued. Allen Buchanan stated the case clearly in describing Rawls´s version of liberal theory as "rules for a vanished Westphalian world."[5] To be precise, Buchanan challenged Rawls´s international argument about a "law of peoples," not all of Rawls´s liberal theory. There is in fact considerable controversy among those largely swayed by Rawls´s earlier theory of justice over whether to accept his later law of peoples.[6] For many of these, the demands of justice as fairness simply must override both the norm of tolerance that Rawls sees as underwriting a strong respect for different ways of life and the fact that the cohesion of actual existing social life is rooted in different historically created solidarities and ways of life. Others struggle more to reconcile respect for difference with the demands of a universalistic appeal to cosmopolitan justice.

But perhaps Rawls accepted too much from nationalist representations of "peoples" as discrete, culturally integrated entities. Nationalists often make strong claims to ethnic purity and cultural uniformity. But in fact part of the importance of nationalism is the ways in which the national bridges a variety of differences. It does this not simply by providing an encompassing culture but by providing an arena for public debate and culture-making.[7]

Certainly greater global solidarity would be a good thing. But many liberal, cosmopolitan arguments rely on three tendentious assumptions. First, that it will be possible to create strong enough solidarities at a global scale to underwrite democratic mutual commitment (or to do so soon enough that pursuing these should have equal or higher priority to strengthening national solidarities and making them more democratic). Second, that justice, respect, and rights are more effectively secured for more human beings by approaching these as ethical universals than as moral obligations situated within particular solidarities and ways of life. And third, that an interest in or commitment to the universal (or the cosmopolitan) is based on the absence of culture (because culture is particularistic bias) rather than itself being a kind of cultural perspective.[8]

I have argued elsewhere about the importance of seeing cosmopolitanism as the presence of particular sorts of culture rather than the absence of culture, and about the extent to which access to the cosmopolitan is distributed on the basis of privilege.[9] What I want to stress here is the extent to which nationalism and democracy may—together—hold more potential for providing political solidarity across lines of cultural difference.

STRUCTURES OF INTEGRATION

A key part of the work that nationalism does is to provide cultural support for structures of social integration. Indeed, it is itself a source of such integration insofar as it structures collective identities and solidarities.[10]

Not everyone would consider this an obvious gain. Starting from the premise that the primary obligation of each human being is to all others, a range of ethical cosmopolitans argue that any smaller-scale solidarity requires specific justification—and starts out under the suspicion of being nothing more than an illegitimate expression of self-interest at the expense of justice for humanity at large.[11] I don´t propose to take up such positions in detail here. Let it suffice to indicate that they are reached by starting with "bare" individuals as equivalent tokens of the universal type, humanity; that they treat the particularities of culture and social relations as extrinsic to and not constitutive of these individuals; that they substitute abstract ethics for politics and particularly for a conception of politics as a world-making and therefore necessarily historically specific process such as that developed in the rhetorical tradition; and finally that they lack any sociological account of how humanity is to be integrated such that the abstract norms they articulate may concretely be achieved. Such a procedure may open up some ethical insights, but it runs the risk of substituting a pure ought for a practical politics. It also deflects our attention from the social, cultural, and historical conditions of democracy.

Democracy depends on social solidarity and social institutions. Neither is given to human beings as a matter of nature; they must be achieved through human imagination and action—in short, through history. As a result, all actually existing examples vary and all are imperfect. It is more helpful to approach them in a spirit of "pragmatic fallibalism" than radical ethical universalism, asking about improvements more than perfection, next steps more than ultimate ends.[12] This doesn't mean that there is no value in utopian dreams or efforts to imagine radically better societies; it does mean both that such dreams will be more helpful if they include attention to the social conditions of solidarity alongside the abstract definitions of justice, and that in making abstract norms guides for practical action we will do well to temper them with recognition of historical circumstances.

Nations, and indeed all structures of social integration, have been achieved with more or less violence. This is neither a source of legitimacy nor a disqualification from it. No one gains rights from the blood of fallen ancestors. Neither does bloodshed render the institutions and solidarities that follow it mere results of force. Nations forged partly in war and in projects of remembering heroic dead exert powerful pulls on the living. It is an important project to try to turn national self-understanding in peaceful directions, but a merely illusory project to imagine that moral objections to past bellicosity or domestic repression render national solidarity unimportant.

National allegiances, moreover, are always in some part the result of symbolic violence and imposition, as for example countries are created in part by skewing resources towards capital cities and making provincials embarrassed by rural accents. In other cases the integration of subaltern populations into national projects has been brutal and severely unequal. But this does not mean that there is necessarily a politically sensible project of undoing those allegiances either in favor of the universal or in order to restore prior local identities—or that this might not itself be an imposition involving new symbolic—or material—violence.

Partitions and secessionist wars are almost universally bloody routes to political autonomy, and if they sometimes become inevitable that does not make them praiseworthy. Moreover, they create new nations which may be as repressive of difference as old ones. Far better to remake national identities and institutions to better accommodate diversity and to support both partial local autonomy and intercultural relations.

Many nationalist ideologies—and indeed many versions of the discursive formation of nationalism itself—mislead in this regard. Nationalist rhetoric is commonly employed to produce the image of populations unifying prepolitically, by culture, religion, or territory. This allows those who employ it to judge contemporary politics—and culture and economics—by the standard of a people understood as always already there, constituted in a kind of primal innocence outside the realm of ordinary politics. The people may be understood simply as given, on ethnic or other cultural grounds, or as the creation of martyrs, heroes, and lawgivers acting outside or above the normal politics of individual and sectional interests. Both images may be evoked at the same time. The important thing is the implication that the nation is established in advance of, separately from, the more quotidian developments which may then be judged as serving or failing to serve its interests.

But in reality nations are always the result of at least partially political histories. That is, not merely are they the result of more or less arbitrary historical circumstances—wars won or lost, mountain ranges that slow the spread of evangelism or commerce. They are also the result of self-constituting collective projects in which culture is created and choices are made. Nations are products not only bases of politics, and they are accordingly objects of new political projects.

Saying that the ideal of prepolitical national unity is an illusion does not make the illusion any less powerful, either in its grips on individual imaginations and emotions or in its capacity to constitute a cultural order. People who have read about "the invention of tradition" are still moved by national anthems and soccer teams, enlist in armies, and understand themselves to have "home" countries when they migrate.[13]

Nations are not the only or necessarily the primary structures of social integration of cultural identity. That they are commonly represented as a kind of "trump card" against other identities, exaggerating national unity and giving short shrift to intranational diversity, is a form of symbolic violence. But local autonomy and cultural diversity may be better pursued through improving structures of national integration rather than abandoning them.

National structures are important in the modern era both because they embody historical achievements and because globalization itself—a key ingredient of the entire modern era—creates a demand for mediating structures between humanity as a whole (or inhumanity as a whole, since that is as often what is achieved on a very large scale) and face-to-face interpersonal relations. Nations are important because integration beyond the level of family and community is important. This requires both culture and institutions. There is no reason to want all to be the same. Moreover, nations are not the only form for such integration—religions are also important and indeed sometimes transnational political movements. But the need for such integration means that nations are not simply "optional"; they may be restructured or replaced but there is no viable way simply to abandon them.

The integration nations help to achieve is of several sorts. They help to bind people together across social classes. They bridge regional and ethnic and sometimes religious differences. They link generations to each other, mobilizing traditions of cultural inheritance mutual obligation. They link the living to both ancestors and future generations. They do this not simply in ideology, but in social institutions which matter to the lives of individuals, families, and communities. Nations are integrated in educational systems, health care systems, and transportation systems. Strengthening these is generally a national and often a state project. Certainly philanthropists moved by care for humanity at large also build schools and clinics and sometimes roads. But, for the most part, these are achievements of nation-states and typically are public institutions (though this very public provision for the common good is currently under challenge). Not least of all, national integration is produced in the formation and sharing of new culture and in political arguments.

Nations accomplish all these linkages imperfectly, leaving room for contention. But if nationalism creates peoples, continued politics can transform them. At best, these are peoples in which the sentiment of common belonging is strong enough that it enables citizens to absorb the frustration of losing political battles over particular policies and leaders while remaining commited to the larger structure of integration. For there is little possibility of collective action to make and remake solidarity that is not also agonistic.[14] World-making politics is inevitably contentious politics, but not for that reason without solidarities.

Among the range of solidarities that have been mobilized in political action, national solidarities

have been distinctively capable of political self-constitution in the making or transformation of states. Nations, at least sometimes, are peoples able to utter (or believe they have uttered) phrases like "we the people" as it appears in the Preamble to the U.S. Constitution:

> We the people of the United States, in order to form a more perfect union, establish justice, insure domestic tranquility, provide for the common defense, promote the general welfare, and secure the blessings of liberty to ourselves and our posterity, do ordain and establish this Constitution for the United States of America.

Such acts of founding are basic to national histories throughout the Americas and present a distinctive counterpart to the idea of nations as ethnic inheritances, as always already there, which is more common in Europe (though in Europe the history of revolutions is a reminder of the role of active creation in nationalism).

To be sure, the founding of a new nation has never been simply the uncoerced and egalitarian project of all potential citizens. On the contrary, elites have commonly driven national projects and claims to unitary national voice have typically occluded not only the cultural diversity within nations but the subjugation of large populations. Indigenous peoples throughout the Americas, and in many countries slaves of African descent, were thus dominated, marginalized, and often in political rhetoric forgotten by national founders. But if independence was not liberation for many in the Americas—or in postcolonies around the world—the new nations, especially where they embraced democracy, did create conditions for continued struggles for fuller citizenship.

The idea of constituting a new country—making new social institutions to integrate people in a solidarity only partially inherited—has profound significance for democracy. Such acts of founding are reminders that the very structures of integration that constitute countries are subject to making—and potentially to democratic will-formation. Democracy, in other words, is something more than electing the least objectionable leaders.

Hannah Arendt situated such acts of revolutionary founding of new countries within the more general human potential for innovative world-making—"natality"—in every act of political speech.[15] Her argument is rooted in a rhetorical tradition that stretches back to ancient Greece but which has been subordinated by dominant perspectives in philosophy and political theory. Politics has been seen as more about power than persuasion, more about perfecting institutional arrangements than nurturing creativity. But Arendt and the rhetorical tradition remind us of a strong sense in which politics can be the creation of new institutional arrangements and indeed the remaking of the world. Politics in this sense is ineluctably historical, culturally specific, and diverse.

If democracy is, following Arendt's lead, about the ways in which people may creatively develop new ways of living together, choose new institutional arrangements, and even found new countries, then it is necessarily not simply a matter of abstract design or the best formal procedures. It is a matter of discerning ways to make the will and well-being of ordinary people more determinative of the very formation of social institutions as well as of specific decisions within them. This can be informed by abstract, universal political theory but it is also necessarily informed by concrete, historically and culturally specific circumstances.

From one side, nationalism is an internationally reproduced discursive formation full of pressures to make each country into an isomorphic token of a global type. There are pressures for conformity: each country should have a recognizable government with ministers and other officials analogous to those in other countries. Each should have a national museum and national folklore, passports and border controls, an authority to issue driving licenses and postage stamps.[16] Countries also face similar problems and learn from each other. But at the same time, in their more historically and culturally specific dimensions, nationalisms mediate between the isomorphic character of constructing tokens of a global type and the historical particularities of tradition and cultural creativity. Distinctive national self-understandings are produced and reproduced in literature, film, political debate—and political grumbling, political jokes, and political insults. These structure the ways in which people feel solidarity with each other (and distinction from outsiders).

Modernist self-understanding commonly exaggerates breaks with history and cultural traditions. Conscious plans and rational choices are favored—even immediate expressions of emotion are in more favor than adherence to tradition. Nationalism, however, is a way of claiming history within a modernist frame. It is typically misleading for it claims history through units of contemporary consciousness and solidarity that did not necessarily exist in the past.

Thus archeologists may speak of Sweden or Sudan when describing sites and cultures millennia older than either nation. Of course, the history that produced both Sweden and Sudan is a matter of imposition and drawing of boundaries by force, not simply of maturation. In different ways, each is troubled today by the international flows and forces of modernity – migrations, money and commodities, media. Each has difficulty with its internal diversity, and leaders in each are tempted to assert untenable ethnic (and sometimes religious) definitions of "proper" national identity. Sweden was shaped by its earlier imperial ambitions as well as later nationalism. Transnational Protestantism informed its constitution which is now being transformed by European unification. Sudan has long been shaped by both pan-African and pan-Arab projects as it is now by transnational Islam. Sudan is also being remade by a geopolitical crisis reverberating throughout northeast Africa, with issues of trade and diplomacy making distant China an important counterpart and human suffering which has brought a humanitarian response on a nearly global scale.

The stories of Sweden and Sudan do not simply pit long-standing, unquestioned, and culturally defined internal unity against new, troubling, and political-economic external forces. Internal diversity is part of the history of each. Some of the lines of diversity predate the history of each (as there were Arabs and Africans, Nubians and Nuer before there was a Sudan). And the history of each is partly a matter of producing what now are taken as defining boundaries (as seemingly obviously unitary Sweden not only includes territories whose integration was contested but doesn't include its former dominions of Estonia, Finland, or Norway). But it is also a matter of producing language, culture, distinctive social institutions, and personal styles.

Nationality situates persons in time, in the world, and in relation to each other. Of course it is not the only identity anyone has. Nationality may be supplemented by a range of other categories of belonging and may be in tension with some—from religion to class. It could be replaced as a primary dimension of belonging; it could be transformed. But simply to imagine overcoming it without attending to the work it does would be a mistake.

NOTES

1. Nationalism is a "discursive formation," in Foucault's sense; see *The Archaeology of Knowledge* and *Power/Knowledge*. That is, it is a way of talking that inescapably exceeds the bounds of any single usage, that endlessly generate more talk, and that embody tensions and contradictions. Nationalism is not simply a settled position, but a cluster of rhetoric and reference that enables people to articulate positions which are not settled and to take stands in opposition to each other on basic issues in society and culture. Nationalist rhetoric provides the modern era with a constitutive framework for the identification of collective subjects, both the protagonists of historical struggles and those who experience history and by whose experience it can be judged good or bad, progress or regress or stagnation. In this, nationalism most resembles another great discursive formation, also constitutive for modernity, individualism. See Calhoun, *Nationalism*.

2. The status of this hyphen is subject to considerable controversy. It is common to speak of "nations" without distinguishing the state from the ostensibly integrated population associated with it. This is in fact hard to avoid without pedantry, and while I shall at certain points make clear that I mean one or the other, like most writers I shall not consistently make clear that the relationship between national identity or integration and state authority or structure is not stable or consistent. As a discursive formation, nationalism continually reproduces the idea that there should be a link between nation and state as well as various forms and dimensions of national identity, integration, distinction, and conflict.

3. John Rawls, *Political Liberalism*, p. 41.

4. Of course it is worth recalling that the 1648 Peace of Westphalia did not transform the world overnight into one of strongly institutionalized nation-states and international relations. It is more a myth or symbol for the project of remaking the world in these terms than a token of such achievement. See Benno Teschke, *The Myth of 1648*.

5. Allen Buchanan, "Rawls' Law of Peoples: Rules for a Vanished Westphalian World," *Ethics* 110, no. 4 (2000): 697–721.

6. Rawls, *A Theory of Justice and The Law of Peoples*; see also Charles R. Beitz, "Rawls' Law of Peoples," *Ethics* 110, no. 4 (2000): 669–96 and Rex Martin and David Reidy (eds.), *Rawls's Law of Peoples: A Realistic Utopia?* (Oxford: Blackwell, 2006).

7. By "encompassing" I mean to echo Louis Dumont's argument about the ways in which culture may bring together dimensions that cannot be logically integrated. National cultures often encompass different subcultures without integrating them and encompass logically contradictory values, creating nonetheless a sense in which they belong as parts of the larger whole. See Dumont, *Homo Hierarchicus* (Chicago, IL: University of Chicago Press, 1966).

8. The best and most careful of such cosmopolitan theoretical visions come from Jürgen Habermas (e.g. *Inclusion of the Other*); and David Held (e.g. *Democracy and the Global Order*). See also essays in Archibugi and Held, *Cosmopolitan Democracy*, Archibugi *et al.*, *Re-Imagining Political Community*, Archibugi, *Debating Cosmopolitics*, and Vertovec and Cohen, *Conceiving Cosmopolitanism*. These cosmopolitan visions are clearly Kantian; for elaboration of that heritage see Bohman and Lutz-Bachmann, *Perpetual Peace: Essays on Kant's Cosmopolitan Ideal*. My

reference here is mainly to these more political theories of cosmopolitanism, not to the accounts of "vernacular cosmopolitanism" in which some anthropologists and historians have urged us to look at the more concrete and often local transactions and cultural productions in which people actually forge relations with each other across lines of difference. See Pollock *et al.,* "Cosmopolitanisms," *Public Culture* 12, no. 3 (2000). In a sense, I pursue in this paper a meeting point between these two perspectives, one which I think is impossible to discern if one focuses only on transcending the nation, imagining the world mainly globally "at large" and relating this to the local and immediate rather than emphasizing the importance of the mediating institutions of which nations and states are among the most important.

9. See Craig Calhoun, *Cosmopolitanism and Belonging* (London: Routledge, forthcoming).

10. Nationalism figures prominently as an example of "categorical" identities in which each individual figures as an equivalent token of the larger type. But this does not exhaust the ways in which national culture matters to the production of solidarity. Common language and frameworks of meaning, for example, may integrate people without suggesting that they are equivalent. Common projects create alliances among otherwise dissimilar people. Communities understand their solidarity to be embeddedness in webs of relationships as well as "categorical" distinctions from other communities. Of course, culture may also figure as ideology underwriting, for better or worse, functional integration among national institutions or nationally organized markets, and direct exercise of power. See Calhoun, *Cosmopolitanism and Belonging.*

11. Martha Nussbaum can serve as an exemplar of such "extreme cosmopolitans" reasoning from the ethical equivalence of individuals. See her *For Love of Country.* See also discussion in Samuel Scheffler, *Boundaries and Allegiances: Problems of Justice and Responsibility in Liberal Thought* (Oxford: Oxford University Press, 2001) and Calhoun, "Belonging in the Cosmopolitan Imaginary."

12. See Richard Bernstein, *The Abuse of Evil* (Cambridge: Polity, 2005), ch. 2.

13. Hobsbawm and Ranger, writing in *The Invention of Tradition,* are thus right about invention but wrong about its implications.

14. To imagine a politics without agonism, a democratic citizenship merely of agreement, is a contradiction in terms, as Chantal Mouffe and others have suggested. See Mouffe, *Dimensions of Radical Democracy* and continued discussion in more recent works.

15. Arendt, *On Revolution; Between Past and Future* (New York: Viking, 1968).

16. This side of nationalism is emphasized by institutionalist theories such as the "world polity" theory of John Meyer and a range of colleagues; for an early statement that helped launch the perspective and informed discussion of "institutional isomorphism," see, Meyer and Rowan, "I Organizations."

SECTION XII

1. What do Omi and Winant mean when they describe race as an ideological construct? As an objective condition?

2. What is a racial formation and how do Omi and Winant think this concept contributes to a critical theory of race?

3. Why does Paul Gilroy use the term "camps" and what is its significance for his argument on behalf of cosmopolitan humanism?

4. What does Kymlicka mean by the term "multiculturalism," why do so many critics see it in decline, and why does he disagree with this claim?

5. Is it possible, as Brubaker encourages us to do, to treat ethnicity without recourse to treating it in terms of ethnic groups? Why does he think it´s important to make an effort to avoid what he refers to as "groupism?"

6. Calhoun begins his essay by claiming that "If nationalism is over, we shall miss it." Why does he think we would miss it? Do you agree or disagree with him? Why?

XIII. CRITICAL THEORY

61. ART IN THE AGE OF MECHANICAL REPRODUCTION

WALTER BENJAMIN

Though associated with members of the Frankfurt School, Walter Benjamin (1892-1940) was an independent scholar without formal institutional affiliations. His thought was influenced by a wide range of intellectual currents, including the neo-Marxism of Theodor Adorno, the more traditional Marxism of Bertolt Brecht, the utopian theory of Ernst Bloch, and the mysticism of Gershom Scholem. First published in 1936, "Art in the Age of Mechanical Reproduction" is one of his most original and widely read works. In this essay, he seeks to explain the impact on art of the introduction of new technologies that allow for the easy reproduction of the work. This is most evident in photography and film. His argument is that in traditional cultures, art contained an aura, which he sees as linked to ritual. In the modern world, that aura is lost as a consequence of various modes of mechanical reproduction. Benjamin does not engage in a critique of this new development but instead seeks to articulate its implications for the society at large.

PREFACE

When Marx undertook his critique of the capitalistic mode of production, this mode was in its infancy. Marx directed his efforts in such a way as to give them prognostic value. He went back to the basic conditions underlying capitalistic production and through his presentation showed what could be expected of capitalism in the future. The result was that one could expect it not only to exploit the proletariat with increasing intensity, but ultimately to create conditions which would make it possible to abolish capitalism itself.

The transformation of the superstructure, which takes place far more slowly than that of the substructure, has taken more than half a century to manifest in all areas of culture the changes in the conditions of production. Only today can it be indicated what form this has taken. Certain prognostic requirements should be met by these statements. However, theses about the art of the proletariat after its assumption of power or about the art of a classless society would have less bearing on these demands than theses about the developmental tendencies of art under present conditions of production. Their dialectic is no less noticeable in the superstructure than in the economy. It would therefore be wrong to underestimate the value of such theses as a weapon. They brush aside a number of outmoded concepts, such as creativity and genius, eternal value and mystery—concepts whose uncontrolled (and at present almost uncontrollable) application would lead to a processing of data in the Fascist sense. The concepts which are introduced into the theory of art in what follows differ from the more familiar terms in that they are completely useless for the purposes of Fascism. They are, on the other hand, useful for the formulation of revolutionary demands in the politics of art.

I

In principle a work of art has always been reproducible. Man-made artifacts could always be imitated by men. Replicas were made by pupils in practice of their craft, by masters for diffusing their works, and, finally, by third parties in the pursuit of gain. Mechanical reproduction of a work of art, however, represents something new. Historically, it advanced intermittently and in leaps at long intervals, but with accelerated intensity. The Greeks knew only two procedures of technically reproducing works of art: founding and stamping. Bronzes, terra cottas, and coins were the only art works which they could produce in quantity. All others were unique and could not be mechanically reproduced. With the woodcut graphic art became mechanically reproducible for the first time, long before script became reproducible by print. The enormous changes which printing, the mechanical reproduction of writing, has brought about in literature are a familiar story. However, within the phenomenon which we are here examining from the perspective of world history, print is merely a special, though particularly important, case. During the Middle Ages engraving and etching were added to the woodcut; at the beginning of the nineteenth century lithography made its appearance.

With lithography the technique of reproduction reached an essentially new stage. This much more direct process was distinguished by the tracing of the design on a stone rather than its incision on a block of wood or its etching on a copperplate and permitted graphic art for the first time to put its products on the market, not only in large numbers as hitherto, but also in daily changing forms. Lithography enabled graphic art to illustrate everyday life, and it began to keep pace with printing. But only a few decades after its invention, lithography was surpassed by photography. For the first time in the process of pictorial reproduction, photography freed the hand of the most important artistic functions which henceforth devolved only upon the eye looking into a lens. Since the eye perceives more

swiftly than the hand can draw, the process of pictorial reproduction was accelerated so enormously that it could keep pace with speech. A film operator shooting a scene in the studio captures the images at the speed of an actor's speech. Just as lithography virtually implied the illustrated newspaper, so did photography fore-shadow the sound film. The technical reproduction of sound was tackled at the end of the last century. These convergent endeavors made predictable a situation which Paul Valéry pointed up in this sentence: "Just as water, gas, and electricity are brought into our houses from far off to satisfy our needs in response to a minimal effort, so we shall be supplied with visual or auditory images, which will appear and disappear at a simple movement of the hand, hardly more than a sign"(*op. cit.*, p. 226). Around 1900 technical reproduction had reached a standard that not only permitted it to reproduce all transmitted works of art and thus to cause the most profound change in their impact upon the public; it also had captured a place of its own among the artistic processes For the study of this standard nothing is more revealing than the nature of the repercussions that these two different manifestations—the reproduction of works of art and the art of the film—have had on art in its traditional form.

II

Even the most perfect reproduction of a work of art is lacking in one element: its presence in time and space, its unique existence at the place where it happens to be. This unique existence of the work of art determined the history to which it was subject throughout the time of its existence. This includes the changes which it may have suffered in physical condition over the years as well as the various changes in its ownership. The traces of the first can be revealed only by chemical or physical analyses which it is impossible to perform on a reproduction; changes of ownership are subject to a tradition which must be traced from the situation of the original.

The presence of the original is the prerequisite to the concept of authenticity. Chemical analyses of the patina of a bronze can help to establish this, as does the proof that a given manuscript of the **Middle Ages** stems from an archive of the fifteenth century. The whole sphere of authenticity is outside technical—and of course, not only technical—reproducibility. . . . Confronted with its manual reproduction, which was usually branded as a forgery, the original preserved all its authority; not so *vis à vis* technical reproduction. The reason is twofold. First, process reproduction is more independent of the original than manual reproduction. For example, in photography, process reproduction can bring out those aspects of the original that are unattainable to the naked eye yet accessible to the lens, which is adjustable and chooses its angle at will. And photographic reproduction, with the aid of certain processes, such as enlargement or slow motion, can capture images which escape natural vision. Secondly, technical reproduction can put the copy of the original into situations which would be out of reach for the original itself. Above all, it enables the original to meet the beholder halfway, be it in the form of a photograph or a phonograph record. The cathedral leaves its locale to be received in the studio of a lover of art; the choral production, performed in an auditorium or in the open air, resounds in the drawing room.

The situations into which the product of mechanical reproduction can be brought may not touch the actual work of art, yet the quality of its presence is always depreciated. This holds not only for the art work but also, for instance, for a landscape which passes in review before the spectator in a movie. In the case of the art object, a most sensitive nucleus—namely, its authenticity—is interfered with whereas no natural object is vulnerable on that score. The authenticity of a thing is the essence of all that is transmissible from its beginning, ranging from its substantive duration to its testimony to the history which it has experienced. Since the historical testimony rests on the authenticity, the former, too, is jeopardized by reproduction when substantive duration ceases to matter. And what is really jeopardized when the historical testimony is affected is the authority of the object. . . .

One might subsume the eliminated element in the term "aura" and go on to say: that which withers in the age of mechanical reproduction is the aura of the work of art. This is a symptomatic process whose significance points beyond the realm of art. One might generalize by saying: the technique of reproduction detaches the reproduced object from the domain of tradition. By making many reproductions it substitutes a plurality of copies for a unique existence. And in permitting the reproduction to meet the beholder or listener in his own particular situation, it reactivates the object reproduced. These two processes lead to a tremendous shattering of tradition which is the obverse of the contemporary crisis and renewal of mankind. Both processes are intimately connected with the contemporary mass movements. Their most powerful agent is the film. Its social significance, particularly in its most positive form, is inconceivable without its destructive, cathartic aspect, that is, the liquidation of the traditional value of the cultural heritage. This phenomenon is most palpable in the great historical films. It extends to ever new positions. In 1927 Abel Gance exclaimed enthusiastically: "Shakespeare, Rembrandt, Beethoven will make films . . . all legends, all mythologies and all myths, all founders of religion, and the very religions . . . await their exposed resurrection, and the heroes crowd each other at the gate."[1] Presumably without intending it, he issued an invitation to a far-reaching liquidation.

III

During long periods of history, the mode of human sense perception changes with humanity's entire mode of existence. The manner in which human sense perception is organized, the medium in which it is accomplished, is determined not only by nature but by historical circumstances as well. The fifth century, with its great shifts of population, saw the birth of the late Roman art industry and the Vienna Genesis, and there developed not only an art different from that of antiquity but also a new kind of perception. The scholars of the Viennese school, Riegl and Wickhoff, who resisted the weight of classical tradition under which these later art forms had been buried, were the first to draw conclusions from them concering the organization of perception at the time. However far-reaching their insight, these scholars limited themselves to showing the significant, formal hallmark which characterized perception in late Roman times. They did not attempt—and, perhaps, saw no way—to show the social transformations expressed by these changes of perception. The conditions for an analogous insight are more favorable in the present. And if changes in the medium of contemporary perception can be comprehended as decay of the aura, it is possible to show its social causes.

The concept of aura which was proposed above with reference to historical objects may usefully be illustrated with reference to the aura of natural ones. We define the aura of the latter as the unique phenomenon of a distance, however close it may be. If, while resting on a summer afternoon, you follow with your eyes a mountain range on the horizon or a branch which casts its shadow over you, you experience the aura of those mountains, of that branch. This image makes it easy to comprehend the social bases of the contemporary decay of the aura. It rests on two circumstances, both of which are related to the increasing significance of the masses in contemporary life. Namely, the desire of contemporary masses to bring things "closer" spatially and humanly, which is just as ardent as their bent toward overcoming the uniqueness of every reality by accepting its reproduction.... Every day the urge grows stronger to get hold of an object at very close range by way of its likeness, its reproduction. Unmistakably, reproduction as offered by picture magazines and newsreels differs from the image seen by the unarmed eye. Uniqueness and permanence are as closely linked in the latter as are transitoriness and reproducibility in the former. To pry an object from its shell, to destroy its aura, is the mark of a perception whose "sense of the universal equality of things" has increased to such a degree that it extracts it even from a unique object by means of reproduction. Thus is manifested in the field of perception what in the theoretical sphere is noticeable in the increasing importance of statistics. The adjustment of reality to the masses and of the masses to reality is a process of unlimited scope, as much for thinking as for perception.

I V

The uniqueness of a work of art is inseparable from its being imbedded in the fabric of tradition. This tradition itself is thoroughly alive and extremely changeable. An ancient statue of Venus, for example, stood in a different traditional context with the Greeks, who made it an object of veneration, than with the clerics of the Middle Ages, who viewed it as an ominous idol. Both of them, however, were equally confronted with its uniqueness, that is, its aura. Originally the contextual integration of art in tradition found its expression in the cult. We know that the earliest art works originated in the service of a ritual—first the magical, then the religious kind. It is significant that the existence of the work of art with reference to its aura is never entirely separated from its ritual function.... In other words, the unique value of the "authentic" work of art has its basis in ritual, the location of its original use value. This ritualistic basis, however remote, is still recognizable as secularized ritual even in the most profane forms of the cult of beauty. ...The secular cult of beauty, developed during the Renaissance and prevailing for three centuries, clearly showed that ritualistic basis in its decline and the first deep crisis which befell it. With the advent of the first truly revolutionary means of reproduction, photography, simultaneously with the rise of socialism, art sensed the approaching crisis which has become evident a century later. At the time, art reacted with the doctrine of *l'art pour l'art*, that is, with a theology of art. This gave rise to what might be called a negative theology in the form of the idea of "purer" art, which not only denied any social function of art but also any categorizing by subject matter. (In poetry, Mallarmé was the first to take this position.)

An analysis of art in the age of mechanical reproduction must do justice to these relationships, for they lead us to an all-important insight: for the first time in world history mechanical reproduction emancipates the work of art from its parasitical dependence on ritual. To a greater degree the work of art reproduced becomes the work of art designed for reproducibility....From a photographic negative, for example, one can make any number of prints; to ask for the "authentic" print makes no sense. But the instant the criterion of authenticity ceases to be applicable to artistic production, the total function of art is reversed. Instead of being based on ritual, it begins to be based on another practice—politics.

V

Works of art are received and valued on different planes. Two polar types stand out: with one, the accent is on the cult value; with the other, on the exhibition value of the work.... Artistic production begins with ceremonial objects destined to serve in a cult. One may assume that what mattered was their existence, not their being on view. The elk portrayed by the man of the Stone Age on the walls of his cave was an instrument of magic. He did expose it to his fellow men, but in the main it was meant for the spirits. Today the cult value would seem to demand that the work of art remain hidden. Certain statues of gods are accessible only to the priest in the cella; certain Madonnas remain covered nearly all year round; certain sculptures on medieval cathedrals are invisible to the spectator on ground level. With the emancipation of the various art practices from ritual go increasing opportunities for the exhibition of their products. It is easier to exhibit a portrait bust that can be sent here and there than to exhibit the statue of a divinity that has its fixed place in the interior of a temple. The same holds for the painting as against the mosaic or fresco that preceded it. And even though the public presentability of a mass originally may have been just as great as that of a symphony, the latter originated at the moment when its public presentability promised to surpass that of the mass.

With the different methods of technical reproduction of a work of art, its fitness for exhibition increased to such an extent that the quantitative shift between its two poles turned into a qualitative transformation of its nature. This is comparable to the situation of the work of art in prehistoric times when, by the absolute emphasis on its cult value, it was, first and foremost, an instrument of magic. Only later did it come to be recognized as a work of art. In the same way today, by the absolute emphasis on its exhibition value the work of art becomes a creation with entirely new functions, among which the one we are conscious of, the artistic function, later may be recognized as incidental . . . . This much is certain: today photography and the film are the most serviceable exemplifications of this new function.

NOTE

1.   Abel Gance, "Le Temps de l'image est venu," *L'Art cinématographique*, Vol. 2, pp. 94 f, Paris, 1927.

62. ONE-DIMENSIONAL MAN

HERBERT MARCUSE

Herbert Marcuse (1898-1979) was one of the key figures associated with the critical theory developed by the members of the Frankfurt School between World Wars I and II. Like so many of his generation, Marcuse was forced to leave Germany because of the rise of Nazism. He settled in the United States, where he remained for the rest of his life, teaching at Brandeis University and later at the University of California, San Diego. During the tumultuous decade of the 1960s, he became an influential intellectual figure for radical students in the New Left. From an early date, his work sought to reveal the lineage of critical theory in the history of German philosophy, especially in the traditions emerging out of Kant and Hegel. In his view, critical theory is primarily concerned with the potential for human freedom, and as such it offers a critique of contemporary social conditions, not from the perspective of utopian thinking, but with an eye to the actual potential for societal transformation. *One-Dimensional Man* (1964) is perhaps his more important and widely read work of social criticism. The selection below is the introduction to that book, in which Marcuse argues that freedom is eroding in advanced industrial societies that are both affluent and democratic—a consequence of the fact that technology and bureaucracy have produced an overly administered society.

1: THE NEW FORMS OF CONTROL

A comfortable, smooth, reasonable, democratic unfreedom prevails in advanced industrial civilization, a token of technical progress. Indeed, what could be more rational than the suppression of individuality in the mechanization of socially necessary but painful performances; the concentration of individual enterprises in more effective, more productive corporations; the regulation of free competition among unequally equipped economic subjects; the curtailment of prerogatives and national sovereignties which impede the international organization of resources. That this technological order also involves a political and intellectual coordination may be a regrettable and yet promising development.

The rights and liberties which were such vital factors in the origins and earlier stages of industrial society yield to a higher stage of this society: they are losing their traditional rationale and content. Freedom of thought, speech, and conscience were—just as free enterprise, which they served to promote and protect—essentially *critical* ideas, designed to replace an obsolescent material and intellectual culture by a more productive and rational one. Once institutionalized, these rights and liberties shared the fate of the society of which they had become an integral part. The achievement cancels the premises.

To the degree to which freedom from want, the concrete substance of all freedom, is becoming a real possibility, the liberties which pertain to a state of lower productivity are losing their former content. Independence of thought, autonomy, and the right to political opposition are being deprived of their basic critical function in a society which seems increasingly capable of satisfying the needs of the individuals through the way in which it is organized. Such a society may justly demand acceptance of its principles and institutions, and reduce the opposition to the

Herbert Marcuse, *One-Dimensional Man: Studies in the Ideology of Advanced Industrial Society*. Boston: Beacon Press, 1964, pp. 1–12. ✦

discussion and promotion of alternative policies *within* the status quo. In this respect, it seems to make little difference whether the increasing satisfaction of needs is accomplished by an authoritarian or a non-authoritarian system. Under the conditions of a rising standard of living, non-conformity with the system itself appears to be socially useless, and the more so when it entails tangible economic and political disadvantages and threatens the smooth operation of the whole. Indeed, at least in so far as the necessities of life are involved, there seems to be no reason why the production and distribution of goods and services should proceed through the competitive concurrence of individual liberties.

Freedom of enterprise was from the beginning not altogether a blessing. As the liberty to work or to starve, it spelled toil, insecurity, and fear for the vast majority of the population. If the individual were no longer compelled to prove himself on the market, as a free economic subject, the disappearance of this kind of freedom would be one of the greatest achievements of civilization. The technological processes of mechanization and standardization might release individual energy into a yet uncharted realm of freedom beyond necessity. The very structure of human existence would be altered; the individual would be liberated from the work world's imposing upon him alien needs and alien possibilities. The individual would be free to exert autonomy over a life that would be his own. If the productive apparatus could be organized and directed toward the satisfaction of the vital needs, its control might well be centralized; such control would not prevent individual autonomy, but render it possible.

This is a goal within the capabilities of advanced industrial civilization, the "end" of technological rationality. In actual fact, however, the contrary trend operates: the apparatus imposes its economic and political requirements for defense and expansion on labor time and free time, on the material and intellectual culture. By virtue of the way it has organized its technological base, contemporary industrial society tends to be totalitarian. For "totalitarian" is not only a terroristic political coordination of society, but also a nonterroristic economic-technical coordination which operates through the manipulation of needs by vested interests. It thus precludes the emergence of an effective opposition against the whole. Not only a specific form of government or party rule makes for totalitarianism, but also a specific system of production and distribution which may well be compatible with a "pluralism" of parties, newspapers, "countervailing powers," etc.

Today political power asserts itself through its power over the machine process and over the technical organization of the apparatus. The government of advanced and advancing industrial societies can maintain and secure itself only when it succeeds in mobilizing, organizing, and exploiting the technical, scientific, and mechanical productivity available to industrial civilization. And this productivity mobilizes society as a whole, above and beyond any particular individual or group interests. The brute fact that the machine's physical (only physical?) power surpasses that of the individual, and of any particular group of individuals, makes the machine the most effective political instrument in any society whose basic organization is that of the machine process. But the political trend may be reversed; essentially the power of the machine is only the stored-up and projected power of man. To the extent to which the work world is conceived of as a machine and mechanized accordingly, it becomes the *potential* basis of a new freedom for man.

Contemporary industrial civilization demonstrates that it has reached the stage at which "the free society" can no longer be adequately defined in the traditional terms of economic, political, and intellectual liberties, not because these liberties have become insignificant, but because they are too significant to be confined within the traditional forms. New modes of realization are needed, corresponding to the new capabilities of society.

Such new modes can be indicated only in negative terms because they would amount to the negation of the prevailing modes. Thus economic freedom would mean freedom *from* the economy—from being controlled by economic forces and relationships; freedom from the daily struggle for existence, from earning a living. Political freedom would mean liberation of the individuals *from* politics over which they have no effective control. Similarly, intellectual freedom would mean the restoration of individual thought now absorbed by mass communication and indoctrination, abolition of "public opinion" together with its makers.

The unrealistic sound of these propositions is indicative, not of their utopian character, but of the strength of the forces which prevent their realization. The most effective and enduring form of warfare against liberation is the implanting of material and intellectual needs that perpetuate obsolete forms of the struggle for existence.

The intensity, the satisfaction and even the character of human needs, beyond the biological level, have always been preconditioned. Whether or not the possibility of doing or leaving, enjoying or destroying, possessing or rejecting something is seized as a *need* depends on whether or not it can be seen as desirable and necessary for the prevailing societal institutions and interests. In this sense, human needs are historical needs and, to the extent to which the society demands the repressive development of the individual, his needs themselves and their claim for satisfaction are subject to overriding critical standards.

We may distinguish both true and false needs. "False" are those which are superimposed upon the individual by particular social interests in his repression: the needs which perpetuate toil, aggressiveness, misery, and injustice. Their satisfaction might be most gratifying to the individual, but this happiness is not a condition which has to be maintained and protected if it serves to arrest the development of the ability (his own and others) to recognize the disease of the whole and grasp the chances of curing the disease. The result then is euphoria in unhappiness. Most of the prevailing needs to relax, to have fun, to behave and consume in accordance with the advertisements, to love and hate what others love and hate, belong to this category of false needs.

Such needs have a societal content and function which are determined by external powers over which the individual has no control; the development and satisfaction of these needs is heteronomous. No matter how much such needs may have become the individual's own, reproduced and fortified by the conditions of his existence; no matter how much he identifies himself with them and finds himself in their satisfaction, they continue to be what they were from the beginning—products of a society whose dominant interest demands repression.

The prevalence of repressive needs is an accomplished fact, accepted in ignorance and defeat, but a fact that must be undone in the interest of the happy individual as well as all those whose misery is the price of his satisfaction. The only needs that have an unqualified claim for satisfaction are the vital ones—nourishment, clothing, lodging at the attainable level of culture. The satisfaction of these needs is the prerequisite for the realization of *all* needs, of the unsublimated as well as the sublimated ones.

For any consciousness and conscience, for any experience which does not accept the prevailing societal interest as the supreme law of thought and behavior, the established universe of needs and satisfactions is a fact to be questioned—questioned in terms of truth and falsehood. These terms are historical throughout, and their objectivity is historical. The judgement of needs and their satisfaction, under the given conditions, involves standards of *priority*—standards which refer to the optimal development of the individual, of all individuals, under the optimal utilization of the material and intellectual resources available to man. The resources are calculable. "Truth" and "falsehood" of needs designate objective conditions to the extent to which the universal satisfaction of vital needs and, beyond it, the progressive alleviation of toil and poverty, are universally valid standards. But as historical standards, they do not only vary according to area and stage of development, they also can be defined only in (greater or lesser) *contradiction* to the prevailing ones. What tribunal can possibly claim the authority of decision?

In the last analysis, the question of what are true and false needs must be answered by the individuals themselves, but only in the last analysis; that is, if and when they are free to give their own answer. As long as they are kept incapable of being autonomous, as long as they are kept indoctrinated and manipulated (down to their very instincts), their answer to this question cannot be taken as their own. By the same token, however, no tribunal can justly arrogate to itself the right to decide which needs should be developed and satisfied. Any such tribunal is reprehensible, although our revulsion does not do away with the question: how can the people who have been the object of effective and productive domination by themselves create the conditions of freedom?

The more rational, productive, technical, and total the repressive administration of society becomes, the more unimaginable the means and ways by which the administered individuals might break their servitude and seize their own liberation. To be sure, to impose Reason upon an entire society is a paradoxical and scandalous idea—although one might dispute the righteousness of a society which ridicules this idea while making its own population into objects of total administration. All liberation depends on the consciousness of servitude, and the emergence of this consciousness is always hampered by the predominance of needs and satisfactions which, to a great extent, have become the individual's own. The process always replaces one system of preconditioning by another; the optimal goal is the replacement of false needs by true ones, the abandonment of repressive satisfaction.

The distinguishing feature of advanced industrial society is its effective suffocation of those needs which demand liberation—liberation also from that which is tolerable and rewarding and comfortable—while it sustains and absolves the destructive power and repressive function of the affluent society. Here, the social controls exact the overwhelming need for the production and consumption of waste; the need for stupefying work where it is no longer a real necessity; the need for modes of relaxation which soothe and prolong this stupefication; the need for maintaining such deceptive liberties as free competition at administered prices, a free press which censors itself, free choice between brands and gadgets.

Under the rule of a repressive whole, liberty can be made into a powerful instrument of domination. The range of choice open to the individual is not the decisive factor in determining the degree of human freedom, but *what* can be chosen and what *is* chosen by the individual. The criterion for free choice can never be an absolute one, but neither is it entirely relative. Free election of masters does not abolish the masters or the slaves. Free choice among a wide variety of goods and services does not signify freedom if these goods and services sustain social controls over a life of toil and fear—that is, if they sustain alienation. And the spontaneous reproduction of superimposed needs by the individual does not establish autonomy; it only testifies to the efficacy of the controls.

Our insistence on the depth and efficacy of these controls is open to the objection that we overrate greatly the indoctrinating power of the "media," and that by themselves the people would feel and satisfy the needs which are now imposed upon them. The objection misses the point. The preconditioning does not start with the mass production of radio and television and with the centralization of their control. The people enter this stage as preconditioned receptacles of long standing; the decisive difference is in the flattening out of the contrast (or conflict) between the given and the possible, between the satisfied and the unsatisfied needs. Here, the so-called equalization of class distinctions reveals its ideological function. If the worker and his boss enjoy the same television program and visit the same resort places, if the typist is as attractively made up as the daughter of her employer, if the Negro owns a Cadillac, if they all read the same newspaper, then this assimilation indicates not the disappearance of classes, but the extent to which the needs and satisfactions that serve the preservation of the Establishment are shared by the underlying population.

Indeed, in the most highly developed areas of contemporary society, the transplantation of social into individual needs is so effective that the difference between them seems to be purely theoretical. Can one really distinguish between the mass media as instruments of information and entertainment, and as agents of manipulation and indoctrination? Between the automobile as nuisance and as convenience? Between the horrors and the comforts of functional architecture? Between the work for national defense and the work for corporate gain? Between the private pleasure and the commercial and political utility involved in increasing the birth rate?

We are again confronted with one of the most vexing aspects of advanced industrial civilization: the rational character of its irrationality. Its productivity and efficiency, its capacity to increase and spread comforts, to turn waste into need, and destruction into construction, the extent to which this civilization transforms the object world into an extension of man's mind and body makes the very notion of alienation questionable. The people recognize themselves in their commodities; they find their soul in their automobile, hi-fi set, split-level home, kitchen equipment. The very mechanism which ties the individual to his society has changed, and social control is anchored in the new needs which it has produced.

The prevailing forms of social control are technological in a new sense. To be sure, the technical structure and efficacy of the productive and destructive apparatus has been a major instrumentality for subjecting the population to the established social division of labor throughout the modern period. Moreover, such integration has always been accompanied by more obvious forms of compulsion: loss of livelihood, the administration of justice, the police, the armed forces. It still is. But in the contemporary period, the technological controls appear to be the very embodiment of Reason for the benefit of all social groups and interests—to such an extent that all contradiction seems irrational and all counteraction impossible.

No wonder then that, in the most advanced areas of this civilization, the social controls have been introjected to the point where even individual protest is affected at its roots. The intellectual and emotional refusal "to go along" appears neurotic and impotent. This is the socio-psychological aspect of the political event that marks the contemporary period: the passing of the historical forces which, at the preceding stage of industrial society, seemed to represent the possibility of new forms of existence.

But the term "introjection" perhaps no longer describes the way in which the individual by himself reproduces and perpetuates the external controls exercised by his society. Introjection suggests a variety of relatively spontaneous processes by which a Self (Ego) transposes the "outer" into the "inner." Thus introjection implies the existence of an inner dimension distinguished from and even antagonistic to the external exigencies—an individual consciousness and an individual unconscious *apart from* public opinion and behavior.[1] The idea of "inner freedom" here has its reality: it designates the private space in which man may become and remain "himself."

Today this private space has been invaded and whittled down by technological reality. Mass production and mass distribution claim the *entire* individual, and industrial psychology has long since ceased to be confined to the factory. The manifold processes of introjection seem to be ossified in almost mechanical reactions. The result is, not adjustment but *mimesis*: an immediate identification of the individual with *his* society and, through it, with the society as a whole.

This immediate, automatic identification (which may have been characteristic of primitive forms of association) reappears in high industrial civilization; its new "immediacy," however, is the product of a sophisticated, scientific management and organization. In this process, the "inner" dimension of the mind in which opposition to the status quo can take root is whittled down. The loss of this dimension, in which the power of negative thinking—the critical power of Reason—is at home, is the ideological counterpart to the very material process in which advanced industrial society silences and reconciles the opposition. The impact of progress turns Reason into submission to the facts of life, and to the dynamic capability of producing more and bigger facts of the same sort of life. The efficiency of the system blunts the individuals' recognition that it contains no facts which do not communicate the repressive power of the whole. If the individuals find themselves, in the things which shape their life, they do so, not by giving, but by accepting the law of things—not the law of physics but the law of their society.

I have just suggested that the concept of alienation seems to become questionable when the individuals identify themselves with the existence which is imposed upon them and have in it their own development and satisfaction. This identification is not illusion but reality. However, the reality constitutes a more progressive stage of alienation. The latter has become entirely objective; the subject which is alienated is swallowed up by its alienated existence. There is only one dimension, and it is everywhere and in all forms. The achievements of progress defy ideological indictment as well as justification; before their tribunal, the "false consciousness" of their rationality becomes the true consciousness.

This absorption of ideology into reality does not, however, signify the "end of ideology." On the contrary, in a specific sense advanced industrial culture is *more* ideological than its predecessor, inasmuch as today the ideology is in the process of production itself.[2] In a provocative form, this proposition reveals the political aspects of the prevailing technological rationality. The productive apparatus and the goods and services which it produces "sell" or impose the social system as a whole. The means of mass transportation and communication, the commodities of lodging, food, and clothing, the irresistible output of the entertainment and information industry carry with them prescribed attitudes and habits, certain intellectual and emotional reactions which bind the consumers more or less pleasantly to the producers and, through the latter, to the whole. The products indoctrinate and manipulate; they promote a false consciousness which is immune against its falsehood. And as these beneficial products become available to more individuals in more social classes, the indoctrination they carry ceases to be publicity; it becomes a way of life. It is a good way of life—much better than before—and as a good way of life, it militates against qualitative change. Thus emerges a pattern of *one-dimensional thought and behavior* in which ideas, aspirations, and objectives that, by their content, transcend the established universe of discourse and action are either repelled or reduced to terms of this universe. They are redefined by the rationality of the given system and of its quantitative extension.

NOTES

1. The change in the function of the family here plays a decisive role: its "socializing" functions are increasingly taken over by outside groups and media. See my *Eros and Civilization* (Boston: Beacon Press, 1955), p. 96ff.
2. Theodor W. Adorno, *Prismen. Kulturkritik and Gesellschaft.* (Frankfurt: Suhrkamp, 1955), p. 24f.

63. TRADITIONAL AND CRITICAL THEORY

MAX HORKHEIMER

As the founding director of the Institute of Social Research, better known as the Frankfurt School, Max Horkheimer (1895–1973) was one of the key exponents of critical theory. Like his close associate Theodor Adorno (1903–1969), he lived in exile in the United States during World War II, but disliking American mass culture, both men returned to Germany after the war. In this 1937 essay, Horkheimer compares what he calls "traditional" theory and critical theory. What he has in mind regarding the former is positivist theory that, in attempting to offer a rigorously scientific account of social life—thus the interest in statistics in empirical research—seeks to divorce theory from ethics and praxis. Critical theory, by contrast, is reflexive theory that locates itself within social life as it seeks to comprehend the world in historical rather than naturalistic terms.

What is "theory"? The question seems a rather easy one for contemporary science. Theory for most researchers is the sum-total of propositions about a subject, the propositions being so linked with each other that a few are basic and the rest derive from these. The smaller the number of primary principles in comparison with the derivations, the more perfect the theory. The real validity of the theory depends on the derived propositions being consonant with the actual facts. If experience and theory contradict each other, one of the two must be reexamined. Either the scientist has failed to observe correctly or something is wrong with the principles of the theory. In relation to facts, therefore, a theory always remains a hypothesis. One must be ready to change it if its weaknesses begin to show as one works through the material. Theory is stored-up knowledge, put in a form that makes it useful for the closest possible description of facts. Poincaré compares science to a library that must ceaselessly expand. Experimental physics is the librarian who takes care of acquisitions, that is, enriches knowledge by supplying new material. Mathematical physics—the theory of natural science in the strictest sense—keeps the catalogue; without the catalogue one would have no access to the library's rich contents. "That is the rôle" of mathematical physics. It must direct generalisation, so as to increase what I have called just now the output of science."[1] The general goal of all theory is a universal systematic science, not limited to any particular subject matter but embracing all possible objects. The division of sciences is being broken down by deriving the principles for special areas from the same basic premises. The same conceptual apparatus which was elaborated for the analysis of inanimate nature is serving to classify animate nature as well, and anyone who has once mastered the use of it, that is, the rules for derivation, the symbols, the process of comparing derived propositions with observable fact, can use it at any time. But we are still rather far from such an ideal situation.

Such, in its broad lines, is the widely accepted idea of what theory is. Its origins supposedly coincide with the beginnings of modern philosophy. The third maximum in Descartes' scientific method is the decision to carry on my reflections in due order, commencing with objects that were the most simple and easy to understand, in order to rise little by little, or by degrees, to knowledge of the most complex, assuming an order, even if a fictitious one, among those which do not follow a natural sequence relative to one another.

The derivation as usually practiced in mathematics is to be applied to all science. The order in the world is captured by a deductive chain of thought.

Those long chains of deductive reasoning, simple and easy as they are, of which geometricians make use in order to arrive at the most difficult demonstrations, had caused me to imagine that all those things which fall under the cognizance of men might very likely be mutually related in the same fashion; and that, provided only that we abstain from receiving anything as true which is not so, and always retain the order which is necessary in order to deduce the one conclusion from the other, there can be nothing so remote that we cannot reach to it, nor so recondite that we cannot discover it.[2]

Depending on the logician´s own general philosophical outlook, the most universal propositions from which the deduction begins are themselves regarded as experiential judgements, as inductions (as with John Stuart Mill), as evident insights (as in rationalist and phenomenological schools), or as arbitrary postulates (as in the modern axiomatic approach). In the most advanced logic of the present time, as represented by Husserl´s *Logische Untersuchungen*, theory is defined "as an enclosed system of propositions for a science as a whole".[3] Theory in the fullest sense is "a systematically linked set of propositions, taking the form of a systematically unified deduction."[4] Science is "a certain totality of propositions . . . , emerging in one or other manner from theoretical work, in the systematic order of which propositions a certain totality of objects acquires definition."[5] The basic requirement which any theoretical system must satisfy is that all the parts should intermesh thoroughly and without friction. Harmony, which includes lack of contradictions, and the absence of superfluous, purely dogmatic elements which have no influence on the observable phenomena, are necessary conditions, according to Weyl.[6]

In so far as this traditional conception of theory shows a tendency, it is towards a purely mathematical system of symbols. As elements of the theory, as components of the propositions and conclusions, there are ever fewer names of experiential objects and ever more numerous mathematical symbols. Even the logical operations themselves have already been so rationalized that, in large areas of natural science at least, theory formation has become a matter of mathematical construction.

The sciences of man and society have attempted to follow the lead of the natural sciences with their great successes. The difference between those schools of social science which are more oriented to the investigation of facts and those which concentrate more on principles has nothing directly to do with the concept of theory as such. The assiduous collecting of facts in all the disciplines dealing with social life, the gathering of great masses of detail in connection with problems, the empirical inquiries, through careful questionnaires and other means, which are a major part of scholarly activity, especially in the Anglo-Saxon universities since Spencer´s time—all this adds up to a pattern which is, outwardly, much like the rest of life in a society dominated by industrial production techniques. Such an approach seems quite different from the formulation of abstract principles and the analysis of basic concepts by an armchair scholar, which are typical, for example, of one sector of German sociology. Yet these divergences do not signify a structural difference in ways of thinking. In recent periods of contemporary society the so-called human studies (*Geisteswissen-schaften*) have had but a fluctuating market value and must try to imitate the more prosperous natural sciences whose practical value is beyond question. . . .

We must go on now to add that there is a human activity which has society itself for its object.[7] The aim of this activity is not simply to eliminate one or other abuse, for it regards such abuses as necessarily connected with the way in which the social structure is organized. Although it itself emerges from the social structure, its purpose is not, either in its conscious intention or in its objective significance, the better functioning of any element in the structure. On the contrary, it is suspicious of the very categories of better, useful, appropriate, productive, and valuable, as these are understood in the present order, and refuses to take them as non-scientific presuppositions about which one can do nothing. The individual as a rule must simply accept the basic conditions of his existence as given and strive to fulfill them; he finds his satisfaction and praise in accomplishing as well as he can the tasks connected with his place in society and in courageously doing his duty despite all the sharp criticism he may choose to exercise in particular matters. But the critical attitude of which we are speaking is wholly distrustful of the rules of conduct with which society as presently constituted provides each of its members. The separation between individual and society in virtue of which the individual accepts as natural the limits prescribed for his activity is relativized in critical theory. The latter considers the overall framework which is conditioned by the blind interaction of individual activities (that is, the existent division of labor and the class distinctions) to be a function which originates in human action and therefore is a possible object of planful decision and rational determination of goals.

The two-sided character of the social totality in its present form becomes, for men who adopt the critical attitude, a conscious opposition. In recognizing the present form of economy and the whole culture which it generates to be the product of human work as well as the organization which mankind was capable of and has provided for itself in the present era, these men identify themselves with this totality and conceive it as will and reason. It is their own world. At the same time, however, they experience the fact that society is comparable to nonhuman natural processes, to pure mechanisms, because cultural forms which are supported by war and oppression are not the creations of a unified, self-conscious will. That world is not their own but the world of capital.

Previous history thus cannot really be understood; only the individuals and specific groups in it are intelligible, and even these not totally, since their internal dependence on an inhuman society means that even in their conscious action such individuals and groups are still in good measure mechanical functions. The identification, then, of men of critical mind with their society is marked by tension, and the tension characterizes all the concepts of the critical way of thinking. Thus, such thinkers interpret the economic categories of work, value, and productivity exactly as they are interpreted in the existing order, and they regard any other

interpretation as pure idealism. But at the same time they consider it rank dishonesty simply to accept the interpretation; the critical acceptance of the categories which rule social life contains simultaneously their condemnation. This dialectical character of the self-interpretation of contemporary man is what, in the last analysis, also causes the obscurity of the Kantian critique of reason. Reason cannot become transparent to itself as long as men act as members of an organism which lacks reason. Organism as a naturally developing and declining unity cannot be a sort of model for society, but only a form of deadened existence from which society must emancipate itself. An attitude which aims at such an emancipation and at an alteration of society as a whole might well be of service in theoretical work carried on within reality as presently ordered. But it lacks the pragmatic character which attaches to traditional thought as a socially useful professional activity.

In traditional theoretical thinking, the genesis of particular objective facts, the practical application of the conceptual systems by which it grasps the facts, and the role of such systems in action, are all taken to be external to the theoretical thinking itself. This alienation, which finds expression in philosophical terminology as the separation of value and research, knowledge and action, and other polarities, protects the savant from the tensions we have indicated and provides an assured framework for his activity. Yet a kind of thinking which does not accept this framework seems to have the ground taken out from under it. If a theoretical procedure does not take the form of determining objective facts with the help of the simplest and most differentiated conceptual systems available, what can it be but an aimless intellectual game, half conceptual poetry, half important expression of states of mind? The investigation into the social conditioning of facts and theories may indeed be a research problem, perhaps even a whole field for theoretical work, but how can such studies be radically different from other specialized efforts? Research into ideologies, or sociology of knowledge, which has been taken over from the critical theory of society and established as a special discipline, is not opposed either in its aim or in its other ambitions to the usual activities that go on within classificatory science . . . .

How is critical thought related to experience? One might maintain that if such thought were not simply to classify but also to determine for itself the goals which classification serves, in other words its own fundamental direction, it would remain locked up within itself, as happened to idealist philosophy. If it did not take refuge in utopian fantasy, it would be reduced to the formalistic fighting of sham battles. The attempt legitimately to determine practical goals by thinking must always fail. If thought were not content with the role given to it in existent society, if it were not to engage in theory in the traditional sense of the word, it would necessarily have to return to illusions long since laid bare.

The fault in such reflections as these on the role of thought is that thinking is understood in a detachedly departmentalized and therefore spiritualist way, as it is today under existing conditions of the division of labor. In society as it is, the power of thought has never controlled itself but has always functioned as a non-independent moment in the work process, and the latter has its own orientation and tendency. The work process enhances and develops human life through the conflicting movement of progressive and retrogressive periods. In the historical form in which society has existed, however, the full measure of goods produced for man's enjoyment has, at any particular stage, been given directly only to a small group of men. Such a state of affairs has found expression in thought, too, and left its mark on philosophy and religion. But from the beginning the desire to bring the same enjoyment to the majority has stirred in the depths of men's hearts; despite all the material appropriateness of class organization, each of its forms has finally proved inadequate. Slaves, vassals, and citizens have cast off their yoke. Now, inasmuch as every individual in modern times has been required to make his own the purposes of society as a whole and to recognize these in society, there is the possibility that men would become aware of and concentrate their attention upon the path which the social work process has taken without any definite theory behind it, as a result of disparate forces interacting, and with the despair of the masses acting as a decisive factor at major turning points. Thought does not spin such a possibility out of itself but rather becomes aware of its own proper function. In the course of history men have come to know their own activity and thus to recognize the contradiction that marks their existence. The bourgeois economy was concerned that the individual should maintain the life of society by taking care of his own personal happiness. Such an economy has within it, however, a dynamism

which results in a fantastic degree of power for some, such as reminds us of the old Asiatic dynasties, and in material and intellectual weakness for many others. The original fruitfulness of the bourgeois organization of the life process is thus transformed into a paralyzing barrenness, and men by their own toil keep in existence a reality which enslaves them in ever greater degree.

Yet, as far as the role of experience is concerned, there is a difference between traditional and critical theory. The viewpoints which the latter derives from historical analysis as the goals of human activity, especially the idea of a reasonable organization of society that will meet the needs of the whole community, are immanent in human work but are not correctly grasped by individuals or by the common mind. A certain concern is also required if these tendencies are to be perceived and expressed. According to Marx and Engels such a concern is necessarily generated in the proletariat. Because of its situation in modern society the proletariat experiences the connection between work which puts ever more powerful instruments into men's hands in their struggle with nature, and the continuous renewal of an out-moded social organization. Unemployment, economic crises, militarization, terrorist regimes—in a word, the whole condition of the masses—are not due, for example, to limited technological possibilities, as might have been the case in earlier periods, but to the circumstances of production which are no longer suitable to our time. The application of an intellectual and physical means for the mastery of nature is hindered because in the prevailing circumstances these means are entrusted to special, mutually opposed interests. Production is not geared to the life of the whole community while heeding also the claims of individuals; it is geared to the power-backed claims of individuals while being concerned hardly at all with the life of the community. This is the inevitable result, in the present property system, of the principle that it is enough for individuals to look out for themselves . . . .

Even the critical theory, which stands in opposition to other theories, derives its statements about real relationships from basic universal concepts, as we have indicated, and therefore presents the relationships as necessary. Thus both kinds of theoretical structure are alike when it comes to logical necessity. But there is a difference as soon as we turn from logical to real necessity, the necessity involved in factual sequences.

The biologist´s statement that internal processes cause a plant to wither or that certain processes in the human organism lead to its destruction leaves untouched the question whether any influences can alter the character of these processes or change them totally. Even when an illness is said to be curable, the fact that the necessary curative measures are actually taken is regarded as purely extrinsic to the curability, a matter of technology and therefore nonessential as far as the theory as such is concerned. The necessity which rules society can be regarded as biological in the sense described, and the unique character of critical theory can therefore be called in question on the grounds that in biology as in other natural sciences particular sequences of events can be theoretically constructed just as they are in the critical theory of society. The development of society, in this view, would simply be a particular series of events, for the presentation of which conclusions from various other areas of research are used, just as a doctor in the course of an illness or a geologist dealing with the earth´s prehistory has to apply various other disciplines. Society here would be the individual reality which is evaluated on the basis of theories in the special sciences.

However many valid analogies there may be between these different intellectual endeavors, there is nonetheless a decisive difference when it comes to the relation of subject and object and therefore to the necessity of the event being judged. The object with which the scientific specialist deals is not affected at all by his own theory. Subject and object are kept strictly apart. Even if it turns out that at a later point in time the objective event is influenced by human intervention, to science this is just another fact. The objective occurrence is independent of the theory, and this independence is part of its necessity: the observer as such can effect no change in the object. A consciously critical attitude, however, is part of the development of society: the construing of the course of history as the necessary product of an economic mechanism simultaneously contains both a protest generated by the order itself, and the idea of self-determination for the human race, that is the idea of a state of affairs in which man´s actions no longer flow from a mechanism but from his own decision. The judgement passed on the necessity inherent in the previous course of events implies here a struggle to change it from a blind to a meaningful necessity. If we think of the object of the theory in separation from the theory, we falsify it and fall into quietism or conformism. Every part of the theory presupposes the critique of the existing order and the struggle against it along lines determined by the theory itself.

The theoreticians of knowledge who started with physics had reason, even if they were not wholly right, to condemn the confusion of cause and operation of forces and to substitute the idea of cause. For the kind of thinking which simply registers facts there are always only series of phenomena, never forces and counterforces; but this, of course, says something about this kind of thinking, not about nature. If such a method is applied to society, the result is statistics and descriptive sociology, and these can be important for many purposes, even for critical theory.

NOTES

1. Henri Poincaré, *Science and Hypothesis,* tr. by W[illiam] J[ohn] G[reenstreet] (London: Walter Scott, 1905), p.145.
2. Descartes, *Discourse on Method,* in *The Philosophical Works of Descartes,* tr. by Elizabeth S. Haldane and G.R.T. Ross (Cambridge: Cambridge University Press, 1931. . . .), Volume 1, p. 92.
3. Edmund Husserl, *Formale and transzendentale Logik* (Halle, 1929), p. 89.
4. Husserl, *op.cit.,* p. 79.
5. Husserl, *op.cit.,* p. 91.
6. Hermann Weyl, *Philosophie der Naturwissenschaft,* in *Handbuch der Philosophie,* Part 2 (Munich-Berlin, 1927), pp. 118ff.
7. In the following pages this activity is called "critical" activity. The term is used here less in the sense it has in the dialectical critique of pure reason than in the sense it has in the dialectical critique of political economy. It points to an essential aspect of the dialectical theory of society.

64. THREE NORMATIVE MODELS OF DEMOCRACY

JÜRGEN HABERMAS

Jürgen Habermas (b. 1929) is the most important second-generation member of the Frankfurt School. During the 1950s, he studied with Theodor Adorno and Max Horkheimer, both of whom had returned to Germany after living in exile in the United States, and he served as Adorno's research assistant. While indebted to their legacies, Habermas devised his own highly original synthesis of social theory influenced not only by his mentors, but by Marx, Weber, Freud, Parsons, and others. In so doing, he developed his own unique perspective as a latter-day defender of the ideals of the Enlightenment. From his first major work, *The Structural Transformation of the Public Sphere* (which was published in German in the early 1960s, but was not translated into English until 1989) to the present, he has been concerned with the fate of democracy—his ideas shaped from the beginning by his reflections on the reconstitution of democratic politics in postwar Germany. In this selection from *The Inclusion of the Other* (1998) he counterposes three distinctive models of democracy. The first two, liberalism and republicanism, have for some time been pitted against each other as competing models. Habermas finds both of them to be problematic, and in their place he offers an alternative that he refers to as deliberative politics, whose central features he describes.

In what follows I refer to the idealized distinction between the "liberal" and the "republican" understanding of politics—terms which mark the fronts in the current debate in the United States initiated by the so-called communitarians. Drawing on the work of Frank Michelman, I will begin by describing the two polemically contrasted models of democracy with specific reference to the concept of the citizen, the concept of law, and the nature of processes of political will-formation. In the second part, beginning with a critique of the "ethical overload" of the republican model, I introduce a third, procedural model of democracy for which I propose to reserve the term "deliberative politics."

I

The crucial difference between liberalism and republicanism consists in how the role of the democratic process is understood. According to the "liberal" view, this process accomplishes the task of programming the state in the interest of society, where the state is conceived as an apparatus of public administration, and society is conceived as a system of market-structured interactions of private persons and their labor. Here politics (in the sense of the citizens' political will-formation) has the function of bundling together and bringing to bear private social interests against a state apparatus that specializes in the administrative employment of political power for collective goals.

On the republican view, politics is not exhausted by this mediating function but is constitutive for the socialization process as a whole. Politics is conceived as the reflexive form of substantial ethical life. It constitutes the medium in which the members of quasi-natural solidary communities become aware of their dependence on one another and, acting with full deliberation as citizens, further shape and develop existing relations of reciprocal recognition into an

Jürgen Habermas, *The Inclusion of the Other: Studies in Political Theory.* Cambridge, UK: Polity, 1998 pp. 239–252. ✦

association of free and equal consociates under law. With this, the liberal architectonic of government and society undergoes an important change. In addition to the hierarchical regulatory apparatus of sovereign state authority and the decentralized regulatory mechanism of the market—that is, besides administrative power and self-interest—*solidarity* appears as a third source of social integration.

This horizontal political will-formation aimed at mutual understanding or communicatively achieved consensus is even supposed to enjoy priority, both in a genetic and a normative sense. An autonomous basis in civil society independent of public administration and market-mediated private commerce is assumed as a precondition for the practice of civic self-determination. This basis prevents political communication from being swallowed up by the government apparatus or assimilated to market structures. Thus, on the republican conception, the political public sphere and its base, civil society, acquire a strategic significance. Together they are supposed to secure the integrative power and autonomy of the communicative practice of the citizens.[1] The uncoupling of political communication from the economy has as its counterpart a coupling of administrative power with the communicative power generated by political opinion- and will-formation.

These two competing conceptions of politics have different consequences.

(a) In the first place, their concepts of the citizen differ. According to the liberal view, the citizen's status is determined primarily by the individual rights he or she has vis-à-vis the state and other citizens. As bearers of individual rights citizens enjoy the protection of the government as long as they pursue their private interests within the boundaries drawn by legal statutes—and this includes protection against state interventions that violate the legal prohibition on government interference. Individual rights are negative rights that guarantee a domain of freedom of choice within which legal persons are freed from external compulsion. Political rights have the same structure: they afford citizens the opportunity to assert their private interests in such a way that, by means of elections, the composition of parliamentary bodies, and the formation of a

government, these interests are finally aggregated into a political will that can affect the administration. In this way the citizens in their political role can determine whether governmental authority is exercised in the interest of the citizens as members of society.[2]

According to the republican view, the status of citizens is not determined by the model of negative liberties to which these citizens can lay claim as private persons. Rather, political rights—preeminently rights of political participation and communication—are positive liberties. They do not guarantee freedom from external compulsion, but guarantee instead the possibility of participating in a common practice, through which the citizens can first make themselves into what they want to be—politically responsible subjects of a community of free and equal citizens.[3] To this extent, the political process does not serve just to keep government activity under the surveillance of citizens who have already acquired a prior social autonomy through the exercise of their private rights and prepolitical liberties. Nor does it act only as a hinge between state and society, for democratic governmental authority is by no means an original authority. Rather, this authority proceeds from the communicative power generated by the citizens' practice of self-legislation, and it is legitimated by the fact that it protects this practice by institutionalizing public freedom.[4] The state's *raison d'être* does not lie primarily in the protection of equal individual rights but in the guarantee of an inclusive process of opinion- and will-formation in which free and equal citizens reach an understanding on which goals and norms lie in the equal interest of all. In this way the republican citizen is credited with more than an exclusive concern with his or her private interests.

(b) The polemic against the classical concept of the legal person as bearer of individual rights reveals a controversy about the concept of law itself. Whereas on the liberal conception the point of a legal order is to make it possible to determine which individuals in each case are entitled to which rights, on the republican conception these "subjective" rights owe their existence to an "objective" legal order that both enables and guarantees the integrity of an autonomous life in common based on equality and mutual respect. On the one view, the legal order is conceived in terms of individual rights; on the other, their objective legal content is given priority.

To be sure, this conceptual dichotomy does not touch on the *intersubjective* content of rights that demand reciprocal respect for rights and duties in symmetrical relations of recognition. But the republican concept at least points in the direction of a concept of law that accords equal weight to both the integrity of the individual and the integrity of the community in which persons as both individuals and members can first accord one another reciprocal recognition. It ties the legitimacy of the laws to the democratic procedure by which they are generated and thereby preserves an internal connection between the citizens' practice of self-legislation and the impersonal sway of the law:

> For republicans, rights ultimately are nothing but determinations of prevailing political will, while for liberals, some rights are always grounded in a "higher law" of transpolitical reason or revelation. . . . In a republican view, a community's objective, common good substantially consists in the success of its political endeavor to define, establish, effectuate, and sustain the set of rights (less tendentiously, laws) best suited to the conditions and *mores* of that community. Whereas in a contrasting liberal view, the higher-law rights provide the transactional structures and the curbs on power required so that pluralistic pursuit of diverse and conflicting interests may proceed as satisfactorily as possible.[5]

The right to vote, interpreted as a positive right, becomes the paradigm of rights as such, not only because it is constitutive for political self-determination, but because it shows how inclusion in a community of equals is connected with the individual right to make autonomous contributions and take personal positions on issues:

> [T]he claim is that we all take an interest in each others' enfranchisement because (i) our choice lies between hanging together and hanging separately; (ii) hanging together depends on

reciprocal assurances to all of having one's vital interests heeded by others; and (iii) in the deeply pluralized conditions of contemporary American society, such assurances are not attainable through virtual representation, but only by maintaining at least the semblance of a politics in which everyone is conceded a voice.[6]

This structure, read off from the political rights of participation and communication is extended to *all* rights via the legislative process constituted by political rights. Even the authorization guaranteed by private law to pursue private, freely chosen goals simultaneously imposes an obligation to respect the limits of strategic action which are agreed to be in the equal interest of all.

(c) The different ways of conceptualizing the role of citizen and the law express a deeper disagreement about the nature of the political process. On the liberal view, politics is essentially a struggle for positions that grant access to administrative power. The political process of opinion- and will-formation in the public sphere and in parliament is shaped by the competition of strategically acting collectives trying to maintain or acquire positions of power. Success is measured by the citizens' approval of persons and programs, as quantified by votes. In their choices at the polls, voters express their preferences. Their votes have the same structure as the choices of participants in a market, in that their decisions license access to positions of power that political parties fight over with a success-oriented attitude similar to that of players in the market. The input of votes and the output of power conform to the same pattern of strategic action.

According to the republican view, the political opinion- and will-formation in the public sphere and in parliament does not obey the structures of market processes but rather the obstinate structures of a public communication oriented to mutual understanding. For politics as the citizens' practice of self-determination, the paradigm is not the market but dialogue. From this perspective there is a structural difference between communicative power, which proceeds from political communication in the form of discursively generated majority decisions, and the administrative power possessed by the governmental apparatus. Even the parties that struggle over access to positions of governmental power must bend themselves to the deliberative style and the stubborn character of political discourse:

> Deliberation . . . refers to a certain attitude toward social cooperation, namely, that of openness to persuasion by reasons referring to the claims of others as well as one´s own. The deliberative medium is a good faith exchange of views—including participants´ reports of their own understanding of their respective vital interests— . . . in which a vote, if any vote is taken, represents a pooling of judgments.[7]

Hence the conflict of opinions conducted in the political arena has legitimating force not just in the sense of an authorization to occupy positions of power; on the contrary, the ongoing political discourse also has binding force for the way in which political authority is exercised. Administrative power can only be exercised on the basis of policies and within the limits laid down by laws generated by the democratic process.

II

So much for the comparison between the two models of democracy that currently dominate the discussion between the so-called communitarians and liberals, above all in the US. The republican model has advantages and disadvantages. In my view it has the advantage that it preserves the radical democratic meaning of a society that organizes itself through the communicatively united citizens and does not trace collective goals back to "deals" made between competing private interests. Its disadvantage, as I see it, is that it is too idealistic in that it makes the democratic process dependent on the virtues of citizens devoted to the public weal. For politics is not concerned in the first place with questions of ethical self-understanding. The mistake of the republican view consists in an ethical foreshortening of political discourse.

To be sure, ethical discourses aimed at achieving a collective self-understanding—discourses in which participants attempt to clarify how they understand themselves as members of a particular nation, as members of a community or a state, as inhabitants of a region, etc., which traditions they wish to cultivate, how they should treat each other, minorities, and

marginal groups, in what sort of society they want to live—constitute an important part of politics. But under conditions of cultural and social pluralism, behind politically relevant goals there often lie interests and value-orientations that are by no means constitutive of the identity of the political community as a whole, that is, for the totality of an intersubjectively shared form of life. These interests and value-orientations, which conflict with one another within the same polity without any prospect of consensual resolution, need to be counterbalanced in a way that cannot be effected by ethical discourse, even though the results of this nondiscursive counterbalancing are subject to the proviso that they must not violate the basic values of a culture. The balancing of interests takes the form of reaching a compromise between parties who rely on their power and ability to sanction. Negotiations of this sort certainly presuppose a readiness to cooperate, that is, a willingness to abide by the rules and to arrive at results that are acceptable to all parties, though for different reasons. But compromise-formation is not conducted in the form of a rational discourse that neutralizes power and excludes strategic action. However, the fairness of compromises is measured by presuppositions and procedures which for their part are in need of rational, indeed normative, justification from the standpoint of justice. In contrast with ethical questions, questions of justice are not by their very nature tied to a particular collectivity. Politically enacted law, if it is to be legitimate, must be at least in harmony with moral principles that claim a general validity that extends beyond the limits of any concrete legal community.

The concept of deliberative politics acquires empirical relevance only when we take into account the multiplicity of forms of communication in which a common will is produced, that is, not just ethical self-clarification but also the balancing of interests and compromise, the purposive choice of means, moral justification, and legal consistency-testing. In this process the two types of politics which Michelman distinguishes in an ideal-typical fashion can interweave and complement one another in a rational manner. "Dialogical" and "instrumental" politics can *interpenetrate* in the medium of deliberation if the corresponding forms of communication are sufficiently institutionalized. Everything depends on the conditions of communication and the procedures that lend the institutionalized opinion- and will-formation their legitimating force. The third model of democracy, which I would like to propose, relies precisely on those conditions of communication under which the political process can be presumed to produce rational results because it operates deliberatively at all levels.

Making the proceduralist conception of deliberative politics the cornerstone of the theory of democracy results in differences both from the republican conception of the state as an ethical community and from the liberal conception of the state as the guardian of a market society. In comparing the three models, I take my orientation from that dimension of politics which has been our primary concern, namely, the democratic opinion- and will-formation that issue in popular elections and parliamentary decrees.

According to the liberal view, the democratic process takes place exclusively in the form of compromises between competing interests. Fairness is supposed to be guaranteed by rules of compromise-formation that regulate the general and equal right to vote, the representative composition of parliamentary bodies, their order of business, and so on. Such rules are ultimately justified in terms of liberal basic rights. According to the republican view, by contrast, democratic will-formation is supposed to take the form of an ethical discourse of self-understanding; here deliberation can rely for its content on a culturally established background consensus of the citizens, which is rejuvenated through the ritualistic reenactment of a republican founding act. Discourse theory takes elements from both sides and integrates them into the concept of an ideal procedure for deliberation and decision making. Weaving together negotiations and discourses of self-understanding and of justice, this democratic procedure grounds the presumption that under such conditions reasonable or fair results are obtained. According to this proceduralist view, practical reason withdraws from universal human rights or from the concrete ethical life of a specific community into the rules of discourse and forms of argumentation that derive their normative content from the validity-basis of action oriented to reaching understanding, and ultimately from the structure of linguistic communication.[8]

These descriptions of the structures of democratic process set the stage for different normative conceptualizations of state and society. The sole presupposition is a public administration of the kind that emerged in the early modern period together with the European state system and in functional interconnection with a capitalist economic system. According to the republican view, the citizens´ political opinion- and will-formation forms the medium through which society constitutes itself as a political whole. Society is centered in the state; for in the citizens´ practice of political self-determination the polity becomes conscious of itself as a totality and acts on itself via the collective will of the citizens. Democracy is synonymous with the political self-organization of society. This leads to a polemical understanding of politics as directed against the state apparatus. In Hannah Arendt´s political writings one can see the thrust of republican arguments: in opposition to the civic privatism of a depoliticized population and in opposition to the acquisition of legitimation through entrenched parties, the political public sphere should be revitalized to the point where a regenerated citizenry can, in the forms of a decentralized self-governance, (once again) appropriate the governmental authority that has been usurped by a self-regulating bureaucracy.

According to the liberal view, this separation of the state apparatus from society cannot be eliminated but only bridged by the democratic process. However, the weak normative connotations of a regulated balancing of power and interests stands in need of constitutional channeling. The democratic will-formation of self-interested citizens, construed in minimalist terms, constitutes just one element within a constitution that disciplines governmental authority through normative constraints (such as basic rights, separation of powers, and legal regulation of the administration) and forces it, through competition between political parties, on the one hand, and between government and opposition, on the other, to take adequate account of competing interests and value orientations. This state-centered understanding of politics does not have to rely on the unrealistic assumption of a citizenry capable of acting collectively. Its focus is not so much the input of a rational political will-formation but the output of successful administrative accomplishments. The thrust of liberal arguments is directed against the disruptive potential of an administrative power that interferes with the independent social interactions of private persons. The liberal model hinges not on the democratic self-determination of deliberating citizens but on the legal institutionalization of an economic society that is supposed to guarantee an essentially nonpolitical common good through the satisfaction of the private aspirations of productive citizens.

Discourse theory invests the democratic process with normative connotations stronger than those of the liberal model but weaker than those of the republican model. Once again, it takes elements from both sides and fits them together in a new way. In agreement with republicanism, it gives center stage to the process of political opinion- and will-formation, but without understanding the constitution as something secondary; on the contrary, it conceives the basic principles of the constitutional state as a consistent answer to the question of how the demanding communicative presuppositions of a democratic opinion- and will-formation can be institutionalized. Discourse theory does not make the success of deliberative politics depend on a collectively acting citizenry but on the institutionalization of corresponding procedures. It no longer operates with the concept of a social whole centered in the state and conceived as a goal-oriented subject writ large. But neither does it localize the whole in a system of constitutional norms mechanically regulating the interplay of powers and interests in accordance with the market model. Discourse theory altogether jettisons the assumptions of the philosophy of consciousness, which invite us either to ascribe the citizens´ practice of self-determination to one encompassing macro-subject or to apply the anonymous rule of law to competing individuals. The former approach represents the citizenry as a collective actor which reflects the whole and acts for its sake; on the latter, individual actors function as dependent variables in systemic processes that unfold blindly because no consciously executed collective decisions are possible over and above individual acts of choice (except in a purely metaphorical sense).

Discourse theory works instead with the *higher-level intersubjectivity* of communication processes that unfold in the institutionalized deliberations in parliamentary bodies, on the one hand, and in the informal networks of the public sphere, on the other. Both within and outside parliamentary bodies geared to decision making, these subjectless modes of communication form arenas in which a more or less rational opinion- and will-formation concerning issues and problems affecting society as a whole can take place. Informal opinion-formation results in institutionalized election decisions and legislative decrees through which communicatively generated power is transformed into administratively utilizable power. As on the liberal model, the boundary between state and society is respected; but here civil society, which provides the social underpinning of autonomous publics, is as distinct from the economic system as it is from the public administration. This understanding of democracy leads to the normative demand for a new balance between the three resources of money, administrative power, and solidarity from which modern societies meet their need for integration and regulation. The normative implications are obvious: the integrative force of solidarity, which can no longer be drawn solely from sources of communicative action, should develop through widely expanded autonomous public spheres as well as through legally institutionalized procedures of democratic deliberation and decision making and gain sufficient strength to hold its own against the other two social forces—money and administrative power.

III

This view has implications for how one should understand legitimation and popular sovereignty. On the liberal view, democratic will-formation has the exclusive function of *legitimating* the exercise of political power. The outcomes of elections license the assumption of governmental power, though the government must justify the use of power to the public and parliament. On the republican view, democratic will-formation has the significantly stronger function of *constituting* society as a political community and keeping the memory of this founding act alive with each new election. The government is not only empowered by the electorate´s choice between teams of leaders to exercise a largely open mandate, but is also bound in a programmatic fashion to carry out certain policies. More a committee than an organ of the state, it is part of a self-governing political community rather than the head of a separate governmental apparatus. Discourse theory, by contrast, brings a third idea into play: the procedures and communicative presuppositions of democratic opinion- and will-formation function as the most important sluices for the discursive rationalization of the decisions of a government and an administration bound by law and statute. On this view, *rationalization* signifies more than mere legitimation but less than the constitution of political power. The power available to the administration changes its general character once it is bound to a process of democratic opinion- and will-formation that does not merely retrospectively monitor the exercise of political power but also programs it in a certain way. Notwithstanding this discursive rationalization, only the political system itself can "act." It is a subsystem specialized for collectively binding decisions, whereas the communicative structures of the public sphere comprise a far-flung network of sensors that respond to the pressure of society-wide problems and stimulate influential opinions. The public opinion which is worked up via democratic procedures into communicative power cannot itself "rule" but can only channel the use of administrative power in specific directions.

The concept of *popular sovereignty* stems from the republican appropriation and revaluation of the early modern notion of sovereignty originally associated with absolutist regimes. The state, which monopolizes the means of legitimate violence, is viewed as a concentration of power which can overwhelm all other temporal powers. Rousseau transposed this idea, which goes back to Bodin, to the will of the united people, fused it with the classical idea of the self-rule of free and equal citizens, and sublimated it into the modern concept of autonomy. Despite this normative sublimation, the concept of sovereignty remained bound to the notion of an embodiment in the (at first actually physically assembled) people. According to the republican view, the at least potentially assembled people are the bearers of a sovereignty that cannot in principle be delegated: in their capacity as sovereign, the people cannot let themselves be represented by others. Constitutional power is founded on the citizens´ practice of self-determination, not on that of their representatives. Against this, liberalism offers the more realistic view that, in the constitutional state, the authority emanating from the people is exercised only "by means of elections and voting and by specific legislative, executive, and judicial organs."[9]

These two views exhaust the alternatives only on the dubious assumption that state and society must be conceived in terms of a whole and its parts, where the whole is constituted either by a sovereign citizenry or by a constitution. By contrast to the discourse theory of democracy corresponds the image of a *decentered* society, though with the political public sphere it sets apart an arena for the detection, identification, and interpretation of problems affecting society as a whole. If we abandon the conceptual framework of the philosophy of the subject, sovereignty need neither be concentrated in the people in a concretistic manner nor banished into the anonymous agencies established by the constitution. The "self" of the self-organizing legal community disappears in the subjectless forms of communication that regulate the flow of discursive opinion- and will-formation whose fallible results enjoy the presumption of rationality. This is not to repudiate the intuition associated with the idea of popular sovereignty but rather to interpret it in intersubjective terms. Popular sovereignty, even though it has become anonymous, retreats into democratic procedures and the legal implementation of their demanding communicative presuppositions only to be able to make itself felt as communicatively generated power. Strictly speaking, this communicative power springs from the interactions between legally institutionalized will-formation and culturally mobilized publics. The latter for their part find a basis in the associations of a civil society distinct from the state and the economy alike.

The normative self-understanding of deliberative politics does indeed call for a discursive mode of socialization for the *legal community*; but this mode does not extend to the whole of the society in which the constitutionally established political system is *embedded*. Even on its own proceduralist self-understanding, deliberative politics remains a component of a complex society, which as a whole resists the normative approach of legal theory. In this regard, the discourse-theoretic reading of democracy connects with an objectifying sociological approach that regards the political system neither as the peak nor the center, nor even as the structuring model of society, but as just *one* action system among others. Because it provides a kind of surety for the solution of the social problems that threaten integration, politics must indeed be able to communicate, via the medium of law, with all of the other legitimately ordered spheres of action, however these may be structured and steered. But the political system remains dependent on other functional mechanisms, such as the revenue-production of the economic system, in more than just a trivial sense; on the contrary, deliberative politics, whether realized in the

formal procedures of institutionalized opinion- and will-formation or only in the informal networks of the political public sphere, stands in an internal relation to the contexts of a rationalized lifeworld that meets it halfway. Deliberatively filtered political communications are especially dependent on the resources of the lifeworld—on a free and open political culture and an enlightened political socialization, and above all on the initiatives of opinion-shaping associations. These resources emerge and regenerate themselves spontaneously for the most part—at any rate, they can only with difficulty be subjected to political control.

NOTES

1. Cf. H. Arendt, *On Revolution* (New York, 1965); *On Violence* (New York, 1970).
2. Cf. F. I. Michelman, "Political Truth and the Rule of Law," *Tel Aviv University Studies in Law* 8 (1988): 283: "The political society envisioned by bumper-sticker republicans is the society of private rights bearers, an association whose first principle is the protection of the lives, liberties, and estates of its individual members. In that society, the state is justified by the protection it gives to those prepolitical interests; the purpose of the constitution is to ensure that the state apparatus, the government, provides such protection for the people at large rather than serves the special interests of the governors or their patrons; the function of citizenship is to operate the constitution and thereby to motivate the governors to act according to that protective purpose; and the value to you of your political franchise—your right to vote and speak, to have your views heard and counted—is the handle it gives you on influencing the system so that it will adequately heed and protect *your* particular, prepolitical rights and other interests."
3. On the distinction between positive and negative freedom see Ch. Taylor, "What is Human Agency?" in *Human Agency and Language: Philosophical Papers 1* (Cambridge, 1985), pp. 15–44.
4. Michelman, "Political Truth and the Rule of Law," p. 284: "In [the] civic constitutional vision, political society is primarily the society not of rights bearers, but of citizens, an association whose first principle is the creation and provision of a public realm within which a people, together, argue and reason about the right terms of social coexistence, terms that they will set together and which they understand as comprising their common good. . . . Hence, the state is justified by its purpose of establishing and ordering the public sphere within which persons can achieve freedom in the sense of self-government by the exercise of reason in public dialogue."
5. Michelman, "Conceptions of Democracy in American Constitutional Argument: Voting Rights," *Florida Law Review* 41 (1989): 446f. (hereafter "Voting Rights").
6. Michelman, "Voting Rights," p. 484.
7. Michelman, "Conceptions of Democracy in American Constitutional Argument: The Case of Pornography Regulation," *Tennessee Law Review* 291 (1989): 293.
8. Cf. J. Habermas, "Popular Sovereignty as Procedure," in *Between Facts and Norms,* trans. W. Rehg (1996), pp. 463–490.
9. Cf. *The Basic Law of the Federal Republic of Germany*, article 20, sec. 2.

65. PERSONAL IDENTITY AND DISRESPECT

AXEL HONNETH

A key representative of what might be seen as the third generation of critical theorists, Axel Honneth (b. 1949) is currently a professor of philosophy at the Johann-Wolfgang Goethe University in Frankfurt and the director of the Institute for Social Research there—making him the current occupant of a position previously held by Max Horkheimer and Jürgen Habermas (see their entries in this section). A former student of Habermas, he was deeply influenced by his mentor's work on communicative ethics. If his philosophical roots lie in G. W. F. Hegel, and in particular his understanding of "recognition," his concern with intersubjectivity has also been shaped by the work of George Herbert Mead and by John Dewey's pragmatist psychology (see their entries in section VI). Recognition is connected to both power and respect, and as such the intersubjective character of recognition/ misrecognition underpins the way that people understand the justness or unjustness of particular social arrangements. From Honneth's perspective, recognition precedes and thus frames any consideration of redistribution, a view that puts him at odds with theorists who grant priority to social structure over intersubjective consciousness. This essay, from his 1995 book, *The Struggle for Recognition*, treats the implications of disrespect for individual identity.

Inherent in our everyday use of language is a sense that human integrity owes its existence, at a deep level, to the patterns of approval and recognition that we have been attempting to distinguish. For up to the present day, in the self-descriptions of those who see themselves as having been wrongly treated by others, the moral categories that play a dominant role are those—such as "insult" or "humiliation"—that refer to forms of disrespect, that is, to the denial of recognition. Negative concepts of this kind are used to designate behaviour that represents an injustice not simply because it harms subjects or restricts their freedom to act, but because it injures them with regard to the positive understanding of themselves that they have acquired intersubjectively. Without the implicit reference to the claims to recognition that one makes to one's fellow human beings, there is no way of using these concepts of "disrespect" and "insult" meaningfully. In this sense, our ordinary language contains empirical indications of an indissoluble connection between, on the one hand, the unassailability and integrity of human beings and, on the other hand, the approval of others. What the term "disrespect" [*Mißachtung*] refers to is the specific vulnerability of humans resulting from the internal interdependence of individualization and recognition, which both Hegel and Mead helped to illuminate. Because the normative self-image of each and every individual human being—his or her "me," as Mead put it—is dependent on the possibility of being continually backed up by others, the experience of being disrespected carries with it the danger of an injury that can bring the identity of the person as a whole to the point of collapse.

Admittedly, all of what is referred to colloquially as "disrespect" or "insult" obviously can involve varying degrees of depth in the psychological injury to a subject. There is a categorial difference between, say, the

Axel Honneth. *The Struggle for Recognition: The Moral Grammar of Social Conflicts.* Cambridge, MA: The MIT Press, 1995, pp. 131–139.✦

blatant degradation involved in the denial of basic human rights, on the one hand, and the subtle humiliation that accompanies a public allusion to a person´s failings, on the other. And the use of a single term threatens to efface this difference. But even just the fact that we have been able to identify systematic gradations for the complementary concept of "recognition" points to the existence of internal differences between individual forms of disrespect. If it is the case that the experience of disrespect signals the withholding or withdrawing of recognition, then the same distinctions would have to be found within the field of negative phenomena as was met with in the field of positive phenomena. In this sense, the distinctions between three patterns of recognition gives us a theoretical key with which to separate out just as many kinds of disrespect. Their differences would have to be measured by the various degrees to which they are able to disrupt a person´s practical relation-to-self by denying him or her recognition for particular claims to identity. Only by proceeding from this set of divisions can one take on the question that neither Hegel nor Mead were able to answer: how is it that the experience of disrespect is anchored in the affective life of human subjects in such a way that it can provide the motivational impetus for social resistance and conflict, indeed, for a struggle for recognition?

In light of the distinctions worked out thus far it would appear sensible to start from a type of disrespect that affects a person at the level of physical integrity. The forms of practical maltreatment in which a person is forcibly deprived of any opportunity freely to dispose over his or her own body represent the most fundamental sort of personal degradation. This is because every attempt to gain control of a person´s body against his or her will—irrespective of the intention behind it—causes a degree of humiliation that impacts more destructively than other forms of respect on a person´s practical relation-to-self. For what is specific to these kinds of physical injury, as exemplified by torture and rape, is not the purely physical pain but rather the combination of this pain with the feeling of being defencelessly at the mercy of another subject, to the point of feeling that one has been deprived of reality. Physical abuse represents a type of disrespect that does lasting damage to one´s basic confidence (learned through love) that one can autonomously coordinate one´s own body. Hence the further consequence,

coupled with a type of social shame, is the loss of trust in oneself and the world, and this affects all practical dealings with other subjects, even at a physical level. Thus, the kind of recognition that this type of disrespect deprives one of is the taken-for-granted respect for the autonomous control of one´s own body, which itself could only be acquired at all through experiencing emotional support as part of the socialization process. The successful integration of physical and emotional qualities of behaviour is, as it were, subsequently broken up from the outside, thus lastingly destroying the most fundamental form of practical relation-to-self, namely, one´s underlying trust in oneself.

Since such forms of basic psychological self-confidence carry emotional preconditions that follow a largely invariant logic associated with the intersubjective balance between fusion and demarcation, this experience of disrespect also cannot simply vary with the historical period or the cultural frame of reference. Whatever the construction of the system of legitimation that tries to justify it, the suffering of torture or rape is always accompanied by a dramatic breakdown in one´s trust in the reliability of the social world and hence by a collapse in one´s own basic self-confidence. By contrast, the other two types of disrespect in our tripartite division are embedded in a process of historical change. Here, what it is that is perceived, in each case, to be a moral injury is subject to the same historical transformations as the corresponding patterns of mutual recognition.

Whereas the first form of disrespect is inherent in those experiences of physical abuse that destory a person's basic self-confidence, we have to look for the second form in those experiences of denigration that can affect a person´s moral self-respect. This refers to those forms of personal disrespect to which an individual is subjected by being structurally excluded from the possession of certain rights within a society. We have initially constructed the term "rights," only roughly, as referring to those individual claims that a person can legitimately expect to have socially met because he or she participates, with equal rights, in the institutional order as a full-fledged member of a community. Should that person now be systematically denied certain rights of this kind, this would imply that he or she is not being accorded the same degree of moral responsibility as other members of society. What is specific to such forms of disrespect, as exemplified by the denial of rights or by social ostracism, thus lies not just in the forcible restriction of personal autonomy but also in the combination with the feeling of not enjoying the status of a full-fledged partner to interaction, equally endowed with moral rights. For the individual, having socially valid rights-claims denied signifies a violation of the intersubjective expectation to be recognized as a subject capable of forming moral judgements. To this extent, the experience of this type of disrespect typically brings with it a loss of self-respect, of the ability to relate to oneself as a legally equal interaction partner with all fellow humans. Thus, the kind of recognition that this type of disrespect deprives one of is the cognitive regard for the status of moral responsibility that had to be so painstakingly acquired in the interactive processes of socialization. This form of disrespect represents a historically variable quantity because the semantic content of what counts as a morally responsible agent changes with the development of legal relations. Therefore, the experience of the denial of rights is always to be measured not only in terms of the degree of universalization but also in terms of the substantive scope of the institutionally established rights.

Finally, this second type of disrespect, which injures subjects with regard to their self-respect, is to be set off from a third type of degradation, one that entails negative consequences for the social value of individuals or groups. Not until we consider these, as it were, evaluative forms of disrespect—the denigration of individual or collective ways of life—do we arrive at the form of behaviour ordinarily labelled "insulting" or "degrading" today. As we saw a person´s "honour" "dignity," or to use the modern term, "status" refers to the degree of social esteem accorded to his or her manner of self-realization within a society´s inherited cultural horizon. If this hierarchy of values is so constituted as to downgrade individual forms of life and manners of belief as inferior or deficient, then it robs the subjects in question of every opportunity to attribute social value to their own abilities. For those engaged in them, the result of the evaluative degradation of certain patterns of self-realization is that they cannot relate to their mode of life as something of positive significance within their community. For individuals, therefore, the experience of this social devaluation typically brings with it a loss of personal self-esteem, of the opportunity to regard themselves as beings whose traits and abilities are esteemed. Thus, the kind of recognition that this

type of disrespect deprives a person of is the social approval of a form of self-realization that he or she had to discover, despite all hindrances, with the encouragement of group solidarity. Of course, one can only relate these kinds of cultural degradation to oneself as an individual person once the institutionally anchored patterns of social esteem have been historically individuated, that is, once these patterns refer evaluatively to individual abilities instead of collective traits. Hence, this experience of disrespect, like that of the denial of rights, is bound up with a process of historical change.

It is typical of the three groups of experiences of disrespect analytically distinguished in this way that their individual consequences are always described in terms of metaphors that refer to states of deterioration of the human body. Psychological studies of the personal after-effects of torture or rape frequently speak of "psychological death." In research concerned with how victims of slavery collectively cope with the denial of rights and exclusion from society, the concept of "social death" is now well established. And with regard to the type of disrespect associated with the cultural denigration of forms of life, one regularly speaks of "scars" and "injuries." These metaphorical allusions to physical suffering and death articulate the idea that the various forms of disregard for the psychological integrity of humans play the same negative role that organic infections take on in the context of the reproduction of the body. The experience of being socially denigrated or humiliated endangers the identity of human beings, just as infection with a disease endangers their physical life. If this interpretation, suggested by our linguistic practice, turns out to be not entirely implausible, then it contains two implicit suggestions that are relevant for our purposes. First, the comparison with physical illness prompts the idea of identifying, for the case of suffering social disrespect as well, a stratum of symptoms that, to a certain extent, make the subjects aware of the state they are in. The hypothesis here is that what corresponds to physical indications here are the sort of negative emotional reactions expressed in feelings of social shame. Second, however, the comparison also provides the opportunity to draw conclusions, on the basis of an overview of the various forms of disrespect, as to what fosters the "psychological health" or integrity of human beings. Seen this way, the parallel to the preventive treatment of illnesses would be the social guarantees associated with those relations of recognition that are able to protect subjects most extensively from suffering disrespect. Although this second comparison will only be of interest to us when we examine the normative implications of this connection between personal integrity and disrespect, the first comparison is already significant for the argument to be developed here. For the negative emotional reactions accompanying the experience of disrespect could represent precisely the affective motivational basis in which the struggled-for recognition is anchored.

Neither in Hegel nor in Mead did we find any indication as to how experiencing social disrespect can motivate a subject to enter a practical struggle or conflict. There was, as it were, a missing psychological link that would lead from mere suffering to action by cognitively informing the person in question of his or her social situation. I would like to defend the thesis that this function can be performed by negative emotional reactions, such as being ashamed or enraged, feeling hurt or indignant. These comprise the psychological symptoms on the basis of which one can come to realize that one is being illegitimately denied social recognition. The reason for this can again be seen in the constitutional dependence of humans on the experience of recognition. In order to acquire a successful relation-to-self, one is dependent on the intersubjective recognition of one's abilities and accomplishments. Were one never to experience this type of social approval at some stage of one's development, this would open up a psychological gap within one's personality, into which negative emotional reactions such as shame or rage could step. Hence, the experience of disrespect is always accompanied by affective sensations that are, in principle, capable of revealing to individuals the fact that certain forms of recognition are being withheld from them. In order to give this complex thesis some plausibility, at least in outline, it would be advisable to connect it to a conception of human emotions of the sort developed by John Dewey in his pragmatist psychology.

In several early essays, Dewey turned against the widespread view that human states of emotional excitation had to be conceived of as expressions of inner feelings. He wanted to show that such a conception, which could still be found in William James,

necessarily overlooks the function of emotions for action by assuming the psychological event to be something "inner" and prior to actions, which it views as something directed "outwards." Against this, Dewey's argument proceeds from the observation that, within the human horizon of experience, insofar as feelings appear at all, they appear in either positive or negative dependence on actions: either they accompany the experience of particularly successful "communications" (with people or things) as bodily states of excitement, or they emerge as the experience of being repelled by a failed, interrupted attempt to execute an action. The analysis of such experiences of being repelled provides Dewey with the key to devising an action-theoretical conception of human emotions. According to this conception, negative feelings such as anger, indignation, and sorrow constitute the affective side of the shift of attention towards one's own expectations that inevitably occurs as soon as one has difficulty making the step one planned to make upon completing an action. Positive feelings such as joy or pride, by contrast, arise when one is suddenly freed from a burdensome state of excitement, because one has been able to find a suitable, successful solution to a pressing action problem. In general, then, Dewey views feelings as the affective reactions generated upon succeeding or failing to realize our intentions.

Starting from this general point, we can differentiate emotions still further once we distinguish more precisely the types of "disruptions" on which habitual human action can founder. Since these disruptions or failures are to be assessed against the background of the orienting expectations that precede the act in each case, we can make an initial, rough division on the basis of two different types of expectations. Routine human actions can come up against obstacles either in the context of expectations of instrumental success or in the context of normative behavioural expectations. Should actions oriented towards success fail as a result of unanticipated obstructions, this leads to "technical" disruptions in the broadest sense. By contrast, should actions guided by norms be repelled by situations because the norms taken to be valid are violated, this leads to "moral" conflicts in the social lifeworld. This second class of disrupted actions constitutes the experiential horizon in which moral emotional reactions are situated practically. They can be understood, in Dewey's sense, as the emotional excitations with which human beings react to having their actions unexpectedly repelled owing to a violation of normative expectations. The differences between the individual feelings can be measured quite elementarily in terms of whether the violation of the norm hindering the action is caused by the subject or by the interaction partner. In the first case, the subject experiences the hindrance to the action in feelings of guilt and, in the second case, in emotions of moral indignation. What is true of both cases, however, is something that Dewey considered to be typical of situations of emotionally experiencing one's action thrown back upon itself, namely, that with the shift of attention to one's own expectations, one also becomes aware of the cognitive components—in this case, moral knowledge—that had informed the planned and (now) hindered action.

The most open of our moral feelings is shame—to the extent that it does not refer simply to the evidently deep-seated shyness about having one's body exposed. In the case of shame, it is not fixed from the outset, which party to the interaction is responsible for violating the norm, a norm that the subject now lacks, as it were, for the routine continuation of an action. As both psychoanalytical and phenomenological approaches have shown, the emotional content of shame consists, to begin with, in a kind of lowering of one's own feeling of self-worth. Ashamed of oneself as a result of having one's action rejected, one experiences oneself as being of lower social value than one had previously assumed. In psychoanalytic terms, this means that what is negatively affected by the action-inhibiting violation of a moral norm is not the super-ego but the subject's ego-ideals. This type of shame—which is only experienced in the presence of a real or imaginary interaction partner, playing as it were the role of witness to the injured ego-ideals—can be caused by oneself or by others. In the first case, one experiences oneself as inferior because one has violated a moral norm, adherence to which had constituted a principle of one's ego-ideals. In the second case, however, one is oppressed by a feeling of low self-esteem because one's interaction partners violate moral norms that, when they were adhered to, allowed one to count as the person that, in terms of one's ego-ideals, one wants to be. Hence,

the moral crisis in communication is triggered here by the agent being disappointed with regard to the normative expectations that he or she believed could be placed on another's willingness to respect him or her. In this sense, the second type of moral shame represents the emotion that overwhelms subjects who, as a result of having their ego-claims disregarded, are incapable of simply going ahead with an action. In these emotional experiences, what one comes to realize about oneself is that one's own person is constitutively dependent on the recognition of others.

In the context of the emotional responses associated with shame, the experience of being disrespected can become the motivational impetus for a struggle for recognition. For it is only by regaining the possibility of active conduct that individuals can dispel the state of emotional tension into which they are forced as a result of humiliation. But what makes it possible for the praxis thus opened up to take the form of political resistance is the opportunity for moral insight inherent in these negative emotions, as their cognitive content. It is only because human subjects are incapable of reacting in emotionally neutral ways to social injuries—as exemplified by physical abuse, the denial of rights, and denigration—that the normative patterns of mutual recognition found in the social lifeworld have any chance of being realized. For each of the negative emotional reactions that accompany the experience of having one's claims to recognition disregarded holds out the possibility that the injustice done to one will cognitively disclose itself and become a motive for political resistance.

Of course, the weakness of this foothold of morality within social reality is shown by the fact that, in these affective reactions, the injustice of disrespect does not inevitably *have* to reveal itself but merely *can*. Empirically, whether the cognitive potential inherent in feeling hurt or ashamed becomes a moral-political conviction depends above all on how the affected subject's cultural-political environment is constructed: only if the means of articulation of a social movement are available can the experience of disrespect become a source of motivation for acts of political resistance. The developmental logic of such collective movements can, however, only be discovered via an analysis that attempts to explain social struggles on the basis of the dynamics of moral experiences.

SECTION XIII

1. Using developments in photography and film in the first half of the twentieth century, Benjamin speculates about the impact of such technological developments on the world of art. What are the implications he sees for art in what he calls the "age of mechanical reproduction"?
2. Do you find convincing Marcuse's argument that freedom is eroding in the world's leading democracies as a result of the impact of technology and bureaucracy? Why or why not?
3. What does Marcuse mean by an "overly administered society"?
4. Summarize in your own words the distinction Horkheimer makes between traditional and critical theory. Do you think theory should be informed by ethics? Why or why not?
5. Habermas contends that historically two particular theories of democracy have constituted competing models: liberalism and republicanism. Compare and contrast these two models.
6. Habermas offers as an alternative to both liberalism and republicanism a theory of democracy he calls "deliberative politics." Summarize this alternative and describe how it differs from the other two.
7. In developing his argument about the role of disrespect in the formation of personal identity, Honneth turns to the work of both Mead and Dewey. Summarize the role these classics then play in Honneth's essay.

XIV. CONTEMPORARY THEORIES OF MODERNITY

66. SHAME AND REPUGNANCE

NORBERT ELIAS

Not too many years before his death, Norbert Elias (1897–1990) was "discovered" by sociology, and since then he has been viewed as one of the most important historical sociologists of the century. Another émigre who left Germany during the Hitler years, Elias published *The Civilizing Process* in 1939, just before the world plunged into war. The timing of its release sealed the fate of the book, as it would be read by only a few, and Elias would teach in England in relative obscurity for decades. This changed in the 1970s; since that time theorists have paid considerable attention to his work. The overarching focus of Elias' work is the way Western civilization has developed and in particular the varied ways that people have been transformed psychologically and behaviorally. Of particular concern to Elias are the ways that self-restraint has become a characteristic feature of the "civilized" person. This selection from *Power and Civility* (Part II of *The Civilizing Process*) offers insights into the ways in which the development of notions of shame and repugnance have been an integral part of this process.

No less characteristic of a civilizing process than "rationalization" is the peculiar moulding of the drive economy that we call "shame" and "repugnance" or "embarrassment". Both these, the strong spurt of rationalization and the (for a time) no less strong advance of the threshold of shame and repugnance that becomes more and more perceptible in the make-up of Western men broadly speaking from the sixteenth century onwards, are different sides of the same transformation of the social personality structure. The feeling of shame is a specific excitation, a kind of anxiety which is automatically reproduced in the individual on certain occasions by force of habit.

Considered superficially, it is fear of social degradation or, more generally, of other people's gestures of superiority. But it is a form of displeasure or fear which arises characteristically on those occasions when a person who fears lapsing into inferiority can avert this danger neither by direct physical means nor by any other form of attack. This defencelessness against the superiority of others, this total exposure to them does not arise directly from a threat from the physical superiority of others actually present, although it doubtless has its origins in physical compulsion, in the bodily inferiority of the child in face of its parents or teachers. In adults, however, this defencelessness results from the fact that

Reprinted by permission of Sage Publications Ltd from Norbert Elias, *Power and Civility*, pp. 292–300. Copyright 1939, ©1969, 1976 by Norbert Elias. English translation copyright ©1982 by Basil Blackwell, Publisher. ✦

the people whose superiority one fears are in accord with one's own superego, with the agency of self-constraint implanted in the individual by others on whom he was dependent, who possessed power and superiority over him. In keeping with this, the anxiety that we call "shame" is heavily veiled to the sight of others; however strong it may be, it is never directly expressed in noisy gestures. Shame takes on its particular coloration from the fact that the person feeling it has done or is about to do something through which he comes into contradiction with people to whom he is bound in one form or another, and with himself, with the sector of his consciousness by which he controls himself. The conflict expressed in shame-fear is not merely a conflict of the individual with prevalent social opinion; the individual's behaviour has brought him into conflict with the part of himself that represents this social opinion. It is a conflict within his own personality; he himself recognizes himself as inferior. He fears the loss of the love or respect of others, to which he attaches or has attached value. Their attitude has precipitated an attitude within him that he automatically adopts towards himself. This is what makes him so defenceless against gestures of superiority by others which somehow trigger off this automatism within him.

This also explains why the fear of transgression of social prohibitions takes on more clearly the character of shame the more completely alien constraints have been turned into self-restraints by the structure of society, and the more comprehensive and differentiated the ring of self-restraints have become within which a person's conduct is enclosed. The inner tension, the excitement that is aroused whenever a person feels compelled to break out of this enclosure in any place, or when he has done so, varies in strength according to the gravity of the social prohibition and the degree of self-constraint. In ordinary life we call this excitement shame only in certain contexts and above all when it has a certain degree of strength; but in terms of its structure it is, despite its many nuances and degrees, always the same event. Like self-constraints, it is to be found in a less stable, less uniform and less all-embracing form even at simpler levels of social development. Like these constraints, tensions and fears of this kind emerge more clearly with every spurt of the civilizing process, and finally predominate over others—particularly the

physical fear of others. They predominate the more, the larger the areas that are pacified, and the greater the importance in the moulding of people of the more even constraints that come to the fore in society when the representatives of the monopoly of physical violence normally only exercise their control as it were standing in the wings—the further, in a word, the civilization of conduct advances. Just as we can only speak of "reason" in conjunction with advances of rationalization and the formation of functions demanding foresight and restraint, we can only speak of shame in conjunction with its sociogenesis, with spurts in which the shame-threshold advances or at least moves, and the structure and pattern of self-constraints are changed in a particular direction, reproducing themselves thenceforth in the same form over a greater or lesser period. Both rationalization and the advance of the shame and repugnance thresholds are expressions of a reduction in the direct physical fear of other beings, and of a consolidation of the automatic inner anxieties, the compulsions which the individual now exerts on himself. In both, the greater, more differentiated foresight and long-term view which become necessary in order that larger and larger groups of people may preserve their social existence in an increasing differentiated society, are equally expressed. It is not difficult to explain how these seemingly so different psychological changes are connected. Both, the intensification of shame like the increased rationalization, are different aspects of the growing split in the individual personality that occurs with the increasing division of functions; they are different aspects of the growing differentiation between drives and drive-controls, between "id" and "ego" or "super-ego" functions. The further this differentiation of individual self-steering advances, the more clearly that sector of the controlling functions which in a broader sense is called the "ego" and in a narrower the "super-ego", takes on a twofold function. On the one hand this sector forms the centre from which a person regulates his relations to other living and non-living beings, and on the other it forms the centre from which a person, partly consciously and partly quite automatically and unconsciously, controls his "inner life", his own affects and impulses. The layer of psychological functions which, in the course of the social transformation that has been described, is gradually differentiated from the drives, the ego or super-ego functions, has in other words, a twofold task within the personality: they conduct at the same time a domestic policy and a foreign policy—which, moreover, are not always in harmony and often enough in contradiction. This explains the fact that in the same socio-historical period in which rationalization makes perceptible advances, an advance in the shame and repugnance threshold is also to be observed. It also explains the fact that here, as always—in accordance with the sociogenetic ground rule—a corresponding process is to be observed even today in the life of each individual child: the rationalization of conduct is an expression of the foreign policy of the same super-ego formation whose domestic policy is expressed in an advance of the shame threshold.

From here many large trains of thought lead off in different directions. It remains to be shown how this increased differentiation within the personality is manifested in a transformation of particular drives. Above all, it remains to be shown how it leads to a transformation of sexual impulses and an advance of shame feelings in the relations of men and women.[1] It must be enough here to indicate some of the main connections between the social processes described above and this advance of the frontier of shame and repugnance.

Even in the more recent history of the West itself, shame feelings have not always been built into the personality in the same way. To mention only one difference, the manner in which they are built in is not the same in a hierarchical society made up of estates as in the succeeding bourgeois industrial order.

The examples quoted earlier, above all those showing differences in the development of shame on the exposure of certain bodily parts,[2] give a certain impression of such changes. In courtly society shame on exposing certain parts is, in keeping with the structure of this society, still largely restricted within estate or hierarchical limits. Exposure in the presence of social inferiors, for example by the king in front of a minister, is placed under no very strict social prohibition, any more than the exposure of a man before the socially weaker and lower-ranking woman was in an earlier phase. Given his minimal functional dependence on those of lower rank, exposure as yet arouses no feeling of inferiority or shame; it can even be taken, as Della Casa states, as a sign of benevolence towards the inferior. Exposure by someone of lower rank before a superior, on the other hand, or even before people of equal rank, is banished more and more from social life as a sign of lack of respect; branded as an offence, it becomes invested with fear. And only when the walls between estates fall away, when the functional dependence of all on all increases and all members of society become several degrees more equal, does such exposure, except in certain narrower enclaves, become an offence in the presence of any other person. Only then is such behaviour so profoundly associated with fear in the individual from an early age, that the social character of the prohibition vanishes entirely from his consciousness, shame appearing as a command coming from within himself.

And the same is true of embarrassment. This is an inseparable counterpart of shame. Just as the latter arises when someone infringes the prohibitions of his own self and of society, the former occurs when something outside the individual impinges on his danger zone, on forms of behaviour, objects, inclinations which have early on been invested with fear by his surroundings until this fear—in the manner of a conditioned reflex—is reproduced automatically in him on certain occasions. Embarrassment is displeasure or anxiety which arises when another person threatens to breach, or breaches, society's prohibitions represented by one's own super-ego. And these feelings too become more diverse and comprehensive the more extensive and subtly differentiated the danger zone by which the conduct of the individual is regulated and moulded, the further the civilization of conduct advances.

It was shown earlier by a series of examples how, from the sixteenth century onwards, the frontier of shame and embarrassment gradually begins to advance more rapidly. Here, too, the chains of thought begin slowly to join up. This advance coincides with the accelerated courtization of the upper class. It is the time when the chains of dependence intersecting in the individual grow denser and longer, when more and more people are being bound more and more closely together and the compulsion to self-control is increasing. Like mutual dependence, mutual observation of people increases; sensibilities, and correspondingly prohibitions, become more differentiated; and equally more subtle, equally more manifold become the reasons for shame and for embarrassment aroused by the conduct of others.

It was pointed out above that with the advancing division of functions and the greater integration of people, the major contrasts between different classes and countries diminish, while the nuances, the varieties of their moulding within the framework of civilization multiply. Here one encounters a corresponding trend in the development of individual conduct and sentiment. The more the strong contrasts of individual conduct are tempered, the more the violent fluctuations of pleasure or displeasure are contained, moderated and changed by self-control, the greater becomes the sensitivity to shades or nuances of conduct, the more finely attuned people grow to minute gestures and forms, and the more complex becomes their experience of themselves and their world at levels which were previously hidden from consciousness through the veil of strong affects.

To clarify this by an obvious example, "primitive" people experience human and natural events within the relatively narrow circle which is vitally important to them—narrow, because their chains of dependence are relatively short—in a manner which is in some respects far more differentiated than that of "civilized" people. The differentiation varies, depending on whether we are concerned with farmers or hunters or herdsmen, for example. But however this may be, it can be stated generally that, insofar as it is of vital importance to a group, the ability of primitive people to distinguish things in forest and field, whether it be a particular tree from another, or sounds, scents or movements, is more highly developed than in "civilized" people. But among more primitive people the natural sphere is still far more a danger zone; it is full of fears which more civilized men no longer know. This is decisive for what is or is not distinguished. The manner in which "nature" is experienced is fundamentally affected, slowly at the end of the Middle Ages and then more quickly from the sixteenth century onwards, by the pacification of larger and larger populated areas. Only now do forests, meadows and mountains gradually cease to be danger zones of the first order, from which anxiety and fear constantly intrude into individual life. And now, as the network

of roads becomes, like social interdependence in general, more dense; as robber-knights and beasts of prey slowly disappear; as forest and field cease to be the scene of unbridled passions, of the savage pursuit of man and beast, wild joy and wild fear; as they are moulded more and more by intertwining peaceful activities, the production of goods, trade and transport; now, to pacified men a correspondingly pacified nature becomes visible, and in a new way. It becomes—in keeping with the mounting significance which the eye attains as the mediator of pleasure with the growing moderation of the affects—to a high degree an object of visual pleasure. In addition, people—more precisely the town-people for whom forest and field are no longer their everyday background but a place of relaxation—grow more sensitive and begin to see the open country in a more differentiated way, at a level which was previously screened off by danger and the play of unmoderated passions. They take pleasure in the harmony of colour and lines, become open to what is called the beauty of nature; their feelings are aroused by the changing shades and shapes of the clouds and the play of light on the leaves of a tree.

And, in the wake of this pacification, the sensitivity of people to social conduct is also changed. Now, inner fears grow in proportion to the decrease of outer ones—the fears of one sector of the personality for another. As a result of these inner tensions, people begin to experience each other in a more differentiated way which was precluded as long as they constantly faced serious and inescapable threats from outside. Now a major part of the tensions which were earlier discharged directly in combat between man and man, must be resolved as an inner tension in the struggle of the individual with himself. Social life ceases to be a danger zone in which feasting, dancing and noisy pleasure frequently and suddenly give way to rage, blows and murder, and becomes a different kind of danger zone if the individual cannot sufficiently restrain himself, if he touches sensitive spots, his own shame-frontier or the embarrassment-threshold of others. In a sense, the danger zone now passes through the self of every individual. Thus people become, in this respect too, sensitive to distinctions which previously scarcely entered consciousness. Just as nature now becomes, far more than earlier, a source of pleasure mediated by the eye, people too become a source of visual pleasure or, conversely, of visually aroused displeasure, of different degrees of repugnance. The direct fear inspired in men by men has diminished, and the inner fear mediated through the eye and through the super-ego is rising proportionately.

When the use of weapons in combat is an everyday occurrence, the small gesture of offering someone a knife at table (to recall one of the examples mentioned earlier) has no great importance. As the use of weapons is restricted more and more, as external and internal pressures make the expression of anger by physical attack increasingly difficult, people gradually become more sensitive to anything reminiscent of an attack. The very gesture of attack touches the danger zone; it becomes distressing to see a person passing someone else a knife with the point towards him.[3] And from the most highly sensitized small circles of high courtly society, for whom this sensitivity also represents a prestige value, a means of distinction cultivated for that very reason, this prohibition gradually spreads throughout the whole of civilized society. Thus aggressive associations, infused no doubt with others from the layer of elementary urges, combine with status tensions in arousing anxiety.

How the use of a knife is then gradually restricted and surrounded, as a danger zone, by a wall of prohibitions, has been shown through a number of examples. It is an open question how far, in the courtly aristocracy, the renunciation of physical violence remains an external compulsion, and how far it has already been converted into an inner constraint. Despite all restrictions, the use of the table knife, like that of the dagger, is still quite extensive. Just as the hunting and killing of animals is still a permitted and commonplace amusement for the lords of the earth, the carving of dead animals at table remains within the zone of the permitted and is as yet not felt as repugnant. Then, with the slow rise of bourgeois classes, in whom pacification

and the generation of inner constraints by the very nature of their social functions is far more complete and binding, the cutting up of dead animals is pushed back further behind the scenes of social life (even if in particular countries, particularly England, as so often, some of the older customs survive incorporated in the new) and the use of the knife, indeed the mere holding of it, is avoided wherever it is not entirely indispensable. Sensitivity in this direction grows.

This is one example among many of particular aspects of the structural transformation of society that we denote by the catchword "civilization". Nowhere in human society is there a zero-point of fear of external powers, and nowhere a zero-point of automatic inner anxieties. Although they may be experienced as very different, they are finally inseparable. What takes place in the course of a civilizing process is not the disappearance of one and the emergence of the other. What changes is merely the proportion between the external and the self-activating fears, and their whole structure. People's fears of external powers diminish without ever disappearing; the never-absent, latent or actual anxieties arising from the tension between drives and drive-control functions become relatively stronger, more comprehensive and continuous. The documentation for the advance of the shame and embarrassment frontiers ... consists in fact of nothing but particularly clear and simple examples of the direction and structure of a change in the human personality which could be demonstrated from many other aspects too. A very similar structure is exhibited, for example, by the transition from the medieval-Catholic to the Protestant superego formation. This, too, shows a pronounced shift towards the internalization of fears. And one thing certainly should not be overlooked in all this: the fact that today, as formerly, all forms of adult inner anxieties are bound up with the child's fears of others, of external powers.

NOTES

1. This particular problem, important as it is, must be left aside for the time being. Its elucidation demands a description and an exact analysis of the changes which the structure of the family and the whole relationship of the sexes have undergone in the course of Western history. It demands, furthermore, a general study of changes in the upbringing of children and the development of adolescents. The material which has been collected to elucidate this aspect of the civilizing process, and the analyses it made possible have

proved too extensive; they threatened to dislocate the framework of this study and will find their place in a further volume.

The same applies to the middle-class line of the civilizing process, the change it produced in bourgeois-urban classes and the non-courtly landed aristocracy. While this transformation of conduct and of the structure of psychological functions is certainly connected in these classes, too, with a specific historical restructuring of the *whole* Western social fabric, nevertheless—as already pointed out on a number of occasions—the non-courtly middle-class line of civilization follows a different pattern to the courtly one. Above all, the treatment of sexuality in the former is not the same as in the latter—partly because of a different family structure, and partly because of the different kind of foresight which middle-class professional functions demand. Something similar emerges if the civilizing transformation of Western religion is investigated. The change in religious feeling to which sociology has paid most attention hitherto, the increased inwardness and rationalization expressed in the various Puritan and Protestant movements, is obviously closely connected to certain changes in the situation and structure of the middle classes. The corresponding change in Catholicism, as shown, for example, in the formation of the power position of the Jesuits, appears to take place in closer touch with the absolutist central organs, in a manner favoured by the hierarchical and centralist structure of the Catholic Church. These problems, too, will only be solved when we have a more exact overall picture of the intertwining of the non-courtly, middle-class and the courtly lines of civilization, leaving aside for the time being the civilizing movement in worker and peasant strata which emerges more slowly and much later.

2. *The Civilizing Process*, vol. 1, pp. 207ff. On the general problem of shame feelings cf. *The Spectator* (1807), vol. 5, no. 373: "If I was put to define Modesty, I would call it, The reflection of an ingenuous Mind, either when a Man has committed an Action for which he censures himself, or fancies that he is exposed to the Censure of others." See also the observation there on the difference of shame feelings between men and women.
3. *The Civilizing Process*, vol. 1, pp. 122ff.

67. SPECTACULAR TIME

GUY DEBORD

The thought of French theorist Guy Debord (1931-1994) was shaped by Marx and subsequent Marxist thinkers, including Lucien Goldman and Henri Lefebvre. A political activist, he was one of the founding members of the Situationist International and an influential figure during the student revolts of May 1968. His major work, *The Society of the Spectacle* (1967), is actually a brief, aphoristic book devoted to specifying what he meant by spectacle and how this term can be seen as characterizing modern life. His central claim is that the spectacle refers to social relations mediated by images. The book contains 221 theses, ranging in length from a sentence to page-long paragraphs. The selection included here is devoted to what he refers to as "spectacular time." Time in contemporary capitalist society is seen as a commodity. If traditional societies could be seen in terms of cyclical time, today it has become "pseudo-cyclical." In these theses, Debord shifts between a focus on what spectacular time means for production and how it shapes modern patterns of consumption. The chapter ends with a fairly traditional Marxist assertion that this alienating type of time can be overcome in "the revolutionary project of realizing a classless society." Stripped of these Marxist claims, Debord's ideas have percolated into some currents of postmodernism.

We have nothing of our own but time, which is enjoyed precisely by those who have no place to stay.

—Baltasar Gracian, *L`Homme de cour*

147

The time of production, commodity-time, is an infinite accumulation of equivalent intervals. It is the abstraction of irreversible time, all of whose segments must prove on the chronometer their merely quantitative equality. This time is in reality exactly what it is in its *exchangeable* character. In this social domination by commodity-time, "time is everything, man is nothing; he is at most the carcass of time" *(Poverty of Philosophy)*. This is time devalued, the complete inversion of time as "the field of human development."

148

The general time of human non-development also exists in the complementary form of *consumable* time which returns as *pseudo-cyclical* time to the daily life of the society based on this determined production.

149

Pseudo-cyclical time is actually no more than the *consumable disguise* of the commodity-time of production. It contains the essential properties of commodity-time, namely exchangeable homogeneous units and the suppression of the qualitative dimension. But being the by-product of this time which aims to retard concrete daily life and to keep it retarded, it must be charged with pseudo-valuations and appear in a sequence of falsely individualized moments.

150

Pseudo-cyclical time is the time of consumption of modern economic survival, of increased survival, where daily life continues to be deprived of decision and remains bound, no longer to the natural order, but to the pseudo-nature developed in alienated labor; and thus this time *naturally* reestablishes the ancient cyclical rhythm which regulated the survival of preindustrial societies. Pseudo-cyclical time leans on the natural remains of cyclical time and also uses it to compose new homologous combinations: day and night, work and weekly rest, the recurrence of vacations.

151

Pseudo-cyclical time is a time *transformed by industry*. The time which has its basis in the production of commodities is itself a consumable commodity which includes everything that previously (during the phase of dissolution of the old unitary society) was differentiated into private life, economic life, political life. All the consumable time of modern society comes to be treated as a raw material for varied new products which impose themselves on the market as uses of socially organized time. "A product which already exists in a form which makes it suitable for consumption can nevertheless in its turn become a raw material for another product" *(Capital)*.

152

In its most advanced sector, concentrated capitalism orients itself towards the sale of "completely equipped" blocks of time, each one constituting a single unified commodity which integrates a number of diverse commodities. In the expanding economy of "services" and leisure, this gives rise to the formula of calculated payment in which "everything's included": spectacular environment, the collective pseudo-displacement of vacations, subscriptions to cultural consumption, and the sale of sociability itself in the form of "passionate conversations" and "meetings with personalities." This sort of spectacular commodity. which can obviously circulate only because of the increased poverty of the corresponding realities, just as obviously fits among the pilot-articles of modernized sales techniques by being payable on credit.

153

Consumable pseudo-cyclical time is spectacular time, both as the time of consumption of images in the narrow sense, and as the image of consumption of time in the broad sense. The time of image-consumption, the medium of all commodities, is inseparably the field where the instruments of the spectacle exert themselves fully, and also their goal, the location and main form of all specific consumption: it is known that the time-saving constantly sought by modern society, whether in the speed of vehicles or in the use of dried soups, is concretely translated for the population of the United States in the fact that the mere contemplation of television occupies it for an average of three to six hours a day. The social image of the consumption of time, in turn, is exclusively dominated by moments of leisure and vacation, moments presented *at a distance* and desirable by definition, like every spectacular commodity. Here this commodity is explicitly presented as the moment of real life, and the point is to wait for its cyclical return. But even in those very moments reserved for living, it is still the spectacle that is to be seen and reproduced, becoming ever more intense. What was represented as genuine life reveals itself simply as more *genuinely spectacular life*.

154

The epoch which displays its time to itself as essentially the sudden return of multiple festivities is also an epoch without festivals. What was, in cyclical time, the moment of a community's participation in the luxurious expenditure of life is impossible for the society without community or luxury. When its vulgarized pseudo-festivals, parodies of the dialogue and the gift, incite a surplus of economic expenditure, they lead only to deception always compensated by the promise of a new deception. In the spectacle, the lower the use value of modern survival-time, the more highly it is exalted. The reality of time has been replaced by the *advertisement* of time.

155

While the consumption of cyclical time in ancient societies was consistent with the real labor of those societies, the pseudo-cyclical consumption of the developed economy is in contradiction with the abstract irreversible time of its production. While cyclical time was the time of immobile illusion, really lived, spectacular time is the time of self-changing reality, lived in illusion.

156

What is constantly new in the process of production of things is not found in consumption, which remains the expanded repetition of the same. In spectacular time, since dead labor continues to dominate living labor, the past dominates the present.

157

Another side of the deficiency of general historical life is that individual life as yet has no history. The pseudo-events which rush by in spectacular dramatizations have not been lived by those informed of them; moreover they are lost in the inflation of their hurried replacement at every throb of the spectacular machinery. Furthermore, what is really lived has no relation to the official irreversible time of society and is in direct opposition to the pseudo-cyclical rhythm of the consumable by-product of this time. This individual experience of separate daily life remains without language, without concept, without critical access to its own past which has been recorded nowhere. It is not communicated. It is not understood and is forgotten to the profit of the false spectacular memory of the unmemorable.

158

The spectacle, as the present social organization of the paralysis of history and memory, of the abandonment of history built on the foundation of historical time, is the *false consciousness of time.*

159

The preliminary condition required for propelling workers to the status of "free" producers and consumers of commodity time was *the violent expropriation of their own time*. The spectacular return of time became possible only after this first dispossession of the producer.

160

The irreducibly biological element which remains in labor, both in the dependence on the natural cycle of waking and sleep and in the existence of irreversible time in the expenditure of an individual life, is a mere *accessory* from the point of view of modern production; consequently, these elements are ignored in the official proclamations of the movement of production and in the consumable trophies which are the accessible translation of this incessant victory. The spectator's consciousness, immobilized in the falsified center of the movement of its world, no longer experiences its life as a passage toward self-realization and toward death. One who has renounced using his life can no longer admit his death. Life insurance advertisements suggest merely that he is guilty of dying without ensuring the regularity of the system after this economic loss; and the advertisement of the *American way of death* insists on his capacity to maintain in this encounter the greatest possible number of *appearances* of life. On all other fronts of the advertising onslaught, it is strictly forbidden to grow old. Even a "youth-capital," contrived for each and all and put to the most mediocre uses, could never acquire the durable and cumulative reality of financial capital. This social absence of death is identical to the social absence of life.

161

Time, as Hegel showed, is the *necessary* alienation, the environment where the subject realizes himself by losing himself, where he becomes other in order to become truly himself. Precisely the opposite is true in the dominant alienation, which is undergone by the producer of an *alien present*. In this *spatial alienation,* the society that radically separates the subject from the activity it takes from him, separates him first of all from his own time. It is this surmountable social alienation that has prohibited and petrified the possibilities and risks of the *living* alienation of time.

162

Under the visible *fashions* which disappear and reappear on the trivial surface of contemplated pseudo-cyclical time, the *grand style* of the age is always located in what is oriented by the obvious and secret necessity of revolution.

163

The natural basis of time, the actual experience of the flow of time, becomes human and social by existing *for man*. The restricted condition of human practice, labor at various stages, is what has humanized and also dehumanized time as cyclical and as separate irreversible time of economic production. The revolutionary project of realizing a classless society, a generalized historical life, is the project of a withering away of the social measure of time, to the benefit of a playful model of irreversible time of individuals and groups, a model in which *independent federated times* are simultaneously present. It is the program of a total realization, within the context of time, of communism which suppressed all that exists independently of individuals.

164

The world already possesses the dream of a time whose consciousness it must now possess in order to actually live it.

68. THE REFLEXIVITY OF MODERNITY

ANTHONY GIDDENS

The former director of the London School of Economics and Political Science and early on a key promoter of Prime Minister Tony Blair's New Labour platform as an instance of "the third way," Anthony Giddens (b. 1938) has taught at Cambridge University as well as in the United States. He is known for his insightful exegetical examinations of both the classical social theorists and contemporary approaches. In this passage from *The Consequences of Modernity* (1990), it is clear that his approach stakes out a position in opposition to postmodernists who have claimed that we have entered a new state of development beyond the modern. On the contrary, Giddens thinks we have entered "late modernity." As he sees it, part of the problem with the idea of postmodernity is that it fails to adequately appreciate how the modern project, although it does develop historically and changes over time, signifies a singular break with tradition. In other words, the stages of modernity are part of a larger whole. Here he focuses on the fact that modernity encourages a reflexivity that is quite unlike what is found in traditional society. He sketches out some of the implications of reflexivity, particularly as it becomes even more implicated in the way that the social system reproduces itself.

THE REFLEXIVITY OF MODERNITY

Inherent in the idea of modernity is a contrast with tradition. As noted previously, many combinations of the modern and the traditional are to be found in concrete social settings. Indeed, some authors have argued that these are so tightly interlaced as to make any generalised comparison valueless. But such is surely not the case, as we can see by pursuing an enquiry into the relation between modernity and reflexivity.

There is a fundamental sense in which reflexivity is a defining characteristic of all human action. All human beings routinely "keep in touch" with the grounds of what they do as an integral element of doing it. I have called this elsewhere the "reflexive monitoring of action," using the phrase to draw attention to the chronic character of the processes involved.[1] Human action does not incorporate chains of aggregate interactions and reasons, but a consistent—and, as Erving Goffman above all has shown us, never-to-be-relaxed—monitoring of behaviour and its contexts. This is not the sense of reflexivity which is specifically connected with modernity, although it is the necessary basis of it.

In traditional cultures, the past is honoured and symbols are valued because they contain and perpetuate the experience of generations. Tradition is a mode of integrating the reflexive monitoring of action with the time-space organisation of the community. It is a means of handling time and space, which inserts any particular activity or experience within the continuity of past, present, and future, these in turn being structured by recurrent social practices. Tradition is not wholly static, because it has to be reinvented by each new generation as it takes over its cultural inheritance from those preceding it. Tradition does not so much resist change as pertain to a context in which there are few separated temporal and spatial markers in terms of which change can have any meaningful form.

In oral cultures, tradition is not known as such, even though these cultures are the most traditional of all. To understand tradition, as distinct from other modes of organising action and experience, demands cutting into time-space in ways which are only possible with the invention of writing. Writing expands the level of time-space distanciation and creates a perspective of past, present, and future in which the reflexive appropriation of knowledge can be set off from designated tradition. However, in pre-modern civilisations reflexivity is still largely limited to the reinterpretation and clarification of tradition, such that in the scales of time the side of the "past" is much more heavily weighed down than that of the "future." Moreover, since literacy is the monopoly of the few, the routinisation of daily life remains bound up with tradition in the old sense.

With the advent of modernity, reflexivity takes on a different character. It is introduced into the very basis of system reproduction, such that thought and action are constantly refracted back upon one another. The routinisation of daily life has no intrinsic connections with the past at all, save in so far as what "was done before" happens to coincide with what can be defended in a principled way in the light of incoming knowledge. To sanction a practice because it is traditional will not do; tradition can be justified, but only in the light of knowledge which is not itself authenticated by tradition. Combined with the inertia of habit, this means that, even in the most modernised of modern societies, tradition continues to play a role. But this role is generally much less significant than is supposed by authors who focus attention upon the integration of tradition and modernity in the contemporary world. For justified tradition is tradition in sham clothing and receives its identity only from the reflexivity of the modern.

The reflexivity of modern social life consists in the fact that social practices are constantly examined and reformed in the light of incoming information about those very practices, thus constitutively altering their character. We should be clear about the nature of this phenomenon. All forms of social life are partly consituted by actors' knowledge of them. Knowing "how to go on" in Wittgenstein's sense is intrinsic to the conventions which are drawn upon and reproduced by human activity. In all cultures, social practices are routinely altered in the light of ongoing discoveries which feed into them. But only in the era of modernity is the revision of convention radicalised to apply (in principle) to all aspects of human life, including technological intervention into the material world. It is often said that modernity is marked by an appetite for the new, but this is not perhaps completely accurate. What is characteristic of modernity is not an embracing of the new for its own sake, but the presumption of wholesale reflexivity—which of course includes reflection upon the nature of reflection itself.

Probably we are only now, in the late twentieth century, beginning to realise in a full sense how deeply unsettling this outlook is. For when the claims of reason replaced those of tradition, they appeared to offer a sense of certitude greater than that provided by preexisting dogma. But this idea only appears persuasive so long as we do not see that the reflexivity of modernity actually subverts reason, at any rate where reason is understood as the gaining of certain knowledge. Modernity is constituted in and through reflexively applied knowledge, but the equation of knowledge with certitude has turned out to be misconceived. We are abroad in a world which is thoroughly constituted through reflexively applied knowledge, but where at the same time we can never be sure that any given element of that knowledge will not be revised.

Even philosophers who most staunchly defend the claims of science to certitude, such as Karl Popper, acknowledge that, as he expresses it, "all science rests upon shifting sand."[2] In science, *nothing* is certain, and nothing can be proved, even if scientific endeavour provides us with the most dependable information about the world to which we can aspire. In the heart of the world of hard science, modernity floats free.

No knowledge under conditions of modernity *is* knowledge in the "old" sense, where "to know" is to be certain. This applies equally to the natural and the social sciences. In the case of social science, however, there are further considerations involved. We should recall at this point the observations made earlier about the reflexive components of sociology.

In the social sciences, to the unsettled character of all empirically based knowledge we have to add the "subversion" which comes from the reentry of social scientific discourse into the contexts it analyses. The reflection of which the social sciences are the formalised version (a specific genre of expert knowledge) is quite fundamental to the reflexivity of modernity as a whole.

Because of the close relation between the Enlightenment and advocacy of the claims of reason, natural science has usually been taken as the preeminent endeavour distinguishing the modern outlook from what went before. Even those who favour interpretative rather than naturalistic sociology have normally seen social science as the poor relation of the natural sciences, particularly given the scale of technological development consequent upon scientific discoveries. But the social sciences are actually more deeply implicated in modernity than is natural science, since the chronic revision of social practices in the light of knowledge about those practices is part of the very tissue of modern institutions.[3]

All the social sciences participate in this reflexive relation, although sociology has an especially central place. Take as an example the discourse of economics. Concepts like "capital," "investment," "markets," "industry," and many others, in their modern senses, were elaborated as part of the early development of economics as a distinct discipline in the eighteenth and early nineteenth centuries. These concepts, and empirical conclusions linked to them, were formulated in order to analyse changes involved in the emergence of modern institutions. But they could not, and did not, remain separated from the activities and events to which they related. They have become integral to what "modern economic life" actually is and inseparable from it. Modern economic activity would not be as it is were it not for the fact that all members of the population have mastered these concepts and an indefinite variety of others.

The lay individual cannot necessarily provide formal definitions of terms like "capital" or "investment," but everyone who, say, uses a savings account in a bank demonstrates an implicit and practical mastery of those notions. Concepts such as these, and the theories and empirical information linked to them, are not merely handy devices whereby agents are somehow more clearly able to understand their behaviour than they could do otherwise. They actively constitute what that behaviour is and inform the reasons for which it is undertaken. There cannot be a clear insulation between literature available to economists and that which is either read or filters through in other ways to interested parties in the population: business leaders, government officials, and members of the public. The economic environment is constantly being altered in the light of

these inputs, thus creating a situation of continual mutual involvement between economic discourse and the activities to which it refers.

The pivotal position of sociology in the reflexivity of modernity comes from its role as the most generalised type of reflection upon modern social life. Let us consider an example at the "hard edge" of naturalistic sociology. The official statistics published by governments concerning, for instance, population, marriage and divorce, crime and delinquency, and so forth, seem to provide a means of studying social life with precision. To the pioneers of naturalistic sociology, such as Durkhiem, these statistics represented hard data, in terms of which the relevant aspects of modern societies can be analysed more accurately than where such figures are lacking. Yet official statistics are not just analytical characteristics of social activity, but again enter constitutively into the social universe from which they are taken or counted up. From its inception, the collation of official statistics has been constitutive of state power and of many other modes of social organisation also. The coordinated administrative control achieved by modern governments is inseparable from the routine monitoring of "official data" in which all contemporary states engage.

The assembling of official statistics is itself a reflexive endeavour, permeated by the very findings of the social sciences that have utilised them. The practical work of coroners, for example, is the basis for the collection of suicide statistics. In the interpretation of causes/motives for death, however, coroners are guided by concepts and theories which purport to illuminate the nature of suicide. It would not be at all unusual to find a coroner who had read Durkheim.

Nor is the reflexivity of official statistics confined to the sphere of the state. Anyone in a Western country who embarks upon marriage today, for instance, knows that divorce rates are high (and may also, however imperfectly or partially, know a great deal more about the demography of marriage and the family). Knowledge of the high rate of divorce might affect the very decision to marry, as well as decisions about related considerations—provisions about property and so forth. Awareness of levels of divorce, moreover, is normally much more than just consciousness of a brute fact. It is theorised by the lay agent in ways pervaded by sociological thinking. Thus virtually everyone contemplating marriage has some idea of how family institutions have been changing, changes in the relative social position and power of men and women, alternations in sexual mores, etc.—all of which enter into processes of further change which they reflexively inform. Marriage and the family would not be what they are today were they not thoroughly "sociologised" and "psychologised."

The discourse of sociology and the concepts, theories, and findings of the other social sciences continually "circulate in and out" of what it is that they are about. In so doing they reflexively restructure their subject matter, which itself has learned to think sociologically. *Modernity is itself deeply and intrinsically sociological.* Much that is problematic in the position of the professional sociologist, as the purveyor of expert knowledge about social life, derives from the fact that she or he is at most one step ahead of enlightened lay practitioners of the discipline.

Hence the thesis that more knowledge about social life (even if that knowledge is as well buttressed empirically as it could possibly be) equals greater control over our fate is false. It is (arguably) true about the physical world, but not about the universe of social events. Expanding our understanding of the social world might produce a progressively more illuminating grasp of human institutions and, hence, increasing "technological" control over them, if it were the case either that social life were entirely separate from human knowledge about it or that knowledge could be filtered continously into the reasons for social action, producing step-by-step increases in the "rationality" of behaviour in relation to specific needs.

Both conditions do in fact apply to many circumstances and contexts of social activity. But each falls well short of that totalizing impact which the inheritance of Enlightenment thought holds out as a goal. This is so because of the influence of four sets of factors.

One—factually very important but logically the least interesting, or at any rate the least difficult to handle analytically—is differential power. The

appropriation of knowledge does not happen in a homogeneous fashion, but is often differentially available to those in power positions, who are able to place it in the service of sectional interests.

A second influence concerns the role of values. Changes in value orders are not independent of innovations in cognitive orientation created by shifting perspectives on the social world. If new knowledge could be brought to bear upon a transcendental rational basis of values, this situation would not apply. But there is no such rational basis of values, and shifts in outlook deriving from inputs of knowledge have a mobile relation to changes in value orientations.

The third factor is the impact of unintended consequences. No amount of accumulated knowledge about social life could encompass all circumstances of its implementation, even if such knowledge were wholly distinct from the environment to which it applied. If our knowledge about the social world simply got better and better, the scope of unintended consequences might become more and more confined and unwanted consequences rare. However, the reflexivity of modern social life blocks off this possibility and is itself the fourth influence involved. Although least discussed in relation to the limits of Enlightenment reason, it is certainly as significant as any of the others. The point is not that there is no stable social world to know, but that knowledge of that world contributes to its unstable or mutable character.

The reflexivity of modernity, which is directly involved with the continual generating of systematic self-knowledge, does not stabilise the relation between expert knowledge and knowledge applied in lay actions. Knowledge claimed by expert observers (in some part, and in many varying ways) rejoins its subject matter, thus (in principle, but also normally in practice) altering it. There is no parallel to this process in the natural sciences; it is not at all the same as where, in the field of microphysics the intervention of an observer changes what is being studied.

NOTES

1. Anthony Giddens, *New Rules of Sociological Method* (London: Hutchinson, 1974).
2. Karl Popper, *Conjectures and Refutations* (London: Routledge, 1962), p. 34.
3. Anthony Giddens, *Constitution of Society* (Cambridge, Eng.: Polity, 1984), ch. 7.

69. REDISTRIBUTION

BRUNO LATOUR

Bruno Latour (b. 1947) is currently a professor at Sciences Po Paris, but for many years he was affiliated with the École Nationale Supérieure des Mines. He is one of the most influential figures associated with new approaches to the study of science. Beginning with *Laboratory Life* (1979, with Steve Woolgar), he has published extensively on science and technology, including *Science in Action* (1987), *The Pasteurization of France* (1988), and *Pandora´s Hope: Essays on the Reality of Science Studies* (1999). He operates from a social constructionist perspective that bears a resemblance to other theoretical approaches—especially ethnomethodology—but offers its own distinctive twists. Actor-network theory (or ANT) was developed by Latour and British colleague, John Law. A particularly intriguing aspect of ANT is the claim that nonhuman entities can be actants—a claim that raises questions about Latour´s understanding of intentionality. The article below, which is an excerpt from *We Have Never Been Modern* (1993), indicates that not all of Latour´s work has been devoted to the study of science per se even if it is deeply embedded in it. In this provocative essay, he argues for a reconsideration of the way the linkages between humans and nature are generally conceptualized, as well as the question of God. In so doing, Latour challenges not only the claims of modernity, but the presumed challenges of postmodernism. His alternative is a call for a "nonmodern constitution."

5.1 THE IMPOSSIBLE MODERNIZATION

I now tackle a most difficult question: the question of the nonmodern world that we are entering, I maintain, without ever having really left it.

Modernization, although it destroyed the near-totality of cultures and natures by force and bloodshed, had a clear objective. Modernizing finally made it possible to distinguish between the laws of external nature and the conventions of society. The conquerors undertook this partition everywhere, consigning hybrids either to the domain of objects or to that of society. The process of partitioning was accompanied by a coherent and continuous front of radical revolutions in science, technology, administration, economy and religion, a veritable bulldozer operation behind which the past disappeared for ever, but in front of which, at least, the future opened up. The past was a barbarian medley; the future, a civilizing distinction. To be sure,

the moderns have always recognized that they too had blended objects and societies, cosmologies and sociologies. But this was in the past, while they were still only premodern. By increasingly terrifying revolutions, they have been able to tear themselves away from that past. Since other cultures still mix the constraints of rationality with the needs of their societies, they have to be helped to emerge from that confusion by annihilating their past. Modernizers know perfectly well that even in their own midst islands of barbarianism remain, in which technological efficacy and social arbitrariness are excessively intertwined. But before long they will have achieved modernization, they will have liquidated those islands, and we shall all inhabit the same planet; we shall all be equally modern, all equally capable of profiting from what, alone, forever escapes the tyranny of social interest: economic rationality, scientific truth, technological efficiency.

Bruno Latour, *We Have Never Been Modern.* Cambridge, MA: Harvard University Press, 1993, pp. 130–145.

Certain modernizers continue to speak as if such a fate were possible and desirable. However, one has only to express it to see how self-contradictory this claim is. How could we bring about the purification of sciences and societies at last, when the modernizers themselves are responsible for the proliferation of hybrids thanks to the very Constitution that makes them proliferate by denying their existence? For a long time, this contradiction was hidden by the moderns' very increase. Permanent revolutions in the State, and sciences, and technologies, were supposed to end up absorbing, purifying and civilizing the hybrids by incorporating them either into society or into nature. But the double failure that was my starting point, that of socialism—at stage left—and that of naturalism—at stage right—has made the work of purification less plausible and the contradiction more visible. There are no more revolutions in store to impel a continued forward flight. There are so many hybrids that no one knows any longer how to lodge them in the old promised land of modernity. Hence the postmoderns' abrupt paralysis.

Modernization was ruthless toward the premoderns, but what can we say about postmodernization? Imperialist violence at least offered a future, but sudden weakness on the part of the conquerors is far worse for, always cut off from the past, it now also breaks with the future. Having been slapped in the face with modern reality, poor populations now have to submit to postmodern hyperreality. Nothing has value; everything is a reflection, a simulacrum, a floating sign; and that very weakness, they say, may save us from the invasion of technologies, sciences, reasons. Was it really worth destroying everything to end up adding this insult to that injury? The empty world in which the postmoderns evolve is one they themselves, and they alone, have emptied, because they have taken the moderns at their word. Postmodernism is a symptom of the contradiction of modernism, but it is unable to diagnose this contradiction because it shares the same upper half of the Constitution—the sciences and the technologies are extrahuman—but it no longer shares the cause of the Constitution's strength and greatness—the proliferation of quasi-objects and the multiplication of intermediaries between humans and nonhumans allowed by the absolute distinction between humans and nonhumans.

However, the diagnosis is not very difficult to make, now that we are obliged to consider the work of purification and the work of mediation symmetrically. Even at the worst moments of the Western imperium, it was never a matter of clearly separating the Laws of Nature from social conventions once and for all. It was always a matter of constructing collectives by mixing a certain type of nonhumans and a certain type of humans, and extracting in the process Boyle-style objects and Hobbes-style subjects (not to mention the crossed-out God) on an ever-increasing scale. The innovation of longer networks is an interesting peculiarity, but it is not sufficient to set us radically apart from others, or to cut us off for ever from our past. Modernizers are not obliged to continue their revolutionary task by gathering their forces, ignoring the postmoderns' predicament, gritting their teeth, and continuing to believe in the dual promises of naturalism and socialism no matter what, since that particular modernization has never got off the ground. It was never anything but the official representation of another much more profound and different work that had always been going on and continues today on an ever-increasing scale. Nor are we obliged to struggle against modernization—in the militant manner of the antimoderns or the disillusioned manner of the postmoderns—since we would then be attacking the upper half of the Constitution alone, which we would merely be reinforcing while remaining unaware of what has always been the source of its vitality.

But does this diagnosis allow any remedy for the impossible modernization? If, as I have been saying all along, the Constitution allows hybrids to proliferate because it refuses to conceptualize them as such, then it remains effective only so long as it denies their existence. Now, if the fruitful contradiction between the two parts—the official work of purification and the unofficial work of mediation—becomes clearly visible, won't the Constitution cease to be effective? Won't modernization become impossible? Are we going to become—or go back to being—premodern? Do we have to resign ourselves to becoming antimodern? For lack of any better option, are we going to have to continue to be modern, but without conviction, in the twilight zone of the postmods?

5.2 FINAL EXAMINATIONS

To answer these questions, we must first sort out the various positions I have outlined in the course of this essay, to bring the nonmodern to terms with the best those positions have to offer. What are we going to retain from the moderns? Everything, apart from exclusive confidence in the upper half of their Constitution, because this Constitution will need to be amended somewhat to include its lower half too. The moderns´ greatness stems from their proliferation of hybrids, their lengthening of a certain type of network, their acceleration of the production of traces, their multiplication of delegates, their groping production of relative universals. Their daring, their research, their innovativeness, their tinkering, their youthful excesses, the ever-increasing scale of their action, the creation of stabilized objects independent of society, the freedom of a society liberated from objects—all these are features we want to keep. On the other hand, we cannot retain the illusion (whether they deem it positive or negative) that moderns have about themselves and want to generalize to everyone: atheist, materialist, spiritualist, theist, rational, effective, objective, universal, critical, radically different from other communities, cut off from a past that is maintained in a state of artificial survival due only to historicism, separated from a nature on which subjects or society would arbitrarily impose categories, denouncers always at war with themselves, prisoners of an absolute dichotomy between things and signs, facts and values.

Westerners felt far removed from the premoderns because of the External Great Divide—a simple exportation, as I have noted, of the Internal Great Divide. When the latter is dissolved, the former disappears, to be replaced by differences in size. Symmetrical anthropology has redistributed the Great Divide. Now that we are no longer so far removed from the premoderns— since when we talk about the premoderns we have to include a large part of ourselves—we are going to have to sort them out as well. Let us keep what is best about them, above all: the premoderns´ inability to differentiate durably between the networks and the pure poles of Nature and Society, their obsessive interest in thinking about the production of hybrids of Nature and Society, of things and signs, their certainty that

transcendences abound, their capacity for conceiving of past and future in many ways other than progress and decadence, the multiplication of types of nonhumans different from those of the moderns. On the other hand, we shall not retain the set of limits they impose on the scaling collectives, localization by territory, the scapegoating process, ethnocentrism, and finally the lasting nondifferentiation of natures and societies.

But the sorting seems impossible and even contradictory in the face of what I have said above. Since the invention of longer networks and the increase in size of some collectives depends on the silence they maintain about quasi-objects, how can I promise to keep the changes of scale and give up the invisibility that allows them to spread? Worse still, how could I reject from the premoderns the lasting nondifferentiation of natures and societies, and reject from the moderns the absolute dichotomy between natures and societies? How can size, exploration, proliferation be maintained while the hybrids are made explicit? Yet this is precisely the amalgam I am looking for: *to retain the production of a nature and of a society that allow changes in size through the creation of an external truth and a subject of law, but without neglecting the co-production of sciences and societies*. The amalgam consists in using the premodern categories to conceptualize the hybrids, while retaining the moderns´ final outcome of the work of purification—that is, an external Nature distinct from subjects. I want to keep following the gradient that leads from unstable existences to stabilized essences—and vice versa. To accomplish the work of purification, but as a particular case of the work of mediation. To maintain all the advantages of the moderns´ dualism without its disadvantages—the clandestineness of the quasi-objects. To keep all the advantages of the premoderns´ monism without tolerating its limits—the restriction of size through the lasting confusion of knowledge and power.

The postmoderns have sensed the crisis of the moderns and attempted to overcome it; thus they too warrant examination and sorting. It is of course impossible to conserve their irony, their despair, their discouragement, their nihilism, their self-criticism, since all those fine qualities depend on a conception of modernism that modernism itself has never really practised. As soon, however, as we add the lower part of the

Constitution to the upper part, many of the intuitions of postmodernism are vindicated. For instance, we can save deconstruction—but since it no longer has a contrary, it turns into constructivism and no longer goes hand in hand with self-destruction. We can retain the deconstructionists´ refusal of naturalization—but since Nature itself is no longer natural, this refusal no longer distances us from the sciences but, on the contrary, brings us closer to sciences in action. We can keep the postmoderns´ pronounced taste for reflexivity—but since that property is shared among all the actors, it loses its parodic character and becomes positive. Finally, we can go along with the postmoderns in rejecting the idea of a coherent and homogeneous time that would advance by goose steps—but without retaining their taste for quotation and anachronism which maintains the belief in a truly surpassed past. Take away from the postmoderns their illusions about the moderns, and their vices become virtues—nonmodern virtues!

Regrettably, in the antimoderns I see nothing worth saving. Always on the defensive, they consistently believed what the moderns said about themselves and proceeded to affix the opposite sign to each declaration.

Antirevolutionary, they held the same peculiar views as the moderns about time past and tradition. The values they defended were never anything but the residue left by their enemies; they never understood that the moderns´ greatness stemmed, in practice, from the very reverse of what the antimoderns attacked them for. Even in their rearguard combats, the antimoderns never managed to innovate, occupying the minor role that was reserved for them. It cannot even be said in their favour that they put the brakes on the moderns´ frenzy—those moderns for whom the antimoderns were always, in effect, the best of stooges.

The balance sheet of this examination is not too unfavourable. We can keep the Enlightenment without modernity, provided that we reintegrate the objects of the sciences and technologies into the Constitution, as quasi-objects among many others—objects whose genesis must no longer be clandestine, but must be followed through and through, from the hot events that spawned the objects to the progressive cool-down that transforms them into essences of Nature or Society.

Is it possible to draw up a Constitution that would allow us to recognize this work officially? We must do

	What is retained	What is rejected
From the moderns	–long networks –size –experimentation –relative universals –final separation between objective nature and free society	–separation between nature and society –clandestineness of the practices of mediation –external Great Divide –critical denunciation –universality, rationality
From the premoderns	–non-separability of things and signs –transcendence without a contrary –multiplication of nonhumans –temporality by intensity	–obligation always to link the social and natural orders –scapegoating mechanism • ethnocentrism • territory –limits on scale
From the post moderns	–multiple times –constructivism –reflexivity –denaturalization	–belief in modernism –critical deconstruction –ironic reflexivity –anachronism

FIGURE 69.1 What is retained and what is rejected

this, since old-style modernization can no longer absorb either other peoples or Nature; such, at least, is the conviction on which this essay is based. For its own good, the modern world can no longer extend itself without becoming once again what it has never ceased to be in practice—that is, a nonmodern world like all the others. This fraternity is essential if we are to absorb the two sets of entities that revolutionary modernization left behind: the natural crowds that we are longer master, the human multitudes that no one dominates any longer. Modern temporality gave the impression of continuous acceleration by relegating ever-larger masses of humans and nonhumans together to the void of the past. Irreversibility has changed sides. If there is one thing we can no longer get rid of, it is those natures and multitudes, both equally global. The political task starts up again, at a new cost. It has been necessary to modify the fabric of our collectives from top to bottom in order to absorb the citizen of the eighteenth century and the worker of the nineteenth. We shall have to transform ourselves just as throughly in order to make room, today, for the nonhumans created by science and technology.

5.3 HUMANISM REDISTRIBUTED

Before we can amend the Constitution, we first have to relocate the human, to which humanism does not render sufficient justice. Here are some of the magnificent figures that the moderns have been able to depict and preserve: the free agent, the citizen builder of the Leviathan, the distressing visage of the human person, the other of a relationship, consciousness, the *cogito*, the hermeneut, the inner self, the thee and thou of dialogue, presence to oneself, intersubjectivity. But all these figures remain asymmetrical, for they are the counterpart of the object of the sciences—an object that remains orphaned, abandoned in the hands of those whom epistemologists, like sociologists, deem reductive, objective, rational. Where are the Mouniers of machines, the Lévinases of animals, the Ricoeurs of facts? Yet the human, as we now understand, cannot be grasped and saved unless that other part of itself, the share of things, is restored to it. So long as humanism is constructed through contrast with the object that has been abandoned to epistemology, neither the human nor the nonhuman can be understood.

Where are we to situate the human? A historical succession of quasi-objects, quasi-subjects, it is impossible to define the human by an essence, as we have known for a long time. Its history and its anthropology are too diverse for it to be pinned down once and for all. But Sartre's clever move, defining it as a free existence uprooting itself from a nature devoid of significance, is obviously not one we can make, since we have invested all quasi-objects with action, will, meaning, and even speech. There is no longer a practico-inert where the pure liberty of human existence can get bogged down. To oppose it to the crossed-out God (or, conversely, to reconcile it with Him) is equally impossible, since it is by virtue of their common opposition to Nature that the modern Constitution has defined all three. Must the human be steeped in Nature, then? But if we were to go looking for specific results of specific scientific disciplines that would clothe this robot animated with neurons, impulses, selfish genes, elementary needs and economic calculations, we would never get beyond monsters and masks. The sciences multiply new definitions of humans without managing to displace the former ones, reduce them to any homogeneous one, or unify them. They add reality; they do not subtract it. The hybrids that they invent in the laboratory are still more exotic than those they claim to break down.

Must we solemnly announce the death of man and dissolve him in the play of language, an evanescent reflection of inhuman structures that would escape all understanding? No, since we are no more in Discourse than we are in Nature. In any event, nothing is sufficiently inhuman to dissolve human beings in it and announce their death. Their will, their actions, their words are too abundant. Will we have to avoid the question by making the human something transcendental that would distance us for ever from mere nature? This would amount to falling back on just one of the poles of the modern Constitution. Will we have to use force to extend some provisional and particular definition inscribed in the rights of man or the preambles of constitutions? This would amount to tracing out once again the two Great Divides, and believing in modernization.

If the human does not possess a stable form, it is not formless for all that. If, instead of attaching it to one constitutional pole or the other, we move it closer to the middle, it becomes the mediator and even the intersection of the two. The human is not a constitutional pole to be opposed to that of the nonhuman. The two expressions "humans" and "nonhumans" are belated results that no longer suffice to designate the other dimension. The scale of value consists not in shifting the definition of the human along the horizontal line that connects the Object pole to the Subject pole, but in sliding it along the vertical dimension that defines the nonmodern world. Reveal its work of mediation, and it will take on human form. Conceal it again, and we shall have to talk about inhumanity, even if it is draping itself in the Bill of Rights. The expression "anthropomorphic" considerably underestimates our humanity. We should be talking about morphism. Morphism is the place where technomorphisms, zoomorphisms, phusimorphisms, ideomorphisms, theomorphisms, sociomorphisms, psychomorphisms, all come together. Their alliances and their exchanges, taken together, are what define the *anthropos*. A weaver of morphisms—isn´t that enough of a definition? The closer the *anthropos* comes to this distribution, the more human it is. The farther away it moves, the more it takes on multiple forms in which its humanity quickly becomes indiscernible, even if its figures are those of the person, the individual or the self. By seeking to isolate its form from those it churns together, one does not defend humanism, one loses it.

How could the *anthropos* be threatened by machines? It has made them, it has put itself into them, it has divided up its own members among their members, it has built its own body with them. How could it be threatened by objects? They have all been quasi-subjects circulating within the collective they traced. It is made of them as much as they are made of it. It has defined itself by multiplying things. How could it be deceived by politics? Politics is its own making, in that it reconstructs the collective through continual controversies over representation that allow it to say, at every moment, what it is and what it wants. How could it be dimmed by religion? It is through religion that humans are linked to all their fellows, that they know themselves as persons. How could it be manipulated by the economy? Its provisional form cannot be assigned without the circulation of goods and obligations, without the continuous distribution of social goods that we concoct through the goodwill of things. *Ecco homo:* delegated, mediated, distributed, mandated, uttered. Where does the threat come from? From those who seek to reduce it to an essence and who—by scorning things, objects, machines and the social, by cutting off all delegations and senders—make humanism a fragile and precious thing at risk of being overwhelmed by Nature, Society, or God.

Modern humanists are reductionist because they seek to attribute action to a small number of powers, leaving the rest of the world with nothing but simple mute forces. It is true that by redistributing the action among all these mediators, we lose the reduced form of humanity, but we gain another form, which has to be called irreducible. The human is in the delegation itself, in the pass, in the sending, in the continuous exchange of forms. Of course it is not a thing, but things are not things either. Of course it is not a merchandise, but merchandise is not merchandise either. Of course it is not a machine, but anyone who has seen machines knows that they are scarcely mechanical. Of course it is not of this world, but this world is not of this world either. Of course it is not in God, but what relation is there between the God above and the God below? Humanism can maintain itself only by sharing itself with all these mandatees. Human nature is the set of its delegates and its representatives, its figures and its messengers. That symmetrical universal is worth at least as much as the moderns´ doubly asymmetrical one. This new position, shifted in relation to the subject/society position, now needs to be underwritten by an amended Constitution.

5.4 THE NONMODERN CONSTITUTION

In the course of this essay, I have simply reestablished symmetry between the two branches of government, that of things—called science and technology—and that of human beings. I have also shown why the separation of powers between the two branches, after allowing for the proliferation of hybrids, could no longer worthily-represent this new third estate. A constitution is judged by the guarantees it offers. The moderns´ Constitution included four guarantees that had meaning only when they were taken together but also kept strictly separate. The first one guaranteed Nature its transcendent dimension by making it distinct from the fabric of Society—thus contrary to the continuous connection between the natural order and the social order found among the premoderns. The second guaranteed Society its immanent dimension by rendering citizens totally free to reconstruct it artificially—as opposed to the continuous connection between the social order and the natural order that kept the premoderns from being able to modify the one without modifying the other. But as that double separation allowed in practice for the mobilization and construction of Nature (Nature having become immanent through mobilization and construction)—and, conversely, made it possible to make Society stable and durable (Society having become transcendent owing to the enrolment of ever more numerous nonhumans), a third guarantee assured the separation of powers, the two branches of government being kept in separate, watertight compartments: even though it is mobilizable and constructed, Nature will remain without relation to Society; Society, in turn, even though it is transcendent and rendered durable by the mediation of objects, will no longer have any relation to Nature. In other words, quasi-objects will be officially banished—should we say taboo?—and translation networks will go into hiding, offering to the work of purification a counterpart that will nevertheless continue to be followed and monitored—until the postmoderns obliterate it entirely. The fourth guarantee of the crossed-out God made it possible to stabilize this dualist and asymmetrical mechanism by ensuring a function of arbitration, but one without presence or power.

In order to sketch in the nonmodern Constitution, it suffices to take into account what the modern Constitution left out, and to sort out the guarantees we wish to keep. We have committed ourselves to providing representation for quasi-objects. It is the third guarantee of the modern Constitution that must therefore be suppressed, since that is the one that made the continuity of their analysis impossible. Nature and Society are not two distinct poles, but one and the same production of successive states of societies-natures, of collectives. The first guanrantee of our new draft thus becomes the nonseparability of quasi-objects, quasi-subjects. Every concept, every institution, every practice

that interferes with the continuous deployment of collectives and their experimentation with hybrids will be deemed dangerous, harmful, and—we may as well say it—immoral. The work of mediation becomes the very centre of the double power, natural and social. The networks come out of hiding. The Middle Kingdom is represented. The third estate, which was nothing, becomes everything.

As I have suggested, however, we do not wish to become premoderns all over again. The nonseparability of natures and societies had the disadvantage of making experimentation on a large scale impossible, since every transformation of nature had to be in harmony with a social transformation, term for term, and vice versa. Now we seek to keep the moderns´ major innovation: the separability of a nature that no one has constructed—transcendence—and the freedom of manoeuvre of a society that is of our own making—immanence. Nevertheless, we do not seek to inherit the clandestineness of the inverse mechanism that makes it possible to construct Nature—immanence—and to stabilize Society durably—transcendence.

Can we retain the first two guarantees of the old Constitution without maintaining the now-visible duplicity of its third guarantee? Yes, although at first this looks like squaring the circle. Nature´s transcendence, its objectivity, and Society´s immanence, its subjectivity, stem from the work of mediation without depending on their separation, contrary to what the Constitution of the moderns claims. The work of producing a nature or producing a society stems from the durable and irreversible accomplishment of the common work of delegation and translation. At the end of the process, there is indeed a nature that we have not made, and a society that we are free to change; there are indeed indisputable scientific facts, and free citizens, but once they are viewed in a nonmodern light they become the double consequence of a practice that is now visible in its continuity, instead of being, as for the moderns, the remote and opposing causes of an invisible practice that contradicts them. The second guarantee of our new draft thus makes it possible to recover the first two guarantees of the modern Constitution but without separating them. All concepts, all institutions, all practices that interfere with the progressive objectivization of Nature—incorporation into a black box—and simultaneously the subjectivization of

Society—freedom of manoeuvre—will be deemed harmful, dangerous and, quite simply, immoral. Without this second guarantee, the networks liberated by the first would keep their wild and uncontrollable character. The moderns were not mistaken in seeking objective nonhumans and free societies. They were mistaken only in their certainly that that double production required an absolute distinction between the two terms and the continual repression of the work of mediation.

Historicity found no place in the modern Constitution because it was framed by the only three entities whose existence it recognized. Contingent history existed for humans alone, and revolution became the only way for the moderns to understand their past—by breaking totally with it. But time is not a smooth, homogeneous flow. If time depends on associations, associations do not depend on time. We are no longer going to be confronted with the argument of time that passes for ever based on a regrouping into a coherent set of elements that belong to all times and all ontologies. If we want to recover the capacity to sort that appears essential to our morality and defines the human, it is essential that no coherent temporal flow comes to limit our freedom of choice. The third guarantee, as important as the others, is that we can combine associations freely without ever confronting the choice between archaism and modernization, the local and the global, the cultural and the universal, the natural and the social. Freedom has moved away from the social pole it had occupied exclusively during the modern representation into the middle and lower zones, and becomes a capacity for sorting and recombining sociotechnological imbroglios. Every new call to revolution, any epistemological break, any Copernican upheaval, any claim that certain practices have become outdated for ever, will be deemed dangerous, or—what is still worse in the eyes of the moderns—outdated!

But if I am right in my interpretation of the modern Constitution, if it has really allowed the development of collectives while officially forbidding what it permits in practice, how could we continue to develop quasi-objects, now that we have made their practice visible and official? By offering guarantees to replace the

Modern Constitution	Nonmodern Constitution
1st guarantee: Nature is transcendent but mobilizable (immanent).	*1st guarantee*: nonseparability of the common production of societies and natures.
2nd guarantee: Society is immanent but it infinitely surpasses us (transcendent)	*2nd guarantee*: continuous following of the production of Nature, which is objective, and the production of Society, which is free. In the last analysis, there is indeed a transcendence of Nature and an immanence of Society, but the two are not separated.
3rd guarantee: Nature and Society are totally distinct, and the work of purification bears no relation to the work of mediation.	*3rd guarantee*: freedom is redefined as a capacity to sort the combinations of hybrids that no longer depend on a homogeneous temporal flow.
4th guarantee: the crossed-out God is totally absent but ensures arbitration between the two branches of government.	*4th guarantee*: the production of hybrids, by becoming explicit and collective, becomes the object of an enlarged democracy that regulates or slows down its cadence.

FIGURE 69.2 Modern/nonmodern constitutions

previous ones, are we not making impossible this double language, and thus the growth of collectives? That is precisely what we want to do. This slowing down, this moderation, this regulation, is what we expect from our morality. The fourth guarantee—perhaps the most important—is to replace the clandestine proliferation of hybrids by their regulated and commonly-agreed-upon production. It is time, perhaps, to speak of democracy again, but of a democracy extended to things themselves. We are not going to be caught by Archimedes´ coup again.

Do we need to add that the crossed-out God, in this new Constitution, turns out to be liberated from the unworthy position to which He had been relegated? The question of God is reopened, and the nonmoderns no longer have to try to generalize the improbable metaphysics of the moderns that forced them to believe in belief.

5.5 THE PARLIAMENT OF THINGS

We want the meticulous sorting of quasi-objects to become possible—no longer unofficially and under the table, but officially and in broad daylight. In this desire to bring to light, to incorporate into language, to make public, we continue to identify with the intuition of the Enlightenment. But this intuition has never had the anthropology it deserved. It has divided up the human and the nonhuman and believed that the others, rendered premoderns by contrast, were not supposed to do the same thing. While it was necessary, perhaps, to increase mobilization and lengthen some networks, this division has now become superfluous, immoral, and—to put it bluntly—anti-Constitutional! We have been modern. Very well. We can no longer be modern in the same way. When we amend the Constitution, we continue to believe in the sciences, but instead of taking in their objectivity, their truth, their coldness, their extraterritoriality—qualities they have never had, except after the arbitrary withdrawal of epistemology—we retain what has always been most interesting about them: their daring, their experimentation, their uncertainty, their warmth, their incongruous blend of hybrids, their crazy ability to reconstitute the social bond. We take away from them only the mystery of their birth and the danger their clandestineness posed to democracy.

Yes, we are indeed the heirs of the Enlightenment, whose asymmetrical rationality is just not broad enough for us. Boyle´s descendants had defined a parliament of mutes, the laboratory, where scientists, mere intermediaries, spoke all by themselves in the name of things. What did these representatives say? Nothing but what the things would have said on their own, had they only been able to speak. Outside the laboratory, Hobbes´s descendants had defined the Republic in which naked citizens, unable to speak all at once, arranged to have themselves represented by one of their number, the Sovereign, a simple intermediary and spokesperson. What did this representative say? Nothing but what the citizens would have said had they all been able to speak at the same time. But a doubt about the quality of that double translation crept in straight away. What if the scientists were talking about themselves instead of about things? And if the Sovereign were pursuing his own interests instead of reciting the script written for him by his constituents? In the first case, we would lose Nature and fall back into human disputes; in the second, we would fall back into the State of Nature and into the war of every man against every man. By defining a total separation between the scientific and political representations, the double translation-betrayal became possible. We shall never know whether scientists translate or betray. We shall never know whether representatives betray or translate.

During the modern period, the critics will continue to sustain themselves on that double doubt and the impossibility of ever putting an end to it. Modernism consisted in choosing that arrangement, nevertheless, but in remaining constantly suspicious of its two types of representatives without combining them into a single problem. Epistemologists wondered about scientific realism and the faithfulness of science to things; political scientists wondered about the representative system and the relative faithfulness of elected officials and spokespersons. All had in common a hatred of intermediaries and a desire for an immediate world, emptied of its mediators. All thought that this was the price of faithful representation, without ever understanding that the solution to their problem lay in the other branch of government.

In the course of this essay, I have shown what happened once science studies re-examined such a division of labour. I have shown how fast the modern Constitution broke down, since it no longer permitted the construction of a common dwelling to shelter the societies-natures that the moderns have bequeathed us. There are not two problems of representation, just one. There are not two branches, only one, whose products can be distinguished only late in the game, and after being examined together. Scientists appear to be betraying external reality only because they are constructing their societies and their natures at the same time. The Sovereign appears to be betraying his constituents only because he is churning together both citizens and the enormous mass of nonhumans that allow the Leviathan to hold up. Suspicion about scientific representation stemmed only from the belief that without social pollution Nature would be immediately accessible. "Eliminate the social and you will finally have a faithful representation," said some. "Eliminate objects and you will finally have a faithful representation," declared others. Their whole debate arose from the division of powers enforced by the modern Constitution.

Let us again take up the two representations and the double doubt about the faithfulness of the representatives, and we shall have defined the Parliament of Things. In its confines, the continuity of the collective is reconfigured. There are no more naked truths, but there are no more naked citizens, either. The mediators have the whole space to themselves. The Enlightenment has a dwelling-place at last. Natures are present, but with their representatives, scientists who speak in their name. Societies are present, but with the objects that have been serving as their ballast from time immemorial. Let one of the representatives talk, for instance, about the ozone hole, another represent the Monsanto chemical industry, a third the workers of the same chemical industry, another the voters of New Hampshire, a fifth the meteorology of the polar regions; let still another speak in the name of the State; what does it matter, so long as they are all talking about the same thing, about a quasi-object they have all created, the object-discourse-nature-society whose new properties astound us all and whose network extends from my refrigerator to the Antarctic by way of chemistry, law, the State, the economy, and satellites. The imbroglios and networks that had no place now have the whole place to themselves. They are the ones that have to be represented; it is around them that the Parliament of Things gathers henceforth. "It was the stone rejected by the builders that became the keystone" (Mark 12:10).

However, we do not have to create this Parliament out of whole cloth, by calling for yet another revolution. We simply have to ratify what we have always done, provided that we reconsider our past, provided that we understand retrospectively to what extent we have never been modern, and provided that we rejoin the two halves of the symbol broken by Hobbes and Boyle as a sign of recognition. Half of our politics is constructed in science and technology. The other half of Nature is constructed in societies. Let us patch the two back together, and the political task can begin again.

Is it asking too little simply to ratify in public what is already happening? Should we not strive for more glamorous and more revolutionary programmes of action, rather than underlining what is already dimly discernible in the shared practices of scientists, politicians, consumers, industrialists and citizens when they engage in the numerous sociotechnological controversies we read about daily in our newspapers? As we have been discovering throughout this essay, the official representation is effective; that representation is what allowed, under the old Constitution, the exploration and proliferation of hybrids. Modernism was not an illusion, but an active performing. If we could draft a new Constitution, we would, similarly, profoundly alter the course of quasi-objects. Another Constitution will be just as effective, but it will produce different hybrids. Is that too much to expect of a change in representation that seems to depend only on the scrap of paper of a Constitution? It may well be; but there are times when new words are needed to convene a new assembly. The task of our predecessors was no less daunting when they invented rights to give to citizens or the integration of workers into the fabric of our societies. I have done my job as philospher and constituent by gathering together the scattered themes of a comparative anthropology. Others will be able to convene the Parliament of Things.

We scarcely have much choice. If we do not change the common dwelling, we shall not absorb in it the other cultures that we can no longer dominate, and we shall be forever incapable of accommodating in it the environment that we can no longer control. Neither Nature nor the Others will become modern. It is up to us to change our ways of changing. Or else it will have been for naught that the Berlin Wall fell during the miraculous year 1989, offering us a unique practical lesson about the conjoined failure of socialism and naturalism.

70. THE POLITICIZATION OF LIFE

GIORGIO AGAMBEN

Italian philosopher Giorgio Agamben (b. 1942) has become an increasingly influential thinker for contemporary social theorists of contemporary politics. Rooted in the classics of philosophy—particularly Aristotle—his thinking has also been shaped by such twentieth-century figures as Martin Heidegger, Walter Benjamin (see selection 61 herein), Carl Schmitt, and, as the beginning of this selection indicates, Michel Foucault (see selection 73). This excerpt derives from what is Agamben's most widely referenced work, *Homo Sacer: Sovereign Power and Bare Life*, which first appeared in Italian in 1995. The term *homo sacer* refers to a person in Roman law who, due to particular offenses, was set apart from the law. This is a person consigned to what he calls "bare life," which in contrast to the political being characteristic of the citizen is indicative of being reduced to the body which is subject to various technologies of power. In this regard, Agamben builds on Foucault's idea of biopolitics, arguing that if bare life was the exception in ancient Rome, it has become normative in modern politics.

1.1 In the last years of his life, while he was working on the history of sexuality and unmasking the deployments of power at work within it, Michel Foucault began to direct his inquiries with increasing insistence toward the study of what he defined as *biopolitics*, that is, the growing inclusion of man's natural life in the mechanisms and calculations of power. At the end of the first volume of *The History of Sexuality*, Foucault, as we have seen, summarizes the process by which life, at the beginning of the modern age, comes to be what is at stake in politics: "For millennia, man remained what he was for Aristotle: a living animal with the additional capacity for political existence; modern man is an animal whose politics calls his existence as a living being into question." Until the very end, however, Foucault continued to investigate the "processes of subjectivization" that, in the passage from the ancient to the modern world, bring the individual to objectify his own self, constituting himself as a subject and, at the same time, binding himself to a power of external control. Despite what one might have legitimately expected, Foucault never brought his insights to bear on what could well have appeared to be the exemplary place of modern biopolitics: the politics of the great totalitarian states of the twentieth century. The inquiry that began with a reconstruction of the *grand enfermement* in hospitals and prisons did not end with an analysis of the concentration camp.

If, on the other hand, the pertinent studies that Hannah Arendt dedicated to the structure of totalitarian states in the postwar period have a limit, it is precisely the absence of any biopolitical perspective. Arendt very clearly discerns the link between totalitarian rule and the particular condition of life that is the camp: "The supreme goal of all totalitarian states," she writes, in a plan for research on the concentration camps, which, unfortunately, was not carried through, "is not only the freely admitted, long-ranging ambition to global rule, but also the never admitted and immediately realized attempt at total domination. The concentration camps are the laboratories in the experiment of total domination, for human nature being what it is, this goal can be achieved only under the extreme circumstances of human made hell" (*Essays*, p. 240). Yet what escapes Arendt is that the process is in a certain sense the inverse of what she takes it to be, and that precisely the radical transformation of politics into the realm of bare life (that is, into a camp) legitimated and necessitated total domination. Only because politics in our age had been entirely transformed into biopolitics was it possible for politics to be constituted as totalitarian politics to a degree hitherto unknown.

The fact that the two thinkers who may well have reflected most deeply on the political problem of our age were unable to link together their own insights is certainly an index of the difficulty of this problem. The concept of "bare life" or "sacred life" is the focal lens through which we shall try to make their points of view converge. In the notion of bare life the interlacing of politics and life has become so tight that it cannot easily be analyzed. Until we become aware of the political nature of bare life and its modern avatars (biological life, sexuality, etc.), we will not succeed in clarifying the opacity at their center. Conversely, once modern politics enters into an intimate symbiosis with bare life, it loses the intelligibility that still seems to us to characterize the juridico-political foundation of classical politics.

* * *

1.2. Karl Löwith was the first to define the fundamental character of totalitarian states as a "politicization of life" and, at the same time, to note the curious contiguity between democracy and totalitarianism:

> Since the emancipation of the third estate, the formation of bourgeois democracy and its transformation into mass industrial democracy, the neutralization of politically relevant differences and postponement of a decision about them has developed to the point of turning into its opposite: a total politicization [*totale Politisierung*] of everything, even of seemingly neutral domains of life. Thus in Marxist Russia there emerged a worker-state that was "more intensively state-oriented than any

absolute monarchy"; in fascist Italy, a corporate state normatively regulating not only national work, but also "after-work" [*Dopolavoro*] and all spiritual life; and, in National Socialist Germany, a wholly integrated state, which, by means of racial laws and so forth, politicizes even the life that had until then been private. (*Der okkasionelle Dezionismus*, p. 33)

The contiguity between mass democracy and totalitarian states, nevertheless, does not have the form of a sudden transformation (as Löwith, here following in Schmitt's footsteps, seems to maintain); before impetuously coming to light in our century, the river of biopolitics that gave *homo sacer* his life runs its course in a hidden but continuous fashion. It is almost as if, starting from a certain point, every decisive political event were double-sided: the spaces, the liberties, and the rights won by individuals in their conflicts with central powers always simultaneously prepared a tacit but increasing inscription of individuals' lives within the state order, thus offering a new and more dreadful foundation for the very sovereign power from which they wanted to liberate themselves. "The 'right' to life," writes Foucault, explaining the importance assumed by sex as a political issue, "to one's body, to health, to happiness, to the satisfaction of needs and, beyond all the oppressions or 'alienation,' the 'right' to rediscover what one is and all that one can be, this 'right'—which the classical juridical system was utterly incapable of comprehending—was the political response to all these new procedures of power" (*La volonté*, p. 191). The fact is that one and the same affirmation of bare life leads, in bourgeois democracy, to a primacy of the private over the public and of individual liberties over collective obligations and yet becomes, in totalitarian states, the decisive political criterion and the exemplary realm of sovereign decisions. And only because biological life and its needs had become the *politically* decisive fact is it possible to understand the otherwise incomprehensible rapidity with which twentieth-century parliamentary democracies were able to turn into totalitarian states and with which this century's totalitarian states were able to be converted, almost without interruption, into parliamentary democracies. In both cases, these transformations were produced in a context in which for quite some time politics had already turned into biopolitics, and in which the only real question to be decided was which form of organization would be best suited to the task of assuring the care, control, and use of bare life. Once their fundamental referent becomes bare life, traditional political distinctions (such as those between Right and Left, liberalism and totalitarianism, private and public) lose their clarity and intelligibility and enter into a zone of indistinction. The ex-communist ruling classes' unexpected fall into the most extreme racism (as in the Serbian program of "ethnic cleansing") and the rebirth of new forms of fascism in Europe also have their roots here.

Along with the emergence of biopolitics, we can observe a displacement and gradual expansion beyond the limits of the decision on bare life, in the state of exception, in which sovereignty consisted. If there is a line in every modern state marking the point at which the decision on life becomes a decision on death, and biopolitics can turn into thanatopolitics, this line no longer appears today as a stable border dividing two clearly distinct zones. This line is now in motion and gradually moving into areas other than that of political life, areas in which the sovereign is entering into an ever more intimate symbiosis not only with the jurist but also with the doctor, the scientist, the expert, and the priest. In the pages that follow, we shall try to show that certain events that are fundamental for the political history of modernity (such as the declaration of rights), as well as others that seem instead to represent an incomprehensible intrusion of biologico-scientific principles into the political order (such as National Socialist eugenics and its elimination of "life that is unworthy of being lived," or the contemporary debate on the normative determination of death criteria), acquire their true sense only if they are brought back to the common biopolitical (or thanatopolitical) context to which they belong. From this perspective, the camp—as the pure, absolute, and impassable biopolitical space (insofar as it is founded solely on the state of exception)—will appear as the hidden paradigm of the political space of modernity, whose metamorphoses and disguises we will have to learn to recognize.

* * *

1.3. The first recording of bare life as the new political subject is already implicit in the document that is generally placed at the foundation of modern democracy: the 1679 writ of *habeas corpus*. Whatever the origin of this formula, used as early as the eighteenth century to assure the physical presence of a person before a court of justice, it is significant that at its center is neither the old subject of feudal relations and liberties nor the future *citoyen*, but rather a pure and simple *corpus*. When John the Landless conceded Magna Carta to his subjects in 1215, he turned his attention to the "archbishops, bishops, abbots, counts, barons, viscounts, provosts, officials and bailiffs," to the "cities, towns, villages," and, more generally, to the "free men of our kingdom," so that they might enjoy "their ancient liberties and free customs" as well as the ones he now specifically recognized. Article 29, whose task was to guarantee the physical freedom of the subjects, reads: "No free man [*homo liber*] may be arrested, imprisoned, dispossessed of his goods, or placed outside the law [*utlagetur*] or molested in any way; we will not place our hands on him nor will have others place their hands on him [*nec super eum ibimis, nec super eum mittimusi*], except after a legal judgment by his peers according to the law of the realm." Analogously, an ancient writ that preceded the *habeas corpus* and was understood to assure the presence of the accused in a trial bears the title *de homine replegiando* (or *repigliando*).

Consider instead the formula of the writ that the act of 1679 generalizes and makes into law: *Praecipimus tibi quod Corpus X, in custodia vestra detentum, ut dicitur, una cum causa captionis et detentionis, quodcumque nomine idem X censeatur in eadem, habeas coram nobis, apud Westminster, ad subjiciendum*, "We command that you have before us to show, at Westminster, that body X, by whatsoever name he may be called therein, which is held in your custody, as it is said, as well as the cause of the arrest and the detention." Nothing allows one to measure the difference between ancient and medieval freedom and the freedom at the basis of modern democracy better than this formula. It is not the free man and his statutes and prerogatives, nor even simply *homo*, but rather *corpus* that is the new subject of politics. And democracy is born precisely as the assertion and presentation of this "body": *habeas corpus ad sub-jiciendum*, "you will have to have a body to show."

The fact that, of all the various jurisdictional regulations concerned with the protection of individual freedom, it was *habeas corpus* that assumed the form of law and thus became inseparable from the history of Western democracy is surely due to mere circumstance. It is just as certain, however, that nascent European democracy thereby placed at the center of its battle against absolutism not *bios*, the qualified life of the citizen, but *zoē*—the bare, anonymous life that is as such taken into the sovereign ban ("the body of being taken...," as one still reads in one modern formulation of the writ, "by whatsoever name he may be called therein").

What comes to light in order to be exposed *apud Westminster* is, once again, the body of *homo sacer*, which is to say, bare life. This is modern democracy's strength and, at the same time, its inner contradiction: modern democracy does not abolish sacred life but rather shatters it and disseminates it into every individual body, making it into what is at stake in political conflict. And the root of modern democracy's secret biopolitical calling lies here: he who will appear later as the bearer of rights and, according to a curious oxymoron, as the new sovereign subject (*subiectus super-aneus*, in other words, what is below and, at the same time, most elevated) can only be constituted as such through the repetition of the sovereign exception and the isolation of *corpus*, bare life, in himself. If it is true that law needs a body in order to be in force, and if one can speak, in this sense, of "law's desire to have a body," democracy responds to this desire by compelling law to assume the care of this body. This ambiguous (or polar) character of democracy appears even more clearly in the *habeas corpus* if one considers the fact that the same legal procedure that was originally intended to assure the presence of the accused at the trial and, therefore, to keep the accused from avoiding judgment, turns—in its new and definitive form—into grounds for the sheriff to detain and exhibit the body of the accused. *Corpus is a two-faced being, the bearer both of subjection to sovereign power and of individual liberties.*

This new centrality of the "body" in the sphere of politico-juridical terminology thus coincides with the more general process by which *corpus* is given such a privileged position in the philosophy and science of the Baroque age, from Descartes to Newton, from Leibniz to Spinoza. And yet in political reflection *corpus* always maintains a close tie to bare life, even when it becomes the central metaphor of the political community, as in *Leviathan* or *The Social Contract*. Hobbes's use of the term is particularly instructive in this regard. If it is true that in *De homine* he distinguishes man's natural body from his political body (*homo enim non modo corpus naturale est, sed etiam civitatis, id est, ut ita loquar, corporis politici pars,* "Man is not only a natural body, but also a body of the city, that is, of the so-called political part" [*De homine*, p. 1]), in the *De cive* it is precisely the body's capacity to be killed that founds both the natural equality of men and the necessity of the "Commonwealth":

> If we look at adult men and consider the fragility of the unity of the human body (whose ruin marks the end of every strength, vigor, and force) and the ease with which the weakest man can kill the strongest man, there is no reason for someone to trust in his strength and think himself superior to others by nature. Those who can do the same things to each other are equals. And those who can do the supreme thing—that is, kill—are by nature equal among themselves. (*De cive*, p. 93)

The great metaphor of the Leviathan, whose body is formed out of all the bodies of individuals, must be read in this light. The absolute capacity of the subjects' bodies to be killed forms the new political body of the West.

SECTION XIV

1. How does Elias assess the role that feelings of shame and repugnance have played in the development of notions of self-restraint? In what ways has this contributed to what he describes as the "civilizing process"?

2. What does Debord mean by "pseudo-cyclical time"? Why does he think that this is an apt characterization of contemporary societies? How is this concept related to the other concept he discusses in his aphorisms, the idea of the spectacle?

3. What, according to Giddens, is reflexivity and why is it a characteristic feature of modernity?

4. According to Giddens, modernity is "deeply and intrinsically sociological." What does he mean by this claim and why does he think this is the case?

5. Latour's provocative thesis is that we have never been modern and are not postmodern. On what grounds does he make this case and what does he offer as a more appropriate depiction of our present condition? Do you find him convincing? Why or why not?

6. What does Agamben mean by "bare life"? How is the concept relevant to campaigns of genocide? How is it relevant to the ways western nations have conducted their "war on terrorism"?

XV. STRUCTURALISM, POSTSTRUCTURALISM, AND POSTMODERNITY

71. THE CORRESPONDENCE BETWEEN GOODS PRODUCTION AND TASTE PRODUCTION

PIERRE BOURDIEU

Pierre Bourdieu (1930–2002) was the chair of sociology at the prestigious Collége de France, and from this position he commanded authority as one of the premier social theorists in the world. He was born in a rural area of the Pyrenees into a family of modest circumstances. This profoundly shaped his political worldview and in particular his understanding of class relations. Influenced by both Marxism and structuralism, his work built on these traditions while simultaneously serving as a corrective to what he saw as a tendency in both paradigms to exhibit a lack of theoretical regard for the role of real-life actors. In developing over the course of his career an alternative theoretical framework, he introduced a number of concepts that have in different ways and to different extents been embraced by many contemporary theorists: habitus; field; social, cultural, and symbolic capital; and reflexivity. His most highly acclaimed work is *Distinction: A Social Critique of the Judgement of Taste* (1984). He shared with Veblen (see essay 25 herein) a conviction that taste is a decidedly social rather than individual faculty, one shaped in particular by specific class locations. Bourdieu goes further by revealing that taste shapes group lifestyles, but it doesn't do so in a vacuum. Rather it occurs in opposition to the tastes of others. This selection from the book attempts to establish the linkages between the creation of cultural objects and the production of taste.

In the cultural market—and no doubt elsewhere—the matching of supply and demand is neither the simple effect of production imposing itself on consumption not the effect of a conscious endeavour to serve the consumer´s needs, but the result of the objective orchestration of two relatively independent logics, that of the fields of production and that of the field of consumption. There is a fairly close homology between the specialized fields of production in which products are developed and the fields (the field of the social classes or the field of the dominant class) in which tastes are determined. This means that the products developed in the competitive struggles of which each of the fields of production is the site, and which are the source of the incessant changing of these products, meet, without having expressly to seek it, the demand which is shaped in the objectively or subjectively antagonistic relations between the different classes or class

Pierre Bourdieu. *Distinction: A Social Critique of the Judgment of Taste.* Cambridge, MA: Harvard University Press. pp. 230–244.✦

fractions over material or cultural consumer goods or, more exactly, in the competitive struggles between them over these goods, which are the source of the changing of tastes. This objective orchestration of supply and demand is the reason why the most varied tastes find the conditions for their constitution and functioning in the different tastes which provide a (short- or long-term) market for their different products.[1]

The field of production, which clearly could not function if it could not count on already existing tastes, more or less strong propensities to consume more or less clearly defined goods, enables taste to be realized by offering it, at each moment, the universe of cultural goods as a system of stylistic possibles from which it can select the system of stylistic features constituting a life-style. It is always forgotten that the universe of products offered by each field of production tends in fact to limit the universe of the forms of experience (aesthetic, ethical, political etc.) that are objectively possible at any given moment.[2] It follows from this, among other things, that the distinction recognized in all dominant classes and in all their properties takes different forms depending on the state of the distinctive signs of class that are effectively available. In the case of the production of cultural goods at least, the relation between supply and demand takes a particular form: the supply always exerts an effect of symbolic imposition. A cultural product—an avant-garde picture, a political manifesto, a newspaper—is a constituted taste, a taste which has been raised from the vague semi-existence of half-formulated or unformulated experience, implicit or even unconscious desire, to the full reality of the finished product, by a process of objectification which, in present circumstances, is almost always the work of professionals. It is consequently charged with the legitimizing, reinforcing capacity which objectification always possesses, especially when, as is the case now, the logic of structural homologies assigns it to a prestigious group so that it functions as an authority which authorizes and reinforces dispositions by giving them a collectively recognized expression.[3] Taste, for its part, a classification system constituted by the conditionings associated with a condition situated in a determinate position in the structure of different conditions,

governs the relationship with objectified capital, with this world of ranked and ranking objects which help to define it by enabling it to specify and so realize itself.[4]

Thus the tastes actually realized depend on the state of the system of goods offered; every change in the system of goods induces a change in tastes. But conversely, every change in tastes resulting from a transformation of the conditions of existence and of the corresponding dispositions will tend to induce, directly or indirectly, a transformation of the field of production, by favouring the success, within the struggle constituting the field, of the producers best able to produce the needs corresponding to the new dispositions. There is therefore no need to resort to the hypothesis of a sovereign taste compelling the adjustment of production to needs, or the opposite hypothesis, in which taste is itself a product of production, in order to account for the quasi-miraculous correspondence prevailing at every moment between the products offered by a field of production and the field of socially produced tastes. The producers are led by the logic of competition with other producers and by the specific interests linked to their position in the field of production (and therefore by the habitus which have led them to that position) to produce distinct products which meet the different cultural interests which the consumers owe to their class conditions and position, thereby offering them a real possibility of being satisfied. In short, if, as they say, "There is something for everyone," if each fraction of the dominant class has its own artists and philosophers, newspapers and critics, just as it has its hairdresser, interior decorator or tailor, or if, as an artist put it, "Everyone sells," meaning that paintings of the most varied styles always eventually find a purchaser, this is not the result of intentional design but of the meeting between two systems of differences.

The functional and structural homology which guarantees objective orchestration between the logic of the field of production and the logic of the field of consumption arises from the fact that all the specialized fields (haute couture or painting, theatre or literature) tend to be governed by the same logic, i.e., according to the volume of the specific capital that is possessed (and according to seniority of possession, which is often associated with volume), and from the fact that the oppositions which tend to be established in each case between the richer and the less rich in the specific capital—the established and the outsiders, veterans and newcomers, distinction and pretension, rear-guard and avant-garde, order and movement etc.—are mutually homologous (which means that there are numerous invariants) and also homologous to the oppositions which structure the field of the social classes (between dominant and dominated) and the field of the dominant class (between the dominant fraction and the dominated fraction).[5] The correspondence which is thereby objectively established between the classes of products and the classes of consumers is realized in acts of consumption only through the mediation of that sense of the homology between goods and groups which defines tastes. Choosing according to one's tastes is a matter of identifying goods that are objectively attuned to one's position and which "go together" because they are situated in roughly equivalent positions in their respective spaces, be they films or plays, cartoons or novels, clothes or furniture; this choice is assisted by institutions—shops, theatres (left- or right-bank), critics, newspapers, magazines—which are themselves defined by their position in a field and which are chosen on the same principles.

For the dominant class, the relationship between supply and demand takes the form of a pre-established harmony. The competition for luxury goods, emblems of "class," is one dimension of the struggle to impose the dominant principle of domination, of which this class is the site; and the strategies it calls for, whose common feature is that they are oriented towards maximizing the distinctive profit of exclusive possessions, must necessarily use different weapons to achieve this common function. On the supply side, the field of production need only follow its own logic, that of distinction, which always leads it to be organized in accordance with a structure analogous to that of the symbolic systems which it produces by its functioning and in which each element performs a distinctive function.

THE LOGIC OF HOMOLOGIES

Thus, the case of fashion, which might seem to justify a model which locates the motor of changing sartorial styles in the intentional pursuit of distinction (the "trickle-down effect") is an almost perfect example of the meeting of two spaces and two relatively autonomous histories. The endless changes in fashion result from the objective orchestration between, on the one hand, the logic of the struggles internal to the field of production, which are organized in terms of the opposition old/new, itself linked, through the oppositions expensive/(relatively) cheap and classical/practical (or rear-guard/avant-garde), to the opposition old/young (very important in this field, as in sport); and, on the other hand, the logic of the struggles internal to the field of the dominant class which oppose the dominant and the dominated fractions, or more precisely, the established and the challengers, in other words—given the equivalence between power (more specifically, economic power) and age, which means that, at identical biological ages, social age is a function of proximity to the pole of power and duration in that position—between those who have the social properties associated with accomplished adulthood and those who have the social properties associated with the incompleteness of youth. The couturiers who occupy a dominant position in the field of fashion only have to follow through the negative strategies of discretion and understatement that are forced on them by the aggressive competition of the challengers to find themselves directly attuned to the demands of the old bourgeoisie who are oriented towards the same refusal of emphasis by a homologous relation to the audacities of the new bourgeoisie; and, similarly, the newcomers to the field, young couturiers or designers endeavouring, to win acceptance of their subversive ideas, are the "objective allies" of the new fractions and the younger generation of the dominant fractions of the bourgeoisie, for whom the symbolic revolutions of which vestimentary and cosmetic outrages are the paradigm, are the perfect vehicle for expressing the ambiguity of their situation as the "poor relations" of the temporal powers.

The logic of the functioning of the fields of cultural-goods production, together with the distinction strategies which determine their dynamics, cause the products of their functioning, be they fashion designs or novels, to be predisposed to function differentially, as means of distinction, first between the class fractions and then between the classes. The producers can be totally involved and absorbed in their struggles with other producers, convinced that only specific artistic interests are at stake and that they are otherwise totally disinterested, while remaining unaware of the social functions they fulfil, in the long run, for a particular audience, and without ever ceasing to respond to the expectations of a particular class or class fraction.

This is especially clear in the case of the theatre, where the correspondence between several relativity autonomous spaces— the space of the producers (playwrights and actors), the space of the critics (and through them the space of the daily and weekly press), and the space of the audiences and relationships (i.e., the space of the dominant class), is so perfect, so necessary and yet so unforeseeable that every actor can experience his encounter with the object of his preference as a miracle of predestination.[6]

Boulevard theatre, which offers tried and tested shows (adaptations of foreign plays, revivals of boulevard "classics" etc.), written to reliable formulae and performed by consecrated actors, and which caters to a middle-aged, "bourgeois" audience that is disposed to pay high prices, is opposed in every respect to experimental theatre, which attracts a young, "intellectual" audience to relatively inexpensive shows that flout ethical and aesthetic conventions. This structure of the field of production operates both in reality, through the mechanisms which produce the oppositions between the playwrights or actors and their theatre, the critics and their newspapers, and in people's minds, in the form of a system of categories shaping perception and appreciation which enable them to classify and evaluate playwrights, works, styles and subjects. Thus, critics occupying opposed positions in the field of cultural production will assess plays in terms of the very same oppositions which engender the objective differences between them, but they will set the terms of these oppositions in opposite hierarchies.

Thus in 1973 Françoise Dorin's play *Le Tournant* (*The Turning*), which dramatizes a boulevard playwright's attempt to start a new career as an avant-grade playwright, aroused reactions which varied in form and content according to the position of the publication in which they appeared, that is, according to how distant the critic and his readership were from the "bourgeois" pole and consequently from Dorin's play. They range from unconditional approval to disdainful silence, via a neutral point (occupied by *Le Monde*), as one moves from right to left, from the Right Bank to the Left Bank, through the field of newspapers and weeklies, from *L'Aurore* to *Le Nouvel Observateur*, and, simultaneously, through the field of readership, which is itself organized in accordance with oppositions corresponding fairly exactly to those defining the field of the theatre. When confronted with an object so clearly organized in terms of the basic opposition, the critics, who are themselves distributed in the field of the press in accordance with the structure which shapes both the classified object and the classification system they apply to it, reproduce—in the space of the judgements whereby they classify both it and themselves—the space within which they are themselves classified. (The whole process constitutes a perfect circle from which the only escape is to objectify it sociologically.)

In the play itself, Françoise Dorin sets "bourgeois" drama (her own), which applies technical skill to produce gaiety, lightness and wit, "typically French" qualities, in opposition to the "pretentiousness" and "bluff," camouflaged under "ostentatious starkness," the dull solemnity and drab decor, which characterize "intellectual" drama. The series of contrasted properties which the right-bank critics pick out—technical skill, joie de vivre, clarity, ease, lightness, optimism, as opposed to tedium, gloom, obscurity, pretentiousness, heaviness and pessimism—reappears in the columns of the left-bank critics, but here the positives are negatives and vice versa, because the hierarchy of qualities is reversed.

As in a set of facing mirrors, each of the critics located at either extreme can say exactly what the critic on the other side would say, but he does so in conditions such that his words take on an ironic value and stigmatize by antiphrasis the very things that are praised by his opposing counterpart. Thus, the left-bank critic credits Mme. Dorin with the qualities on which she prides herself; but when *he* mentions them, to *his* readership, they automatically become derisory (so that her "technique" becomes "a box of tricks," and "common sense" is immediately understood as synonymous with bourgeois stupidity). In so doing, he turns against Mme. Dorin the weapon she herself uses against avant-garde theatre when, exploiting the structural logic of the field, she turns against avant-garde theatre the weapon it likes to use against "bourgeois" chatter and the "bourgeois" theatre which reproduces its truisms and clichés (e.g., Ionesco's descriptions of *The Bald Prima Donna* or *Jacques* as "a sort of parody or caricature of boulevard theatre, boulevard theatre falling apart and going mad").

In each case the same device is used: the critic's relationship of ethical and aesthetic connivance with his readers supplies the leverage to break the connivance of the parodied discourse with its own audience and to turn it into a series of "misplaced" remarks which are shocking and laughable because they are not uttered in the appropriate place and before the right audience. Instead, they become a "mockery," a parody, establishing with their audience the immediate complicity of laughter, because they have persuaded their audience to reject (if it had ever accepted) the presuppositions of the parodied discourse.

As this exemplary case clearly shows, it is the logic of the homologies, not cynical calculation, which causes works to be adjusted to the expectations of their audience. The partial objectifications in which intellectuals and artists indulge in the course of their battles omit what is essential by describing as the conscious pursuit of success with an audience what is in fact the result of the pre-established harmony between two systems of interests (which may coincide in the person of the "bourgeois" writer), or, more precisely, of the structural and functional homology between a given writer's or artist's position in the field of production and the position of his audience in the field of the classes and class fractions. By refusing to recognize any other relationship between the producer and his public than cynical calculation or pure disinterestedness, writers and artists give themselves a convenient device for seeing themselves as disinterested, while exposing their adversaries as motivated by the lust for success at any price, provocation and scandal (the right-bank argument) or mercenary servility (the left-bank argument). The so-called "intellectual lackeys" are right to think and profess that they, strictly speaking, serve no one. They serve objectively only because, in all sincerity, they serve their own interests, specific, highly sublimated and euphemized interests, such as "interest" in a form of theatre or philosophy which is logically associated with a certain position in a certain field and which

(except in crisis periods) has every likelihood of concealing, even from its advocates, the political implications it contains.

Between pure disinterestedness and cynical servility, there is room for the relationships established, objectively, without any conscious intention, between a producer and an audience, by virtue of which the practices and artifacts produced in a specialized and relatively autonomous field of production are necessarily over-determined; the functions they fulfil in the internal struggles are inevitably coupled with external functions, those which they receive in the symbolic struggles between the fractions of the dominant class and, in the long run, between the classes. "Sincerity" (which is one of the pre-conditions of symbolic efficacy) is only possible—and real—in the case of perfect, immediate harmony between the expectations inscribed in the position occupied (in a less consecrated area, one would say "job description") and the dispositions of the occupant; it is the privilege of those who, guided by their "sense of their place," have found their natural site in the field of production. In accordance with the law that one only preaches to the converted, a critic can only "influence" his readers insofar as they grant him this power because they are structurally attuned to him in their view of the social world, their tastes and their whole habitus. Jean-Jacques Gautier, for a long time literary critic of *Le Figaro*, gives a good description of this elective affinity between the journalist, his paper and his readers: a good *Figaro* editor, who has chosen himself and been chosen through the same mechanisms, chooses a *Figaro* literary critic because "he has the right tone for speaking to the readers of the paper," because, without making a deliberate effort, "he naturally speaks the language of *Le Figaro*" and is the paper's "ideal reader." If tomorrow I started speaking the language of *Les Temps Modernes*, for example, or *Saintes Chapelles des Lettres*, people would no longer read me or understand me, so they would not listen to me, because I would be assuming a certain number of ideas or arguments which our leaders don't give a damn about.[7] To each position there correspond presuppositions, a *doxa*, and the homology between the producers' positions and their clients' is the precondition for this complicity, which is all the more strongly required when fundamental values are involved, as they are in the theatre.

ELECTIVE AFFINITIES

This limiting case forces one to question the appearances of the direct effect of demand on supply or of supply on demand, and to consider in a new light all the encounters between the logic of goods production and the logic of taste production through which the universe of appropriate, appropriated things—objects, people, knowledge, memories etc.—is constituted. The limit of these coincidences of homologous structures and sequences which bring about the concordance between a socially classified person and the socially classified things or persons which "suit" him is represented by all acts of co-option in fellow feeling, friendship or love which lead to lasting relations, socially sanctioned or not. The social sense is guided by the system of mutually reinforcing and infinitely redundant signs of which each body is the bearer—clothing, pronounciation, bearing, posture, manners—and which, unconsciously registered, are the basis of "antipathies" or "sympathies"; the seemingly most immediate "elective affinities" are always partly based on the unconscious deciphering of expressive features, each of which only takes on its meaning and value within the system of its class variations (one only has to think of the ways of laughing or smiling noted by ordinary language). Taste is what brings together things and people that go together.

Taste is a match-maker; it marries colours and also people, who make "well-matched couples," initially in regard to taste. All the acts of cooption which underlie "primary groups" are acts of knowledge of others qua subjects of acts of knowledge or, in less intellectualist terms, sign reading operations (particularly visible in first encounters) through which a habitus confirms its affinity with other habitus. Hence the astonishing harmony of ordinary couples who, often matched initially, progressively match each other by a sort of mutual acculturation.[8] This spontaneous decoding of one habitus by another is the basis of the immediate affinities which orient social encounters, discouraging socially discordant relationships, encouraging well-matched relationships, without these operations ever having to be formulated other than in the socially innocent language of likes and dislikes.[9] The extreme imp-robability of the particular encounter between particular people, which masks the probability of interchangeable chance events, induces couples to experience their mutual election as a happy accident, a coincidence which mimics transcendent design ("made for each other") and intensifies the sense of the miraculous.

Those whom we find to our taste put into their practices a taste which does not differ from the taste we put into operation in perceiving their practices. Two people can give each other no better proof of the affinity of their tastes than the taste they have for each other. Just as the art-lover finds a raison d'être in his discovery, which seems to have been waiting for all eternity for the discoverer's eye, so lovers feel "justified in existing," as Sartre puts it, "made *for* each other," constituted as the end and raison d'etre of another existence entirely dependent on their own existence, and therefore accepted, recognized in their most contingent features, a way of laughing or speaking, in short, legitimated in the arbitrariness of a way of being and doing, a biological and social destiny. Love is also a way of loving one's own destiny in someone else and so of feeling loved in one's own destiny. It is no doubt the supreme occasion of a sort of experience of the *intuitus originarius of* which the possession of luxury goods and works of art (made *for* their owner) is an approximate form and which makes the perceiving, naming subject (we know the role of name-giving in love relations), the cause and the end, in short, the raison d'etre, of the perceived subject.

> Le Maître, par un oeil profond, a, sur ses pas,
> Apaisé de l'éden l'inquiète merveille
> Dont le frisson final, dans sa voix seule, éveille
> Pour la Rose et le Lys le mystère d'un nom.[10]

Taste is the form par excellence of *amor fati*. The habitus generates representations and practices which are always more adjusted than they seem to be to the objective conditions of which they are the product. To say with Marx that "the petit bourgeois cannot transcend the limits of his mind" (others would have said the limits of his understanding) is to say that his thought has the same limits as his condition, that his condition in a sense doubly limits him, by the material limits which it sets to his practice and the limits it sets to his thought and therefore his practice, and which make him accept, and even love, these limits.[11] We are now be better placed to understand the specific effect of the "raising of consciousness": making explicit what is given presupposes and produces a suspension of immediate attachment to the given so that the knowledge of probable relationships may become dissociated from recognition of them; and *amor fati* can thus collapse into *odium fati*, hatred of one's destiny.

NOTES

1. Thus E. B. Henning has been able to show that the constitution of a relatively autonomous field of artistic production offering stylistically diversified products depends on the existence of two or more patrons with different artistic needs and an equal power to choose works corresponding to their needs. E. B. Henning, "Patronage and Style in the Arts: A suggestion concerning their Relations," *The Journal of Esthetics and Art Criticism*, 18 (June 1960), 464–471.

2. This system of the ethical, aesthetic or political 'possibles' which are effectively available at a given moment is no doubt an essential dimension of what makes up the historicity of ways of thinking and world views, and the contemporaneity of individuals and groups linked to the same period and place.

3. Advertising for luxury goods systematically exploits the association of a product with a group. In no other field are institutions more overtly defined by their clientele than in the luxury trades, no doubt because here the virtually exclusive function of the products is to classify their owners. The link between the value of emblems and the value of the group which owns them is very clear in the antiques market, in which the value of an object may derive from the social standing of its previous owners.

4. The internalized classifications of taste have to reckon, at every moment, with the classifications objectified in institutions, such as the agencies of cultural consecration and conservation, and with all the objectified hierarchies of which they are always partly the product. But in return, the dominant taxonomies are constantly challenged and revised in the classification struggles through which the different classes or class fractions endeavour to impose their own taxonomy as legitimate, either directly or through the professionals who compete in the specialized fields of production.

5. Rather than elaborate here all the presuppositions of analysis in terms of field (in particular, the interdependence between specific capital and the field in which it is valid and produced its effects I shall merely refer the reader to earlier texts in which these ideas are developed. See, in particular: P. Bourdieu, "Le marché des biens symboliques," *L'Année Sociologique*, 22 (1971), 49–126; "Genèse et structure du champ religieux," *Revue Française de Sociologie*, 12 (1971), 295–334; "Champ du pouvoir, champ intellectual et habitus de classe," *Scolies*, 1 (1971), 7–26; "Le couturier et sa griffe," *Actes*, 1 (1975), 7–36; "L'invention de la vie d'artiste," *Actes*, 2 (1975), 67–93; "L'ontologie politique de Martin Heidegger," *Actes*, 5–6 (1975), 109–156; "The Specificity of the Scientific Field," *Social Science Information*, 14 (December 1975), 19–47; and especially "The Production of Belief," *Media, Culture and Society*, 2 (July 1980), 261–293.

6. See Bourdieu, "Le couturier et sa griffe."

7. See Bourdieu, "The Production of Belief."

8. J.-J. Gautier, *Théâtre d'aujourd'hui* (Paris, Julliard, 1972), pp. 25–26. We may take Gautier at his word when he declares that the efficacy of his reviews stems not from a calculated adjustment to the expectations of his readership but from an objective harmony of view, allowing a perfect sincerity which is essential in order to be believed and therefore effective.

9. Before pointing to all the counter-cases of discord and divorce, one needs to consider how strong the cohesive forces constituted by the harmony of habitus have to be in order to counterbalance the contradictions inherent in the matrimonial enterprise as defined by custom and social law.

10. The intuition of the habitus provides an immediate understanding (which would take some time to justify explicitly) of the fact that, when invited to choose from a list of personalities those whom they would like to invite to dinner, the senior executives and professionals choose more often than all other classes Simone Veil, Giscard, Barre, Françoise Giroud and Chirac, but also Gicquel and Mourousi, whereas the working classes most often choose Coluche, Poulidor, Thévenet and Marchais, while the middle classes most often choose Le Luron, Mitterrand, Princess Caroline of Monaco, Platini and Jauffret (C.S.XLIII). (Veil, Barre, Giroud: ministers in the Giscard presidency. For Giscard, Marchais, Mitterrand, see appendix 4. Roger Gicquel and Yves Mourousi: TV and radio personalities; Coluche, Thierry Le Luron: entertainers; Poulidor, Thévenet: cyclists; Platini: footballer; Jauffret: tennis player—translator.)

11. "The Master's deep gaze has, as he passed, /Calmed the unquiet wonder of Eden, / Whose final shudder, in his voice alone, awakens / For the Rose and the Lily the mystery of a name" (Mallarmé, 'Toast Funèbre', *Oeuvres complètes*, p. 55 [translator]).

72. ADVERTISING

JEAN BAUDRILLARD

Jean Baudrillard (1929-2007), a French social thinker, taught sociology at the University of Nanterre during the tumultuous days of 1968, when student revolts nearly toppled the government of Charles DeGaulle. In the aftermath of those events, Baudrillard left the university, turned from Marxism, and emerged as one of the most radical proponents of postmodernism. Central to his vision of contemporary social life was the notion that our cultures have been thoroughly saturated by the media and entertainment industries such that the differences between the real and the images, signs, and simulations have dissolved. The result was the emergence of what he referred to as "hyperreality." In this essay (published in 1968, at the beginning of his transition from Marxism to postmodernism) he explores from various angles the significance of advertising in shaping modern consumerism.

DISCOURSE ON OBJECTS AND DISCOURSE-AS-OBJECT

Any analysis of the system *of* objects must ultimately imply an analysis of discourse about objects—that is to say, an analysis of promotional `messages´ (comprising image and discourse). For advertising is not simply an adjunct to the system of objects; it cannot be detached therefrom, nor can it be restricted to its `proper´ function (there is no such thing as advertising strictly confined to the supplying of information). Indeed, advertising is now an irremovable aspect of the system of objects precisely by virtue of its disproportionateness. This lack of proportion is the `functional´ apotheosis of the system. Advertising in its entirety constitutes a useless and unnecessary universe. It is pure connotation. It contributes nothing to production or to the direct practical application of things, yet it plays an integral part in the system of objects, not merely because it relates to consumption but also because it itself becomes an object to be consumed. A clear distinction must be drawn in connection with advertising's dual status as a discourse on the object and as an object in its own right. It is as a useless, unnecessary discourse that it comes to be consumable as a cultural object. What achieves autonomy and fulfilment through advertising is thus the whole system that I have been describing at the level of objects: the entire apparatus of personalization and imposed differentiation; of proliferation of the inessential and subordination of technical requirements to the requirements of production and consumption; of dysfunctionality and secondary functionality. Since its function is almost entirely secondary, and since both image and discourse play largely allegorical roles in it, advertising supplies us with the ideal object and casts a particularly revealing light upon the system of objects. And since, like all heavily connoted systems, it is self-referential,[1] we may safely rely on advertising to tell us what it is that we consume *through* objects.

ADVERTISING IN THE INDICATIVE AND IN THE IMPERATIVE

Advertising sets itself the task of supplying information about particular products and promoting their sale. In

From Jean Baudrillard, *The System of Objects*, translated by James Benedict, Verso, London. Copyright © 1996, pp. 164–167, 172–178. Reprinted with permission. ✦

principle this 'objective' function is still its fundamental purpose.[2] The supplying of information has nevertheless given way to persuasion—even to what Vance Packard calls 'hidden persuasion', the aim of which is a completely managed consumption. The supposed threat this poses of a totalitarian conditioning of man and his needs has provoked great alarm. Studies have shown, however, that advertising's pervasive power is not as great as had been supposed. A saturation point is in fact soon reached: competing messages tend to cancel each other out, and many claims fail to convince on account of their sheer excessiveness. Moreover, injunctions and exhortations give rise to all kinds of counter-motivations and resistances, whether rational or irrational, among them the refusal of passivity, the desire not to be 'taken over', negative reactions to hyperbole, to repetition, and so on. In short, the discourse of advertising is just as likely to dissuade as to persuade, and consumers, though not entirely immune, appear to exercise a good deal of discretion when it comes to the advertising message.

Having said this, let us not be misled by the *avowed* aim of that message; while advertising may well fail to sell the consumer on a particular brand—Omo, Simca or Frigidaire—it does sell him on something else, something much more fundamental to the global social order than Omo or Frigidaire—something, indeed for which such brand names are merely a cover. Just as the object's function may ultimately amount merely to the provision of a justification for the latent meanings that the object imposes, so in advertising (and all the more so inasmuch as it is the more purely connotative system) the product designated—that is, its denotation or description—tends to be merely an effective mask concealing a confused process of integration.

So even though we may be getting better and better at resisting advertising in the *imperative*, we are at the same time becoming ever more susceptible to advertising in the *indicative*—that is, to its actual *existence* as a product to be consumed at a secondary level, and as the clear *expression* of a culture. It is in this sense that we do indeed 'believe' in advertising: what we consume in this way is the luxury of a society that projects itself as an agency for dispensing goods and 'transcends itself' in a culture. We are thus taken over at one and the same time by an established agency and by that agency's self-image.

THE LOGIC OF FATHER CHRISTMAS

Those who pooh-pooh the ability of advertising and of the mass media in general to condition people have failed to grasp the peculiar logic upon which the media's efficacy reposes. For this is not a logic of propositions and proofs, but a logic of fables and of the willingness to go along with them. We do not believe in such fables, but we cleave to them nevertheless. Basically, the 'demonstration' of a product convinces no one, but it does serve to rationalize its purchase, which in any case either precedes or overwhelms all rational motives. Without 'believing' in the product, therefore, *we believe in the advertising that tries to get us to believe in it*. We are for all the world like children in their attitude towards Father Christmas. Children hardly ever wonder whether Father Christmas exists or not, and they certainly never look upon getting presents as an effect of which that existence is the cause: rather, their belief in Father Christmas is a rationalizing confabulation designed to extend earliest infancy's miraculously gratifying relationship with the parents (and particularly with the mother) into a later stage of childhood. That miraculous relationship, though now in actuality past, is internalized in the form of a belief which is in effect an ideal extension of it. There is nothing artificial about the romance of Father Christmas, however, for it is based upon the shared interest that the two parties involved have in its preservation. Father Christmas himself is unimportant here, and the child only believes in him precisely because of that basic lack of significance. What children are actually consuming through this figure, fiction or cover story (which in a sense they continue to believe in even after they have ceased to do so) is the action of a magical parental solicitude and the care taken by the parents to continue colluding with their children's embrace of the fable. Christmas presents themselves serve merely to underwrite this compromise.[3]

Advertising functions in much the same way. Neither its rhetoric nor even the informational aspect of its discourse has a decisive effect on the buyer. What the individual does respond to, on the other hand, is advertising's underlying leitmotiv of protection and gratification, the intimation that its solicitations and attempts to persuade are the sign, indecipherable at the conscious level, that somewhere there is an agency (a social agency in the event, but one that refers directly to the image of the mother) which has taken it upon itself to inform him of his own desires, and to foresee and rationalize these desires to his own satisfaction. He thus no more `believes´ in advertising than the child believes in Father Christmas, but this in no way impedes his capacity to embrace an internalized infantile situation, and to act accordingly. Herein lies the very real effectiveness of advertising, founded on its obedience to a logic which, though not that of the conditioned reflex, is nonetheless very rigorous: a logic of belief and regression.[4] . . .

THE FESTIVAL OF BUYING POWER

This gratificatory, infantilizing function of advertising, which is the basis of our belief in it and hence of our collusion with the social entity, is equally well illustrated by its playful aspect. We are certainly susceptible to the reassurance advertising offers by supplying an image that is never negative, but we are equally affected by advertising as a fantastic manifestation of a society capable of swamping the mere necessity of products in superfluous images: advertising as a show (again, the most democratic of all), a game, a *mise en scène*. Advertising serves as a permanent display of the buying power, be it real or virtual, of society overall. Whether we partake of it personally or not, we all live and breathe this buying power. By virtue of advertising, too, the product exposes itself to our view and invites us to handle it; it is, infact, eroticized—not just because of the explicitly sexual themes evoked[5] but also because the purchase itself, simple appropriation, is transformed into a manoeuvre, a scenario, a complicated dance which endows a purely practical transaction with all the traits of amorous dalliance: advances, rivalry, obscenity, flirtation, prostitution—even irony. The mechanics of buying (which is already libidinally charged) gives way to a complete eroticization of choosing and spending.[6] Our modern environment assails us relentlessly, especially in the cities, with its lights and its images, its incessant inducements to status-consciousness and narcissism, emotional involvement and obligatory relationships. We live in a cold-blooded carnival atmosphere, a formal yet electrifying ambience of empty sensual gratification wherein the actual process of buying and consuming is demonstrated, illuminated, mimicked—even frustrated— much as the sexual act is anticipated by dance. By means of advertising, as once upon a time by means of feasts, society puts itself on display and consumes its own image. An essential regulatory function is evident here. Like the dream, advertising defines and redirects an imaginary potentiality. Like the dream's, its practical character is strictly subjective and individual.[7] And, like the dream, advertising is devoid of all negativity and relativity: with never a sign too many nor a sign too few, it is essentially superlative and totally immanent in nature.[8] Our night-time dreams are uncaptioned, whereas the one that we live in our waking hours via the city's hoardings, in our newspapers and on our screens, is covered with captions, with multiple subtitling. Both, however, weave the most colourful of narratives from the most impoverished of raw materials, and just as the function of nocturnal dreams is to protect sleep, so likewise the prestige of advertising and consumption serves to ensure the spontaneous absorption of ambient social values and the regression of the individual into social consensus.

Festival, immanence, positivity—to use such terms amounts to saying that *in the first instance advertising is itself less a determinant of consumption than an object of consumption*. What would an object be today if it were not put on offer both in the mode of discourse and image (advertising) and in the mode of a range of models (choice)? It would be psychologically nonexistent. And what would modern citizens be if objects and products were not proposed to them in the twin dimensions of advertising and choice? They would not be *free*. We can understand the reactions of the two thousand West Germans polled by the Allenbach Demoscopic Institute: 60 percent expressed the view that there was too much advertising, yet when they were asked, `Would you rather have too much advertising (Western style) or minimal—and only socially useful—advertising (as in the East)?´, a majority favoured the first of these options, taking an excess of advertising as indicative not only of affluence but also of freedom—and hence of a basic value.[9] Such is the measure of the emotional and ideological collusion that advertising's spectacular mediation creates between the individual and society (whatever the structures of the latter may be). If all advertising were abolished, individuals would feel frustrated by the empty hoardings. Frustrated not merely by the lack of opportunity (even in an ironic way) for play, for dreaming, but also, more profoundly, by the feeling that they were no longer somehow `being taken care of´. They would miss an environment thanks to which, in the absence of active social participation, they can at least partake of a travesty of the social entity and enjoy a warmer, more maternal and more vivid atmosphere. One of the first demands of man in his progression towards well-being is that his desires be attended to, that they be formulated and expressed in the form of images for his own contemplation (something which is a problem, or becomes a problem, in socialist countries). Advertising fills this function, which is futile, regressive and inessential—yet for that very reason even more profoundly necessary.

GRATIFICATION/REPRESSION: A TWO-SIDED AGENCY

We need to discern the true imperative of advertising behind the gentle litany of the object: `Look how the whole of society simply adapts itself to you and your desires. It is therefore only reasonable that you should become integrated into that society.´ Persuasion is hidden, as Vance Packard says, but its aim is less the `compulsion´ to buy, or conditioning by means of objects, than the subscription to social consensus that this discourse urges: the object is a service, a personal relationship between society and you. Whether advertising is organized around the image of the mother or around the need to play, it always aims to foster *the same tendency to regress to a point anterior to real social processes*, such as work, production, the market, or value, which might disturb this magical integration: the object has not been bought by you, you have voiced a desire for it and all the engineers, technicians, and so on, have worked to gratify your desire. With the advent of industrial society the division of labour severs labour from its product. Advertising adds the finishing touch to this development by creating a radical split, at the moment of purchase, between *products* and consumer *goods*; by interpolating a vast maternal image between labour and the product of labour, it causes that *product* no longer to be viewed as such (complete with its history, and so on), but purely and simply as a good, as an *object*. And even as it separates the producer and the consumer within the one individual, thanks to the material abstraction of a highly differentiated system of objects, advertising strives inversely to re-create the infantile confusion of the object with the desire for the object, to return the consumer to the stage at which the infant makes no distinction between its mother and what its mother gives it.

In reality advertising's careful omission of objective processes and the social history of objects is simply a way of making it easier, by means of the imagination as a social agency, to impose the *real* order of production and exploitation. This is where, behind the psychology of advertising, it behoves us to recognize the demagogy of a *political* discourse whose own tactics are founded on a splitting into two—on the splitting of social reality into a real agency and an image, with the first disappearing behind the second, becoming indecipherable and giving way to nothing more than a pattern of absorption into a material world. When advertising tells you, in effect, that `society adapts itself totally to you, so integrate yourself totally into society´, the reciprocity thus invoked is obviously fake: what adapts to you is an imaginary agency, whereas you are asked in exchange to adapt to an agency that is distinctly real. Via the armchair that `weds the shape of your body´, it is the entire technical and political order of society that weds *you* and takes you in hand. Society assumes a maternal *role* the better to preserve the rule of *constraint*.[10] The immense political role played by the diffusion of products and advertising techniques is here clearly evident: these mechanisms effectively replace earlier moral or political ideologies. Indeed, they go farther, for moral and political forms of integration were never unproblematical and always had to be buttressed by overt repression, whereas the new techniques manage to do without any such assistance: the consumer internalizes the agency of social control and its norms in the very process of consuming.

This effectiveness is reinforced by the status accorded the signs advertising manipulates and the process whereby these are `read´.

Signs in advertising speak to us of objects, but they never (or scarcely ever) explain those objects from the standpoint of a *praxis:* they refer to objects as to a world that is absent. These signs are literally no more than a `legend´: they are there primarily for the purpose of being read. But while they do not refer to the real world, neither do they exactly replace that world: their function is to impose a specific activity, a specific kind of reading. If they did carry information, then a *full* reading, and a transition to the practical realm, would occur. But their role is a different one: to draw attention to the absence of what they designate. To this extent the reading of such signs is intransitive—organized in terms of a specific system of *satisfaction* which is, however, perpetually determined by the absence of reality, that is to say, by *frustration*.

The image creates a void, indicates an absence, and it is in this respect that it is `evocative´. It is deceptive, however. It provokes a cathexis which it then immediately short-circuits at the level of reading. It focuses free-floating wishes upon an object which it masks as much as reveals. The image disappoints: *its function is at once to display and simultaneously to disabuse.* Looking is based on a presumption of contact; the image and its reading are based on a presumption of possession. Thus advertising offers neither a hallucinated satisfaction nor a practical mediation with the world. Rather, what it produces is dashed hopes: unfinished actions, continual initiatives followed by continual abandonments thereof, false dawnings of objects, false dawnings of desires. A whole psychodrama is quickly enacted when an image is read. In principle, this enables the reader to assume his passive role and be transformed into a consumer. In actuality, the sheer profusion of images works at the same time to counter any shift in the direction of reality, subtly to fuel feelings of guilt by means of continual frustration, and to arrest consciousness at the level of a phantasy of satisfaction. In the end the image and the reading of the image are by no means the shortest way to the object, merely the shortest way to another image. The signs of advertising thus follow upon one another like the transient images of hypnagogic states.

We must not forget that the image serves in this way to avoid reality and create frustration, for only thus can we grasp how it is that *the reality principle omitted from the image nevertheless effectively re-emerges therein as the continual repression of desire* (as the spectacularization, blocking and dashing of that desire and, ultimately, its regressive and visible transference onto an object). This is where the profound collusion between the advertising sign and the overall order of society becomes most evident: it is not in any mechanical sense that advertising conveys the values of society; rather, more subtly, it is in its ambiguous *presumptive* function—somewhere between possession and dispossession, at once a designation and an indication of absence—that the advertising sign `inserts´ the social order into its system of simultaneous determination by gratification on the one hand and repression on the other.[11]

Gratification, frustration—two indivisible aspects of social integration. Every advertising image is a key, a *legend*, and as such reduces the anxiety-provoking polysemy of the world. But in the name of intelligibility the image becomes impoverished, cursory; inasmuch as it is still susceptible of too many interpretations, its meaning is further narrowed by the addition of discourse—of a subtitle, as it were, which constitutes a second legend. And, by virtue of the way it is read, the image always refers only to other images. In the end advertising soothes people's consciousness by means of a controlled social semantics—controlled, ultimately, to the point of focusing on a single referent, namely the whole society itself. Society thus monopolizes all the roles. It conjures up a host of images whose meanings it immediately strives to limit. It generates an anxiety that it then seeks to calm. It fulfils and disappoints, mobilizes and demobilizes. Under the banner of advertising it institutes the reign of a freedom of desire, but desire is never truly liberated thereby (which would in fact entail the end of the social order): desire is liberated by the image only to the point where its emergence triggers the associated reflexes of anxiety and guilt. Primed by the image only to be defused by it, and made to feel guilty to boot, the nascent desire is co-opted by the agency of control. There is a profusion of freedom, but this freedom is imaginary; a continual mental orgy, but one which is stage-managed, a controlled regression in which all perversity is resolved in favour of order. If gratification is massive in consumer society, repression is equally massive—and both reach us together via the images and discourse of advertising, which activate the repressive reality principle at the very heart of the pleasure principle.

NOTES

1. See Roland Barthes's account of the system of fashion: *Systéme de la mode* (Paris: Seuil, 1967).

2. We should not forget, however, that the earliest advertisements were for miracle cures, home remedies, and the like; they supplied information, therefore, but information only of the most tendentious kind.

3. One is reminded of the neutral substances or placebos that doctors sometimes prescribe for psychosomatic patients. Quite often these patients make just as good a recovery after the administration of such inactive elements as they do after taking real medicine. What is it that such patients derive or assimilate from the placebo? The answer is the idea of medicine *plus* the presence of the physician: the mother and the father simultaneously. Here too, then, belief facilitates the retrieval of an infantile situation, the result being the regressive resolution of a psychosomatic conflict.

4. Such an approach might well be extended to mass communications in general, though this is not the place to attempt it.

5. Some common leitmotives (breasts, lips) should perhaps be deemed less erotic than `nurturing´ in character.

6. The literal meaning of the German word for advertising, `*die Werbung*´, is erotic exploration. `*Derumworbene Mensch*´, the person won over by advertising, can also mean a person who is sexually solicited.

7. Advertising campaigns designed to alter group behaviour or modify social structures (for example, those against alcohol abuse, dangerous driving, etc.) are notoriously ineffective. Advertising resists the (collective) reality principle. The only imperative that may be effective in this context is `Give!´   for it is part of the reversible system of gratification.

8. Negative or ironic advertisements are mere antiphrasis—a well-known device, too, of the dream.

9. Naturally the existing political situation of the two Germanies must be taken into account, but there can be little doubt that the absence of advertising in the Western sense is a real contributing factor to West German prejudice against the East.

10. What is more, behind this system of gratification we may discern the reinforcement of all the structures of authority (planning, centralization, bureaucracy). Parties, States, power structures—all are able to strengthen their hegemony under cover of this immense mother-image which renders any real challenge to them less and less possible.

11. This account may also be applied to the system of objects, because the object too is ambiguous, because it is never *merely* an object but always at the same time *an indication of the absence of a human relationship* (just as the sign in advertising is an indication of the absence of a real object)—for these reasons, the object may likewise play a powerful integrative role. It is true, however, that the object's practical specificity means that the indication of the absence of the real is less marked in the case of the object than in that of the advertising sign.

73. PANOPTICISM

MICHEL FOUCAULT

Michel Foucault (1926–1984) is a central figure among poststructuralists. Like other French thinkers of his generation, he was profoundly affected by the events of 1968, as well as by his personal experiences with LSD, San Francisco's gay scene in the 1970s, and the advent of the AIDS epidemic (Foucault died of AIDS). Central to Foucault's vision was a concern for the connections between power and knowledge; with his interest in sexuality, he also wanted to understand the body in relation to power/knowledge. In *Discipline and Punish* (1975), he examines the transition in prisons in the late eighteenth and early nineteenth centuries, when torture and other cruel punishments were replaced by more rationalized forms of punishment. Whereas earlier writers have typically described this change as a move toward more humane forms of punishment, Foucault sees it as an example of the growing power of authorities. The Panopticon discussed in this selection from the book is the prime example of the wedding of knowledge and power into a new system of heightened surveillance and control.

Bentham's *Panopticon* is the architectural figure of this composition. We know the principle on which it was based: at the periphery, an annular building; at the centre, a tower; this tower is pierced with wide windows that open onto the inner side of the ring; the peripheric building is divided into cells, each of which extends the whole width of the building; they have two windows, one on the inside, corresponding to the windows of the tower; the other, on the outside, allows the light to cross the cell from one end to the other: All that is needed, then, is to place a supervisor in a central tower and to shut up in each cell a madman, a condemned man, a worker or a schoolboy. By the effect of backlighting, one can observe from the tower, standing out precisely against the light, the small captive shadows in the cells of the periphery. They are like so many cages, so many small theatres, in which each actor is alone, perfectly individualized and constantly visible. The panoptic mechanism arranges spatial unities that make it possible to see constantly and to recognize immediately. In short, it reverses the principle of the dungeon; or rather of its three functions—to enclose, to deprive of light and to hide—it preserves only the first and eliminates the other two. Full lighting and the eye of a supervisor capture better than darkness, which ultimately protected. Visibility is a trap.

To begin with, this made it possible—as a negative effect—to avoid those compact, swarming, howling masses that were to be found in places of confinement, those painted by Goya or described by Howard. Each individual, in his place, is securely confined to a cell from which he is seen from the front by the supervisor; but the side walls prevent him from coming into contact with his companions. He is seen, but he does not see; he is the object of information, never a subject in communication. The arrangement of his room, opposite the central tower, imposes on him an axial visibility; but the divisions of the ring, those separated cells, imply a lateral invisibility. And this invisibility is a guarantee of order. If the inmates are convicts, there is no danger of a plot, an attempt at collective escape, the planning of new crimes for the future, bad reciprocal influences; if they are patients, there is no danger of contagion; if they are madmen there is no risk of their commiting violence upon one another; if they are schoolchildren, there is no copying, no chatter, no waste of time; if they are workers, there are no disorders, no theft, no coalitions, none of those distractions that slow down the rate of work, make it less perfect or cause accidents. The crowd, a compact mass, a locus of multiple exchanges, individualities merging together, a collective effect, is abolished and replaced by a collection of separated individualities. From the point of view of the guardian, it is replaced by a multiplicity that can be numbered and supervised; from the point of view of the inmates, by a sequestered and observed solitude (Bentham, 60–64).

Hence the major effect of the Panopticon: to induce in the inmate a state of conscious and permanent visibility that assures the automatic functioning of power. So to arrange things that the surveillance is permanent in its effects, even if it is discontinuous in its action; that the perfection of power should tend to render its actual exercise unnecessary; that this architectural apparatus should be a machine for creating and sustaining a power relation independent of the person who exercises it; in short, that the inmates should be caught up in a power situation of which they are themselves the bearers. To achieve this, it is at once too much and too little that the prisoner should be constantly observed by an inspector: too little, for what matters is that he knows himself to be observed; too much, because he has no need in fact of being so. In view of this, Bentham laid down the principle that power should be visible and unverifiable. Visible: the inmate will constantly have before his eyes the tall outline of the central tower from which he is spied upon. Unverifiable: the inmate must never know whether he is being looked at at any one moment, but he must be sure that he may always be so. In order to make the presence or absence of the inspector unverifiable, so that the prisoners, in their cells, cannot even see a shadow, Bentham envisaged not only venetian blinds on the windows of the central observation hall, but, on the inside, partitions that intersected the hall at right angles and, in order to pass from one quarter to the other, not doors but zig-zag openings;

for the slightest noise, a gleam of light, a brightness in a half opened door would betray the presence of the guardian.[1] The Panopticon is a machine for dissociating the see/being seen dyad: in the peripheric ring, one is totally seen, without ever seeing; in the central tower, one sees everything without ever being seen.[2]

It is an important mechanism, for it automatizes and disindividualizes power. Power has its principle not so much in a person as in a certain concerted distribution of bodies, surfaces, lights, gazes, in an arrangement whose internal mechanisms produce the relation in which individuals are caught up. The ceremonies, the rituals, the marks by which the sovereign's surplus power was manifested are useless. There is a machinery that assures dissymmetry, disequilibrium, difference. Consequently, it does not matter who exercises power. Any individual, taken almost at random, can operate the machine: in the absence of the director, his family, his friends, his visitors, even his servants (Bentham, 45). Similarly, it does not matter what motive animates him: the curiosity of the indiscreet, the malice of a child, the thirst for knowledge of a philosopher who wishes to visit this museum of human nature, or the perversity of those who take pleasure in spying and punishing. The more numerous those anonymous and temporary observers are, the greater the risk for the inmate of being surprised and the greater his anxious awareness of being observed. The Panopticon is a marvellous machine which, whatever use one may wish to put it to, produces homogeneous effects of power.

A real subjection is born mechanically from a fictitious relation. So it is not necessary to use force to constrain the convict to good behaviour, the madman to calm, the worker to work, the schoolboy to application, the patient to the observation of the regulations. Bentham was surprised that panoptic institutions could be so light: there were no more bars, no more chains, no more heavy locks; all that was needed was that the separations should be clear and the openings well arranged. The heaviness of the old `houses of security´, with their fortress-like architecture, could be replaced by the simple, economic geometry of a `house of certainty´. The efficiency of power, its constraining force have, in a sense, passed over to the other side—to the side of its surface of application. He who is subjected to a field of visibility, and who knows it, assumes responsibility for the constraints of power; he makes them play spontaneously upon himself; he inscribes in himself the power relation in which he simultaneously plays both roles; he becomes the principle of his own subjection. By this very fact, the external power may throw off its physical weight; it tends to the non-corporal; and, the more it approaches this limit, the more constant, profound and permanent are its effects: it is a perpetual victory that avoids any physical confrontation and which is always decided in advance.

Bentham does not say whether he was inspired, in his project, by Le Vaux's menagerie at Versailles: the first menagerie in which the different elements are not, as they traditionally were, distributed in a park (Loisel, 104–7). At the centre was an octagonal pavilion which, on the first floor, consisted of only a single room, the king's *salon*; on every side large windows looked out onto seven cages (the eighth side was reserved for the entrance), containing different species of animals. By Bentham's time, this menagerie had disappeared. But one finds in the programme of the Panopticon a similar concern with individualizing observation, with characterization and classification, with the analytical arrangement of space. The Panopticon is a royal menagerie; the animal is replaced by man, individual distribution by specific grouping and the king by the machinery of a furtive power. With this exception, the Panopticon also does the work of a naturalist. It makes it possible to draw up differences: among patients, to observe the symptoms of each individual, without the proximity of beds, the circulation of miasmas, the effects of contagion confusing the clinical tables; among schoolchildren, it makes it possible to observe performances (without there being any imitation or copying), to map aptitudes, to assess characters, to draw up rigorous classifications and, in relation to normal development, to distinguish `laziness and stubbornness´ from `incurable imbecility´; among workers, it makes it possible to note the aptitudes of each worker, compare the time he takes to perform a task, and if they are paid by the day, to calculate their wages (Bentham, 60–64).

So much for the question of observation. But the Panopticon was also a laboratory; it could be used as a laboratory; it could be used as a machine to carry out experiments, to alter behaviour, to train or correct individuals. To experiment with medicines and monitor their effects. To try out different punishments on prisoners, according to their crimes and character, and to seek the most effective ones. To teach different techniques simultaneously to the workers, to decide which is the best. To try out pedagogical experiments—and in particular to take up once again the well-debated problem of secluded education, by using orphans. One would see what would happen when, in their sixteenth or eighteenth year, they were presented with other boys or girls; one could verify whether, as Helvetius thought, anyone could learn anything; one would follow `the genealogy of every observable idea´; one could bring up different children according to different systems of thought, making certain children believe that two and two do not make four or that the moon is a cheese, then put them together when they are twenty or twenty-five years old; one would then have discussions that would be worth a great deal more than the sermons or lectures on which so much money is spent; one would have at least an opportunity of making discoveries in the domain of metaphysics. The Panopticon is a privileged place for experiments on men, and for analysing with complete certainty the transformations that may be obtained from them. The Panopticon may even provide an apparatus for supervising its own mechanisms. In this central tower, the director may spy on all the employees that he has under his orders: nurses, doctors, foremen, teachers, warders; he will be able to judge them continuously, alter their behaviour, impose upon them the methods he thinks best; and it will even be possible to observe the director himself. An inspector arriving unexpectedly at the centre of the Panopticon will be able to judge at a glance, without anything being concealed from him, how the entire establishment is functioning. And, in any case, enclosed as he is in the middle of this architectural mechanism, is not the director's own fate entirely bound up with it? The incompetent physician who has allowed contagion to spread, the incompetent prison governor or workshop manager will be the first victims of an epidemic or a revolt. " `By every tie I could devise´, said the master of the Panopticon, `my own fate had been bound up by me with theirs´ " (Bentham, 177). The Panopticon functions as a kind of laboratory of power. Thanks to its mechanisms of observation, it gains in efficiency and in the ability to penetrate into men's behaviour; knowledge follows the advances of power, discovering new objects of knowledge over all the surfaces on which power is exercised.

The plague-stricken town, the panoptic establishment—the differences are important. They mark, at a distance of a century and a half, the transformations of the disciplinary programme. In the first case, there is an exceptional situation: against an extraordinary evil, power is mobilized; it makes itself everywhere present and visible; it invents new mechanisms; it separates, it immobilizes, it partitions; it constructs for a time what is both a counter-city and the perfect society; it imposes an ideal functioning, but one that is reduced, in the final analysis, like the evil that it combats, to a simple dualism of life and death: that which moves brings death, and one kills that which moves. The Panopticon, on the other hand, must be understood as a generalizable model of functioning; a way of defining power relations in terms of the everyday life of men. No doubt Bentham presents it as a particular institution, closed in upon itself. Utopias, perfectly closed in upon themselves, are common enough. As opposed to the ruined prisons, littered with mechanisms of torture, to be seen in Piranese's engravings, the Panopticon presents a cruel, ingenious cage. The fact that it should have given rise, even in our own time, to so many variations, projected or realized, is evidence of the imaginary intensity that it has possessed for almost two hundred years. But the Panopticon must not be understood as a dream building: it is the diagram of a mechanism of power reduced to its ideal form; its functioning, abstracted from any obstacle, resistance or friction, must be represented as a pure architectural and optical system: it is in fact a figure of political technology that may and must be detached from any specific use.

It is polyvalent in its applications; it serves to reform prisoners, but also to treat patients, to instruct schoolchildren, to confine the insane, to supervise workers, to put beggars and idlers to work. It is a type of location of bodies in space, of distribution of individuals in relation to one another, of hierarchical organization, of disposition of centres and channels of power, of definition of the instruments and modes of intervention of power, which can be implemented in hospitals, workshops, schools, prisons. Whenever one is dealing with a multiplicity of individuals on whom a task or a particular form of behaviour must be imposed, the panoptic schema may be used. It is—necessary modifications apart—applicable `to all establishments whatsoever, in which, within a space not too large to be covered or commanded by buildings, a number of persons are meant to be kept under inspection´ (Bentham, 40; although Bentham takes the penitentiary house as his prime example, it is because it has many different functions to fulfil—safe custody, confinement, solitude, forced labour and instruction).

In each of its applications, it makes it possible to perfect the exercise of power. It does this in several ways: because it can reduce the number of those who exercise it, while increasing the number of those on whom it is exercised. Because it is possible to intervene at any moment and because the constant pressure acts even before the offences, mistakes or crimes have been committed. Because, in these conditions, its strength is that it never intervenes, it is exercised spontaneously and without noise, it constitutes a mechanism whose effects follow from one another. Because, without any physical instrument other than architecture and geometry, it acts directly on individuals; it gives `power of mind over mind´. The panoptic schema makes any apparatus of power more intense: it assures its economy (in material, in personnel, in time); it assures its efficacity by its preventative character, its continuous functioning and its automatic mechanisms. It is a way of obtaining from power `in hitherto unexampled quantity´, `a great and new instrument of government...; its great excellence consists in the great strength it is capable of giving to *any* institution it may be thought proper to apply it to´ (Bentham, 66).

It's a case of `it's easy once you've thought of it´ in the political sphere. It can in fact be integrated into any function (education, medical treatment, production, punishment); it can increase the effect of this function, by being linked closely with it; it can constitute a mixed mechanism in which relations of power (and of knowledge) may be precisely adjusted, in the smallest detail, to the processes that are to be supervised; it can establish a direct proportion between `surplus power´ and `surplus production´. In short, it arranges things in such a way that the exercise of power is not added on from the outside, like a rigid, heavy constraint, to the functions it invests, but is so subtly present in them as to increase their efficiency by itself increasing its own points of contact. The panoptic mechanism is not simply a hinge, a point of exchange between a mechanism of power and a function; it is a way of making power relations function in a function, and of making a function function through these power relations. Bentham's Preface to *Panopticon* opens with a list of the benefits to be obtained from his `inspection-house´: `*Morals reformed—health preserved—industry invigorated—instruction difused—public burthens lightened*—Economy seated, as it were, upon a rock—the gordian knot of the Poor-Laws not cut, but united—all by a simple idea in architecture!´ (Bentham, 39).

Furthermore, the arrangement of this machine is such that its enclosed nature does not preclude a permanent presence from the outside: we have seen that anyone may come and exercise in the central tower the functions of surveillance, and that, this being the case, he can gain a clear idea of the way in which the surveillance is practised. In fact, any panoptic institution, even if it is as rigorously closed as a penitentiary, may without difficulty be subjected to such irregular and constant inspections: and not only by the appointed inspectors, but also by the public; any member of society will have the right to come and see with his own eyes how the schools, hospitals, factories, prisons function. There is no risk, therefore, that the increase of power created by the panoptic machine may degenerate into tyranny; the disciplinary mechanism will be democratically controlled, since it will be constantly accessible `to the great tribunal committee of the world´.[3] This Panopticon, subtly arranged so that an observer may observe, at a glance, so many different individuals, also enables everyone to come and observe any of the observers. The seeing machine was once a sort of dark room into which individuals spied; it has become a transparent building in which the exercise of power may be supervised by society as a whole.

The panoptic schema, without disappearing as such or losing any of its properties, was destined to spread throughout the social body; its vocation was to become a generalized function. The plague-stricken town provided an exceptional disciplinary model: perfect, but absolutely violent; to the disease that brought death, power opposed its perpetual threat of death; life inside it was reduced to its simplest expression; it was, against the power of death, the meticulous exercise of the right of the sword. The Panopticon, on the other hand, has a role of amplification; although it arranges power, although it is intended to make it more economic and more effective, it does so not for power itself, nor for the immediate salvation of a threatened society: its aim is to strengthen the social forces—to increase production, to develop the economy, spread education, raise the level of public morality; to increase and multiply.

How is power to be strengthened in such a way that, far from impeding progress, far from weighing upon it with its rules and regulations, it actually facilitates such progress? What intensificator of power will be able at the same time to be a multiplicator of production? How will power, by increasing its forces, be able to increase those of society instead of confiscating them or impeding them? The Panopticon's solution to this problem is that the productive increase of power can be assured only if, on the one hand, it can be exercised continuously in the very foundations of society, in the subtlest possible way, and if, on the other hand, it functions outside these sudden, violent, discontinuous forms that are bound up with the exercise of sovereignty. The body of the king, with its strange material and physical presence, with the force that he himself deploys or transmits to some few others, is at the opposite extreme of this new physics of power represented by panopticism; the domain of panopticism is, on the contrary, that whole lower region, that region of irregular bodies, with their details, their multiple movements, their heterogeneous forces, their spatial relations; what are required are mechanisms that analyse distributions, gaps, series, combinations, and which use instruments that render visible, record, differentiate and compare: a physics of a relational and multiple power, which has its maximum intensity not in the person of the king, but in the bodies that can be individualized by these relations. At the theoretical level, Bentham defines another way of analysing the social body and the power relations that traverse it; in terms of practice, he defines a procedure of subordination of bodies and forces that must increase the utility of power while practising the economy of the prince. Panopticism is the general principle of a new `political anatomy´ whose object and end are not the relations of sovereignty but the relations of discipline.

The celebrated, transparent, circular cage, with its high tower, powerful and knowing, may have been for Bentham a project of a perfect disciplinary institution; but he also set out to show how one may `unlock´ the disciplines and get them to function in a diffused, multiple, polyvalent way throughout the whole social body. These disciplines, which the classical age had elaborated in specific, relatively enclosed places—barracks, schools, workshops—and whose total implementation had been imagined only at the limited and temporary scale of a plague-stricken town, Bentham dreamt of transforming into a network of mechanisms that would be everywhere and always alert, running through society without interruption in space or in time. The panoptic arrangement provides the formula for this generalization. It programmes, at the level of an elementary and easily transferable mechanism, the basic functioning of a society penetrated through and through with disciplinary mechanisms.

* * *

There are two images, then, of discipline. At one extreme, the discipline-blockade, the enclosed institution, established on the edges of society, turned inwards towards negative functions: arresting evil, breaking communications, suspending time. At the other extreme, with panopticism, is the discipline-mechanism: a functional mechanism that must improve the exercise of power by making it lighter, more rapid, more effective, a design of subtle coercion for a society to come. The movement from one project to the other, from a schema of exceptional discipline to one of a generalized surveillance, rests on a historical transformation: the gradual extension of the mechanisms of discipline throughout the seventeenth and eighteenth centuries, their spread throughout the whole social body, the formation of what might be called in general the disciplinary society.

A whole disciplinary generalization—the Benthamite physics of power represents an acknowledgement of this—had operated throughout the classical age. The spread of disciplinary institutions, whose network was beginning to cover an ever larger surface and occupying above all a less and less marginal position, testifies to this: what was an islet, a privileged place, a circumstantial measure, or a singular model, became a general formula; the regulations characteristic of the Protestant and pious armies of William of Orange or of Gustavus Adolphus were transformed into regulations for all the armies of Europe; the model colleges of the Jesuits, or the schools of Batencour or Dernia, following the example set by Sturm, provided the outlines for the general forms of educational discipline; the ordering of the naval and military hospitals provided the model for the entire reorganization of hospitals in the eighteenth century. . . .

NOTES

1. In the *Postscript to the Panopticon*, 1791 [1843], Bentham adds dark inspection galleries painted in black around the inspector's lodge, each making it possible to observe two storeys of cells.

2. In his first version of the *Panopticon*, Bentham had also imagined an acoustic surveillance, operated by means of pipes leading from the cells to the central tower. In the *Postscript* he abandoned the idea, perhaps because he could not introduce into it the principle of dis-symmetry and prevent the prisoners from hearing the inspector as well as the inspector hearing them. Julius tried to develop a system of dis-symmetrical listening (Julius, 18).

3. Imagining this continuous flow of visitors entering the central tower by an underground passage and then observing the circular landscape of the Panopticon, was Bentham aware of the Panoramas that Barker was constructing at exactly the same period (the first seems to have dated from 1787) and in which the visitors, occupying the central place, saw unfolding around them a landscape, a city or a battle? The visitors occupied exactly the place of the sovereign gaze.

REFERENCES

Bentham, J., *Works*, ed. Bowring, IV, 1843.
Loisel, G., *Histoire des ménageries*, 11, 1912.

74. ON LIVING IN A LIQUID MODERN WORLD

ZYGMUNT BAUMAN

Zygmunt Bauman (b. 1925), who has lived for many years in England and taught there until his retirement, witnessed as a Polish Jew the authoritarian regimes of both the Nazis and Communists, as they consecutively ruled his native land. He observed first-hand the potent threat of anti-Semitism. While some contemporary intellectuals have seen these ideological movements as anomalies, repudiations of the general trends inherent in modernity, Bauman does not see them as accidents, but rather as emblematic of modernity´s darker side. He has been drawn to postmodern theory, but unlike more radical exponents, he did not think that a complete break had occurred between the worlds of modernity and postmodernity. In recent work, including the selection included here, which is the introduction to his book, *Liquid Life* (2005), he uses the term "liquid" to describe what distinguishes contemporary social life from what preceded it. Liquid modernity—essentially another word for the postmodern condition—is characterized by rapid change that prevents the establishment of established patterns of thought and action, thereby forcing actors to continually adapt and adjust to new circumstances and situations without being able to rely on solid frames of reference.

In skating over thin ice, our safety is in our speed.

Ralph Waldo Emerson, *On Prudence*

"Liquid life" and "liquid modernity" are intimately connected. "Liquid life" is a kind of life that tends to be lived in a liquid modern society. "Liquid modern" is a society in which the conditions under which its members act change faster than it takes the ways of acting to consolidate into habits and routines. Liquidity of life and that of society feed and reinvigorate each other. Liquid life, just like liquid modern society, cannot keep its shape or stay on course for long.

In a liquid modern society, individual achievements cannot be solidified into lasting possessions because, in no time, assets turn into liabilities and abilities into disabilities. Conditions of action and strategies designed to respond to them age quickly and become obsolete before the actors have a chance to learn them properly. Learning from experience in order to rely on strategies and tactical moves deployed successfully in the past is for that reason ill advised: past tests cannot take account of the rapid and mostly unpredicted (perhaps unpredictable) changes in circumstances. Extrapolating from past events to predict future trends becomes ever more risky and all too often misleading. Trustworthy calculations are increasingly difficult to make, while foolproof prognoses are all but unimaginable: most if not all variables in the equations are unknown, whereas no estimates of their future trends can be treated as fully and truly reliable.

In short: liquid life is a precarious life, lived under conditions of constant uncertainty. The most acute and stubborn worries that haunt such a life are the fears of being caught napping, of failing to catch up with fast-moving events, of being left behind, of overlooking "use by" dates, of being saddled with possessions that are no longer desirable, of missing the moment that calls for a change of tack before crossing the point of no return. Liquid life is a succession of new beginnings—yet

Zygmunt Bauman. *Liquid Life*. Cambridge, UK: Polity, 2005 pp. 1–14. ✦

precisely for that reason it is the swift and painless endings, without which new beginnings would be unthinkable, that tend to be its most challenging moments and most upsetting headaches. Among the arts of liquid modern living and the skills needed to practise them, getting rid of things takes precedence over their acquisition.

As the *Observer* cartoonist Andy Riley puts it, the annoyance is "reading articles about the wonders of downshifting when you haven't even managed to upshift yet."[1] One needs to hurry with the "upshifting" if one wants to taste the delights of "downshifting." Getting the site ready for "downshifting" bestows meaning on the "upshifting" bit, and becomes its main purpose; it is by the relief brought by a smooth and painless "downshifting" that the quality of "upshifting" will be ultimately judged ...

The briefing which the practitioners of liquid modern life need most (and are most often offered by the expert counsellors in the life arts) is not how to start or open, but how to finish or close. Another *Observer* columnist, with a tongue only halfway to his cheek, lists the updated rules for "achieving closure" of partnerships (the episodes no doubt more difficult to "close" than any other—yet the ones where the partners all too often wish and fight to close them, and so where there is unsurprisingly a particularly keen demand for expert help). The list starts from "Remember bad stuff. Forget the good" and ends with "Meet someone new," passing midway the command "Delete all electronic correspondence." Throughout, the emphasis falls on forgetting, deleting, dropping and replacing.

Perhaps the description of liquid modern life as a series of new *beginnings* is an inadvertent accessory to a conspiracy of sorts; by replicating a commonly shared illusion it helps to hide its most closely guarded (since shameful, if only residually so) secret. Perhaps a more adequate way to narrate that life is to tell the story of successive *endings*. And perhaps the glory of the successfully lived liquid life would be better conveyed by the inconspicuousness of the graves that mark its progress than by the ostentation of gravestones that commemorate the contents of the tombs.

In a liquid modern society, the waste-disposal industry takes over the commanding positions in liquid life's economy. The survival of that society and the well-being of its members hang on the swiftness with which products are consigned to waste and the speed and efficiency of waste removal. In that society nothing may claim exemption from the universal rule of disposability, and nothing may be allowed to outstay its welcome. The steadfastness, stickiness, viscosity of things inanimate and animate alike are the most sinister and terminal of dangers, sources of the most frightening of fears and the targets of the most violent of assaults.

Life in a liquid modern society cannot stand still. It must modernize (read: go on stripping itself daily of attributes that are past their sell-by dates and go on dismantling/shedding the identities currently assembled/put on)—or perish. Nudged from behind by the horror of expiry, life in a liquid modern society no longer needs to be pulled forward by imagined wonders at the far end of modernizing labours. The need here is to run with all one's strength just to stay in the same place and away from the rubbish bin where the hindmost are doomed to land.

"Creative destruction" is the fashion in which liquid life proceeds, but what that term glosses over and passes by in silence is that what this creation destroys are other forms of life and so obliquely the humans who practise them. Life in the liquid modern society is a sinister version of the musical chairs game, played for real. The true stake in the race is (temporary) rescue from being excluded into the ranks of the destroyed and avoiding being consigned to waste. And with the competition turning global, the running must now be done round a global track.

The greatest chances of winning belong to the people who circulate close to the top of the global power pyramid, to whom space matters little and distance is not a bother; people at home in many places but in no one place in particular. They are as light, sprightly and volatile as the increasingly global and extraterritorial trade and finances that assisted at their birth and sustain their nomadic existence. As Jacques Attali described them, "they do not own factories, lands, nor occupy administrative positions. Their wealth comes from a portable asset: their knowledge of the laws of the labyrinth." They "love to create, play and be on the move." They live in a society `of volatile values, carefree about the future, egoistic and hedonistic´. They "take novelty as good tidings, precariousness as value, instability as imperative, hybridity as "richness."[2] In varying degrees, they all master and practise the art of "liquid life": acceptance of disorientation, immunity to vertigo and adaptation to a state of dizziness, tolerance for an absence of itinerary and direction, and for an indefinite duration of travel.

They try hard, though with mixed success, to follow the pattern set by Bill Gates, that paragon of business success, whom Richard Sennett described as marked by "his willingness to destroy what he has made" and his "tolerance for fragmentation," as "someone who has the confidence to dwell in disorder, someone who flourishes in the midst of dislocation" and someone positioning himself "in a network of possibilities," rather than "paralysing" himself in "one particular job."[3] Their ideal horizon is likely to be Eutropia, one of Italo Calvino´s *Invisible Cities* whose inhabitants, the day they "feel the grip of weariness and no one can any longer bear his job, his relatives, his house and his life," "move to the next city" where "each will take a new job, a different wife, will see another landscape on opening the window, and will spend his time with different pastimes, friends, gossip."[4]

Looseness of attachment and revocability of engagement are the precepts guiding everything in which they engage and to which they are attached. Presumably addressing such people, the anonymous columnist of the *Observer* who hides under the penname of the Barefoot Doctor counselled his readers to do everything they do "with grace." Taking a hint from Lao-tzu, the oriental prophet of detachment and tranquillity, he described the life stance most likely to achieve that effect:

> Flowing like water...you swiftly move along, never fighting the current, stopping long enough to become stagnant or clinging to the riverbank or rocks—the possessions, situations or people that pass through your life—not even trying to hold on to your opinions or world view, but simply sticking lightly yet intelligently to whatever presents itself as you pass by and then graciously letting it go without grasping ...[5]

Faced with such players, the rest of the participants of the game—and particularly the involuntary ones among them, those who don´t "love" or cannot afford "to be on the move"—stand little chance. Joining in the game is not a realistic choice for them—but neither have they the choice of not trying. Flitting between flowers in search of the most fragrant is not their option; they are stuck to places where flowers, fragrant or not, are rare—and so can only watch haplessly as the few that there are fade or rot. The suggestion to "stick lightly to whatever presents itself" and "graciously let it go" would sound at best like a cruel joke in their ears, but mostly like a heartless sneer.

Nevertheless, "stick lightly" they must, as "possessions, situations and people" will keep slipping away and vanishing at a breathtaking speed whatever they do; whether they try to slow them down or not is neither here nor there. "Let them go" they must (though, unlike Bill Gates, with hardly any pleasure), but whether they do it graciously or with a lot of wailing and teeth-gnashing is beside the point. They might be forgiven for suspecting some connection between that comely lightness and grace paraded by those who glide by and their own unchosen ugly torpidity and importance to move.

Their indolence is, indeed, unchosen. Lightness and grace come together with freedom—freedom to move, freedom to choose, freedom to stop being what one already is and freedom to become what one is not yet. Those on the receiving side of the new planetary mobility don´t have such freedom. They can count neither on the forbearance of those from whom they would rather keep their distance, nor on the tolerance of those to whom they would wish to be closer. For them, there are neither unguarded exits nor hospitably open entry gates. They *belong*: those to whom or with whom they belong view their belonging as their non-negotiable and incontrovertible *duty* (even if disguised as their inalienable *right*)—whereas those whom they would wish to join see their belonging rather as their similarly non-negotiable, irreversible and unredeemable *fate*. The first wouldn´t let them go, whereas the second wouldn´t let them in.

Between the start and the (unlikely ever to happen) arrival is a desert, a void, a wilderness, a yawning abyss into which only a few would muster the courage to leap of their own free will, unpushed. Centripetal and centrifugal, gravitational and repelling forces combine to keep the restless in place and stop the discontented short of restlessness. Those hot-headed or desperate enough to try to defy the odds stacked against them risk the lot of outlaws and outcasts, and pay for their audacity in the hard currency of bodily misery and psychical trauma—a price which only a few would choose to pay of their own free will, unforced. Andrzej Szahaj, a most perceptive analyst of the highly uneven odds in contemporary identity games, goes as far as to suggest that the decision to leave the community of belonging is in quite numerous cases downright unimaginable; he goes on to remind his incredulous Western readers that in the remote past of Europe, for instance in ancient Greece, exile from the *polis* of belonging was viewed as the ultimate, indeed capital, punishment.[6] At least the ancients were cool-headed and preferred straight talk. But the millions of *sans papiers*, stateless, refugees, exiles, asylum or bread-and-water seekers of our times, two millennia later, would have little difficulty in recognizing themselves in that talk.

At both extremes of the hierarchy (and in the main body of the pyramid locked between them in a double-bind) people are haunted by the problem of identity. At the top, the problem is to choose the best pattern from the many currently on offer, to assemble the separately sold parts of the kit, and to fasten them together neither too lightly (lest the unsightly, outdated and aged bits that are meant to be hidden underneath show through at the seams) nor too tightly (lest the patchwork resists being dismantled at short notice when the time for dismantling comes—as it surely will). At the bottom, the problem is to cling fast to the sole identity available and to hold its bits and parts together while fighting back the erosive forces and disruptive pressures, repairing the constantly crumbling walls and digging the trenches deeper. For all the others suspended between the extremes, the problem is a mixture of the two.

Taking a hint from Joseph Brodsky's profile of materially affluent yet spiritually impoverished and famished contemporaries, tired like the residents of Calvino's Eutropia of everything they have enjoyed thus far (like yoga, Buddhism, Zen, contemplation, Mao) and so beginning to dig (with the help of state-of-the-art technology, of course) into the mysteries of Sufism, kabbala or Sunnism to beef up their flagging

desire to desire, Andrzej Stasiuk, one of the most perceptive archivists of contemporary cultures and their discontents, develops a typology of the "spiritual lumpenproletariat" and suggests that its ranks swell fast and that its torments trickle profusely down from the top, saturating ever thicker layers of the social pyramid.[7]

Those affected by the "spiritual lumpenproletarian" virus live in the present and by the present. They live to survive (as long as possible) and to get satisfaction (as much of it as possible). Since the world is not their home ground and not their property (having relieved themselves of the burdens of heritage, they feel free but somehow disinherited—robbed of something, betrayed by someone), they see nothing wrong in exploiting it at will; exploitation feels like nothing more odious than stealing back the stolen.

Flattened into a perpetual present and filled to the brim with survival-and-gratification concerns (it is gratification to survive, the purpose of survival being more gratification), the world inhabited by "spiritual lumpenproletarians" leaves no room for worries about anything other than what can be, at least in principle, consumed and relished on the spot, here and now.

Eternity is the obvious outcast. Not infinity, though; as long as it lasts, the present may be stretched beyond any limit and accommodate as much as once was hoped to be experienced only in the fullness of time (in Stasiuk's words, "it is highly probable that the quantity of digital, celluloid and analogue beings met in the course of a bodily life comes close to the volume which eternal life and resurrection of the flesh could offer"). Thanks to the hoped-for infinity of mundane experiences yet to come, eternity may not be missed; its loss may not even be noticed.

Speed, not duration, matters. With the right speed, one can consume the whole of eternity inside the continuous present of earthly life. Or this at least is what the "spiritual lumpenproletarians" try, and hope, to achieve. The trick is to compress eternity so that it may fit, whole, into the timespan of individual life. The quandary of a mortal life in an immortal universe has been finally resolved: one can now stop worrying about things eternal and lose nothing of eternity's wonders—indeed one can exhaust whatever eternity could possibly offer, all in the timespan of one mortal life. One cannot perhaps take the time-lid off mortal life; but one can (or at least try to) remove all limits from the volume of satisfactions to be experienced before reaching that other, irremovable limit.

In a bygone world in which time moved much slower and resisted acceleration, people tried to bridge the agonizing gap between the poverty of a short and mortal life and the infinite wealth of the eternal universe by hopes of reincarnation or resurrection. In our world that knows or admits of no limits to acceleration, such hopes may well be discarded. If only one moves quickly enough and does not stop to look back and count the gains and losses, one can go on squeezing into the timespan of mortal life ever more lives; perhaps as many as eternity could supply. What else, if not to act on that belief, are the unstoppable, compulsive and obsessive reconditioning, refurbishment, recycling, overhaul and reconstitution of identity for? "Identity," after all, is (just as the reincarnation and resurrection of olden times used to be) about the possibility of "being born again"—of stopping being what one is and turning into someone one is not yet.

The good news is that this replacement of worries about eternity with an identity-recycling bustle comes complete with patented and ready-to-use DIY tools that promise to make the job fast and effective while needing no special skills and calling for little if any difficult and awkward labour. Self-sacrifice and self-immolation, unbearably long and unrelenting self-drilling and self-taming, waiting for gratification that feels interminable and practising virtues that seem to exceed endurance— all those exorbitant costs of past therapies—are no longer required. New and improved diets, fitness gadgets, changes of wallpaper, parquets put where carpets used to lie (or vice versa), replacements of a mini with an SUV (or the other way round), a T-shirt with a blouse and monochromatic with richly colour-saturated sofa covers or dresses, sizes of breasts moved up or down, sneakers changed, brands of booze and daily routines adapted to the latest fashion and a strikingly novel vocabulary adopted in which to couch public confessions of intimate soul-stirrings . . . these will do nicely. And, as a last resort, on the vexingly far horizon loom the wonders of gene overhaul. Whatever happens, there is no need to despair. If all those magic wants prove not to be enough or, despite all their user-friendliness, are found too cumbersome or too slow, there are drugs promising an instant, even if brief, visit to eternity (hopefully with other drugs guaranteeing a return ticket).

Liquid life is consuming life. It casts the world and all its animate and inanimate fragments as objects of consumption: that is, objects that lose their usefulness (and so their lustre, attraction, seductive power and worth) in the course of being used. It shapes the judging and evaluating of all the animate and inanimate fragments of the world after the pattern of objects of consumption.

Objects of consumption have a limited expectation of useful life and once the limit has been passed they are unfit for consumption; since "being good for consumption" is the sole feature that defines their function, they are then unfit altogether—useless. Once unfit, they ought to be removed from the site of consuming life (consigned to biodegradation, incinerated, transferred into the care of waste-disposal companies) to clear it for other, still unused objects of consumption.

To save yourself from the embarrassment of lagging behind, of being stuck with something no one else would be seen with, of being caught napping, of missing the train of progress instead of riding it, you must remember that it is in the nature of things to call for vigilance, not loyalty. In the liquid modern world, loyalty is a cause of shame, not pride. Link to your internet provider first thing in the morning, and you will be reminded of that sober truth by the main item on the list of daily news: "Ashamed of your Mobile? Is your phone so old that you're embarrassed to answer it? Upgrade to one you can be proud of." The flipside of the commandment "to upgrade" to a state-of-consumer-correctness mobile is, of course, the prohibition any longer to be seen holding the one to which you upgraded last time.

Waste is the staple and arguably the most profuse product of the liquid modern society of consumers; among consumer society's industries waste production is the most massive and the most immune to crisis. That makes waste disposal one of the two major challenges liquid life has to confront and tackle. The other major challenge is the threat of being consigned to waste. In a world filled with consumers and the objects of their consumption, life is hovering uneasily between the joys of consumption and the horrors of the rubbish heap. Life may be at all times a living-towards-death, but in a liquid modern society living-towards-the-refuse dump may be a more immediate and more energy-and-labour-consuming prospect and concern of the living.

For the denizen of the liquid modern society, every supper—unlike that referred to by Hamlet in his reply to the King's inquiry about Polonius's whereabouts—is an occasion "where he eats" *and* "where he is eaten."[8] No longer is there a disjunction between the two acts. "And" has replaced the "either-or." In the society of consumers, no one can escape being an object of consumption—and not just consumption by maggots, and not only at the far end of consuming life. Hamlet in liquid modern times would probably modify Shakespeare's Hamlet's rule, denying the maggots' privileged role in the consumption of the consumers. He would perhaps start, like the original Hamlet, stating that "We fat all creatures else to fat us, and we fat ourselves..."—but then conclude: "to fat other creatures."

"Consumers" and "objects of consumption" are the conceptual poles of a continuum along which all members of the society of consumers are plotted and along which they move, to and fro, daily. Some may be cast most of the time particularly near to the commodities' pole—but no consumer can be fully and truly insured against falling into its close, too close for comfort, proximity. Only as commodities, only if they are able to demonstrate their own use-value, can consumers gain access to consuming life. In liquid life, the distinction between consumers and objects of consumption is all too often momentary and ephemeral, and always conditional. We may say that role reversal is the rule here, though even that statement distorts the realities of liquid life, in which the two roles intertwine, blend and merge.

It is not clear which of the two factors (attractions of the "consumer" pole, or the repulsion of the "waste" pole) is the more powerful moving force of liquid life. No doubt both factors cooperate in shaping the daily logic and—bit by bit, episode by episode–the itinerary of that life. Fear adds strength to desire. However attentively it focuses on its immediate objects, desire cannot help but remain aware—consciously, half-consciously or subconsciously—of that other awesome stake hanging on its vigour, determination and resourcefulness. However intensely concentrated on the *object* of desire, the eye of the consumer cannot but glance sideways at the commodity value of the desiring *subject*.

Liquid life means constant self-scrutiny, self-critique and self-censure. Liquid life feeds on the self's dissatisfaction with *itself*.

Critique is self-referential and inward directed; and so is the reform which such self-critique demands and prompts. It is in the name of such inward-looking and inward-targeted reform that the outside world is preyed upon, ransacked and ravaged. Liquid life endows the outside world, indeed everything in the world that is not a part of the self, with a primarily instrumental value; deprived of or denied a value of its own, that world derives all its value from its service to the cause of self-reform, and by their contribution to that self-reform the world and each of its elements are judged. Parts of the world unfit to serve or no longer able to serve are either left outside the realm of relevance and unattended, or actively discarded and swept away. Such parts are but the waste from self-reforming zeal, the rubbish tip being their natural destination. In terms of liquid life's reasoning their preservation would be irrational; their right to be preserved for their own sake cannot be easily argued, let alone proved, by liquid life's logic.

It is for that reason that the advent of liquid modern society spelled the demise of utopias centred on society and more generally of the idea of the "good society." If liquid life prompts an interest in societal reform at all, the postulated reform is aimed mostly at pushing society further towards the surrender, one by one, of all its pretences to a value of its own except that of a police force guarding the security of self-reforming selves, and towards the acceptance and entrenchment of the principle of compensation (a political version of a "money back guarantee") in case the policing fails or is found inadequate. Even the new environmental concerns owe their popularity to the perception of a link between the predatory misuse of the planetary commons and threats to the smooth flow of the self-centred pursuits of liquid life.

The trend is self-sustained and self-invigorating. The focusing on self-reform self-perpetuates; so does the lack of interest in, and the inattention to, the aspects of common life that resist a complete and immediate translation into the current targets of self-reform. Inattention to the conditions of life in common precludes the possibility of renegotiating the setting that makes individual life liquid. The success of the pursuit of happiness—the ostensible purpose and paramount motive of individual life—continues to be defied by the very fashion of pursuing it (the only fashion in which it can be pursued in the liquid modern setting). The resulting unhappiness adds reason and vigour to a self-centred life politics; its ultimate effect is the perpetuation of life´s liquidity. Liquid modern society and liquid life are locked in a veritable perpetuum mobile.

Once set in motion, a perpetuum mobile will not stop rotating on its own. The prospects of the perpetual motion arresting, already dim by the nature of the contraption, are made still dimmer by the amazing ability of this particular version of the self-propelling mechanism to absorb and assimilate the tensions and frictions it generates—and to harness them to its service. Indeed, by capitalizing on the demand for relief or cure which the tensions incite, it manages to deploy them as high-grade fuel that keeps its engines going.

A habitual answer given to a wrong kind of behaviour, to conduct unsuitable for an accepted purpose or leading to undesirable outcomes, is education or re-education: instilling in the learners new kinds of motives, developing different propensities and training them in deploying new skills. The thrust of education in such cases is to challenge the impact of daily experience, to fight back and in the end defy the pressures arising from the social setting in which the learners operate. But will the education and the educators fit the bill? Will they themselves be able to resist the pressure? Will they manage to avoid being enlisted in the service of the self-same pressures they are meant to defy? This question has been asked since ancient times, repeatedly answered in the negative by the realities of social life, yet resurrected with undiminished force following every successive calamity. The hopes of using education as a jack potent enough to unsettle and ultimately to dislodge the pressures of "social facts" seem to be as immortal as they are vulnerable...

At any rate, the hope is alive and well. Henry A. Giroux dedicated many years of assiduous study to the chances of "critical pedagogy" in a society reconciled to the overwhelming powers of the market. In a recent conclusion, drawn in cooperation with Susan Searls Giroux, he restates the centuries-old hope:

In opposition to the commodification, privatization, and commercialization of everything educational, educators need to define higher education as a resource vital to the democratic and civic life of the nation. The challenge is thus for academics, cultural workers, students, and labour organizers to join together and oppose the transformation of higher education into a commercial sphere...[9]

In 1989, Richard Rorty spelled out, as desirable and fulfillable aims for the educators, the tasks of "stirring the kids up" and instilling "doubts in the students about the students´ own self-images, about the society in which they belong."[10] Obviously, not all the people employed in the educator´s role are likely to take up the challenge and adopt these aims as their own; the offices and the corridors of academia are filled with two kinds of people—some of them "busy conforming to well-understood criteria for making contributions to knowledge," and the others trying "to expand their own moral imagination" and read books "in order to enlarge their sense of what is possible and important—either for themselves as individuals or for their society." Rorty´s appeal is addressed to the second kind of people, as only in that category are his hopes vested. And he knows well against what overwhelming odds the teacher likely to respond to the clarion call will need to battle. "We cannot tell boards of trustees, government commissions, and the like, that our function is to stir things up, to make our society feel guilty, to keep it off balance," or indeed (as he suggests elsewhere) that higher education" is also not a matter of including or educing truth. It is, instead, a matter of inciting doubt and stimulating imagination, thereby challenging the prevailing consensus."[11] There is a tension between public rhetoric and the sense of intellectual mission—and that tension "leaves the academy in general, and the humanistic intellectuals in particular, vulnerable to heresy hunters." Given that the opposite messages of the promoters of conformity are powerfully backed by the ruling *doxa* and the daily evidence of commonsensical experience, it also, we may add, makes the "humanistic intellectuals" sitting targets for the advocates of the end of history, rational choice, "there is no alternative" life policies and other formulae attempting to grasp and convey the current and postulated impetus of an apparently invincible societal dynamic. It invites charges of unrealism, utopianism, wishful thinking, daydreaming—and, adding insult to injury in an odious reversal of ethical truth, of irresponsibility.

Adverse odds may be overwhelming, and yet a democratic (or, as Cornelius Castoriadis would say, an autonomous) society knows of no substitute for education and self-education as a means to influence the turn of events that can be squared with its own nature, while that nature cannot be preserved for long without "critical pedagogy"—education sharpening

its critical edge, "making society feel guilty" and "stirring things up" through stirring human consciences. The fates of freedom, of democracy that makes it possible while being made possible by it, and of education that breeds dissatisfaction with the level of both freedom and democracy achieved thus far, are inextricably connected and not to be detached from one another. One may view that intimate connection as another specimen of a vicious circle—but it is within that circle that human hopes and the chances of humanity are inscribed, and can be nowhere else.

NOTES

1. See *Observer Magazine*, 3 Oct. 2004.
2. Jacques Attali, *Chemins de sagesse. Traité du labyrinthe* (Fayard, 1996), pp. 79-80, 109.
3. See Richard Sennett, *The Corrosion of Character: The Personal Consequences of Work in the New Capitalism* (W. W. Norton, 1998), p. 62.
4. Italo Calvino, *Le città invisibili*, quoted here after the translation by William Weaver, *Invisible Cities* (Vintage, 1997), p. 64.
5. See `Grace under pressure´, *Observer Magazine*, 30 Nov. 2003, p. 95.
6. Andrzej Szahaj, *E pluribus unum*, (Universitas, 2004), p. 81.
7. See Andrzej Stasiuk, "Duchowy lumpenproletariat" ("Spiritual lumpenproletariat") and "Rewolucja czyli zaglada" ("Revolution, or extermination"), in *Tekturowy Samolot* (Wydawnictwo Czarne, 2002).
8. See Shakespeare, *Hamlet*, Act IV, scene iii.
9. See Henry A. Giroux and Susan Searls Giroux, *Take Back Higher Education* (Palgrave, 2004), pp. 119–20.
10. See Richard Rorty, "The humanistic intellectual: eleven theses," in *Philosophy and Social Hope* (Penguin, 1999), pp. 127-8.
11. In "Education as socialization and as individualization," in *Philosophy and Social Hope*, p. 118.

75. THE POSTMODERN CONDITION: A REPORT ON KNOWLEDGE

JEAN-FRANÇOIS LYOTARD

Jean-François Lyotard's (1924–1998) *The Postmodern Condition*, published in France in 1979, is considered one of the earliest and subsequently most widely cited statements on postmodern culture. As with some other French intellectuals who made the postmodern turn, Lyotard engaged in militant leftist politics during the 1950s and '60s, including being involved with the militants who founded the journal *Socialisme ou Barbarie*. He served as its expert on matters related to the political struggle in Algeria, seeking to determine whether the situation was ripe for socialist revolution. Splitting with that group, he continued his activism with a splinter group called *Pouvoir Ouvrier* (Worker's Power) and played a role in the 1968 movement for radical change. In the aftermath of that year of revolt, he abandoned Marxist politics. All this background is relevant to his understanding of the culture of postmodern society. His beginning assumption is that just as the economies of the developed world were becoming postindustrial, so the culture was entering a new epoch beyond the modern. In this excerpt from the introductory sections of *The Postmodern Condition*, Lyotard calls into question what he refers to as metanarratives, by which he means totalizing accounts of social change and the advancement of knowledge. In particular, he takes aim at accounts promoting ideas of historical progress and treating society as a unified totality.

---

1. THE FIELD: KNOWLEDGE IN COMPUTERISED SOCIETIES

Our working hypothesis is that the status of knowledge is altered as societies enter what is known as the post-industrial age and cultures enter what is known as the postmodern age. This transition has been under way since at least the end of the 1950s, which for Europe marks the completion of reconstruction. The pace is faster or slower depending on the country, and within countries it varies according to the sector of activity: the general situation is one of temporal disjunction which makes sketching an overview difficult. A portion of the description would necessarily be conjectural. At any rate, we know that it is unwise to put too much faith in futurology.

Rather than painting a picture that would inevitably remain incomplete, I will take as my point of departure a single feature, one that immediately defines our object of study. Scientific knowledge is a kind of discourse. And it is fair to say that for the last forty years the "leading" sciences and technologies have had to do with language: phonology and theories of linguistics, problems of communication and cybernetics, modern theories of algebra and informatics, computers and their languages, problems of translation and the search for areas of compatibility among computer languages, problems of information storage and data banks, telematics and the perfection of intelligent terminals, to paradoxology. The facts speak for themselves (and this list is not exhaustive).

These technological transformations can be expected to have a considerable impact on knowledge. Its two principal functions—research and the transmission of acquired learning—are already feeling the effect, or will in the future. With respect to the first function, genetics provides an example that is accessible to the layman: it owes its theoretical paradigm to cybernetics. Many other examples could be cited. As for the second function, it is common knowledge that the miniaturisation and commercialisation of machines is already changing the way in which learning is acquired, classified, made available, and exploited. It is reasonable to suppose that the proliferation of information-processing machines is having, and will continue to have, as much of an effect on the circulation of learning as did advancements in human circulation (transportation systems) and later, in the circulation of sounds and visual images (the media).

The nature of knowledge cannot survive unchanged within this context of general transformation. It can fit into the new channels, and become operational, only if learning is translated into quantities of information. We can predict that anything in the constituted body of knowledge that is not translatable in this way will be abandoned and that the direction of new research will be dictated by the possibility of its eventual results being translatable into computer language. The "producers" and users of knowledge must now, and will have to, possess the means of translating into these languages whatever they want to invent or learn. Research on translating machines is already well advanced. Along with the hegemony of computers comes a certain logic, and therefore a certain set of prescriptions determining which statements are accepted as "knowledge" statements.

We may thus expect a thorough exteriorisation of knowledge with respect to the "knower," at whatever point he or she may occupy in the knowledge process. The old principle that the acquisition of knowledge is indissociable from the training (*Bildung*) of minds, or even of individuals, is becoming obsolete and will become ever more so. The relationships of the suppliers and users of knowledge to the knowledge they supply and use is now tending, and will increasingly tend, to assume the form already taken by the relationship of commodity producers and consumers to the commodities they produce and consume—that is, the form of value. Knowledge is and will be produced in order to be sold, it is and will be consumed in order to be valorised in a new production: in both cases, the goal is exchange.

Knowledge ceases to be an end in itself, it loses its "use-value."

It is widely accepted that knowledge has become the principle [sic] force of production over the last few decades, this has already had a noticeable effect on the composition of the work force of the most highly developed countries and constitutes the major bottleneck for the developing countries. In the postindustrial and postmodern age, science will maintain and no doubt strengthen its preeminence in the arsenal of productive capacities of the nation-states. Indeed, this situation is one of the reasons leading to the conclusion that the gap between developed and developing countries will grow ever wider in the future.

But this aspect of the problem should not be allowed to overshadow the other, which is complementary to it. Knowledge in the form of an informational commodity indispensable to productive power is already, and will continue to be, a major—perhaps the major—stake in the worldwide competition for power. It is conceivable that the nation-states will one day fight for control of information, just as they battled in the past for control over territory, and afterwards for control of access to and exploitation of raw materials and cheap labor. A new field is opened for industrial and commercial strategies on the one hand, and political and military strategies on the other.

However, the perspective I have outlined above is not as simple as I have made it appear. For the merchantilisation of knowledge is bound to affect the privilege the nation-states have enjoyed, and still enjoy, with respect to the production and distribution of learning. The notion that learning falls within the purview of the State, as the brain or mind of society, will become more and more outdated with the increasing strength of the opposing principle, according to which society exists and progresses only if the messages circulating within it are rich in information and easy to decode. The ideology of communicational "transparency," which goes hand in hand with the commercialisation of knowledge, will begin to perceive the State as a factor of opacity and "noise." It is from this point of view that the problem of the relationship between economic and State powers threatens to arise with a new urgency.

Already in the last few decades, economic powers have reached the point of imperilling the stability of the state through new forms of the circulation of capital that go by the generic name of *multi-national corporations*. These new forms of circulation imply that investment decisions have, at least in part, passed beyond the control of the nation-states. The question threatens to become even more thorny with the development of computer technology and telematics. Suppose, for example, that a firm such as IBM is authorised to occupy a belt in the earth's orbital field and launch communications satellites or satellites housing data banks. Who will have access to them? Who will determine which channels or data are forbidden? The State? Or will the State simply be one user among others? New legal issues will be raised, and with them the question: "who will know?"

Transformation in the nature of knowledge, then, could well have repercussions on the existing public powers, forcing them to reconsider their relations (both *de jure* and *de facto*) with the large corporations and, more generally, with civil society. The reopening of the world market, a return to vigorous economic competition, the breakdown of the hegemony of American capitalism, the decline of the socialist alternative, a probable opening of the Chinese market these and many other factors are already, at the end of the 1970s, preparing States for a serious reappraisal of the role they have been accustomed to playing since the 1930s: that of, guiding, or even directing investments. In this light, the new technologies can only increase the urgency of such a re-examination, since they make the information used in decision making (and therefore the means of control) even more mobile and subject to piracy.

It is not hard to visualise learning circulating along the same lines as money, instead of for its "educational" value or political (administrative, diplomatic, military) importance; the pertinent distinction would no longer be between knowledge and ignorance, but rather, as is the case with money, between "payment knowledge" and "investment knowledge"—in other words, between units of knowledge exchanged in a daily maintenance framework (the reconstitution of the work force, "survival") versus funds of knowledge dedicated to optimising the performance of a project.

If this were the case, communicational transparency would be similar to liberalism. Liberalism does not preclude an organisation of the flow of money in which some channels are used in decision making while others are only good for the payment of debts. One could similarly imagine flows of knowledge travelling along identical channels of identical nature, some of which would be reserved for the "decision makers," while the others would be used to repay each person's perpetual debt with respect to the social bond.

2. THE PROBLEM: LEGITIMATION

That is the working hypothesis defining the field within which I intend to consider the question of the status of knowledge. This scenario, akin to the one that goes by the name "the computerisation of society" (although ours is advanced in an entirely different spirit), makes no claims of being original, or even true. What is required of a working hypothesis is a fine capacity for discrimination. The scenario of the computerisation of the most highly developed societies allows us to spotlight (though with the risk of excessive magnification) certain aspects of the transformation of knowledge and its effects on public power and civil institutions—effects it would be difficult to perceive from other points of view. Our hypotheses, therefore, should not be accorded predictive value in relation to reality, but strategic value in relation to the question raised.

Nevertheless, it has strong credibility, and in that sense our choice of this hypothesis is not arbitrary. It has been described extensively by the experts and is already guiding certain decisions by the governmental agencies and private firms most directly concerned, such as those managing the telecommunications industry. To some extent, then, it is already a part of observable reality. Finally, barring economic stagnation or a general recession (resulting, for example, from a continued failure to solve the world's energy problems), there is a good chance that this scenario will come to pass: it is hard to see what other direction contemporary technology could take as an alternative to the computerisation of society.

This is as much as to say that the hypothesis is banal. But only to the extent that it fails to challenge the general paradigm of progress in science and technology, to which economic growth and the expansion of sociopolitical power seem to be natural complements. That scientific and technical knowledge is cumulative is never questioned. At most, what is debated is the form that accumulation takes—some picture it as regular, continuous, and unanimous, others as periodic, discontinuous, and conflictual.

But these truisms are fallacious. In the first place, scientific knowledge does not represent the totality of knowledge; it has always existed in addition to, and in competition and conflict with, another kind of knowledge, which I will call narrative in the interests of simplicity (its characteristics will be described later). I do not mean to say that narrative knowledge can prevail over science, but its model is related to ideas of internal equilibrium and conviviality next to which contemporary scientific knowledge cuts a poor figure, especially if it is to undergo an exteriorisation with respect to the "knower" and an alienation from its user even greater than has previously been the case. The resulting demoralisation of researchers and teachers is far from negligible; it is well known that during the 1960s, in all of the most highly developed societies, it reached such explosive dimensions among those preparing to practice these professions—the students—that there was noticeable decrease in productivity at laboratories and universities unable to protect themselves from its contamination. Expecting this, with hope or fear, to lead to a revolution (as was then often the case) is out of the question: it will not change the order of things in postindustrial society overnight. But this doubt on the part of scientists must be taken into account as a major factor in evaluating the present and future status of scientific knowledge.

It is all the more necessary to take it into consideration since—and this is the second point—the scientists' demoralisation has an impact on the central problem of legitimation. I use the word in a broader sense than do contemporary German theorists in their discussions of the question of authority. Take any civil law as an example: it states that a given category of citizens must perform a specific kind of action. Legitimation is the process by which a legislator is authorised to promulgate such a law as a norm. Now take the example of a scientific statement: it is subject to the rule that a statement must fulfil a given set of conditions in order to be accepted as scientific. In this case, legitimation is the process by which a "legislator" dealing with scientific discourse is authorised to prescribe the stated conditions (in general, conditions of internal consistency and experimental verification) determining whether a statement is to be included in that discourse for consideration by the scientific community.

The parallel may appear forced. But as we will see, it is not. The question of the legitimacy of science has been indissociably linked to that of the legitimation of the legislator since the time of Plato. From this point of view, the right to decide what is true is not independent of the right to decide what is just, even if the statements consigned to these two authorities differ in nature. The point is that there is a strict interlinkage between the kind of language called science and the kind called ethics and politics: they both stem from the same perspective, the same "choice" if you will—the choice called the Occident.

When we examine the current status of scientific knowledge at a time when science seems more completely subordinated to the prevailing powers than ever before and, along with the new technologies, is in danger of becoming a major stake in their conflicts—the question of double legitimation, far from receding into the background, necessarily comes to the fore. For it appears in its most complete form, that of reversion, revealing that knowledge and power are simply two sides of the same question: who decides what knowledge is, and who knows what needs to be decided? In the computer age, the question of knowledge is now more than ever a question of government.

3. THE METHOD: LANGUAGE GAMES

The reader will already have noticed that in analysing this problem within the framework set forth I have favoured a certain procedure: emphasising facts of language and in particular their pragmatic aspect. To help clarify what follows it would be useful to summarise, however briefly, what is meant here by the term *pragmatic*.

A denotative utterance such as "The university is sick," made in the context of a conversation or an interview, positions its sender (the person who utters the statement), its addressee (the person who receives it), and its referent (what the statement deals with) in a specific way: the utterance places (and exposes) the sender in the position of "knower" (he knows what the situation is with the university), the addressee is put in the position of having to give or refuse his assent, and the referent itself is handled in a way unique to denotatives, as something that demands to be correctly identified and expressed by the statement that refers to it.

If we consider a declaration such as "The university is open," pronounced by a dean or rector at convocation, it is clear that the previous specifications no longer apply. Of course, the meaning of the utterance has to be understood, but that is a general condition of communication and does not aid us in distinguishing the different kinds of utterances or their specific effects. The distinctive feature of this second, "performative," utterance is that its effect upon the referent coincides with its enunciation. The university is open because it has been declared open in the above-mentioned circumstances. That this is so is not subject to discussion or verification on the part of the addressee, who is immediately placed within the new context created by the utterance. As for the sender, he must be invested with the authority to make such a statement. Actually, we could say it the other way around: the sender is dean or rector that is, he is invested with the authority to make this kind of statement—only insofar as he can directly affect both the referent, (the university) and the addressee (the university staff) in the manner I have indicated.

A different case involves utterances of the type, "Give money to the university"; these are prescriptions. They can be modulated as orders, commands, instructions, recommendations, requests, prayers, pleas, etc. Here, the sender is clearly placed in a position of authority, using the term broadly (including the authority of a sinner over a god who claims to be merciful): that is, he expects the addressee to perform the action referred to. The pragmatics of prescription entail concomitant changes in the posts of addressee and referent.

Of a different order again is the efficiency of a question, a promise, a literary description, a narration, etc. I am summarising. Wittgenstein, taking up the study of language again from scratch, focuses his attention on the effects of different modes of discourse; he calls the various types of utterances he identifies along the way (a few of which I have listed) *language games*. What he means by this term is that each of the various categories of utterance can be defined in terms of rules specifying their properties and the uses to which they can be put—in exactly the same way as the game of chess is defined by a set of rules determining the properties of each of the pieces, in other words, the proper way to move them.

It is useful to make the following three observations about language games. The first is that their rules do not carry within themselves their own legitimation, but are the object of a contract, explicit or not, between players (which is not to say that the players invent the rules). The second is that if there are no rules, there is no game, that even an infinitesimal modification of one rule alters the nature of the game, that a "move" or utterance that does not satisfy the rules does not belong to the game they define. The third remark is suggested by what has just been said: every utterance should be thought of as a "move" in a game.

This last observation brings us to the first principle underlying our method as a whole: to speak is to fight, in the sense of playing, and speech acts fall within the domain of a general agonistics. This does not necessarily mean that one plays in order to win. A move can be made for the sheer pleasure of its invention: what else is involved in that labor of language harassment undertaken by popular speech and by literature? Great joy is had in the endless invention of turns of phrase, of words and meanings, the process behind the evolution of language on the level of *parole*. But undoubtedly even this pleasure depends on a feeling of success won at the expense of an adversary—at least one adversary, and a formidable one: the accepted language, or connotation.

This idea of an agonistics of language should not make us lose sight of the second principle, which stands as a complement to it and governs our analysis: that the observable social bond is composed of language "moves." An elucidation of this proposition will take us to the heart of the matter at hand.

4. THE NATURE OF THE SOCIAL BOND: THE MODERN ALTERNATIVE

If we wish to discuss knowledge in the most highly developed contemporary society, we must answer the preliminary question of what methodological representation to apply to that society. Simplifying to the extreme, it is fair to say that in principle there have been, at least over the last half-century, two basic representational models for society: either society forms a functional whole, or it is divided in two. An illustration of the first model is suggested by Talcott Parsons (at least the postwar Parsons) and his school, and of the second, by the Marxist current (all of its component schools, whatever differences they may have, accept both the principle of class struggle and dialectics as a duality operating within society).

This methodological split, which defines two major kinds of discourse on society, has been handed down from the nineteenth century. The idea that society forms an organic whole, in the absence of which it ceases to be a society (and sociology ceases to have an object of study), dominated the minds of the founders of the French school. Added detail was supplied by functionalism; it took yet another turn in the 1950s with Parsons's conception of society as a self-regulating system. The theoretical and even material model is no longer the living organism; it is provided by cybernetics, which, during and after the Second World War, expanded the model's applications.

In Parsons's work, the principle behind the system is still, if I may say so, optimistic: it corresponds to the stabilisation of the growth economies and societies of abundance under the aegis of a moderate welfare state. In the work of contemporary German theorists, *systemtheorie* is technocratic, even cynical, not to mention despairing: the harmony between the needs and hopes of individuals or groups and the functions guaranteed by the system is now only a secondary component of its functioning. The true goal of the system, the reason it programs itself like a computer, is the optimisation of the global relationship between input and output, in other words, performativity. Even when its rules are in the process of changing and innovations are occurring, even when its dysfunctions (such as strikes, crises, unemployment, or political revolutions) inspire

hope and lead to belief in an alternative, even then what is actually taking place is only an internal readjustment, and its result can be no more than an increase in the system's "viability." The only alternative to this kind of performance improvement is entropy, or decline.

Here again, while avoiding the simplifications inherent in a sociology of social theory, it is difficult to deny at least a parallel between this "hard" technocratic version of society and the ascetic effort that was demanded (the fact that it was done in name of "advanced liberalism" is beside the point) of the most highly developed industrial societies in order to make them competitive—and thus optimise their "irrationality"—within the framework of the resumption of economic world war in the 1960s.

Even taking into account the massive displacement intervening between the thought of a man like Comte and the thought of Luhmann, we can discern a common conception of the social: society is a unified totality, a "unicity." Parsons formulates this clearly: "The most essential condition of successful dynamic analysis is a continual and systematic reference of every problem to the state of the system as a whole.... A process or set of conditions either 'contributes' to the maintenance (or development) of the system or it is 'dysfunctional' in that it detracts from the integration, effectiveness, etc., of the system." The "technocrats" also subscribe to this idea. Whence its credibility: it has the means to become a reality, and that is all the proof it needs. This is what Horkheimer called the "paranoia" of reason.

But this realism of systemic self-regulation, and this perfectly sealed circle of facts and interpretations, can be judged paranoid only if one has, or claims to have, at one's disposal a viewpoint that is in principle immune from their allure. This is the function of the principle of class struggle in theories of society based on the work of Marx.

"Traditional" theory is always in danger of being incorporated into the programming of the social whole as a simple tool for the optimisation of its performance; this is because its desire for a unitary and totalising truth lends itself to the unitary and totalising practice of the system's managers. "Critical" theory, based on a principle of dualism and wary of syntheses and reconciliations, should be in a position to avoid this fate. What guides Marxism, then, is a different model of society, and a different conception of the function of the knowledge that can be produced by society and acquired from it. This model was born of the struggles accompanying the process of capitalism's encroachment upon traditional civil societies. There is insufficient space here to chart the vicissitudes of these struggles, which fill more than a century of social, political, and ideological history. We will have to content ourselves with a glance at the balance sheet, which is possible for us to tally today now that their fate is known: in countries with liberal or advanced liberal management, the struggles and their instruments have been transformed into regulators of the system; in communist countries, the totalising model and its totalitarian effect have made a comeback in the name of Marxism itself, and the struggles in question have simply been deprived of the right to exist. Everywhere, the Critique of political economy (the subtitle of Marx's *Capital*) and its correlate, the critique of alienated society, are used in one way or another as aids in programming the system.

Of course, certain minorities, such as the Frankfurt School or the group *Socialisme ou barbarie*, preserved and refined the critical model in opposition to this process. But the social foundation of the principle of division, or class struggle, was blurred to the point of losing all of its radicality; we cannot conceal the fact that the critical model in the end lost its theoretical standing and was reduced to the status of a "utopia" or "hope," a token protest raised in the name of man or reason or creativity, or again of some social category such as the Third World or the students—on which is conferred in extremes the henceforth improbable function of critical subject.

The sole purpose of this schematic (or skeletal) reminder has been to specify the problematic in which I intend to frame the question of knowledge in advanced industrial societies. For it is impossible to know what the state of knowledge is—in other words, the problems its development and distribution are facing today—without knowing something of the society within which it is situated. And today more than ever, knowing about that society involves first of all choosing what approach the inquiry will take, and that necessarily means choosing how society can answer. One can decide that the principal role of knowledge is as an indispensable element in the functioning of society, and act in accordance with that decision, only if one has already decided that society is a giant machine.

Conversely, one can count on its critical function, and orient its development and distribution in that direction, only after it has been decided that society does not form an integrated whole, but remains haunted by a principle of oppositions. The alternative seems clear: it is a choice between the homogeneity and the intrinsic duality of the social, between functional and critical knowledge. But the decision seems difficult, or arbitrary.

It is tempting to avoid the decision altogether by distinguishing two kinds of knowledge. One, the positivist kind, would be directly applicable to technologies bearing on men and materials, and would lend itself to operating as an indispensable productive force within the system. The other—the critical, reflexive, or hermeneutic kind—by reflecting directly or indirectly on values or aims, would resist any such "recuperation."

5. THE NATURE OF THE SOCIAL BOND: THE POSTMODERN PERSPECTIVE

I find this partition solution unacceptable. I suggest that the alternative it attempts to resolve, but only reproduces, is no longer relevant for the societies with which we are concerned and that the solution itself is still caught within a type of oppositional thinking that is out of step with the most vital modes of postmodern knowledge. As I have already said, economic "redeployment" in the current phase of capitalism, aided by a shift in techniques and technology, goes hand in hand with a change in the function of the State: the image of society this syndrome suggests necessitates a serious revision of the alternate approaches considered. For brevity's sake, suffice it to say that functions of regulation, and therefore of reproduction, are being and will be further withdrawn from administrators and entrusted to machines.

Increasingly, the central question is becoming who will have access to the information these machines must have in storage to guarantee that the right decisions are made. Access to data is, and will continue to be, the prerogative of experts of all stripes. The ruling class is and will continue to be the class of decision makers. Even now it is no longer composed of the traditional political class, but of a composite layer of corporate leaders, high-level administrators, and the heads of the major professional, labor, political, and religious organisations.

What is new in all of this is that the old poles of attraction represented by nation-states, parties, professions, institutions, and historical traditions are losing their attraction. And it does not look as though they will be replaced, at least not on their former scale, The Trilateral Commission is not a popular pole of attraction. "Identifying" with the great names, the heroes of contemporary history, is becoming more and more difficult. Dedicating oneself to "catching up with Germany," the life goal the French president [Giscard d'Estaing at the time this book was published in France] seems to be offering his countrymen, is not exactly exciting. But then again, it is not exactly a life goal. It depends on each individual's industriousness. Each individual is referred to himself. And each of us knows that our *self* does not amount to much.

This breaking up of the grand Narratives leads to what some authors analyse in terms of the dissolution of the social bond and the disintegration of social aggregates into a mass of individual atoms thrown into the absurdity of Brownian motion. Nothing of the kind is happening: this point of view, it seems to me, is haunted by the paradisaic representation of a lost "organic" society.

A *self* does not amount to much, but no self is an island; each exists in a fabric of relations that is now more complex and mobile than ever before. Young or old, man or woman, rich or poor, a person is always located at "nodal points" of specific communication circuits, however tiny these may be. Or better: one is always located at a post through which various kinds of messages pass. No one, not even the least privileged among us, is ever entirely powerless over the messages that traverse and position him at the post of sender, addressee, or referent. One's mobility in relation to these language game effects (language games, of course, are what this is all about) is tolerable, at least within certain limits (and the limits are vague); it is even solicited by regulatory mechanisms, and in particular by the self-adjustments the system undertakes in order to improve its performance. It may even be said that the system can and must encourage such movement to the extent that it combats its own entropy, the novelty of an unexpected "move," with its correlative displacement of a partner or group of partners, can supply the system with that increased performativity it forever demands and consumes.

It should now be clear from which perspective I chose language games as my general methodological approach. I am not claiming that the *entirety* of social relations is of this nature—that will remain an open question. But there is no need to resort to some fiction of social origins to establish that language games are the minimum relation required for society to exist: even before he is born, if only by virtue of the name he is given, the human child is already positioned as the referent in the story recounted by those around him, in relation to which he will inevitably chart his course. Or more simply still, the question of the social bond, insofar as it is a question, is itself a language game, the game of inquiry. It immediately positions the person who asks, as well as the addressee and the referent asked about: it is already the social bond.

On the other hand, in a society whose communication component is becoming more prominent day by day, both as a reality and as an issue, it is clear that language assumes a new importance. It would be superficial to reduce its significance to the traditional alternative between manipulatory speech and the unilateral transmission of messages on the one hand, and free expression and dialogue on the other.

A word on this last point. If the problem is described simply in terms of communication theory, two things are overlooked: first, messages have quite different forms and effects depending on whether they are, for example, denotatives, prescriptives, evaluatives, performatives, etc. It is clear that what is important is not simply the fact that they communicate information. Reducing them to this function is to adopt an outlook which unduly privileges the system's own interests and point of view. A cybernetic machine does indeed run on information, but the goals programmed into it, for example, originate in prescriptive and evaluative statements it has no way to correct in the course of its functioning—for example, maximising its own performance, how can one guarantee that performance maximisation is the best goal for the social system in every case. In any case the "atoms" forming its matter are competent to handle statements such as these—and this question in particular.

Second, the trivial cybernetic version of information theory misses something of decisive importance, to which I have already called attention: the agonistic aspect of society. The atoms are placed at the crossroads of pragmatic relationships, but they are also displaced by the messages that traverse them, in perpetual motion. Each language partner, when a "move" pertaining to him is made, undergoes a "displacement," an alteration of some kind that not only affects him in his capacity as addressee and referent, but also as sender. These moves necessarily provoke "countermoves"—and everyone knows that a countermove that is merely reactional is not a "good" move. Reactional countermoves are no more than programmed effects in the opponent's strategy; they play into his hands and thus have no effect on the balance of power. That is why it is important to increase displacement in the games, and even to disorient it, in such a way as to make an unexpected "move" (a new statement).

What is needed if we are to understand social relations in this manner, on whatever scale we choose, is not only a theory of communication, but a theory of games which accepts agonistics as a founding principle. In this context, it is easy to see that the essential element of newness is not simply "innovation." Support for this approach can be found in the work of a number of contemporary sociologists, in addition to linguists and philosophers of language. This "atomisation" of the social into flexible networks of language games may seem far removed from the modern reality, which is depicted, on the contrary, as afflicted with bureaucratic paralysis. The objection will be made, at least, that the weight of certain institutions imposes limits on the games, and thus restricts the inventiveness of the players in making their moves. But I think this can be taken into account without causing any particular difficulty.

In the ordinary use of discourse—for example, in a discussion between two friends—the interlocutors use any available ammunition, changing games from one utterance to the next: questions, requests, assertions, and narratives are launched pell-mell into battle. The war is not without rules, but the rules allow and encourage the greatest possible flexibility of utterance.

From this point of view, an institution differs from a conversation in that it always requires supplementary constraints for statements to be declared admissible within its bounds. The constraints function to filter discursive potentials, interrupting possible connections in the communication networks: there are things that should not be said. They also privilege certain classes of statements (sometimes only one) whose predominance characterises the discourse of the particular institution: there are things that should be said, and there are ways of saying them. Thus: orders in the army, prayer in church, denotation in the schools, narration in families, questions in philosophy, performativity in businesses. Bureaucratisation is the outer limit of this tendency.

However, this hypothesis about the institution is still too "unwieldy": its point of departure is an overly "reifying" view of what is institutionalised. We know today that the limits the institution imposes on potential language "moves" are never established once and for all (even if they have been formally defined). Rather, the limits are themselves the stakes and provisional results of language strategies, within the institution and without. Examples: Does the university have a place for language experiments (poetics)? Can you tell stories in a cabinet meeting? Advocate a cause in the barracks? The answers are clear: yes, if the university opens creative workshops; yes, if the cabinet works with prospective scenarios; yes, if the limits of the old institution are displaced. Reciprocally, it can be said that the boundaries only stabilise when they cease to be stakes in the game.

This, I think, is the appropriate approach to contemporary institutions of knowledge.

SECTION XV

1. In his discussion of fashion, what does Bourdieu mean by the "logic of homologies"? Compare and contrast his essay to Simmel on fashion. Compare and contrast it to Veblen on taste.

2. What does Baudrillard mean when he describes the function of advertising as the promotion of gratification and infantilization? Offer an example of what he has in mind. Do you find his argument convincing? Why or why not?

3. Offer a description of Bentham's Panopticon and provide an account of why Foucault would find this architectural composition relevant to his efforts to theorize about the relationship between power and knowledge.

4. Why does Bauman think that the term "liquid" is an apt characterization of the postmodern world? Does he think that a liquid world is preferable to a "solid" world? Do you agree or disagree with him? Why?

5. Compare and contrast Bauman's imagery of a liquid modern world with Marx and Engel's assertion in *The Communist Manifesto* that "all that is solid melts into air."

6. Compare Lyotard's understanding of the nature of the social bond in both modern and postmodern perspectives.

XVI. WORLD SYSTEMS AND GLOBALIZATION THEORY

76. THE THREE INSTANCES OF HEGEMONY IN THE HISTORY OF THE CAPITALIST WORLD-ECONOMY

IMMANUEL WALLERSTEIN

Immanuel Wallerstein (b. 1930) is the most influential exponent of world-systems theory. This macro-sociological theory, rooted in the Marxist tradition, is intent on viewing capitalism as a worldwide system from a perspective that emphasizes the *longue durée* and the operation of long-term cycles of development. This means that rather than viewing capitalism as essentially arising during the nineteenth century's Industrial Revolution, Wallerstein seeks to trace its rise to dominance from 1450 forward, with his more recent writings examining what he sees as the gradual demise of the system. He contends that there have been only two world systems in human history: the world empires of the ancient world and the modern capitalist world-economy that is undergirded by political and military domination. Indeed, he thinks it is a serious mistake to contend that capitalism can be understood solely in economic terms; it is at once an economic and a political system. In this essay, Wallerstein discusses the conceptual salience of "hegemony" in making sense of the way the modern world-system links its core exploiting nations to the nations on the periphery and semi-periphery. He identifies three points at which hegemonic states rose to prominence and notes the significance that wars played in a process that resulted in a restructuring of international relations.

When one is dealing with a complex, continuously evolving, large-scale historical system, concepts that are used as shorthand descriptions for structural patterns are only useful to the degree one clearly lays out their purpose, circumscribes their applicability, and specifies the theoretical framework they presuppose and advance.

Let me therefore state some premises which I shall not argue at this point. If you are not willing to regard these premises as plausible, you will not find the way I elaborate and use the concept of hegemony very useful. I assume that there exists a concrete singular historical system which I shall call the "capitalist world-economy," whose temporal boundaries go from the long sixteenth century to the present. Its spatial boundaries originally included Europe (or most of it) plus Iberian America but they subsequently expanded to cover the entire globe. I assume this totality is a *system*, that is, that it has been relatively autonomous

"The Three Instances of Hegemony in the History of the Capitalist World-Economy" by Immanuel Wallerstein, from *International Journal of Comparative Sociology* XXIV, 1–2, January-April 1983, pp. 100–08. Reprinted by permission of Brill Academic Publishers. ◆

of external forces; or to put it another way, that its patterns are explicable largely in terms of its internal dynamics. I assume that it is a *historical* system, that is, that it was born, has developed, and will one day cease to exist (through disintegration or fundamental transformation). I assume lastly that it is the dynamics of the system itself that explain its historically changing characteristics. Hence, insofar as it is a system, it has structures and these structures manifest themselves in cyclical rhythms, that is, mechanisms which reflect and ensure repetitious patterns. But insofar as this system is historical, no rhythmic movement ever returns the system to an equilibrium point but instead moves the system along various continua which may be called the secular trends of this system. These trends eventually must culminate in the impossibility of containing further reparations of the structured dislocations by restorative mechanisms. Hence the system undergoes what some call "bifurcating turbulence" and others the "transformation of quantity into quality."

To these methodological or metaphysical premises, I must add a few substantive ones about the operations of the capitalist world-economy. Its mode of production is capitalist; that is, it is predicated on the endless accumulation of capital. Its structure is that of an axial social division of labor exhibiting a core/periphery tension based on unequal exchange. The political superstructure of this system is that of a set of so-called sovereign states defined by and constrained by their membership in an interstate network or system. The operational guidelines of this interstate system include the so-called balance of power, a mechanism designed to ensure that no single state ever has the capacity to transform this interstate system into a single world-empire whose boundaries would match that of the axial division of labor. There have of course been repeated attempts throughout the history of the capitalist world-economy to transform it in the direction of a world-empire, but these attempts have all been frustrated. However, there have also been repeated and quite different attempts by given states to achieve hegemony in the interstate system, and these attempts have in fact succeeded on three occasions, if only for relatively brief periods.

The thrust of hegemony is quite different from the thrust to world empire; indeed it is many ways almost its opposite. I will therefore (1) spell out what I mean by hegemony, (2) describe the analogies in the three purported instances, (3) seek to decipher the roots of the thrust to hegemony and suggest why the thrust to hegemony has succeeded three times but never lasted too long, and (4) draw inferences about what we may expect in the proximate future. The point of doing all this is not to erect a Procrustean category into which to fit complex historical reality but to illuminate what I believe to be one of the central processes of the modern world-system.

(1) Hegemony in the interstate system refers to that situation in which the ongoing rivalry between the so-called "great powers" is so unbalanced that one power can largely impose its rules and its wishes (at the very least by effective veto power) in the economic, political, military, diplomatic, and even cultural arenas. The material base of such power lies in the ability of enterprises domiciled in that power to operate more efficiently in all three major economic arenas—agro-industrial production, commerce, and finance. The edge in efficiency of which we are speaking is one so great that these enterprises can not only outbid enterprises domiciled in other great powers in the world market in general, but quite specifically in very many instances within the home markets of the rival powers themselves.

I mean this to be a relatively restrictive definition. It is not enough for one power's enterprises simply to have a larger share of the world market than any other or simply to have the most powerful military forces or the largest political role. I mean hegemony only to refer to situations in which the edge is so significant that allied major powers are *de facto* client states and opposed major powers feel relatively frustrated and highly defensive vis-à-vis the hegemonic power. And yet while I want to restrict my definition to instances where the margin or power differential is really great, I do not mean to suggest that there is ever any moment when a hegemonic power is omnipotent and capable of doing anything it wants. Omnipotence does not exist within the interstate system.

Hegemony therefore is not a state of being but rather one end of a fluid continuum which describes the rivalry relations of great powers to each other. At one end of this continuum is an almost even balance, a situation in which many powers exist, all somewhat equal in strength, and with no clear or continuous groupings. This is rare and unstable. In the great middle of this continuum, many powers exist, grouped more or less into two camps, but with several neutral or swing elements, and with neither side (nor a *fortiori* any single state) being able to impose its will on others. This is the statistically normal situation of rivalry within the interstate system. And at the other end lies the situation of hegemony, also rare and unstable.

At this point, you may see what it is I am describing but may wonder why I am bothering to give it a name and thereby focus attention upon it. It is because I suspect hegemony is not the result of a random reshuffling of the cards but is a phenomenon that emerges in specifiable circumstances and plays a significant role in the historical development of the capitalist world-economy.

(2) Using this restrictive definition, the only three instances of hegemony would be the United Provinces in the mid-seventeenth century, the United Kingdom in the mid-nineteenth, and the United States in the mid-twentieth. If one insists on dates, I would tentatively suggest as maximal bounding points: 1625–72, 1815–73, 1945–67. But of course, it would be a mistake to try to be too precise when our measuring instruments are both so complex and so crude.

I will suggest four areas in which it seems to me what happened in the three instances was analogous. To be sure, analogies are limited. And to be sure, since

the capitalist world-economy is in my usage a single continuously evolving entity, it follows by definition that the overall structure was different at each of the three points in time. The differences were real, the outcome of the secular trends of the world-system. But the structural analogies were real as well, the reflection of the cyclical rhythms of this same system.

The first analogy has to do with the sequencing of achievement and loss of relative efficiencies in each of the three economic domains. What I believe occurred was that in each instance enterprises domiciled in the given power in question achieved their edge first in agro-industrial production, then in commerce, and then in finance.[1] I believe they lost their edge in this sequence as well (this process having begun but not yet having been completed in the third instance). Hegemony thus refers to that short interval in which there is *simultaneous* advantage in all three economic domains.

The second analogy has to do with the ideology and policy of the hegemonic power. Hegemonic powers during the period of their hegemony tended to be advocates of global "liberalism." They came forward as defenders of the principle of the free flow of the factors of production (goods, capital, and labor) throughout the world-economy. They were hostile in general to mercantilist restrictions on trade, including the existence of overseas colonies for the stronger countries. They extended this liberalism to a generalized endorsement of liberal parliamentary institutions (and a concurrent distaste for political change

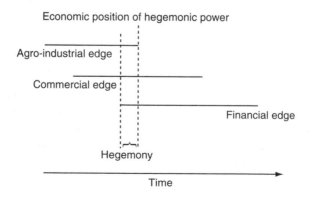

CHART 76.1 Capitalist World-Economy

by violent means), political restraints on the arbitrariness of bureaucratic power, and civil liberties (and a concurrent open door to political exiles). They tended to provide a high standard of living for their national working classes, high by world standards of the time.

None of this should be exaggerated. Hegemonic powers regularly made exceptions to their anti-mercantilism, when it was in their interest to do so. Hegemonic powers regularly were willing to interfere with political processes in other states to ensure their own advantage. Hegemonic powers could be very repressive at home, if need be, to guarantee the national "consensus." The high working-class standard was steeply graded by internal ethnicity. Nevertheless, it is quite striking that liberalism as an ideology did flourish in these countries at precisely the moments of their hegemony, and to a significant extent only then and there.

The third analogy is in the pattern of global military power. Hegemonic powers were primarily sea (now sea/air) powers. In the long ascent to hegemony, they seemed very reluctant to develop their armies, discussing openly the potentially weakening drain on state revenues and manpower of becoming tied down in land wars. Yet each found finally that it had to develop a strong land army as well to face up to a major land-based rival which seemed to be trying to transform the world-economy into a world-empire.

In each case, the hegemony was secured by a thirty-year-long world war. By a world war, I shall mean (again somewhat restrictively) a land-based war that involves (not necessarily continuously) almost all the major military powers of the epoch in warfare that is very destructive of land and population. To each hegemony is attached one of these wars. World War Alpha was the Thirty Years' War from 1618–48, when Dutch interests triumphed over Hapsburg in the world-economy. World War Beta was the Napoleonic Wars from 1792–1815, when British interests triumphed over French. World War Gamma was the long Euroasian wars from 1914–45 when U.S. interests triumphed over German.

While limited wars have been a constant of the operations of the interstate system of the capitalist world-economy (there having been scarcely any year when there was not some war some place within the system), world wars have been, by contrast, a rarity. In fact their rarity and the fact that the number and timing seem to have correlated with the achievement of hegemonic status by one power brings us to the fourth analogy.

If we look to those very long cycles that Rondo Cameron has dubbed "logistics," we can see that world wars and hegemony have been in fact related to them. There has been very little scholarly work done on these logistics. They have been most frequently discussed in the comparisons between the A–B sequences of 1100–1450 and 1450–1750. There are only a few discussions of the logistics that may exist after the latter point in time. But if we take the prime observation which has been used to define these logistics—secular inflation and deflation—the pattern seems in fact to have continued.

It therefore might be plausible to argue the existence of such (price) logistics up to today using the following dates: 1450–1730, with 1600–1650 as a flat peak; 1730–1897, with 1810–17 as a peak; and 1897 to ?, with an as yet uncertain peak. If there are such logistics, it turns out that the world war and the (subsequent) hegemonic era are located somewhere around (just before and after) the peak of the logistic. That is to say, these processes seem to be the product of the long competitive expansion which seemed to have resulted in a particular concentration of economic and political power.

The outcome of each world war included a major restructuring of the interstate system (Westphalia; the Concert of Europe; the U.N. and Bretton Woods) in a form consonant with the need for relative stability of the now hegemonic power. Furthermore, once the hegemonic position was eroded economically (the loss of the efficiency edge in agro-industrial production), and therefore hegemonic decline set in, one consequence seemed to be the erosion of the alliance network which the hegemonic power had created patiently, and ultimately a serious reshuffling of alliances.

In the long period following the era of hegemony, two powers seemed eventually to emerge as the "contenders for the successions"—England and France after Dutch hegemony; the U.S. and Germany after British; and now Japan and western Europe after U.S. Furthermore, the eventual winner of the contending pair seemed to use as a conscious part of its strategy the gentle turning of the old hegemonic power into its "junior partner"—the English vis-à-vis the Dutch, the U.S. vis-à-vis Great Britain . . . and now?

(3) Thus far I have been primarily descriptive. I realize that this description is vulnerable to technical criticism. My coding of the data may not agree with everyone else's. I think nonetheless that as an initial effort this coding is defensible and that I have therefore outlined a broad repetitive pattern in the functioning of the interstate question. The question now is how to interpret it. What is there in the functioning of a capitalist world-economy that gives rise to such a cyclical pattern in the interstate system?

I believe this pattern of the rise, temporary ascendancy, and fall of hegemonic powers in the interstate system is merely one aspect of the central role of the political machinery in the functioning of capitalism as a mode of production.

There are two myths about capitalism put forward by its central ideologues (and, strangely, largely accepted by its nineteenth-century critics). One is that it is defined by the free flow of the factors of production. The second is that it is defined by the non-interference of the political machinery in the "market." In fact, capitalism is defined by the *partially* free flow of the factors of production and by the *selective* interference of the political machinery in the "market." Hegemony is an instance of the latter.

What defines capitalism most fundamentally is the drive for the endless accumulation of capital. The interferences that are "selected" are those which advance this process of accumulation. There are however two problems about "interference." It has a cost, and therefore the benefit of any interference is only a benefit to the extent it exceeds this cost. Where the benefits are available without any "interference," this is obviously desirable, as it minimizes the "deduction." And secondly, interference is always in favor of one set of accumulators as against another set, and the latter will always seek to counter the former. These two considerations circumscribe the politics of hegemony in the interstate system.

The costs to a given entrepreneur of state "interference" are felt in two main ways. First, in financial terms, the state may levy direct taxes which affect the rate of profit by requiring the firm to make payments to the state, or indirect taxes, which may alter the rate of profit by affecting the competitiveness of a product. Secondly, the state may enact rules which govern flows of capital, labor, or goods, or may set minimum and/or maximum prices. While direct taxes always represent a cost to the entrepreneur, calculations concerning indirect taxes and state regulations are more complex, since they represent costs both to the entrepreneur and to (some of) his competitors. The chief concern in terms of individual accumulation is not the absolute cost of these measures, but the comparative cost. Costs, even if high, may be positively desirable from the standpoint of a given entrepreneur, if the state's actions involve still higher costs to some competitor. Absolute costs are only of concern if the loss to the entrepreneur is greater than the medium-run gain which is possible through greater competitiveness brought about by such state actions. It follows that absolute cost is of greatest concern to those entrepreneurs who would do best in open market competition in the absence of state interference.

In general, therefore, entrepreneurs are regularly seeking state interference in the market in multiple forms—subsidies, restraints of trade, tariffs (which are penalties for competitors of different nationality), guarantees, maxima for input prices and minima for output prices, etc. The intimidating effect of internal and external repression is also of direct economic benefit to entrepreneurs. To the extent that the ongoing process of competition and state interference leads to oligopolistic conditions within state boundaries, more and more attention is naturally paid to securing the same kind of oligopolistic conditions in the most important market, the world market.

The combination of the competitive thrust and constant state interference results in a continuing pressure towards the concentration of capital. The benefits of state interference inside and outside the state boundaries is cumulative. In political terms, this is reflected as expanding world power. The edge a rising power's economic enterprises have vis-à-vis those of a competitive rising power may be thin and therefore insecure. This is where the world wars come in. The thirty-year struggle may be very dramatic militarily and politically. But the profoundest effect may be economic. The winner's economic edge is expanded by the very process of the war itself, and the post-war interstate settlement is designed to encrust that greater edge and protect it against erosion.

A given state thus assumes its world "responsibilities" which are reflected in its diplomatic, military, political, ideological, and cultural stances. All conspire to reinforce the cooperative relationship of the entrepreneurial strata, the bureaucratic strata, and with some lag the working-class strata, of the hegemonic power. This power may then be exercised in a "liberal" form—given the real diminution of political conflict within the state itself compared to earlier and later periods, and to the importance in the interstate arena of delegitimizing the efforts of other state machineries to act against the economic superiorities of the hegemonic power.

The problem is that global liberalism, which is rational and cost effective, breeds its own demise. It makes it more difficult to retard the spread of technological expertise. Hence over time it is virtually inevitable that entrepreneurs coming along later will be able to enter the most profitable markets with the most advanced technologies and younger "plant," thus eating into the material base of the productivity edge of the hegemonic power.

Secondly, the internal political price of liberalism, needed to maintain uninterrupted production at a time of maximal global accumulation, is the creeping rise of real income of both the working strata and the cadres located in the hegemonic power. Over time, this must reduce the competitive advantage of the enterprises located in this state.

Once the clear productivity edge is lost, the structure cracks. As long as there is a hegemonic power, it can coordinate more or less the political responses of all states with core-like economic activities to all peripheral states, maximizing thereby the differentials of unequal exchange. But when hegemony is eroded, and especially when the world-economy is in a Kondratieff downturn, a scramble arises among the leading powers to maintain their shares of the smaller pie, which undermines their collective ability to extract surplus via unequal exchange. The rate of unequal exchange thereby diminishes (but never to zero) and creates further incentive to a reshuffling of alliance systems.

In the period leading to the peak of a logistic, which leads towards the creation of the momentary era of hegemony, the governing parable is that of the tortoise and the hare. It is not the state that leaps ahead politically and especially militarily that wins the race, but the one that plods along improving inch by inch its long-term competitiveness. This requires a firm but discreet and intelligent organization of the entrepreneurial effort by the state-machinery. Wars may be left to others, until the climactic world war when the hegemonic power must at least invest its resources to clinch its victory. Thereupon comes "world responsibility" with its benefits but also its (growing) costs. Thus the hegemony is sweet but brief.

(4) The inferences for today are obvious. We are in the immediate post-hegemonic phase of this third logistic of the capitalist world-economy. The U.S. has lost its productive edge but not yet its commercial and financial superiorities; its military and political power edge is no longer so overwhelming. Its abilities to dictate to its allies (western Europe and Japan), intimidate its foes, and overwhelm the weak (compare the Dominician Republic in 1965 with El Salvador today) are vastly impaired. We are in the beginnings of a major reshuffling of alliances.[2] yet, of course, we are only at the beginning of all this. Great Britain began to decline in 1873, but it was only in 1982 that it was openly challenged by Argentina, a middle-ranking military power.

The major question is whether this third logistic will act itself out along the lines of the previous ones. The great difference of this third logistic from the first two is that the capitalist world-economy has now entered into a structural crisis as an historical system. The question is whether this fact will obliterate these cyclical processes. I do not believe it will obliterate them but rather that it will work itself out in part through them.[3]

We should not invest more in the concept of hegemony than is there. It is a way of organizing our perception of process, not an "essence" whose traits are to be described and whose eternal recurrences are to be demonstrated and then anticipated. A processual concept alerts us to the forces at play in the system and the likely nodes of conflict. It does not do more. But it also does not do less. The capitalist world-economy is not comprehensible unless we analyze clearly what are the political forms which it has engendered and how these forms relate to other realities. The interstate system is not some exogenous, God-given, variable which mysteriously restrains and interacts with the capitalist drive for the endless accumulation of capital. It is its expression at the level of the political arena.

NOTES

1. I have described this in empirical detail for the first instance in *The Modern World-System, II: Mercantilism and the Consolidation of the European World-Economy, 1600–1750* (New York: Academic, 1980), ch.2.

2. See my "North Atlanticism in Decline," *SAIS Review*, No.4, Summer, 1982, 21–26.

3. For a debate about this, see the Conclusions of S. Amin, G. Arrighi, A. G. Frank, and I. Wallerstein, *Dynamics of Global Crisis* (New York: Monthly Review Press, 1982).

77. THE COSMOPOLITAN CONDITION: WHY METHODOLOGICAL NATIONALISM FAILS

ULRICH BECK

Most recently a professor at both the University of Munich (where he directs a center on reflexive modernization) and the London School of Economics, Ulrich Beck (b. 1944) is a wide-ranging social theorist who has contributed to our understanding of modernity, particularly the significance of risk in modern societies; to the varied impacts of globalization; and most recently to cosmopolitanism. All of these themes are intertwined in this essay on the "cosmopolitan condition," the specific focus of which is to suggest that the implications of this new social landscape wherein the interconnections across national boundaries expand dramatically. As Beck notes at the outset, cosmopolitanism is a term with varied meanings. He seeks to distinguish his position from what he sees as the normative approach of figures such as Jürgen Habermas, his alternative being to articulate what it means for doing sociological research, which includes how to examine new modes of addressing diversity. In making a case for his version of Cosmopolitan Sociology, Beck takes aim at what he refers to as methodological nationalism, arguing for the necessity of replacing it with a methodological cosmopolitanism.

At the beginning of the 21st century, we are witnessing a global transformation of modernity, which calls for a re-thinking of cosmopolitanism for the social sciences. The newly awakened interest in cosmopolitanism is fed by various sources: globalization research, mobility and migration research, international relations, international law, postcolonial studies, post-feminism, global cultural studies, geography, ethnography, actor-network and science and technology studies, the debates on 'new wars' and human rights as well as mass media communication science, to mention only the most important. In sociology, at present, these analyses are condensing into the paradigm of a 'Cosmopolitan Sociology' (Beck, 2006; Beck and Sznaider, 2006). At its centre there is, on the one hand, the search for new research methods and strategies and, on the other, the question

as to new forms of dealing with otherness in society in an increasingly globalized world. Dealing with otherness includes the otherness of nature and the materiality of threats which is not the focus of this article, but an essential part of the programme of cosmopolitan sociology (Latour, 2003).

Both tendencies can be clearly distinguished from the philosophical-normative cosmopolitanism dominant until now, whose authors (e.g. Jürgen Habermas [2001] and David Held [1995]) read Kant's world citizenship sociologically. Cosmopolitanism is, of course, a contested term; there is no uniform interpretation in the growing literature. The boundaries separating it from competing terms like globalization, transnationalism, universalism, glocalization, etc. are not distinct; but there is an identifiable intellectual movement—working on 'New Cosmopolitanism' or 'Realistic

Cosmopolitanism'—united by at least three interconnected commitments: (1) a shared critique of methodological nationalism; (2) the shared diagnosis that the 21st century is an age of cosmopolitanism; and (3) the shared assumption that for this reason we need some kind of methodological cosmopolitanism.

First, a *shared critique of methodological nationalism*, which subsumes society under the nation-state. There are two dimensions of this: a historical and a systematic understanding of methodological nationalism.

It is evident that, in the 19th century, European sociology was formulated within a nationalist paradigm and that any cosmopolitan sentiments were snuffed out by the horrors of the Great Wars. Responding to the 'ghost of Marx', it was class and in particular the rise of the working class, which was seen as the great social problem and the solidarity of the nation-state was seen as the solution. In the methodological nationalism of Émile Durkheim, fraternity became solidarity and national integration.

Max Weber's sociology involved a comparative study of economic ethics of world religions, but the political inspiration for his sociology was nationalistic. Indeed, in the Freiburg Inaugural Lecture, Weber employed a Darwinistic view of international relations in which he observed that future generations would hold his generation responsible for not creating sufficient 'elbow room' in East Germany to support a strong German state.

In North America, the same national paradigm is evident. Of course, Talcott Parsons adopted a comparative sociological approach and was a student of European social thought, but his sociological interest and approach was American. In his *The System of Modern Societies* (1971: 1), Parsons starts with the admission that the thesis that informs his work

> is that the modern type of society has emerged in a single evolutionary area, the West, which is a century of Europe that fell heir to the Western part of the Roman Empire north of the Mediterranean. The society of western Christendom, then, provided the base for which we shall call the 'system' of modern societies 'took of'.

Most classical sociology today is the study of the 'national society' under the umbrella of 'society'. We should not forget that classical sociology was the product of national struggles, the Franco-German War of 1870 and the First World War at the beginning of the 20th century.

Systematically, methodological nationalism takes the following ideal premises for granted: it equates society with nation-state societies, and sees states and their governments as the cornerstones of a social sciences analysis. It assumes that humanity is naturally divided into a limited number of nations, which on the inside, organize themselves as nation-states, and on the outside, set boundaries to distinguish themselves from other nation-states. It goes even further: this outer delimitation, as well as the competition between nation-states, presents the most fundamental category of political organization. Indeed, the social science stance is rooted in the concept of the nation-state. It is a nation-state outlook on society and politics, law, justice and history, that governs the sociological imagination. And it is exactly this methodological nationalism that prevents the social science from getting at the heart of the dynamics of modernization and globalization, both past and present; the *unintended* result of the radicalization of modernity is a disempowerment of Western states, in sharp contrast to their empowerment before and during the 19th-century wave of globalization (Beck, 2005).

Second, *the shared diagnosis that the 21st century is becoming an age of cosmopolitanism*. In the 1960s, Hannah Arendt (1958) analysed the Human Condition, in the 1970s, Jean-François Lyotard (1984) the Postmodern Condition; now at the beginning of the 21st century we have to discover, map and understand the *Cosmopolitan Condition*.

Third, there is *a shared assumption that for that reason we need some kind of 'methodological cosmopolitanism'*. Of course, there is a lot of controversy about what this means. We can distinguish three phases in how the code word 'globalization' has been used in the social sciences: first, denial; second, conceptual refinement and empirical research; and, third, epistemological shift.

To the extent that the second phase was successful, the insight began to gain ground that the nation-state unit of research has become arbitrary when the distinctions between national and international, local and global, us and them, lose their sharp contours. The question for the research agenda following the epistemological turn is: what happens when the premises and boundaries that define the units of empirical research and theory disintegrate? The answer is that the whole conceptual world of the 'national outlook' becomes disenchanted, stripped of its necessity. We need an alternative which replaces ontology with methodology: what are alternative, non-national units of research? What are post-national concepts of the social and the political? How can we invent a methodology of 'cosmopolitan understanding' in order to decode the multi-ethnic, multi-religious conflicts insight of France, of Germany, and on a global scale? How does cosmopolitanism relate to universalism, relativism, nationalism, etc.? In other words, the sociology for the 21st century has to be reinvented.

As prisoners of methodological nationalism we do not understand Europeanization, we do not understand the new global meta-power game. We do not understand that the nation-state legitimacy of social inequalities is being challenged to its core by universalized human rights, we do not understand the 'global generation' and its transnational fragments, and so on. This is because we are captured by zombie categories, sociology is threatening to become a zombie science, a museum piece of antiquated ideas.

THE COSMOPOLITAN CONDITION

The Cosmopolitan Condition can be explained, for example, in relation to global risks. The experience of global risks—Chernobyl, 9/11, BSE or the mass media, the experience of the Asian tsunami which induced a planetary torrent of sorrow—is an occurrence of abrupt and full confrontation of the apparently excluded other. Global risks tear down national boundaries and jumble together the native with the foreign. The distant other is becoming the inclusive other. Everyday life is becoming cosmopolitan. Human beings must find a meaning of life in the exchange with others and no longer in the encounter with the like. This is what I call 'enforced

cosmopolitanization': global risks activate and connect actors across borders, who otherwise don't want to have anything to do with one another.

I propose, in this sense, that a clear distinction is to be made between the philosophical and normative ideas of cosmopolitanism, on the one hand, and the *impure actual enforced cosmopolitization*, on the other. The crucial point about this distinction is that cosmopolitanism cannot, for example, only become real deductively in a translation of the sublime principles of philosophy, but also and above all through the back door of global risks, unseen, unintended, enforced. Down through history, cosmopolitanism was detained of being elitist, idealistic, imperialistic, capitalist; today, however, we see that reality itself has become cosmopolitan. Cosmopolitanism, then, does not mean—as it did for Immanuel Kant—an asset, a task, that is to order the world. Cosmopolitanization in world risk society opens our eyes to the uncontrollable liabilities that something might happen to us, might befall us and, which at the same time could stimulate us, to make borders transcend new beginnings. Risks cut through the self-absorption of cultures, languages, religions and systems as well as the national and international agenda of politics; they overturn their priorities and create contexts for action between camps, parties and quarrelling nations, which ignore and oppose one another.

What is meant by that can be explained with reference to Hannah Arendt. The existential shock of danger —therein lies the fundamental ambivalence of global risks—opens up unintentionally (and often also unseen and underutilized) the (mis)fortune of a possible new beginning (which is no reason for false sentimentality). How to live in the shadow of global risks? How to live, when old certainties are shattered or are now revealed as lies? Arendt's answer anticipates the ambivalence of risk. The expectation of the unexpected requires that the self-evident is no longer taken as self-evident. The shock of danger is a call for a new beginning. Where there is a new beginning, action is possible. Human beings enter into relations across borders. This common activity by strangers across borders means freedom. All freedom is contained in this ability to begin.

IS THERE A HISTORIC ALTERNATIVE OF POLITICAL ACTION?

It is precisely this question that I have tried to answer in my book *Power in the Global Age* (Beck, 2005). Here I can outline only two premises: (1) world risk society brings a new, historic key logic to the fore: No nation can cope with its problems alone. (2) A realistic political alternative in the global age is possible, which counteracts the loss to globalized capital of the commanding power of state politics. The condition is, that globalization must be decoded not as economic fate, but as a strategic game for world power.

(1) The nation-state, which attempts to deal with global risks in isolation, resembles a drunk man, who on a dark night is trying to find his lost wallet in the cone of light from a street lamp. To the question: Did you actually lose your wallet here?, he replies, 'No, but in the light of the street lamp I can at least look for it.' In other words, global risks are producing 'failed states'—even in the West (latest example: the Iraq war). The state structure evolving under the conditions of world risk society could be characterized in terms of both inefficiency *and* post-democratic authority. A clear distinction, therefore, has to be made between rule and inefficiency. It is quite possible that the end result could be the gloomy perspective, that we have totally ineffective and authoritarian state regimes (even in the context of the Western democracies).

(2) But this is normal sociology. There is a nostalgia and *'kulturkritischer Pessimismus'* built into the foundations of sociological thought which has never disappeared—starting with Max Weber and today including Foucault, system theory and postmodernism. Perhaps this nostalgia can be overcome by the theory of world risk society. My aim is a non-nostalgic New Critical Theory to look at both the past and the future of modernity. The word for this is neither 'utopianism' nor 'pessimism' but 'ambivalence'. Yes, there is a historic alternative of political action. The new global domestic politics that is already at work here and now, beyond the national-international distinction, has become a meta-power game, whose outcome is completely open-ended. It is a game in which boundaries, basic rules and basic distinctions are renegotiated—not only those between the national and the international

spheres, but also those between global business and the state, transnational civil society movements, supranational organizations and national governments and societies. No single player or opponent can ever win on their own; they all are dependent on alliances. This is the way, then, in which the *hazy power game of global domestic politics* opens up its own immanent alternatives and oppositions.

The first one, which is dominant today, gives the priority of power to global capital. The goal of the strategies of capital is, in simplified terms, to merge capital with the state in order to open up new sources of legitimacy in the form of the *neo-liberal state*. Its orthodoxy says: There is only one revolutionary power, which rewrites the rules of the global power order, and that is capital, while the other actors—nation-states and civil society movements remain bound by the limited options of action and power of the national and international order. This dominant coalition of capital and national minimal state is in no position to respond to the challenges of world risk society.

The strategies of action, which global risks open up, overthrow the order of power that has formed in the neo-liberal capital-state coalition: global risks *empower states and civil society movements*, because they reveal new sources of legitimation and options for action for these groups of actors; they *disempower globalized capital*, on the other hand, because the consequences of investment decisions contribute to creating global risks, destabilizing markets and activating the power of that sleeping giant, the consumer. Conversely, the goal of global civil society and its actors is to achieve a connection between civil society and the state, that is, to bring about what I call a *cosmopolitan form of statehood* (including a cosmopolitan form of democracy).

This is not wishful thinking, on the contrary, it is an expression of a *cosmopolitan realpolitik*. In an age of global crises and risks, a politics of 'golden handcuffs'—the creation of a dense network of transnational interdependencies—is exactly what is needed in order to regain *national* autonomy, not least in relation to a highly mobile world economy. The maxims of nation-based realpolitik—that national interests must necessarily be pursued by national means—must be replaced by the maxims of *cosmopolitan realpolitik*: the more cosmopolitan our political structures and activities, the more successful they will be in promoting national interests and the greater our individual power in this global age will be. The historic examples of globally empowered individuals are transnational actor-networks and movements, including terrorist networks.

Global risks are the expression of a new form of global interdependence, which cannot be adequately addressed by way of national politics, nor by the available forms of international co-operation. All the past and present practical experiences of human beings in dealing with uncertainty now exist side by side, without offering any ready solution to the resulting problems. Not only that: key institutions of modernity such as science, business and politics, which are supposed to guarantee rationality and security, find themselves confronted by situations in which their apparatus no longer has purchase and the fundamental principles of modernity no longer automatically hold good. Indeed, the perception of their rating changes—from trustee to suspect. They are no longer seen only as instruments of risk *management*, but also as a *source* of risk.

TRAGIC INDIVIDUALIZATION

As a consequence, everyday life in world risk society is characterized by a new variant of individualization. The individual must cope with the uncertainty of the global world by him- or herself. Here individualization is the default outcome of a *failure* of expert systems to manage risks. Neither science, nor the politics in power, nor the mass media, nor business, nor the law or even the military are in a position to define or control risks rationally. The individual is forced to mistrust the promises of rationality of these key institutions. As a consequence, people are thrown back onto themselves, they are alienated from expert systems but have nothing else instead. *Disembedding without embedding—* this is the formula for this dimension of individualization: the individual, whose senses fail him in the face of ungraspable threats, who, thrown back on himself, is blind to dangers, remains at the same time unable to escape the power of definition of expert systems, whose judgement he cannot, yet must, trust. Sustaining an individual self of integrity in world risk society is indeed a tragic affair.

Of course, there are fundamental ambivalences. I am talking here about only one large transnational fraction of everyday life in world risk society. At the same time we observe the rise of (what might be called) the 'individualization of war': the transnational super-empowerment of the individual vis-à-vis the super-state power But that is a different story.

CONSEQUENCES FOR SOCIOLOGICAL THEORY AND RESEARCH

How does this relate to the basic conceptual ideas of international sociology which have appeared since the 1970s, such as 'world system theory' (Wallerstein, 2004) and 'world polity' (Drori et al., 2006)? Immanuel Wallerstein's 'world system theory' is still captured by an enlarged methodological nationalism, because it presupposes the national-international dualism—as does John Meyer's concept of 'world polity'. Even though both concepts are powerful in producing extremely interesting empirical interpretations, they both ignore the historical fact that the distinction, which underpins their view of the world, namely, that between national and international spheres, is now dissolving. Nonetheless, it was this duality that helped to shape the world of the first modernity, including the key concepts (and theories) of society, state, sovereignty, legitimacy, class, solidarity, generation, and so on.

We then have to ask: How might we conceptualize a world in a set of global dynamics in which the problematic consequences of radicalized modernization effectually eliminate cornerstones and logics of action—certain historically produced fundamental distinctions and basic institutions—of its nation-state order? Thus my theory of 'reflexive or second modernity' is about the unintended consequences and challenges of the *success* of modernity. It is about *more* modernity and the crises it produces, but *not* about *post*-modernity.

How does this renewed cosmopolitan curiosity and sociological imagination relate to the post–Second World War period of sociological thinking? In the 1960s, the *Frankfurt School* and the *Critical Theory* dominated the intellectual movements. In the 1980s, this role was assumed by the *French post-modernists*; and now a cosmopolitan mixture in global sociology could give birth to a cosmopolitan vision for the humanities. This opens up the horizon for a *new Cosmopolitan Critical Theory* which investigates the social and

political grammar of the Cosmopolitan Condition and therefore has a strong standing against the retrogressive idealism of the national perspective in politics, research and theory.

REFERENCES

Arendt, H. (1958) *The Human Condition*. Chicago: University of Chicago Press.

Beck, U. (2005) *Power in the Global Age*. London: Polity Press.

—— (2006) *The Cosmopolitan Vision*. Cambridge: Polity Press.

—— (2007) 'Beyond Class and Nation: Reframing Social Inequalities in a Globalized World', *British Journal of Sociology* 58(4): 680–705.

Beck, U. and N. Sznaider (2006) 'Unpacking Cosmopolitanism for the Social Sciences: A Research Agenda', *British Journal of Sociology*, Special Issue 57(1).

Drori, G.S., J. Meyer and H. Hwang (eds) (2006) *Globalization and Organization: World Society and Organizational Change*. Oxford: Oxford University Press.

Habermas, J. (2001) *The Postnational Constellation*, trans. and ed. M. Pensky. Cambridge, MA: MIT Press.

Held, D. (1995) *Democracy and the Global Order: From the Modern State to Cosmopolitan Governance*. Cambridge: Polity Press.

Latour, B. (2003) 'Is Remodernization Occurring? And if So, How to Prove it? A Commentary on Ulrich Beck', *Theory, Culture & Society* 20(2): 35–48.

Lyotard, J-F. (1984) *The Postmodern Condition*. Manchester: Manchester University Press (original edn 1979).

Parsons, T. (1971) *The Systems of Modern Societies*. Englewood Cliffs, NJ: Prentice-Hall.

Wallerstein, I. (2004) *World-Systems Analysis: An Introduction*. Durham, NC: Duke University Press.

78. DISJUNCTION AND DIFFERENCE IN THE GLOBAL CULTURAL ECONOMY

ARJUN APPADURAI

Despite differences among globalization theorists, there is a general consensus that globalization is a consequence of the reduction in the constraints of geography on economic, political, social, and cultural social arrangements—the result of a process that geographer David Harvey has called "time-space compression." While these various aspects of globalization are interconnected, they also need to be analytically distinguished. In this excerpt from *Modernity at Large* (1996), anthropologist Arjun Appadurai (b. 1949) focuses on globalization's cultural dimensions. More specifically, he is concerned with providing a framework intended to assist in our understanding of disjunctures in the global culture. He does so by defining five "dimensions of cultural flows," giving them the following distinctive names: ethnoscapes, mediascapes, technoscapes, financescapes, and ideoscapes.

It takes only the merest acquaintance with the facts of the modern world to note that it is now an interactive system in a sense that is strikingly new. Historians and sociologists, especially those concerned with translocal processes (Hodgson 1974) and the world systems associated with capitalism (Abu-Lughod 1989; Braudel 1981–84; Curtin 1984; Wallerstein 1974; Wolf 1982), have long been aware that the world has been a congeries of large-scale interactions for many centuries. Yet today's world involves interactions of a new order and intensity. Cultural transactions between social groups in the past have generally been restricted, sometimes by the facts of geography and ecology, and at other times by active resistance to interactions with the Other (as in China for much of its history and in Japan before the Meiji Restoration). Where there have been sustained cultural transactions across large parts of the globe, they have usually involved the long-distance journey of commodities (and of the merchants most concerned with them) and of travelers and explorers of every type (Helms 1988; Schafer 1963). The two main forces for sustained cultural interaction before this century have been warfare (and the large-scale political systems sometimes generated by it) and religions of conversion, which have sometimes, as in the case of Islam, taken warfare as one of the legitimate instruments of their expansion. Thus, between travelers and merchants, pilgrims and conquerors, the world has seen much long-distance (and long-term) cultural traffic. This much seems self-evident.

But few will deny that given the problems of time, distance, and limited technologies for the command of resources across vast spaces, cultural dealings between socially and spatially separated groups have, until the past few centuries, been bridged at great cost and sustained over time only with great effort. The forces of cultural gravity seemed always to pull away from the formation of large-scale ecumenes, whether religious, commercial, or political, toward smaller-scale accretions of intimacy and interest.

Sometime in the past few centuries, the nature of this gravitational field seems to have changed. Partly because of the spirit of the expansion of Western maritime interests after 1500, and partly because of the relatively autonomous developments of large and aggressive social formations in the Americas (such as the Aztecs and the Incas), in Eurasia (such as the Mongols and their descendants, the Mughals and Ottomans), in island-Southeast Asia (such as the Buginese), and in the kingdoms of precolonial Africa (such as Dahomey), an overlapping set of ecumenes began to emerge, in which congeries of money, commerce, conquest, and migration began to create durable cross-societal bonds. This process was accelerated by the technology transfers and innovations of the late eighteenth and nineteenth centuries (e.g., Bayly 1989), which created complex colonial orders centered on European capitals and spread throughout the non-European world. This intricate and overlapping set of Eurocolonial worlds (first Spanish and Portuguese, later principally English, French, and Dutch) set the basis for a permanent traffic in ideas of peoplehood and selfhood, which created the imagined communities (Anderson 1983) of recent nationalisms throughout the world.

With what Benedict Anderson has called "print capitalism," a new power was unleashed in the world, the power of mass literacy and its attendant large-scale production of projects of ethnic affinity that were remarkably free of the need for face-to-face communication or even of indirect communication between persons and groups. The act of reading things together set the stage for movements based on a paradox—the paradox of constructed primordialism. There is, of course, a great deal else that is involved in the story of colonialism and its dialectically generated nationalisms (Chatterjee 1986), but the issue of constructed ethnicities is surely a crucial strand in this tale.

But the revolution of print capitalism and the cultural affinities and dialogues unleashed by it were only modest precursors to the world we live in now. For in the past century, there has been a technological explosion, largely in the domain of transportation and information, that makes the interactions of a print-dominated world seem as hard-won and as easily erased as the print revolution made earlier forms of cultural traffic appear. For with the advent of the steamship, the automobile, the airplane, the camera, the computer, and the telephone, we have entered into an altogether new condition of neighborliness, even with those most distant from ourselves. Marshall McLuhan, among others, sought to theorize about this world as a "global village," but theories such as McLuhan s appear to have overestimated the communitarian implications of the new media order (McLuhan and Powers 1989). We are now aware that with media, each time we are tempted to speak of the global village, we must be reminded that media create communities with "no sense of place" (Meyrowitz 1985). The world we live in now seems rhizomic (Deleuze and Guattari 1987), even schizophrenic, calling for theories of rootlessness, alienation, and psychological distance between individuals and groups on the one hand, and fantasies (or nightmares) of electronic propinquity on the other. Here, we are close to the central problematic of cultural processes in today's world.

Thus, the curiosity that recently drove Pico Iyer to Asia (1988) is in some ways the product of a confusion between some ineffable McDonaldization of the world and the much subtler play of indigenous trajectories of desire and fear with global flows of people and things. Indeed, Iyer's own impressions are testimony to the fact that, if *a* global cultural system is emerging, it is filled with ironies and resistances, sometimes camouflaged as passivity and a bottomless appetite in the Asian world for things Western.

Iyer's own account of the uncanny Philippine affinity for American popular music is rich testimony to the global culture of the hyperreal, for somehow Philippine renditions of American popular songs are both more widespread in the Philippines, and more disturbingly faithful to their originals, than they are in the United States today. An entire nation seems to have learned to mimic Kenny Rogers and the Lennon sisters, like a vast Asian Motown chorus. But *Americanization* is certainly a pallid term to apply to such a situation, for not only are there more Filipinos singing perfect renditions of some American songs (often from the American past) than there are Americans doing so, there is also, of course, the fact that the rest of their lives is not in complete synchrony with the referential world that first gave birth to these songs.

In a further globalizing twist on what Fredric Jameson has recently called "nostalgia for the present" (1989), these Filipinos look back to a world they have never lost. This is one of the central ironies of the politics of global cultural flows, especially in the arena of entertainment and leisure. It plays havoc with the hegemony of Eurochronology. American nostalgia feeds on Filipino desire represented as a hypercompetent reproduction. Here, we have nostalgia without memory. The paradox, of course, has its explanations, and they are historical; unpacked, they lay bare the story of the American missionization and political rape of the Philippines, one result of which has been the creation of a nation of make-believe Americans, who tolerated for so long a leading lady who played the piano while the slums of Manila expanded and decayed. Perhaps the most radical postmodernists would argue that this is hardly surprising because in the peculiar chronicities of late capitalism, pastiche and nostalgia are central modes of image production and reception. Americans themselves are hardly in the present anymore as they stumble into the mega-technologies of the twenty-first century garbed in the film-noir scenarios of sixties' chills, fifties' diners, forties' clothing, thirties' houses, twenties' dances, and so on ad infinitum.

As far as the United States is concerned, one might suggest that the issue is no longer one of nostalgia but of a social *imaginaire* built largely around reruns. Jameson was bold to link the politics of nostalgia to the postmodern commodity sensibility, and surely he was right (1983). The drug wars in Colombia recapitulate the tropical sweat of Vietnam, with Ollie North and his succession of masks—Jimmy Stewart concealing John Wayne concealing Spiro Agnew and all of them transmogrifying into Sylvester Stallone, who wins in Afghanistan—thus simultaneously fulfilling the secret American envy of Soviet imperialism and the rerun (this time with a happy ending) of the Vietnam War. The Rolling Stones, approaching their fifties, gyrate before eighteen-year-olds who do not appear to need the machinery of nostalgia to be sold on their parents' heroes. Paul McCartney is selling the Beatles to a new audience by hitching his oblique nostalgia to their desire for the new that smacks of the old. *Dragnet is* back in nineties' drag, and so is *Adam-12*, not to speak of *Batman* and *Mission Impossible*, all dressed up technologically but remarkably faithful to the atmospherics of their originals.

The past is now not a land to return to in a simple politics of memory. It has become a synchronic warehouse of cultural scenarios, a kind of temporal central casting, to which recourse can be taken as appropriate, depending on the movie to be made, the scene to be enacted, the hostages to be rescued. All this is par for the course, if you follow Jean Baudrillard or Jean-François Lyotard into a world of signs wholly unmoored from their social signifiers (all the world's a Disneyland). But I would like to suggest that the apparent increasing substitutability of whole periods and postures for one another, in the cultural styles of advanced capitalism, is tied to larger global forces, which have done much to show Americans that the past is usually another country. If your present is their future (as in much modernization theory and in many self-satisfied tourist fantasies), and their future is your past (as in the case of the Filipino virtuosos of American popular music), then your own past can be made to appear as simply a normalized modality of your present. Thus, although some anthropologists may continue to relegate their Others to temporal spaces that they do not themselves occupy (Fabian 1983), post-industrial cultural productions have entered a postnostalgic phase.

The crucial point, however, is that the United States is no longer the puppeteer of a world system of images but is only one node of a complex transnational construction of imaginary landscapes. The world we live in today is characterized by a new role for the imagination in social life. To grasp this new role, we need to bring together the old idea of images, especially mechanically produced images (in the Frankfurt School sense); the idea of the imagined community (in Anderson's sense); and the French idea of the imaginary (*imaginaire*) as a constructed landscape of collective aspirations, which is no more and no less real than the collective representations of Émile Durkheim, now mediated through the complex prism of modern media.

The image, the imagined, the imaginary—these are all terms that direct us to something critical and new in global cultural processes: *the imagination as a social practice.* No longer mere fantasy (opium for the masses whose real work is elsewhere), no longer simple escape (from a world defined principally by more concrete purposes and structures), no longer elite pastime (thus not relevant to the lives of ordinary people), and no longer mere contemplation (irrelevent for new forms of desire and subjectivity), the imagination has become an organized field of social practices, a form of work (in the sense of both labor and culturally organized practice), and a form of negotiation between sites of agency (individuals) and globally defined fields of possibility. This unleashing of the imagination links the play of pastiche (in some settings) to the terror and coercion of states and their competitors. The imagination is now central to all forms of agency, is itself a social fact, and is the key component of the new global order. But to make this claim meaningful, we must address some other issues.

HOMOGENIZATION AND HETEROGENIZATION

The central problem of today's global interactions is the tension between cultural homogenization and cultural heterogenization. A vast array of empirical facts could be brought to bear on the side of the homogenization argument, and much of it has come from the left end of the spectrum of media studies (Hamelink 1983; Mattelart 1983; Schiller 1976), and some from other perspectives (Gans 1985; Iyer 1988). Most often, the homogenization argument subspeciates into either an argument about Americanization or an argument about commoditization, and very often the two arguments are closely linked. What these arguments fail to consider is that at least as rapidly as forces from various metropolises are brought into new societies they tend to become indigenized in one or another way: this is true of music and housing styles as much as it is true of science and terrorism, spectacles and constitutions. The dynamics of such indigenization have just begun to be explored systemically (Barber 1987; Feld 1988; Hannerz 1987, 1989; Ivy 1988; Nicoll 1989; Yoshimoto 1989), and much more needs to be done. But it is worth noticing that for the people of Irian Jaya, Indonesianization may be more worrisome than Americanization, as Japanization may be for Koreans, Indianization for Sri Lankans, Vietnamization for the Cambodians, and Russianization for the people of Soviet Armenia and the Baltic republics. Such a list of alternative fears to Americanization could be greatly expanded, but it is not a shapeless inventory: for polities of smaller scale, there is always a fear of cultural absorption by polities of larger scale, especially those that are nearby. One man's imagined community is another man's political prison.

This scalar dynamic, which has widespread global manifestations, is also tied to the relationship between nations and states, to which I shall return later. For the moment let us note that the simplification of these many forces (and fears) of homogenization can also be exploited by nation-states in relation to their own minorities, by posing global commoditization (or capitalism, or some other such external enemy) as more real than the threat of its own hegemonic strategies.

The new global cultural economy has to be seen as a complex, overlapping, disjunctive order that cannot any longer be understood in terms of existing center-periphery models (even those that might account for multiple centers and peripheries). Nor is it susceptible to simple models of push and pull (in terms of migration theory), or of surpluses and deficits (as in traditional models of balance of trade), or of consumers and producers (as in most neo-Marxist theories of development). Even the most complex and flexible theories of global development that have come out of the Marxist tradition (Amin 1980; Mandel 1978; Wallerstein 1974; Wolf 1982) are inadequately quirky and have failed to come to terms with what Scott Lash and John Urry have called disorganized capitalism (1987). The complexity of the current global economy has to do with certain fundamental disjunctures between economy, culture, and politics that we have only begun to theorize.

I propose that an elementary framework for exploring such disjunctures is to look at the relationship among five dimensions of global cultural flows that can be termed (a) *ethnoscapes*, (b) *mediascapes*, (c) *technoscapes*, (d) *financescapes*, and (e) *ideoscapes*. The suffix-scape allows us to point to the fluid, irregular shapes of these landscapes, shapes that characterize international capital as deeply as they do international clothing styles. These terms with the common suffix *-scape* also indicate that these are not objectively given relations that look the same from every angle of vision but, rather, that they are deeply perspectival constructs, inflected by the historical, linguistic, and political situatedness of different sorts of actors: nation-states, multinationals, diasporic communities, as well as subnational groupings and movements (whether religious, political, or economic), and even intimate face-to-face groups, such as villages, neighborhoods, and families. Indeed, the individual actor is the last locus of this perspectival set of landscapes, for these landscapes are eventually navigated by agents who both experience and constitute larger formations, in part from their own sense of what these landscapes offer.

These landscapes thus are the building blocks of what (extending Benedict Anderson) I would like to call *imagined worlds*, that is, the multiple worlds that are constituted by the historically situated imaginations of persons and groups spread around the globe. . . . An important fact of the world we live in today is that many persons on the globe live in such imagined worlds (and not just in imagined communities) and thus are able to contest and sometimes even subvert the imagined worlds of the official mind and of the entrepreneurial mentality that surrounds them.

By *ethnoscapes*, I mean the landscape of persons who constitute the shifting world in which we live: tourists, immigrants, refugees, exiles, guest workers, and other moving groups and individuals constitute an essential feature of the world and appear to affect the politics of (and between) nations to a hitherto unprecedented degree. This is not to say that there are no relatively stable communities and networks of kinship, friendship, work, and leisure as well as of birth, residence, and other filial forms. But it is to say that the warp of these stabilities is everywhere shot through with the woof of human motion, as more persons and groups deal with the realities of having to move or the fantasies of wanting to move. What is more, both these realities and fantasies now function on larger scales, as men and women from villages in India think not just of moving to Poona or Madras but of moving to Dubai and Houston, and refugees from Sri Lanka find themselves in South India as well as in Switzerland, just as the Hmong are driven to London as well as to Philadelphia. And as international capital shifts its needs, as production and technology generate different needs, as nation-states shift their policies on refugee populations, these moving groups can never afford to let their imaginations rest too long, even if they wish to.

By *technoscapes*, I mean the global configuration, also ever fluid, of technology and the fact that technology, both high and low, both mechanical and informational, now moves at high speeds across various kinds of previously impervious boundaries. Many countries now are the roots of multinational enterprise: a huge steel complex in Libya may involve interests from India, China, Russia, and Japan, providing different components of new technological configurations. The odd distribution of technologies, and thus the peculiarities of these technoscapes, are increasingly driven not by any obvious economies of scale, of political control, or of market rationality but by increasingly complex relationships among money flows, political possibilities, and the availability of both un- and highly skilled labor. So, while India exports waiters and chauffeurs to Dubai and Sharjah, it also exports software engineers to the United States—indentured briefly to Tata-Burroughs or the World Bank, then laundered through the State Department to become wealthy resident aliens, who are in turn objects of seductive messages to invest their money and know-how in federal and state projects in India.

The global economy can still be described in terms of traditional indicators (as the World Bank continues to do) and studied in terms of traditional comparisons (as in Project Link at the University of Pennsylvania), but the complicated technoscapes (and the shifting ethnoscapes) that underlie these indicators and comparisons are further out of the reach of the queen of social sciences than ever before. How is one to make a meaningful comparison of wages in Japan and the United States or of real-estate costs in New York and Tokyo, without taking sophisticated account of the very complex fiscal and investment flows that link the two economies through a global grid of currency speculation and capital transfer?

Thus it is useful to speak as well of *financescapes*, as the disposition of global capital is now a more mysterious, rapid, and difficult landscape to follow than ever before, as currency markets, national stock exchanges, and commodity speculations move megamonies through national turnstiles at blinding speed, with vast, absolute implications for small differences in percentage points and time units. But the critical point is that the global relationship among ethnoscapes, technoscapes, and financescapes is deeply disjunctive and profoundly unpredictable because each of these landscapes is subject to its own constraints and incentives (some political, some informational, and some technoenvironmental), at the same time as each acts as a constraint and a parameter for movements in the others. Thus, even an elementary model of global political economy must take into account the deeply disjunctive relationships among human movement, technological flow, and financial transfers.

Further refracting these disjunctures (which hardly form a simple, mechanical global infrastructure in any case) are what I call *mediascapes and ideoscapes*, which are closely related landscapes of images. *Mediascapes* refer both to the distribution of the electronic capabilities to produce and disseminate information (newspapers, magazines, television stations, and film-production studios), which are now available to a growing number of private and public interests throughout the world, and to the images of the world created by these media. These images involve many complicated inflections, depending on their mode (documentary or entertainment), their hardware (electronic or preelectronic), their audiences (local, national, or transnational), and the interests of those who own and control them. What is most important about these mediascapes is that they provide (especially in their television, film, and cassette forms) large and complex repertoires of images, narratives, and ethnoscapes to viewers throughout the world, in which the world of commodities and the world of news and politics are profoundly mixed. What this means is that many audiences around the world experience the media themselves as a complicated and interconnected repertoire of print, celluloid, electronic screens, and billboards. The lines between the realistic and the fictional landscapes they see are blurred, so that the farther away these audiences are from the direct experiences of metropolitan life, the more likely they are to construct imagined worlds that are chimerical, aesthetic, even fantastic objects, particularly if assessed by the criteria of some other perspective, some other imagined world.

Mediascapes, whether produced by private or state interests, tend to be image-centered, narrative-based accounts of strips of reality, and what they offer to those who experience and transform them is a series of elements (such as characters, plots, and textual forms) out of which scripts can be formed of imagined lives, their own as well as those of others living in other places. These scripts can and do get disaggregated into

complex sets of metaphors by which people live (Lakoff and Johnson 1980) as they help to constitute narratives of the Other and protonarratives of possible lives, fantasies that could become prolegomena to the desire for acquisition and movement.

Ideoscapes are also concatenations of images, but they are often directly political and frequently have to do with the ideologies of states and the counterideologies of movements explicitly oriented to capturing state power or a piece of it. These ideoscapes are composed of elements of the Enlightenment worldview, which consists of a chain of ideas, terms, and images, including *freedom, welfare, rights, sovereignty, representation*, and the master term *democracy*. The master narrative of the Enlightenment (and its many variants in Britain, France, and the United States) was constructed with a certain internal logic and presupposed a certain relationship between reading, representation, and the public sphere. (For the dynamics of this process in the early history of the United States, see Warner 1990.) But the diaspora of these terms and images across the world, especially since the nineteenth century, has loosened the internal coherence that held them together in a Euro-American master narrative and provided instead a loosely structured synopticon of politics, in which different nation-states, as part of their evolution, have organized their political cultures around different keywords (e.g., Williams 1976).

As a result of the differential diaspora of these keywords, the political narratives that govern communication between elites and followers in different parts of the world involve problems of both a semantic and pragmatic nature: semantic to the extent that words (and their lexical equivalents) require careful translation from context to context in their global movements, and pragmatic to the extent that the use of these words by political actors and their audiences may be subject to very different sets of contextual conventions that mediate their translation into public politics. Such conventions are not only matters of the nature of political rhetoric: for example, what does the aging Chinese leadership mean when it refers to the dangers of hooliganism? What does the South Korean leadership mean when it speaks of discipline as the key to democratic industrial growth?

These conventions also involve the far more subtle question of what sets of communicative genres are valued in what way (newspapers versus cinema, for example) and what sorts of pragmatic genre conventions govern the collective readings of different kinds of text. So, while an Indian audience may be attentive to the resonances of a political speech in terms of some keywords and phrases reminiscent of Hindi cinema, a Korean audience may respond to the subtle codings of Buddhist or neo-Confucian rhetoric encoded in a political document. The very relationship of reading to hearing and seeing may vary in important ways that determine the morphology of these different ideoscapes as they shape themselves in different national and transnational contexts. This globally variable synaesthesia has hardly even been noted, but it demands urgent analysis. Thus *democracy* has clearly become a master term, with powerful echoes from Haiti and Poland to the former Soviet Union and China, but it sits at the center of a variety of ideoscapes, composed of distinctive pragmatic configurations of rough translations of other central terms from the vocabulary of the Enlightenment. This creates ever new terminological kaleidoscopes, as states (and the groups that seek to capture them) seek to pacify populations whose own ethnoscapes are in motion and whose mediascapes may create severe problems for the ideoscapes with which they are presented. The fluidity of ideoscapes is complicated in particular by the growing diasporas (both voluntary and involuntary) of intellectuals who continuously inject new meaning-streams into the discourse of democracy in different parts of the world.

This extended terminological discussion of the five terms I have coined sets the basis for a tentative formulation about the conditions under which current global flows occur: they occur in and through the growing disjunctures among ethnoscapes, technoscapes, financescapes, mediascapes, and ideoscapes. This formulation, the core of my model of global cultural flow, needs some explanation. First, people, machinery, money, images, and ideas now follow increasingly nonisomorphic paths; of course, at all periods in human history, there have been some disjunctures in the flows of these things, but the sheer speed, scale, and volume of each of these flows are now so great that the disjunctures have become central to the politics of global culture. The Japanese are notoriously hospitable to ideas and are stereotyped as inclined to export (all) and import (some) goods, but they are also notoriously closed to

immigration, like the Swiss, the Swedes, and the Saudis. Yet the Swiss and the Saudis accept populations of guest workers, thus creating labor diasporas of Turks, Italians, and other circum-Mediterranean groups. Some such guest-worker groups maintain continuous contact with their home nations, like the Turks, but others, like high-level South Asian migrants, tend to desire lives in their new homes, raising anew the problem of reproduction in a deterritorialized context.

Deterritorialization, in general, is one of the central forces of the modern world because it brings laboring populations into the lower-class sectors and spaces of relatively wealthy societies, while sometimes creating exaggerated and intensified senses of criticism or attachment to politics in the home state. Deterritorialization, whether of Hindus, Sikhs, Palestinians, or Ukrainians, is now at the core of a variety of global fundamentalisms, including Islamic and Hindu fundamentalism. In the Hindu case, for example, it is clear that the overseas movement of Indians has been exploited by a variety of interests both within and outside India to create a complicated network of finances and religious identifications, by which the problem of cultural reproduction for Hindus abroad has become tied to the politics of Hindu fundamentalism at home.

At the same time, deterritorialization creates new markets for film companies, art impresarios, and travel agencies, which thrive on the need of the deterritorialized population for contact with its homeland. Naturally, these invented homelands, which constitute the mediascapes of deterritorialized groups, can often become sufficiently fantastic and one-sided that they provide the material for new ideoscapes in which ethnic conflicts can begin to erupt. The creation of Khalistan, an invented homeland of the deterritorialized Sikh population of England, Canada, and the United States, is one example of the bloody potential in such mediascapes as they interact with the internal colonialisms of the nation-state (e.g., Hechter 1975). The West Bank, Namibia, and Eritrea are other theaters for the enactment of the bloody negotiation between existing nation-states and various deterritorialized groupings.

It is in the fertile ground of deterritorialization, in which money, commodities, and persons are involved in ceaselessly chasing each other around the world, that the mediascapes and ideoscapes of the modern world find their fractured and fragmented counterpart. For the ideas and images produced by mass media often are only partial guides to the goods and experiences that deterritorialized populations transfer to one another. In Mira Nair's brilliant film *India Cabaret*, we see the multiple loops of this fractured deterritorialization as young women, barely competent in Bombay's metropolitan glitz, come to seek their fortunes as cabaret dancers and prostitutes in Bombay, entertaining men in clubs with dance formats derived wholly from the prurient dance sequences of Hindi films. These scenes in turn cater to ideas about Western and foreign women and their looseness, while they provide tawdry career alibis for these women. Some of these women come from Kerala, where cabaret clubs and the pornographic film industry have blossomed, partly in response to the purses and tastes of Keralites returned from the Middle East, where their diasporic lives away from women distort their very sense of what the relations between men and women might be. These tragedies of displacement could certainly be replayed in a more detailed analysis of the relations between the Japanese and German sex tours to Thailand and the tragedies of the sex trade in Bangkok, and in other similar loops that tie together fantasies about the Other, the conveniences and seductions of travel, the economics of global trade, and the brutal mobility fantasies that dominate gender politics in many parts of Asia and the world at large.

While far more could be said about the cultural politics of deterritorialization and the larger sociology of displacement that it expresses, it is appropriate at this juncture to bring in the role of the nation-state in the disjunctive global economy of culture today. The relationship between states and nations is everywhere an embattled one. It is possible to say that in many societies the nation and the state have become one another's projects. That is, while nations (or more properly groups with ideas about nationhood) seek to capture or co-opt states and state power, states simultaneously seek to capture and monopolize ideas about nationhood (Baruah 1986; Chatterjee 1986; Nandy 1989). In general, separatist transnational movements, including those that have included terror in their methods, exemplify nations in search of states. Sikhs, Tamil Sri Lankans, Basques, Moros, Quebecois—each of these represents imagined communities that seek to create states of their own or carve pieces out of existing states. States, on the other hand, are everywhere seeking to monopolize the moral resources of community, either by flatly claiming perfect coevality between nation and state, or by systematically museumizing and representing all the groups within them in a variety of heritage politics that seems remarkably uniform throughout the world (Handler 1988; Herzfeld 1982; McQueen 1988).

Here, national and international mediascapes are exploited by nation-states to pacify separatists or even the potential fissiparousness of all ideas of difference. Typically, contemporary nation-states do this by exercising taxonomic control over difference, by creating various kinds of international spectacle to domesticate difference, and by seducing small groups with the fantasy of self-display on some sort of global or cosmopolitan stage. One important new feature of global cultural politics, tied to the disjunctive relationships among the various landscapes discussed earlier, is that state and nation are at each other´s throats, and the hyphen that links them is now less an icon of conjuncture than an index of disjuncture. This disjunctive relationship between nation and state has two levels: at the level of any given nation-state, it means that there is a battle of the imagination, with state and nation seeking to cannibalize one another. Here is the seedbed of brutal separatisms—majoritarianisms that seem to have appeared from nowhere and microidentities that have become political projects within the nation-state. At another level, this disjunctive relationship is deeply entangled with the global disjunctures discussed throughout this chapter: ideas of nationhood appear to be steadily increasing in scale and regularly crossing existing state boundaries, sometimes, as with the Kurds, because previous identities stretched across vast national spaces or, as with the Tamils in Sri Lanka, the dormant threads of a transnational diaspora have been activated to ignite the micropolitics of a nation-state.

In discussing the cultural politics that have subverted the hyphen that links the nation to the state, it is especially important not to forget the mooring of such politics in the irregularities that now characterize disorganized capital (Kothari 1989; Lash and Urry 1987). Because labor, finance, and technology are now so widely separated, the volatilities that underlie movements for nationhood (as large as transnational Islam on the one hand, or as small as the movement of the Gurkhas for a separate state in Northeast India) grind against the vulnerabilities that characterize the relationships between states. States find themselves pressed to stay open by the forces of media, technology, and travel that have fueled consumerism throughout the world and have increased the craving, even in the non-Western world, for new commodities and spectacles. On the other hand, these very cravings can become caught up in new ethnoscapes, mediascapes, and, eventually, ideoscapes, such as democracy in China, that the state cannot tolerate as threats to its own control over ideas of nationhood and peoplehood. States throughout the world are under siege, especially where contests over the ideoscapes of democracy are fierce and fundamental, and where there are radical disjunctures between ideoscapes and technoscapes (as in the case of very small countries that lack contemporary technologies of production and information); or between ideoscapes and financescapes (as in countries such as Mexico or Brazil, where international lending influences national politics to a very large degree); or between ideoscapes and ethnoscapes (as in Beirut, where diasporic, local, and translocal filiations are suicidally at battle); or between ideoscapes and mediascapes (as in many countries in the Middle East and Asia) where the lifestyles represented on both national and international TV and cinema completely overwhelm and undermine the rhetoric of national politics. In the Indian case, the myth of the law-breaking hero has emerged to mediate this naked struggle between the pieties and realities of Indian politics, which has grown increasingly brutalized and corrupt (Vachani 1989).

The transnational movement of the martial arts, particularly through Asia, as mediated by the Hollywood and Hong Kong film industries (Zarilli 1995) is a rich illustration of the ways in which long-standing martial arts traditions, reformulated to meet the fantasies of contemporary (sometimes lumpen) youth populations, create new cultures of masculinity and violence, which are in turn the fuel for increased violence in national and international politics. Such violence is in turn the spur to an increasingly rapid and amoral arms trade that penetrates the entire world. The worldwide spread of the AK-47 and the Uzi, in films, in

corporate and state security, in terror, and in police and military activity, is a reminder that apparently simple technical uniformities often conceal an increasingly complex set of loops, linking images of violence to aspirations for community in some imagined world.

Returning then to the ethnoscapes with which I began, the central paradox of ethnic politics in today's world is that primordia (whether of language or skin color or neighborhood or kinship) have become globalized. That is, sentiments, whose greatest force is in their ability to ignite intimacy into a political state and turn locality into a staging ground for identity, have become spread over vast and irregular spaces as groups move yet stay linked to one another through sophisticated media capabilities. This is not to deny that such primordia are often the product of invented traditions (Hobsbawm and Ranger 1983) or retrospective affiliations, but to emphasize that because of the disjunctive and unstable interplay of commerce, media, national policies, and consumer fantasies, ethnicity, once a genie contained in the bottle of some sort of locality (however large), has now become a global force, forever slipping in and through the cracks between states and borders.

But the relationship between the cultural and economic levels of this new set of global disjunctures is not a simple one-way street in which the terms of global cultural politics are set wholly by, or confined wholly within, the vicissitudes of international flows of technology, labor, and finance, demanding only a modest modification of existing neo-Marxist models of uneven development and state formation. There is a deeper change, itself driven by the disjunctures among all the landscapes I have discussed and constituted by their continuously fluid and uncertain interplay, that concerns the relationship between production and consumption in today's global economy. Here, I begin with Marx's famous (and often mined) view of the fetishism of the commodity and suggest that this fetishism has been replaced in the world at large (now seeing the world as one large, interactive system, composed of many complex subsystems) by two mutually supportive descendants, the first of which I call production fetishism and the second, the fetishism of the consumer.

By *production fetishism* I mean an illusion created by contemporary transnational production loci that masks translocal capital, transnational earning flows, global management, and often faraway workers (engaged in various kinds of high-tech putting-out operations) in the idiom and spectacle of local (sometimes even worker) control, national productivity, and territorial sovereignty. To the extent that various kinds of free-trade zones have become the models for production at large, especially of high-tech commodities, production has itself become a fetish, obscuring not social relations as such but the relations of production, which are increasingly transnational. The locality (both in the sense of the local factory or site of production and in the extended sense of the nation-state) becomes a fetish that disguises the globally dispersed forces that actually drive the production process. This generates alienation (in Marx's sense) twice intensified, for its social sense is now compounded by a complicated spatial dynamic that is increasingly global.

As for the *fetishism of the consumer*, I mean to indicate here that the consumer has been transformed through commodity flows (and the mediascapes, especially of advertising, that accompany them) into a sign, both in Baudrillard´s sense of a simulacrum that only asymptotically approaches the form of a real social agent, and in the sense of a mask for the real seat of agency, which is not the consumer but the producer and the many forces that constitute production. Global advertising is the key technology for the worldwide dissemination of a plethora of creative and culturally well-chosen ideas of consumer agency. These images of agency are increasingly distortions of a world of merchandising so subtle that the consumer is consistently helped to believe that he or she is an actor, where in fact he or she is at best a chooser.

The globalization of culture is not the same as its homogenization, but globalization involves the use of a variety of instruments of homogenization (armaments, advertising techniques, language hegemonies, and clothing styles) that are absorbed into local political and cultural economies, only to be repatriated as heterogeneous dialogues of national sovereignty, free enterprise, and fundamentalism in which the state plays an increasingly delicate role: too much openness to global flows, and the nation-state is threatened by revolt, as in the China syndrome; too little, and the state exits the international stage, as Burma, Albania, and North Korea in various ways have done. In general, the state has become the arbitrageur of this *repatriation of difference* (in the form of goods, signs, slogans, and styles). But this repatriation or export of the designs and commodities of difference continuously exacerbates the internal politics of majoritarianism and homogenization, which is most frequently played out in debates over heritage.

Thus the central feature of global culture today is the politics of the mutual effort of sameness and difference to cannibalize one another and thereby proclaim their successful hijacking of the twin Enlightenment ideas of the triumphantly universal and the resiliency particular. This mutual cannibalization shows its ugly face in riots, refugee flows, state-sponsored torture, and ethnocide (with or without state support). Its brighter side is in the expansion of many individual horizons of hope and fantasy, in the global spread of oral rehydration therapy and other low-tech instruments of well-being, in the susceptibility even of South Africa to the force of global opinion, in the inability of the Polish state to repress its own working classes, and in the growth of a wide range of progressive, transnational alliances. Examples of both sorts could be multiplied. The critical point is that both sides of the coin of global cultural process today are products of the infinitely varied mutual contest of sameness and difference on a stage characterized by radical disjunctures between different sorts of global flows and the uncertain landscapes created in and through these disjunctures.

REFERENCES

Abu-Lughod, L. (1989) *Before European Hegemony: The World System A.D. 1250–1350*. New York: Oxford University Press.

Amin, S. (1980) *Class and Nation: Historically and in the Current Crisis*. New York and London: Monthly Review Press.

Anderson, B. (1983) *Imagined Communities: Reflections on the Origin and Spread of Nationalism*. London: Verso.

Barber, K. (1987) Popular Arts in Africa, *African Studies Review* 30 (3, September): 1–78.

Barrier, G. N. (Ed.) (1981) *The Census in British India: New Perspectives*. New Delhi: Manohar.

Barth, F. (Ed.) (1969) *Ethnic Groups and Boundaries*. Boston: Little, Brown.

Baruah, S. (1986) Immigration, Ethnic Conflict and Political Turmoil, Assam 1979–1985, *Asian Survey* 26 (11, November): 1184–1206.

Bayly, C. A. (1989) *Imperial Meridian: The British Empire and the World, 1780–1830*. London and New York: Longman.

Braudel, F. (1981–1984) *Civilization and Capitalism, 15th–18th Century* (3 vols.). London: Collins.

Chatterjee, P. (1986) *Nationalist Thought and the Colonial World: A Derivative Discourse?* London: Zed Books.

Curtin, P. (1984) *Cross-Cultural Trade in World History*. Cambridge: Cambridge University Press.

Deleuze, G., and F. Guattari (1987) *A Thousand Plateaus: Capitalism and Schizophrenia*. B. Massumi (trans.). Minneapolis: University of Minnesota Press.

Fabian, J. (1983) *Time and the Other: How Anthropology Makes Its Object*. New York: Columbia University Press.

Feld, S. (1988) Notes on World Beat, *Public Culture* 1 (1): 31–37.

Gans, E. (1985) *The End of a Culture: Toward a Generative Anthropology*. Berkeley: University of California Press.

Hamelink, C. (1983) *Cultural Autonomy in Global Communications*. New York: Longman.

Handler, R. (1988) *Nationalism and the Politics of Culture in Quebec*. Madison: University of Wisconsin Press.

Hannerz, U. (1987) The World in Creolization, *Africa* 57 (4): 546–559.

——. (1989) Notes on the Global Ecumene, *Public Culture* 1 (2, Spring): 66–75.

Hechter, M. (1975) *Internal Colonialism: The Celtic Fringe in British National Development, 4536–4966*. Berkeley: University of California Press.

Helms, M. W. (1988) *Ulysses' Sail: An Ethnographic Odyssey of Power, Knowledge, and Geographical Distance*. Princeton, N.J.: Princeton University Press.

Herzfeld, M. (1982) *Ours Once More: Folklore, Ideology and the Making of Modern Greece*. Austin: University of Texas Press.

Hobsbawm, E., and T. Ranger (Eds.) (1983) *The Invention of Tradition*. New York: Columbia University Press.

Hodgson, M. (1974) *The Venture of Islam, Conscience and History in a World Civilization*. (3 vols.) Chicago: University of Chicago Press.

Ivy, M. (1988) Tradition and Difference in the Japanese Mass Media, *Public Culture* 1 (1): 21–29.

Iyer, P. (1988) *Video Night in Kathmandu*. New York: Knopf.

Jameson, F. (1983) Postmodernism and Consumer Society. In H. Foster (Ed.) *The Anti-Aesthetic: Essays on Postmodern Culture*. Port Townsend, Wash.: Bay Press, 111–25.

——. (1989) *State Against Democracy: In Search of Humane Governance*. New York: New Horizons.

Kothari, R. (1989) *State against Democracy: In Search of Humane Alternatives*. Delhi: Ajanta Publications. New York: New Horizon Press.

Lakoff, G., and M. Johnson (1980) *Metaphors We Live By*. Chicago and London: University of Chicago Press.

Lash, S., and J. Urry (1987) *The End of Organized Capitalism*. Madison: University of Wisconsin Press.

Mandel, E. (1978) *Late Capitalism*. London: Verso.

Mattelart, A. (1983) *Transnationals and the Third World: The Struggle for Culture*. South Hadley, Mass.: Bergin and Garvey.

McLuhan M., and B. R. Powers. (1989) *The Global Village: Transformations in World, Life and Media in the 2ist Century*. New York: Oxford University Press.

McQueen, H. (1988) The Australian Stamp: Image, Design and Ideology, *Arena* 84 (Spring): 78–96.

Meyrowitz, J. (1985) *No Sense of Place: The Impact of Electronic Media on Social Behavior*. New York: Oxford University Press.

Nandy, A. (1989) The Political Culture of the Indian State, *Daedalus* 118 (4): 1–26.

Nicoll, F. (1989) My Trip to Alice, *Criticism, Heresy and Interpretation* 3: 21–32.

Schafer, E. (1963) *Golden Peaches of Samarkand: A Study of Vang Exotics*. Berkeley: University of California Press.

Schiller, H. (1976) *Communication and Cultural Domination*. White Plains, N.Y.: International Arts and Sciences.

Vachani, L. (1989) Narrative, Pleasure and Ideology in the Hindi Film: An Analysis of the Outsider Formula. M.A. Thesis, Annenberg School of Communication, University of Pennsylvania.

Wallerstein, I. (1974) *The Modern World System*. (2 Vols.) New York and London: Academic Press.

Warner, M. (1990) *The Letters of the Republic: Publication and the Public Sphere in Eighteenth-Century America*. Cambridge, Mass.: Harvard University Press.

Williams, R. (1976) *Keywords*. New York: Oxford University Press.

Wolf, E. (1982) *Europe and the People Without History*. Berkeley: University of California Press.

Yoshimoto, M. (1989) The Postmodern and Mass Images in Japan, *Public Culture* 1 (2) 8–25.

Zarilli, P (1995) Repositioning the Body: An Indian Martial Art and its Pan-Asian Society Publics. In C. A. Breckenridge (Ed.) *Consuming Modernity: Public Culture in a South Asian World*. Minneapolis: University of Minnesota Press.

79. THEORIZING GLOBALIZATION

DOUGLAS KELLNER

In a theoretical perspective on globalization shaped by critical theory, Douglas Kellner (b. 1943) attempts to link the cultural, economic, and political aspects of globalization in what he refers to as a dialectical framework. He is quite clear about the forces driving globalization. They are the interconnected impacts of technological developments—particularly regarding communication technologies and transport advances—and capitalism. Technology and capitalism do not, however, produce a deterministic outcome. Instead, globalization is construed as being both multidimensional and contested. This being the case, globalization needs to be theorized as inherently contradictory, the task being to offer a theoretical account of the tensions between homogenization and fragmentation (an instance of which Benjamin Barber has colorfully described as the tension between McWorld and Jihad). Kellner is interested in the prospects of a progressive political agenda aimed at promoting equality and democracy on a global scale. To that end, he examines the significance of the incipient global movement against capitalist globalization, specifically pointing to the 1999 protests against the World Trade Organization (WTO) in Seattle and subsequent organized protests around the world.

Globalization appears to be the buzzword of the 1990s, the primary attractor of books, articles, and heated debate, just as postmodernism was the most fashionable and debated topic of the 1980s. A wide and diverse range of social theorists are arguing that today's world is organized by accelerating globalization, which is strengthening the dominance of a world capitalist economic system, supplanting the primacy of the nation-state with transnational corporations and organizations, and eroding local cultures and traditions through a global culture.[1] Marxists, world-systems theorists, functionalists, Weberians, and other contemporary theorists are converging on the position that globalization is a distinguishing trend of the present moment.

Moreover, advocates of a postmodern break in history argue that developments in transnational capitalism are producing a new global historical configuration of post-Fordism, or postmodernism, as an emergent cultural logic of capitalism (Harvey 1989; Soja 1989, Jameson 1991; Gottdiener 1995). Others define the emergent global economy and culture as a "network society" grounded in new communications and information technology (Castells 1996, 1997, 1998). For others, globalization marks the triumph of capitalism and its market economy.[2] Some theorists see the emergence of a new transnational ruling elite and the universalization of consumerism (Sklair 2001), while others stress global fragmentation of "the clash of civilizations" (Huntington 1996). Driving "post" discourses into novel realms of theory and politics, Michael Hardt and Antonio Negri (2000) present the emergence of "Empire" as producing fresh forms of sovereignty, economy, culture, and political struggle that open the new millennium to an unforeseeable and unpredictable flow of novelties, surprises, and upheavals.

Reprinted from "Theorizing Globalization," by Douglas Kellner, *Sociological Theory*, Vol. 20, No. 3 (Nov., 2002), pp. 285–305. Reprinted by permission of American Sociological Association. ✦

Indeed, globalization is one of the most hotly debated issues of the present era. For some, it is a cover concept for global capitalism and imperialism and is accordingly condemned as another form of the imposition of the logic of capital and the market on ever more regions of the world and spheres of life. For others, it is the continuation of modernization and a force of progress, increased wealth, freedom, democracy, and happiness. Its defenders present globalization as beneficial, generating fresh economic opportunities, political democratization, cultural diversity, and the opening to an exciting new world. Its critics see globalization as harmful, bringing about increased domination and control by the wealthier overdeveloped nations over the poor underdeveloped countries, thus increasing the hegemony of the "haves" over the "have-nots". In addition, supplementing the negative view, globalization critics assert that globalization produces an undermining of democracy, a cultural homogenization, and increased destruction of natural species and the environment.[3] Some imagine the globalization project—whether viewed positively or negatively—as inevitable and beyond human control and intervention, whereas others view it generating new conflicts and new spaces for struggle, distinguishing between globalization from above and globalization from below (Brecher, Costello, and Smith 2000). In this study, I sketch aspects of a critical theory of globalization that will discuss the fundamental transformations in the world economy, politics, and culture in a dialectical framework that distinguishes between progressive and emancipatory features and oppressive and negative attributes. This requires articulations of the contradictions and ambiguities of globalization and the ways that globalization both is imposed from above and yet can be contested and reconfigured from below. I argue that the key to understanding globalization is theorizing it as at once a product of technological revolution and the global restructuring of capitalism in which economic, technological, political, and cultural features are intertwined. From this perspective, one should avoid both technological and economic determinism and all one-sided optics of globalization as a highly complex, contradictory, and thus ambiguous set of institutions and social relations, as well as one involving flows of goods,

services, ideas, technologies, cultural forms, and people (see Appadurai 1996).

Finally, I will raise the question of whether debates centered around the "post" (e.g., postmodernism, post-industrialism, post-Fordism, and so on) do or do not help elucidate the phenomenon of globalization. I argue in the affirmative, claiming that discourses of the "post" dramatize what is new, original, and different in our current situation, but that such discourses can be and are easily misused. For the discourse of postmodernity, for example, to have any force, it must be grounded in analysis of scientific and technological revolution and the global restructuring of capital, or it is just an empty buzzword (see Best and Kellner 1997, 2001). Thus, to properly theorize postmodernity one must articulate globalization and the roles of technoscience and new technologies in its construction. In turn, understanding how scientific and technological revolution and the global restructuring of capitalism are creating unique historical configurations of globalization helps one perceive the urgency and force of the discourse of the "post."

GLOBALIZATION, TECHNOLOGICAL REVOLUTION, AND THE RESTRUCTURING OF CAPITALISM

For critical social theory, globalization involves both capitalist markets and sets of social relations *and* flows of commodities, capital, technology, ideas, forms of culture, and people across national boundaries via a global networked society (see Castells 1996, 1997, 1998; Held et al. 1999). The transmutations of technology and capital work together to create a new globalized and interconnected world. A technological revolution involving the creation of a computerized network of communication, transportation, and exchange is the presupposition of a globalized economy, along with the extension of a world capitalist market system that is absorbing ever more areas of the world and spheres of production, exchange, and consumption into its orbit. The technological revolution presupposes global computerized networks and the free movement of goods, information, and peoples across national boundaries. Hence, the Internet and global computer networks make possible globalization by producing a technological infrastructure for the global economy. Computerized networks, satellite-communication systems, and the software and hardware that link together and facilitate the global economy depend on breakthroughs in microphysics. Technoscience has generated transistors, increasingly powerful and sophisticated computer chips, integrated circuits, high-tech communication systems, and a technological revolution that provides an infrastructure for the global economy and society (see Gilder 1989, 2000; Kaku 1997; Best and Kellner 2001).

From this perspective, globalization cannot be understood without comprehending the scientific and technological revolutions and global restructuring of capital that are the motor and matrix of globalization. Many theorists of globalization, however, either fail to observe the fundamental importance of scientific and technological revolution and the new technologies that help spawn globalization or interpret the process in a technological determinist framework that occludes the economic dimensions of the imperatives and institutions of capitalism. Such one-sided optics fail to grasp the co-evolution of science, technology, and capitalism and the complex and highly ambiguous system of globalization that combines capitalism and democracy, technological mutations, and a turbulent mixture of costs and benefits, gains and losses.

In order to theorize the global network economy, one therefore needs to avoid the extremes of technological and economic determinism. Technological determinists frequently use the discourse of postindustrial or postmodern society to describe current developments. This discourse often produces an ideal-type distinction between a previous mode of industrial production, characterized by heavy industry, mass production and consumption, bureaucratic organization, and social conformity, and a new postindustrial society, characterized by "flexible production" or post-Fordism, in which new technologies serve as the demiurge to a new postmodernity (Harvey 1989).

For postmodern theorists such as Jean Baudrillard (1993), technologies of information and social reproduction (e.g., simulation) have permeated every aspect of society and created a new social environment. In the movement toward postmodernity, Baudrillard claims that humanity has left behind reality and modern conceptions, as well as the world of modernity. This postmodern adventure is marked by an implosion of technology and the human, which is generating a new posthuman species and postmodern world.[4] For other less extravagant theorists of the technological revolution, the human species is evolving into a novel, postindustrial technosociety, culture, and condition in which technology, knowledge, and information are the axial or organizing principles (Bell 1976).

There are positive and negative models of technological determinism. A positive discourse envisages new technologies as producing a new economy interpreted affirmatively as fabricating a fresh wealth of nations. On this affirmative view, globalization provides opportunities for small business and individual entrepreneurs, empowering excluded persons and social groups. Technophiles claim that new technologies also make possible increased democratization, communication, education, culture, entertainment, and other social benefits, thus generating a Utopia of social progress.

Few legitimating theories of the information and technological revolution, however, contextualize the structuring, implementation, marketing, and use of new technologies in the context of the vicissitudes of contemporary capitalism. The ideologues of the information society act as if technology were an autonomous force and either neglect to theorize the co-evolution of capital and technology or use the advancements of technology to legitimate market capitalism (i.e., Gilder 1989, 2000; Gates 1995, 1999; Friedman 1999). Theorists such as Kevin Kelly, the executive editor of *Wired*, think that humanity has entered a postcapitalist society that constitutes an original and innovative stage of history and economy at which previous categories do not apply.[5] Or, like Bill Gates (1995, 1999), defenders of the new "economy" imagine computer and information technologies producing a "friction-free capitalism," perceived as a highly creative form of capitalism that goes beyond its previous contradictions, forms, and limitations.

By contrast, a negative version of technological determinism portrays the new world system as constituted by a monolithic or homogenizing technological system of domination. German philosopher and Nazi supporter Martin Heidegger talked of the "complete Europeanisation of the earth and man" (Heidegger 1971:15), claiming that Western science and technology were creating a new organization or framework, which he called *Gestell* (or "enframing"), that was encompassing ever more realms of experience. French theorist Jacques Ellul (1964) depicted a totalitarian expansion of technology—what he called *la technique*—imposing its logic on ever more domains of life and human practices. More recently, a large number of technophobic critics have argued that new technologies and global cyberspace constitute a realm of alienation and reification in which humans are alienated from our bodies, other people, nature, tradition, and lived communities (Borgmann 1994, 1999; Slouka 1995; Stoll 1995; Shenk 1997; Virilio 1998).

In addition to technologically determinist and reductive postindustrial accounts of globalization, there are economic determinist discourses that view it primarily as the continuation of capitalism, rather than its restructuring through technological revolution. A large number of theorists conceive globalization simply as a process of the imposition of the logic of capital and neoliberalism on various parts of the world, rather than seeing the restructuring process and the enormous changes and transformations that scientific and technological revolution are producing in the networked economy and society. Capital-logic theorists, for instance, portray globalization primarily as the imposition of the logic of capital on the world economy, polity, and culture, often engaging in economic determinism, rather than seeing the complex new configurations of economy, technology, polity, and culture and the attendant forces of domination and resistance. In the same vein, some critical theorists depict globalization as the triumph of a globalized hegemony of market capitalism, where capital creates a homogenous world culture of commercialization, commodification, administration, surveillance, and domination (Robins and Webster 1999).

From these economistic perspectives, globalization is merely a continuation of previous social tendencies—that is, the logic of capital and domination by corporate and commercial interests of the world economy and culture. Defenders of capitalism, by contrast, present globalization as the triumph of free markets, democracy, and individual freedom (Fukuyama

1992; Friedman 1999). Hence, both positive and negative versions of economic and technological determinism exist. Most theories of globalization, therefore, are reductive, undialectical, and one-sided, either failing to see the interaction between technological features of globalization and the global restructuring of capitalism or failing to articulate the complex relations between capitalism and democracy. Dominant discourses of globalization are thus one-sidedly for or against globalization, failing to grasp the contradictions and the conflicting costs and benefits, upsides and downsides, of the process. Hence, many current theories of globalization do not capture the novelty and ambiguity of the present moment, which involves both innovative forms of technology and economy and emergent conflicts and problems generated by the contradictions of globalization.

In particular, an economic determinism and reductionism that merely depicts globalization as the continuation of market capitalism fails to comprehend the emergent forms and modes of capitalism itself, which are based on novel developments in science, technology, culture, and everyday life. Likewise, technological determinism fails to note how the new technologies and new economy are part of a global restructuring of capitalism and are not autonomous forces that themselves are engendering a new society and economy that breaks with the previous mode of social organization. The postindustrial society is sometimes referred to as the "knowledge society" or "information society," in which knowledge and information are given more predominant roles than in earlier days (see the survey and critique in Webster 1995). It is now obvious that the knowledge and information sectors are increasingly important domains of our contemporary moment, and that the theories of Daniel Bell and other postindustrial theorists are thus not as ideological and far off the mark as many of his critics on the left once argued. In order to avoid the technological determinism and idealism of many forms of this theory, however, one should theorize the information or knowledge "revolution" as part and parcel of a new form of *technocapitalism* marked by a synthesis of capital and technology.

Some poststructuralist theories that stress the complexity of globalization exaggerate the disjunctions and autonomous flows of capital, technology, culture, people, and goods. Thus, a critical theory of globalization grounds globalization in a theory of capitalist restructuring and technological revolution. To paraphrase Max Horkheimer, whoever wants to talk about capitalism must talk about globalization, and it is impossible to theorize globalization without talking about the restructuring of capitalism. The term "technocapitalism" is useful to describe the synthesis of capital and technology in the present organization of society (Kellner 1989a). Unlike theories of postmodernity (e.g., Baudrillard's) or the knowledge and information society, which often argue that technology is *the* new organizing principle of society, the concept of technocapitalism points to both the increasingly important role of technology *and* the enduring primacy of capitalist relations of production. In an era of unrestrained capitalism, it would be difficult to deny that contemporary societies are still organized around production and capital accumulation and that capitalist imperatives continue to dominate production, distribution, and consumption, as well as other cultural, social, and political domains.[6] Workers remain exploited by capitalists, and capital persists as the hegemonic force—more so than ever after the collapse of communism.

Moreover, with the turn toward neoliberalism as a hegemonic ideology and practice, the market and its logic come to triumph over public goods, and the state is subservient to economic imperatives and logic. Yet the term "technocapitalism" points to a new configuration of capitalist society in which technical and scientific knowledge, computerization and automation of labor, and information technology and multimedia play a role in the process of production analogous to the function of human labor-power, mechanization of the labor process, and machines in an earlier era of capitalism. This process is generating novel modes of a societal organization, forms of culture and everyday life, conflicts, and modes of struggle.

The emergence of innovative forms of technology, politics, culture, and economy marks a situation parallel to that confronted by the Frankfurt school in the 1930s. These German theorists, who left Nazi Germany, were forced to theorize the new configurations brought about by the transition from market to state-monopoly capitalism (Bronner and Kellner 1989; Kellner 1989a). In their now classic texts, the Frankfurt school analyzed: the emergent forms of social and economic organization, technology, and culture; the rise of giant corporations and cartels and the capitalist state in "organized capitalism," in both its fascist and "democratic" state capitalist forms; and the culture industries and mass culture that served as new modes of social control, powerful forms of ideology and domination, and novel configurations of culture and everyday life.

Today, critical theorists confront the challenge of theorizing the emergent forms of technocapitalism and novelties of the present era constructed by syntheses of technology and capital in the formation of a new stage of global capitalism. The notion of technocapitalism attempts to avoid technological or economic determinism by guiding theorists to perceive the interaction of capital and technology in the present moment. Capital is generating innovative forms of technology, just as its restructuring is producing novel configurations of a networked global economy, culture, and polity. In terms of political economy, the emergent postindustrial form of technocapitalism is characterized by a decline of the state and the increased power of the market, accompanied by the growing power of globalized transnational corporations and governmental bodies and the declining power of the nation state and its institutions—which remain, however, extremely important players in the global economy, as the responses to the terror attacks of September 11 document.

Globalization is also constituted by a complex interconnection between capitalism and democracy that involves positive and negative features and both empowers and disempowers individuals and groups, undermining and yet creating potential for fresh types of democracy. Yet many theories of globalization present it as either primarily negative, a disaster for the human species, or positive, as bringing a wealth of products, ideas, and economic opportunities to a global arena. Hence, I would advocate development of a critical theory of globalization that would dialectically appraise its positive and negative features. A critical theory is sharply critical of globalization's oppressive effects and skeptical of legitimating ideological discourse, but it also recognizes the centrality of the phenomenon in the present age. And it affirms and promotes globalization's progressive features (such as the Internet, which, as I document below, makes possible a reconstruction of education and more democratic polity, as well as increasing the power of capital), while noting contradictions and ambiguities.

THE CONTRADICTIONS OF GLOBALIZATION

The terrorist acts on the United States on September 11 and the subsequent Terror War dramatically disclose the downsides of globalization—the ways that global flows of technology, goods, information, ideologies, and people can have destructive as well as productive effects. The disclosure of powerful anti-Western terrorist networks shows that globalization divides the world as it unifies, that it produces enemies as it incorporates participants. The events disclose explosive contradictions and the conflicts at the heart of globalization and the fact that the technologies of information, communication, and transportation that facilitate globalization can also be used to undermine and attack it, to generate instruments of destruction as well as production.[7]

The experience of September 11 points to the objective ambiguity of globalization: that positive and negative sides are interconnected, that the institutions of the open society unlock the possibilities of destruction and violence as well as those of democracy, free trade, and cultural and social exchange. Once again, the interconnection and interdependency of the networked world was dramatically demonstrated, as terrorists from the Middle East brought local grievances from their region to attack key symbols of American power and the very infrastructure of New York. Some saw terrorism as an expression of the dark side of globalization, while I would conceive it as part of the objective ambiguity of globalization that simultaneously creates friends and enemies, wealth and poverty, and growing divisions between the "haves" and "have-nots." Yet the downturning of the global economy, intensification of local and global political conflicts, repression of human rights and civil liberties, and general increase in fear and anxiety have certainly undermined the native optimism of globaphiles who perceived globalization as a purely positive instrument of progress and well-being.

The use of powerful technologies as weapons of destruction also discloses current asymmetries of power and emergent forms of terrorism and war, as the new millennium has exploded into dangerous conflicts and interventions. As technologies of mass destruction become more available and dispersed, perilous instabilities have emerged that have elicited policing measures to stem the flow of movements of people and goods both across borders and internally. In particular, the U.S. Patriot Act has led to repressive measures that are replacing the spaces of the open and free information society with new forms of surveillance, policing, and repression.

Ultimately, however, the abhorrent terror acts by Osama bin Laden's network and the violent military response to the al-Qaeda terrorist acts by the Bush Administration may be an anomalous paroxysm, whereby a highly regressive premodern Islamic fundamentalism has clashed with an old-fashioned patriarchal and unilateralist Wild West militarism. It could be that such forms of terrorism, militarism, and state repression will be superseded by more rational forms of politics that globalize and criminalize terrorism and that do not sacrifice the benefits of the open society and economy in the name of security. Yet the events of September 11 may open a new era of Terror War that will lead to the kind of apocalyptic futurist world depicted by cyberpunk fiction (see Kellner forthcoming).

In any case, the events of September 11 have promoted a fury of reflection, theoretical debates, and political conflicts and upheaval that put the complex dynamics of globalization at the center of contemporary theory and politics. To those skeptical of the centrality of globalization to contemporary experience, it is now clear that we are living in a global world that is highly interconnected and vulnerable to passions and crises that can cross borders and can affect anyone or any region at any time. The events of September 11 also provide a test case to evaluate various theories of globalization and the contemporary era. In addition, they highlight some of the contradictions of globalization and the need to develop a highly complex and dialectical model to capture its conflicts, ambiguities, and contradictory effects.

Consequently, I want to argue that in order to properly theorize globalization, one needs to conceptualize several sets of contradictions generated by globalization's combination of technological revolution and restructuring of capital, which in turn generates tensions between capitalism and democracy and "haves" and "have-nots." Within the world economy, globalization involves the proliferation of the logic of capital, but also the spread of democracy in information, finance, investing, and the diffusion of technology (see Friedman 1999; Hardt and Negri 2000). Globalization is thus a contradictory amalgam of capitalism and democracy in which the logic of capital and the market system enter ever more arenas of global life, even as democracy spreads and more political regions and spaces of everyday life are being contested by democratic demands and forces. But the overall process is contradictory. Sometimes globalizing forces promote democracy and sometimes they inhibit it. Thus, both equating capitalism and democracy and simply opposing them are problematic. These tensions are especially evident, as I will argue, in the domain of the Internet and the expansion of new realms of technologically mediated communication, information, and politics.

The processes of globalization are highly turbulent and have generated new conflicts throughout the world. Benjamin Barber (1996) describes the strife between McWorld and Jihad, contrasting the homogenizing, commercialized, Americanized tendencies of the global economy and culture with traditional cultures, which are often resistant to globalization. Thomas Friedman (1999) makes a more benign distinction between what he calls the Lexus and the Olive Tree. The former symbolizes modernization, affluence and luxury, and Westernized consumption; the latter symbolizes roots, tradition, place, and stable community.

Barber's model oversimplifies present world divisions and conflicts and does not adequately present the contradictions within the West or the "Jihad" world, although he postulates a dialectical interpenetrating of both forces and sees both as opposed to democracy. His book does, however, point to problems and limitations of globalization, noting serious conflicts and opponents, unlike Thomas Friedman's harmonizing duality of *The Lexus and the Olive Tree* (1999), which suggests that both poles of capitalist luxury and premodern roots are parts of the globalization process. In an ode

to globalization, Friedman assumes the dual victory of capitalism and democracy, á la Fukuyama, while Barber demonstrates contradictions and tensions between capitalism and democracy within the New World (Dis)Order, as well as the antidemocratic animus of Jihad.

Hence, Friedman (1999) is too uncritical of globalization, caught up in his own Lexus high-consumption lifestyle, failing to perceive the depth of the oppressive features of globalization and the breadth and extent of resistance and opposition to it. In particular, he fails to articulate contradictions between capitalism and democracy and the ways that globalization and its economic logic undermine democracy as well as circulating it. Likewise, he does not grasp the virulence of the premodern and Jihadist tendencies that he blithely identifies with the Olive Tree, or the reasons why many parts of the world so strongly resist globalization and the West.

Consequently, it is important to present globalization as a strange amalgam of both homogenizing forces of sameness and uniformity *and* heterogeneity, difference, and hybridity, as well as a contradictory mixture of democratizing and antidemocratizing tendencies. On the one hand, globalization unfolds a process of standardization in which a globalized mass culture circulates the globe, creating sameness and homogeneity everywhere. On the other hand, globalized culture makes possible unique appropriations and developments everywhere, thus encouraging hybridity, difference, and heterogeneity to proliferate.[8] Every local context involves its own appropriation and reworking of global products and signifies, thus encouraging difference, otherness, diversity, and variety (Luke and Luke 2000). Grasping that globalization embodies these contradictory tendencies at once—that it can be a force of both homogenization and heterogeneity—is crucial to articulating the contradictions of globalization and avoiding one-sided and reductive conceptions.

My intention is to present globalization as conflictual, contradictory, and open to resistance and democratic intervention and transformation, not just as a monolithic juggernaut of progress or domination, as in many discourses. This goal is advanced by distinguishing between "globalization from below" and the "globalization from above" of corporate capitalism and the capitalist state, a distinction that should help us to get a better sense of how globalization does or does not promote democratization.

"Globalization from below" refers to the ways in which marginalized individuals and social movements resist globalization and/or use its institutions and instruments to further democratization and social justice. While on one level globalization significantly increases the supremacy of big corporations and big government, it can also give power to groups and individuals who were previously left out of the democratic dialogue and terrain of political struggle. Such potentially positive effects of globalization include increased access to education for individuals excluded from entry to culture and knowledge and the possible opportunity for oppositional individuals and groups to participate in global culture and politics through access to global communication and media networks and to circulate local struggles and oppositional ideas through these media. The role of new technologies in social movements, political struggle, and everyday life forces social movements to reconsider their political strategies and goals and democratic theory to appraise how new technologies do and do not promote democratization (Kellner 1997, 1999b), social justice, and other positive attributes. Indeed, the movements against capitalist globalization that I would endorse are those that oppose oppressive institutions of capitalist globalization such as the WTO, IMF, and certain transnational corporations and that are for positive values such as social justice, labor and human rights, and ecology.

In their magisterial book *Empire*, Hardt and Negri (2000) present contradictions within globalization in terms of an imperializing logic of "Empire" and an assortment of struggles by the "multitude," creating a contradictory and tension-filled situation. As in my conception, Hardt and Negri present globalization as a complex process that involves a multidimensional mixture of production and effects of the global economy and capitalist market system, new technologies and media, expanded judicial and legal modes of power, sovereignty, and resistance.[9] Combining poststructuralism with "autonomous Marxism," Hardt and Negri stress political openings and possibilities of struggle within *Empire* in an optimistic and buoyant text that envisages progressive democratization and

self-valorization in the turbulent process of the restructuring of capital.

Many theorists, by contrast, have argued that one of the trends of globalization is depoliticization of publics, the decline of the nation-state, and the end of traditional politics (Boggs 2000). While I would agree that globalization is promoted by tremendously powerful economic forces and that it often undermines democratic movements and decision making, I would also argue that there are openings and possibilites for a globalization from below that inflects globalization for positive and progressive ends, and that globalization can thus help promote as well as undermine democracy.[10] Globalization involves both a disorganization and reorganization of capitalism, a tremendous restructuring process, which creates openings for progressive social change and intervention. In a more fluid and open economic and political system, oppositional forces can gain concessions, win victories, and effect progressive changes. During the 1970s, new social movements, new nongovernmental organizations (NGOs), and new forms of struggle and solidarity emerged that have been expanding to the present day (Hardt and Negri 2000; Burbach 2001; Foran forthcoming).

The present conjuncture, I would suggest, is marked by a conflict between growing centralization and organization of power and wealth in the hands of the few and opposing processes exhibiting a fragmentation of power that is more plural, multiple, and open to contestation than was previously the case. As the following analysis will suggest, both tendencies are observable; it is up to individuals and groups to find openings for political intervention and social transformation. Thus, rather than just denouncing globalization or engaging in celebration and legitimation, a critical theory of globalization reproaches those aspects that are oppressive while seizing upon opportunities to fight domination and exploitation and to promote democratization, justice, and a progressive reconstruction of the polity, society, and culture.

Against capitalist globalization from above, there have been a significant eruption of forces and subcultures of resistance that have attempted to preserve specific forms of culture and society against globalization and homogenization and to create alternative forces of society and culture, thus exhibiting resistance and globalization from below. Most dramatically, peasant and guerilla movements in Latin America, labor unions, students, and environmentalists throughout the world, and a variety of other groups and movements have resisted capitalist globalization and attacks on previous rights and benefits.[11] Several dozen people's organizations from around the world have protested World Trade Organization (WTO) policies, and a backlash against globalization is visible everywhere. Politicians who once championed trade agreements like the General Agreement on Tariffs and Trade (GATT) and the North American Free Trade Agreement (NAFTA) are now often quiet about these arrangements. At the 1996 annual Davos World Economic Forum, its founder and managing director presented a warning entitled "Start Taking the Backlash Against Globalization Seriously." Reports surfaced that major representatives of the capitalist system expressed fear that capitalism was getting too mean and predatory, that it needs a kinder and gentler state to ensure order and harmony, and that the welfare state might make a come-back (see *New York Times* 1996:A15).[12] One should take such reports with the proverbial grain of salt, but they do express fissures and openings in the system for critical discourse and intervention.

Indeed, by 1999, the theme of the annual Davos conference centered around making globalization work for poor countries and minimizing the differences between the "haves" and the "have-nots." The growing divisions between rich and poor were worrying some globalizers, as was the wave of crises in Asian, Latin American, and other developing countries. In James Flanigan's report in the *Los Angeles Times* (Flanigan 1999), the "main theme" is to "spread the wealth. In a world frightened by glaring imbalances and the weakness of economies from Indonesia to Russia, the talk is no longer of a new world economy getting stronger but of ways to `keep the engine going'" (p. A13). In particular, the globalizers were attempting to keep economies growing in the more developed countries and capital flowing to developing nations. U.S. Vice President Al Gore called on all countries to spur economic growth, and he proposed a new U.S.-led initiative to eliminate the debt burdens of developing countries. South African President Nelson

Mandela asked: "Is globalization only for the powerful? Does it offer nothing to the men, women and children who are ravaged by the violence of poverty?" (ibid.).

THE GLOBAL MOVEMENT AGAINST CAPITALIST GLOBALIZATION

No clear answer emerged to Mandela's question as the new millennium opened, and with the global economic recession and the Terror War erupting in 2001, the situation of many developing countries has worsened. Yet as part of the backlash against globalization over the past years, a number of theorists have argued that the proliferation of difference and the move to more local discourses and practices define the contemporary scene. In this view, theory and politics should shift from the level of globalization and its accompanying, often totalizing, macrodimensions in order to focus on the local, the specific, the particular, the heterogeneous, and the microlevel of everyday experience. An array of theories associated with poststructuralism, postmodernism, feminism, and multiculturalism focuses on difference, otherness, marginality, the personal, the particular, and the concrete over more general theory and politics that aim at more global or universal conditions.[13] Likewise, a broad spectrum of subcultures of resistance have focused their attention on the local level, organizing struggles around identity issues such as gender, race, sexual preference, and youth subculture.

It can be argued that such dichotomies as those between the global and the local express contradictions and tensions between crucial constitutive forces of the present moment, and that it is therefore a mistake to reject focus on one side in favor of exclusive concern with the other (Cvetkovich and Kellner 1997). Hence, an important challenge for a critical theory of globalization is to think through the relationships between the global and the local by observing how global forces influence and even structure an increasing number of local situations. This requires analysis of how local forces mediate the global, inflecting global forces to diverse ends and conditions and producing unique configurations of the local and the global as the matrix for thought and action in the contemporary world (see Luke and Luke 2000).

Globalization is thus necessarily complex and challenging to both critical theories and radical democratic politics. However, many people operate with binary concepts of the global and the local and promote one or the other side of the equation as the solution to the world's problems. For globalists, globalization is the solution and underdevelopment, backwardness, and provincialism are the problems. For localists, globalization is the problem and localization is the solution. Less simplistically, however, it is the mix that matters, and whether global or local solutions are most fitting depends on the conditions in the distinctive context that one is addressing and the specific solutions and policies being proposed.

For instance, the Internet can be used to promote capitalist globalization or struggles against it. One of the more instructive examples of the use of the Internet to foster movements against the excesses of corporate capitalism occurred in the protests in Seattle and throughout the world against the World Trade Organization (WTO) meeting in December 1999. Behind these actions lay a global protest movement, using the Internet to organize resistance to the WTO and capitalist globalization while championing democratization. Many Web sites contained anti-WTO material, and numerous mailing lists used the Internet to distribute critical material and to organize the protest. This resulted in the mobilization of caravans from all over the United States to take protestors, many of whom had never met and had been recruited through the Internet, to Seattle. There were also significant numbers of international participants in Seattle, which exhibited labor, environmentalist, feminist, anticapitalist, animal rights, anarchist, and other groups organized to protest aspects of globalization and form new alliances and solidarities for future struggles. In addition, protests occurred throughout the world, and a proliferation of material against the extremely secret WTO spread throughout the Internet.[14]

Furthermore, the Internet provided critical coverage of the event, documentation of the various groups' protests, and debate over the WTO and globalization. Whereas the mainstream media presented the protests as "antitrade," featuring the incidents of anarchist violence against property while minimizing police violence against demonstrators, the Internet provided pictures, eyewitness accounts, and reports of police brutality and the generally peaceful and non-violent nature of the protests. While the mainstream media framed the protests negatively and privileged suspect spokespeople such as Patrick Buchanan as critics of globalization, the Internet provided multiple representations of the demonstrations, advanced reflective discussion of the WTO and globalization, and presented a diversity of critical perspectives.

The Seattle protests had some immediate consequences. The day after the demonstrators made good on their promise to shut down the WTO negotiations, Bill Clinton gave a speech endorsing the concept of labor rights enforceable by trade sanctions, thus effectively making impossible any agreement and consensus during the Seattle meetings. In addition, at the World Economic Forum in Davos a month later, there was much discussion of how concessions on labor and the environment were necessary if consensus over globalization and free trade were to be possible. Importantly, the issue of overcoming divisions between the information-rich and poor and improving the lot of the disenfranchised and oppressed—bringing the benefits of globalization to these groups—were also seriously discussed at the meeting and in the media.

More significantly, many activists were energized by the new alliances, solidarities, and militancy and continued to cultivate an antiglobalization movement. The Seattle demonstrations were followed by struggles in April 2000 in Washington, DC, to protest the World Bank and the International Monetary Fund (IMF), and later in the year against capitalist globalization in Prague and Melbourne. In April 2001, an extremely large and militant protest erupted against the Free Trade Area of the Americas summit in Quebec City, and in summer 2001 a large demonstration took place in Genoa.

In May 2002, a surprisingly large demonstration took place in Washington, DC, against capitalist globalization and for peace and justice, and it was apparent that a new worldwide movement was in the making, uniting diverse opponents of capitalist globalization throughout the world. The anticorporate globalization movement favored globalization from below, which would protect the environment, labor rights, national cultures, democratization, and other goods from the ravages of uncontrolled capitalist globalization (Brecher, Costello, and Smith 2000; Steger 2002).

Initially, the incipient antiglobalization movement was precisely that—antiglobalization. The movement itself, however, was increasingly global, was linking together diverse movements into global solidarity networks, and was using the Internet and instruments of globalization to advance its struggles. Moreover, many opponents of capitalist globalization recognized the need for a global movement to have a positive vision and to stand for such things as social justice, equality, labor, civil liberties and human rights, and a sustainable environmentalism. Accordingly, the anticapitalist globalization movement began advocating common values and visions, and began referring to itself in positive terms, like the social justice movement.

In particular, the movement against capitalist globalization used the Internet to organize mass demonstrations and to disseminate information to the world concerning the policies of the institutions of capitalist globalization. The events made clear that protestors were not against globalization per se, but opposed neoliberal and capitalist globalization, rejecting specific policies and institutions that produce intensified exploitation of labor, environmental devastation, growing divisions among the social classes, and the undermining of democracy. The emerging antiglobalization-from-above movements are contextualizing these problems in the framework of a restructuring of capitalism on a worldwide basis for maximum profit with zero accountability and have made clear the need for democratization, regulation, rules, and globalization in the interests of people, not profit.

The new movements against capitalist globalization have placed the issues of global justice and environmental destruction squarely in the center of important political concerns of our time. Hence, whereas the mainstream media failed to vigorously debate or even report on globalization until the eruption of a vigorous antiglobalization movement and rarely, if ever, critically discussed the activities of the WTO, the World Bank, and the IMF, there is now a widely circulating critical discourse and controversy over these institutions. Stung by criticisms, representatives of the World Bank in particular are pledging reform, and pressures are mounting concerning proper and improper roles for the major global institutions, highlighting their limitations and deficiencies and the need for reforms such as debt relief for overburdened developing countries to solve some of their fiscal and social problems.

Opposing capital´s globalization from above, cyberactivists have thus been promoting globalization from below, developing networks of solidarity and propagating oppositional ideas and movements throughout the planet. Opposing the capitalist international of transnational corporate-led globalization, a Fifth International—to use Waterman's (1992) phrase—of computer-mediated activism is emerging that is qualitatively different from the party-based socialist and communist internationals. Such networking links labor, feminist, ecological, peace, and other anticapitalist groups, providing the basis for a new politics of alliance and solidarity to overcome the limitations of postmodern identity politics (see Dyer-Witheford 1999; Burbach 2001; Best and Kellner 2001).

Of course, right-wing and reactionary forces have used the Internet to promote their political agendas as well. In a short time, one can easily access an exotic witch's brew of Web sites maintained by the Ku Klux Klan and myriad neo-Nazi assemblages, including the Aryan Nation and various militia groups. Internet discussion lists also disperse these views, and right-wing extremists are aggressively active on many computer forums as well as radio programs and stations, public-access television programs, fax campaigns, video, and even rock-music productions. These organizations are hardly harmless, having carried out terrorism of various sorts from church burnings to the bombings of public buildings. Adopting quasi-Leninist discourse and tactics for ultratight causes, these groups have successfully recruited working-class members devastated by the developments of global capitalism, which has resulted in widespread unemployment in traditional forms of industrial, agricultural, and unskilled labor. Moreover, extremist Web sites have influenced alienated middle-class youth as well (a 1999 HBO documentary on *Hate on the Internet* provides a disturbing number of examples of how extremist Web sites influenced disaffected youth to commit hate crimes).

Indeed, a recent twist in the saga of technopolitics seems to be that allegedly "terrorist" groups are now increasingly using the Internet and Web sites to promote their causes. An article in the *Los Angeles Times* (2001:A1, A14) reports that groups like Hamas use their Web site to post reports of acts of terror against Israel, rather than calling newspapers or broadcasting outlets. A wide range of groups labeled as "terrorist" reportedly use e-mail, listserves, and Web sites to further their struggles—causes including Hezbollah and Hamas, the Maoist group Shining Path in Peru, and a variety of other groups throughout Asia and elsewhere. For instance, the Tamil Tigers, a liberation movement in Sri Lanka, offers position papers, daily news, and free e-mail service. According to the *Times*, experts are still unclear about "whether the ability to communicate online worldwide is prompting an increase or a decrease in terrorist acts." There have been widespread discussions of how bin Laden's al-Qaeda network used the Internet to plan the September 11 terrorist attacks on the United States, how the group communicated with each other, got funds and purchased airline tickets via the Internet, and used flight simulations to practice their hijacking. In the contemporary era, the Internet can thus be used for a diversity of political projects and goals ranging from education, to business, to political organization and debate, to terrorism.

Moreover, different political groups are engaging in cyberwar as an adjunct to their political battles. Israeli hackers have repeatedly attacked the Web sites of Hezbollah, while pro-Palestine hackers have reportedly placed militant demands and slogans on the Web sites of Israel's army, foreign ministry, and parliament. Pakistani and Indian computer hackers have waged similar cyberbattles against the Web sites of opposing forces in the bloody struggle over Kashmir, while rebel forces in the Phillippines have taunted government troops with cell phone calls and messages and have attacked government Web sites.

The examples in this section suggest how techno-politics makes possible a refiguring of politics, a refocusing of politics on everyday life, and the use of the tools and techniques of new computer and communication technology to expand the field and domain of politics. In this conjuncture, the ideas of Guy Debord and the Situationist International are especially relevant, with their stress on the construction of situations, the use of technology, media of communication, and

cultural forms to promote a revolution of everyday life and to increase the realm of freedom, community, and empowerment.[15] To some extent, the new technologies *are* revolutionary and *do* constitute a revolution of everyday life, but it is often a revolution that promotes and disseminates the capitalist consumer society and involves new modes of fetishism, enslavement, and domination yet to be clearly perceived and theorized.

CONCLUDING COMMENTS

The Internet is thus a contested terrain, used by left, right, and center to promote their own agendas and interests. The political battles of the future may well be fought in the streets, factories, parliaments, and other sites of past struggle, but politics is already mediated by broadcast, computer, and information technologies and will increasingly be so in the future. Those interested in the politics and culture of the future should therefore be clear on the important role of the new public spheres and intervene accordingly, while critical pedagogues have the responsibility of teaching students the skills that will enable them to participate in the politics and struggles of the present and future.

And so, to paraphrase Foucault, wherever there is globalization from above—globalization as the imposition of capitalist logic—there can be resistance and struggle. The possibilities of globalization from below result from transnational alliances between groups fighting for better wages and working conditions, social and political justice, environmental protection, and more democracy and freedom worldwide. In addition, a renewed emphasis on local and grassroots movements has put dominant economic forces on the defensive in their own backyards, and the broadcasting media and the Internet have often called attention to oppressive and destructive corporate policies on the local level, putting national and even transnational pressure for reform upon major corporations. Moreover, proliferating media and the Internet make possible a greater circulation of struggles and new alliances and solidarities that can connect resistant forces that oppose capitalist and corporate-state elite forms of globalization from above (Dyer-Witheford 1999).

In a certain sense, the phenomenon of globalization replicates the history of the United States and most so-called capitalist democracies in which tension between capitalism and democracy has been the defining feature of the conflicts of the past 200 years. In analyzing the development of education in the United States, Samuel Bowles and Herbert Gintis (1986) and Aronowitz and Giroux (1986) have analyzed the conflicts between corporate logic and democracy in schooling, Robert McChesney (1995 and 1997), myself (Kellner 1990, 1992, 2001, forthcoming), and others have articulated the contradictions between capitalism and democracy in the media and public sphere, and Joshua Cohen and Joel Rogers (1983) and many others argue that contradictions between capitalism and democracy are defining features of U.S. polity and history.

On a global terrain, Hardt and Negri (2000) have stressed the openings and possibilities for democratic transformative struggle within globalization, or what they call "Empire." I argue that similar arguments can be made in which globalization is not conceived merely as the triumph of capitalism and democracy working together, as it was in the classical theories of Milton Friedman or more recently in Francis Fukuyama. Nor should globalization be depicted solely as the triumph of capital, as in many despairing antiglobalization theories. Rather, one should see that globalization unleashes conflicts between capitalism and democracy and, in its restructuring processes, creates new openings for struggle, resistance, and democratic transformation.

I would also suggest that the model of Marx and Engels, as deployed in the "Communist Manifesto," could be usefully employed to analyze the contradictions of globalization (Marx and Engels 1978:469ff). From the historical materialist optic, capitalism was interpreted as the greatest, most progressive force in history for Marx and Engels, destroying a retrograde feudalism, authoritarian patriarchy, backwardness and provincialism in favor of a market society, global cosmopolitanism, and constant revolutionizing of the forces of production. Yet capitalism was also presented in the Marxian theory as a major disaster for the human race, condemning a large part of the race to alienated labor and regions of the world to colonialist exploitation and generating conflicts between classes and nations, the consequences of which the contemporary era continues to suffer.

Marx deployed a similar dialectical and historical model in his later analyses of imperialism, arguing, for instance, in his writings on British imperialism in India that British colonialism was a great productive and progressive force in India at the same time as it was highly destructive (Marx and Engels 1978:653ff). A similar dialectical and critical model can be used today that articulates the progressive elements of globalization in conjunction with its more oppressive features, deploying the categories of negation and critique, while sublating (*Aufhebung*) the positive features. Moreover, a dialectical and transdisciplinary model is necessary to capture the complexity and multidimensionality of globalization today, one that brings together in theorizing globalization, the economy, technology, polity, society, and culture, articulating the interplay of these elements and avoiding any form of determinism or reductivism.

Theorizing globalization dialectically and critically requires that we analyze both continuities and discontinuities with the past, specifying what is a continuation of past histories and what is new and original in the present moment. To elucidate the latter, I believe that the discourse of the postmodern is useful in dramatizing the changes and novelties of the mode of globalization. The concept of the postmodern can signal that which is fresh and original, calling attention to topics and phenomena that require novel theorization and intense critical thought and inquiry. Hence, although Manuel Castells (1996, 1997, 1998) does the most detailed analysis of new technologies and the rise of what he calls a networked society, by refusing to link his analyses with the problematic of the postmodern, he cuts himself off from theoretical resources that enable theorists to articulate the novelties of the present that are unique and different from the previous mode of social organization.[16] Consequently, although there is admittedly a lot of mystification in the discourse of the postmodern, it signals emphatically the shifts and ruptures in our era—the novelties and originalities—and dramatizes the mutations in culture, subjectivities, and theory that Castells and other theorists of globalization or the information society gloss over. The discourse of the postmodern in relation to analysis of contemporary culture and society is just jargon, however, unless it is rooted in analysis of the global restructuring of capitalism and analysis of the scientific-technological revolution that is part and parcel of it (see Best and Kellner 1997, 2001).

As I have argued in this study, the term "globalization" is often used as a code word that stands for a tremendous diversity of issues and problems and serves as a front for a variety of theoretical and political positions. While it can function as a legitimating ideology to cover and sanitize ugly realities, a critical globalization theory can inflect the discourse to point precisely to these deplorable phenomena and can elucidate a series of contemporary problems and conflicts. In view of the different concepts and functions of globalization discourse, it is important to note that the concept of globalization is a theoretical construct that varies according to the assumptions and commitments of the theory in question. Seeing the term as a construct helps rob it of its force of nature as a sign of an inexorable triumph of market forces and the hegemony of capital, or, as the extreme right fears, of a rapidly encroaching world government. While the term can both describe and legitimate capitalist transnationalism and supranational government institutions, a critical theory of globalization does not buy into ideological valorizations and affirms difference, hybridity, resistance, and democratic self-determination against forms of global domination and subordination.

Globalization should thus be seen as a contested terrain, with opposing forces attempting to use its institutions, technologies, media, and forms for their own purposes. There are certainly negative aspects to globalization that strengthen elite economic and political forces over and against the underlying population. However, as I suggest above, there are also positive possibilities. Other beneficial openings include the opportunity for greater democratization, increased education and health care, and new possibilities within the global economy that provide entry to members of races, regions, and classes previously excluded from mainstream economics, politics, and culture within the modern corporate order.

Furthermore, there is Utopian potential in the new technologies, as well as the possibility for increased domination and the hegemony of capital. While the first generation of computers were large mainframe systems controlled by big government and big business, later generations of personal computers and networks have created a more decentralized situation in which ever more individuals own their own computers and use them for their own projects and goals. A new generation of wireless communication could enable areas of the world that do not even have electricity to participate in the communication and information revolution of the emergent global era. This would require, of course, something like a Marshall Plan for the developing world, which would necessitate help with disseminating technologies that would also address problems of world hunger, disease, illiteracy, and poverty.

In relation to education, the spread and distribution of information and communication technology signifies the possibility of openings of opportunities for research and interaction not previously accessible to students who did not have the privilege of access to major research libraries or institutions. Although it has its problems and limitations, the Internet makes available more information and knowledge to more people than any previous institution in history. Moreover, the Internet enables individuals to participate in discussions and to circulate their ideas and work in ways that were previously closed off to many excluded groups and individuals.

A progressive reconstruction of education that is done in the interests of democratization would demand access to new technologies for all, helping to overcome the so-called digital divide and divisions of the "haves" and "have-nots" as well as teaching information literacy to provide the skills necessary to participate in the emerging cybersociety (see Kellner 2000). Expanding democratic and multicultural reconstruction of education thus forces educators and citizens to confront the challenge of the digital divide, in which there are divisions between information and technology "haves" and "have-nots," just as there are class, gender, and race divisions in every sphere of the existing constellations of society and culture. Although the latest surveys of the digital divide indicate that the key indicators are class and education and not race and gender, making computers a significant force of democratization of education and society will nonetheless require significant investment and programs to assure that everyone receives the training, literacies, and tools necessary to properly function in a high-tech global economy and culture.[17]

Hence, a critical theory of globalization presents globalization as a product of capitalism and democracy, as a set of forces imposed from above in conjunction with resistance from below. In this optic, globalization generates new conflicts, new struggles, and new crises, which can be seen in part as resistance to capitalist logic. In the light of the neo-liberal projects to dismantle the welfare state, colonize the public sphere, and control globalization, it is up to citizens and activists to create new public spheres, politics, and pedagogies, to use the new technologies to discuss what kinds of society people today want, and to oppose the society against which people resist and struggle. This involves, minimally, demands for more education, health care, welfare, and benefits from the state and a struggle to create a more democratic and egalitarian society. But one cannot expect that generous corporations and a beneficent state are going to make available to citizens the bounties and benefits of the globalized new information economy. Rather, it is up to individuals and groups to promote democratization and progressive social change.

Thus, in opposition to the globalization from above of corporate capitalism, I would advocate a globalization from below, one which supports individuals and groups using the new technologies to create a more multicultural, egalitarian, democratic, and ecological world. Of course, the new technologies might exacerbate existing inequalities in the current class, gender, race, and regional configurations of power and give the major corporate forces powerful new tools to advance their interests. In this situation, it is up to people of good will to devise strategies to use the new technologies to promote democratization and social justice. For as the new technologies become ever more central to every domain of everyday life, developing an oppositional technopolitics in the new public spheres will become more and more important (see Kellner 1995a, 1995b, 1997, 2000). Changes in the economy, politics, and social life demand a constant reconceptualization of politics and social change in the light of globalization and the technological revolution, requiring new thinking as a response to ever-changing historical conditions.

NOTES

1. Attempts to chart the globalization of capital, decline of the nation-state, and rise of a new global culture include the essays in Featherstone (1990), Giddens (1990), Robertson (1991), King (1991), Bird et al. (1993), Gilroy (1993), Arrighi (1994), Lash and Urry (1994), Grewal and Kaplan (1994), Wark (1994), Featherstone, Lash, and Robertson (1995), Axford (1995), Held (1995), Waters (1995), Hirst and Thompson (1996), Axtmann (1998), Albrow (1996), Cvetkovich and Kellner (1997), Kellner (1998), Friedman (1999), Held et al. (1999), Hardt and Negri (2000), Lechner and Boli (2000), Steger (2002), and Stiglitz (2002).

2. See apologists such as Fukuyama (1992) and Friedman (1999), who perceive this process as positive, while others, such as Mander and Goldsmith (1996), Eisenstein (1998), and Robins and Webster (1999) portray it as negative.

3. What appeared at the first stage of academic and popular discourses of globalization in the 1990s tended to be dichotomized into celebratory globophilia and dismissive globophobia. See Best and Kellner (2001). There was also a tendency on the part of some theorists to exaggerate the novelties of globalization, and on the part of others to dismiss these claims by arguing that globalization has been going on for centuries and not that much is new and different. For an excellent delineation and critique of academic discourses on globalization, see Steger (2002).

4. See Baudrillard (1993) and the analyses in Kellner (1989b, 1994).

5. See Kelly (1994, 1998) and the critique in Best and Kellner (1999).

6. In his extreme postmodern stage, Baudrillard (1993) argued that "simulation" had replaced production as the organizing principle of contemporary societies, marking "the end of political

economy" (p. 955). See the critique in Kellner (1989b). In general, I am trying to mediate the economic determinism in some neo-Marxian and other theories of globalization and the technological determinism found in Baudrillard and others.

7. I am not able, in the framework of this paper, to theorize the alarming expansion of war and militarism in the post-September 11 environment. For my theorizing of war and militarism, see Kellner (2002, forthcoming).

8. For example, as Ritzer (1996) argues, McDonald's imposes not only a similar cuisine all over the world, but circulates processes of what he calls "McDonaldization" that involve a production/consumption model of efficiency, technological rationality, calculability, predictability, and control. Yet, as Watson et al. (1997) argue, McDonald's has various cultural meanings in diverse local contexts, as well as different products, organization, and effects. However, the latter source goes too far toward stressing heterogeneity, downplaying the cultural power of McDonald's as a force of a homogenizing globalization and Western corporate logic and system; see Kellner (1999a, 2003).

9. While I find *Empire* an extremely impressive and massively productive text, I am not sure what is gained by using the word "Empire" rather than the concepts of global capital and political economy. While Hardt and Negri (2000) combine categories of Marxism and critical social theory with poststructuralist discourse derived from Foucault and Deleuze and Guattari, they frequently favor the latter, often mystifying and obscuring the object of analysis. I am also not as confident as are they that the "multitude" replaces traditional concepts of the working class and other modern political subjects, movements, and actors, and I find their emphasis on nomads, "New Barbarians," and the poor as replacement categories problematical. Nor am I clear on exactly what forms their poststructuralist politics would take. The same problem is evident, I believe, in an earlier decade's provocative and post-Marxist text by Laclau and Mouffe (1985), who valorized new social movements, radical democracy, and a postsocialist politics without providing many concrete examples or proposals for struggle in the present conjuncture.

10. I am thus trying to mediate in this paper between those who claim that globalization simply undermines democracy and those, such as Friedman (1999), who claim that globalization promotes democratization. I should also note that in distinguishing between globalization from above and globalization from below, I do not want to say that one is good and the other is bad in relation to democracy. As Friedman shows, capitalist corporations and global forces might very well promote democratization in many arenas of the world, and globalization from below might promote special interests or reactionary goals, so I criticize theorizing globalization in binary terms as primarily "good" or "bad." While critics of globalization simply see it as the reproduction of capitalism, its champions, like Friedman, do not perceive how globalization undercuts democracy. Likewise, Friedman does not engage the role of new social movements, dissident groups, or the "have-nots" in promoting democratization. Nor do concerns for social justice, equality, and participatory democracy play a role in his book.

11. On resistance by labor to globalization, see Moody (1997); on resistance by environmentalists and other social movements, see the studies in Mander and Goldsmith (1996). I provide examples below from several domains.

12. Friedman (1999:267ff) notes that George Soros was the star of Davos in 1995, when the triumph of global capital was being celebrated, but that the next year Russian Communist Party leader Gennadi A. Zyuganov was a major media focus when unrestrained globalization was being questioned. Friedman does not point out that this was a result of a growing recognition that divisions between "haves" and "have-nots" were becoming too scandalous and that predatory capitalism was becoming too brutal and ferocious.

13. Such positions are associated with the postmodern theories of Foucault, Lyotard, and Rorty and have been taken up by a wide range of feminists, multiculturalists, and others. On these theorists and postmodern politics, see Best and Kellner (1991, 1997, 2001) and the valorization and critique of postmodern politics in Hardt and Negri (2000) and Burbach (2001).

14. As a December *1 ABC News* story titled "Networked Protests" put it, "Disparate groups from the Direct Action Network to the AFL-CIO to various environmental and human rights groups have organized rallies and protests online, allowing for a global reach that would have been unthinkable just five years ago." As early as March, activists were hitting the news groups and list-serves— strings of e-mail messages people use as a kind of long-term chat—to organize protests and rallies.

    In addition, while the organizers demanded that the protesters agree not to engage in violent action, one Web site urged WTO protesters to help tie up the WTO´s Web servers, and another group produced an anti-WTO Web site that replicated the look of the official site (see RTMark's Web site, ≤http://gatt.org/≥; the same group produced a replica of George W. Bush's site with satirical and critical material, winning the wrath of the Bush campaign). For compelling accounts of the anti-WTO demonstrations in Seattle and an acute analysis of the issues involved, see Hawkens (2000) and Klein (2000).

15. On the importance of the ideas of Debord and the Situationist International to make sense of the present conjuncture, see Best and Kellner (1997:chap.3); on the new forms of the interactive consumer society, see Best and Kellner (2001).

16. Castells claims that Harvey (1989) and Lash (1990) say about as much about the postmodern as needs to be said (Castells 1996:26ff). With due respect to their excellent work, I believe that no two theorists or books exhaust the problematic of the postmodern, which involves mutations in theory, culture, society, politics, science, philosophy, and almost every other domain of experience and is thus inexhaustible (Best and Kellner 1997, 2001). Yet one should be careful in using postmodern discourse to avoid the mystifying elements, a point made in the books just noted as well as in Hardt and Negri (2000).

17. "Digital divide" has emerged as the buzz word for perceived divisions between information technology "haves" and "have-nots" in the current economy and society. A U.S. Department of Commerce report released in July 1999 claimed that the digital divide is dramatically escalating in relation to race, and the Clinton Administration and media picked up on this theme (U.S. Department of Commerce, NTIA 1999). A critique of the data involved in the report emerged, claiming that it was outdated; more recent studies by Stanford University, Cheskin Research, ACNielson, and the Forester Institute claim that education and class are more significant factors than race in constructing the divide (see Cyberatlas for a collection of reports and statistics on the divide).

    In any case, it is clear that there is a gaping division between information-technology "haves" and "have-nots," that this is a major challenge to developing an egalitarian and democratic society, and that something needs to be done about the problem. My contribution involves the argument that empowering the "have-nots" requires the dissemination of new literacies, thus empowering groups and individuals previously excluded from economic opportunities and sociopolitical participation (see Kellner 2000).

REFERENCES

Albrow, Martin. 1996. *The Global Age*. Cambridge, England: Polity Press.
Appadurai, Arjun. 1996. *Modernity at Large*. Minneapolis, MN: University of Minnesota Press.

Aronowitz, Stanley, and Henry Giroux. 1985. *Education Under Siege.* New York: Bergin and Garvey.

Aronson, Ronald. 1983. *The Dialectics of Disaster.* London, England: Verso.

Arrighi, Giovanni. 1994. *The Long Twentieth Century.* London, England, and New York: Verso.

Axford, Barrie. 1995. *The Global System.* Cambridge, England: Polity Press.

Axtmann, Roland, ed. 1998. *Globalization in European Context.* London, England: Cassells.

Barber, Benjamin. 1996. *Jihad vs. McWorld: How Globalism and Tribalism Are Reshaping the World.* New York: Times Books.

Baudrillard, Jean. 1993. *Symbolic Exchange and Death.* London, England: Sage.

Bell, Daniel. 1976. *The Coming of Post-Industrial Society.* New York: Basic Books.

Best, Steven, and Douglas Kellner. 1991. *Postmodern Theory: Critical Interrogations.* London, England, and New York: Macmillan and Guilford.

———. 1997. *The Postmodern Turn.* London, England, and New York: Routledge and Guilford Press.

———. 1999. "Kelvin Kelly's Complexity Theory: The Politics and Ideology of Self-Organizing Systems." *Organization and Environment* 12:141–62.

———. 2001. *The Postmodern Adventure.* London, England, and New York: Routledge and Guilford Press.

Bird, Jon, Barry Curtis, Tim Putnam, and Lisa Tickner, eds. 1993. *Mapping the Futures: Local Cultures, Global Change.* London, England and New York: Routledge.

Boggs, Carl. 2000. *The End of Politics.* New York: Guilford Press.

Borgmann, Albert. 1994. *Across the Postmodern Divide.* Chicago, IL: University of Chicago Press.

———. 1999. *Holding Onto Reality.* Chicago, IL: University of Chicago Press.

Bowles, Samuel, and Herbert Gintis. 1986. *On Democracy.* New York: Basic Books.

Brecher, Jeremy, and Tim Costello. 1994. *Global Village or Global Pillage: Economic Reconstruction From the Bottom Up.* Boston, MA: South End Press.

Brecher, Jeremy, Tim Costello, and Brendan Smith. 2000. *Globalization From Below.* Boston, MA: South End Press.

Bronner, Stephen Eric, and Douglas Kellner, eds. 1989. *Critical Theory and Society: A Reader.* New York: Routledge.

Burbach, Roger. 2001. *Globalization and Postmodern Politics: From Zapatistas to High-Tech Robber Barons.* London, England: Pluto Press.

Castells, Manuel. 1996. *The Information Age: Economy, Society, and Culture. Vol.1, The Rise of the Network Society.* Oxford, England: Blackwell.

———. 1997. *The Information Age: Economy, Society, and Culture. Vol.2, The Power of Identity.* Oxford, England: Blackwell.

———. 1998. *The Information Age: Economy, Society, and Culture. Vol.3, End of Millennium.* Oxford, England: Blackwell.

Cohen, Joshua, and Joel Rogers. 1983. *On Democracy.* New York: Penguin.

Cvetkovich, Ann, and Douglas Kellner. 1997. *Articulating the Global and the Local: Globalization and Cultural Studies.* Boulder, CO: Westview Press. Cyberatlas,< http://cyberatlas.internet.com/big-picture/demographics >.

Drew, Jesse. 1998. "Global Communications in the Post-Industrial Age: A Study of the Communications Strategies of U.S.Labor Organizations." Ph.D. dissertation, University of Texas.

Dyer-Witheford, Nick. 1999. *Cyber-Marx: Cycles and Circuits of Struggle in High-Technology Capitalism.* Urbana and Chicago, IL: University of Illinois Press.

Eisenstein, Zillah. 1998. *Global Obscenities: Patriarchy, Capitalism, and the Lure of Cyberfantasy.* New York: New York University Press.

Ellul, Jacques. 1964. *The Technological Society.* New York: Knopf.

Featherstone, Mike, ed. 1990. *Global Culture: Nationalism, Globalization, and Modernity*. London, England: Sage.

Featherstone, Mike, Scott Lash, and Roland Robertson, eds. 1995. *Global Modernities*. London, England: Sage.

Flanigan, James. 1999. *Los Angeles Times*, February 19.

Foran, John, ed. Forthcoming. *The Future of Revolutions: Rethinking Radical Change in the Age of Globalization*. London, England: Zed Books.

Fredericks, Howard. 1994. "North American NGO Networking Against NAFTA: The Use of Computer Communications in Cross-Border Coalition Building." XVII International Congress of the Latin American Studies Association, pp. 1–24.

Friedman, Thomas. 1999. *The Lexus and the Olive Tree*. New York: Farrar Straus Giroux.

Fukuyama, Francis. 1992. *The End of History and the Last Man*. New York: Free Press.

Gates, Bill. 1995. *The Road Ahead*. New York: Viking.

———.1999. *Business@the Speed of Thought*. New York: Viking.

Giddens, Anthony. 1990. *Consequences of Modernity*. Cambridge, England: Polity Press; Palo Alto, CA: Stanford University Press.

Gilder, George. 1989. *Microcosm*. New York: Simon and Schuster.

———. 2000. *Telecosm*. New York: Simon and Schuster.

Gilroy, Paul. 1993. *The Black Atlantic: Modernity and Double Consciousness*. Cambridge, MA: Harvard University Press.

Gottdiener, Mark. 1995. *Postmodern Semiotics*, Oxford, England: Blackwell.

Grewal, Inderpal, and Caren Kaplan, eds. 1994. *Scattered Hegemonies: Postmodernity and Transnational Feminist Practices*. Minneapolis, MN: University of Minnesota Press.

Hardt, Michael, and Antonio Negri. *Empire*. 2000. Cambridge, MA: Harvard University Press.

Harvey, David. 1989. *The Condition of Postmodernity*. Cambridge, MA: Blackwell.

Hawkens, Paul. 2000. "What Really Happened at the Battle of Seattle." ≤http://www.purefood.org/Corp/PaulHawken.cfm≥.

Heidegger, Martin. 1971. *The Question Concerning Technology*. New York: Harper and Row.

Held, David. 1995. *Democracy and the Global Order*. Cambridge, England: Polity Press; Palo Alto, CA: Stanford University Press.

Held, David, Anthony McGrew, David Goldblatt, and Jonathan Perraton. 1999. *Global Transformations*. Cambridge, England: Polity Press: Palo Alto, CA: Stanford University Press.

Hirst, Paul, and Grahame Thompson. 1996. *Globalization in Question*. Cambridge, England: Polity Press.

Huntington, Samuel. 1996. *The Clash of Civilizations and the Remaking of World Order*. New York: Simon and Schuster.

Jameson, Fredric. 1991. *Postmodernism, or the Cultural Logic of Late Capitalism*. Durham, NC: Duke University Press.

Kaku, Michio. 1997. *Visions: How Science Will Revolutionize the 21st Century*. New York: Anchor Books.

Kellner, Douglas. 1989a. *Critical Theory, Marxism, and Modernity*. Cambridge, England: Polity Press: Baltimore, MD: Johns Hopkins University Press.

———. 1989b. *Jean Baudrillard: From Marxism to Postmodernism and Beyond*. Cambridge, England: Polity Press; Palo Alto, CA: Stanford University Press.

———. 1990. *Television and the Crisis of Democracy*. Boulder, CO: Westview Press.

———. 1992. *The Persian Gulf TV War*. Boulder, CO: Westview Press.

———, ed. 1994. *Jean Baudrillard: A Critical Reader*. Oxford, England: Basil Blackwell.

———. 1995a. *Media Culture*. London, England, and New York: Routledge.

———. 1995b. "Intellectuals and New Technologies." *Media, Culture, and Society* 17:201–17.

———. 1997. "Intellectuals, the New Public Spheres, and Technopolitics." *New Political Science* 41–42:169–188.

———. 1998. "Multiple Literacies and Critical Pedagogy in a Multicultural Society." *Educational Theory* 48:103–122.

———. 1999a. "Theorizing McDonaldization: A Multiperspectivist Approach." pp.186–206 in *Resisting McDonaldization*, edited by Barry Smart. London: Sage Publications.

———. 1999b. "Globalization from Below? Toward a Radical Democratic Technopolitics." *Angelaki* 4:101–13.

———. 2000. "New Technologies/New Literacies: Reconstructing Education for the New Millennium." *Teaching Education* 11:245–65.

———. 2001. *Grand Theft 2000*. Lanham, MD: Rowman and Littlefield.

———. 2002. "Postmodern War in the Age of Bush II." *New Political Science* 24(1):57–72.

———. 2003. *Media Spectacle*. London, England, and New York: Routledge.

———. Forthcoming. "September 11, Terror War, and the New Barbarism." Available online at ≤http://www.gseis.ucla.edu/faculty/kellner/papers/septllkell.htm≥.

Kelly, Kevin. 1994. *Out of Control: The New Biology of Machines, Social Systems, and the Economic World.* New York: Addison Wesley.

———. 1998. *New Rules for the New Economy*. New York: Viking.

King, Anthony D., ed. 1991. *Culture, Globalization, and the World-System: Contemporary Conditions for the Representaion of Identity.* Binghamton, NY: SUNY Art Department.

Klein, Naomi. 2000. "Were the DC and Seattle Protests Unfocused, or Are Critics Missing the Point?" *The Nation* online, July 10. ≤http://past.thenation.com/cgi-bin/framizer.cgi?url:=:http://past.thenation.com/issue/000710/0710klein.shtml≥

Laclau, Ernesto, and Chantel Mouffe. 1985. *Hegemony and Socialist Strategy: Toward a Radical Democratic Politics.* London, England: Verso.

Lash, Scott. 1990. *Sociology of Postmodernism.* London and New York: Routledge.

Lash, Scott, and John Urry. 1994. *Economies of Signs and Space.* London, England: Sage.

Latouche, Serge. 1996. *The Westernization of the World.* Cambridge, England: Polity Press.

Lechner, Frank X, and John Boli. 2000. *The Globalization Reader.* Maiden, MA, and Oxford, UK: Blackwell.

Luke, Allan, and Carmen Luke. 2000. "A Situated Perspective on Cultural Globalization." Pp.275–98 in *Globalization and Education*, edited by Nicholas Burbules and Carlos Torres. London, England, and New York: Routledge.

Mander, Jerry, and Edward Goldsmith. 1996. *The Case Against the Global Economy.* San Francisco, CA: Sierra Club Books.

Marx, Karl, and Frederick Engels. 1978. *The Marx-Engels Reader.* 2d ed. Edited by Robert C. Tucker. New York: W.W. Norton.

McChesney, Robert. 1995. *Telecommunications, Mass Media, and Democracy: The Battle for the Control of U.S.Broadcasting*, 1928–1935. New York and Oxford: Oxford University Press.

———. 1997. *Corporate Media and the Threat to Democracy.* New York: Seven Stories Press.

Moody, Kim. 1988. *An Injury to One.* London, England: Verso.

———. 1997. "Towards an International Social Movement Unionism." *New Left Review* 225:52–72.

Polyani, Karl. [1944] 1957. *The Great Transformation.* Boston, MA: Beacon Press.

Ritzer, George. 1996. *The McDonaldization of Society.* Thousand Oaks, CA: Pine Forge Press.

Robertson, Roland. 1991. *Globalization.* London, England: Sage.

Robins, Kevin, and Frank Webster. 1999. *Times of the Technoculture.* London, England, and New York: Routledge.

Shenk, David. 1997. *Data Smog: Surviving the Information Glut.* New York: HarperCollins.

Sklair, Leslie. 2001. *The Transnational Capitalist Class.* Cambridge: Blackwell.

Slouka, Mark. 1995. *War of the Worlds.* New York: Harper and Row.

Soja, Edward. 1989. *Postmodern Geographies.* London, England: Verso.

Steger, Manfred. 2002. *Globalism: The New Market Ideology.* Lanham, MD: Rowman and Littlefield.

Stiglitz, Joseph E. 2002. *Globalization and Its Discontents.* New York: Norton.

Stoll, Clifford. 1995. *Silicon Snake Oil: Second Thoughts on the Information Highway.* New York: Doubleday.

U.S. Department of Commerce, National Telecommunications and Information Administration (NTIA). 1999. "Falling Through the Net: Defining the Digital Divide." ≤http://www.ntia.doc.gov/ntiahome/fttn99/contents.html≥ (last accessed 29 June 2002).

Virilio, Paul. 1998. *The Virilio Reader.* Edited by James Der Derian. Malden, MA, and Oxford, England: Blackwell Publishers.

Wark, McKenzie. 1994. *Virtual Geography: Living With Global Media Events.* Bloomington and Indianapolis, IN: Indiana University Press.

Waterman, Peter. 1992. "International Labour Communication by Computer: The Fifth International?" Working Paper Series 129, Institute of Social Studies, The Hague.

Waters, Malcolm. 1995. *Globalization.* London, England: Routledge.

Watson, James L., ed. 1997. *Golden Arches East: McDonalds in East Asia.* Palo Alto, CA: Stanford University Press.

Webster, Frank. 1995. *Theories of the Information Society.* London, England, and New York: Routledge.

SECTION XVI

1. What, according to Wallerstein, are the three instances of hegemony in the history of the capitalist world-system, and how did each instance emerge?
2. What does Beck mean by methodological nationalism? Do you agree or disagree with his claim that it is an impediment to understanding globalization?
3. Summarize Beck's understanding of cosmopolitanism in your own words, and provide an example of the cosmopolitan condition.
4. What does Appadurai mean by "mediascapes"? How do they differ from and how are they related to what he refers to as "ideoscapes"?
5. Review Kellner's argument about the growing impact of the global movement that is contesting the direction of contemporary social change brought about by capitalist globalization. Based on your own sense of the political landscape, do you agree or disagree with his assessment of the potential impact of this movement? Explain.

XVII. FURTHER NEW DIRECTIONS IN CONTEMPORARY SOCIAL THEORY

80. THE SUBJECT AND SOCIETAL MOVEMENTS

ALAIN TOURAINE

Alain Touraine (b.1925) is a French social theorist and public intellectual rooted in the democratic socialist tradition. His overarching theoretical project has sought to position his work in contrast to functionalism and as a manifestation of a post-Marxist theory that builds on the Marxist tradition while transcending its limitations and problems. His work represents a unique blend of Marxist and non-Marxist sources. This project has variously been called "sociology of action" and "the self-production of society." Unlike theorists such as Anthony Giddens, who have attempted to link agency and structure in a coherent theoretical framework, Touraine tends to pay little attention to structure per se, treating action as antecedent to structure, which is therefore constitutive of action. In this aspect his work is not entirely distinctive. However, as this essay on social movements illustrates, his concern with collective rather than individual action does serve to distinguish his contribution to theory from those of most theoretical currents. Like resource mobilization theorists, he views contemporary social movements as rational responses to various types of discontent on the part of the subordinated sectors of society. Touraine goes beyond resource mobilization by arguing that progressive social movements contain transformative potential; if successful, they can change the course of social development. In this regard, they can be conceived as subjects of history.

It is initially essential to distinguish three types of collective action. The first type of collective action involves social demands, and occurs at the level of organizations; and the second involves political crisis and occurs at the level of institutions and decision-making centers. The third, which is increasingly important and with which I am concerned, is one that responds to conditions in a deinstitutionalized society in which common beliefs no longer unify and where the Self is fractured. These conditions give rise to societal movements that involve the personal and collective struggle for the unification of the Subject. In contrast with collective action involving social demands, which are based on economic calculation, or those involving political crisis, which lead to political demands, a societal movement relies on a collective determination to acquire a fundamental cultural resource, such as knowledge, recognition, a model of morality, and, most especially, the will to become a Subject.

To make this more concrete, in collective actions involving social demands or under a political crisis, the language is political, even though the collective action may occur in an industry, firm, hospital, university or neighborhood. For example, whenever a recession throws people out of work and lowers wages, a population may rise up with strong demands, but they have few chances of raising consciousness by fostering an understanding of the situation or even an ideology. The actors´ consciousness focuses on their own situation, on calculations for proving the validity of their claims, justifying demands about living standards or the strain of their work, or making comparisons with people in other socioeconomic categories. There is no reference to power relationships, or to the society´s basic cultural orientations. Nor is there a reference to a social Subject, or to conflictive relations about the social uses of a cultural model, or to shared cultural orientations.

THE DISTINCTIVENESS OF SOCIETAL MOVEMENTS

Just as the sociology of rational choice and interests has diligently studied social demands, and functionalist sociology has dwelled on institutions in crises, the third type of collective action requires analyses that center attention on how actors aim to change a society´s key cultural models and how they are managed. Such a movement is recognizable because it brings together three characteristics: a conflict between social actors contending over the social relations whereby a society reproduces itself; a positive reference to the cultural values at stake in the conflict; and an idea as to how the Subject is joined to the societal movement.

It is never easy to detect whether a collective action contains a societal movement, with long-lasting consequences. The long, massive strike of May 1968 (with its demonstration on May 13, for which a million persons turned out) appeared at the time to have been a political crisis with only short-term effects. Yet a quarter of a century afterwards, there is no denying that it changed society and introduced cultural themes

into politics. Therefore, we must consider it to have been a major societal movement with continuing consequences.

A societal movement is based on neither an economic calculation nor political pressure. It relies on the will to acquire a fundamental cultural resource (knowledge, a model of morality such as socialism or equality) and on the will to become a Subject. This will is not expressed in a vacuum—not in the solitude of a personal experience but in social relations and in a way that respects and advances personal and collective freedoms. Societal movements criticize social relations involving inequality, domination, and power, but they go beyond that in appealing to an ethics of collective responsibility.

Many sociologists have concentrated on how societal movements mobilize resources. This approach is useful insofar as a movement´s orientations can be reduced to the collective pursuit of individual interests. But why does the pursuit of individual interests spawn collective action? This question is especially pertinent given the strong temptation to be a free-rider, as Olson (1965) pointed out in his now classical analysis. This we might consider to be a sociology of resource mobilization, and involves actors and their objectives. Also, by focusing on societal movements, I am also not considering rebellions, namely actions taken against suffering, poverty, or slavery. Rebellions are defined by what they reject—by what they designate as unbearable—whereas societal movements have a positive orientation and accompany political, cultural, or social objectives. A rebellion is centered on its own suffering, whereas, in a societal movement, we find both conflict and hope.

In considering the role of hope, idealism, and an altered conscience, which are the seeds of societal movements, I can refer to some concrete examples. These would include: the popular movements that put an end to apartheid in South Africa; the Polish and Czech solidarity movements that prepared the fall of the Soviet system; the Tiananmen uprising; ongoing student actions in Korea, Taiwan, and Iran; and, also, as I indicated, the French student movement of May 1968. Societal movements are the real place where liberation and liberty join together. Although the public (sometimes with the help of the media) have recognized the importance of these movements, sociology has usually resisted interpreting them, except in the most reductionist of ways. A main emphasis in sociology since Olson´s (1965) earlier work has been to state that such movements involve the rational pursuit of ends. This implies that many or most stay out of the conflict so they can benefit from those who take risks without taking risks themselves. But how can we explain that so many men and women have taken risks— have fought and made sacrifices in the hope of achieving goals, a hope in which they themselves could not believe?

As I have defined societal movements as those that are transformative, and infused by shared energy, they involve subjective elements. Although it must be recognized that societal movements, such as the ones I have mentioned, accompany anti-social and sometimes destructive behaviors, it is important not to attach too much importance to such behaviors. The active Subject that lies within the societal movement and its concrete expressions has helped to erode the state´s logic of power and the reproduction of inequality within the state, and, thereby, societal movements have further global consequences.

Two ways of thinking have obscured the very idea of a social movement. The first, which has always prevailed in France, only considers anything having to do with the state´s power as important. Accordingly, only political actions have a broad scope, whereas social actions are always confined in narrow bounds. This, I believe, stems from historical features in France, and the fact that the French demanded, early on, a political democracy but have lagged behind in building a social democracy. The preference of the people in France, and in other Latin countries, for revolutionary radicalism stems from the strong bonds that, in these lands, united the state with the traditional oligarchy and, even more, with the Catholic Church. This has set the revolutionary tone of politics, a tone that has often had (and can still have) ringing effects. As a consequence, so many observers enthusiastically saluted the long workers´ strike in May 1968 but scorned the students´ cultural movement, which they qualified as *petit bourgeois*.

The second way of thinking that has obscured the nature of social movements seems the opposite of the foregoing. It is based on completely splitting the social apart from the political systems. It is then easy to show how, in order to attain its objectives or grow, a political action must mobilize social resources but without a connection with the objectives or conceptions of social actors. This way of thinking is just as political as the first, but it endows politics with a different meaning. From this vantage point, social action is subordinate to political action, which aims specifically at acquiring or maintaining power. Such thinkers see social movements nearly everywhere, since, constantly (especially in democracies), politicians strengthen their hand by presenting themselves as the only actors capable of responding to social pressure. The extreme form of this is Leninism, which, by assigning the political vanguard the central role, places directly under its control movements or organizations, which are soon reduced to being relay mechanisms for the party.

The idea of a societal movement is different from these two conceptions. Above all else, it asserts that, under certain circumstances at least, social actors can define a central social cause and oppose opponents in the name of dominant cultural values, while also defending their particular interests. To talk about a societal movement is to affirm that social actors have preeminence over political authorities. This entails the idea of representative democracy and, in particular, of social democracy, wherein the party is the union´s political muscle. To detect societal movements means inquiring into the conditions under which, at the level of conflicting social relations, actions emerge that have a general scope and are capable of commanding political actors and resources instead of being used by them.

In contrast with political conceptions of a revolutionary or a strategic sort, for which only political action can broaden the scope of demands that are always particularistic, the idea of a societal movement is based on the idea that there exists a central conflict. This is particularly the case in the contemporary world, which we could describe as postindustrial, computerized, and information-based. As I analyze the current situation, social conflicts in our society pit the Subject against the triumph of the marketplace and technology and also against authoritarian communitarian (exclusive) powers. For me, this cultural conflict seems as central as the economic conflict was in industrial society or the political conflict was during the first centuries of the modern era. If we reject the idea of a social movement from the start or use this phrase to refer only to demands or to reactions in a political crisis, we keep ourselves from corroborating, or even understanding, it.

SOCIETAL MOVEMENTS AND THE SUBJECT

A societal movement exists only if it combines a social conflict with a cultural cause defined with reference to a Subject. The Subject has assumed religious and political forms, and even taken on the form of a class or nation. I would like to argue that the Subject can emerge "finally as it is in itself"—as the personal Subject—only in our type of society. In all societies, however, the Subject reveals itself through moral values that oppose the social order. A societal movement defends a way of putting moral values to use that is different from the one its social opponent defends and tries to impose. Moral references and the consciousness of direct conflict with a social opponent who is defined by its way of appropriating common values and cultural resources are two inseparable aspects of a societal movement. This reference to morals should not be confused with claims based on needs or working conditions. Such claims back up demands for modifying the ratio of costs to benefits, whereas the moral discourse of a societal movement refers to freedom, a cause, fairness, justice, and the respect for fundamental rights.

Specifically, as we pass from the depiction of the working-class movement as a reaction to capitalism's contradictions to the image of a working-class movement with a cause that is both defensive and offensive, we see the growing importance of freedom, justice, and social rights. But we must go much further to detect and then understand contemporary societal movements during this transition period involving the postindustrial society. We must give up defining the social actor objectively as a socioeconomic category, because a societal movement does not aim at changing the relative positions of individuals on a scale of revenue or power. It seeks, instead, to rally a dominated, alienated, "fragmented" Subject. In this sense, the word "consciousness" must be used not to refer to the consciousness that a class or nation develops of its own situation but to emphasize the emergence of the actor.

But how does the actor constitute its own self? This question lies at the heart of a sociology that has stopped analyzing systems in order to understand the Subject. For some sociologists, reflection of the Subject upon itself leads it to seek a principle of order and control over the prevailing disorder and arbitrariness. For others, the Subject can assert itself only by referring to common values, a general interest. Sociologists of the first sort are often called "liberals"; those of the second, "communitarians." The first try to discover rules, procedures, and laws; the second, the contents, or substantial definition, of the Good. But the two are not so clearly or fully opposed as it seems, since laws transcribe a conception of the Good, and procedures never stay neutral whenever social interests come into play. The opposition between liberals and communitarians is played out within an objectivist conception of society, even though this conception is more traditional among communitarians (who may be traditionalists or even Tocquevillians). Quite different are those sociologists, such as Habermas (1989) or Taylor (1989), who, in contrast with both liberals and communitarians, assign a central place to the construction of the Subject. What must be added to their different approaches is the idea that the Subject constitutes itself only through social conflict.

Every societal movement has two sides: the one, Utopian; the other, ideological. As Utopian, the actor identifies the self in terms of the Subject's rights. As ideological, the actor concentrates on the struggle with a social opponent. Without a doubt, the class struggle is ideological. It emphasizes social conflict more than shared issues. On the other hand, the student movements of 1964 and 1968 in France were so Utopian that they defined their opponent in excessively vague terms. Even though every societal movement is lopsided, stressing Utopian or ideological aspects at the expense of the other, a societal movement requires both.

In contemporary social thought, we see two conceptions of individualism opposing each other. The one defends the multiplicity of choices offered to the large majority of individuals by our society of consumption and mass communications. For it, the market is the place of freedom, since it takes the place of the power of faith, doctrine, or established hierarchies. Opposite this conception, the second argues for the idea of a personal and collective Subject capable of endowing its situations and experiences with a general meaning. The first conception refers to freedom of choice; the second to autonomy and meaningful life experiences. These two conceptions form the grounds for social movements that, though opposite, both defend the individual.

Nothing sheds a brighter light on the Subject than the analysis of societal movements, because both the Subject and movements involve a moral principle about social relations. A societal movement cannot be reduced to moral protest; nor can the Subject be reduced to the pursuit of individual interests or pleasure. The Subject cannot be separated from a societal movement. They form two sides of a single reality. We thus see how much the idea of the Subject differs from that of conscience, especially when the latter, as classically formulated, means self-control or skeptical self-detachment (as in the case of Montaigne). The Subject is neither a being, nor a place, nor an autonomous space and time. It is a call to protest and to self-assertion.

A societal movement only exists if it succeeds in defining a conflictual social relation and the broad, societal issues underlying this conflict. It thus links together the assertion of an identity, a definition of the opponent, and an understanding of the issues that underlie contention. Can we draw the conclusion that a societal movement is more thoughtful, better controlled, and more responsible than protest or crisis behavior? Not at all. The degree of violence of a collective action has nothing to do with its nature. The violence depends on whether or not there is room for negotiations. A societal movement may assume a revolutionary form; but it stops being a movement only if it loses its autonomy and becomes a social resource in the hands of political leaders whose objectives are quite different from those of the original movement.

At this point, a historical question crops up: can societal movements still exist in societies under the sway of the market economy? Or does the marketplace tend to eliminate what I have called the system of historical action and, consequently, replace societal movements with simple demands or occasional political crises? Many postmodernists, reflecting on the

contemporary global economy, contend that hyper-industrialized societies that have moved beyond historicity can only experience chaos or make adjustments to limited, controlled change. Clearly, this pessimistic view is shortsighted and ignores the human capacity for reflection and for possessing an historical awareness. I take the view that societal movements emerge in all types of societies, and, in particular, they emerge in those endowed with historicity—capable of cognitively, economically, and morally investing in themselves. For that reason, contemporary neoliberalism, even on a near global scale, does not preclude societal movements.

SOCIETAL MOVEMENTS AND DEMOCRACY

One of the reasons why I have analyzed societal movements for such a long time is that I felt it necessary to radically and intellectually criticize revolutionary actions and ideologies, which, from the Reign of Terror to Leninism, have always resulted in essentially totalitarian governments or even in fascism. My central thesis is that we cannot separate the forming of social actors and, therefore, of societal movements from the autonomy of the issues underlying their actions—hence from the political mediation that constitutes democracy's central, indispensable element. The Subject, societal movements, and democracy are as inseparable as historical necessity, revolutionary action, and totalitarianism, which represent their darker side. Societal movements, of whatever sort, bear them within democratic aspirations. They seek to give a voice to those who have no voice and bring them into political and economic decision-making. In contrast, revolutionary actors dream of cultural, ethnic, political, or social purification, of a unified and transparent society, of creating a new mankind, and of eradicating whatever counters a unanimity that soon has no other reason for being than to organize political support for a totalitarian power.

This general conception leads us, as sociologists, to maintain that the presence of a societal movement is linked neither to a revolutionary situation nor to the force of an ideological discourse or line of politics. Rather, it is linked to the actor's capacity for working out a praxis—to a commitment to societal conflict and the defense of societal values, i.e. values that cannot be reduced to interests and, consequently, that cannot lead to the annihilation of one's opponent. A movement's meaning lies neither in the situation where the movement forms nor in the consciousness that ideologists ascribe to it or impose on it. The meaning is in its ability to undertake a certain type of action and place social conflict and issues on a certain level. In opposition to an "economicist" tradition often linked to Marxism, I have constantly defended the idea of a societal movement and a historical actor. In my first study of the working-class movement (Touraine, 1965), I stated that this movement was defending workers' autonomy. We would be caricaturing the study of the consciousness of social movements were we to reduce it to its most ideological forms. In effect, the latter often lie the furthest from praxis; and when they do not, the movement has, in fact, turned into an authoritarian or totalitarian anti-movement. All forms of absolute ideological mobilization—the identification of a social actor with God, Reason, History or the Nation—entail the destruction of societal movements. The latter are open to conflict, debate, and democracy, whereas ideological movements risk replacing plurality with unanimity, conflict with homogeneity, and participation with manipulation. Revolutionary intellectuals and leaders, demagogues and fundamentalists, are the active agents in the destruction of social movements. How can this escape our notice at the end of a century teeming with neo-communitarian movements, the most powerful of which call for a theocratic society?

Nowadays, given the globalization of the economy, we see arising, on the one hand, societal movements for minority rights, immigrant rights, and, more generally, human rights, but we are also witnessing anti-movements, which are giving birth to sects and cults in democratic lands and to new totalitarian movements on a national, ethnic, or religious basis. Here I am using a notion that many commentators—without giving it much thought—have avoided because they wish to ignore the difficulties of comparing the Nazi and communist systems with contemporary nationalist and religious fundamentalist movements. Is it so hard to admit that each totalitarian system, despite its specific aspects, belongs to a general type? Recourse to a "faith," whether Islam, Christianity, or Hinduism, leads to religious warfare, which communism and the revolutionary Mexican system, despite their violently anti-religious campaigns, avoided. Beyond the specific aspects of each totalitarian system, all of them share one characteristic, namely an absolute political power that speaks in the name of a people (a particular historical, national, or cultural group) and an assertion of absolute superiority (as being representative of a reality above politics and the economy). A totalitarian system is always popular, national, and doctrinaire. It subordinates social practices to a power that claims to incarnate the idea that a people represent and defends a faith, race, class, history, or territory.

Obviously, totalitarianism destroys democracy, but it also annihilates social, cultural, and historical movements and actors. It reduces historicity by using economic or cultural resources for constructing a closed mythical identity, itself reduced in practice to the justification of an absolute power. The idea of a people has always been a disguise for an absolutist state. It is no accident that the totalitarian, then authoritarian, governments in the communist countries dependent on the Soviet Union chose to call themselves "people's" republics. Totalitarianism is the central problem of the twentieth century. In like manner, when political activists reject elections or bring excessive moral or material pressure to bear on those who do not share their point of view, they destroy the social movement for which they claim to be speaking. They act like the demagogues (or Red Guards) rather than like the vanguard leading a class, nation or socioeconomic category. In short, a societal movement is praxis and not just a consciousness, and is fully linked to the affirmation that there is no societal movement without democracy, and vice versa.

SOCIAL MOVEMENTS IN A NON-DEMOCRATIC SITUATION

An objection immediately comes to mind. Does this vision not focus solely on developed lands, where modernization is self-sustaining? Does it not overlook situations where democracy does not exist, because of the arbitrary power imposed by a national or foreign state or an oligarchy interested in speculation and social power more than in economic rationality? This is such an important objection that the answers to it serve to guide the analysis of social movements. It calls for two complementary answers.

The first answer is that there can be no development without popular societal movements and democracy. Development results from combining three major factors: the abundance and quality of investment; the distribution of the fruits of growth; and public consciousness of the political unit. In effect, nation and modernization cannot be separated, since a developed economy is a dense, coherent, convergent network of exchanges, transactions, and interactions among all societal sectors. More simply, development supposes a ruling elite accumulating resources and making long-term decisions; but it also requires redistributive and leveling forces, universal participation in the process of modernization, and the reduction of social and cultural privileges. These forces, born out of popular mobilization, have recourse to political institutions. Instead of saying, as many do, that development is a condition for democracy, I contend that democracy is a condition for development. The inability of the Soviet Union to really develop and its increasing paralysis provided evidence in support of this. But is the fast growth of China and of other lands in Asia, or elsewhere, not counter-evidence? We must answer no. In China, we observe the breakup of a totalitarian system and, in the coastal provinces, the rapid growth of a market economy under the leadership of decision-making centers located abroad. This breakup has positive effects, especially coming as it does after the Cultural Revolution´s destructive violence. But if social movements do not form, if democracy is not born, the historical process under way in China will disintegrate into a new authoritarianism or else into chaos. The Soviet Union´s former satellites and former Yugoslavia, too, are looking for a way between democratic development and regression into authoritarianism. Such regression has had tragic consequences in Serbia and has negatively affected Romania and several other ex-Soviet countries. Meanwhile, the communists . . . come back in Poland, Hungary, Bulgaria, and Lithuania, and their success in elections in Russia and elsewhere, cannot—at present—be interpreted as a defeat for democracy and modernization.

Self-sustaining growth is a worthy objective, but this conception must be broadened to take into account other factors. When the dominant mode of development is of a domestic sort, there is a risk that authoritarian agencies will attempt to control the people or reduce them to mere resources. And when the dominant mode of development is of a market sort, social movements inevitably disintegrate into a multitude of pressure groups whose demands make social inequality worse. Can social movements exist in non-democratic situations? Let us push these questions even further. Are there democratic elements, hence movements, whose actions tend toward a despotic or market model instead of a democratic one?

This second answer takes us back to the analysis of the Subject, which can assert itself only through struggling against both the marketplace and commodified community. This means that the Subject arises as a form of opposition and liberation within the world of the marketplace and within the universe of the community. Indeed, societal movements, like the Subject itself, arise within a mode of development or even in forms of social power.

The major historical case is that of collective movements in authoritarian societies ruled by a despotic power, a national oligarchy, or a foreign colonial power. In this case, movements are forced to combine the defense of the oppressed and the demands for democracy with a revolutionary action for destroying the powers that be. Even in democratic lands, the working-class movement has always borne its share of violence in reaction to the violence of employers or governments. The strategy of a collective movement and of its leaders consists in combining actions for breaking with the existing order with democratic actions—the "logic" of the struggle against the powers that be with actions for defending freedom and, thus, political consciousness. This combination often fails. For instance, the labor movement has sometimes been an instrument, lacking autonomy, in the service of a new political power; and, sometimes, it has only defended relatively privileged socioeconomic categories. But these failures, however many times they have happened, must not keep us from realizing that a cultural, historical, or societal movement was present, despite the non-democratic outcome. True, the

Algerian national movement has led to a military dictatorship that quells popular opposition. Nonetheless, it was an anti-colonial movement for national liberation. Nor does the horror of the Reign of Terror detract from the events of June 1789 that introduced democracy in France. A movement is never purely democratic, nor does a revolution ever entirely lack democratic contents.

DESPAIR OR HOPE?

We would weaken the idea of a societal movement were we to reduce it to naming a particular—more ideal than real—type of collective action. It is a concept or theoretical formulation. The idea of a societal movement (and, more broadly, of a social movement) forces us to give up the too easy quests of conservative thought, which looks for factors of integration, and of revolutionary thought, which denounces a system of domination as incapable of being either restrained or reformed.

This idea also protects us against the fragmentation that menaces collective action and, indeed, all aspects of social life. On the one hand, social movements seem to be less focused on being interest groups currently than on efforts for defending social integration from "social fractures" and ruptures of social bonds. The theme of exclusion, which has replaced exploitation, contains this idea. On the other hand, "identity movements" are abounding, in the United States where women, homosexuals, African Americans, and ethnic or national communities are asserting cultural autonomy while also fighting against discrimination, but also in countries obsessed with ideas of purity and homogeneity. The increasing separation between these two types of collective action, which are foreign to each other, is not just a given fact. It is a reality as pathological as the wider separation between the world of instrumentality and the world of identity, a separation that entails the collapse of social and especially political mediation between the economy and cultures.

There is a risk of too easily defining the idea of a societal movement only in terms of its twofold refusal of communitarianism and of economic globalization, and also some risk of considering any pressure group or identity movement as a significant societal movement. It is also important for sociologists to look for such

movements underneath extreme ideologies where they are often hidden. Let us take two opposite examples. In Algeria (and other Islamic countries, Egypt in particular), there are political groups that use Islam to attain power and construct a fundamentally anti-modern, Iranian type of society. To survive, they use the techniques of modernity. However, we should not forget that this also gives expression to an uprooted population, to young people without jobs who use the *trabendo* (black market), or sports, as a means of forcing open the doors of the society of consumption. Those who oppose lay reactions to the dangerous politics of religious mobilization are right up to a point, but they are wrong in that they fail to see that many movements draw their force from the culture and society they defend because they feel threatened. The second example is the 1995 strike in the French public services. The events that took place then cannot be reduced to a defense of vested interests or privileges. They manifested a popular rejection of an economic policy that subordinated all of social life to deficit reduction, considered to be the key for developing a single European currency (which, in and of itself, is supposed to bring prosperity and jobs for all).

Let us try to clear up, at least a little, our confusion by recalling the "natural history" of any movement. It starts when the denunciation of misery goes along with a moral appeal to the dignity of everyone and the solidarity of all. Only thereafter is the opponent identified; and the conflict becomes central, before being institutionalized—as the organized social movement turns into a political force or party, which intervenes in economic and social policy-making. This ultimate phase usually accompanies a return to ideological discourses that, cut off from strategic actions, call for a return either to open conflict or to the denunciation of misery. In each phase, this history may be interrupted. This natural history teaches us useful lessons, even if these are too general to account for the wide diversity of historical situations. But these lessons are of less use for understanding the present than is a historical reflection that pays more attention to the effects of demodernization.

How could the split between the economic and cultural worlds not affect societal movements? The "civil/civic" movements of the seventeenth and eighteenth centuries worked for the creation of a national, republican political order. The working-class move-ment has drawn its strength from its consciousness that it was a means of progress, that it was pulling society "history-wise" through its struggle against the irrationality of capitalistic profit-seeking. These move-ments were borne by collective actors, which we label as social classes because they were defined by their political, economic, or social situations. This linkage between an objective meaning and a consciousness necessarily tears apart in the current situation of demo-dernization. Such movements are becoming increas-ingly moral, while fighting an opponent that is defined less as a power or class than as an agent of "dehumanization" and of domination through globa-lized networks of production, consumption, and com-munication. In this very concrete sense, the identity between the Subject and social movements compels recognition. In industrialized nations particularly, movements are less and less instrumental but more and more expressive.

The awareness of exclusion has spread with pov-erty, segregation, and joblessness. The societal move-ment against exclusion is arising out of the efforts of persons who, working in humanitarian organizations, increasingly think and act in terms not of the crisis of capitalism but of the conditions for the destruction or creation of the individual as Subject. There is no evi-dence that, in France, the leaders of the 1995 protests will be the forerunners of a movement that will orga-nize, undertake a strategic action, and change into a party (as environmentalists have done in Germany). These groups, associations, and movements seem to be constituting themselves as historical, independent actors who mobilize volunteers, who actively use and criticize the media, but who critically stand aloof from a political system that, in their eyes, is subject to the constraints of the international economy. Meanwhile, the weak and threatened sectors of the vast middle class are organizing political actions for defending their vested interests. More diffuse, "everyday" move-ments—which are also more enthusiastic and more generous—are undertaking exemplary actions, decrying the denial of truth and justice, and combining the per-sonal with collective solidarity. How can we not see in them the already constituted force of a new societal movement? To do so fits into a broader reflection on

the conditions for political action and, therefore, for social control over both globalization and technological revolutions, in particular over the effects directly bearing on personality and culture.

Neither liberals nor revolutionaries believe in the capacity of social actions for producing their history through their cultural orientations and social conflicts. In contrast, I maintain that we should recognize the importance of demands for a sense of identity or of strategies for pressing demands. But only the idea of a societal movement enables us to recognize the exis-tence of actions combining a fundamental social con-flict with the pursuit of societal objectives (such as modernization, social integration or the respect for human rights) defined in concrete situations and social relations. The idea of a societal movement is not satisfied with completing a sociology that is mainly oriented toward the quest for social integration. It associates integration with conflict, and, as a conse-quence, takes the central place in analyzing the social organization and social change. It is indispensable for any political sociology.

I am not insisting on placing the idea of the Subject at the center of analysis in order to "desocialize" soci-etal movements, i.e. to separate them from the conflic-tual social relations where they have their origins. On the contrary, this insistence is intended to distinguish a societal movement from the political instruments and ideological apparatuses that keep us from seeing that a societal movement always appeals to the Subject's lib-erty. These appeals are not situated in the social vacuum of natural law, but in the social relations of domina-tion, property, and power. A societal movement is thus both a struggle for and a struggle against.

Societal movements are important not just because they reveal the contradictions within modern societies, which is defined by their historicity, by the concentra-tion of the means for changing society, and by the distance between the rulers and ruled. What best defines a societal movement is the linkage it establishes between cultural orientations and a social conflict bearing demands that are political and societal. If a societal movement does not form, all these elements separate from each other and, doing so, degrade. On the one hand, cultural orientations, when they are split off from social and political conflicts, turn into moral principles of belonging or of exclusion, mechanisms of cultural control, and norms of social conformity. On the other hand, political conflicts, when they are split off from societal movements, are reduced to struggles for power. Finally, demands, left to themselves, tend to reinforce established inequalities, since the most powerful and influential have the most vested interests to defend and are best equipped to press demands. We thus see a juxtaposition of pressure groups; movements of rejection that comprise categories defined as minorities, deviants or foreigners; and a communitarian populism that appeals to an indeterminate people against leaders and intellectuals. Each of these aspects of social or political life could, it initially seems, be studied by itself, but that is impossible. All collective actions bear evidence of an absent or disintegrated societal movement.

Societal movements do not always exist; but they do represent a hypothesis that must be worked out in order to understand contemporary collective life. Sociological positivism that takes as starting point not social relations and historicity but principles of order (whether based on personal interests or communitarian values) provides poor explanations that are insufficient because positivists place nothing between the individual and society. In actual fact, however, neither the individual nor society exists as principles that can be isolated from social relations and processes that constantly join order with change, and integration with conflict.

Our need for these concepts and principles of analysis is all the greater now, in that we are living in a "fragmented" society that has been deprived of a consciousness of itself. Under these conditions, issues and actors of historical change are obscure, and discourses and ideologies lag behind practices or become artificially radicalized practices. Our societies are not just hypermodern; they lack meaning, since they suffer from the dissociation of practices from consciousness, and of acts from discourses. Nowadays, the center of society is an empty field where are scattered the remains of past combats and old discourses, which have become second-hand merchandise acquired by the merchants of power and ideologies. For this reason, the idea of a societal movement must be defended because it interprets this emptiness and gives a coherent meaning to all the behaviours, contradictory with each other, that originate in the disappearance and breakup or breakdown of the former social movements.

REFERENCES

Habermas, J. (1989) *The Structural Transformation of the Public Sphere.* Cambridge, MA: MIT Press.
Olson, M. (1965) *The Logic of Collective Action.* Cambridge, MA: Harvard University Press.
Taylor, C (1996) *Philosophical Arguments.* Cambridge: Cambridge University Press.
Touraine, A. (1965) *Sociologie de l'action.* Paris: Seuil.

81. REAL CIVIL SOCIETIES: DILEMMAS OF INSTITUTIONALIZATION

JEFFREY C. ALEXANDER

Jeffrey C. Alexander (b. 1947) is currently the Lillian Chavenson Saden Professor of Sociology at Yale University and the Director of its Center for Cultural Sociology. His theoretical focus has shifted in recent years. His earlier work constituted an attempt to develop a perspective rooted in but offering a corrective to Parsonian theory that he called neofunctionalism. His more recent work has turned to culture, advancing what he terms a "strong program in cultural sociology." At the same time, he has made a major contribution to our understanding of civil society in a magisterial work, *The Civil Sphere*, a term he uses to link civil society discourse with Habermas' idea of the public sphere. In this selection, which constitutes chapter 2 of that work, he discusses three different perspectives on civil society, with the third representing his position. Central to his understanding of the civil sphere is his claim that it represents a space distinct from other institutional realms, one where both solidarity and justice are promoted, and where the promise of democracy as an ongoing project is played out.

Vital concepts enter social science by a striking process of intellectual secularization. An idea emerges first in practical experiences, from the often overwhelming pressures of moral, economic, and political conflict. Only later does it move into the intellectual world of conceptual disputation, paradigm conflict, research program, and empirical debate. Even after they have made this transition, vital concepts retain significant moral and political associations, and they remain highly disputed. What changes is the terrain on which they are discussed, compromised, and struggled over. The intellectual field, after all, has a very distinctive specificity of its own.

This secularization process created such basic concepts as class, status, race, party, religion, and sect. More recently, we can see a similar process at work with the emergence of such concepts as gender, sexuality, and identity. The subject of this book, civil society, is being subjected to the same kind of secularization today.

Civil society enters into intellectual discourse from the ongoing tumult of social and political life for the second time. We must make every effort to refine it in a theoretical manner so that it will not disappear once again. If we fail, the opportunity to incorporate this idea might disappear from intellectual life for another long period of time. Not only normative theory but moral life itself would be impoverished if this opportunity were missed, and empirical social science would be much the worse as well. There is a new theoretical continent to explore, a new empirical domain waiting to be defined. But we will not be able to make out this new social territory unless we can look at it through new theoretical lenses. Our old conceptual spectacles will not do.

To forge these spectacles is the aim of this book. Its ambition is to develop a set of concepts that can illuminate a new kind of social fact and open up a new arena for social scientific study, one much closer to the spirit and aspirations of democratic life.

Civil society has been conceived in three ideal-typical ways. These have succeeded one another in historical time, though each remains a significant intellectual and social force today. After situating these ideal-types temporally, and evaluating them theoretically, I will introduce the analytical model at the core of this book, a model which aims to define the relationship between civil society and other kinds of institutional spheres. Only by understanding the boundary relations between civil and uncivil spheres can we push the discussion of civil society from the normative into the empirical realm. And only by understanding civil society in a more "realist" manner can we lay the basis for a critical normative theory about the incompleteness of civil society in turn.

CIVIL SOCIETY I

It is well known that in its modern, post-medieval, post-Hobbesian form, "civil society" entered into social understanding only in the late 17th century, with the writings of figures like Locke and James Harrington.[1] Developed subsequently by such Scottish moralists as Adam Ferguson and Adam Smith, by Rousseau and Hegel, and employed energetically for the last time by Tocqueville, "civil society" was a rather diffuse, umbrella-like concept referring to a plethora of institutions outside the state. It included the capitalist market and its institutions, but it also denoted what Tocqueville called voluntary religion (non-established Protestant covenantal denominations), private and public associations and organizations, and virtually every form of cooperative social relationship that created bonds of trust—for example, currents of public opinion, legal norms and institutions, and political parties.

It is vital to see that in this first period of its modern understanding, civil society was endowed with a distinctively moral and ethical force. As Albert Hirschman showed in *The Passions and the Interests*, the civilizing qualities associated with civil society most definitely extended to the capitalist market itself, with its bargaining and trading, its circulating commodities and money, its shopkeepers and private property. Identified by such terms as *le doux commerce*, the processes and institutions of the capitalist market were benignly

conceived—particularly by the progressive thinkers of the day—as helping to produce qualities associated with international peace, domestic tranquility, and increasingly democratic participation. Capitalism was understood as producing self-discipline and individual responsibility. It was helping to create a social system antithetical to the vainglorious aristocratic one, where knightly ethics emphasized individual prowess through feats of grandeur, typically of a military kind, and ascriptive status hierarchies were maintained by hegemonic force. Montesquieu provided high ethical praise for capitalism in this early phase.[2] Benjamin Franklin's influential *Autobiography*, which identifies public virtue with the discipline and propriety of market life, might be said to provide an equally important example of a more popular, more bourgeois, but perhaps not less literary kind.[3]

The decidedly positive moral and ethical tone that CSI attributed to market society underwent a dramatic transformation in the early middle of the nineteenth century. The development of capitalism's industrial phase made Mandeville's famous fable of capitalism's bee-like cooperation seem completely passé.[4] The pejorative association of capitalism with inhumane instrumentality, domination, and exploitation first emerged among radical British political economists like Thomas Hodgskin in the 1820s and 1830s.[5] Marx encountered this Manichean literature in the early 1840s, and he provided it with a systematic economic and sociological theory. His voice, while by far the most important in theoretical terms, was for contemporaries only one among many.

The emerging hatred of capitalism, its identification with all the evils of feudal domination and worse, was expressed among a wide and growing chorus of utopians, socialists, and republicans. It is noteworthy that, for their part, the new industrial capitalists and their liberal economic spokesmen did not shy away from this new view of capitalism as an antisocial force. Brandishing the doctrine of laissez-faire in a decidedly un-Smithean way, their motto seemed to be, "society be damned!" There exists no better representation of this self-understanding of the supposedly inherent and ineradicable antagonism between an evil, egotistical market, and "society" in the moral and collective sense, than Karl Polanyi's *The Great*

Transformation,[6] which dramatically took the side of "society" against the market. Despite its interpretive power and normative force, however, Polanyi's influential book has reinforced the very theoretical understandings I wish to make problematic here.

CIVIL SOCIETY II

In social theory, this dramatic transformation of the moral and social identity of market capitalism had fateful effects on the concept of civil society. As Keane[7] and Cohen[8] were among the first to point out, the connotations of this fecund concept became drastically narrowed. Shorn of its cooperative, democratic, associative, and public ties, in this second version (CSII), civil society came to be pejoratively associated with market capitalism alone.[9] Marx's writings between 1842 and 1845 reflected and crystallized this reduction in a fateful way. Not only does civil society come to be treated simply as a field for the play of egoistical, purely private interests, but it is now viewed as a superstructure, a legal and political arena that camouflages the domination of commodities and the capitalist class. For Marx, industrial capitalism seemed only to consist of markets, the social groups formed by markets, and market-protecting states. Society in the collective and moral sense had dissolved into a morass of particularistic interests. Only the submerged and repressed cooperative ties that defined the proletariat's true economic interest could provide a counter-balancing universalism. Only the collectively-binding social organization of the bourgeoisie's class enemy could sustain a social alternative to selfishness that the ideals of civil society provided only in name.

As Cohen[10] observed in her devastating critique, in Marx's theory of civil society "social, political, private, and legal institutions were treated as the environment of the capitalist system, to be transformed by its logic but without a dynamism of their own." Nothing more clearly illustrates the paradigm shift from CSI to CSII than the accusations Marx made against Hegel, namely, that he had sought, in a reactionary manner, to justify just such a privatized, selfish vision of civil society, that he had identified the civil sphere only with the 'system of needs' that became the mode of production Marx's own work.[11] But Hegel actually never did any such

thing. To the contrary, he sought to rework the liberal line of CSI in a more communal, solidaristic way. It is true that the available linguistic resources and the peculiarities of German history had led Hegel, as it had led Kant before him, to translate the English term, civil society, as *Burgerlich Gesellschaft*, literally 'burger' but more broadly 'bourgeois' or 'middle class' society.[12] But Marx's contention that Hegel, and non-socialists more generally, had identified civil society simply with capitalist class structures was an ahistorical distortion reflecting the sense of crisis that marked the birth of industrial society. For Hegel, the civil sphere was not only the world of economic needs but also the sphere of ethics and law, and other intermediate groupings that we would today call voluntary organizations.[13]

It is not surprising that in this social and intellectual situation, in the middle of the nineteenth century, civil society as an important concept in social theory shortly disappeared. If it was no more than an epiphenomenon of capitalism, then it was no longer necessary, either intellectually or socially. In the context of the ravages of early industrial capitalism, social and intellectual attention shifted to the state. Substantive rather than formal equality became the order of the day. Issues of democratic participation and liberty, once conceived as inherently connected to equality in its other forms, became less important. Strong state theories emerged, among both radicals and conservatives, and bureaucratic regulation appeared as the only counterbalance to the instabilities and inhumanities of market life.[14] In the newly emerging social sciences, mobility, poverty, and class conflict become the primary topics of research and theory. In social and political philosophy, utilitarian and contract theories assumed prominence, along with the neo-Kantian emphasis on justice in terms of formal rationality and proceduralism at the expense of ethical investigations into the requirements of the good life.

The legacy of this century-long distortion of the capitalism-civil society relationship has had regrettable effects. Identifying society with the market, ideologists for the right have argued that the effective functioning of capitalism depends on the dissolution of social controls. Secure in the knowledge that civil society is the private market, that economic processes by themselves will produce the institutions necessary to promote democracy and mutual respect, they have labored right-eously to disband the very public institutions that crystallize social solidarity outside the market place. Such efforts have continued to this day.[15]

Yet if, for the right, the capitalism-civil society identification suggested abolishing society, for the left it suggested abolishing markets and private property itself. If civility and cooperation were perverted and distorted by capitalism, the latter would have to be abolished for the former to be restored. In this way, the big state became the principal ally of the left, and progressive movements became associated not only with equality but with stifling and often authoritarian bureaucratic control.

This was by no means confined to the Marxist left. For thinkers from Walter Lippman and John Dewey to C. Wright Mills, Hannah Arendt, Jürgen Habermas, and most recently Robert Putnam, the disappearance of public life became axiomatic to any thoughtful consideration of twentieth century modernity.[16] Captives of the historical shift in intellectual presuppositions which I have described as CSII, these influential thinkers were unable to think reflexively about it. They were convinced that capitalism was destroying public life, that in democratic mass societies an all-powerful market was pulverizing social bonds, converting citizens into egoists, and allowing oligarchies and bureaucracies full sway. Capitalism and mass societies were conceived as social worlds in which privacy ruled. That this was, in fact, far from the case had become for even the most acute social observers very difficult to see. Because CSI had given way to CSII, they could no longer draw upon the idea of an independent civil sphere. The social conditions that had triggered the demise of CSI still held sway.

In a paradoxical manner, the civil society thinking of Antonio Gramsci, which differed significantly from the reductive understandings of traditional CSII, actually seemed to buttress these fateful lapses in critical democratic thought, whether liberal or socialist. Drawing on a less reductive reading of Hegel, in the early decades of the 20th century Gramsci had developed his own, thoroughly anti-individualistic and anti-economistic approach to civil society. He defined it as the realm of political, cultural, legal, and public life that occupied an intermediate zone between economic relations and political power.[17] With this idea, Gramsci meant to challenge the evolutionary line of Marxist thinking, which held that socialist revolution would be triggered automatically, by a crisis in the economy alone. Broadening Lenin's earlier critique of economism, Gramsci suggested that civil society itself would have to be challenged, and transformed, independently of the strains created by capitalism's economic base. Yet, even while Gramsci challenged the instrumentalism of Marx's thinking about the civil sphere, he reinforced CSII by insisting that, within the confines of capitalist market society, there would never be the space for institutionalizing solidarity of a more universalistic and inclusive kind. Gramsci did not associate civil society with democracy. It was a product of class-divided capitalism understood in the broad sociocultural and economic sense. The values, norms, and institutions of civil society were opposed to the interest of the mass of humanity, even if they did provide a space for contesting their own legitimacy in a public, counter-hegemonic way. Civil society was inherently capitalist. It was a sphere that could be entered into but not redefined. Its discourse could not be broadened and redirected. It was a sphere that would have to be overthrown. In this book, my argument is directed in an opposite way.

RETURN TO CIVIL SOCIETY I?

In recent decades a series of social and cultural events has created the circumstances for a renewed intellectual engagement with civil society. Big state theory has lost its prestige, economically with the falling productivity of command economies, morally and politically with the overthrow of state Communism and bureaucratic authoritarian regimes.[18] Within social science, there is now more interest in informal ties, intimate relationships, trust, cultural and symbolic processes, and the institutions of public life.[19] In political and moral philosophy, there has not only been a return to democratic theory, but renewed interest in Aristotle, Hegel, critical hermeneutics and Pragmatism—all marking a return to investigations of the lifeworld ties of local culture and community.[20]

The problem is that this re-engagement with civil society has largely meant a return to CSI. In *Democracy*

592   PART TWO • THE BRANCHES: CONTEMPORARY SOCIAL THEORY

and Civil Society, a path-breaking work in many ways, John Keane defines civil society broadly as "the realm of social activities," a realm that includes "privately owned," "market-directed," "voluntarily run," and "friendship-based" organizations, phenomena that are by no means necessarily theoretically complementary or practically congenial. Keane goes on to assert, moreover, that such civil activities are at once "legally recognized" and "guaranteed by the state," even as they form an "autonomous [sphere of] social life." Civil society is said to be "an aggregate of institutions whose members are engaged primarily in a complex of non-state activities—economic and cultural production, household life and voluntary association," seemingly private activities that Kane identifies as distinctly "sociable" and at the same time "public spheres."[21] Similarly, when Andrew Arato[22] first employed civil society in his important articles on the Solidarity movement in the early 1980s, he suggested that the civil sphere in its Western form was tied to private property, a traditional understanding that not only contradicts the broad range of references employed by Keane but threatens to render the concept useless for distinguishing democratic from nondemocratic capitalistic societies. A decade later, in their major philosophical rethinking of civil society theory, Cohen and Arato[23] severed this connection, and in its place they offered a substantially improved three-part model of society that went well beyond CSI and CSII. Nonetheless, perhaps by relying so heavily on Hegel, this major work failed to define the civil sphere as distinctive vis-à-vis such arenas as family life, and neglected entirely the relation between the civil sphere and such arenas as culture, religion, ethnicity, and race.[24] Here they were following Habermas, who insists on separating rational discourse in the public sphere from the traditions of cultural life.[25]

The same tendency toward diffuseness marked Alan Wolfe's[26] identification of civil society with the private realm of family and voluntary organization, and Adam Seligman's[27] insistence that it corresponds to the rule of reason in the Enlightenment sense. Carole Pateman[28] claims civil society to be inextricably linked to patriarchal family relations, and Shils[29] and Walzer[30], while disagreeing with Pateman in virtually every other way, likewise revert to an understanding of civil society that reflects its earlier diffuse and

umbrella-like form. Victor Perez-Diaz[31] argues, indeed, that only such a 'maximalist' approach to civil society can maintain the necessary linkages between a democratic public sphere and particular forms of economy, state, family, and cultural life. Though Robert Putnam's model for strengthening democracy through voluntary associations does not focus explicitly on the civil society idea, this neo-Tocquevillian approach looks backward to CSI in very much the same way.[32]

It is most definitely a good thing that the destructive and overly narrow understandings of CSII have been undermined by the recent revival of democratic thought. But social life at the beginning of the twenty-first century is much more complex and more internally differentiated than the early modern societies that generated CSI. The old umbrella understanding will no longer do. We need a much more precise and delimited understanding of the term. Private property, markets, family life, and religious ideals might all be necessary at some point or another to create the capacities of the civil sphere, but they are by no means sufficient to sustain it. Rejecting the reductionism of CSII, but also the diffuse inclusiveness of CSI, we must develop a third approach to civil society, one that reflects both the empirical and normative problems of contemporary life.

TOWARD CIVIL SOCIETY III

We need to understand civil society as a sphere that can be analytically independent, empirically differentiated, and morally more universalistic vis-à-vis the state and the market and from other social spheres as well. Building upon important directional signals from empirical theoretical traditions in sociology and normative traditions in political theory and philosophy... I would like to suggest that civil society should be conceived as a solidary sphere, in which a certain kind of universalizing community comes to be culturally defined and to some degree institutionally enforced. To the degree that this solidary community exists, it is exhibited and sustained by public opinion, deep cultural codes, distinctive organizations—legal, journalistic and associational—and such historically specific interactional practices as civility, criticism, and mutual respect.[33] Such a civil community can never exist as such; it can only be sustained to one degree or another. It is always limited by, and interpenetrated with, the boundary relations of other, noncivil spheres.

The solidarity that sustains the civil sphere amidst the complex and highly conflictual spheres of contemporary life draws from long-standing cultural and institutional traditions that have sustained individual and collective obligation. CSII theories were quite mistaken to link not only individualism (its emergence) but the collective sense of social obligation (its decline) with market society. The individuality that sustains civil society has a long history in Western societies, as a moral force, an institutional fact, and a set of interactional practices. It has a non-economic background in the cultural legacy of Christianity, with its emphasis on the immortal soul, conscience, and confession; in aristocratic liberty and Renaissance self-fashioning; in the Reformation's insistence on the individual relation to God; in the Enlightenment's deification of individual reason; in Romanticism's restoration of expressive individuality. Institutions that reward and model individuality can be traced back to English legal guarantees for private property in the eleventh century; to the medieval parliaments that distinguished the specificity of Western feudalism; to the newly independent cities that emerged in late medieval times and played such a powerful historical role until the emergence of absolutist states. The economic practices of market capitalism, in other words, did not invent either moral or immoral individualism. They should be viewed, rather, as marking a new specification and institutionalization of it, along with other newly emerging forms of social organization, such as religious sect activity, mass parliamentary democracy, and romantic love.[34]

Just as individualism in its moral and expressive forms preceded, survived, and in effect surrounded the instrumental, self-oriented individualism institutionalized in capitalist market life, so did the existence of "society." Civil ties and the enforcement of obligations to a community of others were part of the fundamental structure of many British towns centuries before the appearance of contemporary capitalist life.[35] The notion of a "people" rooted in common lineage, of the community as an ethnos, formed the early basis for an ethically binding, particularist conception of nationhood from at least the fifteenth century.[36] Karl

Polanyi well described the "double movement" that characterized the emergence of industrial capitalism in the nineteenth century, pitting "moral forces" representing "the moral entity 'man'" against the egoistical, impersonal, and degrading practices of the market. The upshot of this struggle was that the "general interests of the community" created "protectionist measures" regulating the conditions of land, labor, and productive organization inside the very bowels of economic life. "Once we rid ourselves of the obsession that only sectional, never general, interest can become effective," Polanyi writes, "as well as the twin prejudice of restricting the interests of human groups to their monetary income, the breadth and depth of the protectionist movement lose their mystery."[37] Still, Polanyi is wrong to describe this "countermovement" as of a "purely practical and pragmatic nature," as producing measures that "simply responded to the needs of an industrial civilization with which market methods were unable to cope."[38] The protectionist movement did not simply grow naturally in response to a moral violation that was there for all to see. Rather, this defensive moral response emerged precisely because there had already existed strongly institutionalized and culturally mandated reservoirs of non-market, non-individualistic force in Western social life. It was from these sources that there emerged protests against capitalism on behalf of "the people."[39]

To identify civil society with capitalism (CSII) is to degrade its universalizing moral implications and the capacity for criticism and repair that the existence of a relatively independent solidary community implies. The civil sphere and the market must be conceptualized in fundamentally different terms. We are no more a capitalist society than we are a bureaucratic, secular, rational one, or indeed a civil one. Yet, to suggest the need to acknowledge the environment outside of economic life is not to embrace the kind of relativism that the pluralism of CSI implies. Michael Walzer has argued eloquently that there are as many spheres of justice as there are differentiated social spheres.[40] Luc Boltanski and Laurent Thevenot, in a parallel argument, suggest that complex societies contain several "regimes of justification," each of which must be respected in its own right.[41] As these American and French theories persuasively remind us, no social sphere, not even the economic, should be conceived in anti-normative terms, as governed only by interest and egoism. They have immanent moral structures in their own right. It remains vital, nonetheless, to specify and differentiate the "regime of justification" or the "sphere of justice" that makes a clear and decisive reference to the common good in a democratic way. This is the criterion of justice that follows from ideals that regulate the civil sphere. The codes and narratives, the institutions, and the interactions that underlay civil solidarity clearly depart from those that regulate the world of economic cooperation and competition, the affectual and intimate relations of family life, and the transcendental and abstract symbolism that form the media of intellectual and religious interaction and exchange.

When the domination of one sphere over another, or the monopolization of resources by elites within the individual spheres themselves, has been forcefully blocked, it has been by bringing to bear the cultural codes and regulative institutions of the civil sphere. This, at least, is the thesis that informs this book. Civil and noncivil spheres do not merely co-exist in a kind of harmonious interchange, as functionalist theories of differentiation from Spencer and Durkheim to Parsons and Luhmann imply. It is not only the pluralization of spheres that guarantees a good society, nor the free play and good will of interlocutors willing to compromise their interests in the face of competing and persuasive claims for moral justification. To maintain democracy, and to achieve justice, it is often necessary for the civil to 'invade' noncivil spheres, to demand certain kinds of reforms, and to monitor them through regulation in turn. In modern times, aggrieved parties have demanded justice by pointing angrily to what they come to see as destructive intrusions into the civil realm, intrusions whose demands they construct as particularistic and self-serving. In response, the forces and institutions of civil society have often initiated repairs that aim to mend the social fabric.

In terms of the normative mandates established by democratic societies, it is the *civil* sphere of justice that trumps every other. The universality that is the ambition of this sphere, its demands to be inclusive, to fulfill collective obligations while at the same time protecting individual autonomy—these qualities have persistently made the civil sphere the court of last resort in modern,

modernizing, and postmodernizing societies.[42] For the last two centuries explicitly, and implicitly for many centuries before, it has been the immanent and subjunctive demands of the civil sphere that have provided possibilities for justice.

As we will see in our later analysis of the tense and shifting boundaries between civil and uncivil spheres, CSIII allows us to revisit the 'capitalism problem' in a more productive way.[43] When exploitation leads to widening class conflict, it signals strains and inequalities in economic life. When class conflict leads to wide public discussion, to the formation of legal trade unions, to urgent appeals for sympathy and support, to scandals and parliamentary investigations, such expansion signals that market conflicts have entered into the civil sphere. In such situations, the mandate of solidarity, the presumptions of collective obligation and autonomy, come face to face with the demands for efficiency and hierarchy. These conflicts are not accidental; they are systematic to every society that opens up a civil sphere, and they make justice a possibility, though not in any sense a necessary social fact. In real civil societies, extending solidarity to others depends on the imagination. The counter-factual "original position" that inspired Rawls' philosophy of justice is assumed in fantasy, as an idealization, via metaphor and symbolic analogy, not through pragmatic experience or logical deduction. It is a matter of cultural struggle, of social movement, of demands for incorporation, of broken and reconstructed dialogue, of reconfiguring institutional life.

Such tense and permeable boundary relationships between capitalist markets and the civil sphere, barely visible during the early reign of CSI, were denied in principle by CSII. Only if we develop a new model, CSIII, can we understand why capitalistic and civil society must not be conflated with one another. If these realms are separated analytically, we gain empirical and theoretical purchase, not only on the wrenching economic strains of the last two centuries, but on the extraordinary repairs to the social fabric that have so often been made in response. Markets are not, after all, the only threats or even the worst threats that have been levied against the democratic possibilities of civil life. Far from the mere existence of plural spheres providing the skeleton key to justice, each of the diverse and variegated spheres of modern societies has created distortions and undermined civil promises. Religious hatreds and repression, gender misogyny and patriarchy, the arrogance of expert knowledge and the secrecy of political oligarchy, racial and ethnic hatreds of every sort—each of these particularistic and anti-civil forces has deeply fragmented the civil domain. The identification of capitalism with civil society, in other words, is just one example of the reductive and circumscribing conflation of civil society with a particular kind of noncivil realm.

Social and cultural movements of every kind, whether old or new, economic or religious, have organized to expose the pretensions of civil society and the hollowness of its promises. The theorists and ideologists who have led these rebellious and critical movements have often concluded, in their desperation and frustration, that civil society has no real force at all. Whether such radical arguments focus on class, gender, race, or religion, their argument is much the same. Justice is impossible; revolution and flight are the only options left. I will suggest that these radical, and radically despairing, arguments for emancipation from civil society are not empirically accurate, even if they are sometimes morally compelling. Generalizing from distorted and oppressive boundary relations, they draw the false conclusion that the civil sphere must invariably be distorted in this manner, not only now but in the future as well. Building on this faulty line of reasoning, they have outlined utopian projects that reject universalizing solidarity as a social goal or have proposed a reconstructed social order in which only peaceable relations will reign. There is no way to avoid conflicts over boundary relations. They reflect the pluralism and complexity that mark modern and postmodern life, especially in its democratic forms. Between civil society and the other social spheres there is a theoretically open and historically indeterminate relation. Sometimes, the power of noncivil spheres has overwhelmed the universalistic aspirations of the civil sphere. At other times, its relative autonomy has provided the possibility for justice.

NOTES

1. Seligman, *Idea of Civil Society*.
2. Hirschman, *Passions and the Interests*.
3. Franklin, *Autobiography and Selection from Other Writings*. Franklin's equivalence of capitalistic thrift with virtue was related to the influence of Puritanism by Max Weber in *Protestant Ethic and the Spirit of Capitalism*, pp. 48–57, and derided by Lawrence in his *Studies in Classic American Literature*, pp. 9–22, for the same association. Neither Weber nor Lawrence, however, highlighted the association of Franklinian virtue with democratic and civil life. See Morgan, *Benjamin Franklin*.
4. See Dumont, *From Mandeville to Marx*.
5. For the manner in which Hodgskin's critique of Ricardo and his innovative concepts adumbrated and facilitated Marx's own radical political economy, see Elie Halévy, *Thomas Hodgskin (1787–1869)*.
6. Polanyi, *Great Transformation*.
7. Keane, *Democracy and Civil Society*.
8. Jean Cohen, *Class and Civil Society*.
9. Easton and Guddat, *Writings of the Young Marx on Philosophy and Society*; and Alexander, *Antinomies of Classical Thought*, pp. 11–40.
10. Jean Cohen, *Class and Civil Society*, pp. 5, 24.
11. K. Marx, "Contribution to the Critique of Hegel's Philosophy of Right."
12. Adam Ferguson, *An Essay on the History of Civil Society*, appeared in 1767; in the German translation that appeared the following year, "civil society" was written as *Burgerliche Gesellschaft* (Bobbio, "Gramsci and the Concept of Civil Society." p. 80).

13. Hegel, *Philosophy of Right*, Part III, section ii: a–c. In addition to Jean Cohen's *Class and Civil Society*, see the argument about Hegel in Jean Cohen and Arato, *Civil Society and Political Theory*, pp. 91–116. For other arguments that develop the nonegoistic interpretation of Hegel, see Pelczynski, *State and Civil Society: Studies in Hegel's Political Philosophy*; and Reidel, *Between Tradition and Revolution*. The problem with these interpretive discussions is that they are so concerned to save Hegel from Marx—and, quite rightly, to provide an alternative to the reductionistic implications of civil society II—that they tend to credit Hegel with too much originality, suggesting, at least by implication, that he virtually invented the nonindividualistic conception of civil society from whole cloth. As the present discussion suggests, however, this underplays the Scottish, British, and French contributions to the earlier creation of civil society I and neglects the importance of discussions by Hegel's non-German contemporaries such as Tocqueville.

14. It was Keane who was the first to present this historical account of strong state versus civil society theory, in "Despotism and Democracy," pp. 35–71.

15. For the historical origins and traces of this conservative conflation, see Polanyi's *Great Transformation*, pp. 135–200, and Hirschman's *Passions and the Interests*, pp. 100–113; for comparisons between historical and contemporary conservative conflations, see Hirschman, *Rhetoric of Reaction: Perversity, Futility, Jeopardy*; and Somers and Block, "From Poverty to Perversity."

16. For a discussion of the disappearing public in the writings of the American pragmatists, see chapter 9 of this book; and for a discussion of Putnam's claims about democratic declension, see the section on "Civil Associations" in chapter 5.

17. Gramsci, *Selections from the Prison Notebooks*, e.g., pp. 12–13 and 234, 263, 268. See also Jean Cohen and Arato, *Civil Society and Political Theory*, pp. 142–174.

18. Alexander, "Bringing Democracy Back In." This intellectual critique of big-state theory from a progressive, civil society perspective first appeared in a series of philosophical articles written by eastern Europeans, e.g., Kolakowski, "Hope and Hopelessness"; Michnik, "New Evolutionism"; Tesar, "Totalitarian Dictatorships."

19. See, for example, Sztompka, *Trust*; Seligman, *Problem of Trust*; and for an earlier and still important treatment, see Barber, *Logic and Limits of Trust*.

20. E.g., Habermas, *Knowledge and Human Interests*; Rorty, *Philosophy and the Minor of Nature*; MacIntyre, *After Virtue*; Nussbaum, *Fragility of Goodness*; Taylor, *Hegel* and *Sources of the Self*.

21. Keane, *Democracy and Civil Society*, pp. 3, 14. The same kind of broad, civil society approach informs such later work by Keane as *Civil Society: Old Images, New Visions*, e.g., pp. 6, 17–19, 53–55. This book presents, at the same time, an informative overview of the wide-ranging international discussions that the revival of civil society has triggered. M. Emirbayer and M. Sheller take up a CSI approach that resembles Keane's, defining it as including "willed communities" and "voluntary associations, on the one hand, and families, schools, churches, and other cultural or socializing institutions, on the other" ("Publics in History," p. 152).

22. Arato, "Civil Society against the State," p. 23.

23. Jean Cohen and Arato, *Civil Society*.

24. For a development of this criticism, see my review of Jean Cohen and Arato, "Return to Civil Society."

25. E.g., Habermas, *Between Facts and Norms*, pp. 352–387. As my argument unfolds, it will become clear that although with the idea of civil society III I am calling for a sharp analytic separation

between civil society and these other spheres, I am in no sense arguing for their empirical separation. The different possibilities for empirical separation and overlap are explored throughout the rest of this book and are presented systematically as a model of "the contradictions of civil society" in chapter 8.

26. A. Wolfe, *Whose Keeper?*

27. Seligman, *Idea of Civil Society*.

28. Pateman, "Fraternal Social Contract," in Keane, *Civil Society and the State*.

29. Shils, "Virtue of Civil Society."

30. Walzer, "Rescuing Civil Society."

31. Perez-Diaz, "Public Sphere and a European Civil Society."

32. Putnam, *Making Democracy Work* and *Bowling Alone*. For a critical discussion of Putnam's ideas in relation to the civil society III alternative which I am proposing here, see the section "Civil Associations" in chapter 5 of this book.

33. Though the cultural and institutional sources of the civil sphere and their interrelation with noncivil spheres form the main topic of this book, I will not have the opportunity to explore such historically specific interactional practices. Such an examination would build upon Freud's understanding, in *Civilization and Its Discontents*, of civilization as a distinctive kind of psychological structure; Elias's analysis of the historical origins of the mannerisms marking civility, in *Civilizing Process* (the dark side of which he explored in "Violence and Civilization"; cf. Keane, "Uncivil Society," in *Civil Society*, pp. 115–156); and Erving Goffman, a great theorist of civil face-to-face relations in contemporary social science, in, e.g., *Presentation of Self in Everyday Life* and *Interaction Ritual*. For contemporary empirical studies of the interactional level of civil society, see Phillips and P. Smith, "Emotional and Behavioral Responses to Everyday Incivility" and "Everyday Incivility"; N. Eliasoph and P. Lichterman, "Culture in Interaction"; and G. Fine and B. Harrington, "Tiny Publics."

34. For the religious origins: Troeltsch, *Social Teaching of the Christian Churches*; Jellinek, *Declaration of the Rights of Man and of Citizens*; M. Weber, "'Churches' and 'Sects' in North America"; and Taylor, *Sources*, esp. pp. 127–142. For individualism in the Renaissance, Reformation, and Enlightenment: J. Burckhardt, *Civilization of the Renaissance in Italy*, esp. pp. 143–174; Greenblatt, *Renaissance Self-Fashioning*; Erikson, *Young Man Luther*, M. Walzer, *Revolution of the Saints*; and Gay, *Enlightenment: An Interpretation*. For the sources of individuality in romanticism, see Taylor, *Sources*, pp. 368–390, and his book *Ethics of Authenticity*. For the eleventh-century roots of English individualism and its reflection in citizenship law, see Somers, "Citizenship and the Place of the Public Sphere"; and Colin Morris, *Discovery of the Individual: 1050–1200*. For medieval parliaments and Western feudalism, see M. Weber, *Economy and Society*, pp. 1038–1039, and, for their relation to individualism in modern times, pp. 1381–1469; and Bendix, *Kings or People*, pp. 200–217. For the distinctiveness of Western cities and individuality, see M. Weber, "The City," 1212–1372. For religious sect activity and individuality, see P. Miller, *Life of the Mind in America*; and M. Weber, "'Churches' and 'Sects'" and "The Protestant Sects and the Spirit of Capitalism," *From Max Weber*, pp. 302–322. For individualism and romantic love, see Bloch, "Untangling the Roots of Modern Sex Roles."

35. Somers, "Citizenship and the Place of the Public Sphere."

36. B. Anderson, *Imagined Communities*; Greenfeld, *Nationalism*; and Brubaker, *Nationalism Reframed*. For discussions that emphasize solidarity but are less focused specifically by the national reference, see M. Weber, *City*, and Bendix, *Kings or People*.

37. Polanyi, *Great Transformation*, pp. 168, 73, and 154.

38. Ibid., pp. 146, 154. At the same time that Polanyi insisted on the purely pragmatic and practical origins of these protest movements, however, he said that they "almost invariably" also involved such concerns as "professional status," "the form of a man's life," and "the breadth of his existence" (p. 154).

39. For discussion of the noneconomic, religious, and political-cultural origins of the collective obligations that generated earlier working- and middle-class critiques of industrial capitalism, see R. Williams, *Culture and Society: 1780–1950*; E. P. Thompson, *Origins of the British Working Class*; Sewell, *Work and Revolution in France*; Joyce, *Visions of the People*; Wilentz, *Chants Democratic*; and Biernacki, *Fabrication of Labor*. More generally, see Hess's discussion of "the semantics of stratification" in his *Concepts of Social Stratification*, pp. 1–9 and 168–174.

40. Walzer, *Spheres of Justice*.

41. Boltanski and Thevenot, *De la justification*.

42. Though this is the same kind of critique as the one Ronald Dworkin leveled against Walzer when *Spheres of Justice* first appeared ("To Each His Own"), I do not agree with Dworkin's argument that the alternative is Rawlsian universalism. Dworkin fails to recognize Walzer's hermeneutic achievement vis-à-vis Rawls, which was, per my argument in chapter 1, to ground justice in cultural meaning. For the most developed statement of this position, see Walzer, *Interpretation and Social Criticism*.

43. In chapter 8, I will develop a model of the temporal, spatial, and functional contradictions of civil society and the three ideal-typical forms of boundary relations that mediate them.

REFERENCES

Alexander, Jeffrey C. 1991. "Bringing Democracy Back In: Universalistic Solidarity and the Civil Sphere." In *Intellectuals and Politics: Social Theory in a Changing World*, ed. C. Lemert., pp. 157–156. London: Sage.

———. 1993. "The Return to Civil Society." *Contemporary Sociology* 22(6): 797–803.

Anderson, Benedict R. 1983. *Imagined Communities: Reflections on the Origin and Spread of Nationalism*. London: Verso.

Arato, Andrew. 1981. "Civil Society against the State: Poland 1980–81. *Telos*" 47: 23.

Barber, Bernard. 1983. *The Logic and Limits of Trust*. New Brunswick, NJ: Rutgers University Press.

Bendix, Reinhard. 1978. *Kings or People: Power and the Mandate to Rule*. Berkeley: University of California Press.

Biernacki, Richard. 1995. *The Fabrication of Labor: Germany and Britain, 1640–1914*. Berkeley: University of California Press.

Bloch, Ruth. 1978. "Untangling the Roots of Modern Sex: A Survey of Four Centuries of Change." *Signs* 4(December): 37–58.

Bobbio, Norberto. 1988. "Gramsci and the Concept of Civil Society." In *Civil Society and the State*, ed. John Keane. London: Verso.

Boltanski, Luc and Laurent Thevenot. 1991. *De la Justification: Les économies de le grandeur*. Paris: Gallimard.

Brubaker, Rogers. 1996. *Nationalism Reframed: Nationhood and the National Question in the New Europe*. New York: Cambridge University Press.

Burkhardt, Jacob. 1958 [1860]. *The Civilization of the Renaissance in Italy*. New York: Harper and Row.

Cohen, Jean L. 1982. *Class and Civil Society: The Limits of Marxian Critical Theory*. Amherst: University of Massachusetts Press.

Cohen, Jean L. and Andrew Arato. 1992. *Civil Society and Political Theory*. Cambridge, MA: MIT Press.

Dumont, Louis. 1977. *From Mandeville to Marx on Mandeville: The Genesis and Triumph of Economic Ideology*. Chicago: University of Chicago Press.

Dworkin, Ronald. 1983. "To Each His Own." *New York Review of Books* 30(6): 6.

Easton, Lloyd and Kurt H. Guddat, eds. 1967. *Writings of the Young Marx on Philosophy and Society*. New York: Doubleday Anchor.

Elias, Norbert. 1982 [1939]. *The Civilizing Process*. New York: Pantheon.

———. 1984. "Violence and Civilization." In *Civil Society and the State: New European Perspectives*, ed. John Keane. London: Verso.

Eliasoph, Nina and Paul Lichterman. 2003. "Culture in Interaction." *American Journal of Sociology* 108 (4): 735–794.

Emirbayer, Mustafa and Mimi Sheller. 1999. "Publics in History." *Theory and Society* 28: 145–197.

Erikson, Eric. 1958. *Young Man Luther: A Case Study in Psychoanalysis and History*. New York: W.W. Norton.

Ferguson, Adam. 1966 [1767]. *An Essay on the History of Civil Society*. Edinburgh: Edinburgh University Press.

Fine, Gary and Brooke Harrington. 2004. "Tiny Publics: Small Groups and Civil Society." *Sociological Theory* 22(3): 341–356.

Franklin, Benjamin. 1952. *The Autobiography and Selection from Other Writings*. New York: Liberty Arts.

Freud, Sigmund. 1961 [1930]. *Civilization and Its Discontents*. Translated and edited by James Strachey. New York: W.W. Norton.

Gay, Peter. 1966. *The Enlightenment: An Interpretation*. New York: W.W. Norton.

Goffman, Erving. 1956. *The Presentation of Self in Everyday Life*. New York: Doubleday Anchor.

———. 1967. *Interaction Ritual: Essays on Face-to-Face Behavior*. New York: Pantheon.

Gramsci, Antonio. 1971. *Selections from the Prison Notebooks of Antonio Gramsci*. New York: International.

Greenblatt, Steven J. 1980. *Renaissance Self-Fashioning: From More to Shakespeare*. Chicago: University of Chicago Press.

Greenfeld, Liah. 1992. *Nationalism: Five Roads to Modernity*. Cambridge, MA: Harvard University Press.

Habermas, Jürgen. 1971. *Knowledge and Human Interests*. Trans. Jeremy J. Shapiro. Boston: Beacon.

———. 1996. *Between Facts and Norms: Contributions to a Discourse Theory of Law and Democracy*, trans. William Rehg. Cambridge, MA: MIT Press.

Halévy, Elie. 1903. *Thomas Hodgskin (1787–1869)*. Paris: Société Nouvelle de Librairie et d'Edition.

Hegel, Georg W.F. 1952 [1821]. *The Philosophy of Right*. New York: Oxford University Press.

Hess, Andreas. 2001. *Concepts of Social Stratification: European and American Models*. London: Palgrave.

Hirschman, Albert O. 1977. *The Passions and the Interests: Political Arguments for Capitalism before Its Triumph*. Princeton, NJ: Princeton University Press.

———. 1991. *The Rhetoric of Reaction: Perversity, Futility, Jeopardy*. Cambridge, MA: Harvard University Press.

Jellinek, Georg. 1901. *The Declaration of the Rights of Man and of Citizens*. Trans. Max Farrand. New York: Holt.

Joyce, Patrick. 1991. *Visions of the People: Industrial England and the Question of Class, 1848–1914*. New York: Cambridge University Press.

Keane, John. 1988. *Democracy and Civil Society: On the Predicaments of European Socialism, the Prospects for Democracy, and the Problem of Controlling Social and Political Power*. London: Verso.

———. 1988. *Civil Society: Old Images, New Visions*. Stanford, CA: Stanford University Press.

Kolakowski, Leszek. 1971. "Hope and Hopelessness." *Survey* 47(3): 37–52.

Lawrence, D.H. 1970 [1923]. *Studies in Classic American Literature*. New York: Viking.

MacIntyre, Alasdair. 1981. *After Virtue: A Study in Moral Theory*. Notre Dame, IN: Notre Dame University Press.

Marx, Karl. 1963 [1843]. "Contribution to the Critique of Hegel's Philosophy of Right, Introduction." In *Karl Marx: Early Writings*, ed. T.B. Bottomore, pp. 41–60. New York: McGraw-Hill.

Michnik, Adam. 1976. "The New Evolutionism." *Survey* 22(3/4): 267–277.

Miller, Perry. 1965. *The Life and Mind in America, from the Revolution to the Civil War*. New York: Harcourt, Brace, and World.

Morgan, Edmund S. 2002. *Benjamin Franklin*. New Haven, CT: Yale University Press.

Morris, Colin. 1972. *The Discovery of the Individual, 1050–1200*. New York: Harper and Row.

Nussbaum, Martha. 1986. *The Fragility of Goodness: Luck and Ethics in Greek Tragedy and Philosophy*. New York: Cambridge University Press.

Pateman, Carole. 1988. "The Fraternal Social Contract." In *Civil Society and the State: New European Perspectives*, ed. John Keane, pp. 101–128. London: Verso.

Pelczynski, Z.A., ed. 1984. *The State and Civil Society: Studies in Hegel's Political Philosophy*. New York: Cambridge University Press.

Pérez-Diaz, Victor. 1998. "The Public Sphere and a European Civil Society." In *Real Civil Societies: Dilemmas of Institutionalization*, ed. Jeffrey C. Alexander. London: Sage.

Phillips, T. and Philip Smith. 2004. "Emotional and Behavioral Responses to Everyday Incivility: Challenging the Fear/Avoidance Paradigm." *Journal of Sociology* 40(4): 378–399.

Polanyi, Karl. 1944. *The Great Transformation: The Political and Economic Origins of Our Time*. Boston: Beacon.

Putnam, Robert D. 1993. *Making Democracy Work: Civic Traditions in Modern Italy*. Princeton, NJ: Princeton University Press.

———. 2000. *Bowling Alone: The Collapse and Revival of American Community*. New York: Simon and Schuster.

Riedel, Manfred. 1984. *Between Tradition and Revolution: The Hegelian Transformation of Political Philosophy*. Trans. Walter Wright. New York: Cambridge University Press.

Rorty, Richard. 1979. *Philosophy and the Mirror of Nature*. Princeton, NJ: Princeton University Press.

Seligman, Adam B. 1992. *The Idea of Civil Society*. New York: Free Press.

———. 1997. *The Problem of Trust*. Princeton, NJ: Princeton University Press.

Sewell, William H., Jr. 1980. *Work and Revolution in France: The Language of Labor from the Old Regime to 1848*. New York: Cambridge University Press.

Shils, Edward. 1991. "The Virtue of Civil Society." *Government and Opposition* 20(Winter): 3–20.

Somers, Margaret. 1993. "Citizenship and the Place of the Public Sphere: Law, Community, and Political Culture in the Transition to Democracy." *American Sociological Review* 58(5): 587–620.

Somers, Margaret and Fred Block. 2005. "From Poverty to Perversity: Ideas, Markets, and Institutions over 200 Years of Welfare Debate." *American Sociological Review* 70(2): 260–287.

Sztompka, Piotr. 1999. *Trust: A Sociological Theory*. New York: Cambridge University Press.

Taylor, Charles. 1975. *Hegel*. Cambridge: Cambridge University Press.

———. 1989. *Sources of the Self: Making of Modern Identity*. Cambridge, MA: Harvard University Press.

———. 1992. *The Ethics of Authenticity*. Cambridge, MA: Harvard University Press.

Tesar, Jan. 1981. "Totalitarian Dictatorships and a Phenomenon of the Twentieth Century and the Possibilities of Overcoming Them." *International Journal of Politics* 11 (Spring): 85–100.

Thompson, E.P. 1964. *The Making of the English Working Class*. New York: Pantheon.

Troeltsch, Ernst. 1960 [1911]. *The Social Teachings of the Christian Churches*. Chicago: University of Chicago Press.

Walzer, Michael. 1965. *The Revolution of the Saints: A Study of the Origins of Radical Politics*. Cambridge, MA: Harvard University Press.

———. 1984. *Spheres of Justice: A Defense of Pluralism and Equality*. New York: Basic Books.

———. 1987. *Interpretation and Social Criticism*. Cambridge, MA: Harvard University Press.

———. 1999. "Rescuing Civil Society." *Dissent* 46(1): 62–67.

Weber, Max. 1927 [1904–05]. *The Protestant Ethic and the Spirit of Capitalism*. New York: Scribner's and Sons.

———. 1958. "The Protestant Sects and the Spirit of Capitalism." In *From Max Weber: Essays in Sociology*, ed. Hans Gerth and C. Wright Mills. New York: Oxford University Press.

———. 1978. *Economy and Society*, Vols. 1 and 2. Edited by Guenther Roth and Claus Wittich. Berkeley: University of California Press.

———. 1985 [1906]. "'Churches' and 'Sects' in North America: An Ecclesiastical Socio-Political Sketch." *Sociological Theory* 3(1): 7–13.

Wilentz, Sean. 1984. *Chants Democratic: New York City and the Rise of the American Working Class, 1788–1850*. New York: Oxford University Press.

Williams, Raymond. 1958. *Culture and Society, 1780–1950*. New York: Harper and Row.

Wolfe, Alan. 1989. *Whose Keeper? Social Science and Moral Obligation*. Berkeley: University of California Press.

82. INTERACTION RITUAL THEORY

RANDALL COLLINS

Randall Collins (b. 1941) established his theoretical career by articulating a formal theory of conflict (see Chapter 39). However, recently he has developed a new theoretical orientation that he calls "interaction ritual theory" (IR). This approach offers a creative appreciation and utilization of two particular theorists: from the classics, Émile Durkheim, and from more recent vintage, Erving Goffman (whom Collins elsewhere has referred to as the most important theorist of the second half of the twentieth century). In this chapter from *Interaction Ritual Chains* (2004), Collins lays out the programmatic features of this theoretical approach, which begins with the claim that the starting point of such a theory is the situation, not the individual. In this respect, he follows Goffman in the first section of this excerpt to make claim to the analytical utility of such a position. In the second section, Durkheim comes into focus as Collins presents his case for the significance of interaction ritual for sociological theory in general. He stresses that IR offers a theory of social dynamics and moreover provides a social psychological account that is sensitive to both cognition and the emotions.

A theory of interaction ritual is the key to microsociology, and microsociology is the key to much that is larger. The small scale, the here-and-now of face-to-face interaction, is the scene of action and the site of social actors. If we are going to find the agency of social life, it will be here. Here reside the energy of movement and change, the glue of solidarity, and the conservatism of stasis. Here is where intentionality and consciousness find their places; here, too, is the site of the emotional and unconscious aspects of human interaction. In whatever idiom, here is the empirical/experiential location for our social psychology, our symbolic or strategic interaction, our existential phenomenology or ethnomethodology, our arena of bargaining, games, exchange, or rational choice. Such theoretical positions may already seem to be extremely micro, intimate, and small scale. Yet we shall see they are for the most part not micro enough; some are mere glosses over what happens on the micro-interactional level. If

we develop a sufficiently powerful theory on the microlevel, it will unlock some secrets of large-scale macrosociological changes as well.

Let us begin with two orienting points. First, the center of microsociological explanation is not the individual but the situation. Second, the term "ritual" is used in a confusing variety of ways; I must show what I will mean by it and why this approach yields the desired explanatory results.

SITUATION RATHER THAN INDIVIDUAL AS STARTING POINT

Selecting an analytical starting point is a matter of strategic choice on the part of the theorist. But it is not merely an unreasoning *de gustibus non disputandum est*. I will attempt to show why we get more by starting with the situation and developing the individual, than by starting with individuals;

and we get emphatically more than by the usual route of skipping from the individual to the action or cognition that ostensibly belongs to him or her and bypassing the situation entirely.

A theory of interaction ritual (IR) and interaction ritual chains is above all a theory of situations. It is a theory of momentary encounters among human bodies charged up with emotions and consciousness because they have gone through chains of previous encounters. What we mean by the social actor, the human individual, is a quasi-enduring, quasi-transient flux in time and space. Although we valorize and heroize this individual, we ought to recognize that this way of looking at things, this keyhole through which we peer at the universe, is the product of particular religious, political, and cultural trends of recent centuries. It is an ideology of how we regard it proper to think about ourselves and others, part of the folk idiom, not the most useful analytical starting point for microsociology.

This is not to say that the individual does not exist. But an individual is not simply a body, even though a body is an ingredient that individuals get constructed out of. My analytical strategy (and that of the founder of interaction ritual analysis, Erving Goffman) is to start with the dynamics of situations; from this we can derive almost everything that we want to know about individuals, as a moving precipitate across situations.

Here we might pause for a counterargument. Do we not know that the individual is unique, precisely because we can follow him or her across situations, and precisely because he or she acts in a familiar, distinctively recognizable pattern even as circumstances change? Let us disentangle what is valid from what is misleading in this statement. The argument assumes a hypothetical fact, that individuals are constant even as situations change; to what extent this is true remains to be shown. We are prone to accept it, without further examination, as "something everybody knows" because it is drummed into us as a moral principle: everyone is unique, be yourself, don´t give in to social pressure, to your own self be true—these are slogans trumpeted by every mouthpiece from preachers´ homilies to advertising campaigns, echoing everywhere from popular culture to the avant-garde marching-orders of modernist and hypermodernist artists and intellectuals. As sociologists, our task is not to go with the flow of taken-for-granted belief—(although doing just this is what makes a successful popular writer)—but to view it in a sociological light, to see what social circumstances created this moral belief and this hegemony of social categories at this particular historical juncture. The problem, in Goffman's terms, is to discover the social sources of the cult of the individual.

Having said this, I am going to agree that under contemporary social conditions, very likely most individuals are unique. But this is not the result of enduring individual essences. The uniqueness of the individual is something that we can derive from the theory of IR chains. Individuals are unique to just the extent that their pathways through interactional chains, their mix of situations across time, differ from other persons´ pathways. If we reify the individual, we have an ideology, a secular version of the Christian doctrine of the eternal soul, but we cut off the possibility of explaining how individual uniquenesses are molded in a chain of encounters across time.

In a strong sense, the individual is the interaction ritual chain. The individual is the precipitate of past interactional situations and an ingredient of each new situation. An ingredient, not the determinant, because a situation is an emergent property. A situation is not merely the result of the individual who comes into it, nor even of a combination of individuals (although it is that, too). Situations have laws or processes of their own; and that is what IR theory is about.

Goffman concluded: "not men and their moments, but moments and their men." In gender-neutral language: not individuals and their interactions, but interactions and their individuals; not persons and their passions, but passions and their persons. "Every dog will have its day" is more accurately "every day will have its dog." Incidents shape their incumbents, however momentary they may be; encounters make their encountees. It is games that make sports heroes, politics that makes politicians into charismatic leaders, although the entire weight of record-keeping, news-story-writing, award-giving, speech-making, and advertising hype goes against understanding how this comes about. To see the common realities of everyday life sociologically requires a gestalt shift, a reversal of perspectives. Breaking such deeply ingrained conventional frames is not easy to do;

but the more we can discipline ourselves to think everything through the sociology of the situation, the more we will understand why we do what we do.

Let us advance to a more subtle source of confusion. Am I proclaiming, on the microlevel, the primacy of structure over agency? Is the structure of the interaction all-determining, bringing to naught the possibility of active agency? Not at all. The agency/structure rhetoric is a conceptual morass, entangling several distinctions and modes of rhetorical force. Agency/structure confuses the distinction of micro/macro, which is the local here-and-now vis-à-vis the interconnections among local situations into a larger swath of time and space, with the distinction between what is active and what is not. The latter distinction leads us to questions about energy and action; but energy and action are always local, always processes of real human beings doing something in a situation. It is also true that the action of one locality can spill over into another, that one situation can be carried over into other situations elsewhere. The extent of that spillover is part of what we mean by macro-patterns. It is acceptable, as a way of speaking, to refer to the action of a mass of investors in creating a run on the stock market, or of the breakdown of an army's logistics in setting off a revolutionary crisis, but this is a shorthand for the observable realities (i.e., what would be witnessed by a micro-sociologist on the spot). This way of speaking makes it seem as if there is agency on the macro-level, but that is inaccurate, because we are taken in by a figure of speech. Agency, if we are going to use that term, is always micro; structure concatenates it into macro.

But although the terms "micro" and "agency" can be lined up at one pole, they are not identical. There is structure at every level. Micro-situations are structures, that is to say, relationships among parts. Local encounters, micro-situations, have both agency and structure. The error to avoid is identifying agency with the individual, even on the micro-level. I have just argued that we will get much further if we avoid reifying the individual, that we should see individuals as transient fluxes charged up by situations. Agency, which I would prefer to describe as the energy appearing in human bodies and emotions and as the intensity and focus of human consciousness, arises in interactions in local, face-to-face situations, or as precipitates of chains of situations. Yes, human individuals also sometimes

act when they are alone, although they generally do so because their minds and bodies are charged with results of past situational encounters, and their solitary action is social insofar as it aims at and comes from communicating with other persons and thus is situated by where it falls in an IR chain.

On the balance, I am not much in favor of the terminology of "agency" and "structure." "Micro" and "macro" are sufficient for us to chart the continuum from local to inter-local connections. The energizing and the relational aspects of interactions, however, are tightly connected. Perhaps the best we might say is that the local structure of interaction is what generates and shapes the energy of the situation. That energy can leave traces, carrying over to further situations because individuals bodily resonate with emotions, which trail off in time but may linger long enough to charge up a subsequent encounter, bringing yet further chains of consequences. Another drawback of the term "agency" is that it carries the rhetorical burden of connoting moral responsibility; it brings us back to the glorification (and condemnation) of the individual, just the moralizing gestalt that we need to break out from if we are to advance an explanatory microsociology. We need to see this from a different angle. Instead of agency, I will devote theoretical attention to emotions and emotional energy, as changing intensities heated up or cooled down by the pressure-cooker of interaction rituals. Instead of emphasizing structure, or taking the other tack of backgrounding it as merely a foil for agency, I will get on with the business of showing how IRs work. . . .

THE SIGNIFICANCE OF INTERACTION RITUAL FOR GENERAL SOCIOLOGICAL THEORY

The Durkheimian model addresses the central questions of social theory; and it has implications that extend to all corners of contemporary microsociology. It asks the basic question: What holds society together? And it answers the question with a mechanism of social rituals. Furthermore, it answers it with a mechanism that varies in intensity: society is held together to just the extent that rituals are effectively carried out, and during those periods of time when the effects of those rituals are still fresh in people's minds and reverberating in their emotions. Society is held together more intensely at some moments than at others. And the "society" that is held together is no abstract unity of a social system, but is just those groups of people assembled in particular places who feel solidarity with each other through the effects of ritual participation and ritually charged symbolism. The total population of France, or the United States, or anywhere else one might consider, consists of pockets of solidarity of different degrees of intensity. A population can be washed by waves of national solidarity on occasion, but these are particular and rather special ritually based events, subject to the same processes of ritual mobilization as more local pockets of solidarity.

This means that the Durkheimian model is entirely compatible with a view of stratification and group conflict. Indeed, it provides key mechanisms for just how stratification and conflict operate. Rephrase the question as, What holds society together as a pattern of stratified and conflicting groups? The answer is social rituals, operating to create and sustain solidarity within those groups. We can elaborate a more complicated answer, and later chapters will do so. Among those complications are these: that some groups have more resources for carrying out their rituals than others, so that some groups have more solidarity and thus can lord it over those who have less; and that these ritually privileged groups have more impressive symbols and fill their members with more emotional energy. We may examine more fine-grained processes of stratification: looking inside the very group that is brought together by participating in a ritual, we can see that some individuals are more privileged than others, by being nearer to the center of the ritual than others. Rituals thus have a double stratifying effect: between ritual insiders and outsiders; and, inside the ritual, between ritual leaders and ritual followers. Rituals are thus key mechanisms, and we might say key weapons, in processes of conflict and domination.

Durkheim famously argued that the utilitarian, economic dimension of life is not basic, but depends upon precontractual solidarity; that rituals provide the basis for a situation of social trust and shared symbolic meanings through which economic exchanges can be carried out. Here I am making a similar argument with regard to social conflict:

conflict is not the primordial condition of social life, a Hobbesian war of all against all, but is analytically derivative of social solidarity. That is to say, effective conflict is not really possible without the mechanisms of social ritual, which generate the alliances and the energies of the partisans, as well as their most effective weapons in dominating others. And the goals of conflict, the things that people fight over, are formed by these patterns of social rituals. The flash-points of conflict, the incidents that set off overt struggle, almost always come from the precedence of symbols and the social sentiments they embody. All this is to say that social conflict, which I and many other theorists have argued is the major process structuring social life, especially on the macro-level of large-scale structures (Collins 1975; Mann 1986–93), requires for its explanation a Durkheimian microsociology of interaction rituals.

The central mechanism of interaction ritual theory is that occasions that combine a high degree of mutual focus of attention, that is, a high degree of intersubjectivity, together with a high degree of emotional entrainment—through bodily synchronization, mutual stimulation/arousal of participants' nervous systems—result in feelings of membership that are attached to cognitive symbols; and result also in the emotional energy of individual participants, giving them feelings of confidence, enthusiasm, and desire for action in what they consider a morally proper path. These moments of high degree of ritual intensity are high points of experience. They are high points of collective experience, the key moments of history, the times when significant things happen. These are moments that tear up old social structures or leave them behind, and shape new social structures. As Durkheim notes, these are moments like the French Revolution in the summer of 1789. We could add, they are moments like the key events of the Civil Rights movement in the 1960s; like the collapse of communist regimes in 1989 and 1991; and to a degree of significance that can be ascertained only in the future, as in the national mobilization in the United States following September 11, 2001. These examples are drawn from large-scale ritual mobilizations, and examples of a smaller scale could be drawn as we narrow our attention to smaller arenas of social action.

Interaction ritual theory is a theory of social dynamics, not merely of statics. Among social theorists there is a tendency to regard ritual analysis as conservative, a worship of traditions laid down in the past, a mechanism for reproducing social structure as it always existed. True enough, ritual analysis has often been used in this vein; and even theories like Bourdieu's, which combine Durkheim with Marx, see a mutually supporting interplay between the cultural or symbolic order and the order of economic power. For Bourdieu, ritual reproduces the cultural and therefore the economic fields. . . . But this is to miss the transformative power of ritual mobilization. Intense ritual experience creates new symbolic objects and generates energies that fuel the major social changes. International ritual is a mechanism of change. As long as there are potential occasions for ritual mobilization, there is the possibility for sudden and abrupt periods of change. Ritual can be repetitive and conservatizing, but it also provides the occasions on which changes break through.

In this respect IR theory mediates between postmodernist and similar theories that posit ubiquitous situational flux of meanings and identities, and a culturalist view that fixed scripts or repertoires are repeatedly called upon. The contrast is articulated by Lamont (2000, 243–44, 271), who provides evidence that there are "cultural and structural conditions that lead individuals to use some criteria of evaluation rather than others." The argument is parallel to my use of IR theory, which pushes the argument at a more micro-situational level: that the operative structural conditions are those that make up the ingredients of interaction ritual; and that cultural repertoires are created in particular kind of IRs, and fade out in others. To show the conditions under which ritual operates in one direction or the other is a principal topic of this book.

Intense moments of interaction ritual are high points not only for groups but also for individual lives. These are the events that we remember, that give meaning to our personal biographies, and sometimes to obsessive attempts to repeat them: whether participating in some great collective event such as a big political demonstration; or as spectator at some storied moment of popular entertainment or sports; or a personal encounter ranging from a sexual experience, to a strongly bonding friendly exchange, to a humiliating insult; the social atmosphere of an alcohol binge, a drug high, or a gambling victory; a bitter argument or an occasion of violence. Where these moments have a high degree of focused awareness and a peak of shared emotion, these personal experiences, too, can be crystalized in personal symbols, and kept alive in symbolic replays for greater or lesser expanses of one´s life. These are the significant formative experiences that shape individuals; if the patterns endure, we are apt to call them personalities; if we disapprove of them we call them addictions. But this usage too easily reifies what is an ongoing flow of situations. The movement of individuals from one situation to another in what I call interaction ritual chains is an up-and-down of variation in the intensity of interaction rituals; shifts in behavior, in feeling and thought occur just as the situations shift. To be a constant personality is to be on an even keel where the kinds of interaction rituals flow constantly from one situation to the next. Here again, IR theory points up the dynamics of human lives, their possibility for dramatic shifts in direction.

IR theory provides a theory of individual motivation from one situation to the next. Emotional energy is what individuals seek; situations are attractive or unattractive to them to the extent that the interaction ritual is successful in providing emotional energy. This gives us a dynamic microsociology, in which we trace situations and their pull or push for individuals who come into them. Note the emphasis: the analytical starting point is the situation, and how it shapes individuals; situations generate and regenerate the emotions and the symbolism that charge up individuals and send them from one situation to another.

Interaction ritual is a full-scale social psychology, not only of emotions and situational behavior, but of cognition. Rituals generate symbols; experience in rituals inculcates those symbols in individual minds and memories. IR provides an explanation of variation in beliefs. Beliefs are not necessarily constant, but situationally fluctuate, as a number of theorists have argued and as researchers have demonstrated (Swider 1986; Lamont 2000). What IR theory adds to contemporary cultural theory in this regard is that what people think they believe at a given moment is dependent upon a kind of interaction ritual taking place in that situation: people may genuinely and sincerely feel the beliefs they express at the moment they express them, especially when the conversational situation calls out a higher degree of emotional emphasis; but this does not mean that they act on these beliefs, or that they have a sincere feeling about them in other everyday interactions where the ritual focus is different. IR theory gives the conditions under which beliefs become salient, by rising and falling in emotional loading. Everyday life is the experience of moving through a chain of interaction rituals, charging up some symbols with emotional significance and leaving others to fade. IR theory leads us into a theory of the momentary flow of internal mental life, an explanation of subjectivity as well as intersubjectivity.

Durkheim held that the individual consciousness is a portion of the collective consciousness. This is tantamount to saying that the individual is socialized from the outside, by social experience carried within. This is surely true, as most social scientists would agree, as far as early childhood socialization is concerned. The argument of IR theory carries this further: we are constantly being socialized by our interactional experiences throughout our lives. But not in a unidirectional and homogeneous way; it is intense interaction rituals that generate the most powerful emotional energy and the most vivid symbols, and it is these that are internalized. Contrary to an implication of Freudian theory and others that stress early childhood experience, socialization once laid down does not endure forever; emotional energies and symbolic meanings fade if they are not renewed. IR theory is not a model of a wind-up doll, programmed early in life, which ever after walks through the pattern once laid down. It is a theory of moment-to-moment motivation, situation by situation. Thus it has high theoretical ambitions: to explain what any individual will do, at any moment in time; what he or she will feel, think, and say

Viewed in the abstract, this may seem like an impossibly high ambition. But consider: there are considerable theoretical resources available for this task. We have Durkheimian theory, which yields an explicit model of what produces sentiments of group membership; of symbols that formulate social values, and through which humans think; and of emotional energies that animate individuals. This theory is cast in

terms of conditions of varying strength, so that we can tell which situations will generate higher or lower levels of solidarity, respect for symbols, and emotional energy. And this model is of wide applicability: it fits not only the great collective events of religion and politics, as Durkheim himself pointed out, but it can be brought to bear on the level of everyday life situation by Goffman's line of application. More and more details of how to apply the Durkheimian ritual theory to everyday life situations are becoming available, as I will attempt to show in later chapters, by drawing on such resources as Meadian symbolic interactionist theory of thinking as internalized conversation, along with contemporary research on conversation and on emotions, and on the ethnography of everyday life. The totality of social life is the totality of situations that people go through in their everyday lives; we have a powerful and wide-ranging model that explains what will happen in those situations. An offshoot of this situational microsociology is the internalization of social life in individuals' subjective experience: the sociology of thinking and feeling.

Why not follow this theoretical research program as far as it will go? Some intellectuals have philosophical commitments that hold them back from taking this path; we do not want a theory that explains everything, and we construct arguments to rule out the possibility of any such a theory succeeding. There are lines of metatheory, going back to Max Weber and to his Neo-Kantian predecessors, which hold that the territory of social science is the realm of human meanings and human freedom, *Geisteszuissenschaft* as opposed to *Naturwissenschaft*, a realm in which deterministic explanations do not apply. But such arguments are hardly conclusive: they try to lay out in advance and by conceptual definition what we can and cannot find along particular lines of investigation. Social theory and research moves along pragmatically, in the real flow of intellectual history; philosophers and metatheorists cannot legislate what we will not be able to explain in the future.

The program of interaction ritual theory is to take the intellectual tools that we have, and to apply them: to all situations, all emotions, all symbols, all thinking, all subjectivity and intersubjectivity. Intellectual life is an exciting adventure when we try to push it as far as we can. There is surely more emotional energy in exploration than in conservatively standing pat and trying to avoid extending our understanding beyond the boundaries set up by intellectual taboos. IR theory, as an intellectual enterprise, is a set of symbolic representations riding on its surge of emotional energy; it is the intellectual version of effervescence that gave elan to Durkheim and his research group, to Goffman and his followers, and to today's sociologists of emotion and process in everyday life. What I attempt to show in this book is some vistas that open up as we ride this intellectual movement into the future.

REFERENCES

Collins, Randall. 1975. *Conflict Sociology: Toward an Exploratory Science.* New York: Academic Press.

Lamont, Michèle. 2000. *The Dignity of Working Men: Morality and the Boundaries of Race, Class, and Immigration.* New York and Cambridge, MA: Russell Sage Foundation and Harvard University Press.

Mann, Michael. 1986–93. *The Sources of Social Power*, 3 vols. Cambridge: Cambridge University Press.

Swidler, Ann. 1986. "Culture in Action." *American Sociological Review*, 51(2): 111–125.

83. QUEER-ING SOCIOLOGY, SOCIOLOGIZING QUEER THEORY

STEVEN SEIDMAN

Steven Seidman (b. 1948) began his career with insightful assessments of classic figures in sociology, but in recent years he has embraced the postmodernist project. Moreover, his own personal politics, which led him to become a political activist in the gay community, have also led him to become a key proponent in sociology of what has become known as "queer theory." His concerns are in part an attempt to redress the theoretical silence on matters related to sexual orientation that has characterized most of the major theorists considered in this collection. Influenced in particular by the path-breaking work on sexuality by Foucault, and clearly operating from a vantage point similar to that of many feminists (including Dorothy Smith), Seidman is intent on bringing queer theory—which has its origins outside of sociology—and sociology into mutually rewarding contact.

I f we follow the recent history and theory of sexuality, we are asked to assume that sexuality is a social fact. What is imagined as sexuality, its personal and social meaning and form, varies historically and between social groups. Indeed, if we are to take seriously Foucault's *The History of Sexuality* (1980), the very idea of sexuality as a unity composed of discrete desires, acts, developmental patterns, and sexual and psychological types is itself a recent and uniquely "modern" Western event. For example, the ancient Greeks imagined a sphere of pleasures *(aphrodisia)* which included eating, athletics, man/boy love, and marriage, not a realm of sexuality (Foucault 1985). This new theorizing figures sex as thoroughly social: bodies, sensations, pleasures, acts, and interactions are made into "sex" or accrue sexual meanings by means of discourses and institutional practices. Framing "sex" as social unavoidably makes it a political fact. Which sensations of acts are defined as sexual, what moral boundaries demarcate legitimate and illegitimate sex, and who stipulates this are political. Paralleling class or gender politics,

sexual politics involve struggles around the formation of, and resistance to, a sexual social hierarchy (Rubin 1983).

The current theorization of sex as a social and political fact prompts a rereading of the history of modern societies and social knowledges. Consider an interpretation of classical sociology from this perspective.

We are familiar with the standard accounts of the rise of sociology. For example, sociology is described as born in the great transformation from a traditional, agrarian, corporatist hierarchical order to a modern, industrial, class-based, but formally democratic system. The so-called classic sociologists acquired their authority because it is claimed that they provided the core perspectives and themes in terms of which social scientists analyze and debate the great problems of modernity. These perspectives include Marx's theorization of capitalism as a class-divided system, Weber's thesis of the bureaucratization of the world, and Durkheim's theory of social evolution as a process of social differentiation. The classics posed the question of

Steven Seidman, "Symposium: Queer Theory/Sociology: A Dialogue." *Sociological Theory*, (July 1994). Copyright © 1994 by The American Sociological Association. Reprinted by permission. ◆

the meaning of modernity in terms of the debates about capitalism, secularization, social differentiation, bureaucratization, class stratification, and social solidarity. If our view of modernity derived exclusively from the sociological classics, we would not know that a central part of the great transformation consisted of efforts to define a sphere of sexuality, to organize bodies, pleasures, desires, and acts as they relate to personal and public life, and that this entailed constructing sexual (and gender) identities, producing discourses and cultural representations, enacting state policies and laws, and conducting religious and familial interventions into personal life. In short, the making of embodied sexual selves and codes has been interlaced with the making of the cultural and institutional life of Western societies.

The standard histories link the rise of the modern social sciences to social modernization (e.g., industrialism, class conflict, and bureaucracy), but are silent about sexual (and gender) conflicts. At the very time when the social sciences materialized, announcing a social understanding of the human condition, they assumed a natural order linking sex, gender, and sexuality. Such silences cannot be excused on the grounds that "sexuality" had not become a site of public organization, conflict, and knowledges. In the eighteenth and nineteenth centuries, there were public struggles focused on the body, desire, pleasure, intimate acts, and their public expression—struggles in the family, the church, the law, and the realm of knowledges and the state. The women's movement flourished in Europe in the 1780s and 1790s, from the 1840s to the 1860s, and between the 1880s and 1920, the key junctures in the development of modern sociology. Struggles over the "women's question" were connected to public conflicts around what today we would call "sexuality." Sexual conflicts escalated in intensity and gained increasing public attention between the 1880s and World War I—the "breakthrough" period of classical sociology. In Europe and the United States, the body and sexuality were sites of moral and political struggle through such issues as divorce, free love, abortion, masturbation, homosexuality, prostitution, obscenity, and sex education. This period experienced the rise of sexology, psychoanalysis, and psychiatry (Birken 1988; Irvine 1990; Weeks 1985). Magnus Hirschfeld created

the Scientific Humanitarian Committee and Institute for Sex Research in Germany. Homosexuality became an object of knowledge. Karl Heinrich Ulrichs, for example, published 12 volumes on homosexuality between 1864 and 1879. One historian estimates that more than 1,000 publications on homosexuality appeared in Europe between 1898 and 1908 (Weeks 1985:67).

What is striking is the silence in classical sociological texts regarding these sexual conflicts and knowledges. For all their aspiration to theorize the human as social, and to sketch the contours of modernity, the classical sociologists offered no accounts of the making of modern bodies and sexualities. Marx analyzed the social reproduction and organization of labor but not the process by which laborers are physically reproduced. Weber sketched what he assumed to be the historical uniqueness of the modern West; he traced the rise of modern capitalism, the modern state, formal law, modern cities, a culture of risk-taking individualism, but had virtually nothing to say concerning the making of the modern regime of sexuality. The core premises and conceptual strategies of classical sociology defined the real and important social facts as the economy, the church, the military, formal organizations, social classes, and collective representations.

Perhaps the classical sociologists' silence on "sexuality" is related to their privileged gender and sexual social position. They took for granted the naturalness and validity of their own gender and sexual experience and status in just the way, as we sociologists believe, any individual unconsciously assumes as natural and good (i.e., normal, healthy, and right) those aspects of one's life that confer privilege and power. Thus, just as the bourgeoisie assert the naturalness of class inequality and of their rule, individuals whose social identity is that of male and heterosexual do not question the naturalness of a male-dominated, normatively heterosexual social order. For the classics, who apparently assumed that their gender and sexually privileged status was natural and deserved, it is hardly surprising that they conceived of the social as a realm of formal organizations, state power, economic classes, and cultural meanings. Thus the classics never examined the social formation of modern regimes of bodies and sexualities. Moreover, their own science of society contributed (unwittingly, we like to think) to the making of this regime whose center is the hetero/homo binary and the heterosexualization of society.

Sociology's silence on "sexuality" was broken when the volume of public sexual conflicts and discourses was turned so high that even sociologists' trained deafness to such sounds was pierced. In early American sociology alone, isolated and still-faint voices speaking to the issue of sexuality can be heard through the first half of the twentieth century. Indeed, sociologists could not entirely avoid addressing this theme in the first few decades of this century. However, the extent to which they did so is remarkable!

Issues such as municipal reform, unionization, economic concentration, the commercialization of everyday life, race relations, and the internationalization of politics were important topics of public debate. At the same time, Americans were gripped by conflicts that placed the body at the center of contention. The women's movement, which in the first two decades of this century was closely aligned to socialist and cultural radical politics, emerged as a national movement. Although the struggle for the right to vote was pivotal, no less important were feminist struggles to eliminate the double standard that permitted men sexual expression and pleasure while pressuring women to conform to Victorian purity norms or suffer degradation if erotic desires were claimed. As women were demanding erotic equality with men, there were public struggles to liberalize divorce, abortion, and pornography; battles over obscenity, prostitution, and marriage were in the public eye (e.g., D'Emilio and Freedman 1988; Peiss 1986; Seidman 1991; Smith-Rosenberg 1990). Sex was being discussed everywhere—in magazines, newspapers, journals, books, the theater, and the courts. In the millions of volumes of sex advice literature published in the early decades of this century, there existed a process of the sexualization of love and marriage (Seidman 1991). Books such as Theodore Van de Velde's *Ideal Marriage* ([1930] 1950), which constructed an eroticized body and intimacy, sold in the hundreds of thousands. Americans were in the first stages of a romance with Freud and psychoanalysis; social radicals such as Max Eastman, Emma Goldman, Edward Boume, and Margaret Sanger connected institutional change to an agenda of sexual and gender

change (Marriner 1972; Simmons 1982; Trimberger 1983). Despite the vigorous efforts of vice squads and purity movements, pornography flourished and obscenity laws were gradually liberalized.

In the first half of this century, sex was put into the public culture of American society in a manner that sociology could not ignore. Yet, through mid-century, sociologists managed to do just that to a considerable degree. The Chicago School studied cab drivers, immigrants, factory workers, and juvenile delinquents, but had little to say about the domain of sexuality. Theorists such as Park, Cooley, Thomas, Parsons, and Ogbum had much to say on urban patterns, the development of the self, political organization, the structure of social action, and technological development—all worthwhile topics—but little or nothing on the making of sexualized selves and institutions. Finally, while sociologists were surveying all other conceivable topics, and while a proliferation of sex surveys was stirring public debate (e.g., K.B. Davis 1929; Dickinson and Beam 1932; Kinsey et al. 1948, 1953), sociologists did not deploy their empirical techniques to study human sexuality.[1]

It took the changes of the 1950s and the public turmoil of the 1960s to make sociologists begin to take sex seriously. The immediate postwar years are sometimes perceived as conservative, but the war, patterns of mobility, prosperity, and social liberalization loosened sexual mores. Indicative of changes in the American culture of the body and sexuality, the 1950s witnessed rock music, the beginnings of the women's movement, the appearance of homophile organizations, and the figures of the beatnik and the rebel, for whom social and sexual transgression went hand in hand. The 1960s made sexual rebellion into a national public drama. The women's movement, gay liberation, lesbian feminism, the counterculture, magazines such as *Playboy* and manuals such as *The Joy of Sex*, and cultural radicals such as Herbert Marcuse and Norman O. Brown made sexual rebellion central to social change.

A sociology of sexuality emerged in postwar America (e.g., Henslin 1971; I. Reiss 1967). This sociology, however, approached sex as a specialty area like organizations, crime, or demography. Sex was imagined as a property of the individual, whose personal expression was shaped by social norms and attitudes. Sex and society were viewed as antithetical; society took on importance as either an obstacle or a tolerant space for sexual release. The idea of a "sexual regime," of a field of sexual meanings, discourses, and practices that are interlaced with social institutions and movements, was absent. Moreover, although sociologists studied patterns of conventional sexuality—most conspicuously, premarital, marital, and extramarital sex—much of this literature was preoccupied with "deviant" sexualities such as prostitution, pornography, and (most impressively) homosexuality.

A sociology of homosexuality emerged as part of the sociology of sex (e.g., Gagnon and Simon 1967a, 1967b; A. Reiss 1964; Sagarin 1969). Sociologists turned to homosexuality as an object of knowledge in the context of the heightened public visibility and politicization of homosexuality. The social context of the rise of a sociology of homosexuality needs at least to be sketched.

Between the early decades of this century and the mid-1970s, homoerotic desire was figured by scientific-medical knowledges into a homosexual identity. Ironically, the framing of homosexuality as a social identity proved to be productive of homosexual subcultures. To put it very schematically, homosexual subcultures evolved from the marginal, clandestine homophile organizations of the 1950s to the public cultures and movements of confrontation and the affirmation of lesbian feminism and gay liberation in the 1970s (Adam 1987; D'Emilio 1983; Faderman 1981). Integral to the transformation of homoerotic desire into a lesbian and gay identity was the insertion of homosexuality into public discourses. From the early 1900s through the 1950s, a psychiatric discourse that figured the homosexual as a pathological personality, a perverse, abnormal human type, dominated public discussion. Kinsey (1948, 1953) challenged this psychiatric model by viewing sexuality as a continuum. Instead of assuming that individuals are either exclusively heterosexual or homosexual, he proposed (with the support of thousands of interviews) that human sexuality is ambiguous with respect to sexual orientation or that most individuals experience both hetero- and homosexual feelings and behaviors. Kinsey's critique of the psychiatric model was met with a hard-line defense of

the model (e.g., Bergler 1956; Bieber et al. 1962; Socarides 1968). At the same time, new social models of homosexuality provided an alternative to both Kinsey and the biological and psychological models of psychiatry. These discourses conceived of homosexuals as an oppressed minority, victims of unwarranted prejudice and social discrimination (e.g., Cory 1951; Hoffman 1968; Hooker 1965; Martin and Lyon 1972). By the early 1970s, the women's and gay liberation movements had fashioned elaborated social concepts of homosexuality that not only sought to normalize homoerotic desire and identities but also criticized the institutions of heterosexuality, marriage and the family, and conventional gender roles (e.g., Altman 1971; Atkinson 1974; Bunch 1975; Rich 1976).

Sociology was positioned ambivalently with regard to the making of homosexuality as a site of political conflict and knowledge. Undoubtedly, the growing national public awareness of homosexuality and the surfacing of social concepts of homosexuality prompted sociologists to conceive of homosexuality as within their domain of knowledge. Sociologists approached homosexuality as a social stigma to be managed; they analyzed the ways in which homosexuals adapted to a hostile society. Through the 1970s, sociologists studied the homosexual (mostly the male homosexual) as a creature of the sexual underworld of hustlers, prostitutes, prisons, tearooms, baths, and bars (e.g., Humphreys 1970; Kirkham 1971; A. Reiss 1964; Weinberg and Williams 1975). My impression is that much of this sociology aimed to figure the homosexual as a victim of unjust discrimination. Nevertheless, sociologists contributed to the public perception of the homosexual as a strange, exotic "other" in contrast to the normal, respectable heterosexual.

Sociological perspectives on sexuality in the 1960s and early 1970s, particularly the labeling theory of Howard Becker (1963), Goffman (1963), and Schur (1971) and the "sexual script" concept of John Gagnon and William Simon (1973), proved influential in shaping knowledges of sexuality and homosexuality. In the late 1970s and early 1980s, however, a new sociology of homosexuality was fashioned, primarily by lesbian- and gay-identified and often feminist sociologists. This new cadre of sociologists took over the conceptual tools of sociology, as well as drawing heavily from feminism and critical social approaches circulating in the lesbian and gay movements, to study gay life (e.g., Harry and Devall 1979; Levine 1979a, 1979b; Murray 1979; Plummer 1975, 1981; Troiden 1988; Warren 1974). This work underscored the social meaning of homosexuality. It contributed to recent gay theory, which has largely neglected sociological research as a distinctive social tradition of sex studies.... The sociology of homosexuality from the early 1970s through the 1980s has not played a major role in recent lesbian and gay theory debates, in part because sociologists did not critically investigate the categories of sexuality, heterosexuality, and homosexuality; they never questioned the social functioning of the hetero/ homosexual binary as the master category of a modern regime of sexuality.... Moreover, sociologists lacked historical perspective while perpetuating an approach that isolated the question of homosexuality from the broader question of modernization and politics....

As homosexuality was being inserted into public discourses and made into an object of knowledge in academic disciplines, a gay theory was developing out-side academe. For example, as sociologists were begin-ning to think of sex as a social fact, knowledges came out of the women's and gay movements, as I men-tioned above. With the formation of homophile groups in the 1950s (e.g., the Mattachine Society and the Daughters of Bilitis), homosexuality was alterna-tively theorized as a property of all individuals or as a property of a segment of the human population. The naturalization of homosexuality was intended to legit-imate homosexuality. Moreover, despite the radicaliza-tion of gay theory in lesbian feminism and gay liberation in the 1970s, few people challenged the view of homosexuality as a natural condition and a key marker of self-identity. A good deal of lesbian feminist and gay liberationist theory simply reversed the dominant sexual hierarchy by asserting the natural-ness and normality of homosexuality. For universalists, normalization was often connected to a political strategy of assimilationism, while the minoritization of homosexuality was often wedded to a separatist agenda or to a politics of difference (e.g., Bunch 1971; Johnston 1973). The notion of homosexuality as a universal category of the self and a sexual identity was hardly questioned, if at all, in the homophile, lesbian

feminist, and gay liberationist discourses (exceptions include Altman 1971; MacIntosh 1968).

As the initial wave of an antihomophobic, gay affirmative politic (roughly from 1968 to 1973) passed into a period of community building, personal empowerment, and local struggles, we can speak of a new period in lesbian and gay theory, the age of social constructionism. Drawing from labeling and phenom-enological theory, and influenced heavily by Marxism and feminism, social constructionists had roots in aca-demia and activism. At the heart of a social construc-tionist perspective is the rejection of the antithesis of sex and society. Sex is viewed as fundamentally social; the categories of sex—especially heterosexuality and homosexuality; but also the whole regime of modern sexual types, classifications, and norms—are under-stood as social and historical facts. With respect to homosexuality, the chief theme was that "homosexu-ality" or (more appropriately) same-sex experiences were not a uniform, identical phenomenon, but that their meaning and social role varied historically. In particular, constructionists argued that "the homo-sexual" cannot be assumed to be a transhistorical iden-tity; instead the category of homosexuality operates as marking a distinct psychological and physical human type or identity only in modern Western societies. Michel Foucault provided the classic statement:

> As defined by ancient civil or canonical codes, sodomy was a category of forbidden acts; their perpetrator was nothing more than the juridical subject of them. The nineteenth-century homo-sexual became a personage, a past, a case history, a life form.... Nothing that went into the total composition was unaffected by his sexuality. It was everywhere present in him: at the root of all his actions ... because it was a secret that always gave itself away (1980:43).

Foucault's thesis of the social construction of "the homosexual" found parallel articulation in the concur-rent work of Jonathan Katz (1976), Carroll Smith-Rosenberg (1975), Randolph Trumbach (1977), and Jeffrey Weeks (1977).

Foucault's genealogical studies of sexuality aimed at exposing a whole sexual regime as a social and poli-tical event. In this regard, Foucault questioned the political strategy of an affirmative lesbian and gay movement on the grounds that it unwittingly reproduced this regime. Foucault's deconstructionist message, however, fell on largely deaf ears in the context of a politics affirming identity and the prodigious efforts at lesbian and gay community building in the 1970s. A good deal of social constructionist studies through the early 1980s sought to explain the origin, social meaning, and changing forms of the modern homosexual (e.g., D'Emilio 1983; Faderman 1981; Plummer 1981). Although this literature challenged essentialist or universalistic understandings of homosexuality, it was often tied to a politics of the making of a homosexual minority. Instead of asserting the homosexual as a natural fact made into a political minority by social prejudice, constructionists traced the social factors that produced a homosexual subject or identity, which functioned as the foundation for the building of a minority, ethnic-like community and politics. Social constructionist studies often functioned as legitimations for the organization of lesbian and gay subcultures into ethnic-like minorities (Epstein 1987; Seidman 1993).[2]

Social constructionist perspectives dominated studies of homosexuality through the 1980s and have been institutionalized in lesbian and gay studies programs in the 1990s, Debates about essentialism (Stein 1992) and the rise, meaning, and changing social forms of homosexual identities and communities are at the core of lesbian and gay social studies. Since the late 1980s, however, aspects of this constructionist perspective have been contested; its own conceptual and political silences and exclusions have been exposed. In particular, discourses that sometimes circulate under the rubric of queer theory, though often impossible to differentiate from constructionist texts, have sought to shift the debate somewhat away from explaining the modern homosexual to questions of the operation of the hetero/homosexual binary, from an exclusive preoccupation with homosexuality to a focus on heterosexuality as a social and political organizing principle, and from a politics of minority interest to a politics of knowledge and difference (Seidman 1993). What is the social context of the rise of queer theory?

By the end of the 1970s, the gay and lesbian movement had achieved such a level of subcultural elaboration and general social tolerance that a politics of cultural and social mainstreaming far overshadowed both the defensive strategies (e.g., the Mattachine Society) and the revolutionary politics of the previous decades. Thus Dennis Altman (1982), a keen observer of the gay movement in the 1970s, could speak of the homosexualization of America. Yet at this very historical moment, events were conspiring to put lesbian and gay life into crisis.

A backlash against homosexuality, spearheaded by the new right but widely supported by neoconservatives and mainstream Republicans, punctured illusions of a coming era of tolerance and sexual pluralism (Adam 1987; Patton 1985; Seidman 1992). The AIDS epidemic both energized the anti-gay backlash and put lesbians and gay men on the defensive as religious and medicalized models which discredited homosexuality were rehabilitated in public discourses. Although the AIDS crisis also demonstrated the strength of established gay institutions, for many lesbians and gay men it underscored the limits of a politics of minority rights and inclusion. Both the backlash and the AIDS crisis prompted a renewal of radical activism, of a politics of confrontation, coalition building, and the need for a critical theory that would link gay empowerment to broad institutional change.

Internal developments similarly prompted a shift in gay theory and politics. Long-simmering internal differences erupted around the issues of race and sex. By the early 1980s, a public culture fashioned by lesbian and gay people of color registered sharp criticisms of mainstream gay culture and politics for its marginalization, devaluation, and exclusion of their experiences, interests, values, and unique forms of life (e.g., their language, writing, political perspectives, relationships, and particular modes of oppression). The concept of lesbian and gay identity that served as the foundation for building a community and organizing politically was criticized as reflecting a white, middle-class experience or standpoint (Anzaldua and Moraga 1983; Beam 1986; Lorde 1984; Moraga 1983; Hemphill 1991). The categories of "lesbian" and "gay" were criticized for functioning as disciplining political forces. Simultaneously, lesbian feminism was further put into crisis by challenges to its foundational concept of sexuality and sexual ethics. At the heart of lesbian feminism, especially in the late 1970s, was an understanding of the difference between men and women anchored in a spiritualized concept of female sexuality and an eroticization of the male that imagined male desire as revealing a logic of misogyny and domination. Being a woman and a lesbian meant exhibiting in one's desires, fantasies, and behaviors a lesbian-feminist sexual and social identity. Many lesbians, and feminists in general, criticized lesbian feminism for marking their own erotic and intimate lives as deviant or male-identified (e.g., Allison 1981; Bright 1984; Califia 1979, 1981; Rubin 1983). In the course of what some describe as the feminist "sex wars," a virtual parade of female and lesbian sexualities (e.g., butch-fems, sadomasochists, sensualists of all kinds) entered the public text of lesbian culture, mocking the idea of a unified lesbian sexual identity (Ferguson 1989; Phelan 1989; Seidman 1992). The intent of people of color and of sex rebels was to encourage social differences to surface in gay and lesbian life, but one consequence was to raise questions about the very foundations of gay culture and politics.

Some people in the lesbian and gay communities reacted to the "crisis" by reasserting a natural foundation for homosexuality (e.g., the gay brain) in order to unify homosexuals in the face of a political backlash, to defend themselves against attacks prompted by the plague, and to overcome growing internal discord. Many activists and intellectuals, however, moved in the opposite direction, affirming a stronger thesis of the social construction of homosexuality, which took the form of radical politics of difference. Although people of color and sex rebels pressured gay culture in this direction, there appeared a new cadre of theorists, influenced profoundly by French poststructuralism and Lacanian psychoanalysis, who have significantly altered the terrain of gay theory and politics (e.g., Butler 1990; de Lauretis 1991; Doty 1993; Fuss 1991; Sedgwick 1990; Warner 1993). If queer theory speaks to a serious epistemic shift, I think it is to this refigured conceptual field.

As the contributors to this symposium make clear, queer theory has accrued multiple meanings, from a merely useful shorthand way to speak of gay, lesbian, bisexual, and transgendered studies to a theoretical sensibility that pivots on transgression or permanent rebellion. I take as central to queer theory its challenge to what has been the dominant foundational concept of both homophobic and affirmative homosexual theory: the assumption of a homosexual subject or identity. I interpret queer theory as contesting this foundation and therefore the very telos of Western homosexual politics.

Modern Western homophobic and gay affirmative theory has assumed a homosexual subject. Dispute materialized over its origin (natural or social), its changing social forms and roles, its moral meaning, and its politics. There has been hardly any serious disagreement regarding the assumption that homosexual theory and politics have as their object "the homosexual" as a stable, unified, and identifiable agent. Drawing from the critique of unitary identity politics by people of color and by sex rebels, and from the poststructural critique of "representational" models of language, queer theorists argue that identities are always multiple or at best composites, with an infinite number of ways in which "identity-components" (e.g., sexual orientation, race, class, nationality, gender, age, ableness) can intersect or combine. Any specific identity construction, moreover, is arbitrary, unstable, and exclusionary. Identity constructions necessarily entail the silencing or exclusion of some experiences or forms of life. For example, the assertion of a black, middle-class, American lesbian identity silences differences in this social category that relate to religion, regional location, subcultural identification, relation to feminism, age, or education. Identity constructs are necessarily unstable because they elicit opposition or indeed produce resistance by those whose experiences, interests, or forms of life are submerged by the assertion of identity. Finally, rather than viewing affirmations of identity as necessarily liberating, queer theorists figure them as disciplinary and regulatory structures. Identity constructions function, if you will, as templates defining selves and behaviors and therefore as excluding a range of possible ways to frame one's self, body, desires, actions, and social relations.

Approaching identities as multiple, unstable, and regulatory may suggest to critics the undermining of gay theory and politics, but for queer theorists it presents new and productive possibilities. Although I detect a strain of anti-identity politics in some queer theory, the aim is not to abandon identity as a category of knowledge and politics but to render it permanently open and contestable as to its meaning and political role. In other words, decisions about identity categories become pragmatic, related to concerns of situational advantage, political gain, and conceptual utility. The gain of figuring identity as permanently open as to its meaning and political use, say queer theorists, is that it encourages the public surfacing of differences or a culture where multiple voices and interests are heard and shape gay life and politics.

Queer theory articulates a related objection to a homosexual theory and politics organized on the ground of the homosexual subject: This project reproduces the hetero-homosexual binary, a code that perpetuates the heterosexualization of society.... Modern Western affirmative homosexual theory may naturalize or normalize the gay subject or even may register it as an agent of social liberation, but it has the effect of consolidating heterosexuality and homosexuality as master categories of sexual and social identity; it reinforces the modern regime of sexuality. Queer theory wishes to challenge the regime of sexuality itself—that is, the knowledges that construct the self as sexual and that assume heterosexuality and homosexuality as categories marking the truth of sexual selves. The modern system of sexuality organized around the heterosexual or homosexual self is approached as a system of knowledge, one that structures the institutional and cultural life of Western societies. In other words, queer theorists view heterosexuality and homosexuality not simply as identities or social statuses but as categories of knowledge, a language that frames what we know as bodies, desires, sexualities, identities; this is a normative language that erects moral boundaries and political hierarchies. Queer theorists shift their focus from an exclusive preoccupation with the oppression and liberation of the homosexual subject to an analysis of the institutional practices and discourses producing sexual knowledges and how they organize social life, with particular attention to the way in which these knowledges and social practices repress differences. In this regard, queer theory is suggesting that the study of homosexuality should not be a study of a minority—the making of the lesbian/gay/bisexual/subject—but a study of those knowledges and social practices which organize "society" as a whole by sexualizing—heterosexualizing or homosexualizing—bodies, desires, acts, identities, social relations, knowledges, culture, and social institutions. Queer theory aspires to transform homosexual theory into a general social theory or one standpoint from which to analyze whole societies.

As of this writing, queer theory and sociology have barely acknowledged one another. Queer theory has largely been the creation of academics, mostly feminists and mostly humanities professors. Sociologists are almost invisible in these discussions.... This is somewhat ironic in light of the gesturing of queer theory towards a general social analysis. Moreover, the silence of sociologists is most unfortunate because queer theory has been criticized for its textualism or "underdeveloped" concept of the social (e.g., Hennessy 1993; Seidman forthcoming; Warner 1993). Sociologists have much to learn from queer theory ... as well as the opportunity to make a serious contribution.

This symposium is intended to bring to an end the mutual neglect between queer theorists and sociologists. It asks the following questions: What is queer theory? How does it speak to sociologists? How does it challenge sociologists to reexamine their paradigms, and how might sociology speak to queer theory? What would a queer theory which seriously engaged sociology look like? The queer-ing of sociology and the sociologizing of queer theory are the twin themes and hopes of this symposium.

A final word about risk and courage is in order. Alan Sica deserves much credit for supporting this symposium, the first of its kind in a sociology journal. It was an act of risk and trust on his part; I hope he has not been disappointed. I have enormous admiration for the contributors. Aside from myself and Ken Plummer, either they are junior faculty members or anticipate entering the job market shortly. Although identifying with a queer standpoint has achieved a level of tolerance and perhaps some cultural currency in the humanities, queer perspectives are barely visible in sociology. These contributors have wagered, perhaps unconsciously but surely bravely, that their contesting of knowledges will be taken on its own terms as part of the ongoing sociological conversation about the understanding and shape of contemporary humanity. Finally, I wish to thank Charles Lemert, whose encouragement of this project and whose respect for "the other" has been as gentle and loving as it has been unyielding and provoking.

NOTES

1. The index of the *American Journal of Sociology* shows that between 1895 and 1965, one article on homosexuality was printed and 13 articles were listed under the heading "Sex"; most of these addressed issues of gender, marriage, or lifestyle. The index of the *American Sociological Review* shows that between 1936 and 1960, 14 articles were published under the heading "Sexual Behavior"; most of these did not address issues of sexuality. One journal article commented on the absence of a sociology of sexuality: "The sociology of sex is quite undeveloped, although sex is a social force of the first magnitude. Sociologists have investigated the changing roles of men and women ... [and] the sexual aspects of marriage. ... Occasionally a good study on illegitimacy or prostitution appears. However, when it is stated that a sociology of sex does not exist, I mean that our discipline has not investigated, in any substantial manner, the social causes, conditions and consequences of heterosexual and homosexual activities of all types" (Bowman 1949:626). Another sociologist, Kingsley Davis (1937, 1939), who later became president of the American Sociological Association, also studied sexuality. Some 20 years after Bowman lamented the absence of a sociology of sexuality, Edward Sagarin reiterated this complaint: "Here and there an investigation, a minor paper, a little data, particularly in the literature of criminology ... and what at the time was called social disorganization ... marked the totality of sex literature in sociology" (1971:384).
2. Placing all innovative homosexual studies in the 1970s and 1980s under the rubric of social constructionism and the project of minority theory simplifies matters. In particular, it signalizes a powerful current of lesbian feminist-inspired theorizing (e.g., Ferguson 1989; MacKinnon 1989; Rich [1980] 1983). Much of this work was concerned less with issues of essentialism and constructionism or the rise of homosexual identities than with analyzing the social forces creating, maintaining, and resisting the institution of heterosexuality. Departing from a tendency in constructionist studies to approach lesbian and gay theory as separate from feminism, this literature insists on tracing the link between a system of compulsory heterosexuality and patterns of male dominance. In this regard ... [a] materialist feminist perspective suggests both a critique of queer theory for isolating sexuality from gender and a critique of feminist sociologists for isolating gender from issues of sexuality.

REFERENCES

Adam, Barry. 1987. *The Rise of a Gay and Lesbian Movement.* Boston: Hall.
Allison, Dorothy. 1981. "Lesbian Politics in the '80s." *New York Native*, December 7–20.
Altman, Dennis. 1971. *Homosexual Liberation and Oppression.* New York: Avon.
———. 1982. *The Homosexualization of America.* Boston: Beacon.
Anzaldua, Gloria and Cherrie Moraga, eds. 1983. *This Bridge Called My Back.* New York: Kitchen Table Press.
Atkinson, Ti-Grace. 1974. *Amazon Odyssey.* New York: Links Books.
Beam, Joseph, ed. 1986. *In the Life.* Boston: Alyson.
Becker, Howard. 1963. *Outsiders.* New York: Free Press.
Bergler, Edmund. 1956. *Homosexuality: Disease or Way of Life?* New York: Hill and Wang.
Bieber, Irving, et al. 1962. *Homosexuality.* New York: Basic Books.
Birken, Lawrence. 1988. *Consuming Desire.* Ithaca: Cornell University Press.
Bowman, Claude. 1949. "Cultural Ideology and Heterosexual Reality: A Preface to Sociological Research." *American Sociological Review* 14: 624–33.

Bright, Susie. 1984. "The Year of the Lustful Lesbian." *New York Native*, July 30–August 12.

Bunch, Charlotte. 1971. "Learning from Lesbian Separatism." *Ms.*, November.

———. 1975. "Lesbians in Revolt." Pp. 29–37 in *Lesbianism and the Women's Movement*, edited by Nancy Myron and Charlotte Bunch. Baltimore: Diane Press.

Butler, Judith. 1990. *Gender Trouble*. New York: Routledge.

Califia, Pat. 1979. "A Secret Side of Lesbian Sexuality." *The Advocate*, December 27.

———. 1981. "What Is Gay Liberation?" *The Advocate*, June 25.

Cory, Daniel Webster (psuedonym of Edward Sagarin). 1951. *The Homosexual in America*. New York: Peter Nevill.

Davis, Katherine Benet. 1929. *Factors in the Sex Life of Twenty-Two Hundred Women*. New York: Harper.

Davis, Kingsley. 1937. "The Sociology of Prostitution." *American Sociological Review* 2: 744–55.

———. 1939. "Illegitimacy and the Social Structure." *American Journal of Sociology* 45: 215–33.

de Lauretis, Teresa. 1991. "Queer Theory: Lesbian and Gay Sexualities." *Differences* 3: iii–xviii.

D'Emilio, John. 1983. *Sexual Politics, Sexual Communities*. Chicago: University of Chicago Press.

D'Emilio, John and Estelle Freedman. 1988. *Intimate Matters*. New York: Harper and Row.

Dickinson, Robert and Laura Bearn. 1932. *A Thousand Marriages*. Baltimore: Williams and Wilkins.

Doty, Alexander. 1993. *Making Things Perfectly Queer*. Minneapolis: University of Minnesota Press.

Epstein, Steven. 1987. "Gay Politics, Ethnic Identity: The Limits of Social Constructionism." *Socialist Review* 93/94 (May–August): 9–54.

Faderman, Lillian. 1981. *Surpassing the Love of Men*. New York. Morrow.

Ferguson, Ann. 1989. *Blood at the Root*. Boston: Pandora.

Foucault, Michel. 1980. *The History of Sexuality*. Vol. 1. New York: Vintage.

———. 1985. *The History of Sexuality*. Vol. 2. New York: Vintage.

Fuss, Diana, ed. 1991. *Inside/Out*. New York: Routledge.

Gagnon, John and William Simon. 1967a. "Homosexuality: The Formulation of a Sociological Perspective." *Journal of Health and Social Behavior* 8: 177–85.

———. 1967b. "The Lesbians: A Preliminary Overview." in *Sexual Deviance*, edited by John Gagnon and William Simon. New York: Harper and Row.

———. 1973. *Sexual Conduct*. Chicago: Aldine.

Goffman, Erving. 1963. *Stigma*. Englewood Cliffs, NJ: Prentice-Hall.

Harry, Joseph and William Devall. 1979. *The Social Organization of Gay Males*. New York: Praeger.

Hemphill, Essex, ed. 1991. *Brother to Brother*. Boston: Alyson.

Hennessy, Rosemary. 1993. "Queer Theory: A Review of the *Differences* Special Issue and Wittig's *The Straight Mind*." *Signs* 18: 964–73.

Henslin, James. 1971. *Studies in the Sociology of Sex*. New York: Appleton-Century-Crofts.

Hoffman, Martin. 1968. *The Gay World*. New York: Basic Books.

Hooker, Evelyn. 1965. "Male Homosexuals and Their Worlds." Pp. 83–107 in *Sexual inversion*, edited by Judd Marmor. New York: Basic Books.

Humphreys, Laud. 1970. *Tearoom Trade*. Chicago: Aldine.

Irvine, Janice. 1990. *Disorders of Desire*. Philadelphia: Temple University Press.

Johnston, Jill. 1973. *Lesbian Nation*. New York: Harper and Row.

Katz, Jonathan. 1976. *Gay American History*. New York: Crowell.

———. 1983. *Gay/Lesbian Almanac*. New York: Harper and Row.

Kinsey, Alfred, Wardell Pomeroy, and Clyde Martin. 1948. *Sexual Behavior in the Human Male*. Philadelphia: Saunders.

———. 1953. *Sexual Behavior in the Human Female*. Philadelphia: Saunders.

Kirkham, George. 1971. "Homosexuality in Prison." Pp. 325–49 in *Studies in the Sociology of Sex*, edited by James Renslin. New York: Appleton-Century-Crofts.

Levine, Martin. 1979a. "Gay Ghetto." *Journal of Homosexuality* 4: 363–77.

———. ed. 1979b. *The Sociology of Male Homosexuality*. New York: Harper and Row.

Lorde, Audre. 1984. *Sister Outsider*. Freedom, CA: Crossing Press.

MacIntosh, Mary. 1968. "The Homosexual Role." *Social Problems* 16: 182–92.

MacKinnon, Catherine. 1989. *Toward a Feminist Theory of the State*. Cambridge, MA: Harvard University Press.

Marriner, Gerald. 1972. "The Estrangement of the Intellectuals in America: The Search for New Life Styles in the Early Twentieth Century." Doctoral dissertation, University of Colorado.

Martin, Dell and Phyllis Lyon. 1972. *Lesbian/Woman*. San Francisco: Glide.

Moraga, Cherrie. 1983. *Loving in the War Years*. Boston: South End Press.

Murray, Stephen. 1979. "The Institutional Elaboration of a Quasi-Ethnic Community." *International Review of Modern Sociology* 9: 165–78.

Patton, Cindy. 1985. *Sex and Germs*. Boston: South End Press.

Peiss, Kathy. 1986. *Cheap Amusements*. Philadelphia: Temple University Press.

Phelan, Shane. 1989. *Identity Politics*. Philadelphia: Temple University Press.

Plummer, Ken. 1975. *Stigma*. London: Routledge.

———. ed. 1981. *The Making of the Modern Homosexual*. London: Hutchinson.

Reiss, Albert, Jr. 1964. "The Social Integration of Queers and Peers." *Social Problems* 9: 102–20.

Reiss, Ira. 1967. *The Social Context of Premarital Sexual Permissiveness*. New York: Holt, Rinehart and Winston.

Rich, Adrienne. 1976. *Of Woman Born*. New York: Norton.

———. (1980) 1983. "Compulsory Heterosexuality and the Lesbian Existence." Pp. 177–205 in *Powers of Desire*, edited by Ann Snitow, Christine Stansell, and Sharon Thompson. New York: Monthly Review Press.

Rubin, Gayle. 1983. "Thinking Sex." Pp. 267–319 in *Pleasure and Danger*, edited by Carole Vance. Boston: Routledge.

Sagarin, Edward. 1969. *Odd Man In*. Chicago: Quadrangle Books.

———. 1971. "Sex Research and Sociology: Retrospective and Prospective." Pp. 377–408 in *Studies in the Sociology of Sex*, edited by James Henslin. New York: Appleton-Century-Crofts.

Schur, Edwin. 1971. *Labeling Deviant Behavior*. New York: Random.

Sedgwick, Eve. 1990. *The Epistemology of the Closet*. Berkeley: University of California Press.

Seidman, Steven. 1991. *Romantic Longings*. New York: Routledge.

———. 1992. *Embattled Eros*. New York: Routledge.

———. 1993. "Identity and Politics in a Postmodern Gay Culture: Some Conceptual and Historical Notes." Pp. 105–42 in *Fear of a Queer Planet*, edited by Michael Warner. Minneapolis: University of Minnesota Press.

———. Forthcoming. "Deconstructing Queer Theory, or the Under-Theorizing of the Social and the Ethical." In *Social Postmodernism*, edited by Linda Nicholson and Steven Seidman. Cambridge, UK: Cambridge University Press.

Simmons, Christina. 1982. "Marriage in the Modern Manner: Sexual Radicalism and Reform in America, 1914–1941." Doctoral dissertation, Brown University.

Smith-Rosenberg, Carroll. 1975. "The Female World of Love and Ritual: Relations between Women in Nineteenth-Century America." *Signs* 9: 1–29.

———. 1990. "Discourses of Sexuality and Subjectivity: The New Woman, 1870–1936." Pp. 264–80 in *Hidden from History*, edited by Martin Duberman, Martha Vicinus, and George Chauncey, Jr. New York: Penguin.

Socarides, Charles. 1968. *The Overt Homosexual*. New York: Grune and Stratton.

Stein, Edward, ed. 1992. *Forms of Desire*. New York: Routledge.

Trimberger, Ellen Kay. 1983. "Feminism, Men and Modern Love: Greenwich Village, 1900–1925." Pp. 131–52 in *Powers of Desire*, edited by Ann Snitow, Christine Stausell, and Sharon Thompson. New York: Monthly Review Press.

Troiden, Richard. 1988. *Gay and Lesbian Identity*. New York: General Hall.

Trumbach, Randolph. 1977. "London's Sodomites: Homosexual Behavior and Western Culture in the Eighteenth Century." *Journal of Social History* 11: 1–33.

Van de Velde, Theodore. (1930) 1950. *Ideal Marriage*. Westport, CT: Greenwood.

Warner, Michael (ed.). 1993. Introduction. *Fear of a Queer Planet*. Minneapolis: University of Minnesota Press.

Warren, Carol. 1974. *Identity and Community in the Gay World*. New York: Wiley.

Weeks, Jeffrey. 1977. *Coming Out*. London: Quartet.

———. 1985. *Sexuality and Its Discontents*. London: Routledge.

Weinberg, Martin and Colin Williams. 1975. "Gay Baths and the Social Organization of Impersonal Sex." *Social Problems* 23: 124–36.

84. MATERIALS FOR AN EXPLORATORY THEORY OF THE NETWORK SOCIETY

MANUEL CASTELLS

Manuel Castells (b. 1942) is one of the foremost contemporary theorists of urbanization, globalization, and the impact of technology on contemporary social life. In his most recent work, he argues that we have entered an Information Age characterized by a global network society predicated in large part on advances in informational technologies. In this essay, Castells notes that although networks are not new forms of organization, a situation has emerged in recent decades wherein a network society comes to constitute the characteristic social structure of the new society. This transformation has made possible greater flexibility and decentralization of power compared to the preceding era of industrial society. The impact of network society is far-reaching, extending not simply to the realm of economic production but also filtering into patterns of consumption, power relations, the ways individuals experience the world, interpersonal relationships, and culture. In short, what he outlines is a reframing of sociological theory in an effort to capture the most significant technological and social changes of the past four decades.

INTRODUCTION

The network society is a specific form of social structure tentatively identified by empirical research as being characteristic of the Information Age. By social structure I understand the organizational arrangements of humans in relationships of production/consumption, experience, and power, as expressed in meaningful interaction framed by culture. By Information Age I refer to a historical period in which human societies perform their activities in a technological paradigm constituted around microelectronics-based information/communication technologies, and genetic engineering. It replaces/subsumes the technological paradigm of the Industrial Age, organized primarily around the production and distribution of energy. . . .

THE NETWORK SOCIETY: AN OVERVIEW

In the last two decades of the twentieth century a related set of social transformations has taken place around the world. While cultures, institutions, and historical trajectories introduce a great deal of diversity in the actual manifestations of each one of these transformations, it can be shown that, overall, the vast majority of societies are affected in a fundamental way by these transformations. All together they constitute a new type of social structure that I call the network society for reasons that hopefully will become apparent. I shall summarize below the main features of these transformations, in a sequential order that does not imply hierarchy of causation in any way.

We have entered *a new technological paradigm*, centred around microelectronics-based, information/

Excerpted from "Materials for an Exploratory Theory of the Network Society," by Manuel Castells, *British Journal of Sociology*, Vol. No. 51, No. 1, (January/March 2000), pp. 5–24, ISSN 0007 1315. Copyright © 2000 by London School of Economics. Reprinted by permission of Taylor and Francis, Ltd., <http://www.tandf.co.uk/journals> (now published by Blackwell Publishing). ✦

communication technologies, and genetic engineering. In this sense what is characteristic of the network society is not the critical role of knowledge and information, because knowledge and information were central in all societies. Thus, we should abandon the notion of "Information Society," which I have myself used sometimes, as unspecific and misleading. What is new in our age is a new set of information technologies. I contend they represent a greater change in the history of technology than the technologies associated with the Industrial Revolution, or with the previous Information Revolution (printing). Furthermore, we are only at the beginning of this technological revolution, as the Internet becomes a universal tool of interactive communication, as we shift from computer-centred technologies to network-diffused technologies, as we make progress in nanotechnology (and thus in the diffusion capacity of information devices), and, even more importantly, as we unleash the biology revolution, making possible for the first time, the design and manipulation of living organisms, including human parts. What is also characteristic of this technological paradigm is the use of knowledge-based, information technologies to enhance and accelerate the production of knowledge and information, in a self-expanding, virtual circle. Because information processing is at the source of life, and of social action, every domain of our eco-social system is thereby transformed.

We live in a *new economy*, characterized by three fundamental features. First, it is *informational*, that is, the capacity of generating knowledge and processing/managing information determine the productivity and competitiveness of all kinds of economic units, be they firms, regions, or countries. While it took two decades for the new technological system to yield its productivity dividend, we are now observing substantial productivity growth in the most advanced economies and sectors, in spite of the difficulty in measuring informational productivity with the categories of the industrial era.

Second, this new economy is *global* in the precise sense that its core, strategic activities, have the capacity to work as a unit on a planetary scale in real time or chosen time. By core activities I mean financial markets, science and technology, international trade of goods and services, advanced business services, multinational production firms and their ancillary networks,

communication media, and highly skilled speciality labour. Most jobs are in fact not global, but all economies are under the influence of the movements of their globalized core. Globalization is highly selective. It proceeds by linking up all that, according to dominant interests, has value anywhere in the planet, and discarding anything (people, firms, territories, resources) which has no value or becomes devalued, in a variable geometry of creative destruction and destructive creation of value.

Third, the new economy is *networked*. At the heart of the connectivity of the global economy and of the flexibility of informational production, there is a new form of economic organization, the *network enterprise*. This is not a network of enterprises. It is a network made from either firms or segments of firms, and/or from internal segmentation of firms. Large corporations are internally de-centralized as networks. Small and medium businesses are connected in networks. These networks connect among themselves on specific business projects, and switch to another network as soon as the project is finished. Major corporations work in a strategy of changing alliances and partnerships, specific to a given product, process, time, and space. Furthermore, these co-operations are based increasingly on sharing of information. These are information networks, which, in the limit, link up suppliers and customers through one firm, with this firm being essentially an intermediary of supply and demand, collecting a fee for its ability to process information.

The unit of this production process is not the firm, but the business project. The firm continues to be the legal unit of capital accumulation. But since the value of the firm ultimately depends on its valuation in the stock market, the unit of capital accumulation (the firm) itself becomes a node in a global network of financial flows. In this economy, the dominant layer is the global financial market, where all earnings from all activities and countries end up being traded. This global financial market works only partly according to market rules. It is shaped and moved by information turbulences of various origins, processed and transmitted almost instantly by tele-communicated, information systems, in the absence of the institutional regulation of global capital flows.

This new economy (informational, global, networked) is certainly capitalist. Indeed, for the first time in history, the whole planet is capitalist, for all practical purposes (except North Korea, but not Cuba or Myanmar, and certainly not China). But it is a new brand of capitalism, in which rules for investment, accumulation, and reward, have substantially changed (see Giddens and Hutton 2000). Besides, since nothing authorizes capitalism as eternal, it is essential to focus on the characteristics of the new economy because it may well outlast the mode of production where it was born, once capitalism comes under decisive challenge and/or plunges into a structural crisis derived from its internal contradictions (after all, statism died from its self-inflicted flaws).

Work and employment are substantially transformed in/by the new economy. But, against a persistent myth, there is no mass unemployment as a consequence of new information technologies. The empirical record is conclusive on this matter (Carnoy 2000). Yet, there is a serious unemployment problem in Europe, unrelated to technology, and there are dramatic problems of under-employment in the developing world, caused by economic and institutional backwardness, including the insufficient diffusion and inefficient use of information technologies. There is a decisive transformation of work and employment. Induced by globalization, and the network enterprise, and facilitated by information/communication technologies, the most important transformation in employment patterns concerns the development of flexible work, as the predominant form of working arrangements. Part-time work, temporary work, self-employment, work by contract, informal or semi-formal labour arrangements, and relentless occupational mobility, are the key features of the new labour market. Feminization of paid labour leads to the rise of the "flexible woman," gradually replacing the "organization man," as the harbinger of the new type of worker. The key transformation is the individualization of labour, reversing the process of socialization of production characteristic of the industrial era, still at the roots of our current system of industrial relations.

The work process is interconnected between firms, regions, and countries, in a stepped up spatial division of labour, in which networks of locations are more important than hierarchies of places. Labour is fundamentally divided in two categories: self-programmable labour, and generic labour. Self-programmable labour is equipped with the ability to retrain itself, and adapt to new tasks, new processes and new sources of information, as technology, demand, and management speed up their rate of change. Generic labour, by contrast, is exchangeable and disposable, and co-exists in the same circuits with machines and with unskilled labour from around the world. Beyond the realm of employable labour, legions of discarded, devalued people form the growing planet of the irrelevant, from where perverse connections are made, by fringe capitalist business, through to the booming, global criminal economy. Because of this structural divide in terms of informational capacities, and because of the individualization of the reward system, in the absence of a determined public policy aimed at correcting structural trends, we have witnessed in the last 20 years a dramatic surge of inequality, social polarization, and social exclusion in the world at large, and in most countries, particularly, among advanced societies, in the USA and in the UK (see UNDP 1999; Hutton 1996; Castells 2000, for sources).

Shifting to the *cultural realm*, we see the emergence of a similar pattern of networking, flexibility, and ephemeral symbolic communication, in a culture organized primarily around an integrated system of electronic media, obviously including the Internet. Cultural expressions of all kinds are increasingly enclosed in or shaped by this electronic hypertext. But the new media system is not characterized by one-way, undifferentiated messages through a limited number of channels that constituted the world of mass media. And it is not a global village. Media are extraordinarily diverse, and send targeted messages to specific segments of audiences responding to specific moods of audiences. They are increasingly inclusive, bridging from one another, from network TV to cable TV or satellite TV, radio, VCR, video, portable devices, and the Internet. The whole set is coming together in the multimedia system, computer-operated by the digitalized set-top box that opens up hundreds of channels of interactive communication, reaching from the global from the local. While there is oligopolistic concentration of multimedia groups, there is, at the same time, market segmentation, and the rise of an interactive audience, superseding the uniformity of the mass audience. Because of the inclusiveness and flexibility of this system of symbolic exchange, most cultural expressions are enclosed in it, thus inducing the formation of what I call a culture of "real virtuality." Our symbolic environment is, by and large, structured by this flexible, inclusive hypertext, in which many people surf each day. The virtuality of this text is in fact a fundamental dimension of reality, providing the symbols and icons from which we think and thus exist.

This growing enclosure of communication in the space of a flexible, interactive, electronic hypertext does not only concern culture. It has a fundamental effect on *politics*. In almost all countries, media have become the space of politics. To an overwhelming extent people receive their information, on the basis of which they form their political opinion and structure their behaviour, through the media and particularly television and radio. Media politics needs to convey very simple messages. The simplest message is an image. The simplest, individualized image is a person. Political competition increasingly revolves around the personalization of politics. The most effective political weapons are negative messages. The most effective negative message is character assassination of opponents´ personalities, and/or of their supporting organizations. Political marketing is an essential means to win political competition, including, in the information age, media presence, media advertising, telephone banks, targeted mailing, image making and unmaking. Thus, politics becomes a very expensive business, way beyond the means of traditional sources of political financing, at a time when citizens resist giving more of their tax money to politicians. Thus, parties and leaders use access to power as ways to obtain resources for their trade. Political corruption becomes a systemic feature of information age politics. Since character assassination needs some substance from time to time, systemic political corruption provides ample opportunity, as a market of intermediaries is created to leak and counter-leak damaging information. The politics of scandal takes centre stage in political competition, in close interaction with the media system, and with the co-operation of judges and prosecutors, the new stars of our political soap operas. Politics becomes a horse race, and a tragicomedy motivated by greed, backstage manoeuvres, betrayals, and, often, sex and violence—a genre increasingly indistinguishable from TV scripts.

As with all historical transformations, the emergence of a new social structure is linked to a redefinition of the material foundations of our life, of *time and space*, as Giddens (1984), Lash and Urry (1994), Thrift (1990), and Harvey (1990), among others, have argued. I propose the hypothesis that two emergent social forms of time and space characterize the network society, while coexisting with prior forms of time and space. These are timeless time and the space of flows. In contrast to the rhythm of biological time characteristic of most of human existence, and to clock time characterizing the industrial age, timeless time is defined by the use of new information/communication technologies in a relentless effort to annihilate time. On the one hand, time is compressed (as in split second global financial transactions, or in the attempt to fight "instant wars"), and on the other hand, time is de-sequenced, including past, present, and future occurring in a random sequence (as in the electronic hypertext or in the blurring of life-cycle patterns, both in work and parenting).

The space of flows refers to the technological and organizational possibility of organizing the simultaneity of social practices without geographical contiguity. Most dominant functions in our societies (financial markets, transnational production networks, media systems, etc.) are organized around the space of flows. And so do an increasing number of alternative social practices (such as social movements) and personal interaction networks. However, the space of flows does include a territorial dimension, as it requires a technological infrastructure that operates from certain locations, and as it connects functions and people located in specific places. Yet, the meaning and function of the space of flows depend on the flows processed within the networks, by contrast with the space of places, in which meaning, function, and locality are closely interrelated.

The central power-holding institution of human history, *the state*, is also undergoing a process of dramatic transformation. On the one hand, its sovereignty is called into question by global flows of wealth, communication, and information. On the other hand, its legitimacy is undermined by the politics of scandal and its dependence on media politics. The weakening of its power and credibility induce people to build their own systems of defence and representation around their identities, further de-legitimizing the state. However, the state does not disappear. It adapts and transforms itself. On the one hand, it builds partnerships between nation-states and shares sovereignty to retain influence. The European Union is the most obvious case, but around the world there is a decisive shift of power toward multi-national and transnational institutions, such as NATO, IMF/World Bank, United Nations agencies, World Trade Organization, regional trade associations, and the like. On the other hand, to regain legitimacy, most states have engaged in a process of devolution of power, decentralizing responsibilities and resources to nationalities, regions, and local governments, often extending this de-centralization to non-governmental organizations. The international arena is also witnessing a proliferation of influential, resourceful non-governmental organizations that interact with governments, and multinational political institutions. Thus, overall the new state is not any longer a nation-state. The state in the information age is a network state, a state made out of a complex web of power-sharing, and negotiated decision-making between international, multinational, national, regional, local, and non-governmental, political institutions.

There are two common trends in these processes of transformation that, together, signal a new historical landscape. First, none of them could have taken place without new information/communication technologies. Thus, while technology is not the cause of the transformation, it is indeed the indispensable medium. And in fact, it is what constitutes the historical novelty of this multidimensional transformation. Second, all processes are enacted by organizational forms that are built upon networks, or to be more specific, upon information networks. Thus, to analyse the emerging social structure in theoretically meaningful terms, we have to define what information networks are, and elaborate on their strategic role in fostering and shaping current processes of social transformation.

SOCIAL STRUCTURE AND SOCIAL MORPHOLOGY: FROM NETWORKS TO INFORMATION NETWORKS

A network is a set of interconnected nodes. A node is the point where the curve intersects itself. Networks are very old forms of social organization. But they have taken on a new life in the Information Age by becoming information networks, powered by new information technologies. Indeed, networks had traditionally a major advantage and a major problem, in contrast to other configurations of social morphology, such as centralized hierarchies. On the one hand, they are the most flexible and adaptable forms of organization, able to evolve with their environment and with the evolution of the nodes that compose the network. On the other hand, they have considerable difficulty in co-ordinating functions, in focusing resources on specific goals, in managing the complexity of a given task beyond a certain size of the network. Thus, while they were the natural forms of social expression, they were generally outperformed as tools of instrumentality. For most of human history, and unlike biological evolution, networks were outperformed by organizations able to master resources around centrally defined goals, achieved through the implementation of tasks in rationalized, vertical chains of command and control. But for the first time, the introduction of new information/communication technologies allows networks to keep their flexibility and adaptability, thus asserting their evolutionary nature. While, at the same time, these technologies allow for co-ordination and management of complexity, in an interactive system which features feedback effects, and communication patterns from anywhere to everywhere within the networks. It follows an unprecedented combination of flexibility and task implementation, of co-ordinated decision making, and de-centralized execution, which provide a superior social morphology for all human action.

Networks de-centre performance and share decision-making. By definition, a network has no centre. It works on a binary logic: inclusion/exclusion. All there is in the network is useful and necessary for the existence of the network. What is not in the network does not exist from the network's perspective, and thus must be either ignored (if it is not relevant to the network's task), or eliminated (if it is competing in goals or in performance). If a node in the network ceases to perform a useful function it is phased out from the network, and the network rearranges itself as cells do in biological processes. Some nodes are more important than others, but they all need each other as long as they are within the network. And no nodal domination is systemic. Nodes increase their importance by absorbing more information and processing it more efficiently. If they decline in their performance, other nodes take over their tasks. Thus, the relevance, and relative weight of nodes does not come from their specific features, but from their ability to be trusted by the network with an extra share of information. In this sense, the main nodes are not centres, but switchers, following a networking logic rather than a command logic, in their function vis-à-vis the overall structure.

Networks, as social forms, are value-free or neutral. They can equally kill or kiss: nothing personal. They process the goals they are programmed to perform. All goals contradictory to the programmed goals will be fought off by the network components. In this sense, a network is an automaton. But, who programmes the network? Who decides the rules that the automaton will follow? Social actors, naturally. Thus, there is a social struggle to assign goals to the network. But once the network is programmed, it imposes its logic to all its members (actors). Actors will have to play their strategies within the rules of the network. To assign different goals to the programme of the network (in contrast to perfect the programme within the same set of goals), actors will have to challenge the network from the outside and in fact destroy it by building an alternative network around alternative values. Or else, building a defensive, non-network structure (a commune) which does not allow connections outside its own set of values. Networks may communicate, if they are compatible in their goals. But for this they need actors who possess compatible access codes to operate the switches. They are the switchers or power-holders in our society (as in the connections between media and politics, financial markets and technology, science and the military, and drug traffic and global finance through money laundering).

The speed and shape of structural transformations in our society, ushering in a new form of social organization, come from the widespread introduction of information networks as the predominant organizational form. Why now? The answer lies in the simultaneous availability of new, flexible information technologies and a set of historical events, which came together by accident, around the late 1960s and 1970s. These events include the restructuring of capitalism with its emphasis on deregulation and liberalization; the failed restructuring of statism unable to adapt itself to informationalism; the influence of libertarian ideology arising from the countercultural social movements of the 1960s; and the development of a new media system, enclosing cultural expressions in a global/local, interactive hypertext. All processes, interacting with each other, favoured the adoption of information networks as a most efficient form of organization. Once introduced, and powered by information technology, information networks, through competition, gradually eliminate other organizational forms, rooted in a different social logic. In this sense, they tend to assert the predominance of social morphology over social action. Let me clarify the meaning of this statement by entering into the heart of the argument, that is, by examining how specifically the introduction of information networks into the social structure accounts for the set of observable transformations as presented in the preceding section. Or, in other words, how and why information networks constitute the backbone of the network society.

THE ROLE OF INFORMATION NETWORKS IN SHAPING RELATIONSHIPS OF PRODUCTION, CONSUMPTION, POWER, EXPERIENCE, AND CULTURE

Information networks, as defined above, contribute, to a large extent, to the transformation of social structure in the information age. To be sure, this multidimensional transformation has other sources that interact with the specific effect of information networks, as mentioned above. Yet, in this analysis, I will focus on the specificity of the interaction between this new social morphology and the evolution of social structure. I will be as parsimonious as possible, trying to avoid repetition of arguments and observations already presented in this text.

A social structure is transformed when there is simultaneous and systemic transformation of relationships of production/consumption, power, and experience, ultimately leading to a transformation of culture. Information networks play a substantial role in the set of transformations I have analysed in my work and summarized here. This is how and why.

RELATIONSHIPS OF PRODUCTION

Although I suppose information networks will shape, eventually, other modes of production, for the time being we can only assess their effect in the capitalist mode of production. Networks change the two terms of the relationship (capital, labour) and their relationship. They transform capital by organizing its circulation in global networks and making it the dominant sphere of capital the one where value, from whichever origin, increases (or decreases) and is ultimately realized. Global financial markets are information networks. They constitute themselves into a collective "capitalist," independent from any specific capitalist (but not indifferent to), and activated by rules that are only partly market rules. In this sense, capital in the Information Age has become a human-made automaton, which, through mediations, imposes its structural determination on relationships of production. More specifically, global financial markets and their management networks constitute an automated network, governed by interactions between its multiple nodes, propelled by a combination of market logic, information turbulences, and actors´ strategies and bets (see Castells 2000).

Relationships between capital and labour (all kinds of capital, all kinds of labour) are organized around the network enterprise form of production. This network enterprise is also globalized at its core, through telecommunications and transportation networks. Thus, the work process is globally integrated, but labour tends to be locally fragmented. There is simultaneous integration of production and specification of labour's contribution to the production process. Value in the production process depends essentially on the position occupied by each specific labour or each specific firm in the value chain. The rule is individualization of the relationship between capital and labour. In a growing number of cases, self-employment, or payment in stocks, leads to workers becoming holders of their own capital; however, any individual capital is submitted to the movements of the global automaton. As labour comes to be defined by a network of production and individualized in its relationship to capital, the critical cleavage within labour becomes that between networked labour and switched-off labour which ultimately becomes non-labour. Within networked labour, it is the capacity to contribute to the value-producing chain that determines the individual bargaining position. Thus labour's informational capacity, by ensuring the possibility of strategic positioning in the network, leads to a second, fundamental cleavage, between self-programmable labour and generic labour. For self-programmable labour, its individual interest is better served by enhancing its role in performing the goals of the network, thus establishing competition between labour and co-operation between capital (the network enterprize) as the structural rule of the game. Indeed game theory and rational choice theory seem to be adequate intellectual tools to understand socio-economic behaviour in the networked economy. While for generic labour, its strategy is survival: the key issue becomes not be degraded to the realm of discarded or devalued labour, either by automation or globalization, or both.

In the last analysis, the networking of relationships of production leads to the blurring of class relationships. This does not preclude exploitation, social differentiation and social resistance. But production-based, social classes, as constituted, and enacted in the Industrial Age, cease to exist in the network society.

RELATIONSHIPS OF CONSUMPTION

Relationships of consumption (that is, the culturally meaningful, differential appropriation of the product) are determined by the interplay between relationships of production and culture. Who does what, in a given value production system, determines who gets what. What is valued as appropriation is framed by culture. The networking of production relationships, and the consequent individualization of labour, leads on the one hand to increasing differentiation and thus inequality in consumption. It also leads to social polarization and social exclusion following the opposition between self-programmable labour and generic labour, and between labour and devalued labour. The ability of networks to connect valuable labour and territories, and to discard dispensable labour and territories, so enhancing their performance through reconfiguration, leads to cumulative growth and cumulative decline. The winner-takes-all system is, in the consumption sphere, the expression of value creation by/in the networks.

On the other hand, the fragmentation of culture, and the individualization of positions in relationships of production, lead jointly to a growing diversification of consumption patterns. Mass consumption was predicated upon standardized production, stable relationships of production, and a mass culture organized around predictable senders and identifiable sets of values. In a world of networks, self-programmable individuals constantly redefine their life styles and thus their consumption patterns; while generic labour just strives for survival.

As culture is similarly fragmented and constantly recombined in the networks of a kaleidoscopic hypertext, consumption patterns follow the variable geometry of symbolic appropriation. Thus, in the interplay between relationships of production and cultural framing, relationships of production define levels of consumption, and culture induces consumption patterns and life styles.

RELATIONSHIPS OF POWER

The most direct impact of information networks on social structure concerns power relationships. Historically, power was embedded in organizations and institutions, organized around a hierarchy of centres. Networks dissolve centres, they disorganize hierarchy, and make materially impossible the exercise of hierarchical power without processing instructions in the network, according to the network's morphological rules. Thus, contemporary information networks of capital, production, trade, science, communication, human rights, and crime, bypass the nation-state, which, by and large, has stopped being a sovereign entity, as I argued above. A similar process, in different

ways, takes place in other hierarchical organizations that used to embody power ("power apparatuses" in the old Marxist terminology), such as churches, schools, hospitals, bureaucracies of all kinds. Just to illustrate this diversity, churches see their privilege as senders of belief called into question by the ubiquitous sending and receiving of messages in the interactive hypertext. While religions are flourishing, churches have to enter the new media world in order to promote their gospel. So doing, they survive, and even prosper, but they open themselves up to constant challenges to their authority. In a sense, they are secularized by their co-existence with profanity in the hypertext, except when/if they anchor themselves in fundamentalism by refusing to bend to the network, thus building self-contained, cultural communes.

The state reacts to its bypassing by information networks, by transforming itself into a network state. So doing, its former centres fade away as centres becoming nodes of power-sharing, and forming institutional networks. Thus, in the war against Yugoslavia, in spite of US military hegemony, decision-making was shared in various degrees by NATO governments, including regular video-conferences between the leaders of the main countries where key decisions were taken. This example goes beyond the former instances of traditional military alliances, by introducing joint war-making in real time. NATO was reinforced by NATO's state members, when these states, including the USA, entered the new world of shared sovereignty. But individual states became weakened in their autonomous decision-making. The network became the unit.

Thus, while there are still power relationships in society, the bypassing of centres by flows of information circulating in networks creates a new, fundamental hierarchy: the power of flows takes precedence over the flows of power.

RELATIONSHIPS OF EXPERIENCE

If power relationships are the ones most directly affected by the prevailing networking logic, the role of networks in the transformation of relationships of experience is more subtle. I will not force the logic of the analysis. I do not believe that we must see networks everywhere for the sake of coherence. Yet, I think it could be intriguing to elaborate tentatively on the links between networking and the transformation of relationships of experience.

This transformation, empirically speaking, revolves around the crisis of patriarchalism, and its far-reaching consequences for family, sexuality and personality. The fundamental source of this crisis is women's cultural revolution, and men's resistance to reverse their millennial privileges. Additional sources are the feminization of labour markets (undermining male domination in the family and in society at large), the revolution in reproductive technology, the self-centring of culture, the individualization of life patterns and the weakening of the state's authority to enforce patriarchalism. What networks have to do with all this?

There is one direct connection between the networking of work and the individualization of labour, and the mass incorporation of women to paid labour, under conditions of structural discrimination. Thus, new social relationships of production, translate into a good fit between the "flexible woman" (forced to flexibility to cope with her multiple roles) and the network enterprise. Networks of information and global communication are also critical in diffusing alternative life styles, role models and, more importantly, critical information, for instance about self-control of biological reproduction. Then, there is an additional, meaningful connection. The disintegration of the patriarchal family does not [leave] people, and children, isolated. They reconfigure life-sharing forms through networking. This is particularly true of women and their children, relying on a form of sociability and solidarity tested by millennia of living "underground." But also men, and men and women after going their own ways, come to rely on networks (sometimes around children of multiple marriages) to both survive and reinvent forms of togetherness. This trend shifts the basis of interpersonal relationships from nuclei to networks: networks of individuals and their children—which, by the way, are also individuals. What is left of families are transformed in partnerships which are nodes of networks. Sexuality is decoupled from the family, and transformed into consumption/images, stimulated and simulated from the electronic hypertext. The body, as proposed by

Giddens some time ago, becomes an expression of identity (1991). It is individualized and consumed in sexual networks. At the level of personality, the process of socialization becomes customized, individualized, and made out of composite models. The autonomous ability to reprogramme one's own personality, in interaction with an environment of networks, becomes the crucial feature for psychological balance, replacing the strengthening of a set personality, embedded in established values. In this "risk society" (Beck 1992), the management of anxiety is the most useful personal skill. Two conflicting modes of interpersonal interaction emerge: on the one hand, self-reliant communes, anchored in their non-negotiable sets of beliefs; and on the other hand, networks of ever shifting individuals.

These are social networks, not information networks. So, in a way, they are a fundamental part of our societies, but not necessarily a feature of the network society—unless we extend the meaning of the concept beyond what I propose: information networks-based social structure. However, as communication technology, biological technology, transgender networking, and networks of individuals develop in parallel, as key elements of social practice, they are interacting, and influencing each other. Thus, the Internet is becoming a very instrumental tool of management of new forms of life, including the building of on-line communities of support and collective learning.

I see, however, a much stronger connection between networks and relationships of experience through the cultural transformations induced by communication networks, as experience becomes practice by its rooting in cultural codes.

NETWORKS AND CULTURAL TRANSFORMATION

Culture was historically produced by symbolic interaction in a given space/time. With time being annihilated and space becoming a space of flows, where all symbols coexist without reference to experience, culture becomes the culture of real virtuality. It takes the form of an interactive network in the electronic hypertext, mixing everything, and voiding the meaning of any specific message out of this context, except that is for fundamental, non-communicable values external to the hypertext. So, culture is unified in the hypertext but interpreted individually (in line with the "interactive audience" school of thought in media theory). Culture is constructed by the actor, self-produced and self-consumed. Thus, because there are few common codes, there is systemic misunderstanding. It is this structurally induced cacophony that is celebrated as postmodernity. However, there is one common language, the language of the hypertext. Cultural expressions left out of the hypertext are purely individual experiences. The hypertext is the vehicle of communication, thus the provider of shared cultural codes. But these codes are formal, voided of specific meaning. Their only shared meaning is to be a node, or a blip, in the network of communication flows. Their communicative power comes from their capacity to be interpreted and re-arranged in a multi-vocality of meanings, depending on the receiver, and on the interactor. Any assigned meaning becomes instantly obsolete, reprocessed by a myriad of different views and alternative codes. The fragmentation of culture and the recurrent circularity of the hypertext, leads to the individualization of cultural meaning in the communication networks. The networking of production, the differentiation of consumption, the decentring of power, and the individualization of experience are reflected, amplified, and codified by the fragmentation of meaning in the broken mirror of the electronic hypertext—where the only shared meaning is the meaning of sharing the network.

CONCLUSION: SOCIAL CHANGE IN THE NETWORK SOCIETY

Social structures are sets of organizational regularities historically produced by social actors, and constantly challenged, and ultimately transformed by deliberate social action. The network society is no exception to this sociological law. Yet, the characteristics of specific social structures impose constraints on the characteristics of their transformation process. Thus, the recurrence and flexibility of information networks, their embedded ability to bypass, ignore or eliminate instructions alien to their programmed goals, make social change in the network society a very tricky task. This is because, apparently, nothing must be changed—

any new input can theoretically be added to the network, like free expression in the global media system. Yet, the price for the addition is to accept implicity the programmed goal of the network, its ancillary language and operating procedures. Thus, my hypothesis is that there is little chance of social change within a given network, or network of networks. Understanding by social change, the transformation of the programme of the network, to assign to the network a new goal, following a different set of values and beliefs. This is in contrast to reprogramming the network by adding instructions compatible with the overarching goal.

Because of the capacity of the network to find new avenues of performance by switching off any non-compatible node, I think social change, under these circumstances, happens primarily through two mechanisms, both external to dominant networks. The first is the denial of the networking logic through the affirmation of values that cannot be processed in any network, only obeyed and followed. This is what I call cultural communes, that are not necessarily linked to fundamentalism, but which are always centred around their self-contained meaning. The second is alternative networks, that is networks built around alternative projects, which compete, from network to network, to build bridges of communication to other networks in society, in opposition to the codes of the currently dominant networks. Religious, national, territorial, and ethnic communes are examples of the first type of challenge. Ecologism, feminism, human rights movements are examples of alternative networks. All use the Internet and electronic media hypertext, as dominant networks do. This is not what makes them networks or communes. The critical divide lies in the communicability or non-communicability of their codes beyond their specific self-definition. The fundamental dilemma in the network society is that political institutions are not the site of power any longer. The real power is the power of instrumental flows, and cultural codes, embedded in networks. Therefore, the assault to these immaterial power sites, from outside their logic, requires either the anchoring in eternal values, or the projection of alternative, communicative codes that expand through networking of alternative networks. That social change proceeds through one way or another will make the difference between fragmented communalism and new history making.

REFERENCES

Arquilla, John and Rondfeldt, David. 1999. *The Emergence of Noopolitik*. Santa Monica, CA: Rand, National Defense Research Institute.

Barber, Benjamin. 1995. *Jihad vs. McWorld*. New York: Times Books.

Beck, Ulrich. 1992. *Risk Society: Towards a New Modernity*. London: Sage.

Calhoun, Craig (ed.). 1994. *Social Theory and the Politics of Identity*. Oxford: Blackwell.

Carnoy, Martin. 2000. *Work, Family and Community in the Information Age*. New York: Russell Sage.

Castells, Manuel. 2000. "Information Technology and Global Capitalism," in A. Giddens and W. Hutton (eds.), *On the Edge*. London: Jonathan Cape.

Croteau, David and Hoynes, William. 1997. *Media/Society: Industries, Images, and Audiences*. Thousand Oaks, CA: Pine Forge Press.

De Kerckhove, Derrick. 1997. *"Connected Intelligence."* Toronto: Somerville House.

Dutton, William H. 1999. *Society on the Line: Information Politics in the Digital Age*. Oxford: Oxford University Press.

Giddens, Anthony. 1984. *The Constitution of Society: Outline of a Theory of Structuration*. Cambridge: Polity Press.

———. 1991. *Modernity and Self-Identity: Self and Society in the Late Modern Age*. Stanford: Stanford University Press.

Giddens, Anthony, and Hutton, Will (eds.). 2000. *On the Edge*. London: Jonathan Cape.

Graham, Stephen, and Marvin, Simon. 1996. *Telecommunications and the City: Electronic Spaces, Urban Places*. London: Routledge.

Hage, Jerald, and Powers, Charles. 1992. *Postindustrial Lives: Roles and Relationships in the 21st Century*. London: Sage.

Hall, Peter (Sir). 1998. *Cities in Civilization*. New York, Pantheon.

Harvey, David. 1990. *The Condition of Postmodernity*. Oxford: Blackwell.

Held, David, and McGrew, Anthony, Goldblatt, David, and Perraton, Jonathan. 1999. *Global Transformations: Politics, Economics, and Culture*. Stanford: Stanford University Press.

Hutton, Will. 1996 [1995]. *The State We're In*. London: Jonathan Cape.

Lash, Scott, and Urry, John. 1994. *Economies of Signs and Space*. London: Sage.

Lyon, David. 1999. *Postmodernity*. Buckingham: Open University Press.

Mansell, Robin, and Silverstone, Roger (eds.). 1996. *Communication by Design: The Politics of Information and Communication Technologies*. Oxford: Oxford University Press.

Scott, Allen. 1998. *Regions and the World Economy. The Coming Shape of Global Production, Competition, and Political Order*. New York: Oxford University Press.

Subirats, Marina. 1998. "Con diferencia: las mujeres frente al reto de la autonomía." Barcelona: Icaria.

Thrift, Nigel J. 1990. "The Making of Capitalism in Time Consciousness," in J. Hassard (ed.), *The Sociology of Time*. London: Macmillan.

Touraine, Alain. 1993 [1973]. *Production de la societé*. Paris: Seuil.

———. 1997. *Pourrons-nous vivre ensemble? Egaux et differents*. Paris: Fayard.

Turkle, Sherry. 1995. *Life on the Screen, Identity in the Age of Internet*. New York: Simon and Schuster.

United Nations Development Programme. 1999. *1999 Human Development Report: Globalization with a Human Face*. New York: UNDP-United Nations.

Webster, Juliet. 1996. *Shaping Women's Work: Gender, Employment, and Information Technology*. London: Longman.

Wellman, Barry (ed.). 1999. *Networks in the Global Village*. Boulder, CO: Westview Press.

85. MOBILE SOCIOLOGY

JOHN URRY

John Urry (b. 1946) is a British theorist whose sociological interests have been varied. His theoretical contributions have always been located within and shaped by a variety of concrete research projects. His early work focused on power, while subsequent work has examined urban and regional development, changes in the nature of contemporary capitalism, and the increasing significance of consumerism and tourism. More recently, he has turned his attention to complexity theory. Urry describes "Mobile Sociology" as a manifesto that urges greater appreciation of "diverse mobilities of peoples, objects, images, information, and wastes." In focusing attention on movement and fluidity, his argument bears a resemblance to that of Arjun Appadurai. What makes his essay distinctive is that it calls for further reflection on the very notion of society, which has been since sociology's formative period its presumed central object of inquiry. Picking up on Margaret Thatcher's infamous remark that "there is no such thing as society," he enters into a discussion of what we mean by society, in the process urging a greater self-reflexivity on the part of theorists.

At the present moment of history the network of social relations spreads over the whole world, without any absolute solution of continuity. This gives rise to the difficulty . . . of defining what is meant by the term `society´ . . . If we say that our subject is the study and comparison of human societies we ought to be able to say what are the unit entities with which we are concerned.

(A. R. Radcliffe-Brown 1952: 193)

A *self does* not amount to much, but no self is an island; each exists in a fabric of relations that is now more complex and mobile than ever before.

(J-F Lyotard 1984: 15)

INTRODUCTION

In this article I outline some categories relevant for developing sociology as a `discipline´ as we enter the next century. I argue for a sociology concerned with the diverse mobilities of peoples, objects, images, information, and wastes; and of the complex interdependencies between, and social consequences of, these diverse mobilities.

Elsewhere I have shown how mobilities are transforming the historic subject-matter of sociology which within the `west´ has focused upon individual societies and their generic characteristics (Urry 2000). In *Sociology Beyond Societies* I develop a `post-societal´ agenda for sociology elaborating how various global `networks and flows´ undermine endogenous social structures that possess the power to reproduce themselves. New rules of sociological method are necessitated by the apparently declining powers of national societies since it is they that have historically provided the intellectual and organizational context for sociology. Some of the diverse mobilities that are materially transforming the `social as society´ into the `social as mobility´ include imaginative travel, movements of images and information, virtual travel, object travel and corporeal travel (see Urry 2000: ch. 3). The consequence of such diverse mobilities is to produce what Beck terms the growth of `inner mobility´ for which coming and going, being both here and there at the same time, has become much more globally normal (1999: 75–6).

In this article I show how mobilities crisscrossing societal borders in new temporal-spatial patterns constitute a novel agenda for sociology, of mobility. Much twentieth-century sociology has been based upon the study of occupational, income, educational and social mobility. This literature regarded society as a uniform surface and failed to register the geographical intersections of region, city and place, with the social categories of class, gender and ethnicity. Further, there are crucial flows of people within, but especially beyond, the territory of each society, and these flows relate to many different desires, for work, housing, leisure, religion, family relationships, criminal gain, asylum seeking and so on. Moreover, not only people are mobile, but so too are many `objects´, `images´, `informations´ and `wastes´. Mobility is thus to be understood in a horizontal rather than a vertical sense, and it applies to a variety of actants and not just to humans.

Bauman's vertical metaphor of `gardening´ to characterize modern societies is pertinent here (1987). He suggests that a gardening state has replaced earlier `gamekeeper´ states that were not involved in giving society an overall shape and were uninterested in detail. By contrast the gardening state presumes exceptional concern with pattern, regularity and ordering, with what is growing and with what should be weeded out. Legislators have been central to careful tendering by the gardening state, with using their reason to determine what is, and is not, productive of order. The social sciences have been part of that application of reason to society through facilitating the husbandry of societal resources, identifying what is and what is not to be cultivated and determining what are the exact conditions of growth of particular plants.

However, the new global order appears to involve a return to the gamekeeper state and away from that of the gardener. The gamekeeper was concerned with regulating mobilities, with ensuring that there was sufficient stock for hunting in a particular site but not with the detailed cultivation of each animal in each particular place. Animals roamed around and beyond the estate, like the roaming hybrids that currently wander

in and especially across national borders. States are increasingly unable or unwilling to garden their society, only to regulate the conditions of their stock so that on the day of the hunt there is appropriate stock available for the hunter. As Beck has recently argued: `capital, culture, technology´ and politics merrily come together to roam *beyond* the regulatory power of the national state´ (1999: 107).

The former East European societies were `gardening´ societies. Following the Second World War, the individual societies of central and eastern Europe constructed exceptionally strong frontiers both from the `West´ and especially from each other. Cultural communication into and out of such societies was exceptionally difficult. The Cold War chilled culture as well as politics. So although such societies were internationally linked via the hegemony of the USSR, there was a parallel emphasis upon cultural involution and the reinforcement of strongly reinforced national networks. It constituted an interesting social laboratory based upon the concept of `society´.

But what happened was that regional frontiers of each society were transgressed, they were got around through various fluid-like movements. The attempt to freeze the peoples and cultures of `Eastern Europe´ could not be sustained. The Berlin Wall was of course the most dramatic example of this attempted gardening the people of a society. But through the 1960s, forms of communication and later of leisure travel noticeably increased. Both peoples and objects especially began to flow across the carefully constructed borders, often involving what has been termed the `invisible hand of the smuggler´ (Braun et al. 1996: 1). Objects of the `West´ became used and talked about in multiple informal ways, helping the citizens of such societies to form new bases of personal identity, new ways of collectively remembering and new images of self and society. Many citizens went to inordinate lengths to learn about and to acquire objects that were immutable in their western-ness. Thus these societies became surrounded by hordes of `animals´ (consumer goods, images, western ideas and so on) which increasingly crossed into and over the land that had been so carefully husbanded. Their populations chased after the animals and trampled underfoot the carefully tended plants (another kind of `animal farm´! See Urry 2000: ch. 2).

In the next section I consider `sociology` and `society` in more detail, before turning briefly to global networks and fluids. I consider how notions of complexity can analyse intensely mobile hybrids that roam across the globe and help to create a self-reproducing global order. I conclude with some observations about the implications of this mobile order for `sociology`, the science of `society`.

'THERE IS NO SUCH THING AS SOCIETY'

When former British Prime Minister Margaret Thatcher famously declared that `there is no such thing as society`, sociologists led the charge to critique her claim. They declared that there are obviously societies and that Thatcher's claim indicated the wrongness of her policies based upon trying to reduce the societal to the interests of `individual men and women and their families`. However, the riposte to Thatcher from the sociological community was not fully justified since it is actually unclear just what is meant by `society`. Although there is something `more` in social life than `individual men and women and their families`, exactly what this surplus amounts to is not so obvious (see Albertsen and Diken 1999: ch. 2, for extensive discussion).

Sociological discourse has indeed been premised upon `society` as its object of study (Billig 1995: 52–3; Hewitt 1997: Urry 2000: ch. 1). This was especially so from the 1920s onwards as sociology was institutionalized, especially within the American academy. MacIver and Page's standard *Society: An Introductory Analysis* argues that sociology is `"about" social relationships, the network of relationships we call society` (1950: v). The radical Gouldner in *The Coming Crisis of Western Sociology* talks of `Academic Sociology's emphasis on the potency of society and the subordination of men [sic] to it` (1972: 52). Wallerstein summarizes the overall situation: `no concept is more pervasive in modern social science than society` (1987: 315; note that the major exception to this is Luhmann's analysis of autopeitic systems, see 1990: ch. 1; 1995). This construction of the discourse of sociology around the concept of society in part stemmed from the apparent autonomy of American society throughout the twentieth century and is thus to universalize the American societal experience.

However, what most of these formulations neglect to specify is how `society` connects to the system of nations and nation-states. Billig argues that: `the "society" which lies at the heart of sociology's self-definition is created in the image of the nation-state` (1995: 53). Interestingly American-based theories of society have frequently ignored the `nationalist` basis of American and indeed of all western societies. They have typically viewed nationalism as surplus to society that only needs deployment in situations of `hot` extremism, situations which supposedly do not describe societies of the `west` (Billig 1995: 52–4).

In theorizing society, sovereignty, national citizenship and social governmentality lie at its core. Each `society` is a sovereign social entity with a nation-state that organizes the rights and duties of each societal member or citizen. Most major sets of social relationships flow within the territorial boundaries of the society. The state possesses a monopoly of jurisdiction or governmentality over members living within the territory or region of the society. Economy, politics, culture, classes, gender and so on are societally structured. In combination they constitute a clustering or a `social structure`. Such a structure organizes and regulates the life-chances of each member of the society in question.

This societal structure is not only material but also cultural, so that its members believe they share some common identity that is bound up in part with the territory that the society occupies or lays claim to. And *contra* the argument of much sociology, central to most such societies is a vernacular nationalism that articulates the identities of each society through its mundane differences from the other. These include the waving of celebratory flags, singing national anthems, flying flags on public buildings, identifying with one's own sportsheroes, being addressed in the media as a member of a given society, celebrating independence day and so on (Billig 1995),

However, societies are never entirely self-reproducing entities. Sociology has a tendency to treat what is `outside` the society as an unexamined environment. But no society, even in the heyday of the nation-state earlier this century, has been separate from the very systems of such states and from the notion of national identity that mobilizes sovereign societies. As Calhoun points out: `No nation-state ever existed entirely unto itself' (1997:118; Wallerstein 1991: 77). It is through this interdependence that societies are constituted as partially self-regulating entities, significantly defined by their banal or vernacular differences from each other.

Over the past two centuries this conception of society has been central to North American and West-European notions of what it is to possess the rights and duties of social citizenship. To be human meant that one is a member or citizen of a particular society. Historically and conceptually there has been a strong connection between the idea of humanness and of membership of a society. Society here means that ordered through a nation-state, with clear territorial and citizenship boundaries and a system of governance over its particular citizens. Conceptually and historically there has been an indivisible duality, of citizens and societies. Rose characterizes this model as government from 'the social point of view' (1996: 328; see Marshall and Bottomore 1992). There is a nationalisation of social responsibility with societal governmentality effected through new forms of expertise, particularly that of the sociology as the science of such societies and of the appropriate forms of social citizenship (Knorr Cetina 1997).

In this account 'society' and its characteristic social divisions of especially social class are strongly interconnected with the 'nation-state'. Mann shows that societies, nations and states have been historically intertwined (1993: 737). They developed together and should not be conceptualized as billiard balls existing only in external relations with one another. Mann evocatively talks of the sheer patterned messiness of the social world and of the mutually reinforcing intersections of class and nation, as societies developed their 'collective powers' especially over nature.

Sociology as a specific academic practice was the product of this particular historical moment, of an emergent industrial capitalism in Western Europe and North America. It took for granted the success of modern societies in their spectacular overcoming of nature. Sociology specialized in describing and explaining the character of these modern societies based upon industries that enabled and utilized dramatic new forms of energy and resulting patterns of social life. As such sociology adopted one or other versions of a tradition-modernity divide that implied that a revolutionary change had occured in North Atlantic rim societies between 1700–1900. These modern societies were presumed to be qualitatively different from the past. Sociology was thus based upon the acceptance and enhancement of the presumed division of academic labour stemming from the Durkheimian identification of the region of the social to be investigated and explained autonomously (Durkheim 1952 [1897]). Until recently this academic division between a world of natural facts and one of social facts made good sense as a strategy of professionalization for sociology. This sphere was parallel to, but did not challenge or confront, those physical sciences that dealt with an apparently distinct and analysable nature (see Macnaghten and Urry 1998).

Each society was sovereign, based upon a social governmentality. The concerns of each society were to be dealt with through national policies, especially from the 1930s onwards through a Keynesian welfare state that could identify and respond to the risks of organized capitalism (Lash and Urry 1987; 1994). These risks were seen as principally located *within* the geographical borders and temporal frames of each society. And solutions were devised and implemented within such societal frontiers. National societies were based upon a concept of the citizen who owed duties to, and received rights from, their society through the core institutions of the nation-state. This 'societal' model applied to the dozen or so societies of the North Atlantic rim. Most of the rest of the world was subject to domination by these societies of the North Atlantic rim.

In the next section I consider further this system which contemporary changes have put into question and which suggest that Thatcher was right when she said there is no such thing as society. But that there may not be such a thing as society is not because of the power of individual human subjects, but because of their weakness in the face of 'inhuman' fluid and mobile processes of globalization. Wallerstein points out that: 'What is fundamentally wrong with the concept of society is that it reifies and therefore crystallizes social phenomena whose real significance lies not in their solidity but precisely in their fluidity and malleability' (1991: 71).

GLOBAL NETWORKS AND FLUIDS

A useful starting point here is Mann's description of the contemporary world

> Today, we live in a global society. It is not a unitary society, . . . nor is it an ideological community or a state, but it is a single power network. Shock waves reverberate around it, casting down empires, transporting massive quantities of people, materials and messages, and finally, threatening the ecosystem and atmosphere of the planet. (1993: 11)

He makes a number of points here: there is no unified global society but there are exceptional levels of global interdependence; unpredictable shock waves spill out `chaotically´ from one part to the system as a whole; there are not just `societies´ but massively powerful `empires´ roaming the globe; and there is mass mobility of peoples, objects and dangerous human wastes.

What then are appropriate metaphors to make sense of these transformations? Mol and Law argue that there are three distinct metaphors of space or social topologies, regions, networks and fluids (1994; Urry 2000: ch. 2). First, there are *regions* in which objects are clustered together and boundaries are drawn around each particular regional cluster. Second, there are *networks* in which relative distance is a function of the relations between the components comprising the network—the invariant outcome is delivered across the entire network that often crosses regional boundaries. And third, there is the metaphor of the *fluid* that flows: `neither boundaries nor relations mark the difference between one place and another. Instead, sometimes boundaries come and go, allow leakage or disappear altogether, while relations transform themselves without fracture. Sometimes, then, social space behaves like a fluid´ (Mol and Law 1994: 643).

The sociological concept of society is based upon the metaphor of a region, namely that `objects are clustered together and boundaries are drawn around each particular cluster´ (Mol and Law 1994: 643). And one way to study globalization is through seeing it involved in inter-regional competition with `society´. Globalization could be viewed as the replacing of one region, the bounded nation-state-society of the `west´, with another, that of global economy and culture. And as both economy and culture are increasingly globalized, so the old dominant region of society appears to become relatively less powerful. In the fight between these two regions it looks as though the global region will win out and defeat the societal region (see Robertson 1992).

But this is only one way of understanding globalization. Globalization can also be viewed not as one larger region replacing the smaller region of each society, but as involving alternative metaphors of *network* and *fluid* (Mol and Law 1994; Waters 1995; Albrow 1996; Castells 1996, 1997; Eade 1997; Held et al. 1999; Beck 1999). The globalization literature has described the wide variety of new *machines* and *technologies* that dramatically compress or shrink time-space. These technologies carry people, information, money, images and risks, and flow within and across national societies in increasingly brief moments of time. Such technologies do not derive directly and uniquely from human intentions and actions. They are intricately interconnected with machines, texts, objects and other technologies. The appropriate metaphor to capture these intersections of peoples and objects is not that of a vertical structure that typically involves a centre, a concentration of power, vertical hierarchy and a formal or informal constitution. Castells argues, by contrast, that we should employ the metaphor of network, `the unit is the network´ (1996: 198).

> Networks constitute the new social morphology of our societies, and the diffusion of networking logic substantially modifies the operation and outcomes in processes of production, experience, power and culture . . . the network society, characterized by the pre-eminence of social morphology over social action. (Castells 1996: 469)

Castells defines a network as a set of interconnected nodes, the distances between social positions are shorter where such positions constitute nodes within a network as opposed to those which lie outside the particular network. Networks are to be viewed as dynamic open structures, so long as they are able to effect communication with new nodes and to innovate (Castells 1996:470–1). Much economic geography has detailed the apparently increased significance of such networks within the contemporary economy, at the intra-firm level, at the inter-film and inter-organizational level and at the firm-community levels (see Amin and Thrift 1992; Cooke and Morgan 1993; Messner 1997).

Network here does not mean purely *social* networks since the ʻconvergence of social evolution and information technologies has created a new material basis for the performance of activities throughout the social structure. This material basis, built in networks, earmarks dominant social processes, thus shaping social structure itself' (Castells 1996: 471). Networks thus produce complex and enduring connections across space and through time between peoples and things (see Murdoch 1995: 745). They spread across time and space which is hugely important, since according to Law, if ʻleft to their own devices *human actions and words do not spread very far at all*' (1994: 24). Different networks possess different reaches or abilities to bring home distant events, places or people, to overcome the friction of regional space within appropriate periods of time (Emirbayer and Sheller 1999: 748). This requires mobilizing, stabilizing and combining peoples, actions or events elsewhere into a stable network, an immutable mobile (Latour 1987). Accountancy, for example, is particularly effective at reducing the variety of activities in distant regions to a common set of figures, the flows of information, that can be instantaneously translated back to other parts of the network and especially to its control and command headquarters (Murdoch 1995: 749).

By contrast with the immutable mobiles of accountancy, Mol and Law show how the networks and flows involved in the measurement of haemoglobin levels are less secure (1994: 647–50). They ask how it is possible to produce regional maps of such comparative haemoglobin levels—analogous to accountants producing regional maps of the relative profitability of different plants of a global company. They argue that this requires a network constituted across many different regions, comprising appropriate technologies, measuring machines and people with suitable medical and technical skills. However, such a network is problematic to establish because in parts of the world there are inadequate numbers of machines to undertake appropriate measurement and, even where they do exist, they may not be appropriately maintained (see Messner 1997, more generally on network failure). Where a successful network thus gets established across a number of regions, this transforms the configurations of space and time that are no longer ʻregional'. In a network established for measuring haemoglobin levels, two hospitals can be

proximate although they are geographically hundreds of kilometres apart from each other. They constitute nodes within that particular set of network flows.

There are two further aspects of networks to distinguish here, namely, scapes and flows. *Scapes* are the networks of machines, technologies, organizations, texts and actors that constitute various interconnected nodes along which *flows* can be relayed. Such scapes reconfigure the dimensions of time and space. Once particular scapes have been established, then individuals and especially corporations within each society will normally try to become connected to them through being constituted as nodes within that particular network. They will seek to develop their own hub airport or at least have regular flights to such airports; they will wish their local schools to be plugged into the internet; they will try to attract satellite broadcasting; they may even seek to reprocess nuclear waste products, and so on. Between certain nodes along some scapes extraordinary amounts of information may flow, of financial, economic, scientific and news data and images, into which some groups are extermely well plugged-in while others are effectively excluded. What becomes significant is what Brunn and Leinbach term ʻrelative' as opposed to ʻabsolute' location (1991: xvii). This creates novel inequalities of flow as opposed to the inequalities of stasis. Graham and Marvin maintain that what is involved here is a rewarping of time and space by advanced telecommunication and transportation structures, as scapes pass by some areas and connect other areas along information and transport rich ʻtunnels' (1996: 60). Social and spatial distances are no longer homologous (Beck 1999: 104).

So far I have talked rather generally of global networks criss-crossing the regional borders of society, thus bringing out some aspects of contemporary ʻde-territorialization' (Lefebvre 1991: 346–8). These notions will now be made more precise by distinguishing between two different kinds of such networks, *global networks* and what I will call *global fluids*.

Numerous ʻglobal' enterprises, such as American Express, McDonalds, Coca Cola, Disney, Sony, BA and so on, are organized on the basis of a *global network* (see Ritzer 1992; 1995; 1997). Such a network of technologies, skills, texts and brands ensures that more or less the same product is delivered in more or less the same way in every country in which the enterprise operates. Such products are produced in predictable, calculable, routinized and standardized environments. These companies have produced enormously effective networks based upon immutable mobiles with few Tailings´. Such networks depend upon allocating a very large proportion of resources to branding, advertising, quality control, staff training and the internalization of the corporate image, all of which cross societal boundaries in standardized patterns so maintaining constancy. Distance is measured in terms of the time taken to get to the next McDonalds, the next Disney park, the next BA hub airport and so on, that is, from one node in this global network to the next. Such global networks can also be found within oppositional organizations such as Greenpeace. Like other global players it devotes much attention to developing and sustaining its brand identity throughout the world. Greenpeace's brand identity has `such an iconic status that it is a world-wide symbol of ecological virtue quite above and beyond the actual practical successes of the organization´ within particular societies (Szerszynski 1997: 46).

Second, there are *global fluids*, the heterogeneous, uneven and unpredictable mobilities of people, information, objects, money, images and risks, that move chaotically across regions in strikingly faster and unpredictable shapes. Such global fluids (as opposed to networks) demonstrate (see Deleuze and Guattari 1986, 1988; Lefebvre 1991; Mol and Law 1994; Auge 1995; Kaplan 1996; Shields 1997) no clear point of departure or arrival, just de-territorialized movement or mobility (rhizomatic rather than arboreal). They are relational in that they productively effect relations between the spatially varying features of a scape that would otherwise remain functionless. Fluids move in particular directions at certain speeds but with no necessary end-state or purpose. They possess different properties of viscosity and, as with blood, can be thicker or thinner and hence move in different shapes at different speeds. They move according to certain temporalities, over each minute, day, week, year and so on. Most importantly, fluids do not always keep within the scape—they may move outside or escape like white blood corpuscles through the `wall´ of the blood vessel into tinier and tinier capillaries; hence their power is diffused through these various fluids into very many often minute capillary-like relations of

domination/subordination. Different fluids spatially intersect in the `empty meeting grounds´ of the non-places of modernity, such as motels, airports, service stations, the internet, international hotels, cable television, expense account restaurants and so on.

I have thus set out some characteristics of global networks and fluids. Because these are inhuman hybrids, conceptions of agency that specifically focus upon the capacities of humans to attribute meaning or sense or to follow a social rule are inappropriate. This is not to suggest that humans do not do such things, not to suggest that humans do not exert agency. But they only do so in circumstances which are not of their own making; and it is those circumstances—the enduring and increasingly intimate relations of subjects *and* objects—that are of paramount significance. This means that the human and physical worlds are elaborately intertwined and cannot be analysed separately from each other, as society and as nature, or humans and objects. Also agency is not a question of humans acting independently of objects in terms of their unique capacities to attribute meaning or to follow rules. If then there is not autonomous realm of human agency, so there should not be thought of as a distinct level of *social* reality that is the unique outcome of humans acting in and through their specific powers. Various writers have tried to develop the thesis of the dialectic of individuals making society and society making individuals (Berger and Luckmann 1967). But such a dialectic would only be only plausible if we mean by society something trivial, that is pure social interactions abstracted from the networks of intricate relationships with the inhuman. Since almost all social entities do involve networks of connections between humans and these other components, so there are no uniquely *human* societies as such. Societies are necessarily hybrids.

More generally, Laclau and Mouffe show the impossibility of society as a valid object of discourse (1985). What we can ask stitches a `society´ together when inhuman networks criss-cross it in strikingly new ways at ever-faster speeds? The classic philosophical-sociological debates as to the respective virtues of methodological individualism versus holism, or in their later manifestations, structurationism versus the dualism of structure, are unhelpful here. They do not deal with the complex consequences of diverse mobilities; the intersecting sensuous relations of humans with diverse objects; the timed and spaced quality of relations stretching across societal borders; and the complex and unpredictable intersections of many `regions, networks and flows`. To describe these as either `structure` or as `agency` does injustice to the complexity of such relations. Luhmann summarizes: `There can be no "intersubjectivity" on the basis of the subject` (1995: xli). The ordering of social life is contingent, unpredictable, irreducible to human subjects and is only made possible by extra-somatic assets (as opposed to the pure sociality of baboon society: Law 1994). Knorr Cetina outlines the necessity of analysing `sociality with objects` (1997).

In the next section I consider whether notions of `complexity` can illuminate such inhuman, mobile intersecting hybrids—is complexity the basis of `post-social` knowledge?

COMPLEX MOBILITIES

The `complex` nature of both physical and social systems means that they are characterized by a very large number of elements that interact physically and informationally over time and result in positive and negative feedback loops (see Byrne 1998; Cilliers 1998; Wallerstein 1998; Thrift 1999, on recent social science applications of chaos/complexity theory). Such systems interact dissipatively with their environment and have a history that evolves irreversibly through time. Emergent, unintended and non-linear consequences are generated within such systems, consequences that are patterned but unpredictable, distant in time and/or space from where they originate and involving potential system bifurcation.

In the physical sciences complexity theory uses mathematical formulae and computer algorithms to characterize the enormously large number of iterative events. In certain experiments, the analysis of increases in the reproduction patterns of gypsy moths showed, through resulting changes in population size, dramatic non-linear changes in the quality of the system. Changes in the parameter resulted in transformations in the system; in certain contexts, order generates chaos. The more complex the system the more likely it is that small fluctuations will be critical (see Prigogine and Stengers 1984).

This iterative character of systems has been insufficiently interrogated within sociology (although see Mingers 1995: Eve, Horsfall, Lee 1997). Partly this is because of the presumed a-temporal character of the social world, rather than the seeing of all social hybrids as necessarily historical (as are physical hybrids; see Adam 1990). But it has also stemmed from the baleful consequences of the divide between structure and agency. In sociological thought the millions of individual interative actions are largely subsumed under the notion of `structure` (such as the class structure, or the structure of gender relations or social structure) which is seen as `ordered` and reproduced through continuous iteration. The concept of structure solves the problem of iteration for sociology. However, social systems do change and sociology then draws upon the concept of agency to argue that some sets of agents can on occasions manage to escape such a structure and effect change in it. If social systems change then this is seen to result from agency.

Certain authors have however seen the limitations of this formulation, including those that emphasize the performativity of gender through the stylized repetition of actions over time (Butler 1990); Giddens develops the `duality of structure` to account for the recursive character of social life (1984). Now recursive is like iteration; and Giddens undoubtedly advances the ways in which we understand how `structures` are both drawn on, and are the outcome of, countless iterative actions by knowledgeable agents. However, Giddens insufficiently examines the `complex` character of these iterative processes, of how order can generate chaos, unpredictability and non-linearity. So although there is recurrence, such recurrent actions may produce non-equilibrium, non-linearity and, if the parameters change dramatically, a sudden branching of the social world. And this is the crucial point; such complex change may have nothing necessarily to do with agents actually seeking to change that world. The agents may simply keep carrying out the same recurrent actions or what they conceive to be the same actions. But it is through iteration over time that they may generate unexpected, unpredictable and chaotic outcomes, often the very opposite of what the human agents involved may seek to realize. Moreover, of course, agents are not just humans but will be a variety of human and non-human actants that constitute the typical mobile, roaming hybrids (where states at best `regulate the game´ rather than `tend the garden´; see Urry 2000: ch. 8).

One social science example of complexity thinking is Marx's analysis of the unfolding `contradictions´ of capitalism (see Elster 1978). Marx argues that individual capitalists seek to maximize their profits and hence pay their particular workers as little as possible or make them work increasingly long hours. The `exploitation´ of the workforce will continue unless states, or collective actions by trade unions, prevent it, or workers die prematurely. The consequences of such endlessly repeated actions reproduces the capitalist system since substantial profits are generated, so offsetting what Marx hypothesized as the law of the declining rate of profit. The realization of such profits has the effect of reproducing the class relations of capital and wage-labour integral to the ordering of the capitalist system.

However, the very process of sustaining order through each capitalist exploiting their particular workers, results in three system contradictions, of overproduction, of an increasingly revolutionary workforce and the smashing down of Chinese walls and the internationalization of the proletariat. Thus the outcomes of capitalist order are, over time and millions of iterations, the opposite of what capitalists appeared to be reproducing through exploiting their local workforce. Millions of iterations produce chaos out of order, non-linear changes and a potentially catastrophic branching of the capitalist system (see Read and Harvey 1992). Much sociology has sought to explain why these predictions have not materialized. However, Marx's inability to predict social revolution can be regarded by contemporary theory as comprehensible since relatively small perturbations in the system can produce a very different branching of the social world from what he envisaged a century or so ago.

Moreover, Marx's analysis brings out the key significance of *local* forms of information, and more generally of what Kwa terms a baroque rather than a romantic conception of complex wholes (1998). Cilliers describes how any emergent complex system is the result of a rich interaction of simple elements each of which `only respond [s] to the limited information each is presented with´ (1998: 5). Thus, according to Marx, each capitalist operates under conditions that

are far from equilibrium; they can only respond to `local´ sources of information since relevant information carries across only a limited temporal and spatial range. Moreover, local struggles by groups of workers against the conditions of their exploitation had the longer-term effect, through complex iteration, of reproducing the capitalist system, albeit in a quite different form. In the end such struggles prevented such an exploitation of the workforce that social revolution of the sort Marx predicted would have resulted. The struggles of workers, based upon local knowledge, had the effect of re-establishing social order, but at a higher `social welfare´ level.

Capitalism, we now know, has indeed broken down many Chinese walls and has gone global. Can complexity provide some illumination into such a global capitalism? Is an emergent level of the `global´ developing that is recursively self-producing, where its outputs constitute inputs into an autopoietic circular system of `global´ objects, identities, institutions and social practices? And if there is, what are its complex properties, how are chaos and order combined in the global? First, we can note that billions of individual actions occur, each of which is based upon exceptionally localized forms of information. Most people most of the time act iteratively in terms of local information, knowing almost nothing about the global connections or implications of what they are doing. However, these local actions do not remain simply local since they are captured, represented, marketed, circulated and generalized elsewhere. They are carried along the scapes and flows of the emerging global world, transporting ideas, people, images, monies and technologies to potentially everywhere. Indeed such actions may jump the scapes, since they are fluid-like and difficult to keep within particular channels (such as the internet jumping from military to road protestor communications).

The consequences for the global level are nonlinear, large-scale, unpredictable and partially ungovernable (baroque rather than romantic: see Kwa 1998). Small causes at certain places produce massive consequences elsewhere. Consider a pile of sand; if an extra grain of sand is placed on top it may stay there or it may cause a small avalanche. The system is self-organized but the effects of local changes can vary enormously (Cilliers 1998: 97). The heap will maintain itself at the critical height and we cannot know in advance what will happen to any individual action or what its consequence will be for the pile of sand.

The emergent global order is one of constant disorder and disequilibrium. The following are some recent examples of where millions of actions based upon local knowledge have, through iteration, resulted in unpredictable and non-linear consequences at the emergent global level (see Urry 2000: ch. 2 on each of these). For US military communications in the event of a nuclear war there developed the arpanet/internet, but which has then provided a scape which has generated extraordinary flows of image, information and non-military communications throughout the world (internet use has grown faster than any previous new technology). In 1989 there was the almost instantaneous collapse of all of `communist' Eastern Europe, once it was seen that the particular local centre of the Kremlin was unable and unwilling to prevent such an occurrence. The apparently `rational' decision of millions of individual people to exercise their right to drive has resulted in carbon gas discharges that threaten the long-term survival of the planet (even where most motorists are aware of such consequences). And omnipotent consumerism has almost everywhere generated religious fundamentalism. Barber apocalyptically describes the emergent global order as being locked in a major conflict between the consumerist `McWorld' on the one hand, and the identity politics of the `Jihad', on the other (1996). There is a `new world disorder' in which McWorld and Jihad depend upon, and globally reinforce, each other.

There is a kind of spiralling global disequilibrium that threatens existing public spheres, civil society and democratic forms. There are of course forms of global governance designed to dampen down some of these forms of disequilibrium, but mostly they are based upon national governments acting within particular *local* contexts. Baker has elaborated on how the relationship between the centre and the periphery, or what he calls the `centriphery', functions to create both order and turbulence in social life (1993). He suggests that the centriphery functions as an attractor, which is defined as the space to which the trajectory of any particular system is over time attracted (Byrne 1998: 26–9; Cilliers 1998: 96–7). In this case the centriphery is a

dynamic pattern that is repeated at many different levels, involving flows of energy, information and ideas that simultaneously create both centres and peripheries. The trajectory of social systems is irreversibly attracted to the centriphery.

Baker further argues that

> Today, particular multinational industries center vast amounts of human activity, locating specific aspects of their enterprise in different continents. In each of these cases, the exchange of goods and services binds and lubricates a dynamic relationship between the center and the periphery. As centering progresses, it deepens the periphery.... Because centering and peripheralizing involve the transformation of energy and information and, thus, the creation of entropy, the process is irreversible. (1993: 140)

A specific form taken by the strange attractor of the centriphery is that of `glocalization', whereby there is a parallel irreversible process of globalization-deepening-localization-deepening-globalization and so on. Both are bound together through a dynamic relationship, as huge flows of resources move backwards and forwards between the global and the local. Neither the global nor the local can exist without the other. They develop in a symbiotic, irreversible and unstable set of relationships, in which each gets transformed through billions of world-wide iterations. Small perturbations in the system can result in unpredictable and chaotic branching of such a system, as has happened with what Imken terms the `non-linear, asymmetrical, chaotically-assembled ... new artificial life-form of the global telecommunications *Matrix'* (Imken 1999: 92).

CONCLUSION

I have thus illustrated how `complexity' systems can assist in the analysis of mobile hybrids. How though does this leave `sociology' which would seem to be cast adrift once we leave the relatively safe boundaries of bounded societies? Most of the tentative certainties that sociology has cautiously erected would appear to dissolve with the structure of feeling entailed by complexity. These developments seem to imply a post-disciplinary social/cultural/political science with no particular space or role for individual disciplines (see Sayer 1999). Why should `sociology` analyse these intersecting complex mobilities that have travelled onto the intellectual stage in such a powerful fashion (see Thrift 1999, on the new *complex* `structure of feeling` within the academy, management science and `new age`)?

First, most other disciplines are subject to extensive forms of discursive normalization, monitoring and policing that make them poor candidates for post-disciplinary reconfiguration. Indeed theories, methods and data may be literally expelled from such disciplines since they are viewed as too `social` and outside the concerns of that particular policed discipline (see Urry 1995: ch. 2). There are many examples of how sociology provides a place of temporary intellectual dwelling for those marginalized by discursive normalization in adjacent disciplines. Moreover, sociology's discursive formation has often demonstrated a relative lack of hierarchy, a somewhat unpoliced character, an inability to resist intellectual invasions, an awareness that all human practice is socially organized, a potential to identify the social powers of objects and nature, and an increasing awareness of spatial and temporal processes. While all these wreak havoc with any remaining notion of society *tout court*, sociology could develop a new agenda for a discipline that is losing its central concept of human `society`. It is a discipline organized around networks, mobility and horizontal fluidities. More generally, Diken advocates the `more "mobile" theorizing` that will be necessary to deal with emerging hybrid entities, as well as with so-called societies (1998: 248).

Dogan and Pahre show the importance of `intellectual mobility` for innovation in the social sciences (1990). Their extensive research demonstrates that innovation does not principally result from those scholars who are firmly entrenched within disciplines, nor from those practising rather general `interdisciplinary` or `post-disciplinary` studies. Rather innovation results from academic mobility across clear disciplinary borders, a mobility that generates `creative marginality`. It is this marginality, resulting from scholars moving from the centre to the periphery of their discipline and then crossing its frontiers that produces new productive hybridities in the social sciences. These can constitute institutionalized sub-fields (such as medical sociology) or more informal networks (such as historical sociology;

see Dogan and Pahre 1990: ch. 21). This creative marginality results from complex, overlapping and disjunctive processes of migration, processes which can occur across disciplinary and/or geographical and/or social borders (in the case of the `Frankfurt School` it was all three; Dogan and Pahre 1990: 73–4). Intellectual mobilities are good for the social sciences, so it would seem (see Diken 1998, as well). Sociology has often been the beneficiary of the `creative marginality` of such creative `in-migrants`.

Further, most important developments in sociology have at least indirectly stemmed from social movements with `emancipatory interests` fuelling a new or reconfigured social analysis. Examples of such mobilized groupings which at different historical moments have included the working class, farmers, the professions, urban protest movements, student's movement, women's movement, immigrant groups, environmental NGOs, gay and lesbian movement, `disabled` groups and so on. The emancipatory interests of these groupings are not always directly reflected within sociology; more they have had a complex and refracted impact. But in that sense, sociology has been `parasitic` upon these movements, thus demonstrating how the `cognitive practices` of such movements have helped to constitute `public spaces for thinking new thoughts, activating new actors, generating new ideas` within societies (Eyerman and Jamison 1991: 161; Urry 1995: ch. 2). Societies were organized through debate occuring within a relatively delimited national, public sphere. The information and knowledge produced by its universities centrally formed those debates and delimited possible outcomes. Disciplines were particularly implicated in contributing knowledge to such a public sphere, and indeed in constituting that sphere as part of a national civil society (Cohen and Arato 1992; Emirbayer and Sheller 1999).

However, the increasingly mediatized nature of contemporary civil societies transforms all of this. It is not so much that the mass media reflects what goes on elsewhere, so much as what happens in and through the media *is* what happens elsewhere. The sphere of public life that provided the context for knowledge produced within the academy is now increasingly mediatized (see Dahlgren 1995). Thrift describes the cosmopolitan mediatization of complexity science, especially as organized in and through the Santa Fe

Institute (Thrift 1999). Debate is concerned as much with image, meaning, and emotion, as it is with written texts, cognition and science. The global economy of signs, of globally circulating information and images, is transforming the public sphere into an increasingly denationalized, visual and emotional public stage (Urry 2000: ch. 7; Knorr Cetina 1997).

And on that mediated public stage, many social groupings are appearing, developing partially, imperfectly and contingently, a kind of globalizing civil society. This is summarized within the World Order Models Project. Falk documents the widespread growth of trans-national citizens associations, world-wide shifts towards democratization and non-violence, huge difficulties for national states in maintaining popularity and legitimacy, and the more general growth of diverse global trends (1995; and see Archibugi, Held, Kohler 1998). Falk concludes that: `such cumulative developments are facilitating the birth and growth of global civil society´ (Falk 1995: 35). And it is this set of social transformations that could constitute the social base for the sociology of mobilities I have elaborated in this article. The social basis of a `global civil society´ and its emancipatory interests may result in a `sociology of mobilities´ of the sort I have outlined here, as we move chaotically into the next century.

REFERENCES

Adam, B. 1990 *Time and Social Theory*, Cambridge: Polity.

Albertsen, N. and Diken, B. 1999 *Moving Ontologies/Mobile Sociologies*, mimeo, Sociology Dept., Lancaster University.

Albrow, M. 1996 *The Global Age*, Cambridge: Polity.

Amin, A. and Thrift, N. 1992 `Neo-Marshallian nodes in global networks´, *International Journal of Urban and Regional Research* 16: 571–87.

Archibugi, D., Held, D. and Kohler, M. (eds.) 1998 *Re-Imagining Political Community*, Cambridge: Polity.

Auge, M. 1995 *Non-Places*, London: Verso.

Baker, P. 1993 `Chaos, order, and sociological theory´, *Sociological Inquiry* 63: 123–49.

Barber, B. 1996 *Jihad vs McWorld*, New York: Ballantine.

Bauman, Z. 1987 *Legislators and Interpreters*, Cambridge: Polity.

Beck, U. 1999 *What Is Globalization?* Cambridge: Polity.

Berger, P. and Luckmann, T. 1967 *The Social Construction of Reality*, London: Allen Lane.

Billig, M. 1995 *Banal Nationalism*, London: Sage.

Braun, R., Dessewfly, T., Scheppele, K., Smejkalova, J., Wessely, A., Zentai,V. 1996 *Culture without Frontiers*, Internationales Forschungszentrum Kulturwissenschaten, Vienna: Research Grant Proposal.

Brunn, S. and Leinbach, R. (eds.) 1991 *Collapsing Space and Time: Geographic Aspects of Communications and Information*, London: HarperCollins.

Butler, J. 1990 *Gender Trouble*, New York: Routledge.

Byrne, D. 1998 *Complexity Theory and the Social Sciences*, London: Routledge.

Calhoun, C. 1997 *Nationalism*, Buckingham: Open University Press.

Castells, M. 1996 *The Rise of the Network Society*, Oxford: Blackwell.

———. 1997 *The Power of Identity*, Oxford: Blackwell.

Cilliers, P. 1998 *Complexity and Post-modernism*, London: Routledge.

Cohen, J. and Arato, A. 1992 *Civil Society and Political Theory*, Cambridge: MIT Press.

Cooke, P. and Morgan, K. 1993 `The John Urry network paradigm: new departures in corporate and regional development´, *Environment and Planning D. Society and Space* 11: 543–64.

Dahlgren, P. 1995 *Television and the Public Sphere*, London: Sage.

Deleuze, G. and Guattari, F. 1986 *Nomadology*, New York: Semiotext(e).

———. 1988 *A Thousand Plateaus.Capitalism and Schizophrenia*, London: Athlone Press.

Diken, B. 1998 *Strangers, Ambivalence and Social Theory*, Aldershot: Ashgate.

Dogan, M. and Pahre, R. 1990 *Creative Marginality*, Boulder: Westview Press.

Durkheim, E. [1897] 1952 *Suicide*, London: Routledge.

Eade, J. (ed.) 1997 *Living the Global City*, London: Routledge.

Elster, J. 1978 *Logic and Society*, Chichester: Wiley.

Emirbayer, M. and Sheller, M. 1999 `Publics in history´, *Theory and Society* 28: 145–97.

Eve, R., Horsfall, S. and Lee, M. (eds.) 1997 *Chaos, Complexity, and Sociology*, California: Sage.

Eyerman, R. and Jamison, A. 1991 *Social Movements. A Cognitive Approach*, Cambridge: Polity.

Falk, R. 1995 *On Human Governance*, Cambridge: Polity.

Giddens, A. 1984 *The Constitution of Society*, Cambridge: Polity.

Gouldner, A. 1972 *The Coming Crisis of Western Sociology*, London: Heinemann.

Graham, S. and Marvin, S. 1996 *Telecommunications and the City*, London: Routledge.

Held, D., McGrew, A., Goldbatt, D. and Perraton, J. 1999 *Global Transformations*, Cambridge: Polity.

Hewitt, R. 1997 *The Possibilities of Society*, Albany: SUNY Press.

Imken, O. 1999 `The convergence of virtual and actual in the Global Matrix´, in M. Crang, P. Crang, J. May (eds.), *Virtual Geographies*, London: Routledge.

Kaplan, C. 1996 *Questions of Travel*, Durham, US: Duke University Press.

Knorr Cetina, K. 1997 `Sociality with objects´, *Theory, Culture and Society* 14: 1–30.

Kwa, C. 1998 `Romantic and baroque conceptions of complex wholes in the sciences´, mimeo, University of Amsterdam.

Ladau, E. and Mouffe, C. 1985 *Hegemony and Socialist Strategy*, London: Verso.

Lash, S. and Urry, J. 1987 *The End of Organized Capitalism*, Cambridge: Polity.

———. 1994 *Economics of Science and Space*, London: Sage.

Latour, B. 1987 *Science in Action*, Milton Keynes: Open University Press.

Law, J. 1994 *Organizing Modernity*, Oxford: Basil Blackwell.

Lefebvre, H. 1991 *The Production of Space*, Oxford: Blackwell.

Luhmann, N. 1990 *Essays on Self Reference*, New York: Colombia University Press.

———. 1995 *Social Systems*, Stanford: Stanford University Press.

Lyotard, J-F. 1984 *The Postmodern Condition*, Manchester: Manchester University Press.

MacIver, R. and Page, C. 1950 *Society: An Introductory Analysis*, London: Macmillan.

Macnaghten, P, and Urry, J. 1998 *Contested Natures*, London: Sage.

Mann, M. 1993 *The Sources of Social Power: Vol.2.* Cambridge: Cambridge University Press.

Marshall, T. H. and Bottomore, T. 1992 *Citizenship and Social Class*, London: Pluto.

Messner, D. 1997 *The Network Society: Economic Development and International Competitiveness as Problems of Social Governance*, London: Cass.

Mingers, J. 1995 *Self Producing Systems*, New York: Plenum.

Mol, A. and Law, J. 1994 `Regions, networks and fluids: anaemia and social topology´, *Social Studies of Science* 24: 641–71.

Murdoch, J. 1995 `Actor-networks and the evolution of economic forms: combining description and explanation in theories of regulation, flexible specialization, and networks´, *Environment and Planning A*, 27: 731–57.

Prigogine, I. and Stengers, L. 1984 *Order out of Chaos*, New York: Bantam.

Radcliffe-Brown, R. 1952 *Structure and Function in Primitive Society*, London: Cohen and West.

Reed, M. and Harvey, D. 1992 `The new science and the old: complexity and realism in the social sciences´, *Journal for the Theory of Social Behaviour* 22: 353–80.

Ritzer, G. 1992 *The McDonaldization of Society*, London: Pine Forge.

——. 1995 *Expressing America*, London: Pine Forge.

——. 1997 "McDisneyization" and "post-tourism": complementary perspectives on contemporary tourism, in C. Rojek and J.Urry (eds.), *Touring Cultures*, London: Routledge.

Robertson, R. 1992 *Globalization*, London: Sage.

Rose, N. 1996 `Reconfiguring the territory of government´, *Economy and Society* 25: 327–56.

Sayer, A. 1999 `Long live postdisciplinary studies´. Sociology and the curse of disciplinary parochialism/imperialism´, British Sociological Association Conference, Glasgow, April.

Shields, R. 1997 `Flow as a new paradigm´, *Space and Culture* 1: 1–4.

Szerszynski, B. 1997 `The varieties of ecological piety´, *Worldviews: Environment, Culture, Religion* 1: 37–55.

Thrift, N. 1999 ` The place of complexity´, *Theory, Culture and Society* 16: 31–70.

Urry, J. 1995 *Consuming Places*, London: Routledge.

——. 2000 *Sociology Beyond Societies*, London: Sage.

Wallerstein, I. 1987 `World-systems analysis´, in J. Turner and A. Giddens (eds.), *Social Theory Today*, Cambridge: Polity.

——. 1991 *Unthinking Social Science*, Cambridge: Polity.

——. 1998 `The heritage of sociology, the promise of social science´, Presidential Address, 14th World Congress of Sociology, Montreal, July.

Waters, M. 1995 *Globalization*, London: Routledge.

SECTION XVII

1. How does Touraine differentiate his idea of social movements from what he describes as "revolutionary actions and ideologies"?

2. Summarize Alexander's Civil Society III and describe the ways in which it is similar to and different from Civil Society I and II.

3. Why does Collins think that the proper starting point for sociological analysis ought to be the situation rather than the individual? In this regard, relate his theoretical approach to that of Durkheim, who factors prominently in this essay.

4. Summarize in your own words what Collins means by interaction ritual and interaction ritual chains. In advancing his thesis, how does Collins make use of theorists contained in this collection such as Goffman and Bourdieu?

5. What is queer theory and what does Seidman think it can do in reshaping mainstream sociology?

6. What does Castells see as the distinctive impacts of information networks on all aspects of contemporary social relationships, including "relationships of production, consumption, power, experience and culture"?

7. How does Urry think we can rectify certain problematic aspects of the way sociologists have traditionally conceived of society by focusing on the idea of mobility? Do you agree or disagree with his thesis?

8. Compare and contrast Castell's theory of network society with Urry's call for a mobile sociology. Do you think these theories are complementary or at odds with each other?